Dictionary of Literary Biography

Dictionary of Literary Biography Documentary Series

1 Sherwood Anderson, Willa Cather, John Dos Passos, Theodore Dreiser, F. Scott Fitzgerald, Ernest Hemingway, Sinclair Lewis, edited by Margaret A. Van Antwerp (1982)

2 James Gould Cozzens, James T. Farrell, William Faulkner, John O'Hara, John Steinbeck, Thomas Wolfe, Richard Wright, edited by Margaret A. Van Antwerp (1982)

3 Saul Bellow, Jack Kerouac, Norman Mailer, Vladimir Nabokov, John Updike, Kurt Vonnegut, edited by Mary Bruccoli (1983)

4 Tennessee Williams, edited by Margaret A. Van Antwerp and Sally Johns (1984)

5 American Transcendentalists, edited by Joel Myerson (1988)

6 Hardboiled Mystery Writers: Raymond Chandler, Dashiell Hammett, Ross Macdonald, edited by Matthew J. Bruccoli and Richard Layman (1989)

7 Modern American Poets: James Dickey, Robert Frost, Marianne Moore, edited by Karen L. Rood (1989)

8 The Black Aesthetic Movement, edited by Jeffrey Louis Decker (1991)

9 American Writers of the Vietnam War: W. D. Ehrhart, Larry Heinemann, Tim O'Brien, Walter McDonald, John M. Del Vecchio, edited by Ronald Baughman (1991)

10 The Bloomsbury Group, edited by Edward L. Bishop (1992)

11 American Proletarian Culture: The Twenties and The Thirties, edited by Jon Christian Suggs (1993)

12 Southern Women Writers: Flannery O'Connor, Katherine Anne Porter, Eudora Welty, edited by Mary Ann Wimsatt and Karen L. Rood (1994)

13 The House of Scribner, 1846–1904, edited by John Delaney (1996)

14 Four Women Writers for Children, 1868–1918, edited by Caroline C. Hunt (1996)

15 American Expatriate Writers: Paris in the Twenties, edited by Matthew J. Bruccoli and Robert W. Trogdon (1997)

16 The House of Scribner, 1905–1930, edited by John Delaney (1997)

17 The House of Scribner, 1931–1984, edited by John Delaney (1998)

18 British Poets of The Great War: Sassoon, Graves, Owen, edited by Patrick Quinn (1999)

19 James Dickey, edited by Judith S. Baughman (1999)

See also DLB 210, 216, 219, 222, 224, 229, 237, 247, 253, 254, 263, 269, 273, 274, 280, 284, 288, 291, 294, 298, 301, 304

Dictionary of Literary Biography Yearbooks

1980 edited by Karen L. Rood, Jean W. Ross, and Richard Ziegfeld (1981)

1981 edited by Karen L. Rood, Jean W. Ross, and Richard Ziegfeld (1982)

1982 edited by Richard Ziegfeld; associate editors: Jean W. Ross and Lynne C. Zeigler (1983)

1983 edited by Mary Bruccoli and Jean W. Ross; associate editor Richard Ziegfeld (1984)

1984 edited by Jean W. Ross (1985)

1985 edited by Jean W. Ross (1986)

1986 edited by J. M. Brook (1987)

1987 edited by J. M. Brook (1988)

1988 edited by J. M. Brook (1989)

1989 edited by J. M. Brook (1990)

1990 edited by James W. Hipp (1991)

1991 edited by James W. Hipp (1992)

1992 edited by James W. Hipp (1993)

1993 edited by James W. Hipp, contributing editor George Garrett (1994)

1994 edited by James W. Hipp, contributing editor George Garrett (1995)

1995 edited by James W. Hipp, contributing editor George Garrett (1996)

1996 edited by Samuel W. Bruce and L. Kay Webster, contributing editor George Garrett (1997)

1997 edited by Matthew J. Bruccoli and George Garrett, with the assistance of L. Kay Webster (1998)

1998 edited by Matthew J. Bruccoli, contributing editor George Garrett, with the assistance of D. W. Thomas (1999)

1999 edited by Matthew J. Bruccoli, contributing editor George Garrett, with the assistance of D. W. Thomas (2000)

2000 edited by Matthew J. Bruccoli, contributing editor George Garrett, with the assistance of George Parker Anderson (2001)

2001 edited by Matthew J. Bruccoli, contributing editor George Garrett, with the assistance of George Parker Anderson (2002)

2002 edited by Matthew J. Bruccoli and George Garrett; George Parker Anderson, Assistant Editor (2003)

Concise Series

Concise Dictionary of American Literary Biography, 7 volumes (1988–1999): *The New Consciousness, 1941–1968; Colonization to the American Renaissance, 1640–1865; Realism, Naturalism, and Local Color, 1865–1917; The Twenties, 1917–1929; The Age of Maturity, 1929–1941; Broadening Views, 1968–1988; Supplement: Modern Writers, 1900–1998.*

Concise Dictionary of British Literary Biography, 8 volumes (1991–1992): *Writers of the Middle Ages and Renaissance Before 1660; Writers of the Restoration and Eighteenth Century, 1660–1789; Writers of the Romantic Period, 1789–1832; Victorian Writers, 1832–1890; Late-Victorian and Edwardian Writers, 1890–1914; Modern Writers, 1914–1945; Writers After World War II, 1945–1960; Contemporary Writers, 1960 to Present.*

Concise Dictionary of World Literary Biography, 4 volumes (1999–2000): *Ancient Greek and Roman Writers; German Writers; African, Caribbean, and Latin American Writers; South Slavic and Eastern European Writers.*

Dictionary of Literary Biography® • Volume Three Hundred Seven

Brazilian Writers

Brazilian Writers

Edited by
Monica Rector
University of North Carolina at Chapel Hill
and
Fred M. Clark
University of North Carolina at Chapel Hill

A Bruccoli Clark Layman Book

THOMSON
™
GALE

Detroit • New York • San Francisco • San Diego • New Haven, Conn. • Waterville, Maine • London • Munich

Dictionary of Literary Biography
Volume 307: Brazilian Writers

LIBRARY OF CONGRESS CATALOGING-IN-PUBLICATION DATA

Brazilian writers / edited by Monica P. Rector.
  p. cm. — (Dictionary of literary biography ; v. 307)
"A Bruccoli Clark Layman Book."
Includes bibliographical references and index.
  ISBN 0-7876-6844-3 (hardcover : alk. paper)
  1. Brazilian literature—Bio-bibliography—Dictionaries. 2. Brazilian literature—History and criticism—Dictionaries. 3. Authors, Brazilian—Biography—Dictionaries. I. Rector, Mônica. II. Title. III. Series.

PQ9506.B73 2004
869.09'981'03—dc22   2004018640

Contents

Contents

Plan of the Series

The advisory board, the editors, and the publisher of the *Dictionary of Literary Biography* are joined in endorsing Mark Twain's declaration. The literature of a nation provides an inexhaustible resource of permanent worth. Our purpose is to make literature and its creators better understood and more accessible to students and the reading public, while satisfying the needs of teachers and researchers.

To meet these requirements, *literary biography* has been construed in terms of the author's achievement. The most important thing about a writer is his writing. Accordingly, the entries in *DLB* are career biographies, tracing the development of the author's canon and the evolution of his reputation.

The purpose of *DLB* is not only to provide reliable information in a usable format but also to place the figures in the larger perspective of literary history and to offer appraisals of their accomplishments by qualified scholars.

The publication plan for *DLB* resulted from two years of preparation. The project was proposed to Bruccoli Clark by Frederick G. Ruffner, president of the Gale Research Company, in November 1975. After specimen entries were prepared and typeset, an advisory board was formed to refine the entry format and develop the series rationale. In meetings held during 1976, the publisher, series editors, and advisory board approved the scheme for a comprehensive biographical dictionary of persons who contributed to literature. Editorial work on the first volume began in January 1977, and it was published in 1978. In order to make *DLB* more than a dictionary and to compile volumes that individually have claim to status as literary history, it was decided to organize volumes by topic, period, or

genre. Each of these freestanding volumes provides a biographical-bibliographical guide and overview for a particular area of literature. We are convinced that this organization—as opposed to a single alphabet method—constitutes a valuable innovation in the presentation of reference material. The volume plan necessarily requires many decisions for the placement and treatment of authors. Certain figures will be included in separate volumes, but with different entries emphasizing the aspect of his career appropriate to each volume. Ernest Hemingway, for example, is represented in *American Writers in Paris, 1920–1939* by an entry focusing on his expatriate apprenticeship; he is also in *American Novelists, 1910–1945* with an entry surveying his entire career, as well as in *American Short-Story Writers, 1910–1945, Second Series* with an entry concentrating on his short fiction. Each volume includes a cumulative index of the subject authors and articles.

Between 1981 and 2002 the series was augmented and updated by the *DLB Yearbooks*. There have also been nineteen *DLB Documentary Series* volumes, which provide illustrations, facsimiles, and biographical and critical source materials for figures, works, or groups judged to have particular interest for students. In 1999 the *Documentary Series* was incorporated into the *DLB* volume numbering system beginning with *DLB 210: Ernest Hemingway.*

We define literature as the *intellectual commerce of a nation:* not merely as belles lettres but as that ample and complex process by which ideas are generated, shaped, and transmitted. *DLB* entries are not limited to "creative writers" but extend to other figures who in their time and in their way influenced the mind of a people. Thus the series encompasses historians, journalists, publishers, book collectors, and screenwriters. By this means readers of *DLB* may be aided to perceive literature not as cult scripture in the keeping of intellectual high priests but firmly positioned at the center of a nation's life.

DLB includes the major writers appropriate to each volume and those standing in the ranks behind them. Scholarly and critical counsel has been sought in deciding which minor figures to include and how full their entries should be. Wherever possible, useful references are made to figures who do not warrant separate entries.

Each *DLB* volume has an expert volume editor responsible for planning the volume, selecting the figures for inclusion, and assigning the entries. Volume editors are also responsible for preparing, where appropriate, appendices surveying the major periodicals and literary and intellectual movements for their volumes, as well as lists of further readings. Work on the series as a whole is coordinated at the Bruccoli Clark Layman editorial center in Columbia, South Carolina, where the editorial staff is responsible for accuracy and utility of the published volumes.

One feature that distinguishes *DLB* is the illustration policy–its concern with the iconography of literature. Just as an author is influenced by his surroundings, so is the reader's understanding of the author enhanced by a knowledge of his environment. Therefore *DLB* volumes include not only drawings, paintings, and photographs of authors, often depicting them at various stages in their careers, but also illustrations of their families and places where they lived. Title pages are regularly reproduced in facsimile along with dust jackets for modern authors. The dust jackets are a special feature of *DLB* because they often document better than anything else the way in which an author's work was perceived in its own time. Specimens of the writers' manuscripts and letters are included when feasible.

Samuel Johnson rightly decreed that "The chief glory of every people arises from its authors." The purpose of the *Dictionary of Literary Biography* is to compile literary history in the surest way available to us–by accurate and comprehensive treatment of the lives and work of those who contributed to it.

The *DLB* Advisory Board

Introduction

Scholars generally divide literature written in Latin America into two large epochs, the colonial and the national. In Brazil the colonial era covers the period from discovery in 1500, including colonization and expansion of the country, up to the establishment of nationhood with independence in 1822. The national period begins with the political break from Portugal early in the nineteenth century, as writers and intellectuals began to search for a national identity. Literary historians, however, do not always agree on what constitutes the first truly Brazilian work. Some perceive in certain pieces written throughout the colonial period a developing nationalist sentiment that distinguishes the writing from that of Portugal. Others see the works of the colonial era as an extension of Portuguese literature and believe that a Brazilian literature was possible only after the country had gained its political independence and could establish a national identity.

Although the development of literature in Brazil followed European movements and trends throughout the colonial period, a cultural identity that was noticeably different from the Portuguese gradually emerged in the colony. As the population grew and more areas of the country came to be inhabited, new ethnic groups, especially the African, arrived, and a racial mixture unique to Brazil developed. Literary works with traits and characteristics peculiar to the colony portrayed the realities of the New World. Writers who had little or no contact with Portugal began to express a worldview more identifiable with the new land than with Europe. This worldview was the manifestation of a common experience in the colony of persons who shared an historical origin that had been modified over the course of generations. Brazil became a mixture of the Portuguese, the indigenous populations, and the various African groups brought in as slaves for the workforce. Although the indigenous and African elements had an impact on the emerging culture, the eventual product remained essentially European in social and cultural terms.

The Colonial Period

During the colonial period literary and artistic models were imposed by the colonizers on the young country. Portugal maintained a firm control over the import of printed materials into Brazil, which received its first printing press only in the early nineteenth century. The literary movements of the continent—the Renaissance, the baroque, and the neoclassical—influenced the writers in the American colonies as they made their first timid attempts at self-expression.

At the time of the discovery of Brazil, Portugal was experiencing the impact of the radically new directions in human thought and culture of the Renaissance. Portuguese writers and artists, however, were slow in giving up the worldview of the Middle Ages, in which the focus was on the divine rather than on the human. The mixture of medievalism and humanism that characterized Portuguese culture in the fifteenth century found its way to Brazil through the missionary groups, especially the Jesuits, who became some of the first important writers and educators in the colony.

The first known Brazilian document is a letter written in 1500 by the scribe Pero Vaz de Caminha to King Manuel I of Portugal. This document, in which Caminha describes the encounter with the new land, reveals the tone that characterizes the early letters and chronicles written by travelers and priests in Brazil: a sense of awe and amazement at the natural wonders and the inhabitants. This vision of the New World was a European one, registering and judging everything from the viewpoint of the medieval and Renaissance ideologies that dominated the Portuguese mind in the sixteenth century. This Eurocentric vision dominated writing in Brazil up to the early nineteenth century, when writers and intellectuals, with a new sense of nationhood, rejected Portuguese models and searched for inspiration from within. Throughout the nineteenth century, however, the European influence remained strong; it simply shifted from Portugal to France. In the early twentieth century, Brazilian artists once again attempted cultural liberation, this time through the modernist movement.

Literary works in sixteenth-century Brazil were few and sporadic. Conditions in the colony were not favorable to the development of coherent literary and artistic expression. The various settlements were isolated at great distances from each other, and time and effort were expended on colonization and protection of the land from other European countries eager for its resources. Cultural and intellectual development was secondary to the colonial mission, which was registered in the few documents remaining from the period. Several writers, including Pêro de Magalhães Gândavo, Gabriel Soares de Sousa, Ambrósio Fernandes Brandão, Fernão Cardim, and Vicente do Salvador, wrote descriptive treatises and histories of the new land. The most important Brazilian literary figure of the sixteenth century, José de Anchieta, was born in the Canary Islands and went to Brazil in 1553. He left a considerable body of writing, including sermons, letters, poetry, and theatrical works. The literary elements in Anchieta's work, as was the case with most of the missionaries who wrote during the colonial period, including Manuel da Nóbrega, seemed incidental to his mission of converting the indigenous peoples to Christianity and watching over the moral and spiritual lives of the colonists. Bento Teixeira, generally considered the first Brazilian poet, wrote the short epic poem *Prosopopéia* (1601), which praises Jorge de Albuquerque Coelho, governor of Pernambuco. The work reveals the strong influence of Portugese poet Luís de Camões's epic *Os Lusíadas* (1572, The Lusiads).

The cultural center of Brazil in the seventeenth century was Bahia. The second half of the century was dominated by the baroque spirit, in which the human being, caught between the liberating forces of Renaissance humanism and the rigid doctrines of the Middle Ages, was portrayed through artistic use of contrast, antithesis, and paradox. The themes and tone of Gregório de Matos Guerra's poetry—from the ardent religious and sensual love poems to his satirically mordant verses on life in the colony—capture the baroque spirit. The Iberian influence, especially the extravagance of Spanish poet Luis de Góngora (whose elaborate style came to be known as *gongorismo*), was strongly felt among the writers of the colony. Antônio Vieira, although born in Portugal, spent much of his life in Brazil with the Jesuits. His sermons and letters include anti-Gongoristic references; Vieira insisted on clarity of style in his religious mission. He also preached against the Dutch, who attacked northern Brazil twice in the seventeenth century (1624–1625 and 1630), the cruel treatment of African slaves, and enslavement of the native populations. Other important writers of the seventeenth century include Manuel Botelho de Oliveira, who wrote poems and plays in the baroque style, and Eusébio de Matos and Nuno Marques Pereira, whose works are characterized by a moralistic tone. André João Antônio and Sebastião da Rocha Pita continued the tradition of historical and descriptive prose established in the sixteenth century.

The baroque influence continued well into the eighteenth century as the economic and cultural center of Brazil shifted from the northeastern coast to the central highlands of Minas Gerais after gold was discovered there in 1695. The colony, however, began to undergo several changes that favored the growth of cultural activities. The economic boom in Minas Gerais spawned a new generation of intellectuals, most of whom were educated in Europe but harbored strong sentiments of being Brazilian. Sebastião de Carvalho, marquês de Pombal, expelled the Jesuits from the Portuguese empire, marking the end of a tradition that had had far-reaching effects in all spheres of life in the colony, including the social, political, spiritual, educational, and cultural. The capital was moved from Bahia to Rio de Janeiro, terminating the cultural dominance of Bahia over the colony and creating a new cultural axis of Minas Gerais–Rio de Janeiro.

One of the first important manifestations of the Enlightenment in Brazil throughout the first half of the eighteenth century was the foundation of academies modeled on the contemporary literary societies of Europe. Several such societies emerged in the colony, including some stable organizations with members who shared a common mission, others that held ephemeral meetings organized to mark special occasions, and some that convened regular literary gatherings. The most important academies included the Academia dos Esquecidos (Academy of the Forgotten Ones) in Salvador, the Academia dos Felizes (Academy of the Happy Ones) in Rio de Janeiro, and the Academia dos Seletos (Academy of the Chosen Ones) in the same city. Literary historians consider the surviving works by members of these academies to be mediocre and secondary in importance to the establishment of the first communal spirit of thinkers and artists in Brazil. The academy members shared their ideas and works, which showed an increasingly nativist sentiment. This sentiment was later transformed into nationalist fervor, leading to independence.

The second half of the eighteenth century in Brazil was dominated by *Arcadismo* (Arcadianism), a neoclassical movement of Italian origin. Brazilian *Arcadismo* had its beginnings in Claúdio Manuel da Costa's *Obras poéticas* (1768, Poetic Works). The Arcadian poets, like their European counterparts, assumed the names of shepherds in their verses and cultivated the pastoral style. Influenced by the theories of the Encyclopedists, their poetry, both lyric and epic, is characterized by simplicity and clarity, often incorporating aspects of Brazilian nature. The important poets of Brazilian Arcadianism include Tomás Antônio Gonzaga, José Basílio da Gama, Cláudio Manuel da Costa, Inácio José de Alvarenga Peixoto, and José de Santa Rita Durão.

Although not a tightly knit group, the poets were united in their desire to combat the excesses of baroque poetry. Some shared similar political interests and were involved in the ill-fated Inconfidência Mineira (Minas Conspiracy) of 1789, an early attempt at gaining independence from Portugal.

The National Period

The national period in Brazilian literature begins with the movement for independence from Portugal (proclaimed in 1822) and corresponds to the literary movement of Romanticism, which was a reaction against neoclassical values. Romanticism, with its origins in England and Germany, had a profound impact on Western culture and is often considered to be the beginning of the modern period. Romantic writers perceived art, life, and reality in a radically different manner from the writers of the neoclassical period. The neoclassical emphasis on order, tranquility, harmony, and objectivity gave way to the exuberance and chaos of creative freedom and subjectivity. In Brazil the concepts of political and artistic freedom merged as artists explored the country and its past in search of a national identity independent from that of Portugal.

Brazil became the seat of the Portuguese Empire when King João VI fled the approaching armies of Napoleon Bonaparte and moved his court to Rio de Janeiro in 1808. The monarch instituted many changes in the colony that ultimately led to the formation of a national consciousness and identity and prepared Brazil for independence. The political and administrative structure of the country became more organized; schools and libraries were constructed as the educational system was improved; the ports were opened to trade and commerce with countries other than Portugal; public services were improved; a printing press was established; and artistic and scientific missions were invited to the country.

Literary historians have traditionally identified a pre-Romantic period (1808–1836) and four loosely defined phases of Brazilian Romanticism, which dominated the arts until the 1870s. The period from 1808 to 1836 was a time of transition in which characteristics of Romanticism began to appear in the works of Brazilian writers who looked more to France and England and less to Portugal for inspiration.

Brazilian literature written from 1836 to 1840 is characterized by remnants of neoclassicism mixed with an emerging nationalism and reaction against the Portuguese influence. In this first phase poetry, which already had a solid foundation and tradition in the colony, flourished, and the novel and theater began to emerge as national genres. Domingos Gonçalves de Magalhães's publication of *Suspiros poéticos e saudades* (1836, Poetic Sighs and Yearnings) marks the beginning of Romanticism in Brazil. In 1836 Gonçalves de Magalhães and Manuel Araújo de Porto Alegre collaborated on the literary journal *Niterói-Revista Brasiliense,* the objective of which was the propagation of the notions of Romanticism and the definition of a national culture in Brazil. In 1838 actor João Caetano dos Santos staged Gonçalves de Magalhães's tragedy *Antônio José* (1838) and Luís Carlos Martins Pena's comedy *O juíz de paz da roça* (1842, The Country Judge), considered the first national plays. Caetano dos Santos's productions were enthusiastically received by a growing theater public.

French, English, and North American writers strongly influenced the second group of Brazilian Romantics (1840–1850). The writings of François-René de Chateaubriand and James Fenimore Cooper left their mark on writers who used the Brazilian Indian as a nationalistic symbol in their struggle to produce a truly Brazilian literature. Writers also focused on Brazilian nature as they idealized the native into the noble savage. Antônio Gonçalves Dias poeticized the Indian in notable poems such as "I-Juca-Pirama" (1851, He Who Must Be Killed), while José de Alencar captured the national past and future in Indianist novels such as *O Guarani* (1857) and *Iracema* (1865). Alencar established the novel, often serialized in newspapers in the nineteenth century, as a genre in Brazil. He wrote novels of various types, including the regional, historical, and urban. The regional novel, also cultivated by Bernardo Joaquim da Silva Guimarães, persisted through the last decades of the nineteenth century and made a strong reappearance in the 1930s with writers in the Northeast. The second phase of Romanticism was also marked by an increase in journalistic activities and a growing enthusiasm for the theater. Gonçalves Dias's historical play *Leonor de Mendonça* was staged in 1847, and Martins Pena's comedies continued to attract audiences to the theater.

The years 1850 to 1860 were characterized by themes derived from English, French, and Spanish influences, particularly George Gordon, Lord Byron, Alphonse de Lamartine, and José de Espronceda. Poets during this period expressed negative feelings of disillusionment and cynicism in extremely subjective and individualistic verses. Lyric poetry dominated in the works of writers such as Manuel Antônio Álvares de Azevedo, Luís José Junqueira Freire, Luís Nicolau Fagundes Varela, and Casimiro José Marques de Abreu. Alencar, Joaquim Manuel de Macedo, Guimarães, and João Franklin da Silveira Távora solidified a tradition in the novel through their Indianist, historical, and regional works that explored various aspects of the nation and contributed to the creation of a sense of national identity. Manuel Antônio de Almeida's *Memórias de um sargento de milícias* (translated as *Memoirs of a Militia Sergeant,* 1999), serialized in 1854–1855, stands out at this time for its realism and humorous treatment of life in Rio de Janeiro in the early nineteenth century.

Romantic literature in Brazil reached its peak in the 1850s and 1860s. Around 1870 a new generation of writers, influenced by the liberal and social aspects of Romanticism, began to define a new aesthetic that focused on social issues such as the abolition of slavery. The Paraguayan War (1864–1870) had contributed to a greater sense of national identity as Brazilian writers began to face the immediate problems of their national reality. The exaggerated sentimentalism and subjectivism of Romanticism began to yield to the objectivity of realism in the novel and Parnassianism in poetry. In 1872 Alfredo d'Escragnolle Taunay published his novel *Inocência* (Innocence), which continued the line of the regional novel. The Romantic plot of the work, however, is well balanced by a descriptive realism portraying the life and customs of rural Brazil. Antônio de Castro Alves, one of the last great Romantic poets, captured the social concerns of liberalism in his fiery verses that advocated the abolitionist cause in works such as *A cachoeira de Paulo Afonso* (Paulo Afonso's Waterfall), published posthumously in 1876, and *Os escravos* (The Slaves), published posthumously in 1883. Because of its elevated ideals, Castro Alves's poetry is referred to as *condoreirismo,* after the high-flying condor; his verse pointed the way to the more objective spirit of Parnassianism, which focused on form rather than on emotional content, or "art for art's sake."

Brazil underwent major social and political changes with the abolition of slavery in 1888 and the declaration of the Republic in 1889. Realism and naturalism began to dominate prose as Parnassianism provided the poetic reaction against the excesses of Romanticism. Throughout the 1880s poets such as Antônio Mariano Alberto de Oliveira, Raimundo da Mota Azevedo Correia, Olavo Bilac, and Augusto dos Anjos captured in formally polished and objective verses the materialism of an age in which ideas from biology and the social sciences were incorporated into literature. The environmentalism of Hippolyte-Adolphe Taine and the positivism of Auguste Comte had a great impact on Brazilian intellectual life, while French writers such as Emile Zola influenced Brazilian novelists with their scientific approach to observation and experimentation. The human being was seen as a product of heredity and environment in the novels of the most accomplished of the naturalist writers in Brazil, Aluísio Azevedo, such as *O mulato* (1881; translated as *Mulatto,* 1990), *Casa de pensão* (1884, The Boarding House), and *O cortiço* (1890; translated as *A Brazilian Tenement,* 1926).

Other important novelists of the last decades of the nineteenth century include Raul Pompéia, Herculano Inglês de Sousa, Júlio Ribeiro, and Adolfo Caminha. Pompéia is known for his treatment of the harsh realities of life in a boys' boarding school in *O Ateneu* (1888), Inglês de Sousa for his anticlericalism in *O missionário* (1888, The Missionary), Ribeiro for the erotic scenes of *A carne* (1888, Flesh), and Caminha for his open treatment of homosexuality in *Bom-crioulo* (1895, The Good Mulatto).

Joaquim Maria Machado de Assis stands out for his writings that are in direct contrast to the dominant philosophy and aesthetic of positivism and naturalism in the last two decades of the nineteenth century. Considered the most important of all Brazilian writers, Machado de Assis is an anachronistic figure who has been embraced by writers and critics for his emphasis on a concept of the human being more in tune with the twentieth than with the nineteenth century. Although he also wrote theater and poetry, he is best remembered for his short stories and the novels of his mature period, *Memórias póstumas de Brás Cubas* (1881, The Posthumous Memoirs of Bras Cubas; translated as *Epitaph of a Small Winner,* 1952), *Quincas Borba* (1891; translated as *Philosopher or Dog?* 1954), and *Dom Casmurro* (1899; translated, 1953). Machado de Assis's fiction, characterized by a sardonic humor, uses irony, paradox, and antithesis to portray a relativistic view of human nature. Often narrated in the first person, his works focus on the human being's futile and anguished search for absolute truths. His characters, mostly from the upper-middle class of Rio de Janeiro, are psychologically credible individuals who are often in situations in which the line between illusion and reality is fragile. Machado de Assis's use of metafictional devices, such as the narrator's direct address of the reader and digressions in which the text discusses itself as a text, places his work closer to twentieth-century than to nineteenth-century fiction.

Realism, naturalism, and Parnassianism dominated Brazilian literature until the last decade of the nineteenth century. The last years of that century and the first decades of the twentieth were a time of a hybrid situation in literature and the arts as symbolism provided a reaction against Parnassianism without totally replacing it. The two coexisted, along with remnants of Romanticism. Although several poets are known for both their Parnassian and symbolist verses, the black poet João da Cruz e Sousa is considered the Brazilian symbolist par excellence. His verses in volumes such as *Broquéis* (1893, Shields), *Missal* (1893), and *Faróis* (1900, Beacons) capture his personal anguish in a musical language characterized by sensual metaphors and symbols. The illogical, the irrational, and the search for essences distinguish Cruz e Sousa's poetry from the materialism and objectivism of Parnassianism. Although symbolism was not a well-defined movement in Brazil, it had an impact that continued into the twentieth century in the works of poets such as Alphonsus de Guimarães and Vicente de Carvalho.

Literary critic and historian Tristão de Ataíde has labeled the period extending from the early years of the twentieth century to the Semana de Arte Moderna (Week of Modern Art)–the official beginning of Brazilian modernism in 1922–as *pré-modernismo* (premodernism). This period was a time of consolidation of the Republic in politics and increased interest in a national Brazilian culture. Although the important Parnassian and symbolist poets of the previous century continued to dominate the literary scene, several new and innovative writers emerged. Important novelists of the period include Henrique Maximiliano Coelho Neto, José Pereira da Graça Aranha, Afonso Henriques de Lima Barreto, and José Bento Monteiro Lobato. Graça Aranha's *Canaã* (1902), Coelho Neto's *Banzo* (1918), and Lobato's *Urupês* (1918) explore rural life and consolidate the line of regionalist fiction established in the nineteenth century. Lima Barreto portrays social issues of urban life in novels such as *Triste fim de Policarpo Quaresma* (1915, The Sad End of Policarpo Quaresma).

Euclides da Cunha's *Os sertões* (1902, The Hinterlands; translated as *Rebellion in the Backlands,* 1944) marked an important new direction in the treatment of rural life in Brazil. Although outdated today in its sociological approach, *Os sertões* offers a vigorously objective treatment of the physical and human geography of the hinterlands. The work is divided into three parts; the first two, "A terra" (The Land) and "O homem" (The Man), present the backdrop for the third section, "A luta" (The Battle), in which Cunha portrays the federal government's long and bloody campaign at Canudos, a village in the interior of the state of Bahia, against the popular leader Antônio Conselheiro and his handful of followers in 1897.

Although the Semana de Arte Moderna in São Paulo in 1922 is recognized as the official beginning of Brazilian modernism, the movement had several important antecedents. Artists and writers had planted the seeds of renovation and innovation earlier in the century with various exhibitions, the creation of new journals, articles that attempted to create a sense of modernity, and books that exhibited modernist characteristics. Lasar Segall and Anita Malfatti introduced expressionism in painting as Vitor Brecheret captured the modern spirit in his sculptures. Young writers such as Oswald de Andrade and Mário de Andrade, both active in the organization of the Semana de Arte Moderna, and Manuel Bandeira rebelled against the worn-out literary traditions that dominated in Brazil

during the first two decades of the twentieth century. Seminal publications that contributed to the emergence of the modernist spirit in poetry include Mário de Andrade's *Há uma gota de sangue em cada poema* (There Is a Drop of Blood in Every Poem), Bandeira's *A cinza das horas* (The Ash of the Hours), Paulo Menotti del Picchia's *Moisés* and *Juca Mulato,* and Guilherme de Almeida's *Nós* (We), all published in 1917.

Although artists and intellectuals were united in their desire for the modernization of Brazilian art and literature in the various concerts, exhibitions, and literary readings of the Semana de Arte Moderna, differences in philosophy and approaches to change emerged within a few years. The 1920s were marked by an agitated political and artistic life. As the government experienced various intense moments, different groups and successive generations of artists and writers developed divergent opinions and ideas as the modernist movement spread to the major urban centers of Brazil.

The lines dividing the groups are not always clear, and some artists appear aligned with different currents throughout their careers. The basic philosophy of the groups was similar in that they all focused on the modernization of Brazilian art and life. Differences arose over the importance of how to achieve this goal; some artists embraced influences from abroad, while others rejected these influences in favor of a more nationalistic approach in their definition of a national culture. The main groups included the Dynamists in Rio de Janeiro, with writers and artists such as Graça Aranha, Guilherme de Almeida, Renato Almeida, and Heitor Villa-Lobos; the Primitivists in São Paulo, with Oswald de Andrade and Raul Bopp, centered around the review *Antropofagia* (Cannibalism); the Nationalists in São Paulo, with Plínio Salgado, Menotti del Picchia, and Cassiano Ricardo Leite; the Spiritualists in Rio de Janeiro, with Tasso da Silveira, Murilo Araújo, and, later, Cecília Meireles, centered around the review *Festa;* and the Desvairistas (Hallucinationists), inspired by Mário de Andrade in São Paulo.

Poetry dominated the 1920s in terms of innovation and change. Sometimes referred to as the "heroic phase" of modernism, the period was characterized by an aggressive rejection of the stagnant tenets of Parnassianism and symbolism. Poets explored freer verse forms and elevated the colloquial language to literary status in order to capture the realities of modern life in Brazil. Mário de Andrade's *Paulicéia desvairada* (1922; translated as *Hallucinated City,* 1968) and Oswald de Andrade's *Pau Brasil* (1925, Brazilwood) reflect the spirit of experimentation of this first phase of the modernist movement.

The influence of the Semana de Arte Moderna continued into the 1930s in the poetry of Bandeira,

Vinícius de Morais, and Carlos Drummond de Andrade, whose verses reflected a growing concern with social as well as aesthetic issues. Regionalism in both poetry and prose took on new life after sociologist Gilberto de Mello Freyre returned from his studies in the United States and organized the Congresso Regionalista (Regionalist Congress) of Recife in 1926. The repercussions of this congress echoed well into the 1930s in the poetry of Jorge de Lima and the prose of a generation of writers emerging in northeastern Brazil, including Graciliano Ramos, José Lins do Rêgo, Rachel de Queiroz, and Jorge Amado. Other trends in prose fiction include the psychological novel, developed by Erico Veríssimo, Otávio de Faria, and Cyro dos Anjos, and the novel centered on urban life, developed by Marquês Rebelo (pseudonym of Edy Dias da Cruz).

The term *neomodernismo* (neomodernism) has been used to refer to the period 1945 to 1964. With the end of World War II the fascist dictatorship of Getúlio Vargas also ended, and a democratic government assumed political power in the country. The date 1945 also corresponds to the emergence of the "Generation of 1945," which began a conscious revision of the tenets of modernism. The generation, mostly composed of poets, recognized the emergence of a new world order and the need for new poetic forms to express new realities. The important poets of the Generation of 1945 include Péricles Eugênio da Silva Ramos, Lêdo Ivo, and João Cabral de Melo Neto.

Several new prose writers who reshaped the novel began to publish in the mid 1940s. João Guimarães Rosa redefined regionalist fiction in his short stories and one novel, *Grande sertão: veredas* (1956, Great Backlands: Paths; translated as *The Devil to Pay in the Backlands,* 1963). Adonias Filho offered a new vision of reality in the Northeast in his psychologically penetrating novels such as *Memórias de Lázaro* (1952; translated as *Memories of Lazarus,* 1969) and *Corpo vivo* (1962, Live Body). Clarice Lispector gave introspective fiction new dimensions in her stories and novels, including *Perto do coração selvagem* (1944; translated as *Close to the Wild Heart,* 1990) and *A paixão segundo G. H.* (1964; translated as *The Passion According to G. H.,* 1985). Autran Dourado is often identified with this group for his experimental narrative devices and artistic language. Rubem Braga and Fernando Sabino, both known for their short fiction, especially in the area of the *crônica* (chronicle), began publishing in the 1940s and maintained active and distinguished literary careers throughout the remainder of the twentieth century.

Nelson Rodrigues, along with the Polish-born director Zbigniew Ziembinski, modernized the Brazilian theater with *Vestido de noiva* (translated as *The Wedding Gown,* 1978), which premiered in 1943. Rodrigues continued to write controversial plays about life in the Zona Norte (North Zone) of Rio de Janeiro until his death in 1980. His texts offered innovative staging techniques and often focused on sexual themes involving patriarchal families.

The last half of the twentieth century presents a variety of trends in Brazilian poetry, prose, and theater. In the 1950s the brothers Haroldo and Augusto de Campos, along with Décio Pignatari, questioned the limits of language in their concrete poetry. The writers of the Concrete Poetry movement, which was a part of a larger international movement, experimented with the formal association of words in a poem and with the visual and spatial organization of letters and words on the page. Mário Chamie continued these linguistic experiments with his Poesia-Praxis throughout the 1960s. From 1964 to 1985 Brazil was ruled by a military dictatorship that, at times, heavily censored literature and the arts.

In the late 1960s a cultural movement known as Tropicália (also called Tropicalismo) brought together musicians and movie and theater directors; it also had links to Concrete Poetry. Musicians Gilberto Gil and Caetano Veloso spearheaded the movement, which was cut short by the dictatorship. The *cinema novo* (new cinema) of Gláuber Rocha and the theatrical group Teatro Oficina, directed by José Celso Martinez Correia, were inspired by the Tropicália movement.

New names emerged in the theater reflecting a variety of interests in themes both urban and rural. Writers such as Jorge Andrade, Ariano Suassuna, and Alfredo Dias Gomes, as well as later figures such as Plínio Marcos, focused on the problems of the urban poor. Gianfrancesco Guarnieri and Augusto Boal experimented with new theatrical techniques and devices as they explored political themes in drama that drew heavily on the epic theater of Bertolt Brecht. Under the military dictatorship several women playwrights, including Consuelo de Castro and Leilah Assunção, began to deal with social issues and the question of freedom for the female and for the individual in general.

Although Brazilian literature tended to be restricted to its national boundaries before 1980, this tendency changed toward the end of the twentieth century. There has been more contact with the Spanish-speaking neighbors of Brazil, both in political and cultural terms, because of the development of Mercosul (an abbreviation for Mercado Comum do Sul, Common Market of the South), an economic bloc created in 1995. Brazilian attitudes toward the rest of Latin America, which previously verged on a sense of disdain, evolved into a sense of pride at being a part of the South American continent. The study of Spanish has spread and the number of Spanish American literary works translated into Portuguese has increased.

Brazil has achieved a greater sense of cultural identity separate from its Portuguese origins. Concern for the colonial past has been replaced by a preoccupation with the realities created by globalization. Discussions of the nature of literature have been replaced by discussions of the conditions of its existence. The advent of technology has had an impact on literature and literary language, which has tended to approximate that of cinematography, television, and even the computer. Movement, visibility, and simultaneity of time and space have gained new dimensions in literature. As the printing press created a revolution in the fifteenth century, the latter part of the twentieth century had its own revolution in the postmodern obsession with the visual image. Cultural production has been transformed on a massive scale as it has become more organized along the lines of financial markets.

Literary quality has been sacrificed at times because of these markets, as can be noted in the best-sellers lists of popular magazines such as *Veja* and *Isto É* and in the reviews appearing in the literary supplements of the major Brazilian newspapers. The media have sometimes created popular tastes, and trends are often more important than traditional literary values. This tendency intensified beginning in the 1970s with the success of works such as Veríssimo's *Incidente em Antares* (1971, Incident in Antares), Antônio Callado's *Bar Don Juan* (1971; translated as *Don Juan's Bar,* 1972), Ignácio Loyola Brandão's *Zero* (1975; translated, 1983) Ivan Angelo's *A festa* (1976; translated as *The Celebration,* 2003), and Fernando Gabeira's *O que é isso, companheiro?* (1979). Gabeira's book was of particular interest at the time because of its political content.

More women writers have made their way into the Brazilian literary canon since the 1970s. Their works have attracted the interest of publishers and scholars. Writers such as Sônia Coutinho consider themselves postfeminists, while authors such as Patrícia Melo have moved into traditionally male-dominated genres such as the police novel. The older generation of women writers, including Lya Fett Luft, Nélida Piñon, Adélia Prado, and Lygia Fagundes Telles, have continued to write and evolve as artists, and some have become members of the previously all-male Academia Brasileira de Letras (Brazilian Academy of Writers). The novels of Luft (the subject of an entry by Carmen Chaves Tesser in *DLB 145: Modern Latin-American Fiction Writers, Second Series*) explore the experiences of the German immigrant in Brazil from a feminine point of view. Prado's poetry, with its religious tones, portrays the intimate details of a woman's everyday life. Piñon has explored her Galician roots in view of the Brazilian

patriarchal family in novels such as *A república dos sonhos* (1984; translated as *The Republic of Dreams,* 1989). She was elected the fourth female member of the Academia Brasileira de Letras in 1989 and became the first female president of the academy in 1996. Telles's *As meninas* (1973, The Girls; translated as *The Girl in the Photograph,* 1982) reflects the existential crisis of the Brazilian middle class in the 1960s, while her later novels have explored more-contemporary political and feminine issues.

The focus on persons of African descent and their position and problems in contemporary Brazilian society began with Carolina Maria de Jesus's *O quarto de despejo* (1960; translated as *Beyond All Pity,* 1970). Since the 1980s several Afro-Brazilian writers have emerged, including Maria Conceição Evaristo, Miriam Alves, and Esmeralda Ribeiro. These authors explore social and political themes, especially as they relate to persons of African descent.

More-established authors, such as Carlos Heitor Cony, Adriano Espínola, Rubem Fonseca, and Dalton Trevisan continued to publish throughout the final years of the twentieth century. Their later works, however, lack the shock value of their earlier ones. Osman Lins's and Murilo Rubião's fiction occupies an important place in Brazilian literature of the last three decades of the twentieth century. Lins began his career with an introspective type of regional fiction, which later evolved into a highly intellectualized narrative. Rubião was a pioneer in literature of the fantastic, which finally attracted other Brazilian writers in the 1970s. João Antônio's *Malagueta, perus e bacanaço* (1963, Pepper, Cocks and Good Times) initiated experiments with various types of writing, including parody, which Fonseca uses in his *E do meio mundo prostituto só amores guardei ao meu charuto* (1997, And from the Middle of the Whorish World I Kept Only My Cigar). Cony, Espínola, Fonseca, and João Antônio incorporate the marginalized elements of Brazilian society into their writing with the intent of making the reader uncomfortable enough to take notice of the country's social ills.

Throughout the first four decades of the twentieth century it was possible to classify Brazilian prose fiction clearly into the regional and the urban and into the traditional and the avant-garde. Brazilian literature of the second half of the twentieth century, however, is characterized by a hybrid quality combining premodernist, modernist, and postmodernist traits. Narrative was influenced by techniques borrowed from cinema, and authors experimented with intertextuality in which the notion of originality became blurred. Themes often centered around urbanization and technology, which, although they were sometimes believed to hold the promise of a better future for humanity, were seen as the source of many social ills. The individual was portrayed as perceiving reality through fragmented bits and pieces of information that left him with a feeling of isolation and anonymity. Authors captured their characters and situations in an often abstract language that broke with traditional narrative discourse. Sérgio Sant'Anna's *A senhorita Simpson* (1989, Miss Simpson), Caio Fernando Abreu's *Morangos mofados* (1982, Moldy Strawberries) and *Triângulo das águas* (1983, Triangle of the Waters), Fonseca's *A grande arte* (1983; translated as *High Art,* 1986), and Raduan Nassar's *Um copo de cólera* (1978, A Cup of Anger) present these hybrid qualities.

Fonseca's work, which belongs to the genre of the police novel, has generally appealed to a large reading public. The language of his narrative, however, reveals elements of postmodernist literature in his use of metalanguage and a mixture of direct discourse and interior monologue. Nassar combines literary with cinematographic and theatrical devices. Established authors, such as Amado in his *O sumiço da santa* (1988; translated as *The War of the Saints,* 1995), combine modern prose techniques while maintaining a nationalistic and regionalistic flavor. Amado's novel mixes melodramatic elements with the exotic aspects of the Bahian Carnaval and folklore, producing a narrative that appeals to his large reading public.

Brazilian writers have often worked in journalism, which throughout the twentieth century provided a space for their literary talents in the form of the *crônica*. This genre, which is difficult to classify in terms of literature, has undergone many modifications throughout the second part of the twentieth century as newspapers have often made a point of hiring famous writers to contribute on a regular basis. Some of the more important names involved with the *crônica* include Drummond and Affonso Romano de Sant'Anna. Sant'Anna, in particular, has used the genre with artistic dexterity to inform a large public of important social and political issues. Writers' *crônicas* are often collected and published as books, which have been well received not only by the reading public but also by literary critics. Other important writers who have worked in the *crônica* genre include Luís Fernando Veríssimo, Arnaldo Jabor, and Marcelo Coelho.

Some Brazilian writers have gained an international audience through translations of their books. Amado's novels continue to appear in paperback editions in most of the major languages of the world. Paulo Coelho has become popular in the United States and Europe with his books that deal with magical worlds and supernatural happenings. Brazilian academics have criticized his works, claiming that they appeal to a vast public as easy reading rather than for their aesthetic qualities. Coelho, however, was elected to the Academia Brasileira de Letras. Children's literature, which has had a large market in Brazil with the works of writers such as Ana María Machado, Ruth Rocha, and Marina Colasanti, has also attracted international attention through the award-winning books of Lygia Bojunga.

Brazil has passed through several periods of social, economic, and political crisis, culminating in the military dictatorship that ruled the country from 1964 to 1985 and had an often negative impact on the arts and intellectual life. The government focused its attention on industrialization of the major urban centers in the 1960s. A large middle class emerged, and women stepped forward into positions of prominence at all levels of social and political life. Both the middle class and women in general struggled throughout the remainder of the century to maintain their newly found way of life. With access to new and better positions in the workplace and to education, women slowly began to occupy a larger place in the Brazilian literary canon.

Women writers have worked to overcome stereotypical images of the female in what has been a strongly patriarchal society. Traditionally depicted as either wife or prostitute, or as either angel or demon, women have searched for a female identity in relation to others. Ana Maria Miranda's works, such as *Desmundo* (1996) and *Amrik* (1997), exemplify this search.

The period of military dictatorship was marked by governmental censorship, which of necessity generated creative devices for the portrayal of forbidden themes, ranging from political protest to homosexuality. With the establishment of a democratic form of political rule, however, marginalized elements of society found new and more-open forms of expression. Technology and industrialization created in Brazil the same problems that have plagued most developing countries. Authors have questioned where the country is in terms of globalization, and they have explored the social and political directions that Brazil has taken. Such preoccupations are seen in João Ubaldo Ribeiro's *Viva o povo brasileiro* (1984, Long Live the Brazilian People; translated as *An Invincible Memory,* 1989) and in Márcio Souza's *Lealdade* (1997, Loyalty). As Brazil entered a democratic phase in 1985, some writers turned to the historical novel to reinterpret the history of the country. Urban life has been a central concern in contemporary fiction as writers perceive the city as a place of great social problems and inequities. Paulo Lins's *Cidade de Deus* (1997, City of God), for example, explores the criminal activities of the slums of Rio de Janeiro.

Publications in the first years of the twenty-first century have focused on the search for a national identity in the cultural multiplicity that characterizes contemporary Brazil. Works such as *Para entender o Brasil*

(2001, To Understand Brazil), edited by Marisa Sobral and Luiz Antonio Aguiar, attempt to accomplish this goal through interviews with writers and other intellectuals, who generally pose questions rather than offer answers when asked to describe and define Brazilian culture. Anthologies, such as *Os cem melhores contos brasileiros do século* (2000, The One Hundred Best Brazilian Short Stories of the Century), allow authors to speak on the issue of national identity through their artistic voices. Current literary activities reflect the general creative search that has characterized Brazilian literature since its beginnings in the colonial period. Although it is difficult to define Brazilian culture in precise terms, it is easy to recognize a culture unique to its South American geographical space and well differentiated from its European origins.

—*Monica P. Rector*

Acknowledgments

This book was produced by Bruccoli Clark Layman, Inc. R. Bland Lawson and C. Bryan Love were the in-house editors.

Production manager is Philip B. Dematteis.

Administrative support was provided by Carol A. Cheschi.

Accountant is Ann-Marie Holland.

Copyediting supervisor is Sally R. Evans. The copyediting staff includes Phyllis A. Avant, Caryl Brown, Melissa D. Hinton, Philip I. Jones, Rebecca Mayo, Nadirah Rahimah Shabazz, Joshua Shaw, and Nancy E. Smith.

Pipeline manager is James F. Tidd Jr.

Editorial associate is Jessica R. Goudeau.

In-house vetter is Catherine M. Polit.

Permissions editor is Amber L. Coker.

Layout and graphics supervisor is Janet E. Hill. The graphics staff includes Zoe R. Cook and Sydney E. Hammock.

Office manager is Kathy Lawler Merlette.

Photography editors are Mark J. McEwan and Walter W. Ross.

Digital photographic copy work was performed by Joseph M. Bruccoli.

Systems manager is Donald Kevin Starling.

Typesetting supervisor is Kathleen M. Flanagan. The typesetting staff includes Patricia Marie Flanagan and Pamela D. Norton.

Walter W. Ross is library researcher. He was assisted by the following librarians at the Thomas Cooper Library of the University of South Carolina: Elizabeth Suddeth and the rare-book department; Jo Cottingham, interlibrary loan department; circulation department head Tucker Taylor; reference department head Virginia W. Weathers; reference department staff Laurel Baker, Marilee Birchfield, Kate Boyd, Paul Cammarata, Joshua Garris, Gary Geer, Tom Marcil, Rose Marshall, and Sharon Verba; interlibrary loan department head Marna Hostetler; and interlibrary loan staff Bill Fetty, Nelson Rivera, and Cedric Rose.

Dictionary of Literary Biography® • Volume Three Hundred Seven

Brazilian Writers

Dictionary of Literary Biography

Adonias Filho
(Adonias Aguiar Filho)
(27 November 1915 – 2 August 1990)

Mark A. Lokensgard
St. Mary's University of San Antonio

See also the Adonias Filho entry in *DLB 145: Modern Latin-American Fiction Writers, Second Series.*

BOOKS: *Renascimento do homem* (Rio de Janeiro: Schmidt, 1937);

Tasso da Silveira e o tema da poesia eterna (São Paulo: Panorama, 1940);

Os servos da morte (Rio de Janeiro: J. Olympio, 1946);

Memórias de Lázaro (Rio de Janeiro: O. Cruzeiro, 1952); translated by Fred P. Ellison as *Memories of Lazarus* (Austin: University of Texas Press, 1969);

Jornal de um escritor (Rio de Janeiro: Ministério de Educação e Cultura, 1954);

Modernos ficcionistas brasileiros, volume 1 (Rio de Janeiro: O. Cruzeiro, 1958);

Cornélio Pena (Rio de Janeiro: AGIR, 1960);

Corpo vivo (Rio de Janeiro: Civilização Brasileira, 1962);

O bloqueio cultural: O intelectual, a liberdade, a receptividade (São Paulo: Martins, 1964);

O forte (Rio de Janeiro: Civilização Brasileira, 1965);

Modernos ficcionistas brasileiros, volume 2 (Rio de Janeiro: Tempo Brasileiro, 1965);

A nação grapiuna: Adonias Filho na Academia, by Adonias Filho and Jorge Amado (Rio de Janeiro: Tempo Brasileiro, 1965);

Léguas de promissão (Rio de Janeiro: Civilização Brasileira, 1968);

O romance brasileiro de trinta (Rio de Janeiro: Bloch, 1969);

Luanda, Beira, Bahia (Rio de Janeiro: Civilização Brasileira, 1971);

Volta Redonda: O processo brasileiro de mudança, by Adonias Filho and Octales Gonzalez (Rio de Janeiro: Image, 1972); translated by Richard J. Spock as *Volta Redonda: The Brazilian Process of Change* (Rio de Janeiro: Image, 1972);

Uma nota de cem (Rio de Janeiro: Ouro, 1973);

As velhas (Rio de Janeiro: Civilização Brasileira, 1975);

Sul da Bahia, chão de cacau: Uma civilização regional (Rio de Janeiro: Civilização Brasileira, 1976);

Fora da pista (Rio de Janeiro: Civilização Brasileira, 1978);

O largo da palma (Rio de Janeiro: Civilização Brasileira, 1981);

Auto de Ilhéus (Rio de Janeiro: Civilização Brasileira, 1981);

Noite sem madrugada (São Paulo: Difusão, 1983);

O homem de branco (Rio de Janeiro: Bertrand Brasil, 1987).

Edition: *Os servos da morte,* third edition, with essay by Afrânio Coutinho (Rio de Janeiro: Ouro, 1967).

OTHER: Cornélio Pena, *Os romances completos de Cornélio Pena,* introduction by Adonias Filho (Rio de Janeiro: Aguilar, 1958);

"Catete: Amor no Catete," in *A cidade e as ruas: Novelas cariocas* (Rio de Janeiro: Lidador, 1964);

"O nosso Bispo," in *O assunto é padre* (Rio de Janeiro: AGIR, 1968);

"A ficção de Guimarães Rosa," in *Guimarães Rosa: Estudos* (Lisbon: Instituto Luso-Brasileiro, 1969).

SELECTED PERIODICAL PUBLICATION–
UNCOLLECTED: "Experiência de um romancista," *Minas Gerais Suplemento Literário,* 9 (9 February 1974): 2–3.

Adonias Filho speaking to the Academia Brasileira de Letras, 29 April 1966 (frontispiece for Os servos da morte,
1967; Thomas Cooper Library, University of South Carolina)

The importance of the Northeast in Brazilian literature, particularly the state of Bahia, is reflected in the works of Adonias Filho, who approaches his subject in a manner considerably different from his more famous contemporary Jorge Amado. While Amado's novels are colorful and generally present the poor in a sympathetic and optimistic manner, Adonias Filho's fiction tends toward a somber and pessimistic portrayal of life in northeastern Brazil. His prose conveys an oppressive, almost suffocating feeling as he represents the consequences of his home state's cacao-growing economy, authoritarian-style politics, and harsh poverty.

Adonias Aguiar Filho was born on 27 November 1915 on the São João *fazenda* (plantation) in the town of Itajuípe, Bahia. His parents, Raquel Bastos de Aguiar and Adonias Aguiar, owned a cacao plantation, and Adonias Filho's childhood exposure to this industry had a marked influence on his work. After primary schooling, Adonias Filho, like many of his wealthy contemporaries, was sent to study in the capital city of Salvador. He enrolled in the Ginásio Ipiranga (Ipiranga Secondary School), studying there at the same time as Amado. At fourteen, he interrupted his studies and

returned to the *fazenda,* taking up the reading of Romantic authors such as Camilo Castelo Branco, Joaquim Manuel de Macedo, and José de Alencar. A year later he returned to school, completing his studies in 1934. He published *crônicas* (chronicles), stories, and articles in the school newspaper, and after graduation he began to publish in the *Diário de Notícias* (News Daily) and in *O Imparcial* (The Impartial) a newspaper in Bahia.

While Adonias Filho published pieces in periodicals such as the *Jornal do Comércio* (Journal of Commerce), the *Estado de São Paulo* (State of São Paulo) and the *Folha da Manhã* (Morning Paper), he also worked on translations of works by George Sand, Robert de Traz, and Jacob Wasserman; he translated the last of these authors in collaboration with Octávio de Faria. His first long work of fiction, apparently completed in the early 1940s, was the novel "Cachaça" (Sugar Cane Rum), which he destroyed before showing it to anyone. In 1942 Adonias Filho earned a bachelor of law degree from the Faculdade de Direito do Distrito Federal (Federal Law School), and two years later he married Rosita Galiano, with whom he had two children, Rachel and Adonias. He founded the short-lived publishing house

Editora Ocidente in 1944, and from 1946 to 1950 he directed the Editora A Noite.

Adonias Filho published his first novel, *Os servos da morte* (The Servants of Death), in 1946. The work is the first of three that deal with the cacao subregion of the Northeast. The author uses his childhood experiences as the basis for creating a tragic sense of life that pervades this and several other novels. The setting of *Os servos da morte* is the Fazenda Baluarte (Plantation Fortress/Bastion). It is a place permeated by rage and bitter revenge. The protagonist, Paulino Duarte, almost more animal than human, lives there with his wife, Elisa, and four children. To punish the brutal Paulino for her unhappy life, Elisa has a child by another man, Angelo. Angelo torments Paulino until Paulino's last days, and then he finally goes insane, leading him to cause the murder of his sister-in-law's daughter. The girl's mother, Claudia, is similarly caught in the cycle of inextinguishable hate. The atmosphere is not unlike that of a Greek tragedy, with the elements of the landscape—wind, plants, and earth—almost taking the role of accomplices. Critic Francisco de Assis Brasil has noted that *Os servos da morte* and Adonias Filho's other two cacao novels, *Memórias de Lázaro* (1952; translated as *Memories of Lazarus*, 1969) and *Corpo vivo* (1962, Living Body), document the conquest of a brutal land. All of these novels feature a crude, harsh world inhabited by primitive characters.

Djalma Viana was the pseudonym Adonias Filho used when writing for *Letras e Artes* (Letters and Art), a literary supplement to the newspaper *A Manhã* (The Morning), from 1943 to 1954. The literary criticism he wrote under this name is often polemical in nature. Djalma Viana makes no effort to be impartial, defending his preferences for writers such as Carlos Drummond de Andrade, Graciliano Ramos, Raquel de Queiroz, Eugênio Gomes, and his alter ego, Adonias Filho. At the same time he criticizes other important writers: Amado, Antônio Cândido, Fernando Sabino, and Otto Lara Resende.

In 1950 Adonias Filho made an unsuccessful run for a federal congressional seat in his home state of Bahia. He then moved to Rio de Janeiro, where he wrote literary criticism for the *Jornal de Letras* (Journal of Letters), which was under the direction of the Condé brothers. In 1952 Adonias Filho published his second novel situated in the cacao region of Bahia, *Memórias de Lázaro*. The setting for this novel, the Vale do Ouro (the Valley of Gold), is similar to the Fazenda Baluarte of *Os servos da morte* in that both are sealed spaces that draw the characters into lives of darkness and violence. The narrator of *Memórias de Lázaro*, Alexandre, is the son of Abílio, who is originally from Ilhéus, and Paula, a demented woman who died during childbirth. Alexan-

dre is literally raised in a cave by Jerônimo, a mentor who represents the brutal mind-set of the people in the Vale do Ouro. Alexandre continually thinks about life away from the valley and even begins walking the road that brought his father from Ilhéus, but he is inexplicably drawn back to his primitive birthplace.

In 1953 Adonias Filho wrote a play, "A hora certa" (The Right Time), which, like his first novel, he destroyed. In 1954 he published fragments of his critical journal in *Jornal de um escritor* (Diary of a Writer). He also began dedicating himself to Brazil's cultural institutions, serving as director of the Serviço Nacional do Teatro (National Theater Service) from 1954 to 1956, with a small interruption to direct the Instituto Nacional do Livro (National Book Institute).

In 1958 Adonias Filho published his literary criticism in an organized manner with the first volume of *Modernos ficcionistas brasileiros* (Modern Brazilian Fiction Writers). He continued writing criticism for the *Jornal de Letras* and the literary section of the magazine *O Cruzeiro*, and he also contributed to the Portuguese newspaper *O Diário Popular* (The Popular Journal). His eponymous book about writer Cornélio Pena was published in 1960 as part of the didactic series Nossos Clássicos.

As part of his continued dedication to Brazilian cultural institutions, Adonias Filho served as the director of the Biblioteca Nacional (National Library) from 1961 to 1964, and he continued to serve at the library in various administrative capacities until 1971. He published *Corpo vivo* in 1962. This novel completes the cacao trilogy, and like the preceding two volumes, it takes place in an isolated environment, this time Camacã. The protagonist, Cajango, sees his family wiped out by armed bandits as a child and is raised by his Brazilian Indian uncle, Inuri. Inuri instills a sense of revenge in Cajango, who grows up preparing to avenge his family's death. However, Cajango finds love with Malva, who awakens his more human instincts and allows him to leave the cycle of violence, thus ending the cacao trilogy on an optimistic and romantic note.

Adonias Filho published his fourth novel, *O forte* (The Fort), in 1965. Although situated in the state of Bahia, the novel differs from the cacao trilogy in that its main characters come to greater levels of consciousness rather than being drawn into cycles of violence. Fort São Pedro in Salvador looms large in the imagination of the protagonist, Jairo, who as an adolescent heard stories about its past from Olegário, the Afro-Brazilian grandfather of the woman who becomes his lover, Tibiti. Olegário's stories about the fort interweave aspects of Brazilian history from the conquest of the Indians to the Dutch invasion to the battles of the "War of Canudos." The stories also serve as a kind of racial

ADONIAS FILHO

JORNAL DE UM ESCRITOR

SERVIÇO DE DOCUMENTAÇÃO

MINISTÉRIO DA EDUCAÇÃO E CULTURA

OS CADERNOS DE CULTURA

*Title page for Adonias Filho's 1954 book including fragments
of his critical journal (Biblioteca Nacional de Chile)*

memory for their narrator. Meanwhile, Olegário's beautiful and musically talented granddaughter suspects that her paternal heritage is an explosive family secret, and she eventually discovers the truth: her father was a Frenchman, a musician who gave her whiter skin than the rest of her family as well as her talent for music. Furthermore, she learns that her father died at her grandfather's hands during a fight. Olegário prophesies that Tibiti and Jairo must see each other again. The prophecy comes true years later, when Jairo, an engineer with a career in building roads throughout Brazil, returns to his hometown assigned to demolish the fort. Both Jairo and Tibiti are married to other people and have children, but they nevertheless pledge their love to each other.

The second volume of *Modernos ficcionistas brasileiros* also appeared in 1965. On 28 April 1965 Adonias Filho's friend Amado officially received him for his induction into the Academia Brasileira de Letras (Brazilian Academy of Letters), their literary differences proving no obstacle to their long friendship. In 1967 Adonias Filho traveled to Mozambique and Angola at the invitation of the Portuguese government for the

Second Congress of the Portuguese-Speaking Countries.

Adonias Filho's first collection of novellas, *Léguas da promissão* (The Promised Leagues), was published in 1968. This book won several prizes, including awards from the PEN-Clube do Brasil and the Instituto Nacional do Livro. The stories poeticize the relationship between Bahia and its people. For example, in "O túmulo das aves" (The Birds' Tomb) an old man sees the meaning of death in the flight of birds over a river and resolves to bequeath his land to a Gypsy-like black man and an outlaw. In "O pai" (Father) the patriarch of a rural family is buried in the corral by his three children in a ceremony attended by the ranch's dogs and sheep; they imagine that from his grave he will hear the horses leap and continue giving life to the ranch.

In 1969 Adonias Filho published a volume of criticism, *O romance brasileiro de trinta* (The Brazilian Novel of the 1930s). In 1971 he published his novel *Luanda, Beira, Bahia* (Luanda, Bank, Bahia). In this book the author used his trips to Africa for inspiration and linked his home state with the former Portuguese colonies on the continent, telling the stories of people in Brazil, Mozambique, and Angola who all live in cities called Salvador and Ilhéus.

From 1972 to 1974 Adonias Filho served as the president of the Associação Brasileira de Imprensa (Brazilian Association of the Press). His next novel, *As velhas* (1975, The Old Women), won him a second prize from the Instituto Nacional do Livro. This novel focuses on four old *baianas* (Bahians) who appear fragile but who have a kind of primitive, telluric strength. One of the four, the Pataxó Indian Tari Januária, vows to recover the bones of her deceased husband, Pedro Cobra; this vow leads to a journey through the Bahian jungle to complete the mission. Throughout the novel, narratives that tie the living to the land and to the deceased recur. For example, another old woman, the black, tall, and proud Zonga, describes seeing her mother promising her father's corpse that their daughter will want for nothing. Adonias Filho's characters continue a tradition with their shared relationships to the land based on stories and promises.

Adonias Filho published an essay in book form in 1976 with *Sul da Bahia, chão de cacau: Uma civilização regional* (South of Bahia, Cacao Ground: A Regional Civilization). In this work the author treats the land that he has dealt with so many times in his fiction. He further reveals why the region came to dominate his imagination, noting that the cultivation of cacao was a sort of war against nature, the violence of which extended to the people involved in it. He also makes clear that the cacao trilogy takes place between the second and third cacao economic cycles, between pioneers creating new plantations and a consolidation of the crop's importance.

In 1978 Adonias Filho published his first work of children's literature, *Fora da pista* (Off the Road). This work was followed in 1981 by a collection of novellas titled *O largo da palma* (Palmtree Plaza, or A Palm's Width). These novellas represent a break in Adonias Filho's fiction, as the six stories are centered around a public plaza in the capital city of Salvador, contrasting with his usual focus on rural life in Bahia. (Although *O forte* also takes place in Salvador, its references to the past give it a more rural and primitive atmosphere.) The characters struggle with poverty and unhappiness, and their plights are treated with dramatic lyricism and dark humor. Adonias Filho also published for the first time a dramatic work, *Auto de Ilhéus* (Morality Play from Ilhéus), in 1981.

Adonias Filho published his last novel, *Noite sem madrugada* (Dawnless Night), in 1983. This work, a detective story set in Rio de Janeiro, revealed a willingness to experiment with new settings and genres. The book is not, however, a classic mystery or crime novel. The protagonists are a couple falsely accused of a crime, not through any kind of sinister conspiracy, but rather through error, blindness, and political expediency. Thus, the author moves beyond plot intricacies to create a psychological drama through which he makes pointed criticisms of society.

Adonias Filho spent the last years of his life in the town of his birth, Itajuípe, Bahia, on his ranch, the Fazenda Aliança (Alliance Plantation). There he suffered a sudden, fatal stroke on 2 August 1990. Two days later his body was laid to rest in the Mausoleum of the Brazilian Academy of Letters in Rio de Janeiro.

Literary critics have noted that Adonias Filho continued a tradition of fiction shaped by religious themes, a tradition that includes Lúcio Cardoso, Jorge de Lima, and Pena. The prevailing features of this type of religiously influenced fiction, sometimes compared by critics to the works of American novelist William Faulkner, include the use of monologue and an emphasis on the power of forces beyond characters' control, such as grace or destiny.

Adonias Filho's style, which incorporates techniques from the vanguard movements of early-twentieth-century Europe, is different from the more conventional realism of the northeastern Brazilian novelists of the 1930s. In fact, his work has been called "neo-regionalist" by a number of critics in efforts to distinguish it from earlier regionalist literature. The critic Assis Brasil, however, is of the opinion that the term "magic realism" is more apt, emphasizing the author's creation of a fictional world that is more connected to

Cover for Adonias Filho's award-winning first collection of novellas portraying the relationship between Bahia and its people (Joint University Libraries, Nashville, Tennessee)

primal and primitive emotions than to clear geographical or historical contexts.

Some disagreement has also resulted from efforts to situate Adonias Filho in Brazilian literary history. Many critics see Adonias Filho as part of the post-1945 third phase of Brazilian modernism, a period in which many authors attempted to reduce the emphasis on linguistic and cultural differences among regions in order to create a more universal literature. Assis Brasil, however, places him within a phase of "new Brazilian literature" that began in 1956, the year of such events as the emergence of concrete poetry and the debuts of important prose works by Samuel Rawet, Geraldo Ferraz, and João Guimarães Rosa. Either way, Adonias Filho's rhythmic, compelling prose narratives exploring and defining essential aspects of Brazilian culture secured for him an important place among Brazil's best novelists.

Interview:

Edla Van Steen, "Adonias Filho," in *Viver e escrever* (São Paulo: L & PM, 1981), pp. 241–248.

References:

M. Fátima Albuquerque, "The Brazilian Nationalist Myth in Adonias Filho's *Corpo vivo*," *Portuguese Studies*, 3 (1987): 149–158;

Francisco de Assis Brasil, *Adonias Filho: ensaio* (Rio de Janeiro: Organizações Simões, 1969);

Alfredo Bosi, *História concisa da literatura brasileira*, third edition (São Paulo: Cultrix, 1997);

Sílvio Castro, "A moderna prosa de ficção: Adonias Filho," in his *A revolução da palavra* (Petrópolis, Brazil: Vozes, 1976), pp. 252–263;

Castro, "Literatura e ideologia em Adonias Filho," *Rassegna Iberistica*, 40 (1991): 15–32;

Susan Hill Connor, "From Anti-Hero to Hero: The Rebirth Archetype," *Luso-Brazilian Review*, 16 (Winter 1979): 224–232;

Thomas Deveny, "Narrative Techniques in Adonias Filho's *Memórias de Lázaro*," in *From Linguistics to Literature: Romance Studies Offered to Francis M. Rogers*, edited by Bernard H. Bichakjian (Amsterdam: Benjamins, 1981), pp. 321–327;

Elsa Dias dos Santos, "Adonias Filho: a Trilogia do Cacau," *Letras de hoje: estudos e debates de lingüística, literatura e língua Portuguesa*, 34 (1999): 101–110;

Fred P. Ellison, "The Schizophrenic Narrator and the Myth of Renewal in *Memórias de Lázaro*," in *From Linguistics to Literature: Romance Studies Offered to Francis M. Rogers*, edited by Bernard H. Bichakjian (Amsterdam: Benjamins, 1981), pp. 155–166;

Maria do Carmo Lanna Figueiredo, "A construção da tenda ficcional em *Léguas de promissão* de Adonias Filho," *Cadernos de Lingüística e Teoria da Literatura*, 7 (1985): 133–148;

Figueiredo, "Percorrendo as *Léguas de promissão*," *Luso-Brazilian Review*, 22 (Summer 1985): 33–49;

Cyro de Mattos, "O Chão de Cacau: Adonias Filho," *Minas Gerais Suplemento Literário*, 24 (1991): 6–7;

Raimundo de Menezes, *Dicionário literário brasileiro*, second edition (Rio de Janeiro: Livros Técnicos e Científicos, 1978);

José Rodrigues de Paiva, "Níveis de Consciência no Romance: uma Leitura de *O forte* de Adonias Filho," *Cadernos de Literatura*, 16 (1983): 51–58;

Maria da Conceição Paranhos, *Adonias Filho: representação épica da forma dramática* (Salvador: Fundação Casa de Jorge Amado, 1989);

Daphne Patai, "Adonias Filho: The Myth of Malevolence," in her *Myth and Ideology in Contemporary Brazilian Fiction* (Rutherford, N.J.: Fairleigh Dickinson University Press, 1983), pp. 167–190;

Adeítalo Manoel Pinho, "Adonias Filho e Djalma Viana, uma crítica de duas faces," *Letras de hoje: estudos e debates de lingüística, literatura e língua Portuguesa*, 37 (2001): 9–16;

Manuel Simões, "Introdução à narrativa de Adonias Filho," *Studi di Letteratura Ispano-americana*, 11 (1981): 73–89.

José de Alencar
(1 May 1829 – 12 December 1877)

Eduardo F. Coutinho
Universidade Federal do Rio de Janeiro

BOOKS: *O Marquês do Paraná: traços biográficos* (Rio de Janeiro, 1856);

Cinco minutos (Rio de Janeiro, 1857);

O guarany (Rio de Janeiro: Garnier, 1857);

O demônio familiar (Rio de Janeiro: Garnier, 1857);

A noite de S. João (Rio de Janeiro, 1857);

O Rio de Janeiro: verso e reverso (Rio de Janeiro: Empreza Nacional do Diario, 1857);

Cinco minutos; A viuvinha (São Paulo: Melhoramentos, 1858);

As azas de um anjo: comédia em um prólogo, quatros actos e um epílogo (Rio de Janeiro: Soares & Irmão, 1860);

Carta aos eleitores da província do Ceará (Rio de Janciro, 1860);

As minas de prata, 6 volumes (Rio de Janeiro, 1862–1866);

Lucíola: um perfil de mulher (Rio de Janeiro & Paris: Garnier, 1862);

Mãi: drama em quatro actos (Rio de Janeiro, 1862);

Diva: perfil de mulher (Rio dc Janeiro & Paris: Garnier, 1864);

Ao imperador: cartas políticas de Erasmo (Rio de Janeiro, 1865);

Iracema: lenda do Ceará (Rio de Janeiro: Vianna, 1865); translated by Isabel Burton as *Iraçéma, the Honey Lips: A Legend of Brazil* (London: Bickers, 1886);

Ao imperador: novas cartas políticas de Erasmo ([Rio de Janeiro], 1866);

Ao povo: cartas políticas de Erasmo (Rio de Janeiro: Pinheiro, 1866);

Ao Visconte de Itaborahy (Rio de Janeiro: Pinheiro, 1866);

Páginas de atualidade: os partidos (Rio de Janeiro, 1866);

A côrte do leão (Rio de Janeiro: Pinheiro, 1867);

A expiação (Rio de Janeiro, 1867);

O Marquês de Caxias: biografia (Rio de Janeiro: J. Villeneuve, 1867);

Uma these constitucional; a Princeza Imperial e o Príncipe Consorte no Conselo de Estado (Rio de Janeiro, 1867);

O systema representativo (Rio de Janeiro: Garnier, 1868);

Questão de habeas-corpus (Rio de Janeiro: Perseverança, 1868);

José de Alencar (frontispiece for Discursos parlamentares, *1977; Thomas Cooper Library, University of South Carolina)*

Discussão do voto de graças: discurso proferido na sessão de 9 de agosto de 1869 (Rio de Janeiro: Santos Cardoso, 1869);

O gaúcho, 2 volumes (Rio de Janeiro: Garnier, 1870);

A pata da gazela: romance brasileiro (Rio de Janeiro: Garnier, 1870);

A viagem imperial: Câmara dos Deputados, sessão de 9 de maio de 1871 (Rio de Janeiro: J. Villeneuve, 1871);

Discursos proferidos na sessão de 1871 na Câmara dos deputados (Rio de Janeiro: Perseverança, 1871);

O tronco do ipê, 2 volumes (Rio de Janeiro: Garnier, 1871);

Til, 4 volumes (Rio de Janeiro: Garnier, 1872);

Sonhos d'ouro, 2 volumes (Rio de Janeiro: Garnier, 1872);

Alfarrábios: crônicas dos tempos coloniais, 2 volumes (Rio de Janeiro: Garnier, 1873)—comprises volume 1, *O Garatuja;* and volume 2, *O ermitão da Glória; A alma do Lázaro;*

A guerra dos mascates: chronica dos tempos coloniaes, 2 volumes (Rio de Janeiro: Garnier, 1873, 1874);

Voto de graças: discurso que devia proferier na sessão de 20 de maio (Rio de Janeiro: Pinheiro, 1873);

Ubirajara: lenda tupi (Rio de Janeiro & Paris: Garnier, 1874); translated by J. T. W. Sadler as *Ubirajara, a Legend of the Tupy Indians* (London: Massey, n.d.; São Paulo: Seccao de Obras, 1922);

O jesuíta: drama em quatros actos (Rio de Janeiro: Garnier, 1875); translated by Edgardo R. de Britto as *The Jesuit, Poet Lore,* 30, no. 4 (1919): 475–547;

Senhóra, 2 volumes (Rio de Janeiro: Garnier, 1875); translated by Catarina Feldmann Edinger as *Senhora: Profile of a Woman* (Austin: University of Texas Press, 1994);

O sertanejo, 2 volumes (Rio de Janeiro: Garnier, 1875);

A propriedade (Rio de Janeiro: Garnier, 1883);

Esboços juridicos (Rio de Janeiro: Garnier, 1883);

Como e porque sou romancista (Rio de Janeiro: G. Leuzinger, 1893);

Encarnação: romance (Rio de Janeiro: G. Leuzinger, 1893);

O que tinha de ser: narrativa (Rio de Janeiro: F. Briguiet, 1912);

Teatro completo, 2 volumes (Rio de Janeiro: Ministério da Educação e Cultura, Fundação Nacional de Arte, Serviço Nacional de Teatro, Departamento de Documentação e Divulgação, 1977)—includes two previously unpublished plays: *O crédito* and *O que é o casamento?*

Editions and Collections: *Cartas sobre "A Confederação dos Tamoios"* (Rio de Janeiro: Empreza Typographica Nacional do Diario, 1856);

Diatribe contra timonice do Jornal de Timon Maranhense acerca da "História geral do Brasil" do Senhor Varnhagen (Lisbon, 1859);

Ao correr da pena (São Paulo, 1874);

Obras de ficção, 16 volumes, with prologues, biographical studies, and criticism by various authors, illustrated by Tomás Santa Rosa (Rio de Janeiro: J. Olympio, 1951);

Obra completa, 4 volumes, general introduction by M. Cavalcanti Proenca, edited by Tristão de Alencar Araripe Júnior and others (Rio de Janeiro: J. Aguilar, 1958–1960);

Pareceres de José de Alencar, introduction by Fran Martins, edited by Martins and Luis Cruz de Vasconcelos,

Publicações do Arquivo Nacional, volume 47 (Rio de Janeiro, 1960);

A polêmica Alencar-Nabuco, edited by Afrânio Coutinho (Rio de Janeiro: Edições Tempo Brasileiro, 1965);

Discursos parlamentares (Brasília: Câmara dos Deputados, 1977).

The author of novels, poetry, plays, criticism, and journalism, José de Alencar is one of Brazil's most outstanding and productive writers. Alencar garnered popular and critical attention for his novels, and he is considered by many critics to be the father of the Brazilian novel, but his role in Brazilian literary history is even larger than that. Living in a period in which Brazilian literature was seeking a national identity after more than three centuries of Portuguese colonization, Alencar developed in his works a taste for Brazilian themes and motives and devoted himself so fully to the representation of his country's life that critics often call him the patriarch of Brazilian literature. Alencar produced his works under the aegis of Romanticism, but his Romantic spirit is marked by a nationalistic and patriotic vein best expressed in the exaltation of local color, of which the Indianist current is the best example.

José Martiniano de Alencar was born in Mecejana, Ceará, on 1 May 1829. His father was a senator of the Brazilian empire, and his family, of great wealth, had a long political tradition in Ceará, having been involved in several revolutions (his grandmother, Bárbara Pereira de Alencar, had even been a heroine in the 1817 Pernambuccan Revolution, in which outlying areas revolted against the centralization of power at Rio de Janiero). Alencar's childhood in Ceará was marked by scenes of life in the backlands that he later represented in several of his novels. At the age of nine, Alencar crossed the backlands from Ceará to Bahia, a trip he would never forget and that often recurred in his works.

From 1840 to 1843 Alencar went to school in Rio de Janeiro, where he developed his interest in the humanities. During this time he had opportunities to witness the political meetings his father held at home, which he later described in his *Como e porque sou romancista* (How and Why I Am a Novelist, 1893). In 1846 he moved to São Paulo to study law, but his true interests were in the study of literature, rhetoric, philosophy, and history. Alencar devoted much time to the reading of literary masterpieces and became a great admirer of figures such as Honoré de Balzac, François-René de Chateaubriand, Victor Hugo, Alexandre Dumas *père,* and George Gordon, Lord Byron. At that time the Romantic movement had reached Brazil, and a strong concern was raised in intellectual circles about the existence of a Brazilian literature. Brazilian Romanticism began with the publication of *Suspiros poéticos e saudades* (1836, Poetic Sighs and Longings) by Domingos Gonçalves de Magalhães, who also founded the review *Niterói: Revista Brasiliense* (Niterói: A Brazilian Review) in Paris in 1836. Eight years later the Brazilian novel was established with the publication of Joaquim Manuel de Macedo's *A moreninha* (The Little Brunette), which Alencar, a student in the São Paulo Law School when the book appeared, immediately recognized as the Brazilian model for the genre. A few years later Antônio Gonçalves Dias, the great Romantic poet of Brazilian Indianism, made his debut.

These distinctive works marked the emergence of a nationalist and patriotic ideology, rooted in the independence period (circa 1822), and sharpened and restated by Brazil's first Romantic writers. This ideology, which was fundamental to Alencar's intellectual and artistic development, began to have an impact on him early in his life as he gathered information about the Brazilian oral tradition and landscape and applied himself to the study of the colonial past. In 1848 Alencar went to Recife to complete his degree in law, but he wound up graduating in 1850 from the law school in São Paulo. The year after graduation he moved back to Rio de Janeiro and devoted himself to journalism and literature. As a journalist for the *Correio Mercantil* (Mercantile Post) and later for the *Diário do Rio de Janeiro* (Rio de Janeiro Daily News), he enriched his view of court life and analyzed Brazilian social and political problems. At this time he began using the pseudonym "Erasmus" in order to protect himself from the powerful targets of his criticism.

Alencar's experience writing for newspapers opened the path for his career as a novelist. Alencar began publishing newspaper chronicles in 1854, when he replaced Franciso Otaviano at the *Correio Mercantil,* and he also published chronicles in the *Diário do Rio de Janeiro.* His weekly chronicles from 1854 and 1855 were eventually gathered into a book titled *Ao correr da pena* (1874, Writing at Random). Alencar wrote his weekly chronicles and the novels he published in the *Diário do Rio de Janeiro* at the same time, and he used his readers' feedback to help him in the elaboration of his fiction. In his weekly commentaries Alencar transformed prosaic everyday episodes into poetic stories. By using different literary devices, he abandoned the typical journalistic tone, giving his writing a special touch that delighted his readers. Although he was poetic and idealistic in his chronicles, he was also often cunning and sarcastic, and these qualities caused the loss of his job at the newspaper. After one of his chronicles was censored because it criticized one of the newspaper's patrons, he wrote a letter of resignation, cited

by Afrânio Coutinho in "Ensaio e crônica" (1971), in which he said: "I always thought that the weekly review of a newspaper was independent and did not have to be sympathetic with its major political line, especially when the writer assumes the responsibility of his articles by signing them." Alencar became a congressman representing Ceará in 1861 and was eventually recommended as a senator, but his criticism of Brazilian politics, especially those later collected in *Ao imperador: cartas políticas de Erasmo* (1865, Political Letters of Erasmus) and *Ao imperador: novas cartas políticas de Erasmo* (1866, New Political Letters of Erasmus), irritated the emperor, who decided to put an end to Alencar's political career. During this period, in 1864, Alencar married Georgiana Cochrane, a daughter of physician Thomás Cochrane.

Alencar's work in the literary world began with the publication of his *Cartas sobre "A Confederação dos Tamoios"* (Letters on "The Confederation of the Tamoios") in 1856, which launched one of the most famous debates in Brazilian Romanticism. These letters, written in reference to Gonçalves de Magalhães's Indianist poem "A Confederação dos Tamoios" (1856), were not only a criticism of Magalhães's poem because Alencar considered the epic genre to be outdated and inadequate for representing the vitality and political eagerness of a nascent Brazilian literature, but also a reappraisal of Indianism, an ideology stemming from nationalism that would later constitute the basis for several of Alencar's novels. In the letters Alencar raises the figure of the Indian as a nationalistic symbol because the Indian was the native inhabitant of the country.

Alencar's greatest successes were novels. He focused on this genre because of the possibilities he believed it offered and because of the success it was attaining in Europe and even in Brazil, where Macedo's *A moreninha* had been widely appreciated. Alencar wrote a preface for his *Sonhos d'ouro* (1872, Golden Dreams) in which he divided what he called "the organic period of Brazilian literature" into three phases and categorized the works he had published to that point according to these phases. The first phase is the primitive or "aboriginal" phase, composed of myths and legends from the wilderness, which corresponded to the infancy of the Brazilian people. He placed his novel *Iracema: lenda do Ceará* (1865; translated as *Iraçéma, the Honey Lips: A Legend of Brazil,* 1886) into this phase. The second period, represented by the contact of the Europeans with the American land, covered the three centuries of colonization and ended with political independence in 1822. It included the novels *O guarany* (1857) and *As minas de prata* (1862–1866, The Silver Mines), which are set in that time. The third period corresponded to Alencar's lifetime. In the works of this phase, Alencar intended to portray Brazilian life with special emphasis on the features and qualities that characterized it in opposition to European life. His books belonging to this phase are divided into two groups: those that portray Brazilian customs and traditions, *O gaúcho* (1870), *O tronco do ipê* (1871), *Til* (1872), and *O sertanejo* (1875), and those that deal with the conflict between national spirit and foreign influence, *Lucíola: perfil de mulher* (1862, Lucíola: Profile of a Woman), *Diva: perfil de mulher* (1864, Diva: Profile of a Woman), *A pata da gazela* (1870, The Gazelle's Hoof), *Sonhos d'ouro,* and *Senhóra* (1875; translated as *Senhora: Profile of a Woman,* 1994).

Although Alencar's categories have been contested by several critics, they express his effort to produce a body of work that offers a panorama of Brazilian life from its beginnings to his own time. Alencar's classification was so firmly rooted in the development of Brazilian history that it served as a point of departure for later classifications made by writers such as Machado de Assis and Mário de Andrade. Thus, while later critics have proposed different classifications, they typically pay tribute to Alencar's efforts. Among these critics is Heron de Alencar, who, in an essay in *A literatura no Brasil* (1968, Literature in Brazil), divides Alencar's works into three groups: historical novels, urban novels, and regionalist novels. Although it may seem strange that Heron de Alencar includes the Indianist novels within his grouping of historical novels, he justifies this move by pointing out Alencar's intention of representing Brazil before the arrival of Europeans through the figure of the Indian.

The Indian novels that, according to Heron de Alencar, compose a subgroup of the historical novels are *O guarany, Iracema,* and *Ubirajara: lenda tupi* (1874; translated as *Ubirajara, a Legend of the Tupy Indians,* n.d/ 1922); they are some of Alencar's most significant and well-known works. The Indians, those who inhabited the Brazilian land when the Portuguese arrived, have a long tradition in Brazilian literature, a fact that contrasts with the secondary role usually attributed to them by both the colonial and postcolonial periods. The Indian is present from the first manifestations of Brazilian literature to the present time, appearing in every genre, frequently as protagonist. The Indian's importance, however, was particularly pronounced during the time of Romanticism, when the abundant use of the Indian gave birth to the trend called Indianism that had as its main authors Gonçalves Dias in poetry and Alencar in prose fiction. The *bon sauvage* (noble savage) was a symbol of the purity of American nature as opposed to the devastating ambition and lack of scruples of the European conqueror. Although the Indianist movement had its roots in the works of Chateaubriand, an author who was admired by and exerted a strong influence on Alencar,

it found a special profile in Brazil, particularly through Alencar's fiction, where the escapism typical of this type of literature was replaced by a nationalistic yearning. The idealization of the Indian, which in Chateaubriand's works had been associated with the opposition between "natural" and "civilized" man, gained new meaning in Alencar's works: the Indian was not only the native element, but also the inhabitant of the land at the time of discovery, and therefore the only ethnic group capable of representing the nation's past, a past that had to be exalted to oppose European colonization. With the fusion of the nativist and the historical, the Indian was transformed into a nationalistic symbol, the embodiment of Brazilian identity in opposition to the Portuguese and the African. Moved by a strong will to define a national literature different from that of Portugal, Alencar took the idealization of the Indian to extremes, creating figures that hold a place of honor in the gallery of major Brazilian literary characters, conferring upon them an unprecedented stature. Yet, in spite of the interest he expressed for the Indian's culture, the figure of the Indian present in Alencar's works is mainly an European construction, conceived in the manner of Chateaubriand: the Indians' physical traits are supposedly realistic, extracted from the reports of settlers and historians, but their values are those of medieval knights, anachronistic and alien to their context. This paradox in Alencar's fiction confers upon the Indian great dynamism and vivacity: he is, on the one hand, exalted as never before in Brazilian literature for being a symbol of the American continent as opposed to the European, but, on the other hand, he is almost entirely conceived with the values of the culture against which he is set in contrast.

The first of the Indianist novels, *O guarany,* was published in 1857 in feuilleton in *Diário do Rio de Janeiro* and in the same year as a book. It immediately met with success. The chapters that came out in feuilleton were read avidly every day, and the book version quickly sold out. By this time Alencar had already published the novel *Cinco minutos* (1857, Five Minutes) and part of *A viuvinha* (1858, The Little Widow) in the *Diário do Rio de Janeiro,* but the difference between his new novel and the two previous ones was significant. Although the former were well-constructed works, *O guarany* was a mature novel that revealed the author's skill in narrative technique. What mostly caught the public's attention, however, was the plot of the novel—a love story, set in the seventeenth century, between a settler's daughter, Cecília, and an Indian man, Peri, who saves her life more than once. Fascinated by Cecília's beauty, so different from that of the women he is accustomed to seeing, Peri falls madly in love with her and dedicates himself entirely to serving and worshiping her. As time goes by, the seemingly insurmountable barriers that separate them are gradually overcome. Going through a series of adventures in the typical Romantic fashion, Peri little by little gains the confidence of Cecília's family. At the end of the novel Peri is urged by Cecília's father to take her to town in order to keep her away from the fight taking place between the settlers and the Aimoré Indians, enemies of Peri's tribe. The final scene of the novel is a metaphor of the union of the settlers and the new land: caught by a tremendous flood, Cecília and Peri, the latter already baptized, climb to the top of a palm tree, where, though unwilling to admit it, they recognize their mutual love.

Published eight years later, but preceded by several other novels of a different sort, Alencar's second Indian novel, *Iracema,* is a highly poetic type of narrative. Much more accomplished than *O guarany, Iracema* is considered by several critics to be one of the masterpieces of nineteenth-century Brazilian literature. The subject of the book is a legend that deals with the founding of Ceará, Alencar's native state. Above all, the novel is a song of praise of America, of which the title character's name is an anagram. Like *O guarany,* the novel features star-crossed lovers, but in this story the lovers are an Indian female and a white male settler, and their affair is richer in detail than that of their predecessors. Despite the novel's nationalistic tone, there is a tendency toward Christianity and a sympathy toward European civilization. Iracema, the young Indian maiden, a symbol of the virgin American land, falls in love with the white warrior Martim and abandons her tribe to live with him. After a period of intense happiness, however, Martim, possessed by a nostalgia for his own land, tires of his life with Iracema, who, overcome with sorrow, becomes ill and dies after giving birth to their child, Moacir (which in Tupi means "the son of pain"). The child, the product of the fusion of the two races, is the first citizen of the state of Ceará. The end of the narrative brings Martim back with his son, after a long absence, to the land where he will found the Christian village that, according to the legend, will flourish.

Alencar was criticized for his excessive idealization of the Indian in *O guarany* and *Iracema,* so he tried in his third Indian novel, *Ubirajara,* to approach the Indian's culture from a more realistic perspective. Hence, he offers his reader a narrative entirely set in the jungles where the white man has no access. Contrary to his aim, however, the Indian is more mythicized than ever before. Despite the fact that the author leaves aside his concern with Christianity and with the process of civilization, his treatment of the characters often reveals his Eurocentrism. The story is based on an Indian legend that deals with the union of two tribes, and the description of the Indian customs and traditions is pre-

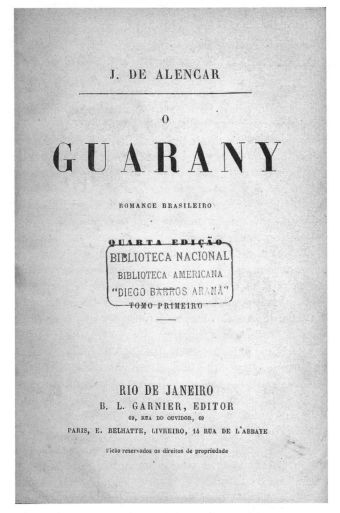

Title page of Alencar's first Indianist novel, featuring a love story between a settler's daughter and an Indian man (Biblioteca Nacional de Chile)

dominantly objective. The values attributed to them and the way they act, however, reveal the Europeanization through which they have gone in the process of literary transfiguration. Therefore, *Ubirajara* actually features the same contradictions already pointed out in Alencar's other Indianist novels: the existence of a pure and noble savage, who is the symbol of the American land, but at the same time a figure constructed with values from the European culture. Alencar's broad panorama of the native origins and hybrid formation of the Brazilian character is extended to colonial times in several other novels in which the historical narrative model prevails: *As minas de prata,* published in six volumes between 1862 and 1866, *A guerra dos mascates* (The War of the Mascates), published in two volumes in 1873 and 1874, and *Alfarrábios: crônicas dos tempos coloniais* (1873, Alfarrábios: Chronicles of Colonial Times), which comprises the novels *O Garatuja* (The Scribbler), *O ermitão da Glória* (The Hermit of Glória, and *A alma do Lázaro* (Lazarus's Soul). These works are closely related to the historical novels of European Romanticism and were influenced by authors such as Sir Walter Scott and Alexandre Herculano. They were inspired by the nationalistic feeling typical of Romanticism, which was concerned with the exaltation of a people's legendary past, and were produced simultaneously with the Indian novels. The most accomplished of all of these novels, *As minas de prata,* deals with El Dorado, a myth of national significance that attracted waves of people to the Brazilian backlands and resulted in its settlement in colonial times. Set in the seventeenth century, the story is based on the search for silver mines in the Jacobina backlands in the state of Bahia. Settlers and adventurers were determined to find and take possession of the mines, which led them into a series of conflicts and misunderstandings. *As minas de prata* is based on historical documents and chronicles of the colonial period, and Alencar reconstructs the atmosphere of the time of the arrival of the general-governor Diogo de Meneses, mixing historical episodes and characters with purely fictional ones. But what gives the novel its special flavor are the protagonists' love stories, marked in the typical Romantic manner by a series of fortunate and unfortunate episodes.

Also based on an historical episode, a dispute among peddlers which took place in Recife and Olinda in the eighteenth century, *A guerra dos mascates* is a satire in which Alencar does not spare any of his colleagues, particularly those who criticized his works. By mingling historical and fictitious characters, Alencar produces a typical roman à clef in which there can be identified several important figures of the social and political life of his time, including the emperor himself. Also among Alencar's targets is Romanticism, whose metaphors and commonplaces are grotesquely stressed. The merit of *A guerra dos mascates,* however, lies in the author's technique and especially in his vigorous and detailed portrayal of the Brazilian social life of the time.

Alfarrábios, the other publication listed among Alencar's historical works, is a set of three novels. The first one, *O Garatuja,* is based on an episode taken from Baltazar da Silva Lisboa's *Anais do Rio de Janeiro* (Chronicles from Rio de Janeiro): the exorcizing of the magistrate Pedro Mustre Portugal by the prelate Manuel de Sousa Almada. *O Garatuja* is a dynamic picaresque narrative set in the city of Rio de Janeiro before the arrival of the Portuguese royal family. Its satirical tone and detailed descriptions of the city's customs and social atmosphere resemble Manuel Antônio de Almeida's masterpiece *Memórias de um sargento de milícias* (1854–1855; translated as *Memoirs of a Militia Sergeant,* 1999). *O*

ermitão da Glória and *A alma do Lázaro* are a result of Alencar's readings of historical documents. The first of these novels deals with episodes of piracy and struggles among corsairs at the time when Frenchmen kept a trading post in Cabo Frio for the exploitation and smuggling of brazilwood, and the second is a story told by an old fisherman based on the diary of a leper.

The second of Heron de Alencar's novel groupings—the urban novel—corresponds to the third stage of Alencar's classification and comprises works that take place in the author's time. The main conflict in these novels is between national spirit and foreign influence, and the setting is the court, that is, the city of Rio de Janeiro. Brazilian reality is represented from the point of view of Rio de Janeiro because the attention of the Brazilian provinces was turned to that city, the place from which national decisions and models came. The novels of this group, the social urban narratives, are elaborate, and most are centered around a female character. It is not by chance that some are titled with the name of a woman *(Lucíola, Diva),* and four of the nine novels that make up this group carry as part of their titles the expression "perfil de mulher" (profile of a lady). The feminine profiles generally are drawn according to the Romantic view of women's social and emotional behavior. Brazilian social and cultural life, however, is portrayed with a realism that ranges from the description of simple family parties, to the narration of vivid street episodes, to ordinary professional occurrences. The settings are filled with well-dressed people who use perfume from Paris and whose lives consist of attending the opera and parties, strolling in the English fashion, and dining in luxurious hotels. Alencar depicts an emerging society undermined by the corrupting power of money and the desire for social status, in which financial interests mingle with matrimonial objectives. The plots focus on love, specifically the role of women with regard to love and marriage. In these urban novels, love is depicted as a powerful force that restores the balance between the emotional ideal and society; it redeems those who have been led astray by a vile social ethic. Along with a strong understanding of women's emotional independence, a fact seen by many critics as well ahead of Alencar's time, these novels project an equally Romantic psychology that dissects feelings and equates temperament and individual behavior with good manners, social status, and social changes. Everything is subject to love's restoring and humanizing power, in which emotional honesty counts as much as moral balance, a conception that fits perfectly with the Romantic ideal of morality.

In accordance with the Romantic tradition, Alencar's heroines protest marriages of convenience, a regular feature of their authoritarian society, and claim the need for evading such circumstances and seeking refuge in their inner lives. Although represented in a different way in each novel, this protest is present in each of the urban narratives, and it is usually associated with the Romantic desire for freedom. This aspect of the urban novels has been responsible for some of the recent reappraisals of Alencar's work, especially on the part of feminist critics.

Among the social novels with an urban setting, *Senhóra* stands out as a European Romantic model that treats the past and present of Brazilian society in a lyrical and ideal vision of life. In this book, considered one of the author's masterpieces, Alencar criticizes Brazilian society through his depiction of a marriage of convenience. The protagonist, Aurélia Camargo, is a young lady of humble origin who inherits tremendous wealth and decides to take revenge on her former fiancé, who left her for a rich woman. Without revealing her identity, Aurélia offers him a large dowry to marry an unknown lady. Hesitant at the beginning, but pressed by a difficult financial situation, he decides to accept the offer, but with the condition of receiving part of the dowry in advance. On the wedding night he is received with disgust by Aurélia, who shows him the receipt with which she bought him. A year later he manages to pay his debt to his wife in exchange for his freedom; however, by this time they have fallen in love with each other, and she asks him not to leave her. His behavior during their time together has redeemed him of his baseness and venality. Despite its realist traits, with themes of interest and corruption in human relationships, the novel ends with the triumph of love and redemption in the Romantic tradition. The titles of the parts into which the narrative is divided capture these themes: "Preço" (Price), "Quitação" (Release), "Posse" (Possession), "Resgate" (Redemption).

Another novel that stands out among the urban narratives because of Alencar's careful attention to form and thematic structure is *Lucíola,* the first novel to bear the "profile of a woman" subtitle. The story of *Lucíola* is that of Alexandre Dumas *fils*'s *La dame aux camélias* (1852, The Lady of the Camellias), that is, of a prostitute who tries to redeem herself by means of a pure love. Alencar, however, gives his story a different tone by stressing the contrast between his heroine's true inner feelings and the life she has led. Lúcia, a young lady from a poor family, was forced to sell her body to save her parents from dying of yellow fever. She became prey to an unscrupulous man and later to a procuress, and she eventually became one of the most famous prostitutes in the city. However, she falls in love with a young lawyer who has just arrived from his native province. Considering herself unworthy of his love, she tries to bring him close to her younger sister,

whom she has raised as her daughter, hoping that he might marry her. Falling fatally ill at the end, Lúcia dies with the firm conviction that the lawyer loved her and would take good care of her sister for the rest of his life. Combining love and death, a relationship commonly explored in Romanticism, and alternating between realistic descriptions (that are sometimes a bit daring for the time) and Romantic idealism, Alencar once again draws a highly critical portrait of his society, creating a trend in Brazilian fiction that was taken up and further developed by Machado de Assis.

Unlike *Lucíola,* which, despite its romantic ending, may be seen as a challenge to the conventions of a patriarchal society, *Diva* has as its protagonist a typical middle-class girl who expresses great concern about the role expected of her in society. Throughout the narrative Diva reveals a complex, strong, and paradoxical personality that causes some perplexity, not only among the other characters of the novel, but also among readers. The work anticipates some psychological theses that later became central to realist and naturalist fiction in Brazil. Having received a rigid puritanical education, the protagonist develops a strange feeling of hatred for a young doctor who once had to touch her naked body to cure her of a disease. Long after this episode, now an adult, she meets him again, and he falls in love with her. A conflict is then established between a man in love and a woman who, although in love with him, believes that what she feels is hatred. The entire novel focuses on this relationship and ends when both parties, having overcome their conflicted feelings, resign themselves to their mutual passion. Criticism of society is also present in this novel: bourgeois values and transgression is represented once again by the triumph of love over any sort of conventionality.

Two other urban novels in which the psychological vein is strongly present are *A pata da gazela* and *Encarnação* (Incarnation), which was published posthumously in 1893. The former features a case of fetishism in which a gallant young man one day finds a woman's boot and creates incredible fantasies about its owner to the point that he falls in love with the image he creates. The later, more elaborate novel is the story of a widower who creates a morbid cult around his dead wife: not only has he preserved her room exactly the way it was while she was alive, but he also has made two statues of her that he worships daily. One day he falls in love with a neighbor and marries her, but he feels so guilty for his sentiments that he tries to commit suicide. After the protagonist is shown suffering a great deal from his feelings of guilt, a fire destroys his first wife's room, and he is saved by the love and dedication of his second wife. Alencar's criticism of society in this novel focuses on bourgeois habits and the cult of appearances.

As in the other novels, love is the vital force that saves and redeems people. With *Encarnação,* Alencar closes his cycle of urban novels, providing his readers with an impressive gallery of characters and a wide panorama of the life of Rio de Janeiro in the nineteenth century.

Alencar's third group of novels, those characterized as regionalist, presents a shift from the more general national approach; yet, here too there is a strong preoccupation with the exaltation of Brazilian landscape and the recording of aspects of Brazilian culture as opposed to those of Europe. In each of these works—*O gaúcho, Til, O tronco do ipê,* and *O sertanejo*—a certain region's daily routine is described in detail. More conservative than their urban counterparts, rural societies better preserved the roots of the earliest periods of colonization, and Alencar dwells on these aspects of rural culture. As in the Indianist narratives, myth and legend are present in the regionalist novels, with the difference that they are treated as a part of rural man's imagination. Predominant is the author's intention of giving an accurate evaluation of both people and landscapes in rural societies, leading to a type of narrative that approximates the historical novel. The well-articulated plots are a chronicle of life in the provinces, centered upon characters representative of the region. They are a study of characters and their relationships not only to the landscape but to other people. The geographical descriptions that form the settings of these narratives are not realistic enough for them to be called fully regionalist, but Alencar's interpretations had their foundations in reality, and it is possible to identify the real locations behind the settings. Thus, the reader can clearly recognize the pampas of Rio Grande do Sul, the hinterland of São Paulo and Rio de Janeiro, and the backlands of Ceará as the settings of the four novels that compose this group. At the two geographical extremes, the northeast and the south, Alencar portrays the crudeness of traditions and customs; at the center, he presents a more developed, aristocratic atmosphere that shares the traditions and customs of a court undergoing changes. He also makes very clear the differences between the city and its surroundings on the one hand, and the countryside on the other, as can be observed by comparing *Sonhos d'ouro,* which takes place in a semi-rural area that is now part of the city of Rio de Janeiro, with *O tronco do ipê,* which is set in a genuinely rural part of Brazil.

Although Alencar had never been to Rio Grande do Sul, his first regionalist novel, *O gaúcho,* published in two volumes in 1870, is set in that area. The novel was a great success with the reading public, in large part because of its elaborate structure marked by a large amount of action and suspense, but it was highly criticized for its inaccuracies in the portrayal of the region.

Alencar created the setting of his story based on documents and reports rather than on firsthand experience at a time when regionalist narratives of a more realistic vein were being developed in Brazil. Yet, leaving aside the issue of its faithfulness to real life, Alencar's *O gaúcho* has among its many merits the fact that it anticipated a whole literary cycle that would later, in the first half of the twentieth century, play a significant role in both Brazilian and Argentinean literature—the so-called *gaúcho* cycle, in which the gaucho, a cowboy from southern Brazil, Uruguay, or Argentina, is idealized as a local Romantic hero. Manuel Canho, the protagonist of *O gaúcho,* is a rough sketch of later figures such as Ricardo Guiraldes's Don Segundo Sombra and even José Hernández's Martín Fierro. Canho is a highly complex figure that, due to his split personality and to the circumstances of his life, has been often compared with William Shakespeare's Hamlet. Canho's troubles, including his constant oscillations in his relationship with Catita, a typical Romantic heroine, grant the novel a vigorous dynamism that also accounts for its appeal to the public. The novel transcended the boom of regionalist fiction and continues to be widely read.

O tronco do ipê is set in a region familiar to Alencar—the Paraíba River valley, the area of coffee plantations in the state of Rio de Janeiro. As activities on the plantation where the main story takes place are described, the figure of the African slave is introduced and represented in stereotypical ways: either as a playful trickster or as associated with witchcraft. The antithesis between the city and the countryside is stressed in this novel, expressed by the contrast between the refinement of urban habits and the authenticity and spontaneity of rural life. The two main female characters in the story—Alice and Adélia—represent this opposition. The plot, inspired by the story of *Hamlet,* is centered upon a young man, Mário, who nourishes an aversion for his life because of the suspicion that he lives on the property of the man who killed his father. The situation becomes more complicated when he falls in love with Alice, the landowner's daughter, whose life he saves. The entire narrative is developed around his vacillating between accepting and refusing her affection. The purity and sincerity of her feelings for him finally triumph, but the typical romantic happy ending is only achieved at the last minute, when the old African slave and his wife reveal the secret of the hero's origins. The catalpa *(ipê),* the Brazilian national tree that gives title to the novel, is a symbol of the country's vitality and capacity for renewal. Most of the major episodes of the narrative occur under its shade or near its roots, including the opening and closing scenes of the novel.

Alencar's next novel, *Til,* is set in the region of Piracicaba in the state of São Paulo. Here the atmosphere of *O tronco do ipê*–created by the social relations between landowners and rural workers–is further developed, but an emphasis is placed on the cultural habits and customs of the people and upon the peculiarities of their daily lives. In this novel, people's beliefs and superstitions, as well as their popular games and religious practices, are described in detail, and even the regional cuisine is presented almost in the form of recipes. Although the plot of *Til* is not as strong as that of the other regionalist novels, the work stands out for its elaborate descriptions of Brazilian rural life and has served, more perhaps than the other narratives of the series, as a basis for folkloric studies.

 O sertanejo, the last of Alencar's regionalist narratives, resulted from a trip the author took to his native land for medical reasons. This trip was a return to his past, and as such the novel is full of nostalgia and childhood recollections. The heroes of this narrative come from the place where Alencar was raised and are like the humble and fearless men whose temperament he knew so well. The original inspiration for the novel is the writer's childhood, when he became emotionally carried away every time he heard the popular verse narrative *Boi Espácio* (The Ox Espácio). In fact, Alencar saved for posterity a version of that tale in the animal Boi Dourado (the Golden Ox), a sort of character in the novel. Looking for a theme in the collective memory, he went back to the seventeenth- and eighteenth-century practice of raising cattle in wild, open spaces, and thereby created a model that eventually prevailed in Brazilian fiction.

 The story of *O sertanejo* is based on the relationship between D. Flor, a wealthy landowner's daughter, and Arnaldo, the hero of the tale, a poor but noble man endowed with every virtue, who worships D. Flor and manages to prevent her from marrying two suitors who are pretenders: the son of a wealthy landowner who sold his properties to live in a city, and a cousin she does not like. Arnaldo is portrayed as a typical man from the backlands, raised in contact with nature. At the same time, however, he is mythicized and transformed into a kind of demigod; like Peri from *O guarani,* he becomes an idealized symbol of his land. As such, he is often set in contrast to D. Flor's first pretender, who exchanges his farms for life in a city. D. Flor and Arnaldo complement each other, representing the male and the female principles of their land. Since Alencar's descriptions of both the landscape and customs are made with knowledge derived from his experience, the inaccuracies of which he was accused in *O gaúcho* are not present in this work. The setting is so faithfully portrayed that the book often has been used in studies of history and folklore. These aspects of the book are frequently idealized in a manner typical of Romanticism:

Alencar in 1861, the year he entered parliament as a representative of Ceará (from José de Alencar, Discursos parlamentares, 1977; Thomas Cooper Library, University of South Carolina)

nature is always green and prosperous and man's cultural habits are exalted. *O sertanejo* ends with the promise of a second volume that never appeared.

 With novels ranging from Indianist and historical to urban and regionalist, Alencar left one of the most complete portraits of Brazilian life ever produced. Writing at a time when Brazilian literary manifestations were evolving from a formative phase to a dynamic period of struggle for autonomy, and at a time when the reading public was increasing considerably, Alencar was a kind of synthesizer of Brazilian Romanticism, the writer through whom all the efforts, theories, and criticism of preceding writers converged. From him came models and ideas that were doubly productive because they were both attacked and followed. He redefined Brazilian literature and, at the same time, pointed out its authentic nature, characterized from the remote past by its concern with reality–seen as diversity and the essential unity of habits and traditions. More than any author before him, he exploited the Brazilian landscape and its people's way of life. Alencar's preoccupation with the construction of a national literature was not, however, restricted to the treatment of Brazilian subjects; rather, it also included a way of expressing these subjects, a way that had evolved from the language of the original Portuguese settlers. Alencar searched for a style that corresponded more closely to the language spoken in Brazil, a style that critics now consider to be eminently Brazilian.

Beginning with *Cartas sobre "A Confederação dos Tamoios,"* Alencar expressed his interest in style, yet he never proposed the existence of a Brazilian language different from peninsular Portuguese. His intention, however, was to create a style that would express the lexical and syntactical peculiarities of Brazilian Portuguese—hence, his criticism of the normative character of grammar based on the classical authors of Portuguese literature. Alencar knew these writers' works and studied them carefully as part of the process of creating his very own style, which was carefully developed to meet the demands of his narrative form and to clearly transmit Brazilian everyday speech. Alencar's style not only incorporates a number of words of Tupi origin and a more relaxed type of syntax—which allows, for example, the construction of sentences beginning with object pronouns—but it is also endowed with a special rhythm and musicality not found in any previous writer in Portuguese. These elements give his prose a particular tone that Machado de Assis recognized and described with words that assured Alencar a place of honor in Brazilian literature:

> Nenhum escritor teve em mais alto grau a alma brasileira. E não é só porque houvesse tratado assuntos nossos. Há um modo de ver e de sentir que dá a nota íntima da nacionalidade, independente da face externa das cousas. . . . O nosso Alencar juntava a esse dom a natureza dos assuntos, tirados da vida ambiente e da história local. Outros o fizeram também; mas a expressão do seu gênio era mais vigorosa e mais íntima.

> (No writer held so high Brazilian soul. And it is not only because he dealt with our subjects. There is a way of seeing and feeling which is eminently national, independently from the external side of things. . . . Our Alencar added to this special gift the nature of his subjects, extracted from actual life and local history. Others have done that too; but the expression of Alencar's genius was more vigorous and intimate.)

Alencar's constant reflection on his own writing has aroused the interest of critics over the years. Of all the Brazilian Romantic writers, he was the one who most openly discussed and questioned his own works. His entire trajectory as a writer was accompanied by keen critical reflections in the form of prefaces and polemics, and his chronicles also often served as vehicles for his constant self-criticism. It is said that Alencar's career started with a polemic and ended with another one: the first one was *Cartas sobre "A Confederação*

dos Tamoios," and the last one, with Joaquim Nabuco, was about his theatrical and fictional works, titled *A polêmica Alencar-Nabuco* (1965). Both of these texts have been published in critical editions, the former by José Aderaldo Castello and the latter by Coutinho. Whereas in the first polemic Alencar presented a sketch of what his Indianist novels might be like, in the last he drew a firm defense of the national character of Brazilian literature and of the autonomy of the Brazilian style. While Nabuco treats Alencar's works according to a critical filter based on European models, Alencar defends himself by stressing the need for constructing a Brazilian literary canon that would contribute to the grandeur of the recently formed nation. For Alencar, literature was crucial for the projection of the nation's image, and as such it should present a proper profile. The creation of a national literature was Alencar's mission. Hence, Alencar was preoccupied with searching for particularities that could confer a special character to his own works, making them distinct and therefore tantamount to that which was being produced in Europe.

One of Alencar's most significant prefaces was that to *Sonhos d'ouro,* which he titled "Bênção paterna" (Paternal Blessing). This preface, which constitutes a kind of *ars poetica,* poses the question of the existence or nonexistence of a Brazilian literature and presents a defense of local color, raising a vehement protest against the importation of models. Alencar inveighs against those critics who have no standards by which to evaluate literature and affirms that their preoccupation should lie in the structure and the content of the works rather than in language itself. He defends the public as the true and legitimate critic of literary works, and he ends by offering to this public a general and analytical classification of his own efforts. Some of these topics are further developed in the "letter" he writes as a postscript to *Senhóra,* where he specifies his position on verisimilitude, plot structure, and the psychology of his characters, and in the postcript to the second edition of *Iracema,* where he demonstrates his full domain. Alencar's self-criticism, however, was not complete until the posthumous publication in 1893 of his literary autobiography *Como e porque sou romancista.* Written four years before his death, when he was already ill, Alencar reveals episodes of his literary career that he had never before discussed publicly, expresses his predilection for the novel genre, makes explicit his literary influences, and places his works within the framework of Romanticism.

Although Alencar's success largely stemmed from his novels, his plays, written mostly at the beginning of his career, were also well received by the public, who filled the theaters to see them performed. Despite the public's favorable response, however, critics did not show much enthusiasm for Alencar's plays, finding in them an artificiality and solemnity of style as well as a lack of spontaneity. Alencar's was a type of moralizing theater that dealt with social and political themes of the moment. *As azas de um anjo* (1860, The Wings of an Angel), for example, was inspired by the author's desire to find a solution to the human questions raised in *La dame aux camélias*. The rehabilitation of the lost woman is possible, as critic Décio de Almeida Prado affirms, but at the cost of the renunciation of physical love. Marriage is allowed to the heroine, but not carnal communion. As such, both moral requirements will be attained: punishment for the fault committed, and a new opportunity for the one who repents. *Mãi* (1862, Mother) presents Alencar's desire to correct a serious social problem: slavery. In this play, a young medical student, apparently white, suddenly discovers that the slave who has served him since his early childhood is his real mother. His reaction, contrary to what might be expected, is of pure joy, followed by a happy ending in which both his fiancée and her father accept his racial background. An ending of this sort in a country where slavery was still a reality may seem strange, but it represents the author's moral feelings: if prejudices are unjust, ignore them; if reality is immoral, correct it. The function of art for Alencar was to establish norms, and his characters are often as idealistic as himself.

As a playwright Alencar was no less versatile than as a novelist, and he moved with ease from writing bourgeois comedies to writing historical dramas. His best productions belong to these less ambitious types of theater. Of the former type an example is *O demônio familiar* (1857, The Familiar Demon), which offers a critical view of the bourgeois life in which marriage is the goal for women and social position for men. The main character of this four-act comedy of petty sentimental intrigues is a young scoundrel, a kind of clumsy Figaro, whose major artistic faults are those of being a bit artificial and too conscious of his own mission in the play. *O jesuíta* (1875; translated as *The Jesuit,* 1919), the last of Alencar's plays, is an example of a well-structured historical drama, written in accordance with the precepts of the genre. It is a play that maintains its tension from beginning to end and combines several different ingredients: a love story, a tale of mystery and secrets, a noble and patriotic cause (the country's independence), and a moral idea (the relationship between the ends and the means).

By the time Alencar died of lung disease, probably tuberculosis, in Rio de Janeiro on 12 December 1877, he had produced many works of high quality that assured him a place of honor in Brazilian literature. Machado de Assis once told Alencar that against the conspiracy of silence, he would have on his side the conspiracy of posterity, and Assis was prophetic. For many years after his death, Alencar's works received little recognition or praise from literary critics, who seemed unimpressed with the grandeur of his heroines and heroes and generally considered his works most appropriate for young ladies because of their Romantic sentimentality. Yet, at the same time, Alencar was highly valued by the general public; he remained wildly popular, and the number of editions and reprints of his works exceeded any prediction.

The only favorable critical study of Alencar's works in the nineteenth century was Tristão de Alencar Araripe Júnior's *José de Alencar* (1882), a brilliant and sensitive essay that is still an important reference in the study of Alencar's fiction. Only in 1929, more than fifty years after his death, was Alencar's critical fortune to change. In that year, the Brazilian Academy of Letters organized a series of lectures on his work by eminent critics and published them in an issue of its journal. Two later works also played a significant role in the rise of Alencar's critical fortunes: *Obras de ficção de José de Alencar* (Fictional Works of José de Alencar), which features a series of critical essays on the writer, published in sixteen volumes by José Olympio in 1951, and *Obra completa* (Complete Works), published by Aguilar in 1958–1960. The Aguilar collection includes the author's complete works and a number of unpublished texts, and it was organized according to the author's son, Mário de Alencar.

Over the years many excellent critical works on José de Alencar, often focusing on his role in consolidating Brazilian literature, have appeared. Alencar was not only Brazil's first great novelist, but he was also the writer who, as Alceu de Amoroso Lima has argued, first expressed a complete consciousness of the national character of Brazilian literature. With Alencar, the Brazilian landscape and its people's way of life not only became part of literature, but they came to be the very subject of literary works. Alencar's aesthetic doctrine was based on the notion of Brazil's literary independence. His ideas constituted the first step in the construction of the country's national literature, and his fiction and drama are the expression of this ideal, making him the patriarch of Brazilian literature.

References:

Heron de Alencar, "José de Alencar e a ficção romântica," in *A literatura no Brasil,* second edition, volume 2: *Romantismo,* edited by Afrânio Coutinho (Rio de Janeiro: Sul Americana, 1969), pp. 217–300;

Tristão de Alencar Araripe Júnior, *José de Alencar* (Rio de Janeiro: Fauchon, 1882);

José Aderaldo Castello, *A polêmica. Sobre a "Confederação dos Tamoios"* (São Paulo: Faculdade de Filosofia, 1953);

Afrânio Coutinho, "Ensaio e crônica," in his *A Literatura no Brasil,* second edition, volume 6: *Teatro, conto, crônica, a nova literatura* (Rio de Janeiro: Sul Americana, 1971), pp. 105–128;

Coutinho, *A tradição afortunada (o espírito de nacionalidade na crítica brasileira)* (Rio de Janeiro & São Paulo: J. Olympio, Editora da Universidade do São Paulo, 1968);

Coutinho and J. Galante de Sousa, eds., *Enciclopédia de Literatura Brasileira,* 2 volumes (Rio de Janeiro: Fundação de Assistênca ao Estudante, 1989);

Fábio Freixeiro, *Alencar: os bastidores e a posteridade* (Rio de Janeiro: Museu Histórico Nacional, 1977);

Gilberto Freyre, *José de Alencar* (Rio de Janeiro: J. Olympio, 1962);

Alceu de Amoroso Lima, *Estudos literários* (Rio de Janeiro: Aguilar, 1966);

J. M. Machado de Assis, *Páginas recolhidas* (Rio de Janeiro: Garnier, n.d.);

Raimundo de Menezes, *José de Alencar: literato e político,* second edition (Rio de Janeiro: Livros Técnicos e Científicos, 1977);

Pedro Paulo Montenegro, "Prosa e narrativa em José de Alencar," in *História da Literatura Brasileira,* volume 2, edited by Sílvio Castro (Lisbon: Publicações Alfa, 1999), pp. 127–152;

Artur Mota, *José de Alencar* (Rio de Janeiro: Briguiet, 1921);

Décio de Almeida Prado, "Evolução da literatura dramática," in *A Literatura no Brasil,* second edition, volume 6: *Teatro, conto, crônica, a nova literatura,* edited by Coutinho (Rio de Janeiro: Sul Americana, 1971), pp. 7–38;

M. Cavalcanti Proença, *José de Alencar na Literatura Brasileira* (Rio de Janeiro: Civilização Brasileira, 1966);

Revista do Academia Brasileira de Letras, special Alencar issue, no. 89 (May 1929).

Manuel Antônio de Almeida

(17 November 1831 – 28 November 1861)

Vivaldo A. Santos
Georgetown University

BOOKS: *Memórias de um sargento de milícias,* 2 volumes, as "Um Brasileiro" (Rio de Janeiro: Tipografia Brasiliense, 1854, 1855); republished as *Memórias de um sargento de milícias: romance de costumes brasileiros,* 2 volumes, introduction by Francisco Joaquim Bethencourt da Silva (Rio de Janeiro: Carioca, 1876); translated by Ronald W. Souza as *Memoirs of a Militia Sergeant,* with foreword by Thomas H. Holloway and afterword by Flora Süssekind (Oxford: Oxford University Press, 1999);

Tese de doutoramento (Rio de Janeiro: M. Barreto, 1855);

Dous amores: drama lyrico em 3 actos, poesia imitação do italiano de Piave, music by Rafaela Rozwadowska (Rio de Janeiro: B. X. Pinto de Sousa, 1861).

Editions and Collections: *Memórias de um sargento de milícias,* 2 volumes (Pelotas: Tipografia do Comércio, 1862, 1863);

Memórias de um sargento de milícias: romance de costumes brasileiros, introduction by José Veríssimo (Rio de Janeiro. Garnier, 1900);

Memórias de um sargento de milícias, introduction by Mário de Andrade, illustrated by F. Acquarone (São Paulo: Livraria Martins, 1941);

Memórias de um Sargento de Milícias, edited by Cecília de Lara (Rio de Janeiro: Livros Técnicos e Científicos, 1978);

Obra dispersa: crítica, crônica, correspondência, teatro. Antologia complementar, com testemunhos de contemporâneos e juízos críticos pré-modernistas sobre Memórias de um sargento de milícias, edited by Bernardo de Mendonça (Rio de Janeiro: Graphia, 1991).

OTHER: Louis Friedel, *Gondicar ou o Amor de Cristão,* translated by Almeida, *Tribuna Católica,* nos. 25–27, 29–32, 34–38, 40–41, and 47–48 (1852);

Charles Ribeyrolles, *Brasil pitoresco,* translated by Almeida, Francisco Ramos Paz, Remígio de Sena Pereira, Joaquim Machado de Assis, and Rinaldo Montoro (Rio de Janeiro: Tipografia Nacional, 1859);

Manuel Antônio de Almeida (from Obra Dispersa, *1991; Hodges Library, University of Tennessee)*

Paulo Feval, *O rei dos mendigos,* translated by Almeida (Rio de Janeiro: Correio Mercantil, 1860);

Lírica nacional, edited by Almeida (Rio de Janeiro: Diário do Rio de Janeiro, 1862).

SELECTED PERIODICAL PUBLICATIONS–
UNCOLLECTED: "Civilização dos Indígenas," *Jornal do Comércio,* 12 February 1852;

"A fisiologia da voz," *Correio Mercantil,* 9 July 1854;

"Amor de criança," *Correio Mercantil,* 16 July 1854;

"O nome," *Correio Mercantil,* 30 July 1854;

"O riso," *Correio Mercantil,* 13 August 1854;

"As flores e os perfumes," *Correio Mercantil,* 27 August 1854;

"As Muletas de Sixto V," *Correio Mercantil,* 3 September 1854;

"Uma história triste," *Correio Mercantil,* 24 September 1854;

"Carta," *O Paraíba,* 2 December 1857;

"A Independência dos Jornais," *O Paraíba,* 12 December 1858.

Manuel Antônio de Almeida occupies an unusual position in Brazilian Romantic fiction. His *Memórias de um sargento de milícias* (1854, 1855; translated as *Memoirs of a Militia Sergeant,* 1999) is considered one of the best novels ever written in Brazil. Almeida's distinctive literary style, in contrast to that of his Romantic contemporaries, made him an important precursor of realism.

Manuel Antônio de Almeida, nicknamed "Maneco," was born in Rio de Janeiro on 17 November 1831. He was the second son of Portuguese immigrants, Lieutenant Antônio de Almeida and his wife, Josefina Maria. The poor social condition of the Almeida family is known, but few details of Almeida's childhood and early schooling have survived. Almeida's father died when he was about twelve years old, leaving his mother to struggle to provide for her two sons and two daughters. During his early teenage years Almeida was a student at the Colégio São Pedro de Alcântara (Sâo Pedro de Alcântara School); he also studied drawing at the Academia de Belas Artes (Academy of Fine Arts). At the age of seventeen Almeida passed the entrance exam to the Faculdade de Medicina (Medical School), a modest school of medicine in Rio de Janeiro that was attended by Brazilians who did not have the social and financial advantages that would enable them to study in the more prestigious schools in São Paulo and Olinda. He started his medical studies in 1849, but he missed two years of school because of financial reasons. He graduated in 1855. Despite his degree in medicine, Almeida never practiced in that profession.

Almeida's medical studies were interrupted by events that led to his early career in journalism. His mother died in 1852, while he was at the Faculdade de Medicina, and he had to assume the responsibility of taking care of his brothers and sisters. Thus, for economic reasons Almeida began working for the newspaper *Correio da Manhã* (Morning News). Subsequently, the dilettante Almeida translated French author Louis Friedel's novel *Gondicar, épisode des croisades* for the newspaper *Tribuna Católica.* On 12 February 1852 Almeida waded into controversy when he published "Civiliza-ção dos Indígenas" (The Civilization of the Indigenous Peoples) in the *Jornal do Comércio* (The Daily Commercial). This essay was written in response to Francisco Adolfo Varnhagen's article "Memorial Orgânico" (Organic Memorial), which appeared in the Rio de Janeiro magazine *Guanabara.* Almeida attacks Varnhagen's desire to recolonize native Brazilians through a protective policy in the name of civilization: "O autor quer que eduquemos à força os nossos selvagens e que quinze anos depois, quando já não precisem mais de tutela, façamos deles prestantes cidadãos e cristãos!" (The author wants us to educate our natives by force so that fifteen years from now, when they don't need our tutelage, we can make them useful citizens and Christians!). Here Almeida denigrates Varnhagen's position by associating it with that of the Portuguese colonizers of Brazil.

During 1852 Almeida was granted a permanent position at the *Correio Mercantil* (The Commerce News), the most prestigious newspaper in Brazil. In 1854 he started a literary section of the paper titled "Páginas Menores" (Minor Pages), where, together with José de Alencar and other writers, he published short pieces of fiction. At this newspaper Almeida also started the "Revista Bibliográfica" (Bibliographic Journal), a portion of the newspaper dedicated to literary criticism.

Almeida launched his career as an author at a time when the literary scene was dominated by the traditional Romantic conception of literature. The majority of Almeida's Brazilian contemporaries, such as Alencar, Joaquim Manuel de Macedo, Bernardo de Guimarães, and Teixeira e Souza, attempted to follow the sentimental and idealist aesthetics of European Romanticism as established by writers such as Jean-Jacques Rousseau, François-René de Chateaubriand, Sir Walter Scott, Victor Hugo, Almeida Garrett, and Alexandre Herculano. The Brazilian Romantic writers were engaged in two major trends. One was the development of an urban literature favoring Rio de Janeiro's petite bourgeoisie, making the "carioca" (a native of the city of Rio de Janeiro) family of the mid nineteenth century a popular literary topic. Although the authors of such works carefully constructed realistic fictional spaces and plot developments, their characters are products of Romanticism, idealized and artificial. Such is the case of the urban novels of Manuel de Macedo (*A Moreninha* [1844, The Light Brown-Skinned Girl]) and Alencar (*Senhóra* [1875; translated as *Senhora: Profile of a Woman,* 1994], *Diva: perfil de mulher* [1864, Diva: Profile of a Woman], and *Lucíola: um perfil de mulher* [1862, Lucíola: Profile of a Woman]). The other major Romantic approach of Almeida's time involved using historical or Indianist themes to construct a Brazilian national identity. Alencar's novels, which are strongly influenced by Scott and James Fenimore Cooper, are examples of this type of literature. Alencar attempted to reconstruct a Brazilian past through the depiction of colonial society and the idealization of the native, as seen in his Indianist novels *O guarany* (1857), *Iracema: lenda do Ceará* (1865; translated as *Iracéma, the Honey Lips: A Legend of Brazil,* 1886), and *Ubirajara* (1874; translated as *Ubirajara, a Legend of the Tupy Indians,* n.d./1922).

Almeida, however, took a different path from his contemporaries. *Memórias de um sargento de milícias,* his only novel, is his most significant contribution to Brazilian literature. The first installment of the narrative appeared anonymously in the *Correio Mercantil* on 27 June 1852. Further installments were published, also anonymously, in weekly chapters or *folhetins* (feuilletons) that appeared in the Sunday literary supplement "A Pacotilha" between 27 June 1852 and 31 July 1853.

While *Memórias de um sargento de milícias* did not achieve recognition in the literary milieu of the time, its popularity among average newspaper readers motivated Almeida to turn his serialized narrative into a book, the first volume of which was published in 1854, a year after the final chapters appeared in the newspaper. The second volume of *Memórias de um sargento de milícia* was published the following year. These two volumes, simply signed "Um Brasileiro" (A Brazilian), were produced by Tipografia Brasiliense, a publishing house owned by Maximiniano Gomes Ribeiro. The fact that the book is attributed to "Um Brasileiro" shows the spirit of nationalism that characterized Almeida's generation after Brazil gained its independence from Portugal in 1822.

Almeida's book publication of *Memórias de um sargento de milícia* was a disappointment. It ended up lost among piles of other texts produced by the publishing house and was completely ignored by the public. Although the first edition failed, one clandestine edition was published in 1862 in Pelotas by the Tipografia do Comércio, which was owned by Joaquim F. Nunes, indicating that there was some interest in the novel. Among the various editions of *Memórias de um sargento de milícia* published over the years, two deserve special attention. The third edition, which came out in 1862–1863 under the auspices of Quintino Bocaiúva, revealed the author's real name on the cover for the first time. Another important feature of this edition is the fact that it was revised by the famous author Machado de Assis. The familiarity between Almeida and Assis went back to 1858, when Assis was an apprentice at the Tipografia Nacional and Almeida was the director. Another noteworthy edition is the one from 1876 in which a subtitle is added to describe the kind of narrative that the *Memórias de um sargento de milícia* is: *Romance de costumes brasileiros* (Novel of Brazilian Manners). This subtitle, however, was dropped from all editions of the novel published after 1941.

One possible reason for the early failure of *Memórias de um sargento de milícia* might be its unusual style. It was only around 1880, when the aesthetics of realism and naturalism became prevalent, that Almeida's novel began attracting more attention. Critics began to reevaluate the work according to new aesthetic models that valued a sense of objectivity and observation over idealism. In 1900 José Veríssimo, a major Brazilian literary critic, wrote the introduction to the edition published by H. Garnier. Veríssimo considered the *Memórias de um sargento de milícia:*

um dos mais característicos da nossa literatura, um dos menos intencional e mais naturalmente me dãã uma forte impressão de nacionalismo. . . . Não conheço quem no romance brasileiro tenha revelado tão singular talento em descrever, senão criar tipos tão nacionais e tão vivos

(one of the most characteristic books of our literature, one of the least intentional and one that most naturally gives me a strong sense of nationalism. . . . I don't know who in the history of the Brazilian novel has revealed such a singular talent to describe, if not to create characters so national and so lively.)

Almeida finally became part of the Brazilian literary canon with the recognition of his work by the modernist generation in the 1930s, including writers such as Luís Felipe Vieira Souto, Xavier Marques, and Astrogildo Pereira, and later Marques Rebelo and Mário de Andrade. Andrade placed *Memórias de um sargento de milícia* in the picaresque tradition in his famous preface for the illustrated edition of the book published by Livraria Martins in São Paulo in 1941. This edition was the first to carry the author's full, unabbreviated name.

Memórias de um sargento de milícia is the story of Leonardo, who lives in Rio de Janeiro during the time of King João VI. The king arrived with the royal court in 1808 and returned to Portugal in 1821. The reader follows Leonardo's comic adventures among thugs and gypsies, his short time in the army as a private, his sudden promotion to sergeant, and his transfer to the military reserve. The novel ends on a happy note with Leonardo's marriage to Luisinha, a widow he has loved since his teenage years.

The ambiguous title of *Memórias de um sargento de milícia* refers to either the life story of Leonardo, the protagonist, or the memoirs of Antônio César Ramos, a Portuguese soldier who lived in Rio when the narrative takes place and who was supposedly Almeida's informant. Although the book isn't an historical novel, it

Title page for Almeida's most successful work, featuring realistic and picaresque elements that were embraced by the modernist generation of the 1930s (Biblioteca Nacional de Chile)

reveals a keen interest in documenting aspects of life in Rio de Janeiro during the first decades of the nineteenth century. The realistic aspects of the novel are apparent in the opening chapter, where the precise time setting is announced—"Era no tempo do rei" (It was back in the time of the king)—followed by a detailed description of the life of bailiffs in the city of Rio de Janeiro.

Different from his contemporaries who chose to portray the carioca elite, Almeida chose to depict the lower classes and their vices, popular figures, local places, traditional festivities, religion, and family and social relations. The exploration of popular culture, including descriptions of traditional dances, music, religious festivities, rituals, and superstitions, is one of the strengths of the novel. Andrade, a folklorist himself, said that *Memórias de um sargento de milícia* revealed that Almeida "tinha em grau elevadíssimo a bossa do folclorista, e estava consciente disso pois confessa francamente, no livro, trazer entre as suas intenções a de fixar costumes" (had the superior talent of a folklorist, and

he was conscious of that since he openly confesses in the book that one of his intentions was to preserve customs).

Unlike the majority of Romantic heroes that are depicted as noble and superior against all the negative forces of the universe, Almeida's protagonist, Leonardo, comes from the lower strata of society and always needs somebody to help him out of his difficulties. This characteristic has caused some critics to link *Memórias de um sargento de milícia* to the traditional Spanish picaresque novel. For example, Antonio Candido says that Almeida's objectivity breaks "a tensão romântica entre o Bem, e o Mal por meio de um nivelamento divertido de atos e caracteres" (the romantic tension between good and evil by a sort of funny leveling of the action and the characters). He also claims that Leonardo is one of the first "malandros" (rogues) from the folkloric tradition to enter Brazilian literature. Despite the novel's realistic qualities, the characters in *Memórias de um sargento de milícia* are superficial and closer to caricature. Since the book emphasizes actions, the characters lack psychological depth. Leonardo's actions, for example, are more intuitive than rational.

Critical studies of *Memórias de um sargento de milícia* have pointed out that Almeida's objective view of Rio de Janeiro's everyday life and customs and his use of colloquial language that breaks with traditional Romantic rhetoric made him an *avant la lettre* realist. This description seems especially appropriate when, as Agripino Grieco suggests, "se consideramos que, em 1854, Flaubert ainda não havia publicado a *Madame Bovary* e o Naturalismo de Zola ainda levaria umas décadas para tomar seu lugar nas letras francesas" (we consider that, in 1854, Flaubert had not yet published *Madame Bovary* and Zola's naturalism would still take a couple of decades to take its place in French literature). Additionally, humor and irony are important in *Memórias de um sargento de milícia*. Leonardo's tricks and unexpected turns are a powerful satire of nineteenth-century Brazilian political and social habits. All these elements have assured Almeida an important position in the development of the Brazilian novel in the nineteenth century.

The other works Almeida produced during his short life comprise newspaper *crônicas* (chronicles), scattered poems, his lyric drama *Dous amores* (1861, Two Lovers), and some pieces of literary criticism. Many of these works are collected in a 1991 anthology titled *Obra dispersa: crítica, crônica, correspondência, teatro,* edited by Bernardo de Mendonça.

In 1855 Almeida was elected member of the first carnival association in Rio de Janeiro, the "Congresso das Sumidades Carnavalescas" (The Congress of the Carnavalesque Celebrities). From 1857 to 1860 Almeida was the director of the Imperial Academia de

Música e Ópera (Royal Academy of Music and Opera). He also served from 1857 to 1859 as the director of the Tipografia Nacional, where in 1858 he met Assis. That year Almeida became secretary of the Sociedade Propagadora de Belas-Artes (Association for the Dissemination of the Fine Arts), which inaugurated the still-existing Liceu de Artes e Ofícios (School of Arts and Crafts), where he taught geometry. In 1859 Almeida became secretary of the treasury, but he left the position to move with his sisters, one of them severely ill, to Nova Friburgo, away from his creditors. Almeida's financial circumstances at this time were extremely poor. In Nova Friburgo he worked for a short time as a translator. In 1861 he returned to Rio de Janeiro to pursue a political career, hoping to improve his economic situation. Not long after returning to the city, Almeida set off for Campos to discuss the details of his candidacy for state representative. On the night of 28 November 1861, the ship he was on, the *Hermes,* collided with a cliff, and 37 of its 90 passengers drowned. Almeida's body was never found.

References:

Nola Kortner Aiex, "Memórias de um Sargento de Milícias as Menippean Satire," *Romance-Quarterly,* 28, no. 2 (1981): 199–208;

Mário de Andrade, "Memórias de Um Sargento de Milícias," in his *Aspectos da literatura brasileira* (São Paulo: Martins/Instituto Nacional do Livro/ Ministério da Educação, 1972), pp. 25–130;

Machado de Assis, "O Futuro de 15 de Fevereiro de 1863," in his *Crônicas, volume 1: 1859–1863* (Rio de Janeiro: W. M. Jackson, 1944);

Celia Berrettini, "El primer asomo de la picaresca en la literatura brasileña," *Sin-Nombre,* 13, no. 2 (1983): 59–66;

Alfredo Bosi, *História Concisa da Literatura Brasileira* (São Paulo: Cultrix, 1994);

Antonio Candido, "Dialética da Malandragem," in his *O Discurso e a Cidade* (São Paulo: Duas Cidades, 1993), pp. 19–54; translated by Howard S. Becker as "Dialectic of Malandroism," in *Antonio Candido: On Literature and Society* (Princeton: Princeton University Press), pp. 79–103;

Candido, "Manuel Antônio de Almeida: O romance em moto-contínuo," in his *Formação da literatura brasileira,* volume 2 (Belo Horizonte: Itatiaia, 1981), pp. 215–220;

José Aderaldo Castello, *Aspectos do romance brasileiro* (Rio de Janeiro: Ministério da Educação, 1960);

Walnície Nogueira Galvão, *"No tempo do rei,"* in her *Saco de gatos* (São Paulo: Livraria Duas Cidades/Secretaria da Cultura, Ciêna e Tecnologia do Estado de São Paulo, 1976), pp. 27–33;

Eugênio Gomes, *Aspectos do romance brasileiro* (Salvador: Publicações da Universidade da Bahia, 1958);

Agripino Grieco, *Evolução da prosa brasileira* (Rio de Janeiro: Ariel, 1933);

Reginaldo Guimarães, *O folclore na ficção brasileira: roteiro das "Memórias de um sargento de milícias"* (Rio de Janeiro: Cátedra/Instituto Nacional do Livro/ Ministério da Educação, 1977);

Maria José da Trindade Negrão, *Nossos Clássicos: Manuel Antônio de Almeida* (Rio de Janeiro: AGIR, 1966);

John M. Parker, "The Nature of Realism in *Memórias de um Sargento de Milícias,"* *Bulletin of Hispanic-Studies,* 48 (1971): 128–150;

Marques Rebelo, *Para conhecer melhor Manuel Antônio de Almeida* (Rio de Janeiro: Bloch, 1973);

Rebelo, *Vida e obra de Manuel Antônio de Almeida* (São Paulo: Martins, 1943);

João Cezar de Castro Rocha, "Do malandro ao antropófago: por uma epistemologia da ausência," *Mester,* 24, no. 1 (1995): 173–184;

Roberto Schwarz, "Pressupostos, salvo engano, de 'Dialética da Malandragem,'" in his *Que Horas São?* (São Paulo: Companhia das Letras, 1987), pp. 129–155;

Nelson Werneck Sodré, *História da literatura brasileira: seus fundamentos econômicos* (Rio de Janeiro: J. Olympio, 1960);

José Veríssimo, "Um velho romance brasileiro," in *Estudos brasileiros,* second series (Rio de Janeiro: Laemmert, 1894).

Papers:

A collection of Manuel Antônio de Almeida's papers is held at the Fundação Biblioteca Nacional (National Brazilian Library) in Rio de Janeiro.

Jorge Amado
(10 August 1912 – 6 August 2001)

Alain-Philippe Durand
University of Rhode Island

See also the Amado entry in *DLB 113: Modern Latin-American Fiction Writers, First Series.*

BOOKS: *Lenita,* by Amado, Dias da Costa, and Edison Carneiro (Rio de Janeiro: Coelho Branco Filho, 1930);

O paiz do carnaval (Rio de Janeiro: Schmidt, 1931);

Cacau (Rio de Janeiro: Ariel, 1933);

Suor (Rio de Janeiro: Ariel, 1934);

Jubiabá (Rio de Janeiro: J. Olympio, 1935); translated by Margaret Neves (New York: Avon, 1984);

Mar morto (Rio de Janeiro: J. Olympio, 1936); translated by Gregory Rabassa as *Sea of Death* (New York: Avon, 1984);

Capitães da areia (Rio de Janeiro: J. Olympio, 1937); translated by Rabassa as *Captains of the Sands* (New York: Avon, 1988);

A estrada do mar (Estância, Brazil: Popular, 1938);

ABC de Castro Alves (São Paulo: Martins, 1941);

Vida de Luiz Carlos Prestes, el caballero de la esperanza (Buenos Aires: Claridad, 1942);

Brandão entre o mar e o amor, by Amado, José Lins do Rêgo, Graciliano Ramos, Aníbal Machado, and Rachel de Queiroz (São Paulo: Martins, 1942);

Terras do sem fim (São Paulo: Martins, 1943); translated by Samuel Putnam as *The Violent Land* (New York: Knopf, 1945);

São Jorge dos Ilhéus (São Paulo: Martins, 1944); translated by Clifford E. Landers as *The Golden Harvest* (New York: Avon, 1992);

Bahia de Todos os Santos (São Paulo: Martins, 1945);

Homens e coisas do Partido Comunista (Rio de Janeiro: Horizonte, 1946);

Seara vermelha (São Paulo: Martins, 1946);

O amor de Castro Alves (Rio de Janeiro: Povo, 1947); republished as *O amor do soldado* (São Paulo: Martins, 1958);

O mundo da paz (Rio de Janeiro: Vitória, 1950);

Os subterrâneos da liberdade, 3 volumes (São Paulo: Martins, 1954);

Jorge Amado (frontispiece for Bobby J. Chamberlain, Jorge Amado, *1990; Thomas Cooper Library, University of South Carolina)*

Gabriela, cravo e canela (São Paulo: Martins, 1958); translated by James L. Taylor and William L. Grossman as *Gabriela, Clove and Cinnamon* (New York: Knopf, 1962; London: Chatto & Windus, 1963);

Os velhos marinheiros (São Paulo: Martins, 1961)—comprises "A morte e a morte de Quincas Berro D'Agua," translated by Barbara Shelby Merello as *The Two Deaths of Quincas Wateryell* (New York: Knopf, 1965), and "A completa verdade sobre as discutidas aventuras do Comandante Vasco Moscoso de Aragão," translated by Harriet de Onís as *Home Is the Sailor* (New York: Knopf, 1964);

O mistério dos MMM, by Amado, João Guimarães Rosa, Viriato Correia, Dinah Silveira de Queiroz, Lúcio Cardozo, Herberto Salles, José Condé, Antonio Calledo, Orígenes Lessa, and Rachel de Queiroz (Rio de Janeiro: O Cruzeiro, 1962);

Os pastores da noite (São Paulo: Martins, 1964); translated by de Onís as *Shepherds of the Night* (New York: Knopf, 1967);

Dona Flor e seus dois maridos, história moral e de amor (São Paulo: Martins, 1966); translated by de Onís as *Dona Flor and Her Two Husbands* (New York: Knopf, 1969; London: Weidenfeld & Nicolson, 1969);

Tenda dos milagres (São Paulo: Martins, 1969); translated by Merello as *Tent of Miracles* (New York: Knopf, 1971);

Tereza Batista cansada de guerra (São Paulo: Martins, 1972); translated by Merello as *Tereza Batista: Home from the Wars* (New York: Knopf, 1975);

O gato malhado e a andorinha Sinhá (Rio de Janeiro: Record, 1976); translated by Merello as *The Swallow and the Tomcat* (New York: Delacorte/Friede, 1982);

Tieta do Agreste: pastora de cabras (Rio de Janeiro: Record, 1977); translated by Merello as *Tieta the Goat Girl* (New York: Knopf, 1979);

Farda, fardão, camisola de dormir (Rio de Janeiro: Record, 1979); translated by Helen R. Lane as *Pen, Sword, Camisole* (Boston: Godine, 1985);

O menino grapiúna (Rio de Janeiro: Record, 1981);

A bola e o goleiro (Rio de Janeiro: Record, 1984);

Tocaia Grande (Rio de Janeiro: Record, 1984); translated by Rabassa as *Showdown* (New York: Bantam, 1988);

O sumiço da santa: uma história de feitiçaria (Rio de Janeiro: Record, 1988); translated by Rabassa as *The War of the Saints* (New York: Bantam, 1995);

Chapada Diamantina, by Amado and others (Rio de Janeiro: AC & M, 1989);

Navegação de cabotagem: apontamentos para um livro de memórias que jamais escreverei (Rio de Janeiro: Record, 1992); translated in part by Alfred Mac Adam in *The Oxford Book of Latin American Essays,* edited by Ilan Stavans (New York: Oxford University Press, 1997);

Memorial Mãe Menininha do Gantois, by Amado, Caetano Veloso, and Nizan Guanaes (Salvador: Memorial Mãe Menininha do Gantois, 1993);

Discursos (Salvador: Fundação Casa de Jorge Amado, 1993);

A descoberta da América pelos turcos: romancinho (Rio de Janeiro: Record, 1994);

Carnaval, texts by Amado, Arnaldo Jabor, and Roberto da Matta, photography by Claudio Edinger (São Paulo: Dórea Books and Art, 1996); translated as *Carnaval* (Heaton Moor, Stockport, U.K.: Dewi Lewis, 1996);

O milagre dos pássaros (Rio de Janeiro: Record, 1997);

Mágica Bahia / Mágica Bahía, by Amado, Antonio Risério, and Renato Pinheiro (Salvador: Fundação Casa de Jorge Amado, Bustamante, 1997);

Contrabandista (Lisbon: EXPO 98, 1998);

Salvador, texts by Amado, António Vieira, and Wilson Rocha, edited, with photography, by Mário Cravo Neto (Salvador: Aries Editora, 1999);

Rua Alagoinhas 33, Rio Vermelho: a casa de Zélia e Jorge Amado, texts by Amado, Gilberbert Chaves, and Paloma Jorge Amado Costa, photography by Adenor Gondim, art by Pedro Costa (Salvador: Fundação Casa de Jorge Amado, Fazcultura, Programa Estadual de Incentivo à Cultura, Governo da Bahia, Secretaria da Cultura e Turismo, Secretaria da Fazenda, 1999).

Collection: *Obras,* 20 volumes (São Paulo: Martins, 1944–1975).

Jorge Amado was one of the rare Latin American writers who made a living from his writing. In his seventy-year-long career, the Brazilian author wrote more than forty books, of which he sold twenty million copies in Brazil alone. Although most of his works are novels, Amado also wrote in a wide range of other genres, including poetry, drama, political pamphlets, memoirs, short stories, and travel accounts. His works have been translated into as many as forty-six languages, and many have been adapted for television and cinema. An institution and source of national pride in Brazil, Amado's reputation spread worldwide, and several times he was considered as a potential nominee for the Nobel Prize in literature.

Amado was widely known as the writer of the people. Most of his books deal with the struggles and exploitation of the working class and the poor of his native Bahia in the northeast of Brazil. Amado's characters are a mixture of good and bad, bloody killers and good-hearted villains, street kids and workers, prostitutes and circus owners, landlords and political leaders, musicians, poets, and religious men. Amado's works share an emphasis on Brazilian popular culture and folklore, including representative elements such as *Carnaval* and the Afro-Brazilian religious cult of *candomblé.* Most critics agree that Amado was a politically conscious writer close to the communist ideology, a social

*Cover for the 1944 edition of Amado's first three
novels (Biblioteca Nacional de Chile)*

realist whose works can be divided into two distinct periods. His writings during the period of 1931 to 1958 are characterized by a strong sociopolitical emphasis; they consistently denounce the disparity between the upper and lower classes, and the exploitation of the poor by the rich. His works from the post-1958 period continue to denounce the oppression of the underclass, but they do so in a lighter, more satirical and humorous tone.

Jorge Amado was born on 10 August 1912 in Ilhéus, Bahia, the son of João Amado de Faria, a cocoa plantation owner, and Eulália Leal Amado de Faria. Amado was almost killed before he was a year old when his father was the target of an assassination attempt. Amado spent his early childhood on the plantation, and the violent environment in which he was raised became the source of inspiration for several characters and actions in his novels. In 1922 Amado entered the Antônio Vieira boarding school, which was run by Jesuits in Salvador, the capital city of Bahia. It was during his stay at this religious institution that Amado discovered the classical Portuguese authors as well as

English novelist Charles Dickens, who became a life-long favorite. However, Amado found his school environment oppressive. Two years later, while at home for Christmas break, a depressed Amado asked to change schools, but his father refused. Consequently, instead of returning to Bahia for the start of the new term in March 1924, the already free-minded student decided to run away. He traveled on his own across the region and joined his grandfather José Amado, with whom he stayed for two months in Itaporanga, Sergipe.

In March 1925 Amado returned to Bahia, enrolling at the Ipiranga boarding school. In contrast to the strict and severe Jesuits at Antônio Vieira, the director of Ipiranga, Isaías Alves de Almeida, provided his pupils with a more flexible atmosphere. This new setting gave Amado the opportunity to spend most of his time on his favorite activities: reading and writing. During his stay at Ipiranga, Amado learned to appreciate Brazilian modernist Oswald de Andrade and French writers such as Honoré de Balzac, Guy de Maupassant, and Emile Zola. He also made his first attempts at writing fiction and journalistic articles while spending time with a group of nonconformist young men who shared his literary curiosity. Amado wrote for the school newspaper *A Pátria* (The Nation), launched the literary review *A Folha* (The Paper), and contributed articles as a reporter for the city newspaper *Diário de Bahia* (Bahia Daily). This literary activity led to the first publication of Amado's fiction, a short story titled "Lenita" (1930) that he composed with his friends Dias de Costa and Edison Carneiro.

Upon the completion of his secondary education in 1930, Amado moved to Rio de Janeiro (then the capital of the country), where he was sent by his father to study law. Amado enjoyed the city, making many friends while living on Copacabana Avenue and later in Ipanema. He continued to write; for five years he contributed to reviews and newspapers, including the Bahian review *ETC,* and *Boletim de Ariel* (The Ariel Bulletin), *Diário de Notícias* (Daily News), *Literatura* (Literature), *Rio-Magazine,* and *A Manhã* (The Morning News) in the capital. During this time Amado was also busy writing his first novel, *O paiz do carnaval* (1931, The Land of Carnival), which was published with the help of friends. This book, which earned some praise for the young writer, tells the story of Paulo Rigger, a young dandy who returns to his native Brazil after seven years of studying law in Paris. He is the son of a rich cocoa plantation owner who has recently died. The reader follows Rigger and his acquaintances to Ilhéus, then to Bahia, site of his father's farm, and finally to Rio de Janeiro. In the end the protagonist decides to return to Europe, embarking in the middle of the *Carnaval* season. Rigger's rediscovery of his country is an allegorical journey: it is a search for an identity for both the Brazilian people and Amado himself.

Amado married his first wife, Matilde Garcia Rosa, in December 1933, and they had a child, Lila, in 1935. That year Amado graduated from law school, but he never bothered to pick up his diploma. During this time he continued writing. His second novel, *Cacau* (1933, Cacao), was the first in a series of three books revolving around the cocoa industry. *Cacau* exposes the conflicts, hardships, and violence that divide the cocoa plantation owners and workers in the city of Ilhéus. The novel clearly denounces the poverty and economic abuse that rural workers had to endure on the plantations. The publication of this novel was an unequivocal statement of Amado's sympathy for the Communist Party. On the one hand, *Cacau* had a good commercial reception that established Amado on the national literary scene. On the other hand, it created the first in a long series of conflicts between Amado and various Brazilian dictatorships, beginning with Getúlio Vargas's government, which banned *Cacau* shortly after its publication. By that time Amado already was finishing his third novel, which he began writing in 1929. *Suor* (1934, Sweat) is similar to *Cacau* in the sense that it continues to depict the misery and exploitation of the lower class. Whereas the previous work takes place in the rural interior of Bahia, however, this novel unfolds in the urban setting of Salvador, the capital of the state.

Amado next published *Jubiabá* (1935; translated, 1984), which, after *O país do carnaval*, was the second novel in a series devoted to the city of Salvador. This book tells the story of the picaresque-like character Antonio Balduíno, known as Baldo, who embodies the sorrows and the hopes of the Brazilian poor, especially the population of African descent. Balduíno is a lost black child who rapidly escapes the home of his Portuguese hosts to live off the streets, leading a gang of young beggars. Over the course of the narrative he takes on many vocations, including professional boxer, tobacco plantation worker, circus employee, and docker. Balduíno spends some of his time in bars, improvising and writing samba songs. He has a love for the bohemian lifestyle and for black women, with whom he enjoys great success. Although he seduces many such women throughout the novel, his sincere but platonic love goes to Lindinalva, the white daughter of his childhood host who dies as a prostitute, unaware of Balduíno's lifelong commitment to her.

Most of the proletarian themes that characterized Amado's previous works are present in *Jubiabá*. For instance, the novel ends with a successful strike that allows Balduíno and his fellow workers to gain new recognition and improvements of their working conditions. Compared with Amado's previous efforts,

however, *Jubiabá* was written in a more sophisticated and symbolic literary style. Balduíno's role as labor agitator in scenes that depict drinking and prostitution is an obvious testament to Zola's works, and yet, unlike the endings of Zola's novels, which reestablish power to the rich owners, the conclusion of *Jubiabá* offers victory in the solidarity of the working class.

For some critics Amado's use of aspects of Brazilian popular culture make *Jubiabá* his masterpiece of the 1930s. For example, aspects of Afro-Brazilian folklore are introduced in the narrative through the title character, an old black man who conducts *candomblé* ceremonies, a type of African spirit worship brought by slaves to Brazil in the 1550s. These same critics praise Amado for being the first Brazilian novelist to strongly promote Bahian African culture and religion and for being the first to write a novel with a main character of African descent. Others, however, have denounced the way Amado describes a *candomblé* ceremony in the novel and accuse him of turning the Afro-Brazilian cult into an exotic, primitive, and erotic show. In the story, however, Jubiabá seems to possess mysterious powers that allow him to cure people of their ills.

Amado wrote two more books in the 1930s, *Mar morto* (1936; translated as *Sea of Death,* 1984) and *Capitães da areia* (1937; translated as *Captains of the Sands,* 1988). Both novels confront two realities of northeastern Brazil: the close relationship of the people with the sea and the misery that plagues a large portion of the population. *Mar morto* is the tragic love story between a mulatto sailor, Guma, and the young and pure Lívia. *Capitães da areia,* on the other hand, recounts the adventures of a group of homeless children whose leader is fourteen-year-old Pedro Bala. These kids work together during the day, fighting and committing various, sometimes violent, crimes in order to survive; when they return to the abandoned warehouse that serves as their shelter at night, however, they are portrayed as children with typical emotions, beliefs, hopes, and fears. *Mar morto* and *Capitães da areia* mix social analysis with a new, more poetic and lyrical style.

Several elements contributed to the immense popularity that Amado rapidly attained in Brazil in the 1930s: his consistent populist approach and the high quality of his storytelling; the many references to popular culture and folklore; his controversial writing style that mixes literary forms with the most accessible (and often vulgar) spoken language; and his direct political and sexual references. Amado's growing popularity, along with the communist themes of his novels and his association with the leftist Aliança Nacional Libertadora (National Liberation Alliance), was seen as a threat to the Vargas regime. As a result, Amado was arrested and jailed for two months in Rio de Janeiro in 1936.

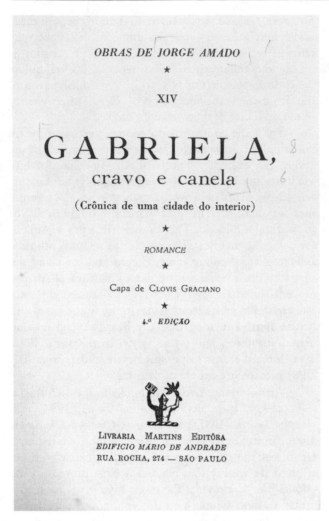

OBRAS DE JORGE AMADO

★

XIV

GABRIELA,
cravo e canela

(Crônica de uma cidade do interior)

★

ROMANCE

★

Capa de Clovis Graciano

★

4.ª EDIÇÃO

LIVRARIA MARTINS EDITÔRA
EDIFÍCIO MÁRIO DE ANDRADE
RUA ROCHA, 274 — SÃO PAULO

*Title page for Amado's popular 1958 novel featuring his first
strong and sensual female protagonist (Daniel
Library, The Citadel)*

Upon his release he embarked on a long journey across the Americas, visiting Uruguay, Argentina, Chile, Peru, Ecuador, Colombia, Guatemala, Mexico, Cuba, and the United States. During these travels he met Mexican painter Diego Rivera and American writer Michael Gold, whose *Jews Without Money* (1930) had a strong impact on the writing of *Suor*.

Amado attempted to return home through Manaus, where he was immediately imprisoned on 6 November 1937. Three days later several of his novels were burned publicly by order of the government. In January 1938 Amado was returned to Rio de Janeiro and released. That same year the government officially banned his books. Amado moved first to São Paulo, then to Estância, and in 1941, faced with an increasingly menacing political climate, Amado decided to move to Argentina. Throughout these agitated times he remained busy, collaborating with newspapers and writ-

ing two biographies. The first was *ABC de Castro Alves* (1941, ABC of Castro Alves), focusing on the poet who fought for the abolition of slavery and for improving the conditions of the poor. The second was *Vida de Luiz Carlos Prestes, el caballero de la esperanza* (1942, Life of Luiz Carlos Prestes, The Knight of Hope), which was published in Spanish in Buenos Aires. This book features the story of the founder of the Brazilian Communist Party.

Amado spent 1942 in Uruguay, where he wrote the novel that is considered his masterpiece. *Terras do sem fim* (1943; translated as *The Violent Land,* 1945) is set in the cocoa region of southern Bahia. It recounts the violent struggles for territorial supremacy between two powerful landowners and their families: the brothers Sinhô and Juca Badaró and Colonel Horácio da Silveira. *Terras do sem fim* shifts Amado's usual political message to the background in order to develop a much richer and complex narrative style. In this work Amado allows his writing to flow freely, which results in incredibly powerful, realistic characters. Several subplots involving approximately two hundred characters surround the main conflict. For example, Virgílio Cabral, an ambitious young lawyer hired by Horácio to defend his interests, leaves his mistress and former prostitute Margot (who then becomes Juca Badaró's lover) to have a passionate affair with Ester, Horácio's charming wife. When the colonel eventually finds out, he orders Virgílio's execution. Meanwhile, Amado creates an imposing female character in Sinhô Badaró's sister, the strong Don'Ana. The only survivor of her family, she marries the gambler João Magalhães and takes over the business. Other interesting and authentic characters include the authoritative Juca Badaró, who makes all his decisions—including the ordering of murders—based on randomly selected readings in the Bible; the witchdoctor Jeremias, who lives alone in the forest and who has "remédio para males do corpo e para males do amor" (remedies for bodily ills and for lovers' ailments); and the three sisters, Maria, Lucia, and Violeta, who turn to prostitution in order to survive.

The critics have often described *Terras do sem fim* as a lyrical epic whose frontier plot is reminiscent of the best western motion pictures, and it is generally considered to be Amado's most universal work. Indeed, the themes and conflicts at the center of this Bahian drama in many ways reflect the history of humanity and therefore resonated not just with Brazilians and other Latin Americans but with people around the world. The parallelisms of the birth of cities with the destinies of various generations along with the use of magical realism in *Terras do sem fim* may be seen as precursors of Colombian Gabriel García Márquez's novels, in particular *Cien años de soledad* (1968; translated as *One Hundred Years of Solitude,* 1970).

Amado returned to Brazil at the end of 1942. Briefly imprisoned, he was released and confined to residency in Salvador. While in the capital city of Bahia, he worked for the newspaper *O Imparcial* (The Impartial) and continued to write. Not yet finished with the cocoa cycle, in 1944 Amado published *São Jorge dos Ilhéus* (Saint George of Ilhéus; translated as *The Golden Harvest,* 1992), a sequel to *Terras do sem fim.* The action begins after Colonel Horácio da Silveira's victory over the Badaró family in the cocoa war. Horácio is now in control of the majority of the region, including the forest that had been the object of everyone's desire. Other characters who appeared in *Terras do sem fim* return in *São Jorge dos Ilhéus:* Don'Ana and her husband, João Magalhães; Maneca Dantas; and Antônio Víctor. This time, however, the plot does not tell the stories of two local colonels in search of territorial supremacy. Instead, Horácio faces a new kind of adversary: rich exporters who control prices, best represented in the novel by Carlos Zude and a mysterious American named Karbanks. This new setting represents the opposition between two systems: on one side, the archaic feudalism of the colonels who have sentimental and real attachments to the land, the region, and the plantations; and on the other, the modern imperialistic exporters who are well-organized businessmen. These outsiders do not care for the land and are only interested in profit. In the book Amado emphasizes the fact that both the colonels and the businessmen exploit the working class. In the end the capitalist Zude claims a total victory, but Amado makes sure to promote his own political vision through other characters. Zude's wife, Julieta, befriends the poet Sérgio Moura and the mechanic Joaquim. The latter is presented as a well-traveled idealist who gives lessons of hope and of a Marxist economy for a better, communist future.

In 1944 Amado was officially divorced from Matilde Garcia Rosa. That year he spent most of his time in the state of Bahia, first in Periperi and then in Salvador. During his stay in Periperi he wrote *Bahia de Todos os Santos* (1945, Bahia of All Saints), an unconventional text that is presented as a guide to the streets and mysteries of the city of Salvador. In 1945 Amado moved to São Paulo where he worked as a translator for the publishing house Editora Brasiliense and for the newspaper *Folha da Manhã* (The Morning News). Amado married his second wife, Zélia Gattai, on 8 July 1945, just before becoming director of the daily *Hoje,* and that year he also met and became a friend of Chilean poet Pablo Neruda. During this period Amado benefited from the overthrow of the Vargas government. This moment was favorable for the Brazilian Commu-

nist Party, and Amado was elected congressman from the state of São Paulo on the party's ticket.

While assuming his new functions in Rio de Janeiro, Amado was writing his next novel. Often compared by the critics to John Steinbeck's *The Grapes of Wrath* (1939), *Seara vermelha* (1946, Red Harvest) is Amado's first work that entirely takes place outside of Bahia. Divided into two parts, the novel marks a return of the author to a strong communist propaganda. The first section follows the long and difficult journey of the Jerónimo family. A new proprietor forces these farmers off the land they had cultivated in northeast Brazil for twenty years, and they decide to move to the promised land of São Paulo in search of a better life. The story depicts the sufferings the family has to endure, including the deaths of several relatives on the way to their new home. The second section of *Seara vermelha* revolves solely around one of Jerónimo's sons. Juvêncio (also known as Neném) leaves the family's household and becomes a political activist in Natal, where he ends up leading communist uprisings. Amado's own responsibilities in the Brazilian Communist Party probably had a great influence on the writing of *Seara vermelha,* which features strong criticism of Brazil's latifundiary system.

Amado's son João Jorge was born in Rio on 25 November 1947. That year, which marked the centenary of the birth of poet Castro Alves, Amado published the play *O amor de Castro Alves* (1947, The Love of Castro Alves; republished as *O amor do soldado* [1958, The Love of the Soldier]). By 1948 the Brazilian Communist Party was declared illegal, and Amado had to leave his seat in the congress. He immediately went into a voluntary exile, taking his family to various European countries. Their first stop was France, where Amado established residency in Paris in March. There he met the great thinkers, artists, and poets of the time: Jean-Paul Sartre, Simone de Beauvoir, Louis Aragon, Paul Eluard, Pablo Picasso, and Fernand Léger. Sartre and de Beauvoir developed a long friendship with the Amados, who in 1960 invited them to Salvador. In August 1948 Amado traveled to Poland, where he participated as vice president in the World Congress of Artists and Writers for Peace. After the Congress, Amado began a tour of Europe, visiting Italy, Czechoslovakia, Germany, Belgium, Switzerland, the Soviet Union, Sweden, Norway, Denmark, the Netherlands, Hungary, and Bulgaria. On 19 December 1949 Amado's daughter, Lila, died of a sudden illness in Rio. In 1950 Amado moved to Prague, where he wrote a travel account of his experiences in Eastern European countries titled *O mundo da paz* (1950, The World of Peace). In 1951 the Stalin Prize was awarded to Amado in Moscow. On 19 August 1951 his daughter Paloma was born in Prague. The fol-

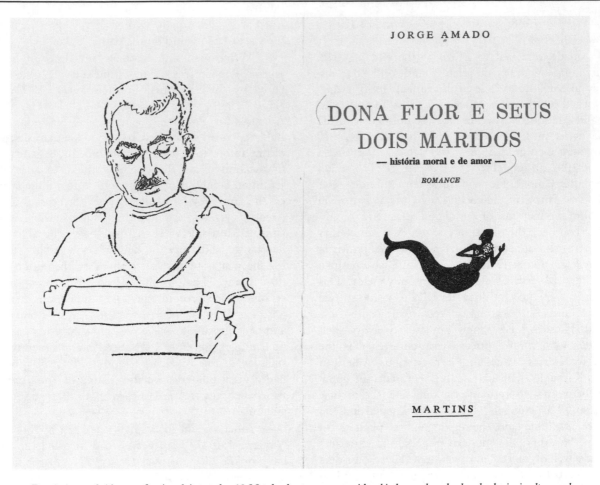

JORGE AMADO

(DONA FLOR E SEUS DOIS MARIDOS

— história moral e de amor —)

ROMANCE

MARTINS

Frontispiece and title page for Amado's popular 1966 tale about a woman with a kind, mundane husband who is simultaneously involved in a relationship with the ghost of her passionate, unfaithful, and abusive former husband (Young Library, University of Kentucky)

lowing year Amado traveled to China and Mongolia before returning to Brazil in 1953.

One result of Amado's years in exile was the simultaneous publication in Brazil and in Europe of *Os subterrâneos da liberdade* (1954, The Freedom Underground). Published in three volumes, it is Amado's longest and most political text. The narrative is based on the Vargas dictatorship that lasted from 1937 to 1940. Amado praises the clandestine communist fight of the people against the government while touching on some of the most cruel details of Vargas's rule such as imprisonment and torture. Amado's original plan to write two more volumes of this political epic to cover the post-1941 years was impeded by serious events unfolding in Eastern Europe. The death of Joseph Stalin in 1953 in the Soviet Union was followed by a period of transition that comprised Nikita Khrushchev's political takeover and the invasion of Hungary by Soviet troops in order to stop a people's revolt. By this time several members of the Brazilian Communist Party, including Amado, asked for the opening of a public debate on the redefining of socialist ideology and objectives. Tired of being ignored by a party that was intent on following the lines drawn by Moscow, many Brazilian intellectuals left the Communist Party. Amado virulently criticized the Soviet invasion of Hungary and joined his Brazilian comrades in requesting a new debate, but it is not clear to this day if he ever really resigned from the party. This political turmoil had a direct impact on Amado's work.

Most critics agree that Amado's next book, *Gabriela, cravo e canela* (1958; translated as *Gabriela, Clove and Cinnamon,* 1962), marks a definite change in his career. Although the novelist on several occasions insisted on the unity of his work, it is clear that all Amado's novels written after *Os subterrâneos da liberdade* differ from those before it on two major points: the political propaganda is relegated to a position of secondary importance and, most of all, Amado advances to the fore his sense of humor. The result of this new direction was a huge commercial success for *Gabriela, cravo e canela,* which sold more copies than any other book in Brazil at the time, going through six editions in four months, and earning several literary prizes for Amado, including the Prêmio Machado de Assis from the Instituto Nacional do Livro (National Book Institute) and the PEN Club do Brasil's Prêmio Luísa Cláudio de Souza. It was also adapted for Brazilian television. The *telenovela* (miniseries) based on *Gabriela, cravo e canela* that was produced by TV Globo in 1975 was a tremendous success.

Gabriela, cravo e canela takes place in 1925 in Ilhéus, the center of the cocoa industry, at a time of great prosperity and growing modernity. Nacib, a Brazilian bar owner of Syrian origin, desperately seeks a new cook and finds Gabriela, a gorgeous mulatto girl dressed in tatters, fleeing the drought of the arid Northeast. Nacib soon succumbs to Gabriela's irresistible charms and marries her in what becomes a passionate and tumultuous relationship. Nacib, however, is not the only man in town who falls for Gabriela's beauty and cooking. His bar becomes the city's main attraction, and his cook is the center of attention. Gabriela, accustomed to living in total freedom before her marriage, has a difficult time adapting to Nacib's rules, especially to the monogamous behavior expected in marriage. Nacib inevitably catches her cheating on him and has no choice but to have the marriage annulled to restore his honor. Life is not the same, however, and Nacib cannot live long without Gabriela. Incapable of resisting her, he finally hires Gabriela back and restores their personal relationship.

Gabriela, cravo e canela features Amado's first strong and sensual female protagonist whose extraordinary personality eclipses all the other characters. Thanks to his heroine, the novel is a refreshing depiction of the daily realities of the people of the region. It is also often described by critics as a novel where human relationships take precedence over political controversies and a work that gives priority to a kind of storytelling through which a sense of the joy of life is transmitted. There is a definite emphasis on laughter over tears, love and sex over ideological discourses, social satire over social realism, and freedom over restriction. Although the novel proved popular, Amado's new emphasis was not embraced by everyone. Some critics immediately accused the writer of becoming too capitalistic, and of turning to a more simplistic style of writing—sometimes labeled pornographic—to achieve commercial success over literary quality.

In 1959 Amado was inducted as a dignitary of Axé Opô Afonjá, a large *candomblé* center in Salvador, and he was unanimously elected to the Academia Brasileira de Letras (Brazilian Academy of Letters) two

years later. Shortly after this election he declined an offer to serve as Brazilian ambassador to Cairo. His father died in 1962, and that year he traveled to Cuba, accepting an invitation from the Unión de Escritores y Artistas Cubanos (Union of Cuban Writers and Artists), and from there he went on to visit Mexico. After his return to Brazil, Amado finally realized a longtime dream of settling his family in Salvador. In September 1963 the Amados moved into a brand-new home, located at 33 Alagoinhas Street in the district of Rio Vermelho.

Through these years Amado continued publishing. *Os velhos marinheiros* (1961, The Old Sailors) features two works. The short narrative "A morte e a morte de Quincas Berro D'Agua" (translated as *The Two Deaths of Quincas Wateryell,* 1965) tells the story of Joaquim Soares da Cunha, a family man and public functionary who decides one day to leave everything behind and to become Quincas Berro D'Agua. Quincas is a drunk who embraces a bohemian lifestyle before apparently dying in the seediest part of town. During what is presented as his wake Quincas's four best friends (who are notorious barflies) show up and take him for a night on the town. In this novelette Amado reveals his skill in his ability to maintain ambiguous language so that it is never clear if Quincas is dead or alive throughout the night. The readers are forced to come up with their own interpretations.

The novella "A completa verdade sobre as discutidas aventuras do Comandante Vasco Moscoso de Aragão" (The Complete Truth on the Debated Adventures of Captain Vasco Moscoso de Aragão; translated as *Home Is the Sailor,* 1964) completes *Os velhos marinheiros* and develops the same kind of duality found in its companion piece. In this case, however, two narrators propose different interpretations of the adventures of the main character, Vasco Moscoso de Aragão. Vasco claims to be a retired sea captain, but one narrator suspects him of being an impostor. The chain of events Amado describes gives the readers an opportunity to judge for themselves. When a ship arrives in Bahia with its captain missing, Vasco, who happens to be the only licensed captain in town, is recalled from retirement. His mission is to take the boat up north, to the city of Belém, where he arrives and safely disembarks. Vasco's order to anchor the vessel in perfect weather shortly after his arrival reinforces one narrator's view of the captain as a fake. Yet, a violent storm hits the port the following night. All ships but Vasco's are damaged, which seems to prove Vasco's good faith.

The two stories of *Os velhos marinheiros,* and "A morte e a morte de Quincas Berro D'Agua" in particular, won Amado almost unanimous acclaim. His mastery at using ambiguity and his command of plot

Cover for Amado's 1988 novel that celebrates Brazilian culture
and satirizes the policies of the military dictatorship that ruled
Brazil until 1985 (Thomas Cooper Library,
University of South Carolina)

socioeconomic system. Critics, however, did not like *Os pastores da noite* as much as they had enjoyed *Os velhos marinheiros*. They commonly found the plot simplistic and complained that the novel gave the impression of capitalizing on poverty.

In January 1965 Amado traveled to Paris, where he stayed three months to finish his latest novel, *Dona Flor e seus dois maridos* (1966; translated as *Dona Flor and Her Two Husbands,* 1969), which became a social phenomenon in Brazil and achieved enormous international success. In Amado's oeuvre the fame of this novel is matched only by *Gabriela, cravo e canela. Dona Flor e seus dois maridos* tells the story of Flor, a young Bahian woman, who is married to Vadinho, a great lover but an incorrigible drunk and rogue. Flor endures Vadinho's challenging personality until the day a drinking spree results in his death. Now a young and beautiful widow, Flor finds a new, more responsible husband in the well-established and respected pharmacist Doctor Teodoro Madureira. Yet, if Flor is reassured by her husband's devotion and faithfulness, she soon misses the passion that only Vadinho could provide. Flor is caught in a major dilemma when Vadinho returns to her as a ghost. Flor's initial reaction is to try to get rid of him, but she changes her mind when she realizes how much she misses him. With the pharmacist unaware of Vadinho's ghostly return, the novel concludes with a love triangle that fulfills all of Flor's desires.

Dona Flor e seus dois maridos reveals Amado's genius for storytelling and results in an entertaining mixture of parody and magic realism. It is also a return to a constant theme in Amado's fiction: the idealization of typically marginal characters from the Bahian lower classes. Readers found the characters of this novel convincing because many are based on real people from among Amado's friends. *Dona Flor e seus dois maridos* was adapted for cinema and theater. A motion picture, directed by Luís Carlos Barreto and starring Brazilian star Sônia Braga, was released in Latin America, Europe, and the United States in 1976, and there was also a Hollywood remake, *Kiss Me Goodbye* (1982), directed by Robert Mulligan and starring Sally Field, James Caan, and Jeff Bridges. A musical adaptation appeared on Broadway in 1979, and in 1997, TV Globo produced a miniseries based on the novel.

Between 1967 and 1970, Amado traveled to various European countries during the last five months of every year except 1968, which was a rare complete year in Brazil. However, Amado's many comings and goings during these years did not hamper his writing. The highly anticipated *Tenda dos milagres* (translated as *Tent of Miracles,* 1971) was published in 1969 with an initial printing of seventy-five thousand copies. *Tenda dos milagres* deals with a topic still controversial in Brazil:

structure silenced those reviewers who had previously criticized Amado for what they saw as unorganized and overly flamboyant texts.

Amado's next novel, *Os pastores da noite* (1964; translated as *Shepherds of the Night,* 1967), is divided into three distinct episodes that take place in the poorest neighborhoods of Salvador. Once again, the author deals with characters from the lowest classes who have in common their misery and hopes for a better future: vagabonds, drunks, cheaters, prostitutes, rogues, and scoundrels. This novel is also illustrative of Amado's increasing interest in magical realism, especially as represented in Afro-Brazilian issues such as *candomblé.* Amado sees these rituals as a possible solution for social discrepancies. Indeed, according to Amado, the gathering and inclusion of people of different races and social backgrounds in a deeply rooted cultural and religious cult show that all Brazilians can take their destinies into their own hands and solve their problems. Amado believed in people and in their capacity to control the racial relationships and the social situation of people of African descent. The protagonist, Pedro Archanjo, is a self-educated Bahian mulatto who publishes a series of anthropological studies on Afro-Brazilian culture during the first three decades of the twentieth century. Archanjo's writings contest the racist theories elaborated by scholars of the time and advocates mixed marriages. Ignored for years, Archanjo's work is discovered by James D. Levenson, a renowned American professor from Columbia University, during a visit to Brazil. This rediscovery results in a sudden national interest in Archanjo's books. Throughout the novel Amado reflects on the exploitation of the Afro-Brazilian community and on the hypocrisy that has always surrounded racial issues in Brazil. A motion picture based on the novel, directed by Nélson Pereira dos Santos, premiered in 1977.

In April 1971 Amado and his wife undertook a long journey to the United States and Canada. The Amados sailed across the Pacific Ocean, disembarked in Los Angeles, and crossed the United States from coast to coast. Amado's main reasons for this trip were to visit his American publisher Alfred Knopf and to give a series of informal talks at Pennsylvania State University, where he was a writer-in-residence from September to December 1971. Shortly after his return to Brazil, Amado had to deal with the death of his mother in March 1972. In the following years the novelist, always accompanied by his wife, traveled frequently between Brazil and Europe. They spent time in London and Paris, on the Mediterranean coast, and in Lisbon and Rome, where Amado received a prize from the Instituto Italo-Latino Americano (Italian Institute of Latin America) in 1976. During this time Amado did most of his writing at the house of his friend Zitelmann Oliva in Bahia while in Brazil, and in a London apartment on Harrowby Street while in Europe.

Amado's next two novels have young promiscuous girls turned prostitutes as protagonists. *Tereza Batista cansada de guerra* (1972; translated as *Tereza Batista: Home from the Wars,* 1975) recounts, from the perspective of several narrative voices, the adventures of Tereza Batista, who is sold by her starving family at the age of thirteen to the vile Justiniano Duarte da Rosa. She eventually escapes her sadistic owner by killing him, and she takes various roles in the remainder of the novel. Tereza ends up as a dynamic prostitute who, in an episode reminiscent of Balduíno's social fight in Jubiabá, leads a strike in favor of her profession. Organized prostitution is also at the center of *Tieta do Agreste: pastora de cabras* (1977; translated as *Tieta the Goat Girl,* 1979). The main character, Tieta, is expelled from home by her father, who condemns his daughter's promiscuity. She leaves her rural native town of Agreste

for the big city of São Paulo, where she becomes Madame Antoinette, the owner of one of the most popular houses of prostitution in the city. In the last episodes of the novel Tieta returns to her village to champion successfully several causes for her people. Although the protagonists of *Tereza Batista cansada de guerra* and *Tieta do Agreste* suffer an initial rejection by their relatives and eventually turn to prostitution, Amado depicts both Tereza and Tieta as likable, ambitious, and even powerful women. Nevertheless, just as *Gabriela, cravo e canela* generated the very first accusations of sexual stereotyping of women in Amado's works, the characters of Tereza and Tieta attracted criticism from academics, especially feminists, who began to describe Amado as a misogynist who exploits his female protagonists by always reducing them to male fantasies, making them champions of the only two skills that seem to be available to them: sex and cooking.

In 1979 Amado traveled to Africa, visiting Senegal and Angola as a guest of the countries' respective presidents, Léopold Sédar Senghor and Agostinho Neto. That same year *Farda, fardão, camisola de dormir* (translated as *Pen, Sword, Camisole,* 1985) was published. This novel, set during World War II, is another example of Amado's preference for multiple complex narrative voices. It depicts the hard-fought struggles that pit candidates for a recently open seat to the Brazilian Academy of Letters against each other. The novel also offers a glance at an aspect of the writer's life since Amado had been a member of the Academy of Letters since 1961.

By 1981 Amado's prolific and successful literary career had stretched over fifty years. He celebrated this landmark with the publication of his childhood memoirs, *O menino grapiúna* (1981, The Coastal Child). As an adult Amado always maintained a lively, childlike imagination. Hence, the novelist was able to address readers from all backgrounds and all ages, including children, for whom he wrote a few short stories. Among his works for children is *O gato malhado e a andorinha Sinhá* (1976; translated as *The Swallow and the Tomcat,* 1982), which was originally written in 1948 in honor of Amado's son, João Jorge. The publication of another children's book, *A bola e o goleiro* (1984, The Ball and the Goal Keeper), follows a certain logic: as an author so closely identified with the Brazilian people and popular culture, it only made sense that Amado finally wrote on the theme of soccer, which, along with *Carnaval,* is the most important and venerated institution in Brazil.

In 1984 Amado returned to an old favorite theme of his, that of the cocoa wars in northeast Brazil at the turn of the century. *Tocaia Grande* (1984, The Big Ambush; translated as *Showdown,* 1988), like *Terras do sem fim,* is a frontier novel with picaresque and fantastic elements. Its title refers to the initial ambush that allows one landowner to take control of an entire region. In the tradition of the best westerns, the novel chronicles the rise of an entire city, Irisópolis. Amado's storytelling develops many characters of various nationalities and races involved in many conflicts and plots. It is a story that captures the violence, vulgarity, and sexual promiscuity that characterize the survival of men in inhospitable locales. *Tocaia Grande* is also a denunciation of the rewriting of historical events. If the actions in the novel are faithfully reported by an anonymous narrator, they are completely changed by the journalist characters who report the events.

The publication of *Tocaia Grande* preceded long-awaited political change in Brazil. In 1985 a civilian government returned, ending a prolonged series of military dictatorships. The politically outspoken Amado especially enjoyed the moment, even though his incredible national and international popularity had generally protected him from dictators. The opening of the Fundação Casa de Jorge Amado (Jorge Amado Foundation's House) in Salvador da Bahia in 1987 confirmed Amado's place as a Brazilian institution.

During the 1980s and the early 1990s Amado continued to spend long periods of time in London and Paris, where he did most of his writing. His enormous popularity in Brazil made it impossible for him to have there the quietness and privacy he needed for his craft. *O sumiço da santa: uma história de feitiçaria* (1988, The Saint's Disappearance: A Magic Tale; translated as *The War of the Saints,* 1995) was written in Paris between the summer of 1987 and the summer of 1988. Some critics argue that in this novel Amado took advantage of the freedom provided by the restored democracy. According to this point of view Amado was finally free to include culturally diversified and controversial themes in his narrative. *O sumiço da santa* is the novelist's tribute to Afro-Brazilian culture and a severe (but humorously satirical) criticism of the racial discrimination that was common practice in Brazil during the military dictatorship. The narrative is recounted from the perspective of an omniscient narrator with strong ties to the author. In fact, at the end of the novel, Amado directly addresses, through his author-narrator, readers and critics, including those who constantly attached (sometimes contradictorily) his works and style. Amado's focus on an action in Salvador over forty-eight hours, the disappearance of the precious statue of Saint Barbara of the Thunder, allows him to address the most important representations of Afro-Brazilian culture: *candomblé, capoeira* (a mixture of dance and martial art), samba music, and *Carnaval.* Amado uses many fictional Bahian characters such as a devout Catholic named Adalgisa

and a novice practitioner of *candomblé* named Manela, along with representations of real people such as singer Caetano Veloso and Mãe Menininha dos Gantois, a *candomblé* dignitary. Again Amado uses multiple voices to develop several important Brazilian themes, such as the fusion of Catholicism and *candomblé,* the definition and nature of race, and the power of minority standpoints.

Two books printed in the early 1990s provided many insights on the novelist's personal life. In 1990 Amado published simultaneously in France and in Brazil a series of interviews with his French translator and dear friend Alice Raillard. This book, *Conversando com Alice Raillard* (Conversations With Alice Raillard), was originally written in French and was translated into Portuguese by Annie Dymetman. The publication of *Navegação de cabotagem: apontamentos para um livro de memórias que jamais escreverei* (1992, Coastal Navigation: Notes for a Book of Memoirs That I Will Never Write) coincided with the author's eightieth birthday. This book tells the author's life story in a series of journal entries that do not appear in chronological order. Consequently, the large index of names at the end of the book is most helpful for the reader. These memoirs feature many amusing anecdotes that marked the novelist's life. The accounts of the many travels Amado took around the world are especially interesting and enjoyable. For example, Amado recounts a trip to Ulaanbaater, the capital of Mongolia, that he undertook with Cuban poet Nicolás Guillén and their spouses in 1952. The Amados and the Guilléns, who had difficulty understanding their English interpreter, asked for another who could speak French or Spanish, but they were informed by their host, the minister of culture, that no one in the entire republic had mastered these two languages. Nonetheless, the next day a shy and frightened French interpreter was brought to them. It seems that shortly after the request by the Amados and the Guilléns the whole country had been searched by the national police force, who eventually found a young elementary-school teacher who knew French. Without any explanation he was taken to the capital city, where he was ordered to serve as interpreter for the Latin American guests. It happened that the teacher had taught himself French by reading over and over the only four texts available in this language at the National Library: a grammar manual, Alexandre Dumas *père's Les Trois mousquetaires* (1844; translated as *The Three Musketeers,* 1846) and *Le Comte de Monte-Cristo* (1844–1845; translated as *The Count of Monte-Cristo,* 1846), as well as a book on French wine and cheese. After Amado's visit the novice interpreter became director of the newly created Department of French at the Mongolian Ministry of Foreign Affairs.

Amado at work (from O sumiço da santa: uma história de feitiçaria, *1988;
Thomas Cooper Library, University of South Carolina)*

First published in a French translation in 1992, *A descoberta da América pelos turcos* (1994, The Discovery of America by the Turks) was Amado's humorous and original way to mark the celebrations surrounding the five hundredth anniversary of the discovery of the Americas. Obviously, the Turks did not discover the Americas, and Amado's title is not meant to be taken literally. The book is about the Syrian-born Jamil Bichara's discovery of the Brazilian town of Itabuna at the beginning of the twentieth century. Bichara is surrounded by two spiritual characters, Allah and Shatan (God and Satan according to Islam), who fight over who will influence his love life. Another best-seller, *A Descoberta da América pelos turcos* was seen by some critics as yet another example of Amado's story-telling genius and of his ability to insert humor and jokes in what otherwise appear to be serious topics.

In the 1990s Amado did not travel as much as in the past, although he did return to Europe and the Middle East on several occasions to be awarded various honors, including honorary doctorates from universities in France, Israel, Italy, and Portugal. He also attended in 1998 the annual Paris Book Exhibition, which was dedicated to Brazilian authors. In Brazil,

Amado remained active both in the developing of his cultural foundation and his writing. He published a book featuring a short story, *O milagre dos pássaros* (1997, The Miracle of Birds), and beginning with *Chapada Diamantina* (1989, Diamantina Highlands), he co-authored or prefaced a series of books documenting important aspects of the city and region of Bahia with text and photographs: *Carnaval* (1996; translated as *Carnaval*, 1996), *Mágica Bahia / Mágica Bahía* (1997, Magical Bahia), *Salvador* (1999), and *Rua Alagoinhas 33, Rio Vermelho: a casa de Zélia e Jorge Amado* (1999, 33 Alagoinhas Street, Rio Vermelho: Home of Zélia and Jorge Amado).

After 1998 Amado spent most of his time in his house, surrounded by family and friends. Somewhat weakened by heart problems that resulted in several hospitalizations and surgeries, the beloved Brazilian writer continued to receive prizes and honors. For instance, in 1997 the third volume of the prestigious series *Cadernos de Literatura Brasileira* (Journal of Brazilian Literature) was dedicated to Amado's work, and that same year, Amado was the theme of Salvador's *Carnaval*. In 2000 some of the most renowned Brazilian singers, including Gilberto Gil, Fafa de Belém, and Veloso, recorded a tribute in song to the writer titled

Jorge Amado: Letra e música. The Nobel Prize in literature is an honor, however, that Amado never received, although he was regularly mentioned as a possible recipient. Some critics believe that the awarding of the Nobel Prize in literature to José Saramago in 1998 meant that the award was unlikely to go to another author of Portuguese expression in the years immediately following. For Amado it was soon too late. On 6 August 2001, shortly before his eighty-ninth birthday, the novelist was rushed to a hospital in Salvador, where he died of a heart attack. Brazilian president Fernando Henrique Cardoso declared three days of national mourning, and thousands of people filed past the novelist's open casket on the day of his funeral. Following his demands, Amado was cremated, and his ashes were spread around a mango tree in the garden adjoining his house.

Critics continue to debate Amado's long literary career. For some, Amado was a major writer of the twentieth century, a great storyteller who mastered all forms of expression. These commentators are seduced by the author's ability to combine the most serious themes with humorous and sometimes magical descriptions of the daily realities of common people. They also admire the novelist's ability to develop incredibly complex narratives and to create so many different characters. According to these critics, Amado's expertise in Bahian culture, as well as in street dialects and ways of life, enhance the credibility of his protagonists.

Other critics argue that Amado was a promising writer who sold out to capitalism, claiming that he followed the success of *Gabriela, cravo e canela* by consistently using the same recipe to produce best-selling works. The author was often accused of writing simplistic novels featuring melodrama, gossip, and sex, elements that contributed to the popularity of Brazilian *telenovelas,* including those that were adaptations of his own books. In *Navegação de cabotagem* Amado responded to a critic who had called him "the novelist of whores and vagabonds," saying (with characteristic wit) that it was the best description of his work. Also, Amado's work has frequently been labeled as pornographic and misogynous. For some, his inclination to constantly insert sexual scenes or illustrations in his novels reflects his desire to have the ingredients thought to guarantee a best-seller. Amado has also been criticized for simplifying and idealizing serious unresolved issues such as race relations in Brazil.

The critical debate surrounding Jorge Amado makes it clear that his works have left few people unmoved. Although Amado has detractors, his exceptional national and international fame and his personal accomplishments, including an array of prestigious awards and honors, speak for his importance in Brazilian literary history.

Letters:
Jorge Amado: documentos (Lisbon: Europa-América, 1964).

Interview:
Conversando com Alice Raillard, translated from French into Portuguese by Annie Dymetman (Rio de Janeiro: Record, 1990).

References:
Alfredo Wagner Berno de Almeida, *Jorge Amado, política e literatura: un estudo sobre a trajetória intelectual de Jorge Amado* (Rio de Janeiro: Campus, 1979);

Piers Armstrong, *Third World Literary Fortunes: Brazilian Culture and Its Reception* (Lewisburg, Pa.: Bucknell University Press, 1999);

Bahia, a cidade de Jorge Amado: atas do ciclo de palestras A Bahia de Jorge Amado (Salvador: Casa de Palavras, 2000);

Juarez da Gama Batista, *O barroco e o maravilhoso no romance de Jorge Amado* (João Pessoa, Brazil: Chaves, 1973);

David Brookshaw, *Race and Color in Brazilian Literature* (Metuchen, N.J.: Scarecrow Press, 1986);

Keith H. Brower, Earl E. Fitz, and Enrique Martínez-Vidal, eds., *Jorge Amado: New Critical Essays* (New York: Routledge, 2001);

Cadernos de literatura brasileira, no. 3: *Jorge Amado* (São Paulo: Instituto Moreira Salles, 1997);

Nelson Cerqueira, *A política do partido comunista e a questão do realismo em Jorge Amado* (Salvador: Fundação Casa de Jorge Amado, 1988);

Bobby J. Chamberlain, *Jorge Amado* (Boston: Twayne, 1990);

Paloma Jorge Amado Costa, *ABC dos 50 anos de amor de Zélia e Jorge* (São Paulo: Maltese, 1995);

Costa, *As frutas de Jorge Amado ou o livro de delícias de Fadul Abdala* (São Paulo: Companhia das Letras, 1997);

Mark J. Curran, *Jorge Amado e a literatura de cordel* (Salvador: Fundação Cultural do Estado da Bahia / Rio de Janeiro: Fundação Casa de Rui Barbosa, 1981);

Eduardo de Assis Duarte, *Jorge Amado: romance em tempo de utopia* (Rio de Janeiro: Record, 1996);

Fred P. Ellison, "Jorge Amado," in his *Brazil's New Novel—Four Northeastern Masters: José Lins do Rêgo, Jorge Amado, Graciliano Ramos, and Rachel de Queiroz* (Berkeley: University of California Press, 1954), pp. 83–108;

Zélia Gattai, *Um chapéu para viagem* (Rio de Janeiro: Record, 1982);

Ilana Seltzer Goldstein, *O Brasil best seller de Jorge Amado: literatura e identidade nacional* (São Paulo: Serviço Nacional de Aprendizagem Comercial, 2003);

Alvaro Cardoso Gomes and Sonia Regina Rodrigues Neves, *Jorge Amado,* third edition (São Paulo: Nova Cultural, 1990);

Jorge Amado: ensaios sobre o escritor (Salvador: Universidade Federal da Bahia, 1982);

Giulia Lanciani, ed., *Jorge Amado: Ricette narrative* (Rome: Bulzoni, 1994);

Luis Costa Lima, "Jorge Amado," in *A literatura no Brasil,* second edition, volume 6, edited by Afrânio Coutinho (Rio de Janeiro: Sul Americana, 1968), pp. 304–332;

Suênio Campos de Lucena, "Jorge Amado," in her *21 escritores brasileiros: uma viajem entre mitos e motes* (São Paulo: Escrituras, 2001), pp. 13–17;

Antonio Manzatto, *Teologia e literatura: reflexão teológica a partir da antropologia contida nos romances de Jorge Amado* (São Paulo: Loyola, 1994);

Giorgio Marotti, *Black Characters in the Brazilian Novel,* translated by Maria O. Marotti and Harry Lawton (Los Angeles: Center for Afro-American Studies, University of California, 1987), pp. 325–388;

José de Barros Martins, ed., *Jorge Amado, povo e terra: 40 anos de literatura* (São Paulo: Martins, 1971);

José Paulo Paes, *De Cacau a Gabriela: um percurso pastoral* (Salvador: Fundação Casa de Jorge Amado, 1991);

Daphne Patai, *Myth and Ideology in Contemporary Brazilian Fiction* (Rutherford, N.J.: Fairleigh Dickinson University Press / London: Associated University Presses, 1983), pp. 111–140;

Vera Rollemberg, ed., *Um grapiúna no país do carnaval* (Salvador: Fundação Casa de Jorge Amado, 1992);

Rosane Rubim and Maried Carneiro, *Jorge Amado, 80 anos de vida e obra: subsídios para pesquisa* (Salvador: Fundação Casa de Jorge Amado, 1992);

Alvaro Salema, *Jorge Amado, o homem e a obra: presença em Portugal* (Lisbon: Europa-América, 1982);

Aluysio Mendonça Sampaio, *Jorge Amado, o romancista* (São Paulo: Maltese, 1996);

Izatil Benício dos Santos, *Jorge Amado: retrato incompleto* (Rio de Janeiro: Record, 1993);

Malcolm Noel Silverman, "Algumas observações sobre as personagens na obra de Jorge Amado," in his *Moderna ficção brasileira,* translated into Portuguese by João Guilherme Linke (Rio de Janeiro: Civilização Brasileira, 1978), pp. 137–157;

Miécio Táti, *Jorge Amado: vida e obra* (Belo Horizonte, Brazil: Itatiaia, 1961);

Paulo Tavares, *O baiano Jorge Amado e sua obra* (Rio de Janeiro: Record, 1980);

Tavares, *Criaturas de Jorge Amado: dicionário biográfico de todas as personagens imaginárias, seguido de índice onomástico das personalidades reais ou lendárias mencionadas, de elenco dos animais e aves com nomes próprios e de roteiro toponímico da obra de ficção de Jorge Amado, totalizando 4.910 verbetes,* revised second edition (Rio de Janeiro: Record, 1985);

Tempo Brasileiro, special Amado issue, 74 (July–September 1983);

Jon S. Vincent, "Jorge Amado, Jorge Desprezado," *Luso-Brazilian Review,* supplementary issue, 15 (Summer 1978): 11–17.

Papers:

Collections of Jorge Amado's manuscripts and other papers are held by the Academia Brasileira de Letras (Brazilian Academy of Letters) in Rio de Janeiro and the Fundção Casa de Jorge Amago (Jorge Amado House Foundation) and Universidade Federal da Bahia (Federal University of Bahia) in Salvador.

Jorge Andrade
(Aluísio Jorge Andrade Franco)
(21 March 1922 – 13 March 1984)

Sabrina Karpa-Wilson
Indiana University

BOOKS: *Pedreira das almas: peça em dois atos e quatro quadros* (São Paulo: Anhembi, 1958);

A moratória (Rio de Janeiro: AGIR, 1959);

Pedreira das almas; O telescópio, introduction by Paulo Mendonça (Rio de Janeiro: AGIR, 1960);

A escada e Os ossos do barão (São Paulo: Brasiliense, 1964);

Vereda da salvação: peça em 2 atos (São Paulo: Brasiliense, 1965);

Rasto atrás: peça em 2 partes, preface by Delmiro Gonçalves (São Paulo: Brasiliense, 1966);

Senhora na boca do lixo: peça em três atos (Rio de Janeiro: Civilização Brasileira, 1968);

Marta, a árvore e o relógio: dez peças, with essays by Antônio Cândido, Osman Lins, Lourival Gomes Machado, Sábato Magaldi, Richard Morse, Décio de Almeida Prado, and Anatol Rosenfeld (São Paulo: Perspectiva, 1970);

Milagre na cela (Rio de Janeiro: Paz e Terra, 1977);

Labirinto (Rio de Janeiro: Paz e Terra, 1978);

O incêndio (São Paulo: Global, 1979).

PLAY PRODUCTIONS: *A moratória,* São Paulo, Teatro Maria Della Costa, 6 May 1955;

O telescópio, Rio de Janeiro, Teatro Nacional de Comédia, 1957;

Pedreira das almas, São Paulo, Teatro Brasileiro de Comédia, 1958;

A escada, São Paulo, Teatro Brasileiro de Comédia, 1961;

Os ossos do barão, São Paulo, Teatro Brasileiro de Comédia, 8 March 1963;

Vereda da salvação, São Paulo, Teatro Brasileiro de Comédia, 8 July 1964;

Senhora na boca do lixo, Lisbon, Companhia Amélia Rey-Colaço, 1966;

Rasto atrás, Rio de Janeiro, Teatro Nacional de Comédia, 26 January 1967;

A receita, São Paulo, Primeira Feira Paulista de Opinião, 1968;

A zebra, Rio de Janeiro, Feira Brasileira de Opinião, 1978;

Milagre na cela, Rio de Janeiro, Grupo de Barr, 1981.

PRODUCED SCRIPTS: *Os ossos do barão,* television, TV Globo, 1973–1974;

Exercício findo, television, TV Globo, 1974;

O grito, television, TV Globo, 1975–1976;

As gaivotas, television, TV Tupi, 1979;

Dulcinéia vai à guerra, television, TV Bandeirantes, 1980–1981;

O fiel e a pedra, television, TV Cultura, 1981;

O velho diplomata, television, TV Cultura, 1981;

Memórias do medo, television, TV Cultura, 1981;

Os adolescentes, television, Bandeirantes, 1981–1982;

Senhora na boca do lixo, television, TV Cultura, 1982;

A escada, television, TV Cultura, 1982;

Ninho de serpentes, television, Bandeirantes, 1982;

Sabor de mel, television, Bandeirantes, 1983;

Mulher diaba, television, Bandeirantes, 1983.

OTHER: *O mundo composto, Realidade,* 80 (November 1972);

A zebra, in *Feira Brasileira de Opinião* (São Paulo: Global, 1978).

Jorge Andrade is generally viewed as a key figure in the development of the modern Brazilian stage. The play for which he is best known, *A moratória* (1955, The Moratorium), launched his career as a playwright and returned national themes to a theatrical establishment that had relied heavily on European classics. Following in the footsteps of Nelson Rodrigues's *Vestido de noiva* (1943, Wedding Gown), Andrade's play also introduced innovative narrative and staging techniques that influenced future Brazilian theatrical texts and productions. Less widely known and discussed, but just as important for a full understanding of contemporary Brazilian theater, is Andrade's complete ten-play cycle,

Marta, a árvore e o relógio (1970, Martha, the Tree and the Clock), of which *A moratória* is a part. Written between 1951 and 1969, a period in which Brazil underwent intense political, economic, and social change, the cycle incorporates national history, autobiographical experience, and a concern with the workings of theater itself to produce a highly cohesive and powerful body of plays. Andrade's sustained, in-depth examination of personal and collective memory—and of the role theater plays in the shaping and transmission of memory—was unprecedented in the history of Brazilian drama.

Aluísio Jorge Andrade Franco was born in Barretos, a small town in the interior of the state of São Paulo, on 21 March 1922, the eldest son of Ignacio Lima Franco and Albertina Andrade Franco. His parents were descendants of the Junqueiras, a traditional family that had migrated from Minas Gerais to São Paulo some two hundred years earlier. At the time of Andrade's birth his family enjoyed significant prosperity as coffee planters. Seven years later their circumstances changed, as the international impact of the United States's stock market crash of 1929 and the Brazilian Revolution of 1930 brought financial ruin to many members of the Brazilian coffee aristocracy. The Andrade property, which at its largest had covered almost 73,000 hectares, shrank to 148.

The crisis of the Brazilian coffee aristocracy caused dramatic scenes within the Andrade family, episodes that were deeply etched in the playwright's memory and eventually surfaced in different forms in his plays. For example, at the age of seven Andrade witnessed his once-imposing grandfather break down, threatening invisible enemies with a gun while his wife and daughter struggled to take the weapon away from him. The playwright later dubbed the event "Pietà Fazendeira" (Planter Pietà) and identified it as the memory that determined the thematic focus of his dramaturgy. Andrade included this episode in an early version of *A moratória,* but it was cut from performances of the play because it was considered by the director of the first production, Gianni Ratto, too melodramatic and untheatrical, and it never made it into print. Nevertheless, the economic and emotional trajectory of Andrade's family clearly had a major impact on his writing, becoming the structural and thematic center of his early plays and one of the primary narrative lines of his ten-play cycle. Some critics have argued that Andrade's obsessive focus on the decline of the coffee elite was fueled largely by nostalgia, and he has been compared to nostalgic writers of historical family cycles such as José Lins do Rêgo. Andrade's approach to this period in his family's and nation's history, however, grows increasingly critical in his later plays.

Andrade's tumultuous relationship with his father also became a recurring theme in his plays. As the eldest son, Andrade was expected to take over the family farm and carry on the rural family tradition, but he was an introspective child who loved to read and showed little inclination for the rigors of rural life. Andrade's desire to take a different path became a source of ongoing and traumatic friction with his father. He later worked these experiences into dramatic plots turning on generational conflict, particularly conflict between a father and his intellectual son.

During his nine difficult years working on his father's plantation, Andrade embarked on several different occupational courses with little success. He enrolled in and soon abandoned a course of study at the prestigious Faculdade de Direito de São Paulo (São Paulo Law School), law being the expected professional avenue for the sons of wealthy landowning families. He also worked at a bank for a short period and failed an entrance exam for military school in Ceará. In 1950 he fled his father's farm for São Paulo, where he experienced an epiphany. He went to see a production of a Tennessee Williams play and was so taken by the experience that he approached the famous actress Cacilda Becker. Becker encouraged him to enroll in the Escola de Artes Dramáticas (School of Dramatic Arts), which proved to be a major turning point in his life, launching his career in drama.

In 1956 Andrade married Helena de Almeida Prado, who was from one of the oldest, most traditional families of São Paulo, a so-called *quatrocentão* (four-hundred-year family), a descendant of the sixteen aristocratic families who were presumably part of the original colonizing expedition to the São Paulo region in the early sixteenth century. His wife's family became a rich source of material for his plays, several of which focus on *quatrocentões* who, despite or because of economic decline, evade their present circumstances through an obsession with lineage and past grandeur. Furthermore, some of Andrade's plots are embellished transpositions of stories told to him by his wife's relatives. Such is the case with *A escada* (1964, The Stairs) and *Os ossos do barão* (1964, The Baron's Bones).

Andrade's writing career can be roughly divided into two periods. The first period began in 1951 with a play he wrote as a class exercise at the School of Dramatic Arts, *O telescópio* (1960, The Telescope), and ends with the 1970 publication of *Marta, a árvore e o relógio.* These years of Andrade's career were largely dedicated to the writing of his ten-play cycle, variously dubbed the "Ciclo do Marta" (Cycle of Marta), "Ciclo do passado" (Cycle of the Past), "Ciclo paulista" (*Paulista* Cycle), "Ciclo da memória" (Cycle of Memory), and "Ciclo da experiênca pessoal" (Cycle of Personal Expe-

JORGE ANDRADE
"

PEDREIRA DAS ALMAS
O TELESCÓPIO

INTRODUÇÃO DE
PAULO MENDONÇA

CAPA DE
MILTON RIBEIRO

1 9 6 0
Livraria AGIR *Editôra*
RIO DE JANEIRO

Title page for the book featuring two of Jorge Andrade's early plays, including the first book publication of O telescópio *(Joint University Libraries, Nashville, Tennessee)*

rience). Most of these plays deal with one of the two social groups with which Andrade's life was entangled, alternately focusing on the decline of the coffee elite and the fate of the *quatrocentões*. This split perspective allows for a wide range of plot possibilities while retaining cohesion in terms of broader themes: social, political, and economic change as seen through the stories of individual families; the conflict, felt at both a personal and national level, between a nostalgia for the past and a need to live in the present and work for the future; and Brazilian social and economic inequalities and injustices.

Andrade apparently had a play cycle in mind early on, and he proceeded to write his plays according to a basic plan that evolved over the years. At first, he intended to write a four-play cycle that he dubbed

"Raízes da terra" (Roots of the Earth). These plays were to focus on the formation, development, and decline of the *paulista* (those living in São Paulo) landowning families. After his marriage to Helena, his plan was broadened to include the *quatrocentão* focus, and it eventually expanded into the ten-play *Marta, a árvore e o relógio*. The plays included in the final version of the cycle were written in a different order than that in which they appear in the definitive 1970 edition, for which they were rearranged by the author according to an internal chronological logic.

Andrade's first produced play was *O telescópio*, which tells the story of a ruined coffee planter who watches impotently as his children fight over their inheritance. The main characteristics of Andrade's intended "Roots of the Earth" cycle are all here: the decline of the coffee elite, nostalgia for the past, and conflicts between an older and younger generation and between rural and urban ways of life. In *O telescópio* the conflict is polarized with little room for psychological complexity. The older generation is portrayed as honest, hardworking, and basically good, while the younger generation is seen as lazy, selfishly ambitious, and conniving. The telescope of the title serves as an organizing symbol: used by the father to stargaze and escape a harsh reality, it is destroyed when his oldest son, returning drunk from town, steps on it, thus signaling the destruction of the old by the new and the inevitability of decadence.

Andrade's next play, *A moratória,* worked through the same basic themes but added psychological depth, richer historical background, and innovative use of space and time. The narrative structure and the stage are divided into two spaces and two time periods: 1929 on the old family farm, and 1932 in a modest home in town after the farm has been lost. The central cast of characters is the father, in denial about his losses and waiting for a moratorium so that he can regain the farm, a self-sacrificing mother, a misfit son, and a daughter who sews to support the family. All embody characteristics that recur in Andrade's characters. For example, the misfit son is a precursor of Vicente, the playwright son featured in several later plays, and the mother and daughter exhibit a female courage and strength that will be epitomized in the symbolic character of Martha, after whom the entire cycle is named. Finally, the father, who appears in several plays in the cycle, is the desperate patriarch of "Pietà Fazendeira." In comparison with *O telescópio, A moratória* is more clearly and heavily based on autobiographical premises. Andrade continued this trend in future texts.

After *A moratória,* Andrade received a fellowship from the American government to study theater in the United States. There he met American playwright

Arthur Miller, who, according to Andrade, advised him to try to discover why men are what they are and not what they would like to be, and write about the difference. Andrade took this advice to heart, since his dramatic plots frequently focus on disappointment and a sense of failure.

First, however, Andrade wrote *Pedreira das almas* (1958, Quarry of Souls), in which he moves back in time to 1842 in order to trace the *paulista* beginnings of the families depicted in *O telescópio* and *A moratória*. Like Andrade's own family, the characters of *Pedreira das almas* migrate from Minas Gerais to São Paulo in search of a better life after the end of the Minas gold rush. Where Andrade's first two plays are realistic dramas, reminiscent of Anton Chekhov or Arthur Miller, this third play has been compared to Greek tragedy. During the Liberal Revolt of 1842 in Minas Gerais, a group of people led by one of the rebels decides to leave their dying town for the promised land of São Paulo. They are opposed by the matriarch of the town and her followers, who do not want to leave their ancestors and roots behind. When the imperial forces invade the town looking for the rebel leader, the matriarch's son is killed and his body denied burial. This event brings the town together against the repressive invading troops, and in the end all but the matriarch and her daughter leave for the new land. Once again, the past is pitted against the present and the future, and old values against new ideas, but unlike in *O telescópio,* the new is seen in a positive light, as offering the possibility of hope and renewal. *Pedreira das almas* also introduces the theme of political oppression, which appeared again in later plays, notably in those written after 1964.

In 1960 Andrade wrote the realistic drama *A escada,* in which he shifted his viewpoint from a rural to an urban setting, and from the coffee elite to the *quatrocentões*. In this play a once wealthy, traditional family now lives in an apartment building, and the elderly parents shuffle up and down the building's stairs, alternately living with one or another of their children. The patriarch dreams of recuperating land once owned by a baron ancestor, now a thriving urban neighborhood, while his children face the need to put their parents in a nursing home. Vicente, the playwright character who is a stand-in for Andrade himself, makes his first appearance in this play. The urban, *quatrocentão* focus of *A escada* continues in *Os ossos do barão* (1963), Andrade's biggest box-office success, which he later turned into a popular soap opera. The only comedy of *Marta, a árvore e o relógio,* it tells a story of class reconciliation through romance: a poor Italian immigrant turned wealthy industrialist plots to marry his son to the daughter of a traditional *paulista* family, luring the *quatrocentões* to his home through an ad announcing the sale of their

revered ancestor's bones. With the next play in the cycle, *Senhora na boca do lixo* (Lady in the Garbage Pit; staged in Lisbon in 1966 and Rio de Janeiro in 1968), Andrade returns to more serious themes. An impoverished *quatrocentona* smuggles goods from Europe in order to maintain her lifestyle, while her daughter struggles to adapt to a new, more humble reality. Although criticized for featuring caricatures and implausible, melodramatic situations, the play was another commercial success.

Andrade returns to a rural setting in *Vereda da salvação* (Path of Salvation, produced in 1964; published 1965), one of the playwright's best-known plays, but this time he depicts the experience of a different social class. Based on a real event that occurred in the interior of Minas Gerais, the play dramatizes the massacre of a group of sharecroppers who were caught up in a wave of religious fanaticism brought on by their impoverished conditions. Andrade conceived *Vereda da salvação* on a continuum with the plays that focus on the landowning class, noting in a June 1964 interview for *Visão* (Vision) magazine that its characters belong to the same larger social landscape. The play, a strong indictment of social and economic inequalities, was an utter failure at the box office in July 1964. The reception of the play was telling of the political climate of the time. Appearing shortly after the March 1964 military coup that overthrew populist president João Goulart and installed a military dictator, Humberto Castello Branco, in the presidency, the play was rejected by an elitist, wealthy public, who found echoes of communist rhetoric in its preoccupation with the "agrarian question." Meanwhile, observers on the Left took exception to what they considered to be the "alienation" of Andrade's sharecropper characters. Not until a 1993 production at the Teatro Serviço Social do Comércio-Anchieta in São Paulo did the play enjoy a reception that recognized its merits as a moving social and political drama.

The last three plays of *Marta, a árvore e o relógio* deepen Andrade's autobiographical explorations and his examination of metatheatrical concerns. Andrade turned away from realism toward more expressionist techniques and to epic theater. *Rasto atrás* (Backward Tracks, published in 1966; produced in 1967) may be considered a dramatized autobiography because it traces the life of Vicente, the playwright character from *A escada,* from his birth in 1922, the year Andrade was born, to 1965. The text works through psychological conflicts that were the author's own, namely the difficult relationship between the intellectual protagonist and his father, a farmer and hunter who can neither understand nor accept his son's bookish pursuits. At forty-three years old, the tormented Vicente returns to his

Jorge Andrade
Marta, a Árvore e o Relógio

Editôra Perspectiva   São Paulo

*Title page for Andrade's 1970 ten-play cycle, in which he portrays
social, political, and economic changes in mid-twentieth-century
Brazil through the stories of individual families
(Howard-Tilton Memorial Library,
Tulane University)*

cally complex, probing the processes of history, art, and the self in abstract, sometimes cryptic language. *As confrarias* is set in late-eighteenth-century Minas Gerais, during the *Inconfidência Mineira* (an unsuccessful conspiracy against the Portuguese colonial government), and follows the travails of Martha, who knocks at the doors of several religious brotherhoods in search of a burial site for her son, José, who was executed by the Portuguese colonial government. José was an actor who became involved in the anticolonial conspiracy, and through his story the play explores the political and social role of actors and the theater in general. The work expounds on the need to connect theatrical practice with political reality, particularly in times of oppression. The brotherhoods' behavior, rejecting Martha's pleas and refusing to bury the body out of selfish fear and greed, dramatizes the venality of religious institutions, while the cruelty and repressive measures of the colonial administration bring to mind the repressive actions of the dictatorship under which Andrade was writing.

As confrarias is the only play in the cycle in which Martha, one of the three elements of the cycle's title, appears as the protagonist. In the other plays a character named Martha either makes a brief appearance or is mentioned by other characters. Some of these Marthas appeared in the original versions of the plays, but others were inserted when Andrade revised the texts for the 1970 publication of the cycle. In preparing this edition, the playwright made some important adjustments to several of the texts, with the purpose of establishing greater cohesion among the plays. Many of his changes involve the three components of the title, Martha, the tree, and the clock, which function as symbols in the major thematic lines of the plays. Martha, both in *As confrarias* and elsewhere, embodies a host of positive qualities, including action, renewal, and realism against the stagnation and escapism of those who would cling to the past, and courage and strength in the face of corruption and injustice. She might be construed as a kind of muse to both Vicente and Andrade himself. The tree functions as a metaphor for origins, rural tradition, and genealogy, but also in *Pedreira das almas* as a symbol of change. The presence in several plays of a clock without hands suggests stagnation, an inability to transcend the past, but at cycle's end the repaired family clock signals movement forward. This symbolism is rich in suggestions about the complexity of the dialogue between past and present, and between tradition and transformation in Andrade's work.

O sumidouro is Andrade's most clearly metatheatrical text. It is essentially a dialogue between Vicente, the playwright, and the protagonist of the play he is in the process of writing, the famous seventeenth-century

hometown in search of self-knowledge through reconciliation with his father, but he is assailed by memories of formative events from different periods of his life. The play follows the meanderings of Vicente's memory, rendered through a fragmented, nonlinear narrative. Film and slide projectors are used to capture the jumbled, associative processes of memory, introducing into Brazilian theater a major technique of contemporary stagecraft.

As confrarias (The Brotherhoods) and *O sumidouro* (The Sinkhole) were completed for the 1970 edition of the cycle and have not yet been staged. They are perhaps Andrade's most explicitly political plays after *Vereda da salvação,* and they are textually and theatri-

paulista bandeirante (explorer) Fernão Dias. Vicente writes about Dias's last expedition to search for gold and precious stones at the behest of the Portuguese king. He is especially interested in Dias's relationship with his son by an Indian woman, José Dias, and in the *bandeirante*'s decision to sacrifice his own son for the sake of the expedition's success. Vicente challenges Fernão Dias's decision, urging his character to reexamine his actions and role as a pawn of the corrupt Portuguese government, and to reevaluate his relationship with José. In turn, Dias questions Vicente's motivations for writing, insinuating that the playwright too may be looking for something he cannot find. Hence, Andrade once again returns to the father/son plot, this time to offer alternative interpretations of some of the national myths enshrined in history books. As in *As confrarias,* a key episode in Brazilian history is examined through a critical lens that brings the past to bear incisively on a present fraught with its own lies and deceptions.

The short second phase of Andrade's writing career has received little attention or praise. After 1970, declaring himself disillusioned with theater in Brazil, Andrade turned to writing soap operas and journalistic pieces. He did write some new plays, however, dedicating himself more to contemporary issues, but critics generally consider these texts to be of lesser literary interest than his earlier work. His best-known play from this period is *Milagre na cela* (Miracle in the Cell; published in 1977, produced in 1981), which tells the story of a nun tortured and raped by a police commissioner during the military dictatorship installed in 1964. Like several of his other plays of this period, *Milagre na cela* was poorly received by critics, who saw it as a superficial and clichéd treatment of the subject of institutionalized torture. Other dramatic texts from this phase of his career, many of which are one-act plays, include *As colunas do templo* (The Temple Columns; written in 1952, revised in 1968, and adapted for television as *Exercício findo* in 1974), *A receita* (The Prescription; performed in 1968), *A zebra* (The Zebra; performed in 1978), *O mundo composto* (The Composed World; published in 1972), *A Loba* (The Female Wolf; written in 1978 but never performed or published), *O incêndio* (The Fire; published in 1979), and *A corrente* (The Chain; written and performed in 1981).

Jorge Andrade died in São Paulo on 13 March 1984. In reputation he remains one of the most productive and incisive Brazilian playwrights of all time. Surprisingly, there have been few in-depth studies and only infrequent attempts at serious productions of his dramatic works. Recently, however, some scholars and theater companies have rediscovered Andrade and his works. In 1994 a "Ciclo de Debates" (Cycle of Debates) to discuss Andrade's work was organized in São Paulo, and productions of *Vereda da salvação* and *Rasto atrás,* in 1993–1994 and 1995–1996, respectively, received prizes in Rio de Janeiro and São Paulo. Additionally, two recent studies of plays from *Marta, a árvore e o relógio* thoroughly examine issues central to Andrade's dramaturgy: Catarina Sant'Anna's *Metalinguagem e teatro* (1997) and Luiz Humberto Martins Arante's *Teatro da memória: história e ficção na dramaturgia de Jorge Andrade* (2001). There is little doubt that Andrade's drama deserves this renewed attention. With their sustained scrutiny of history, use of personal and collective memory, and explorations of the possibilities of theater, Andrade's works still have much to say to today's audiences.

References:

Luiz Humberto Martins Arrantes, *Teatro da memória: história e ficção na dramaturgia de Jorge Andrade* (São Paulo: Anablume/Fundação de Amparo à Pesquisa do Estado de São Paulo, 2001);

João Roberto Faria, "A dramaturgia de Jorge Andrade," in *O teatro na estante: estudos sobre dramaturgia brasileira e estrangeira* (Cotia, São Paulo: Ateliê, 1998), pp. 143–157;

Mário Guidarini, *Jorge Andrade na contramão da história* (Florianópolis: Editora da Universidade Federal de Santa Catarina, 1992);

Sábato Antônio Magaldi, *Panorama do teatro brasileiro,* third edition (São Paulo: Global, 1997);

Décio de Almeida Prado, "A escada," in *Teatro em progresso: crítica teatral, 1955–1964* (São Paulo: Martins, 1964), pp. 221–225;

Prado, "Os ossos do barão," in *Teatro em progresso: crítica teatral, 1955–1964* (São Paulo: Martins, 1964), pp. 257–260;

Prado, "Vereda da salvação," in *Teatro em progresso: crítica teatral, 1955–1964* (São Paulo: Martins, 1964), pp. 291–296;

Catarina Sant'Anna, *Metalinguagem e teatro: a obra de Jorge Andrade* (Cuiabá: Editora de Universidade Federal de Mato Grosso, 1997).

Papers:

Some of Jorge Andrade's dramatic writings are held at the Acervo da Seção de Artes Cênicas do Centro Cultural São Paulo (Collection of the Scenic Arts Section of the São Paulo Cultural Center).

Mário de Andrade

(9 October 1893 – 25 February 1945)

Maria Luci De Biaji Moreira
College of Charleston

BOOKS: *Há uma gota de sangue em cada poema,* as Mário Sobral (São Paulo: Pocai, 1917);

Paulicéia desvairada (São Paulo: Casa Mayença, 1922); translated by Jack E. Tomlins as *Hallucinated City* (Nashville: Vanderbilt University Press, 1968);

A escrava que não é Isaura (São Paulo: Lealdade, 1925);

Primeiro andar: contos (São Paulo: A. Tisi, 1926);

Losango cáqui, ou, Afetos militares de mistura com os porquês de eu saber alemão (São Paulo: A. Tisi, 1926);

Amar, verbo intransitivo: idílio (1923–1924) (São Paulo: A. Tisi, 1927); translated by Margaret Richardson Hollingsworth as *Fräulein* (New York: Macaulay, 1933);

Clã do jaboti: poesia (São Paulo: E. Cúpolo, 1927);

Macunaíma: o herói sem nenhum caráter (São Paulo: E. Cúpolo, 1928); translated by E. A. Goodland as *Macunaíma* (New York: Random House, 1984; London: Quartet, 1985);

Ensaio sobre música brasileira (São Paulo: I. Chiarato, 1928);

Compêndio de história da música (São Paulo: I. Chiarato, 1929); revised as *Pequena história da música* (São Paulo: Martins, 1942);

Remate de males (São Paulo: E. Cúpolo, 1930);

Modinhas imperiais, ramalhete de 15 preciosas modinhas de salão brasileiras, do tempo do Império . . . (São Paulo: L. G. Miranda, 1930);

Música, doce música: estudos de crítica e folclore (São Paulo: L. G. Miranda, 1933);

Belazarte (São Paulo: Piratininga, 1934);

O Aleijadinho e Álvares de Azevedo (Rio de Janeiro: Revista Acadêmica, 1935);

A música e a canção populares no Brasil ([Rio de Janeiro?]: Ministério das Relações Exteriores, Divisão de Cooperação Intelectual, 1936); translated by Luiz Victor Le Cocq d'Oliveira as *Popular Music and Song in Brazil* (Rio de Janeiro: Imprensa Nacional, 1943);

Namoros com a medicina: ensaios sobre a terapêutica musical (Pôrto Alegre: Globo/Barcellos, Bertaso, 1939);

Mário de Andrade in his library, 1935 (from Telê Porto Ancona Lopez, ed., A imagem de Mário, 1984; Collection of Maria Luci De Biaji Moreira)

A expressão musical nos Estados Unidos, Lições da vida americana, no. 3 (Rio de Janeiro: Leuzinger, 1940);

Música do Brasil: desenho de Portinari (Curitiba, São Paulo & Rio de Janeiro: Guaíra, 1941);

A nau catarineta (São Paulo: Departamento de Cultura, 1941);

Poesias (São Paulo: Martins, 1941);

O movimento modernista (Rio de Janeiro: Casa do Estudante do Brasil, 1942);

Lasar Segall (São Paulo: Ministério da Educação, 1943);

O baile das quatro artes (São Paulo: Martins, 1943);

Aspectos da literatura brasileira (Rio de Janeiro: Imprensa Nacional, 1943);

Os filhos da Candinha (São Paulo: Martins, 1943);

Padre Jesuíno do Monte Carmelo, Serviço do Patrimônio Histórico e Artístico Nacional, Publicações, no. 14 (Rio de Janeiro: Ministério da Educação e Saúde, 1945);

Lira paulistana; O carro da miséria (São Paulo: Martins, 1946);

Curso de filosofia e história da arte (São Paulo: Centro de Estudos Folclóricos, 1955);

O turista aprendiz, edited, with an introduction and notes, by Telê Porto Ancona Lopez (São Paulo: Duas Cidades/Secretaria da Cultura, Ciência e Tecnologia, 1976);

Quatro pessoas: edição-crítica do romance inacabado de Mário de Andrade, 2 volumes, edited by Maria Zélia Galvão de Almeida (São Paulo, 1984);

O empalhador de passarinho (São Paulo: Martins, n.d.).

Editions and Collections: *Obras completas,* 20 volumes (São Paulo: Martins, 1944–1965)—comprises volume 1, *Obra imatura* (1960); volume 2, *Poesias completas* (1955); volume 3, *Amar, verbo intransitivo: idílio* (1944); volume 4, *Macunaíma* (1944); volume 5, *Os contos de Belazarte* (1947); volume 6, *Ensaio sôbre a música brasileira* (1962); volume 7, *Música, doce música* (1963); volume 8, *Pequena história da música* (1944); volume 9, *Namoros com a medicina* (1956); volume 10, *Aspectos da literatura brasileira* (n.d.); volume 11, *Aspectos da música brasileira* (1965); volume 12, *Aspectos das artes plásticas no Brasil* (1965); volume 13, *Música de feitiçaria no Brasil,* edited, with an introduction and notes, by Oneyda Alvarenga (1963); volume 14, *O baile das quatro artes* (1963); volume 15, *Os filhos da Candinha* (1963); volume 16, *Padre Jesuíno do Monte Carmelo* (1963); volume 17, *Contos novos* (1947); volume 18, *Danças dramáticas do Brasil,* 3 volumes, edited by Alvarenga (1959); volume 19, *Modinhas imperiais* (1964); and volume 20, *O empalhador de passarinho* (1948);

Mário de Andrade: ficção, edited by Manoel Cavalcanti Proença (Rio de Janeiro: AGIR, 1960);

Mário de Andrade: Poesia, edited by Dantas Motta (Rio de Janeiro: AGIR, 1961);

Mário de Andrade: ensaios e textos comentados sobre autores contemporâneos brasileiros e portugueses, edited by Luísa Enoé Cabral Schutel (Rio de Janeiro: EDUCOM, 1976);

Poesias completas (São Paulo: Círculo do Livro, 1976);

Táxi e crônicas no Diário Nacional, edited by Telê Porto Ancona Lopez (São Paulo: Duas Cidades/Secretaria da Cultura, Ciência e Tecnologia, 1976);

O banquete, edited by Jorge Coli and Luiz Carlos da Silva Dantas (São Paulo: Duas Cidades, 1977);

Mário de Andrade, edited by João Luiz Lafetá (São Paulo: Abril, 1982);

Poesias completas, edited by Diléa Zanotto Manfio (Belo Horizonte: Itatiaia / São Paulo: Editora da Universidade de São Paulo, 1987);

Macunaíma: o herói sem nenhum caráter, edited by Lopez (Paris: Asociación Archivos de la Literatura Latinoamericana del Caribe y Africana del Siglo XX / Brazil: Conselho Nacional de Pesquisas, 1988);

Os melhores contos, edited by Lopez (São Paulo: Global, 1988);

Os melhores poemas de Mário de Andrade, edited by Gilda de Mello e Souza (São Paulo: Global, 1988);

Poço e outras histórias, edited by Lopez (São Paulo: Ática, 1989);

A gramatiquinha de Mário de Andrade: Texto e contexto, edited by Edith Pimentel Pinto (São Paulo: Duas Cidades, 1990);

Será o Benedito!: artigos publicados no suplemento em rotogravura de O Estado de S. Paulo (Setembro 1937 – Novembro 1941), edited by Lopez (São Paulo: Editora da Pontifícia Universidade Católica de São Paulo/Giordano, 1992);

A arte religiosa no Brasil: crônicas publicadas na Revista do Brasil em 1920, edited by Claudéte Kronbauer (São Paulo: Experimento/Giordano, 1993);

Fotógrafo e turista aprendiz (São Paulo: Instituto de Estudos Brasileiros, Universidade de São Paulo, 1993);

Música e jornalismo: diário de S. Paulo, edited, with an introduction and notes, by Paulo Castagna (São Paulo: Editora de Humanismo, Ciência e Tecnologia/Editora da Universidade de São Paulo, 1993);

Vida literária, edited by Sonia Sachs (São Paulo: Editora de Humanismo, Ciência e Tecnologia/Editora da Universidade de São Paulo, 1993);

Balança, trombeta e battleship, ou, O descobrimento da alma, edited by Lopez (São Paulo: Instituto Moreira Salles/Instituto de Estudos Brasileiros, 1994);

Introdução à estética musical, edited, with an introduction and notes, by Flávia Camargo Toni (São Paulo: Editora de Humanismo, Ciência e Tecnologia, 1995);

Macunaíma: o herói sem nenhum caráter, edited, with an introduction and notes, by Jorge Henrique Bastos (Lisbon: Antígona, 1998).

OTHER: "Luciano Gallet," in Luciano Gallet, *Estudos de Folclore,* edited by Andrade (Rio de Janeiro: C. Wehrs, 1934);

"Os compositores e a língua nacional," in *Anais do Primeiro Congresso da Língua Nacional Cantada* (São Paulo: Departamento de Cultura da Prefeitura de São Paulo, 1938), pp. 95–168;

"A pronúncia cantada e o problema brasileiro, através de discos," in *Anais do Primeiro Congresso da Língua Nacional Cantada*, pp. 189–208;

Portinari, includes biographical and critical sketches by Andrade and Manuel Bandeira (Rio de Janeiro: Serviço Gráfico do Ministério da Educação e Saúde Pública, 1939);

Manuel Antônio de Almeida, *Memórias de um sargento de milícias (1854–1855),* introduction by Andrade (São Paulo: Martins, 1941);

Victor Seroff, *Dmitri Shostakovich,* translated by Guilherme Figueiredo, preface by Andrade (Rio de Janeiro: Cruzeiro, 1945);

José Lins do Rêgo, *Riacho doce,* preface by Andrade (Rio de Janeiro: J. Olympio, 1956);

Antologia da poesia negra de expressão portuguesa, precedida de Cultura negro-africana e assimilação, edited by Andrade (Paris: P. J. Oswald, 1958);

Literatura africana de expressão portuguesa, 2 volumes, edited by Andrade ([Paris?]: Argel, 1967).

SELECTED PERIODICAL PUBLICATIONS–UNCOLLECTED: "Cultura musical," *Revista do Arquivo Municipal de São Paulo,* 26 (1936);

"Festa de Bom Jesus do Pirapora e o samba rural paulista," *Revista do Arquivo Municipal de São Paulo,* 41 (1937);

"Samba rural paulista," *Revista do Arquivo Municipal de São Paulo,* 91 (1937).

Poet, novelist, essayist, musicologist, ethnographer, folklorist, linguist, art and literary critic, and director of the São Paulo Department of Culture, Mário de Andrade was the spiritual guide of the Brazilian literary vanguard and one of the mentors and leaders of the revolutionary 1922 Semana de Arte Moderna (Week of Modern Art). He is known for his association with the Week of Modern Art as much as for *Macunaíma: o herói sem nenhum caráter* (Macunaíma: The Hero With No Character, 1928; translated as *Macunaíma,* 1984), his masterpiece. The man, the researcher, and the artist cannot be separated from one another. Andrade played a crucial role as instigator and organizer of the most significant literary movement of twentieth-century Brazil: modernism. Embodying the movement that he helped to create, he became a permanent presence on the Brazilian literary scene.

Mário Raul de Morais Andrade was born on 9 October 1893 in São Paulo, the son of Carlos Augusto Andrade and Maria Luísa Leite Moraes de Andrade.

He never married and lived his entire life at his parents' home. His father and his maternal grandfather, Joaquim de Almeida Leite Moraes, had traveled together to the Amazon region in 1881. As a result of this trip, Moraes wrote *Apontamentos de viagem* (1883, Notes of a Voyage), describing their itinerary. The same route appears later in *Macunaíma,* Andrade's most important book.

Andrade once said that he wrote his first poem, "Fiori de-lá-pa," in 1904, with words that he had invented himself. The inspiration came after seeing a disaster at the Central Station in São Paulo. His mother was unhappy with his recitation and did not consider the work a poem. Nevertheless, it marked the opening of his life as a poet. Andrade believed that nobody becomes a poet or a writer but is born one, and he felt that he was born a poet and writer, like his father and maternal grandfather. In addition to his natural talent, however, many of Andrade's works show the influence of Guillaume Apollinaire, Blaise Cendrars, and Filippo Tommaso Marinetti.

As a student Andrade's main interest was the Portuguese language. In 1910 he began attending the College of Philosophy at the University of São Paulo, where he remained for one year. Although he never finished college, his passion for literature had been awakened. The following year he began musical studies at the Conservatório Dramático e Musical de São Paulo (Conservatory of Theater and Music of São Paulo), finishing five years later. He was a disciplined pianist, practicing nine hours a day. One year later he became a monitor at the conservatory. With the death of his fourteen-year-old brother Renato in 1913, Andrade left the city to spend four months at the family's farm in Araraquara, northwest of the state of São Paulo, in an emotional crisis. Upon his return, he decided to be a music teacher instead of a pianist because his hands had begun to tremble. Moreover, he was also determined to be a poet.

The year 1917 was marked by losses and gains for Andrade. His father died, he graduated from the conservatory, and he met the future modernists Anita Malfatti, Oswald de Andrade (no relation), Guilherme de Almeida, and Emiliano Di Cavalcanti. That same year Andrade published his first book, *Há uma gota de sangue em cada poema* (There Is a Drop of Blood in Each Poem), under the pseudonym Mário Sobral. Using Parnassian and symbolist techniques, the poet presents himself as a pacifist, trying to understand humanity from a utopian socialist viewpoint. The influences of Victor Hugo, Emile Verhaeren, Jules Romains, Abílio Manuel Guerra Junqueiro, and Paul Claudel are clear. The poems in the collection have an animistic formulation and a social and political agenda. The animistic approach encompasses the expression of life and collective human feelings, putting the artist close to humankind and not disdaining popular lyricism. Andrade expresses a strong Catholic orientation and opposes World War I. In "Devastação" (Devastastion) he criticizes the war and denounces the futility of the soldiers' sacrifices. In "Guilherme" (William), Christ's brotherhood as a basic element of life is identified. (Critics, however, do not consider "Guilherme" a relevant work.) In his first book of poetry Andrade eschews Romantic lyricism and tries to tell the story of humanity and its challenges.

In the 1920s Andrade began to write for several magazines and newspapers, including *Papel e tinta, Revista do Brasil, Ilustração brasileira, Klaxon, Ariel, América brasileira, Estética, A Revista nova, Revista de antropofagia, Revista do Brasil, Terra roxa e outras terras, A Manhã, Diário nacional,* and *Verde*. In 1922 he started teaching the history of music and aesthetics at the Conservatório Dramático e Musical de São Paulo and became an art critic for the São Paulo newspaper *A Gazeta* and the magazines *A Cigarra* and *O Echo*. In the 1930s and 1940s Andrade contributed to *Revista nova, Festa, Revista brasileira de música, Diário de São Paulo, Revista do Arquivo Municipal de São Paulo, Diário de notícias, Folha de São Paulo,* and *O Estado de São Paulo*.

The year 1922 was the highlight of Andrade's literary life. With Oswald de Andrade he was a leader of the Week of Modern Art (13–17 February), the most important event of his intense public life. This week was a Brazilian response to what Mário de Andrade and other young intellectuals had discovered in the free spirits of Jean Cocteau, Marinetti, Cendrars, and Jean Epstein. They were looking toward a new art form, already established in Europe, that rejected traditional artistic values. Andrade and his peers also wanted an authentic art, thematically based on the peoples, traditions, and folklore of the country that would express the soul of Brazil.

The Week of Modern Art was considered extravagant, peculiar, and nonsensical by traditionalists at the time. Three events held on 13, 15, and 17 February at the Teatro Municipal in São Paulo offered a preview of what modern art in Brazil would be. The city's young intellectuals introduced their progressive ideas to the public. Many contemporaries of Andrade participated in the attack on the conservatism of Brazilian art. Malfatti exhibited her paintings; Victor Brecheret showed his sculptures; Heitor Villa-Lobos played his music; and Andrade, Carlos Drummond de Andrade (no relation), and Manuel Bandeira recited their poetry. Mário de Andrade inaugurated the Week of Modern Art by reading *A escrava que não é Isaura* (The Slave Who Is Not Isaura), a modern poetic speech that was not published

Title page for the first edition of Andrade's groundbreaking novel that draws heavily on the folklore of Brazil and employs the idiomatic Portuguese commonly spoken by Brazilians (from Lopez, ed., Macunaíma, *critical edition, 1988; Thomas Cooper Library, University of South Carolina)*

until 1925. It features a passionate and provocative argument against the old style still in use in Brazilian literature. He also recited "Ode ao burguês" (Ode to the Bourgeoisie), which was included in his *Paulicéia desvairada* (translated as *Hallucinated City*, 1968), published five months after the Week of Modern Art. The public was shocked at the modernists' audacity, their free-verse poetry, and their new concept of the plastic arts. As a creator and activist, Andrade was one of the most prominent figures in the creation of a new cultural mentality in Brazilian society.

Paulicéia desvairada is considered the bible of the Brazilian modernist movement. It is the first formal poetry of the movement and marks the changed direction of Brazilian poetry, exploding on the scene with a new form and style. Andrade attacks the rigidity of prior literary schools. In essence, *Paulicéia desvairada* is a superficial meditation on the behavior of middle-class people born in São Paulo, the *paulistas,* more an expression of Andrade's youthful feelings than an example of mature and deep reasoning. The work presents a surrealistic ode to his hallucinated and beloved city of São Paulo through poems that attack the middle class and the hypocrisy of the government. Andrade used Brazilian elements and nuances in the Portuguese language, because he considered them more appropriate for expressing Brazilian feelings than the academic, European variety of Portuguese largely used by the Parnassian poets of the time.

In *Paulicéia desvairada,* Andrade uses unarticulated speech, breaks with established metrical patterns, rejects traditional logic, and invents words. At the same time he impregnates his verses with irony, compassion, and mockery embedded in a discourse guided by reflection, emotion, and lyric impulse. Poems such as "O trovador" (The Minstrel) bring new expression, form, and freedom to obscure feelings of the unconscious. *Paulicéia desvairada* also reflects political and social concerns and dissatisfactions, as in "O rebanho" (The Flock) and "Ode ao burguês." Critics at the time felt the book was overloaded with senselessness, absurdity, and irrationality; even the title and the colorful cover irritated them. *Paulicéia desvairada* is an ovation and a jeer at the same time. The poems of the collection, with their modernist spirit, had an enormous influence on Brazilian poetry and prose after 1922.

In 1927 Andrade published *Amar, verbo intransitivo* (To Love, an Intransitive Verb); although it is not a novel in terms of the chronological development of the story and complexity of plot and characters, it is presented as a novel. In one chapter Andrade tells the story of an adolescent sexual initiation and criticizes the hypocrisy of São Paulo society. He does not use a systematic structural pattern, and his personality is always present. The real and the imaginary are superimposed on the narrative, and Andrade plays with objects, beings, and facts, adopting a free form of writing.

In *Clã do jaboti* (1927, The Jabuti Clan), Andrade returned to poetry mixed with popular traditions. By that time modernism, with nationalist characteristics, had already been established in Brazil. For Andrade, to be Brazilian was to have an aesthetic presupposition, as shown in two lines from "O poeta come amendoim" (The Poet Eats Peanuts): "Brasil que eu amo porque é o ritmo do meu braço aventuroso" (Brazil that I love because it is the rhythm of my venturesome arm); "Brasil que eu sou porque é minha expressão muito engraçada . . ." (Brazil that I am because it is my most amusing expression . . .). In this work he condenses his concept of Brazilians—a mixture of races, religious syncretism, linguistic uncertainties, lethargy, and lack of worries. Irony impregnates the poem with the jocose tone peculiar to modernism.

Andrade had a peculiar way of creating his works. One of his techniques was to collect information far ahead of the actual writing. He traveled to sites that interested him, performing research and taking notes, in order to learn about a subject first and write the proposed work later. With this technique in mind, Andrade took several trips. In 1924 he traveled to the state of Minas Gerais to become acquainted with its baroque architecture and culture. In 1927 he took his first ethnographic trip, traveling to the Amazon and Peru. The result of this trip was *O turista aprendiz* (The Apprentice Tourist), first published in *Diário nacional* in 1928 and in book form in 1976. During 1928 and 1929 Andrade made his second ethnographic trip, this time to northeast Brazil, where he collected popular music and folk dances. Working as a self-taught scholar, he read such great authors as José Vieira Couto de Magalhães, Rui Barbosa, José Honório Rodrigues, and Capistrano de Abreu, making personal notes in the margins of the books and numbering them with bibliographical indications.

Even though it is said that Andrade wrote *Macunaíma* in one day, he had done long and exhaustive research on Brazilian myths, legends, popular dances, and stories long before writing the book, using his particular method of research. After reading Theodor Koch-Grünberg's five-volume collection of myths and legends of South America and Amerindian indigenous culture, *Vom Roroima zum Orinoco: Ergebnisse einer Reise in Nordbrasilien und Venezuela in den Jahren 1911–1913* (From Roraima to the Orinoco: Account of a Journey in Northern Brazil and Venezuela in the Years 1911–1913, 1917–1928), Andrade perceived that Koch-Grünberg's Indian Makunaima resembled typical Brazilian men and women in terms of character and personality. Andrade then created the hero Macunaíma as a synthesis of Brazilians. When writing *Macunaíma,* he used his notes on Koch-Grünberg's work; in a few days he finished the book, afterward destroying all his original notes.

Although most critics have overlooked Andrade's prose, concentrating instead on his poetry, *Macunaíma* has undeniable historical importance in modern Brazilian fiction, and it is his most frequently cited work. The book brings together elements of epic, rhapsody, lyric, history, mythology, folklore, and the popular language spoken in Brazil. *Macunaíma* had enormous repercussions, becoming perhaps the most controversial work ever written in Portuguese.

Drawing on the style of the fifteenth-century chronicles, *Macunaíma* is the story of an Indian who comes from the Amazon jungle to São Paulo looking for his lost talisman. Macunaíma is the Brazilian hero, "o herói da nossa gente" (the hero of our people).

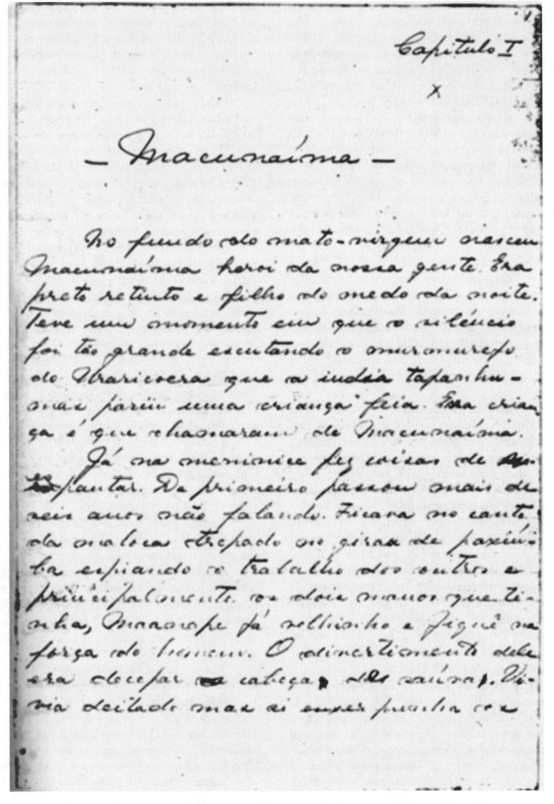

First page of the manuscript of Macunaíma *(from Lopez, ed.,* Macunaíma, *critical edition, 1988;*
Thomas Cooper Library, University of South Carolina)

Descended from the Tapanhumas, he was born in the Amazon jungle. From a young age he enjoys sexual pleasure with Sofara, his brother's wife. When Macunaíma is with Sofara, he experiences several metamorphoses: one day he is a prince; on another he is a white man, a fish, and so on. In his walk across the forest he encounters Ci, the mother of the forest. A child is born from his relationship with Ci, but it is poisoned and dies along with the mother. Before her death Ci gives Macunaíma a *muiriquitã* (talisman), a symbol of intense spiritual and eternal unification between two persons or entities. The talisman represents the union of nature and the Brazilian people. After Ci's death, Macunaíma flees into the forest and loses the talisman when fighting the monster Capei. Hearing that the talisman is in São Paulo, he and his brothers travel to the city, where Macunaíma learns that it now belongs to a giant named Venceslau Pietro Pietra. He attempts to recover it, but he cannot fight Pietra. After frustrated attempts to recover his talisman, Macunaíma journeys to Rio de Janeiro for an African Brazilian ritual, evoking African *orishas* (gods and goddesses) to help him against his opponent, who almost dies of violent strokes received in São Paulo because of the power of the *orishas*.

When Macunaíma returns to São Paulo, he tries to learn Portuguese. He notes that the *paulistas*—or Brazilians—speak one language and write another, meaning that the written and spoken varieties of Portuguese are so different that they seem to be two separate languages. He and his brothers also try to assimilate themselves into the urban civilization of São Paulo. Finally, after many fantastic adventures, Macunaíma returns to the forest with his talisman. On his way, he loses it again, and his enemies destroy him and all of his Indian brothers. He dies and becomes a useless constellation in the sky. Macunaíma represents the average Brazilian, with positive qualities and faults, as well as the native Indian destroyed by modern culture. The hero Macunaíma is the synthesis of a people formed by diverse ethnic and racial origins.

Macunaíma is filled with fantastic and picaresque narratives derived from folktales developed around Amerindian myths. By using folktales, Andrade was able to write without a linear structure and move between the possible and impossible, the real and unreal, the conscious and unconscious, and the objective and subjective. Despite the complex and subjective nature of the work, the characters are not deeply developed. They are present because they are necessary at a particular moment in the narrative; when no longer needed, they are discarded. Repetition, a device found in ancient rhapsodies, is a constant in the work and is used to provide an oral tone to the text. In *Macunaíma,*

Andrade exemplifies what his colleague Oswald de Andrade had proposed in the *movimento antropofágico* (anthropophagic movement): the development of a national culture without rejecting other cultures—in other words, taking what was good from foreign art but keeping national roots.

Andrade was more formal when writing essays and articles. Before becoming well known as a poet and writer, he had earned a solid reputation as a musicologist. He was a professor of music history at the conservatory and a musical theorist. In his writings on this subject he emphasizes the social function of music and seeks to determine the nature of music. *Ensaio sobre música brasileira* (1928, Essay on Brazilian Music) systematizes the most important directions of Brazilian music as a means of national expression. As Andrade comments in this book, Brazilian music had been established with a specific identity a century earlier. He pleads the case for *brasileiridade* (Brazilianness)—an artisanal element in national production in which composers of good quality and solidity use music as a political venue. Andrade was more interested in directing his thoughts to the musician than to the music itself. As in other books, he expresses the idea that the artist needs intellectual freedom in order to have creative possibilities. In *Ensaio sobre música brasileira* he also maintains that the national element in music, as well as in the other arts, is fundamental to an artist, who must be engaged as an individual and as a collective agent of emotions and intentions at the same time. For Andrade, the ultimate function of contemporary music was to evoke the spirit of the listener's own people.

In *Ensaio sobre música brasileira,* Andrade also compares music and poetry. For him, music does not have the power to create precise images, and for this reason it is unique. Music transmits vague feelings through which listeners create images. Poetry, on the other hand, transmits concrete images. The poem is situated between the plastic arts and music, and music gives magic to the words, resulting in a perfect artistic combination.

Music was for Andrade the result of an individual creative factor allied with nationalism since a musician is a social and national individual or entity. Andrade was aware of the power that a musician could have on listeners; for this reason the musician's social role was important. In "Terapêutica musical" (1936, Musical Therapy), collected in *Namoros com a medicina: ensaios sobre a terapêutica musical* (1939, Encounters with Medicine: Essays on Music Therapy), Andrade associates the concept of music with kinesthesia, or the undistinguished sensations that make a person aware of internal or external bodily conditions. He points out that music has the ability to organize itself in the listener's psyche without demanding intellectual understanding. Rhythm has the power to reduce the listener to passive obedience, while melody and harmony draw an active response from the listener. This combination of forces could be used to make music a socially powerful instrument.

In 1935 Andrade created the Department of Culture for the city of São Paulo and was its first director. He oversaw the creation of playgrounds, public libraries, and children's libraries and planned a new county library building (named after him), which still stands. Andrade later participated in the project of the Serviço do Patrimônio Histórico e Artístico Nacional (National Office of Historic and Artistic Preservation), an organization responsible for maintaining artistic and historical documents and buildings. The purpose of this service, created through Andrade's intervention, was to protect important historical landmarks as national monuments, avoiding their demolition or remodeling without governmental authorization.

Andrade moved to Rio de Janeiro in 1938 to work as director of the Institute of Art at the Universidade Federal do Distrito Federal, today the Universidade Federal do Rio de Janeiro. The next year he moved back to São Paulo, feeling the need to return to his roots and to the place where he felt comfortable. In 1939 he created the Sociedade de Etnologia e Folclore de São Paulo (Ethnology and Folklore Society of São Paulo) and became its first president. He then organized the Primeiro Congresso Nacional de Língua Cantada (First National Congress of Song). In 1942 he became an associate founder of Sociedade de Escritores Brasileiros (Society of Brazilian Writers).

In 1942, twenty years after the Week of Modern Art, Andrade delivered a lecture titled "O movimento modernista" (The Modernist Movement), published that same year in book form. In it he evaluates the modernist movement and the period from 1922 to 1930 as a heroic time, with both achievements and failures. He points out the mistake the modernists made by not addressing more specifically the social problems of Brazil at the time. Andrade analyzes the movement as a prediction of and a preparation for the national spirit. He also indicates that the Week of Modern Art reflected the society of the age: a society that was living a dichotomy between conservative ethics and political liberalism that demanded a new spirit to renovate the national intelligentsia. São Paulo had changed dramatically since the late 1800s. The city had factories and rapid transportation and communication. Foreigners and European immigrants fed the progress of commerce and industry. The Communist Party had been created in the early 1920s. The Coluna Prestes (Prestes Column), a political movement led by Carlos Prestes

Retrato de Mário de Andrade *(1927, Portrait of Mário de Andrade), by Lasar Segall (b. 1891, Vilnius – d. 1957, São Paulo), oil on canvas (Coleção de Artes Visuais, Instituto de Estudos Brasileiros, Universidade de São Paulo; from Nelly Novaes Coelho,* Mário de Andrade para a jovem geração, *1970; Thomas Cooper Library, University of South Carolina)*

(originally an army captain and later secretary of the Communist Party) that opposed the government, had been defeated after more than a decade of skirmishes. Prestes had become a national hero for left-wing intellectuals and deeply influenced Andrade and his fellow writers. Many changes were taking place in Brazil, but not in the arts, because the bourgeoisie was satisfied with the Parnassian tradition. The modernist conception was held by Andrade and a small group of intellectuals who compelled the public to change Brazilian art. The power of the Week of Modern Art was stronger than Andrade and his few young fellow artists, who had interacted with a hissing public at their open revolt against Parnassians in 1922.

Andrade's contribution goes beyond his fiction and nonfiction works, extending to the Portuguese language as an instrument expressing both his essence and that of Brazil. A nationalist, he wanted to free the country from the linguistic purism of Portugal. In the 1800s José de Alencar had already raised this issue, trying to *abrasileirar* (Brazilianize) Portuguese—to accommodate the Portuguese language to the Brazilian way, or to create a Brazilian idiom as the national language.

Illustration by Carybé from the fiftieth-anniversary edition of Macunaíma *(from Antônio Bento, ed.,* Macunaíma: ilustrações do mundo do herói sem nenhum caráter de Carybé, *1979; Collection of Maria Luci De Biaji Moreira)*

Andrade's nationalistic thoughts regarding the language coincided with those of Alencar. Andrade, however, did not want to create a new language but rather to capture the essence of the popular language in literary texts. He did not want the consecration of grammatical mistakes but the creation of a more natural Brazilian language, without the influence of European Portuguese. Nevertheless, this "new" way to express Brazilian feelings through popular language was not new. Some constructions, phrases, and words of popular employ and used by Andrade are also found in medieval Portuguese texts. The European Portuguese language had evolved in a different way from the Brazilian variety. Linguistic forces compel transplanted languages—such as Brazilian Portuguese—to the stagnation of archaic forms and to the creation of new ones at the same time. As a diligent linguist, Andrade was aware that many linguistic constructions spoken in several parts of Brazil was the same as that found in medieval texts. His merit consists in collecting and assembling the characteristics of Brazilian popular language, establishing a close proximity between Brazilian thought and popular nationalism, and changing the literary Brazilian Portuguese language.

Andrade helped to modernize the literary scene in Brazil not only through his works but also through his personal correspondence with several intellectuals. His letters clarify his extensive and varied kinds of writing. Andrade made a point of paying attention to those writing to him, especially neophytes. This receptive attitude was in reaction to his own experience of sending a short story to Vicente de Carvalho for evaluation in 1914. Carvalho never responded to his request. In 1921 Andrade began a correspondence with Bandeira that continued until Andrade's death in 1945. Carlos Drummond de Andrade, Oswald de Andrade, Tarsila do Amaral, Fernando Sabino, and Augusto Meyer are among those friends with whom Mário de Andrade corresponded for many years. When he died of a heart attack on 25 February 1945, he left contributions in several artistic fields, including *Lira paulistana* (1946, Paulistan Lyre), which was in press at the time of his death, and an unfinished book of short stories, *Contos novos* (New Stories), which was published in 1947 as part of the series of his *Obras completas* (Complete Works).

Mário de Andrade's achievements rest on the fact that he made popular expression an aesthetic part of literature. He searched for Brazilian psychological, social, aesthetic, folk, and ethnographic values, and he succeeded in helping to create a characteristic Brazilian literature and a persona who symbolized the average

Brazilian citizen. By moving beyond his limits as writer and researcher, Andrade became an original and authentic influence on the national arts and culture. The impact of his prose and poetry constituted the nucleus of the modernist movement. Through his creative nature he helped to free Brazil from its subservience to European culture, intelligence, and imagination as represented in the Parnassian and naturalistic works of the time. Andrade conferred on Brazilian literature and art in general a national consciousness, an appreciation of the Brazilian intelligentsia, a prerogative to perform aesthetic research on the popular arts, and the freedom to create. He reacted against "Lusitanisms" (signs of Portuguese influence), favoring Brazilian colloquialisms in literary language, and he attempted to broaden people's way of thinking. Finally, through an immanent universalism within a sense of immanent localism, Andrade changed nationalistic attitudes that were traditionally organized and established, re-creating them in a most genuine and modern Brazilian way.

Letters:

Cartas de Mário de Andrade a Manuel Bandeira, preface and notes by Manuel Bandeira (Rio de Janeiro: Simões, 1958);

Setenta e uma cartas de Mário de Andrade, edited by Lygia Fernandes (Rio de Janeiro: São José, 1963);

Mário de Andrade escreve cartas a Alceu, Meyer e outros, edited by Fernandes (Rio de Janeiro: Editora do Autor, 1968);

Macunaíma e a viagem grandota: cartas inéditas de Mário Andrade, edited by Carlos Heitor Castello Branco (São Paulo: Quatro Artes, 1970);

Itinerários: cartas a Alphonsus de Guimaraens Filho (São Paulo: Duas Cidades, 1974);

Cartas a um jovem escritor: de Mário de Andrade a Fernando Sabino (Rio de Janeiro: Record, 1981); enlarged as *Cartas a um jovem escritor e suas respostas* (Rio de Janeiro: Record, 2003);

Cartas a Murilo Miranda (1934-1945), edited by Raúl Antelo (Rio de Janeiro: Nova Fronteira, 1981);

Mário de Andrade, cartas de trabalho: correspondência com Rodrigo Mello Franco de Andrade (1936-1945), introduction and notes by Lélia Coelho Frota, Publicações da Secretaria do Patrimônio Histórico e Artístico Nacional, no. 33 (Brasília: Ministério da Educação e Cultura/Fundação Nacional Pró-Memória, 1981);

Correspondente contumaz: cartas a Pedro Nava, 1925-1944, edited by Fernando da Rocha Peres (Rio de Janeiro: Nova Fronteira, 1982);

A lição do amigo: cartas de Mário de Andrade a Carlos Drummond de Andrade, annotated by Carlos Drummond de Andrade (Rio de Janeiro: J. Olympio, 1982);

Cartas: Mário de Andrade, Oneyda Alvarenga (São Paulo: Duas Cidades, 1983);

Cartas de Mário de Andrade a Álvaro Lins, commentaries by José César Burba and Marco Morel (Rio de Janeiro: J. Olympio, 1983);

Cartas de Mário de Andrade a Prudente de Moraes Neto, 1924/36, edited by Georgina Koifman (Rio de Janeiro: Nova Fronteira, 1985);

A lição do guru: cartas a Guilherme Figueiredo, 1937-1945 (Rio de Janeiro: Civilização Brasileira, 1989);

Mário de Andrade: cartas a Anita Malfatti, edited by Marta Rossetti Batista (Rio de Janeiro: Forense Universitária, 1989);

Querida Henriqueta: cartas de Mário de Andrade a Henriqueta Lisboa, edited, with an introduction and notes, by Lauro Palú (Rio de Janeiro: J. Olympio, 1990);

Cartas de Mário de Andrade a Luís da Câmara Cascudo, introduction and notes by Veríssimo de Melo (Belo Horizonte: Villa Rica, 1991);

Mário de Andrade e(m) Campos dos Goitacazes: cartas de Mário de Andrade a Alberto Lamego, 1935-1938, edited by Arthur Soffiati (Niterói: Editora Universitária Universidade Federal Fluminense, 1992);

"Tudo está tão bom, tão gostoso—": Postais a Mário de Andrade, edited by Marcos Antonio de Moraes (São Paulo: Editora de Humanismo, Ciência e Tecnologia/Editora da Universidade de São Paulo, 1993);

Carta ao pintor moço (São Paulo: Boitempo, 1995);

Mário e o pirotécnico aprendiz: cartas de Mário de Andrade e Murilo Rubião, edited, with an introduction and notes, by Moraes (São Paulo: Instituto de Estudos Brasileiros/Giordano / Belo Horizonte: Editora da Universidade Federal de Minas Gerais, 1995);

Portinari, amico mio: cartas de Mário de Andrade a Cândido Portinari, edited, with an introduction and notes, by Annateresa Fabris (Rio de Janeiro: Projeto Portinari / Campinas: Editora Autores Associados/Mercado de Letras, 1995);

Correspondência Mário de Andrade & Tarsila do Amaral, edited, with an introduction and notes, by Aracy Amaral, Coleção correspondência de Mário de Andrade, no. 2 (São Paulo: Editora da Universidade de São Paulo/Instituto de Estudos Brasileiros, 1999);

Correspondência Mário de Andrade & Manuel Bandeira, edited, with an introduction and notes, by Moraes, Coleção correspondência de Mário de Andrade, no. 1 (São Paulo: Editora da Universidade de São Paulo/Instituto de Estudos Brasileiros, 2000);

Carlos & Mário: correspondência completa entre Carlos Drummond de Andrade (inédita) e Mário de Andrade, edited by Frota, preface and notes by Silviano Santiago (Rio de Janeiro: Bem-Te-Vi, 2002).

References:

Henrique L. Alves, *Mário de Andrade* (São Paulo: Editora do Escritor, 1973; revised and enlarged edition, São Paulo: Instituição Brasileira de Difusão Cultural, 1983);

Antônio Bento, *Macunaíma: ilustrações do mundo do herói sem nenhum caráter de Carybé* (Rio de Janeiro: Livros Técnicos e Científicos Editora, 1979);

Nelly Novaes Coelho, *Marío de Andrade para a jovem geração* (São Paulo: Saraiva, 1970);

Jorge Coli, "Mário de Andrade e a Música," in *Mário de Andrade hoje,* edited by Carlos E. O. Berriel (São Paulo: Ensaio, 1990), pp. 41–65;

Afrânio Coutinho, *An Introduction to Literature in Brazil,* translated by Gregory Rabassa (New York & London: Columbia University Press, 1969);

Marta Morais da Costa and others, *Estudos sobre o modernismo* (Curitiba: Criar Edições, 1982);

"Eu sou trezentos, sou trezentos-e-cincoenta": uma "autobiografia" de Mário de Andrade (São Paulo: Instituto de Estudos Brasileiros, Universidade de São Paulo/ Secretaria Municipal de Cultura, Prefeitura de São Paulo, 1992);

Maria Helena Grembccki, *Mário de Andrade e L'Esprit nouveau* (São Paulo: Instituto de Estudos Brasileiros, Universidade de São Paulo, 1969);

Lucia Helena, *Uma literatura antropofágica,* second edition (Fortaleza: Edições Universidade Federal do Ceará, 1983);

Victor Knoll, *Paciente arlequinada: uma leitura da obra poética de Mário de Andrade* (São Paulo: Editora de Humanismo, Ciência e Tecnologia, 1983);

Alceu de Amoroso Lima, *Poesia brasileira contemporânea* (Belo Horizonte: P. Bluhm, 1941);

Telê Porto Ancona Lopez, "Cronologia Geral da Obra de Mário de Andrade," *Boletim Bibliográfico* (1970): 117–149;

Lopez, "A margem e o texto: contribuição para o estudo de Macunaíma," *Boletim Bibliográfico* (1970): 9–73;

Lopez, *Mário de Andrade: ramais e caminhos* (São Paulo: Duas Cidades, 1972);

Lopez, ed., *Entrevistas e depoimentos: Mário de Andrade* (São Paulo: T. A. Queiroz, 1983);

Lopez, ed., *A imagem de Mário: fotobiografia de Mário de Andrade* (Rio de Janeiro: Alumbramento/ Livroarte, 1984);

Vasco Mariz, *Três musicólogos brasileiros: Mário de Andrade, Renato Almeida, Luiz Heitor Correa de Azevedo* (Rio de Janeiro: Civilização Brasileira, 1983);

O modernismo no Museu de Arte Brasileira: Pintura (São Paulo: Fundação Armando Alvares Penteado, 1993);

João Pacheco, *Poesia e prosa de Mário de Andrade* (São Paulo: Martins, 1970);

Manoel Cavalcanti Proença, *Roteiro de Macunaíma* (São Paulo: Anhembi, 1955);

Antônio Simões dos Reis, *Mário de Andrade: bibliografia sobre sua obra* (N.p.: Ministério da Educação e Cultura, n.d.);

Adrien Roig, "Ensaio de interpretação de *Paulicéia Desvairada,*" in his *Modernismo e realismo: Mário de Andrade, Manuel Bandeira e Raul Pompéia* (Rio de Janeiro: Presença, 1981), pp. 69–213;

Carlos Sandroni, *Mário contra Macunaíma: cultura e política em Mário de Andrade* (São Paulo: Vértice / Rio de Janeiro: Instituto Universitário de Pesquisas do Rio de Janeiro, 1988);

Affonso Romano de Sant'Anna, "Mário de Andrade e o conhecimento de seu destino," in his *O desemprego do poeta* (Belo Horizonte: Estante Universitária, 1962);

Homero Senna, *República das letras: entrevistas com 20 grandes escritores brasileiros,* third edition (Rio de Janeiro: Civilização Brasileira / São José dos Campos: Universidade do Vale do Paraíba, 1996);

Gilda de Mello e Souza, *O tupi e o alaúde: uma interpretação de Macunaíma* (São Paulo: Duas Cidades, 1979);

José I. Suárez and Jack E. Tomlins, *Mário de Andrade: The Creative Works* (Lewisburg, Pa.: Bucknell University Press / London: Associated University Presses, 2000).

Oswald de Andrade
(José Oswald de Sousa Andrade)
(11 January 1890 – 22 October 1954)

K. David Jackson
Yale University

BOOKS: *Théâtre Brésilien: Mon coeur balance (comédie en 4 actes); Leur âme (pièce en 3 actes et 4 tableaux),* by Andrade and Guilherme de Almeida, Théâtre Brésilien (São Paulo: Asbahr, 1916);

A trilogia do exílio: Os condemnados (São Paulo: Monteiro Lobato, 1922); revised as *Alma, Os condenados,* volume 1 (Pôrto Alegre: Globo, 1941);

Memórias sentimentaes de João Miramar (São Paulo: Independência, 1924); translated by Albert G. Bork and Ralph Niebuhr as *Sentimental Memoirs of John Seaborne, Texas Quarterly,* 15, no. 4 (Winter 1972): 112–160;

Pau Brasil: Cancioneiro de Oswald de Andrade, preface by Paulo Prado (Paris: Sans Pareil, 1925);

Os romances do exílio: A estrêlla de absyntho (São Paulo: Hélios, 1927); revised as *A estrêla de absinto, Os condenados,* volume 2 (Pôrto Alegre: Globo, 1941);

Primeiro caderno do alumno de poesia Oswald de Andrade (São Paulo: Mayença, 1927);

Serafim Ponte Grande (Rio de Janeiro: Ariel, 1933); translated by K. David Jackson and Albert G. Bork as *Seraphim Grosse Pointe,* afterword by Haroldo de Campos (Austin: New Latin Quarter, 1979);

O homem e o caválo: espetáculo em 9 quadros (São Paulo: Edição do Autor, 1934);

A escada vermelha (São Paulo: Editora Nacional, 1934); revised as *A escada, Os condenados,* volume 3 (Pôrto Alegre: Globo, 1941);

Teatro: A morta; O rei da vela (Rio de Janeiro: J. Olympio, 1937);

Marco zero, 2 volumes (Rio de Janeiro: J. Olympio, 1943, 1945)—comprises volume 1, *A revolução melancólica;* and volume 2, *Chão;*

Poesias reunidas, preface by Paulo Prado (São Paulo: Gaveta, 1945);

Ponta de lança (São Paulo: Martins, 1945);

A arcádia e a inconfidência (São Paulo: Revista dos Tribunais, 1945);

Oswald de Andrade (from Maria Eugênia da Gama Alves Boaventura, O salão e a selva: uma biografia ilustrada de Oswald de Andrade, *1995; Heard Library, Vanderbilt University)*

A crise da filosofia messiânica (São Paulo: Revista dos Tribunais, 1950);

Um homem sem profissão, memórias e confissões, volume 1: *Sob as ordens de mamãe, 1890–1919,* preface by Antonio Cândido (Rio de Janeiro: J. Olympio, 1954);

A marcha das utopias (Rio de Janeiro: Ministério de Educação e Cultura, 1966);

O perfeito cozinheiro das almas deste mundo: diário coletivo da garçonnière de Oswald de Andrade, introduction by Mário da Silva Brito and Haroldo de Campos, transcription by Jorge Schwartz (São Paulo: Ex Libris, 1987).

Collections: *Oswald de Andrade: Trechos escolhidos,* edited by Haroldo de Campos (Rio de Janeiro: AGIR, 1967);

Obras completas, 10 volumes (Rio de Janeiro: Civilização Brasileira, 1970–1974);

Obras completas de Oswald de Andrade (São Paulo: Secretaria de Estado da Cultura de São Paulo, Globo, 1990–   ).

Brazilian writer and intellectual Oswald de Andrade is one of the principal figures of literary modernism. Especially important is his authorship of the most important manifesto in twentieth-century Latin American letters and intellectual history, the "Manifesto Antropófago" (1928; translated as "Cannibal Manifesto" in *Obras Completas de Oswald de Andrade,* 1991). Andrade is normally referred to in Brazil as "Oswald," both because given names are preferred in Brazilian culture and because of the many "Andrades" who were active in the modernist movement. A graduate of the Faculdade de Direito de São Paulo (São Paulo Law School), Andrade used his wit to promote a program of national modernization beginning with the Semana de Arte Moderna (Modern Art Week) of 1922, a gathering of young, innovative artists in São Paulo. Andrade's works and ideas were shaped by his contact with Europe, particularly the Parisian vanguard of the 1920s, and by his radical revision of the relationship between Europe and Brazil. According to the "Manifesto Antropófago," Brazil will invert its colonial position, changing from a peripheral country to an industrial center of production and exporter of aesthetic materials. A complex man whose life mirrored the major artistic and cultural trends of his day, Andrade saw his life as a dramatic series of opposites, alternating episodes of Nietzschean risks and Dostoevskyian suffering. He was known for his wit and unforgiving humor, which he aimed at friend and foe alike, particularly during his long career as a journalist. Examples of Andrade's sense of humor may be seen in his pocket dictionary, in which he took "famous names" and morphed them into satirical descriptions: the Brazilian critic Tristão de Ataíde is "Tristinho de Alaúde" (Sad Little Coffin), and Swiss-French poet Blaise Cendrars, who was wounded in World War I, is "Blaise Sans Bras" (Blaise Without Arms).

Andrade first came to public attention as a journalist for *O Pirralho* (The Short Kid) between 1911 and 1917, then as a promoter and participant in the Modern Art Week of 1922. In the 1920s Andrade wrote manifestos and geographical, lyrical, and concise poetry in the style of Cendrars, and he introduced the Cubist fragmentary novel. In vanguard magazines he attacked vestiges of patriarchal, colonial society and promoted a radical reordering of sociopolitical thought. Becoming a Marxist in the 1930s, Andrade wrote plays exposing decadence and corruption, employing vanguard language that foreshadowed a new national theater. In polemical essays and journalism throughout the 1940s he continued to defend the aesthetic and social program of the modernist vanguard and to promote a national project of modernization in letters, arts, architecture, and design.

In plans for his memoirs, which he began along with a diary on 19 June 1948, Andrade divided his life into four major phases of intellectual development. The general title he chose for his memoirs was *Um homem sem profissão, memórias e confissões* (A Man Without a Profession, Memoirs and Confessions), but he only wrote the first of the four intended volumes: volume one, *Sob as ordens de mamãe, 1890–1919* (1954, Following Mother's Orders, 1890–1919); volume two, "O modernismo, 1920–1930" (Modernism, 1920–1930); volume three, "Nas fileiras de Marx, 1930–1945" (In Marx's Columns, 1930–1945); and volume four, "Antropofagia, 1945–   " (Cannibalism, 1945–   ). The title of his last planned volume emphasizes the fundamental importance of modernist aesthetics and avant-garde social thought in his life and works.

José Oswald de Sousa Andrade was born in São Paulo at noon on 11 January 1890. His father was José Oswald Nogueira de Andrade, from Baependi, Minas Gerais. After moving to São Paulo in 1881, he married Andrade's mother, D. Inês Inglês de Sousa, who was born in Óbidos, Pará, and raised in Pernambuco. Andrade was the second of their nine children. Andrade's recollections of his introverted early years involve a pious, strict, and traditional family life. The moral basis for Andrade's later criticisms of society perhaps lies in a combination of this rigid formative period and his early strong Catholicism. Brazilian scholar Benedito Nunes traces Andrade's interest in philosophy to São Bento academy, which he began attending in 1903 and where he first became interested in writing, especially rhymes and children's songs. During these years in São Paulo he also became fascinated with the novelties of the new century, including the "light" (that is, electric) company and streetcars. Furthermore, an early visit to the circus deeply impressed him and perhaps inspired the sense of spectacle that informed his works. A model for a literary career was immediately available to Andrade in his famous maternal uncle, novelist Herculano Marcos Inglês de Sousa. After graduating from São Bento in 1908, Andrade wrote his first journalistic articles for the *Diário Popular* (Popular Diary). He entered law school in 1909 and in 1911 founded his first magazine, *O Pirralho,* featuring caricatures of local personalities and a satirical style. The magazine continued through 1917.

With a voyage to France, England, and Italy in 1912, Andrade discovered the social and literary activity of Paris, with its Cubist salons and vanguard poetry. He read the "Manifeste Futuriste" (Futurist Manifesto), the statement of Italian author and critic Filippo Tommaso Marinetti, and became acquainted with the works of French composer Erik Satie, French writer and artist Jean Cocteau, and Spanish artist Pablo Picasso. He was impressed by the sexual and social freedoms of Paris, and he returned to Brazil with a young student named Kamiá, who gave birth to his first son, Oswald de Andrade Jr. (Nonê), on 14 January 1914.

Writing in *O Pirralho,* Andrade took up the topic of a national art style, wrote satires in Italian-Paulistano dialect, and in 1916 published two plays in French that he co-authored with Brazilian poet Guilherme de Almeida. That year he also began a diary of his European trip using the name João Miramar, a pseudonym that he used off and on for years, especially in the 1920s. In 1916 excerpts from these memoirs appeared in several magazines, and during that year Andrade met American dancer Isadora Duncan in São Paulo. In 1917 Andrade made the acquaintance of Mário de Andrade, who later became the humanist voice and intellectual conscience of the modernist movement. Andrade introduced Mário de Andrade in the influential newspaper article "O meu poeta futurista" (My Futurist Poet), which appeared in the *Jornal do Commercio* on 27 May 1921. Andrade also defended from a negative review by prominent author and journalist Monteiro Lobato the 1917 individual art exhibit of Anita Malfatti, a young painter influenced by German expressionism and recently returned from the New York Independent School of Art. Andrade graduated from law school in 1918 and publicly announced the existence of his modernist group. In 1919 he discovered the sculptor Victor Brecheret at the Palácio das Indústrias, whose works played an important role in the development of modernist aesthetics.

During these years Andrade maintained a *garçonnière* (Gentleman's Club) as a meeting place for a premodernist group. These meetings were frequented by a witty young student from the interior called "Deisi," who charmed the group with her quick, satirical iconoclasm. After a turbulent romance, Deisi and Andrade were married shortly before her death on 24 August 1919. The diary of the *garçonnière,* titled *O perfeito cozinheiro das almas deste mundo: diário coletivo da garçonnière de*

O, *Perfeito Cozinheiro*
das
Almas deste Mundo,...

Diário coletivo da garçonnière de

OSWALD de ANDRADE

São Paulo, 1918

Edição fac-similar

Textos de
Mário da Silva Brito
e
Haroldo de Campos

Transcrição tipográfica de
Jorge Schwartz

Editora Ex Libris

Title page for the 1987 facsimile edition of the collective diary of Andrade's premodernist group (1918–1919). This book is considered one of the major documents of early literary modernism (Howard-Tilton Memorial Library, Tulane University).

Oswald de Andrade (The Perfect Cookbook of the Souls of this World: The Collective Diary of the *garçonnière* of Oswald de Andrade), has become one of the major documents of early literary modernism after the publication of a meticulous facsimile edition in 1987. Composed between 1918 and 1919, the scrapbook-size volume of more than two hundred pages contains poems built with rubber stamps, objects, postcards, and witticisms expressing an incipient modernist outlook. Anyone who passed through the *garçonnière* could contribute to the open book. In 1920 Andrade was editor of the bimonthly magazine *Papel e Tinta* (Paper and Ink), which was dedicated to satire and caricatures and helped form a modernist group of artists and writers.

At the São Paulo Week of Modern Art in February 1922, Andrade read portions of his first novel, *Os condemnados* (1922, The Condemned), the first book in *A trilogia do exílio* (The Trilogy of Exile), a panoramic story of premodern life in São Paulo. Later that year he contributed a column, "Escolas & Idéias" (Schools & Ideas), to the short-lived vanguardist magazine *Klaxon*

(Car Horn). In June 1922 he met painter Tarsila do Amaral, a plantation owner's daughter, and the couple left for Paris, where she had studied, in December. In her studio near the Place Clichy, Tarsila introduced Andrade to artists such as Cendrars, Satie, Cocteau, Ferdinand Léger, André Lhote, Albert Gleizes, Jules Supervielle, Valéry Larbaud, and Igor Fyodorovich Stravinsky, as well as visiting Brazilian artists such as Heitor Villa-Lobos.

In an important lecture at the Sorbonne in 1923, Andrade served as an official representative of the Brazilian embassy in discussing the international dimension of what his title refers to as "L'effort intellectuel du Brésil contemporain" (The Intellectual Contribution of Contemporary Brazil). Returning briefly to Brazil at the end of the year, Andrade and Tarsila were introduced to Olívia Guedes Penteado, a patron of the arts—including the modernist group—who had constructed a special salon where sculptures and paintings by artists such as Léger, Picasso, Lhote, Georges Braque, Constatin Brancusi, Lasar Segall, Victor Brecheret, and Tarsila, were displayed. In March 1924 Cendrars arrived for a first visit to Brazil, and in a symbolic voyage of rediscovery Andrade and Tarsila drove him to the colonial cities of Minas Gerais. The trip involved the recovery of the colors, styles, and baroque forms of the colonial interior, features Brazilian artists and poets began incorporating into their works.

The five-year period from 1923 to 1928 was the most intense and significant phase of Andrade's intellectual development and artistic production. His first "invention" in the Cubist style, the novel *Memórias sentimentae de João Miramar* (1924; translated as *Sentimental Memoirs of John Seaborne,* 1972), was revised in Italy in 1923 and published in São Paulo with a cover illustration by Tarsila. Based on Andrade's diary of his voyage to Europe, this fragmented memoir of his literary persona provides a portrait of the artist as a young Brazilian man. Written in 163 prose fragments with satirical titles, the book describes the infancy, European travels, and return to Brazil of a sensitive youth who narrates with an equal sense of discovery and alienation. *Memórias sentimentae de João Miramar* is particularly critical of the generic experiences and attitudes of his generation. Composed in Cubist syntax, full of displacements and language play, the novel requires active reader participation. Andrade's playful experimentation also involves a mixing of literary genres, as the numbered fragments take the form of letters, diaries, interviews, speeches, and poems. Humor and parody are the main vehicles that convey social criticism. The novel is composed with self-conscious satire, beginning with a preface composed by one of the characters who represents a school of conservative literary taste associated with

Brazilian statesman-author Rui Barbosa. The theme of the novel is the formation of a new national artistic consciousness through the hero's changing critical perspectives and self-awareness.

Andrade's first major manifesto, the "Manifesto da Poesia Pau Brasil," was published in the *Correio da Manhã* (Morning Mail) in Rio de Janeiro on 18 March 1924. The manifesto was the principal document to establish an aesthetic for national modernism in the aftermath of the 1922 Week of Modern Art. The modernists saw in their own moment a dividing line between the colonial Brazil of the past and an as-yet-undefined future, and they found in their daily environment and culture sufficient aesthetic materials to promote social happiness and sustain a modern national identity. For them the future was embedded in contemporary aspects of Brazilian culture. For example, Andrade's manifesto finds "aesthetic facts" in the colors of the slums, Afro-Brazilian recipes and dances, carnival, speech, and the poetry of everyday life. In a country of immigrants the Brazilian language is described as "a contribuição milionária de todos os erros" (the millionaire-contribution of all the errors). To be modern is to place the newspaper and the skyscraper alongside the energy of shamans, legends, and the Museu Nacional (National Museum). The modern Brazilian of the times should be "sentimental, intelectual, irônico, ingênuo" (sentimental, intellectual, ironic, ingenuous). Brazilwood, which was the first colonial product exported to Europe, and other vegetation evoked in the manifesto constitutes the background for paintings in a "Pau Brasil" (Brazilwood) style by Tarsila and Segall. "Pau Brasil" is also used as an aesthetic term, applied to Tarsila's colorful geometric Cubist "portraits" of Brazilian life in this period.

In 1924 Andrade published poems in the *Revista do Brasil* (Journal of Brazil) that became part of his major collection of poetry, *Pau Brasil* (1925, Brazilwood). This book was published in Paris at Au Sans Pareil and features a cover based on the Brazilian flag, illustrations by Tarsila, and a dedication to Cendrars. Andrade uses documentary, ready-made, and objet trouvé techniques in his streamlined, synthetic verse. Structured as a concise history of Brazil, the volume begins with a program-manifesto, taken from the "Manifesto da Poesia Pau Brasil," featuring guidelines for aesthetic and national modernization. The first section of poetry, "História do Brasil" (History of Brazil), quotes passages from Pero Vaz de Caminha's letter of discovery of Brazil (1500) and select other chronicles of discovery, reproduced for ironic and satirical effects. Andrade became fond of such uses of copy and referentiality in his compositions. The chronological historical sequence of *Pau Brasil* continues with poems about colonization, a section on carnival, an excursion through urban São Paulo, a voyage to the colonial cities of Minas Gerais, and the return to Brazil of a transatlantic passenger, the poet himself arriving at a customs post in Santos. Beginning with the theme of carnival, the poems derive from Andrade's personal experiences with the modernist group, particularly the 1924 automobile excursion to the colonial cities of Minas Gerais. Throughout the collection Andrade maintains an aesthetic of surprise and invention in poems that are "snapshots" of a synthetic reality, conveyed with humor and satire. The point is to see things with "new eyes" in an attitude of creative innocence. In a few poems Andrade uses extreme semiotic concision, producing works of only two or three lines in which, for example, a train divides Brazil "como un meridiano" (like a meridian).

At this time Andrade was in contact with Portuguese modernists, and a polemical description of his Parisian agenda sent to the young Portuguese writer António Ferro, who had lectured in Brazil in 1922, was published in the Lisbon magazine *Contemporânea* in 1925. In 1926 Andrade and Tarsila married, and the couple, jointly called "Tarsiwald" by Mário de Andrade, received many celebrated artists, writers, and composers and traveled frequently between São Paulo and Paris. Visitors in São Paulo included Le Corbusier, Josephine Baker, and Benjamin Péret. Tarsila moved her Parisian studio to 19 boulevard Bertheir. In 1926 she had her first individual exhibit at the Galérie Percier, rue de Boétie (Percier Gallery, Boétie Street). At this time Andrade met Valéry Larbaud, translator of James Joyce into French, and became acquainted with Joyce's novel *Ulysses* (1922). Visitors to Tarsila's atelier included Léger, Cocteau, Supervielle, Jules Romains, and Brancusi, who dedicated to the couple a catalogue for his 1926 New York exposition. A Thomas Cook trip to the Middle East that year with Tarsila and others is reflected in Andrade's second "novel of invention," *Serafim Ponte Grande* (1933; translated as *Seraphim Grosse Pointe,* 1979), which he composed in fragments. Although belonging aesthetically to the 1920s, the work was published with a Marxist preface rejecting much of the novel as the "sentimental barometer of the bourgeoisie." Serafim is an antiheroic character, more aggressive and cynical than João Miramar, whose travel adventures enact some principles of Andrade's "Manifesto Antropófago." He is a modest employee of a federal public department who suddenly becomes rich with funds taken from a group of revolutionaries. He sets sail on a libertine voyage to Africa, Europe, and the Middle East, consisting of a series of burlesque adventures. Serafim's satirical humor culminates in an outright rebellion against social norms and conventions in the final fragment, "Os antropófagos" (The Cannibals).

Cover for Andrade's 1927 novel, the second in A trilogia do exílio (The Trilogy of Exile) (from Maria Augusta Fonseca, Oswald de Andrade, 1890–1954: biografia, 1990; Ralph Brown Draughon Library, Auburn University)

While traveling the oceans by transatlantic liner, Serafim claims there is a plague onboard and puts in at port only to take on supplies. Although Andrade had used ironic fragments in the *Memórias sentimentaes de João Miramar,* his approach in *Serafim Ponte Grande* was more experimental. The fragments of the novel are written as parodies, each section mocking a different literary style from the past such as travel narratives, romantic cloak-and-dagger stories, realist novels, and several subgenres such as diaries, letters, telegrams, and postcards. The novel also includes an "Errata" in which the author condemns the book and gives written permission for it to be "deformado en todas as línguas" (deformed in all languages). An adaptation for theater was performed in Rio de Janeiro by Pessoal do Cabaré in the 1980s.

In 1927 Andrade published a second volume of poetry, *Primeiro caderno do alumo de poesia Oswald de Andrade* (First Notebook of the Poetry Student Oswald de Andrade), in an ingenuous, simple style. The cover, designed by Tarsila, is based on a Parisian grade-school notebook. Some of the poems are based on children's rhymes, and classics of Romantic poetry are parodied. Andrade begins the volume with what has been called the shortest poem in the Portuguese language: the title is "Amor" (Love), printed in red ink in the first edition, and the text is one word, "Humor" (Humor). This collection of poems continues the national theme of Pau Brasil, but with a self-conscious and self-deprecating style, mixing personal reflections and experience with national material. During this time Andrade finished the second novel of *A trilogia do exílio, A estrêlla de absyntho* (1927, The Star of Absinthe).

The first half of 1928 was the high mark in Andrade's achievements as a modernist. On his birthday in January he received a gift of Tarsila's celebrated painting "Abaporu," which means "Man Who Eats" in Tupy, the language of the Tupinambás, and in May he published his renowned "Manifesto Antropófago" in the first issue of the *Revista de Antropofagia* (Cannibal Magazine), a publication edited by Antônio de Alcântara Machado. The theme of cannibalism had already appeared in Brazil with a canvas by Rego Monteiro titled "O Antropófago" (1921, The Cannibal) that depicts an Indian chewing on a femur, and it also appeared in the *Revista de Antropofagia* and in a Portuguese edition of the sixteenth-century memoirs of Hans Staden titled *Meu captiveiro entre os selvagens do Brazil* (1925, My Captivity among the Savages of Brazil), edited by Monteiro Lobato, who was a close acquaintance of Andrade. Staden's memoirs were illustrated by forty woodcuts printed in black and red that depicted life among the Tupinambás, and those featuring cannibalism are reproduced in the Brazilian magazine.

"Manifesto Antropófago" was eventually recognized as the most significant expression of Latin American intellectual autonomy in the twentieth century. The modern Brazilian is cast in the guise of a Tupinambá cannibal who devours arriving Europeans, absorbing their values and transforming them into native material. The manifesto offers a new calendar, dated from the ingestion of Bishop Sardinha by the Caetés in 1554. The rite of ritual consumption is the broad metaphor Andrade chooses for his view of society and his critical revision of Western ethics and religion. Unlike the European intellectual's search for primitivism, the Brazilian claims a direct relationship to a cannibal reality. The natural legal, religious, and economic systems of the tribe are promoted as utopian solutions to the problems plaguing Western society, such as crime, repression, and poverty. Andrade finds Surrealist language in a Tupy poem to the full moon, quoted in Couto de Magalhães's *O selvagem* (1881, The Savage). Borrowing

language from Sigmund Freud and William Shakespeare, Andrade proposes that Brazil's indigenous primitivism will totemize the taboos of Western culture, invoking the slogan "Tupy or not Tupy, that is the question." A more radical second "dentição" (dentition) of the *Revista de Antropofagia,* printed as a special page in the *Diário de São Paulo* (São Paulo Daily) from March to June 1929, features attacks on the Catholic Church as well as on the legal code of patriarchal society. Among the ambitious works based on European models that Andrade planned at this time but never completed was the "Ballet Brésilien," which was to have a text by Andrade, setting by Tarsila, and music by Villa-Lobos, and for which a four-page précis survives. At some point in 1929 Andrade and Tarsila divorced.

In 1930 Andrade began an experiment with Marxism and the Partido Comunista do Brasil (Brazilian Communist Party), following his intense, dynamic companion Patrícia Galvão, known as Pagu, whom he married in April 1930. In Pagu's radical novel *Parque Industrial* (1933; translated as *Industrial Park,* 1993), Andrade appears as a character who converts from the bourgeoisie to the working class. In 1931 the couple had a son, Rudá, and they collaborated on the eight issues of the journal *O Homem do Povo* (Man of the People). The political agenda and militant avant-garde tone of the journal caused it to be attacked and closed by law students. Each issue featured a questionnaire asking "Who is the biggest living bandit in Brazil?" followed by names of politicians, priests, and well-known national figures. In the journal Andrade wrote provocatively that the most profound mental activity ever produced by the São Paulo Law School was hazing. Pagu contributed a column, "Mulher do povo" (Woman of the People), in which she deftly attacks the dominant sexual morality. Andrade attacks the government of President Getúilo Vargas, whom he calls the "anão Vargas" (dwarf Vargas), and the labor policies of minister Lindolfo Collor, whom he calls the "Sinistro do Trabalho" (Sinister of Labor). In a 1933 speech to the union of bakers Andrade criticized the Brazilian policy to nationalize labor for its effects on poor foreign workers and its evisceration of union and management relations. In 1931 Pagu and Andrade traveled to Montevideo to visit the leader of the Brazilian Communist Party, Luiz Carlos Prestes, and in 1933 Pagu left Brazil to travel around the world as a reporter, via China, Moscow, and Paris. During this period Andrade finished the final volume of *A trilogia do exílio, A escada vermelha* (1934), and he published three innovative and challenging plays, *O homem e o caválo* (1934), full of disjointed characterization, violence and social attacks, followed by *A morta* and *O rei da vela* (1937, The Candle King).

Andrade next began writing a series of novels titled *Marco zero,* which he likened to a social mural, of which two were later published, *A revolução melancólica* (1943) and *Chão* (1945). After an affair with pianist Pilar Ferrer, Andrade married the writer Julieta Bárbara in 1935. The financially limited couple received in their home foreign intellectuals such as French sociologist Roger Bastide and the Italian poet Guiseppe Ungaretti, who had arrived in São Paulo as professors at the recently created university. Andrade also traveled with Bastide and Claude Lévi-Strauss. During this time Andrade supported a group of young Brazilian intellectuals led by Paulo Emílio Salles Gomes in the creation of the journal *Movimento* (Movement). The circle expanded into a "Clube do Quarteirão" (Block Club) that included such figures as Flávio de Carvalho, Malfatti, Sérgio Milliet, Geraldo Ferraz, and Décio de Almeida Prado. Andrade remained active as an irreverent journalist during this period, defending modernism and attacking the fascist Integralists of Vargas's "Estado Novo" (New State). With his finances depleted, Andrade offered for sale the last properties that he owned in the district of Cerqueira Cesar. He also owned paintings by Giorgio de Chirico and Picasso that he attempted to sell at bargain prices.

Published in 1937, the play *O rei da vela* illustrates how Andrade continued to use a modernist aesthetic in the realm of Marxist criticism. The title refers to the transfer of the landed coffee aristocracy's wealth to the incipient industrialization and raw capitalism of the city. The play concerns the world of pawnshops and usury, illustrating the bankruptcy, misery, and desperation of a class that has to borrow to survive. The main character, Abelard I, is a loan shark who has cut the supply of electricity, forcing the population to buy candles, for which he has the monopoly. Andrade's reliance on underlying literary and historical references is seen in the allusion to the fourteenth-century French romance of Abelard and Heloise, a story featuring a tragic, grotesque denial of Eros that is directly related to the decadent situation in Brazil. The rural aristocracy has estates but no money, and the urban capitalists have cash but no social standing. Thus, Abelard I arranges a marriage to Heloisa, daughter of a colonel, notwithstanding her lesbianism. The decadence of institutions is revealed through economic and sexual deviance, and Abelard casts debtors into a large cage in his office. The layered relationships between urban decadence and the dependency of a mortgaged class involve people who are ultimately revealed to be puppets of foreign capital in the person of an American businessman, the homosexual Mr. Jones, who is responsible for Abelard's suicide and whose only line in the play is "Good Business!" *O rei da vela* became one of the most famous

Cover for Andrade's 1933 novel about Serafim, an antiheroic figure whose travels lead to a series of burlesque adventures (*from Maria Augusta Fonseca,* Oswald de Andrade, 1890–1954: biografia, *1990; Ralph Brown Draughon Library, Auburn Univeristy*)

plays in Brazilian drama after it was produced by Teatro Oficina in São Paulo in 1967.

In 1939 Andrade sailed with his wife for Stockholm as a representative of the PEN Club, but the voyage was interrupted by World War II. The couple had a close escape from France and returned to Brazil via Portugal, where Andrade was interviewed in the press. In 1940 Andrade became a candidate for a vacancy in the Academia Brasileira de Letras (Brazilian Academy of Letters) but lost to poet Manuel Bandeira. During this time Andrade entertained many young critics, including Antônio Cândido, and attempted a reconciliation with Mário de Andrade, which was rebuffed.

In the early 1940s Andrade, disillusioned with organized causes, left the Communist Party and began a prolific period dedicated to poetry, essays, and philosophical studies. He published a major book of essays, *Ponta de lança* (1945, Tip of the Lance), followed by several essays and even university theses. With his essay of sociopolitical theory titled *A arcádia e a inconfidência* (1945, Arcadia and the Uprising in Minas), he unsuccessfully competed for a chair in literature at the Universidade de São Paulo and became a *livre docente*

(Doctor of Letters), although he never taught. The last great love of his life, Maria Antonieta d'Alkmin, was hired as a secretary for the publication of *Marco zero*, and the couple was married on 19 June 1944 in a ceremony that Andrade described as "últimas núpcias" (last nuptials). Andrade's long poem "Cântico dos cânticos para flauta e violão" is dedicated to Maria. In 1946 the couple had a daughter, Antonieta Marília, and in 1948 they had a son, Paulo Marcos, who died in an accident at age nineteen. Andrade's complete poetry, titled *Poesias reunidas*, was published in a luxurious edition in 1945. The title parodies the advertisement for the Indústrias Reunidas (United Industries) of the industrialist Matarazzo in São Paulo. In the summer of 1949, Andrade hosted Albert Camus and traveled with him in southern Brazil. Camus left his positive impressions of Andrade and expresses enthusiasm for "Antropofagia" in his diary.

Andrade's longest poem, *O santeiro do Mangue,* begun in 1935, is written in the form of an opera set in Rio de Janeiro. It is an imaginative work that may be considered a companion to Mário de Andrade's grandiose poem-oratorio "As enfibraturas do Ipiranga" (1922, The Moral Fibrature of Ipiranga). Because of its ideological aggression and linguistic obscenities, the poem was censored, although a mimeographed version circulated in the late 1960s. The poem is set in the Mangue, a zone of prostitution and decadence that had been the subject of many well-known Brazilian works, including poems by Bandeira and Vinícius de Moraes and paintings by Emiliano Di Cavalcanti. Once again Andrade constructs a theatrical text that refers to many literary, historical, and religious antecedents. His biting view of society in the Mangue produces characters styled after English poet George Gordon, Lord Byron; Gustave Flaubert's Madame Bovary; Brazilian composer Antônio Carlos Gomes; and Brazilian writer Antônio de Castro Alves, with the statue of Christ of Corcovado directing from on high. The poem contains scatological language and violent attacks on organized religion and imperialism, while it celebrates popular culture through the work of a poor sculptor of wooden saints.

In 1950 Andrade became a candidate for a chair in philosophy with a second thesis, *A crise da filosofia messiânica* (The Crisis of Messianic Philosophy). In this essay he develops a theory of man and society with an emphasis on utopian thought and the production of social leisure and happiness, ideas derived from the "Manifesto Antropófago." One of Andrade's final philosophical essays, *A marcha das utopias* (1966), is a study of societies and utopian thinkers as seen from the perspective of the natural, autochthonous philosophy of "Antropofagia." Against the repressed world of patriarchy, Andrade proposes for Brazil an open matriarchal society. Citing Michel de Montaigne's essay on Brazilian cannibals titled "De Cannibales" (The Cannibals), published in his *Essais de Messire Michel Seigneur de Montaigne* (1580; translated as *The Essays, or, Morall, Politike and Militarie Discourses of Lo: Michaell de Montaigne,* 1603), Andrade finds examples in primitive man for the renewal of Western society, particularly the absence of illness and dementia as well as the open expression of revenge and affection. In the messianism of the colonizers of Brazil, Andrade sees the origin of all the illusions that lead to slavery, whereas the revolt and stoicism of the tribe show a new path to the modern discovery of the "technological primitive" and the conquest of leisure and social happiness. In 1950 Andrade was an unsuccessful candidate for the state legislature. The memoirs, begun in 1948, appeared with the first volume of *Um homem sem profissão: Sob as ordens de mamãe.* After a long illness, Andrade died on 22 October 1954 in São Paulo. He was buried in the Cemitério da Consolação.

Although largely forgotten or ignored at the time of his death, Oswald de Andrade's works were rediscovered in the 1960s. With the revival of studies of the modernist movement in the 1970s, influenced by the seminal essays of Haroldo de Campos, Antônio Candido, Décio Pignatari, and other prominent intellectuals, Andrade became almost universally known in Brazil. Andrade's irreverent satire and striking conceptual originality stem from a complex personality thought now to belong to an audacious genius who created a lasting model for national modernization. Two complete editions of Andrade's works appeared in the 1970s and 1990s, and there were also significant performances of his plays, stage adaptations of his novels, and short movies and videos based on his life and works. Among his works, the "Manifesto Antropófago" in particular has reached an international readership and is esteemed an influential document of postcolonial thought. A United Nations Educational, Scientific, and Cultural Organization Archives volume of scholarly editions and studies titled *Oswald de Andrade: Obra Incompleta* (Oswald de Andrade: Incomplete Works) is scheduled to appear in 2005. Additionally, in the 1990s two biographies were published, Maria Augusta Fonseca's *Oswald de Andrade, 1890–1954: biografia* (1990, Oswald de Andrade, 1890–1954: Biography) and Maria Eugênia da Gama Alves Boaventura's *O salão e a selva: uma biografia ilustrada de Oswald de Andrade* (1995, The Salon and the Jungle: An Illustrated Biography of Oswald de Andrade). These treatments of Andrade's life and works highlight his acceptance as one of the most original and unforgettable figures in early-twentieth-century Brazilian social, political, and literary history.

Biographies:

Maria Augusta Fonseca, *Oswald de Andrade, 1890–1954: biografia* (São Paulo: Secretaria de Estado da Cultura, Art Editora, 1990);

Maria Eugênia da Gama Alves Boaventura, *O salão e a selva: uma biografia ilustrada de Oswald de Andrade* (São Paulo: Ex Libris / Campinas, Brazil: Unicamp, 1995).

References:

Adria Frizzi, "Life and Letters of a Chameleon: The Carnival of Memoirs in *Serafim Ponte Grande*," *Luso-Brazilian Review,* 23, no. 2 (1986): 61–69;

David George, *Anthropophagy and the New Brazilian Theater,* dissertation, University of Minnesota, 1981;

Hans Ulrich Gumbrecht, "Biting You Softly: A Commentary on Oswald de Andrade's *Manifesto Antropófago*," *Nuevo Texto Crítico,* 12, nos. 23–24 (1999): 191–198;

K. David Jackson, "Three Glad Races: Primitivism and Ethnicity in Brazilian Modernist Literature," *Modernism and Modernity,* 1, no. 2 (1994): 89–112;

Jackson, ed., *One Hundred Years of Invention: Oswald de Andrade and the Modern Tradition in Latin American Literature* (Austin: Department of Spanish and Portuguese, University of Texas at Austin/Abaporu Press, 1990);

Richard Morse, "Triangulating Two Cubists: William Carlos Williams and Oswald de Andrade," *Latin American Literary Review,* 14, no. 27 (1986): 175–183;

Benedito Nunes, *Oswald, cannibal* (São Paulo: Perspectiva, 1979);

Luciana Stegagno Picchio, "Brazilian Anthropophagy: Myth and Literature," *Diogenes,* no. 144 (Winter 1988): 116–139;

Marcos Reigota, "Brazilian Art and Literature, Oswald de Andrade's Contribution to Global Ecology," in *Literature of Nature: An International Sourcebook,* edited by Patrick D. Murphy, Terry Gifford, and Katsunori Yamazato (Chicago: Fitzroy Dearborn, 1998), pp. 359–365;

Jeffrey Schnapp, "Biting the Hand that Feeds You: On the 70th Anniversary of the Manifesto antropófago," *Nuevo Texto Crítico,* 12, nos. 23–24 (1999): 243–247;

Vicky Unruh, "From Idle Pursuits to Critical Voracity: *Memórias Sentimentais de João Miramar* and *Serafim Ponte Grande*," in *Latin American Vanguards: The Art of Contentious Encounters* (Berkeley: University of California Press, 1995), pp. 114–122, 197–205;

Beth Joan Vinkler, "The Anthropophagic Mother/Other: Appropriated Identities in Oswald de Andrade's 'Manifesto Antropófago,'" *Luso-Brazilian Review,* 34, no. 1 (1997): 105–111.

Papers:

A collection of Oswald de Andrade's papers is held at the Fundo Oswald de Andrade (Oswald de Andrade Foundation), Centro de Documentação Cultural Alexandre Eulalio, Universidade Estadual de Campinas, at Campinas, São Paulo.

Aluísio Azevedo

(14 April 1857 – 11 January 1913)

Regina Santos
University of North Carolina at Chapel Hill

BOOKS: *Uma lágrima de mulher* (São Luís: Frias, 1880);

O mulato (São Luís: Tipografia de *O País,* 1881); translated by Murray Graeme MacNicoll as *Mulatto,* edited by Daphne Patai, introduction by Patai and MacNicoll (Rutherford, N.J.: Fairleigh Dickinson University Press, 1990);

A flor de liz: opera comica em 3 actos, by Azevedo and Artur Azevedo (Rio de Janeiro: Domingos de Magalhães, 1882);

Mistério da Tijuca (Rio de Janeiro: Garnier, 1883); republished as *Girândola de amores* (Rio de Janeiro: Garnier, 1900);

Casa de pensão (Rio de Janeiro: Faro & Lino, 1884);

Filomena Borges (Rio de Janeiro: Tipografia da *Gazeta de Notícias,* 1884);

Memórias de um condenado (Ouro Prêto: Tipografia de *O Liberal Mineiro,* 1886); republished as *A Condessa Vésper* (Rio de Janeiro: Garnier, 1902);

O homem (Rio de Janeiro: A. de Castro Silva, 1887);

Fritzmac, by Aluísio Azevedo and Artur Azevedo (Rio de Janeiro: L. Braga, 1889);

O cortiço (Rio de Janeiro: Garnier, 1890); translated by Harry W. Brown as *A Brazilian Tenement* (New York: R. M. McBride, 1926);

O coruja (Rio de Janeiro: Garnier, 1890);

O esqueleto (Mistérios da casa de Bragança), by Aluísio Azevedo and Olavo Bilac, as Vítor Leal (Rio de Janeiro: Tipografia da *Gazeta de Notícias,* 1890);

Demônios (São Paulo: Teixeira & Irmão, 1893);

A mortalha de Alzira (Rio de Janeiro: Fauchon, 1894);

O livro de uma sogra (Rio de Janeiro: Domingos de Magalhães, 1895);

Pégadas (Rio de Janeiro: Garnier, 1897);

Obras completas de Aluísio Azevedo, 14 volumes, edited by M. Nogueira da Silva (Rio de Janeiro: F. Briguiet, 1937–1944)—comprises volume 1, *Uma lágrima de mulher* (1939); volume 2, *O mulato* (1941); volume 3, *A Condessa Vésper* (1939); volume 4, *Girândola de amores* (1939); volume 5, *Casa de pensão* (1944); volume 6, *Philomena Borges* (1938); volume 7, *O homem* (1938); volume 8, *O coruja* (1940); volume

Aluísio Azevedo (Arquivo da Academia Brasileira de Letras)

9, *O cortiço* (1939); volume 10, *O esqueleto* (1939); volume 11, *A mortalha de Alzira* (1940); volume 12, *O livro de uma sogra* (1941); volume 13, *Demônios* (1937); and volume 14, *O touro negro* (1938);

Casa de orates: comédia em 3 atos, by Aluísio Azevedo and Artur Azevedo (Rio de Janeiro: Edição da Sociedade Brasileira de Autores Teatrais, 1956);

O Japão, edited by Luiz Dantas (São Paulo: R. Kempf, 1984);

Mattos, Malta ou Matta? Romance ao correr da pena (Rio de Janeiro: Nova Fronteira, 1985).

Editions and Collections: *Trechos escolhidos,* edited by Josué Montello (Rio de Janeiro: AGIR, 1963); *Aluísio Azevedo: literatura comentada,* edited by Antônio Dimas (São Paulo: Abril, 1980).

Edition in English: *The Slum,* translated, with a foreword, by David H. Rosenthal, afterword by Affonso Romano de Sant'Anna (Oxford & New York: Oxford University Press, 2000).

Inspired and influenced by Emile Zola and José Maria de Eça de Queirós, Aluísio Azevedo introduced the literary movement of naturalism into Brazil with his novel *O mulato* (1881; translated as *Mulatto,* 1990). He earned his reputation as a writer for his portrayal of Brazilian society through detailed descriptions of groups rather than analyses of individual characters. Azevedo was also an artist, and he worked in Rio de Janeiro as an illustrator and caricaturist. His vibrant and detailed examination of a society characterized by vitality and disarray places his work within the socially engaged literature of the late nineteenth century.

Aluísio Tancredo Gonçalves de Azevedo was born in São Luís in the state of Maranhão, in northern Brazil, on 14 April 1857. His parents, Davi Gonçalves de Azevedo and Emília Amália Pinto de Magalhães, were from Portugal. Aluísio's older brother was Artur Azevedo, who became one of the most popular and notable dramatists in Brazil at the end of the nineteenth century. Because Aluísio's mother had left her first husband, and divorce was illegal in Brazil at that time, his parents were not able to marry until the death of his mother's first husband. Davi Gonçalves de Azevedo, who served as the Portuguese vice consul in São Luís, recognized Aluísio as his legitimate son in 1864.

As a youth Azevedo showed great interest in drawing and painting, which influenced the techniques he used years later in depicting the characters of his novels. In 1864 he began taking classes with Joaquim Raimundo César, and shortly thereafter he attended a school directed by José Antônio Pires. At the age of thirteen Azevedo went to work in a store owned by one of his father's friends, Davi Freire, at Praia Grande. In 1870 he quit this job to study at the Liceu Maranhense, which was directed by Sotero dos Reis. At this point Azevedo began to study painting with the Italian artist Domingos Tribuzzi.

At the age of nineteen Azevedo decided to move to Rio de Janeiro (where Artur, his brother, was already becoming known for his plays) in order to study at the Imperial Academy of Fine Arts. There he earned his living by drawing illustrations and caricatures for magazines. One of his first caricatures, *Os trinta botões* (The Thirty Buttons), which was intended to ridicule the figure of the artist and caricaturist Rafael Bordalo Pinheiro, appeared in *O Fígaro* in 1876 and earned Azevedo some popularity. He had to compete, however, with famous European caricaturists who had established themselves in Rio de Janeiro, including the German Henrique Fleiuss and the Italian Angelo Agostini.

When his father died in 1878, Azevedo returned to São Luís to attend to family business. There he started writing for the humorous newspaper *A Flecha* (The Arrow) under the pseudonym Pitibri. In 1879 he applied for a grant from the government of Maranhão to study painting in Rome. Because of his anticlerical position, however, his request was denied. In the following year Azevedo published his first novel, *Uma lágrima de mulher* (1880, A Woman's Tear), which he had originally intended to be a drama. Although he was severely criticized for his use of Romantic rhetoric and ideology in this work, *Uma lágrima de mulher* includes the kind of social and personal conflicts that he developed in his later works.

After the publication of his first novel, Azevedo and some friends created an anticlerical periodical, *O Pensador* (The Thinker). In 1880 Azevedo also created the first daily newspaper in São Luís, titled *Pacotilha,* with his future brothers-in-law, Libânio Vale and Vítor Lobato. The humorous pieces, stories, and journalistic attacks in both periodicals on the clergy and slavery aroused considerable animosity in the city and, as a result, provoked a lawsuit brought against Azevedo in 1881 by Francisco José Batista, a local priest. The author was acquitted. Azevedo's anticlerical views have their roots in the society of São Luís itself, where religion served to strengthen and maintain provincial proslavery attitudes even after slavery had been abolished in 1888.

Azevedo's second novel, *O mulato,* published in 1881, is considered a landmark of naturalism in Brazil. Naturalism is based on the notion that knowledge about what exists and about how things work is best achieved through the sciences rather than through personal revelation or religious tradition. The human being is seen as the product of natural selection. There are no immaterial souls standing apart from the physical world. According to this point of view, human beings' actions are determined by various biological, social, genetic, and environmental factors. They cannot act outside this framework or outside the causal connections that link them in every respect to the rest of the world. The characters of a naturalist narrative are usually individuals of either the middle or lower classes, and many times they are portrayed as poor, ignorant, and illiterate. Their world is usu-

Front cover of the 1996 edition of the 1990 translation of Azevedo's O mulato *(1881), the novel that introduced literary naturalism to Brazil (Thomas Cooper Library, University of South Carolina)*

ally monotonous and unjust. Within this world, however, they try to find the meaning of life by seeking adventure and heroism through acts of passion, violence, love, and goodness. Naturalist writers such as Zola describe their characters as conditioned and controlled by their environment and heredity. To a certain extent Brazilian naturalists do the same, but they give a humanitarian value to their characters, as if to compensate for their lack of material possessions. The tension lies in these authors' desire to portray the strict and severe reality of the world but at the same time to reaffirm the dignity and the importance of mankind.

The influences of naturalism on *O mulato* make it a distinctive novel among Azevedo's works. It is marked by a strong sense of determinism, and the protagonist, Raimundo da Silva (the mulatto of the title), is portrayed as a positivist. Azevedo's gift for detailed and vivid descriptions of society created much controversy. Notable themes of the novel include racism, abolitionism, and anticlericalism.

O mulato earned Azevedo a bad reputation among the citizens of São Luís, whose narrow-mindedness and racism he had attacked. In the late nineteenth century the last years of the Second Empire and the establishment of the Republic of Brazil in 1889 marked a significant transitional period in the structure of Brazilian society. The abolition of slavery in 1888 created changes in racial and social values, both urban and provincial. *O mulato* was considered by conservative factions of the provincial city of São Luís to be a blatant attack on them. Azevedo criticized mainly the excessive emphasis on and misuse of religion in society, which he considered the source of spiritual infirmities and mental disorders. Such characteristics can be observed in *O mulato* in the character of Ana Rosa and reappear in Father Angelo in the novel *A mortalha de Alzira* (The Shroud of Alzira), first serialized under the pseudonym Vítor Leal in the *Gazeta de Notícias* in 1891 and published in book form under Azevedo's own name in 1894. The anticlerical themes of these two novels are similar, highlighting the priests' greed for material wealth, their inability to control their sex drive, and their use of prayer and the Mass to control or impress their parishioners.

In *O mulato* there is a clear conflict between the protagonist, Raimundo, and the social circle of his father's family, made up of Portuguese immigrants. Raimundo is the son of a rich farmer, José Pedro da Silva, and a slave, Domingas. After his father's death Raimundo goes to Portugal and a few years later decides to study law. Upon graduating, he travels throughout Europe and then leaves for Rio de Janeiro, where he stays for one year. He returns to Maranhão to sell some property he inherited from his father and stays in the house of his uncle, Manoel Pescada. Here Raimundo falls in love with his cousin, Ana Rosa. Her father and her grandmother, Maria Bárbara, refuse to agree to the marriage of Raimundo and Ana Rosa because Raimundo is the son of a slave. Raimundo, however, has no knowledge of his racial origin. His mother had gone insane when José Pedro da Silva's wife, Quitéria Inocência, tortured her. Although Quitéria Inocência is a jealous wife, she also betrays her husband with the local priest, Diogo. When her husband finds out about her adultery, he kills her. As a rich man, he is not punished for his crime. The priest, however, has Raimundo's father killed in revenge. Fearing that the son will later learn the truth about his father's murder, Diogo also later plans the murder of Raimundo.

O mulato portrays the regional characteristics of Maranhão in a harsh light but at the same time presents an exuberant view of popular customs, such as the celebration of the traditional Festa de São João. The novel also reveals Azevedo's attempt to view Brazil through the scope of Western scientific thought and to match Brazilian reality to European theories. He relied on naturalist techniques to depict the city and its inhabitants, and no one escaped his detailed and often grotesque characterization. Azevedo's effort to apply scientific determinism in the novel also provides an insight into the difficulties of such a process.

Although Azevedo made use of naturalist techniques and their underlying scientific principles, he rejected determinist notions in depicting his mulatto protagonist, Raimundo. Although racially marked as a mulatto, Raimundo does not possess the degenerate characteristics or traits attributed to people of mixed race by scientific determinists. He is portrayed as an intelligent, scientifically astute, and modern man who was educated at the University of Coimbra in Portugal. Raimundo's behavior is not attributed to his racial heritage, since he becomes aware of the fact that he is a mulatto only as an adult. In contrast, Azevedo portrays several of the white members of the local society in a negative manner.

It is difficult to pinpoint specific literary sources for *O mulato*. Apparent similarities have been noted between Azevedo's novel and Queirós's *O crime do padre Amaro* (1876; translated as *The Sin of Father Amaro*, 1963) and *O primo Basílio* (1878; translated as *Cousin Bazilio*, 1953). Some critics have even accused Azevedo of plagiarism. Although he read and was influenced by Queirós's naturalism and his novelistic technique, there is no basis for such an accusation.

With the money Azevedo earned from the publication of *O mulato* in 1881, he decided to return to Rio de Janeiro, where his work had been well received and where he hoped to make a living as a writer. During this time he wrote several novels and collaborated on plays with his brother Artur and also with Emílio Rouède. The novels include *Mistério da Tijuca* (Mystery of Tijuca), serialized in 1882, published in book form the following year, and republished as *Girândola de amores* (Circle of Love) in 1900; and *Memórias de um condenado* (1886, Memoirs of One Condemned), republished as *A Condessa Vésper* (Countess Vesper) in 1902. These two novels were probably written around the same time. Both are original in their incorporation of social themes dealing with Brazilian society and its people.

Mistério da Tijuca opens with the kidnapping of the character Gregório, a central figure in the novel. The plot is complex, and there is a preoccupation with the origin and status of Gregório, as well as with those persons closely associated with him. His past is a mystery and is revealed only when his kidnapper, the count of São Francisco, tells the young man part of the story of his family. The theme of illegitimacy in Azevedo's writing recurs when it is revealed that Gregório's father was a bigamist whose Brazilian wife had a daughter by him named Clorinda.

In *Mistério da Tijuca*, Azevedo explores another theme that appears in his later works—the difference in the way men and women think about love. Although he maintains the tension of the novel through the mystery surrounding Gregório and his activities in Rio de Janeiro, the narrative focuses on an overview of the role of women in Brazilian and Portuguese society. Azevedo's female characters are, in general, figures with important positions in the volatile and complex social context of Rio de Janeiro. His concern with marriage as a failed component of society can be seen in *Mistério da Tijuca*, in which he denounces sexist morality, which concedes all rights to the husband, and portrays the adulterous woman as the victim of a marriage arranged against her will.

Critics have sometimes divided Azevedo's novels into "serious" works and what they consider to be his "pulp" fiction. The former category refers to such works as *O mulato*, *Casa de pensão* (The Boardinghouse, serialized, 1883; published in book form, 1884), *O homem* (1887, The Man), *O coruja* (The Raven, serialized, 1885; published in book form, 1890), *O cortiço* (1890, The Slum; translated as *A Brazilian Tenement*, 1926), and *O livro de uma sogra* (1895, The Book of a Mother-in-Law). The latter category refers to such sensationalist works as *Uma lágrima de mulher*; *A Condessa Vésper*; *Girândola de amores*; *Filomena Borges* (1884); *O esqueleto (Mistérios da casa de Bragança)* (1890, The Skeleton [Mysteries of the House of Bragança]), written with Olavo Bilac and published under the pseudonym Leal; and *A mortalha de Alzira*. These serialized "pulp" novels were quite popular among the reading public of the time. Azevedo developed his skills at character delineation in his "pulp" fiction. The women in these works are especially noteworthy for their strength and independence of thought, characteristics not often seen in female characters in Brazilian novels before Azevedo's time. Even within the limits of the social determinism of naturalism, they are individuals who think for themselves and make their own decisions.

Casa de pensão presents a transition in Azevedo's work as he moved from the patriarchal society of

Maranhão to the microcosm of the boardinghouses of Rio de Janeiro. The novel is considered a roman à clef based on the "Capistrano Affair," a famous crime that had occurred in the capital and captivated the interest of the population of the city. A young man from the provinces, João Capistrano da Cunha, was murdered by the owner of one of the city's better-known boardinghouses under circumstances that were argued at length in the local press. Azevedo, who had lived in one of these boardinghouses and had closely observed the lives of the other tenants, was inspired by this event. *Casa de pensão* is more than a simple recounting of a sensationalist event in Rio de Janeiro. On the contrary, it is a vividly descriptive narrative of life in a boardinghouse that assumes almost human dimensions at certain points in the story.

In *Casa de pensão,* Amâncio de Vasconcelos, a young man from Maranhão, moves to Rio de Janeiro with the intention of studying medicine. He lives with a friend of his family, Luís Campos; his wife, Maria Hortência; and his sister-in-law. Meanwhile, Amâncio meets an old friend, Paiva Rocha, and from this point on he changes his style of life, becoming a bohemian. He misses classes, and he often arrives home late and drunk. Although Maria Hortência is secretly attracted to Amâncio, Campos and his family do not approve of the kind of life he leads, and as a consequence, he moves to a boardinghouse owned by João Coqueiro and his wife, Brizard. Amâncio becomes involved with João's sister, Amélia, and also becomes a victim of the corrupting environment of the boardinghouse. To escape the situation, he plans to visit his mother, who had just been widowed. João discovers his plan, however, and convinces the police to arrest him, accusing Amâncio of having seduced his sister. After a difficult trial Amâncio is found not guilty, but João, who does not agree with the verdict, kills him with a shotgun. Most of the action in the novel is linked to Amâncio as Azevedo attempts to depict through his situation the values of a corrupted and hypocritical society. The setting serves as a catalyst to motivate the action in the novel.

In 1883, when *Casa de pensão* was published, the reading public of Brazil was still small, and novels often appeared in installments in newspapers before they were published as books. After the publication of *Casa de pensão,* Azevedo had several of his plays performed, and he published more serialized works throughout the decade.

In 1888 Azevedo's mother died at the age of seventy. Two years later he published *O cortiço,* which is considered to be his masterpiece. When he published the novel, he had an ambitious plan in mind to write five novels that would serve as panoramic portrayals of Brazilian society from 1820 to 1890. His plan was modeled on Honoré de Balzac's *La Comédie humaine* (1842–1846, 1848, 1855, The Human Comedy; translated as *La Comédie humaine,* 1895–1900) and Zola's *Les Rougon Macquart* (1871–1893; translated as *The Rougon-Macquarts,* 1896–1900). Only the first book of Azevedo's series, *O cortiço,* was published. At that time Brazil was undergoing a crucial moment in its history, with the emancipation of the slaves in 1888, the collapse of the Second Empire in 1889, and the fall of the political dynasty inherited from Portugal.

In *O cortiço,* Azevedo reveals his genius for timing, his instinct for complex plot organization, and his skill at establishing counterpoint among characters and incidents. The influence of his training as a professional illustrator has been noted in his character descriptions in this work. Before writing a novel he would go to the places where his characters lived and spend some time sketching the people there, so that he could capture the nuances of his characters' personalities in his prose. This technique is seen in his preoccupation with exact descriptions of the different types that emerge in the narrative. It is said that Azevedo used to dress as a laborer and mingle with working-class people to draw his sketches. On one occasion, he and his companion were attacked by some workers who mistook them for policemen.

O cortiço represents society through several character types, including the hardworking Portuguese immigrant, the sultry mulatta, the greedy Portuguese bourgeois, and blacks and persons of mixed race who live in the same working-class neighborhood of Rio de Janeiro. The novel, which focuses on social struggle, is characterized by an intricate interplay of story lines, detailed observation, and the accurate portrayal of everyday speech. The narrative concentrates on the economic and social trajectory of four characters: João Romão, who manages to become rich while exploiting the inhabitants of the area; his mistress, Bertoleza, a former slave; Jerônimo, a Portuguese immigrant who is slowly seduced and destroyed by life in this tropical society; and Miranda, a rich immigrant who lives on the edge of the neighborhood, has a noble title, and looks down on the lives of the inhabitants of the neighborhood.

O cortiço is a narrative of social and economic problems, exemplified by the circumstances of the workers who are exploited by those in power. Although Azevedo presents the stories of several different characters, there are two main narrative lines. The first concerns the rise of João from a penny-pinching shopkeeper and landlord to a rich capitalist.

The second centers on the love affair between the vivacious mulatta Rita Baiana and the sweet-natured, brawny Jerônimo. Jerônimo and João represent two alternative immigrant responses to Brazil. The former is transformed by Rita from a thrifty and prudent European into a sensual Brazilian. João, in contrast, is dazzled not by the light and sexual heat of the tropics but by the glitter of gold. Like Jerônimo, who left his wife for Rita, João leaves his lover, Bertoleza, to become engaged to another woman, the rich, refined, and sheltered Zulmira. Bertoleza's suicide provides the stunning conclusion to the novel. As in *O mulato,* the question of race plays a central role in *O cortiço.* Azevedo reveals the prejudice of most whites of the time as he attacks bigotry in his society.

Azevedo published *O livro de uma sogra* in 1895. This novel, which deals with the question of marriage, differs from his other works. Critics consider it to be more experimental in its narrative techniques. The principal female character, Olympia, is a mother-in-law whom Azevedo uses to express his own views on marriage. Olympia, who is worried about the marriage of Palmira, her daughter, to Leandro, decides to write a guide for married couples. The examples she gives, however, are taken from her own failed marriage. In her treatise on the psychology and physiology of marriage Olympia criticizes all of the usual aspects of relationships between men and women. The novel, which presents an intriguing view of the institution of marriage, is not, however, a continuation of the determinism found in *O homem* and *O cortiço.*

Throughout his novels Azevedo's characters generally emerge as social prototypes rather than as individuals. They are closely linked to the themes of the novels and provide the author with a means of conveying his opinions on the social issues and problems of the time. Azevedo explores a large range of topics, such as traditional Portuguese patterns in Brazilian society, slavery and its consequences, the position and role of women in society, and the politics of the old Empire in conflict with the new Republic. The environment in which the action of his novels takes place, generally the cities of Rio de Janeiro and São Luís, plays an important role in shaping and determining the behavior of the characters.

After an intense sixteen years involved in the literary life of Brazil, Azevedo abandoned writing in 1895. That year, with the help of the writer Graça Aranha, he applied for a diplomatic position and was named vice consul to Vigo, Spain. In 1897 he decided to sell the rights to his literary works to the publisher Garnier. In a letter to a friend (quoted in David H. Rosenthal's foreword to his 2000 translation of *O*

Dust jacket, illustrated by Eli Malvina Heil, for the 2000 translation of Azevedo's O cortiço (1890), the novel about life in a working-class neighborhood in Rio de Janeiro that is considered his masterpiece (Richland County Public Library)

cortiço) he explained his decision to leave his career as a writer: "Qual é o propósito da escrita? Para quem? Nós não temos leitores. Uma tiragem de duzentas cópias leva anos para se esgotar. . . . Eu estou farto com a literatura!" (What's the usage of writing? For whom? We have no readers. A printing of two thousand copies takes years to sell out. . . . I've had it up to here with literature!).

Azevedo, along with the novelist Joaquim Maria Machado de Assis, was one of the founding members of the Brazilian Academy of Letters. He was inducted into the academy in 1897. That same year he took up diplomatic duties in Yokohama. During the journey from San Francisco to Japan, his ship almost foundered in severe storms. Azevedo also served as a diplomat in Spain, England, and several South American countries, including Argentina (1899), where he met Pastora Luquez, with whom he decided to live. He adopted her son, Pastor, who became a writer in Spanish and Portuguese, as well as her daughter, Zulema.

Azevedo later served as consul in cities in Uruguay (1903) and Italy (1906). In 1908 he was named consul to Asunción, Paraguay. That same year his brother Artur died. Five years later, on 11 January 1913, Azevedo died of myocarditis in Buenos Aires, Argentina, where he was a commercial attaché. His remains were transferred to Brazil in 1919.

Aluísio Azevedo's reputation as a writer rests on his literary portraits of the Brazilian society of his time, in which he reveals and satirizes the prejudices and habits of the people of São Luís. He shows his opposition to the conservatism and power of the clergy, which, in his view, was responsible for social apathy and lack of action. Azevedo is appreciated for his vivid and dynamic prose that captures a society in an historical moment of great change and transformation, struggling with the reality of its situation and seeking economic stability. As is typical in naturalistic writing, Azevedo's characters are products of their environment, but at the same time the analytical view of naturalism is tempered by the emotionalism of Romanticism in his books.

References:

Alfredo Bosi, *História concisa da literatura brasileira,* thirty-third edition (São Paulo: Cultrix, 1994);

David Brookshaw, *Race and Color in Brazilian Literature* (Metuchen, N.J.: Scarecrow Press, 1986);

Sheldon C. Klock Jr., *Themes in the Novels of Aluísio Azevedo* (Toronto: York, 1999);

Raimundo de Menezes, *Aluísio Azevedo, uma vida de romance,* second edition (São Paulo: Martins, 1958);

Josué Montello, *Aluísio Azevedo e a polêmica d' "O mulato"* (Rio de Janeiro: J. Olympio, 1975);

Herberto Sales, *Para conhecer melhor Aluísio Azevedo* (Rio de Janeiro: Bloch, 1973);

Affonso Romano de Sant'Anna, *Análise estrutural de romances brasileiros* (Petrópolis: Vozes, 1973).

Manuel Antônio Álvares de Azevedo

(12 September 1831 – 25 April 1852)

Vivaldo A. Santos
Georgetown University

BOOKS: *Discurso recitado no dia 11 de agosto de 1849, na sessão acadêmica, commemoradora do anniversário da creação dos cursos jurídicos do Brasil* (Rio de Janeiro: Americana, 1849);

Lira dos vinte anos, 2 volumes, edited by Jacy Monteiro (Rio de Janeiro: Tipografia Americana, 1853, 1855); enlarged as *Obras de Manoel Antonio Álvares de Azevedo,* 3 volumes (Rio de Janeiro: Garnier, 1862);

O Conde Lopo (Rio de Janeiro: Rio Leuzinger, 1866);

O livro de Fra Gondicário, published by Pires de Ameida in *Jornal do Comércio* (1903–1905).

Editions and Collections: *Obras de Manoel Antônio Álvares de Azevedo,* edited by Jacy Monteiro (Rio de Janeiro: Garnier, 1862);

A Noite na taverna. Contos phantasticos por Álvares de Azevedo (Rio de Janeiro: Maia & Ramos, 1878)—includes biography by J. M. de Macedo;

O Conde Lopo: poema inédito (Rio de Janeiro: Leuzinger, 1886);

Noite na taverna, Macário, introduction by Edgard Cavalheiro (São Paulo: Martins, 1952);

Álvares de Azevedo: poesias completas, introduction by Péricles Eugênio da Silva Ramos (São Paulo: Edição Saraiva, 1957);

Macário, Noites na taverna e Poemas malditos, introduction by Hildon Rocha (Rio de Janeiro: Alves, 1983);

Noite na taverna, introduction by Rocha (Rio de Janeiro: Alves, 1991);

Poesias completas, preface by Attilio Milano and Cavalheiro (Rio de Janeiro: Ediouro, 1991);

Noites na taverna, edited by Célia A. N. Passoni (São Paulo: Núcleo, 1993);

Lira dos vinte anos, edited by Maria Lúcia Dal Farra (São Paulo: Martins Fontes, 1996);

Macário, introduction by Marco Lucchesi (Rio de Janeiro: Artium, 1998);

Macário: teatro, edited by Marcelo Backe (Pôrto Alegre, Brazil: Mercado Aberto, 1998);

Obra completa, edited by Alexei Bueno (Rio de Janeiro: Nova Aguilar, 2000).

Manuel Antônio Álvares de Azevedo (Arquivo da Academia Brasileira de Letras)

Manuel Antônio Álvares de Azevedo is frequently identified with the so-called ultra-Romantics, a group of Brazilian Romantic poets that includes Bernardo de Guimarães, Casimiro de Abreu, and Fagundes Varela. These poets are grouped by their obsessive pursuit of writing and a common style featuring contradictions and exaggerated emotions. Their works, which feature themes of pessimism, doubt, despair, abandon, love, and death, were heavily influenced by George Gordon, Lord Byron, and Alfred de Musset.

Azevedo and the ultra-Romantics form the second of the three phases of Brazilian Romantic literature. Their predecessors, the National Romantics, had worked to establish a national literature, influenced by the spirit of the country's independence from Portugal in 1822. For example, the man generally considered to be the founder of Brazilian Romanticism, Gonçalves de Magalhães, author of *Suspiros poéticos e saudades* (1836, Poetical Sights and Longing), used for the epigraph of the literary magazine *Niterói, Revista Brasiliense* (1836) the phrase "Tudo pelo Brasil, e para o Brasil" (Everything by Brazil, and for Brazil). The literature of the first Brazilian Romantics was characterized by, and generally limited to, lyric poetry (featuring love, the idealization of women, and the celebration of poetic genius), religious themes, and Indianism (the search for a Brazilian identity through the cult of the native, as seen in José de Alencar's works). Azevedo and the ultra-Romantic poets also stand apart from the later group of Romantics called "Condoreiros." This third group of Brazilian Romantics was highly influenced by the works of Victor Hugo, who expanded lyric themes to philosophy and to political and social ideals, such as republicanism, the end of slavery, rights and justice, and education.

Manuel Antônio Álvares de Azevedo was born on 12 September 1831 in São Paulo, Brazil, to Inácio Manoel Álvares de Azevedo, a lawyer, and Maria Luísa Carlota Silveira da Mota. The second of nine children, Azevedo moved with his parents to Rio de Janeiro when his father accepted a position teaching law in 1833. From 1840 to 1844 Azevedo was a boarding student at the Colégio Stoll (Stoll School). In 1845 he began attending the most prestigious school of his time, the Colégio Pedro II (Pedro II School), where he studied humanities. During this time he learned French, English, and Latin and became acquainted with European literature.

There are few records of Azevedo's literary work before the age of sixteen. One is a reference, recorded by Vicente de Paulo Vicente de Azevedo in *O noivo da morte,* to poems that he destroyed at a young age. Azevedo said: "Acontece, às vezes, que depois de lê-los (os versos) eu os atiro fora; às vezes, rasgo-os, mas ao menos antes me haviam eles concedido sonhar" (It happens, sometimes, that after I read them [the verses], I get rid of them; sometimes, I rip them up, but at least they have allowed me to dream). Azevedo's only surviving early works are a collection of verses titled "Três liras" (Three Lyres) that he gathered together in a notebook in 1845, and a collection of poems titled "Flores murchas" (Wilted Flowers) that was found among his papers. None of these poems were ever published, but the *Flores murchas* notebook is held at the Biblioteca Nacional (National Library) in Rio de Janeiro.

Azevedo attended the Faculdade de Direito de São Paulo (São Paulo Law School), where he excelled in his law studies, but he also devoted his time to literature, writing prolifically. At the same time he had the typical experiences and fell into the typical vices afforded by the freedom of student life: dancing, alcohol, tobacco, and idealized first loves that he later extolled in his poems. During this time he became friendly with writers Guimarães and Aureliano Lessa, and these friendships helped him develop the gregarious side of his personality and his sarcastic sense of humor. An active participant in the cultural milieu of São Paulo, he founded the literary association Ensaio Filosófico Paulistano (São Paulo Philosophical essay [Society]). Some of his political and social commentaries about education and the Republic were delivered as speeches to this group.

All of Azevedo's work that made it to print was published after his death at age twenty, and his place in literary history has been evaluated not simply on what he wrote but also on the potential he represented. Antonio Candido, in his *Formação da literatura brasileira: momentos decisivos* (1981, Formation of Brazilian Literature: Decisive Moments), described Azevedo as: "um caso de notável possibilidade artística sem correspondente oportunidade ou capacidade de realização" (a unique case of artistic possibility without equal opportunity or capacity of realization). Some critics believe that Azevedo lacked the necessary self-reflection of an artist and accuse him of naiveté. Conversely, other critics credit his creativity and impressive knowledge and love of literature, reflected in his ambition and ability to work in different genres. Although Azevedo's eclecticism has led to criticism of his works in terms of their overall weakness and lack of development, his shortcomings can be explained largely by the brevity of his life and by the fact that his work was organized and published after his death, without his supervision.

Examples of Azevedo's diverse interests can be seen in his poetry, narrative prose, experimental work with mixed literary styles, and pieces of literary criticism on world literature, including "Literatura e civilização em Portugal" (Literature and Civilization in Portugal), "Lucano," "George Sand," and "Jacques Rolla," all of which are published in *Obra completa* (2000, Complete Works). Azevedo was particularly proud of being able to read many different texts in their original languages. He once said, "Quem pode ir às fontes, não bebe a água das sarjetas" (Those who can go to the fountain, don't drink the water from the gutter). In his poem "Idéias íntimas" (Intimate Ideas), published in *Lira dos vinte anos* (1853, 1855, Poetry of the Twenties), he indicates the variety of his reading when he claims: "Junto do leito meus poetas dormem / O Dante, a Bíblia, Shakespeare e Byron / Na mesa confundidos" (At my bedside my poets sleep / Dante, the Bible, Shakespeare, Byron / All confused upon the table). Azevedo's interest in world literature shaped his place in Brazilian Romanticism. His contemporaries who endeavored to affirm Brazilian identity consistently ran the risk of limiting and encapsulating their fictional universe, while Azevedo moved in the opposite direction.

The complexity of Azevedo's work can be seen in *Lira dos vinte anos,* the only book he prepared for publication, although it did not go to press until after his death. In *Lira dos vinte anos* dreamworlds meet the real world, idealized love meets the mundane, and the sacred meets the satanic. In the preface to the second part of *Lira dos vinte anos,* Azevedo reveals that his literary ambiguities were to some extent a conscious choice in order to distance himself from the traditional aesthetics of Romanticism. His conception of literature was a discursive construction that he felt placed him in the tradition of Johann Wolfgang von Goethe's *Die Leiden des jungen Werthers* (1774; translated as *The Sorrows of Werther,* 1779) and *Faust* (part one, 1808; translated as *Faust* in *Faust; and Schiller's Song of the Bell,* 1823; part two, 1832; translated in *Faust Rendered into English Verse,* 1838) and Byron's *Parisina and Giaour* (1816), *Cain* (1821), and *Don Juan* (1819–1824), a literary genealogy that was important to the development of modern literature.

One characteristic of Azevedo's work is its darkness. Often his poetry conveys a sense of the precariousness of human existence that earned him, in the history of Brazilian literature, the titles "Poeta da morte" (The Poet of Death), "Poeta da solidão" (The Poet of Solitude), and "Noivo da morte" (Death's Fiancée). His obsession with death made him the best representation of the *mal du siècle* in Brazilian Romanticism, which is characterized by extreme melancholy, exasperation, dreams, and the bohemian life. Death is a central theme in *Lira dos vinte anos,* particularly in the first part of the book. This dark theme is evident in poems such as "Se eu morresse amanhã" (If I were to die tomorrow):

Se eu morresse amanhã, viria ao menos
Fechar meus olhos minha triste irmã;
Minha mãe de saudades morreria
Se eu morresse amanhã!

(If I were to die tomorrow, would my sad sister
At least close my eyes;
My mother would die missing me
If I were to die tomorrow!)

Here the poet feels impotent in life, and the futility of his efforts in love is projected into a fascination with death. What prevails, then, is love for death, which, together with the mother's and sister's love, becomes a form of escape from reality. Similarly, the last verses of "Lembrança de morrer" (Memories of dying), also

from *Lira dos vinte anos,* offer the speaker's renunciation of life, where the only significance of existence is placed, above all, on the poetic condition:

Descansem o meu leito solitário
Na floresta dos homens esquecida
À sombra de uma cruz, e escrevam nela:
Foi poeta—sonhou—e amou na vida.

(Let my lonely bed rest
in the forgotten forest of men
in the shadow of a cross, and write on it:
he was a poet—he dreamed—and he loved in life.)

This poem is clearly designed to evoke sympathy for the poet's suffering. Beyond his exploration of dark themes, Azevedo is considered the first Brazilian writer to treat the prosaic as poetic. He incorporates into his poems everyday images such as a washerwoman, a smoking pipe, dirty clothes, geckos, and money. These images had not been seen in Brazilian poetry before. Additionally, Azevedo's ability to shift from dramatic and hopeless to jovial and playful is seen in "O poeta moribundo" (The Dying Poet), in which the poet's mocking of his existential drama makes death seem less ominous. In "O vagabundo" (Vagabond), from the second part of *Lira dos vinte anos,* his sense of humor also prevails: "Eu durmo e vivo ao sol como um cigano, . . . Sou pobre, sou mendigo e sou ditoso!" (I sleep and live in the sunlight like a gypsy, . . . I am poor, I am homeless and I am lucky!).

Azevedo also frequently focuses on love in his work. The verses of his "Soneto" (Sonnet) illustrate the traditional idealization of love in Romantic poetry, a prominent feature of the first part of *Lira dos vinte anos.* "Soneto" expresses a belief, marked by a religious tone, in love as transcendent and redeeming.

Azevedo sometimes uses his sense of humor and satirical spirit to destroy the idea of a mythical and idealized love. An example may be seen in the unromantic scenario created in "Namoro a cavalo" (Courting by Horse), from the third part of *Lira dos vinte anos.* The poet rents a horse to pay a visit to his beloved, and along the way he falls on the rain-soaked ground. The scared horse runs off, but the poet persists in his quest, despite being completely covered in mud.

Furthermore, while women are described as angelic in many of the love poems of *Lira dos vinte anos,* Azevedo also provides some mundane representations of women that serve to demystify romantic love. For example, in "É ela!" (It's She!), the poet attempts to idealize a washerwoman before realizing that her love for him is merely a figment of his imagination. In this burlesque the traditional pale and sleeping virgin is replaced by a snoring working-class woman who sleeps

ÁLVARES DE AZEVEDO

OBRA COMPLETA

Organização
ALEXEI BUENO

Textos Críticos
JACI MONTEIRO
MACHADO DE ASSIS
SÍLVIO ROMERO
JOSÉ VERÍSSIMO
AGRIPINO GRIECO
RONALD DE CARVALHO
MÁRIO DE ANDRADE
MANUEL BANDEIRA
ANTONIO CANDIDO
JOSÉ GUILHERME MERQUIOR
LUCIANA STEGAGNO-PICCHIO
WELLINGTON DE ALMEIDA SANTOS

RIO DE JANEIRO, EDITORA NOVA AGUILAR S.A., 2000

Title page for an edition of Azevedo's complete works (Glenn G. Bartle Library, State University of New York at Binghamton)

not amid flowers under the stars but rather with the iron that she uses in her trade. Also, the piece of paper that the poet believes to be a love poem for him is just a roll of dirty clothes:

> É ela! É ela!—repeti tremendo;
> Mas cantou nesse instante uma coruja . . .
> Abri cioso a página secreta . . .
> Oh! Meu Deus! Era um rol de roupa suja!

> (It is she! It's she!—I repeated trembling;
> but an owl hooted at this moment . . .
> I jealously opened the secret page . . .
> Oh! My God! It was a roll of dirty clothes!)

Although Azevedo started law school in São Paulo in 1848, he was unable to finish his studies when he contracted enteritis, an intestinal disease, shortly before the last year of his studies. He died from this illness (not only from tuberculosis, as many believe) on 25 April 1852, in Rio de Janeiro.

The posthumously published works of Azevedo, *O poema do frade* (The Friar's Poem), *Macário,* and *Noites na taverna* (Nights in the Tavern), all of which were published in *Obras de Manoel Antonio Álvares de Azevedo* (1862, Works of Manuel Antônio Álvares de Azevedo), as well as *O Conde Lopo* (1866, Count Lopo) and *O livro de Fra Gondicário* (1903–1905, Fra Gondicário's Book), are considered weak in terms of their artistic value. Published by Azevedo's friends, these works are raw, having never gone through a process of authorial revision. Drafts of literary works written by an adolescent, they lack refinement and originality.

The influence of Byron is revealed in Azevedo's penchant for verbosity, continuous digressions, and sarcasm, and in his portrayals of blasphemy and rebellion. While a fascination with Byron contributed to Azevedo's special place in Brazilian literature by inspiring his use of humor, it also damaged his writings, which often lack originality, concision, and personal creativity. The value in these works lies more in Azevedo's artistic potential as "O Byron brasileiro" (the Brazilian Byron), as many critics have called him, than in the writings themselves.

O Conde Lopo, for instance, is a romantic cliché that tells the story of a poet whose life is marked by tragedy after murdering his fiancée in a fit of jealousy. Written in free verse, the long narrative poem belongs to the tradition of fantastic literature, populated by ghosts and skeletons in an ambience of terror. *O poema do frade* is a metrical poetic narrative about the love affairs of a licentious young man named Jônatas, his girlfriend, and a prostitute. This long poem is characterized by a confusion of themes, verbosity, and digressions, problems it shares with the surviving fragment of Azevedo's lost book, *O livro de Fra Gondicário.*

Noites na taverna, however, demonstrates some literary development on the part of Azevedo. Although the text is still heavily influenced by Byron, it offers a sense of fantasy and imagination that reveals Azevedo's creative capacity. The text consists of narratives by five different friends sitting at a table in a tavern. The stories, marked by a satanic spirit, are sensational, featuring murders, incest, cannibalism, revenge, fratricide, and necrophilia. The innovations of *Noites na taverna* reside in the aspects of modern prose the work anticipates, such as double narration, the intersection of different story lines, and the combination of the fantastic with the realistic.

Finally, *Macário* represents Azevedo's experiment in the dramatic genre. A mix of metaphysical themes and incidents from everyday life, the play tells the story of three figures: Macário, an irreverent and skeptical atheist in the tradition of Byron; Penseroso, whose personality is defined by moderation, the sentimental, and the nationalist spirit; and Satan. The story originates in a hostel in São Paulo and later moves to Italy.

Noteworthy aspects of *Macário* include: the presence of the city of São Paulo as a poetic theme, Macário's criticism of the picturesque and national representation of nature in literature that was dear to most Brazilian Romantic writers, and the unfolding of Azevedo's personality in the divergent characters Macário and Penseroso, who embody the two different styles of most of Azevedo's works. According to Candido in "A educação pela noite," the elaborateness of *Macário* makes the play better for reading than for performance.

Despite his death at an early age, Manuel Antônio Álvares de Azevedo left an important legacy to Brazilian literature. His intellectual desire and curiosity, which stretched beyond that of most poets of his and preceding generations, gave him an important place in nineteenth-century literature. His aesthetic view, which was distant from the focus on "local color" that dictated the nationalistic tone of Brazilian Romanticism, and his conveyance of universal themes through particular settings, characters, and actions, place him stylistically close to great Brazilian writers such as Machado de Assis, the most acclaimed writer of nineteenth-century Brazilian Realism, and João Guimarães Rosa and Clarice Lispector of the twentieth century. Hence, Azevedo was a precursor to the great writers who would give Brazilian literature a place within the ranks of world literature.

Letters:

Cartas de Álvares de Azevedo, edited by Vicente de Paulo Vicente de Azevedo (São Paulo: Academia Paulista de Letras, 1976).

Biographies:

Vicente de Paulo Vicente de Azevedo, *O noivo da morte* (São Paulo: Clube do Livro, 1970);

Azevedo, *Álvares de Azevedo desvendado* (São Paulo: Martins/Instituto Nacional do Livro, Ministério da Educação e Cultura, 1977).

References:

João Severino Albuquerque, "A Brazilian Intermediary in the Transmission of European Romantic Ideas: Álvares de Azevedo," *Romance Notes,* 23, no. 3 (1983): 220–226;

Cilaine Alves, *O belo e o disforme: Álvares de Azevedo e a ironia romântica* (São Paulo: Editoria da Universidade do São Paulo/Fundação de Amparo à Pesquisa do Estado de São Paulo, 1998);

Mário de Andrade, "Amor e medo," in his *Aspectos da literatura brasileira* (São Paulo: Martins/Instituto Nacional do Livro, Ministério da Educação e Cultura, 1972);

Antonio Candido, "Álvares de Azevedo, ou Ariel e Caliban," in his *Formação da literatura brasileira: momentos decisivos,* sixth edition, volume 2 (Belo Horizonte: Itatiaia, 1981), pp. 178–193;

Candido, "A educação pela noite," in his *A educação pela noite e outros ensaios* (São Paulo: Ática, 1987), pp. 11–22;

Modesto Carone, "Álvares de Azevedo, um poeta urbano," *Remate-de-Males,* 7 (1987): 1–6;

Afrânio Coutinho, "The Romantic Movement," in his *An Introduction to Literature in Brazil,* translated by Gregory Rabassa (New York: Columbia University Press, 1969), pp. 119–151;

Jamil Almansur Haddad, *Álvares de Azevedo, a maçonaria e a dança* (São Paulo: Conselho Estadual de Cultura, Comissão de Literatura, 1960);

Samuel Putnam, "Tristful Tavern and a Condor Bard," in his *Marvelous Journey: A Survey of Four Centuries of Brazilian Writing* (New York: Knopf, 1948), pp. 115–135;

Hildon Rocha, *Álvares de Azevedo, anjo e demônio do romantismo* (Rio de Janeiro: J. Olympio, 1982);

Donald O. Warrin, "On the Function of the Poetic Sign in Álvares de Azevedo," *Luso-Brazilian Review,* 17 (1980): 93–105.

Papers:

Some of Manuel Antônio Azevedo's early letters and poems are held in the manuscripts section of the Biblioteca Nacional (National Library) in São Paulo.

Manuel Bandeira

(19 April 1886 – 13 October 1968)

Bruce Dean Willis
University of Tulsa

BOOKS: *A cinza das horas* (Rio de Janeiro: Privately printed, 1917);

Carnaval (Rio de Janeiro: Tipografia do *Jornal do Commercio,* 1919);

Poesias (Rio de Janeiro: Editora da *Revista da Língua Portuguesa,* 1924)—includes *O ritmo dissoluto;*

Libertinagem (Rio de Janeiro: Paulo, Pongetti, 1930);

Estrela da manhã (Rio de Janeiro: Privately printed, 1936);

Crônicas da província do Brasil (Rio de Janeiro: Civilização Brasileira, 1937);

Poesias escolhidas (Rio de Janeiro: Civilização Brasileira, 1937);

Guia de Ouro Prêto (Rio de Janeiro: Ministério da Educação e Saúde, 1938; revised edition, Rio de Janeiro: Casa do Estudante do Brasil, 1957);

Noções de história das literaturas (São Paulo: Editora Nacional, 1940; revised and enlarged, 1946; revised and enlarged, 2 volumes, 1954)—Brazilian section translated by Ralph Edward Dimmick as *A Brief History of Brazilian Literature* (Washington, D.C.: Pan American Union, 1958);

Poesias completas (Rio de Janeiro: Civilização Brasileira, 1940)—includes *Lira dos cinqüent'anos;* revised and enlarged edition (Rio de Janeiro: Casa do Estudante do Brasil, 1948)—includes *Belo belo;* revised and enlarged as *Poesias* (Rio de Janeiro: J. Olympio, 1954)—includes *Opus 10;*

Discurso de posse de Manuel Bandeira; Resposta de Ribeiro Couto: Academia Brasileira, 30 de novembro de 1940 (Rio de Janeiro: Bedeschi, 1941);

Apresentação da poesia brasileira, seguida de uma pequena antologia, preface by Otto Maria Carpeaux (Rio de Janeiro: Casa do Estudante do Brasil, 1946); revised and enlarged as *Apresentação da poesia brasileira, seguida de uma antologia de versos* (Rio de Janeiro: Casa do Estudante do Brasil, 1954; revised, 1957);

Oração de Paraninfo, proferida em 1945 na cerimônia de colação de grau dos bacharéis da Faculdade de Filosofia da Uni-

Drawing of Manuel Bandeira by Luís Jardim (from Stefan Baciu, Manuel Bandeira de corpo inteiro, *1966; Thomas Cooper Library, University of South Carolina)*

versidade do Brasil (Rio de Janeiro: Pongetti, 1946);

Mafuá do malungo (Barcelona: J. Cabral de Melo Neto, 1948; enlarged edition, Rio de Janeiro: São José, 1954);

Poesias escolhidas (Rio de Janeiro: Pongetti, 1948);

Literatura hispano-americana (Rio de Janeiro: Pongetti, 1949);

Gonçalves Dias: esboço biográfico (Rio de Janeiro: Pongetti, 1952);

Opus 10 (Niterói: Hipocampo, 1952);

De poetas e de poesia (Rio de Janeiro: Ministério da Educação e Cultura, 1954);

Itinerário de Pasárgada (Rio de Janeiro: Edicões *Jornal de Letras*, 1954);

Mário de Andrade: animador da cultura musical brasileira (Rio de Janeiro: Teatro Municipal, 1954);

50 poemas escolhidos pelo autor (Rio de Janeiro: Ministério da Educação e Cultura, 1955);

Francisco Mignone (Rio de Janeiro: Teatro Municipal, 1956);

Obras poéticas (Lisbon: Minerva, 1956);

Flauta de papel (Rio de Janeiro: Alvorada, 1957);

Poesia e prosa, 2 volumes, edited by Sérgio Buarque de Holanda and Francisco de Assis Barbosa (Rio de Janeiro: J. Aguilar, 1958)–includes *Estrela da tarde;*

Estrela da tarde (Rio de Janeiro: Dinamene, 1960);

Pasárgada (Rio de Janeiro: Cem Bibliógrafos do Brasil, 1960);

Castro Alves (Santiago: Centro Brasileiro de Cultura, Embajada del Brasil en Santiago de Chile, 1962);

Poesia e Vida de Gonçalves Dias (São Paulo: Editora das Américas, 1962);

Estrela da tarde (Rio de Janeiro: J. Olympio, 1963)–com prises *Estrela da tarde, Duas canções do tempo do beco, Louvações, Composições, Ponteios, Preparação para a morte,* and *Auto sacramental do divino Narciso;*

Preparação para a morte (Rio de Janeiro: A. Willième & A. Grosso, 1965);

Andorinha, andorinha, edited by Carlos Drummond de Andrade (Rio de Janeiro: J. Olympio, 1966);

Os reis vagabundos, e mais 50 crônicas (Rio de Janeiro: Editora do Autor, 1966);

Colóquio unilateralmente sentimental: crônicas (Rio de Janeiro: Record, 1968).

Editions and Collections: *Antologia poética* (Rio de Janeiro: Editora do Autor, 1961; enlarged edition, Rio de Janeiro: Sabiá, 1972);

Estrela da vida inteira: poesias reunidas (Rio de Janeiro: J. Olympio, 1966); revised and enlarged as *Estrela da vida inteira: poesias reunidas e poemas traduzidos* (Rio de Janeiro: J. Olympio, 1986); selections translated by Candace Slater as *This Earth, That Sky: Poems,* introduction and notes by Slater, Latin

American Literature and Culture, no. 1 (Berkeley: University of California Press, 1989);

Meus poemas preferidos (Rio de Janeiro: De Ouro, 1966);

Poesia completa e prosa, introduction by Bandeira and Sérgio Buarque de Holanda (Rio de Janeiro: J. Aguilar, 1967);

Poesias, edited, with a preface, by Adolfo Casais Monteiro (Lisbon: Portugália, 1968);

Poesia, edited by Alceu Amoroso Lima (Rio de Janeiro: AGIR, 1970);

Seleta em prosa e versa, edited by Emanuel de Moraes (Rio de Janeiro: J. Olympio, 1971);

Testamento de Pasárgada: antologia poética, edited by Ivan Junqueira (Rio de Janeiro: Nova Fronteira, 1980; revised and enlarged, 2003);

Prosa, edited by Antonio Carlos Villaça (São Paulo: AGIR, 1983);

Os melhores poemas de Manuel Bandeira, edited by Francisco de Assis Barbosa (São Paulo: Globo, 1984);

Poemas de Manuel Bandeira com motivos religiosos, edited, with an introduction, by Edson Nery da Fonseca, preface by Gilberto Freyre (Rio de Janeiro: Philobiblion, 1985);

Berimbau e outros poemas, edited by Elias José (Rio de Janeiro: J. Olympio, 1986);

Carnaval, edited by Júlio Castañon Guimarães and Rachel Teixeira Valença (Rio de Janeiro: Nova Fronteira/Fundação Casa de Rui Barbosa, 1986);

Vou-me embora pra Pasárgada: poemas escolhidos, edited by Moraes (Rio de Janeiro: J. Olympio, 1986);

A cinza das horas; Carnaval; O ritmo dissoluto, edited by Guimarães and Valença (Rio de Janeiro: Nova Fronteira, 1994);

Vou-me embora pra Pasárgada e outros poemas, edited by Maura Sardinha (Rio de Janeiro: Ediouro, 1996);

Seleta de prosa, edited by Guimarães (Rio de Janeiro: Nova Fronteira, 1997);

Libertinagem; Estrela da manhã, edited by Giulia Lanciani (Paris: UNESCO / Nanterre: Asociación Archivos de la Literatura Latinoamericana del Caribe y Africana del Siglo XX, Université de Paris X, 1998);

Melhores crônicas de Manuel Bandeira, edited, with a preface, by Eduardo Coelho (São Paulo: Global, 2003).

Editions in English: *Recife,* translated by Eddie Flintoff (London: Rivelin Grapheme, 1984);

Selected Poems, translated by David R. Slavitt (Riverdale-on-Hudson, N.Y.: Sheep Meadow Press, 2002).

OTHER: *Antologia dos poetas brasileiros: fase simbolista,* edited by Bandeira (Rio de Janeiro: Imprensa Nacional, 1937);

Antologia dos poetas brasileiros da fase romântica, edited by Bandeira (Rio de Janeiro: Imprensa Nacional, 1937);

Antologia dos poetas brasileiros da fase parnasiana, edited by Bandeira (Rio de Janeiro: Ministério da Educação e Saúde, 1938);

Gilberto Freyre, *Olinda: 2o guia pratico, historico e sentimental de cidade brasileira,* illustrated by Bandeira (Recife: Drechsler, 1939);

Hildebrando Lima and Gustavo Barroso, *Pequeno dicionário brasileiro da língua portuguêsa,* second edition, revised and enlarged by Bandeira, José Baptista da Luz, and Antenor Nascentes (Rio de Janeiro: Civilização Brasileira, 1939);

Portinari, includes biographical and critical sketches by Bandeira and Mário de Andrade (Rio de Janeiro: Ministério da Educação, 1939);

Antero de Quental, *Sonetos completos e poemas escolhidos,* edited, with a preface, by Bandeira (Rio de Janeiro: Livros de Portugal, 1942);

Glória de Antero, by Bandeira and Jaime Cortesão (Lisbon: Cadernos da Seara Nova, 1943);

Obras-primas da lírica brasileira, edited by Bandeira, notes by Edgard Cavalheiro (São Paulo: Martins, 1943; revised and enlarged, 1957);

Antônio Gonçalves Dias, *Obras poéticas de A. Gonçalves Dias,* 2 volumes, edited by Bandeira (São Paulo: Editora Nacional, 1944);

Antologia de poetas brasileiras bissextos contemporâneos, edited, with biobibliographical sketches, by Bandeira (Rio de Janeiro: Z. Valverde, 1946);

José Albano, *Rimas de José Albano,* edited, with a preface, by Bandeira (Rio de Janeiro: Pongetti, 1948);

M. Said Ali, *Versificação portuguésa,* preface by Bandeira (Rio de Janeiro: Imprensa Nacional, 1948);

Deolinda Tavares, *Poemas,* edited by Bandeira, Freyre, and Murilo Mendes (Rio de Janeiro: Casa do Estudante do Brasil, 1949);

Cartas de Mário de Andrade a Manuel Bandeira, preface and notes by Bandeira (Rio de Janeiro: Organização Simões, 1958);

Gonçalves Dias, *Gonçalves Dias: Poesia,* edited by Bandeira (Rio de Janeiro: AGIR, 1958);

"Em louvor das letras hispano-americanas," in *3 Conferências sobre cultura hispano-americana,* by Bandeira, Augusto Tamayo Vargas, and Cecília Meireles (Rio de Janeiro: Ministério da Educação e Cultura, 1959);

Poesia do Brasil: seleção e estudos da melhor poesia brasileira de todos os tempos, edited by Bandeira and José Guilherme Merquior (Pôrto Alegre: Editora do Autor, 1963);

Rio de Janeiro em prosa & verso, by Bandeira and Carlos Drummond de Andrade (Rio de Janeiro: J. Olympio, 1965);

Antônio de Castro Alves, *Poesias completas,* preface by Bandeira (Rio de Janeiro: De Ouro, 1966);

Antologia dos poetas brasileiros: fase moderna, 2 volumes, edited by Bandeira and Walmir Ayala (Rio de Janeiro: De Ouro, 1967);

Lasar Segall, *Mangue,* text by Bandeira, Jorge de Lima, and Mário de Andrade (Rio de Janeiro: Philobiblion, 1977).

TRANSLATIONS: Clifford Whittingham Beers, *Um espírito que se achou a si mesmo* (São Paulo: Editora Nacional, 1934);

Elionor Glyn, *Tudo se paga* (Rio de Janeiro: Civilização Brasileira, 1935);

Alfred Assollant, *Aventuras maravilhosas do Capitão Corcoran* (São Paulo: Editora Nacional, 1936);

Poemas traduzidos, edited by Bandeira (Rio de Janeiro: R. A. Editora, 1945; revised and enlarged, Rio de Janeiro: Globo, 1948; revised and enlarged, Rio de Janeiro: J. Olympio, 1956);

Friedrich von Schiller, *Maria Stuart* (Rio de Janeiro: Civilização Brasileira, 1955);

Jacques Maritain, *Reflexões sôbre os Estados Unidos* (Rio de Janeiro: Editora Fundo de Cultura, 1959);

José Zorrilla, *D. João Tenório* (Rio de Janeiro: Serviço Nacional de Teatro, 1960);

William Shakespeare, *Macbeth* (Rio de Janeiro: J. Olympio, 1961);

Frédéric Mistral, *Mirèia* (Rio de Janeiro: Delta, 1962);

Carl Spitteler, *Prometeu e Epimeteu* (Rio de Janeiro: Delta, 1963);

Gabriel Cacho, *Edith Stein na câmara de gas: teatro* (Petrópolis: Vozes, 1965);

Antonio Gala, *Os verdes campos do Eden: história dramática em duas partes* (Petrópolis: Vozes, 1965);

Omar Khayyam, *Rubaiyat,* from the French translation of Franz Toussaint (Rio de Janeiro: De Ouro, 1965).

Manuel Bandeira was one of the most influential, innovative, and productive of twentieth-century Brazilian poets. Embraced by the Brazilian people, he built on his symbolist and vanguardist background to develop his own stylistics that transcended any one literary movement. Bandeira's mix of melancholy with humor, eroticism with spirituality, and the quotidian with the escapist endeared his verses to a public who found them worthy of memorization and recitation. As a man of letters, he was a distinguished voice in the essential dialogue of his era: *modernismo,* an attempt to redefine and modernize Brazilian language and arts. Bandeira also wrote essays about Brazilian history and arts, published many translations and anthologies, and was paramount in promoting interest in Spanish American literature. During his later years he was the best-known Brazilian poet, as is attested by a plethora of photographs, portraits, caricatures, busts, and versions of his poems set to music. His relationships with other poets over the course of several generations as apprentice, friend, critic, and mentor portray the articulation and development of twentieth-century Brazilian poetry.

Manuel Carneiro de Sousa Bandeira Filho was born on 19 April 1886 in Recife, capital and largest city of the state of Pernambuco, along the northeastern coast of Brazil. His parents were Manuel Carneiro de Sousa Bandeira, an engineer, and Francelina Ribeiro de Sousa Bandeira. Although his family moved to Rio de Janeiro when he was four and the young Bandeira spent two formative summers in Petrópolis (north of Rio de Janeiro), the family returned in 1892 to Recife, the place that is most associated in his work with his childhood memories. After four more years in Recife the family again moved to Rio de Janeiro, Bandeira's residence for most of the rest of his life. He was fascinated by life in the street, especially in the Laranjeiras district of the city. At school he developed an interest in the classics, such as Luís de Camões's *Os Lusíadas* (1572; translated as *The Lusiad, or, Portugals Historicall Poem*, 1655), and was even able to recite a stanza of that epic to the much impressed famous novelist Joaquim Maria Machado de Assis on a streetcar one day. The influence of his father was deeply felt by the young Bandeira, who in 1903, after completing his high-school education and publishing his first poem, went to São Paulo to study architecture at his father's bidding.

In 1904 Bandeira was diagnosed with tuberculosis, the factor that most affected his life and work. He quit his architectural studies and for the next decade sought, in a series of Brazilian locales, climatic conditions favorable to the treatment of his disease, all the while reading and writing. He entered a poetry contest in 1910 (in the end, no prize was awarded) and began to experiment with free verse at that time. In 1913 Bandeira traveled to Clavadel Sanatorium in Switzerland, where he met and befriended Paul-Eugène Grindel (who took the pseudonym Paul Eluard in 1914), who lent him books by such French writers as Paul Claudel. While in Europe, Bandeira attempted to publish a first book, "Poemetos melancólicos" (Melancholy Little Poems), in Portugal. It was never published, and the original poems were lost, but the title was indicative of the general tone and style of many of his later works. The outbreak of World War I in Europe in 1914 precipitated Bandeira's return to Brazil, where he set up residence in Rio de Janeiro. He lived constantly with

Ink caricature of Bandeira by Cicero Dias (from Stefan Baciu, Manuel Bandeira de corpo inteiro, *1966, Thomas Cooper Library, University of South Carolina)*

the specter of his own death from tuberculosis; yet, in the next few years he suffered the deaths of his mother (1916); his only sister, Maria (1918); his father (1920); and an older brother, Antônio (1922).

Bandeira financed the publication of his first book, *A cinza das horas* (Ash of the Hours), in 1917. With the attention to fixed form, emotional state, and vivid imagery found in the poems, the collection embodies the influence of the Parnassians and symbolists, the main poetic groups in late-nineteenth- and early-twentieth-century Brazil. A melancholy tone and continental Portuguese grammar prevail throughout, although there are early signs of what later became Bandeira's trademark irony and use of Brazilian colloquialisms. The first poem, "Epígrafe" (Epigraph), contrasts the poet's comfortable upbringing ("Sou bem-nascido" [I am well born]) with the onslaught of his disease ("Veio o mau gênio da vida" [The evil spirit of life came]) to frame the title image of the collection:

Ardeu em gritos dementes
Na sua paixão sombria . . .
E dessas horas ardentes
Ficou esta cinza fria.
—Esta pouca cinza fria. . . .
([My heart] burned in demented howls
In its dark passion . . .

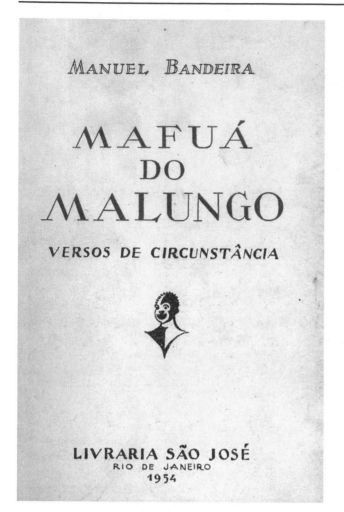

Title page for the enlarged edition of Bandeira's 1948 poetry collection, originally published by the poet João Cabral de Melo Neto (Joint University Libraries, Nashville)

And from these burning hours
Remain these cold ashes.
—These few cold ashes. . . .)

    This tone of despair, characterized by the limitations of disease and also of traditional poetry, strongly influenced *Carnaval* (1919, Carnival) and *O ritmo dissoluto* (Freed Rhythm), published in *Poesias* (1924). *Carnaval* holds loosely to the themes suggested by the title, elaborated in a series of poems about commedia dell'arte characters, but the collection is most remembered for such works as "Os sapos" (The Toads) and "Vulgívaga," innovative and iconoclastic poems that support the key modernist figure Mário de Andrade's epithet for Bandeira, the "St. John the Baptist of modernism." "Os sapos" parodies the Parnassian and symbolist styles through the boasts of a toad chorus, but the chorus is abandoned for the sobbing of a far-off, lonely little frog, suggesting the poet's frustration with the

structural pomp of the predominant Brazilian poetry. In 1922 the poem was recited, although not by Bandeira, at the pivotal Semana de Arte Moderna (Week of Modern Art) in São Paulo, where it was received, as was most of the week's program, by the bourgeois audience's boos and hisses. The frankly erotic "Vulgívaga," in which the poetic voice is that of an experienced woman remembering her diverse lovers, is representative of Bandeira's portrayal of the poetic muse. The experienced woman is generally interpreted to be poetry, who rewards the most daring and experimental of those who would love her. Nonetheless, the meter and rhyme of the poem are still fixed:

> Fui de um . . . Fui de outro . . . Éste era médico . . .
> Um, poeta . . . Outro, nem sei mais!
> Tive em meu leito enciclopédico
> Todas as artes liberais.

> (I belonged to one . . . and another . . . this one was a doctor . . .
> One was a poet . . . another one, I don't remember!
> I welcomed in my encyclopedic bed
> all the liberal arts.)

    With *O ritmo dissoluto* Bandeira inaugurated the importance of everyday elements and childhood memories in his poetry. He had begun residing on Rua do Curvelo in Rio de Janeiro in 1920, a street that he claimed carried him back to his childhood and made palpable for him the humility of everyday life. "Na Rua do Sabão" (Soap Street), "Meninos carvoeiros" (Little Coal Men), and "Balõezinhos" (Balloons) exemplify the poet's adoption of a child-like sense of wonder in recollection of scenes from his youth that influenced many of his best-known poems. The prosaic diction in "Balõezinhos" exemplifies Bandeira's first published free-verse poems: "Sente-se bem que para eles ali na feira os balõezinhos de cor são a única mercadoria útil e verdadeiramente indispensável" (It feels good that for them [the children] there in the fair the little colored balloons are the only useful and truly indispensable merchandise). As in "Balõezinhos," the flexibility of free verse is instrumental to the "Balada de Santa Maria Egipcíaca" (Ballad of St. Mary of Egypt), in which the unsettling effect of the saint's disrobing is heightened by the varying rhyme and rhythm, as in the last strophe: "Santa Maria Egipcíaca despiu / O manto, e entregou ao barqueiro / A santidade da sua nudez" (Saint Mary of Egypt let fall / her robe, and gave unto the boatman / the sanctity of her nudity). "Berimbau" (the name of a folk musical instrument), along with "Debussy," from *Carnaval,* typifies Bandeira's penchant for musical experimentation. In "Berimbau" indigenous Brazilian words stressed on the last syllable dictate a striking rhythm.

The pinnacle of Bandeira's early success was *Libertinagem* (1930, Libertinism), which emphasized key stylistic and thematic tendencies that had only been glimpsed previously: irony, humor, colloquial speech, and everyday life. Moreover, the almost complete abandonment of meter in this collection represented a decisive formal break from Bandeira's previous works and showed the deeply felt influence of the artistic renovation of *modernismo*. These formal and thematic liberties are evoked by the title of the collection and through contrast to the faults of outdated, stifling lyricism, enumerated in the battle cry of the collection, "Poética" (Poetics):

Estou farto do lirismo comedido
Do lirismo bem comportado
Do lirismo funcionário público com livro de ponto expediente protocolo
e manifestações de apreço ao sr. diretor.

(I've had it with modest lyricism
well-behaved lyricism
lyricism of the bureaucrat with his book of protocol
and manifestations of appreciation for mr. director.)

The lengthy "Evocação do Recife" (Evocation of Recife), a mosaic of childhood memories tinged with the aura of a golden age, contrasts with the technical language and ironic brevity of "Pneumotórax" (Pneumothorax), one of Bandeira's best-known poems and a salient example of the *poema piada* (joke poem). "Pneumotórax" is often cited as a summary of Bandeira's life-long struggle in the shadow of tuberculosis; yet, the poem is just as memorable for its crystallization of Bandeira's melancholy humor:

Febre, hemoptise, dispnéia, e suores noturnos.
A vida inteira que podia ter sido e que não foi.
Tosse, tosse, tosse.
. . . .
–O senhor tem uma escavação no pulmão esquerdo e o pulmão direito infiltrado.
–Então, doutor, não é possível tentar o pneumotórax?
–Não. A única coisa a fazer é tocar um tango argentino.

(Fever, coughing blood, heavy breathing, night sweats.
An entire life that could have been and wasn't.
Cough, cough, cough.
. . . .
–You've got a hole in your left lung and fluid in your right.
–So, doctor, is it not possible to try a pneumothorax?
–Nope. The only thing to do is play an Argentine tango.)

"Porquinho-da-índia" (Guinea Pig), a lesson in love for the young Bandeira, is later summarized in the brief "Madrigal tão engraçadinho" (Such a Funny Little Madrigal): "Teresa, você é a coisa mais bonita que eu vi até hoje na minha vida, inclusive o porquinho-da-índia que me deram quando eu tinha seis anos" (Teresa, you are the most beautiful thing I have seen in my life, including the guinea pig they gave me when I was six years old).

Libertinagem also includes a found poem, "Poema tirado de uma notícia de jornal" (Poem Taken from a Newspaper Article), some travel poems, and the prose poem "Noturno da Rua da Lapa" (Nocturne on Lapa Street), but probably the most beloved work in the collection is "Vou-me embora pra Pasárgada" (Off to Pasárgada), which Bandeira claimed had the longest gestation of all his works. The popular phrase "vou-me embora" sums up a common, restless attitude that Bandeira links to the mythical Pasárgada (the name comes from an antique map of Persia that the poet had seen in his youth) through the colloquial pronunciation of "para" as "pra":

Vou-me embora pra Pasárgada
Lá sou amigo do rei
Lá tenho a mulher que eu quero
Na cama que escolherei
Vou-me embora pra Pasárgada
. . . .
É outra civilização
Tem um processo seguro
De impedir a concepção

(I'm off to Pasárgada
There I'm the friend of the king
There I can have the woman I want
In the bed of my choosing
I'm off to Pasárgada
. . . .
It's another civilization
They have a guaranteed way
of impeding conception)

Pasárgada began to turn up in popular speech as a term for an Eldorado-like imaginary paradise, as well as in the names of housing developments, a yacht, and a bookstore, as Bandeira himself observed. Most importantly, the name became a popular reference to Bandeira, appearing in the titles of publications about his work and in Bandeira's own title for his autobiographical *Itinerário de Pasárgada* (1954, Itinerary of Pasárgada).

In the 1930s Bandeira wrote newspaper pieces on arts and history and worked on the poems for his next collection, *Estrela da manhã* (1936, Morning Star), which continued to develop the thematic and stylistic accomplishments of *Libertinagem*. The title poem explores the

MANUEL
BANDEIRA

POESIA E PROSA

Introdução geral por
Sérgio Buarque de Holanda e Francisco de Assis Barbosa

869.89914
B214
t.1

VOLUME I
POESIA

Notas preliminares de
João Ribeiro, Alceu Amoroso Lima, Antônio Olinto,
Mário de Andrade, Múcio Leão, Wilson Castelo Branco,
Carlos Drummond de Andrade, Sérgio Milliet, Fernando Góis,
Ledo Ivo, Paulo Mendes Campos, Sousa Rocha.

Marginália à Poesia de Manuel Bandeira
por
Onestaldo de Pennafort

EDITÔRA JOSÉ AGUILAR, LTDA. RIO DE JANEIRO, D.F., 1958

*Title page for the first volume in the two-volume collection
of Bandeira's poetry and prose (Morris Library,
Southern Illinois University at Carbondale)*

theme of unconditional love seen in "Vulgívaga" and "Porquinho-da-India," expressing the poet's desperate search for the morning star, no matter what her condition: "Procurem por toda parte / Pura ou degradada até a última baixeza / Eu quero a estrela da manhã" (Look for her everywhere / Pure or degraded to the ultimate baseness / I want the morning star). As in many of Bandeira's love poems, the female lover can also be interpreted here as poetry. The nature of the poetic subject is the theme of the two-line "Poema do beco" (Poem of the Alley), which again expresses the poet's frustrations with limitations, although in this case he paradoxically suffers the limits of one of his own favorite poetic subjects, the alley: "Que importa a paisagem, a Glória, a baía, a linha do horizonte? / —O que eu vejo é o beco" (What matter the landscape, the Glória district, the bay, the line of the horizon? / —What I see is the alley). Other works in the collection include the prose poem

"Tragédia brasileira" (Brazilian Tragedy); the sound-and-rhythm experiment "Trem de ferro" (Iron Horse); "Momento num café" (Moment in a Café), a commentary on death; and "Rondó dos cavalinhos" (Rondeau of the Little Horses), a cynical commentary on world events in which Bandeira's friend Alfonso Reyes, an influential writer and the Mexican ambassador to Brazil, makes a cameo appearance.

Estrela da manhã also includes one of Bandeira's best-known poems, "Balada das três mulheres do sabonete Araxá" (Ballad of the Three Women on the Araxá Soap Wrapper), a light-hearted fantasy inspired by a picture on the packaging of a brand of soap. The poet wonders what these women would be like if they were real and even reacts to contrived events concerning them, all the while producing an intricate intertextuality, with oft-recited, even clichéd, lines from the works of such writers as Arthur Rimbaud, William Shakespeare, and the Brazilian poets Luis Delfino and Olavo Bilac.

> A mais nua é doirada borboleta.
> Se a segunda casasse, eu ficava safado da vida, dava pra beber e nunca mais telefonava.
> Mas se a terceira morresse . . . Oh, então, nunca mais a minha vida outrora teria sido um festim!

> (The most nude is a golden butterfly.
> If the second one were to get married, I would really be pissed off at life, I'd start drinking and I'd never use the phone again.
> But if the third one died . . . Oh, then, never again would my life as I know it be festive!)

The preposterously profound expression of sentiment, sliding between formal and informal registers, contrasts with the purely graphic, commodified, and mass-produced picture of the women, producing one of the most felicitous expressions of Bandeira's characteristically ironic style.

In 1937 Bandeira published *Crônicas da província do Brasil* (Chronicles of the Brazilian Provinces), in which he developed a variety of regional and personal themes within the formal prose parameters of the uniquely Brazilian *crônica,* a genre somewhere in between a newspaper column and an essay. Some of his topics include Brazilian architecture and speech, the cities of Bahia and Recife, the Candomblé religion, writers such as Andrade and Elizabeth Barrett Browning, and the Brazilian painters Tarsila do Amaral and Cândido Portinari. In "Leituras de mocinhas" (Readings for Adolescent Girls) Bandeira considers a list of titles proposed for such a population. He wrote *crônicas* and critical essays on music, literature, the plastic arts, and cinema during most of his professional career, although they were only beginning to be compiled during the last decade of his life.

Bandeira turned fifty in the productive year of 1936, and the import of his status and fame in Brazilian letters was commemorated by his friends and colleagues in *Homenagem a Manuel Bandeira* (Homage to Manuel Bandeira), a collection including poems, analyses, commentaries, and impressions by thirty-three of the leading writers of the time. Shortly thereafter Bandeira began to earn money from his poetry, the most money he had ever had at one time up to that date. In 1938 he was named to a position as professor of literature at the Colégio Pedro II in Rio de Janeiro and also to a seat on the advisory board of the Departamento do Patrimônio Histórico e Artístico Nacional (Department of National Historic and Artistic Patrimony). Several of his didactic works were published during this time by the Ministério da Educação (Ministry of Education), including two anthologies of Brazilian poets and his *Guia de Ouro Prêto* (1938, Guide to Ouro Prêto), an illustrated text about that colonial city in the state of Minas Gerais.

A highlight of Bandeira's career was his induction in 1940 to the Academia Brasileira de Letras (Brazilian Academy of Letters). Coming just a few years after the publication of *Homenagem a Manuel Bandeira,* his induction solidified his fame and led to the publication that same year of *Poesias completas,* which included his own commemoration of his fifty years, *Lira dos cinqüent'anos* (Lyre of Fifty Years). *Lira dos cinqüent'anos* displays Bandeira's continuing love for formal variety in six sonnets, a haiku, and "Cantar de amor" (Song of Love), a poem written in the style and idiom of a medieval Portuguese *cantiga* (ballad). The collection includes several of his best-remembered poems, including the whimsical "Mozart no céu" (Mozart in Heaven), in which the famous composer becomes "o mais moço dos anjos" (the youngest angel). The structurally intriguing "Última canção do beco" (Last Song of the Alley), in which Bandeira evokes and then exorcises the scene of so many of his memories of Rio de Janeiro, features seven strophes composed of seven lines of seven syllables each. "Testamento" (Testament) inaugurates Bandeira's well-known but universally ignored self-assessment as a minor poet: "Sou poeta menor, perdoai!" (I am a lesser poet, pardon!). There are also two uncharacteristically optimistic poems, "Canção do vento e da minha vida" (Song of the Wind and of My Life) and "Belo belo" (Lovely Lovely), commentaries on the plenitude to be found in simple pleasures and natural phenomena.

Bandeira left Colégio Pedro II for a position teaching Spanish American literature at the Faculdade Nacional de Filosofia (Universidade do Brasil) in 1943.

MANUEL BANDEIRA

ESTRÊLA
DA
VIDA INTEIRA

poesias reunidas

LIVRARIA

EDITÔRA

Title page for the 1966 edition of Bandeira's collected poems, enlarged in 1986 (Thomas Cooper Library, University of South Carolina)

His encyclopedic knowledge of versification and Western literature and languages was showcased in *Poemas traduzidos* (1945, Translated Poems), which features his translations of a wide range of forms and styles by sixty poets (in most cases, one poem by each), including Johann Wolfgang von Goethe, José Asunción Silva, Jorge Luis Borges, Rainer Maria Rilke, Heinrich Heine, E. E. Cummings, Langston Hughes, Emily Dickinson, Basho, Rubén Darío, and Federico García Lorca. After winning the Instituto Brasileiro de Educação e Cultura (IBEC) poetry prize in 1946, Bandeira published *Mafuá do malungo* (1948, Friends at the Fair), a playful collection of poetry of circumstance, onomastic poems, and poems in the style endorsed by two of the most important contemporary poets in Brazil: Carlos Drummond de Andrade, who wrote the preface, and João Cabral de Melo Neto, who published the book from his Barcelona office.

The title "Belo belo," a reference to a popular song, was reprised for the title poem in the collection *Belo belo,* included in the 1948 edition of *Poesias completas.* But the second "Belo belo" diametrically contrasts with the earlier one from *Lira dos cinqüent'anos;* in the first one the poet says, "Tenho tudo quanto quero" (I have all I want), while in the second he says, "Tenho tudo que não quero" (I have all I don't want). This melancholy tone also pervades "A Mário de Andrade ausente" (To Mário de Andrade, Absent), a tersely poignant eulogy for his great friend, who had died in 1945. Bandeira praises and echoes his Chilean contemporary Pablo Neruda's cry of love for wounded Spain under dictator Francisco Franco in "No vosso e em meu coração" (In Your and in My Heart). He also puts forth revised ideas about his poetics in "A realidade e a imagem" (Reality and Image) and "Nova poética" (New Poetics), both of which revolve around the key image of mud and imply that the reader of poetry should become somewhat uncomfortable and shaken from complacency by an unexpected immediacy.

In 1949, after six years of teaching Spanish American literature, Bandeira published *Literatura hispano-americana,* a work that proved to be essential in fomenting interest among Brazilians for the literatures of their Latin American neighbors. In 1952 he published *Opus 10,* a work he later described as a paltry little thing written for his fans; nonetheless, it includes a few of his best poems, such as "Boi morto" (Dead Ox), a hallucinatory meditation on time and change, and "Consoada" (Late Supper), depicting the poet's resigned meeting with Death, personified as "a Indesejada" (the Undesired).

Itinerário de Pasárgada, an autobiographical prose poetics published in 1954, is unique in Brazilian letters. Written at the request of younger writers, it ranges from insights on the inspirations behind Bandeira's own works to in-depth analyses of poems that influenced him:

> Mas ao mesmo tempo compreendi, ainda antes de conhecer a lição de Mallarmé, que em literatura a poesia está nas palavras, se faz com palavras e não com idéias e sentimentos, muito embora, bem entendido, seja pela força do sentimento ou pela tensão do espírito que acodem ao poeta as combinações de palavras onde há carga de poesia.

> (I perceived, even before understanding the lesson of Mallarmé, that poetry is in the words, it is made with words and not ideas and feelings, although it must be recognized that the force of the feeling or the tension of the spirit delivers to the poet those word combinations that have poetic charge.)

He compares selected verses from the initial and later versions of the Brazilian Romantic poet Antônio de Castro Alves's poem "Mocidade e morte" (Youth and Death), originally titled "O tísico" (The Consumptive), noting the effects of phonemic and semantic changes. Many such examples lead Bandeira to affirm that "cotejos como esses me foram ensinando a conhecer os valores plásticos e musicais dos fonemas; me foram ensinando que a poesia é feita de pequeninos nadas e que, por exemplo, uma dental em vez de uma labial pode estragar um verso" (comparisons such as these taught me to understand the plastic and musical values of phonemes; they taught me that poetry is made of little nothings and that, for example, a dental consonant instead of a labial one can ruin a verse). He also confesses that, accustomed as he was to rhyme and meter, learning free verse was a "conquista difícil" (difficult conquest) aided by reading prose translations, menus, recipes, and even hair-treatment formulas. He insists that in authentic free verse, "o metro deve estar de tal modo esquecido que o alexandrandino mais ortodoxo funcione dentro dele sem virtude de verso medido" (meter is forgotten to such an extent that the most orthodox alexandrine works without the virtue of being a measured verse).

In 1958 the José Aguilar publishing house brought out the two-volume *Poesia e prosa* (Poetry and Prose), which approximated Bandeira's complete works. Volume one features his poetry up to that time, including the collection *Estrela da tarde* (Evening Star), published separately in 1960. This collection is characteristically eclectic, with six traditional sonnets as well as six concrete poems in the graphic style of the Brazilian vanguard concretist group (although these poems were later augmented and detached from *Estrela da tarde* in the 1966 collection *Estrela da vida inteira: poesias reunidas* [Star of a Whole Life: Collected Poems]). Bandeira loved to experiment with form and could move gracefully between the rigid composition requirements of a sonnet such as "A ninfa" (The Nymph) and the loose but nonetheless recognizably connotative characteristics of a concrete poem such as "Rosa tumultuada" (Turbulent Rose). A standout poem in *Estrela da tarde* is "Passeio em São Paulo" (A Walk through São Paulo), which evokes the presence of Bandeira's great friend Mário de Andrade and questions the passage of time by quoting from Andrade's *Paulicéia desvairada* (1922; translated as *Hallucinated City,* 1968). Another intertextual piece in the collection is "Antologia" (Anthology), which recontextualizes verses from Bandeira's own poems–including "Pneumotórax," "Consoada," and "Vou-me embora pra Pasárgada"–into a singular summation of his attitudes toward life and death.

Volume two of *Poesia e prosa* gathers many of Bandeira's *crônicas* and skillful analyses of the works of art—literary, plastic, musical, and architectural—of his contemporaries and forebears. It includes *Flauta de papel* (1957, Paper Flute), *Gonçalves Dias: esboço biográfico* (1952, Biographical Sketch of the Writer Gonçalves Dias), and writings grouped under the titles *Ensaios literários* (Literary Essays) and *Crítica de artes* (Fine Arts Criticism). Some of Bandeira's voluminous correspondence with such literary luminaries as Gilberto Freyre, Drummond, and Jorge de Lima is also included in the second volume of *Poesia e prosa*. These letters display the writer's deeper personal convictions and reactions to his cultural milieu; for example, in one letter Bandeira asks Drummond to clarify one of his verses; in a letter to Antônio de Alcántara Machado he wittily scolds the members of the Anthropophagy movement, an important subgroup of the vanguard modernists, for not living up to their original promise.

In the 1960s Bandeira continued to be an active translator, especially of plays, and a popularizer of Brazilian poetry in a series of radio presentations. In 1965 several of his anthologies of Brazilian poets were republished, along with his translation of the *Rubaiyat* of Omar Khayyam (from the French translation of Franz Toussaint). That same year, *Preparação para a morte* (Preparation for Death) came out in a limited edition. In the title poem, after enumerating the many miracles that life manifests, Bandeira concludes, "—Bendita a morte, que é o fim de todos os milagres" (—Blessed be death, the end of all miracles). In this and other poems from the collection he accepts death as a rest and a reunion with all the family members and friends who, since his diagnosis with tuberculosis in 1904, he never thought he would outlive.

In 1966, the year of Bandeira's eightieth birthday, Brazilian president Humberto Castelo Branco awarded him the Ordem de Mérito Nacional (Order of National Merit). The Academia Brasileira de Letras organized a special session in Bandeira's honor, and the José Olympio firm published *Estrela da vida inteira,* a collection of his complete poetry, and *Andorinha, andorinha* (Swallow, Swallow), a collection of *crônicas* and critical essays edited by his friend Drummond. *Estrela da vida inteira* includes several reorganized sections, including *Duas canções do tempo do beco* (Two Songs from the Time of the Alley), which comprises ten poems. The first four poems are characterized by corporeal imagery and an intensely felt desire; the desire is thwarted in the title songs and in "O fauno" (The Faun) but joyously fulfilled in "Nu" (Naked):

Baixo até o mais fundo
De teu ser, lá onde

Front cover for the 1966 collection of Bandeira's crônicas (chronicles) and critical essays, edited by the poet Carlos Drummond de Andrade (William T. Young Library, University of Kentucky)

Me sorri tu'alma,
Nua, nua, nua. . . .

(I dive to the depths
of your being, there where
your soul smiles at me,
naked, naked, naked. . . .)

In the final years of his life Bandeira was named Cidadão Carioca (Honored Citizen of Rio de Janeiro) and received the Moinho Santista Prize. He was the subject of several interviews, photo sessions, caricatures, portraits, and musical and sculptural tributes. Upon his death in Rio de Janeiro on 13 October 1968 he was buried in the mausoleum of the Academia Brasileira de Letras. Since his death there have been many reprintings and new editions of his works, as well as of his correspondence. The centenary of Bandeira's birth was celebrated in 1986 with new editions, exhibits, and conferences and the inauguration of the Espaço Cultural Pasárgada (Pasárgada Cultural Center) in Recife.

The general assessment of Manuel Bandeira's place in Brazilian and in Lusophone (Portuguese-speaking) letters recognizes two fundamental ironies. The disease that diverted Bandeira's course of life away from architecture and into poetry and that constantly haunted him with premonitions of his own death could not impede him from living eighty-two years and building a literary legacy. Since the condition of living with tuberculosis influenced his early works in particular, it colored his style with a melancholy humor that sharpened his sense of the grace and dignity of everyday life as well as his ability to adapt his poetic voice to register a child's sense of wonder. These stylistic tendencies often produced an ironic detachment in his poems, a product of his life with tuberculosis. The second irony pits Bandeira's vast knowledge of poetics and his talent for formal experimentation against the fact that many of his best-known poems, such as "Pneumotórax," "Evocação do Recife," and "Balada das três mulheres do sabonete Araxá," are those free-verse poems that best register the idiosyncrasies of spoken Brazilian Portuguese. It has been argued that only someone with precisely such structural poetic talent could be capable of effectively expressing the nuanced cadences of free verse. Bandeira's greatest legacy is thus his multifaceted celebration of poetic expression in all aspects of life.

Letters:

Itinerários: cartas a Alphonsus de Guimaraens Filho, by Bandeira and Mário de Andrade (São Paulo: Duas Cidades, 1974);

Correspondência Mário de Andrade & Manuel Bandeira (São Paulo: Editora da Universidade de São Paulo/ Instituto de Estudos Brasileiros, 2000);

Correspondência de Cabral com Bandeira e Drummond, edited by Flora Süssekind (Rio de Janeiro: Nova Fronteira/Casa de Rui Barbosa, 2001).

References:

Stefan Baciu, *Manuel Bandeira de corpo inteiro* (Rio de Janeiro: J. Olympio, 1966);

Manuel Bandeira, "Cronologia de Manuel Bandeira," in his *Estrela da vida inteira: poesias reunidas e poemas traduzidos* (Rio de Janeiro: J. Olympio, 1986), pp. xxi–xlvii;

Sônia Brayner, "O humour bandeiriano ou as Histórias de um Sabonete," *Minas Gerais: suplemento literário,* 8 September 1979, pp. 4–5;

Dorine Daisy D. de Cerqueira, "A ironia e o humor na poesia de Manuel Bandeira," *Iris,* 2 (1989): 59–71;

David William Foster, "Manuel Bandeira's 'Poética': A Structural Approach to Its *Escritura*," *Hispania,* 63 (1980): 316–320;

Homenagem a Manuel Bandeira (Rio de Janeiro: Typographicas do *Jornal do Commercio,* 1936; reprinted, São Paulo: Metal Leve, 1986);

Inventário do arquivo Manuel Bandeira (Rio de Janeiro: Ministério da Cultura/Fundação Casa de Rui Barbosa, 1986);

Maria Manuel Lisboa, "Manuel Bandeira: sexualidade e subversão," *Colóquio: Letras,* 115–116 (1990): 73–88;

Tulo Hostílio Montenegro, "A tuberculose da vida e obra de Manuel Bandeira," *Revista interamericana de bibliografia=Review of Inter-American Bibliography,* 19 (1969): 278–300;

Maximiano de Carvalho e Silva, ed., *Homenagem a Manuel Bandeira, 1986–1988* (Niterói: UFF-Sociedade Sousa da Silveira / Rio de Janeiro: Presença, 1989);

Gilberto Mendonça Teles, "A utopia poética de Manuel Bandeira," in his *A escrituração da escrita: teoria e prática do texto literário* (Petrópolis: Vozes, 1996), pp. 217–272.

Olavo Bilac

(16 December 1865 – 28 December 1918)

Maria Angélica Lopes
University of South Carolina

BOOKS: *Poesias* (São Paulo: Teixeira & Irmão, 1888; enlarged edition, Rio de Janeiro: H. Garnier, 1902);

Crônicas e novelas (Rio de Janeiro: Cunha & Irmão, 1894);

Contos para velhos, as Bob (Rio de Janeiro: Casa Mont'Alverne, 1897);

Sagres: commemoração da descoberta do caminho da India (Rio de Janeiro: Tipografia *Jornal do Comércio,* 1898);

Critica e fantasia (Lisbon: A. M. Teixeira, 1904);

Poesias infantis (Rio de Janeiro: F. Alves, 1904);

Livro de composição para o curso complementar das escolas primárias, by Bilac and Manoel José do Bomfim (Rio de Janeiro: Laemmert, 1904);

Livro de leitura para o curso complementar das escolas primárias, by Bilac and Bomfim (Rio de Janeiro: Laemmert, 1904);

Theatro infantil: comedias e monólogos em prosa e em verso, by Bilac and Henrique Coelho Netto (Rio de Janeiro: F. Alves, 1905);

Tratado de versificação, by Bilac and Passos (Rio de Janeiro: F. Alves, 1905);

Conferências literárias (Rio de Janeiro: Kosmos, 1906; enlarged edition, Rio de Janeiro: F. Alves, 1912);

Contos pátrios: educação moral e cívica para as crianças, by Bilac and Coelho Netto (Rio de Janeiro: F. Alves, 1906);

7 de março de 1906: 26 anniversario de sua fundação, by Bilac and Aloysio de Castro (Rio de Janeiro: L. de Rennes, 1906);

A patria brazileira (para os alumnos das escolas primarias), by Bilac and Coelho Netto (Rio de Janeiro: F. Alves, 1911);

Atravez do Brazil (narrativa): livro de leitura para o curso medio das escolas primárias, by Bilac and Bomfim (Rio de Janeiro: F. Alves, 1913);

Ironia e piedade (Rio de Janeiro: F. Alves, 1916; enlarged, 1921);

Bocage: conferencia realisada no Theatro Municipal de S. Paulo em 19-3-17 (Porto, Portugal: Renascença Portuguesa, 1917);

Olavo Bilac (Arquivo da Academia Brasileira de Letras)

A defesa nacional (Rio de Janeiro: Liga da Defesa Nacional, 1917);

Tarde (Rio de Janeiro: F. Alves, 1919);

Ultimas conferências e discursos (Rio de Janeiro: F. Alves, 1924);

Sanatorium, by Bilac and Carlos Azeredo Magalhães, notes and preface by R. Magalhães Jr. (São Paulo: Clube do Livro, 1977);

Vossa insolência: crônicas, edited, with an introduction, by Antonio Dimas (São Paulo: Letras, 1996);

O esqueleto: mistério da casa de Bragança, by Bilac and Pardal Mallet, as Victor Leal (Rio de Janeiro: Casa da Palavra, 2000).

Editions and Collections: *Bom humor,* edited by Eloy Pontes (Rio de Janeiro: Casa Mandarino, 1939);

Poesia, edited by Alceu Amoroso Lima (Rio de Janeiro: AGIR, 1957);

As mais belas poesias de Olavo Bilac, edited by José Régio (Lisbon: Artis, 1966);

Os melhores poemas de Olavo Bilac, edited by Marisa Lajolo (São Paulo: Global, 1985);

Poesias, introduction by Josué Montello (Belo Horizonte: Itatiaia, 1985);

Obra reunida, edited, with an introduction, by Alexei Bueno (Rio de Janeiro: Aguilar, 1996);

Antologia poética, edited by Paulo Hecker Filho (Pôrto Alegre: L & PM, 1997);

O caçador de esmeraldas e outros poemas, edited by Maura Sardinha (Rio de Janeiro: Ediouro, 1997);

O dinheiro: ensaio, notes by Sergio Faraco (Pôrto Alegre: Aberto, 1997);

Poesias, edited, with a preface, by Ivan Teixeira (São Paulo: Martin Fontes, 1997);

O pássaro cativo: poesias infantis (Pôrto Alegre: Aberto, 1998).

OTHER: *Brésil: guide des Etats-Unis du Brésil,* by Bilac, Sebastião Guimarães Passos, and Antonio Francisco Bandeira Jr., translated by Roberto Gomes (Rio de Janeiro: Bilac, Passos & Bandeira, 1904);

Discursos pronunciados na sessão commemorativa do tricentenario da publicação do D. Quixote, by Bilac and others (Rio de Janeiro: Typografia do *Jornal do Commercio* de Rodrigues, 1905);

Baptista Cepellos, *Os bandeirantes,* preface by Bilac (São Paulo: Fanfulla, 1906);

Joaquim Manuel de Macedo, *Lições de historia do Brasil para uso das escolas de instrucção primária,* tenth edition, edited by Bilac (Rio de Janeiro & Paris: H. Garnier, 1907);

Hilário Ribeiro, *Grammatica elementar e lições progressivas de composição,* revised edition, edited by Bilac (Rio de Janeiro & Paris: H. Garnier, 1907);

Passos, *Diccionario de rimas,* second edition, revised and enlarged by Bilac (Rio de Janeiro: F. Alves, 1913);

Diadems and Fagots, includes two sonnets and two fragments by Bilac, translated by John Meem (Santa Fe: Privately printed, 1921);

Bandeira do Brasil: história, simbolismo, glórias e leis, by Bilac and others (Rio de Janeiro: Bloch, 1939);

Wilhelm Busch, *Juca e Chico: historia de dois meninos em sete travessuras,* translated by Bilac (Rio de Janeiro: F. Alves, n.d.).

Olavo Bilac is a representative figure of Brazilian Parnassian poetry. His poems are characterized by technical perfection and a high level of inspiration. He was a precocious writer, and his work was recognized early by such major critics as Sílvio Romero, José Verissimo, and Joaquim Maria Machado de Assis, as well as by contemporary readers who eagerly bought his books. Bilac's poems have never gone out of print. He was also a lifelong and prolific journalist whose *crônicas* (short pieces written for newspapers), published in major Rio de Janeiro newspapers, were read throughout Brazil. A concerned patriot, from a young age Bilac wrote and spoke against injustices ranging from the mistreatment of children to the institution of slavery, which was abolished in Brazil in 1888. He was a committed opponent of slavery and a friend of the great abolitionist José do Patrocínio, for whose newspaper, *Gazeta de Notícias,* he wrote. A Republican since his student days, Bilac wrote the lyric for the anthem to the Brazilian flag shortly after the Republic was proclaimed in 1889. Although for many years he was a clever satirist who did not spare public figures or institutions deserving of opprobrium, in his later years Bilac concerned himself more with constructing than destroying. As an established poet, member of the Academia Brasileira de Letras (Brazilian Academy of Letters), and government official, he advanced such important causes as literacy, public education, and military service. Toward this end he delivered speeches, wrote articles in periodicals, and co-authored books with such eminent writers as Henrique Coelho Netto and Manoel José do Bomfim.

Bilac's reputation as a poet and public figure suffered a brief eclipse after his death in 1918 because of the young modernists' iconoclastic antipathy to Parnassian poetry. Critical opinion at the end of the twentieth and beginning of the twenty-first century, however, has reaffirmed his literary eminence. In his *História da inteligência brasileira* (1976–1979) critic Wilson Martins docs not hesitate to assign to Bilac the highest position in Brazilian poetry, unrivaled before or since the poet's time. Present-day poets cite Bilac's importance for their own art and still recite his patriotic poems.

Olavo Brás Martins dos Guimarães Bilac was born in Rio de Janeiro on 16 December 1865, the first son of Brás Martins dos Guimarães Bilac, a physician, and Delvina de Paula dos Guimarães Bilac. Both parents were from Bahia, a state famous for its natural beauty, history, literature, and art. Prophetically, the poet's full name forms an alexandrine line in Portuguese. The name Bilac, however, is a cognomen deriving from a mispronunciation. As a young child the poet's paternal grandfather was called *velhaco* (rascal) by his Portuguese godfather, who mixed his *b*s and *v*s, and this mispronounced nickname became his and his descendants' surname. Shortly before Olavo was born, his father, an army surgeon, left for duty in the War of the Triple Alliance that Argentina, Brazil, and Uruguay were fighting against Paraguay. In his *crônicas,* poems, and stories the adult Bilac often mentions the difficult times before his father came back from the war as a hero. The war helped to define the future poet's patriotic sensibility.

In 1880 Bilac enrolled in medical school in Rio de Janeiro, the capital of the country at that time, but he left school in 1886. In 1887 he moved to São Paulo to study law but did not graduate. At nineteen he had published his first "serious" sonnet in the *Gazeta de Notícias,* to which he was to contribute throughout his life. In 1888 Bilac published *Poesias* (Poems) in São Paulo. The prologue, the poem "Profissão de fé" (Profession of Faith), extols the purity of language of the Portuguese classics, as well as the formal perfection emphasized by the French Parnassians. More than half of the book consists of the thirty-five sonnets that make up "Via láctea" (Milky Way), recognized as some of the best love poetry in the Portuguese language. The personal tone of these sonnets is unmistakable; yet, they are also reminiscent of the sixteenth-century Portuguese poet Luís de Camões. Another series of poems in *Poesias,* "Panóplias" (Panoplies), includes pieces on Greco-Roman antiquity and some Indianist poems, including "Morte do Tapir" (Death of the Indian Brave). This poem links Bilac's Parnassian concern for form with Romanticism as he honors the nineteenth-century Indianist poet Antônio Gonçalves Dias as the greatest of Brazilian poets. Years later, when Bilac was elected to the Academia Brasileira de Letras in 1897, he chose Gonçalves Dias as his patron. The poems in "Sarças de fogo" (Burning Bushes), the third part of *Poesias,* also mix antiquity with Brazilian themes in a highly lyrical language. Some of the pieces honor contemporary poets and writers. *Poesias* unites Bilac's two most characteristic features: his rigorously constructed verse and his ardent sensuality.

Although *Poesias* was greeted with enthusiasm for the uniformly high level of inspiration, sentiment, and technique in the poems, some critics accused Bilac of impassivity—a trait to which the Parnassian poets aspired. In "Profissão de fé" Bilac extols the poet's service to the "serena deusa, / Serena Forma!" (serene goddess, / Serene Form!) without changing the "cor da face / E o tom da voz!" (color of my face / Or the tone of my voice!), even if threatened by "bárbaros" (barbarians). Bilac's condemnation of shoddy verse was a lifelong concern; from the beginning he worked painstakingly to polish and perfect his own poetry. Unlike his Romantic predecessors, he did not believe that emotion alone could produce a good poem. Even though he focused heavily on form, his poetry is faithful to his ardent and sensual temperament and is anything but impassive.

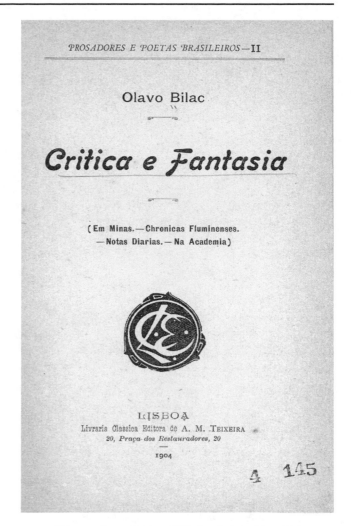

Title page for a collection of Bilac's crônicas *(chronicles) originally published in São Paulo and Rio de Janeiro newspapers under various pseudonyms (Joint University Libraries, Nashville)*

Bilac is considered to be one of the great erotic poets in the Portuguese language. He was a confirmed bachelor and a proponent of divorce (the right to which was included in the Republican constitution). As a young man, though, he had been engaged to a friend's sister, Amélia Mariano de Oliveira. Although the young couple was perceived to be deeply in love, her brother and father turned against Bilac, and the engagement was broken. The poet's letters to Amélia were published in 1954 as *O noivado de Bilac, com a correspondência inédita do poeta à sua noiva, D. Amélia de Oliveira* (Bilac's Engagement, with His Unpublished Letters to His Fiancée, Miss Amélia de Oliveira).

Among Bilac's writings on the topic of technical accuracy, "A Alberto de Oliveira" (To Alberto de Oliveira), from *Ultimas conferências e discursos* (1924, Last Conferences and Speeches), stands out. In this eulogy

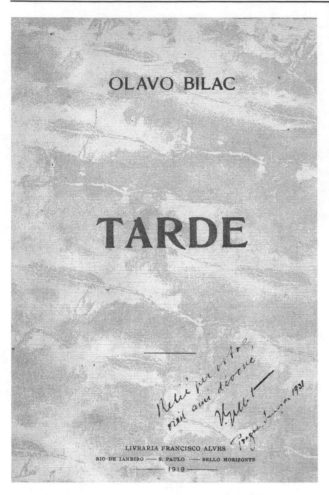

OLAVO BILAC

TARDE

LIVRARIA FRANCISCO ALVES
RIO DE JANEIRO — S. PAULO — BELLO HORIZONTE
1919

Title page for Bilac's final volume of poetry, published in the year following his death on 28 December 1918 (Lauinger Library, Georgetown University)

for his Parnassian master, Bilac makes clear that, notwithstanding the importance of intricate, formal perfection to many of his poems, actual feelings were at their core; without these feelings there would be no poetry. According to Bilac, true popular poetry was formally simple in its greatness. His readers sensed his coherence and sincerity, and throughout his life he had a healthy readership. His concern with form did not preclude attention to realism (as was the case with other Parnassian poets), especially in his prose. Bilac's outlook in his *crônicas* is critical and observant as he reflects on daily life in Rio de Janeiro and in the rest of the country, on international matters, and on the arts, especially literature. He was pragmatic in his attempts to find solutions to major Brazilian problems; he suggested, for example, compulsory military service as a means for improving literacy in Brazil.

As one of the founding members of the Academia Brasileira de Letras in 1897, Bilac favored the august body's dedication to a national language and literature,

a dedication that matched his personal credo. In 1902 he added a major series of poems to the 1888 edition of *Poesias* and published the definitive edition of the collection. The new poems, including "Alma inquieta" (Troubled Soul), "As viagens" (Voyages), and the justly famous "O caçador de esmeraldas" (The Emerald Seeker), reveal the same high quality of the earlier volume. "O caçador de esmeraldas" is a romanticized treatment of an historical figure, Fernão Dias Pais, a seventeenth-century explorer who became legendary in Brazilian history and literature. This *bandeirante* (an early explorer to the interior of Brazil in search of precious stones and minerals) had spent years in his search for emeralds. The poem presents his death as an ironically triumphal scene: Dias Pais believes that he has found the green stones. In reality, they are the much less valuable green tourmalines. Three centuries later emeralds were discovered in Brazil only a few miles from the area where Dias Pais had painstakingly searched.

An industrious writer, Bilac collaborated with colleagues on different books, sometimes for fun and sometimes in a serious didactic effort directed at the young people of Brazil. Several of these collaborations were published serially in newspapers, such as the novel *Sanatorium*. Bilac was identified posthumously as the co-author, under the pseudonym Jaime de Ataíde, with Carlos Azeredo Magalhães. This curious autobiographical novel, which features members of Bilac's literary group, depicts his political exile in the early 1890s in the historical city of Ouro Preto, capital of Minas Gerais, where he found a safe haven from Floriano Peixoto, the harsh and vengeful president of Brazil whom Bilac had criticized in journalistic pieces and who had sent him to jail in Rio de Janeiro for six months. *Sanatorium,* serialized in the *Gazeta de notícias* in 1894–1895, was republished in 1977.

In 1904 Bilac published *Crítica e fantasia* (Criticism and Fantasy), which showed him to be an informed and sensitive critic. The volume is a collection of *crônicas* that he had written over the course of several years under various pseudonyms for newspapers in Rio de Janeiro and São Paulo. A voracious reader and an eloquent writer, Bilac resembled his fellow *cronistas* of the Brazilian Belle Epoque in his awareness of the social and cultural aspects of his city and nation, including foreign influences.

In 1906 Bilac published *Conferências literárias* (Literary Speeches). His eloquence and enthusiasm made him a sought-out speaker at a time when attending lectures was a popular social activity. Such an interest matched the ongoing modernization of Rio de Janeiro, which included the razing of the downtown area known as Morro do Castelo (Castle Hill); the widening of the major thoroughfare, Avenida Rio Branco (Rio Branco Avenue); and the construction of the neoclassical Theatro Municipal (Municipal Theater), the Biblioteca Nacional (National Library), and the Museu Nacional de Belas Artes (National Museum of Fine Arts). With a keen sense of history, Bilac was able to depict the life of the city. Thus, in his lectures he offered pertinent and pleasant lessons about the past and present civilization of the region to an interested public. As a journalist he also traced a path between earlier celebrated figures, including writers, and his own time. In contrast with his satirical daily journalistic verses against bumbling or corrupt politicians, Bilac's lectures and articles revealed his gratitude and admiration toward his elders and contemporaries, such as Oliveira and Machado de Assis, the president of the recently founded Academia Brasileira de Letras. In 1897 Bilac had replaced Machado de Assis as a writer at the important newspaper *Gazeta de Notícias.*

Ironia e piedade (1916, Irony and Compassion) is a collection of *crônicas* of the previous decade in which Bilac evinces his awareness of important Brazilian and foreign matters and personalities. Like his other *crônicas,* they are masterful and even today engage the reader.

Bilac's biographers and critics stress his many revisions of his poems. He was, indeed, the "goldsmith" prescribed by Parnassianism, for which prosody and rhyme were important components of poetry. Bilac was well read and possessed an immense vocabulary, which included arcane Indo-European words as well as indigenous and African ones. As a conscientious technician, he wanted to pass on his skills. In 1913 he revised and republished Sebastião Guimarães Passos's *Diccionario de rimas* (1904, Dictionary of Rhymes) to aid apprentice poets and students.

Although he was concerned with language and form, Bilac condemned grammarians who pontificated on minor linguistic points. He respected and believed in the strength and agility of an ever-evolving language with its natural proclivities. Paradoxically, though, he was traditional in his view of Brazilian Portuguese as bound to the European model, in contrast to the opinion of the modernist generation that succeeded his own. Bilac's respect for the rules of prosody and rhyme enabled him to produce effective, pliant verse. In *Tratado de versificação,* co-authored with Passos in 1905, he examines the different poetic genres through Brazilian examples in an anthology that includes several contemporary poets.

Although Bilac was a Parnassian poet, his concern for formal perfection and classical subjects did not preclude a Romantic enthusiasm for his nation. He devoted a great deal of his time and energy to patriotic causes. The sonnet "Pátria," other poems such as "A

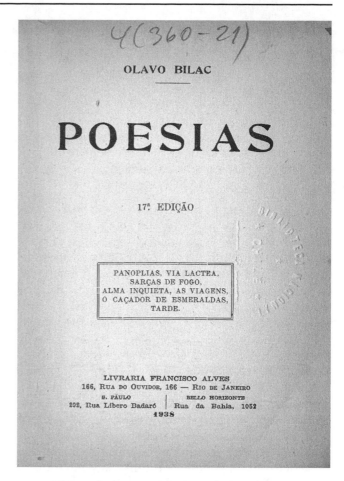

Title page for the seventeenth edition of Bilac's first poetry collection, originally published in 1888, enlarged in 1902, and enlarged again in 1925 to include the posthumously published Tarde *(Biblioteca Nacional de Chile)*

pátria" (To the Fatherland), and the short essay "Pátria" show his love for his country and a concern for the education of its youth and the well-being of its adults. The sonnet "Língua portuguesa" (Portuguese Language) reminds the reader of the historical and literary importance of the language spoken by Brazilians.

The graceful architecture, magnificent beaches, mountains, and the lush Floresta da Tijuca (Tijuca Forest, a planted urban forest) in Rio de Janeiro nurtured Bilac's aesthetic sense. He shared the *nativista* (nativist) sentiment of the Romantics who had preceded him. This enthusiasm for the beauty and bounty of the land was as old as the country itself, having begun with Pero Vaz de Caminha in his letter to King Manoel I of Portugal in May 1500. Caminha equated the crystalline waters, astounding flora, and gentle natives of the new land with Eden.

Throughout colonial days such a descriptive mode was dominant in Brazilian poetry, fiction, and essays, side by side with a satirical mode. European Romanticism strengthened the descriptive vein in early-nineteenth-century Brazilian literature, which emphasized local color and exotic locales. Description became an important component of both poetry and prose. The first major Brazilian novelist, José de Alencar, placed equal emphasis on the psychological aspects and the settings of his novels, which portrayed distinct geographical areas of the large nation. Contemporary poets followed in the same vein, extolling their country as a paradise, complete with the noble savage.

As Auguste Comte's positivism influenced the Brazilian intelligentsia in the late 1800s, the spontaneous and even child-like wonder at nature shifted into a different gear. Reverence for nature became a means of trying to instill patriotism and character in both children and adults. Proclaimed in 1889, the Brazilian Republic was strongly influenced by the didactic aspects of positivistic ideology. The new flag symbolized the beauty and natural wealth of the country with its green forests, gold, and sun under the Southern Cross. The motto on the flag, "Ordem e Progresso" (Order and Progress), coaxed Brazilians to elevate themselves and their country through moral and pragmatic virtue. Such sentiments were reinforced by Bilac's lyric for the flag anthem, "Bendita sejas, bandeira do Brasil" (Blessed You Are, Flag of Brazil), which offers a melodious meditation on Brazilians' duty toward their country. His own sense of duty led him to accept such important official positions as general inspector of Rio de Janeiro schools and director of the Pedagogium. Bilac was a member of the presidential committee charged with preparing the First Pan American Congress in Buenos Aires, in 1901, and a delegate to the same conference the next year. He also traveled in Europe and was well esteemed in Portugal.

Bilac was elected "Prince of Brazilian Poets" through a nationwide contest organized by *Fon-Fon,* a popular magazine. He died of pulmonary edema on 28 December 1918. He had just read the proofs of his final poetry volume, *Tarde* (Evening), which was published posthumously in 1919. The collection presents exquisite and melancholic poetry in which regret for the end is tempered by the celebration of a well-lived life. The sonnet "Frutidor" (Golden Fruit) typifies this spirit.

Olavo Bilac's importance for Brazilian literature is not limited to the excellence and popularity of his poetry. Through his journalistic activity, books, and speeches he influenced and helped to mold Brazilian culture as the country moved from monarchy to a republican form of government. Although sometimes derided by cynics, Bilac's patriotic writings have been effective in establishing guidelines for the civic education of young Brazilians. His are the just laurels of a national poet.

Letters:

Elmo Elton, ed., *O noivado de Bilac, com a correspondência inédita do poeta à sua noiva, D. Amélia de Oliveira* (Rio de Janeiro: Organização Simões, 1954).

Bibliographies:

Claude Hulet, ed., *Latin American Poetry in English Translation: A Bibliography* (Washington, D.C.: Pan American Union, 1965);

Hensley C. Woodbridge, "A Bibliography of Brazilian Poetry in English Translation: 1965–1977," *Luso-Brazilian Review,* 15 supplement (1978): 161–188.

References:

Manuel Bandeira, *A Brief History of Brazilian Literature,* translated, with an introduction and notes, by Ralph Edward Dimmick (Washington, D.C.: Pan American Union, 1958; reprinted, New York: Charles Frank, 1964);

David Miller Driver, *The Indian in Brazilian Literature* (New York: Hispanic Institute in the United States, 1942);

David W. Foster and Virginia Ramos Foster, eds., *Modern Latin American Literature,* volume 2 (New York: Ungar, 1975);

Wilson Martins, *História da inteligência brasileira,* 7 volumes (São Paulo: Cultrix, 1976–1979);

Flora Süssekind, *Cinematograph of Words: Literature, Technique, and Modernization in Brazil,* translated by Paulo Henriques Britto (Stanford: Stanford University Press, 1997).

Augusto Boal
(16 March 1931 –)

Alessandra M. Pires
University of Georgia

BOOKS: *A revolução na América do Sul* (São Paulo: Massao Ohno, 1961);

Arena conta Zumbi, by Boal and Gianfrancesco Guarnieri (São Paulo, 1965);

Arena conta Tiradentes, by Boal and Guarnieri (São Paulo: Sagarana, 1967);

Categorías de teatro popular (Buenos Aires: Cepe, 1972);

3 obras de teatro (Argentina: Noé, 1973)—comprises *El gran acuerdo internacional del Tío Patilludo, Torquemada,* and *Revolución en América del Sur;*

Teatro del oprimido y otras poéticas políticas (Buenos Aires: Ediciones de la Flor, 1974); translated as *O teatro do oprimido e outras poéticas políticas* (Rio de Janeiro: Civilização Brasileira, 1975); Spanish version translated by Charles A. McBride and Maria-Odilia Leal McBride as *Theater of the Oppressed* (New York: Urizen, 1979; London: Pluto, 1979);

Ejercicios y juegos para el actor y para el no actor con ganas de decir algo a través del teatro (Buenos Aires: Ediciones de Crisis, 1975); translated as *200 Exercícios e jogos para o ator e o não-ator com vontade de dizer algo através do teatro* (Rio de Janeiro: Civilização Brasileira, 1977); translated from the 1978 French edition by Adrian Jackson as *Games for Actors and Non-Actors* (London & New York: Routledge, 1992); first Brazilian edition revised and enlarged as *Jogos para atores e não atores* (Rio de Janeiro: Civilização Brasileira, 1998);

Técnicas latinoamericanas de teatro popular: una revolución copernicana al revés (Buenos Aires: Corregidor, 1975)—comprises *Categorías de teatro popular* and *Técnicas latinoamericanas de teatro popular;* translated by Vanda Maria de Barros as *Técnicas latinoamericanas de teatro popular: uma revolução copernicana ao contrário* (Coimbra, Portugal: Centelha, 1977); enlarged as *Técnicas latino-americanas de teatro popular: uma revolução copernicana ao contrário, com o anexo, Teatro do oprimido na Europa* (São Paulo: Editora de Humanismo, Ciência e Tecnologia, 1979);

Milagre no Brasil (Lisbon: Plátano, 1976; Rio de Janeiro: Civilização Brasileira, 1977);

Teatro popular de nuestra América (Cuernavaca, Mexico: Mascarones, 1976);

Ao quisto chegou!? (Lisbon: Estampa, 1977);

Crônicas de nuestra América (Rio de Janeiro: Codecri, 1977);

A deliciosa e sangrenta aventura latina de Jane Spitfire, espiã e mulher sensual!: intriga! ação! suspense! mistério!!! (Rio de Janeiro: Codecri, 1977);

Murro em ponta de faca (São Paulo: Editora de Humanismo, Ciência e Tecnologia, 1978);

Stop: c'est magique! (Rio de Janeiro: Civilização Brasileira, 1980);

O corsário do rei (Rio de Janeiro: Civilização Brasileira, 1985);

The Sartrouville Experience: Theory, Practice, Three Hypotheses (Devon, U.K.: Dartington College of Arts, 1985);

Augusto Boal (Rio de Janeiro: Ministério da Cultura, Instituto Nacional de Artes Cênicas, Biblioteca Edmundo Moniz, 1986);

Teatro de Augusto Boal, 2 volumes (São Paulo: Editora de Humanismo, Ciência e Tecnologia, 1986, 1990)—comprises volume 1, *A revolução na América do Sul, As aventuras do Tio Patinhas,* and *Murro em Ponta de Faca;* and volume 2, *Historias de nuestra América, A lua pequena e a caminhada perigosa,* and *Torquemada;*

Méthode Boal de théâtre et de thérapie (l'arc-en-ciel du désir), translated by Márcia Fiani (Paris: Ramsay, 1990); translated by Jackson as *The Rainbow of Desire: The Boal Method of Theatre and Therapy* (London & New York: Routledge, 1995); original Portuguese version published as *O arco-íris do desejo: método Boal de teatro e terapia* (Rio de Janeiro: Civilização Brasileira, 1996);

O suicida com medo da morte: romance (Rio de Janeiro: Civilização Brasileira, 1992);

Aqui ninguém é burro!: graças e desgraças da vida carioca (Rio de Janeiro: Revan, 1996);

Teatro legislativo: versão beta (Rio de Janeiro: Civilização Brasileira, 1996); translated by Jackson as *Legislative Theatre: Using Performance to Make Politics* (London & New York: Routledge, 1998);

Augusto Boal leading a drama workshop in Germany, 1977 (from Hamlet and the Baker's Son: My Life in
Theatre and Politics, *2001; Thomas Cooper Library, University of South Carolina)*

Hamlet e o filho do padeiro: memórias imaginadas (Rio de
Janeiro: Record, 2000); translated by Jackson and
Candida Blaker as *Hamlet and the Baker's Son: My
Life in Theatre and Politics* (London & New York:
Routledge, 2001);

O teatro como arte marcial (Rio de Janeiro: Garamond,
2003).

Edition in English: *Documents on the Theatre of the
Oppressed,* translated by Robert Cannon and others, edited by Anthony Hozier (London: Red Letters, 1984).

PLAY PRODUCTIONS: *Marido magro, mulher chata,*
São Paulo, Teatro de Arena, 1957;

José do parto à sepultura, São Paulo, Teatro de Arena,
1962;

Arena canta Bahia, São Paulo, Teatro de Arena, 1965;

Arena conta Zumbi, by Boal and Gianfrancesco Guarnieri,
São Paulo, Teatro de Arena, 1965;

Arena conta Tiradentes, by Boal and Guarnieri, São Paulo,
Teatro de Arena, 1966;

A lua muito pequena e a caminhada perigosa, São Paulo,
Teatro Ruth Escobar, 1968;

Chiclete com banana, São Paulo, Teatro de Arena, 1969;

Teatro jornal, São Paulo, Teatro de Arena, 1970;

Torquemada, Buenos Aires, 1971;

Murro em ponta de faca, São Paulo, Teatro de Arena, 1978;

O corsário do rei, Rio de Janeiro, 1985.

OTHER: Nikolai Vasil'evich Gogol, *O inspetor geral:
comédia em 5 atos,* translated by Boal and Gianfrancesco Guarnieri, preface by Boal (São Paulo:
Brasiliense, 1966);

"Teatro del Oprimido: Una experiencia de teatro educa-
tivo en el Peru," in *Popular Theater for Social Change
in Latin America: Essays in Spanish and English,* edited
by Gerardo Luzuriaga (Los Angeles: UCLA
Latin American Center, 1978), pp. 24–41;

"El teatro popular," in *Teatro popular y cambio social en América Latina: panorama de una experiencia,* edited by Sonia Gutiérrez (San José, Costa Rica: Editorial Universitaria Centro Americana, 1979), pp. 43–65;

"Theory and Practice of the Theatre of the Oppressed," in *Tot lering en vermaak: 9 manieren voor 10 jar vormingstheater,* edited by Dina van Berlaer-Hellemans and Marianne van Kerkhoven (Antwerp: Soethoudt, 1980), pp. 83–90.

SELECTED PERIODICAL PUBLICATIONS–
UNCOLLECTED: "Catégories du théâtre populaire," *Travail théâtral,* 6 (1972): 3–26;

"Il y a plusieurs manières de faire du théâtre populaire: je les préfère toutes," *Travail théâtral,* 18–19 (1975): 161–171;

"Invisible Theatre," *Adult Education and Development,* 12 (1979): 29–31;

"The Cop in the Head: Three Hypotheses," *Drama Review,* 34 (Fall 1990): 35–42;

"Vindicated: A Letter from Augusto Boal," *Drama Review,* 38 (Fall 1994): 35–36.

Augusto Boal has been internationally recognized as a pioneer in creating what he calls *o teatro do oprimido* (the theater of the oppressed). His original scenic-acting method of this name has been performed in many different settings, from prisons and psychiatric hospitals to schools at various levels of education. The *teatro do oprimido* is defined as a pedagogical acting method that transcends ordinary stage frontiers to become an element contributing to social transformation.

Augusto Pinto Boal was born in Rio de Janeiro on 16 March 1931. His parents, Albertina Pinto Boal and José Augusto Boal, were originally from Portugal. After immigrating to Brazil in 1914, returning to Portugal briefly to marry Albertina in 1925, Boal's father worked as a baker in the family business in a Rio de Janeiro suburb, where Boal's uncles, also Portuguese immigrants, were partners. Boal has three siblings: Albertino, Augusta, and Aida.

Boal graduated with a degree in chemical engineering from the Universidade Federal do Rio de Janeiro (Federal University of Rio de Janeiro) when he was twenty-one. He then decided to move to the United States, where he attended the School of Dramatic Arts at Columbia University in the early 1950s. Having specialized in stage directing, Boal was invited to accept the position of director of the Teatro de Arena (Arena Theater) in São Paulo. He remained in the city working at this theater from 1956 to 1971.

In 1964 Brazil suffered a military coup d'état, followed by a more repressive coup in 1968. Because of

Title page for the first edition of the work in which Boal enunciated his concept of teatro do oprimido *(theater of the oppressed), published in Spanish in 1974 and in Portuguese the following year (Thomas Cooper Library, University of South Carolina)*

Boal's cultural and political activities, he was arrested and tortured in 1971 and was forced to abandon his activities at the Teatro de Arena. He exiled himself and his family, going first to Argentina, where he resided until 1976, when he moved to Paris. He remained active in Paris for ten years promoting the creation of various centers for the *teatro do oprimido.*

During the 1960s, while still directing at the Teatro de Arena, Boal experimented with a new technique, known as *spect-ator* (spect-actor). Initially, he invited members of the audience to comment on the play at the end of every performance. It is said, however, that a spectator herself came up with the idea for the *spect-ator* technique by deciding to go on the stage in order to have her suggestion viewed and, therefore, better comprehended. The *spect-atores* began to act on the changes they envisioned instead of just proposing them as an abstract notion. The *spect-ator* is thus an active participant in a play, "an activated spectator, an audience member who takes part in the action," as Mady Schutzman and Jan Cohen-Cruz note in *Playing Boal: Theatre, Therapy, Activism* (1994). Boal was primarily concerned with leading the public toward active thought during and after every performance.

Between 1968 and 1971 at the Teatro de Arena, Boal developed another technique, known as the *sistema curinga* (joker system). This method encouraged actors to use fact and fiction without distinction, switching roles with each other during the play in an attempt to interchange all the characters. The *curinga* addressed the audience and was ready to transform him- or herself into any of the characters.

In 1973 Boal continued to build his terminology based on his ideas for a revolutionary approach to the theater. He proposed *teatro imagem* (image theater), a "technique that privileges physical theatre over the spoken word," as Schutzman and Cohen-Cruz explain it. The main concern of *teatro imagem* is to address current events. Boal suggested that those events ought to be introduced in a fashion that addressed current social concerns, allowing audience members to interact by assuming the actors' roles on the stage. Schutzman and Cohen-Cruz write that *teatro imagem* is primarily defined by "a series of wordless exercises in which participants create embodiments of their feelings and experiences. Beginning with a selected theme, participants 'sculpt' images onto their own and others' bodies. These frozen images are then 'dynamized,' or brought to life, through a sequence of movement-based and interactive exercises." An example of *teatro imagem* is the racial stereotyping that pervades societies. Such a performance could take place on the street or in the heart of a city; it did not need to be restricted to theatrical space.

The *spect-ator* technique, *sistema curinga,* and *teatro imagem* illustrate the relevance of the human body in Boal's research. Throughout his career the body has remained an essential tool that allows for comprehension of the world and the multiple social and political problems in it. In Boal's aesthetics the theater itself, in order to tell a truth and be truthful to its own quest, must be a "bodily struggle," as he writes in *Hamlet e o filho do padeiro: memórias imaginadas* (2000; translated as *Hamlet and the Baker's Son: My Life in Theatre and Politics,* 2001). The active presence of bodies during performances reveals the difficulty of telling a given truth, part of the daily trouble of societies, which to Boal cannot be considered mere fiction. Therefore, the theater assumes an important role as an educational tool in which Aristotelian catharsis takes on another meaning;

in Boal's terms, it moves individuals toward liberation. Whereas in Aristotle's definition catharsis acted on passive spectators, inducing them to suffer and learn as part of the theatrical process, in Boal's theory catharsis works dynamically. Traditionally, the spectator had to endure the effects of catharsis and was not able to interact—that is, to have a voice.

Boal was also influenced by Paulo Freire's *Pedagogia do oprimido* (1970; translated as *Pedagogy of the Oppressed,* 1970). He said that he was inspired by Freire's title to create his own *teatro do oprimido,* the subject of his book first published in Spanish as *Teatro del oprimido y otras poéticas políticas* (1974, Theater of the Oppressed and Other Poetic Policies; translated as *Theater of the Oppressed,* 1979) and in Portuguese as *O teatro do oprimido e outras poéticas políticas* (1975). In *Hamlet and the Baker's Son,* Boal defines his philosophy of the *teatro do oprimido:* "The Theatre of the Oppressed did political events, it was politics; it withdrew into the intimacy of internalized oppression, it was psychotherapy; in schools, it was pedagogy; in the cities, it legislated. The Theatre of the Oppressed superimposed itself onto other social activities, invaded other fields and allowed itself to be invaded." One of the main novelties in Boal's aesthetics lies in the combination of multiple fields of knowledge that work with the individual—that is, the author experiments with ordinary people. The result, Boal expects, is the consequent engaging of these people with current facts because they are reminded at all times that social and political problems exist and should be reflected upon.

In 1975 Boal published *Técnicas latinoamericanas de teatro popular: una revolución copernicana al revés* (Latin American Techniques of Popular Theater: A Copernican Revolution in Reverse), which he wrote while in Peru. It was published in Portuguese two years later as *Técnicas latino-americanas de teatro popular: uma revolução copernicana ao contrário.* He explained in *Hamlet and the Baker's Son* that his Peruvian students spoke forty-seven mother tongues, having "Spanish as a stepmother," a situation to which Boal himself could relate. In need of a means to communicate with the students, he approached images. As the students created images of their desire, new techniques were born. This dramatic method in Peru allowed the people to be in charge of their own desires. Once empowered by their new attitude, they discovered the possibility of raising questions about society and their own issues as a community.

In 1975 Boal also published *Ejercicios y juegos para el actor y para el no actor con ganas de decir algo a través del teatro* (Exercises and Games for the Actor and the Non-Actor with the Desire to Say Something through the Theater; translated as *Games for Actors and Non-Actors,* 1992), published two years later in Portuguese as *200 Exercícios e*

Scene from a 1978 São Paulo performance of Boal's play Murro em ponta de faca *(1978, Blows at Knifepoint), which portrays his experiences as an exile during the period of military rule in Brazil (from* Hamlet and the Baker's Son: My Life in Theatre and Politics, *2001; Thomas Cooper Library, University of South Carolina)*

jogos para o ator e o não-ator com vontade de dizer algo através do teatro. This work presents the basis for the exercises that a person involved with the theater should follow. Boal summarizes his terminology and introduces material relating to theater production for both the professional and the nonprofessional. He reintroduces the complete terminology of the *teatro do oprimido,* its structure as well as the actor's interpretation.

Boal's play *Murro em ponta de faca* (1978, Blows at Knifepoint) portrays his experience while in exile. In *Hamlet and the Baker's Son* he observes that the play is a "circular one, in which I am no one: I am all of them, I am the one who commits suicide and also those who survive." In 1978 and 1979 he continued to work with the *teatro do oprimido,* giving workshops that led to the creation of the Centre d'Etude et de Diffusion des Techniques Actives d'Expression (CEDITADE). His Argentinean wife, Cecilia, initially an actress in his company, became a psychoanalyst during these years in Paris. The exile lasted until 1986, when Boal was invited to move back to Brazil and develop a theater program tailored to teach underprivileged children at public schools.

In 1989 another of Boal's dramatic techniques, *teatro foro* (forum theater), served as a tool in Luiz Inácio Lula da Silva's political campaign for the presidency of

Brazil in the year 2002. (Lula won the election and took office in January 2003.) In *teatro foro* the spectators trade places with the actors, having as the ultimate goal the proposal of new alternatives to a given situation. In an interview with Cohen-Cruz published in *Playing Boal,* Boal explains in detail how he and his actors went into the streets during one of Lula's earlier presidential campaigns and acted out different situations: "We did forum theatre, inventing situations where the protagonist was Lula. We would go to a square and an actor would play Lula and the spectators were invited to replace Lula and show what they would do in his place."

As a cultural and political figure Boal was a candidate for office in the Câmara dos Vereadores (Chamber of Deputies) of Rio de Janeiro in 1992. Because of the strategic launching of his campaign, he won the election. During his term, as he had done previously on Lula's campaign, Boal used the methodology of the *teatro foro* in order to understand some of the local problems. After four years of struggling in the Câmara dos Vereadores, Boal realized that the *teatro foro* did not suffice to cope with the social and economic reality; he decided to turn the population's desire into law by creating a new technique, *teatro legislativo* (legislative theater), which was the conclusion of his previous

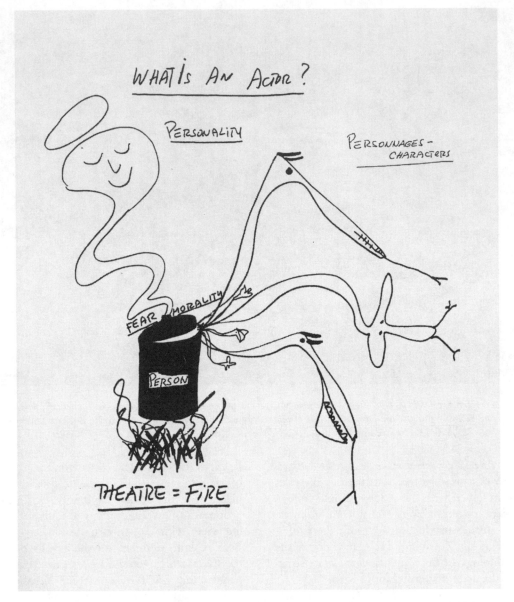

Undated drawing by Boal for a theater workshop (from Hamlet and the Baker's Son: My Life in
Theatre and Politics, *2001; Thomas Cooper Library, University of South Carolina)*

researches in the social field. The notion of *teatro legisla-tivo* appears linked to *teatro foro,* being a development of the techniques of the latter to determine what types of legislation were required to solve problems at the community level. In *Hamlet e o filho do padeiro,* Boal remarks that he had previously accomplished similar experiments in Munich, Paris, London, and Bradford.

The core of Boal's techniques extracted from the *teatro do oprimido* was called the *arco-íris do desejo* (rainbow of desire), a term that became the title of another major work, first published in French translation as *Méthode Boal de théâtre et de thérapie (l'arc-en-ciel du désir)* (1990; translated as *The Rainbow of Desire: The Boal Method of Theatre and Therapy,* 1995). The Portuguese version was

published in 1996 as *O arco-íris do desejo: método Boal de teatro e terapia.* According to Schutzman and Cohen-Cruz in *Playing Boal,* the *arco-íris do desejo* denotes "the name of a specific TO [Theatre of the Oppressed] exercise in Boal's therapeutic repertoire and, for a while, referred to his whole body of therapeutic techniques." *O arco-íris do desejo* has been regarded as Boal's third fundamental work, in which he proposes the therapeutic element as one of considerable concern in his aesthetics. He does not believe his ideas are far from the psychological domain; nonetheless, he has insisted on their theatrical element and the consequent necessity of their staging. The fundamental characteristic of the *arco-íris do desejo* remains, however, the social concern. Realizing that social structures prevent individuals from expressing their whole selves, Boal announced the necessity of democratizing therapy by taking it into all social domains, such as prisons, streets, schools, and theaters. In *O arco-íris do desejo* he develops a technique called *flic dans la tête* (cop in the head). He first coined this term in the 1980s when living in Paris. *Flic dans la tête* was the title of a workshop that he led for two years in an attempt to prove that all individuals create a system of inner censorship that will generate their own repression. As Boal explains in *The Rainbow of Desire*, "the cops are in our head, but their headquarters and barracks must be on the outside." The goal of this workshop was the removal of the cops in the head of the participants.

In *O arco-íris do desejo*, Boal elaborates in detail the concept of the *flic dans la tête* and presents three hypotheses pertinent to it: osmosis, metaxis, and analogical induction. The first hypothesis pertains to the propagation of values, tastes, and ideas that are deeply rooted in society. Boal uses the example of black children in the northern United States who, when asked to choose between a black and a white doll, picked the white one as the standard of beauty. His desire is to fight against this type of preconceived and constructed idea. Metaxis deals with the creation by *spect-atores* of realities that reflect their own oppressed world. When that happens, according to Boal in *The Rainbow of Desire*, "we see the phenomenon of *metaxis:* the state of belonging completely and simultaneously to two different, autonomous worlds." Boal attempts to separate these two worlds, rendering them completely autonomous. The autonomy thus created encourages individuals to act in their own lives with the same liberation. Analogical induction operates by presenting different images to the participants, images that reflect the other participants' reality. By multiplying the possible situations, using the technique of analogy, one can produce a critical analysis from a new perspective. As Boal puts it in *The Rainbow of Desire*, "We do not interpret it, we explain nothing, we only offer multiple points of reference."

In 2000 Boal published his autobiography, *Hamlet e o filho do padeiro.* In it he describes his familial background, his childhood, and his early years in Brazilian theater, as well as his exile from and return to Brazil.

Augusto Boal has traveled worldwide to introduce his theater to a large audience by means of workshops and conferences at various universities in which he demonstrates such concepts as *teatro foro, teatro imagem, teatro legislativo,* the *sistema curinga,* the *arco-íris do desejo,* and the *spect-ator.* His innovative readings on theater have placed him at the forefront of Brazilian literature as one of the voices conveying its Latin roots all over the planet. Boal's writings stand out simultaneously as universal and as deeply concerned with their Brazilian origins. His dramatic theories are intended for any audience motivated by sociopolitical issues.

Interviews:

Michael Taussig and Richard Schechner, "Boal in Brazil, France, and the USA: An Interview with Augusto Boal," *Drama Review,* 34 (Fall 1990): 50–56;

Douglas L. Paterson, "We Are All Theater: An Interview with Augusto Boal," *High Performance,* 19 (Summer 1996): 18–23.

References:

Severino João Albuquerque, "Conflicting Signs of Violence in Augusto Boal's *Torquemada,*" *Modern Drama,* 29 (September 1986): 452–459;

Judith I. Bisset, "Victims and Violators: The Structure of Violence in *Torquemada,*" *Latin American Theatre Review,* 15 (Spring 1982): 27–34;

Franc Chamberlain, ed., "Working Without Boal: Digressions and Developments in the Theatre of the Oppressed," *Contemporary Theatre Review,* 3, no. 1 (1995);

Jan Cohen-Cruz, "Boal at NYU: A Workshop and Its Aftermath," *Drama Review,* 34 (Fall 1990): 43–49;

Paulo Freire, *Pedagogy of the Oppressed,* translated by Myra Bergman Ramos (New York: Herder & Herder, 1970);

Paul Heritage, "The Courage to Be Happy: Augusto Boal, Legislative Theatre, and the 7th International Festival of the Theatre of the Oppressed," *Drama Review,* 38 (Fall 1994): 25–36;

Andy Lavender, "Theatrical Utopia," *New Statesman and Society,* 8 (20 January 1995): 32;

Gerado Luzuriaga, "Augusto Boal and His Poetics of the Oppressed," *Discurso: revista de estudios iberoamericanos,* 8, no. 1 (1990): 53–66;

Barbara Norden, "The Cop in the Head," *New Statesman and Society,* 5 (27 March 1992): 33–34;

Douglas L. Paterson, "A Role to Play for the Theatre of the Oppressed," *Drama Review,* 38 (Fall 1994): 37–49;

Mady Schutzman, "Activism, Therapy, or Nostalgia? Theatre of the Oppressed in NYC," *Drama Review,* 38 (Fall 1994): 77–83;

Schutzman and Cohen-Cruz, "Theatre of the Oppressed Workshops with Women," *Drama Review,* 34 (Fall 1990): 66–76;

Schutzman and Cohen-Cruz, eds., *Playing Boal: Theatre, Therapy, Activism* (London & New York: Routledge, 1994).

Lygia Bojunga

(26 August 1932 –   )

Eliana Yunes
Pontifícia Universidade Católica do Rio de Janeiro

BOOKS: *Os colegas,* as Lygia Bojunga Nunes (Rio de Janeiro: Sabiá, 1972); translated by Ellen Watson as *The Companions* (New York: Farrar, Straus & Giroux, 1989);

Angélica, as Nunes (Rio de Janeiro: AGIR, 1975);

A bolsa amarela, as Nunes (Rio de Janeiro: AGIR, 1976);

A casa da madrinha, as Nunes (Rio de Janeiro: AGIR, 1978);

Corda bamba, as Nunes (Rio de Janeiro: Civilização Brasileira, 1979);

O sofá estampado, as Nunes (Rio de Janeiro: Civilização Brasileira, 1980);

Tomie Ohtake: 7 cartas e 2 sonhos, by Bojunga, as Nunes, and Tomie Ohtake (Rio de Janeiro: Berlendis & Vertecchia, 1983);

Tchau, as Nunes (Rio de Janeiro: AGIR, 1984);

O meu amigo pintor, as Nunes (Rio de Janeiro: J. Olympio, 1987); translated by Giovanni Pontiero as *My Friend the Painter* (San Diego: Harcourt Brace Jovanovich, 1991);

Nós três, as Nunes (Rio de Janeiro: AGIR, 1987);

Livro: um encontro com Lygia Bojunga Nunes, as Nunes (Rio de Janeiro: AGIR, 1988);

Fazendo Ana paz, as Nunes (Rio de Janeiro: AGIR, 1991);

Paisagem, as Nunes (Rio de Janeiro: AGIR, 1992);

O abraço (Rio de Janeiro: AGIR, 1995);

Seis vezes Lucas (Rio de Janeiro: AGIR, 1995);

Feito à mão (Rio de Janeiro: Casa Lygia Bojunga, 1996);

A cama (Rio de Janeiro: AGIR, 1999);

O Rio e eu (Rio de Janeiro: Salamandra, 1999);

Retratos de Carolina (Rio de Janeiro: Casa Lygia Bojunga, 2002).

Lygia Bojunga (photograph by Peter Lopez; from the dust jacket for My Friend the Painter, *1991; Richland County Public Library)*

In 1982 the International Board on Books for Youth gave the prestigious Hans Christian Andersen Award, considered the Nobel Prize of children's literature, to Lygia Bojunga, the first author writing in Portuguese to receive the prize. Although she had already published six innovative works by this time, none had been translated into any of the major languages of the world. A short version translated into English by Bojunga and one French translation were all that the jury for the Hans Christian Andersen Award had on which to judge her works. Bojunga, who had begun publishing ten years earlier with a book for children, *Os colegas* (1972; translated as *The Companions,* 1989), was surprised by this unusual international recognition for a Brazilian writer.

Lygia Bojunga was born in Pelotas, in the southern state of Rio Grande do Sul, on the border with Uruguay, on 26 August 1932. Her father, who was in the military, moved the family to Rio de Janeiro in 1940. His career took the family to Belo Horizonte for a short time during Bojunga's adolescence, but she spent most of her youth in Copacabana in Rio de Janeiro. In a rare statement to the press in the 1980s the writer spoke of her early interest in literature, beginning at age seven. Later, she was studying to enter medical school when she won first place in auditions given by the theatrical director Paschoal Carlos Magno. She gave up her plans to become a physician and joined the professional acting company of Henriette Morineau.

This experience led Bojunga not only to perform but also to translate, adapt, and write. As she stated, "meu encontro com *o fazer* literário me pegou de surpresa; foi tão forte tão cheio de afinidades que, quando me dei conta, eu tinha assumido por completo minha vocação de escritora" (my encounter with *making* literature caught me by surprise; it was such a strong experience, filled with such possibilities, that before I realized it I was already totally dedicated to being a writer). She went on radio and then on television to one of the most important theatrical series for children, *Teatrinho Trol*, presented on Sunday afternoons. The theater was to have an even greater impact later in her life.

Determined to dedicate herself to writing, Bojunga decided to move to the mountains a few hours outside of Rio de Janeiro to be closer to nature. Here she met and married an Englishman and opened a small rural school that they operated from 1964 to 1969, during the first phase of the military dictatorship in Brazil. Her husband, Peter, however, had wanderlust, so the couple left Brazil and traveled around the world while he worked as a supervisor for the International Air Transport Association (IATA). During their trips Bojunga generally wrote by hand in a notebook.

Even though the dictatorship imposed harsh censorship measures on writers, the 1970s were a promising period for literature in Brazil. The government required the reading of national authors in the schools, including José Bento Monteiro Lobato, Ofélia and Narbal Fontes, Maria Dupret, Origines Lessa, Câmara Cascudo, and Cecília Meireles. At this time several writers emerged who experimented with fiction for young people. This group, mostly writing for a journal dedicated to children, *Recreio* (Recreation), included Ana Maria Machado, Ruth Rocha, and Joel Rufino e Ziraldo. Several new illustrators of books for children worked with these writers.

Bojunga, however, was not a part of the group that worked for *Recreio*. She shunned publicity, refusing to give interviews or be photographed. She dispensed with parties celebrating the publication of her works, and she never went to schools to promote them. This situation is interesting since she began her professional life as an actress.

Bojunga has received prizes for all of her books published in Brazil. *Os colegas,* her first book, is a story about individual freedom that features animal charac-

Dust jacket for the 1989 translated edition of Bojunga's first book, Os colegas *(1972), a children's story about individual freedom (Richland County Public Library)*

ters. *Angélica,* which came out in 1975 and was well received by the critics, discusses the directions in life taken by a disillusioned stork upon discovering that her status among the animals is based on a lie: storks do not deliver babies. Bojunga's third work, *A bolsa amarela* (1976, The Yellow Purse), which was popular with young readers, narrates the story of a young girl who, by means of a yellow purse thrown away by an aunt, experiences her three greatest wishes: to be a child, to grow up, and to become a writer. The book deals with family relationships, school, childhood repressions, and the joy of the imagination that allows for anything to happen.

When Bojunga published *A casa da madrinha* (The Godmother's House) in 1978 and *Corda bamba* (an idiomatic expression meaning to find oneself in a dangerous situation with no protection) in 1979, Brazilian children's literature reached a new level of maturity. She demonstrated that authors writing for children could use the same stylized diction present in works for adults, as long as the content was kept at a level accessible to the child. In these two works Bojunga deals with the social and cultural impact on children who are abandoned and those who are overly protected.

Dust jacket for the 1991 English-language edition of Bojunga's O meu amigo pintor *(1987), about a boy who must come to terms with the suicide of an artist he has befriended (Richland County Public Library)*

In 1982, the year that Bojunga won the Hans Christian Andersen Award, she and her husband moved to England, where, as she says, she discovered that the writer is a citizen of her language: "comecei então a alternar meu tempo entre Londres e Rio: mas não ouvir a minha língua vai ficando uma penalidade cada vez maior e eu ando esticando cada vez mais o meu tempo do Rio . . ." (I began then to divide my time between London and Rio: but not hearing my own language became a great burden and I began to prolong my time in Rio on each trip . . .).

Prior to her travels Bojunga left a sixth book, *O sofá estampado* (1980, The Printed Sofa), in press in Brazil. The book, which concerns the relationship of young people with the medium of television, is a courageous criticism of television programming. Although critical of the medium, Bojunga is not propagandistic in tone. On the contrary, her narrative is allegorical and metaphorical in its approach to the problem as she discusses the lack of communication that television fosters, even among people who love each other.

After Bojunga won the Hans Christian Andersen Award, her works were translated into twenty languages, including English. The success of international recognition did not change her rhythm of writing; she continued to publish books at about the same rate. For a special volume in the series *Arte para crianças* (Art for Children), Bojunga wrote the text for *Tomie Ohtake: 7 cartas e 2 sonhos* (1983, Tomie Ohtake: 7 Letters and 2 Dreams), a book illustrated by Tomie Ohtake, a well-known Japanese-Brazilian artist. In 1984 she published *Tchau* (Ciao), a small book that is somewhat different from her previous novellas. The work is a collection of four short stories linked by the recurrence of the notion of saying good-bye, as the title suggests. In simple, colloquial language Bojunga explores difficult situations of separation involving a mother and daughter, friends, and sisters.

O meu amigo pintor (1987; translated as *My Friend the Painter,* 1991) is the story of a reclusive artist, a former political prisoner, who tells his secrets and stories to a child living in the same building. The youth observes the life of the artist and perceives his prejudices, relationships, and solitude up to the moment of his suicide. Bojunga handles the painful issue of suicide in a delicate and subtle manner for her young readers. Her stage adaptation of the story as *O pintor* (The Painter) won two important theatrical awards in 1986, the Molière Prize (France) and the Mambembe Prize (Brazil).

Nós três (We Three), also published in 1987 and adapted for the stage in 1989, is presented through the eyes of an adolescent who accompanies a sculptress, a friend of her mother, on a trip to the beach. The child intuits the artist's obsessive passion for her model. The strong emotional involvement kills the woman at the end of the narrative.

Livro: um encontro com Lygia Bojunga Nunes (1988, Book: An Encounter with Lygia Bojunga Nunes) is a mixture of literature, autobiography, reading theory, and Proustian reflections on the formation of the reader. The work is composed of six stories that present the love affair between a reader and literature. Narrated in the first person under her own name, the stories have the tone of a memoir and may be seen as depicting the relationship between Bojunga and her model reader. The work, which has the structure of a theatrical monologue, was a success in Brazil and Portugal. This particular type of writing represented Bojunga's renewed contact with the stage. The experiment fascinated her, and in 1991 she published *Fazendo Ana paz* (Making Peace with Ana), which features a similar mixture of autobiography and fiction. She uses the narrative as a space in which to come to grips with her past and find some sense of closure. She admits that she is not successful and presents the story as unfinished.

Bojunga's next book, *Paisagem* (Landscape), much anticipated by critics, was published in 1992. In this work she establishes an elaborate theory of reading and writing through an exchange of correspondence with a young reader in London.

Bojunga admitted in a 1995 interview that the face-to-face contact with her public afforded by the stage was better than the visibility created by an interview: "Não é isso (teatralização do texto literário) que ando querendo fazer. O que eu quero agora é investigar melhor essa nova forma de me relacionar com meus leitores . . . eles passam de leitor para espectador; eu largo a escrita e conto meu livro ao vivo" (This [the theatricalization of the literary text] is not what I want to do. What I want to do now is to research better this new way of creating a relationship with my readers . . . they go from being my reader to being my spectator; I stop writing and narrate my book in the flesh). This process kept Bojunga occupied for three years.

Bojunga began to publish again in 1995 with two new books. Both *Seis vezes Lucas* (Six Times Lucas) and

O abraço (The Embrace) were daring works for the genre of children's literature. In the first, a young boy experiences the breakup of his home because of his parents' childish behavior and is forced to grow up quickly. *O abraço* is an even more daring but masterful work. Bojunga deals with the issue of child molestation in a story told by a young woman facing her attacker. Even the author's most supportive critics were hesitant in their acceptance of the book; they did not criticize its literary quality but questioned the treatment of such a theme in a work for children. Bojunga has never commented on or responded to reviews or analyses of her writing.

Until 1996 Bojunga published all her works with her first two publishers, AGIR and José Olympio. That year she finally fulfilled her lifelong dream of setting up her own publishing firm, Casa Lygia Bojunga (House of Lygia Bojunga), which published her next book, *Feito à mão* (Handmade). She was involved in every aspect of the production of this autobiographical work, including even the selection of the paper and the binding.

Bojunga published two books in 1999, *O Rio e eu* (Rio and I) and *A cama* (The Bed). The Rio of the first title is Rio de Janeiro, which the writer has loved since her childhood. She transforms it into the city of her dreams in a flowing narrative that vacillates between love and hate for the streets and neighborhoods that once enchanted her. She establishes an even-tempered but emotional dialogue with the city, which becomes a protagonist, as she describes a society that lives in a mixture of wealth and poverty. The style that emerges in the narrative is a combination of the autobiographical, the lyrical, and the magical. In *A cama* a bed serves as the protagonist, with whom the narrator carries on a dialogue. The bed is a two-hundred-year-old family heirloom that is about to be passed from father to son in a poor family. *A cama* is the first work by Bojunga that is identified as a novel on the cover.

Bojunga spent six years working on *Retratos de Carolina* (2002, Portraits of Carolina), which, like *Feito à mão,* is autobiographical in nature. She has discussed how she and her main character, Carolina, are fused in the narrative: "Aqui eu me misturo com a Carolina, viro personagem também: queria ver se dava pra ficar todo mundo morando junto na mesma casa: eu, a Carolina, e mais os outros personagens: na casa que eu inventei" (Here I become fused with Carolina, I become a character also; I wanted to see if we all–I, Carolina, and the other characters–could live in the house that I invented).

An issue that clearly stands out in Bojunga's work is the question of reading and the formation of the reader. She explores this issue in her narratives through titles and themes that revolve around her own reading, the processes of writing, the failure of schools in teaching, and the importance of language as a liberating force. Diaries play an important role in some of her works, linking the acts of writing and reading.

Bojunga's works seem to mature with the readers she addresses in each successive book. In *Os colegas* she speaks to a reader aged seven or eight. Each following work then becomes more complex as she increases her expectations of the reader. From one narrative to the next, up to *Retratos de Carolina,* she poses new questions, problems, and conflicts through allegorical situations. Because of this pattern of development, critics have constantly asked if her work was ever really intended for children. For Bojunga this question is not important. Although adults and children perceive and interpret life in different ways, an interesting story has something for readers of all ages.

Lygia Bojunga's works provide good examples of the artistic possibilities inherent in the delicate and difficult genre of children's literature. In her narratives, which appeal also to adults, she uncovers prejudices and power structures in lucid, playful writing that offers various levels of interpretation. In a style reminiscent of Lobato that respects young people's sensibilities and intelligence, Bojunga has created works that inspire a happiness in reading. Her writings have earned her a place among the best Brazilian writers of children's literature.

References:

Amélia Lacombe, *Lygia Bojunga* (Rio de Janeiro: AGIR, 1989);

Marta Morais, "Narrar e criar: Lygia Bojunga Nunes," *Proleitura,* 2, no. 8 (1995): 4–8;

Morais, "Por que ler Bojunga," *Proleitura,* 2, no. 9 (1996): 6–10;

Morais, "Transpondo a dor em cor, a letra em palco: textos de Lygia Bojunga Nunes," *Letras,* 41–42 (1992–1993): 51–61;

Eliana Yunes, "A maioridade da literatura infantil brasileira," *Revista tempo brasileiro: literatura infanto-juvenil,* 63 (1980): 106–130.

Rubem Braga
(12 January 1913 – 17 December 1990)

Richard Vernon
University of North Carolina at Chapel Hill

BOOKS: *Direito comercial: lições rudimentares* (Niterói: Dias Vasconcelos, 1932);

O conde e o passarinho: chronicas (Rio de Janeiro: J. Olympio, 1936);

Falências e concordatas (lições rudimentares), second edition (São Paulo: Livraria acadêmica/Saravia, 1938);

O morro do isolamento: crônicas de Rubem Braga (São Paulo: Brasiliense, 1944);

Com a F.E.B. na Itália: crônicas (Rio de Janeiro: Zelio Valverde, 1945);

Um pé de milho: crônicas (Rio de Janeiro: J. Olympio, 1948);

O homem rouco: crônicas (Rio de Janeiro: J. Olympio, 1949);

Três "primitivos" (Rio de Janeiro: Ministério da Educação e Saúde, Serviço de Documentação, 1953);

A borboleta amarela: crônicas (Rio de Janeiro: Privately printed, 1955);

A cidade e a roça: crônicas (Rio de Janeiro: J. Olympio, 1957);

Ai de ti, Copacabana (Rio de Janeiro: Editôra do Autor, 1960);

A traição das elegantes (Rio de Janeiro: Sabiá, 1967);

Caderno de guerra de Carlos Scliar: 1944–1945, Itália, illustrations by Carlos Scliar, text by Braga (Rio de Janeiro: Sabiá, 1969);

Rio de Janeiro, photography by Bruno Furrer and Peter Solmssen, text by Braga (São Paulo: Brunner, 1973);

Os trovões de antigamente: crônicas (Lisbon: "Livros do Brasil," 1973);

O livro de versos (Recife: Pirata, 1980);

Crônicas do Espírito Santo (Vitória: Fundação Ceciliano Abel de Almeida/Universidade Federal do Espírito Santo, Secretaria de Estado da Educação e Cultura, 1984);

Recado de primavera (Rio de Janeiro: Record, 1984);

As boas coisas da vida (Rio de Janeiro: Record, 1988);

Uma fada no front, edited by Carlos Reverbel, illustrated by Joaquim de Fonseca (Pôrto Alegre: Artes e Ofícios, 1994);

Casa dos Braga: memória de infância (Rio de Janeiro: Record, 1997);

Rubem Braga (from O verão e as mulheres, *1986; Thomas Cooper Library, University of South Carolina)*

Um cartão de Paris, edited by Domício Proença Filho (Rio de Janeiro: Record, 1997).

Editions and Collections: *50 crônicas escolhidas* (Rio de Janeiro: J. Olympio, 1951);

100 crônicas escolhidas (Rio de Janeiro: J. Olympio, 1958);

200 crônicas escolhidas (Rio de Janeiro: Record, 1978);

Conheça o escritor brasileiro Rubem Braga, edited by Lygia Marina Moraes (Rio de Janeiro: Record, 1978);

Os melhores contos de Rubem Braga, introduction by Davi Arrigucci Jr. (São Paulo: Global, 1985).

OTHER: Fannie Hurst, *Corações humanos: a esquina do pecado,* translated by Braga (Rio de Janeiro: Civilização Brasileira, 1941);

Os ingleses, antigos e modernos, edited by Braga (Rio de Janeiro: Companhis editora leitura, 1944);

Os Russos, antigos e modernos, edited by Braga (Rio de Janeiro: Companhis editora leitura, 1944);

A. J. Cronin, *Sob a luz das estrêlas: romance,* sixth edition, translated by Braga (Rio de Janeiro: J. Olympio, 1954);

Antoine de Saint-Exupéry, *Terra dos homens,* seventh edition, translated by Braga (Rio de Janeiro: J. Olympio, 1964);

O libro de bâlso das contos inglêses, edited by Braga (Rio de Janeiro: Ouro, 1965);

Saint-Exupéry, *Sagarana,* ninth edition, translated by Braga (Rio de Janeiro: J. Olympio, 1966);

Pero Vaz de Caminha, *Carta a El Rey Dom Manuel,* edited by Braga (Rio de Janeiro: Sabiá, 1968);

Chico Anísio, *Obatizado da vaca,* preface by Braga (Rio de Janeiro: J. Olympio, 1974);

Guy Pinheiro de Vasconcellos, *Passagens pelo absurdo,* preface by Braga (Rio de Janeiro: Dazibao, 1989);

Oscar Wilde, *Fantasma de canterville: uma novela e tres cantos,* fourth edition, translated by Braga (São Paulo: Scipione, 1991);

Edmond Rostand, *Cyrano de Bergerac,* eighth edition, translated by Braga (São Paulo: Scipione, 1993).

Rubem Braga's years of literary activity span from the late 1920s until his death in 1990, but he wrote with the greatest intensity from the mid 1930s to 1960. He is distinctive among Brazilian writers in that he earned a prestigious position in Brazilian literary history solely through the genre of the *crônica* (chronicle). He is considered the premier Brazilian *cronista* (writer of *crônicas*) of the twentieth century, having written more than fifteen thousand *crônicas*. Braga reached his readers through his regular, often autobiographical, mass-media publications, and his books are actually collections of *crônicas* previously published in magazines and newspapers. As a journalist, Braga did not consider himself to be a "man of letters," but he associated with many of Brazil's most famous modernist writers, wrote a few poems, and infused a heavy dose of lyricism into the majority of his *crônicas*.

The modern *crônica* is frequently described as a short story, often occurring within a single scene, with minimal characterization, plot, and action, but *crônicas* can also take the form of an essay or social reflection, and in this way many are akin to the newspaper editorial. Like the editorial, the *crônica* is published in newspapers, magazines, and other periodicals. Afrânio Coutinho, in *A literatura no Brasil* (1986, Literature in Brazil), classifies the genre into five types: the narrative, which is the kind most like a short story; the metaphysical, philosophic, or meditational *crônica;* the poem in prose or lyrical *crônica,* in which the author attributes special meaning to the subject matter; the commentary *crônica* in which the author provides a subjective commentary on some recent happening; and the informational *crônica,* which is a relation of facts with very little commentary. The *crônicas* of Braga fall principally under the poem-in-prose category, although examples of each kind can be found in his body of work.

For the reader, the value of the *crônica* is often found in its personal, subjective (and at times fictional) nature, which contrasts sharply with the objective, factual reporting that dominates news publications. Though many Brazilian poets and writers of fiction have published *crônicas* (including Olavo Bilac, the famous Parnassian poet, and Machado de Assis, the dominant Brazilian novelist of the nineteenth century), their fame was based on other, "more literary" genres, while the *crônica* traditionally has been viewed as a method of earning a wage—an ephemeral subliterature. Yet, through both the quantity and quality of his work, Braga is credited with elevating the genre of the *crônica* to the level of legitimate literature.

Rubem Braga was born on 12 January 1913 in Cachoeiro de Itapemirim, a city in the Brazilian coastal state of Espírito Santo. His father was Francisco de Carvalho Braga, the first prefect of Cachoeiro, and his mother was Rachel Cardoso Coelho Braga. Braga was a precocious writer and began his journalistic career in 1928 by writing *crônicas* for the *Correio do Sul* (Southern Courier), a local paper founded by his brothers Jerônimo and Armando. He began studying law in 1929 in Rio de Janeiro, transferred to Belo Horizonte in 1931, and completed his degree there in 1932.

Although Braga was educated for law, it was a career path he never followed, being wholly captivated by journalism. While a student in Belo Horizonte in 1931 he worked first as a reporter and then again as a *cronista* for the *Diário da Tarde* (Afternoon Daily). In the preface to *Uma fada no front* (1994, A Fairy in Front) Carlos Reverbel relates that Braga confessed his early *crônicas* were written "na mesa de redação entre um telegrama a traduzir e um reportagem a fazer" (on the editing table between translating a telegram and writing a news story). That year he moved to São Paulo to cover the Constitutionalist Revolution against Getúlio Vargas's presidency for the *Diários Associados* (Associated Dailies), which was the first, and at the time only, chain of newspapers in Brazil. Braga's articles, which were sympathetic to the revolutionaries, attracted the attention of the Vargas regime, and he was charged with espionage and imprisoned for a short time.

As a reporter and *cronista* in 1933 for the *Diário de São Paulo* (São Paulo Daily), Braga worked with and befriended the writer Antônio de Alcântara Machado and the modernist giant, Mário de Andrade. The *Diário de São Paulo* was, like the *Diário da Tarde,* a branch of the Diários Associados. During this time Braga's literary production was his daily *crônica,* written in São Paulo and published the very next day in all the newspapers of the Diários Associados, which meant that it was printed simultaneously in many major cities such as São Paulo, Rio de Janeiro, Recife, Porto Alegre, and Belo Horizonte. Such a young writer reaching such a vast audience on a daily basis was unprecedented.

In 1935 Braga left São Paulo for Rio de Janeiro to work for the *Diário de Noite* (Night Daily) on invitation from Alcântara Machado, who had already begun working for that paper. His stay in Rio de Janeiro, however, was short: after Machado's death he moved again, this time to Recife, where he worked as an editor for the police page of the *Diário de Pernambuco* and established a new paper, *Folha do Povo* (People's Page), with a platform in opposition to the increasingly dictatorial Vargas regime. Braga then moved to Rio de Janeiro, where he went to work for the leftist paper *A Manhã* (The Morning), but after the attempted communist coup of 1935, the paper was closed.

In 1936 Braga published his first book, *O conde e o passarinho* (The Count and the Little Bird), a collection of twenty-eight previously published *crônicas.* The principal themes of these early *crônicas* are social injustice and the trespasses of the Vargas regime. The publication is a watershed for the genre as it is the first time a *cronista* removed his or her *crônicas* from the empheral and transitory form of newsprint and gave them the respectable permanance of the book format. *O conde e o passarinho* was well received, but because of it Braga was branded subversive, and the next few years of his life were characterized by less regular employment and repression by the Vargas regime.

The year *O conde e o passarinho* was published, Braga moved again to Belo Horizonte, where he wrote *crônicas* for the *Folha de Minas* (Minas Page). During his time in Belo Horizonte he married Zora Seljan, a writer. The following year they had a son, Roberto, Braga's only child. The couple separated in the mid 1940s.

In 1937 Braga was again in São Paulo, where he was one of the founders of *Problemas* (Problems), a leftist paper to which many of the country's premier socialist thinkers contributed. He was in the home of famous modernist poet and novelist Oswald de Andrade when they heard the radio proclamation of the establishment of the Estado Novo (New State), the dictatorial regime of Gertúlio Vargas that lasted until 1945.

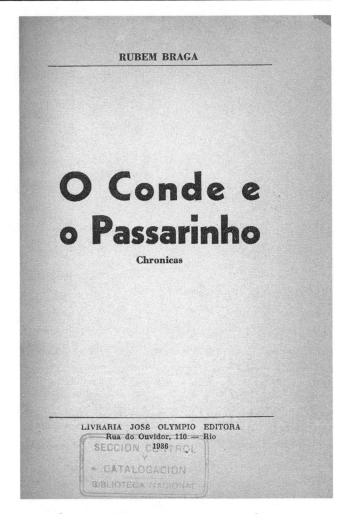

Title page for Braga's first book, a collection of crônicas
(Biblioteca Nacional de Chile)

Upon arriving in Porto Alegre in 1939, Braga was again arrested as a subversive, but he was quickly released through the influence of friends. In 1944 his second book, *O morro do isolamento* (Mound of Isolation), was published. Like *O conde e o passarinho,* the book is a collection of *crônicas* previously published in various publications, but it also includes four poems. The famous Brazilian modernist poet Manuel Bandeira thought the poems of sufficient merit to be included in his *Antologia de poetas bissextos contemporâneos* (Anthology of Contemporary Bissextile Poets), published in 1946.

In 1944 Braga was sent with the Brazilian Expeditionary Force to Italy as a war correspondent for the *Diário Carioca* (Rio de Janeiro Daily). He remained in Europe until the end of the war, and upon his return to Brazil he published his third book, a collection of *crônicas* based on his wartime experience in Italy titled *Com a F.E.B. na Itália* (1945, With the B.E.F. in Italy). Rather than cover the larger military accomplishments of the Brazilian troops, Braga's *crônicas* are centered on the

Cover for Braga's 1944 book featuring a collection of crônicas *and four poems (Heard Library, Vanderbilt University)*

daily life of the soldier—the difficulties and contradictions of such a life. He states in the preface that his initial intent when chosen as a war correspondent was to create "uma narrative popular, honesta e simples da vida e dos feitos de nossos homens na Itália. Uma espécie de crônica da FEB, à boa moda portuguesa antiga" (a popular narrative, honest and simple, of the life and the doings of our men in Italy. A kind of chronicle of the BEF, in the good old Portuguese fashion). Lack of access to information and periodic separation from the troops themselves kept Braga from accomplishing his goal, but the words *popular, honest,* and *simple* are still applicable to *Com a F.E.B. na Itália* and most of Braga's other *crônicas.*

Braga continued to work as a reporter and *crônista.* In 1946 he covered the first election of President Juan Domingo Perón in Argentina. His fourth book, *Um pé de milho* (A Stalk of Corn), was published in 1948; it consists of *crônicas* written between 1933 and 1947. The title is indicative of one of Braga's principal themes: the value of the quotidian. His *crônicas* often take the point of view that even the simplest objects and everyday happenings of life have a valuable story. In

the *crônica* from which his 1948 collection takes its title, Braga tells of a solitary stalk of corn that grows spontaneously in his small urban garden:

> Um pé de milho sozinho, em um canteiro, espremido, junto do portão, numa esquina de rua—não é um número numa lavoura, é um ser vivo e independente. . . . É alguma coisa de vivo que se afirma com ímpeto e certeza. Meu pé de milho é um belo gesto da terra.

> (A stalk of corn alone, in a corner, squeezed, next to the gate, on a street corner—is not a number in a field, it is a living and independent being. . . . It is something alive that affirms itself with impetus and certainty. My stalk of corn is a beautiful gesture of the earth.)

In 1949 Braga had another collection of *crônicas* published under the title *O homem rouco* (The Hoarse Man). This volume is composed of writings from April 1948 to July 1949. The man of the title is Braga himself. Coutinho writes in the sixth volume of *A literatura no Brasil* that Braga is the most subjective of Brazilian *cronistas.* Braga offers himself undisguised as first-person narrator of the majority of his *crônicas.* In fact, he was never comfortable with the idea of writing his own memoirs, as he thought that such a product would be not only dry but redundant in light of his many autobiographical *crônicas.*

In 1950 Braga lived in Paris as a correspondent for the *Correio de Manhã* (Morning Courier). Indicative of the popularity of Braga's work in book form as well as mass media, the following year the publishing house José Olympio printed *50 crônicas escolhidas* (50 Selected *Crônicas*), selections of Braga's *crônicas* from previously published books overseen by the author himself. In the 1958 edition the number of *crônicas* grew to 100, and the 1978 edition featured 200.

Braga spent 1953 writing *crônicas* for the large Brazilian magazine *Manchete* (Headline), and in the following year he published his sixth book, *Três "primitivos"* (Three Primitives). In 1955 he experienced a temporary change of career. Braga was a friend of João Café Filho, who had been elected vice president to Vargas in 1950 and became the Brazilian president in 1954 after Vargas's suicide. Café Filho named Braga chief Brazilian consul in Santiago, Chile, in 1955. Braga asked to be dismissed from the post in November of that year. His request coincided with Café Filho's leaving office because of poor health.

From 1955 to 1960 four more new collections of *crônicas* were published. *A cidade e a roça* (1957, The City and the Country) features some of Braga's most famous works, including "Recado ao Senhor 903" (A Note to Mr. 903), which takes a comical look at human relationships in an urban environment. *Crônicas* such as "O Cajueiro" and "Homem no Mar" have been anthologized in many school textbooks.

In 1960 Braga was named ambassador to Morocco, a post he occupied until 1963 when he asked to be dismissed. In 1968 Braga, together with Fernando Sabino and Otto Lara Resende, established Editora Sabiá, a publishing house that introduced such authors as Gabriel García Márquez, Pablo Neruda, and Jorge Luis Borges to Brazilian audiences.

Throughout the 1960s new editions of Braga's previous books were published. The only wholly new collection was *A traição das elegantes* (The Treachery of the Elegant) in 1967, which consists of 60 *crônicas* originally written for the magazine *Manchete* and the *Diário de Notícias*.

In 1968 Braga published a modern version of Pero Vaz de Caminha's *Carta a El Rey Dom Manuel* (Letter to King Dom Manuel). The original *Carta a El Rey Dom Manuel* was written in 1500 by Caminha, a captain in Pedro Alvares Cabral's discovery fleet. The letter is Caminha's communication to the Portuguese king and is considered Brazil's first piece of literature in Portuguese.

Braga published no more books until 1980, when a small volume of poetry titled *O livro de versos* (The Book of Verse) was printed. *O livro de versos* features fourteen poems, including the four poems published in *Morro do isolamento*. Between 1980 and his death in 1990 Braga published three more collections of *crônicas*, the last being *As boas coisas da vida* in 1988.

Braga died on 17 December 1990 from throat cancer. He declined undergoing difficult operations and treatments that might have prolonged his life a short while longer. Since his death, new collections of his *crônicas* continue to be published through the efforts of friends and his son Roberto.

Rubem Braga's popularity and success on all levels can be attributed to a distinct style that mixes accessibility with literary depth and complexity. His *crônicas* are personal and subjective, yet simultaneously reflect universal human experience. In his introduction to *Os melhores contos de Rubem Braga* (1985, The Best Short Stories by Rubem Braga), Davi Arrigucci Jr., perhaps the most dedicated Braga scholar, expresses the appeal of Braga's work. Arrigucci writes that Braga's *crônicas* conceal the author's art beneath an unconcerned, apparently simplistic prose that seems to wander without direction or destination; beneath the author's seemingly easy and haphazard style hides a prose obtained through hard labor and at great cost, featuring linguistic gems, a vocabulary in which each word is handpicked and precisely located, and a language that is unparalleled in Brazilian literature for its naturalness.

References:

Davi Arrigucci Jr., "Onde andará o velho Braga?" in his *Achados e perdidos* (São Paulo: Polis, 1979), pp. 159–166;

Frederico Barboso, "Estudo do livro *Os melhores contos de Rubem Braga*," in *Literatura para a FUVEST 98*, edited by António de Castro, José de Paula Ramos Jr., and Ivan Teixeira (São Paulo: Anglo, 1997);

Afrânio Coutinho, "Ensaio e crônica," in *A literatura no Brasil*, third edition, volume 6, edited by Afrânio Coutinho and Eduardo de Faria Coutinho (Rio de Janeiro: J. Olympio / Niterói: Editora da Universidade Federal Fluminense, 1986), pp. 117–143;

Jorge de Sá, *Rubem Braga* (Rio de Janeiro: AGIR, 1994).

João Cabral de Melo Neto

(6 January 1920 – 9 October 1999)

Celso Lemos de Oliveira
University of South Carolina

BOOKS: *Pedra do sono* (Recife: Privately printed, 1942);

O engenheiro (Rio de Janeiro: Amigos da Poesia, 1945);

Psicologia da composição com a fábula de Anfion e Antiode (Barcelona: Livro Inconsútil, 1947);

O cão sem plumas (Barcelona: Livro Inconsútil, 1950);

Joan Miró (Rio de Janeiro: Ministério da Educação e Saúde, 1952);

Poemas reunidos (Rio de Janeiro: Orfeu, 1954);

O rio, ou relação da viagem que faz o Capibaribe de sua nascente a cidade do Recife (São Paulo: Comissão do IV Centenário da Cidade de São Paulo, Serviço de Comemorações Culturais, 1954);

Morte e vida Severina: auto de natal pernambucano (São Paulo: Luzes, 1955);

Pregão turístico (Recife: A. Magalhães, 1955);

Aniki Bobó (Recife: A. Magalhães, 1955);

Duas aguas: poemas reunidos (Rio de Janeiro: J. Olympio, 1956)—includes *Uma faca só lâmina,* translated by Kerry Shawn Keys as *A Knife All Blade; or, Usefulness of Fixed Ideas* (Camp Hill, Pa.: Pine Press, 1980);

Poemas reunidos (Rio de Janeiro: Orfeu, 1958);

Quaderna (Lisbon: Guimarães, 1960);

Dois parlamentos (Madrid: Editora do Autor, 1961);

Serial: poesia, 1959–1961 (Rio de Janeiro: Editora do Autor, 1961);

Terceira feira (Rio de Janeiro: Editora do Autor, 1961);

Poemas escolhidos (Lisbon: Portugália, 1963);

Antologia poética (Rio de Janeiro: Editora do Autor, 1965);

Morte e vida Severina (São Paulo: Teatro da Universidade Católica de São Paulo, 1965);

A educação pela pedra (Rio de Janeiro: Editora do Autor, 1966);

Morte e vida Severina e outros poemas em voz alta (Rio de Janeiro: Editora do Autor, 1966);

Funeral de um Lavrador (São Paulo: Musical Arlequim, 1967);

Museu de tudo: poesia, 1966–1974 (Rio de Janeiro: J. Olympio, 1975);

João Cabral de Melo Neto (frontispiece for Benedito Nunes, João Cabral de Melo Neto, *1971; Thomas Cooper Library, University of South Carolina)*

Brazilian Painting and Poetry=Pintura e poesia brasileiras, by Cabral and Reynaldo Fonseca (Rio de Janeiro: Spala, 1979);

A escola das facas: poesia, 1975–1980 (Rio de Janeiro: J. Olympio, 1980);

Poesia e composição: a inspiração e o trabalho de arte (Coimbra, Portugal: Fenda, 1982);

Auto do frade: poema para vozes (Rio de Janeiro: J. Olympio, 1984);

Agrestes: poesia, 1981–1985 (Rio de Janeiro: Nova Fronteira, 1985);

Crime na Calle Relator (Rio de Janeiro: Nova Fronteira, 1987);

Museu de tudo e depois, 1967–1987 (Rio de Janeiro: Nova Fronteira, 1988);

Poemas pernambucanos (Recife: Nova Fronteira/Centro Cultural José Mariano, Sindicato da Indústria do Açúcar no Estado de Pernambuco, 1988);

Sevilha andando (Rio de Janeiro: Nova Fronteira, 1989);

Primeiros poemas, edited by Antonio Carlos Secchin (Rio de Janeiro: Universidade Federal do Rio de Janeiro, 1990).

Editions and Collections: *Poesias completas, 1940–1965* (Rio de Janeiro: Sabiá, 1968);

João Cabral de Melo Neto, edited by José Fulaneti de Nadal, notes and analyses by Samira Youssef Campedelli and Benjamin Abdala Jr. (São Paulo: Abril, 1982);

Poesia crítica: antologia (Rio de Janeiro: J. Olympio, 1982);

Os melhores poemas de João Cabral, edited by Antonio Carlos Secchin (Rio de Janeiro: Global, 1985);

Poesia completa, 1940–1980, preface by Oscar Lopes (Lisbon: Imprensa Nacional/Casa da Moeda, 1986);

Poemas sevilhanos (Rio de Janeiro: Nova Fronteira, 1992);

Obra completa, edited by Marly de Oliveira (Rio de Janeiro: Aguilar, 1994);

Serial e antes, preface by Cabral and Oliveira (Rio de Janeiro: Nova Fronteira, 1997);

A educação pela pedra e depois (Rio de Janeiro: Nova Fronteira, 1997);

Entre o sertão e Sevilha, edited by Maura Sardinha (Rio de Janeiro: Ediouro, 1997);

Idéias fixas de João Cabral de Melo Neto, edited, with a preface, by Félix de Athayde (Rio de Janeiro: Fundação Biblioteca Nacional/Nova Fronteira, 1998);

Prosa (Rio de Janeiro: Nova Fronteira, 1998);

João Cabral de Melo Neto, edited by Laura Sandroni and Luiz Raul Machado (Rio de Janeiro: Nova Fronteira, 2002).

Edition in English: *Selected Poetry, 1937–1990,* translated by Elizabeth Bishop and others, edited by Djelal Kadir (Hanover, N.H.: University Press of New England, 1994).

RECORDING: *Antologia poética de João Cabral de Melo Neto,* read by Cabral, Somlivre 444.6001, 1984.

OTHER: Angel Crespo, *Grabados populares del nordeste del Brasil,* prologue by Cabral (Madrid: Servicio de Propaganda y Expansión Comercial de la Embajada del Brasil, 1963);

O arquivo das Indias e o Brasil: documentos para a história do Brasil existentes no Arquivo das Indias de Sevilha, edited by Cabral, preface by José Honório Rodrigues (Rio de Janeiro: Ministério das Relações Exteriores, 1966);

Maria Ignez Corrêa da Costa, *Gentíssima,* preface by Cabral (Rio de Janeiro: Record, 1968);

Murilo Mendes, *Antologia poética,* edited by Cabral (Rio de Janeiro: Fontana, 1976);

Açúcar bruto, poetry by Cabral, text by Gerson Camarotti and others, photography by Paula Simas (Brasília: Editora Universidade de Brasília, 1997);

Marly de Oliveira, *Antologia poética,* edited, with a preface, by Cabral (Rio de Janeiro: Nova Fronteira, 1997).

João Cabral de Melo Neto, the last great Brazilian poet of the twentieth century, is almost invariably referred to as a *poeta pernambucano*–that is, a poet from the northeastern state of Pernambuco, the landscape and atmosphere of which he frequently drew on in his poetry. He was born in Recife on 6 January 1920 to a traditional family that owned a sugarcane farm. The second son of Luis Antonio Cabral de Melo and Carmen Leão Cabral de Melo, he lived on two sugarcane plantations, first in Poço do Aleixo, in São Lourenço da Mata, and afterward in Pascoval and Dois Irmãos, both in the municipality of Moreno. Growing up with farmworkers, Cabral was moved by their condition and their needs. Whenever they went to the nearby town, these illitcrate workers brought back booklets called *literatura de cordel* (string literature) that Cabral read to them. He portrays these farm laborers in such poems as "A descoberta da literatura" (The Discovery of Literature), from *A escola das facas* (1980, The School of Knives).

Among Cabral's relatives were such writers as the poet Manuel Bandeira, a cousin from his father's side of the family, and the sociologist Gilberto Freyre, a cousin from his mother's side. These older men perhaps played some part in the young man's career. Like Bandeira, Cabral moved to Rio de Janeiro when young and soon became a leading poet of his generation. Like Freyre, he held the view that the multiracial population of Brazil was an historical advantage. Cabral's was a distinguished family that valued intellectual achievements. In a short autobiographical account included in the recording *Antologia poética de João Cabral de Melo Neto* (1984), Cabral says that his paternal grandfather, a real patriarch, insisted that his grandchildren be born in a special room in the house in Recife, the capital of Pernambuco. But in Cabral's case the room was not prepared in time, and he was delivered in a room filled with images of saints, something like a private chapel. He claims that he was actually born on 6 January 1920, as stated on his birth certificate, but his family said the correct date was 9 January.

In 1930 Cabral's family moved from their sugarcane plantation to Recife, where he began his elementary education at the Colégio de Ponte d'Uchoa of the Irmãos Maristas (Marist Brothers), studying afterward at the Conde da Boa Vista. He had no higher education. As a youth in Recife, Cabral was an ardent soccer player and in 1935 was a juvenile champion for the Santa Cruz Futebol Clube. He was also a member of the América Futebol Clube, which had been founded by his family before he was born. (Shortly after his death the *Folha de São Paulo* of 11 October 1999 published a photograph of the poet taken only a few days earlier, proudly holding up the official shirt of the America Club of Recife.) But Cabral was already writing poetry as a teenager and at age sixteen abandoned soccer for his intellectual pursuits, including poetry.

When he was only seventeen, Cabral wrote two poems on the Italian dramatist Luigi Pirandello. They are slight works but interesting for what they anticipate in a career that was to last half a century. The familiar idea that life is theater (as in Pirandello's *Sei personaggi in cerca d'autore,* 1921; translated as *Six Characters in Search of an Author,* 1922) is neatly laid out in unrhymed free verse that is hard to approximate in English. Before long Cabral began to write formal poetry in quatrains and other familiar verse forms. Almost from the beginning he was attracted to the Surrealism of such French poets as Guillaume Apollinaire. In 1937, when Cabral wrote his poems on Pirandello, Surrealism had been part of the European artistic scene for almost a generation, and Apollinaire himself had been dead since 1918. It was still avantgarde in a remote place such as Recife, however, far up the Atlantic coast from Rio de Janeiro, the Brazilian capital, which had a strong infusion of French cultural life.

Cabral's first job was with the Associação Comercial (Commercial Association) of Pernambuco in 1937; afterward, he worked for the Departamento do Estado (Department of Statistics) of Pernambuco. At the age of eighteen he started going to the Café Lafayette in Recife, where he gathered with the painter Vicente do Rego Monteiro and other writers and artists, some of whom had lived in Europe.

In 1940 Cabral moved with his family to Rio de Janeiro, where he got in touch with Carlos Drummond de Andrade and Jorge de Lima, who were among the finest poets in Brazil. In 1941 Cabral participated in the Congresso de Poesia (Poetry Con-

gress) in Recife, presenting the lecture "Considerações sobre o poeta dormindo" (Considerations about a Sleeping Poet). He was only twenty-two when he published his first book, *Pedra do sono* (1942, The Stone of Sleep). This book is in effect a manifesto directed against the Parnassian ideal of poetry, impersonal and anti-Romantic, which had long been fashionable in Brazil. The title of the book is Surrealist, and Cabral liked to intertwine the words *sono* (sleep) and *sonho* (dream).

At this time Cabral was recruited by the Força Expedicionária Brasileira (FEB) for obligatory military service but was released because of poor health. Deciding to remain in Rio de Janeiro, he successfully passed a required exam and was made assistant of the Departamento Administrativo do Serviço Pùblico (Department of Administration of Public Services). He also frequented intellectual gatherings at the Café Amarelinho and the Café Vermelhinho in downtown Rio de Janeiro. Before long he became a respected poet.

Cabral belonged to a group of young Brazilian poets who began calling themselves the Generation of 1945—meaning that they came into their own around 1945, at the end of World War II. He is one of the few whose reputations have survived from that period, and nowadays he might be ranked in the company of several poets of a preceding generation—perhaps the most important that Brazil has known, including Bandeira and Drummond. Flora Süssekind has edited Cabral's correspondence with Bandeira and Drummond as *Correspondência de Cabral com Bandeira e Drummond* (2001), and the result is a volume that brings together the three poets in a fascinating way.

Cabral's correspondence with Drummond began in 1940. By that time Cabral was already publishing verse in the "little magazines," and these publications would have given him some prestige among his elders. Drummond addressed him at first as simply "Meu caro poeta" (My dear poet). Back in Recife, Cabral, encouraged by this cordiality, continued to write to "Caro amigo Carlos Drummond de Andrade" (Dear friend Carlos Drummond de Andrade). In 1942 Cabral sent a copy of *Pedra do sono* to Drummond. He also sent the older poet the manuscript of a poem in four parts called "Os Quatro Elementos" (1942, The Four Elements), which was not published until it was included in Süssekind's edition of the correspondence. One is tempted to think that Cabral had T. S. Eliot's *Four Quartets* (1943) in mind; Eliot's sequence is also based on the four elements of air, earth, water, and fire in exactly the same order, and the last poem, "Little Gidding," was finished at the same time as Cabral's sequence.

In 1945 Cabral published *O engenheiro* (The Engineer), consisting of poems written between 1942 and 1945. Although this book includes Surrealist poems such as "As Nuvens" (The Clouds), he was already moving toward a new objective concept of poetry involving the rational control of the emotions. That same year he passed the examination that admitted him to the Instituto Rio Branco, the college for diplomats. His admission marked the beginning of a career in the diplomatic service; Cabral was to become a government representative, as many other Latin American literary figures did for their own countries, such as his fellow Brazilian Vinícius de Moraes, the Chilean Pablo Neruda, and the Mexicans Octavio Paz and Carlos Fuentes. In December 1945 Cabral started working for the cultural department of the Ministério das Relações Exteriores (Ministry of Foreign Relations), known as Itamaraty for the building in Rio de Janeiro that first housed the ministry. He then worked for the political department and the Comissão de Organismos Internacionais (Committee of International Institutions). In the following year he married Stella Maria Barbosa de Oliveira, the granddaughter of the writer and lawyer Rui Barbosa. They had five children, the first of whom was born in December 1946.

Cabral's first diplomatic post, in 1947, was with the Brazilian consulate in Barcelona, a city that profoundly influenced his poetry. He created a small publishing house, Livro Inconsútil, which brought out Spanish and Brazilian poetry, including two of his own books, *Psicologia da composição com a fábula de Anfion e Antiode* (1947, Psychology of Composition, with the Story of Anfion and Antiode) and *O cão sem plumas* (1950, The Featherless Dog). Cabral seems to have found life in Barcelona much to his liking. In 1948 he wrote to Bandeira:

> Aqui tenho tido oportunidades fabulosas de comprar algumas pinturinhas. Conheço um imbecil amigo do marechal Pétain, e a quem procuram todos os refugiados franceses quando necessitam de gaita. Tenho podido comprar, assim, desenhos de Picasso, Modigliani, Van Gogh; um pastel de Degas, um pequeno óleo de Bonnard. Tenho em negúcios um curiosíssimo desenho do Douanier e um pequeno óleo de Manet. Mas não pudemos ainda chegar a um acordo em questão de preços. Para que o Manet não fosse parar em mãos estranhas, sugeri ao Osório que o comprasse. Ele o viu, disse que gostara, mas não quis comprar a pintura porque, na hora de fugir para cá, o proprietário cortou a pintura (que se mantem intacta) do chassis. Por isso ele disse que o quadro estava defeituoso....

Manuscript page from Cabral's poem that was published in 1947 in Psicologia da composição com a fábula de Anfion e Antiode *(from Benedito Nunes,* João Cabral de Melo Neto, *1971; Thomas Cooper Library, University of South Carolina)*

(Here I have had fabulous opportunities for buying some small paintings. I know an idiot friend of Marshall Pétain, and all the French refugees look for him when they need money. I have been able to buy drawings by Picasso, Modigliani, Van Gogh; a pastel by Degas, a small oil painting by Bonnard. I have been negotiating a very curious drawing by Douanier and a small oil painting by Manet. In order for the Manet not to get in the wrong hands, I suggested to Osorio to buy it. He had seen it and liked it but did not want to buy it, because the owner, at the time when he had to escape, removed it from the frame [even though it is intact]. Because of that he thought the painting was defective. . . .)

This episode gives one an idea of life in postwar Spain, when refugees from France survived by selling works of art that they had managed to smuggle out when they escaped the German occupation. A junior diplomat such as Cabral certainly had an advantage at the time. As the artists' names suggest, he had exquisite taste in painting. Selden Rodman, who visited Cabral in Asunción, Paraguay, in the early 1970s, recalls in *Tongues of Fallen Angels* (1974) how he was impressed by Cabral's modern house and its decor, the "cultural baggage" that he carried to places sometimes remote from the usual centers of modernist art.

Cabral's correspondence with Bandeira, then considered the leading poet in Brazil, lasted until 1958. In February 1948 Bandeira received a copy of *Psicologia da composição com a fábula de Anfion e Antiode* and responded warmly:

> Acuso o recebimento de sua carta de 17 e da Psicologia da Composição. Estou encantado, encantado. Com o poeta e com o impressor. Você sabe bem o que quer e realiza bem o que quer: *rigoroso horizonte!* O Vinícius escreveu-me de Hollywood: "acabei de receber o livrinho do João Cabral, que achei de primeira. Está de longe o melhor de todos esses novos."

> (I acknowledge receiving your letter dated the 17th and the *Psychology of Composition*. I am amazed, amazed. With the poet and with the printing. You know very well what you want and you carry out well what you want: *rigorous horizon!* Vinícius [de Moraes] wrote to me from Hollywood: "I have just received the book from Joao Cabral, which I think is first-class. He is by far the best of these new ones.")

"Rigorous horizon" is a phrase from the Spanish poet Jorge Guillén; Cabral used it as the epigraph for *Psicologia da composição com a fábula de Anfion e Antiode*. Moraes, an established poet, eventually became famous through his association with bossa nova during the 1950s and 1960s. In 1948 he was living in Los Angeles as the Brazilian vice consul.

In 1950 Cabral was stricken with a headache that never left him as he grew older; drugs relieved the pain only briefly. This suffering changed his life, making him bitter and even antisocial. But in his stoicism he managed to transform his pain into a poem, "Monumento à aspirina" (Monument to Aspirin), included in *A educação pela pedra* (1966, Education through Stone).

In Barcelona, Cabral befriended the artist Joan Miró, about whom he published a small book (actually a long essay), *Joan Miró* (1952), with reproductions of original works by the Catalan artist. Although it is only thirty-two pages long, it demonstrates Cabral's remarkable grasp of Miró's place in modern art. The poet-diplomat was well aware of the literature on Miró already published by various French and American as well as Spanish critics. Cabral's text was republished in the collection *Prosa* (1998, Prose).

Cabral's interest in Miró during his first residence in Barcelona seems to have been associated with his interest in two French writers, Raymond Queneau and Jacques Prévert. A letter to Bandeira in 1949 makes this association clear:

> Conhece v. a obra de Jacques Prevert? Acabo de ler, emprestado por Mirü seu livro *Paroles*. Que poeta! Este livro me fez notar uma coisa: como gosto de poesia posterior à Guerra se vai aproximando de certas maneiras da poesia brasileira. O fenômeno deve estar aproximado daquelo outro que se nota em França: fome de novella norte-americana. Pois aqui na Espanha também, o poeta que mais interessa aos jóvens não-catolizantes e não-fascistas é Neruda. Creio que há em nós americanos uma ausência de retórica e um contato direto com a coisa que os europeus desconhecem. Prévert, neste sentido, é quase americano. (Evidentemente, quando falo na ausência retórica em nós, não penso nem em Schmidt, nem em Lêdo, nem em Jorge de Lima, nem em Emílo Moura, etc.)

> (Do you know the work of Jacques Prévert? I just finished reading his book *Paroles,* which I borrowed from Miró. What a poet! This book made me notice one thing: how I like the postwar poetry; it is getting closer to certain ways of Brazilian poetry. This phenomenon must be getting close to that other one that is noticed in France: hunger for North American novels. Because here in Spain also the poet who is most admired by the young people who are non-Catholic and non-fascist is Neruda. I think that there is in us Americans an absence of rhetoric and a direct contact with things that Europeans do not know. Prévert, in this sense, is almost an American. [Evidently, when I speak of the absence of rhetoric in us, I am not referring to either Schmidt or Ledo, or Jorge de Lima, or Emilio Moura, etc.])

In this remarkable passage Cabral mentions several living Brazilian poets of some fame whom he tends to reject as rhetoricians. In the letter he goes on to quote brief passages of verse from Bandeira, Drummond, and Moraes, poets with whom he obviously aligns himself. Cabral seems to say that Brazilian poets at their best have more in common with North American poets than with Europeans.

Cabral's correspondence with Drummond was not as extensive as that with Bandeira. After the first few years, during the 1940s, it dwindled to occasional short notes and telegrams, and in 1957 it came to an end. This cessation seems rather surprising, because the poets and their wives always expressed themselves in affectionate terms to each other. Drummond, for many years a civil servant in a government ministry, was at least as busy as Cabral. Drummond seldom traveled and seemed content to live in Rio de Janeiro, even though some of his finest poems are set in the state of Minas Gerais, where he grew up. In 1951 Cabral took special notice of Drummond's great poem "A Mesa" (1951, The Table), which was later translated by the poet Elizabeth Bishop.

Cabral was next posted to the Brazilian mission in London, where he stayed from 1950 to 1952.

There he was accused of being subversive and a communist and was forced to return to Rio de Janeiro on a sabbatical in 1953. He had a temporary job with a newspaper, *A vanguarda,* but his journalistic work did not interfere with his poetry. He published *O rio, ou relação da viagem que faz o Capibaribe de sua nascente a cidade do Recife* (1954, The River; or, Account of the Journey Made by the Capibaribe from Its Source to the City of Recife) and received the Prêmio José de Anchieta (José de Anchieta Prize) during the fourth-centenary celebrations in São Paulo in 1954. That same year Cabral was invited to participate in the International Congress of Writers, also in São Paulo, and a volume of his works titled *Poemas reunidos* (Collected Poems) was published in Rio de Janeiro. In 1955 he resumed his diplomatic career after charges against his political activity were dismissed by the Supremo Tribunal Federal (Federal Supreme Court). The year was a happy one for Cabral: a daughter, Isabel, was born, and he received the Prêmio de Poesia Olavo Bilac (Olavo Bilac Poetry Prize) given by the Academia Brasileira de Letras (Brazilian Academy of Letters).

In 1955 Cabral published his best-known work, *Morte e vida Severina: auto de natal pernambucano* (Death and Life of a Severino: A Pernambucan Christmas Play), a painful story about a poor man from northeast Brazil who, having lost his piece of land to a drought and a rich farmer, has nowhere to go. The story of Severino is an allegory. The name comes from the Latin *severo,* which means severe or rigorous, like the land he tried to farm, the *sertão*—a dry land where only low bushes grow. He represents the people of this harsh region, where droughts are constant and hardly anything grows. Severino wanders from the *sertão* in the hinterland to the coast in the vicinity of Recife, trying to find conditions in which to survive; it is a scene of despair. But a child is born—a sign of survival and hope—and so he abandons the idea of suicide. Cabral wrote this work as if it were an Iberian play called an *auto* (a short play). It was to be performed at Christmas; the newborn child represents the nativity of Christ. The religious theme is mixed with elements from the popular culture of northeast Brazil. This poetic drama is written in what is called *media velha* or *redondilha,* lines with seven syllables.

Morte e vida Severina had been commissioned by the playwright and theater director Maria Clara Machado. Because of the structure of the play, she was unable to stage it and sent it back to Cabral, who decided to reduce the stage directions and publish it as a poem in *Duas aguas: poemas reunidos* (1956, Two Waters: Collected Poems). In 1960, however, *Morte e vida Severina* was staged with music by Chico Buarque

de Hollanda, first in Brazil and then in Europe. The musical setting that this gifted young composer provided for the play had much to do with its success in Europe and Brazil. It is produced from time to time, and much of the score was recorded in 1966 on a long-playing record in Brazil. *Morte e vida Severina* is known in the United States only through a partial translation by Bishop, who lived in Brazil for many years and was acquainted with Cabral. She finished only three of the eighteen sections of the work, but they have been reprinted several times, and Djelal Kadir included them in his bilingual anthology of Cabral's works, *Selected Poetry, 1937–1990* (1994).

As no leftist connections had ever been proved against him, Cabral returned to Barcelona in 1956 to undertake historical research in the Arquivo das Indias (Archives of the Indies) in Seville. The research was later published as *O arquivo das Indias e o Brasil: documentos para a história do Brasil existentes no Arquivo das Indias de Sevilha* (1966, The Archives of the Indies and Brazil: Documents on the History of Brazil in the Archives of the Indies in Seville). In 1958 Cabral moved to Marseille and received the prize as best author in the Festival de Teatro do Estudante (Student Theater Festival) in Recife. In 1960 *Quaderna* was published in Lisbon, indicating Cabral's growing international reputation. Before long he was to go to Madrid as first secretary of the Brazilian embassy, but in 1961, the year he published *Dois parlamentos* (Two Parliaments), he was appointed to work with the state minister of agriculture, Romero Cabral da Costa; therefore, Cabral moved to the new capital of Brasília. But the government of President Jânio da Silva Quadros ended after a few months, and Cabral was sent back to Spain. The consulate was moved from Seville to Cadiz, where he lived until 1964, meanwhile traveling throughout the world on diplomatic missions.

In 1964 Cabral was appointed councillor for the delegation of Brazil at the Geneva office of the United Nations. There his fifth child, João, was born. In 1966 Cabral moved to Bern. That year, *Morte e vida Severina* was presented by the Teatro da Universidade Católica de São Paulo (TUCA), the theater group of the Catholic University of São Paulo in France, first at the Festival de Nancy, then at the Théatre des Nations in Paris, and subsequently in Portugal in Lisbon, Coimbra, and Porto. At the festival in Nancy, Cabral received the "best living author" prize. In 1967 he returned to Barcelona as general consul.

Cabral's *Poesias completas, 1940–1965* (Complete Poetry, 1940–1965) was published in 1968, the year in which he was elected a member of the Academia Brasileira de Letras, filling the opening left by the death of the writer and journalist Assis Chateaubri-

Carlos Miranda as Severino and Paulo Autran as Mestre Carpina in a performance (circa late 1960s) of Cabral's 1955 verse drama Morte e vida Severina *(Death and Life of a Severino), an allegorical tale of a poor man who loses his drought-stricken land to a rich farmer (from Benedito Nunes,* João Cabral de Melo Neto, *1971; Thomas Cooper Library, University of South Carolina)*

In 1974 Cabral received an important award from the government of Brazil, the Grã-Cruz da Ordem do Rio Branco (Great Cross of the Order of Rio Branco). In 1975, the year he published *Museu de tudo: poesia, 1966–1974* (Museum of Everything: Poetry, 1966–1974), Cabral received a prize from the Associação Paulista de Críticos de Arte (Association of Art Critics of São Paulo). *Museu de tudo* is an important miscellaneous volume of eighty-three poems, with subjects ranging from admired poets (W. H. Auden, Dylan Thomas, Paul Valéry, Rainer Maria Rilke, and Moraes) to brief tributes to noted Brazilians (the architect Oscar Niemeyer and Cabral's cousin Freyre, the sociologist), evocations of the Pernambuco coast, and Brazilian soccer as experienced from abroad. According to a friend, Cabral's enthusiasm for soccer was so great that, during the World Cup matches of 1978, he flew from Senegal to Rio de Janeiro to watch the games played in Argentina, simply because they were not being televised in Senegal. A poem from *Museu de tudo* titled "Retrato de Andaluza" (Portrait of an Andalusian) illustrates Cabral's love for Spain, his favorite diplomatic posting, and for Andalusia in particular; in it he praises a lady born in Cadiz who is now living in Seville.

Cabral also received awards from Senegal, the Grande Oficial do Mérito and the Grande Oficial da Ordem do Leão. These came to him about the time that he was posted to Quito, Ecuador, in 1979, where he served as the Brazilian ambassador until 1981. In 1980 a bibliographical exhibition of Cabral's work was inaugurated in Pernambuco. His *A escola das facas,* published that same year, is considered by some readers to be a love poem dedicated to two regions in two countries, Pernambuco in Brazil and Andalusia in Spain. The next year Cabral became the Brazilian ambassador to Honduras, and soon the Universidade Federal do Rio Grande do Norte granted him the degree of doctor honoris causa.

Cabral's last post in a foreign country was in Porto. While serving in Portugal, he received the Prêmio Golfinho de Ouro (Gold Dolphin Prize) of the state of Rio de Janeiro and published *Auto do frade: poema para vozes* (1984, Play of a Monk: Poem for Voices), written in Honduras. This work deals with the death in 1824 of the Carmelite Frei Caneca (Friar Caneca), leader of a popular revolutionary movement in northeast Brazil. He was supposed to be hanged, but the executioner refused to do so, saying that he saw Frei Caneca "flying through the sky." Finally, the *oficial da justiça* (officer of justice) decided that a group of twelve men would execute Frei Caneca so that nobody would feel directly responsible for his death. *Auto do frade* is one of Cabral's most ambitious works–

and. In 1969 Cabral was sent to the embassy in Asunción, Paraguay, and that same year he was appointed a member of the Hispania Society of America. Three years later he was sent to Senegal as ambassador; at this time he was also appointed to the embassies of three other African countries. One would expect a diplomat such as Cabral to have become a cosmopolitan after living in several countries on three continents. But the evidence of his poetry suggests otherwise. His residence in Senegal from 1972 to 1978 did not lead to much poetry of consequence–only a handful of short poems. While he was posted there, however, the president of Senegal was Léopold Sédar Senghor, a francophone poet of world stature, and one might assume that they had literary conversations of a high order. Cabral moved with ease among several modern languages, and he was influenced most by writers in French and English.

a play for many voices that runs to sixty pages. In "João Cabral de Melo Neto: 'Literalist of the Imagination'" (1992) John M. Parker translates the title as "The Friar's Way," and he points out that the title in Portuguese suggests "auto-da-fé" with good reason, because the subject is the martyrdom of Frei Caneca. One might assume that, growing up in Recife, Cabral would have been familiar with the historical episode involving Frei Caneca. His treatment of the story, involving various choral groups, is reminiscent of Eliot's play about the martyrdom of St. Thomas Becket, *Murder in the Cathedral* (1935), and perhaps Paul Claudel's *Jeanne d'Arc au bûcher* (1939, Joan of Arc at the Stake), which Cabral would have known about in Europe.

Because Cabral's and Drummond's correspondence essentially ended in 1957, it is surprising to find in *Correspondência de Cabral com Bandeira e Drummond* a final letter from Drummond to Cabral, written in April 1984, concerning *Auto do frade.* The elder Drummond was eighty-two at this time and was to live three more years.

Meu caro João:

Está comigo o exemplar especial do *Auto do frade,* com sua dedicatória cordial.

Recebi-o com alegria, pois quebra um silêncio de muitos anos, para o qual não encontro outra explicação senão . . . a falta de explicação. Sempre estranhei e lamentei o afastamento a que nos vimos submetidos, e que não foi motivado por qualquer desentedimento ou desavença entre nós. Ainda bem que as coisas voltam ao natural, e podemos restaurar aquele velho e bom contato, do qual conservo as melhores recordações de amizade e confiança mutual.

O *Auto do frade* é uma criação engenhosa, que entrelaça habilmente história e poesia, de modo a alcançar plenamente o objetivo teatral e edificante, uma obra literária calcada na vida. Parabéns por mais essa vitória.

Com Dolores mando um abraço carinhoso para Stela. E para você a melhor lembrança amiga do seu velho,
Carlos

(My dear João:

I have with me the special book, the *Auto do frade,* with your dedication to me.

I received it with joy, because it breaks the silence of many years, for which I find no explanation except . . . lack of explanation. I always found it strange and lamented the separation in which we involved ourselves, which was not due to any disagreement or misunderstanding between us. Fortunately things went back to normal, and we couldn't re-establish our old contact, from which I keep the best memories of mutual trust.

The *Auto do frade* is an ingenious creation that weaves together history and poetry to reach a theatrical purpose, a literary work based on real life. Congratulations for one more victory.

Along with Dolores I send you an affectionate hug to Estela [Stella Maria, Cabral's first wife]. And to you the best wishes from your old friend,
Carlos)

Cabral must have hoped that *Auto do frade* would be well received, and no doubt he was especially pleased by this response from his old friend Drummond.

In 1984 *Antologia Poética de João Cabral de Melo Neto,* a recording of Cabral reading from his own works, was released in Rio de Janeiro. It consists of two records and was produced by Marilda Pedroso. According to her account of the event, she was a guest for twelve "indescribable days" at the Brazilian embassy in Quito, and during that time Cabral recorded some of his "extraordinary" poetry. Back in Rio de Janeiro, background music for his recitations was composed and performed by Egberto Gismonti, a well-known composer. The music varies from solo guitar to a small orchestra playing in the minimalist idiom familiar in the United States. Toward the end of the third side Cabral delivers a short autobiographical account of his youth, his days as a soccer player, and his career as a diplomat. He says to his listener, "me perdoe a voz de sacristão" (forgive me for having the voice of a sacristan). One of the poems that he reads on the recording is titled "Paisagem pelo telefone" (Landscape by Telephone), from *Quaderna.* It brings together various aspects of his poetry—the Pernambuco littoral, the intense light that pervades the scene, and the white sails, all the whiter because of the nearby *salinas* (salt marshes). "Paisagem pelo telefone" is also a love poem written with Cabral's characteristic kind of humor.

Cabral continued his literary career with great success. He received the Prêmio Moinho Recife (Moinho Recife Prize) in 1984, and in the following year he published an important book of poems titled *Agrestes: poesia, 1981–1985. Agreste* might be translated as a rustic area typical of northeast Brazil. Cabral's admiration for such North Americans poets as Marianne Moore and Bishop is apparent in this collection, which includes three poems in homage to Moore. In 1986 he received another degree of doctor honoris causa, this time from the Universidade Federal de Pernambuco, but otherwise it was a sad year for Cabral: his wife, Stella Maria, died. He soon married the poet Marly de Oliveira, with whom he had two sons and a daughter.

After returning to Rio de Janeiro, Cabral published *Crime na Calle Relator* (1987, Crime on Relator Street) and received a prize from the União Brasileira de Escritores (Brazilian Writers' Union). In Recife he published an anthology, *Poemas pernambucanos* (1988, Poems from Pernambuco), and the second volume of his complete poetry, *Museu de tudo e depois, 1967–1987* (1988, Museum of Everything and Afterward, 1967–1987). There were more prizes—the Bienal Nestlé de Literature for his life's work and the Prêmio Lily de Carvalho from the Associação Brasileira de Críticos de Letras (ABCL) in Rio de Janeiro.

In 1989 Ashley Brown and Celso de Oliveira visited Cabral in his apartment overlooking the Praia do Flamengo in Rio de Janeiro. The conversation touched on many writers and artists, some of whom Cabral had celebrated in his poems, but probably none was as important to him as Valéry, author of "Le Cimetiére marin" (1920; translated as "The Graveyard by the Sea," 1928), whom he briefly discussed. Valéry's famous poem, Brown thought, stood behind some of Cabral's poems about the Pernambuco littoral and its nearby cemeteries, a supposition that the poet verified. Brown, a professor of English, knew Cabral's poem "Ao Reverendo George Crabbe" (To the Reverend George Crabbe), from *Agrestes,* and was impressed that such an unlikely English poet would appeal to a Brazilian. But then Brown remembered that Crabbe was also a poet of the seaside (in his case, Aldeburgh, in Suffolk) and made this analogy in the essay "Cabral de Melo Neto's English Poets" (1991). Cabral often wrote about authors (usually poets) and painters whom he admired, and in a sense his poems represent a modernist ideal of art, formal and austere, that he developed in youth.

Cabral finally retired from his diplomatic career in 1990. The Universidade Federal do Rio de Janeiro published his *Primeiros poemas* (First Poems) that same year. After 1990 Cabral's wife helped him to write because he suffered from an incurable degenerative disease as well as from depression. The year before his retirement he published an important collection titled *Sevilha andando* (1989, Walking Seville), for which he received the Pedro Nava prize in 1991. The eighty poems in this collection are mostly short and more formal than his other verse. Most of them are written in quatrains or couplets, sometimes arranged in groups of four or eight. Although the book lacks a formal structure, the title suggests its procedure—a series of strolls through a beloved city seen from many perspectives, visual and sometimes literary.

Parker points out that Seville "has become a composite metaphor for many qualities which the poet admires, and which he otherwise found in isolated objects, places, or people." Parker traces a connection between the city and Cabral's recurring praise of the feminine, noting that *Sevilha andando* is dedicated to the poet's second wife, Marly. As a state of mind and inspiration, Cabral was able to evoke Seville easily from his home in Brazil, where he spent his last decade after retiring from the diplomatic service. He touches on this attitude in "Sevilha em Casa" (Seville at Home):

> Tenho Sevilha em minha casa.
> Não sou eu que estou *chez* Sevilha.
> E Sevilha em mim, minha sala.
> Sevilha e tudo o que ela afia.
>
> Sevilha veio a Pernambuco
> porque Aloísio lhe dizia
> que o Capibaribe e o Guadalquivir
> são de uma só maçonaria.
>
> (I have Seville in my house.
> It isn't that I am *chez* Seville.
> It is Seville in me, in my *sala*.
> Seville and all that she touches.
>
> Seville came to Pernambuco
> because Aloísio used to say
> that the Capibaribe and the Guadalquivir
> are made of the very same substance.)

In these two quatrains (half of the short poem) Cabral projects a state of mind into time and geographical space. "Aloísio" refers to Aluísio Azevedo, a late-nineteenth-century naturalistic novelist and later a diplomat. He was the author of several novels, of which the best were probably *O Mulato* (1881; translated as *Mulatto,* 1990) and *Casa de Pensão* (1883, The Boardinghouse). They were widely read at one time, and Cabral would probably have known them in his youth. Azevedo the diplomat (like Cabral) would have known the Capibaribe and the Guadalquivir, two rivers that are linked in "Sevilha em Casa" to establish a poetic analogy. The Capibaribe flows through Pernambuco to reach the Atlantic at Recife; the Guadalquivir flows past Seville and into the Atlantic on the other side of the ocean. Here, as nearly always, Cabral writes with great economy and condenses what could be a large subject into a few lines.

Another poem from *Sevilha andando* that is remarkable for its economy of treatment is "O *Aire* de Sevilha" (The *Air* of Seville):

> Mal cantei teu ser e teu canto
> enquanto te estive, dez anos.
>
> Cantaste em mim e ainda tanto,
> cantas em mim teus dois mil anos.

Agora há um cantar diferente
delanchado como a *madeleine*

de Proust, que precipitava
a vida que já não lembrava.

Essa *madeleine* à mão está
e não depende mais do chá

que lhe servia certos dias
a certo menino uma tia,

nem como o chão tropeçante
do patio da Casa Guermantes:

tenho-o comigo todo o dia,
hoje o que é o *aire* de Sevilha.

(I hardly sang your presence and your song
during the time I lived there, those ten years.

You sang in me and still persist,
Singing in me two thousand years.

Now there is another kind of singing
set in motion like the *madeleine*

of Proust, which brought back
the life that could not be remembered.

This *madeleine* is right at hand
and does not depend on the tea

that on certain days
an aunt served to a certain boy,

nor even the rough paving-stones
in the courtyard of the Guermantes mansion:

I carry it with me every day,
what is today the *air* of Seville.)

Undated caricature of Cabral by Moura (from Benedito Nunes,
João Cabral de Melo Neto, *1971; Thomas Cooper
Library, University of South Carolina)*

This poem, like many others in *Sevilha andando,* personifies the city. But in the third couplet the poet puts the subject into the literary context of Marcel Proust's *A la recherche du temps perdu* (1913–1927; translated as *Remembrance of Things Past,* 1922–1932). Cabral uses the famous scene, early in the novel, when the narrator dips a little cake called a madeleine into a cup of tea and has an illuminating memory of his boyhood, when his aunt Léonie sometimes did the same thing for him on Sunday mornings. The sensation evokes an entire world, the small town called Combray where the narrator spent much of an idyllic boyhood. At the end of the novel the last scene (in itself almost three hundred pages in length) takes place in a great modern house built by the Prince de Guermantes, the present head of a noble family whose members have played a large part in the novel. The time is now shortly after World War I, and most of the surviving characters have aged, so much so that the narrator hardly recognizes them. As he enters the courtyard of the mansion, paved with uneven stones, he stumbles and recovers his balance. When he does so, he has another sensation that evokes a memory of a similar situation that took place, long ago, in Venice. Then the two images, of Combray and Venice, merge in his imagination. In "O *Aire* de Sevilha," Cabral juxtaposes the two scenes (the madeleine and the entrance to the Guermantes mansion) in a remarkable way. The figure of speech established by the novel takes over the poem and suggests something of the importance that Seville had for Cabral.

Another aspect of Seville that finds its way into Cabral's poetry is bullfighting. Parker suggests that the bullfighter is a surrogate figure for the poet: he "constantly exposes himself to danger while being in control of the situation." "Touro Andaluz" (Andalusian Bull), a poem in ten rhymed couplets (the rhymes are impossible to reproduce in English), is slightly different from most of those in *Sevilha andando.* The subject has been familiar since Ernest Hemingway celebrated it in *The Sun Also Rises* (1926), *Death in the Afternoon* (1932), and a few of his short stories. Because

*Front cover of the first of two volumes of Cabral's
collected poetry published in 1997 (University
of Massachusetts, Dartmouth Library)*

bullfighting is characteristic of Spain and parts of
Spanish America but not Brazil, it is interesting that
Cabral joins certain French and American writers who
were attracted to the subject. But it is for him simply
part of the life of Seville, and he does not create a mys-
tique out of it in the manner of Hemingway.

Most poets have a second art, music or one of
the visual arts. Eliot and Auden were close to music,
William Butler Yeats to painting, and in their different
ways they played off the language of poetry against
the language or even the structural devices of the
other artistic medium. In Cabral's case the second
medium was obviously painting. In the two volumes
of his collected poetry published in 1997, *Serial e antes*
(Serial and Before) and *A educação pela pedra e depois*
(Education through Stone and Afterward), one finds
poems about Pablo Picasso, André Masson, Piet Mon-
drian, and Paul Klee, along with several poems about
poets. The cover of Cabral's *Crime na Calle Relator* features an early Wassily Kandinsky painting.

In a special section on Cabral following his
death, the *Jornal do Brasil* (23 October 1999) published
a poem titled "O papel em branco" (which may be
translated as "The Blank Paper") alongside a photograph of Cabral standing with Rio de Janeiro's Praia
do Flamengo (Flamengo Beach) in the background.
The poem was written and first published in a newspaper in 1943, but it was strangely overlooked and
never included in any of Cabral's books, including the
two 1997 volumes of his collected poems. In retrospect, "O papel em branco" seems like the genesis of
many of the poems and motifs in Cabral's subsequent
work, as Süssekind points out in the accompanying
article in the *Jornal do Brasil*. The word *branco* (white)
occurs frequently in Cabral's work, and in this poem
it appears a dozen times. Composed of twenty quatrains, "O papel em branco" begins:

> Esta folha branca
> Me prescreve o sonho;
> Me incita ao verso
> Nítido e preciso.
>
> Não é a morte
> Que a faz deserta;
> E branca de vida
> Ainda por nascer.
>
> (This white sheet
> Prescribes the dream to me;
> It incites me toward verse
> Clean and precise.
>
> It is not death
> That makes it deserted;
> It is the white of life
> Yet to be born.)

As a young poet Cabral might have thought of
himself as an heir to the practices of earlier Latin
American modernists, for instance the Nicaraguan
Rubén Darío, whose "Sinfonía en gris mayor" (1891,
Symphony in Gray Major) was a "response" to the
quatrain poems in French poet Théophile Gautier's
Emaux et camées (1852; translated as *Enamels and Cameos
and Other Poems*, 1903). One of Gautier's poems in
Emaux et camées is "Symphonie en blanc majeur" (Symphony in White Major), in which even the white of
the page contributes to the total effect. Cabral's "O
papel em branco" is somewhat reminiscent of
Gautier's poem, and indeed it is almost a credo: "This
white sheet / . . . incites me toward verse / Clean and
precise." Whatever his antecedents, Cabral belongs to
a well-established body of poets whose main theme is
creativity itself, which might include the act of writing
the poem at hand. One could cite Samuel Taylor Cole-

ridge, Stéphane Mallarmé, and Wallace Stevens as other members of this group. At the same time Cabral's allegiance to a stretch of northeastern Brazil was always a source of creative vitality. For instance, in *A educação pela pedra* the imagery is largely based on the great stretches of *sertão* in the backcountry of Pernambuco. But a counterimage cuts across this image— the rivers that unexpectedly emerge, the subject of several poems in this volume. Some of them are written with a two-part structure; the verse line resembles blank verse in English.

As an international figure João Cabral de Melo Neto was honored increasingly for his life's work. Five times in a row the Academia Brasileira de Letras submitted his name to the Nobel Foundation as a candidate for the prize in literature, but he never received it. The Prêmio Luís de Camões, which Cabral won for his entire body of work in 1991, was awarded by the joint governments of Brazil and Portugal. In the early 1990s he also received the Neustadt International Prize for Literature from the University of Oklahoma; the Grã-Cruz da Ordem de Isabel, a Católica (Great Cross of the Order of Isabel, the Catholic); and the Queen Sophia Prize for Ibero-American literature.

After blindness struck him in 1994, Cabral became reclusive. Losing his sight made him a bitter man, and thenceforth he maintained close relations only with his family and a few friends, rarely giving interviews. He died on 9 October 1999, a few months before turning eighty. Cabral was fittingly buried in the uniform of the Academia Brasileira de Letras, with the flag of the America Soccer Club draped over his body, in the Mausoléu dos Imortais (Mausoleum of the Immortals) in the São João Baptista cemetery in Rio de Janeiro.

Letters:

Correspondência de Cabral com Bandeira e Drummond, edited by Flora Süssekind (Rio de Janeiro: Nova Fronteira/Casa de Rui Barbosa, 2001).

References:

António José Ferreira Afonso, *João Cabral de Melo Neto: uma teoria da luz* (Braga, Portugal: Associação Portuguesa de Pais e Amigos do Cidadão Deficiente Mental de Braga, 1995);

Eugênio de Andrade and others, *O TUCA no Porto* (Porto, Portugal: Plano, 1966);

João Alexandre Barbosa, *A imitação da forma: uma leitura de João Cabral del Melo Neto* (São Paulo: Duas Cidades, 1975);

Eli Nazareth Bechara, *Cabral: dois momentos no tecer da manhã* (São José do Rio Prêto: Universidade Estadual Paulista, 1991);

Assis Brasil, *Manuel e João: dois poetas pernambucanos* (Rio de Janeiro: Imago, 1990);

Ashley Brown, "Cabral de Melo Neto's English Poets," *World Literature Today,* 65 (Winter 1991): 62–64;

Alice F. L. A. Cafezeiro, *A estrutura semântica em "Tecendo a Manhã," de João Cabral de Melo Neto* (Petrópolis: Vozes, 1966);

André Camlong, *Le vocabulaire poétique de João Cabral de Melo Neto* (Toulouse: Cahier 1, Centre d'Etude Lexicologique, Université de Toulouse, 1978);

Modesto Carone Netto, *A poética do silêncio: João Cabral de Melo Neto e Paul Celan* (São Paulo: Perspectiva, 1979);

Antônio da Costa Ciampa, *A estória do Severino e a história da Severina* (São Paulo: Editora Brasiliense, 1987);

Angel Crespo and Pilar Gómez Bedate, *Realidad y forma en la poesía de Cabral de Melo* (Madrid: Revista de Cultura Brasileña, 1964);

Lauro Escorel, *A pedra e o rio: uma interpretação da poesia de João Cabral de Melo Neto* (São Paulo: Duas Cidades, 1973);

Folha de São Paulo, special Cabral section, 11 October 1999;

John A. Gledson, "Sleep, Poetry and João Cabral's 'False Book': A Revaluation of *Pedra do Sono,*" *Bulletin of Hispanic Studies,* 55 (1978): 43–58;

Aguinaldo José Gonçalves, *Transição e permanência: Miró/ João Cabral, da tela ao texto* (São Paulo: Iluminuras, 1989);

Jornal do Brasil, special Cabral section, 23 October 1999;

Luiz Costa Lima, *O espaço da percepção* (Petrópolis: Vozes, 1968);

Lima, *Lira e antilira (Mário, Drummond, Cabral)* (Rio de Janeiro: Editora Civiliazaço Brasileira, 1968; revised edition, Rio de Janeiro: Topbooks, 1995);

Danilo Lôbo, *O poema e o quadro: o picturalismo na obra de João Cabral de Melo Neto* (Brasília: Thesaurus, 1981);

Napoleão Lopes Filho, *Interpretação silenciosa de dois poemas de João Cabral de Melo Neto* (Lisbon: Ocidente, 1964);

Zila Mamede, *Civil geometria: bibliografia crítica, analítica e anotada de João Cabral de Melo Neto, 1942–1982* (São Paulo: Nobel, 1987);

Rosa Maria Martelo, *Estrutura e transposição: invenção poética e reflexão metapoética na obra de João Cabral de Melo Neto* (Porto, Portugal: Fundação Eng. Antonio de Almeida, 1988);

Nancy Maria Mendes, "Ironia, sátira, paródia e humor na poesia de João Cabral de Melo Neto," dissertation, Universidade Federal de Minas Gerais, 1980;

Arnaldo Nogueira, "João Cabral de Melo Neto," *Jornal do Brasil,* 27 July 2003;

Benedito Nunes, *João Cabral de Melo Neto* (Petrópolis: Vozes, 1971);

Célia Therezinha Guidão da Veiga Oliveira, *O lexema seda num poema de João Cabral de Melo Neto* (Petrópolis: Vozes, 1971);

Marly de Oliveira, *O deserto jardim, 1989–1990* (Rio de Janeiro: Nova Fronteira, 1990);

John M. Parker, "João Cabral de Melo Neto: 'Literalist of the Imagination,'" *World Literature Today,* 66 (Autumn 1992): 609–616;

Marta Peixoto, *Poesia com coisas: uma leitura de João Cabral de Melo Neto* (São Paulo: Perspectiva, 1983);

Ormindo Pires Filho, *A contestação em João Cabral de Melo Neto* (Recife: Ministério da Educação e Cultura/Instituto Joaquim Nabuco de Pesquisas Sociais, 1977);

Antônio Lázaro de Almeida Prado, "Rosa tetrafoliar: uma leitura de *A educação pela pedra,* a partir de seus módulos poético-gerativos," *Revista de letras do Instituto de Letras, Historia e Psicologia de Assis,* 18 (1976): 155–183;

Selden Rodman, *Tongues of Fallen Angels* (New York: New Directions, 1974);

Maria Lúcia Pinheiro Sampaio, "Os meios de expressão na obra de João Cabral de Melo Neto," dissertation, Universidade de São Paulo, 1972;

Sampaio, "A palavra na obra de João Cabral de Melo Neto," *Revista de letras do Instituto de Letras, Historia e Psicologia de Assis,* 17 (1975);

Sampaio, *Processos retóricos na obra de João Cabral de Melo Neto* (São Paulo: Editora de Humanismo, Ciência e Tecnologia, 1978);

Luiz Santa Cruz, *A metapoética de João Cabral através de Joaquim Cardoso* (Rio de Janeiro: Senhor, 1962);

Antonio Carlos Secchin, *João Cabral: a poesia do menos* (São Paulo: Duas Cidades, 1985);

Secchin, *Morte e vida Cabralina* (Rennes, France: Université de Rennes II, 1991);

Marta de Senna, *João Cabral: tempo e memória* (Rio de Janeiro: Antares, 1980);

Anazildo Vasconcelos da Silva, *Lirica modernista e percurso literário brasileiro* (Rio de Janeiro: Editora Rio, 1978);

Angélica Maria Santos Soares, *O poema, construção às avessas: uma leitura de João Cabral de Melo Neto* (Rio de Janeiro: Tempo Brasileiro, 1978).

Consuelo de Castro
(16 January 1946 –   )

Sandra R. G. Almeida
Universidade Federal de Minas Gerais

BOOKS: *A última greve* (São Paulo: Martins, 1963);
Caminho de volta: peça em tres atos (Pôrto Alegre: Tapa, 1974);
À prova de fogo (São Paulo: Editora de Humanismo, Ciência e Tecnologia, 1977);
O porco ensangüentado (Pôrto Alegre: Vanguarda, 1978);
A cidade impossível de Pedro Santana: peça em 3 atos (São Paulo: Vanguarda, 1978);
O grande amor de nossas vidas (São Paulo: Promoção do Departamento de Artes e Ciências Humanas da Secretaria Estadual de Cultura, Comissão Teatro São Paulo, 1981);
Urgência e ruptura (São Paulo: Perspectiva/Secretaria de Estado da Cultura, 1989)–comprises *À prova de fogo, À flor da pele, Caminho de volta, O grande amor de nossas vidas, Louco circo do desejo, Script-tease, Marcha a ré,* and *Aviso prévio; Aviso prévio* translated as *Walking Papers,* in *Three Contemporary Brazilian Plays in Bilingual Edition,* edited by Elzbieta Szoka and Joe W. Bratcher (Austin, Tex.: Host, 1988);
Only you: uma história de amor (São Paulo: Veredas, 2001).

PLAY PRODUCTIONS: *À flor da pele,* São Paulo, Teatro Paiol, 1969;
Caminho de volta, São Paulo, Teatro Aliança Francesa, October 1974;
À prova de fogo, São Paulo, Cidade Universitária, 1975;
O porco ensangüentado, Rio de Janeiro, Teatro Glaucio Gil, 1975;
O grande amor de nossas vidas, São Paulo, Teatro Paiol, 1978;
A corrente, by Castro, Lauro César Muniz, and Jorge Andrade, Rio de Janeiro, Serviço Nacional de Aprendizagem, 1981;
Louco circo do desejo, São Paulo, Teatro Macksoud Plaza, 1985;
Ao sol do novo mundo, São Paulo, Teatro Brasileiro de Comédia, 1986;
Uma caixa de outras coisas, by Castro and Antônio Abujamra, São Paulo, Teatro Brasileiro de Comédia, October 1986;

Aviso prévio, São Paulo, Teatro Paiol, October 1987;
O kotô, São Paulo, Espaço Off, October 1988;
Only you, São Paulo, Teatro Ruth Escobar, 8 March 2001.

PRODUCED SCRIPTS: "Implosão," television, TV Cultura, 1976;
"Último capítulo," television, TV Cultura, 1976.

SELECTED PERIODICAL PUBLICATIONS–UNCOLLECTED: *À flor da pele: peça em 3 atos, Revista de Teatro,* no. 382 (1971): 25–54;
O caminho de volta: peça em 3 atos, Revista de Teatro, no. 410 (1976): 37–80.

Consuelo de Castro is among the most prominent contemporary Brazilian playwrights. She has written more than thirty plays and scripts, many of which have never been produced because the military regime in Brazil in the 1960s and 1970s banned any literary production deemed subversive. Nevertheless, Castro has been awarded several prizes from national government offices and theater critics. A strong voice against political oppression and social injustices, Castro wrote many of her plays to expose the evils of society, challenging the authoritarian regime, the capitalist system, and the patriarchal society that she deems responsible for the individual's destruction and annihilation. Besides her productive career as a playwright, Castro has also written several scripts for television, including "Implosão" (1976) and "Último capítulo" (1976), both of which were broadcast on TV Cultura.

Castro belongs to a group of playwrights committed to social change who during the late 1960s and early 1970s produced plays that primarily focus on the political situation in Brazil. This group, which includes Leilah Assunção, Isabel Câmara, Antônio Bivar, and José Vicente, was greatly influenced by Plínio Marcos, a writer whose work explores the lives of the underprivileged in Brazil and introduced to Brazilian theater theoretical and theatrical innovations from Europe and

*Cover for the first edition of Castro's play, written in 1968,
about the plight of students protesting in an effort to
create a more liberal and less repressive society
(Heard Library, Vanderbilt University)*

America. Critic Renata Pallottini refers to the theater of this period as "porcupine dramaturgy" because the plays are mostly about two antagonists whose conflict involves an endless struggle of attraction and repulsion. As several critics have pointed out, Castro's presence in Brazilian theater is also highly relevant in that she is at the beginning of a line of women playwrights who emphasize the plight of women characters, exploring their oppression and constraint in social roles. While rejecting the label of feminist, Castro foregrounds in her plays various situations in which women figure as central characters and have to cope with the demands of an oppressive and sexist society.

Consuelo de Castro was born on 16 January 1946 in Araguari, a small town in the state of Minas Gerais, where her parents, Affonso de Oliveira Castro and Dalva Santana Castro, lived. Castro later moved to São Paulo and began her literary career in 1963 with the publication of a book of poems titled *A última greve* (The Last Strike). In 1964 she began to study social sci-

ences at the University of São Paulo, one of the most prestigious Brazilian universities; that year a revolution in Brazil installed a military dictatorship that lasted almost twenty years. Castro did not finish her degree, but her experiences as a student during the controversial 1960s supplied the material for her first play, *À prova de fogo* (Fire Proof; produced 1975, published 1977), which was written in 1968 and originally titled *A invasão dos bárbaros* (The Invasion of the Barbarians). The play was immediately censored before it was presented to the public. In 1974, however, it won the second prize from a federal institution that sponsors Brazilian theater—the Serviço Nacional de Teatro (National Theater Service [SNT]). In 1975 the still-censored *À prova de fogo* was performed secretly on the campus of the University of São Paulo, and in 1985 it finally received its first official performance.

À prova de fogo portrays a period of turmoil in which students all over the world fought against the rigid structure of universities, the capitalist system, and the bourgeoisie, trying to build a more liberal and less repressive society in social, sexual, and economic terms. In Brazil the students also protested against the authoritarian military regime. The plot is based on a real event, the occupation of the University of São Paulo's School of Philosophy by students in 1968. In the play a group of students take over a university building and begin a conflict with the police. Instead of focusing on the occupation itself, however, Castro exposes the clash among the various characters within the movement, people with divergent viewpoints on how best to conduct their political resistance. According to some critics, the work also features a discussion of the role of women in society, exposing how despite occupying a space in the public sphere in the struggle for social justice, women are still bound to a patriarchal society that denies them the same privileges and rights men have politically, socially, and—above all—sexually. The outcome of the play is tragic for the students who are arrested, especially for the women who are faced with double standards and suffer discrimination in an overtly sexist society. The students' fight for liberation is unable to account for the change in women's role in society. The two female characters in the play end up being punished for what is considered social and sexual transgression.

The next play Castro wrote, *À flor da pele* (Skin Deep; produced 1969, published 1971), was the first of her plays to be produced, and it was received with acclaim and remains her most popular play. *À flor da pele* was even made into an award-winning movie in Brazil. The plot centers exclusively around two characters who expose their innermost conflicts and angst, which is the reason this play is considered an example of the so-called new or porcupine dramaturgy. Castro not only brings to the fore the clash of values between the characters, but she also unveils a deeper critique of their political and social circumstances. À flor da pele analyzes the relationship between Marcelo, a theater teacher and playwright who now only writes for television soap operas, and his younger lover, Verônica, a brilliant but unstable actress. The entire play is an endless confrontation between the lovers, punctuated by accusations and verbal abuse from both sides. In the play Castro explores a generation gap and issues of personal choice, the role of the writer, and the woman's position in contemporary society. Verônica exposes Marcelo by revealing their affair to his wife and daughter, and she questions his conformity to the status quo by criticizing the mediocrity of his recent work. In contrast, Marcelo, who obviously wants things to remain as they are, accuses her of being a hysteric and a rebel without a clear and reasonable cause. As in À prova de fogo, the ending of À flor da pele brings the demise of the female character–Verônica, like Ophelia, the character she is supposed to play, ends up killing herself.

O porco ensangüentado (The Bloody Pig; published, 1978) was written in 1972, and, despite receiving an award in 1974 from SNT, it was only produced in 1975 after several cuts by censors. The play is primarily about women and the role of marriage in society. The five female characters around which the play revolves provide a vivid portrayal of the alienation with which women are faced, many of them living solely in the shadow of their husbands and showing a frivolous or hypocritical outlook on life. These women are unable to develop any kind of bond or solidarity among themselves and are forced to deal with competition, rivalry, and violence. In the play Castro reveals the bleak side of human relationships, focusing on how women fail to interact with each other, how society fosters their alienation, and how they take a destructive path in their social dealings.

Caminho de volta (1974, Path of Return; published, 1976), like À flor da pele, was produced in the same year it was written, and it was received with great acclaim from the public and critics. This play focuses on individual aspirations and alienation in capitalist society. Marisa da Penha sees a sudden change in her social life when she begins to work for an advertising agency. Trying to shed her misery and shake up the status quo, Marisa does not hesitate to prostitute herself to help the company get an account from a customer. Here Castro draws from her experience working in the advertising industry to portray the hypocrisy of the workplace. She continues to show her concern with the lives of women and their lack of options for a better life in a repressive, consumer-oriented society. Cabecinha, Marisa's boyfriend from the poor suburb where she once lived,

seems at first to be the only character with some sense of morality. He reveals in the end, however, a deeply ingrained sexist behavior, clearly expressing his belief in the dichotomous division of women into "saints" and "whores." Marisa, on the other hand, remains completely alienated regarding her exploitation. Her only concern is to do whatever is needed so that she does not have to return to the poverty in which she once lived. Her efforts are fruitless, however, because under the circumstances her return home is inevitable.

Castro's next play, A cidade impossível de Pedro Santana (The Impossible Town of Pedro Santana; published, 1978), was written in 1975 and, despite receiving a public reading in 1977 at the Ruth Escobar Theater in São Paulo and a prize from SNT, was censored for its subversive content. It has never been produced in any official way. At this time Castro became extremely frustrated with being awarded prizes from governmental agencies while simultaneously having her plays censored and barred from production. She eventually refused to accept any more prizes from national offices as long as her plays were banned.

In many ways A cidade impossível de Pedro Santana offers the story of O porco ensangüentado from the perspective of the male characters. The central character is Pedro Santana, who has just left the asylum to which he was confined in the earlier play. He is an architect who plans to build an ideal town for workers, but he succumbs to madness as he understands the impossibility of realizing his dream. The play illustrates the ways in which individual ideals and aspirations for a better society are thwarted. Castro also focuses on madness, an issue that she broached in O porco ensangüentado and continued to feature in later works. With the exception of Ordália, the retarded young woman with whom the delusional Pedro gets along, the characters are conniving symbols of their exploitative and duplicitous society.

In O grande amor de nossas vidas (1978, The Great Love of Our Lives; published, 1981) Castro focuses on the family unit for the first time, exploring the living conditions of a dysfunctional family from the lower classes and the hate and violence that dominate the interaction among its members. Above all, the play shows the oppression of the female characters within the family unit, which is a microcosm for social evils. The women are simultaneously the victims of a repressive and stratified society and the ones who maintain the workings of this society. As with several of the female characters in Castro's other plays, the women here are submissive, alienated, and unaware of their exploitation. Also, Castro again reveals her fascination with the theme of madness, which returns in the form of an absent mad son.

Urgência e Ruptura
Consuelo de Castro

313 16

EDITORA PERSPECTIVA   secretaria de estado da cultura.

Title page for the collection of Castro's plays in which she divides her work into two distinct phases ("urgency" and "rupture") reflecting both her growth as a dramatist and the effect of changing censorship policies in Brazil on her plays (Heard Library, Vanderbilt University)

After working with Lauro César Muniz and Jorge Andrade on *A corrente* (1981, The Current), a small play in three acts, or "links," as the writers call them, Castro did not return to drama until 1985 with *Louco circo do desejo* (Mad Ring of Desire; published, 1989). Instead of focusing on the crude reality of Brazilian society, Castro explores love, human relationships, and existential problems in this play. *Louco circo do desejo* marks what Castro calls a "ruptura" (rupture), a break with the cycle of plays she wrote earlier. In a collection of her plays published in 1989, *Urgência e ruptura* (Urgency and Rupture), Castro divides her work into two distinctive phases. *Urgência* (Urgency) includes her initial plays

written between 1968 and 1978: *À prova de fogo, À flor da pele, Caminho de volta,* and *O grande amor de nossas vidas.* These works convey a sense of immediacy and pressure in relation to the social problems in Brazilian society. They also correspond to a period of intense struggle with censorship in the most oppressive years of the military dictatorship in Brazil. On the other hand, the second phase, *Ruptura,* includes the plays written from 1978 to 1988, marking Castro's freedom from censors and featuring her reflections on the social inequalities in Brazil together with a profound existential concern. In this phase Castro begins experimenting with form and distancing herself from the traditional formula of the well-made play composed of exposition, development, and denouement.

In *Louco circo do desejo,* Castro again portrays a relationship between an older man and a younger woman. Fábio is a rich executive, and Selly is a dancer in a strip club and a prostitute. What is supposed to be just a fling becomes a serious love affair that reveals the highly prejudiced society in which the characters live. Fábio finally realizes the futility of his existence but is unable to accommodate Selly in his high-class social environment. This play shows how individuals' compliance with the rules of a socially stratified and prejudiced society hinders their search for happiness.

In Castro's next play, *Ao sol do novo mundo* (1986, Under the Sun of a New World), she returns once more to the old theme of madness as emblematic of the individual's inability to cope with social reality. Like Pedro from *A cidade impossível de Pedro Santana,* Lélio has an impossible dream of a new world. He believes that the earth does not move but rather remains in a state of paralysis—a metaphor that reflects an ingrained conflict between the old and the new, between the freedom to which Lélio aspires and the confines of a conservative society endorsed by his traditional and bourgeois family.

Another work in *Urgência e ruptura, Script-tease,* has never been produced, but it did receive a public reading shortly after it was written in 1985. This play deals with the role of the writer through the portrayal of a woman playwright who has become a conformist scriptwriter for television. She remembers, through action occurring on a different level in the theater, her past as an idealist writer. Another play, *Aviso prévio* (1987; published, 1989; translated as *Walking Papers,* 1988), differs from Castro's others in its innovative portrayal of archetypal representations of characters in which gender roles are blurred. The loose plot explores a variety of apparently disconnected situations.

Marcha a ré (1989, Reverse Gear), a play that exists only in manuscript form, continues Castro's innovation, adding choreography and special staging devices and blending mythical stories with mundane realities. In a similar vein, two other unpublished plays, *Uma caixa de outras coisas* (1986, One Box with Many Other Things), written with Antônio Abujamra, and *O kotô* (1988, The Stump), combine theater and dance in fragmented and episodic structures.

Castro's most recent play, *Only you* (2001), came out after a long hiatus in her career as a playwright, during which time she dedicated herself to human-rights organizations such as the group Tortura Nunca Mais (Torture Never More). *Only you* brings back the conflict between an older man and a younger woman, and the clashes between these characters clearly evoke some of the issues dealt with in *À flor da pele*. Also, as in *Script-tease,* the role of the writer and the importance of social commitment are analyzed. Like Marcelo from *À flor da pele* and Verônica from *Script-tease,* André is a writer who abandons his dream of a career as a playwright and turns to writing scripts for television. Júlia enters his life, however, and forces him to face some of the issues that were once significant for him, reminding him of his political position during the dictatorship and the corruption of his ideals in his life choices.

As several critics have pointed out, Consuelo de Castro's prolific work addresses social and political issues that are relevant in Brazilian society. Her plays have earned for her a prominent place in Brazilian theater, which traditionally has been committed to social change. Castro's work displays a thematic unity that can be traced to her strong commitment to describing the conflicts and contradictions of a repressive society that frustrates the expectations of individuals and suffocates women in a pattern of double oppression on the grounds of gender and class.

References:

Alcides João de Barros, "A situação social de mulher no teatro de Consuelo de Castro e Leilah Assunção," *Latin American Review,* 9, no. 2 (1976): 13–20;

Eliana Goulart Berg, "The Discourse of Cruelty and the Absurd and the Representation of Difference in the Theatre of Women Playwrights in Latin America," dissertation, University of Wisconsin, Madison, 1998;

Judith Bissett, "La revolución y el papel de la mujer en el teatro de Consuelo de Castro y Pilar Campesino," *Latin American Review,* 33, no. 1 (1999): 45–53;

Sábato Magaldi, *Moderna dramaturgia brasileira* (São Paulo: Perspectiva, 1998);

Margo Milleret, "Acting Radical: The Dramaturgy of Consuelo de Castro," in *Latin American Women Dramatists: Theater, Texts and Theories,* edited by Catherine Larson and Margarita Vargas (Bloomington: Indiana University Press, 1998), pp. 89–109;

Renata Pallottini, "A mulher na dramaturgia brasileira," in *Feminino singular: a participação da mulher na literatura brasileira contemporânea,* edited by Nelly Novaes Coelho (São Paulo: Gumercindo Rocha Dorea/Arquivo Municipal de Rio Claro, 1989), pp. 102–121;

Magda Bianchini Cavalcanti e Silva, "Consuelo de Castro and Brazilian Theater in the 1960s and 1970s," dissertation, University of North Carolina at Chapel Hill, 2000;

Elza Cunha Vincenzo, *Um teatro de mulher: dramaturgia feminina no palco brasileiro contemporâneo* (São Paulo: Editora de Universidade de São Paulo/Perspectiva, 1998).

Antônio de Castro Alves

(14 March 1847 – 6 July 1871)

Mark A. Lokensgard
St. Mary's University of San Antonio

BOOKS: *Espumas flutuantes* (Salvador: C. de Lellis Masson, 1870);

Gonzaga ou A revolução de Minas (Rio de Janeiro: A. A. da Cruz Coutinho, 1875);

A cachoeira de Paulo Afonso (Salvador: Imprensa Econômica, 1876);

Vozes d'Africa: navio negreiro (Rio de Janeiro: S. J. Alves, 1880);

Os escravos (Rio de Janeiro: S. J. Alves, 1883);

Ultimas estrofes (Salvador: Diário da Bahia, 1895);

Correspondência e crítica, edited, with a preface, by Alfredo Mariano de Oliveira (Rio de Janiero: H. Antunes, 1920);

Consuelo, de Castro Alves, seguida de linha cançonetas, monólogos, lundús, recitativos, modinhas . . . (São Paulo: Casa Endrizzi, n.d.).

Editions and Collections: *Obras completas de Castro Alves,* 2 volumes, edited by M. Said Ali (Rio de Janeiro: Laemmert, 1898);

Poesias, preface by Homero Pires (Salvador: R. dos Santos, 1913);

Espumas flutuantes: nova edição, correcta e augmentada, edited by Alfredo Mariano de Oliveira (Rio de Janeiro: Garnier, 1919);

Obras completas de Castro Alves, 2 volumes, edited by Afrânio Peixoto (São Paulo: F. Alves, 1921);

Obras completas de Castro Alves, 2 volumes, introduction by Agripino Grieco, biographical essay by Bandeira Duarte (Rio de Janeiro: Z. Valverde, 1943);

Poemas revolucionários, edited, with a preface, by Fernando Góes (São Paulo: Editôra Universitária, 1945);

Poesias escolhidas, edited, with a preface and notes, by Pires (Rio de Janeiro: Nacional, 1947);

Poesias completas, edited by Frederico José da Silva Ramos, introduction by Jamil Almansur Haddad (São Paulo: Saraiva, 1953);

Espumas flutuantes, Vozes d'Africa, Navio negreiro: poesias (Rio de Janeiro: H. Antunes, 1960);

Obra completa, edited, with an introduction, by Eugênio Gomes (Rio de Janeiro: J. Aguilar, 1960);

Antônio de Castro Alves (from Pedro Calmon, Castro Alves: o homem e a obra, *1973; Thomas Cooper Library, University of South Carolina)*

Espumas flutuantes, Navio negreiro, Vozes d'Africa (São Paulo: Edições "O Livreiro," 1962);

Poemas escolhidos de Castro Alves, edited, with a preface, by Haddad (São Paulo: Cultrix, 1967);

Poesias completas: Espumas flutuantes, Os escravos, A cachoeira de Paulo Afonso, Poesias diversas, preface by Manuel Bandeira (Rio de Janeiro: De Ouro, 1969);

Espumas flutuantes, facsimile edition (Salvador: Instituto Nacional do Livro, 1970);

Antologia póetica, edited by Gomes and Hildon Rocha, critical and bibliographic essay by Gomes (Rio de Janeiro: Aguilar, 1971);

Espumas flutuantes, edited, with an introduction, by Ivo Barbieri (Rio de Janeiro: Editora Expressão e Cultura, 1974);

Castro Alves, edited by Marisa Lajolo and Samira Campedelli (São Paulo: Abril, 1980);

Os melhores poemas de Castro Alves, edited by Lêdo Ivo (São Paulo: Global, 1983);

Castro Alves: antologia poética, edited by Maria Chaves de Mello, critical essays by Fernando Whitaker da Cunha and J. Galdino (Rio de Janeiro: Barrister's, 1987);

Os escravos, facsimile of 1921 *Obras completas de Castro Alves* edition (Rio de Janeiro: F. Alves, 1988);

Canto da esperança: poesia social, libertária e lírica, edited, with an introduction and notes, by Rocha (Rio de Janeiro: Nova Frontera, 1990);

Melhores poesias, edited by Célia A. N. Passoni (São Paulo: Núcleo, 1996);

Antologia poética, edited by Antônio Carlos Secchin (Rio de Janeiro: Ministério da Cultura, Funatre, 1997);

Castro Alves: poesias, edited by Maria da Graça Mascarenhas (Rio de Janeiro: Oderbrecht / Brasília: Fundação Banco do Brasil, 1997);

Poesias de Castro Alves: antologia comentada, edited by Lizir Arcanjo Alves (Salvador: Secretaria da Cultura e Turismo do Estado da Bahia, Fundação Cultural do Estado, 1997);

Espumas flutuantes e Os escravos, edited by Luiz Dantas and Pablo Simpson (São Paulo: Martins, 2000).

Editions in English: *Navio negreiro,* translated by Karl-Heinz Hansen (Salvador: Progresso, 1959);

The Major Abolitionist Poems, edited and translated, with an introduction, by Amy A. Peterson, World Literature in Translation, no. 5 (New York: Garland, 1990).

Antônio de Castro Alves is widely considered to embody two important tendencies of his era: the liberal, republican mentality that made him a vociferous abolitionist, and a dramatic, occasionally melodramatic tendency in his poetry typical of the youthful energy and idealism of the Romantics. His life is also widely seen as fitting the Romantic mold, with his passionate loves and his untimely death at age twenty-four. Known as the "cantor dos escravos" (poet of the slaves) because of his unwavering opposition to slavery and his use of African and Afro-Brazilian themes in his poetry, Alves is widely read in Brazil. In 1971 commemorations throughout the country marked the centennial of his

death. He died before the founding of the Brazilian Academy of Letters, which made him the patron of its seventh academic chair.

Antônio Frederico de Castro Alves was born on 14 March 1847 on the Cabaceiras ranch in the region of Cachoeira in the state of Bahia. His parents were Antônio José Alves, a physician, and Clélia Brasília da Silva de Castro Alves, daughter of José Antônio da Silva Castro, one of the heroes in the Bahian struggle for independence. His father had moved to the interior of the state for health reasons; ill health and madness were recurring themes in the poet's life and family. Castro Alves's oldest sibling, José Antônio, who showed great promise as a poet, suffered from mental illness and died at the age of eighteen. A younger brother, Guilherme, born in 1852 and also a promising poet, suffered similarly and died in 1887.

Castro Alves's first published poem, "A destruição de Jerusalém" (The Destruction of Jerusalem), appeared in the *Jornal do Recife* in 1862. Written in the same Romantic style Castro Alves was to use throughout his life, the poem details the fall of the Holy City to Nebuchadnezzar, when the Jews failed to heed the warnings of the prophet Jeremiah. The prophet is scorned and derided by the city, which falls because its corruption and wickedness provoked God's wrath. "A destruição de Jerusalém" may be understood as a kind of commentary on how Castro Alves saw his role in society. As an abolitionist he acted as a kind of prophet, warning Brazil of the evils it continued to perpetuate by allowing slavery and trying to prevent the moral and spiritual collapse of the country.

Castro Alves's plans for law school were soon thwarted when, owing to a failing grade in geometry, he was allowed to enroll only as an auditor. As a poet, however, he began to become more known; more of his work began to appear in both student publications and well-known periodicals. His first abolitionist poem, "A canção do africano" (The African's Song), was published on 17 May 1863 in *A primavera* (The Spring), an academic journal. Centering on a slave couple housed in miserable quarters with their infant son, it is a somewhat sentimental poem that lacks the emotional and rhetorical force of Castro Alves's later abolitionist verse. The inferiority of the poem may explain why he left it out of a later plan for his book *Os escravos* (1883, The Slaves). In his 1921 edition of Castro Alves's works, *Obras completas de Castro Alves* (Complete Works of Castro Alves), critic Afrânio Peixoto included "A canção do africano" as part of *Os escravos* on historical and thematic grounds.

The year 1863 also marked the stage debut of the Portuguese actress Eugênia Câmara in Recife. Castro Alves was not intimidated by the fact that she was his

GONZAGA

OU

A REVOLUÇÃO DE MINAS

Drama historico brazileiro

POR

A. DE CASTRO ALVES

Precedido de uma carta do Exm. Sr. Conselheiro José de
Alencar e de outra do Illm. Sr. Machado de Assis

RIO DE JANEIRO
NA LIVRARIA DO EDITOR
A. A. DA CRUZ COUTINHO
75   Rua de S. José   75
1875

Reprodução do frontespicio da edição original do *Gonzaga*.

*Title page for the first edition of Castro Alves's play, first performed
in 1867, about the Inconfidência Mineira (Minas Conspiracy), an
eighteenth-century revolt in the state of Minas Gerais
against Portuguese rule (Homer Babbidge Library,
University of Connecticut)*

senior by ten years and began a passionate relationship with her that lasted five years. Several of his poems—"A uma atriz" (To an Actress), "A Eugênia Câmara," and "A atriz Eugênia Câmara"—are explicitly dedicated to her; many others were probably inspired by her, and Câmara also proved to be an inspiration to Castro Alves's work as a playwright.

In October 1864 Castro Alves began to feel pulmonary weakness, the first signs of tuberculosis. He composed the poem "O tísico" (The Consumptive) at this time, later changing the title to "Mocidade e morte" (Youth and Death). He finally managed to enter law school the following year, and he began to find public success with his recitation and publication of "O século" (The Century). This poem was Castro Alves's first clear expression in verse of *condoreirismo,* the belief in a common destiny for Latin America that took the Andean condor as a unifying symbol. The poem exalts José Bonifácio de Andrada e Silva, one of the architects of Brazilian independence, as well as Benito Juárez of

Mexico, linking them in the struggle to create a just political order in the Americas.

Castro Alves showed his willingness to fight for his belief beyond debates by enlisting, along with many other students, in a volunteer battalion that was to be sent to fight in the War of the Triple Alliance. Argentina, Brazil, and Uruguay had agreed to fight Paraguay in May 1865, after disputes over territory and the seizure by Paraguay of a Brazilian ship. Castro Alves became the unofficial spokesman for the young idealists, giving a public recital in Recife of his poem "Aos estudantes voluntários" (To the Student Volunteers). The victory by Brazilian troops in Uruguaiana in September, however, seemed decisive, and the volunteer troops were never sent. The war dragged on, nevertheless, for another five years, provoking much internal debate and unrest in Brazil. Castro Alves participated actively in these political debates, most notably clashing with the poet and activist Tobias Barreto in 1866 about the war with Paraguay and other issues. Castro Alves also continued working on his poems for *Os escravos.*

In September 1866 Castro Alves recited "Pedro Ivo." The hero of the poem is Pedro Ivo Veloso da Silveira, the leader of the Revolução Praieira, a liberal revolt in 1848 in Pernambuco that culminated in an attack on Recife. Ivo was defeated in this uprising, one of many that hampered the first decade of governance for the emperor, Dom Pedro II. Castro Alves's lionizing of Ivo further raised his profile as the voice of Brazil's youthful and liberal elite, longing for the establishment of a republic. In hindsight, "Pedro Ivo" proved to be prophetic when one considers that the poet declares that his glance is fixed on "Oitenta e Nove" (eighty-nine), which refers to the year of the French Revolution in the previous century but could also be the corresponding year of the nineteenth century, when the republic of Brazil was finally established.

Republican and liberal ideals continued to grow in importance in Castro Alves's writings from this time until his death. In May 1867 he traveled with Câmara to Bahia with the idea of producing the play he had finished the year before, *Gonzaga ou A revolução de Minas* (1875, Gonzaga or the Revolution of Minas). The play deals with the Inconfidência Mineira, a thwarted eighteenth-century attempt at independence in Minas Gerais that today is viewed as the first act of separatist activity in Brazil. The death of one of the main participants, Tiradentes, is commemorated annually on 21 April.

While working to produce the play, Castro Alves's other works gained him further fame as the poetic champion of liberal ideas. He read his poem "Ode ao dous de julho" (Ode to July Second) in Salvador on 2 July 1867. This poem commemorates in epic

Undated self-portrait by Castro Alves (frontispiece for Pedro Calmon, Castro Alves: o homem e a obra, *1973; Thomas Cooper Library, University of South Carolina)*

terms the declaration of the Confederation of the Equator in 1824. Progressive thinkers in Bahia, later joined by separatists in Rio Grande do Norte, Ceará, and Paraíba, formed the confederation in an attempt to break away from the empire of Brazil, rejecting the constitution of 1824 that had established a constitutional monarchy and a small, elite electorate in the country. Castro Alves thus also carried on family ideals; his maternal grandfather, José Antônio da Silva Castro, had been one of the heroes of this unsuccessful attempt to found a republic. At his recitation of "Ode ao dous de julho" in the São João Theater, Castro Alves was hailed with great applause.

The following month, in the same theater, Câmara read Castro Alves's "O livro e a América" (The Book and America). In this poem he foresees a great future for the continent, linking together two pivotal events of the fifteenth century, the first voyage of Christopher Columbus and the invention of the printing press by Johannes Gutenberg. Similarly, the poem exalts those who write and produce books, comparing books to seeds in the souls of the nation's people. Finally, on 7 September 1867, the anniversary of Brazil's declaration of independence from Portugal in 1822, *Gonzaga ou A revolução de Minas* received its pre-

miere. Castro Alves was literally crowned with laurels and paraded on the shoulders of the public.

Castro Alves sought greater recognition for his play, which could only be had only in the larger cities of the south. In February 1868 he and Câmara left Bahia for Rio de Janeiro. There he read his play to the writer José de Alencar, who wrote favorably of the work to the author Joaquim Maria Machado de Assis. Machado's open letter of response to Alencar, published in the *Correio mercantil,* convinced the *Diário do Rio de Janeiro* to host a reading by Castro Alves for an audience of journalists, intellectuals, and politicians. Despite the positive reaction, he was unable to get the play produced in the city.

Castro Alves had better luck in São Paulo, where he was able to convince one of the premier actors in Brazil, Joaquim Augusto, to take the lead role, that of the revolutionary Tiradentes. Castro Alves went so far as to publish the poem "Ao ator Joaquim Augusto" (To the Actor Joaquim Augusto) in October 1868 as part of the campaign. Finally, the securing of funding from the baron of Iguape for Câmara's acting company for the São Paulo production meant that the play would go on. Several performances were given to applause and critical acclaim, even from the politically conservative *Diário*

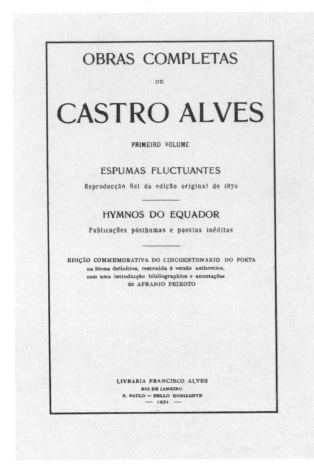

OBRAS COMPLETAS
DE
CASTRO ALVES

PRIMEIRO VOLUME

ESPUMAS FLUCTUANTES
Reproducção fiel da edição original de 1870

HYMNOS DO EQUADOR
Publicações pósthumas e poesias inéditas

EDIÇÃO COMMEMORATIVA DO CINCOENTENARIO DO POETA
na fórma definitiva, restituida á versão authentica,
com uma introducção bibliographica e annotações
de AFRANIO PEIXOTO

LIVRARIA FRANCISCO ALVES
RIO DE JANEIRO
S. PAULO — BELLO HORIZONTE
— 1921 —

*Title page for the first volume of the commemorative edition,
published fifty years after the author's death, of Castro
Alves's complete works (Homer Babbidge Library,
University of Connecticut)*

de São Paulo. Castro Alves's fame and standing increased, and he was warmly received in São Paulo by such contemporaries as Rui Barbosa, Joaquim Nabuco, and Carlos Ferreira.

Shortly after this time, however, Castro Alves's fortunes took a downturn. His relationship with Câmara ended. Most likely as a result, he lost interest in reading and began to write only sporadically. His physical health suffered next: having taken up hunting, he suffered an unfortunate accident on one outing and wounded himself in the left foot, requiring amputation and leaving him weak. He returned to Bahia in 1869 suffering further from tuberculosis but carrying the manuscript for his only book to be published in his lifetime, *Espumas flutuantes* (1870, Floating Foam). In 1870, in considerably worse health, he returned to the *sertão,* the Brazilian backlands of his childhood, in the hope that its purer air would aid his recovery.

Espumas flutuantes shows considerable diversity in poetic genres. As Ivo Barbieri has noted in his 1974

critical edition of the collection, the poems range from photograph-like description ("Immensis orbibus anguis") to abstract allegory ("A meu irmão Guilherme de Castro Alves" [To My Brother Guilherme de Castro Alves]); from fantastic narratives ("O hóspede" [The Guest]) to the bucolic ("Aves de arribação" [Birds of Passage]); and from dramatic epic ("O adeus de Teresa" [Teresa's Farewell]) to burlesque ("Canção do boêmio" [The Bohemian's Song]). Nevertheless, certain themes emerge, such as the figure of the antihero, doomed to a life outside of society and its acceptance because of the individuality of his vision. Similarly, even among poems that vary widely in purpose, disparate elements are linked by metaphor; an element is given, followed by a proposed key to understanding the first element: a storm is a galloping charger, a ship is a cemetery, and so forth.

As his health deteriorated, Castro Alves did as his father before him had done and went to the interior of the state, for the drier air of the backlands. The town to which he traveled now bears his name. Around the end of 1870, his health improved somewhat, and he returned to Salvador, where he read "A Cachoeira de Paulo Afonso" (1876, Paulo Afonso's Waterfall) to his poet and journalist friends. The poem was the first in a series that was published posthumously as a fragment of *Os escravos.* Many of Castro Alves's poems have themes of rivers and waterfalls, inspired by the period of his childhood spent in São Félix, a small town beside the Paraguaçu River in Bahia. Both praise for the beauty of the region and denunciation of the injustice of slavery are common topics for the poems of this book, as seen from some titles: "Na margem" (On the Bank), "O nadador" (The Swimmer), "O barco" (The Boat), "A senzala" (The Slave Quarters), "Sangue de africano" (African Blood), and "História de um crime" (Story of a Crime).

In Salvador, Castro Alves fell in love with Agnese Trinci Murri, an opera singer originally from Florence who had been hired as his sisters' voice teacher. Several poems, starting with "A violeta" (The Violet), are dedicated to her. His last recitation was of his "No 'Meeting du Comité du Pain'" (At the "Meeting of the Bread Committee"). This poem calls for the people of the New World to rise up and throw off oppression. The poet sees that the original ideals of the French Revolution and of the Enlightenment have weakened in the face of tyranny, and he appeals to France to continue to live up to those ideals, symbolized in bread for the poor.

Sensing that his life was drawing to a close, in May 1871 Castro Alves wrote "Virgem dos últimos amores" (Virgin of Last Loves). The verses include echoes of Antônio Gonçalves Dias's Indianist poem "I-

Juca-Pirama" (1851). In both the hero is a native Brazilian warrior who has been captured by an enemy tribe and is to be sacrificed. Dias's hero proves his courage and is deemed worthy of being sacrificed, thus redeeming himself in his father's eyes. Castro Alves focuses on the custom of granting a worthy prisoner of war a bride before his execution, and his hero is thus granted a final, bittersweet love before his death.

Castro Alves's illness finally proved too great, and he died at the age of twenty-four on 6 July 1871. His early death did not end public interest in his work. On the contrary, it helped to solidify his image as young, energetic, and idealistic. All of his books, with the exception of *Espumas flutuantes,* were published posthumously. Occasionally, this publication history has led to disagreements on the organization and exact transcription of his poems among various editors and compilers, but these disagreements have proven to be minor and no impediment to his veneration.

Antônio de Castro Alves's image is actually much as he wished it be: the talented poet was also a respectable artist, producing drawings and some oil paintings in the course of his short life. One of the most reproduced images of Castro Alves is, in fact, his self-portrait. For Brazilians, he remains one of their best-loved and most celebrated poets, representing to them the youthful and dynamic aspects of their nation.

Letters:

Correspondência, ineditos e dispersos (Salvador: Progresso, 1956).

References:

Norlândio Meirelles de Almeida, *Polêmica em torno de uma poesia de Castro Alves* (São Paulo: Pannartz, 1990);

Vicente de Azevedo, *O poeta da liberdade: Castro Alves* (São Paulo: Clube do Livro, 1971);

Frederico Pessoa de Barros, *Poesia e vida de Castro Alves* (São Paulo: Editora das Américas, 1962);

Alfredo Bosi, *História concisa da literatura brasileira,* third edition (São Paulo: Cultrix, 1981);

Pedro Calmon, *Castro Alves: o homem e a obra* (Rio de Janeiro: J. Olympio, 1973);

Calmon, ed., *Para conhecer melhor Castro Alves* (Rio de Janeiro: Bloch, 1974).

Marina Colasanti
(26 September 1937 –   )

Susan Canty Quinlan
University of Georgia

BOOKS: *Eu sozinha* (Rio de Janeiro: Record, 1968);

Nada na manga, introduction by Fausto Cunha (Rio de Janeiro: Nova Fronteira, 1973);

Zooilógico: mini contos fantásticos (Rio de Janeiro: Imago, 1975);

A morada do ser (Rio de Janeiro: F. Alves, 1978);

Uma idéia toda azul (Rio de Janeiro: Nórdica, 1979);

A nova mulher (Rio de Janeiro: Nórdica, 1980);

Mulher daqui pra frente (Rio de Janeiro: Nórdica, 1981);

Doze reis e a moça no labirinto do vento (Rio de Janeiro: Nórdica, 1982);

E por falar em amor (Rio de Janeiro: Salamandra, 1984);

A menina arco-íris (Rio de Janeiro: Rocco, 1984);

Uma estrada junto ao rio (São Paulo: Cultrix, 1985);

O lobo e o carneiro no sonho da menina (São Paulo: Cultrix, 1985);

Contos de amor rasgados (São Paulo: Círculo do Livro, 1986);

O verde brilha no poço (São Paulo: Melhoramentos, 1986);

O imaginário a dois: textos escolhidos, by Colasanti and Affonso Romano de Sant'Anna (Rio de Janeiro: Art Bureau, 1987);

Um amigo para sempre (São Paulo: Quinteto, 1988);

Aqui entre nós (Rio de Janeiro: Rocco, 1988);

Ofélia, a ovelha (São Paulo: Melhoramentos, 1989);

Será que tem asas? (São Paulo: Quinteto, 1989);

Intimidade pública (Rio de Janeiro: Rocco, 1990);

A mão na massa (Rio de Janeiro: Salamandra, 1990);

Agosto 1991: estávamos em Moscou, by Colasanti and Sant'Anna (São Paulo: Melhoramentos, 1991);

Entre a espada e a rosa (Rio de Janeiro: Salamandra, 1992);

Ana Z. aonde vai você? (São Paulo: Ática, 1993);

Rota de colisão (Rio de Janeiro: Rocco, 1993);

Um amor sem palavras (São Paulo: Melhoramentos, 1995);

De mulheres sobre tudo (Rio de Janeiro: Ediouro, 1995);

O homem que não parava de crescer (Rio de Janeiro: Ediouro, 1995);

Eu sei, mas não devia (Rio de Janeiro: Rocco, 1996);

Longe como o meu querer (São Paulo: Ática, 1997);

Marina Colasanti (frontispiece for the second edition of Zooilógico: mini contos fantásticos, *1985; Thomas Cooper Library, University of South Carolina)*

Gargantas abertas (Rio de Janeiro: Rocco, 1998);

O leopardo é um animal delicado (Rio de Janeiro: Rocco, 1998);

Um espinho de marfim e outras histórias (Pôrto Alegre: L & PM, 1999);

Cada bicho seu capricho (São Paulo: Global, 2000);

Esse amor de todos nós (Rio de Janeiro: Rocco, 2000);

O menino que achou uma estrela (São Paulo: Global, 2000);

Penélope manda lembranças (São Paulo: Ática, 2001);

A casa das palavras, e outras crônicas (São Paulo: Ática, 2002).

RECORDING: *A moça tecelã e outras histórias,* read by Colasanti, Luz da Cidade LCJ002, 2000.

TRANSLATIONS: Konrad Lorenz, *Civilização e pecado: os oito erros capitais do homem* (Rio de Janeiro: Artenova, 1974);

Alberto Moravia, *A romana* (São Paulo: Abril, 1982).

To understand contemporary women's writing in Brazil, one needs to be aware of the writing of Marina Colasanti; throughout her essay-writing career she has been a spokeswoman for the cultural transformation that has occurred since the late 1960s in Brazil. She has been steadfast in her struggle for gender parity and women's rights and remains outspokenly feminist in her outlook and thinking. Colasanti has also contributed greatly to the development and recognition of quality children's literature in Brazil. Like many intellectuals of her generation, her artistic and philosophical expression has taken many forms.

Marina Colasanti was born on 26 September 1937 in Asmara, Eritrea, at that time an Italian colony. Her parents were Manfredo Colasanti, an Italian and Brazilian stage and screen actor, and Elisa del Bone Colasanti. The family moved to Libya in 1938 and then to Livorno, Italy, at the beginning of World War II. In 1948 they immigrated to Brazil. Colasanti was raised in the Arpoador section of Ipanema, Rio de Janeiro, along with her brother, Arduíno, a world-champion long-board surfer and occasional movie star. She studied painting with Catarina Baratelle from 1952 to 1958, when she began showing her artwork in various galleries and salons throughout Brazil. In 1960 she began her formal studies at the Escola Nacional de Belas Artes (National School for Fine Arts) in Rio de Janeiro. Studying under the direction of Orlando da Silva, a master printmaker, Colasanti concentrated on metal engraving and also taught portraiture and etching.

Colasanti's career can be divided into several overlapping stages that demonstrate her knowledge and creativity on many artistic levels. Today she is best known as a writer in a genre she helped to invent, the *micro conto* or *mini conto* (microtext or minitext), works consisting of one or two short paragraphs of fiction. She also writes children's fables that appeal to both children and adults. Colasanti is also one of the foremost essayists on contemporary women's issues in Brazil and is an acclaimed feminist. She has had a long career as a journalist and television personality as well as that of a painter and illustrator. The many facets of Colasanti's life underscore her multiple influences on the cultural and social fabric of Brazilian life, not only for the cultural elite but also for the underprivileged and working classes.

In 1962 Colasanti joined the editorial staff of *Caderno B,* the arts section of the *Jornal do Brasil,* for which she wrote columns, *crônicas* (chronicles—short, semifictitious vignettes of daily life), and book reviews. She also worked as an illustrator and edited the children's section of the paper. She maintained her collaboration with this important newspaper until 1994 as a writer and illustrator. During the late 1960s and early 1970s Colasanti edited the weekly magazine *Segundo tempo,* a feature of the *Jornal dos esportes,* and wrote for such magazines as *Senhor, Fatos e fotos, Ele e ela, Fairplay, Claúdia,* and *Joía.* In 1968 she published her first book, *Eu sozinha* (By Myself), a semi-autobiographical series of short, contemplative pieces written in the form of a diary expressing the despair and loneliness of a single woman in a large city. In 1971 Colasanti married the writer Affonso Romano de Sant'Anna, with whom she had two daughters, Fabiana and Alessandra.

Colasanti's second book of short stories, *Nada na manga* (1973, Nothing Up My Sleeve), reflects the structure of *Eu sozinha.* Both books narrate experiences of censorship and self-censorship and of feeling silenced and invisible. In *Eu sozinha* the reader finds one of Colasanti's best-known quotes, repeated frequently in feminist studies on Brazilian women's literature: "Quem disse que não podia? Fui eu, é claro. Sou sempre eu quem diz as coisas contra, de medo da esperança. Porque às vezes penso que se esperasse tudo a que tenho direito, não agüentaria o impacto, por pura falta de costume" (Who said I couldn't? I did, of course. It is always I who speaks in contradictions, who is afraid of hope. Because sometimes I think that if I expressed everything I had a right to, I would not be able to stand the impact [of my words] for lack of experience).

Colasanti's writing style, controlled and objective rather than passionate and emotional, allows for scathing critiques of personal suffering. These characteristics of her style are most likely derived from her work in journalism. From her earliest publications, during the Brazilian military dictatorship of the late 1960s and early 1970s, Colasanti's self-reflective style allowed her works to slip past the censor's eye even though they promoted social change. Middle-class women in particular were beginning to question the status quo, especially after the first United Nations global conference on women's rights, held in Mexico City in 1975. Brazilian women were facing the prospect of returning to the workforce in order to combat the steady decline in earnings because of the end of the "economic miracle" that occurred after the worldwide oil crisis of 1974 and the accompanying rise in inflation. Brazil at this time was entering a new, somewhat uncertain phase, and Colasanti began to shape new game plans to help explain the uncharted directions women's lives were taking. In the 1970s and 1980s her essays and chronicles spoke to this new order. In an unpublished 1996 interview she stated,

> I would publish short informational pieces on breast cancer, reproductive alternatives, rape counseling, discriminatory practices in the work place, women's nutritional needs and the like in short stories or short articles written in a simple clear language published in women's magazines like *Nova* or *Cláudia.* I was hoping to educate those lower class women in the public health care system about the options available to them and to assure readers that they could take control of their own lives.

Many middle-class Brazilians left these magazines for their maids or housekeepers. In addition, they were found in beauty salons and doctors' offices throughout Brazil.

With the publication of *Zooilógico: mini contos fantásticos* (Illogical Zoo: Fantastic Minitexts) in 1975, Colasanti broke new ground with her minitexts or mini-*crônicas.* The book is structured around animals, animal activities, and the art of writing. Chapter titles include "O leão" (The Lion), "O tigre" (The Tiger), and "O camelo" (The Camel), as well as "História com princípio meio e fim" (A Story with a Beginning, Middle, and End) and "História só com princípia e fim" (A Story with Just a Beginning and End). Thematically elaborating the texts is the job of the reader as well as the author. The story "O circo" (The Circus) provides an example:

> Todos se surpreenderam com a chegada do homen barbudo que escreveu Circo em folhas grandes de papel e as colocou nos quatro cantos da sala. Mas a surpresa transformou-se em pânico quando os leões entraram e, sob o chicote do barbudo, acabaram com a festa.

> (Everyone was surprised with the arrival of the bearded man who wrote Circus on huge sheets of paper and hung them in the four corners of the room. Nevertheless, surprise gave way to panic when the lions entered and, in time to the beat of the bearded man's whip, ended the party.)

"Circus" illustrates the process of filling in meaning on levels that are either collective or based on personal experiences. Is the bearded man a metaphor for the military government? Is he symbolic of the universal male oppressor? Is the image of the circus an inverted notion of fun, or does it recall the idea of ancient Roman circuses, places of emotional and actual slaughter? The possibilities of multiple meanings are vast and enriching.

From 1975 until 1982 Colasanti worked as an editor for the advertising agency Agência Estructural, responsible for creating advertising campaigns in the media of television, radio, and magazines. She won more than twenty advertising awards for her work at this agency. In 1976 she joined the publishing house Editora Abril, where she served as an editor at large for more than eighteen years, working mostly on the magazine *Nova,* the most widely read women's magazine in Brazil. She remained at Abril until 1992, after serving briefly as the editor of *Cláudia* and earning three journalistic prizes. Colasanti began appearing on television in 1977 as an editor and newscaster for the program *Primeira Mão* (Firsthand) on TV Rio, as an interviewer for the program *Olho por Olho* (Eye to Eye) on TV Tupi, and as an editor and newscaster for the cultural program *Os mágicos* (The Magicians) on TVE Brasil.

Colasanti's next book, *A morada do ser* (1978, The Dwelling of the Self), is based on the Heideggerian idea that language is the dwelling of the soul. Language becomes an architectonic structuring principle throughout the stories. The actual edifice of the book consists of apartment numbers rather than chapters, with entries into the lives of multiple protagonists struggling to survive in a hostile urban environment. Most notable in this work is the use of the fantastic, which serves to demonstrate the uselessness of words in understanding the human soul. This refined use of fantasy points to the unparalleled success of Colasanti's books of fairy tales, the first of which was published soon after *A morada do ser.*

Apart from her adult fiction, Colasanti has published several books of fairy tales, which have been the most frequently translated of her works and have received many national and international prizes. *Uma idéia toda azul* (1979, An All Blue Idea) received more than five literary prizes in 1979. Colasanti merges fantasy with reality in order to establish relationships among the different levels of understanding represented by the unconscious, the conscious, and the preconscious. These relationships provide vehicles for the processing of information, reflection, and fantasy in the development of children. Children and, by extension, adults can thereby determine that fantasy and reality are two sides of the same coin; fantasy becomes the vehicle to transform and clarify reality. Fairy tales help to address issues of interior reality and allow for an understanding of problems, if not always solutions to them. Colasanti's fairy tales can be seen as therapeutic for all kinds of readers.

Colasanti's extensive list of children's books is a testament to her concern about transforming gender misunderstandings at an earlier age. Her works express a sensitivity to the notion that in order for change to occur at all levels of society, it must be inclusive and not necessarily demanding. What works for her is the blurring of boundaries between genders and genres, creating a reading public that includes all ages and socioeconomic levels.

Most of Colasanti's nonliterary writing for adult readers has focused on the role of women in modern society. Her female characters often reflect conventional Brazilian value systems that seem to offer plausible solutions for daily conundrums but only pretend to explain why women's voices have been seldom heard or understood and how women communicate differently from men. Generally, in the quest to discover their own identities, Colasanti's female characters are confronted with new and challenging experiences far removed from contemporary Brazilian reality. Each of her books demonstrates the work of the chronicler whose task it is to report and question the incidents of daily life, pointing out the inequalities and injustices. In a sense, as Peggy Sharpe notes, Colasanti takes the conventional form of the essay and turns it into a vehicle for change for both the writer and the reader.

In her monthly column "De olho ao precoceito" (Looking at Preconceptions) Colasanti published what some critics have called articles on the pedagogy of hope—a reference to Paulo Freire's 1970 book *Pedagogia do oprimido* (translated as *Pedagogy of the Oppressed,* 1970). These essays, which appeal to the female experience, call into question discussions of gender and the relationship between men and women in an attempt to explain and reconcile their differences. Many of these articles have been published in Colasanti's essay collections, which include *A nova mulher* (1980, The New Woman), *Mulher daqui pra frente* (1981, Woman from Now On), *E por falar em amor* (1984, And Speaking about Love), and *Aqui entre nós* (1988, Here Between Us).

Colasanti's essays are based primarily on the idea that Brazilian women are subjects, not objects, in a state of transition, moving rapidly toward redefining their social, cultural, and political spaces. One of her most common themes involves the notion of collective female experiences resulting from gender oppression. Colasanti's ideas are not necessarily essentialist; she is cognizant of her own upper-middle-class origins and intellectual background. She does not attempt to impose her own experiences as a norm but rather tries to find a collective commonality that will speak across socio-economic, racial, and gender barriers. She tries to reach women at all social levels in Brazil. She speaks, however, from her own experience and acknowledges that identity construction is a fluid process that is always in a state of regeneration.

Colasanti's work in television continued in the 1980s and 1990s. In 1982 she wrote a screenplay,

Front cover of the second edition, published in 1985, of the 1975 collection in which Colasanti introduced her mini contos, works of fiction only one or two paragraphs long (Thomas Cooper Library, University of South Carolina)

Crescendo em amor e guerra (Growing in Love and War), for the critically acclaimed and award-winning *telenovela* (Brazilian prime-time soap opera) *Malu mulher,* broadcast on the Globo television network. She served as the anchor for the movie program *Sábado forte* from 1985 to 1988. From 1992 to 1993 she was the host of the program *Imagens da Itália* (Images of Italy), sponsored by the Istituto Italiano di Cultura (Italian Institute of Culture) and shown on TVE Brasil.

In 1985 Colasanti was nominated to the Conselho Nacional dos Direitos da Mulher (National Council for the Rights of Women). She also served on the board of directors of the Paço das Artes museum in São Paulo and was the president of the Associação dos Amigos da Escola de Artes Visuais do Parque Lage (Association of Friends of the Parque Lage School of Visual

Arts) in Rio de Janeiro. Colasanti kept up her journalistic work in this period as well, contributing short stories in 1986 to *Revista Manchete,* a photojournalistic review with articles along the lines of *Life* magazine.

Marina Colasanti's most important contributions to Brazilian literature are her crafting of the minimalist genre of the *micro conto* and her uncompromising stance in support of the voices of women in the formation of the Brazilian literary canon. In her essay "Por que nos perguntamos se existimos?" (Why Do They Ask Us if We Exist?), published in Sharpe's *Entre resistir e identificar-se: para uma teoria da prática da narrativa brasileira de autoria feminina* (1997, Between Resistance and Identity: Toward a Theory of the Practice of Narrative by Brazilian Women Writers), she posits that Brazilian women writers have been strongly influenced by feminism, which allows for a new relationship to the writing process than the one established by male authors. Colasanti possesses an uncanny ability to express her ideas in multiple genres, assuring her place in Brazilian letters as one of the foremost writers of her generation.

References:
Nellie Novaes Coelho, *Dicionário crítica da literature infantil e juvenil brasileira, 1882–1982* (São Paulo: Quiron, 1983), pp. 661–667;

Sylvia Paixão, "Clarice Lispector e Marina Colasanti: Mulheres de jornal," in *Cronistas do Rio,* edited by Beatriz Resende (Rio de Janeiro: J. Olympio, 1995), pp. 99–116;

Loida Pereira Peterson, "Feminine Space in Short Stories of Lídia Jorge, Marina Colasanti and Orlanda Amarílis," dissertation, University of North Carolina at Chapel Hill, 2001;

Susan Canty Quinlan, *The Female Voice in Contemporary Brazilian Narrative* (New York: Peter Lang, 1991), pp. 1–5;

Peggy Sharpe, "Imagens e poder: construindo a obra de Marina Colasanti," in *Entre resistir e identificar-se: para uma teoria da prática da narrativa brasileira de autoria feminina,* edited by Sharpe (Goiânia: UFG / Florianópolis: Editora Mulheres, 1997), pp. 43–55;

Sharpe, "A Tropical Utopia? The Brazilian Fairy Tales of Marina Colasanti," in *Daughters of Restlessness: Women's Literature at the End of the Millennium,* edited by Sabine Coelsch-Foisner, Gerhild Reisner, and Hanna Wallinger (Heidelberg: C. Winter, 1998), pp. 71–79.

João da Cruz e Sousa

(24 November 1861 – 19 March 1898)

Marta Almeida
Yale University

BOOKS: *Trópos e phantasias,* by Cruz e Sousa and Virgílio Várzea (Desterro: Regeneração, 1885);

Broquéis (Rio de Janeiro: Magalhães, 1893);

Missal (Rio de Janeiro: Magalhães, 1893);

Evocações (Rio de Janeiro: Aldina, 1898);

Faróis, edited by Nestor Vítor (Rio de Janeiro: Instituto Profissional, 1900);

Últimos sonetos (Paris: Aillaud, 1905);

Poemas inéditos, editcd, with an introduction and notes, by Uelinton Farias Alves (Florianópolis: Papa-Livro, 1996).

Editions and Collections: *Obras completas,* 2 volumes, introduction and notes by Nestor Vítor (Rio de Janeiro: Anuário do Brasil, 1923, 1924);

Obras, 2 volumes, introduction by Fernando Goés (São Paulo: Cultura, 1943);

Poesias completas de Cruz e Souza, introduction by Tasso da Silveira (Rio de Janeiro: Z. Valverde, 1944; revised edition, Rio de Janeiro: Edições de Ouro, 1965);

Obras poéticas, preface by José Cândido de Andrade Muricy (Rio de Janeiro: Nacional, 1945);

Poesia, edited by Silveira (Rio de Janeiro: AGIR, 1957);

Sonetos da noite, edited by Silveira de Sousa (Florianópolis: Livro de Arte, 1958);

Poemas escolhidos, edited, with an introduction, by Massaud Moises (São Paulo: Cultrix, 1961);

Obra completa, edited, with an introduction and notes, by Andrade Muricy (Rio de Janeiro: J. Aguilar, 1961); revised and updated by Alexei Bueno (Rio de Janeiro: Nova Aguilar, 1995);

Poesia completa (Florianópolis: Fundação Catarinense de Cultura, 1981);

Cruz e Sousa, edited, with a biographical study and notes, by Aguinaldo José Gonçalves (São Paulo: Abril, 1982);

Últimos sonetos, edited by Adriano da Gama Kury, literary study by Julio Castañon Guimarães (Florianópolis: Editora da Universidade Federal de Santa Catarina, 1984);

João da Cruz e Sousa (from David T. Haberly, Three Sad Races, *1983; Thomas Cooper Library, University of South Carolina)*

Missal; Broquéis, edited by Ivan Teixeira (São Paulo: Martins, 1993);

Poesia completa, edited, with an introduction, by Zahidé Lupinacci Muzart (Florianópolis: Fundação Catarinense de Cultura/Fundação Banco do Brasil, 1993);

Cruz e Sousa: melhores poemas, edited by Flávio Aguiar (São Paulo: Global, 1998);

Dispersos: poesia & prosa, edited by Iaponan Soares and Zilma Gesser Nunes (São Paulo: Editora Universidade Estadual Paulista/Giordano, 1998).

For most Brazilian critics the name of the black poet João da Cruz e Sousa is intimately associated with the advent of symbolism in Brazilian literature in 1893. The powerful imagery in his first poems and prose expresses themes reflecting his personal experience, including Catholic faith, racial conflict, and love. Toward the end of Cruz e Sousa's life, when he fell ill from tuberculosis, the tone of his poetry became more somber as he faced the prospect of his approaching death with sadness for the insanity of his beloved wife, anger at his fate, and self-pity for his misery.

João da Cruz e Sousa was born in Desterro (now Florianópolis), in the province of Santa Catarina, on 24 November 1861. His father, Guilherme, was a slave, and his mother, Carolina Eva da Conceição, was a freedwoman who worked as a laundress. The family lived and worked on a farm, where the young and talented boy was taught to read and write by the wife of the owner. Later, the farm owners paid for his schooling; he received the kind of education reserved for the white elite. Cruz e Sousa studied with the German-born naturalist Fritz Müller, who corresponded with Charles Darwin. Müller did not share the dominant view of the time that the black race was intellectually inferior to the white race, a view that Darwin's ideas about natural selection had been distorted to support. Müller saw as much potential and effort in Cruz e Sousa as in any white student.

Cruz e Sousa lived up to the expectations of his teachers. At the age of eight he enjoyed reading, and he wrote and recited poetry during parties at the mansion of the farm owners. After finishing school in 1874, he taught at the Ateneu Provincial Catarinense (Santa Catarina Provincial Academy) and then worked as a journalist. He founded the literary journal *Colombo* and in 1882 joined the staff of the *Tribuna popular.* Cruz e Sousa's intellectual standing, however, did not change his status as an underpaid young black man. Even his friends called him the son of a simian, and his father called him "the man of Darwin."

Cruz e Sousa faced misery and poverty throughout his life. He also experienced a sense of abandonment since his protectors died when he was still a child, leaving him misplaced as a black and unwanted by most of white society. He confronted racism and prejudice in his birthplace when jobs that he was perfectly capable of doing were denied him because the white ruling class could not conceive of having a black man in a position of authority.

In "Psicologia do Feio" (Psychology of the Ugly), from *Broquéis* (1893, Shields), Cruz e Sousa establishes a contrast between blackness and whiteness that comes from the awareness of physical distinctions rather than from prejudice. In a passage about his realization of his identity, which came to him in confronting white men, the awareness of his otherness emerges: "Tu vens exata e diretamente do Darwin, da forma ancestral comum dos seres organizados. . . . Entretanto, eu gosto de ti, ó Feio! Porque és a escalpelante ironia da Formosura . . . porque negas a infalível, a absoluta correção das Formas perfeitas e consagradas . . ." (You come exactly and directly from Darwin, from the ancestral form common to organized beings. . . . And yet, I love you, oh Ugly creature! Because you are the cutting irony of Beauty . . . because you deny the infallible and absolute correction of the perfect and consecrated Forms . . .). What makes Cruz e Sousa's notion of black identity even more remarkable is the fact that the Africa he knew came from books that dealt with North Africa and Egypt, with images of serpents and Nubian princesses. Not until the middle of the twentieth century did historians write accurately about the predominantly Angolan origins of the slaves in Brazil.

Cruz e Sousa's works denouncing racism resemble what has been recently termed testimonial writing. In "Consciência tranquila" (Tranquil Conscience), from "Outras evocações," a section of *Broquéis,* he uses the technique of stream of consciousness to describe the treatment that black women received from their masters. The thoughts are presented as flowing through the mind of the white master: "Mandei afogar. . . . E devo ter algum remorso disso? Por quem? Por quê? Por quem? Meu filho? Como? Feito por um civilizado num bárbaro, num selvagem? Remorso por tão pouco?" (I told her to drown the baby. . . . Should I feel remorse? For whom? Why? For whom? My child? Made by a civilized in a barbarian, in a savage? Remorse for so little?).

In 1884 a representative of the government of Santa Catarina made Cruz e Sousa the public prosecutor of Laguna, but local politicians pressured him and prevented him from accepting the job. It was understood that a white man would not take orders from a black man. In 1885 Cruz e Sousa edited the illustrated newspaper *O moleque* (The Black Boy). The title was given to the paper to challenge the proslavery status of Brazilian society at that time.

During this time Cruz e Sousa took a trip to Rio Grande do Sul, where he had an affair with a blond pianist who figured in his early poetry and prose works, such as "Lenda dos Campos" (Legend of the Fields), from *Missal* (1893). Whiteness was often associated with chaste love, as is seen in the image of "o loiro cadáver branco de uma virgem noiva, morta de amor" (the blond, white body of a maiden who was engaged, and died from love).

In 1890 Cruz e Sousa left Desterro for Rio de Janeiro, only to find that the intellectuals in that city—

namely, the poets of the day, who quickly adopted him and greeted him as the "Black Poet" and the "Black Swan"—did not find much merit in his work. In 1891 he and some friends began publishing a literary journal in Rio de Janeiro. The first issue honored Antônio de Castro Alves on his death. Cruz e Sousa contributed to other magazines with small circulations but never moved to a more stable position in journalism. He felt stigmatized and powerless to change his condition, even though he knew that he was the intellectual equal or even the superior of his bohemian friends in Rio de Janeiro, not to mention those from Santa Catarina, which was a small province at that time.

Cruz e Sousa attempted to explain his relationship with symbolism. As quoted in José Cândido de Andrade Muricy's introduction to *Obra completa* (1961, Complete Works), the poet wrote, "Eu quero me organizar, criar uma nova forma, nem prosa nem verso, outro drama, outra mágica, outro movimento . . ." (I want to get organized, create a new form, neither prose nor verse, another drama, another magic, another movement . . .). Various tendencies ran parallel to symbolism at the end of the nineteenth century, including realism, Parnassianism, and the beginnings of modernism. Eduardo Portella describes Cruz e Sousa's poetry as having traits of the Parnassians' works, in terms of meter and a preference for the sonnet. Unlike other intellectuals, however, the symbolists were not interested in science, progress, or the impact of industrialization, which had left a mark on the realists and Parnassians. The symbolists reacted against materialism and the detachment of science by turning toward more-personal and subjective impressions. Later, with Sigmund Freud's findings demonstrating the power of the unconscious, the ideas of the symbolists gained more ground. French symbolism, especially the works of Charles Baudelaire and Stéphane Mallarmé, had a strong impact on the poetry and poetic prose of Cruz e Sousa.

The characteristics of symbolist writing, according to Afrânio Coutinho, are seen especially in content, tone, the role of the individual, and the specific use of language. The content of symbolist writing is spiritual, mystic, and subconscious. There is a renewed interest in the individual rather than in the universal. The highly poetic tone emphasizes imagination and fantasy. The poet attempts to escape reality, and intuition is cherished more than logic. The language is complex, colorful, and exotic. Cruz e Sousa reveals these traits in his masterpieces, *Broquéis* and *Missal,* both published in 1893, six years after he completed them.

Cruz e Sousa's poetry acquires social significance as the personal story of his ethnic marginality becomes intermingled with his innovative poetic language. In

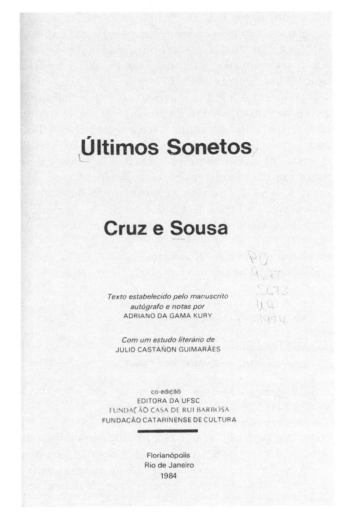

Title page for the scholarly edition of Cruz e Sousa's final poetry collection, originally published posthumously in 1905 (Thomas Cooper Library, University of South Carolina)

"Emparedado" (Walled), from *Broquéis,* he verbalizes his anger against people with racist ideas: "Deus meu! Por uma questão banal da química biológica do pigmento ficam alguns mais rebeldes e curiosos fósseis preocupados, a ruminar primitivas erudições, perdidos e atropelados pelas longas galerias submarinas de uma sabedoria infinita, esmagadora, irrevógavel!" (God of mine! Because of a mere question of the biological chemical of pigment, some rebellious and curious fossils are concerned, ruminating primitive erudition, lost and run over by long-submerged galleries of a wisdom that is infinite, crushing, and unchangeable!).

The Brazilian sociopolitical situation of the final decades of the nineteenth century that culminated in the abolition of slavery in 1888 and the proclamation of the republic in 1891 had a deep impact on Cruz e Sousa. He was acquainted with the work of the major abolitionists, such as Castro Alves and Tobias Barreto. He participated in readings of abolitionist plays and once, during a trip to Bahia, delivered a speech against slavery in such an inflamed way that a spectator (unaware that Cruz e Sousa had never been a slave) was moved to offer him money to buy his freedom. These events seem to confirm that, even if he was not considered an activist in the abolitionist cause, he participated in the movement and shared its ideals. In "Pandemonium," from *Faróis* (1900, Beacons), an abolitionist poem that resembles Castro Alves's "O navio negreiro" (1880, The Slave Ship), there are many references to the terror that slavery created. The description of a woman in the poem is probably an allusion to Cruz e Sousa's own mother, who had been a slave:

Eis que te reconheço escravizada
Divina Mãe, na Dor acorrentada.

Que reconheço a tua boca presa
Pela mordaça de uma sede acesa.

(And I recognize you enslaved
Divine Mother, in your fettered pain.

I recognize your mouth
Closed by the muzzle of a burning thirst.)

"Grito de Guerra" (War Cry), from the posthumously published *Últimos sonetos* (1905, Last Sonnets), is dedicated to the masters who freed their slaves, like the farmer of the plantation where Cruz de Sousa was born.

In 1892 Cruz de Sousa met Gavita Rosa Gonçalves, an educated black woman who worked as a seamstress. She turned out to be the great love of his life and a source of inspiration for his poetry. They married in 1893 and had four children within a short period of time. The family lived in extreme poverty, which seemed to have drained Gavita's energy; she suffered occasional bouts of insanity. Cruz e Sousa now found himself between two cultures. On the one hand were the African deities that haunted the insane dreams of his beloved Gavita. Unlike many blacks in Brazil, Cruz e Sousa seemed ignorant of the rituals and deities that slaves brought from Africa to Brazil. On the other hand was the religion expressed in his poetry, usually described as ethereal and full of the high aspirations of Catholicism. The wise white men who had first developed his intellect and initiated him into the symbols and myths of Catholicism were the same ones who later segregated him as an adult.

In "Antífona" (Antiphon), from *Broquéis,* a poem dedicated to Gavita, a parallel is drawn between the mystery of the transformation of bread and wine into the flesh and blood of Christ during Communion and Cruz e Sousa's personal transformation from man into poet. This parallel is seen in his plea to the "Infinitos espíritos dispersos" (Infinite and dispersed spirits) to inspire him and help him to create his poetry. The way to this sublime state of attainment, however, is through pain and carnal experience. In *Three Sad Races: Racial Identity and National Consciousness in Brazilian Literature* (1983) David T. Haberly describes four levels of symbolic conflict in Cruz e Sousa's poetry—the celestial, the Catholic, the carnal, and the infernal. "Antífona," considered by many anthologists to be the epitome of Brazilian symbolism, embodies these levels. The celestial is seen in the lines "Ó Formas alvas, brancas, Formas claras / De luares, de neves, de neblinas! . . ." (Oh, white, alabaster Forms, bright Forms / of moonlights, snows, and mists! . . .); the Catholic, in "Incensos dos turíbulos das aras . . ." (Incense burning on altars . . .); the carnal, in "De carnes de mulher, delicadezas . . ." (Of flesh of women, delicacies . . .); and the infernal, in the lines "Nos turbilhões quiméricos do Sonho / Passe, cantando, ante o perfil medonho / E o tropel cabalístico da Morte . . ." (In the vain whirlwinds of Dream / Let it pass, singing, before the dreaded face / and cabalist hordes of Death . . .). From another perspective, Secchin (1988) finds in Cruz e Sousa a fascination for the body and eroticism in the sense that by denying the carnal instincts, he ends up valuing them.

Cruz e Sousa's use of language is symbolist. He coined new words, as in "Balada dos Loucos" (Ballad of the Insane), from *Broquéis,* in which he describes the continuous mumbling of "barbarian prayers" uttered by his wife during her periods of insanity as derived from witches. The environment surrounding the couple is unfriendly and contaminated by their sadness and his wife's insanity: "Naquela paisagem extravagante parecia passar o calafrio aterrador, a glacial sensação de um hino Negro cantado e dançado agoureiramente por velhas e espectrais feiticeiras nas trevas . . ." (In that fantastic landscape there seems to be a frightening chill, the glacial sensation of a Black hymn sung and danced in a way that predicted something evil by old and ghostly witches in the shadows . . .). The word *agoureiramente* comes from *agouro* (omen, prediction). Cruz e Sousa creates an adverb from a noun, giving the verbs *sing* and *dance* the function of predicting something evil. The adjective *espectral* (spectral, ghostly) is followed by the noun *feiticeiras* (witches), giving the noun a dream-like meaning. The mere presence of the ghostly witches suggests the evil of the "paisagem extravagante" in which he and his wife walk. Cruz e Sousa combines adjectives often used to describe the landscape with two that are not generally used in this context, *envenenada* (poisoned) and *maligna* (malign). In doing so, he provides the surrounding environment with human feelings and emotions: "Essa paisagem rude, bravia, envenenada e maligna" (This rude, wild, poisoned and malign scenery).

Cruz e Sousa combined symbolic language with synesthesia, and, absorbed in his own sensations, he sometimes strengthened his poetic language with onomatopoeia. This use of onomatopoeia can be seen in the humorous "Questão Brocardo" (Question Axiom), from "O livro derradeiro" (The Last Book), part of *Broquéis:*

> –Pife, pufe, pafe, pefe
> Pafe, pefe, pife, pufe–
> A cacholeta no chefe–
> –Pife, pufe, pafe, pefe
> Estoure como um tabefe. . . .
>
> (–Pife, pufe, pafe, pefe
> Pafe, pefe, pife, pufe–
> The blow on the head of the boss–
> –Pife, pufe, pafe, pefe
> Echoes like a slap. . . .)

With the combination of consonants and vowels Cruz e Sousa imitates the sound of slapping someone, in this case, a hated boss. Alliteration is used in "Arte," also from "O livro derradeiro":

> Como eu vibro este verso, esgrimo e torço
> Tu, Artista sereno, esgrime e torce:
> Emprega apenas um pequeno esforço
> Mas sem que a Estrofe a pura idéia force.
>
> (How I tremble [writing] this verse, how I fence and cheer
> You, serene Artist, fence and cheer:
> You employ only a small effort
> But without the Strophe forcing the pure idea.)

Cruz e Sousa portrays the art of creating a poem in terms of the art of fencing, in which one trembles, twists, and forces one's way through. This idea is reinforced by the use of words that include the combination of a vowel and *r* or a consonant and *r*.

When trying to explain the significance of his poetry, Cruz e Sousa referred to the intensity of his feelings toward people, events, and places depicted in his poems. At times he extends his use of symbolism, complicating his work and making it confusing and hermetic. Close readings of his texts, however, reveal that this apparent confusion is usually synthesized into a powerful message. Being a father and a husband gave him a new perspective on blacks. His wife's insanity brought him pain and anxiety that he translated into poetry and prose. Cruz e Sousa wrote some of his best poetry about this new twist of fate in his life, showing how depressed and helpless he felt. Tuberculosis, which

Dust jacket for the 2000 edition of Cruz e Sousa's complete works (Bruccoli Clark Layman Archives)

affected many of the urban poor at that time, ended up destroying him and his family. At the end of his life Cruz e Sousa was in debt, and his family barely survived with the help of friends. His poverty was a blow to his dignity and self-esteem.

The tone of Cruz e Sousa's poems changes in "O livro derradeiro," in which he deals with feelings of humiliation and fear of the illness that eventually took him and his family. More than ever, a world of restlessness and the torment of the soul are present. This conflict between his sensibility and the oppression he felt is shown in the last stanza of "Escárnio Perfumado" (Perfumed Mockery):

> Pois fico só e cabisbaixo, inerme,
> A noite andar-me na cabeça, em roda,
> Mais humilhado que um mendigo, um verme. . . .
>
> (Then I am alone, head down, motionless,
> The night inside my head and around
> More humiliated than a beggar, a worm. . . .)

In 1898 Cruz e Sousa was sent to a sanatorium in the state of Minas Gerais to be treated for tuberculosis. He died on 19 March 1898 from the illness, without ever having seen his last child. His wife succumbed in 1901 to the same disease, as did all his children eventually. Cruz e Sousa owes the preservation and diffusion of his work to his friend Nestor Vítor, who edited *Faróis* and *Últimos sonetos* and compiled *Obras completas* (1923, 1924), the first edition of the writer's complete works. Smaller editions of Cruz e Sousa's works were published by friends and minor publishing companies during the twenty years following his death.

After his death, Cruz e Sousa received the honors and the credit that he so industriously pursued in life. In *A poesia afro-brasileira* (1943, Afro-Brazilian Poetry) the French sociologist and ethnographer Roger Bastide drew attention to his work, comparing the Brazilian poet to Mallarmé. Cruz e Sousa's life of extreme poverty and his struggle with continuous discrimination added a dimension to his poetry that impressed Bastide as genuine and true. Not until 1961, the centenary of Cruz e Sousa's birth, was *Obra completa,* the scholarly edition of his complete works, published, allowing literary critics the opportunity to see his poems and poetic prose pieces within their historical context.

João da Cruz e Sousa's art and personal testimony constitute an extraordinary contribution to Brazilian literature. In *Cruz e Sousa, o poeta do Desterro* (1998, Cruz e Sousa, the poet from Desterro), a documentary released a hundred years after the poet's death, movie director Sylvio Back presents him from a new perspective to new generations. The title of the movie has a double meaning, since *desterro* is both the name of Cruz e Sousa's hometown and a word meaning "banished

from one's own country." Now, however, Cruz e Sousa has the status of a role model, and his poetry is included in literary anthologies.

Letters:

Cartas de Cruz e Sousa, edited, with an introduction and notes, by Zahidé Lupinacci Muzart (Florianópolis: Letras Contemporâneas, 1993).

References:

Roger Bastide, *A poesia afro-brasileira* (São Paulo: Martins, 1943);

Zila Bernd, *Introdução à literatura negra* (São Paulo: Brasiliense, 1988);

David Brookshaw, "Quatro poetas negros brasileiros," *Estudos afro-asiáticos,* 1 (1978): 30–43;

Afrânio Coutinho, *Introdução à literatura brasileira* (Rio de Janeiro: São José, 1959);

Coutinho, introduction to *Cruz e Sousa,* edited by Coutinho, Fortuna crítica, no. 4 (Rio de Janeiro: Civilização Brasileira/Instituto Nacional do Livro, 1979);

Carmen Fernandes, "Estudo temático estilístico de Cruz e Sousa," *Boletim do Instituto Luis de Camões,* no. 8 (1974): 215–234;

David T. Haberly, *Three Sad Races: Racial Identity and National Consciousness in Brazilian Literature* (Cambridge & New York: Cambridge University Press, 1983);

Claude Levi-Strauss, "Race and Culture," *International Social Science Journal,* 23, no. 4 (1971): 608–625;

Wilson Martins, "O simbolismo brasileiro," *Suplemento literário de São Paulo,* 10 February 1976, p. 3.

Euclides da Cunha

(20 January 1866 – 15 August 1909)

Carmen Chaves Tesser
University of Georgia

BOOKS: *Os sertões: campanha de canudos* (Rio de Janeiro: Laemmert, 1902); partially translated by R. B. Cunningham-Graham as *A Brazilian Mystic: Being the Life and Miracles of Antonio Conselheiro* (London: Heinemann, 1920; New York: Dodd, Mead, 1920); translated by Samuel Putnam as *Rebellion in the Backlands* (Chicago: University of Chicago Press, 1944);

Portuguese Self-Taught (Thimm's System) with Phoenetic Pronunciation (Philadelphia: McKay, 1904);

Relatório da comissão mixta brasileiro-peruana de reconhecimento do Alto Purús (Rio de Janeiro: Imprensa Nacional, 1906);

Castro Alves e seu tempo: discurso proferido no centro académico onze de agosto, de S. Paulo (Rio de Janeiro: Imprensa Nacional, 1907);

Perú versus Bolívia (Rio de Janeiro: Alves, 1907);

Contrastes e confrontos, preface by Jose Pereira de Sampaio (Bruno) (Porto, Portugal: Emprêsa Literária e Tipográfica, 1907);

À marjem da história (Porto, Portugal: Chardeon, 1909);

Canudos (diário de uma expedição), introduction by Gilberto Freyre (Rio de Janeiro: J. Olympio, 1939).

Editions and Collections: *Obra completa,* 2 volumes, edited by Afrânio Coutinho (Rio de Janeiro: Aguilar, 1966; revised, 1995);

Peru versus Bolívia (São Paulo: Cultrix, 1975);

Os sertões: campanha de Canudos, edited by Walnice Nogueira Galvão (São Paulo: Ática, 1998).

OTHER: Alberto Rangel, *Inferno verde: scena e scanarios do Amazonas,* preface by Cunha (Genova: SAI Cliches Celluloide Bacigalupi, 1908).

In 1943 Brazilian Academy of Letters member Afrânio Peixoto, writing a preface for a 1944 English edition of *Os sertões* (1902, The Backlands; partially translated as *A Brazilian Mystic: Being the Life and Miracles of Antonio Conselheiro,* 1920; translated as *Rebellion in the Backlands,* 1944), explains Euclides da Cunha's originality as a product of his engineering background, his

Euclides da Cunha (from Ronald de Carvalho, Pequena Historia da Literatura Brasileira, *1937; Thomas Cooper Library, University of South Carolina)*

training in mathematics and geography, and his military career: "In place of that bookish erudition which is common with those who set out to win fame in literature, he had a knowledge of nature gained through his previous studies which was to make of him an outstanding figure in our national letters." Others claim that Cunha's embrace of European positivism as an explanation for social and cultural changes in nineteenth-century Brazil put him in sharp contrast with the Romantic writers of the time. Hence, *Os sertões,* his masterpiece, is vital to any literary discussion of the period.

Although students of Latin American literature in general, and of Brazilian letters in particular, have never neglected the study of Euclides da Cunha, only in 1981, when Mário Vargas Llosa published his *La guerra del fin del mundo* (The War of the End of the World), a novel based on *Os sertões,* did the Brazilian essayist finally take a place among the greats of world literature. Today, the "Culto a Cunha" (Cunha Cult), a phrase used by anthropologist Regina Abreu in her presentation at the Semana Euclidiana (Euclidian Week) celebration, revolves around both his controversial writings and his tumultuous life and tragic death. Cunha's biography reads like a romantic novel, contrasting sharply with his exact and scientific writings. He was typical of the nineteenth-century Romantic hero who is passionate about his life and his work, but who is drawn by his own impulses and events toward a tragic destiny. Readers of *Os sertões* have pointed to the sharp contrast between Cunha's personal life and his scientific description of "O Homem" (The Man) in his classic essayistic novel.

Euclides Rodrigues Pimenta da Cunha was born in the Fazenda da Saudade in the region of Cantagalo, Rio de Janeiro, on 20 January 1866, the son of Manuel Rodrigues Pimenta da Cunha and Eucóxia Moreira da Cunha. Cunha's mother died when he was three years old, leaving him and his one-year-old sister, Adélia, to be reared by aunts. Cunha began his studies in the Colégio Caldeira (Caldeira School), one of the best available primary schools, which was directed by the Portuguese political exile Francisco José Caldeira da Silva. In 1877 Cunha moved with his father to Bahia where he studied in the Colégio Bahia (Bahia School), and in 1879, when he was thirteen years old, the precocious adolescent moved to Rio de Janeiro to live with his uncle, Antônio Pimenta da Cunha. In Rio de Janeiro he studied in four different schools: the Anglo-American School, the Vitório da Costa, the Meneses Vieira, and the Aquino (Aquinas). In the last of these schools he began his writing career by contributing to the school's newspaper, *O Democrata* (The Democrat), offering his thoughts on nature and ecology, topics he would return to again and again throughout his writing career. At Aquino he began writing poetry in a small notebook that he titled "Ondas" (Waves). Cunha also wrote poetry, although few of his poems were published during his lifetime. While at Aquino he also demonstrated great affinity for mathematics and the physical and biological sciences.

In 1885 Cunha began studying engineering at the Polytechnic School in Rio de Janeiro, but for finan-

cial reasons he had to transfer to the Military School in Praia Vermelha, in the state of Rio de Janeiro. The young cadet joined the republican antimilitaristic movement. He was expelled from the military school in 1888 for insubordination and showing a lack of respect for the minister of war, Tomás Coelho. Cunha was arrested and sent to the military hospital to be treated for mental fatigue. Appearing before the military court, Cunha reaffirmed his republican ideology and was transferred to the São João Fort military prison to await his sentence. Through the intervention of friends and colleagues, Cunha received a pardon from King Pedro II, but he did not return to the school until 1889, after the Proclamação da República Brasileira (Proclamation of the Brazilian Republic), the bloodless separation of Brazil from the Portuguese empire. During the year's hiatus from his studies, Cunha wrote for the newspaper *A Província de São Paulo* (The Province of São Paulo) under the pseudonym Proudhon.

During his studies at the military school, Cunha wrote essays for the republican newspaper *Democracia* (Democracy), defending positivism and attacking those who wanted the return of the Portuguese Empire. On 10 September 1890 he married Anna Emília Ribeiro, the daughter of Major Frederico Solon Sampaio Ribeiro, and in 1891 he graduated with degrees in mathematics, physical and natural sciences, and civil engineering. Always the journalist, he began writing for *Gazeta de Notícias* (News Gazette), where he developed some socialist theories. In 1892 Cunha, promoted to first lieutenant, began working on the Central Brazilian railroad project. At this time he initiated what would be a long-term relationship with the newspaper *A Província de São Paulo* (The Province of São Paulo), later known as *O Estado de São Paulo* (The State of São Paulo).

In 1896 Cunha retired from active military duty and began working as a civil engineer in São Paulo, taking charge of building projects for bridges, roads, and public buildings. In 1897 he joined the newspaper *O Estado de São Paulo* as a correspondent. He accompanied War Minister Marechal Bittencourt to the backlands of Bahia to cover the rebellion of Canudos for the paper. The articles that he submitted formed the basis for his most famous work, *Os sertões.* During the next two years he continued to write essays for the paper while developing the manuscript for his first novel. Also, during his coverage of the Canudos Rebellion he kept a detailed "war diary" featuring scientific descriptions of not only the surroundings but also the people he encountered and their culture. Once the Canudos Rebellion ended, Cunha returned to São José do Rio Pardo in 1898 to join his wife, Anna, and their two sons, Solon and Euclides Filho (Quidinho). That same year he published what he called "an excerpt of an unpublished book" in *O Estado de São Paulo,* bringing to light the first samples of *Os sertões.* He also presented the study "Climatologia bahiana" (Bahian Climatology) at the Instituto histórico de São Paulo (Historic Institute of São Paulo). Both *Os sertões* and "Climatologia bahiana" are laced with imaginative language that prompted their later classification as fiction.

During 1899 and 1900 Cunha oversaw construction in São José, including the bridge over the river Pardo, and he also finished the manuscript for *Os sertões.* Also, in *Revista Brasileira* (Brazilian Magazine), Cunha published "A guerra do sertão" (The War in the Backlands). His reputation as a positivist continued to grow, and he made friends and enemies alike through his publications. In December 1900, at the request of his friend Júlio de Mesquita, then editor of *O Estado de São Paulo,* Cunha published the article "O Brasil no século XIX" (Brazil in the XIX Century), describing in minute detail the many advances in culture, science, and engineering in the young republic.

Cunha developed *Os sertões* slowly. As a scientist, Cunha was careful to investigate minute details in order properly to base his argument on the accepted scholarship of the time. As an engineer, he carefully structured the text with the precision of a bridge builder. Finally, in 1902 he financed the publication by Laemmert of the first edition (totaling one thousand copies). The book met with great critical enthusiasm and sold out within weeks.

Cunha introduced *Os sertões* by citing French philosopher Hippolyte-Adolphe Taine and his theory of determinism. Using this theoretical framework, Cunha subdivided the text in three parts. The three sections of *Os sertões*–"A terra" (Land), "O homem" (Man), and "A luta" (Struggle)–reflect the writer's scientific knowledge, which is greatly influenced by European positivism. "A terra" offers a detailed description of the region–geological formations, climate, and flora. "O homem" gives the reader an ethnographic study of the Brazilian people and the initial phase of their biological identity. Preoccupied with miscegenation, Cunha "proves" that the *jagunço* (the backland ruffian) is not guilty of rebellion but rather is the product of racial, geographical, and historical factors that create a kind of semibarbaric existence. Thus, the *jagunço's* rebellious spirit is a "natural" consequence of his racial makeup. In this section of the text Cunha describes the leader of the rebellion, Antônio Conselheiro, who followed mystical traditions. After the first two sections provide context, the author tells the conflict of Canudos and in a way justifies the struggle. He considers Conselheiro to be nothing more than a natural product of his environ-

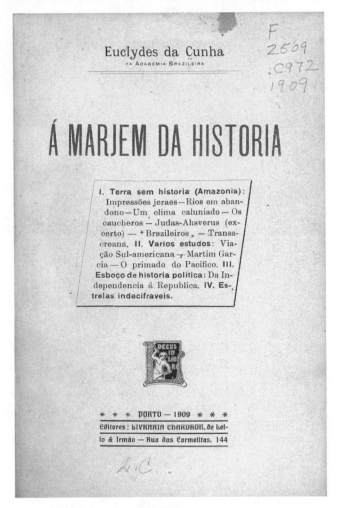

Title page for Cunha's collection of essays about the development of the Amazon region (Amelia Gayle Gorgas Library, University of Alabama)

ment. Cunha represented the views of his elite contemporaries, who saw a struggle between the "primitive" citizens of the interior and the "civilized" citizenry of the coastal areas. The apparent contradictions in his observations about Conselheiro became the fabric of ideological inquiry still in vogue at the beginning of the twenty-first century. That is, Cunha's essay becomes one of the first texts to problematize and attempt to define identity in general and Brazilian identity in particular. An example of its influence may be seen in *A Writer's Reality* (1991), where Vargas Llosa describes his reaction when he first encountered Cunha's text: "For me all of this was like seeing in a small laboratory the pattern of something that had been happening all over Latin America since the beginning of our independence."

Although there is undeniable racism in Cunha's text, such as his view of the degeneration of the races in America because of miscegenation, the author also

EUCLIDES DA CUNHA

PERU
VERSUS
BOLÍVIA

Introdução, cotejo e estabelecimento do texto
pelo Prof. ROLANDO MOREL PINTO, da disciplina
de Língua Portuguesa da Faculdade de Filosofia, Letras e Ciências Humanas da Universidade
de São Paulo.

EDITORA CULTRIX
SÃO PAULO
Em convênio com o INSTITUTO NACIONAL DO LIVRO
MINISTÉRIO DA EDUCAÇÃO E CULTURA

*Title page for a 1975 paperback edition of Cunha's collection of
eight articles originally written for the* Jornal do Comérci
*(Journal of Commerce) (Harold B. Lee Library,
Brigham Young University)*

thousand corrections. Editions six through eleven (1923–1929) were published in Paris. In 1929 publisher Francisco Alves brought out another Brazilian edition and continued publishing the book until its twenty-seventh edition in 1968. Since the text has become public domain, many publishers have brought out classroom and annotated scholarly editions. Moreover, the text has been translated into more than a dozen different languages, including Spanish, French, Italian, Japanese, Chinese, and Russian.

The immediate success of the book gave Cunha some notoriety among Brazilian literary circles. On 21 September 1903 he was elected to the Academia Brasileira de Letras (Brazilian Academy of Letters) to occupy the Castro Alves chair number 7, vacated by the death of its founder, Valentim Magalhães. On 20 November of the same year he was elected to the Instituto de história e geografia de São Paulo (Historic and Geographic Institute of São Paulo). In 1904 the "writer-engineer," as the popular Cunha came to be known, was named to chair the Comissão do Purus (Commission of the Purús), which was charged with writing a detailed report of the border regions between Brazil and Peru. This Comissão Mista (Mixed Commission) met during the months of August and September, and in October 1905 Cunha wrote the report, which was published as *Relatório da comissão mixta brasileiro-peruana de reconhecimento do Alto Purús* (1906).

The first edition of *Contrastes e confrontos* (Contrasts and Confrontations), a collection of articles published between 1901 and 1904 in *O Estado de São Paulo* and *El País* (The Country), was published in Portugal in 1907, just as Cunha began working as an engineer for the federal government. For the next two years he continued to publish journalistic prose in the national press, and he edited a collection of eight articles written for the *Jornal do Comércio* (Journal of Commerce) that was published by Francisco Alves as *Perú versus Bolívia* (1907).

But as his career as a writer, engineer, and statesman was blooming, Cunha was forced to accept the fact that his wife, Anna, was unfaithful. He had been away from home for one year, and Anna had fallen in love with Dilermando de Assis, a handsome young man from Pôrto Alegre, Rio Grande do Sul. An expert marksman, Assis was only four years older than Cunha's oldest son, Solon.

Although his personal life was crumbling, Cunha continued in 1909 to work on his writing, polishing the manuscript for *À marjem da história* (The Edge of History), a collection of essays about the development of the people, culture, and history of the Amazon region. In addition to this manuscript, Cunha had begun outlining a new book, "Um paraíso perdido" (A Lost Par-

saw that not all barbarism lay on the side of the rebels. He saw civilization as more than the political and military establishment of Brazil, including the rural population and culture. Cunha's primary purpose was to re-create the peasant revolt against the republic, but what he achieved has been recognized as the first attempt within Brazilian letters to probe beneath the surface of Brazilian reality and to expose forbidden topics of discussion, such as race and miscegenation. For the student of late-nineteenth-century Brazilian literature, Cunha provides an important backdrop against which to measure current efforts to describe and define Brazilian identity in terms of what is African; what is European or North American (that is, foreign); and what is really "native," meaning "authentically Brazilian," an inherently problematic idea.

With each new edition of *Os sertões,* Cunha carefully revised the manuscript, adding details and correcting grammatical errors. In 1904 he finished what he introduced as the definitive edition, with some two

adise). In May he took a competitive exam for a position in the Colégio Pedro II to teach logic. Obtaining second place, he was named to a teaching post and began this new phase of his life on 21 July.

On 14 August 1909 Cunha's wife Anna took the children and left the couple's home to begin a new life with Assis. The next day, distraught over his condition and suffering from poor health, Cunha set out to avenge his betrayal. Cunha entered Assis's house, gun in hand, ready to kill his rival. The young marksman, however, was the victor in the struggle. Cunha was killed, Assis was acquitted of the murder, and Assis then married Anna. Years later, Solon, Cunha's oldest son, tried to restore honor to the family name by pulling out a gun and attempting to kill his stepfather. Once again, Assis was successful in defending himself. He killed Solon, and again he was acquitted for acting in self-defense. These compelling historical facts have enhanced the "Cunha Cult" as admirers try to restore Cunha's honor within the context of Brazil's patriarchal structure.

Cunha's writing style is typical of his time: baroque, characterized by antithesis, hyperbole, paradox, and an inordinate use of adjectives and repetition. Critics have noted that these characteristics point to his extraordinary facility with the Portuguese language. A journalist at heart, Cunha was able to combine journalistic and poetic prose to create an extraordinarily artistic discourse. Furthermore, although he was constrained by the ideology, political developments, and discursive style of his time, he was the first man of letters to take a critical look at his culture and to begin to question it. His important contributions to Brazilian literary history are undeniable.

References:

Regina Abreu, *Coisas boas p'ra pensar* (São José do Rio Pardo: Casa Euclidiana, 1998);

Lilia Mortiz Schwarcz, *O espetáculo das raças: cinetistas, instituições e questão racial no Brasil, 1870–1930* (São Paulo: Companhia das Letras, 1993);

Carmen Chaves Tesser, "Euclides da Cunha," in *Encyclopedia of the Essay,* edited by Taci Chevalier (Chicago & London: Fitzroy Dearborn, 1997), pp. 199–200;

Mário Vargas Llosa, *A Writer's Reality,* edited by Myron I. Lichtblau (Syracuse, N.Y.: Syracuse University Press, 1991).

Alfredo Dias Gomes

(19 October 1922 – 18 May 1999)

Robert N. Anderson
University of North Carolina at Chapel Hill

BOOKS: *A comédia dos moralistas* (Salvador: Fênix Gráfica, 1937);

O pagador de promessas (São Paulo: AGIR, 1959); translated by Stanley Richards as *Journey to Bahia: Dias Gomes' Brazilian Prize Play O pagador de promessas* (Washington, D.C.: Brazilian American Cultural Institute, 1964); translated by Oscar Fernández as *Payment as Pledged,* in *The Modern Stage in Latin America: Six Plays,* edited by George Woodyard (New York: E. P. Dutton, 1971);

A invasão; A revolução dos beatos (Rio de Janeiro: Civilização Brasileira, 1962);

O bem-amado—Odorico, o bem-amado, e os mistérios de amor e da morte (Rio de Janeiro: Civilização Brasileira, 1963);

O berço do herói (Rio de Janeiro: Civilização Brasileira, 1965); translated by Leon Lyday as *The Cradle of the Hero, Modern International Drama,* 11, no. 2 (1978);

O Santo Inquérito (Rio de Janeiro: Civilização Brasileira, 1965);

Dr. Getúlio, sua vida e sua glória, by Dias Gomes and Ferreira Gullar (Rio de Janeiro: Civilização Brasileira, 1968);

O túnel (Rio de Janeiro: Civilização Brasileira, 1968);

Amor em campo minado (Rio de Janeiro: Civilização Brasileira, 1969);

As primícias (Rio de Janeiro: Civilização Brasileira, 1977);

O rei de Ramos (Rio de Janeiro: Civilização Brasileira, 1978);

Campeões do mundo (Rio de Janeiro: Civilização Brasileira, 1979);

Sucupira, ame-a ou deixe-a: venturas e desventuras de Zeca Diabo e sua gente na terra de Odorico, o bem-amado (Rio de Janeiro: Civilização Brasileira, 1982);

Odorico na cabeça: contos (Rio de Janeiro: Civilização Brasileira, 1983);

Derrocada (Rio de Janeiro: Record, 1993);

Decadência, ou, O procurador de Jesus Cristo: romance (Rio de Janeiro: Bertrand Brasil, 1995);

Alfredo Dias Gomes (Arquivo da Academia Brasileira de Letras)

Apenas um subversivo (Rio de Janeiro: Bertrand Brasil, 1998).

Editions and Collections: *Os heróis vencidos,* Coleção Dias Gomes, no. 1 (Rio de Janeiro: Bertrand Brasil, 1989)—comprises *Pagador de promessas* and *O Santo Inquérito;*

Os falsos mitos, edited by Antonio Mercado, Coleção Dias Gomes, no. 2 (Rio de Janeiro: Bertrand Brasil, 1990)—comprises *A revolução dos beatos, O bem-amado,* and *O berço do herói;*

Os caminhos da revolução, edited by Mercado, Coleção Dias Gomes, no. 3 (Rio de Janeiro: Bertrand Brasil, 1991)—comprises *A invasão, O túnel, Amor em campo minado,* and *Campeões do mundo;*

Espetáculos musicais, edited by Mercado, Coleção Dias Gomes, no. 4 (Rio de Janeiro: Bertrand Brasil, 1992)—comprises *Vargas, As primícias,* and *O rei de Ramos;*

Peças da juventude, edited by Mercado, Coleção Dias Gomes, no. 5 (Rio de Janeiro: Bertrand Brasil, 1994)—comprises *Pé-de-cabra, Eu acuso o céu,* and *Os cinco fugitivos do juízo final.*

PLAY PRODUCTIONS: *Pé-de-cabra,* Rio de Janeiro, Teatro Serrador, 7 August 1942;
João Cambão, Pelotas (theater unknown), 1943;
Amanhã será outro dia, Rio de Janeiro (theater unknown), 1943;
Zeca Diabo, Rio de Janeiro, Teatro Regina, January 1944;
Dr. Ninguém, São Paulo, Teatro Santana, May 1944;
Os cinco fugitivos do juízo final, Rio de Janeiro, Teatro Glória, 8 September 1954;
O pagador de promessas, São Paulo, Teatro Brasileiro de Comédia, 29 July 1960;
A invasão, Rio de Janeiro, Teatro do Rio, 25 October 1962;
A revolução dos beatos, São Paulo, Teatro Brasileiro de Comédia, 17 September 1963;
O Santo Inquérito, Rio de Janeiro, Teatro Jovem, 23 September 1966;
Odorico, o bem-amado, Recife, Teatro Santa Isabel, 4 May 1968;
Dr. Getúlio, sua vida e sua glória, Pôrto Alegre, Teatro Leopoldina, 10 August 1968; revised as *Vargas,* Rio de Janeiro, Teatro João Caetano, 3 October 1983;
The Cradle of the Hero, University Park, Pennsylvania, Playhouse, 1976;
O rei de Ramos, Rio de Janeiro, Teatro João Caetano, 31 March 1979;
Campeões do mundo, Rio de Janeiro, Teatro Vila-Lobos, 4 November 1980;
Amor em campo minado, Recife, Teatro Santa Isabel, 12 July 1984;
Meu reino por um cavalo, Rio de Janeiro, Teatro Nelson Rodrigues, 1990.

PRODUCED SCRIPTS: *O testa de ferro,* television, TV Excelsior, 1963;
A ponte dos suspiros, as Stela Calderón, television, Rede Globo, 1969;
Verão vermelho, television, Rede Globo, 1969–1970;
Assim na terra como no céu, television, Rede Globo, 1970–1971;
Um grito no escuro, television, Rede Globo, 1971;
Bandeira 2, television, Rede Globo, 1971–1972;
O bem-amado, television, Rede Globo, 1973;
O espigão, television, Rede Globo, 1974;
O marginal, motion picture, by Dias Gomes, Carlos Manga, and Lauro César Muniz, Carlos Manga Produções Cinematográficas, 1974;

Saramandaia, television, Rede Globo, 1976–1977;
Sinal de alerta, television, Rede Globo, 1978–1979;
O Santo Inquérito, television, Rede Globo, 1979;
O bem-amado, television, Rede Globo, 1979–1984;
Roque Santeiro, television, Rede Globo, 1985–1986;
Expresso Brasil, television, Rede Globo, 1987;
Mandala, television, Rede Globo, 1987–1988;
O boi santo, television, Rede Globo, 1988;
O pagador de promessas, television, Rede Globo, 1988;
Araponga, television, 1990–1991;
As noivas de Copacabana, television, 1993;
Decadência, television, 1994;
Fim do mundo, television, 1996;
Dona Flor e seus dois maridos, television, adapted by Dias Gomes from Jorge Amado's 1966 novel, 1998.

Alfredo Dias Gomes is one of the most important playwrights of twentieth-century Brazil. In 2001 he was voted seventh in the Artes Cênicas (Scenic Arts) category of *IstoÉ* magazine's Brasileiro do Século (Brazilian of the Century) poll for his contribution to the theatrical renaissance of the 1950s; for his relentless resistance to government censorship, corruption, and indifference to poverty; and for his role in revolutionizing the *telenovela* (or *novela,* prime-time soap opera). Known as Dias Gomes or even just Dias to his friends, he wrote in many dramatic forms, but he was a master of sociopolitical satire.

When Carlos Lacerda, governor of the state of Guanabara, blocked the staging of *O berço do herói* (1965, The Cradle of the Hero) in 1963, he called Dias Gomes "pornográfico e subversivo" (pornographic and subversive). The playwright appears to have owned up to only part of that accusation by the title of his autobiography, *Apenas um subversivo* (Just a Subversive), published one year before his untimely death in 1999. Progressive politics, innovative art, and a bohemian spirit have often traveled together in Brazil, especially in the case of the Cariocas (residents of Rio de Janeiro), who have made the Lapa district of Rio de Janeiro their home, from the days of the establishment of the theater district nearby during the early nineteenth century to the times of poet Manuel Bandeira, the composer Heitor Villa-Lobos, and the popular musician Noel Rosa in the early twentieth century. The tawdry cabarets, the late-night restaurants, and the many corner bars—impromptu stages for guitarists, poets, would-be actors, and amateur politicos—were Dias Gomes's turf during his early career. He was a Bahian by birth and had lived in São Paulo, but he seemed a Carioca at heart.

Alfredo de Freitas Dias Gomes was born on 19 October 1922 in Salvador, Bahia, the second son of Plínio Alves Dias Gomes, an engineer who had worked

Front cover of the 1976 paperback edition of Dias Gomes's 1959 play about a farmer from the interior of the state of Bahia who makes a pilgrimage to the state capital, Salvador (Robert Scott Small Library, College of Charleston)

on railroad construction in the Amazon region, and Alice Ribeiro de Freitas Gomes. Their home was on Rua do Bom Gosto (Good Taste Street), which always caused the playwright amusement. Dias Gomes was three when his father died, and his mother, Alice, soon had to struggle to support her family. A native of the small nearby port town of Cachoeira, she had been trained only in the skills needed to be a good middle-class housewife. Guilherme, Dias Gomes's older brother, was determined to help his mother, so he studied medicine and entered the army medical corps. This career move required the family to move to Rio de Janeiro in 1935.

In his autobiography Dias Gomes notes that his brother was a medical doctor by occupation but a writer by calling; Guilherme's devotion to his family, though, put his economic goals ahead of his creative urges. He exercised a tremendous influence on Dias Gomes as a role model, a yardstick to measure up to, and a creative inspiration; as Dias Gomes wrote, Guilherme was his

"bússola" (compass). Their mother was an avid opera fan, and accompanying her to performances gave the future playwright his first exposure to the professional theater. He had, however, already staged skits with his cousins for family gatherings.

Dias Gomes's school experiences were generally unhappy. He disliked the dogmatic rigidity of the school he attended in Bahia, which was run by Marist priests. He was finally expelled when he vocally resisted the advances of a pederast priest. Later, in Rio de Janeiro, Dias Gomes attended the Colégio Vera Cruz, co-owned by the futurist writer and Integralist Plínio Salgado, but he rebelled against the inculcation of the Integralists' fascism. Dias Gomes credits his early school years for his later agnostic views on religion and his left-wing political convictions.

Dias Gomes wrote his first play, *A comédia dos moralistas* (The Comedy of the Moralists), in 1937, when he was fifteen. He published it in a limited edition with the help of his uncle. The play, a critique of bourgeois morals set during Carnaval, was never performed. The script did, however, win a contest sponsored by the Serviço Nacional do Teatro (National Theater Service) for the União Nacional dos Estudantes (National Students' Union). More important than the accolades at the time was the cash prize, which Dias Gomes's family sorely needed, now that his brother was married and out of the home.

Dias Gomes's checkered scholastic career continued as he shelved his artistic ambitions and sought to enter the Academia Militar (Military Academy). In his autobiography he recounts that his motives were economic; he banked on a comfortable career that would eventually make him general, "just as long as he did not die young," he thought. He studied hard but failed the entrance exam because of a "tornado that swept his brain" as a result of sleep deprivation. Dias Gomes then entered the Escola Preparatória de Cadetes (Preparatory School for Cadets) in the southern city of Pôrto Alegre in order to put his military career back on track. The school's commander, however, counseled him to leave school as he lacked the slightest calling for the soldier's profession.

Dias Gomes had a passion for physics, so he tried studying engineering at University College in Rio de Janeiro. He soon lost interest and enrolled in the law school of Colégio Pedro II. At this time he took his first stabs at political activism, protesting the government of the populist-fascist dictator Getúlio Vargas. He also saw Orson Welles's movie *Citizen Kane* (1941), which inspired him to write a few plays and begin a novel, all of which were of little critical importance, however. Dias Gomes also took his first job as a radio scriptwriter for Rádio Vera Cruz. At the age of eighteen he was personally content with his transition from presumptive cadet to an unattached youth in the cultural and social whirlpool of Rio de Janeiro. There he made lifelong friendships with comic writers José Wanderley and Mário Lago, his partners in the nightlife of the city. Dias Gomes joined the mounting popular protest against Vargas's neutrality in World War II and in support of the Allies. This conviction led indirectly to his first theatrical success, when he came between the two greatest Brazilian actors of the day.

In 1942 Dias Gomes wrote two plays. *Ludovico* was a light comedy about an elderly man married to an eighteen-year-old girl. *Amanhã será outro dia* (Tomorrow Is Another Day) was an antifascist play about a French refugee in Brazil. Through a family connection Dias Gomes was able to show the text of *Ludovico* to Henrique Pongetti, the premier writer of comedies of the day. Pongetti liked the play and sent it to Jayme Costa, a famous comic actor, who was inclined to stage the play, pending revision. Dias Gomes also showed *Amanhã será outro dia* to Costa, who was uncomfortable with this play, given his pro-Vargas sentiments and unwillingness to draw political fire. Costa, however, saw talent in the budding playwright, and he asked the young man to write a comic reply to Joracy Camargo's *Deus lhe pague* (1932, May God Pay You), the most popular play of the Brazilian stage in the 1930s and 1940s. The result, Dias Gomes's *Pé-de-cabra* (1942, Goat's Foot [The Devil]), was more of a satire than a reply to Camargo's play, and Costa was again hesitant about committing to it.

At about the same time, Dias Gomes approached Procópio Ferreira, another grand old man of the theater and Costa's rival in popularity. Ferreira was more sympathetic to the ideas of *Pé-de-cabra*, but he, too, was reticent about staging it at that time. He wanted to know if Dias Gomes had any comedies. It was clear that the theatergoing public wanted light comedies as an escape from the anxiety of a world at war. Moreover, everyone knew that Vargas's Departamento de Imprensa e Propaganda (DIP, the Department of Press and Propaganda) could step in and censor or close any show, causing economic loss to the theater house. When Dias Gomes showed *Pé-de-cabra* to Ferreira, he mentioned that it was promised to Costa. After reading the play, Ferreira wanted to stage it, Costa notwithstanding. Dias Gomes felt somewhat like a traitor, but Costa had indeed hesitated. Despite opening to rave reviews, the play was closed for a time by the DIP and was only allowed to continue with cuts to satisfy the censors. The DIP had accused the play of being "Marxist." Dias Gomes affirmed that he had never read Karl Marx, but the censor's attention inspired him to start reading the philosopher's work.

Thus did Dias Gomes join the theatrical elite of Rio de Janeiro. While *Pé-de-cabra* was still on the marquee, he began writing other plays for Ferreira: *João Cambão* (1943), *Zeca Diabo* (1944, Joe Devil), and *Dr. Ninguém* (1944, Dr. Nobody) were all staged; two others, *Eu acuso o céu* (1943, I Blame Heaven) and *Um pobre gênio* (1943, A Poor Genius), were eventually presented on radio.

All this activity took place against the backdrop of World War II. The effect of the war on Brazil was mostly in the form of threats of torpedoes and shelling by German craft offshore, until 1943, when the tide shifted in favor of the Allies and Vargas raised an expeditionary force to fight on their side in Italy. The day had finally arrived for *Amanhã será outro dia*. It was Dias Gomes's third play to be staged, after *Pé-de-cabra* and *João Cambão*. His self-satisfaction was shaken when Guilherme, his older brother, died suddenly of an unexplained illness. In addition to bearing his own grief, Dias Gomes now had to act as his mother's sole provider. He sent her back to Bahia for a time to be with family, and he moved to São Paulo in 1945 to work at playwright Oduvaldo Vianna's new radio station as an editor.

This move was a calculated risk for a newly established playwright: Rio de Janeiro, not São Paulo, was the theatrical center of Brazil. Dias Gomes was away from Rio de Janeiro during a critical period in the development of the Brazilian theater. The modernist movement finally came to the Brazilian stage, some twenty years late, with the 1943 production of Nelson Rodrigues's *Vestido de noiva* (published, 1946; translated as *The Wedding Dress*, 1980), directed by Zbigniew Ziembinski and with set design by Tomás Santa Rosa. This production caused an aesthetic revolution, loosening the stranglehold of light comedies and melodramas on the Brazilian theater. The change was also structural, as Dias Gomes noted in his autobiography, as it spurred amateur groups on and elevated the importance of the director.

Dias Gomes's time spent in São Paulo was a sort of artistic incubation, while it was a busy time in his personal life. His work as a writer and editor for Rádio Pan-Americana led him to read widely in world literature, since part of his work was to adapt classics for presentation on radio. He channeled his natural anarchic tendencies into the start of a long-lasting affiliation with the Partido Comunista Brasileiro (PCB, the Brazilian Communist Party). Dias Gomes continued his carousing and womanizing, but while at Rádio Pan-Americana, he met Madalena Theoto, with whom he lived for two years. While still living with Theoto, he met and fell in love with radio actress and announcer Janete Clair, whom he married in 1950. In this period Dias Gomes wrote three novels and began a fourth, all of little importance in his estimation, other than to confirm that his talent lay more in dramaturgy.

São Paulo in the 1940s was an incubator in other ways. An entire generation of future television actors got

ALFREDO DIAS GOMES

A INVASÃO

+

A REVOLUÇÃO
DOS BEATOS

teatro

nota introdutória
de
FLÁVIO RANGEL

EDITÔRA CIVILIZAÇÃO BRASILEIRA S. A.
RIO DE JANEIRO

Title page for the 1962 volume comprising Dias Gomes's play about poor Cariocas (residents of Rio de Janeiro) squatting in abandoned buildings and his communist play that was closed by public protest (Joint University Libraries, Nashville)

Paulo, his politics led to his being blacklisted, this time because of his participation in a clandestine delegation to the Soviet Union. The blacklisting created job instability and economic insecurity for the whole family. Thanks to his network of friends and colleagues, however, Dias Gomes always seemed to land on his feet.

Dias Gomes's life underwent a profound change, as did the political life of the nation, when Vargas committed suicide while in office on 24 August 1954. Not only did the country have a new president, but the new theatrical generation was taking over as well. New actors, who later dominated the stage, and new directors, such as Bibi Ferreira, daughter of Procópio Ferreira, were coming into their own. Several Italian directors, fleeing the economic troubles of postwar Italy, came to Brazil, bringing the influence of neorealism to the Brazilian stage and screen. Everywhere, student drama groups, spin-off companies, and small-capacity *teatros de bolso* (pocket theaters) were springing up.

The aesthetic revolution in Brazilian theater begun with Rodrigues's *Vestido de noiva* was maturing, receiving an infusion from the mix of nationalism and modernism that dominated civic life in the 1950s. Modernism now expressed Brazilian topics in such key plays as Jorge Andrade's *A moratória* (1955, The Moratorium), which combined an important sociohistorical topic with innovative stagecraft; Ariano Suassuna's *Auto da compadecida* (1957; translated as *The Rogue's Trial*, 1963), which mixed Northeastern folklore, the popular circus, and the medieval mystery play into a social satire; and Gianfrancesco Guarnieri's *Eles não usam black-tie* (1958, They Don't Wear Black-Tie), which brought a portrayal of urban working-class realities to the "selective realism" of the arena stage.

In this context Dias Gomes wrote and eventually had staged his best-known play, *O pagador de promessas* (1959, The Payer of Promises; translated as *Journey to Bahia*, 1964). *O pagador de promessas* arose from several elements: a fascination with popular religiosity, a nostalgia for the Bahia of Dias Gomes's youth, the appeal at the time of all things Brazilian, and a mistrust of social constraints. More precisely, the playwright remembered the promise his mother had made to attend mass in every church in Salvador if Our Lord of the Good Death would allow Guilherme to enter the medical corps. (She soon fulfilled that promise with the young Dias Gomes in tow.) The play did not come, as the author has noted, from a need to preach ideology or propagandize for the Left or against the Church; it came from an interior need to understand the world. Dias Gomes underscored that he never submitted his plays to the cultural committee of the PCB for review or comment; his first obligation was always to the quality of the drama. In his autobiography he stated a prin-

their start in the Paulista radio business. (Television, of course, was not yet on the scene at that time.) Industrialist Franco Zampari founded the Teatro Brasileira de Comédia (TBC, Brazilian Theater of Comedy) in 1948. While Zampari's intent was to stage world-class productions of international drama in the city, the TBC nevertheless greatly elevated the technical skill and quality of the Brazilian theater and sowed the seeds for São Paulo's participation in the theatrical renaissance of the 1950s. Several notable actors and directors got their start with the TBC or its spin-offs, including internationally acclaimed actress Fernanda Montenegro.

Dias Gomes returned to Rio de Janeiro in 1948 and continued to work in radio. His reasons for working in radio were mostly economic, as before, and, as in São

ciple in relation to *O pagador de promessas* that indeed broadly applies to his drama, noting "an awareness . . . of being exploited and impotent to use the freedom that, in principle, is granted to me." It follows that survival involves partial or total submission to the social organization; the alternative is death or destruction.

O pagador de promessas went through several rewrites. Widely praised, the play was adapted as a motion picture in 1962 and has been staged in various foreign productions. Dias Gomes had hoped that the Teatro dos Sete, directed by Gianni Rato and based in the Teatro Municipal (Municipal Theater), would stage the play, but a delay led the author to take the play to the TBC, where Flávio Rangel finally directed it in 1960. Rangel, a young director and Dias Gomes's personal choice, had worked with another new playwright, Guarnieri, and with the TBC as it emerged from its snobbish cosmopolitanism and began favoring Brazilian authors.

Zé-do-Burro (Burro Joe), the protagonist of *O pagador de promessas,* is a farmer from the interior of Bahia. He made a promise to St. Barbara if she would cure his burro—hence his nickname. He pledged to divide his lands among his farmhands and make a pilgrimage to Salvador, a distance of seven leagues, carrying a cross on his back to deliver to the Church of St. Barbara there. Upon Zé-do-Burro's arrival, though, the priest at the church does not let him bring the cross inside because of an important detail. Lacking a church or shrine to St. Barbara at home, Zé-do-Burro made his promise in a household practicing the Candomblé faith, in which St. Barbara is a syncretic representation of the Yoruba goddess Iansã. The devotee is obstinate in his desire to fulfill his promise, but the priest is equally unyielding in permitting such heterodoxy. Most of the action of the play occurs as Zé-do-Burro and his wife, Rosa, wait on the steps of the church for a change. Zé-do-Burro becomes a cause célèbre and a notorious distraction, first among the neighborhood and eventually among the police and the press. At the climax he is shot during a scuffle and dies, a simple man turned tragic hero, as critic Sábato Magaldi notes in *Panorama do teatro brasileiro* (1976). The people carry Zé-do Burro into the church on the cross; he pays his promise in death, unable to do so while living, "in the same ironic spirit manipulated by the Greek tragedies," adds Magaldi.

The religious conflict in the play exemplifies the potential clash between popular religiosity and the orthodoxy of the conservative elements of the Church. Beyond this conflict, though, *O pagador de promessas* presents a theme common in the Brazilian theater of the second half of the twentieth century: the conflict between the modern and the premodern. Usually, such a treatment demystifies modernity as the repository of all truth and perfection and redeems the premodern ethos as the bearer of popular virtues and even national authenticity. This position was a reaction to the late-nineteenth- and early-twentieth-century intellectual stance. Generally, though, the effect is not to privilege the premodern over the modern in a battle of good versus evil but rather to juxtapose social forces and note the outcome. The characters in *O pagador de promessas,* therefore, embody and give expression to various currents within the social organization. They are basically types who also function both as farcical counterpoints to the tragic plot and as a chorus.

Magaldi pronounced *O pagador de promessas* a success even before it opened, and indeed it proved to be. The play gave Dias Gomes his second wind and thrust him into the spotlight once again. A second production was staged in 1962 in Rio de Janeiro under the direction of José Renato, and the motion-picture adaptation, adapted and directed by Anselmo Duarte, was released that same year. The success of the movie at the Cannes Film Festival and elsewhere led to a later revival of the play at the TBC. In 1962 Dias Gomes also premiered *A invasão* (The Invasion), a naturalistic play based on the contemporary news of poor Cariocas invading abandoned buildings after being driven from hillside slums by floods and mud slides. The following year he premiered *A revolução dos beatos* (The Revolution of the Holy Men), a play so frankly communist that it had to be closed owing to public outcry, despite good reviews. In 1962 Dias Gomes wrote *O bem-amado* (The Beloved One), based on the true story of a small-town politician who fulfilled a campaign promise to build a municipal cemetery and then waited for someone to die so he could dedicate it. As the delay dragged on, the opposition and townsfolk began to cry "boondoggle." The challenge in the play becomes how to expedite the day of the inauguration of the cemetery. Dias Gomes also worked in some parody of the grandiosity of Lacerda, then governor of Guanabara. The play eventually became the basis for a 1973 *telenovela.*

The coup of 1 April 1964 interrupted this fervent period of Dias Gomes's career, as it did the life of the country in general. The civil-military alliance that ousted the president, João Goulart, also took over the media, including Rádio Nacional, where Dias Gomes then worked. He dodged police attempts to apprehend him and other prominent "communists"—the code word for any opponent of the new regime. The real communists did indeed fare badly under the "Revolução" (Revolution), as supporters called the coup. In the 1950s the PCB had already suffered a crisis when Soviet leader Nikita Khrushchev made public the violent excesses of Joseph Stalin. Many left the party; others went through crises of conscience and reformulated their beliefs, still others simply rationalized the contradictions. In the late 1950s and early 1960s the party strategically aligned itself with the "developmentalist" ideology of the urban economic elite and the bourgeoisie. The PCB was nevertheless a target of the right-wing coup. Party members soon found themselves abandoned by their centrist allies and mercilessly hunted, tortured, and "disappeared" by the dictatorship.

At the same time, the Brazilian theater found itself under assault as never before, even under Vargas. The theater was a public art form and had the power to reach large numbers of people in a direct way. The present generation was also nationalistic and left-leaning. After the coup the theater shifted its emphasis from representation and analysis of Brazilian social problems to a frontal critique of the dictatorship, rallying resistance to it. The Teatro de Arena of São Paulo and the newly formed Teatro Opinião were prominent in this phase, but many authors, actors, and directors lent their voices to the cause, Dias Gomes among them. This resistance, of course, drew fire, culminating in the infamous Ato Institucional Número 5 (AI-5, Institutional Act No. 5), which institutionalized the president's dictatorial powers. AI-5 and subsequent decrees allowed those in control of the state to operate in any way they chose, including subjecting virtually the entire cultural life of the country to prior censorship.

Dias Gomes had written *O berço do herói* in 1963, but publication of the play was delayed until 1965, and its stage debut was delayed even longer. By 1965 he had also written *O Santo Inquérito* (The Holy Inquisition), which premiered in 1966. The two plays thus straddled 1964, the year of the coup. *O berço do herói* is a social satire about the fall from grace of a local hero who is supposed to have distinguished himself with the expeditionary force in World War II but is later found out to have deserted. *O Santo Inquérito,* written as it was after the coup, is a more forceful condemnation of the contemporary political situation. The topic of the play is, in fact, the Inquéritos Policiais Militares (IPMs, Military Police Inquiries). Direct denunciation of the status quo was hardly possible, though, so various playwrights, Dias Gomes included, hit upon the device of the historical allegory. The government was nationalistic enough (and the censors were dim enough) to allow retellings of Brazilian history and legend, carefully crafted, of course, to draw parallels with the present. Dias Gomes chose the legend of Branca Dias, a young "New Christian" woman, who was burned by the Santo Inquérito in colonial Brazil. The choice of topic was reinforced by Arthur Miller's *The Crucible* (1953), an allegory of McCarthyism set during the Salem witch trials.

Curiously, *O berço do herói* had a more tortuous history than *O Santo Inquérito.* Under the direction of Antônio Abujamra, *O berço do herói* was to open at the Teatro Princesa Isabel in Rio de Janeiro when it was banned by the state censors on the scheduled day of its premiere, even though the text had been previously approved. This sort of erratic censorship was a familiar form of government harassment, causing psychological and economic harm to theater professionals. Still, Dias Gomes fought to understand why his play had first been approved and then denied. In response to the playwright's inquiries, Governor Lacerda branded him "pornográfico e subversivo." In truth, the play had wounded the sensibilities of the military, dealing as it did with the topic of desertion. Not only was the play prohibited, but a planned motion-picture version was too. A television adaptation, titled *Roque Santeiro* (Roque, the Saint-Maker), aired in 1985–1986, after the military had left power, and enjoyed great success.

O Santo Inquérito, however, was not banned. The play was directed by Ziembinski at the Teatro Jovem in Rio de Janeiro in 1966. The production was an aesthetic success but a box-office flop. It was successfully restaged ten years later in São Paulo by Rangel and also in Lisbon by the Grupo de Campolide. In 1968 Dias Gomes contributed *O túnel* (The Tunnel) to José Celso Martinez Corrêa's invitational Feira Brasileira de Opinião (Brazilian Opinion Fair), for which the leading playwrights of Brazil were asked to represent what they thought of their country in the form of a one-act play. Dias Gomes's vision was an experiment in theater of the absurd in which Brazil was a traffic jam headed into a dark tunnel. The entire festival was banned, however, as was an attempt to restage *A revolução dos beatos.*

Dias Gomes's next major project was a retelling of the Vargas story, *Dr. Getúlio, sua vida e sua glória* (1968, Dr. Getúlio, His Life and His Glory), inspired aesthetically by the *samba enredo* (story samba) of the Carnaval parades in Rio de Janeiro. Dias Gomes collaborated with poet Ferreira Gullar on the play, writing part of it in verse. Dias Gomes had long been intrigued by the larger-than-life figure of Vargas and had been disturbed by his suicide; he came to view Vargas as a tragic figure. The aesthetic and intellectual challenge of the play was to represent the mythic figure (Vargas had been immensely popular—and that is where the Carnaval samba came in) measured against the historical record of Vargas's fascist and authoritarian tendencies. A revised version, *Vargas,* directed by Rangel, with sets by Rato, music by Edu Lobo and Francisco "Chico" Buarque de Hollanda, and an all-star cast, played successfully at the Teatro João Caetano in Rio de Janeiro in 1983.

In 1968 the Russian invasion of Czechoslovakia, the consolidation of the Brazilian dictatorship under AI-5, the failure of the Left to prevent the installation of the right-wing government, and the beginning of armed leftist guerrilla resistance all made Dias Gomes rethink his relationship with the PCB. He opted against armed struggle and began to wonder what mistakes the Brazilian Left had made in the years before the military coup. Dias Gomes gave dramatic form to these doubts in *Amor em campo minado* (Love in a Minefield), originally titled *Vamos soltar os demônios* (Let's Let the Demons Out), which was published in 1969 but not staged until 1984. Such self-appraisal became common among leftists worldwide in the 1980s and 1990s, but it was not welcome in 1968, when the Left was on the defensive in Brazil.

Soon thereafter, Dias Gomes received an offer to write *telenovelas* for Rede Globo. His wife, Janete, had already established a productive career writing *novelas*. Her husband was not the only "serious" writer to make the move to television at about this time: Guarnieri had been writing for television since the early 1960s. Stage actors had long worked in television as a bread-and-butter job. Dias Gomes had often drawn a parallel between radio and television. As government repression deepened, motion-picture and theater professionals found their work increasingly precarious. The motive for writing for television was thus primarily economic, but Dias Gomes also saw it as a challenge. He saw this work as an opportunity to bring change to a medium that had a vast capacity for alienation but reached an immense popular audience, including the working poor. This view might have appeared as a rationalization to his critics, who saw his questioning of the PCB and move to television as politically incorrect, had he not turned out to be right. The move of such writers as Dias Gomes and Guarnieri to the small screen in fact spurred changes in Brazilian televised drama in the course of the 1970s and 1980s: *novelas* broached such taboo subjects as divorce, child abuse, and corruption; settings shifted from a strict regimen of exotic or upper-class ambience to more- commonplace locales in various parts of the country. The programs started to address regional, class, racial, and ecological themes. Dias Gomes was able to bring into millions of Brazilian homes adaptations of several of his plays, including the formerly prohibited *O berço do herói* as *Roque Santeiro*. The *telenovelas* of this early stage included *A ponte dos suspiros* (1969, The Bridge of Sighs, 1969), *Verão vermelho* (1969–1970, Red Summer), *Assim na terra como no céu* (1970–1971, On Earth as It Is in Heaven), and *Bandeira 2* (1971–1972).

Alice, Dias Gomes's mother, who had lived with the family since his marriage to Janete in 1950, died in the early 1970s. In this period Dias Gomes made a definitive departure from the PCB. The self-described nonconformist had always had difficulty in submitting to the strict discipline and hierarchy of the party. Even so, his reputation as a "subversive" followed him into his later career. He recalled many overreactions on the part of the censors, the IPMs. Once, during an IPM interrogation,

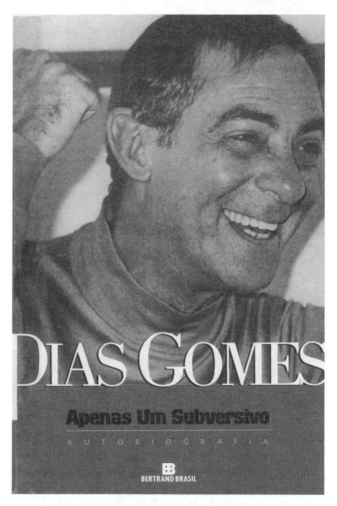

Front cover of Dias Gomes's 1998 autobiography, published the year before his death in an automobile accident (Heard Library, Vanderbilt University)

instead of asking him to squeal on his comrades, the officer asked Dias Gomes to reveal who had killed Nívea, a character in *Assim na terra como no céu,* an episode that was a mainspring in the plot of the *novela.* Another time, a censor had cut an innocuous scene in *Saramandaia* (1976–1977). When Dias Gomes confronted the censor, the official conceded that the dialogue was inoffensive, "but it was what [Dias Gomes] was thinking at the time that was the problem."

Some of the reaction was based on the unprecedented success of the 1973 *novela* adaptation of *O bemamado.* The play had received its theatrical debut at the Teatro dos Amadores in the Northeastern state of Pernambuco in 1968, and it had played in regional theaters until staged in Rio de Janeiro in 1970 under the direction of Rato, with Procópio Ferreira in the role of the title character, Odorico Paraguaçu. The television version of the saga of the imaginary Bahian town of Sucupira, its corrupt mayor, and the foibles of its citizenry was able to poke fun at the "system" despite the many constraints imposed by the censors. The *novela,* the first to be broadcast in color in Brazil, was directed by Cinema Novo director Leon Hirshman with a cast featuring some of the best actors from the stage and screen, including Paulo Gracindo in the lead role. The world of Sucupira was such a phenomenon that *O bem-amado* returned as a television series that ran from 1979 to 1984.

As the pace of work in television eased in the second half of the 1970s, Dias Gomes had time to return to the theater. (The pace of new productions of his earlier stage works had not let up, however, especially for favorites such as *O pagador de promessas* and *O Santo Inquérito.*) He spent a semester as writer-in-residence at Pennsylvania State University at the invitation of Leon Lyday. There *O berço do herói* finally received its premiere in 1976, in the form of Lyday's translation, *The Cradle of the Hero.* Dias Gomes then wrote *As primícias* (1977, The First Fruits), which explored the medieval notion of *jus primae noctis* (right of the first night, the nobleman's right to the commoner's bride on the first night of marriage) as a metaphor for the persistence of censorship under President Ernesto Geisel's "détente" in domestic Brazilian politics. Dias Gomes experimented with the genre of the musical in *O rei de Ramos* (1979, The King of Ramos), in collaboration with musicians Buarque and Francis Hime. Based on the *novela Bandeira 2* and dealing with the world of the illegal *jogo do bicho* (animal game) lottery in Brazil, this musical was, as Dias Gomes pointed out, probably the first time a *novela* had spawned a play and not vice versa. *O rei de Ramos* was a box-office success, despite lukewarm reception by the critics, and it was later adapted for the cinema by Fábio Barreto, in neorealist style with many other changes, as *O rei do Rio* (1985, The King of Rio).

The office of the federal censor was finally abolished in 1979, and Dias Gomes charted a new post-censorship course that year with *Campeões do mundo* (Champions of the World). The problem for the Brazilian performing arts in general in the 1980s was to sustain revolutionary art while moving beyond an "art of resistance," with its coded metaphor and allegory and its focus on the particularities of authoritarian governmental repression (censorship, torture, and so forth). A great personal pleasure of *Campeões do mundo* for Dias Gomes was the chance to collaborate with his three children. Daughter Denise composed the theme song, and she and her brothers, Guilherme and Alfredo, performed it.

The late 1970s, however, brought the sad end of a thirty-year partnership and love affair, when Janete suc-

cumbed to intestinal cancer. She had had a stellar career as a screenwriter, and the couple had raised a happy family. Dias Gomes eventually married a young actress, Maria Bernadeth Lyzio, with whom he had two daughters, Mayra and Luana. During the 1980s and 1990s most of Dias Gomes's new projects were in television, although concentrated more on miniseries and dramas. He continued to reflect deeply on the relation of politics to art, as in a treatment of the collapse of Soviet communism in the novel *Derrocada* (1993, Defeat) and an exploration of the stagnation of art, politics, and morality in the postdictatorship period in the novella *Decadência* (1994, Decadence). Dias Gomes received his highest mainstream literary honor in 1991, when he was elected into the Academia Brasileira de Letras (Brazilian Academy of Letters). His fruitful career was cut short suddenly when he was killed in a taxi accident on 18 May 1999. He was not wearing a seat belt.

Alfredo Dias Gomes never abandoned his faith in political theater. In his autobiography he affirms that he wrote drama

sem impor minha visão particular, mas fornecendo elementos para que o espectador conluísse e formalizasse sua própria visão, já que, no meu entender, não cabe ao teatro—que é o reino da mentira—ditar verdades. Cabe-lhe, sim, armar o espectador para que ele possa, por si mesmo e fora do teatro, encontrá-las. . . . Sim, o teatro não pode transformer o mundo, mas por seu intermédio podemos, sem dúvida, transmitir a consciência da necessidade dessa transformação.

(without imposing my personal vision, but rather furnishing elements so that the spectator would come to a conclusion and formalize his own vision, since, as I understand it, it is not up to the theater—which is the kingdom of falsehood—to dictate truths. It is, however, up [to the theater] to arm the spectator so that he can, of his own accord and outside of the theater, find them. . . . Yes, the theater cannot transform the world, but through it we can, no doubt, transmit the awareness for the need for its transformation.)

References:

Sábato Magaldi, *Moderna dramaturgia brasileira* (São Paulo: Perspectiva, 1998);

Magaldi, *Panorama do teatro brasileiro,* second edition (Brasília: Serviço Nacional de Teatro, 1976);

Jan Michalski, *O palco amordaçado: 15 anos de censura teatral no Brasil* (Rio de Janeiro: Avenir, 1979);

Décio de Almeida Prado, *Teatro em progresso: crítica teatral, 1955–1964* (São Paulo: Martins, 1964).

Autran Dourado

(18 January 1926 –   )

Carmen Chaves Tesser
University of Georgia

See also the Dourado entry in *DLB 145: Modern Latin-American Fiction Writers, Second Series.*

BOOKS: *Teia* (Belo Horizonte: Edifício, 1947);

Sombra e exílio (Belo Horizonte: J. Calazans, 1950);

Tempo de amar (Rio de Janeiro: J. Olympio, 1952);

Três histórias na praia (Rio de Janeiro: Ministério da Educação e Cultura, 1955);

Nove histórias em grupos de três (Rio de Janeiro: J. Olympio, 1957);

A barca dos homens (Rio de Janeiro: Editora do Autor, 1961; revised edition, Rio de Janeiro: Expressão e Cultura, 1973);

Uma vida em segrêdo (Rio de Janeiro: Civilização Brasileira, 1964; revised edition, Rio de Janeiro: Editora Expressão e Cultura, 1973; revised edition, Rio de Janeiro: Difel, 1977)–includes *História de uma história;* first edition translated by Edgar H. Miller Jr. as *A Hidden Life* (New York: Knopf, 1969);

Ópera dos mortos (Rio de Janeiro: Civilização Brasileira, 1967; revised edition, Rio de Janeiro: Difel, 1977); translated by John M. Parker as *The Voices of the Dead* (London: P. Owen, 1980; New York: Taplinger, 1981);

O risco do bordado (Rio de Janeiro: Expressão e Cultura, 1970; revised edition, Rio de Janeiro: Expressão e Cultura, 1974); translated by Parker as *Pattern for a Tapestry* (London: P. Owen, 1984);

Solidão solitude (Rio de Janeiro: Civilização Brasileira, 1972);

Uma poética de romance (São Paulo: Perspectiva, 1973); revised and enlarged as *Uma poética de romance: matéria de carpintaria* (São Paulo: Difel, 1976);

Os sinos da agonia (Rio de Janeiro: Expressão e Cultura, 1974); translated by Parker as *The Bells of Agony* (London: P. Owen, 1988);

Novelário de Donga Novais (Rio de Janeiro: Difel, 1976);

Armas & corações (Rio de Janeiro: Difel, 1978);

Autran Dourado, circa 1973 (photograph by Inês Autran Dourado Barbosa; used by permission)

Três histórias no internato: conto, edited by Heitor Megale and Marilena Matsuoka (São Paulo: Nacional, 1978);

As imaginações pecaminosas (Rio de Janeiro: Record, 1981);

O meu mestre imaginário (Rio de Janeiro: Record, 1982);

Lucas Procópio (Rio de Janeiro: Record, 1984);

A serviço del-Rei (Rio de Janeiro: Record, 1984);

Violetas e caracóis (Rio de Janeiro: Guanabara, 1987);

Um artista aprendiz (Rio de Janeiro: J. Olympio, 1989);

Monte da Alegria (Rio de Janeiro: F. Alves, 1990);

Um cavalheiro de antigamente (São Paulo: Siciliano, 1992);

Ópera dos fantoches (Rio de Janeiro: F. Alves, 1994);

Vida, paixão e morte do herói (São Paulo: Global, 1995);

Confissões de Narciso (Rio de Janeiro: F. Alves, 1997);

Gaiola aberta: tempos de JK e Schmidt (Rio de Janeiro: Rocco, 2000);

Breve manual de estilo e romance (Belo Horizonte: Editora Universidade Federal de Minas Gerais, 2003).

Editions and Collections: *Uma vida em segrêdo,* edited, with a biobibliography, introduction, and notes, by Diva Vasconcellos da Rocha (Rio de Janeiro: Edições de Ouro, 1978);

Novelas de aprendizado (Rio de Janeiro: Nova Fronteira, 1980)–comprises *Teia* and *Sombra e exílio;*

Autran Dourado, edited by Angela Maria de Freitas Senra (São Paulo: Abril, 1983);

Autran Dourado, edited by João Luiz Lafetá (São Paulo: Global, 1997).

OTHER: Godofredo Rangel, *Vida ociosa,* preface by Dourado (Rio de Janeiro: Casa de Palavra/ Fundação Casa de Rui Barbosa, 2000).

In August 2000 the Ministério da Cultura (Ministry of Culture) of Portugal announced that the Prêmio Camões (Camões Prize) for literature was to be given to Autran Dourado for his "neo-Baroque style of Iberian origin" and for his "pronounced capacity for storytelling." For the Brazilian novelist this prize represented the "crown jewel" of his career as a writer that began in 1947 with the publication of the short novel *Teia* (Web). Ever since, Dourado's work has met with positive critical acclaim. His novels have been translated into many languages, and *Ópera dos mortos* (1967, Opera of the Dead; translated as *The Voices of the Dead,* 1980) is one of the representative universal works of literature designated by the United Nations Educational, Scientific, and Cultural Organization (UNESCO).

Waldomiro Freitas Autran Dourado was born on 18 January 1926 in Patos de Minas, in the colonial state of Minas Gerais, to Telêmaco Autran Dourado, a judge, and Alice Freitas Autran Dourado. History and its vestiges in the architecture of his hometown fascinated the precocious boy, as well as stories told by the old-timers who seemed immortal to him. All of these character types and many of the remembered places were to appear later in Dourado's writings. He attended the law school of the Universidade de Minas Gerais in Belo Horizonte, where he and his friends Fernando Sabino, Paulo Mendes Campos, Otto Lara Resende, and Sábato Magaldi founded a literary magazine, *Edifício.* Although the magazine produced only four issues, Dourado used it as an aegis for the publication of *Teia* in 1947. That same year he married Maria Lúcia Christo, a French teacher and translator. The couple had four children: Inês, Ofélia, Henrique, and Lúcio.

Dourado's inaugural novel, a publication financed by his mother, features some of the techniques and themes that he continued to develop throughout his literary career: gothic mood, family intrigue, secrets, small-town gossip, and rural settings that create a hermetic web. The reader is forced to follow a guilt-ridden narrator who lives in a boardinghouse owned by a malevolent caretaker. *Teia* has dubious literary value other than pointing toward what was to become Dourado's polished, mature style in later years.

Sombra e exílio (1950, Shadow and Exile) was published after Dourado had graduated from law school and begun working as a journalist. The novel presents a dysfunctional triangle among the protagonist, Rodrigo; his mother; and his estranged wife, Marta. Like the protagonist in *Teia,* Rodrigo is young and conflicted and has an unfulfilled desire for a male figure, the absent father. Both of these early novels are Surrealist and Kafkaesque. They were republished together much later as *Novelas de aprendizado* (1980, Novels of Apprenticeship).

Dourado was twenty-six years old when he published his third novel, *Tempo de amar* (1952, A Time for Loving). The protagonist, Ismael, is a young, anguished intellectual who has to live within the confines of a small town. As the narrator describes Ismael's stifling surroundings, the reader is drawn into the psychological drama that takes place. In a technique he was to perfect in later works, Dourado employed intertextuality as part of the structure of his narrative; thus, Ismael and his father parallel the biblical Abraham and his firstborn son, Ishmael.

In 1954 Dourado began working for Juscelino Kubitschek de Oliveira, first governor of Minas Gerais and later president of Brazil, with whom he worked for the next six years. During this time Dourado kept a meticulous journal that was the inspiration for his *Gaiola aberta: tempos de JK e Schmidt* (Open Birdcage: The Age of JK and Schmidt), published in 2000. While working as a press secretary for Kubitschek, Dourado published *Três histórias na praia* (1955, Three Stories at the Beach). In this book he experiments with different points of view. A single episode is described by three people: a man, a child, and a woman. Reminiscent of William Faulkner's *As I Lay Dying* (1930) in structure, *Três histórias na praia* breaks with the closed and stifling settings of Dourado's earlier books.

Dourado's Brazil was in a period of euphoria. A new capital was about to be built, and the "giant" seemed to be awakening to the world when the young journalist published his *Nove histórias em grupos de três* (1957, Nine Stories in Groups of Three). This collection includes the three stories from *Três histórias na praia* in addition to six new ones. The second group of three stories, all first-person narratives, includes "A glória do ofício" (The Glory of Work), in which Dourado painstakingly illustrates intertextuality through an allegory. The last three stories, "Histórias do internato" (Boarding School Stories), highlight the lives of students at the Colégio de São Mateus. Particularly important in these stories is the introduction of characters that later return in Dourado's novels and other short stories, such as João da Fonseca Nogueira and Martim. *Nove histórias em grupos de três* won critical praise as well as the Prêmio Artur Azevedo (Artur Azevedo Prize) from the Instituto Nacional do Livro (National Book Institute) in Brazil.

When Dourado published *A barca dos homens* (The Ship of Mankind) in 1961, he was already recognized as a fine writer and an established literary figure among the critics, but this volume also gave him popularity among the Brazilian reading public. As Dourado himself has explained, *A barca dos homens* is a pastiche of Portuguese literary figures that includes fictitious accounts from sixteenth-century navigators. Unlike his earlier narratives, this novel includes eroticism as a device for reflection on the human soul.

In 1964, as Brazil shifted into a military dictatorship that was to become one of the most repressive regimes in the history of the country, Dourado published a small volume, *Uma vida em segrêdo* (A Life in Secret; translated as *A Hidden Life,* 1969). This narrative focuses on the life of Biela, a wealthy woman who moves to the city of Duas Pontes (Two Bridges) to live with her cousins. Many critics have compared Dourado's expertly crafted text with Gustave Flaubert's "Un Coeur simple" (1877, A Simple Heart), a comparison that often angers the Brazilian writer, although Dourado acknowledges his love of books and his insatiable reading as a child and an adolescent. Importantly, *Uma vida em segrêdo* features the introduction of Duas Pontes, which is also the setting for many of Dourado's later novels. The narrative and characterization have provided a model for later writers. Suzana Amaral adapted *Uma vida em segrêdo* as a motion picture of the same title in 2001.

In 1967 Dourado published a new novel, *Ópera dos mortos,* the story of the spinster Rosalina, the last remaining member of the Cota family. The family and the mansion where Rosalina lives are shadows of their once-great opulence. Rosalina lives with her servant in the cavernous mansion that no longer means wealth or aristocracy but rather symbolizes the decay in the culture of the time. The house, the town, and the characters all seem to enter into a dizzying confluence. It is difficult to separate the narrative thread from the setting and its symbolism. Reminiscent of Faulkner's short story "A Rose for Emily" (1931), Dourado's novel introduces more characters in the Cota family who return to Duas Pontes in later works. In other novels the closed environment of the town becomes disturbed when an outsider breaches its seal.

Dourado's next novel, *O risco do bordado* (1970; The Embroidery Pattern; translated as *Pattern for a Tapestry,* 1984) continues the development of his narrative style as well as his narrative devices. He considers the pattern indicated by the title as a preestablished design: "Só Deus sabe por inteiro o risco do bordado" (Only God knows the whole pattern of the tapestry). But he knows that the colors and the hues will not be preestablished. In this novel the embroidery becomes a metaphor for the creative act of writing a text. Nogueira, the adolescent from "Histórias do internato," returns to Duas Pontes. The reader finds out at the end of the novel that twenty years have gone by, and the strands of the narrative come together as Nogueira, the narrator, ties the last knots in the embroidery. Although the pieces are "tied together neatly," the despair surrounding the inhabitants of this small town cannot be patched, and the reader is left with the same anxiety that the narrator experiences.

Two years after *O risco do bordado* came out, Dourado published *Solidão solitude* (1972, Solitude). The title, inspired by a poem by Mário de Andrade, brings together twelve short stories, only three of which are new. The other nine are those already published as *Nove histórias em grupos de três*. The three new stories reveal adult fears and feelings: a poet meets his idol, Andrade; a widower has a strange relationship with his mistress; and a couple commits suicide.

As Dourado perfected his novelistic talent, he also taught a course on literary theory at the Universidade Católica do Rio de Janeiro (Catholic University of Rio de Janeiro). He began to analyze his own writing, and he published his analyses and explanations of the writing process based on notes from this course as *Uma poética de romance* (1973, A Poetics of the Novel), later revising the text with more analyses and republishing it as *Uma poética de romance: matéria de carpintaria* (1976, A Poetics of the Novel: A Matter of Carpentry). In these two books of criticism Dourado explains what he calls "a carpintaria" (the carpentry) of novel writing: blocks are placed carefully as a foundation, to be followed by other blocks that will finally "build" the novel. Significantly, his first publication, a literary journal, was titled *Edifício* (Edifice), almost a foreshadowing of his metaphor for writing.

In 1974 Dourado published *Os sinos da agonia* (translated as *The Bells of Agony,* 1988). In this text he incorporates stream of consciousness as a guiding device as well as the already established multiple-perspective device. Continuing the development of the fictitious town of Duas Portes and its inhabitants, Dourado weaves their psychological traumas as they engage in everyday activities. More than in his other works, Dourado uses different language registers as well as fiction and nonfiction to give the novel various levels of discourse and a depth and richness not present in his other works. In describing eighteenth-century Minas Gerais and the golden age of this colonial state, Dourado employs the myth of Phaedra and Hippolytus but adds Euripides, Seneca the Younger, and Jean Racine as the "readers," or critics. With these classical allusions Dourado is able to enter into reflections on race, cus-

Dust jackets for Dourado's 1987 novel (Violets and Snails), one of his works that uses figures from Brazilian and Portuguese literary history to explore the theme of insanity, and his 1989 novel (An Apprentice Artist), the autobiography of his fictional alter ego that describes through the experiences of one man the development of the art of fiction through the "ages of a man" (Bruccoli Clark Layman Archives)

toms, and culture that had not appeared in his earlier books as explicitly.

In 1976 Dourado published *Novelário de Donga Novais,* in which he coins the word *novelário* as a synthesis between the novella and *novelos* (skein of yarn or string). Thus, the narrator, Donga Novais, unravels his story through everyday sayings well known to the Brazilian reader. Novais is a timeless, sleepless, ageless sage who sees all and forgets nothing. From his window he sees and describes Duas Pontes.

Armas & corações (1978, Arms and Hearts) is a collection of four novellas focusing on crimes of passion and their consequences. Most of the characters are familiar to the reader. They are the same types that appear in every small town, and Duas Pontes is no exception in this regard. What is somewhat different in this collection is the depiction of crime and a bit of violence not seen before in Dourado's prose. Three years later Dourado published *As imaginações pecaminosas* (1981, Sinful Imaginations). The underlying thread throughout the ten stories in this volume is the change that takes place in "facts" when people's imagination and gossip take over. Moreover, the narrator

explains the power of family name and honor as a guide to gossip. Dourado further clarified his thinking about the power of families in another book of literary reflection, *O meu mestre imaginário* (1982, My Imaginary Master). In this text he deals with the nature of apprenticeship in any trade, including that of the writer.

In 1984 Dourado published *A serviço del-Rei* (In the King's Service), a novel loosely based on his experience as press secretary to Kubitschek. Unlike Dourado's other books, this one is a farce in the classical sense. The novel combines politics, literature, and the art and mastery of apprenticeship in the story of the press secretary João, who learns the art of trickery from Saturniano de Brito. The novel also gives the reader another perspective on the "first families" of Duas Pontes and their familial intrigue.

When *Lucas Procópio* was published in 1984, the Cota family of Duas Pontes was well ingrained in the Brazilian imagination. The title character, Lucas, is the paternal grandfather of Rosalina (from *Ópera dos mortos*), and he demonstrates the power of family relationships, love, and insanity. Lucas is a pathetic dreamer and idealist. Physically and psychologically, he is like Miguel de Cervantes'

Don Quixote; however, as Lucas's story unfolds, it is an inversion of the Spanish hero's.

Dourado continues his reflection on sanity and insanity in his next novel, *Violetas e caracóis* (1987, Violets and Snails). Like many of the earlier titles, *Violetas e caracóis* relies on irony to introduce many figures from the "glorious" past of Brazilian and Portuguese literary history. In his elaboration of the theme of insanity Dourado unravels the musings of the diplomat and writer Afonso Arinos, the protagonist of the novel. In the end, sanity and insanity become entangled in the web of circumstances.

In 1989 Dourado published *Um artista aprendiz* (An Apprentice Artist), dedicated to Artur Versiani Veloso, his high-school philosophy teacher, and to Godofredo Rangel, a respected novelist already alluded to in *O meu mestre imaginário*. *Um artista aprendiz* is a biography of the character Nogueira, Dourado's alter ego. He describes Nogueira's coming-of-age as a man, a writer, and a political figure. *Um artista aprendiz* describes the art and craft of writing as it developed through the "ages of a man," but in this case, the man in question is a fictitious character.

In 1990 Dourado published *Monte da Alegria* (Hill of Happiness), continuing the symbolism and metaphorical images employed in his earlier works. More than in his other narratives, Dourado reflects on issues of religion in this text. Hagiography becomes psychology; church history becomes fiction; and the protagonist appears both as a messianic figure and as a mendicant preacher. This novel, unlike his others up to this point, did not receive much critical praise. Indeed, most critics find it less carefully crafted than Dourado's earlier works.

Two years later Dourado published *Um cavalheiro de antigamente* (1992, A Gentleman from Older Times). In this book the reader reencounters Lucas Procópio's son and Rosalina's father, João Capistrano Honório Cota. Through the voice of an alienated and melancholic old man, the narrative centers on Dourado's concerns about life and death, love and hate, and reality and appearances. The multiple perspectives come not from different voices but rather from memories now clouded by time and age. Multiple perspectives guided through strings shape the underlying themes in *Ópera dos fantoches* (1994, Puppet Opera). In this text Dourado also goes back to some of his earlier literary tapestry to find characters, plots, and manipulations. The puppets are not only characters but also a metaphor for outside manipulation.

Dourado published *Confissões de Narciso* (Narcissus's Confessions), perhaps his most introspective narrative, in 1997. Based on Stendhal's *De l'amour* (1822; translated as *On Love*, 1914), it is the diary of the protagonist, Tomás de Sousa Albuquerque, who commits suicide. His wife finds his diary shortly after his death and discovers that her husband was obsessed with a Don Juan complex. This short novel presents Dourado's usual preoccupations with the dilemmas of love and hate and life and death through the eyes of a self-absorbed and self-centered character for whom emotions are nothing more than machine-like behavior. Unlike Dourado's earlier prose, which is characterized by a heavy baroque style, the language in *Confissões de Narciso* is direct and simple. The narrative is well crafted and reflects the thinking of a mature writer.

Dourado's *Gaiola aberta: tempos de JK e Schmidt* was published in 2000. This volume is a rewriting, in memoir style, of the diary and notes that Dourado kept during his time as press secretary to Kubitschek. In comments to Ana Cecília Martíns published in the *Jornal do Brasil* (31 August 2000), Dourado states, "Neste livro eu mexo com a relação entre escritor e poder, e pinto um retrato humano de JK que talvez seja demasiadamente humano" (In this book I deal with the relation between writer and power, and I paint a human picture of JK that is perhaps too human). Dourado attempts to undo the myth surrounding Kubitschek that he admittedly helped to create. This book, although based on fact, does not differ much from the already established craftsman's model of unraveling a story from an historical precedent.

In 2003 Dourado published *Breve manual de estilo e romance* (Brief Manual on Style and the Novel), in which he reiterates his views on writing, reading, and literature. The reader again finds the admonition that good writing can be developed only through the reading of good literature.

Autran Dourado has created an entire world in the fictional Duas Pontes. This imaginary city is as much a part of the Brazilian imagination as is Yoknapatawpha County, Mississippi, in Faulkner's fiction. The characters that Dourado created have matured, as has his narrative style. They are well known and have become those long-ago relatives that everyone seems to have and revere, even while uncovering the usual mischief and insanity. Dourado's narrative art combines lucid use of language with intertextual manipulations that envelop and place the reader within the writer's fictional world.

References:

José Castello, "Diário amoroso: Autran Dourado derruba clichés em novela enxuta," *Isto É,* no. 1444 (4 June 1997);

Ana Cecília Martíns, "Aquitetura literária," *Jornal do Brasil,* 31 August 2000;

Carmen Chaves McClendon, "A arte de carpintaria e a narrativa poética de Autran Dourado," *Chasqui: revista de literatura latinoamericana,* 15 (1985): 19–24;

McClendon, "A Rose for Rosalina: From Yoknapatawpha to *Ópera dos Mortos,*" *Comparative Literature Studies,* 19 (1982): 450–458;

McClendon, "*Violetas e caracóis* e a interpretação da loucura," *Hispania,* 73 (1990): 291–293.

Carlos Drummond de Andrade

(31 October 1902 – 17 August 1987)

Jon M. Tolman
University of New Mexico

BOOKS: *Alguma poesia* (Belo Horizonte: Pindorama, 1930);

Brejo das almas: poemas (Belo Horizonte: Amigos do Livro, 1934);

Sentimento do mundo (Rio de Janeiro: Pongetti, 1940);

Poesias (Rio de Janeiro: J. Olympio, 1942)—includes *José;*

Confissões de Minas (Rio de Janeiro: Americ-Edit., 1944);

O gerente (Rio de Janeiro: Horizonte, 1945);

A rosa do povo (Rio de Janeiro: J. Olympio, 1945);

Poesia até agora (Rio de Janeiro: J. Olympio, 1948)—includes *Novos Poemas;*

A máquina do mundo (Rio de Janeiro: Martins, 1949);

Claro enigma (Rio de Janeiro: J. Olympio, 1951)—includes "A máquina do mundo";

Contos de aprendiz (Rio de Janeiro: J. Olympio, 1951; enlarged edition, 1958);

A mesa (Niterói: Hipocampo, 1951);

Passeios na ilha: divagações sôbre a vida literária e outras matérias (Rio de Janeiro: Simões, 1952);

Viola de bolso (Rio de Janeiro: Ministério da Educação e Saúde, Serviço de Documentação, 1952); revised and enlarged as *Viola de bolso novamente encordoada* (Rio de Janeiro: J. Olympio, 1955);

Fazendeiro do ar & Poesia até agora (Rio de Janeiro: J. Olympio, 1954);

Soneto da buquinagem (Rio de Janeiro: Philobiblion, 1955);

Ciclo (Recife: Gráfico Amador, 1957)—includes *A vida passada a limpo;*

Fala amendoeira (Rio de Janeiro: J. Olympio, 1957);

A bolsa & a vida: crônicas em prosa e verso (Rio de Janeiro: Editora do Autor, 1962);

Lição de coisas: poesia (Rio de Janeiro: J. Olympio, 1962);

Cadeira de balanço: crônicas (Rio de Janeiro: J. Olympio, 1966);

José & Outros (Rio de Janeiro: J. Olympio, 1967);

Versiprosa: crônica da vida cotidiana e de algumas miragens (Rio de Janeiro: J. Olympio, 1967);

Boitempo & A falta que ama (Rio de Janeiro: Sabiá, 1968);

Carlos Drummond de Andrade (*frontispiece for* The Minus Sign: Selected Poems, *translated by Virginia de Araujo, 1980; Thomas Cooper Library, University of South Carolina*)

Caminhos de João Brandão: crônicas (Rio de Janeiro: J. Olympio, 1970);

O poder ultra jovem, e mais 79 textos em prosa e verso (Rio de Janeiro: J. Olympio, 1972);

As impurezas do branco (Rio de Janeiro: J. Olympio, 1973);

Menino antigo (Boitempo II) (Rio de Janeiro: J. Olympio, 1973);

De notícias & não notícias faz-se a crônica: histórias, diálogos, divagações (Rio de Janeiro: J. Olympio, 1974);

Amor, amores (Rio de Janeiro: Alumbramento, 1975);

Os dias lindos: crônicas (Rio de Janeiro: J. Olympio, 1977);

Discurso da primavera e algumas sombras (Rio de Janeiro: J. Olympio, 1977);

A visita (São Paulo: Privately printed, 1977);

O marginal Clorindo Gato (Rio de Janeiro: Avenir, 1978);

70 historinhas: antologia (Rio de Janeiro: J. Olympio, 1978);

Esquecer para lembrar (Boitempo III) (Rio de Janeiro: J. Olympio, 1979);

Nudez (Recife: Escola de Artes, 1979);

A paixão medida (Rio de Janeiro: Alumbramento, 1980);

Contos plausíveis (Rio de Janeiro: J. Olympio/Editora JB, 1981);

Crônica das favelas cariocas (Rio de Janeiro: Privately printed, 1981);

O elefante (Rio de Janeiro: Record, 1983);

Boca de luar (Rio de Janeiro: Record, 1984);

Em certa casa da rua Barão de Jaguaribe: ata de natal comemorativa dos 20 anos do Sabadoyle (1984) (Rio de Janeiro: Sabadoyle, 1984);

Corpo (Rio de Janeiro: Record, 1984);

Crônicas de Carlos Drummond de Andrade sob pseudônimo Antônio Crispim e Barba Azul (Belo Horizonte: Revista do Arquivo Público Mineiro, 1984);

Amar se aprende amando: poesia de convívio e de humor (Rio de Janeiro: Record, 1985);

Amor, sinal estranho: antologia poética (Rio de Janeiro: Lithos, 1985);

História de dois amores (Rio de Janeiro: Record, 1985);

O observador no escritório (Rio de Janeiro, 1985);

Saudação a Plínio Doyle (Rio de Janeiro: Sabadoyle, 1986);

Tempo, vida, poesia: confissões no rádio (Rio de Janeiro: Record, 1986);

O avesso das coisas (Rio de Janeiro: Record, 1987);

Crônicas, 1930–1934 (Belo Horizonte: Governo do Estado de Minas Gerais, Secretaria de Estado da Cultura, 1987);

Moça deitada na grama (Rio de Janeiro: Record, 1987);

Poesia errante: derrames líricos (e outros nem tanto, ou nada) (Rio de Janeiro: Record, 1988);

Auto-retrato e outras crônicas, edited by Fernando Py (Rio de Janeiro: Record, 1989);

O amor natural (Rio de Janeiro: Record, 1992);

O sorvete e outras histórias (São Paulo: Atica, 1993);

A vida passada a limpo (Rio de Janeiro: Record, 1994);

A cor de cada um (Rio de Janeiro: Record, 1996);

Criança dagora é fogo! (Rio de Janeiro: Record, 1996);

Farewell (Rio de Janeiro: Record, 1996);

A senha do mundo (Rio de Janeiro: Record, 1996);

Vó caiu na piscina (Rio de Janeiro: Record, 1996);

Conversa de livraria, 1941 e 1948 (Pôrto Alegre: AGE / São Paulo: Giordano, 2000);

Quando é dia de futebol, edited by Luis Mauricio Graña Drummond and Pedro Augusto Graña Drummond (Rio de Janeiro: Record, 2002).

Editions and Collections: *50 poemas escolhidos pelo autor* (Rio de Janeiro: Ministerio da Educacão e Cultura, Servico de Documentacão, 1956);

Poemas (Rio de Janeiro: J. Olympio, 1959);

Antologia poética (Pôrto Alegre: Editora do Autor, 1962);

Obra completa, edited by Afrânio Coutinho, critical study by Emmanuel de Moraes (Rio de Janeiro: Aguilar, 1964; enlarged edition, 1967); revised and enlarged as *Poesia completa e prosa* (Rio de Janeiro: Aguilar, 1973); revised and enlarged as *Poesia e prosa* (Rio de Janeiro: Aguilar, 1979; revised and enlarged, 1988);

Reunião: 10 livros de poesia, introduction by Antônio Houaiss (Rio de Janeiro: J. Olympio, 1969);

Seleta em prosa e verso, critical study and notes by Gilberto Mendonça Teles (Rio de Janeiro: J. Olympio, 1971);

Minas & Drummond (Belo Horizonte: Conselho de Extensão da Universidade Federal de Minas Gerais, 1973);

Nova reunião: 19 livros de poesias (Rio de Janeiro: J. Olympio, 1983);

60 anos de poesia, edited, with an introduction, by Arnaldo Saraiva (Lisbon: Jornal, 1985); enlarged as *65 anos de poesia,* edited by Saraiva (Lisbon: Jornal, 1989);

Obra poética, 6 volumes (Mem Martins, Portugal: Publicações Europa-América, 1985–1990);

Histórias para o rei: conto, edited by Luzia de Maria (Rio de Janeiro: Record, 1997);

A palavra mágica: poesia, edited by Maria (Rio de Janeiro: Record, 1997);

As palavras que ninguém diz: crônica, edited by Maria (Rio de Janeiro: Record, 1997);

Poesia completa: conforme as disposições do autor, 2 volumes, edited by Teles, introduction by Silviano Santiago (Rio de Janeiro: Aguilar, 2001);

100 poemas, edited by Manuel Graña Etcheverry (Belo Horizonte: Editora Universidade Federal de Minas Gerais, 2002);

Prosa seleta (Rio de Janeiro: Aguilar, 2003).

Editions in English: *In the Middle of the Road: Selected Poems,* edited and translated by John Nist (Tucson: University of Arizona Press, 1965);

Souvenir of the Ancient World, translated by Mark Strand (New York: Antaeus, 1976);

The Minus Sign: Selected Poems, translated by Virginia de Araujo (Redding Ridge, Conn.: Black Swan, 1980; Manchester, U.K.: Carcanet, 1981);

Travelling in the Family: Selected Poems, edited by Thomas Colchie and Strand, additional translations by

Elizabeth Bishop and Gregory Rabassa (Hopewell, N.J.: Ecco Press, 1986).

RECORDINGS: *Carlos Drummond de Andrade,* read by Drummond, Festa FP-7002, 1963;

Antologia poética, read by Drummond, Polygram do Brasil 518 502-4, 1978;

Vinícius de Moraes; Carlos Drummond de Andrade, read by Drummond and Vinícius de Moraes, Philips 6842 134, 1981;

Manuel Bandeira; Carlos Drummond de Andrade, read by Drummond and Manuel Bandera, Festa LPP-001, n.d.

OTHER: *Quadrante,* 2 volumes, by Drummond and others (Rio de Janeiro: Editora do Autor, 1962–1963);

Rio de Janeiro em prosa & verso, by Drummond and Manuel Bandeira (Rio de Janeiro: J. Olympio, 1965);

Vozes da cidade: crônicas de Carlos Drummond de Andrade, Cecília Meireles, Genolino Amado, Henrique Pongetti, Maluh de Ouro Prêto, Manuel Bandeira, Rachel de Queiroz (Rio de Janeiro: Record, 1965);

Manuel Bandeira, Andorinha, Andorinha, edited by Drummond (Rio de Janeiro: J. Olympio, 1966);

Minas Gerais, edited by Drummond (Rio de Janeiro: Editora do Autor, 1967);

Elenco de crônistas modernos: Carlos Drummond de Andrade, Clarice Lispector, Fernando Sabino, Manuel Bandeira, Paulo Mendes Campos, Rachel de Queiroz, Rubem Braga (Rio de Janeiro: Sabiá, 1971);

Cândido Portinari, D. Quixote: 21 desenhos de Cândido Portinari, commentary by Drummond (Rio de Janciro: Diagraphics, 1972);

Pedro Nava, Bau De Ossos: Memorias, annotated by Drummond (Rio de Janeiro: J. Olympio, 1973);

Para gostar de ler, 6 volumes, by Drummond and others (São Paulo: Atica, 1977–1984);

O pipoqueiro da esquina, text by Drummond (Rio de Janeiro: Codecri, 1981);

Leila Diniz: "uma mulher solar" (Domingos Oliveira), text by Drummond and others (Rio de Janeiro: CODECRI, 1982);

Mata atlântica=Atlantic Forest, poetry by Drummond, translated by Aíla de Oliveira Gomes (Rio de Janeiro: Chase Banco Lar/Assessoria de Comunicação e Marketing, 1984);

Quatro vozes, by Drummond and others (Rio de Janeiro: Record, 1984);

Pantanal, poetry by Drummond, translated by Gomes (Rio de Janeiro: Chase Banco Lar/Assessoria de Comunicação e Marketing, 1985);

Bandeira, a vida inteira: poemas de Carlos Drummond de Andrade, textos extraídos da obra de Manuel Bandeira (Rio de Janeiro: Alumbramento/Instituto Nacional do Livro, 1986);

Hugo Rodrigo Octavio, *O prazer das imagens: fotografias de Hugo Rodrigo Octavio,* text by Drummond and others (São Paulo: Metal Leve/Hamburg, 1987);

Drummond, Arte em exposição, poetry by Drummond, translated by Gomes, introduction by Affonso Romano de Sant'Anna (Rio de Janeiro: Salamandra/Record, 1990);

O mês modernista, by Drummond and others, edited by Homero Senna (Rio de Janeiro: Fundação Casa de Rui Barbosa, 1994);

Rua da Bahia, by Drummond and Nava (Belo Horizonte: Editora Universidade Federal de Minas Gerais, 1996);

Looking for Poetry: Poems by Carlos Drummond de Andrade and Rafael Alberti and Songs from the Quechua, translated by Mark Strand (New York: Knopf, 2002).

TRANSLATIONS: François Mauriac, *Uma gota de veneno* (Rio de Janeiro: Pongetti, 1943);

Pierre Choderlos de Laclos, *As relações perigosas* (Pôrto Alegre: Globo, 1947);

Honoré de Balzac, *Os camponeses* (Pôrto Alegre: Globo, 1954);

Marcel Proust, *A fugitiva* (Rio de Janeiro, 1958);

Federico García Lorca, *Dona Rosita, a solteira; ou, A linguagem das flores* (Rio de Janeiro: Agir, 1959);

Jean-Théodore Descourtilz, *Beija-flores do Brasil* (Rio de Janeiro: Biblioteca Nacional, 1960);

Maurice Maeterlinck, *O pássaro azul* (Rio de Janeiro: Delta, 1962);

Molière, *Artimanhas de Scapino* (Rio de Janeiro: Serviço de Documentação do Ministério da Educação e Cultura, 1962);

Knut Hamsun, *Fome* (Rio de Janeiro: Delta, 1963).

Carlos Drummond de Andrade is one of the most important twentieth-century Brazilian poets. He began writing poetry seriously in the mid 1920s and quickly became one of the best-known modernists in the country. He succeeded in reinventing himself decade after decade, maintaining his position of preeminence until his death in 1987. Drummond's complete published poetry comprises some nineteen volumes. He sent original poems to hundreds of fans who wrote to him or sent him samples of their own verse, and he took the time to send poetry and respond to letters from secondary schools all over Brazil. These occasional poems, if collected, would probably total several hundred additional pages.

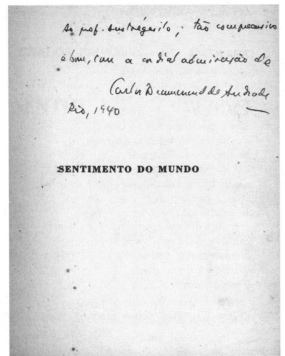
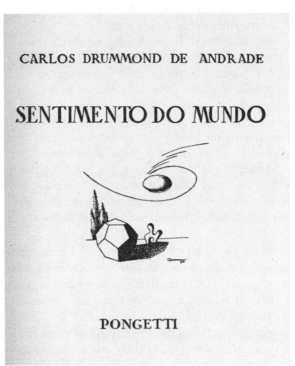

Title page for Drummond's third poetry collection, published in 1940, with the half-title page inscribed by the author
(Northern Regional Library Facility, University of California, Berkeley)

In addition to poetry, Drummond produced an astonishing range of work in prose: short stories, essays, and *crônicas* (chronicles). The chronicle is a short prose work produced exclusively for newspapers and may be almost anything, from a short-short story or a whimsical essay to a piece of social commentary. Drummond earned a steady income from these pieces, publishing for many years in the *Correio da Manhã* when it was in its heyday and later in the *Jornal do Brasil*. He was notoriously secretive about his private life and rarely gave interviews, but his essays occasionally offer insight into his creative process. *O observador no escritório* (1985, The Observer in his Office) purports to be his autobiography, but it is singularly uninformative. A godsend for scholars is *Carlos & Mário: correspondência completa entre Carlos Drummond de Andrade (inédita) e Mário de Andrade* (Carlos & Mário: Complete Correspondence between Carlos Drummond de Andrade [Unpublished] and Mário de Andrade), published in 2002 as part of the commemoration of the centenary of Drummond's birth. Drummond initiated correspondence with the poet and critic Mário de Andrade shortly after the latter's visit to Minas Gerais in 1924, and Andrade was Drummond's most trusted friend and mentor until his death in 1945. Drummond's letters reveal a completely different man from

the taciturn, efficient, sardonic, shy persona he presented to the world.

Carlos Drummond de Andrade was born on 31 October 1902 in the mining town of Itabira do Mato Dentro, in the interior of the central-southern state of Minas Gerais. Minas Gerais became an important part of the Portuguese empire when massive deposits of gold were discovered there in the seventeenth century. Later, other minerals were discovered, and when Drummond was growing up, an English mining company (excavating iron ore) was an important part of daily life. Born into an important local ranching family, Drummond was the ninth son of Carlos de Paula Andrade. Drummond's father owned four ranches and a great deal of property in Itabira and was a dominant local political figure. His mother, Julieta Augusta Drummond de Andrade, a cousin of his father, was a delicate, shy woman.

The family moved from Itabira to Belo Horizonte, the state capital, in 1920. Drummond's father divided his properties among his surviving sons and spent the final decade of his life in retirement before dying in 1931. Julieta Augusta was not in the best of health either and spent the years 1941 to 1948 as a special patient in the Hospital São Lucas in Belo Horizonte. Drummond was devoted to his mother, but he had a contentious relationship with his father, and this quarrel became the focal point of an important theme in the poet's work. In his early writings he referred to himself as Drummond or Carlos Drummond, implicitly rejecting his paternal heritage. His father spared no expense in educating his bookish son and at various times showed great tolerance for his escapades, but he was apparently an inarticulate man who could find no way of expressing his love, either through language or physical contact. Julieta Augusta was affectionate and voluble, writing frequent letters from her hospital apartment to her surviving children but most especially to Drummond. "Suas mãos" (Her Hands), from *Boitempo* (Cowtime & Beloved Absence), published in *Boitempo & A falta que ama* (1968), is one of his tributes to her.

As a member of an important oligarchic family at the beginning of the twentieth century, Drummond grew up surrounded by reminders of slavery, abolished only in 1888 in Brazil (the family's servants were all former slaves), privilege, and the peculiar Brazilian social matrix in which mulatto lower-class workers and artisans in a small town were likely to be related to members of the upper class. For example, a man who exercised a kind of adoptive paternal role for the young Carlos, or Carlito, as he was called, was Alfredo Duval, a mulatto wood carver of figures of saints and religious tableaux who lived near the Andrade family in Itabira. Duval was probably Drummond's older half brother. He was both a religious man and an ardent radical, and some of Drummond's own heterodox view of the world may have been formed in Duval's house, where the boy spent a great deal of time. When Drummond moved to Rio de Janeiro, he took one of Duval's statuettes with him, and there is a reference to Duval in "Confidência do itabirano," from *Sentimento do mundo* (1940, Sense of the World).

In a society where wealthy landowners lived with their wives and legitimate children in close proximity to slave (and later servant) concubines and their children, it was traditional that young white men be initiated sexually by black women in the household. Some of these same women might have wet-nursed the boys who later became their lovers. The result was a complex web of affection, lust, exploitation, and guilt. In Drummond's case, there is evidence that his upbringing was in no way different from that of thousands of other white men, and the subject is emphasized in several poems. In "Canto negro" (Black Song), from *Claro enigma* (1951, Transparent Enigma), he writes:

Meu preto, o bom era o nosso.
O mau era o nosso. E amávamos
a comum essência triste
que transmutava os carinhos

numa visguenta doçura
de vulva negro-amaranto
barata! que vosso preço,
ó corpos de antigamente,
somente estava no dom
de vós mesmos ao desejo,
num entregar-se sem pejo
de terra pisada. . . .

(Black friend, the good was ours.
The bad was ours. And we loved
the common sad essence
that transmitted caresses
in a sticky sweetness
of black-purple vulva
cheap! Because your price,
oh bodies of yesteryear,
was only in the gift
of yourselves to desire,
surrender without shame
of trodden earth. . . .)

In "Negra" (Black Woman), from *Boitempo,* Drummond writes:

A negra para tudo
a negra para todos
a negra para capinar plantar
regar
colher carregar empilhar no paiol
ensacar
lavar passar remendar costurar cozinhar
rachar lenha
limpar a bunda dos nhozinhos
trepar.

(The black woman for everything
the black woman for everyone
the black woman to hoe plant
irrigate
harvest carry pile up in the barn
fill sacks
wash iron mend sew cook
split wood
clean little masters' butts
fuck.)

The concatenation of verbs piles up in a symbolic mountain of obligations.

Another important influence on the young Drummond was his reading of satirical reviews from Rio de Janeiro, such as *Fon-Fon* and *Careta,* and especially a children's magazine called *Tico-Tico* (Sparrow), which offered readers a serialized translation of Daniel Defoe's *Robinson Crusoe* (1719–1722). The story of a civilized man trapped on an isolated island appealed greatly to the young Carlito's sense that he, too, was trapped in Itabira and Minas Gerais, condemned to the small-mindedness and inconsequentiality of provincial life. It takes an effort of imagination to understand how truly isolated a town such as Itabira must have been at the beginning of the twentieth century. It was far from Belo Horizonte, even farther from Rio, and impossibly far from Europe. The town sat in a valley, surrounded by mountains of iron ore, so the psychological isolation was compounded by a sense of encirclement.

The magazines of Rio de Janeiro offered to a provincial child's eyes a sense of metropolitan life. Reading *Robinson Crusoe* was a formative experience. Drummond's concept of the relationship between the individual and society and the individual and the world was shaped by what he read in Defoe's novel. Drummond's work features many references to islands. In *Confissões de Minas* (1944, Confessions of Minas) he says, "Por que será que o homem civilizado sonha tanto com a ilha deserta? . . . Cada um de nós constrói dentro de si mesmo a sua ilha pessoal e vai vivendo como pode, no tumulto da cidade, que, na aparente solidariedade de suas casas e ruas, esconde a estranha composição de milhares de almas opostas e inconciliáveis, vegetando orgulhosamente em ilhas inacessíveis" (Why is it that civilized man dreams so much about desert islands? . . . Each of us constructs inside himself his personal island and lives in it as he can in the tumult of the city, which, in the apparent solidarity of its houses and streets, hides the strange composition of thousands of opposing and irreconcilable souls, proudly vegetating in inaccessible islands).

In 1918 Drummond's father sent him to the Colégio Anchieta in Nova Friburgo, in the interior of the state of Rio de Janeiro. There he first heard about Marxism, as the students demanded of newcomers whether they were maximalists or minimalists. Drummond answered that he was neither; he was an anarchist. The Colégio Achieta was an important secondary school, with students from all over Brazil. Discipline was rigid, but Drummond took to the regimen of the school and excelled in his studies. In 1919, however, just before the end of the term, he ran afoul of a Portuguese instructor and was expelled for "intellectual insubordination." This episode seems to have had a lasting influence on Drummond's worldview. If he was a skeptic before, he afterward vacillated between agnosticism and atheism, and he never reconciled with the church. The injustice of his expulsion seems to have confirmed a growing conviction that society was governed by arbitrary and capricious rules. Throughout his life Drummond was insubordinate, instinctively rejecting authority.

In 1920 Drummond accompanied his family to Belo Horizonte, and he quickly found a circle of like-minded young men who gathered at the bookstore Livraria Alves and at the Café Estrela. He loved the freedom of the capital and the opportunities it provided for flirtation and discussion of new ideas with his friends. The owner of the Livraria Alves was willing to order the latest in European literature from Paris, and the young men congregated there every time a new crate arrived. Unemployed, Drummond tried to alleviate his growing discomfiture at living on the paternal dole by publishing occasional book and movie reviews in local newspapers, beginning an almost ten-year relationship with the *Diário de Minas* that was to be important in launching the modernist movement in Minas Gerais. The men who met at the Livraria Alves and the Café Estrela became the intellectual elite of Minas Gerais, and several, like Drummond, became nationally prominent.

Minas Gerais was an important political and economic actor in the First Republic of Brazil (1889–1930). When the eventually successful revolution of 1930 broke out, Minas Gerais sided with the rebels, led by Getúlio Vargas, who was from the far southern state of Rio Grande do Sul. In so doing, Minas Gerais guaranteed itself an important role in the new government. Many men from Drummond's generation and circle of friends became important national political figures. Gustavo Capanema, a schoolmate, was named Vargas's minister of education and public health in 1934, and he brought Drummond to Rio de Janeiro with him to be his chief of staff.

In 1920 Drummond discovered two other passions: movies and the young women, some of them shop girls, who also frequented the Odeon cinema, the finest in Belo Horizonte. One of these girls was Dolores Dutra de Morais, one of seven daughters from a lower-middle-class family that lived near the Andrades. Dolores was a typist, and her father was a night watchman. Drummond dated her for five years, in spite of his parents' disapproval and the bafflement of his friends. He was hardly monogamous, however, and had affairs with several attractive, intellectually challenging young women of his own class. Drummond attended the School of Odontology and Pharmacy in Belo Horizonte and graduated in 1925 with a degree in pharmacy.

Drummond's reasons for marrying Dolores have never been elucidated. In a 20 May 1925 letter to Mário de Andrade he said of his impending marriage, "I feel a mixture of nervousness, dejection, happiness (disillusioned happiness), and several other things. . . ." Andrade was alarmed and replied on 27 May, advising Drummond to break off his engagement to avoid "the deliberate misfortune of two people." Drummond responded on 19 July, indicating that Andrade's letter had arrived the day after his marriage. The marriage endured, but it was not without drama because of Drummond's many affairs. Once, many years later,

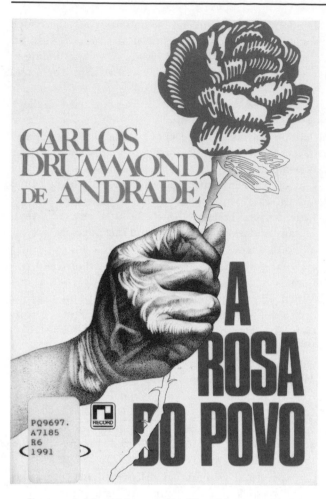

Front cover of the 1991 paperback edition of the poetry collection originally published to great acclaim in 1945 (Dinand Library, College of the Holy Cross)

part this interest was in reaction to Parnassianism, the dominant poetic style in Brazil since the 1880s, which exalted form, logic, and lucidity. The post-symbolist aestheticism and world-weary pose of Wilde and the decadents appealed to these young men who feigned contempt for the provincialism of Belo Horizonte and disdain for underdeveloped Brazil. France's skepticism fitted well into this attitude. Andrade argued that this decadence was a dead end and convinced Drummond to change his attitude, avoid Gallicisms and Lusitanisms (signs of Portuguese influence), and incorporate Brazilian vernacular language into his poetry. The tone of the letters exchanged between the two poets at this time is cordial, uninhibited, and brotherly, with Andrade assuming the role of a wiser, elder brother. In spite of Andrade's tutelage, there are many decadence-tinged poems in Drummond's first two collections, *Alguma poesia* (1930, Some Poetry) and *Brejo das almas* (1934, Soul Swamp).

Alguma poesia is aggressively experimental and iconoclastic, but *Brejo das almas* has a more pessimistic, fin de siècle tone. Most of the poems in *Alguma poesia* were written from 1924 to 1929 and were first published in various vanguard journals. Drummond later said of this early poetry,

> Meu primeiro livro, *Alguma poesia* (1930), traduz uma grande inexperiência do sofrimento e uma deleitação ingênua com o próprio indivíduo. Já em *Brejo das almas* (1934), alguma coisa se compôs, se organizou; o individualismo será mais exacerbada mas há também uma consciência crescente da sua precariedade e uma desaprovação tácita da conduta (ou falta de conduta) espiritual do autor. Penso ter resolvido as contradições elementares da minha poesia num terceiro volume, *Sentimento do mundo* (1940).

> (My first book, *Alguma poesia* (1930), expresses a great inexperience with suffering and a naive enjoyment of individuality. In *Brejo das almas* (1934), some things were fixed, organized; my individualism may be more exaggerated but there is also a growing awareness of its instability and a tacit disapproval of the spiritual conduct [or lack of conduct] of the author. I think I have solved the elementary contradictions of my poetry in a third volume, *Sentimento do mundo* [1940].)

Drummond's professional situation stabilized when his friend Alberto Campos got him a job as chief editor at the *Diário de Minas*. As editor, Drummond revealed the qualities that were to make him a model administrator. He was efficient, conscientious, thorough, and well organized, qualities that led his friend Capanema to bring him into state government in 1934. Later Capanema was named *interventor* in Minas Gerais, and Drummond went with him as his chief of staff.

Dolores threatened to divorce him because of his open flaunting of his mistress, Lygia Fernandes. Drummond responded that he would kill himself if she left him. Dolores relented, and they continued together until his death.

Drummond had begun corresponding with Manuel Bandeira, already a famous poet, in 1924. Bandeira, who began his poetic career as a Parnassian, was an early convert to the radical new modernist movement that had coalesced in 1922 in the Semana de Arte Moderna (Week of Modern Art, 13–17 February) in São Paulo. The members of the Belo Horizonte intelligentsia were intensely curious about modernism, and they got their chance to find out about it firsthand in April 1924, when a delegation of intellectuals, writers, and artists from São Paulo came to Belo Horizonte in the company of the Swiss writer Blaise Cendrars. Drummond met Andrade at this time.

Drummond's group was enthralled by the European decadents, Oscar Wilde, and Anatole France. In

(The revolutionary Vargas government replaced elected governors of states with special appointees known as *interventores*.)

In Drummond's personal life things were not going well. Dolores had an ectopic pregnancy that almost killed her, and the fetus had to be aborted. This misfortune was followed in 1927 by the birth of a son, Carlos Flávio, who lived for a mere thirty minutes. Drummond was desolated, but he referred to the tragedy rarely in his work and in letters to family and close friends. In "O que viveu meia hora" (He Who Lived a Half Hour), from *A paixão medida* (1980, Measured Passion), the poet says,

> Nascer para não viver
> só para ocupar
> estrito espaço numerado
> ao sol-e-chuva
> que meticulosamente vai delindo
> o número. . . .
>
> (To be born to not live
> only to occupy
> a strictly numbered space
> in the sun-and-rain
> which meticulously dissolves
> the number. . . .)

Finally, a healthy daughter, Maria Julieta, was born to the couple on 4 March 1928. She became the joy of Drummond's life, and he was a doting father and, later, grandfather to her children. Although he was becoming nationally famous, and his exceptional job skills guaranteed him employment, his income as a government official, even combined with fees for freelance journalism, was always insufficient for a comfortable lifestyle.

Drummond's letters to Andrade from this period reveal a hesitant, fearful man who refused a big promotion to the general editorship of *Diário da Noite,* a major São Paulo daily, because he was unsure of himself. Drummond dithered about publishing his poems, which until this time had circulated in manuscript form. Eventually he gathered his courage, publishing *Alguma poesia* to immense acclaim in 1930 and uprooting his family in 1934 at the invitation of Capanema to move to Rio de Janeiro. Drummond was tentative in publishing his early work, generally self-financing limited editions (500 copies of *Alguma poesia,* 200 of *Brejo das almas,* and 150 of *Sentimento do mundo*) that he sent to friends and selected critics. Only when the books became established did he finally accept a contract with the famous José Olympio Editora to publish his work commercially.

In 1928 Drummond published "No meio do caminho" (In the Middle of the Road) in the *Revista de antropofagia* (Cannibal Review) of São Paulo. The poem created a sensation and became a kind of emblem of the literary vanguard, even for a general public not generally concerned with formal literature. The short, ten-line poem seems innocuous enough, but it divided the literary community and the community at large into two camps–those who "got it" and those who not only did not get it but had no desire to do so. The first stanza reads, "No meio do caminho tinha uma pedra / tinha uma pedra no meio do caminho / tinha uma pedra / no meio do caminho tinha uma pedra" (In the middle of the road there was a rock / there was a rock in the middle of the road / there was a rock / in the middle of the road there was a rock). The repeating lines expressed in simple, conversational Portuguese are the antithesis of the arcane, melodic verses of the Parnassians and symbolists. Taken literally, the words are almost gibberish, but the metaphysical implications of Drummond's rock echo through his work and gain new meaning with each new iteration. The second stanza begins, "Nunca me esquecerei desse acontecimento / na vida de minhas retinas tão fatigadas" (I shall never forget this event / as long as my exhausted retinas have life). These lines seem to reveal a vestige of Drummond's flirtation with fin de siècle pessimism but hint at the meaning hidden beneath the expressionless surface of the rock. Drummond had an instinctive suspicion of global systems, be they religious or ideological in nature, because they all require that the inquirer surrender himself to the solution.

One distinctive feature of Drummond's poetry is the dialogue he maintained with himself for several decades, expressing a synthesis or conclusion only to repudiate or modify it later, as in "No meio do caminho." His body of work is one of the most exhaustively studied in Brazilian literature, and many scholars have attempted to devise schemes to explain the underlying unity connecting his different periods. All of his poetry attempts in one way or another to explain the mystery of human existence as social beings and to explore the perplexity of contemporary man attempting to solve the problem of his own identity, lacking the traditional certainties of religion, family, and class.

In "Poema de sete faces" (Seven Faceted Poem), the first poem in *Alguma poesia,* Drummond expresses what is an enduring theme in his poetry: awkwardness, gaucherie, and off-centeredness. The seven facets of the title are expressed in seven stanzas, an odd number for a decidedly odd poem: "Quando nasci, um anjo torto / desses que vivem na sombra / disse: Vai, Carlos! Ser gauche na vida" (When I was born, a twisted angel / one of those who live in the shadow / said: Go, Carlos! Be gauche in life). These first lines use one of Drummond's favorite devices, alter egos. Carlos is one alter ego, Carlitos another, and one whole book is dedicated to a third, José. Drummond used pseudonyms for a variety of purposes throughout his life.

A well-known stanza from "Poema de sete faces" encapsulates Drummond's fundamental orientation toward the world, at least in his first two volumes of poetry:

> Mundo mundo vasto mundo,
> se eu me chamasse Raimundo
> seria uma rima, não seria uma solução.
> Mundo mundo vasto mundo,
> mais vasto é meu coração.

> (World world vast world,
> if I were named Raimundo
> it would be a rhyme; it would not be a solution.
> World world vast world
> my heart is more vast.)

In his isolation the poet retreats from the overwhelming world and concentrates on himself and what he can control, his own words. In the final stanza there is an awkward, sardonic explanation for the perhaps too revealing words that preceded it: "Eu não devia te dizer / mas essa lua / mas esse conhaque / botam a gente comovido como o diabo" (I shouldn't tell you this / but that moon / but this cognac / get a guy all shook up.)

Even in this first poem the reader gains some insight into why many of Drummond's poems are still enjoyable long after they were written. The language is colloquial, simple, and straightforward and retains its freshness. Drummond's concession to the nationalism of the first modernist era, a period of poets who believed that they should be writing poetry about Brazil and who are no longer read, was merely to situate himself in the contemporary urban landscape, using contemporary Brazilian speech.

"Infância" (Childhood), the following poem in *Alguma poesia,* presents a theme that runs throughout Drummond's poetry for the next fifty years: his family and his place in it and, through it, with the world. As he was to do for decades, he portrays his father as a silent, enigmatic figure who refuses to communicate with his son: "Meu pai montava a cavalo, ia para o campo. / Minha mãe ficava sentada cosendo" (My father would get on his horse and ride off. / My mother stayed home sewing). The poem concludes with another apparently egotistical affirmation: "E eu não sabia que minha história / era mais bonita que a de Robinson Crusoé" (And I didn't know that my life / was prettier than Robinson Crusoe's). This idea is simply a restatement of the "vast world" argument in "Poema de sete faces." Other Minas Gerais poems in *Alguma poesia* include "Família" (Family), "Igreja" (Church), "Lanterna

mágica" (Cinema), "Cidadezinha qualquer" (Any Town), "Iniciação amorosa" (Lesson in Love), "Cabaré mineiro" (Minas Bar), "Sesta" (Siesta), and "Romaria" (Pilgrimage).

Some of the poems in *Alguma poesia* are pure exercises in vanguard attempts to *épater le bourgeois.* "No meio do caminho" perhaps fits this description since it has become a metaphor among the middle class for stupid, meaningless modern art. "Sinal de apito" (Traffic Whistle) is a found poem, phrases from a traffic manual arranged in verse form. "Quadrilha" (Square Dance) is a serious joke poem about love, or rather, love lost: "João amava Teresa que amava Raimundo / que amava Maria que amava Joaquim que amava Lili / que não amava ninguém" (John loved Teresa who loved Raymond / who loved Mary who loved Jack who loved Lilly / who didn't love anyone). As the partners change in the dance, they all end up in unexpected places: John goes to the United States, Teresa ends up in a convent, Raymond dies in an accident, Mary becomes an old maid, Jack commits suicide, and Lilly marries someone who is not in the poem.

In *Brejo das almas* the spirit of "Quadrilha" is continued in a more sarcastic, cynical vein. "Necrológio dos desiludidos do amor" (Autopsy of Disillusioned Lovers) seems to be based on sensationalist tabloid stories:

> Os desiludidos do amor
> estão desfechando tiros no peito.
> Do meu quarto ouço a fuzilaria.
> As amadas torcem-se de gozo.
> Oh quanta matéria para os jornais.

> (Disillusioned lovers
> are shooting themselves in the chest.
> I hear the fusillade from my room.
> Their women are beside themselves with pleasure.
> So much material for the papers.)

The sarcastic, pseudomilitary term "fusillade" is used for the suicides, and it is followed by more exaggeration. The dead had "grandes corações" (enormous hearts) and "vísceras imensas" (immense intestines). They are competently boxed in appropriate coffins, "paixões de primeira e de segunda classe" (first- and second-class passions), as if they were taking a train. The play on words between "caixões" (coffins) and "paixões" (passions) was actually suggested by a reader of the first edition, in which Drummond had used the obvious "caixões."

Brejo das almas is in general a darker work than *Alguma poesia.* The later collection includes several poems about violent death, and suicide, which Drummond had mentioned before, is now openly discussed.

Many of the poems express a frustrated or tormented sexuality. In "Poema patético" (Pathetic Poem) the poet uses a refrain–"Que barulho é esse na escada?" (What is that noise on the stairs?)–to frame stanzas that focus on the pathos of everyday life in the city, with its anonymous tragedies and the necessary promiscuity of living in apartment buildings: "Que barulho é esse na escada? / E o amor que está acabando, / é o homem que fechou a porta / e se enforcou na cortina" (What is that noise on the stairs? / It is love ending, / and the man who closed the door / and hanged himself with the curtains).

In "Não se mate" (Don't Kill Yourself) Drummond employs his alter ego Carlos, reinforcing an autobiographical connection as he argues himself out of suicide. Frustrated love is not worth it, and repressed impulses are simply small noises inside the head. Drummond uses "recalques" for repression, a term that came into vogue with the popularity of Sigmund Freud's theories of the unconscious. In a 1931 interview Drummond said, "Espiritualmente, a minha geração está diante de três rumos, ou de três soluções–Deus, Freud e o comunismo. A bem dizer, os rumos são dois apenas: uma ação católica, fascista, e organizada em 'Defesa do Ocidente' de um lado. E do outro lado o paraíso moscovita, com a sua terrível e por isso mesmo envolvente sedução" (Spiritually, my generation confronts three paths, or three solutions: God, Freud, and communism. In reality, there are only two paths: a Catholic action, fascist and organized in defense of the West on one side, and on the other the Muscovite paradise with its terrible, and for that reason, embracing seduction). Drummond seems to have embraced both Freud and communism; fascism and Brazil's right-wing Catholic-action movement repelled him.

There is a series of references in *Alguma poesia* and *Brejo das almas* to women and eroticism. At the beginning of Drummond's career critics spoke of a "sexual tension" in his poetry, but these occasional erotic verses and poems were not considered central to his work. Now that his complete poetry is available for examination, these instances are clear hints of a deep current of sexuality that was always present, occasionally manifesting itself in the early poems and finally breaking out as a major theme in his mature poetry. *O amor natural* (Natural Love) was a bombshell when published posthumously in 1992. The poems are frankly, shockingly erotic.

Drummond's first erotic allusion comes in the third stanza of "Poema de sete faces": "O bonde passa cheio de pernas: / pernas brancas pretas amarelas. / Para que tanta perna, meu Deus, pergunta o meu coração. / Porém meus olhos não perguntam nada" (The trolley passes by full of legs: / white black yellow

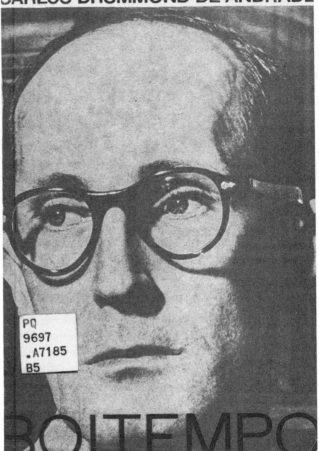

Front cover of the 1968 poetry collection that was the first in a series of three similarly titled collections drawing on Drummond's childhood in Minas Gerais (Joint University Libraries, Nashville)

legs. / My God, why are there so many legs, my heart inquires. / But my eyes have no questions). These remarks are inoffensive enough, but their meaning is unmistakable. "Iniciação amorosa" narrates a youthful sexual experience with a washerwoman, who comes to the narrator in his hammock, and once again the poet tries to hide his awkwardness with a joke: ". . . me deu as maminhas / que eram só minhas" (. . . she gave me her nipples / that were all for me). At the end of "O procurador do amor" (Agent of Love), from *Brejo das almas,* the poet says, "E faço este verso perverso, / inútil, capenga e lúbrico" (And I write this perverse verse / useless, crippled and lubricious). The psychological picture that emerges from *Brejo das almas* is one of a person tormented by his sexuality.

Drummond remained Capanema's chief of staff in the Ministry of Education and Public Health until 1945. Capanema had Vargas's confidence and was able to survive attempts to oust him from office, especially from the far right. An especially tolerant man, Capanema chose subordinates for their talent, not for their political opinions. As the Vargas regime wavered between the Allies and the Axis powers in the years preceding World War II, the Ministry of Education and Public Health was a haven for intellectuals and creative spirits of all kinds. Drummond became the target of conservatives, who saw him as presiding over a communist conspiracy in the ministry. Although Drummond once sent Capanema a letter of resignation, the minister refused to accept it. This situation helps to explain why Drummond, who despised Vargas and his fascist Estado Novo (New State, 1937–1945), continued to work in his government. He owed his loyalty to Capanema, not Vargas.

In Rio de Janeiro, Drummond had installed his family in a house on Avenida Princesa Isabel near the Tunel Novo (New Tunnel), an engineering feat completed in 1906. The tunnel linked Copacabana and Botafogo and permitted the rapid urbanization of Copacabana, until then a relatively remote suburb of Rio de Janeiro. One early result of this new urban experience is the poem "Morro da Babilônia" (Babylon Slum), from *Sentimento de Mundo. Morro* (hill) is a term used in Rio de Janeiro for its *favelas* (slums) because they are predominantly located on the slopes of the granite hills that structure the city. The Morro da Babilônia is one of the most infamous slums because of its violence. It is located between Copacabana and Botafogo (near Drummond's house), and its gangsters find easy access to the beaches and luxury hotels located in the same area. Even in the 1930s the Morro was feared, as Drummond observes:

> À noite, do morro
> descem vozes que criam o terror
> . . . Mas as vozes do morro
> não são propriamente lúgubres.
> Há mesmo um cavaquinho bem afinado
> que domina os ruídos da pedra e da folhagem
> e desce até nós, modesto e criativo,
> como a gentileza do morro.
>
> (At night from the slum
> voices fall that create terror
> . . . But the voices of the slum
> are not exactly mournful.
> In fact there is a well-tuned ukelele
> that overcomes the noises of stone and foliage
> and comes to us, modest and diverting,
> like a favor from the slum.)

At first Drummond, who was quite well known in Belo Horizonte, was mystified by the standoffishness of his new neighbors. He quickly grew to love the freedom Rio de Janeiro offered, however, and spent his weekends walking with Maria Julieta on the city's spectacular beaches. The separation from his roots in Minas Gerais allowed him to purge himself of the last traces of fin de siècle mannerisms and to focus his attention outward, toward society and the world. In so doing he gave voice to his social poetry, a modality that dominated his work until the 1950s. Drummond was always acutely aware of the ways that class and race interacted in Brazil, and in Rio de Janeiro he felt suffocated by the apparatus of repression deployed by the Vargas government. He was also keenly interested in events in Europe. Together, social inequality and injustice in Brazil and the rise of Nazi Germany in Europe confirmed his socialist beliefs.

Drummond was alone in his turn toward social poetry. His modernist companions were worn out with vanguardism by the late 1920s and adopted an inward-looking pre-existentialist poetics. Typical voices in the "Generation of 1930" were Cecília Meireles, Jorge de Lima, Augusto Frederico Schmidt, and Murilo Mendes. The formerly proscribed sonnet and other traditional forms, along with rhyme, were again widely cultivated. Although Drummond welcomed this enrichment of poetic expression, his decision to concentrate on social concerns demonstrates that he was always self-directed in his poetic orientation, depending less on outside influences, whether from Brazil or Europe, than on his own innate sense of direction.

Drummond's radical new orientation was announced in the eponymous first poem of *Sentimento do mundo,* a manifesto of sorts:

> Tenho apenas duas mãos
> e o sentimento do mundo,
> mas estou cheio de escravos,
> minhas lembranças escorrem
> e o corpo transige
> na confluência do amor.
>
> (I have just two hands
> and a sense of the world,
> but I am full of slaves,
> my memories slide
> and my body compromises
> in the intersection of love.)

The two hands are the instruments of a laborer, or a poet in this case, an intellectual worker. Throughout *Sentimento do mundo* and *A rosa do povo* (1945, The People's Rose) Drummond emphasizes the hands as a metaphor for brotherhood. This image is made explicit in "Mãos dadas" (Holding Hands):

> Não serei o poeta de um mundo caduco.
> Também não cantarei o mundo futuro.
> Estou preso à vida e olho meus companheiros.

. . . O presente é tão grande, não nos afastemos.
Não nos afastemos, vamos de mãos dadas.

(I shall not be the poet for a decrepit world.
I also shall not sing the future world.
I am tied to life and I look at my comrades.
. . . The present moment is so large, let us not separate.
Let us not separate, let us go together holding hands.)

"Mundo grande" (Large World) is a response to the stanza beginning "Mundo mundo vasto mundo" in "Poema de sete faces." That stanza concludes, "mais vasto é meu coração" (my heart is more vast). Now Drummond says, "Não, meu coração não é maior que o mundo. / E muito menor. . . . Meu coração não sabe. / Estúpido, ridículo e frágil é meu coração" (No, my heart is not greater than the world. / It is much smaller. . . . My heart does not know. / Stupid, ridiculous and fragile is my heart). At the conclusion of this later poem the poet consoles himself with the knowledge that the world is ever expanding, growing, and changing and that his own heart can grow "entre o fogo e o amor" (between fire and love). The final verse affirms faith in the future, one that will be built together: "nós" (we) shall build it. Throughout his poetry Drummond strains to bridge the gap between himself, a member of the elite, and the voiceless members of the working class. He realizes that they will never read his words and are unaware of his efforts on their behalf.

Drummond recognized that an elite should not impose a socialist utopia, nor could it speak for the people. This awareness was notably lacking in the Brazilian Communist Party, which was Stalinist: rigid, authoritarian, and intolerant. Given Drummond's instinctive repudiation of authority, it is unsurprising that his relationship with the party was contentious and brief. Like many intellectuals in the West, Brazilian communists of conscience became affiliated with the party because it offered an organized, worldwide means of manifesting their objections to the status quo. In Brazil there was enormous admiration for the Soviet Union's resistance to Nazi Germany's invasion and the heroic defense of Stalingrad. Luís Carlos Prestes, a founder of the Brazilian Communist Party, was widely admired for his stoic endurance and integrity during nine years of imprisonment by the Vargas government.

A rosa do povo has several poems celebrating the Soviet Union, including "Carta a Stalingrado" (Letter to Stalingrad), "Com o russo em Berlim" (With the Russians in Berlin), and "Telegrama de Moscou" (Telegram from Moscow). In "Carta a Stalingrado" the poet says,

Stalingrado, miserável monte de escombros, entretanto resplandescente!

As belas cidades do mundo contemplam-te em pasmo e silêncio
. . . Stalingrado, quantas esperanças!
Que flores, que cristais e músicas o teu nome nos derrama!
Que felicidade brota de tuas casas!

(Stalingrad, wretched pile of ruins, but resplendent!
The beautiful cities of the world observe you in silence and astonishment
. . . Stalingrad, so many hopes!
What flowers, what crystals and music your name spreads!
What happiness springs from your houses!)

The naive enthusiasm of this poem is repeated in "Com o russo em Berlim."

Brazilian intellectuals and writers who fell out with the Communist Party usually did so because they could not accept its attempts to censor their writing and control their behavior. In order to remain in good standing with the party, writers were required to submit their manuscripts to a party committee for approval before they were published. In Drummond's case, after resigning from the Ministry of Education and Public Health, he was pleased to be on the editorial board of the *Tribuna Popular,* the Communist Party's newspaper, but he grew restive when nothing he wrote was published as he had written it. He finally broke with the paper, fell from grace, and was shunned by active party members, who began referring to him as a turncoat. Pablo Neruda, the famous Chilean communist poet who had insisted on meeting Drummond on a visit to Rio de Janeiro, now publicly called him a traitor.

Aside from the overtly political and dated poems, much of Drummond's social poetry still reverberates because it addresses the human condition. "Congresso internacional do medo" (International Congress of Fear), from *Sentimento do mundo,* describes the situation of those who live in societies dominated by repression and fear:

Provisoriamente não cantaremos o amor,
que se refugiou mais abaixo dos subterrâneos.
Cantaremos o medo, que esteriliza os abraços,
não cantaremos o ódio porque esse não existe,
existe apenas o medo, nosso pai e nosso companheiro. . . .

(Provisionally we shall not sing of love;
it has taken refuge below underground.
We shall sing of fear, which sterilizes hugs,
we shall not sing of hate because it does not exist,
only fear exists, our father and our comrade. . . .)

Drummond returned some years later to the generalized sense of fear that dominated Brazil during the Estado Novo in "O medo" (Fear), from *A rosa do povo.* The Vargas regime created the usual organs of repres-

Carlos Drummond de Andrade

The Minus Sign

SELECTED POEMS

Translated by Virginia de Araújo

BLACK SWAN BOOKS

Title page for the 1980 collection of Drummond's poetry
in English translation (Thomas Cooper Library,
University of South Carolina)

sion, domestic espionage, and censorship. The poet
says,

Em verdade temos medo.
Nascemos escuro.
. . . E fomos educados para o medo
Cheiramos flores de medo
Vestimos panos de medo.
. . . Faremos casas de medo,
duros tijolos de medo,
medrosos caules, repuxos,
ruas só de medo e calma.

(Truly we are afraid.
We are born obscure.
. . . And we were educated to fear
we sniff flowers of fear
we wear fear.
. . . We shall make fear houses,

with hard fear bricks,
fearful stems, fountains,
streets full of fear and calm.)

"Os ombros suportam o mundo" (Your Shoulders
Support the World), from *Sentimento do Mundo*, expresses
a desire for solidarity in the face of suffering, hunger,
and death:

Teus ombros suportam o mundo
e ele não pesa mais que a mão de uma criança.
As guerras, as fomes, as discussões dentro dos edifícios
provam apenas que a vida prossegue. . . .
Chegou um tempo em que não adianta morrer.
Chegou um tempo em que a vida é uma ordem.
A vida apenas, sem mistificação.

(Your shoulders support the world
and it does not weigh more than the hand of a child.
Wars, hunger, arguments inside of buildings
only prove that life moves on. . . .
A time has come when dying does not solve anything.
A time has come when life is obligatory.
Life itself, without mystification.)

A distillation of this sense of burden is expressed in
"Carrego comigo" (I Carry with Me), from *A rosa do
povo*. The poet says that he has carried with him a
"small package" for dozens of years, hundreds of years.
He has carried it so long that he no longer remembers
how he came by it, but he does not dare open it. It
burns in his hands but is pleasing to touch; it both fasci-
nates and saddens him. The package presents a mad-
dening mystery that demands to be solved; yet, he
carries it along, tempted to throw it away. Instead, he
resigns himself to the burden the package presents and
paradoxically consoles himself with its company. He
concludes the poem by saying, "Não estou vazio, / não
estou sozinho, / pois anda comigo / algo indescritível" (I
am not empty, / I am not alone, / since something indescribable / accompanies me).

The famous poem "José"–from *José*, first published in *Poesias* (1942)–expresses Everyman's perplexity at modern life. As in other poems in this cycle,
Drummond admires the endurance of the poor and
their acceptance of life regardless of their situation:

Está sem mulher . . .
já não pode beber,
já não pode fumar,
cuspir já não pode,
a noite esfriou,
o dia não veio . . .
e tudo acabou
e tudo fugiu
e tudo mofou
e agora, José?

(Your wife is gone . . .
you can't drink,
you can't smoke,
spitting is not permitted,
the night has gotten cold,
the morning didn't come . . .
and everything ended
and everything disappeared
and everything ruined
what now, Joe?)

This list of prohibitions is a part of living in fear, but it is also a part of modern times, in which everything has been objectified and there is no solidarity among men. Instead, there are political parties and other mechanisms of separation.

In "A mão suja," also from *José,* Drummond uses a Macbeth-like image of filthy hands to express his sense of class guilt, which underlies his social poetry: "Minha mão está suja, / Preciso cortá-la. / Não adianta lavar. / A água está podre" (My hand is dirty. / I need to cut if off. / Washing won't help. / The water is rotten). The dirt on his hand is vile, not soil or coal black that can be washed off. It is the dirt from exploiting slaves and field hands. In a famous play on words that typifies Drummond's technique of *palavra-puxa-palavra* (word suggestion), he writes, "Era sujo pardo, / pardo, tardo, cardo" (It was a brown filth, / brown, retarded, filthy). *Pardo* in Portuguese is the word used for the color of mulattos. *Cardo,* which otherwise means "thistle," is here used as a synonym for *encardido* (filthy).

Objectification, moral bankruptcy, and isolation are the themes of the long meditative poem "Nosso tempo" (Our Time), from *A rosa do povo.* Drummond begins with a short two-line stanza that frames the meditation that follows: "Este é o tempo de partido, / tempo de homens partidos" (This is the time of the party, / the time of sundered men). Once again, Drummond plays with words, since "partido" means both a political party and "split" or "broken." The poet seeks "a precária síntese" (the precarious synthesis) to the confusion and universal discord of modern life but finds nothing.

The second section of "Nosso tempo" begins by restating the confusion of modern society, "Este é tempo de divisas, / tempo de gente cortada. / De mãos viajando sem braços, / obscenos gestos avulses" (This is a time of emblems, / a time of cut people. / Of hands traveling without arms, / of obscene random gestures). The emblems are those of tribes and nations, symbols of their divisions. The picture that emerges from the verses recalls Pablo Picasso's painting *Guernica* (1937), with its shattered bodies. Once again, the poet emphasizes that words and their meanings have become disconnected: "Símbolos obscuros se multiplicam" (obscure symbols multiply).

Drummond uses long, sprawling verses in the fifth section of "Nosso tempo" to describe the insane machinery of capitalism and mass societies, in which individuals are reduced to consuming units. The leitmotiv and organizing word is "escuta" (listen). Listen to the dreadful lunch hour in the city. At lunchtime the offices disgorge hordes of hungry mouths that fill the cafés and bars, while the homeless, the "subterrâneos da fome" (hungry underground denizens), cry for a little soup. Everything is a transaction, and business silently occupies all the spaces of the city. Listen at the end of the workday to the anonymous masses who once again slouch along the streets to their homes: "Homem depois de homem, mulher, criança, homem, / roupa, cigarro, chapéu, roupa, roupa, roupa, / homem, homem, mulher, homem, mulher, roupa, homem . . ." (One man after another, woman, child, man, / clothes, cigarette, hat, clothes, clothes, clothes, / man, man, woman, man, woman, clothes, man . . .). Individuals are reduced to generic man-woman-child units, or worse, simple hangers for articles of dress as they form a silent army moving in what they imagine is a city. "Nosso tempo" concludes with a short coda (the eighth section) in which Drummond states his personal manifesto:

O poeta
declina de toda responsabilidade
na marcha do mundo capitalista
e com suas palavras, intuições, símbolos e outras armas
promete ajudar a destruí-lo
como uma pedreira, uma floresta,
um verme.

(The poet
declines all responsibility
in the capitalist world's march
and with his words, intuitions, symbols and other weapons
promises to contribute to its destruction
like a quarry, a forest,
a worm.)

Poems about Minas Gerais and his family are an intermittent presence in Drummond's early works, but the perspective afforded by his complete works shows that this thematic complex is one of his most important. Drummond himself recognized this in his own thematic anthology, *Antologia poética* (1962), in which he created a section of poems titled "A família que me dei" (The Family I Gave Myself). In *Claro enigma* there is a suite of poems about Minas Gerais, and in the 1960s the poet seems to have decided to embark on a monumental Proustian project to re-create his childhood in Minas Gerais as the capstone to his distinguished career. *Boitempo* was the first of his memoir-like collections, and it was followed by *Menino antigo (Boitempo II)* (1973, Old Child) and *Esquecer para lembrar (Boitempo III)* (1979, Forget so as to Remember). Drummond knew Marcel Proust's work well, and in fact he translated Proust's *Albertine disparue* (1925) as *A fugitiva* (1958, The Fugitive). Most critics regard the *Boitempo* collections as minor poetry, especially as compared with the magnificent poems of *Claro enigma, Fazendeiro do ar* (1954, Air Rancher), and *A vida passada a limpo* (Life, Final Draft), which was first published in *Ciclo* (1957, Cycle). Undeniably, most of the poetry in the *Boitempo* collections is simply descriptive and anecdotal, but there are occasional poems of great beauty, and they offer glimpses into the private life of a notoriously secretive man.

In "Confidência do itabirano," from *Sentimento do mundo,* Drummond concludes with the following stanza: "Tive ouro, tive gado, tive fazendas. / Hoje sou funcionário público / Itabira é apenas uma fotografia na parede. / Mas como dói!" (I had gold, I had cattle, I had ranches. / Today I am a bureaucrat / Itabira is just a photograph on the wall. / But how it hurts!). When the poet says that he had gold, cattle, and ranches, he is referring metaphorically to his ancestors, or to himself as the last in a line of Andrades. As the real Itabira fades from the photograph on the wall in his various residences in Rio de Janeiro, Drummond replaces the images with memories that he can charge with emotion and detail. He laboriously reassembles his family and its retainers. Occasionally he would write to cousins in Itabira requesting objects or photographs of places and persons he did not remember well. In his early work Itabira is a specific historical and geographic place, but in the *Boitempo* volumes it becomes a refuge of memory and affection.

"Viagem na família" (translated as "Travelling in the Family" in *Travelling in the Family: Selected Poems,* 1986), from *José,* has been widely translated and studied. The poem is about Drummond's father, and a haunting refrain runs through it: "Porém nada dizia" (However, he said nothing). The poet in the guise of the boy he once was walks with the ghost of his silent father both through Itabira and through time: "Pisando livros e cartas, viajamos na família" (Stepping on books and letters we traveled in the family). Throughout the poem the father does not speak, despite his son's exhortations. Some fifteen poems in Drummond's mature work are dedicated to his father, and gradually the poet worked his way toward acceptance and reconciliation. One moving poem that expresses his reconciliation with his father is the sonnet "Encontro" (Meeting), from *Claro enigma,* which precedes "A mesa" (The Table), a poem about a family gathering. Drummond writes,

Meu pai perdi no tempo e ganho em sonho.
Se a noite me atribui poder de fuga,
sinto logo o meu pai e nele ponho
o olhar, lendo-lhe a face, ruga a ruga.
Está morto, que importa? . . .

(I lost my father in time and I recover him in dreaming.
If the night gives me the power of escape,
I immediately feel my father and I put
my sight on him, reading his face, wrinkle by wrinkle.
He is dead, so what? . . .)

Drummond's acceptance of his paternal name, Andrade, was another way to express his reconciliation with his father. In a section of *Boitempo* titled "Notícias de Clã" (News of the Clan) he begins with a series of poems about his family name. "Que há no Andrade" (What is it in Andrade), he asks, and answers that it is a *quebracho,* a tough kind of tree, otherwise known as *braúna:* "Que há no Andrade / diferente dos demais? / Que de ferro sem ser laje? / braúna sem ser árvore?" (What is it in Andrade / that makes it different from other names? / What iron without being stone? / What quebracho without being tree?). The iron in question comes from the hills surrounding Itabira, whose streets are paved in hematite. As Drummond said in "Confidência do itabirano" (An Itabaran's Confession), from *Sentimento do mundo,* "Noventa por cento de ferro nas calçadas. / Oitenta por cento de ferro nas almas" (Ninety percent iron in the streets. / Eighty percent iron in souls).

The year 1945 was a watershed in Drummond's life. He published *A rosa do povo* to great acclaim. He resigned from the Ministry of Education and Public Health and temporarily attempted to earn a living as a journalist. His disagreements with the Communist Party and his resignation from the editorial staff of *Tribuna Popular* left him briefly unemployed. Drummond was rescued by his friend Rodrigo Melo Franco de Andrade, who called him to work in the newly organized Patrimônio Histórico e Artístico Nacional (PHAN), an agency that had as its objective the preservation of historic buildings and artistic treasures. Drummond's task was to supervise the agency's archive, and once again his talent for administration and meticulous organization made him outstanding. The Secretaria do Patrimônio Histórico e Artístico Nacional (SPHAN), as it is now known, still uses Drummond's classification system. He stayed at the SPHAN until his retirement in 1962, making a total of thirty-five years as a federal public servant. In 1945 Drummond also began contributing to the literary supplement of *Correio da manhã,* which eventually led him to accept a contract to publish his famous *crônicas* with the Rio de Janeiro newspaper until 1969, when he began writing for the *Jornal do Brasil.*

The mid to late 1940s marked a period of considerable turbulence in Drummond's public life. The modernist movement had split along ideological lines (Marxist versus fascist) in the 1920s, and these fundamental fault lines continued to divide the Brazilian intelligentsia in the 1940s. Drummond helped to found the Associação Brasileira de Escritores (Brazilian Writer's Association) and the União dos Trabalhadores Intelectuais (Union of Intellectual Workers), always working with a congenial group of leftist friends, but the machinations and backstabbing involved in organizing the agenda of these organizations became increasingly distasteful to the poet. His public break with the Communist Party in 1945 was a serious blow to his belief in the ability of intellectuals to affect public policy, and his verse during these years took a radical new stance, embracing the introspection that had always been latent in his poetry.

Claro enigma begins with a poem of renunciation in which Drummond repudiates the symbols of his social engagement. In "Dissolução" (Dissolution) he says his attitude is now one of acceptance. Instead of reaching out, even to ignite a light against the darkness, he is content to wait with his arms crossed:

> Escurece, e não me seduz
> tatear sequer uma lâmpada.
> Pois que aprouve ao dia findar,
> aceito a noite.
> . . . Braços cruzados. . . .
>
> (It grows dark and I am not tempted
> even to grope for a lamp.
> Since it pleased the day to end,
> I accept the night.
> . . . Crossed arms. . . .)

Later in the poem Drummond says, "mais vasto é o céu" (the heavens are larger), explicitly rejecting his belief in the world and its problems. He renounces "aquele agressivo espírito" (that aggressive spirit) and says that this attitude will endure: "Esta rosa é definitiva, / ainda que pobre" (This rose is definitive, / though poor). In the last stanza of "Dissolução" he expresses a widely quoted sentiment: "Imaginação, falsa demente, / já te desprezo. E tu, palavra . . ." (Imagination, demented and false, / I now despise you. And you, word . . .).

"Dissolução" is followed by a series of sonnets in which Drummond expresses pessimism and acceptance of impermanence. He speaks of "esse travode angústia" (those bitter dregs of anguish) in his songs. He asks whether "mereço esperar mais do que os outros" (I deserve to expect more than others) and, in "Confissão" (Confession), confesses that he did not love his fellow man enough or even love himself enough. All that

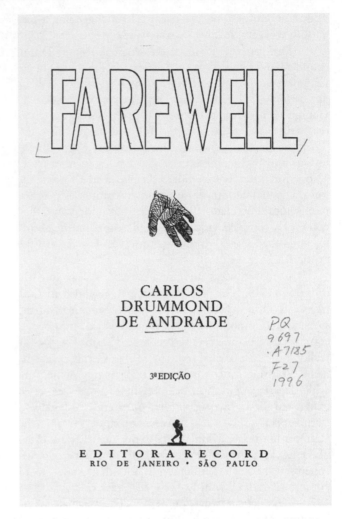

Title page for the 1996 collection of poems that Drummond left ready for publication at the time of his death in 1987 (Thomas Cooper Library, University of South Carolina)

remains in the future for his life and work is that rock in the middle of the road from "No meio do caminho," he writes in "Legado" (Legacy). In "Cantiga de enganar" (Song of Deceit) Drummond creates a changing refrain negating the world: "O mundo não vale o mundo, meu bem. . . . O mundo, meu bem, não vale a pena. . . . O mundo não tem sentido . . ." (The world is not worth the world, my love. . . . The world, my love, is not worth the trouble. . . . The world makes no sense . . .). The poet writes in "Oficina irritada" (Irritated Workshop) that his work, "irritante e impuro" (irritating and impure), will not be remembered, and he compares it to a dog urinating in chaos and to shooting at a wall. The introductory section of *Claro enigma* ends with a poem titled "Aspiration," in which Drummond states that he no longer aspires to love, "a simples rosa do sexo" (the simple rose of sex), or even to maternal adoration. Rather, he aspires only to a "fiel indiferença" (faithful indifference) that in its obdurate refusal to choose is capable of suggesting a conclusion without the injustice of rewards.

The permanence of the rock metaphor in Drummond's work, alluded to in "Legado," is the subject of the last poem in *Novos poemas* (New Poems), published in *Poesia até agora* (1948, Poetry Thus Far). Appropriately titled "O enigma" (The Mystery), this prose poem portrays rocks as originally having the power of movement and thought. They are stopped, however, startled by some sort of mysterious and frightening barrier that freezes them in place: "No esforço de compreender, chegam a imobilizar-se de todo. E na contenção desse instante, fixam-se as pedras—para sempre—no chão" (In their effort to understand, they come to a complete stop. And in the containment of that instant, the stones freeze themselves—forever—in the ground).

In many ways the long poem "A máquna do mundo" (1949, The World Machine), included in *Claro enigma,* is Drummond's most complete statement of the stone and its importance to his life and work. The poem is composed in blank-verse tercets that describe the poet as walking along a rocky road in Minas Gerais, when he hears "um sino rouco" (a hoarse bell) ringing in the gathering darkness, and the world machine opens itself to his exhausted view, "majestosa e circunspecta" (majestic and circumspect). The magnificent machine recalls the attempts in the late Middle Ages to portray the great chain of being as a series of interlocking and superimposed spheres. One such description is found in canto 33 of *Paradiso* (Paradise) from Dante's *La Divina Commedia* (circa 1310–1314, The Divine Comedy). The machine offers Drummond a "total explicaçao da vida" (total explanation of life), but he refuses it, disdaining the solution offered to his imagination, and the machine silently folds in upon itself, while he, hands dangling, continues his wandering, meditating on what he has lost. Drummond's youthful passion for knowledge has given way to a hard-won self-reliance, and he is offended by the gratuitousness of the answer to his search for meaning. Like other modern men, the poet must make his own accommodation to life, without the consolation of received truth.

Drummond's pessimism in the early poems of *Claro enigma* gives way to a section of poems on love and a famous suite of poems about his childhood in Minas Gerais, but the book ends on the resignation expressed in "A máquina do mundo." *Fazendeiro do ar, A vida passada a limpo,* and *Lição de coisas* (1962, Lesson from Things) are short collections of poetry with a clearly crepuscular air. By the early 1960s the poet was beginning a new and exuberant phase in his erotic poetry, and he was embarking on the detailed and affectionate poems that were later published in the *Boitempo* series. In the late 1950s Drummond had come under attack by the new generation of vanguard writers of the concrete-poetry movement. He emerged vir-

tually unscathed from the fuss that repudiated virtually the whole modernist generation except for Oswald de Andrade, but he was irritated and responded with two concrete poems, titled "Isto e aquilo" (This and That) and "F" (both from *Lição de coisas*), as a demonstration that he understood the message.

Drummond's daughter, Maria Julieta, had married Argentine lawyer Manuel Graña Etcheverry in 1949 and moved to Buenos Aires, where she directed the Center for Brazilian Studies. She remained in Argentina until 1983. Drummond's trips to Buenos Aires for the births of his three grandsons were his only direct exposures to a foreign capital and culture; he detested Argentina. Maria Julieta's health began to deteriorate in the early 1970s, and she had a mastectomy in 1979. After three years of remission the cancer returned, and, divorced from Etcheverry, she began a relationship with a friend and neighbor of Drummond's, Octavio Mello Alvarenga, who supported her as she slowly wasted away. This period in the poet's life was a perplexing, bittersweet time. He was constantly winning awards of one kind or another, but he reacted by becoming almost a recluse, refusing interviews and declining some prizes that he felt he did not merit. He repeatedly refused induction into the Brazilian Academy of Letters. Famous writers tried to meet with him on trips to Rio de Janeiro, but he generally avoided them. When Drummond was in Buenos Aires, Jorge Luís Borges tried to set up a meeting, which Drummond avoided. Brazil had entered a new and prolonged period of military dictatorship in 1964, and as a famous communist and leftist, Drummond was repeatedly called in by the military police for interviews. More of his friends and family members were dying year by year. At the end of 1964 Álvaro Moreyra and Meireles died, followed in 1965 by Schmidt. In 1968 Drummond's dear friend Bandeira died. In August 1983 Drummond underwent prostate surgery, and in 1984 his companion from his early days in Belo Horizonte, Pedro Nava, committed suicide. The poet was desolated.

At the end of 1984 it was clear that Maria Julieta's cancer was terminal, and Drummond's own health was failing. This time the problem was heart disease, which slowly worsened. The poet gathered his failing energies to organize one last collection of poems that he left ready for publication when he died, appropriately titled *Farewell,* which was published posthumously in 1996. Maria Julieta entered a hospital for the last time in early August 1987, and died on the fifth of that month. Drummond collapsed during her burial ceremony, and he died shortly thereafter, on 17 August 1987.

In the years since his death, Carlos Drummond de Andrade's reputation has grown, looming over the work of his contemporaries, talented as they may have been. In part the lasting impact of Drummond's poetry perhaps lies in his perceptive teasing out of contemporary man's existential disquiet from the many strands that make up the tapestry of modern life. In his reluctance to accept received wisdom, his struggle against solitude while surrounded by a metropolis, and his instinctive embrace of those less fortunate, Drummond exemplifies the best of the modern spirit. Another secret of his lasting popularity is his resolute avoidance of "literary" discourse. His poetic language is direct, simple, and colloquial.

Letters:

A lição do amigo: cartas de Mário de Andrade a Carlos Drummond de Andrade, annotated by Drummond (Rio de Janeiro: J. Olympio, 1982);

Correspondência de Cabral com Bandeira e Drummond, edited by Flora Süssekind (Rio de Janeiro: Nova Fronteira/ Casa de Rui Barbosa, 2001);

Carlos & Mário: correspondência completa entre Carlos Drummond de Andrade (inédita) e Mário de Andrade, edited by Lélia Coelho Frota, preface and notes by Silviano Santiago (Rio de Janeiro: Bem-Te-Vi, 2002).

Bibliography:

Fernando Py, *Bibliografia comentada de Carlos Drummond de Andrade (1918–1930)* (Rio de Janeiro: J. Olympio, 1980); revised and enlarged as *Bibliografia comentada de Carlos Drummond de Andrade: 1918–1934* (Rio de Janeiro: Casa de Rui Barbosa, 2002).

Biography:

José Maria Cançado, *Os sapatos de Orfeu: biografia de Carlos Drummond de Andrade* (São Paulo: Scritta, 1993).

References:

Rita de Cássia Barbosa, *Poemas eróticos de Carlos Drummond de Andrade* (São Paulo: Editora Atica, 1987);

Sônia Brayner, *Carlos Drummond de Andrade: coletânea* (Rio de Janeiro: Civilização Brasileira, 1977);

Maria Consuelo Cunha Campos, *Mineiridade* (Rio de Janeiro: Achiamé, 1980);

Joaquim-Francisco Coelho, *Terra e família na poesia de Carlos Drummond de Andrade* (Belém: Universidade Federal do Pará, 1973);

José Eduardo da Fonseca, *O telurismo na literatura brasileira e na obra de Carlos Drummond de Andrade* (Belo Horizonte: Seção de Publicações do Departmento de Letras Vernáculas da Faculdade de Letras da Universidade Federal de Minas Gerais, 1970);

Othon Moacyr Garcia, *Esfinge clara: palavra-puxa-palavra em Carlos Drummond de Andrade* (Rio de Janeiro: São José, 1955);

John Gledson, *Poesia e poética de Carlos Drummond de Andrade* (São Paulo: Duas Cidades, 1981);

Inventário do arquivo Carlos Drummond de Andrade (Rio de Janeiro: Fundação Casa de Rui Barbosa/Arquivo-Museu de Literatura Brasileira, 1998);

Lausimar Laus, *O mistério do homem na obra de Drummond* (Rio de Janeiro: Tempo Brasileiro, 1978);

Hélcio Martins, *A rima na poesia de Carlos Drummond de Andrade* (Rio de Janeiro: J. Olympio, 1968);

José Guilherme Merquior, *Verso universo em Drummond,* translated by Marly de Oliveira (Rio de Janeiro: J. Olympio, 1975);

Emanuel de Moraes, *Drummond: rima, Itabira, mundo* (Rio de Janeiro: J. Olympio, 1972);

Geneton Moraes Neto, *O dossiê Drummond* (São Paulo: Globo, 1994);

Dilman Augusto Motta, *A metalinguagem na poesia de Carlos Drummond de Andrade,* second edition (Rio de Janeiro: Presença, 1976);

Sérgio Ribeiro Rosa, *Pedra engastada no tempo* (Pôrto Alegre: Cultura Contemporânea, 1978);

Affonso Romano de Sant'Anna, *Drummond: o gauche no tempo* (Rio de Janeiro: Lia, 1972);

Silviano Santiago, *Carlos Drummond de Andrade* (Petrópolis: Vozes, 1976);

Vivaldo Andrade dos Santos, "A figuração intima da modernidade: uma leitura poesia de Carlos Drummond de Andrade," dissertation, University of California, Berkeley, 2000;

Donald Schüler, *A dramaticidade na poesia de Drummond* (Pôrto Alegre: Editora da Universidade Federal do Rio Grande do Sul, 1979);

Iumna Maria Simon, *Drummond: uma poética do risco* (São Paulo: Atica, 1978);

Gilberto Mendonça Teles, *Drummond, a estilística da repetição,* second edition (Rio de Janeiro: J. Olympio, 1976).

Rubem Fonseca

(11 May 1925 –   )

Carmen Chaves Tesser
University of Georgia

BOOKS: *Os prisioneiros* (Rio de Janeiro: GRD, 1963);
A coleira do cão (Rio de Janeiro: GRD, 1965);
Lúcia McCartney (Rio de Janeiro: Olivé, 1967);
O caso Morel (Rio de Janeiro: Artenova, 1973);
Feliz ano novo (Rio de Janeiro: Artenova, 1975);
O cobrador (Rio de Janeiro: Nova Fronteira, 1979);
A grande arte (Rio de Janeiro: F. Alves, 1983); translated by Ellen Watson as *High Art* (New York: Harper & Row, 1986; London: Collins, 1986);
Bufo & Spallanzani (Rio de Janeiro: F. Alves, 1985); translated by Clifford E. Landers (New York: Dutton, 1990);
Vastas emoções e pensamentos imperfeitos (São Paulo: Companhia das Letras, 1988); translated by Landers as *Vast Emotions and Imperfect Thoughts* (Hopewell, N.J.: Ecco Press, 1998); republished as *The Lost Manuscript* (London: Bloomsbury, 1998);
Agosto (São Paulo: Companhia das Letras, 1990);
Romance negro e outras histórias (São Paulo: Companhia das Letras, 1992);
O selvagem da ópera (São Paulo: Companhia das Letras, 1994);
O buraco na parede (São Paulo: Companhia das Letras, 1995);
História de amor (São Paulo: Companhia das Letras, 1996);
E do meio do mundo prostituto só amores guardei ao meu charuto (São Paulo: Companhia das Letras, 1997);
Histórias de amor (São Paulo: Companhia das Letras, 1997);
A confraria dos espadas (São Paulo: Companhia das Letras, 1998);
O doente Molière (São Paulo: Companhia das Letras, 2000);
Secreções, excreções e desatinos (São Paulo: Companhia das Letras, 2001);
Pequenas criaturas (São Paulo: Companhia das Letras, 2002);
Diário de um fescenino (São Paulo: Companhia das Letras, 2003).

Rubem Fonseca (photograph © Miriam Berkley; from the dust jacket of the American edition of Bufo & Spallanzani, *1990; Richland County Public Library)*

Collections: *O homem de fevereiro ou março* (Rio de Janeiro: Artenova, 1973);
Contos reunidos (São Paulo: Companhia das Letras, 1994);
Romance negro, Feliz ano novo e outras histórias, edited by Maura Sardinha (Rio de Janeiro: Ediouro, 1996);
Livro de ocorrências: seleta (Rio de Janeiro: Agora, 1998).

PRODUCED SCRIPTS: *Relatório de um homem casado,* motion picture, Embrafilme/Flávio Tambellini Produções Cinematográficas, 1974;
A Extorsão, motion picture, by Fonseca and Flávio R. Tambellini, CIC/Flávio Tambellini Produções Cinematográficas, 1975;
Stelinha, motion picture, Embrafilme, 1990;

A grande arte (released in the United States and Canada as *Exposure*), motion picture, Alpha Filmes/J & M Entertainment, 1991;

Bufo & Spallanzani, motion picture, by Fonseca, Patrícia Melo, and Tambellini, Quanta Centro de Produções, 2001;

O homem do ano, motion picture, Conspiração Filmes, 2003.

OTHER: Álvaro Pacheco, *Seleção de poemas de Álvaro Pacheco,* edited by Fonseca, Odylo Costa Filho, and Fábio Lucas (Rio de Janeiro: Artenova, 1984).

An award-winning novelist, short-story writer, screenwriter, and former policeman, Rubem Fonseca offers his reading public an honest, though brutal, view of contemporary Brazil with his shocking portrayals of urban reality. James Polk, reviewing *Vast Emotions and Imperfect Thoughts* (1998), the translation of Fonseca's *Vastas emoções e pensamentos imperfeitos* (1988), in *The New York Times Book Review* (23 August 1998), claims that Fonseca is a "writer of joyful excess." For the reader who has followed Fonseca's career through his period of censorship, Polk's phrase seems to capture the essence of the novelist. Viewed in the context of postmodernism, Fonseca has the capacity to portray in words the breakdown of the usual order of things. His texts invert and subvert a Brazilian ideological background based on the positivistic mantra of "order and progress" by forcing the reader to witness the fragile balance between violence and eroticism.

José Rubem Fonseca was born on 11 May 1925 in Juiz de Fora, in the state of Minas Gerais, where he lived for the first seven years of his life. When he was eight years old, the family moved to Rio de Janeiro, where he still lives. Fonseca claims to have sold ties from a kiosk in the city to fund his studies. On New Year's Eve 1952 he joined the 16th Distrito Policial (Police District) in São Cristóvão, a working-class suburb north of Rio de Janeiro. His police work not only took him to the streets but also required him to write daily crime reports. He witnessed firsthand some of the episodes that he later described in gruesome detail in many of his stories. Along with nine other policemen, Fonseca had the opportunity to study in the United States during the 1953–1954 academic year. He spent the time at New York University studying business administration.

Upon his return to Brazil, Fonseca continued to work at the 16th Distrito Policial until 1958. Five years later he published his first collection of short stories, *Os prisioneiros* (1963, The Prisoners), establishing for himself a place among controversial contemporary writers

specializing in urban narratives. It is not enough for Fonseca to portray urban life; he "joyfully" shocks by presenting what is base, violent, nauseating, and repulsive. The reader is both repelled and attracted by the macabre narratives. An overview of Fonseca's books (some of which are collections of previously published work) demonstrates a literary progression coinciding loosely with the author's own maturation within the context of his changing culture.

Os prisioneiros was published the year before the military coup of 1964. The collection of eleven short stories clearly establishes the pattern that Fonseca followed throughout the development of his narrative style: short, staccato sentences punctuate the violence in an impressionistic way. With this collection Fonseca established himself as a quasi photographer of the details of urban life. The everyday speech of his characters is filled with obscenities that in just a few years gave the military censors some points to criticize and banish from his prose. The book met with critical enthusiasm and assured that when Fonseca's second book, *A coleira do cão* (The Dog's Collar), was published in 1965, his readership was established. Once again, in this second collection of short stories, he presents characters facing the banality of urban life and surviving through wit, violence, and psychological manipulation of self and others. The characters might have been, and often were, based on tabloid descriptions of crime and violence. They were the victims and the perpetrators that Fonseca had met during his time as a policeman.

Lúcia McCartney was published in 1967, three years into the Brazilian military dictatorship. In the first edition one of the stories is titled "Relato de ocorrência em que qualquer semelhança não é mera coincidência" (Report of a Happening in Which Any Similarity Is Not a Mere Coincidence). In later editions the story is simply titled "Relato de ocorrência" (Report of a Happening). In an award-winning article in the *Folha de São Paulo* (25 June 1995), Mário César Carvalho posits that the original title for this story could be applied to many of Fonseca's stories. Many of the characters that appear in the stories, as well as the plots themselves, are based on real people and events. Indeed, some of the characters bear the actual names of people who worked with him during his police years. In developing both plot and characters, Fonseca leads and misleads his readers with parenthetical expressions, such as those found in the title story in *Lúcia McCartney:* "Diálogo, possível (Mas inventado)" (Possible Dialogue [But Invented]), which is followed by "Diálogo (Verdadeiro)" (Dialogue [True]). Fonseca's stories are filled with dialogue between someone named or referred to by a pronoun and "I." The first person, whether in narrative or dialogue, is a constant in his prose.

Dust jacket for the 1990 translation of Fonseca's 1985 intertextual novel, in which the protagonist is writing a narrative with the same title (Richland County Public Library)

As Fonseca's abrupt and aggressive style began to take hold of the Brazilian imagination, the military government began to take measures to assure that Brazilians read only those texts that were supposed to maintain national well-being without affront to moral values. The first such measures came in the form of the Lei de Segurança Nacional (Law of National Security) and the Lei da Imprensa (Law of the Press). These two laws were intended to keep "subversive" material from reaching the reading public. In 1968 Ato Institucional Número 5 (Institutional Act Number 5) came into effect. This act gave the government the power to imprison writers who did not follow the literary norms seen as being in the best interest of society. Fonseca, along with other writers, fell victim to the government's repression and persecution. He reflects, in his violent style, on this situation in *O caso Morel* (1973, The Morel Case). In this book, Fonseca's first novel, the reader finds once again the conflict in an artist's reality, an

intellectual word game, and an intertextuality that appears as a code to be broken by readers who share a common classical background. Just as *O caso Morel* arrived at bookstores, Fonseca organized an anthology of previously published short stories and published it in an inexpensive edition titled *O homem de fevereiro ou março* (1973, The February or March Man). In 1975 a movie version of *O caso Morel* was to begin production under the direction of Suzana Amaral, but funding that seemed available during preparations suddenly became scarce.

Feliz ano novo (Happy New Year) was published in time for Christmas 1975. The book appeared with a festive plastic cover featuring a ready-made holiday card filled with messages of good tidings in several languages. This apparently inoffensive Christmas present brought to light narratives with dehumanized characters clinically described as they murder, tear flesh, and crush bones. The title story, "Feliz ano novo," depicts a bourgeois New Year's Eve party that becomes the target of brutal criminals who stop at nothing to get the gold worn by the fancy rich ladies. The initial presentation of the story demonstrates once again Fonseca's ability to invert the normal order of things. The three criminals are at home, hungry, and watching on television the festivities that are taking place in many homes. The televised celebrations give them the idea for the night's "entertainment."

In the stories in *Feliz ano novo* Fonseca seems to be answering interview questions–questions that he poses to himself. He summarizes his feelings about interviews and about life itself in "O intestino grosso" (The Large Intestine), in which the character "Author" gives advice to a reporter who agrees to listen to his "sete palavras de graça" (seven free words): "Adote uma árvore e mate uma criança"(Adopt a tree and kill a child). Apart from the play on words typical of Fonseca's style (for example, "de graça"–free, funny, of grace), the reader is also shocked by the juxtaposition of an ecological allusion with a violent act. In May 1976, after three editions (thirty thousand copies) had been sold, *Feliz ano novo* was banished from "the Brazilian territory" by the Polícia Federal (Federal Police) for its pornographic content that was "contrary to moral values and good customs."

The fate of *Feliz ano novo* has become emblematic of the military repression exercised during the dictatorship. The book resulted in a lengthy court battle for Fonseca, which has been analyzed by Deonísio da Silva in *O caso Rubem Fonseca: violência e erotismo em Feliz ano novo* (1983, The Ruben Fonseca Case: Violence and Eroticism in *Feliz Ano Novo*). Fonseca waited four years before publishing a new collection of short stories, *O cobrador* (1979, The Conductor), in which the title story features a toothless character that had already appeared in *Feliz ano novo*. A theme is explicitly stated in *O cobrador:* "Quando não se tem dinheiro é bom ter músculos e ódio" (When one does not have money it is good to have muscles and hate). Fonseca, however, seems to demonstrate that muscles and hate are not sufficient without teeth. Here one could consider the word *teeth* and its symbolic connotations of identity, aggression, frustration, castration, defense, and anger. As many critics have said, to lose one's teeth is to be disarmed, defenseless. Teeth are also part and parcel of word articulation, and without words one has no voice, in a metaphorical sense. By the time *O cobrador* was published in 1979, the military dictatorship was beginning the first steps toward *abertura* (opening), leading to a less repressive regime.

For his own intellectual survival Fonseca perfected the art of wordplay, as evidenced by his next book, *A grande arte* (1983; translated as *High Art,* 1986), which was adapted in 1991 as a motion picture, released by Miramax in the United States and Canada as *Exposure*. Fonseca wrote the screenplay for the movie, which was directed by Walter Salles Jr. For the reader used to Fonseca's prose and wordplay, the title of *A grande arte* presents a possible comic interpretation: "a grande arte" translates not only as "high art"–in itself an ironic term for the art of "cutting" (the knife fighting that is the subject of the book)–but also as "great mischief." Mandrake, the protagonist and narrator, is an attorney suffering from "sanguephobia" (blood phobia). Because of circumstances he excels in the "high art" of cutting, at the same time traveling between "high" society and its artistic values and "low" society and its values. As has become typical in Fonseca's prose, the base street language of urban characters is presented through a background of classical allusions and symbolism. Indeed, violence and brutality come in a sequential crescendo culminating in a final scene of Eros versus Thanatos as an emblem of life itself: "Eu mato para viver" (I kill to live).

With *Bufo & Spallanzani* (1985; translated, 1990) Fonseca underscores a technique that he began developing in his first books: the presence of the authorial voice within the narrative, either in the person of the protagonist, the narrator, or the interplay between the two. In *Bufo & Spallanzani* he employs a protagonist who is also the narrator and is himself writing a manuscript titled "Bufo & Spallanzani." The use of constant flashbacks and an intricate intertextual game provide the framework for the development of the narrative into five parts. Within this preestablished frame Fonseca creates a pastiche of a police narrative as a patchwork quilt sewn together by the presence of the narrator/author/protagonist. As the narrative develops, each piece of the

patchwork comes apart in a dizzying play of sex and violence. The narrative opens just as Brazil is entering a new democratic phase, and the country enthusiastically awaits the future of a "cultura nova" (new culture). A movie adaptation of *Bufo & Spallanzani,* with a screenplay by Fonseca, Patrícia Melo, and Flávio R. Tambellini (who also directed), was shown at the Festival do Rio, the Rio de Janeiro movie festival, in October 2000 and released in 2001.

Fonseca's next book, *Vastas emoções e pensamentos imperfeitos,* was published in 1988, when Brazilians were preparing for new democratic and direct elections. The text, using the ploy of a "found manuscript," continues Fonseca's reflections on metalanguage and intertextuality. The protagonist is obsessed with the idea of filming Soviet writer Isaac Babel's fiction as presented in the manuscript. An innovation in this book is the presentation of explicit motion-picture narrative superimposed on another narrative passage. This book, like *Bufo & Spallanzani,* presents steps taken by Fonseca in the preparation of *Agosto* (August), published in 1990, the year that President Fernando Collor de Mello took office. (He was forced to resign two years later amid charges of corruption.)

In *Agosto* Fonseca continues to use the framework of police work, violence, and sex but also focuses on an historical event now quite removed from the Brazilian imagination: the era of President Getúlio Vargas and Vargas's suicide in 1954. Fonseca uses all of the techniques of the earlier stories but now manipulates the perception of an historical event from several different perspectives. The code of police behavior becomes confused with the "rules" of narrative development, and these rules become intertwined with corruption at all levels of society. Once again, Fonseca seems to enjoy manipulating his reader. In this case, however, he further compresses the narrative into a well-defined historical context.

What makes *Romance negro e outras histórias* (1992, Black Novel and Other Stories) a different step in Fonseca's narrative development is not only the addition of a new set of vaguely familiar characters but also the emphasis on settings and situations, such as a meeting of writers and professors, a hospital, and a meat-filled meal in the presence of vegetarians. Each of the situations becomes an emblem, and each is developed with the precision that Fonseca earlier applied to character development. In this book the settings are the characters.

In 1994 Fonseca published *Contos reunidos* (Collected Stories) and *O selvagem da ópera* (The Savage of the Opera), which brings to light yet a different time frame and a different idea. The protagonist is nineteenth-century Brazilian composer Carlos Gomes. Fonseca

HIGH ART

Rubem Fonseca

Translated from the Portuguese
by Ellen Watson

1817

HARPER & ROW, PUBLISHERS, New York
Cambridge, Philadelphia, San Francisco, London
Mexico City, São Paulo, Singapore, Sydney

Vast Emotions and Imperfect Thoughts

Rubem Fonseca

Translated by Clifford E. Landers

THE ECCO PRESS

Title pages for the 1986 translation of Fonseca's knife-fighting novel A grande arte *(1983) and for the 1998 translation of Fonseca's*
Vastas emoções e pensamentos imperfeitos *(1988), about a man obsessed with adapting Soviet writer*
Isaac Babel's fiction for the cinema (Thomas Cooper Library, University of South Carolina)

deeply explores the human psyche by describing the tribulations of the creative genius in re-creating his own environment. In this case, Gomes and the re-creation of Brazilian culture serve as a metaphor for artistic creation. Fonseca's movie-like language and fast-paced narrative do not leave out the characteristic violence.

Followers of Fonseca's literary trajectory recognize his painstaking compression of themes, times, types, and language. In *O buraco na parede* (1995, Hole in the Wall) his cinematographer's lens becomes sharper. Now current events become minutiae, and even characters become physically small, as in the story "O anão" (The Dwarf), as well as small in their actions. The hole in the wall, the camera lens, or, in terms of literary theory, the "gaze," all focus on the smallest particles that combine to define the culture of violence.

Fonseca's *Histórias de amor* (Love Stories) and *E do meio do mundo prostituto só amores guardei ao meu charuto* (And from the Middle of the Whorish World I Kept Only My Cigar) were both published in 1997. The

former volume presents almost a scientific study of different kinds of love, all illustrating some perversion. The characters in relationships each have to deal with human imperfections; however, they are not able to do so without resorting to violent acts. In the second book Fonseca revisits characters with whom the reader has become familiar—the writer Gustavo, from *Bufo & Spallanzani,* and the lawyer Mandrake, from *A grande arte.* The two discuss eroticism, reflect on the art of writing and loving, and ponder the elements of desire—all developed amid the disclosure of a refined passion for good cigars. The Freudian allusion will not be lost on the reader who is used to looking beyond and beneath Fonseca's words for emblems.

In 1998 Fonseca published *A confraria dos espadas* (The Brotherhood of the Swords), in which he unabashedly studies large topics such as life, death, and liberty while trying his hand at something new—the macabre. In his earlier books Fonseca manipulated violence, sex, and brutality within the controlled environment of the narrative. In *A confraria dos espadas* he takes the reader through a review of beauty as a metaphor for the macabre. Many critics have seen this book as Fonseca's weakest. The consensus seems to be that he was trying to find a different voice.

The beginning of the new millennium brought two new books from the Brazilian storyteller. In 2000 Fonseca published *O doente Molière* (The Sick Molière) and, in the following year, *Secreções, excreções e desatinos* (Secretions, Excretions, and Madness). In these books Fonseca reworks the techniques that he has perfected: history as context for mischief, and human fluids as metaphors for life, love, and soul. *O doente Molière,* based on the life and death of the seventeenth-century French dramatist, is told from the perspective of an anonymous *marquês* who tries to solve the mystery of the death of the playwright. The narrator, the only fictitious character in the novel, provides Fonseca with the artifice for creating a text that mirrors Molière's own caustic comedic style while presenting the baser side of human nature. *Secreções, excreções e desatinos* once again exemplifies the mastery of the storyteller, with short sentences, fast and shocking dialogue, scatological themes, and violence. Beginning with "Copromancia," featuring a man obsessed by his own excrement, Fonseca seems to be recollecting all his former characters and situations. This time, however, he does so as a fortune-teller who knows and sees the future of the human soul. In 2002 Fonseca published *Pequenas criaturas* (Small Creatures), a collection of short stories interspersed with essays, which earned him the 2002 Prêmio Jabuti (Jabuti Prize) in literature. This collection displays his continuing fas-

cination with the morbid details that surround characters in their daily lives. In 2003 his *Diário de un fescenino* (Diary of a Fescenine), became a favorite of the reading public. Written with the structure of a diary, the satirical narrative is strongly critical of Brazilian cultural values. On 13 May 2003 Fonseca received the Prêmio Luis de Camões (Luis de Camões Prize), awarded by both the Brazilian and the Portuguese governments, for his career achievements.

Rubem Fonseca continues to be controversial in his themes and language. His works are fine examples of well-crafted short stories in the context of Brazilian urban literature. Many contemporary Brazilian writers have been influenced by Fonseca, who, more than anything else, exemplifies "joyful excess," as Polk characterized his work in 1998.

References:

Mário Cesar Carvalho, "A verdadeira história policial de Rubem Fonseca," *Folha de São Paulo,* 25 June 1995, pp. 5–10;

Afrânio Coutinho, *O erotismo na literatura: o caso Rubem Fonseca* (Rio de Janeiro: Cátedra, 1979);

Deonísio da Silva, *O caso Rubem Fonseca: violência e erotismo em Feliz ano novo* (São Paulo: Alfa-Omega, 1983);

Silva, *Nos bastidores da censura: sexualidade, literatura e repressão pós-64* (São Paulo: Estação Liberdade, 1989);

Carmen Chaves Tesser, *Las máscaras de la apertura: un contexto literario* (Mexico: Universidad Nacional Autónoma de México, 1998).

Antônio Gonçalves Dias

(10 August 1823 – 3 November 1864)

Jon M. Tolman
University of New Mexico

BOOKS: *Leonor de Mendonça: drama original em três atos e cinco quadros* ([Rio de Janeiro], [1846]);
Primeiros cantos: poesías (Rio de Janeiro: Laemmert, 1847);
Segundos cantos e Sextilhas de frei Antão (Rio de Janeiro: Monteiro, 1848);
Últimos cantos: poesias (Rio de Janeiro: Brito, 1851);
Vocabulario da lingua geral usada hoje em dia no alto-amazonas: offercido ao Instituto historico e geographico do Brazil, pelo socio effectivo (Rio de Janeiro: Laemmert, 1854);
Dicionário da língua tupy: chamada lingua geral dos indigenas do Brazil (Leipzig: Brockhaus, 1857);
Os tymbiras: poema americano (Leipzig: Brockhaus, 1857);
Cantos: collecção de poesias (Leipzig: Brockhaus, 1857);
Obras póstumas, 6 volumes, edited by Antônio Henriques Leal (São Luís do Maranhão: Matos, 1868–1869).

Editions and Collections: *Poesias completas e prosa escolhida,* edited by Manuel Bandeira and Antônio Houaiss (Rio de Janeiro: Aguilar, 1959);
Antônio Gonçalves Dias: poemas, edited by Péricles Eugênio da Silva Ramos (São Paulo: Cultrix, 1968);
Teatro Completo (Rio de Janeiro: Ministério de Educação e Cultura, Fundação Nacional de Arte, Serviço Nacional de Teatro, 1979);
Teatro de Gonçalves Dias, edited by Luis Antonio Giron (São Paulo: Livraria Martins Fontes, 2004).

Antônio Gonçalves Dias (from Ronald de Carvalho, Pequena Historia da Literatura Brasileira, *1937; Thomas Cooper Library, University of South Carolina)*

Antônio Gonçalves Dias occupies an unusual place in Brazilian literature. He began his ascent in the literary world within a year of the first edition of his *Primeiros cantos* (1847, First Songs), and his popularity increased with each new volume of poems and endures to this day. Brazil's literary historians generally regard him as the country's most important nineteenth-century poet. His collected poems went through two editions in Europe before his death, and they were translated into French, English, and Spanish to wide acclaim.

Nothing about the circumstances of Antônio Gonçalves Dias's birth in the remote Amazonian state of Maranhão on 10 August 1823 suggested that he might have a promising future. He was the illegitimate son of a Portuguese merchant, João Manuel Gonçalves Dias, and an illiterate mestiza servant, Vicência Ferreira. Shortly after Gonçalves Dias's birth his father, a Portuguese loyalist during Brazil's struggle for independence, fled the city of Caxias for two years. During this time Gonçalves Dias lived with his mother in what he called a "choupana" (grass shack). Some critics have suggested his childhood led him to identify with Brazil's Indians, and the exuberance of nature in the Amazon deeply affected him.

At a young age Gonçalves Dias became familiar with discrimination because of his marginal social status as both an illegitimate child and a "half-breed." Gonçalves Dias's mother was perhaps a *cafusa,* a mixture of Indian, Portuguese, and black. His father was a type of merchant referred to as a *tendeiro,* a pejorative term derived from the word *tenda,* a tent or stall, implying a sort of traveling salesman or small shopkeeper. Gonçalves Dias himself applied the term to his father and others of his class. Brazilian society in the nineteenth century was rigidly stratified, with prestige and power vested in a landed oligarchy. The only occupations that had social status were those of planter or rancher, doctor, lawyer, and, in some cases, priest. Merchants and other intermediate classes were tolerated but did not engage in refined social discourse. After the Portuguese royal court established itself in Rio de Janeiro in 1808, Brazil's preexisting social structure was overlaid with artificially created titles of nobility that successive emperors granted to those who distinguished themselves. Gonçalves Dias grew up outside the most powerful and respectable social circles. Because he had no inheritance or other independent source of income, he struggled with finances his whole life. As an adult his problems were largely self-inflicted: he was constantly out of money because of his extravagance, in spite of generous commissions and salaries from the imperial government and Dom Pedro II himself, who came to regard him as a friend and protégé.

When Gonçalves Dias's father returned to Caxias in 1825, he renewed his relationship with Vicência and assumed paternity for young Gonçalves Dias, seeing to his education and later putting him to work in his store. In 1829 João Manuel Gonçalves Dias abandoned Vicência and married a white woman of status, Adelaide Ramos de Almeida. He brought Gonçalves Dias with him to the new marriage. Gonçalves Dias had a problematic relationship with his stepmother, but a cordial one with his half brothers and sisters. He also maintained his relationship with Vicência. For example, when he was sure he was dying in 1864, Gonçalves Dias's thoughts turned to his mother. He wrote to his best and oldest friend, Teófilo de Carvalho Leal in São Luís, for assurance that she would be looked after.

In 1837 João Manuel Gonçalves Dias, sick with tuberculosis, decided to return to Portugal for treatment. He took his son with him, intending to enroll him in the University of Coimbra, Portugal's oldest and most prestigious university. João Manuel Gonçalves Dias died in São Luís before embarking, however, and Gonçalves Dias was forced to return to Caxias, where he discovered that he was excluded from his father's will. Furthermore, Adelaide was not inclined to spend anything on her bastard stepson.

Although the situation seemed desperate, the charismatic boy had attracted the attention and sympathy of several of his father's friends and his former teachers. They jointly raised enough money to pay for his passage to Portugal. Faced with this sponsorship, Adelaide agreed to pay Gonçalves Dias's tuition and living costs at the University of Coimbra.

In Coimbra, Gonçalves Dias discovered that his provincial education had left him with deficits in several subjects, and he was forced to spend a year in remedial study. During that year he endeared himself to a group of fellow students from Maranhão. The most important of these was Teófilo. When Adelaide, pressed for funds, demanded Gonçalves Dias return to Brazil, his new friends, all from wealthy families, assumed responsibility for his expenses. Gonçalves Dias was grateful for this support, but he also was deeply embarrassed at having to accept charity. Adelaide finally offered some assistance, sending him money from time to time. Early on Gonçalves Dias perceived that he was superior to most of the other students and felt that he was destined for greatness. This sense of his own worth sustained him through periodic bouts of depression and hard times.

In 1840 Gonçalves Dias was accepted into the University of Coimbra, and he settled into a routine of studies, discussions in taverns, and love affairs. He embarked on a crash course in European literature and civilization, reading the great writers of the day, including the Portuguese poets Alexandre Herculano, Almeida Garrett, and A. F. de Castilho, and the French poets Victor Hugo, Alphonse de Lamartine, François-René de Chateaubriand, Alfred de Vigny, Alexander Dumas *père,* and Pierre Jean de Béranger. Additionally, the great German and English Romantics were available to him in translation. For a person with Gonçalves Dias's sense of being an outsider, belief in his own superiority, love of the Amazon, and general idealism and passion, Romanticism was irresistible. He embraced ideas of the *poéte maudit* (cursed poet), the theme of unrequited love, and an almost pantheistic adoration of wild nature and the sea. Gonçalves Dias was also fascinated by medievalism, and, like other American Romantics, he felt that Indians could serve as avatars of national identity in place of knights and crusades. In 1841 and 1842 he began contributing to literary journals, including the *Gazeta Literária* (Literary Gazette) and *O Trovador* (To the Troubador), and he met Herculano and Garrett in Lisbon.

In the period from 1843 to 1844, Gonçalves Dias traveled widely in Portugal, continued his studies, and formed and cultivated lifelong friendships. The poems he wrote during this time were later included in *Primeiros cantos.* For the most part, they are derivative

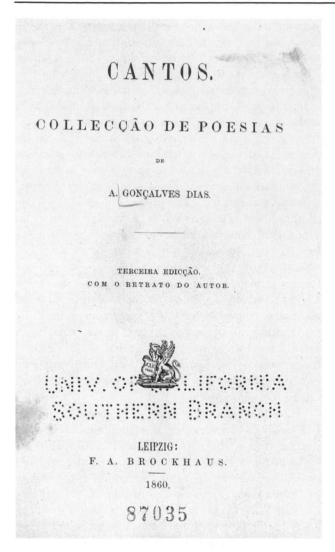

CANTOS.

COLLECÇÃO DE POESIAS

DE

A. GONÇALVES DIAS.

TERCEIRA EDIÇÇÃO.
COM O RETRATO DO AUTOR.

LEIPZIG:
F. A. BROCKHAUS.
1860.

87035

A collection of poems, published during a period in which Gonçalves Dias was traveling to conduct a government study of European public education (Young Research Library, University of California, Los Angeles)

works, the efforts of an apprentice. Today only two or three of these poems are still read: "Canção do exílio" (Song of Exile), "A escrava" (The Slave), and sometimes "O canto do Piaga" (The Shaman's Song). "Canção do exílio" became Gonçalves Dias's signature poem, one almost all literate Brazilians know since it is a standard part of the school curriculum. Although an early piece, the poem has qualities typical of Gonçalves Dias's later lyrics. His choice of title is apropos because his best poetry often follows song or ballad form and uses intense imagery and simple language to distill deeply felt emotions. "Canção do exílio" also reveals how well Gonçalves Dias had learned poetic craft. Using an unusual sprung rhyme ending in words accented on the last syllable, he makes his song memorable while expressing a most characteristic Luso-

Brazilian sentiment, an intense longing or nostalgia expressed in the Portuguese language by the word *saudade*. Interestingly, the emotion is evoked without actually using the word itself: "Minha terra tem palmeiras / Onde canta o sabiá / As aves que aqui gorjeiam, / Não gorjeiam como lá" (My land has palm trees / Where the thrush sings / The birds who sing here / Don't sing like they do there). Gonçalves Dias's epigraph for the poem quoting Johann Wolfgang von Goethe's "Mignon" (1795) is appropriate, since many of his songs are strikingly similar in tone and feeling to Goethe's lyrics.

For modern readers Romantic conventions of expression often seem florid or absurdly exaggerated, and many of Gonçalves Dias's lyric poems are written in this overblown style. There are, however, many poems, "Canção do exílio" among them, where Gonçalves Dias's language is direct, simple, and contemporary. Furthermore, Gonçalves Dias's Portuguese in his prose works was always very Brazilian: colloquial and direct. He contended that since Brazil's population was already twice that of Portugal, there was no reason Brazilians should imitate Portuguese diction and syntax. On this issue he was quite modern in his thinking. The debate over "Brazilian" versus "Portuguese" grammar would span the nineteenth century and continue through the first twenty-five years of the twentieth century, when it was finally settled in the 1920s and 1930s by the modernists, who incorporated Brazilian colloquial language into formal discourse.

Another piece from *Primeiros cantos,* "A escrava," is Gonçalves Dias's only poem about slavery. Although it is inferior to "Canção do exílio," it shows Gonçalves Dias's trademark song structure and sense of the dramatic. The poem is divided into two parts. The first part involves a long lyrical idyll set in the Congo, where young Alsgá frolics with an unidentified lover in primeval nature; the second part is a short, brutal epilogue showing Alsgá as a terrified slave. Gonçalves Dias's description of the Congo and use of African terms fit easily within Romantic notions of the exotic and the tropical.

"O canto do Piaga," written in São Luís in 1846 and published in *Primeiros cantos,* is Gonçalves Dias's first great Indian poem. Structured in three movements, the poem describes a horrific vision in which the tribe's *piaga,* or shaman, is shown Portuguese ships coming to destroy the Tupi nation. The poem equates the Portuguese destroyers to instruments of Satan ("Anhangá" in Tupi): "Não sabeis o que o monstro procura? / Não sabeis a que vem, o que quer? / Vem matar vossos bravos guerreiros, / Vem roubar-vos a filha, a mulher!" (Don't you know what the monster seeks? / Don't you know why he comes, what he wants? / He comes to kill your brave warriors, / He comes to steal your daughter, your wife!).

In this poem Gonçalves Dias first employed a poetic device rare in Portuguese poetry, the anapestic foot. This short-short-long rhythm is well suited to poetry depicting Indian culture because it imitates the beating of a drum. It is unknown where Gonçalves Dias learned the technique, but it is common in English poetry with its accented-syllabic verse structure. The anapestic foot became a staple of Gonçalves Dias's Indian poems, and he learned to manipulate it with great effect by incorporating it into traditional forms of Portuguese verse featuring quatrains with consonant rhyme on even verses: "Ó guerreiros da Taba sagrada / Ó guerreiros da Tribo Tupi / Falam deuses nos cantos do Piaga, / Ó guerreiros meus cantos ouvi" (Warriors of the sacred tribe / Warriors of the Tupi nation / Gods speak in the shaman's songs / Warriors, hear my songs).

In 1845, after seven years abroad, Gonçalves Dias returned to Caxias with a law degree in hand. He was now a sophisticated and worldly young man who quickly discovered that he had no future in his hometown, where his social deficits were held against him. After a miserable year in Caxias he left for São Luís, where his friends from Coimbra welcomed him. There he met Teófilo's cousin Ana Amélia Ferreira do Vale, at the time a precocious adolescent. She later became his ideal and unattainable woman, the source of some of his best lyric poems.

In June 1846 Gonçalves Dias's friend Teófilo secured for him passage to Rio de Janeiro. He arrived bearing letters of introduction, hoping to secure support from classmates from Coimbra. He had borrowed some money from friends in São Luís, but he rapidly spent a large portion of it in extravagant living. This extravagance allowed him to shine on the social scene, however, and he secured the publication of *Primeiros cantos* in January 1847. There was little reaction to *Primeiros cantos* in Brazil until an enthusiastic review by Herculano appeared in a Rio de Janeiro newspaper, the *Revista Universal Lisbonense,* on 30 November 1847.

Although Gonçalves Dias gained employment in late 1847 at a secondary school in the provincial city of Niterói, he continued to work assiduously on poetry and drama. Around this time he began writing his American epic, "Os Tymbiras," a project on which he worked until his death. He published four cantos in Europe as *Os tymbiras: poema americano* (1857, The Timbiras: American Poem). In later correspondence he indicated that he had completed the poem, writing a total of sixteen cantos, but if he did so, the originals were lost in the shipwreck that ended his life. "Os Tymbiras" narrates the saga of a tribe of Indians from Gonçalves

Dias's native Maranhão who are forced to migrate to the Amazon and eventually are exterminated. "Os Tymbiras" is little regarded by critics and readers, who generally prefer Gonçalves Dias's shorter Indian poems.

Gonçalves Dias was extremely productive between 1847 and 1851. In June 1848 he published his *Segundos cantos* (Second Songs) together with the medieval exercise *Sextilhas de frei Antão* (Friar Anton's Sextains). As he began attracting attention for his literary works, Gonçalves Dias embarked on a career as a journalist in 1848, working full-time for the *Jornal do Comércio* (Commercial Journal) and part-time for the *Correio Mercantil* (Business Mail), the *Correio da Tarde* (Afternoon Mail), and the *Gazeta Oficial* (Official Gazette), reporting on politics. In 1849 he was appointed as a professor of Latin and Brazilian history in the Colégio Pedro II, the finest secondary school in nineteenth-century Brazil. Gonçalves Dias simply added this job to his other activities, and he also founded the literary journal *Guanabara* (named after the Indian word for the region around Rio de Janeiro) with Manuel de Macedo and Manuel Araújo Porto Alegre. When Gonçalves Dias and his coeditors presented the first issue of the journal to Don Pedro, who was keenly interested in natural sciences, Gonçalves Dias was named Cavaleiro da Ordem da Rosa (Cavalier of the Order of the Rose). The poem "Meditação" (Meditation), featured in *Guanabara,* led to an imperial commission to compare Brazilian Indians with indigenous peoples elsewhere. Gonçalves Dias's work in this area resulted in a pioneering ethnographic study, *Brasil e Oceania,* which was read in nine consecutive sessions of the Instituto Histórico (Historical Institute) between 20 August 1852 and June 1853, and ethnography, comparative education, and history became his focus for the balance of his career.

Throughout the nineteenth century Rio de Janeiro was pestilential, and a devastating yellow-fever epidemic swept the city in 1850. Yellow fever was not stamped out until the public hygiene and sanitation campaigns of Oswaldo Cruz at the end of the century. Gonçalves Dias contracted yellow fever at this time, and it was added to a growing list of health problems he suffered. Literary historians have pondered the role illness may have played in Gonçalves Dias's frequent depression. In his letters to friends he often complained of his ailments. Over the course of his life Gonçalves Dias survived an astonishing array of usually fatal illnesses, often recovering quickly. By 1850 he was suffering from arthritis and one or more venereal diseases.

Gonçalves Dias's venereal disease was the result of a frantic and indiscriminate love life that began during his student days and continued in Rio de Janeiro. In the Brazilian capital Gonçalves Dias became a gallant who participated actively in the nightlife of the imperial court, and he attracted a remarkable series of female admirers. His many infatuations yielded a series of memorable love poems, and Brazilian literary historians have made efforts to identify many of his lovers. Gonçalves Dias's attitude toward women seems to have been a combination of cynicism in practice and romantic idealism in theory. Representative love poems written from this time are "Olhos verdes" (Green Eyes) and "Pensas tu, bela Anarda" (So You Think, Anarda), both published in *Obras póstumas* (1868–1869, Posthumous Works). "Olhos verdes" is an ingenious if archaic conceit on the seductiveness of green eyes. The poem serves as a kind of gloss on the epigraph, a stanza by Portuguese Renaissance poet Luís de Camões: "Eles verdes são: / E tem por usança, / Na cor esperança, / E nos obras, não" (Her eyes are green: / and they usually / show hope in their color / but not in their acts). Gonçalves Dias says that the woman in question has green, green eyes, sea-green eyes, that give hope in good times. They are eyes for which the poet pines and in which he loses all notion of himself. The poet tells his friends to remember after he is gone that he died for love and for a pair of green eyes. In "Pensas tu, bela Anarda," Gonçalves Dias once again offers an old approach to love, but the speaker is a cynic who tells the young woman that while she may think poets—like butterflies—live on air, perfume, and ambrosia, she should not think them such fools. Such romantic attitudes are fine for poetry, the speaker says, but he, sinner that he is, prefers kissing to swooning. The language Gonçalves Dias uses is intentionally crude, as if a young dandy were patronizing a naive young woman.

These love poems are of a piece with *Sextilhas de frei Antão,* with which they simultaneously were composed. The *sextilha* is a medieval six-verse stanza, and today these verses are difficult reading. Technically brilliant, the poems seem to be more of a demonstration of poetic technique than the relation of any deeply felt experience. It appears that Gonçalves Dias was moved to write the *sextilhas* as a proof of his linguistic virtuosity after critics dismissed his play *Beatriz Cenci,* written in 1843 and rejected by the Conservatório Dramático in 1846, as inauthentic and full of errors in Portuguese. In *Segundos cantos e Sextilhas de frei Antão,* Gonçalves Dias maintained that he had found the *sextilhas* in historical documents, and that the author had been a Dominican friar.

"A tempestade" (The Tempest) is another poem from this period that primarily seems to be a demonstration of poetic technique. It describes the coming of a storm, its climax, and decline. It begins with two-syllable verses, and each stanza that follows adds a syllable up to the climax, which features verses of eleven syllables in length; the denouement follows with each stanza reducing verse length until the poem ends with verses of two syllables. Proof of the poet's virtuosity lies in the variety of verses and rhymes and in the fact that the exactitude and beauty of the descriptions of each moment in the storm's progress are rendered so that the feeling invoked is of inspiration rather than tedium. These poems have made their way into anthologies since the 1850s because they convincingly demonstrate that not all Romantic poets were poor technicians.

In 1851 Gonçalves Dias published *Últimos cantos* (Last Songs), bringing to a close the greater part of his poetic activity. This collection features what is generally considered to be his finest Indian poem, "I-Juca-Pirama" (a Tupi phrase that, according to Gonçalves Dias, roughly translates to "he who must be killed"). Developed in ten tableaux, the poem is a portrait of a vanished people who embodied ideals only dimly perceptible in mid-nineteenth-century Brazilian society. One critic, Lúcia Miguel Pereira, has attributed the composition and success of "I-Juca-Pirama" to the fact that at that moment, when society was dominated by a despotic rural oligarchy that used slavery as a means of supplying cheap sugar and other goods to Europe, Brazil needed heroes. Gonçalves Dias, and later José de Alencar, offered up stoic, noble, larger-than-life Indian characters who owed more to Greece than to the sad reality of a conquered, annihilated people.

The characters in "I-Juca-Pirama" and similar poems are more like avatars than individuals; they have no inner life. Gonçalves Dias and other Brazilian Indianist authors clearly read Michel de Montaigne's essays and the works of Chateaubriand, but Indianism in Brazil was quite different from the European depictions of the noble savage. Chateaubriand saw New World savages as an antidote to the evils of industrialization and urbanization, while Brazil was an agrarian plantation society. Gonçalves Dias's heroes are not innocent children playing in the fields of Tupã. They are noble, but they are also warriors and cannibals. Their ideal is war without quarter, and they believe only the brave are worthy of being eaten. Cowards are shunned by both their own families and their enemies.

The young warrior in "I-Juca-Pirama" is torn between filial devotion and his tribe's ideal of dying bravely in confronting one's enemies. He is captured by the tribe called Timbiras and confesses, crying, that he must return to his blind, sick father. The Timbiras release him, believing him a coward, and he returns to his father, where he is cursed because the only outcomes the tribe accepts are victory or honorable death. The young warrior then attacks the Timbira village by himself and redeems his honor, allowing his father to reconcile with him before both die. According to the poem, the story of the apparent coward turned hero becomes a Timbira legend, passed down from generation to generation.

Another Indian poem from *Últimos cantos* still read today is "Marabá." The poem recounts the story of a beautiful, light-skinned, blue-eyed mestiza, or "marabá." Both the Portuguese and Indians shun her. The similarities between the circumstances of this character and those of Gonçalves Dias make the poem especially poignant. Finally, "Canção do Tamoio" (Song of the Tamoio) is another popular poem from *Últimos cantos*. It purports to be a lullaby sung by a mother to her newborn son. She extols the virtues of stoicism, bravery, and sacrifice: "Não chores, meu filho; / Não chores, que a vida / É luta renhida" (Don't cry my son; / Don't cry; life is / Unending strife).

In spite of his many professional activities and a busy social life, by 1851 Gonçalves Dias was depressed and bored with life in Rio de Janeiro. A commission from the imperial government to retrieve colonial documents and to study the state of public education in the northern provinces compelled him to travel to São Luís late that year. From 1851 onward Gonçalves Dias was consumed with one official mission or another, and his poetic activity declined markedly. From 1851 to 1864 his literary production was sporadic; most of his poems from this period were written during time spent in Maranhão and the Amazon in 1861–1862. These literary efforts were collected and published by his friend Antônio Henriques Leal as part of *Obras póstumas* in 1868–1869. Yet, despite the overall drop in his literary activity in these years, Gonçalves Dias's lyric poetry written after 1851 forms an important part of his legacy. While Gonçalves Dias also wrote several plays, he never succeeded in getting them onstage in Brazil. Eventually his *Boabdil,* which he completed in 1850, was translated into German and produced in Dresden in 1857, but he was busy in Berlin and did not go to see it.

Gonçalves Dias's trip to the North in 1851 began well and ended disastrously. His volubility in love and his constancy in fulfilling his professional obligations, both distinctive characteristics of his life, converged in significant ways during this period. In São Luís he stayed with Teófilo and his family, and he inevitably renewed his acquaintance with Ana Amélia, whom he had not seen for four years. Ana Amélia had matured into a beautiful young woman. Gonçalves Dias was attracted to her, and his interest was reciprocated. Meanwhile, between romantic interludes Gonçalves Dias undertook his research. Although many of his colleagues regarded imperial commissions as sinecures and performed their duties haphazardly, Gonçalves Dias dutifully wrote his reports, copied the documents he could find, and collected artifacts, exhausting himself in the process. He persevered in his obligations, often in spite of overwhelming difficulties.

Gonçalves Dias continued courting Ana Amélia, naively assuming that his special status in the family would overcome his social liabilities. He wrote a formal letter to her mother, Dona Lourença, asking for her daughter's hand in marriage, and departed for the Northeast to continue his research. While in Recife he received a peremptory refusal from Ana Amélia's mother. Devastated, he informed Ana Amélia of what had happened. She proposed that they elope, but Gonçalves Dias accepted the refusal out of respect for Teófilo's family. There is some evidence that Ana Amélia later reproached him for his cowardice, but given Gonçalves Dias's relationship with Teófilo and the rest of the family, it is not difficult to understand that a deep sense of obligation and duty would not permit him to affront them by eloping with one of the most eligible young women of São Luís. Ana Amélia eventually married a local businessman and moved on with her life. Later, when her husband died, she married again. Everything that is known about her reveals a sensible, practical woman who accepted her status and role in society.

Gonçalves Dias, on the other hand, self-destructed. He returned to Rio de Janeiro, looked up Olímpia da Costa, a woman from a good family who was in love with him, and proposed to her. They were married in 1853. Still in love with Ana Amélia, however, Gonçalves Dias offered his new bride only benevolent indifference, and the marriage immediately unraveled. Gonçalves Dias made no effort to hide his interest in other women, and Olímpia responded with jealousy and reproach.

In his letters to friends Gonçalves Dias constantly complained about Olímpia, expressing his desperate desire to be free of her and her paranoid jealousy. In public, however, their marriage continued, and he maintained relatively cordial relations with her father, Cláudio Luiz da Costa, a successful doctor. Throughout his life he kept Olímpia in a style appropriate for her class and sent her presents on her birthdays and other occasions, sometimes very expensive ones. At the end of his life Gonçalves Dias and Olímpia maintained separate residences when he was in Rio de Janeiro, but they kept up appearances in public. There is ample evidence that Olímpia loved Gonçalves Dias deeply, and her desperate attempts to be with him were the subject of crude jokes by his friends. On his last, fatal trip to São Luís, Olímpia tried to follow him, but his decision in Recife to go directly to Europe prevented her from catching up.

GONÇALVES
DIAS

POESIA COMPLETA
E PROSA ESCOLHIDA

MANUEL BANDEIRA
A Vida e a Obra do Poeta. A Poética de Gonçalves Dias

ANTÔNIO HOUAISS
O Texto dos Poemas

ALEXANDRE HERCULANO
Futuro Literário de Portugal e do Brasil
(Prólogo aos Cantos)

RIO DE JANEIRO, EDITÔRA JOSÉ AGUILAR LTDA., 1959

*Title page for an important mid-twentieth-century collection
of Gonçalves Dias's works (Hodges Library,
University of Tennessee)*

During this period Gonçalves Dias contracted another disease, tuberculosis. Tuberculosis was epidemic in Rio de Janeiro, but Gonçalves Dias thought his wife had given him the disease, a conclusion that was almost certainly wrong. Tuberculosis seems to have run in his family, killing both his father and a half brother. Additionally, Olímpia lived a long and productive life after his death, and there is no evidence she was ever tubercular. Gonçalves Dias's belief in his wife's guilt in this matter is, however, indicative of his mindset during this period.

The shock of losing Ana Amélia seems to have imbued Gonçalves Dias's lyricism with tragic intensity. Sixteen poems he composed between 1851 and 1856 were included in the European edition of his poetry, *Cantos: collecção de poesias* (1857, Cantos: Collection of Poems), under the rubric "Novos cantos" (New Songs). One of these poems, "Se se morre de amor" (Can One Die of Love?), was written in Recife in the immediate

aftermath of his receiving the letter of refusal from Ana Amélia's mother. This poem begins with an epigraph from Friedrich Schiller's *Die Räuber* (1781; translated as *The Robbers,* 1792) and expounds a romantic theory of love. A measure of the seriousness of the subject is that the poem is written in ten-syllable lines that give it a stately, measured rhythm. In the first two stanzas the poet explains what love is not: it is not the excitement of the dance, beauty, grace, dress, and decoration, which are all "enganos de amor" (love's tricks). These things lead to infatuation, but infatuation is not lethal. The third stanza propounds that true love is life itself, an expansive opening up to greatness, beauty, virtue, the infinity of the universe, even God himself; those who have this kind of love can die from it.

The poem proceeds in a series of crescendos, each metaphor more exaggerated than the one before: "Conhecer o prazer e a desventura / No mesmo tempo, e ser no mesmo ponto / O ditoso, o misérrimo dos entes / Isso é amor, e desse amor se morre!" (To know pleasure and sadness / At once, and be at the same time / The happiest and most miserable of persons / That is love, and one dies of that love!). The fourth stanza describes love as a cult of devotion to the beloved. This sort of adoration is a commonplace of romantic love: a woman placed upon a pedestal engenders fear and trembling from the poet who dares approach her. The speaker places himself in a position of supplicant, unable to give voice to his love because of fear that "olhos profanes" (profane glances) will spoil the sanctuary where he hides his devotion. The speaker develops a kind of special sense of his beloved, perceiving her thoughts and emotions, but he is unable even to touch the hem of her dress.

The fifth stanza discusses what happens when a true union exists but the lovers are separated by destiny. The sixth stanza describes the wreckage that results from the sundering of this union: death, or worse, vegetating, living only to be buried in native soil. Here Gonçalves Dias employs the image of the exiled wanderer, an idea that had a powerful influence on the Romantic imagination. For example, Charles Robert Maturin's famous Gothic novel *Melmoth the Wanderer* (1820) is based on the medieval figure of the Wandering Jew. The image and the emotion of suffering that the book evoked was incorporated into notions of the Romantic hero. It is clear from his correspondence that Gonçalves Dias regarded his sojourns in Rio de Janeiro and Europe as a kind of exile from his happiness in São Luís. When he felt his death approaching, his belief that he was living in exile explains why he desperately wanted to return to Maranhão.

The seventh stanza of "Se se morre de amor" describes the situation of "Esse, que sobrevive a própria ruína" (He, who survives his own ruin) and envies the dead: "Esse, que à dor tamanha não sucumbe, / Inveja a quem na sepultura encontra / Dos males seus o desejado termo!" (He who does not succumb to such pain / Envies he who finds in the grave / The end of his suffering!). Like Melmoth, the speaker is condemned to relive in solitude the remembered moments of happiness, simultaneously assuaging and intensifying his pain.

In 1855 Ana Amélia and her husband were in Lisbon, where they had come after his bankruptcy in São Luís. At the same time Gonçalves Dias traveled from Paris to Lisbon as part of his research, and he and Ana Amélia accidentally crossed paths in the streets. Ana Amélia apparently refused to acknowledge him and passed him by, while Gonçalves Dias stood rooted to the ground. When he got over his consternation, he wrote "Ainda uma vez–adeus!" (Once again–Goodbye!). This poem is an explanation for his behavior and describes the grief he feels because his difficult sacrifice was neither understood nor appreciated. The chance encounter in Lisbon was apparently the last time Ana Amélia and Gonçalves Dias met. Although in subsequent visits to São Luís, Gonçalves Dias always stayed with Teófilo's family, he did not make contact with Ana Amélia. Furthermore, there is no evidence that she ever read his explanation of things or any of the other poems dedicated to her.

There was clearly a divergence between Gonçalves Dias's generally shoddy treatment of his wife and his many lovers and his apparently deep and sincere feelings for Ana Amélia. With Ana Amélia, Gonçalves Dias apparently carried into his personal life the notion of a distant, idealized love object on whom to confer his amorous attentions, and in many ways he seems to have sacrificed his personal happiness and well-being in the bargain. Critics have theorized that Gonçalves Dias crammed more work and travel into his life than was healthy as an anodyne, his frantic busyness serving as a way of avoiding introspection. In a letter to his friend Guilherme Schür Capanema dated 3 May 1857 he refers to his activities as "un meio de matar ou de subjugar a todo custo o pensamento" (a means of killing or subjugating, at all cost, thinking).

There is no doubt of the painful sincerity expressed in "Ainda uma vez–adeus!" There is a naive, endearing quality to his bewilderment and hurt. He begins by saying "Enfim te vejo!" (At last I see you!), and proceeds to tell the woman that he has never stopped loving her, imposing exile on himself and living among strangers. He speaks of his depression, of how her memory saved him from suicide. He has lived in hope they might meet again, and in that moment she turns away from him: "Mas que tens? Não me conhe-

ces? / De mim afastas teu rosto? / . . . / Nenhuma voz me diriges!" (What is wrong? Don't you know me? / Do you turn your face from me? / . . . / You say nothing to me!). Gonçalves Dias alludes to those who came between them, and his acceptance of the situation is explained as part of his desire to spare her from gossip. He now perceives he was wrong: "Erro foi, mas não foi crime" (It was a mistake, not a crime).

Gonçalves Dias was made an official in the Secretaria de Negócios Estrangeiros (Foreign Ministry) in 1852. Since both he and Olímpia were in poor health, Gonçalves Dias conceived of a trip to Europe for treatment and recuperation. At the time there was a general belief that the tropics were unhealthy and that the northern climate of Europe had restorative powers. The mid nineteenth century was a transitional time in medicine; scientific methods did not come until later. Louis Pasteur's germ theory did not become widely disseminated until the 1870s, and it remained controversial until the end of the century. Consequently, there were fads for mineral baths, bizarre concoctions of all sorts, and treatments that in most cases made diseases worse. For example, mercury was widely used to treat syphilitic lesions.

To finance the trip Gonçalves Dias proposed a study of European public education that was accepted by the government. The family arrived in Lisbon in July 1854. From there they went to Paris. Although Gonçalves Dias was vehemently opposed to having children, Olímpia had become pregnant before they left Brazil. A sickly daughter, Joana, was born in November 1854. In March 1856 Gonçalves Dias was able to free himself of his wife and child–something he deeply desired–by sending them back to Brazil with friends. Joana died of pneumonia shortly after arriving in Rio de Janeiro. Gonçalves Dias continued his work, visiting almost every capital in Europe.

By January 1859 Gonçalves Dias was back in the Amazon. Olímpia desperately wanted to accompany him on his new assignment, a scientific expedition to the Northeast and the North, but she was refused. The "Comissão das borboletas" (Butterfly Commission), as critics called it, was a disaster. The problem was that exploring the backlands of Brazil at this time was tantamount in difficulty to similar projects in Africa or the Lewis and Clark expedition in the United States: ideas that seemed brilliant in the salons of London; Paris; Washington, D.C.; and Rio de Janeiro were impractical in the field. Of the group of scientific experts involved at the beginning, only Gonçalves Dias and one other member of the expedition actually finished the project, exploring the Rio Negro and the Madeira after wandering through the interior of the Northeast. Gonçalves Dias assiduously collected artifacts and got along well with the Indians he met along the way. His attitude toward the indigenous people he met during his voyages was remarkably modern. Scholars lament the fact that most of his reports and the material artifacts he assembled have been lost. Although Gonçalves Dias accomplished his mission, the effect it had on his health was disastrous, as he contracted malaria in Ceará.

In the poems written in 1861–1862 and collected in *Obras póstumas,* Gonçalves Dias frequently returns to the theme of love and the moment of his and Ana Amélia's last meeting. These poems generally are inferior to "Ainda uma vez–adeus!," but "Como! És Tu?" (What, Is It You?) is exceptional. The poet imagines Ana Amélia in her wedding dress, apparently happy but hiding inner turmoil: "Pálida, pálida a fronte / Olhos em pranto a nadar!" (Pallid, pallid your forehead / And your eyes almost crying!). To the poet's consternation and disbelief, she walks away from him to go to her marriage: "Sei que te aguardam no templo / Deixa-me aqui a chorar; / Fazes somente o que fiz, / Não fazes mais que imitar!" (I know they wait for you in the church, / Leave me here crying; / You only do what I did, / You do nothing more than imitate me!" This passage alludes to Gonçalves Dias's own precipitous marriage after receiving the response from Ana Amélia's mother. The poet ends by blessing his lost lover: "Vai! Sê feliz! Adeus!" (Go! Be happy! Goodbye!).

In another poem from this period, "Não me deixes" (Don't Leave Me), Gonçalves Dias composes a much more objective–but no less poignant–ballad on love. The anguish of impossible love is expressed as a parable of a flower in love with a brook, pleading with the water not to leave her until at last she is carried away in the stream, exclaiming, "Não me deixaste, não!" (You didn't leave me after all!). This distinctively Brazilian use of the double negative (não . . . não) is striking for the time. In "Não me deixes" all the Romantic rhetorical flourishes and posturing are pared away, leaving the simplest possible language to evoke a powerful emotional response: "Debruçada nas águas dum regato / A flor dizia em vão; / À corrente, onde bela se mirava . . . / 'Ai, não me deixes, não!'" (Bent over the waters of a brook / The flower cried in vain / To the stream, where, beautiful, she observed herself . . . / "Please don't leave me!").

By late 1861 Gonçalves Dias was back in Rio de Janeiro, deathly ill, depressed, and bitter about the failure of the backlands expedition, even though he still enjoyed enormous respect in intellectual circles. In his capacity as a physician, Olímpia's father advised him to seek treatment in Rio de Janeiro. Gonçalves Dias, however, determinedly began his return to São Luís, but his health deteriorated so badly on the voyage to Recife that he decided to consult a doctor there. The doctor

was alarmed: Gonçalves Dias had heart disease, a bad liver, hepatitis, and a flare-up of his venereal disease, not to mention his other ailments. The doctor recommended that he go immediately to Europe for treatment, and this time he followed professional advice. He tried to secure passage on a small merchant sailing ship preparing to depart for Europe, but the captain was afraid he would die on the voyage and initially refused to accept him. Gonçalves Dias pleaded with him, however, and he was finally accepted as a passenger on the condition that he provide for his own food and medicine. The voyage lasted fifty-five days instead of the normal twenty-five because of doldrums in midpassage. A sailor died en route, and the ship was quarantined in Marseille out of fear of tropical disease. Somehow, a rumor started that it was Gonçalves Dias who had died, and the press in Brazil and Europe published emotional tributes to the great poet, who was greatly amused by this premature obituary praise.

Nevertheless, Gonçalves Dias was quite sick, and once in Europe, he underwent a round of treatments and embarked on visits to spas. He recovered briefly but relapsed in 1864. His situation was so dire that he contemplated throat surgery because his congenital tuberculosis had invaded his larynx. At the end he was unable to speak. He finally secured return passage to São Luís on another sailing ship. A second difficult voyage of more than fifty days was a struggle, and Gonçalves Dias was bedridden for most of the voyage. When the ship hit a reef off the coast of Maranhão, Gonçalves Dias was too feeble to save himself. All his unpublished manuscripts as well as other documents collected in Europe were lost with him.

A complex, deeply flawed man, Antônio Gonçalves Dias was a polymath genius. He excelled in several distinct lines of work, ranging from journalism to ethnography. In fact, he may be viewed as the father of ethnography in Brazil, although most of his work in this area has been lost. Meanwhile, his poetry has endured and become an important part of Brazilian culture. Gonçalves Dias's greatest contributions to Brazilian literary history are undoubtedly his later Indian poems–most notably "I-Juca-Pirama"–and the intense lyric poems occasioned by losing Ana Amélia do Vale. In the years since his death, Gonçalves Dias's literary star has grown brighter, while the names and works of many of his contemporaries, famous at the time, have slowly dimmed. His poems are still read for pleasure, and scholars study his works for what they say about the attitudes and values of those in nineteenth-century Brazil. His Indianist poems helped shape Brazilians' notions of indigenous people and helped to make cannibalism comprehensible to Brazilians as a positive cultural act, not a source of shame. These poems clearly

provided a foundation for the theory of cultural cannibalism espoused by vanguardists in the 1920s.
Gonçalves Dias's deep love of Brazil was instrumental
in shaping the country's self-image, and the presence of
his poems in Brazilian grade-school and middle-school
textbooks continues his influence on the culture.

Bibliography:

Marilene Rosa Nogueira da Silva, *Bibliografia de
Gonçalves Dias* (Rio de Janeiro: Imprensa Nacional, 1942).

References:

Fritz Ackermann, *Die Versdichtung des Brasilianers Antônio
Gonçalves Dias* (Hamburg: Evert, 1938);

Manuel Bandeira, *Poesía e vida de Gonçalves Dias* (São
Paulo: Editôra das Américas, 1962);

Alfredo Bosi, "Gonçalves Dias," in his *História concisa da
literatura brasileira* (São Paulo: Cultrix, 1970), pp.
11–119;

Antônio Cândido, "Gonçalves Dias consolida o romantismo," in *Formação da literatura brasileira: momentos
decisivos,* volume 2 (São Paulo: Martins, 1959), pp.
81–96;

Otto Maria Carpeaux, *Pequena bibliografia crítica da literatura brasileira* (Rio de Janeiro: Ministério da Edu-

cação e Cultura, Serviço de Documentação, 1951;
revised, 1955);

Othon Moacyr Garcia, *Luz e fogo no lirismo de Gonçalves
Dias* (Rio de Janeiro: Livraria de São José, 1956);

Henrique de Campos Ferreira Lima, *Gonçalves Dias em
Portugal* (Coimbra: Coimbra Editora, 1942);

Lúcia Miguel Pereira, *A vida de Gonçalves Dias: contendo o
diario inédito da viagem de Gonçalves Dias ao rio Negro,
com 11 ilustrações fora do texto* (Rio de Janeiro: J.
Olympio, 1943);

Manoel de Sousa Pinto, *Gonçalves Dias em Coimbra*
(Coimbra: Coimbra Editora, 1931);

Cassiano Ricardo, "Gonçalves Dias e o indianismo," in
A literatura no Brasil, volume 1, edited by Afrânio
Coutinho (Rio de Janeiro: Sul-Americana, 1955),
pp. 659–736;

Marilene Nogueira da Silva, *Gonçalves Dias e Castro Alves*
(Rio de Janeiro: A Noite, 1943).

Papers:

Collections of Antônio Gonçalves Dias's correspondence and other papers are held in the Antônio Henriques Leal archive at the Instituto Histórico and at the
Biblioteca Nacional, both in Rio de Janeiro.

Gianfrancesco Guarnieri

(6 August 1934 –)

Robert N. Anderson
University of North Carolina at Chapel Hill

BOOKS: *Gimba, Presidente dos Valentes: peça em 1 prólogo e 2 tempos* (Rio de Janeiro: Edição da Sociedade Brasileira de Autores Teatrais, 1959);

A semente: peça em 3 atos (São Paulo: Massao Ohno, 1961);

Arena conta Zumbi, by Guarnieri and Augusto Boal, music by Edu Lôbo (São Paulo, 1965);

Eles não usam black-tie: peça em 3 atos e 6 quadros (São Paulo: Brasiliense, 1966);

Arena conta Tiradentes, by Guarnieri and Boal (São Paulo: Sagarana, 1967);

Castro Alves pede passagem (São Paulo: Palco+Platéia, 1971);

Um grito parado no ar; Botequim, ou Céu sobre a chuva (São Paulo: Monções, 1973);

Ponto de partida: fábula em um ato (São Paulo: Brasiliense, 1976);

Teatro de Gianfrancesco Guarnieri, 3 volumes (Rio de Janeiro: Civilização Brasileira, 1978)—comprises volume 1: *Eles não usam black-tie, Gimba;* volume 2: *A semente;* and volume 3: *O filho do Cão, O cimento;*

Teatro de Gianfrancesco Guarnieri: textos para televisão (São Paulo: Editora de Humanismo, Ciência e Tecnologia; Editora da Universidade de São Paulo, 1988)—comprises *As pessoas da sala de jantar, O pivete, Gino, Solidão, Édipo,* by Guarnieri; and *Carga pesada* (2 episodes), *A procura, Perdão,* and *Dadá,* by Guarnieri and Fernando Peixoto.

Editions and Collections: *Gianfrancesco Guarnieri,* edited by Maria Helena Pires Martins (São Paulo: Abril Educaçao, 1980);

Gianfrancesco Guarnieri, edited by Décio de Almeida Prado (São Paulo: Global, 1986).

PLAY PRODUCTIONS: *Eles não usam black-tie,* São Paulo, Teatro de Arena, 22 February 1958;

Gimba, Presidente dos Valentes, São Paulo, Teatro Maria Della Costa, 17 March 1959;

O filho do Cão, São Paulo, Teatro de Arena, 31 January 1961;

A semente, São Paulo, Teatro de Arena, 27 April 1961;

Gianfrancesco Guarnieri (frontispiece for Simon Khoury, Atrás da máscara, *1984; Howard-Tilton Memorial Library, Tulane University)*

Arena conta Zumbi, São Paulo, Teatro de Arena, 1 May 1965;

Arena conta Tiradentes, São Paulo, Teatro de Arena, 21 April 1967;

Castro Alves pede passagem, Salvador, Teatro Castro Alves, 18 May 1971;

Botequim ou Céu sobre a chuva, Brasília, Sala Martins Pena, 3 April 1973;

Um grito parado no ar, Curitiba, Teatro Guaíra, 3 April 1973;

Ponto de partida, São Paulo, Teatro TAIB, 23 September 1976.

PRODUCED SCRIPTS: *O cimento,* television, TV Excelsior, 1962;
As pessoas da sala de jantar, television, TV Tupi, 1972;
Gino, television, TV Globo, 1975;
Solidão, television, TV Globo;
"A procura" and "Perdão, Dadá," television, *Carga pesada,* by Guarnieri and Fernando Peixoto, TV Globo;
Eles não usam black-tie, motion picture, story and screenplay by Guarnieri and Leon Hirszman, Embrafilme, 1981; released in the U.S. as *They Don't Wear Black Tie,* New Yorker Films, 1983.

OTHER: *Janelas abertas,* in *Feira Brasileira de Opinião,* edited by Ruth Escobar (São Paulo: Global, 1978), pp. 89–110.

SELECTED PERIODICAL PUBLICATION–
UNCOLLECTED: *Arena conta Zumbi, Revista de teatro,* no. 378 (1970): 31–59.

One of the pillars of the renaissance of Brazilian theater of the 1950s, Gianfrancesco Guarnieri is a respected actor, writer, director, and arts administrator in theater, television, and motion pictures. Guarnieri is best known for his work in political theater with the Teatro de Arena de São Paulo (Arena Theater of São Paulo) between 1956 and 1971. Teatro de Arena was one of the most important theatrical companies in postwar Brazil. It gathered an unusually talented group of artists from a variety of fields for the purpose of creating a Brazilian political theater. The company brought theater-in-the-round to South America and spearheaded intellectual resistance to the 1964 military coup that deposed João Goulart and installed General Castello Branco in the presidency. Teatro de Arena launched not only Guarnieri's career but also those of Augusto Boal, Milton Gonçalves, and Fernanda Montenegro, to mention a few internationally known names from screen and stage, as well as a dozen or so playwrights and actors who achieved local fame.

In the award-winning 1981 motion-picture adaptation of Guarnieri's *Eles não usam black-tie* (They Don't Wear Black Tie), internationally acclaimed Brazilian actress Fernanda Montenegro played the steely matriarch Romana opposite Guarnieri's Otávio, the uncompromising patriarch of the play. In the penultimate scene in which the couple sorts beans while fighting back tears, one of the most moving scenes in all Brazilian cinema, both actors deliver intimate performances that are both tender and resolute. Interestingly, Guarnieri had played the character of Otávio's son, Tião, in the theatrical production of the play in 1958, but by the time the motion-picture version was produced, he was able to play the father. This shift in roles is a fitting measure of Guarnieri's long career as a playwright, screenwriter, actor, and advocate of both the worker and the arts, a man who brought the complexities of the human condition to political theater.

Gianfrancesco Sigfrido Benedetto Martinenghi de Guarnieri was born into a family of musicians in Milan, Italy, on 6 August 1934. His mother, Elsa Martinenghi, was a harpist in the orchestra of the Teatro Scala di Milano (Scala di Milano Theater), and his father, Edoardo, was an orchestral musician and conductor who cofounded the I Vittoriale String Quartet. Guarnieri's political training began in his family life. His father opposed the Fascists and consequently left Italy for Brazil with his wife and young son in 1936. In Brazil, Guarnieri's parents reestablished their musical careers, and Guarnieri was raised in a milieu of performers. The Guarnieris settled initially in the Cosme Velho district of Rio de Janeiro, where Guarnieri spent his childhood. His father became a conductor for the Orquestra Sinfónica Brasileira (Brazilian Symphonic Orchestra), and his mother was a musician.

By the time Guarnieri was eighteen, his family was living in São Paulo, where his parents continued their musical careers with the Orquestra Sinfónica do São Paulo (São Paulo Symphony Orchestra), and where his father was director of the Teatro Municipal (Municipal Theater). Guarnieri got his own start in the theater during his student years at the University of São Paulo, where he was also an activist in the student movement.

Guarnieri began his career as an artist at an important time in the theatrical landscape. Brazil's premier theater company of the mid twentieth century, the Teatro Brasileiro de Comédia (Brazilian Comedy Theater), supported the formation of Escola de Arte Dramática (School of Dramatic Art) in order to provide a source of trained talent for it and other professional companies. In 1952 director José Renato Pécola headed up a group of Escola de Arte Dramática graduates in forming the Teatro de Arena. Arena, unlike the Teatro Brasileiro de Comédia, had an economic, aesthetic, and social agenda. Pécola was familiar with the work of Margo Jones, whose *Theatre-in-the-Round* was published in 1951. The company could stage plays at a tenth of the cost of similar Teatro Brasileiro de Comédia productions because of their smaller space and its technical simplicity. Moreover, Arena in its first two years had little or no fixed overhead and had mobility that allowed it to seek out its desired audiences. The company was initially a cooperative, so there was no price-inflating

Cover for the first edition of Guarnieri's successful play, published in 1966, depicting the ways in which a labor struggle divides a family. The play was turned into a motion picture in 1981 (Joint University Libraries, Nashville).

profit. Presumably, all of these savings were reflected in lower ticket prices, which helped make the theater more accessible to the general public.

In 1955 a group of leftist student activists at the University of São Paulo that included Guarnieri founded the Teatro Paulista do Estudante (Paulista [from São Paulo] Student Theater). The Teatro Paulista do Estudante had a more overtly political purpose than either Arena or the Teatro Brasileiro de Comédia. The student group viewed theater not only as a means of consciousness-raising but also as a means of invigorating a broadly conceived national culture so that Brazilians might resist foreign exploitation. Teatro Paulista do Estudante had a political mission and a view of the role of theater within that mission. From the beginning this included the promotion of a national dramaturgy. In late 1955 Arena merged with the Teatro Paulista do Estudante, forming a company that retained the Arena name. The merger moved Arena more squarely into the realm of political and nationalist theater.

In 1956 Pécola contracted Boal as Arena's artistic director. In retrospect, Guarnieri has acknowledged that Boal's leadership was key for Arena during its most fruitful period because he tackled the Arena problem, which was how to reconcile the distancing effects of the theater-in-the-round with the theatrical representation of Brazilian culture. Commercial and popular success came slowly. In early 1958, when financial difficulty appeared ready to doom Arena, Pécola chose *Eles não usam black-tie* as the company's final production. Guarnieri had written the play in 1956, as he puts it, "sem compromisso, sem pretensão" (without obligation or pretense), as a way of passing sleepless nights. He had no intention of staging it professionally. Despite the seemingly suicidal gesture of opening the play during Carnaval on 22 February, *Eles não usam black-tie* was a critical and commercial success. It ran for the entire 1958 season and ensured the stability of Arena for years to come.

The play is in three acts, each with two parts. The action centers on two weeks in the life of a working-class family in a Rio de Janeiro hillside slum, or *favela*. The family includes a father and mother named Otávio and Romana and their two sons, Tião and Chiquinho. Most of the action takes place in the family's home. At the beginning of act 1, Maria, Tião's girlfriend, reveals that she is pregnant with his child, and the two make plans to get married within the month. The same evening, Otávio discusses with Tião the possibility of a general strike at the factory where they both work. Otávio is a seasoned labor campaigner and has strong views on labor-management relations as well as politics and economics in general. He is a Marxist more by faith than reason, and he believes in the potential of the solidarity of the working class to improve the lives of the *favelados*. Meanwhile, Romana is the archetypal mother. She is strong, even aggressive, and has the respect of the men in her family. She does not, however, share the depth of Otávio's political convictions.

Slowly the audience learns that Tião was raised in the city by godparents whom he served as a houseboy. He never has become reaccustomed to life in the *favela*. Otávio speculates that Tião is afraid of being poor. His future bride, Maria, is a trained seamstress and by implication a serious, hardworking woman. At the couple's engagement party the rift between Tião and Otávio over the coming strike widens, and Tião and his buddy Jesuíno agree to cross the picket line after discussing "safer" alternatives to striking. The scene offers contrasting characterizations of a cowardly Jesuíno and a more forthright Tião, who is willing to risk the anger of his coworkers for the sake of his family's security. As union leaders are imprisoned and intimidated, however, Tião and Maria begin to diverge on their views of the strike and their solidarity with their community, with Maria beginning to side with Otávio. During the strike Tião crosses the picket line overtly, while Jesuíno is beaten up trying to sneak in. Tião has secured his job and the good graces of the factory management, but he has lost the respect of his community in the process. His father throws him out of the house, which he more or less expected, but, to his surprise, Maria refuses to come with him. The play ends with Romana drying her eyes and sorting beans—three cupfuls rather than the usual four.

Part of the success of *Eles não usam black-tie* stemmed from its realism: audiences saw character types and situations that they recognized from daily life. The characters wear everyday clothing, speak and gesture in colloquial ways, drink coffee, and sort beans. The real aesthetic breakthrough of the play came in putting this realism in the Arena space with a sparse set and no scenic backdrops.

Over the next six years Guarnieri continued to write and stage realist plays focused on Brazil's "classes populares" (popular classes). In 1961 Arena produced Guarnieri's *A semente* (The Seed), another drama about a working-class family in a labor conflict. Guarnieri took realism to the Italian proscenium stage in a 1959 production of *Gimba: Presidente dos Valentes* (Gimba: President of the Toughs). Like *Eles não usam black-tie*, *Gimba, Presidente dos Valentes* deals with solidarity and betrayal among the urban poor. Gimba is a renowned outlaw who returns home to "retire" with his girlfriend Guiô. The couple befriends a youngster, Tico. Gimba is betrayed by another youth, Gabiró, who is jealous of both his fame and his relationship with Guiô. The production of *Gimba* was lavish in its scenic realism, replete with representations of the hillside slums that are the setting of the play.

In 1958 Guarnieri married his first wife, journalist Cecília Thompson, a Brazilian of Scottish descent, with whom he had two sons, Flávio, born in 1959, and Paulo, born in 1961. Flávio and Paulo are both established stage actors in their own right. Guarnieri and Cecília divorced after approximately seven years of marriage.

In 1962 Guarnieri began writing for television with the drama *O cimento* (Cement), and he has returned to this kind of work several times over the course of his career. In the early 1960s Arena experimented with staging versions of classics of Western drama, selected and adapted always with a view to the social commentary they offered. Guarnieri and Boal call this phase "Nacionalização dos Clássicos" (Nationalization of the Classics). In the 1964 production of Molière's *Le Tartuffe, ou L'Imposteur* (1669, Tartuffe, or The Imposter), Guarnieri played the lead role opposite Vanya

Sant'Anna. They fell in love in real life, and she eventually became Guarnieri's second wife. They had three children, Claudio Luis ("Cacau"), Fernando Henrique, and Mariana. These children later appeared in plays with their father.

On the heels of the 1964 right-wing coup in Brazil, Guarnieri and Arena changed directions toward rallying the intellectual and artistic vanguard against the newly installed military dictatorship. To avoid censorship Guarnieri and others hit on the idea of presenting "allegorical" drama. For the most part Arena offered highly analogical historical plays, plots offering past events as thinly disguised representations of present realities. Furthermore, Arena was inspired by the musical and epic political theater of Bertolt Brecht and his collaborators, composer Kurt Weil and director-designer Irwin Piscator. Many of the songs from the political musicals from this period are now bossa nova standards.

Guarnieri began to collaborate on political musicals, most notably the *Arena conta* (Arena Tells) series. *Arena conta Zumbi* (Arena Tells about Zumbi) opened on 1 May 1965–Dia do Trabalho (Labor Day)–and had the longest run of any Arena production. The play enjoyed critical acclaim, both at the time of its first run and during revivals, and it has to be included on any short list of important and influential leftist cultural production during the years of military rule. Boal accords *Arena conta Zumbi* a position of privilege in Arena's repertoire because it provided necessary chaos in the theater. In Boal's usage "chaos" is the destruction of a system of conventions deemed necessary for the imposition of his new system of performance, "O Sistema Coringa" (the Joker System). The Joker System combines the mixing of fact and fiction and role-swapping among the actors with theatrical elements reminiscent of Brechtian theater, including the presence of a character called "the Joker" whose role is to comment on the dramatic action and its context. *Arena conta Zumbi* had a deep effect on Boal and the Arena team by bringing together in one work two tendencies already present in Arena's productions: realism and Brechtian technique. It was not, however, a Joker play per se, but it facilitated the creation of the Joker System.

In a broad sweep *Arena conta Zumbi* covers the founding and growth of Palmares; the famous *quilombo*, or maroon society, established in the interior of Brazil's Northeast by fugitive slaves; the attacks by colonial Dutch and Portuguese forces; the vicissitudes of Portuguese policy toward the maroon state; and the final attack by the backwoods mercenary Domingos Jorge Velho, which was commissioned by the colonial government, with the support of Portuguese landowners. The play was based on a novel by João Felício dos Santos

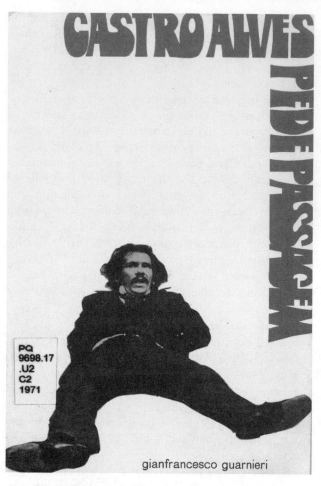

gianfrancesco guarnieri

*Cover for Guarnieri's 1971 play, a series of vignettes depicting the
life of Brazil's favorite poet of the Romantic era (Howard-Tilton
Memorial Library, Tulane University)*

titled *Ganga-Zumba* (1962), a fictionalized account of the history of Palmares. Both the novel and the play it inspired begin with the arrival of King Zambi in Brazil and end with the death of its last ruler, Ganga Zumba, or Zumbi. The play follows the novel closely in both fact and fiction, appropriating some of its characterization, depiction of events, dialogue, and even linguistic expression. The play highlights an aesthetic of the exotic, sensual, and popular. Although the play includes many events and characters found in the novel and the historical record, faithfulness to these documents is subordinated to parallels with contemporary repression and the resistance to it through self-sacrifice. The set and costumes called for by the play reinforce the connection of the story with the present. The stage is bare except for several carpeted platforms, and the cast wears sweatshirts of various colors and white jeans. Critics have noted that the presentation resembles a bunch of students in a middle-class living room, in stark contrast to the play's historical setting, the wilderness of seventeenth-century Brazil. The cast interchanges roles,

reinforcing the impression of a bunch of kids role-playing, contributing to a sense of "chaos" typical of Arena's repertoire.

While there were many productions connected with *Arena conta Zumbi* in terms of aesthetic concept and style, spirit, or personnel, *Arena conta Tiradentes,* a musical co-authored by Guarnieri and Boal, was the sole instance of Arena's complete application of the Joker System. *Arena conta Tiradentes* (Arena Tells about Tiradentes) opened on Tiradentes Day (21 April) 1967.

In 1968 political repression intensified. President Artur da Costa e Silva took unto himself emergency powers in what has been called the "golpe dentro do golpe" (coup within the coup). The infamous Institutional Act Number 5 (AI-5) gave the president power to restrict legislative and judicial bodies and abrogate basic civil liberties for the indefinite future. AI-5 and subsequent decrees allowed those in control of the state to operate in any way they chose. The political climate hampered Guarnieri's development as a playwright during this period, and two of his plays, *Animália* (1968) and *Marta Saré* (1968), were affected by censorship. Guarnieri's association with Arena ended by 1970.

In May 1971 *Castro Alves pede passagem* (Castro Alves Asks Permission to Pass), written and directed by Guarnieri, opened at the Teatro Castro Alves in Salvador. The play, whose title repeats the introductory banners carried by the Carnaval parade groups, is a series of vignettes depicting the life of Salvadoran Antônio Castro Alves, Brazil's favorite poet of the Romantic era. Castro Alves was an upper-middle-class student, a bohemian, and a womanizer. He was also a political progressive who argued for the abolition of slavery. Castro Alves's activities before he died of tuberculosis at a young age made him a figure that resonated with the youth of the counterculture and the political left. Because he was a respected member of Brazil's literary canon, however, a play focusing on him could not easily be attacked by censors. *Castro Alves pede passagem* launched a line of plays that Guarnieri called Teatro de Ocasião (Theater of the Occasion), which he described as "não exatamente a história que eu gostaria de estar contando, mas a possível naquele instante" (not exactly the story I would like to be telling, but that which is possible at that moment). Guarnieri intended Teatro de Ocasião as a critique of the "irracionalismo" (irrationalism) he saw invading the theater. On the most basic level Teatro de Ocasião is a label that could also be applied to *Animália* and *Marta Saré*.

Teatro de Ocasião had as its expressed aim the reaffirmation of rational dramatic discourse at a time when the dictatorship appeared to have silenced or subverted it. Working within the constraints of the time and following his own aesthetic goals, Guarnieri created plays that were highly poetic and metaphorical. The government censors had become aware of the use of historical analogy and had effectively silenced most of such veiled criticism. Consequently, Teatro de Ocasião was formulated as an abstract, often lyrical inquiry into what the theater and the spoken word could accomplish. Guarnieri seemed unaware, however, of the fundamental contradiction in his project: when engagé theater is so constrained by either censorship or frustration that verbal expression is limited to a "um grito parado no ar" (a cry suspended in the air), the resulting theatrical discourse is practically the same as that of the "irrational" sort of theater that Guarnieri was criticizing.

In addition to *Castro Alves pede passagem,* Guarnieri's Teatro de Ocasião includes *Botequim ou Céu sobre a chuva* (Corner Bar or the Sky above the Rain) and *Um grito parado no ar,* which opened simultaneously in April 1973. Another example of Teatro de Ocasião is "Basta" (Enough), a one-act play written in 1973 that was prohibited in 1974 and is still unpublished and unperformed. Finally, *Ponto de partida* (1976, Point of Departure) is perhaps the most beautiful and enduring work of Teatro de Ocasião. It is certainly the most accessible of these works.

Subtitled *fábula em um ato* (a fable in one act), *Ponto de partida* is almost pure allegory. The indeterminate setting is suggestive of a village in the Middle Ages. The parallel with Brazil of the 1970s is schematic—the play offers a vivid portrait of authoritarianism. The drama is linked to events of contemporary Brazil through the veiled representation of the death of São Paulo journalist Vladimir Herzog. Herzog was found dead on 24 October 1975 after security police had interrogated him. The official story was that the journalist had hanged himself, but public pressure and a civil court ruling implicated the police in the death. The Herzog case received international attention, but it was only one of several such hangings to come to light during the mid 1970s. In *Ponto de partida* the body of a man named Birdo is found hanging in the village square. At the request of the victim's father, Ainon, a local lord named D. Félix opens an inquest into the death. D. Félix is inclined to agree with the assertion of his wife, Aida, that the death was a suicide, but he orders that the body not be moved until the case is resolved.

Ainon describes his son as a wanderer, poet, and thinker. Birdo is characterized by those who loved him as a man of the people, not only a singer and poet but one who was willing to lend a hand where needed. He was a free spirit, full of the joy of living, but always ready to denounce injustice when he encountered it. One of the many characters who cared about Birdo was a crazy goatherd, Dôdo. Another was D. Félix and

Aida's daughter, Maíra, who reveals to Ainon that she is bearing Birdo's child. As the inquest proceeds, Ainon suspects murder. Dôdo denies any knowledge of the case, taking refuge in his visions. Aida attempts to convince D. Félix to drop the inquest, but her husband perceives that all is not as it seems. Aida insinuates privately and publicly that Ainon is trying to undermine her husband's authority. Meanwhile, Maíra seeks to determine what the goatherd knows. Increasingly suspicious that her father killed Birdo, she privately confronts him. In her testimony Aida makes the case for suicide: that Birdo was insane, depressed, and guilt-ridden. In desperation Maíra reveals publicly that she is carrying Birdo's child and accuses her parents of murder. D. Félix summarily closes the investigation and forbids any further discussion of the matter. Dôdo later admits to Ainon that he saw Aida and her henchmen hanging Birdo's body in the square. Maíra's parents abort her baby, and she retires to the square where she vows to remain with Birdo's body "until these times end and human beings rediscover what is left of their humanity." The power of *Ponto de partida* derives from the simplicity of the plot and the beauty and power of the spoken word.

Guarnieri diversified his career during the slow process of redemocratization in Brazil. He flourished with his writing for television, a medium for which he continues to write and act. Guarnieri also has acted in motion pictures, including the aforementioned *Eles não usam black-tie,* which won the Leone d'Oro (Golden Lion) in the 1982 Venice Film Festival, and he played the Italian immigrant Enrico in Tizuka Yamasaki's 1980 movie *Gaijin: Caminhos da liberdade* (Gaijin: Paths to Freedom). Additionally, Guarnieri has served in the public sector as an arts administrator in São Paulo, bringing to reality some of the visions for popular arts he nurtured during his Arena years.

Guarnieri's legacy to the Brazilian stage is in two related phenomena: his thematic depth as a playwright and his breadth of ability as a "man of the theater." Perhaps no one—not even Boal—did more to galvanize the political theater of postwar Brazil. After the stunning success of *Eles não usam black-tie,* Guarnieri did not stick with the realism of Arena's early phase. He did not adhere to the widely held belief that realism was the only valid aesthetic for socialist art. Hence, from play to play his style ranged from realism to epic musical theater to allegorical symbolism to comedy. In the process he developed a gallery of memorable characters, including archetypal matriarchs and patriarchs, Peter Pans and princesses. Especially prominent is a nuanced treatment of father-child relationships. Guarnieri's dramas reveal the complexity of human relationships underlying political and social issues. In his programmatic writ-

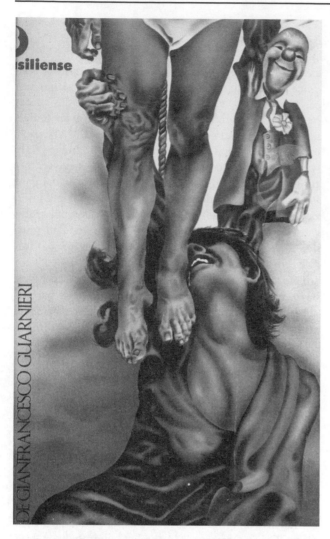

DE GIANFRANCESCO GUARNIERI

Cover for Guarnieri's 1976 play Ponto de partida, *a fábula
(fable) featuring the suspicious death of a São Paulo journalist
(Lauinger Library, Georgetown University)*

ners than Gianfrancesco Guarnieri, who worked as writer, director, performer, and musical collaborator in the theater, cinema, and television. His versatility explains his impact on the twentieth-century theater of political consciousness. Not only did he write dramatic texts, he shaped how they came to life in performance. Guarnieri's mild speech and friendly manner belie his experience in the turbulent times of the 1960s and 1970s, when he confronted a military dictatorship with the spoken word as his main weapon, defending what he considered most sacred: the power of speech and freedom of expression.

Interview:

Simon Khoury, "Gianfrancesco Guarnieri," in his *Atrás da máscara,* volume 1 (Rio de Janeiro: Civilização Brasileira, 1984), pp. 11–72.

References:

Leonor Amarante, "Guarnieri promete decentralizar a cultura e a própria Secretaria," *Revista de Teatro,* no. 450 (1984): 3–4;

Robert Anderson, *Realism, Allegory and the Strangled Cry: Theatrical Semiosis in the Drama of Gianfrancesco Guarnieri* (Valencia, Spain: Albatrós Hispanófila, 1998);

Augusto Boal, *Theatre of the Oppressed,* translated by Charles A. McBride and Maria-Odilia Leal McBride (New York: Urizen Books, 1979; New York: Theatre Communications Group, 1985); revised as *Theatre of the Oppressed,* translated by Charles A. McBride, Maria-Odilia Leal McBride, and Emily Fryer (London: Pluto, 2000);

"O Brasileiro do Século," *Terra–Isto É Online* (10 October 2001) <http://www.terra.com.br/istoe/biblioteca/brasileiro/>;

Margo Milleret, "Acting into Action: Teatro Arena's *Zumbi,*" *Latin American Theatre Review,* 21, no. 1 (1987): 19–27;

Edélcio Mostaço, *Teatro e política: Arena, Oficina e Opinião* (São Paulo: Proposta, 1982);

A página oficial de Gianfrancesco Guarnieri <http://www.geocities.com/broadway/8793/pl.html>;

Cecília Thompson, *CECILIA* (25 July 2002) <http://www.geocities.com/broadway/8731/>.

ings and interviews Guarnieri is often doctrinaire in his Marxism, but in his drama he always allows human beings to complicate his presentation of politics.

While there were eight dramatists ranked ahead of him in the scenic arts category of the "O Brasileiro do Século" (Brazilian of the Century) poll in *Isto É* (That's Right), few–not even Alfredo Dias Gomes or Nelson Rodrigues–have been more diverse practitio-

Jorge de Lima

(23 April 1893 – 15 November 1953)

Zilá Bernd
Universidade Federal do Rio Grande do Sul

BOOKS: *XIV alexandrinos* (Rio de Janeiro: Artes Gráficas, 1914);

A comédia dos erros (Rio de Janeiro: J. Ribeiro dos Santos, 1923);

O mundo do menino impossível (Maceió: Casa Trigueiros, 1925);

Poemas (Maceió: Casa Trigueiros, 1927);

Salomão e as mulheres (Rio de Janeiro: Paulo, Pongetti, 1927);

Essa negra fulô (Maceió: Casa Trigueiros, 1928);

Dois ensaios (Maceió: Casa Ramalho, 1929);

Novos poemas (Rio de Janeiro: Pimenta de Mello, 1929);

Poemas escolhidos (Rio de Janeiro: Adersen, 1932);

Anchieta (Rio de Janeiro: Civilização Brasileira, 1934);

O anjo (Rio de Janeiro: Cruzeiro do Sul, 1934);

Calunga (Pôrto Alegre: Globo, 1935);

Tempo e eternidade, by Lima and Murilo Mendes (Pôrto Alegre: Globo/Barcellos, Bertaso, 1935);

Quatro poemas negros (Cambuquira: Editora do *Jornal Cambuquira,* 1937);

A tunica inconsútil (Rio de Janeiro: Cooperativa Cultural Guanabara, 1938);

A mulher obscura (Rio de Janeiro: J. Olympio, 1939);

Poemas negros, preface by Gilberto Freyre (Rio de Janeiro: Editora da *Revista Acadêmica,* 1947);

Livro dos sonetos (Rio de Janeiro: Livros de Portugal, 1949);

Vinte sonetos (Rio de Janeiro: V. P. Brumlik, 1949);

Guerra dentro do beco (Rio de Janeiro: Editora a Noite, 1950);

Obra poética, edited by Otto Maria Carpeaux (Rio de Janeiro: G. Costa, 1950)–includes *Anunciação e encontro de Mira-Celi;*

Castro Alves–Vidinha (Rio de Janeiro: Artesanato Cristo Operário, 1952);

As ilhas (Niterói: Hipocampo, 1952);

Invenção de Orfeu (Rio de Janeiro: Livros de Portugal, 1952);

Antologia de sonetos (Rio de Janeiro: Artesanato Cristo Operário, 1953);

Jorge de Lima (frontispiece for the 1967 edition of Invenção de Orfeu, *1952; Thomas Cooper Library, University of South Carolina)*

Marcel Proust, essai, translated by Luís de Oliveira Guimarães (Rio de Janeiro: Tupa, 1953);

Poema do cristão (Rio de Janeiro: Artesanato Cristo Operário, 1953);

Obra completa, edited by Afrânio Coutinho, introduction by Waltensir Dutra and Euríalo Canabrava (Rio de Janeiro: J. Aguilar, 1959)–includes *Diário.*

Editions and Collections: *Poesia,* edited by Luiz Santa
   Cruz (Rio de Janeiro: AGIR, 1958);

Antologia de Jorge de Lima, edited, with a preface, by
   António Relordão Navarro (Porto, Portugal:
   Sousa & Almeida, 1965);

Invenção de Orfeu, introduction and notes by M. Cavalcanti Proença (Rio de Janeiro: Edições de Ouro,
   1967);

Anchieta, introduction by Afrânio Coutinho (Rio de
   Janeiro: Edições de Ouro, 1967);

Antología poética, edited by Paulo Mendes Campos (Rio
   de Janeiro: Sabiá, 1969);

Os melhores contos rústicos de Portugal (Rio de Janeiro:
   Edições de Ouro, 1970);

Jorge: 80 anos, edited by Rubens Jardim (São Paulo,
   1973);

Poesia, 4 volumes (Rio de Janeiro: J. Aguilar, 1974);

Poesia completa, 2 volumes, introduction by Santa Cruz,
   preliminary note by João Gaspar Simões (Rio de
   Janeiro: Nova Fronteira, 1980);

Jorge de Lima: poesias esquecidas, edited, with an introduction, by Moacir Medeiros de Sant' Ana (Maceió:
   Edufal, 1983);

O poeta insólito: fotomontagens de Jorge de Lima, edited by
   Ana Maria Paulino (São Paulo: Instituto de Estudos Brasileiros, Universidade de São Paulo,
   1987);

Os melhores poemas, edited by Gilberto Mendonça Teles
   (São Paulo: Global, 1994);

Novos poemas; Poemas escolhidos; Poemas negros (Rio de
   Janeiro: Lacerda, 1997);

Poesia completa, edited by Alexei Bueno, critical studies
   by Marco Lucchesi and others (Rio de Janeiro: J.
   Aguilar, 1997).

Edition in English: *Poems,* translated by Melissa S. Hull
   (Rio de Janeiro, 1952).

OTHER: Agnelo Rodrigues de Melo, *Primeira serie das
   caretas de Judas Isgorogota,* preface by Lima
   (Maceió, 1922);

Estêvão Cruz, *Teoria da literatura para uso das escolas, e de
   acôrdo com os programas oficiais vigentes,* preface by
   Lima (Pôrto Alegre: Globo/Barcellos, Bertaso,
   1935);

Ivani Ribeiro, *Aleluia,* preface by Lima (N.p., 1937);

Aventuras de Malasarte, translated and adapted by Lima
   and Matheos de Lima (Rio de Janeiro: Editora a
   Noite, 1946);

Georges Bernanos, *Sol de Satã,* translated by Lima (Rio
   de Janeiro: AGIR, 1947);

Zhak Konfino, *Perfis e silhuetas: contos iugoslavos,* translated and adapted by Lima (Rio de Janeiro: Konfino, 1947);

Antologia poética, preface by Lima (Pôrto Alegre: Edição
   do Centro Acadêmico Santo Tomás de Aquino,
   Faculdade de Filosofia, 1951).

Jorge de Lima's work comprises not only the
poetry responsible for his acclaim as the greatest Brazilian poet of regional literature but also essays and novels. The writer spent his childhood in the small inland
city of União dos Palmares, in the northeastern state of
Alagoas, and later worked as a physician there. He had
close contact with the people and manifestations of popular culture, influences that contributed to the hybrid
nature of his work. The use of popular elements in his
erudite creations gave Lima's poetics a profundity
rarely displayed in Brazilian literature. His deep religious convictions imbued his most famous work,
Invenção de Orfeu (1952, Invention of Orpheus), with a
transcendental character that earned him the title of
"prince of Brazilian poets."

Son of João Mateus de Lima and Delmira Somões
de Mateus Lima, Jorge Mateus de Lima was born in
União dos Palmares on 23 April 1893. The small town,
which at that time was simply called União, is located
in the mountainous region known as the Serra da
Barriga. Palmares, the famous seventeenth-century refuge for *quilombo* (runaway slaves), was located there.
The elements of this aspect of Brazilian history and the
subsequent legends relating to it had a decisive influence on Lima, inspiring his extensive series of *poemas
negros* (black poems). In an interview given to Homero
de Sena in 1945 he acknowledged the fact that he
became interested in poetry as a child when he visited
the Serra da Barriga. The landscape and stories captured his young imagination, "Tanto assim que, já
homem feito, foram esses os temas que fui buscar para
alguns de meus poemas da fase que poderia chamar
'nordestina' de minha poesia" (So much so that years
later, being a grown-up man already, it was exactly
those themes that I searched for in some of my poems
belonging to what I could call the "northeastern" phase
of my poetry).

In 1900 Lima moved to Maceió, the capital of
Alagoas, to study in the Instituto Alagoano. Two years
later he began to take classes at a school run by the
Marists. Although he began publishing poems in 1907,
he became known only after the publication of the sonnet "O acendedor de lampiões" (The Lamplighter) in
1910.

In Rio de Janeiro, Lima entered medical school in
1911 and graduated in 1914. The following year he
returned to Maceió and began to work as a physician.
In 1919 he was elected deputy of the state of Alagoas.
Four years later Lima's first book of essays, *A comédia
dos erros* (1923, The Comedy of Errors), was published;

it was not greeted as enthusiastically as his literary works were later received.

Lima married Adila Alves de Lima in 1925, and the couple had their first child, Mário Jorge, one year later. Meanwhile, Lima began to experiment with poetic language, as is seen in *Poemas* (Poems), published in 1927. The focus on language that characterizes this collection remained a constant in all of his poetic creations. His essays in *A comédia dos erros* did not give heed to Brazilian modernism, which had emerged as an organized movement the year before. In *O mundo do menino impossível* (1927, The World of the Spoiled Child), however, Lima followed the tenets of the new literary movement. Nevertheless, only after having published the poem *Essa negra fulô* (That Negress Fulô) in 1928 did he become acknowledged and admired by the Brazilian modernists. Carlos Polvina Cavalcanti has written that *Essa negra fulô* "foi um abre-alas da nova poesia negra que Jorge de Lima comandava comum espírito de uma autêntica democracia racial" (was the pioneer in a new black poetry led by Jorge de Lima with an authentic spirit of racial democracy). The poem became so famous that critic Tristão de Athayde declared it the most representative work of modern poetry in Brazil.

In 1929 Lima published *Novos poemas* (New Poems) and *Dois ensaios* (Two Essays). *Novos poemas* includes "Essa negra fulô," which had originally been published in a limited edition, and several poems with regional and folkloric themes. By this time he had moved with his family to Rio de Janeiro, where he worked as a physician for several years. His office served not only as a place to see his patients but also as a gathering spot for the local intelligentsia.

In 1934 Lima published *Anchieta,* a lyrical biography of the sixteenth-century Jesuit priest José de Anchieta, and *O anjo* (The Angel), an attempt at a hyperrealistic novel. By this time Lima had converted to Catholicism, which was a pivotal event in his poetic production. As Hamilton Nogueira notes, with his religious conversion "Jorge de Lima ampliou o campo de suas experiências. O mundo lhe aparecia com outro sentido, e as coisas visíveis passaram a ter um sentido novo, sacral" (Jorge de Lima extended the limit of his experiences. The world began to be seen from a different perspective, and the visible things then assumed a new, sacred meaning). Lima's work entered a mystical phase, and with his friend the poet Murilo Mendes he wrote *Tempo e eternidade* (1935, Time and Eternity). The poets' purpose, stated in the dedicatory line—"Restauremos a poesia em cristo" (Let us restore poetry in Christ)—becomes more intense in Lima's *A túnica inconsútil* (1938, The Seamless Tunic).

In 1936 Lima won a prize in Buenos Aires for his 1935 novel *Calunga* (Calunga is a divinity of the Bantu

Front cover for the 1967 edition of Lima's best-known work, an epic poem in ten cantos, originally published in 1952 (Thomas Cooper Library, University of South Carolina)

cult), although he missed a chance at being elected to the Academia Brasileira de Letras (Brazilian Academy of Letters). *Calunga* represents an incursion of the writer into the social novel as a means of denouncing the exploitation of poor rural workers by large landowners. Critics of the time received the novel enthusiastically and considered it, as Cavalcanti notes, a book of "libertação de de contradições, razão de ser do poeta múltiplo, multígeno, multiforme" (liberation and contradictions, which is what motivates the multiple, multifarious, and multiform poet).

Starting in 1939, Lima's works began to catch the attention of readers outside of Brazil. *Poemas* was rendered into Spanish that year, with a preface by Georges Bernanos; in 1945 *Calunga* was also translated into Spanish. Lima's most-translated work is "Essa negra fulô," which has been published in Spanish, German, English, and Hungarian editions. *Anunciação e encontro de*

O POETA INSÓLITO

Fotomontagens de
JORGE DE LIMA

Front cover of a posthumous collection of modernist photomontages by Lima, published in 1987 (Thomas Cooper Library, University of South Carolina)

Mira-Celi (The Annunciation and Encounter of Mira-Celi), first published in *Obra poética* (1950, Poetic Works), was translated into Spanish in 1950. *Anunciação e encontro de Mira-Celi,* which Lima wrote in 1942, comprises fifty-nine numbered poems in which elements of the supernatural create an enchanting and deeply religious poetry. The work is thematically linked to Lima's earlier religious poems. The greatest symbol of *Anunciação e encontro de Mira-Celi* is hope, as the poet writes: "Todos os séculos e dentro de todos os séculos—todos os poetas, / desde o início, foram cristãos pela esperança que continham" (All centuries, and within all centuries—all poets / from the beginning were Christians because of the hope they cherished).

Lima's *A mulher obscura* (1939, The Dark Woman) is a mystical novel that lacks the social engagement of *Calunga*. In 1940 he was acknowledged by the Aca-

demia Brasileira de Letras with its most important award for poetry, Grande Prêmio de Poesia da Academia Brasileira de Letras. Lima was also invited to fill the chair in Brazilian literature at the Universidade do Brasil. Despite these accolades and his having become nationally and internationally known for his work as a poet, professor, physician, and lecturer, Lima fell into a deep depression. The poet himself wrote, as Cavalcanti records, "Eu me sentia preso de uma profunda depressão e de uma amargura que não chegava a explicar a mim mesmo" (I felt I was stuck in a deep depression and possessed by a bitterness that even I could not explain). He had the support of his friends, such as Mendes, to overcome the crisis, which may have been caused by great stress resulting from Lima's deep involvement in so many different activities. During this period he had also begun to translate important books on French philosophy and literature, including works by the Catholic philosopher Jacques Maritain and by Bernanos.

In 1944 Lima once more missed the chance of being elected to the Academia Brasileira de Letras. The following year he decided to dedicate himself to politics and became a União Democrática Nacional (UDN, the National Democratic Union) candidate for the city council. Two years later he published *Poemas negros* (1947), which was illustrated by the artist Lasar Segall and prefaced by the sociologist Gilberto Freyre. Critics were unanimous in emphasizing Lima's spirit of democratization as well as the ethnic and aesthetic equality that his poems established between blacks and whites. As Freyre affirmed in his preface, Lima was now one of the most important poetic interpreters of life in northeastern Brazil, which was deeply influenced by the culture of the African slaves. Lima was also an outstanding interpreter of the condition of black people in Brazil in general, as his works sensitively explore the burden of slavery borne by Brazilian blacks.

In the 1940s Lima also turned to painting and enjoyed remarkable success in that field of artistic expression. His tremendous sensitivity led him to create with virtuosity in all the artistic forms to which he dedicated himself. At the same time his poetry became increasingly intense and metaphysical, requiring erudition on the part of the reader to grasp the complicated symbols and intertextual references. Lima's family life was enriched at this time by the birth of his grandchildren, who brought him much joy and satisfaction.

In 1948, overcome by stress, Lima suffered a breakdown and spent several days at the clinic Casa de Repouso do Alto da Boa Vista. There he wrote *Livro dos sonetos* (Book of Sonnets), which was published the following year. Otto Maria Carpeaux edited Lima's poetry and published *Obra poética* in 1950. This volume presented to the public Lima's collected poems, including those written in his youth.

Guerra dentro do beco (War in the Alley), although published in 1950, was written probably between 1941 and 1942. This novel explores the concept of the demonic. In 1952 Lima published *Castro Alves–Vidinha* (Castro Alves–A Short Life), created from a series of lectures that the author had prepared on the nineteenth-century Brazilian poet Antônio de Castro Alves, whose dominant theme had been slavery and the life led by Brazilians subjected to the horrors of that system. Lima showed himself extremely skillful in transforming a mere compilation of essays into a rich and multidimensional treatment of the life and works of Castro Alves. Through this book Castro Alves's name came to be incorporated in the works of popular poets whose booklets were sold in marketplaces all over Brazil. In 1952 Lima also published one of his most important works, *Invenção de Orfeu,* which was illustrated by the famous Brazilian artist Fayga Ostrower. An epic poem composed of ten cantos, *Invenção de Orfeu* is considered to be a synthesis of Lima's literary works. Mendes wrote that the work initiated a new phase of Gongorism (the elaborate writing style associated with the works of the Baroque-era Spanish poet Luis de Góngora y Argote) transplanted into a Brazilian context and that he was not sure if it represented an isolated work or one that would influence future poets. Mendes was sure, however, that, because of the complexity of the poem, analysis would require the work of many critics over a period of years. Whereas some people regard *Invenção de Orfeu* as a work focusing on "Brazilianness," others think of it as an ecumenical one. The cantos capture the chaos of the contemporary world through a fable in which elements of fantasy intervene. At first, Lima had intended to give the work the title "Canção geral" (General Song), but he abandoned this idea since the Chilean Pablo Neruda had published a famous work with the same title, *Canto general* (1950).

In 1952 Lima returned to his homeland and friends in Maceió. That same year, he became seriously ill and suffered a long and painful sickness. He died on 15 November 1953 in Rio de Janeiro. The testimony of friends, colleagues, and relatives revealed the stoicism with which he tolerated the pain of his last months.

Lima remained firm in his Christian faith to the end. Before his death he wrote a final work made up of his thoughts and meditations. Titled *Diário,* it was included in the posthumous publication of his complete works, *Obra completa* (1959).

Jorge de Lima's career as a writer involved him in several important trends in the first half of the twentieth century. He participated actively in these movements, making important contributions as he experimented with language and thematic content. He began to write under the influence of the Parnassians and then moved to modernist regionalism, black poetry, religious poetry, and even abstract verse. The richness and variety of Lima's work, including poetry and prose, have guaranteed his position in twentieth-century Brazilian literature. He left an important legacy to Brazilian poetry in works characterized by an enormous hunger for the universal, particularly those poems of his mystic, postregionalist phase. In Lima's opinion, poetry was a type of knowledge; it was magic and thinking at the same time, and it was an aspect of the religious. He dealt with social and human issues through his poetry, writing poems that were well received by a large public. Lima also explored hermeneutic and metaphysical subjects in his religious poetry. The content of these works cannot be explained easily; they appeal more to the reader's intuition and acceptance of the mysterious and the ineffable. Lima saw his poetry as a means of bringing together people separated by hate, intolerance, and wars and as a way of leading them to the divine.

Interview:

Homero de Sena, "Opinião e tendências dos escritores," *Revista de O Jornal,* 29 July 1945.

References:

Alfredo Bosi, "Jorge de Lima," in his *História concisa da literatura brasileira,* second edition (São Paulo: Cultrix, 1976), pp. 502–508;

Carlos Polvina Cavalcanti, *Vida e obra de Jorge de Lima* (Rio de Janeiro: Correio da Manhã, 1969);

Miriam Möller, "Orfeu na invenção de Jorge de Lima," M.A. thesis, Universidade Federal do Rio Grande do Sul, 1995.

Afonso Henriques de Lima Barreto

(13 May 1881 – 1 November 1922)

Marco G. Silva

University of North Carolina at Chapel Hill

BOOKS: *Recordações do escrivão Isaías Caminha* (Lisbon: Livraria Clássica, 1909);

As aventuras do Dr. Bogóloff, 2 issues (Rio de Janeiro: A. Reis, [1912]);

Numa e a nympha: romance da vida contemporanea, escripto especialmente (Rio de Janeiro: A Noite, 1915);

Triste fim de Polycarpo Quaresma (Rio de Janeiro: Revista dos Tribunais, 1915); translated by Robert Scott-Buccleuch as *The Patriot* (London: Collings, 1978);

Vida e morte de M. J. Gonzaga de Sá (São Paulo: Revista do Brasil, 1919); translated by Rosa Veloso Dwyer and John P. Dwyer as *The Life and Death of M. J. Gonzaga de Sá,* in *Lima Barreto: Bibliography and Translations,* edited by Maria Luisa Nunes (Boston: G. K. Hall, 1979);

Histórias e sonhos: cantos (Rio de Janeiro: Schettino, 1920);

Os Bruzundangas (Rio de Janeiro: Jacintho Ribeiro dos Santos, 1922);

Bagatelas (Rio de Janeiro: Empresa de Romances Populares, 1923);

Clara dos Anjos (Rio de Janeiro: Mérito, 1948); translated by Earl Fitz in *Lima Barreto: Bibliography and Translations,* edited by Maria Luisa Nunes (Boston: G. K. Hall, 1979);

O diário íntimo (São Paulo & Rio de Janeiro: Mérito, 1953);

Feiras e mafuás (São Paulo & Rio de Janeiro: Mérito, 1953);

Marginália (Rio de Janeiro: Mérito, 1953);

Três contos (Rio de Janeiro: Cem Bibliógrafos do Brasil, 1955);

Coisas do reino de Jambom: sátira e folclore, preface by Olívío Montenegro (São Paulo: Brasiliense, 1956);

Correspondência ativa e passiva (São Paulo: Brasiliense, 1956);

Impressões de leitura: crítica, preface by M. Cavalcanti Proença (São Paulo: Brasiliense, 1956);

O cemitério dos vivos: memorias, preface by Eugênio Gomes (São Paulo: Brasiliense, 1956);

Afonso Henriques de Lima Barreto (frontispiece for Francisco de Assis Barbosa, A vida de Lima Barreto: 1881–1922, *1952; Thomas Cooper Library, University of South Carolina)*

Vida urbana: artigos e crônicas, preface by Antônio Houaiss (São Paulo: Brasiliense, 1956);

O homen que sabia javanês, edited by Austregésilo de Athayde (São Paulo: Clube do Livro, 1965);

A nova Califórnia: contos (São Paulo: Brasiliense, 1979).

Editions and Collections: *Triste fim de Polycarpo Quaresma* (São Paulo: Moderna, 1985);

Aventuras do Dr. Bagoloff (Rio de Janeiro: Expressão e cultura, 2001).

Afonso Henriques de Lima Barreto was a prolific and talented twentieth-century writer whose creative work for many decades was highly criticized for a lack of style. Recent reevaluations of his novels and short stories, however, have led critics to recognize their aesthetic and literary value, establishing Lima Barreto as an important writer in the Brazilian literary canon.

Afonso Henriques de Lima Barreto was born on 13 May 1881 in Rio de Janeiro, just before the abolition of slavery in Brazil in 1888. Lima Barreto's father, João Henriques de Lima Barreto, was a Portuguese immigrant who first worked as a typesetter for the Imprensa Nacional Brasileira (Brazilian National Press) and later as a clerk in a mental institution in Rio de Janeiro. His mother, Amália Augusta, was a former slave who died when Lima Barreto was only seven. She was responsible for guiding her son's first steps toward a formal education. Although Lima Barreto was born a poor mulatto, he was free, and his talent and education provided opportunities for success.

In 1891 Lima Barreto began his primary studies in the Liceu Popular Niteroiense (Popular School in Niterói), where he continued until 1894. With the financial help of his godfather, viscount of Ouro Preto, the minister of the empire, he was able to complete his secondary education in Rio de Janeiro at the Ginásio Nacional Pedro II (Pedro II National Academy), now known as the Colégio Pedro II (Pedro II High School). Lima Barreto decided to enter the Polytechnic School in 1897 to study engineering, but he was forced to drop his studies in 1902 to support his family after his father was institutionalized with a serious mental illness.

Lima Barreto debuted as a writer in 1902, publishing work in his high school newspaper. His family moved to a simple house in Engenho de Dentro, an outlying neighborhood of Rio de Janeiro. Shortly afterward Lima Barreto decided to apply for the position of civil servant in the office of the Secretariat of War; after a public competition he was hired for the job in 1903. His monthly income was modest, however, and times were difficult for the family.

In 1904 Lima Barreto wrote the first version of the novel *Clara dos Anjos* (1948; translated, 1979) under extremely unfavorable conditions. Although it was the first novel he wrote, it was actually one of the last to be published. The novel is set in the suburbs of Rio de Janeiro. It tells the story of the young mulatta daughter of mailman Joaquim dos Anjos, Clara, who is seduced by the unscrupulous Cassi Jones, a young white man who is supposedly the descendant of English nobles. Cassi's father condemns his son's many romantic adventures and refuses to talk to him because of his bad reputation. When Cassi targets Clara as his next conquest, even the clear disapproval of Clara's parents and

godfather cannot stop the young man's advances. Clara does not believe the bad things that people say about Cassi, and her naiveté further stimulates his interest. With the help of Clara's dentist, Cassi and Clara begin exchanging love letters. After Cassi's sexual conquest of Clara, he moves to São Paulo, where he presumably has accepted a job, leaving a pregnant Clara behind. Desperate and considering an abortion, Clara tells her mother the truth. Clara's mother tries to talk to Cassi's parents about the situation, but they treat her like a poor mulatta who is trying to take advantage of a noble white family.

Clara dos Anjos features many depictions of racial prejudice. For example, a mulatto character named Leonardo Flores is a poet who, despite being extremely talented, is exploited because of his racial status. Many of the characters of *Clara dos Anjos* are typical poor people from the suburbs of Rio de Janeiro, and the dialogue clearly illustrates Lima Barreto's knowledge of colloquial language.

At the beginning of 1905 Lima Barreto started writing the novel *Recordações do escrivão Isaías Caminha* (Memoirs of the Clerk Isaías Caminha), which became his first published novel, going to press in Lisbon in 1909. *Recordações do escrivão Isaías Caminha* is a highly autobiographical narrative. The story is one of a young mulatto, Isaías, who goes to Rio de Janeiro to study and work. After struggling against social prejudice, Isaías acquires a simple job in the office of the newspaper *O globo* (The Globe), directed by Loberant (an anagram for *beltrano,* the equivalent of "John Doe"). Isaías quickly finds that unscrupulous literary critics, dishonest journalists, and pedantic grammarians run the paper. Through his work Isaías is able to testify to much of the nonsense of his time. After Floc, one of the literary critics, commits suicide, Isaías becomes a reporter and, little by little, adapts himself to the system.

In 1905 Lima Barreto also published a series of articles in the periodical *Correio da Manhã* (Morning Post), and he contributed many pieces to the magazine *Fon Fon* until 1907. He never had problems publishing scornful chronicles of urban folklore, humorous articles, and satires, even when they were designed to expose the most prestigious men and powerful institutions of his time. In 1907 Lima Barreto and some friends launched their own magazine, *Floral,* which only lasted for four issues.

In 1907 Lima Barreto wrote the novel *Vida e morte de M. J. Gonzaga de Sá* (translated as *The Life and Death of M. J. Gonzaga de Sá,* 1979), which was not published until twelve years later. The title of this novel is deceptive because the reader is hardly informed about either the life or the death of Manuel Joaquim Gonzaga de Sá.

Instead, the narrative features a conversation between the sexagenarian Gonzaga de Sá and his young friend Augusto Machado, a mulatto who may be seen as one of Lima Barreto's alter egos. The conversation is actually a type of soliloquy where the characters point out the absurdity of life in Brazil. Gonzaga de Sá criticizes the aristocracy and the inefficiency, archaism, and uselessnessness of the bureaucracy. The irony of this situation is that Gonzaga de Sá himself is a bureaucrat of the "Secretariat of Men of Letters" and a descendent of the aristocratic Salvador de Sá. Over the course of the novel Lima Barreto presents the major themes that marked his work: a critical view of the government and the exposure of racial discrimination and society's hypocrisy. Lima Barreto's later short story "Os três gênios da Secretaria" (1921, The Three Geniuses of the Secretariat) is closely related to this novel.

In 1915 Lima Barreto published two important novels: *Triste fim de Polycarpo Quaresma* (The Sad End of Policarpo Quaresma) and *Numa e a nympha* (Numa and the Nymph). In these novels the female characters are surprisingly superior to their male counterparts, especially since Lima Barreto was notorious for his satirical views on women's issues. *Triste fim de Polycarpo Quaresma* tells the story of Major Policarpo Quaresma, a hot-tempered and proud nationalist with romantic ideas of Brazil. After trying various ways to make social and political changes in Brazil, Quaresma participates in a revolt for which he is imprisoned and supposedly executed in the end. The novel stresses the corruption, inefficiency, incompetence, and laziness of the Brazilian social and political system.

Numa e a ninfa is also a novel with a strong political tone. Lima Barreto portrays civilian and military characters' struggles for money and power after Marshal Hermes da Fonseca takes the presidency of Brazil. Numa Pompílio de Castro is one of these characters, a "happy and good" man who, as member of the Chamber of Representatives, is actually a cynical and stupid person. The novel features an extensive gallery of types, including members of the ruling class, politicians, doctors, and foreigners. Among the foreigners is Dr. Gregory Bogóloff, a Russian language expert who becomes the director of the Ministério da Agricultura Brasileira (Brazilian Ministry of Agriculture) because of his title.

Lima Barreto's ability to expose Brazilian society's weaknesses may be seen in one of his most famous short stories, "Nova Califórnia" (New California), published in 1915 along with "O homem que sabia javanês" (The Man Who Knew Javanese) as a part of *Triste fim de Polycarpo Quaresma*. A criticism of human greed, "Nova Califórnia" relates the story of a mysterious alchemist in the city of Tubiacanga. The alchemist completes a successful experiment: he is able to transform human bones into gold. He invites three community members—a druggist, a farmer, and a collector—to witness the experiment. Soon after the demonstration the alchemist disappears and someone starts desecrating tombs at the local cemetery. The police arrest the perpetrators, who happen to be two of the witnesses of the experiment. The druggist manages to escape, and as soon as the population finds out that he has run away, they invade his house and force him to reveal the formula. They all then rush to the cemetery, desecrating the tombs in order to get as many bones as possible for the miraculous transformation. What follows is a war among the inhabitants of the city that results in the cemetery, in a single night, having an unprecedented number of corpses. The only person uninvolved in the confusion and turmoil, an infamous drunkard, ends up being the only survivor as the city is transformed into a ghost town.

Lima Barreto was a mixture of writer, journalist, and bureaucrat, and his stories often have a veiled moral tone. He was a clever creator of types and situations that conveyed his sense of morality. Furthermore, as an acute observer of Brazilian society at the beginning of the twentieth century, especially the society of Rio de Janeiro, Lima Barreto records changes in customs, innovations, trends, and even the architecture of the city. His newspaper pieces offer a realistic picture of the city's suburbs and its inhabitants. Although Lima Barreto often expresses an acceptance of the rapid progress of Brazil, a nostalgic tone emerges at times.

As a mulatto, Lima Barreto understood from a very early age the stigma of racism. With the end of slavery in 1888, racial prejudice and discrimination were major problems in Brazil. Most of his novels and short stories are autobiographical in the sense that he relates his own life experiences and his thoughts about racial discrimination. Lima Barreto always wanted to be understood by a public he tried to reach by exploring familiar themes. He was not recognized as an important author during his lifetime, however, and he was often criticized for his "lack of style." This attitude about his work was reflected in the fact that his first two applications for membership to the Academia Brasileira de Letras (Brazilian Academy of Letters) were denied. He subsequently made a third application, which he later withdrew. Lack of critical recognition did not prevent Lima Barreto from exercising his talent as a writer, however, and with *A vida e morte de M.J. Gonzaga de Sá* he did receive an honorable mention in the competition for the Premio Literario da Academia de Letras (Academy of Letters Literary Prize) for the best book of 1919.

With its critical representations of Brazilian society at the beginning of the twentieth century, Lima

Barreto's work belongs to the premodernist period of Brazilian literature. In Brazil, premodernism was a literary period characterized by innovations, including the use of a Portuguese dialect close to its spoken form and a focus on the country's social problems. Many ideas from realism and naturalism were still reflected in the literature of the time. Lima Barreto represented a country in transition from the liberal politics that incorporated slavery to a questionable democratic system. He was a sharp critic of the utopian nationalism of the time. His style, similar to the journalistic style adopted by different writers after the Week of Modern Art in 1922, was considered too ordinary and simple by critics.

Social analysis and humor are important ingredients in most of Lima Barreto's works, and these qualities are especially evident in his social satire titled *Os Bruzundangas* (1922). Bruzundanga is a fictitious country resembling early-twentieth-century Brazil. It is dominated by a racist elite and fraught with poverty and an obsession with social status and wealth. Lima Barreto exposes and criticizes the fictional country's cultivation of outdated literary values. The book is the diary of a Brazilian man's life in Bruzundanga, an account of his familiarization with the country's literature, especially the *Samoyède* tradition. This particular literary school, promulgated by writers from the ruling class and featuring false, monotonous, and uncultured principles, has the power to affect the country's unstable economy based on the cultivation of coffee in the province of Kaphet.

Besides criticizing Bruzundanga's obsession with titles of nobility and college degrees—mainly by showing that most of those in Bruzundanga who claim to possess such titles and honors are neither nobles nor scholars—Lima Barreto attacks the country's unfair constitution, its corrupt politicians, its lack of democratic values, its scientific underdevelopment, its illogical cultural values, its armed forces, and its chaotic international affairs. In the process he presents caricatures of Brazilian politicians such as Venceslau Brás and the baron of Rio Branco. *Os Bruzundangas* constitutes a critical view of the social, political, economic, and cultural aspects of Brazilian society.

The Brazilian education system was also a target of Lima Barreto's criticism, especially with regard to the education of women. He was one of the first public figures to support women's right to vote in Brazil. Another target of his literary attacks was the Brazilian republican movement that led to the dictatorship of President Floriano Peixoto and a militaristic approach to Brazilian politics. Among the other topics explored by Lima Barreto were the Brazilian coffee policy, the chaotic reurbanization of Rio de Janeiro, and his cul-

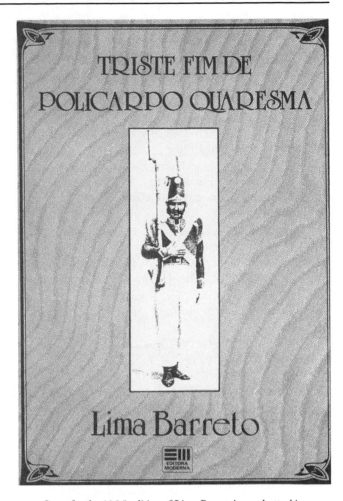

Cover for the 1985 edition of Lima Barreto's novel attacking the Brazilian social and political system ('Thomas Cooper Library, University of South Carolina)

ture's general corruption, intellectual emptiness, and social alienation.

Lima Barreto had started exhibiting the first symptoms of health problems related to alcoholism in 1912 while writing the two parts of *As aventuras do Dr. Bogóloff* (The Adventures of Dr. Bogóloff) for the magazine *Riso*. The disease did not yet affect his work, and he continued writing his articles and chronicles for newspapers and magazines. In 1919 Lima Barreto suffered a stroke and was institutionalized, and this horrific experience was used as a basis for the first chapters of his memoir *O cemitério dos vivos* (The Cemetery of the Living), published in 1953 as a single volume along with *O diário íntimo* (A Personal Diary). Depressed and alcoholic, Lima Barreto died of a heart attack on 1 November 1922 in Rio de Janeiro.

Afonso Henriques de Lima Barreto's body of work is broad in scope. Lima Barreto was a critic of his age, a man who raised his voice against a society filled with injustice, false values, and corruption. He was a man who easily could have been devoured by these conditions, but he became a writer who prevailed and established a place as one of Brazil's most important early-twentieth-century writers.

References:

Luís Alberto de Abreu, *Lima Barreto, ao terceiro dia* (São Paulo: Caliban, 1996);

Anoar Aiex, *As idéias sócio-literárias de Lima Barretto* (São Paulo: Vértice, [1990]);

Enéias Atanásio, *O mulato de Todos os Santos* (Piraquara, 1982);

Francisco de Assis Barbosa, *A vida de Lima Barreto, 1881–1922* (Rio de Janeiro: J. Olympio, 1952); revised as *Aldebarã; ou A vida de Lima Barreto, 1881–1922* (Rio de Janeiro: Edições de Ouro, 1967);

Paula Beiquelman, *Por que Lima Barreto* (São Paulo: Brasiliense, 1981);

Maria Zilda Ferreira Cury, *Um mulato no reino de Jambom: as classes sociais na obra de Lima Barreto* (São Paulo: Cortez, 1981);

Cury, *Visão de mundo em Lima Barreto* (Belo Horizonte: Universidade Federal de Minas Gerais, Faculdade de Letras, 1980);

Carmem Lúcia Negreiros de Figueiredo, *Lima Barreto e o fim do sonho republicano* (Rio de Janeiro: Tempo Brasileiro, 1995);

Figueiredo, *Trincheiras de sonho: ficção e cultura em Lima Barreto* (Rio de Janeiro: Tempo Brasileiro, 1998);

Idilva Maria Pires Germano, *Alegorias do Brasil: imagens de brasilidade em Triste fim de Policarpo Quaresma e Viva o povo brasileiro* (São Paulo: Annablume / Fortaleza: Governo do Estado do Ceará, Secretaria de Cultura e Desporto, 2000);

Robert Deupree Herron, "The Individual, Society, and Nature in the Novels of Lima Barreto," dissertation, University of Wisconsin–Madison, 1971;

Eliane Vasconcellos Leitão, *Entre a agulha e a caneta: a mulher na obra de Lima Barreto* (Rio de Janeiro: Lacerda Editores, 1999);

Clóvis Meira, *Três faces de Lima Barreto* (São Paulo: Scortecci, 1994);

R. J. Oakley, *The Case of Lima Barreto and Realism in the Brazilian "Belle Epoque"* (Lewiston, N.Y.: Edwin Mellen Press, [1998]);

Hélcio Pereira da Silva, *Lima Barreto, escritor maldito* (Rio de Janeiro: Civilização Brasileira, 1981).

Osman Lins

(5 July 1924 – 8 July 1978)

Regina Igel
University of Maryland

See also the Lins entry in *DLB 145: Modern Latin-American Fiction Writers, Second Series.*

BOOKS: *O visitante* (Rio de Janeiro: J. Olympio, 1955);
Os gestos (Rio de Janeiro: J. Olympio, 1957);
O fiel e a pedra (Rio de Janeiro: Civilização Brasileira, 1961; revised edition, São Paulo: Martins, 1967, 1971);
Marinheiro de primeira viagem (Rio de Janeiro: Civilização Brasileira, 1963);
Lisbela e o prisioneiro (São Paulo: Letras e Artes, 1964);
Um mundo estagnado (Recife: Universidade Federal de Pernambuco, 1966);
Nove, novena (São Paulo: Martins, 1966); translated by Adria Frizzi as *Nine, Novena* (Los Angeles: Sun & Moon Press, 1995);
Guerra do "Cansa-Cavalo" (Petrópolis: Vozes, 1967);
Capa-verde e o natal (São Paulo: Comissão Estadual de Teatro, 1968);
Guerra sem testemunhas: o escritor, sua condição e a realidade social (São Paulo: Martins, 1969);
Avalovara (São Paulo: Melhoramentos, 1973); translated by Gregory Rabassa (New York: Knopf, 1980);
Santa, automóvel e soldado (São Paulo: Duas Cidades, 1975);
Lima Barreto e o espaço romanesco (São Paulo: Ática, 1976);
A rainha dos cárceres da Grécia (São Paulo: Melhoramentos, 1976); translated by Frizzi as *The Queen of the Prisons of Greece* (Normal, Ill.: Dalkey Archive Press, 1995);
O diabo na noite de Natal (São Paulo: Pioneira, 1977);
Do ideal e da glória: problemas inculturais brasileiros (São Paulo: Summus, 1977);
La Paz Existe? by Lins and Julieta de Godoy Ladeira (São Paulo: Summus, 1977);
Casos especiais de Osman Lins (São Paulo: Summus, 1978)— comprises "A ilha no espaço," "Quem era Shirley Temple?" and "Marcha fúnebre";
Evangelho na taba: outros problemas inculturais brasileiros (São Paulo: Summus, 1979);
A ilha no espaço (São Paulo: Moderna, 1997).

Osman Lins (from the back cover of Casos especiais de Osman Lins, *1978; Alderman Library, University of Virginia)*

OTHER: Henrik Pontoppidan, *O urso polar e outras novelas,* translated by Lins (Rio de Janeiro: Delta, 1963);
Graciliano Ramos, *Alexandre e outros heróis,* afterword by Lins (São Paulo: Martins/Record, 1975);
Missa do galo: variações sobre o mesmo tema, edited by Lins (São Paulo: Summus, 1977).

Brazilian literature has changed since the emergence of Osman Lins, regarded by many as one of the most important twentieth-century writers in Brazil.

Breaking with traditional narrative techniques, he created new paths in fiction. He wrote with a provocative wisdom and an all-embracing passion for writing. An accomplished author, Lins can best be described as a verbal goldsmith, a perfectionist who weighed and measured words and their sounds and meanings within a context, be it surrealistic, realistic, erotic, or simply descriptive. He was also a staunch defender of the best possible literary application of the Portuguese language as used in Brazil and a stylist who would not exchange his sense of tradition for the sake of popular trends. Yet, he created new ways of telling stories through experiments with narrative structure and a relentless pursuit of the art of writing. Lins's published works include novels, short stories, chronicles, essays, travel narratives, and radio, television, and stage plays. His literary legacy offers a clear vision of literature as a craft as well as a conduit for the interpretation of the afflictions involving humankind. He raised a distinct voice of denunciation against the social ills plaguing his country.

Osman da Costa Lins was born on 5 July 1924 in Vitória de Santo Antão, a small town in the state of Pernambuco, in northeastern Brazil. In that city he wrote many of his works, including in them his ubiquitous persona as a *pernambucano* (someone born and raised in Pernambuco), as he liked to characterize himself formally and informally. Lins's mother died when he was only two weeks old. After five years as a widower, his father, Teófanes Costa Lins, a tailor by profession, married a fifteen-year-old woman, with whom he had two more sons and two daughters. Osman was cared for by his paternal grandmother, Joana Carolina Lins, and by his father's sister, Laura Figueiredo, who moved into her mother's house along with her husband, Antonio Figueiredo. Osman grew up in a family environment, but without the physical presence of his biological mother.

One of the consequences of the absence of Lins's mother was an Oedipal trait in his outlook on the world and in his literary creativity. In several interviews he stated that since he never saw her, not even in pictures, he felt the need to search for her face everywhere around him. Apparently, he tried to soften his anguished search for her by bestowing some of the female characters in his works with characteristics that, through descriptions by family members, he imagined as having belonged to his mother: a maternal inclination toward children, protective behavior toward animals, and devotion to religion.

Among the people who assisted in Lins's upbringing, three men had a strong influence on his career as a writer: his father, his uncle, and a teacher he had in elementary and secondary schools. From his father Lins learned how to adapt the skills of a tailor—taking measurements, chalk tracing, and cutting fabric—to his literary endeavors. His novels and short stories emerge from a careful search for the right words and a cautious inquiry into the adequacy of terms, as well as their musicality within a related context, as if imitating a tailor involved in the many aspects of making clothing. In spite of his economical usage of adjectives and measured distribution of metaphoric modifiers, Lins's writing echoes the convolutions of the baroque style, repeating its conceptual, visual, and, to a certain extent, playful traits. *Avalovara* (1973; translated, 1980) is one of his novels in which the baroque manner triumphs, just as in the earlier story collection *Nove, novena* (1966; translated as *Nine, Novena,* 1995). Both works present circumvolutions in the narrative process resulting from the selection of alternate texts. A profusion of realistic and surrealistic images is accompanied by the replication of sounds, description of smells, and presentation of allegories whose interpretation may present a challenge to first-time readers.

The second man to play an active role in Lins's formative years was his uncle Antonio, his aunt Laura's husband. Figueiredo was a traveler and explorer, roaming the northeastern region of the country in search of gold, trading in cattle, or looking for new businesses. Returning home, he would recount episodes that had happened to him or to cowboys and other dwellers of the backcountry whom he had met, or he would describe the popular beliefs and superstitions prevailing among peasants. As a boy, Lins was fascinated by his uncle's narratives, incorporating and adapting many of them in his novels, short stories, and plays. As for the teacher who had influenced him from an early age, José de Aragão Bezerra Cavalcanti, Lins praised that former seminarian as the person to whom he owed his sense of discipline in the selection of readings and the assimilation of what he had learned from books. This same sense of discipline prevailed alongside Lins's preference for order and method when he was creating his complex fictional works.

The men and women of influence in Lins's life unfold through many characters in his writings. In the title of "Retábulo de Santa Joana Carolina" (St. Joana Carolina's Retable), a story in *Nove, novena,* he pays homage to his paternal grandmother. In Teresa, a character in the novel *O visitante* (1955, The Visitor), and in Cecília, from *Avalovara,* he reproduces some of the traits perceived in his aunt Laura, such as her naiveté and personal interest in people. Figueiredo's generosity and selfishness are displayed in Bernardo, from *O fiel e a pedra* (1961, The Pointer and the Stone); the Treasurer, from *Avalovara;* and Dudu, from *A rainha dos cárceres da Grécia* (1976; translated as *The Queen of the Prisons of*

Greece, 1995). Lins also incorporated his own experiences as a young boy growing up in Pernambuco, a period that provided him with firsthand knowledge of the rural cosmogony, which is represented in many of his novels and short stories, particularly in *Nove, novena* and *Avalovara.*

After his high-school graduation Lins opted to go to Recife, the capital of Pernambuco. There he hoped to continue with his studies and earn his living, which he accomplished with the help of an uncle already living there. This uncle provided his nephew with a job as an accountant at the school where he was working. Lins was introduced by his uncle to such writers as Mário Sette and Mário Motta, with whom Lins was to maintain a friendship for the rest of his life. Taking advantage of a vacancy in the local branch of the Banco do Brasil (Bank of Brazil), Lins applied for the job, went through the necessary screening process, and was accepted. He worked at the bank, in various branches, for twenty years. Those two decades of work were carried on through boredom and disappointment within the restrictions of an occupation that, for Lins, became merely a means of financial support.

Feeling more secure, nevertheless, Lins proposed marriage to his sweetheart of many years, his cousin Maria do Carmo, whom he married in 1947. The young couple continued living in Recife, where their three daughters were born. (Lins and Maria were later divorced.) In spite of his contemplative and reflective spirit, Lins was delighted with life in a bigger city. To be sure, Recife at that time was not a cosmopolitan location, but it was a far cry from Vitória de Santo Antão. He thrived there, participating in many cultural affairs, having received enthusiastic support from fellow writers to start submitting works for publication and also to enter them in literary contests. In the meantime, the popularity of the radio and the possibilities it presented for the expansion of culture attracted Lins's attention. He had his first play performed on radio, an adaptation of Sophocles' *Oedipus Rex,* followed by adaptations of William Shakespeare's *Hamlet* and of a short story by the Brazilian master Joaquim Maria Machado de Assis. Lins used to argue that his experience in radio could be seen as a pattern to be followed by other writers. Because radio had many resources that could enhance a literary text (sound, music, and speech tonalities), a writer should take advantage of this technology to reach more people. Lins's defense of radio as a means of communication recurs through the character Marie de France in *A rainha dos cárceres da Grécia,* when a voice-over breaks into the text imitating a speaker who announces one more defeat in Marie's struggle to have her worker's rights recognized by bureaucrats.

Front cover of Lins's experimental 1973 novel regarded as the Brazilian equivalent of the French nouveau roman (Bruccoli Clark Layman Archives)

Besides activities at the local radio station, which included the daily reading of his own short articles, Lins was writing a short story that was to turn into the novel *O visitante.* After submitting the manuscript to a literary contest sponsored by a local newspaper, he received the second prize. In 1954 he resubmitted it to another contest, the Concurso Fábio Prado (Fábio Prado Competition) in São Paulo, and won first place. The award was a great honor for Lins and, by extension, his contemporary writers. One of them, Ariano Suassuna, published a series of three articles in the newspapers of Recife praising his fellow citizen Lins.

O visitante is a traditional novel in the sense that Lins followed a time-honored narrative structure: the plot has a beginning, middle, and ending. This sequence is presented without further enhancement or surprises; in the same way the plot is also rather banal: Celina, a vulnerable and lonely woman, is seduced by Arthur, a lascivious and smart schoolteacher. Rosa, Celina's only friend, tries to alert her against the teacher, but he, perceiving Rosa's intention, separates the friends. The book, which was successful with critics and the public at large, reveals the amount of Machado de Assis's influence on Lins's writing at the time, mainly through the irony applied to the narrative structure. Instead of chapters, the book is divided into "cadernos" (notebooks), an ironic reference to the schoolteacher. In a 1954 interview with Mauritônio Meira, Lins observed that in this novel he employed a three-fold narrative technique, pointing out that one of the characters is presented from the inside out, through his reasoning and emotions; another character is formulated from the outside, through gestures, attitudes, and words; and a third one, with the exception of two chapters in the book, is presented through indirect references, since this character is absent for most of the narrative.

Lins did not usually have any trouble disclosing his writing method and his views on his work in general. According to his own assertions about his career, *O fiel e a pedra,* which followed *O visitante,* should be regarded as a literary area of convergence for his writings up to that time and, at the same time, as a platform from which his creativity would take different paths. Both novels can be regarded as belonging to the same dimension of Lins's writing abilities, but *O fiel e a pedra* is richer than the earlier novel, in terms of the amount of erudition brought into the plot. *O fiel e a pedra* combines aspects of Virgil's *Aeneid* with a contemporary situation peculiar to the backcountry of Pernambuco, family struggles regarding a piece of land and some cattle. While in Virgil's epic Aeneas tries to solve problems related to imperial Rome, the humble Bernardo of *O fiel e a pedra* brings solutions to local conflicts through dignified behavior and through his silent and strong presence in most of the conflicts. Pensive and contemplative, Bernardo's actions are strong and persuasive, despite his many extended periods of silence. The humanist basis of the *Aeneid* finds a counterpart in Bernardo, since the man is a decent hero who is able to confront, on his own terms, the malignant Nestor Benicio, the opposite of his namesake Nestor in Virgil's epic. Their confrontation re-creates, in the midst of the *sertão* (the interior of Pernambuco), the Trojan War, within the geographic limits of the area and the ideological outlook of the time. Lins's appreciation for the classics also prompted him to use a line from book 2 of the *Aeneid* as the epigraph of the play *Guerra do "Cansa-Cavalo"* (1967, The Cansa-Cavalo War).

Lins's contribution to Brazilian fiction can be discerned in two areas, the traditional and the innovative. The traditional works include *O visitante* and *O fiel e a pedra.* Both are characterized by an omniscient narrative voice that reveals the states of consciousness and emo-

tions of the characters; the author coordinates time and space within the confines of the plot, developed with a sequence of beginning, middle, and end. Lins's innovative writings convey a rupture with traditional ways of narrating, beginning a journey of experiments in the technique of storytelling. Three works of fiction in which Lins distances himself from the traditional way of telling a story by favoring experimentation are *Nove, novena, Avalovara,* and *A rainha dos cárceres da Grécia.*

Nove, novena comprises, as the title implies, nine short stories (or novellas): "O pássaro transparente" (The Transparent Bird), "O ponto no círculo" (A Point in the Circle), "Pentágono de Hahn" (Hahn's Pentagon), "Os confundidos" (The Confused), "Retábulo de Santa Joana Carolina," "Conto barroco ou Unidade tripartita" (Baroque Tale; or, Tripartite Unity), "Pastoral," "Noivado" (Engagement), and "Perdidos e achados" (Lost and Found). Baroque-era retables, altarpieces that Lins viewed during his visits to Europe, are reflected in these stories as the background of emotions, struggles, sexual encounters, romantic involvements, social criticism, and self-discoveries. For the literary craft that pervades the narratives, this 1966 collection has been dubbed a precursor of *Avalovara.* The stories prefigure the novel chiefly in the echoes of the baroque emerging in periphrastic constructions, as in "Perdidos e achados," in which a collective critical voice emerges during one of the periodic floods that plagued the city of Recife. Fragmentation, a deviating path from more-traditional ways of narrating, is evident in "Conto barroco ou Unidade tripartita," in which Lins deconstructs reality by inserting the theme of death through the interplay of hypothetical characters and possible situations lived by them.

In "Retábulo de Santa Joana Carolina" Lins develops, explores, and resuscitates several facets of baroque art and literature. The story, which revolves around the life of Lins's paternal grandmother, also uses resources typical of medieval times, such as iconography. (A circle with a central dot represents nature; a circle divided in four parts conveys both the wheel of fortune and the wheel of an oxcart; the upper part of a pitchfork characterizes the devil or malignant forces; and so on.) The life of Joana Carolina is explored through the narratives and reminiscences of her living and dead relatives, friends, and acquaintances, demonstrating Lins's ability to connect the past and the present in a smooth texture of events detached from time and space. Like any retable, the altarpiece that guards the statue of St. Joana Carolina is protected by words and symbols, erected by Lins to honor the memory of the woman who cared for him in his youth.

In 1966, the same year that *Nove, novena* was published in São Paulo, *O visitante* was published for the first time in Portugal, and *Um mundo estagnado* (A Stagnated World), an essay collection, was published in Recife. The intensity of publications, writing, travels, and research kept Lins busy for the rest of his life. In the following decade he was to see the publication in Portugal of *O fiel e a pedra* and a French edition of *Nove, novena,* titled *Retable de sainte Joana Carolina* (1971), for the story in the collection about his grandmother. Lins's knowledge of French and his deep interest in following the itineraries of his books led him to collaborate closely with his translators.

In 1969 Lins published *Guerra sem testemunhas: o escritor, sua condição e a realidade social* (War without Witnesses: The Writer, His Conditions and Social Reality), an essay collection in which he describes the double role of the writer in society. An author is at the same time a vigilant observer and denouncer of social malaises and a worker in the field of literature struggling to realize himself. In the ten essays Lins makes strong remarks about the need for the writer to be part of society, in a combatant's dress, and not a mere collector of interesting facts that he transforms into fiction. Written and published during a time of political, social, and artistic repression on the part of the military dictatorship then ruling in Brazil, the collection showed Lins's courage and determination in expressing his views on the writer's mission as he saw it.

During this period Lins prepared courses in Brazilian literature at the Universidade de Marilia (University of Marilia), a prestigious institution in the interior of the state of São Paulo. Although teaching was not what he most wanted to do, he thrived on the contact with his students. Finally came the time when he placed a priority on his literary craft. He stayed for two more years at the university and in 1974 ceased teaching, dedicating himself wholly to his writings. He completed his doctorate in letters at the Universidade de Marilia in 1973, the year of the publication of *Avalovara*. The next year he signed a contract in Germany for the publication of *Avalovara* in German, followed by English and Swedish versions of the novel. *Avalovara* was becoming recognized in many countries and praised as the Brazilian equivalent of the French *nouveau roman*. Lins became renowned as a representative of radical changes in Brazilian literature.

Avalovara is the predictable and at the same time unpredictable story of Abel, a bank clerk and an unpublished writer born in Pernambuco. He is engaged in a constant search for the imponderable, having spent his entire life seeking after the quintessential object of his desire, the knowledge of paradise on earth. The novel revolves around three plots centered in Europe, Recife, and São Paulo. In each of these geographic sites Abel tries to seduce a woman who becomes his bridge

toward knowledge. In Europe he meets Roos, who, in his imagination, is the incarnation of a city, with its atmosphere of mysteries and lack of a spiritual direction. For Abel, Roos and an urban map are the same entities, and her name, as he indicates, is an acronym formed by the names of the cities of Ravenna, Oviedo, Orleans, and Salzburg. If he were to attain the happiness of seducing her, he would find knowledge and grace, the supreme ideals summarized in the union of matter and spirit. Roos, however, rejects Abel. He tries several times to convince her of his love, but to no avail. Thus, Roos, whose name means *rose* in Dutch, has an ephemeral but intense and thorny intervention in Abel's life. In the grand mural of symbols that *Avalovara* conveys, Roos could possibly represent the everlasting Oedipal want felt by Latin Americans for Mother Europe, with her mysterious medieval and gloomy smile or her contorted baroque features. Although Abel has been nurtured by European arts and architecture, the ambitions of Europe, or Roos, are directed elsewhere, away from an insignificant Latin American student. His and Roos's relationship lasts for the duration of an academic semester. When Europe/Roos rejects him, he withdraws.

Upon his return to his hometown of Recife, Abel is relentless in pursuing his ideal. Then he meets Cecilia, a social worker. Within six months they have intercourse, she becomes pregnant, and she dies shortly afterward in a road accident. Afterward, Abel becomes a bitter, frustrated man. The story of his life, including his involvement with Cecilia, is narrated following an archetypal pattern of Greek mythological legends, premonitions, and visions. Still suffering from his loss, Abel leaves the northeastern region and migrates toward southern Brazil. In São Paulo he meets a woman who is represented in the text by a circle with a pair of tiny horns, with a dot in the center of the circle. This unnamed woman becomes the essence and the sum of Abel's two previous lovers. With her he reaches the platform of sublime bliss, having finally reached paradise through a spiritual exchange and carnal knowledge. Their entire acquaintance has the duration of a single afternoon.

The literary energy of *Avalovara* is supported by a palindrome of Latin origin, more than two thousand years old. The meaning of this word puzzle is still controversial, as is the reason for its creation; it is believed that it was originally used as a talisman. The palindrome was found inscribed in a little square stone in Pompeii in 1936. The chief peculiarity is that the words can be read not only from left to right and vice versa (as in a typical palindrome) but also from top to bottom and in the opposite direction, with the same spelling in all directions:

Thus, what would normally be called "chapter 1" is titled "S," for the *S* in *SATOR*. Lins imagined a spiral line printed over the palindrome in such a way that, at the crossing of the spiraled line with each of the twenty-five letters corresponding to the chapters, the ensuing text would "reveal" a segment of the narrative. The novel has been dubbed "the novel of the square and the spiral" for the conjunction of these two elements and for their respective functions—the spiral representing the passing of time, the square conveying the space in which the plot is developed. Time and space converge in the novel as inseparable from each other, in spite of the plurality of settings and the different times in which the actions take place.

The title *Avalovara* itself is a token of the sublimations, mutations, separations, and unions that occur in the novel. Avalovara is a name derived from Avalokiteçvara, a cosmic entity in Mahayana Buddhism from which the sun, the moon, the winds, and the earth are derived. Lins also configured the image of a gigantic bird that, flying among the narratives in *Avalovara,* may represent fiction itself and the abundant progeny of elements (metaphors, allegories, association of ideas, and dissociation of actions) that it engenders.

Avalovara clearly represents a rupture with traditional narrative technique. It distances itself from any current or past structural means of correspondence between narrative, reader, and author, breaking into paths that have been neglected by other Brazilian authors. Lins's contribution to the creation of new literary applications of the Portuguese language has undoubtedly had consequences. Not only was his novel not understood by a reasonable number of critics at the time of its publication, *Avalovara* still retains the aura of being difficult, hermetic, and complicated. It may be so at a first glance, but it surely allures and envelops readers with enough maturity to accept the challenges inherent to reading the novel.

In 1975 Lins published *Santa, automóvel e soldado* (Saint, Automobile and Soldier), a collection of three plays. That same year a short story, "A ilha no espaço" (An Island in Space), later collected in *Casos especiais de Osman Lins* (1978, Special Cases of Osman Lins), was adapted for television broadcast. The story concerns a tenant living in a high-rise apartment. He notices that all the tenants are gradually leaving their residences, while he resists the invisible stress to move out. The protagonist's own family insists that they should all move out too, for the building is insecure, although nobody seems to know why people are leaving. The protagonist lets his family go, but he stays behind, alone. "A ilha no espaço" can be read as a statement against the censorship that was then mutilating or destroying the lives of Brazilians represented by the res-

Cover for the 1978 collection (Special Cases of Osman Lins) that includes "A ilha no espaço" (An Island in Space), which has been interpreted as a denunciation of the destructive effect on Brazilian life of the military dictatorship then in power (Alderman Library, University of Virginia)

SATOR
AREPO
TENET
OPERA
ROTAS

Since its discovery the palindrome has received many translations, such as the following: "Arepo, the sower, holds the wheels during his work"; "Sator, the shepherd, has his works in progress"; "The peasant carefully holds the world in its orbit"; and "The peasant carefully maintains his plow on the furrows." This last translation was selected by Lins as the leitmotiv for *Avalovara,* as if foretelling and embracing a terrestrial force that is imbued in the novel.

The structure of *Avalovara* emphasizes each of the letters that composes the palindrome as if they were chapters in the sequence of stories told by the narrator.

idents of the apartment building, a microcosm of the country under military rule.

Lins continued his pattern of breaking away from literary tradition with *A rainha dos cárceres da Grécia,* published in 1976. It is a less elaborate novel than *Avalovara,* but in the plotting and language Lins explores new realms of fiction writing. The story is about a woman who, destitute, alone, and sick, is denied her constitutional rights to receive help from the Brazilian welfare system to treat her health. She walks painfully through the bureaucratic labyrinths of her own country, which insists on relegating her and her fellow workers to oblivion. The simplicity of such a banal story conceals complex structural situations, starting with the artifice that the chronicle of the female protagonist, Maria de França, is actually an unfinished novel that was left after the sudden death of the author, Julia Marquezim Enone (her last name is a palindrome). A former suitor of Julia, a high-school teacher, finds the manuscript and decides, after much pondering about the appropriateness of taking charge of someone else's writings, to analyze and eventually publish the work. Although at first he is able to keep some distance from the object of his scrutiny, he slowly becomes engulfed in the story of Maria until he and she—his objective eye and her personal struggle—become one body of writing, the analysis superimposed on the fiction, and vice versa. The crisscross of the texts, the convergence of the study of the novel and the novel itself, is one of the many folds in the narration of the story of Maria.

A rainha dos cárceres da Grécia features an obvious refinement in the art of narrating, since Lins creates a story within another story, hiding from the readers' eyes the basic story, which is, conceivably, in the book left by Julia. Her manuscript becomes a pretext for Lins's narrative within the context of the destitute woman's life. The bulk of *A rainha dos cárceres da Grécia,* like a chronicle, is dated and situated in real and contemporary places, since it follows, step by step, the stubbornness of a frail woman in her attempt to penetrate the absurdity of Brazilian bureaucracy.

Lins died of skin cancer at the age of fifty-four on 8 July 1978 in São Paulo, where he had lived since 1962. At his bedside were his three daughters from his first marriage and his second wife, the writer Julieta de Godoy Ladeira. The year before his death, a collection of his essays was published as *Do ideal e da glória: problemas inculturais brasileiros* (1977, On the Ideal and Glory: Brazilian Un-cultural Issues). In these essays Lins reiterates his criticism of Brazilians' lack of contributions to intellectual, creative, scholarly, and educational advancement.

Osman Lins's constant struggle against the chaotic political and cultural situation in Brazil was part of his being as a writer. He believed in his role as a participant in society through his books. He was not discouraged by the lack of a response from the leaders of society to his appeals for a less suffocating environment as he pronounced them in daily articles published in several newspapers. At the time of his death he had just begun writing a book with a working title that speaks loudly about his convictions: "Uma cabeça levada em triunfo" (A Triumphant Head).

Interviews:

Mauritônio Meira, *Flan,* June 1954;

Edla van Steen, "An Interview with Osman Lins," translated by Adria Frizzi, *Review of Contemporary Fiction,* 15 (Fall 1995): 161–172.

References:

Ana Luiza Andrade, *Osman Lins: crítica e criação* (São Paulo: Editora de Humanismo, Ciência e Tecnologia, 1987);

Regina Dalcastagnè, *A garganta das coisas: movimentos de Avalovara, de Osman Lins* (Brasília: Editora da Universidade de Brasília, 2000);

Maria Teresa Dias, "Fortuna Crítica," *Cult,* 5 (2001);

Ermelinda Ferreira, "O retrato perdido na origem da criação da personagem osmaniana," *Estudos de literatura brasileira contemporânea* (September–October 2001);

Regina Igel, *Osman Lins: uma biografia literária* (São Paulo & Brasília: T. A. Queiroz/Instituto Nacional do Livro, 1988);

Julieta de Godoy Ladeira, "A força de Osman Lins," *Estado de Minas Gerais,* 24 August and 24 September 1978;

Ladeira, "Hidden Facets in the Work of Osman Lins," in *A South American Trilogy: Osman Lins, Felisberto Hernández, Luis Fernando Vidal,* edited by Luis Ramos-García, translated by Fred Ellison and others (Austin, Tex.: Studia Hispanica, 1982), pp. 9–15;

Moisés Massaud, "Um grande romance," *Estado de São Paulo: suplemento literário,* 7 April 1962;

Candace Slater, "A Play of Voices: The Theater of Osman Lins," *Hispanic Review,* 49 (Summer 1981): 285–295;

Ariano Suassuna, "O romance de um pernambucano," *Folha da Manhã,* 12, 17, and 18 March 1953.

Clarice Lispector

(10 December 1925? – 9 December 1977)

Eliana Yunes
Pontifícia Universidade Católica do Rio de Janeiro

See also the Lispector entry in *DLB 113: Modern Latin-American Fiction Writers, First Series.*

BOOKS: *Perto do coração selvagem* (Rio de Janeiro: Noite, 1944); translated by Giovanni Pontiero as *Near to the Wild Heart* (New York: New Directions, 1990; Manchester, U.K.: Carcanet, 1990);

O lustre (Rio de Janeiro: AGIR, 1946);

A cidade sitiada (Rio de Janeiro: Noite, 1949; revised edition, Rio de Janeiro: Alvaro, 1964);

Alguns contos (Rio de Janeiro: Ministério da Educação e Saúde, 1952);

Laços de família (Rio de Janeiro: Alves, 1960); translated by Pontiero as *Family Ties* (Austin: University of Texas Press, 1972; Manchester, U.K.: Carcanet, 1985);

A maçã no escuro (Rio de Janeiro: Francisco Alves, 1961); translated by Gregory Rabassa as *The Apple in the Dark* (New York: Knopf, 1967; London: Virago, 1985);

A legião estrangeira (Rio de Janeiro: Editora do Author, 1964); translated by Ponticro as *The Foreign Legiom: Stories and Chronicles* (Manchester, U.K.: Carcanet, 1986; New York: New Directions, 1992);

A paixão segundo G.H. (Rio de Janeiro: Editora do Autor, 1964); translated by Ronald W. Sousa as *The Passion according to G.H.* (Minneapolis: University of Minnesota Press, 1985);

O mistério do coelho pensante (Rio de Janeiro: Alvaro, 1967);

A mulher que matou os peixes (Rio de Janeiro: Sabiá, 1968); translated by Earl E. Fitz as "The Woman Who Killed the Fish," *Latin American Literary Review,* 11 (Fall–Winter 1982): 89–101;

Uma aprendizagem; ou, O livro dos prazeres, romance (Rio de Janeiro: Sabiá, 1969); translated by Richard A. Mazzara and Lorri A. Parris as *An Apprenticeship; or, The Book of Delights* (Austin: University of Texas Press, 1986);

Felicidade clandestina (Rio de Janeiro: Sabiá, 1971);

Clarice Lispector (from the dust jacket for The Foreign Legion, *translated by Giovanni Pontiero, 1986; Richland County Public Library)*

A imitação da rosa (Rio de Janeiro: Artenova, 1973);

Água viva (Rio de Janeiro: Artenova, 1973); translated by Fitz and Elizabeth Lowe as *The Stream of Life* (Minneapolis: University of Minnesota Press, 1989);

A via crucis do corpo (Rio de Janeiro: Artenova, 1974);

Onde estiveste de noite? (Rio de Janeiro: Artenova, 1974);

A vida íntima de Laura (Rio de Janeiro: J. Olympio, 1974);

De corpo inteiro: Reis Velloso, Ney Braga, Dr. J. D. Azulay, Nelida Pinon, Jorge Amado (Rio de Janeiro: Artenova, 1975);

Visão do esplendor: impressões leves (Rio de Janeiro: Alves, 1975);

A hora da estrela (Rio de Janeiro: J. Olympio, 1977); translated by Pontiero as *The Hour of the Star* (Manchester, U.K.: Carcanet, 1986);

Quase de verdade (Rio de Janeiro: Rocco, 1978);

Para não esquecer (São Paulo: Ática, 1978);

Um sopro de vida: Pulsações (Rio de Janeiro: Nova Fronteira, 1978);

A bela e a fera (Rio de Janeiro: Nova Fronteira, 1979);

A descoberta do mundo (Rio de Janeiro: Nova Fronteira, 1984); translated by Pontiero as *Discovering the World* (Manchester, U.K.: Carcanet, 1992); selections from the translation republished as *Selected Crônicas* (New York: New Directions, 1996);

Como nasceram as estrelas: doze lendas brasileiras (Rio de Janeiro: Nova Fronteira, 1987).

Collection: *Seleta de Clarice Lispector,* edited by Renato Gordeiro Gomes (Rio de Janeiro: J. Olympio, 1975).

Editions in English: *The Apple in the Dark,* translated by Gregory Rabassa (Austin: University of Texas Press, 1986);

Soulstorm: Stories, translated by Alexis Levitin (New York: New Directions, 1989)—comprises translations of selected stories from *A via crucis do corpo* and *Onde estiveste de noite?*

TRANSLATION: Oscar Wilde, *O retrato de Dorian Gray* (Rio de Janeiro: Ouro, 1974).

Since her death Clarice Lispector has emerged as one of the most important twentieth-century Brazilian writers, and her fame has spread beyond Brazil. The author stated on many occasions that it was impossible to separate her life from her writing, and her biographers have found many instances in which documented facts about her life parallel characters and incidents in her novels and short stories. The search for a personal identity and for a sense of wholeness as a human being and as a woman led Lispector unintentionally to include autobiography in her fiction; in works such as *Água viva* (1973; translated as *The Stream of Life,* 1989) and *Um sopro de vida: Pulsações* (1978, A Breath of Life: Throbbings) there is an obvious struggle on the part of the writer to distance herself from her fictional creations.

Haia Lispector was born in Tchetchelnik, a Ukrainian village, when her parents, Pinkas and Mania Krimgold Lispector, were about to leave Russia. Her date of birth is in doubt; most sources give 10 December as the day, but the year varies among 1920, 1921, 1922, and 1925. The country was dominated by the Bolsheviks and had experienced a civil war; hunger and illness were widespread, and anti-Semitism was increasing. Mania, who was ill, had gotten pregnant in accordance with a superstition that having a child would restore a woman's health. The family—which included two other girls, Tania and Elisa—immigrated to Brazil and, in an attempt to adapt to their new country, changed their names and began to speak Portuguese at home. Haia, who would always refer to herself as a Brazilian, took the name Clarice; her parents became Pedro and Marian. Clarice spent most of her infancy and part of her adolescence in the city of Recife, where she was enrolled in a public school. The family's financial situation was precarious, and the mother was wasting away from her illness; she died in 1930. Lispector records many memories of this period in her short-story collection *Felicidade clandestina* (1971, Clandestine Happiness). In a deposition for the Museum of Image and Sound in 1976 she declared that she became a voracious reader at an early age and enjoyed the romantic novels of Delly (pseudonym of Jeanne-Marie and Frédéric Petitjean de la Rosière), as well as Brazilian and world classics by authors such as José de Alencar, Eça de Queirós, and Fyodor Dostoevsky.

In 1933 the family moved to Rio de Janeiro, where Lispector enrolled in the Colégio Sílvio Leite. In 1938 she entered the Colégio Andrews to prepare for law school; she chose this career with the goal of humanizing the Brazilian prison system. During this time she discovered the works of Katherine Mansfield, which had an impact on her writing. She enrolled in law school in 1939.

At age nine Lispector had sent some short theatrical and prose texts to the newspaper *O Diário de Pernambuco;* but her first work was not published until 1940, when the short story "Triunfo" (Triumph) appeared in the Rio de Janeiro journal *Pan.* Later that year two more stories were published in the weekly *Vamos Ler!* Also in 1940 Lispector's father died.

On 23 January 1943 Lispector married a former fellow law student, Maury Gurgel Valente, who had interrupted his studies to prepare for a diplomatic career. Encouraged by her professor, Santiago Dantas, she looked for work at Rio de Janeiro newspapers and was hired as an editor and translator by *A Noite.* There she met the writer Lúcio Cardoso, with whom she became close friends, and began writing her first novel. In his *Diário completo* (1970, Complete Journal) Cardoso comments on her sense of discipline. Frustrated when she tried to organize on paper things she had seen and felt earlier, Lispector began carrying a notebook in her purse so that she could jot down her impressions and

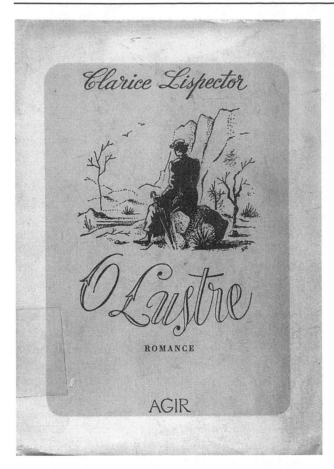

Cover for Lispector's second novel (1946, The Splendor), about a woman who submerges herself in memories of her lonely childhood (Arquivo da Academia Brasileira de Letras)

later transfer them to her works. In this way she completed her novel. Lispector graduated from law school in December 1943.

Lispector had difficulty finding a publisher for her novel but finally reached an agreement with her newspaper to bring out the work. *Perto do coração selvagem* (translated as *Near to the Wild Heart,* 1990) appeared in 1944, the year in which she and her husband left for Belém do Pará for six months and then went on to his first diplomatic assignment in Naples. In Naples, where she did volunteer work in hospitals with Brazilian soldiers, Lispector learned that the novel had won the prestigious Graça Aranha Prize.

Perto do coração selvagem resembles a diary of the early years of Lispector's marriage. Joana loses her mother in childhood and her father in adolescence; she marries a young lawyer but finds marriage stifling and imprisoning. Facts and events are intermingled with feelings and sensations and transformed into a personal type of writing that does not follow the logic of external linearity. Critics have often seen the influence of James Joyce on Lispector's style in the novel; at the time she

wrote *Perto do coração selvagem* she had read one of Joyce's works at Cardoso's suggestion. Some critics have considered Lispector's novel a personal confession typical of feminine writing; others describe her style as a form of magic realism. The novel ends with a promise: "um dia virá que todo o meu movimento será criação, nascimento, eu romperei todos nãos que existem dentro de mim" (a day will come in which all my movements will be a creation, a birth, I will shatter all the no's that exist in me).

As a diplomat's wife Lispector found much of her time consumed by social activities with people whose values she often did not share. She suffered from homesickness, and her desire to write diminished. She explained in a 1946 letter to her sisters: "A vida começa a parar por dentro, e não se tem mais tempo de trabalhar ou ler . . . o pior é que estou ficando embotada: às vezes nem entendo o que leio . . . passo meses sem olhar se quer meu trabalho, faço tudo na ponta dos dedos sem me misturar a nada" (Life has begun to stop in me, and there is no time to work or to read . . . the worst is that I am becoming numb: at times I do not understand what I read . . . I spend months without even looking at my work, I do everything at hand without becoming involved).

Virgínia, the protagonist of Lispector's second novel, *O lustre* (1946, The Splendor), submerges herself in memories of a lonely childhood and feels incapable of communicating with others; she is killed by being run over by an automobile. Lucrécia, the protagonist of Lispector's third novel, *A cidade sitiada* (1949, City under Siege), marries and moves to a large city. Although she is involved in social activities and has a rich cultural life, she is lonely and homesick for her family and friends, but she hides her feelings. Lispector considered the two novels "cacete, sinceramente" (boring, really); the critics did not have a much better opinion of them.

Lispector and Gurgel Valente's first son, Pedro, was born in Bern in 1949. In 1951 Gurgel Valente was assigned to a post in London, and the family spent six months there. While Lispector was pregnant with their second son, Paulo, in 1952, her husband was transferred to Washington, D.C. The family lived in the U.S. capital until 1959, when Lispector separated from her husband and returned to Rio de Janeiro with her sons. There she wrote the column "Feira de Utilitidades" for the newspaper *Correio da Manhã* in 1959–1960 under the pseudonym Helen Palmer. In 1960 she began another column for the newspaper *Diário da Noite.* That same year she published the short-story collection *Laços de família* (translated as *Family Ties,* 1972). The stories, which had first appeared in the periodicals *Senhor* and *Cadernos de Cultura,* are unified by anguished protagonists who feel imprisoned in their relationships; almost all of them experience a temptation to flee into ecstasy or madness.

The sense of evasion of external reality that characterizes Lispector's earlier works continues in the novel *A maçã no escuro* (1961; translated as *The Apple in the Dark,* 1967). The male protagonist, Martim, abandons a successful social life to search for an authentic sense of identity. Lispector uses free indirect discourse to achieve a stream-of-consciousness effect. The critics were enthusiastic about the work: Affonso Romano de Sant'Anna noted that "a personagem organiza sua alma pela linguagem" (the character organizes his soul through language), and José Guilherme Merquior wrote that "oferece a vitória do valor sobre o fato, estando autor e leitor empenhados na construção do significado humano" (the book offers the victory of value over fact, both the author and the reader being engaged in the construction of human meaning).

In 1964 Lispector published one of her densest works of fiction, the novel *A paixão segundo G.H.* (translated as *The Passion according to G.H.,* 1985). The plot is minimal; the narrator, identified only by her initials, tries "vomitar o eu" (to vomit up the I) and "comungar o lado desconhecido e selvagem" (to commune with the unknown, wild side), and at times she involves the reader in the narrative. Caught between the fear and the desire of finding herself, G.H. searches for meaning in the smallest of details; in one scene she eats the crushed body of a cockroach in an act of communion with life. The reader, rather than being repulsed by the act, accompanies the narrator in her experiences of the vile aspects of existence and accepts the complex ambiguity of her feelings. As G.H. says: "Criar não é imaginação, é correr o grande risco de se ter a realidade" (To create is not imagination, it is to run the great risk of having to face reality). In his analysis of the work, critic Alfredo Bosi comments: "Não há mais eu e mundo, mas um Ser de que um e outro participam" (There is no longer an I and the work, but rather a Being in which one and the other participate).

In September 1966 Lispector took a tranquilizer and fell asleep holding a lit cigarette. Her bed caught on fire, and she suffered serious burns on her hands and legs but was saved from death by her son Paulo. In 1967 she began to write intimate personal *crônicas* (short literary columns) for the *Jornal do Brasil;* the columns continued until 1973. She also conducted interviews for the magazine *Manchete.*

While Lispector was working on *A maçã no escuro,* her son Paulo had asked her to write a story for him "right away." Taking the page of typescript from the typewriter, she wrote her first work for children, *O mistério do coelho pensante* (1967, The Mystery of the Pensive

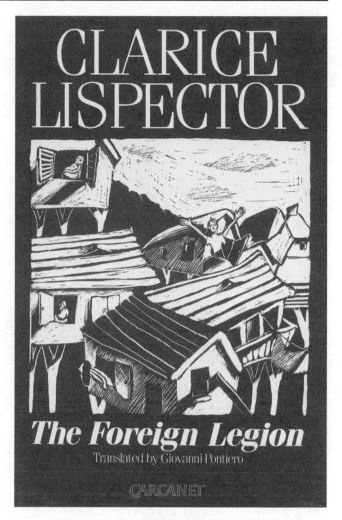

Dust jacket for the British edition of the English translation of Lispector's 1964 short-story collection (Richland County Public Library)

Rabbit), about a rabbit she had given the boys that had escaped from its cage. The book concludes: "Se você quiser adivinhar o mistério, Paulinho experimente você mesmo franzir o nariz para ver se dá certo. É capaz de você descobrir a solução porque menino e menina entendem mais de coelho do que pai e mãe. Quando você descobrir, me conta" (If you want to guess the mystery, dear Paul, try wrinkling your nose to see if that works. You could solve the mystery because little boys and little girls understand the rabbit better than dad or mom. When you solve it, tell me).

In 1968 Lispector published another children's book, *A mulher que matou os peixes* (translated as "The Woman Who Killed the Fish," 1982), in which she confesses that she got so caught up in her writing that she forgot to feed the goldfish one of her sons left in her care when he went on a trip: "O cachorro late, o gato mia, mas o peixe é tão mudo como uma árvore e não

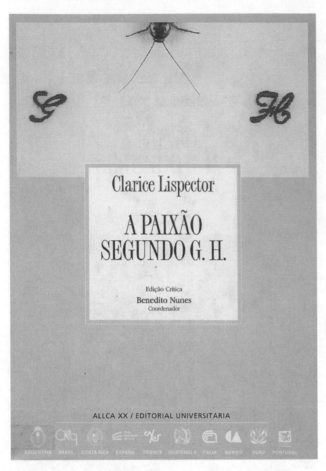

Cover for Lispector's 1964 novel (translated as The Passion According to G.H., *1985), a dense work in which the narrator eats a dead cockroach in an attempt to commune with the viler aspects of existence (Arquivo da Academia Brasileira de Letras)*

author cut passages that made it too autobiographical. The first version was titled "Atrás do pensamento, monólogo com a vida" (Behind Thought, a Monologue with Life); Lispector titled the second version "Objeto gritante" (Striking Object) and changed the protagonist's profession from writer to painter.

In the children's book *A vida íntima de Laura* (1974, Laura's Intimate Life) Lispector returns to a character she had used in an earlier story for adults: a hen. "Eu queria tanto que Laura pudesse falar. . . . Talvez ela pudesse explicar que gosto tem minhoca. . . . Você sabe que Deus gosta de galinha? E sabe como é que eu sei que ele gosta? É o seguinte: se Ele não gostasse de galinha Ele simplesmente não fazia galinha no mundo. Deus gosta de você também, senão Ele não fazia você" (I so wanted Laura to be able to speak. . . . Perhaps she could explain what a worm tastes like . . . Do you know that God likes hens? And do you know how I know this? It's like this: if he did not like hens, he would simply not create hens. God likes you also, or he wouldn't have made you). In this work Lispector adds a new element to her writing: a warm sense of humor.

During a financial crisis Lispector wrote a series of erotic stories that were collected as *A via crucis do corpo* (1974, The Body's Path of the Cross). She also translated works by Oscar Wilde, Jack London, Agatha Christie, Edgar Allan Poe, Jonathan Swift, and Bella Chagall and conducted interviews with writers and other well-known personalities for the weekly magazine of a newspaper. On receiving a substantial monetary award in 1976 from the Fundação Cultural de Brasília, she expressed her concern for others who were worse off than she: "Não consigo senão pensar nisto—crianças morrem de fome, crianças mortas de fome" (I cannot help but think of this—children dying of hunger, children dead of hunger).

Lispector's final work, *A hora da estrela* (1977; translated as *The Hour of the Star,* 1986), is her most socially oriented writing. Dreaming of a better life in the south, Macabéa moves from northeastern Brazil to Rio de Janeiro, where she becomes a low-paid worker. Her boyfriend, also a migrant, is less naive and better able to survive in the harsh urban setting. At the end of the novel Macabéa crosses the street with her eyes on the headlights of an oncoming automobile; she is struck by the car and dies. The narrator comments: "Não vos assusteis, morrer é só um instante, passa logo, eu sei porque acabei de morrer com a moça" (Don't be afraid, to die is only an instant, it passes quickly, I know because I just died with this young woman).

Lispector never remarried, nor was she involved in an amorous relationship after leaving her husband. Although she disliked being alone, it became increasingly difficult for her to maintain relationships with

tinha voz para reclamar e me chamar. . . . Então me dêem perdão. Eu também fiquei muito zangada com a minha distração e peço muito que vocês me desculpem" (The dog barks, the cat meows, but the fish is as silent as a tree and has no voice with which to complain and call me. . . . So, please forgive me. I also became irritated with my distraction, and now I ask you to pardon me).

In *Uma aprendizagem; ou, O livro dos prazeres* (1969; translated as *An Apprenticeship; or, The Book of Delights,* 1986) fragments of Lispector's most intimate and confessional *crônicas* are transferred to the voice of the character Lori, a concrete replacement for the vague "she" of the author's journalistic texts. Lori says: "'Se eu fosse eu' parecia representar o maior perigo de viver, parecia a entrada nova do desconhecido" ("If I were I" seemed to represent the greatest danger of living and seemed to be a new entrance to the unknown). Before appearing in 1973, *Água viva* went through three versions as the

anyone other than her readers. She died on 9 December 1977 of ovarian cancer.

In *Quase de verdade* (Almost the Truth), which appeared posthumously in 1978, Lispector gives her dog, Ulysses, a voice: he "late para Clarice uma história bem latida" (barks a well-barked story for Clarice). Like Monteiro Lobato, who made children's literature an accepted genre in Brazil, Lispector playfully experiments with words in the manner of a child. Many of the images in the book are the result of the careful attention she had paid to conversations with her children.

Lispector's *crônicas* were collected after her death as *A descoberta do mundo* (1984; translated as *Discovering the World,* 1992). In one column she remarks, "Quanto a me delatar, realmente isto é fatal, não digo nas colunas, mas nos romances. Estes não são autobiográficos nem de longe, mas fico sabendo por quem os lê que eu me delatei" (As for my revealing myself, this is truly fatal, not in my columns but in my novels. These are not the least bit autobiographical, but through those who read them I have come to know that I have revealed myself). In the various columns she discusses her family, her immigration to Brazil, her girlhood in Recife, and the cities in which she lived as the wife of a diplomat. She also reveals the difficulties she had with her writing and her relationships with friends, secretaries, and maids. She is, however, silent about one of the most painful aspects of her life: her older son, Pedro, developed schizophrenia as he entered adolescence. She wrote in a letter to her son Paulo: "Pedro não está nada bem e isto me tira a alegria de viver" (Pedro is not well and this takes away my joy of living).

Clarice Lispector left a body of work that assures her position as one of the most important women writers of her time and one of the foremost Brazilian writers of the twentieth century. Her novels, short stories, and chronicles have been translated into many languages and are studied in universities around the world.

Interviews:

"Entrevista," *Revista Textura,* 3 (May 1974);

"Entrevista a Júlio Lerner. TV Cultura. São Paulo, fevereiro de 1977," *Revista Shalon,* 296 (1992).

Bibliography:

Diane E. Marting, *Clarice Lispector: A Bio-bibliography* (Westport, Conn.: Greenwood Press, 1993).

Biographies:

Teresa Cristina Monteiro Ferreira, "Eu sou uma pergunta: uma biografia de Clarice Lispector," M.A. thesis, Pontifícia Universidade Católica do Rio de Janeiro, 1995;

Nádia Batella Gotlib, *Clarice, uma vida que se conta* (São Paulo: Ática, 1995).

References:

Cláudia Pazos Alonso and Claire Williams, eds., *Closer to the Wild Heart: Essays on Clarice Lispector* (Oxford: Legenda, European Humanities Research Centre, University of Oxford, 2002);

Maria Julieta Drummond de Andrade, "Em forma de pomba," in her *Um buquê de alcachofras* (Rio de Janeiro: J. Olympio, 1981), pp. 24–26;

Maria José Somerlate Barbosa, *Clarice Lispector: mutações faiscantes = Sparkling Mutations* (Belo Horizonte: Gam, 1997);

Barbosa, *Clarice Lispector: Spinning the Webs of Passion* (New Orleans: University Press of the South, 1997);

Raimunda Bedasee, *Violência e ideologia feminista na obra de Clarice Lispector* (Salvador: EDUFBA, 1999);

Ivaldo Santos Bittencourt, *Neo-análise da produção literária em Clarice Lispector* (Recife: Editora Universitária, Universidade Federal de Pernambuco, 1987);

Olga Borelli, *Clarice Lispector: esboço para um possível retrato* (Rio de Janeiro: Nova Fronteira, 1981);

Assis Brasil, *Clarice Lispector: ensaio* (Rio de Janeiro: Organização Simões, 1969);

Samira Campedelli and Benjamin Abdala Jr., *Clarice Lispector* (São Paulo: Abril Educação, 1981);

Lúcio Cardoso, "Sobre Clarice," in his *Diário completo* (Rio de Janeiro: J. Olympio, 1970), pp. 139–141;

Hélène Cixous, *Reading with Clarice Lispector,* edited and translated by Verena Andermatt Conley (London: Harvester Wheatsheaf, 1990; Minneapolis: University of Minnesota Press, 1990);

Eleonora Cróquer Pedrón, *El gesto de Antígona o la escritura como responsabilidad: Clarice Lispector, Diamela Eltit y Carmen Boullosa* (Santiago: Cuarto Propio, 2000);

Simone Ribeiro da Costa Curi, *A escritura nômade em Clarice Lispector* (Chapecó: Argos, 2001);

Marie-Ange Depierre, *Une petite liberté: Récits; suivi de Dire oui à Clarice Lispector* (Montreal: Triptyque, 1989);

Nilson Dinis, *A arte da fuga em Clarice Lispector* (Londrina: UEL, 2001);

Júlio Diniz, "O olhar (do) estrangeiro: uma possível leitura de Clarice Lispector," in his *Feminino e literatura* (Rio de Janeiro: Revista Tempo Brasileiro, 1990), pp. 29–50;

Américo António Lindeza Diogo, *Da vida das baratas: leitura de* A paixão segundo G.H., *de Clarice Lispector* (Braga: Angelus Novus, 1993);

Earl E. Fitz, *Clarice Lispector* (Boston: Twayne, 1985);

Fitz, *Sexuality and Being in the Poststructuralist Universe of Clarice Lispector: The Différance of Desire* (Austin: University of Texas Press, 2001);

Laura Freixas, *Clarice Lispector* (Barcelona: Omega, 2001);

Márcia Lígia Guidin, *Roteiro de leitura: "A hora da estrela" de Clarice Lispector* (São Paulo: Ática, 1996);

Gabriela Hofmann-Ortega Lleras, *Die produktive Rezeption von Thomas Manns Doktor Faustus: Einzeltextanalysen zu João Guimarães Rosa, Clarice Lispector, Michel Tournier und Danièle Sallenave* (Heidelberg: Winter, 1995);

Ricardo Iannace, *A leitora Clarice Lispector* (São Paulo: FAPESP, 2001);

Neiva Pitta Kadota, *A tessitura dissimulada: o social em Clarice Lispector* (São Paulo: Estação Liberdade, 1997);

Dany Al-Behy Kanaan, *Escuta e subjetivação: a escritura de pertencimento de Clarice Lispector* (São Paulo: Casa do Psicólogo/EDUC, 2002);

Eliane Vasconcellos Leitão, *Inventário do arquivo Clarice Lispector* (Rio de Janeiro: El Ministério, 1994);

Elena Losada Soler, Antonio Maura, and Wagner Novaes, *Clarice Lispector, la escritura del cuerpo y el silencio* (Barcelona: Proyecto A Ediciones, 1997);

Ivo Lucchesi, *Crise e escritura: uma leitura de Clarice Lispector e Vergílio Ferreira* (Rio de Janeiro: Forense-Universitária, 1987);

Lícia Manzo, *Era uma vez: Eu—a não-ficção na obra de Clarice Lispector* (Juiz de Fora: Ed. UFJF, 2001);

Lina Meruane, "La gallina hueca, carencia y deseo femenino en la obra de Clarice Lispector," *EURE,* 28 (September 2001): 45–54;

Ana Miranda, *Clarice Lispector: o tesouro de minha cidade* (Rio de Janeiro: Relume-Dumará/Prefeitura Rio Arte, 1996);

João Alfredo de Sousa Montenegro, *História e ontologia em A hora da estrela de Clarice Lispector* (Rio de Janeiro: Tempo Brasileiro, 2001);

Alexandre Moraes, *Clarice Lispector: em muitos olhares* (Vitória: UFES, 2000);

Mara Negrón-Marrero, *Une genèse au "féminin": Etude de La pomme dans le noir de Clarice Lispector* (Amsterdam & Atlanta: Rodopi, 1997);

Cláudia Nina, *A palavra usurpada: exílio e nomadismo na obra de Clarice Lispector* (Pôrto Alegre: EDIPUCRS, 2003);

Edgar Cézar Nolasco, *Clarice Lispector: nas entrelinhas da escritura* (São Paulo: Annablume, 2001);

Nicolino Novello, *O ato criador de Clarice Lispector* (Rio de Janeiro: Presença, 1987);

Benedito Nunes, *O drama da linguagem: uma leitura de Clarice Lispector* (São Paulo: Ática, 1989);

Nunes, *Leitura de Clarice Lispector* (São Paulo: Quíron, 1973);

Nunes, *O mundo de Clarice Lispector* (Manaus: Edições Governo do Estado do Amazonas, 1966);

Solange Ribeiro de Oliveira, *A barata e a crisálida: o romance de Clarice Lispector* (Rio de Janeiro: J. Olympio & Instituto Nacional do Livro, Fundação Nacional Pró-Memória, 1985);

Montserrat Ordóñez, *Clarice Lispector: La mirada múltiple* (Bogotá: Centro Colombo-Americano, 1990);

Marta Peixoto, "Family Ties: Female Development in Clarice Lispector," in *The Voyage In: Fictions of Female Development,* edited by Elizabeth Abel, Marianne Hirsch, and Elizabeth Langland (Hanover, N.H.: Published for Dartmouth College by University Press of New England, 1983);

Peixoto, *Passionate Fictions: Gender, Narrative, and Violence in Clarice Lispector* (Minneapolis: University of Minnesota Press, 1994);

Hélio Pellegrino, "Clarice: A Paixão do real," in his *A burrice do demônio* (Rio de Janeiro: Rocco, 1988), pp. 193–196;

Teresinka Pereira, *Estudo sôbre Clarice Lispector* (Coimbra, Portugal: Nova Era, 1975);

Regina Lúcia Pontieri, *Clarice Lispector: uma poética do olhar* (São Paulo: Ateliê, 1999);

Pontieri, ed., *Leitores e leituras de Clarice Lispector* (São Paulo: Hedra, 2004);

Telma Maria Silva Rêgo, *Sobre a possibilidade de uma leitura sartreana em Clarice Lispector* (São Luís do Maranhão: SIOGE, 1993);

Francisco Aurélio Ribeiro, *A literatura infanto-juvenil de Clarice Lispector* (Vitória: Nemar, 1993);

Yudith Rosenbaum, *Clarice Lispector* (São Paulo: Publifolha, 2002);

Rosenbaum, *Metamorfoses do mal: uma leitura de Clarice Lispector* (São Paulo: FAPESP, 1999);

Igor Rossoni, *Zen e a poética auto-reflexiva de Clarice Lispector: uma literatura de vida e como vida* (São Paulo: UNESP, 2002);

Olga de Sá, *Clarice Lispector: a travessia do oposto* (São Paulo: Annablume, 1993);

Sá, *A escritura de Clarice Lispector* (Petrópolis: Vozes, 1979);

Cristina Santos, *Bending the Rules in the Quest for an Authentic Female Identity: Clarice Lispector and Carmen Boullosa* (New York: Peter Lang, 2004);

Jeana Laura da Cunha Santos, *A estética da melancolia em Clarice Lispector* (Florianópolis: UFSC, 2000);

Roberto Corrêa dos Santos, *Clarice Lispector* (São Paulo: Atual, 1986);

Santos, *Lendo Clarice Lispector* (São Paulo: Atual, 1986);

Irmgard Scharold, *Epiphanie, Tierbild, Metamorphose, Passion und Eucharistie: Zur Kodierung des "Anderen" in den Werken von Robert Musil, Clarice Lispector und J. M. G. Le Clézio* (Heidelberg: Winter, 2000);

Heike Schmitz, *Von Sturm und Geisteswut: Mystische Spuren und das Kleid der Kunst bei Ingeborg Bachmann und Clarice Lispector* (Königstein: Helmer, 1998);

Carlos Mendes de Sousa, *Clarice Lispector, figuras da escrita* (Minho: Universidade de Minho, Centro de Estudos Humanísticos, 2000);

Claire Varin, *Clarice Lispector: Rencontres Brésiliennes* (Laval, Quebec: Trois, 1987);

Varin, *Langues de Feu: Essais sur Clarice Lispector* (Laval, Quebec: Trois, 1990);

Nelson Vieira, *Ser judeu e escritor: três casos brasileiros. Samuel Rawet, Clarice Lispector, Moacyr Scliar* (Rio de Janeiro: CIEC, Centro Interdisciplinar de Estudos Contemporâneos, Escola de Comunicação/Universidade Federal do Rio de Janeiro, 1990);

Telma Maria Vieira, *Clarice Lispector: uma leitura instigante* (São Paulo: Annablume, 1998);

Berta Waldman, *Clarice Lispector: a paixão segundo C.L.,* revised and enlarged edition (São Paulo: Escuta, 1993);

Eliana Yunes, "A assunção do sujeito segundo Clarice," in *Dos Contos, em Cantos. Coleção Psicanálise da Criança: coisa de Criança,* edited by Jandyra Kondera Mengarelli (Salvador: Ágalma, 1998), pp. 83–94;

Regina Zilberman and others, *Clarice Lispector: a narração do indizível* (Pôrto Alegre: Instituto Cultural Judaico Marc Chagall/Artes e Ofícios/EDIPUCRS, 1998).

Papers:

The Clarice Lispector Archives are in the Fundação Casa de Rui Barbosa in Rio de Janeiro. Her letters to Lúcio Cardoso are in the Cardoso archives in the Fundação Casa de Rui Barbosa. Her letters to Elisa and Tânia Kauffman are in the Biblioteca Nacional, Rio de Janeiro. Lispector's "Depoimento a Affonso Romano de Sant'Anna, Marina Colasanti e João Salgueiro," 20 October 1976, is in Coleção Depoimentos no. 7, Museu da Imagem e do Som, Rio de Janeiro.

José Bento Monteiro Lobato

(18 April 1882 – 5 July 1948)

Eliana Yunes
Pontifícia Universidade Católica do Rio de Janeiro

BOOKS: *Urupês* (São Paulo: Revista do Brasil, 1918);

Problema vital (São Paulo: Revista do Brasil, 1918);

O Sacy-perêrê (São Paulo: Nacional, 1918);

Cidades mortas (São Paulo: Revista do Brasil, 1919);

Idéias de Jeca Tatu (São Paulo: Revista do Brasil, 1919);

A menina do narizinho arrebitado (São Paulo: Monteiro Lobato, 1920);

Negrinha (São Paulo: Revista do Brasil, 1920);

Os negros, ou, Elle e o outro (São Paulo: O. Ribeiro, 1921);

A onda verde: jornalismo (São Paulo: Monteiro Lobato, 1921);

O saci (São Paulo: Monteiro Lobato, 1921);

Fábulas (São Paulo: Monteiro Lobato, 1922);

O macaco que se fez homem (São Paulo: Monteiro Lobato, 1923);

Mundo da lua (São Paulo: Monteiro Lobato, 1923);

O garimpeiro do Rio das Garças (São Paulo: Nacional, 1924);

Los ojos que sangran, translated by B. Sánchez Saez (Buenos Aires: Tor, 1924);

O choque das raças ou O presidente negro: romance americano do anno de 2228 (São Paulo: Nacional, 1926);

How Henry Ford Is Regarded in Brazil, translated by Aubrey Stuart (Rio de Janeiro: São Paulo Editora, 1926);

Aventuras de Hans Staden: meu captiveiro entre os selvagens do Brasil (São Paulo: Nacional, 1927);

Mr. Slang e o Brasil: colloquios com o inglez da Tijuca (São Paulo: Nacional, 1927);

Peter Pan (São Paulo: Editora Brasiliense, 1930);

Ferro: a solucão do problema siderurgico do Brasil pelo processo Smith (São Paulo: Nacional, 1931);

As reinações de Narizinho (São Paulo: Nacional, 1931);

América (São Paulo: Nacional, 1932);

Viagem ao céu (São Paulo: Nacional, 1932);

As caçadas de Pedrinho (São Paulo: Nacional, 1933);

Contos pesados (São Paulo: Nacional, 1933)—comprises *Urupês, Negrinha,* and *O macaco se fez homem;*

História do mundo para as crianças (São Paulo: Companhia Editora Nacional, 1933);

Drawing of José Bento Monteiro Lobato inscribed to Edgard Cavalheiro (frontispiece for Cavalheiro, Monteiro Lobato: vida e obra, *1955; Joint University Libraries, Nashville)*

Na antevéspera: reações mentaes dum ingenuo (São Paulo: Nacional, 1933);

Novas reinações de Narizinho (São Paulo: Nacional, 1933);

Emília no país da gramática (São Paulo: Nacional, 1934);

Aritmética da Emília (São Paulo: Nacional, 1935);

Contes leves: Cidades mortas e outros (São Paulo: Nacional, 1935);

Geografia de Dona Benta (São Paulo: Nacional, 1935);

História das invenções (São Paulo: Nacional, 1935);

Dom Quixote das crianças (São Paulo: Nacional, 1936);

O escândalo do petróleo: depoimentos apresentados a Comissão de Inquerito sobre o petróleo, by Lobato and Hilario Freire, compiled by Essad Bey, preface and commentary by Lobato (São Paulo: Nacional, 1936);

Memórias da Emília (São Paulo: Nacional, 1936);

Histórias de Tia Nastácia (São Paulo: Nacional, 1937);

O poço do Visconde: geologia para as crianças (São Paulo: Nacional, 1937);

Serões de Dona Benta (São Paulo: Nacional, 1937);

O minotauro: maravilhosas aventuras dos netos de Dona Benta na Grecia antiga (São Paulo: Nacional, 1939);

O picapau amarelo (São Paulo: Nacional, 1939);

O espanto das gentes (São Paulo: Nacional, 1941);

A reforma da natureza (São Paulo: Nacional, 1941);

A chave do tamanho: historia da maior reinação do mundo onde Emília reduz temporariamente o tamanho das criaturas humanas (São Paulo: Nacional, 1942);

Os doze trabalhos de Hércules, 2 volumes (São Paulo: Editora Brasiliense, 1944);

O touro de Creta (São Paulo: Editora Brasiliense, 1944);

Prefácios e entrevistas (São Paulo: Editora Brasiliense, 1946);

A casa da Emília (Buenos Aires: Codex, 1947);

O centaurinho (Buenos Aires: Codex, 1947);

Uma fada moderna (Buenos Aires: Codex, 1947);

A lampreia (Buenos Aires: Codex, 1947);

La nueva Argentina, as Miguel P. García (Buenos Aires: Acteon, 1947);

No tempo de Nero (Buenos Aires: Codex, 1947);

Zé Brasil (Rio de Janeiro: Vitória, 1947);

Conferências, artigos e crônicas (São Paulo: Editora Brasiliense, 1959);

Literatura do Minarete (São Paulo: Editora Brasiliense, 1959);

Críticas e outras notas (São Paulo: Editora Brasiliense, 1965).

Editions and Collections: *Urupês, outros contos e coisas,* edited, with a preface, by Artur Neves (São Paulo: Nacional, 1943);

Obras completas, 30 volumes (São Paulo: Editora Brasiliense, 1946–1947; revised and enlarged, 34 volumes, 1956–1959; revised and enlarged, 35 volumes, 1961–1965);

Textos escolhidos, edited by José Carlos Barbosa Moreira (Rio de Janeiro: AGIR, 1962);

Monteiro Lobato, edited by Marisa Lajolo (São Paulo: Abril, 1981);

Contos escolhidos, edited by Lajolo (São Paulo: Editora Brasiliense, 1989).

Edition in English: *Brazilian Short Stories,* introduction by Isaac Goldberg (Girard, Kans.: Haldeman-Julius, 1925).

SELECTED TRANSLATIONS: Lewis Carroll, *Alice no país das maravilhas* (São Paulo: Nacional, 1931);

Hans Christian Andersen, *Contos de Andersen* (São Paulo: Nacional, 1932);

Jacob Grimm and Wilhelm Grimm, *Contos de Grimm* (São Paulo: Nacional, 1932);

Carroll, *Alice no país do espelho* (São Paulo: Nacional, 1933);

Carlo Collodi, *Pinocchio* (São Paulo: Nacional, 1933);

Rudyard Kipling, *Kim* (São Paulo: Nacional, 1934);

Charles Perrault, *Contos de fadas* (São Paulo: Nacional, 1934);

Mark Twain, *Aventuras de Huck* (São Paulo: Nacional, 1934);

H. G. Wells, *O homem invisivel* (São Paulo: Nacional, 1934);

Herman Melville, *Moby Dick: a fera do mar,* translated by Lobato and Adalberto Rochsteiner (São Paulo: Nacional, 1935);

Ernest Hemingway, *Por quem os sinos dobram* (São Paulo: Nacional, 1941);

Hemingway, *Adeus às armas* (São Paulo: Nacional, 1942);

Ilya Ehrenburg, *A queda de Paris* (São Paulo: Nacional, 1944);

Richard Wright, *Filho nativo: tragedia de um negro americano* (São Paulo: Nacional, 1944);

Will Durant, *História da filosofia: vida e idéias dos grandes filósofos* (São Paulo: Nacional, 1945);

Hendrik Willem Van Loon, *A história da Biblia* (São Paulo: Nacional, 1945).

Stories for children, which have existed since time immemorial, generally begin with "Once upon a time. . . ." The narratives of José Bento Monteiro Lobato, considered the founder of children's literature in Brazil, break with this traditional pattern. His stories are not escapist, nor are they psychoanalytical fantasies. Annoyed one day by the stories he was reading to his four children, he thought about narratives without any literary pretense that could fascinate and, at the same time, inform and sharpen children's critical abilities. At that moment Lobato decided that he was going to become the Latin American Hans Christian Andersen, which possibly would have happened had his native language been Spanish or had his native land in the decades of the 1920s and 1930s been more advanced in industrial development.

Front cover for Lobato's 1918 book on an impish figure popular in Brazilian folklore (from Carmen Lucia de Azevedo, Marcia Camargos, and Vladimir Sacchetta, eds., Monteiro Lobato: furacão na Botocúndia, *1998; Bruccoli Clark Layman Archives)*

Lobato was not only a writer but also an editor, a literary agent, the owner of a publishing house, a critic, a journalist, and, above all, a man totally dedicated to his country. In his opinion, books should be marketable items like automobiles and electrical appliances. His best-known phrase was "Um país se faz com homens e com livros" (A country is made with men and with books).

Born in Taubaté, close to the city of São Paulo, on 18 April 1882, José Bento Monteiro Lobato was the son of José Bento Marcondes Lobato and Olympia Monteiro Lobato. After the death of both parents, Lobato and his sisters, Esther and Judith, were raised by their maternal grandfather, José Francisco Monteiro, Visconde de Tremembé. Lobato grew up on a farm, riding horseback, fishing in the river, climbing trees, and frightened by the ghost stories he was told in the country. His grandfather's library, with its thick illus-

trated volumes, fascinated the boy. He was taught to read and write at home and then attended several different schools in the area.

In 1900 Lobato was sent to São Paulo to study law, the typical career for children of the elite at that time. He enjoyed art and literature more than the law, and during his years in school he contributed to several newspapers and magazines. Written under various pseudonyms, these early pieces reveal a precocious astuteness and perspicacity. Lobato and a group of fellow students, with whom he remained friends throughout his entire life, formed a literary group called O Cenáculo (The Cenaculum) and met regularly in the Café Guarany. The young people named the house in which they lived O Minarete (The Minaret) and declared that it was a place "onde só se come o pão do espírito" (where one only eats the bread of the spirit). The literary background of the group, which had an interest in national themes and issues, was shaped by the late-nineteenth-century movement known as Parnassianism.

After he graduated from law school in 1904, Lobato returned to Taubaté, where he married Maria da Pureza Natividade in 1908. The couple had four children, Martha, Edgard, Guilherme, and Ruth, who all died young. With the help of his grandfather Lobato obtained a job as public prosecutor in the town of Areias, and he began his long career as an author, writing stories and letters to his friends. His correspondence with Godofredo Rangel, collected as *A barca de Gleyre: quarenta anos de correspondência literária entre Monteiro Lobato e Godofredo Rangel* (1944, Gleyre's Boat: Forty Years of Literary Correspondence between Monteiro Lobato and Godofredo Rangel), perhaps offers the most authentic portrait of Lobato the man, who was both loved and hated and was a polemical figure throughout his life.

When his grandfather died in 1911, Lobato inherited the farm and all its problems. He became aware of the reality of rural Brazilian society, which resisted any type of agricultural modernization. He took care of the land, planting crops and buying equipment to keep the farm going, but the political situation and economy wiped out his efforts. In 1914, as World War I broke out across Europe, Lobato began his opposition to what he thought was his greatest enemy: the ignorant and lazy rural inhabitant, who was supported by governmental neglect. That year he published the article "Velha praga" (Old Plague), which catapulted him to fame. The piece surprisingly won the support of the rural oligarchy, which was in financial ruin, and it had political repercussions. The main character of the work, the country bumpkin Jeca Tatu, became Lobato's most famous creation, emblematic of the author's sincere revisions of his own judgments and opinions throughout his life. In portraying the backwardness of the rural population, Lobato came into conflict with the Romantic, nationalistic notions of writers who idealized the rural population's resistance to modernization.

With his work and his ideas, Lobato became a popular figure in intellectual and political circles. He moved his family to São Paulo in 1917, where he became involved in a polemic that still perturbs scholars of Brazilian literature. He wrote a negative newspaper article, "Paranóia ou mistificação" (Paranoia or Mystification), about an exhibit of works by the painter Anita Malfatti, who was active and important in the emerging artistic movement of modernism at the time. Lobato did not attack Malfatti's talent so much as he did the formal aspects of her painting that he felt distanced it from the general public. The article put Lobato into conflict with Oswald de Andrade and Mário de Andrade, the leaders of modernism and organizers of the Semana de Arte Moderna (Week of Modern Art) of 1922.

At the height of the controversy over "Paranóia ou mistificação," Lobato bought the magazine *Revista do Brasil* in 1918 and quickly became an important force in the cultural life of the country. As editor he invested in the modernization of all aspects of the magazine, including printing and graphics. He published his first book, *Urupês* (a type of fungus that the author uses as a metaphor for the peasant), in 1918. The work is a collection of stories in which Lobato deals with the prejudices, ignorance, complacency, and poverty of the Brazilian peasant.

Determined to change the country and to make money with books, Lobato revolutionized and expanded the system of distribution for about fifty bookstores. He mailed out a circular to the owners of around 1,200 businesses, including drugstores, stationery shops, tobacco kiosks, newsstands, and bazaars, suggesting that they could increase their profits through the sale of books along with their usual merchandise. Lobato did not limit himself to the area of sales; he also became involved in almost every aspect of book production, such as the quality of the graphics, the appeal of the title, the illustrations, and critical remarks that accompanied the release of a book. He also paid careful attention to the publicity that polemics and scandals brought to his books. He was responsible for the appearance in print of works by several important Brazilian writers, including Paulo Menotti del Picchia and Graça Aranha.

Around this time Lobato became interested in finding solutions to the problems of the poor Brazilian educational system. He published his opinions in various newspaper articles and in the book *Problema vital* (1918, Vital Problem), in which he discusses the economy, politics, and public administration in Brazil. He reformulated his views on the peasantry as expressed in "Velha praga." Lobato's involvement with the campaign for improving sanitary conditions in São Paulo was at the root of his change of view; he now focused on the tuberculosis, malnutrition, and hookworm among the peasants. He published *Cidades mortas* (Dead Cities) in 1919 and *Negrinha* (Little Black Girl) in 1920.

As Rangel notes in a 1919 letter, *Problema vital* took Lobato away from literature and from his time for reading and writing. His research for the newspaper *O estado de São Paulo,* however, had given him the idea for a book on the folkloric figure of Saci-pererê, *O Sacy-pererê* (1918), and helped him to realize his desire to write for younger readers. He published *A menina do narizinho arrebitado* (The Little Girl with the Turned-Up Nose) in 1920. The work, presented in short episodes, is set in an imaginary place where a grandmother invites her grandchildren for a vacation. She tells them fantastic stories about the world and charms them into imaginary voyages that seem real.

Before Lobato's children's literature could gain national popularity, the publishing house of the *Revista do Brasil* went bankrupt. The revolution of 1924, an economic situation that made obtaining credit difficult, and an electrical-energy crisis contributed to the failure of the company. With the sale of a lottery house that he owned with a partner, Lobato was able to open the Companhia Editora Nacional (National Publishing Company) in 1925, one of the first great publishing firms in Brazil. He also began writing a popular series of stories with a cast of characters who have become a fixture in Brazilian children's literature. Lobato's works in this genre constitute a complete pedagogical compendium for teachers and parents, who have found in these imaginative pieces an effective tool for making the learning experience attractive and fun for young people.

Influenced by the impact of his books on young readers, Lobato realized the importance of school in the national culture and wrote a series of informative books on grammar, arithmetic, geography, history, and science. In these works he tempered an obvious didactic purpose with the playful, artistic aspects of the spoken language. With characters such as Dona Benta, aided by Emília, the doll who takes "talking pills" and serves as Lobato's alter ego, the books entertained and instructed generations of Brazilian youth. Through Emília the writer employed a technique that became central to some of the later modernist writers, such as Mário de Andrade in his *Macunaíma:*

Advertisement for Lobato's first children's book, from the 16 January 1921 issue of O estado de São Paulo
(*from Edgard Cavalheiro,* Monteiro Lobato: vida e obra, *1955;*
Joint University Libraries, Nashville)

o herói sem nenhum caráter (1928, Macunaíma: The Hero With No Character; translated as *Macunaíma,* 1984): he absorbed and adapted different cultures to the Brazilian situation of the period while creating highly original works. Important titles in this series include *Emília no país da gramática* (1934, Emília in the Country of Grammar), *Aritmética da Emília* (1935, Arithmetic of Emília), and *Geografia de Dona Benta* (1935, Geography of Dona Benta). The analytical focus of the texts has guaranteed their timelessness and popularity in Brazil.

In Rio de Janeiro, Lobato wrote *Aventuras de Hans Staden: meu captiveiro entre os selvagens do Brasil* (1927, Adventures of Hans Staden: My Captivity Among the Savages of Brazil), based on the notes of a German navigator who was captured and almost eaten by the Tapuia Indians. By this time Lobato's new publishing firm had gained national recognition, and he decided to collect the episodes of his writings for children in the volume *As reinações de Narizinho* (1931, Nazarinho's Pranks). The work sold a record 150,000 copies within a year, 30,000 of these going to the state of São Paulo for the public-school system.

Lobato published one book after the other, some dealing with fact and some with fiction. These works were intended to provoke his young readers to think and talk freely about subjects ranging from war, history, and economy to popular knowledge. His works as a whole present a break with the naive aspects of European children's literature. Lobato was bold in his approach to writing for children, and he passed this boldness along to his young readers while tempering it with the ponderings of nonstereotypical characters such as the old black grandmother who becomes the narrator of *Histórias de Tia Nastácia* (1937, Stories of Aunt Nastácia).

Lobato's children's literature constitutes an essay on social democracy. Told from a third-person point of view, his stories move between the dissonant voice of childhood and that of the adult narrator, creating a filter through which the reader can critically and objectively judge the world captured in the text. Lobato valued the literary text not only for its power of imagination but also as a vehicle for critical judgment. At times in a realistic manner and at others through allegory, he deals with political, religious, philosophical, and moral issues in his writing for children. Both *História do mundo para as crianças* (1933, History of the World for Children) and *História das invenções* (1935, History of Inventions) are imbued with the concept of the evolution of the human race and nature. Using magical devices for travel through time and space, Lobato traces the development of humanity and focuses on the positive aspects of the enlightenment of successive generations, scientific advances, and the

social responsibility of the individual. There is a certain contradiction in Lobato's thought reflected in these works: thanks to education, art, and science, the individual can change and better himself, while the general population remains mired in the pessimistic traditionalism perpetuated by inept and corrupt governments caught up in politics.

In 1936 Lobato published a short work for children, *Memórias da Emília* (Memories of Emília), and *Dom Quixote das crianças* (Don Quixote for Children), an adaptation of Miguel de Cervantes' *Don Quixote* (1605, 1615). *Memórias da Emília* is a critical, theoretical work in which, through the voice of some of his previous characters, Lobato analyzes the notion of autobiography. In *Serões de Dona Benta* (Evenings with Dona Benta) and *O poço do Visconde* (The Viscount's Well), both published in 1937, Lobato, without losing sight of his young readers, deals with the national political issue of petroleum. He focuses on the shame and senselessness of war in *A chave do tamanho* (1942, The Key of Size) and uses nonsense in *A reforma da natureza* (1941, Nature's Reform).

Lobato's books for children and adults began to have an effect on his life in the 1930s and 1940s. Works such as *O choque das raças ou O presidente negro* (1926, The Shock of the Races; or, The Black President), *Mr. Slang e o Brasil* (1927, Mr. Slang and Brazil), *América* (1932), and *O escândalo do petróleo* (1936, The Petroleum Scandal) had already created polemical situations for the author, who had spent some time in the United States as a commercial attaché for Brazil in 1927. While there, he had become enthusiastic about the North American system of free enterprise. For Lobato, however, this system had a devastating effect on the economy and politics in Brazil. He lost the resources of Companhia Editora Nacional in the stock market in New York, and on his return to Brazil he had to sell the firm and live from what he earned as an author. He invested in his translations of works by writers such as Jacob and Wilhelm Grimm, Andersen, Charles Perrault, and Lewis Carroll.

With the female characters in his children's literature, Lobato, who placed a high value on the family, distanced himself from dominant patriarchal attitudes and combated conservatism and prejudice. This stance angered some sections of Brazilian society, especially the Church, and resulted in the burning of his books and their prohibition in schools. The dictatorship of the Estado Novo (New State) under Getúlio Vargas, whom Lobato publicly defied, pressured the press to keep his name out of the news in 1939. Lobato, however, was committed to his ideas, and his enemies could not stop him. With his small estate used up, he finally ended up in prison in 1941 for

Front cover of the 1932 book that Lobato wrote as a result of his experience as a commercial attaché for Brazil in the United States in 1927 (from Carmen Lucia de Azevedo, Marcia Camargos, and Vladimir Sacchetta, eds., Monteiro Lobato: furacão no Botocúndia, *1998; Bruccoli Clark Layman Archives)*

three months because of a letter that he wrote to Vargas concerning the problem of petroleum in Brazil. Lobato did not ask for special favors while imprisoned; he spent his time teaching other prisoners to read and write, and he continued to write against the government. He became the spokesman for the prisoners as he learned firsthand another side of his Brazilian society.

Lobato was invited to become a member of the Academia Brasileira de Letras (Brazilian Academy of Letters) in 1944. He refused this honor, offered by the well-known poets Cassiano Ricardo and Menotti Del Picchia, because Vargas had also been elected a full member. Lobato published some new works, including *O picapau amarelo* (1939, The Yellow Woodpecker), *O minotauro* (1939, The Minotaur), and *Os doze trabalhos de Hércules* (1944, The Twelve Labors of Hercules). He also lost his two sons, Edgard and Guilherme, during

this period. He continued to wage a battle in the press against North American economic liberalism and monopolies, which supported a quality of life that he admired but at the cost of weaker economies in countries such as Brazil. Lobato broke with the cultural organization that supported a cooperative effort between Brazil and the United States, the União Cultural Brasil–Estados Unidos. He stated in a letter that he felt deceived by the United States, which fought fascism in Europe but supported the Brazilian dictatorship. With his juvenile works under suspicion of including communist propaganda, Lobato's life became more difficult. He was an agnostic, but he began to show an interest in spiritualism, and he began to correspond with such noted communists as Carlos Prestes.

Lobato went into voluntary exile in Argentina in 1946. There he wrote and published *La nueva Argentina* (1947, The New Argentina) under the pseudonym Miguel P. García and *O garimpeiro do Rio das Garças* (1924, The Prospector of the Rio das Garças), *Uma fada moderna* (1947, A Modern Fairy), *A lampreia* (1947, The Lamprey), *No tempo de Nero* (1947, In the Times of Nero), *A casa da Emília* (1947, Emily's House), and *O centaurinho* (1947, The Little Centaur) under his own name. He returned to Brazil in 1947 weakened, but still a beloved name among young and adult readers. With Caio Prado Jr., Lobato founded the publishing house Editora Brasiliense and prepared a definitive edition of his works. In a letter to his friend Rangel he asserted that his most important accomplishment in life was having directed various generations to literature. That same year Lobato published *Zé Brasil,* in which he demonstrated that, in addition to problems of public health, the country also suffered from flaws in its social and economic infrastructure.

The legacy Lobato left to Brazilian culture through his many letters, interviews, lectures, and journalistic writings cannot compare with the mark made by his literature for children. He experimented with all aspects of writing for young people, and in his works he attempted to create a utopian place, Sítio do Picapau Amarelo (Yellow Woodpecker Farm), where his readers could think and react without the usual restrictions placed on them. Lobato firmly believed that fantasy was not simply an escape from everyday reality but rather a device by which to present the real in a critical manner. He was convinced that literature was a perfect place to teach language and cultural differences and that learning could be an enjoyable and interesting adventure for children.

Lobato died on 5 July 1948, leaving a strong mark on children's literature and Brazilian culture in general through his many publications. His works have remained popular with young readers of all social classes. Parents and educators, themselves influenced as children by the imagination of this man who was devoted to his country and its youth, have assured his place in Brazilian literature.

José Bento Monteiro Lobato's works influenced succeeding generations in Brazil. His readers include those who, during the dictatorship of the 1970s, recovered through the new Brazilian children's literature their critical capacity and ability to resist as they grew up in a generation silenced by fear. The censors did not pay much attention to children's literature and were unaware that through it there emerged some of the best allegorical denunciations of governmental abuses of that time. Both Ana Maria Machado and Lygia Bojunga Nunes, who won the important Hans Christian Andersen Prize in children's literature, have stated that Lobato's writing had a great impact on their lives and works.

Letters:

A barca de Gleyre: quarenta anos de correspondência literária entre Monteiro Lobato e Godofredo Rangel, preface by Edgard Cavalheiro (São Paulo: Nacional, 1944);

A correspondência entre Monteiro Lobato e Lima Barreto, edited by Cavalheiro (Rio de Janeiro: Ministério da Educação e Cultura, 1955);

Cartas escolhidas, 2 volumes (São Paulo: Editora Brasiliense, 1959);

Conversa entre amigos: correspondência escolhida entre Anísio Teixeira e Monteiro Lobato, edited by Aurélio Vianna and Priscila Fraiz (Salvador: Fundação Cultural do Estado da Bahia, 1986).

References:

Edgard Cavalheirio, *Monteiro Lobato: vida e obra,* 2 volumes (São Paulo: Nacional, 1955);

Paulo Dantas, *Presença de Lobato* (São Paulo: Editora do Escritor, 1973);

Dantas, ed., *Vozes do tempo de Lobato: depoimento* (São Paulo: Traço, 1982);

Teresinha Aparecida Del Fiorentino, *Prosa de ficção em São Paulo: produção e consumo, 1900–1922* (São Paulo: Editora de Humanismo, Ciência e Tecnologia/Secretaria de Estado da Cultura, 1982);

Alice Mitika Koshiyama, *Monteiro Lobato: intelectual, empresário, editor* (São Paulo: T. A. Queiroz, 1982);

Marisa Lajolo, "Jeca Tatu em três tempos," in *Os pobres na literatura brasileira,* edited by Roberto Schwarz (São Paulo: Editora Brasiliense, 1983);

Lajolo and Regina Zilberman, *Literatura infantil brasileira: história e histórias* (São Paulo: Ática, 1984);

Humberto Marini Filho, "O caipira e o neoliberal: o estranho caso de Jeca Tatu e Mr. Slang: uma interpretação da obra adulta de Monteiro Lobato," M.A. thesis, Universidade do Estado de Rio de Janeiro, 1997;

Marini Filho, "O estranho caso de Monteiro Lobato com a identidade nacional: interpretação da obra adulta," dissertation, Universidade do Estado de Rio de Janeiro, 2000;

Carlos Morais, *Grandes vultos da nossa história* (São Paulo: Abril, 1980);

Cassiano Nunes, *O sonho americano de Monteiro Lobato* (São Paulo: Edart, 1964);

Nunes, *O último sonho de Monteiro Lobato* (São Paulo: Edart, 1964);

Nelson Palma Travassos, *Minhas memórias dos Monteiros Lobatos* (São Paulo: Edart, 1964);

Zinda Maria Carvalho de Vasconcellos, *O universo ideológico da obra infantil de Monteiro Lobato* (São Paulo: Traço, 1982);

Eliana Yunes, *Presença de Monteiro Lobato* (Rio de Janeiro: Divulgação e Pesquisa, 1982);

Zilberman, ed., *Atualidade de Monteiro Lobato: uma revisão crítica* (Pôrto Alegre: Mercado Aberto, 1983).

Joaquim Maria Machado de Assis

(21 June 1839 – 29 September 1908)

Paul B. Dixon
Purdue University

BOOKS: *Queda que as mulheres têm para os tolos* (Rio de Janeiro: Brito, 1861);

Desencantos: fantasia dramática (Rio de Janeiro: Brito, 1861);

A festa da caridade: poesias distribuidas e recitadas no beneficio a favor dos azylos da infancia desvalida de Portugal no theatro Lyrico Fluminense, na noite de 26 de julho de 1862 (Rio de Janeiro: Pinheiro, 1862);

Teatro (Rio de Janeiro: Tipografia do Diário do Rio de Janeiro, 1863);

Quase ministro: comédia em um ato (Rio de Janeiro: Tipografia da Escola, 1864);

Crisálidas (Rio de Janeiro: Garnier, 1864);

Os deuses de casaca: comédia (Rio de Janeiro: Tipografia do Imperial Instituto Artístico, 1866);

Os trabalhadores do mar (Rio de Janeiro: Perseverança, 1866);

Falenas (Rio de Janeiro: Garnier / Paris: Belhatte, 1870);

Contos fluminenses (Rio de Janeiro: Garnier, 1870);

Ressurreição (Rio de Janeiro: Garnier, 1872);

Histórias de meia-noite (Rio de Janeiro: Garnier, 1873);

Higiene para uso dos mestre-escolas (Rio de Janeiro: Tipografia Cinco de Março, 1873);

A mão e a luva (Rio de Janeiro: Gomes de Oliveira, 1874); translated by Alberto I. Bagby Jr. as *The Hand and the Glove,* foreword by Helen Caldwell (Lexington: University of Kentucky Press, 1970);

Americanas (Rio de Janeiro: Garnier, 1875);

Helena (Rio de Janeiro: Garnier, 1876); translated by Caldwell (Berkeley & London: University of California Press, 1984);

Iaiá Garcia (Rio de Janeiro: G. Vianai, 1878); translated by R. L. Scott-Buccleuch as *Yayá Garcia* (London: Owen, 1976);

Memórias póstumas de Brás Cubas (Rio de Janeiro: Tipografia Nacional, 1881); translated by William L. Grossman as *Epitaph of a Small Winner* (New York: Noonday Press, 1952);

(frontispiece for Memorias póstumas de Brás Cubas, *1951; Biblioteca Nacional de Chile)*

Tu só, tu, puro amor: comédia (Rio de Janeiro: Lombaerts, 1881);

Papéis avulsos (Rio de Janeiro: Lombaerts, 1882);

Histórias sem data (Rio de Janeiro: Garnier, 1884);

Terras: compilação para estudo (Rio de Janeiro: Imprensa Nacional, 1886);

Quincas Borba (Rio de Janeiro: Garnier, 1891); translated by Clotilde Wilson as *Philosopher or Dog?* (New York: Noonday Press, 1954);

Várias histórias (Rio de Janeiro: Laemmert, 1896);

Páginas recolhidas (Rio de Janeiro: Garnier, 1899);

Dom Casmurro (Rio de Janeiro: Garnier, 1899); translated by Caldwell, introduction by Waldo Frank (New York: Noonday Press, 1953);

Poesias completas (Rio de Janeiro: Garnier, 1901)–includes *Chrysalidas, Phalenas, Americanas,* and *Occidentaes;*

Esaú e Jacó (Rio de Janeiro: Garnier, 1904); translated by Caldwell as *Esau and Jacob,* introduction by Caldwell (Berkeley: University of California Press, 1965);

Relíquias de casa velha (Rio de Janeiro: Garnier, 1906);

Memorial de Aires (Rio de Janeiro: Garnier, 1908); translated by Caldwell as *Counselor Ayres' Memorial,* introduction by Caldwell (Berkeley & London: University of California Press, 1972).

Collection: *Obra completa,* 3 volumes, edited by Afrânio Coutinho (Rio de Janeiro: Nova Aguilar, 1959).

Editions in English: *The Psychiatrist and Other Stories,* translated by William L. Grossman and Helen Caldwell (Berkeley: University of California Press, 1963; London: Owen, 1963);

The Devil's Church and Other Stories, translated by Jack Schmitt and Lorie Ishimatsu (Austin & London: University of Texas Press, 1977);

Iaiá Garcia, translated by Alberto I. Bagby Jr. (Lexington: University of Kentucky Press, 1977);

The Wager: Aires' Journal, translated, with an introduction, by R. L. Scott-Buccleuch (London: Owen, 1990);

Dom Casmurro: Lord Taciturn, translated, with an introduction, by Scott-Buccleuch (London: Owen, 1992);

Dom Casmurro, translated, with a foreword, by John Gledson, afterword by João Adolfo Hansen (New York & Oxford: Oxford University Press, 1997);

The Posthumous Memoirs of Brás Cubas, translated by Gregory Rabassa, foreword by Enylton de Sá Rego, afterword by Gilberto Pinheiro Passos (New York & Oxford: Oxford University Press, 1997);

Quincas Borba, translated by Rabassa, introduction by David T. Haberly, afterword by Celso Favaretto (New York & London: Oxford University Press, 1998);

Esau and Jacob, translated by Elizabeth Lowe, edited, with a foreword, by Dain Borges, afterword by Carlos Felipe Moisés (New York: Oxford University Press, 2000).

Among Latin American fiction writers of the nineteenth century, Joaquim Maria Machado de Assis (usually called "Machado de Assis" or simply "Machado") is without peer. Machado de Assis emerged from undistinguished biographical and literary origins with a brilliant and subtle voice that set him apart from his contemporaries and pointed the way to the Ibero-American literary boom of the twentieth century. As a maturing writer Machado de Assis bristled at the servile imitation of European realism and natural-

ism so prevalent among the Brazilian writers of his day. Instead, he sought models among the playful ironists of the eighteenth century and earlier. According to the Mexican novelist Carlos Fuentes, Machado de Assis's adherence to the early traditions of the novel made him the legitimate heir of Miguel de Cervantes. Paradoxically, Machado de Assis's devotion to past models made him an important precursor of future trends. Through self-reference, irony, the rejection of strict verisimilitude, and an emphasis on the relativity of events and actions, the Brazilian author, more than any other Latin American of his century, cleared ground for Jorge Luis Borges and his successors.

The narrator of Machado de Assis's novel *Dom Casmurro* (1899, Lord Taciturn; translated, 1953) expresses a preference for reading books with omissions because such works allow him to use his imagination to fill in what he does not find on the pages. Interestingly, the biography of Machado de Assis allows for this mode of reading. The facts of his life offer a vague outline of a genius who came out of the shadows to achieve near-universal admiration and the highest status of his country's intellectual establishment. Yet, the personal vision of the man–his motives, passions, and private engagement with the world–remains out of reach. Hence, Machado de Assis has been the subject of much speculation as scholars attempt to discover the person behind the opus.

Machado de Assis's many literary texts in virtually every genre are the most readily available documents from his life, and it is therefore understandable that biographers often have been inclined to call these texts into service in their attempts to explain the writer. However, the intersection between literature and biography is especially problematic in the case of Machado de Assis: are the literary works consonant with the writer's life, as has generally been assumed? The fact that many characters are concerned with climbing the social ladder, or that narrators tend to be skeptical and relativistic, suggests that they were designed to reflect known aspects of Machado de Assis's persona. However, it could just as easily be shown that the texts obey a law of inversion with respect to the author's life. Machado de Assis was a writer from humble origins who preferred to deal with wealthy protagonists, and a man with a model marriage who wrote constantly about adultery. Machado de Assis was a person whose social and economic ascendancy relied primarily on merit, but he preferred to portray a fictional world where fortunes are made or broken by favors, circumstance, and even blind luck. The sketchy surviving facts about Machado de Assis and the problematic relationship between his life and work make a literary biogra-

Title page for a 1938 edition of Machado de Assis's 1873
collection of short stories that includes "A parasita azul"
(The Blue Parasite), one of his first experiments with
ambiguity (Biblioteca Nacional de Chile)

phy of Machado de Assis a tenuous and problematic enterprise.

Joaquim Maria Machado de Assis was born on 21 June 1839 in Rio de Janeiro on Quinta do Livramento (a semirural property), part of a large estate referred to as Morro do Livramento (Livramento Hill). According to the certificate from his baptism, which occurred on 13 November 1839, his parents were Francisco José de Assis, "pardo" (a dark-skinned freeman), and Maria Leopoldina Machado, a Portuguese woman from the Azorian island of São Miguel. Machado de Assis's grandparents on his father's side were both freed slaves, and his parents are listed as "agregados" (dependents) of Dona Maria José de Mendonça Barroso, the Portuguese widow of a noted military figure and imperial senator, Bento Barroso Pereira. This designation indicates that Machado de Assis's parents lived on the rich woman's property and under her protection in exchange for contributing their services to her household. Professionally, Francisco José de Assis worked as a painter and installer of gold leaf, and Maria Leopoldina Machado is variously described as a laundry woman, seamstress, and embroiderer.

Mendonça Barroso was Machado de Assis's godmother, an arrangement that was a typical means of formalizing the relationship between dependents and their benefactors. Normally, this situation meant that a child such as Machado de Assis would have circulated freely between the humble abode of his parents and the opulent house of his godmother. The boy's early years, therefore, would have been characterized by intimate relationships with people of different racial and economic backgrounds. Those searching for the seeds of Machado de Assis's keen eye toward class distinctions and his ambition for social ascension, therefore, might find them in his early childhood.

Machado de Assis had a sister two years younger who died of measles at four years of age. Tuberculosis claimed the boy's mother when he was nine years old. Some of Machado de Assis's first published works were poems, characterized by a derivative and immature Romanticism, in which he mourns the death of his sister and mother. In 1854 Machado de Assis's father married Maria Inês da Silva, a laundress and candy maker who was also of mixed ancestry. Machado de Assis's relationship with his stepmother has been the subject of considerable speculation. There appears to have been little or no contact between the two during Machado de Assis's adult life. Renard Pérez gives her credit for much of the boy's early education, but R. Magalhães Júnior claims that Machado de Assis saw the woman as the usurper of his father's affections. Scholars have tended to view the distance between Machado de Assis and his stepmother as revealing Machado de Assis's ingratitude or obsessive drive to leave his origins behind, but there is little evidence to support this position. If Machado de Assis did not maintain ties with his stepmother, it could simply be because no real ties were established in the first place. By the time his father's second marriage occurred, Machado de Assis was fifteen years old and bent on launching his career as a writer. It seems plausible that he could have been striking out on his own in other ways as well, perhaps no longer even residing in the household. Different biographers provide different dates on the death of Machado de Assis's father, but the event seems to have occurred while he was still in his teens. Unlike with his mother and sister, he apparently never wrote of his father's passing.

There is very little documentary evidence about Machado de Assis's early education. He may have gained limited access to the resources of a girl's school by selling candies there with his stepmother. Additionally, according to Magalhães, he may have learned

French from the immigrant employee at a neighbor's bakery. Such details, however, merely could belong to the considerable corpus of legend surrounding the author. Artur Azevedo, a fellow writer, friend, and coworker, probably provides one of the more reliable bits of anecdotal evidence, stating that Machado de Assis only went to school long enough to learn to read and write. Remarks by Machado de Assis himself acknowledge that Padre Silveira Sarmento, who was both a priest and a teacher, served as a mentor to him in some capacity for an indefinite period of time. Although the details are sketchy, what cannot be doubted is that Machado de Assis learned much, and that he was mostly self-taught. Lacking the resources for a private library of any size, he frequented the public ones, most notably Rio de Janeiro's Gabinete Português de Leitura (Portuguese Reading Salon), where he is known to have been a member for most of his life. Machado de Assis's zeal for independent learning later became evident as he taught himself German while in his fifties and began a serious study of Greek near the end of his life.

Much of Machado de Assis's early learning occurred on the job. Stories of his earliest employment—as an altar boy, a candy vendor, a cashier, and a typesetter—are difficult to verify, although Machado de Assis did acknowledge his experience in the printing trade. At the beginning of his career as a writer, it is hard to distinguish between those instances when he was working as an unpaid volunteer and those when his efforts were remunerated. By choosing the route of the amateur collaborator, however, Machado de Assis made the best possible choice, for it put him in contact with highly influential intellectuals and initiated a chain of opportunities from which he would benefit for the rest of his life.

Early on, Machado de Assis was drawn to the Francisco de Paula Brito's bookstore, located on the Largo do Rocio. Paula Brito was actually much more than a bookseller, and his bookstore much more than a bookstore. Paula Brito, a mulatto, was sometimes a poet, a printer, a publisher, and always a socializer. According to Ubiratan Machado:

> Paula Brito, above all, was an admirable human being. A born conciliator, he had a leader's charisma and knew how to have his way even with arrogant imperial politicians. Assiduous frequenters of the bookstore and its discussion group, the Petalógica, liberals and conservatives, forgot their political intrigues and squabbles, and thought only of having a few good laughs.

The Petalógica was a society of liars, and its discussions had the sole rule that everything said had to be a prevarication. Machado de Assis became a member of the Petalógica, perused the books in the shop, and contributed to Paula Brito's periodicals. Eventually, he worked for Paula Brito as a cashier and a proofreader. Most important, however, he rubbed elbows with established writers. Primarily through the convivial space of Paula Brito's bookstore, Machado de Assis became friends with popular novelist and playwright Joaquim Manuel de Macedo; Romantic poets Casimiro de Abreu and Antônio Gonçalves Dias; Brazil's most prominent novelists, José de Alencar and Manuel Antônio de Almeida; and other notable players on the intellectual scene. The importance of these contacts for Machado de Assis's career cannot be overestimated. In Brazil extended family connections traditionally have been one of the principal means by which people establish themselves in society. Lacking significant contacts of this kind, Machado de Assis needed another kind of network, and he found exactly what he needed among the bookshelves of downtown Rio de Janeiro.

Machado de Assis's contributions to small magazines began when he was only fifteen with a sonnet praising a married woman named Petronilha that appeared in *Periódico dos Pobres* (Periodical of the Poor). A year later he began regularly publishing poems in a more prestigious journal, *Marmota Fluminense* (Marmot from Rio de Janeiro), which was published by Paula Brito. These works were laments of unrequited love, poems of mourning for departed family members, encomiums written to friends or mentors, or parodies written in ersatz archaic language. In general, they are romantic, facile, and unoriginal. There are only two remarkable things about these early poems. The first is that they represent their author's drive and sense of direction. Machado de Assis learned how to launch a career as a writer, and set about establishing himself in that career with a maturity that is not apparent in the poems themselves. The second remarkable aspect of the poems is that works of such low quality could have marked the beginning of an outstanding writing career.

From the solid roots of his association with *Marmota Fluminense,* which continued until 1861, Machado de Assis began to contribute to other periodicals such as *O Paraíba* (The Paraíba [River]), published in neighboring Petrópolis, and the *Correio Mercantil* (Mercantile Courier). In 1859 he was one of the founding organizers of *O Espelho* (The Mirror), a short-lived monthly. As these associations developed, Machado de Assis began writing less poetry and applied himself more to writing prose. His first literary essay, "O passado, o presente e o futuro da literatura" (The Past, Present, and Future of Literature), which appeared in 1858, was a powerful beginning to a distinguished career in the genre. In the essay Machado de Assis deals with literary nationalism, calling for an end to subservience to Portuguese mod-

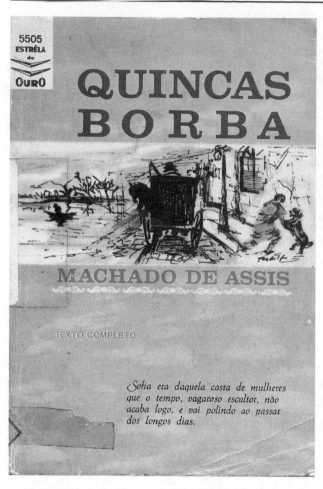

*Cover for a 1964 edition of Machado de Assis's 1891 novel
describing the plight of the material and intellectual heir of a
semidemented philosopher (Biblioteca Nacional de Chile)*

abandoned poetry, however. When he outgrew Romanticism his poetry improved, and he was later recognized for writing one of the most famous sonnets in the Portuguese language. It took years of infelicitous versifying, however, before he achieved that honor.

In 1860 Machado de Assis accepted a position on the staff of *O Diário do Rio de Janeiro* (Rio de Janeiro Daily), a liberal newspaper that had been suspended for its vigorous opposition to some of the policies of the monarch, Dom Pedro II. Machado de Assis was hired by a friend of the group at Paula Brito's store, Quintino Bocaiúva, a journalist, critic, and playwright who became a distinguished politician when Brazil became a republic. This appointment marks Machado de Assis's transition from the status of amateur contributor to professional writer. He reported on debates from the senate, wrote theater criticism, and maintained a column of commentaries on politics, culture, and current events. He remained at *O Diário do Rio de Janeiro* for seven years but continued collaborating with other organs such as *O Cruzeiro* (The Southern Cross) and *A Semana Ilustrada* (The Illustrated Weekly).

Machado de Assis's first books are almost completely ignored by modern readers. Published at obscure houses in limited quantities, they seem today like tentative experiments from an author who has not yet found his own voice. Among the early volumes are translations such as *Queda que as mulheres têm para os tolos* (1861, Destruction that Women Have for Fools), which is, according to Ubiratan Machado, a version of an essay by the Belgian author Victor Hénaux about social hypocrisy, and *Os trabalhadores do mar* (1866, The Sea Workers), an adaptation of a play by Victor Hugo. Another publication, *Higiene para uso dos mestre-escolas* (1873, Hygiene for the Use of Master-Schools), is a textbook. Machado de Assis's early dramatic efforts, *Desencantos* (1861, Disenchanteds), *Teatro* (1863, Theater), *Quase ministro* (1864, Almost Minister), and *Os deuses de casaca* (1866, The Dress-Coat Gods), reveal an ambitious young playwright enamored with the parlor-style comedies of his day, a talented writer of dialogue struggling to assemble interesting plots.

Theater was the most popular of all literary enterprises at the time, and it would be surprising if Machado de Assis had not become involved in this genre. Two of his plays, *O caminho da porta* (The Way of the Door) and *O protocolo* (Protocol), were performed at the Ateneu Dramático (Dramatic Academy) within three months of each other in 1862. When the two plays were published together in a book titled *Teatro*, correspondence between Machado de Assis and Bocaiúva was included as a preface. This material showed that Machado de Assis recognized his dramatic writing had limitations and that Bocaiúva thought the

els but simultaneously warning against superficial and false national models such as exotic Indianism. According to Pérez, the essay "shows fine analytical gifts, astounding in a young man of 19 years, especially considering the intellectual poverty that surrounded him."

More often, Machado de Assis's prose took the form of the *crônica,* a column of commentary on current issues. He wrote *crônicas* for various publications, sometimes under his own name and sometimes under pseudonyms. Analyzing a set of the twenty-year-old Machado de Assis's *crônicas,* Luís Augusto Fischer finds them to be politically courageous, rhetorically sophisticated, and culturally enlightened. While certainly not the form that made his reputation, it was the genre to which Machado de Assis most consistently dedicated himself. As he gravitated toward prose after his early attempts at poetry, Machado de Assis found a mode of writing to which his temperament seemed more suited. Thus, while his early poems are noteworthy for their poor quality, his early prose seems impressive for its strength and maturity. Machado de Assis never fully

plays were well written and valuable as literary texts but cold and lacking in dramatic power. Two other plays were performed in the next three years.

Despite his limitations as a playwright, Machado de Assis wrote some perceptive dramatic criticism and was recognized as an important man of the theater. Evidence for this claim resides in the fact that in 1864 he was invited, along with others such as Macedo and Alencar, to be a member of the Conservatório Dramático Brasileiro (Brazilian Dramatic Conservatory). In this capacity he briefly wrote recommendations for a censorship board. For many years Machado de Assis continued to write drama sporadically, and his plays continued to be performed and published. *Tu só, tu, puro amor* (You Only, You, Pure Love), a noteworthy example from 1881, celebrates the three-hundreth anniversary of Portugal's greatest poet, Camões. Machado de Assis never achieved his desires, however, either in terms of public acceptance or of his own satisfaction with his drama.

In 1863 Machado de Assis became an associate of the *Jornal das Famílias* (Family Journal), which brought yet another new direction in his literary activities. He began to publish short stories, normally under pseudonyms. This genre would prove to be one of the most fruitful of his career, being represented by more than two hundred texts.

Machado de Assis's first book of poetry, *Crisálidas* (Chrysalises), appeared in 1864, published by Livraria Garnier, the publisher of almost all of Machado de Assis's major books. The collection brought together the best of Machado de Assis's published poems, works primarily in the mode of amorous Romanticism with occasional references to current affairs within Brazil or on the international scene. Translations of some French poetry and even a few verses by friends rounded out the volume. The book was generally well received by the public.

By this time Machado de Assis had achieved some fame in Brazil. The doyens of the literary establishment began to treat him as one of their own. For example, when Alencar, the country's greatest novelist, discovered the extraordinary talent of the Bahian poet Antônio de Castro Alves, he wrote asking Machado de Assis to be Alves's guide and mentor when he came to Rio de Janeiro, confident that his endorsement would assure success in the capital. Calling Machado de Assis "the primary Brazilian critic," Alencar made this request: "Be the Virgil of this young Dante, conduct him through the forbidding paths through which one must go to disappointment, indifference, and finally, glory, which are the three grand circles of *the divine comedy* of talent."

In March 1867 Machado de Assis was named Cavaleiro da Ordem da Rosa (Cavalier of the Order of the Rose) by the Brazilian government. The honor indirectly boosted his career as a writer. The government distributed these prizes liberally to achievers, and they ultimately became little more than a stamp of approval from the government for official service. It is no accident, therefore, that in the same year that he was named Cavaleiro da Ordem da Rosa, Machado de Assis was named assistant to the director of the *Diário Oficial* (Official Diary), an authorized record of government proceedings. In Brazil, as in many other countries, such bureaucratic positions were an implicit sponsorship for writers. Placing few demands on a person's time, talent, and creative energy, the posts provided a stable income and an opportunity for continued creative endeavor in one's "spare time."

While Machado de Assis had been a professional writer for some time, he had not necessarily earned a decent living. Staff journalists were paid little, and freelancers were assumed to work for little more than the satisfaction of seeing their names in print. Royalties from publications cannot have amounted to much when there were so few readers: a printing of a thousand copies for a book was typical. With few exceptions, Brazilian writers have struggled to survive if their only source of income is their craft. Official positions, therefore, provided a sense of security that stimulated creativity. Machado de Assis left *O Diário do Rio de Janeiro* after obtaining his bureaucratic position. This decision probably was not merely a matter of needing to find time for his new duties. *O Diário do Rio de Janeiro* had been taken over by conservatives, his friend Bocaiúva was no longer on the staff, and it is possible—if not probable—that Machado de Assis had lost his enthusiasm for the job.

Having achieved a measure of financial stability, the twenty-eight-year-old Machado de Assis turned his thoughts to marriage. For some time he had been a friend of Faustino Xavier de Novais, a Portuguese poet who had become a part of Machado de Assis's group of intellectual associates. Carolina de Novais joined her brother in Rio de Janeiro, meeting Machado de Assis the year he received his prize and government post. Five years older than Machado de Assis, Carolina was literate, articulate, and elegant. According to Magalhães, she needed to care for her brother, who suffered from mental illness and was in poor condition financially. Machado de Assis regularly visited his ailing friend, and shortly after meeting Carolina the two were engaged to be married. The marriage took place on 12 November 1869, and in the meantime Carolina's brother died. It is easy to perceive Machado de Assis's choice of a white Portuguese woman as his spouse as

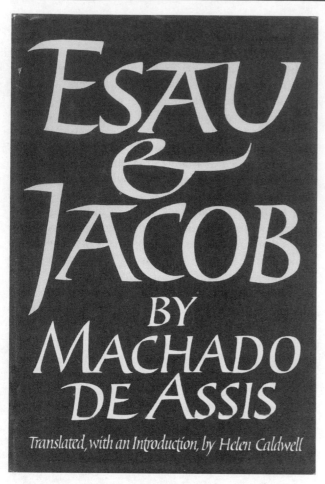

Dust jacket for the 1965 English translation of Machado de Assis's 1904 satire on the political turmoil surrounding the establishment of the republic in Rio de Janeiro in 1889 (Thomas Cooper Library, University of South Carolina)

and give a preview of the psychological insight, light-hearted satire, and keen sense of irony that are hallmarks of the author's great stories. "Linha reta e linha curva" (Straight Line and Curved Line), for example, narrates two approaches to wooing a young woman. First, the protagonist attempts to court her in a sincere, straightforward manner and is rebuffed. Then, a few years later, when the woman has completely forgotten him, he pretends that he has no interest in her and succeeds in winning her heart.

When critics gave his first collection of stories a positive reception, Machado de Assis resolved to give the novel a try. In 1872 he published *Ressurreição* (Resurrection), arriving at the literary form that is considered (perhaps along with the short story) his greatest strength. This novel Romantically treats an anguished young man who is about to marry a young widow but finally calls off the marriage out of jealousy. In the preface to the first edition, Machado de Assis quotes Shakespeare: "Our doubts are traitors, / And make us lose the good we oft might win, / By fearing to attempt." He then declares, "I did not try to write a novel of manners; rather, I aimed for the outline of a situation and the contrast of two personalities. With these simple elements I hoped to create the interest of the book." This statement may be said to provide a key for understanding Machado de Assis's fictional aesthetic throughout his career. Everything must begin with questions of the human heart, conflicts or contrasts relating to the character of the actors. Local color, customs, and landscapes are secondary. While this first novel is of minor stature compared to later works, it provides an important prelude; taking into account that its dominant theme is that of jealousy, *Ressurreição* appears today as a sort of rehearsal for *Dom Casmurro*.

In 1873 Machado de Assis published another collection of short stories, *Histórias de meia-noite* (Midnight Stories), a book dominated by a long text titled "A parasita azul" (The Blue Parasite). This story features a spoiled young man who returns to Brazil only reluctantly from France, eventually finding love and—in the process—a renewed appreciation for his homeland. It is one of Machado de Assis's first ambiguous stories, because it is not clear whether the impetuous near-suicide with which the protagonist wins the girl's heart is sincerely undertaken or feigned. Shortly after the publication of *Histórias de meia-noite,* Machado de Assis received a different government appointment for a higher salary in the higher ranks of the Secretaria de Agricultura (Secretariat of Agriculture), and he left the Diário Oficial. Three years later he was promoted to the position of section head within the department.

Relentlessly continuing to write for periodicals, including the *Revista Ocidental* (Occidental Magazine) in

evidence of his drive for social ascent, although it was hardly unique behavior among Brazilians. Furthermore, Machado de Assis's mother was Portuguese, and from a psychological standpoint it is perhaps unsurprising that he would choose a similar wife. Machado de Assis's marriage is now celebrated in Brazil as a perfect example of a couple's mutual devotion.

Machado de Assis's marriage coincided with the publication of his second book of poetry, *Falenas* (1870, Nocturnal Butterflies), which features poetry in the Romantic vein, expressing an interest in nature and, in a series of "Chinese" poems, showing increased exoticism. The collection is generally considered insignificant. That year Machado de Assis also published his first collection of short stories, *Contos fluminenses* (Short Stories from Rio de Janeiro). Although they are also written in the Romantic mode and hardly comparable to the stories of the more mature Machado de Assis, the texts of *Contos fluminenses* show a vigorous, lively style

Lisbon, Machado de Assis produced *A mão e a luva* (translated as *The Hand and the Glove,* 1970), his second novel, in 1874. This narrative first appeared in installments in the magazine *O Globo* (The Globe). The novel is about a poor but ambitious young woman whose desires to improve her station in life are aided by her wealthy godmother. She is courted by two young men: one is a thoroughly romantic character, sensitive, but poor and moody, and the other confident, better situated, and similarly ambitious. She chooses the more financially promising of the two.

In 1875 Machado de Assis published another book of poetry, *Americanas* (Female Americans), which is a curiosity in that it introduced in many of its pieces the very theme that Machado de Assis had warned Brazilian writers against abusing in their efforts to discover national qualities–the Indian. But Machado de Assis's efforts go beyond mere exoticism, exploring psychology and social dynamics under the guise of Indianism. An interesting example is "Niâni," in which the protagonist is betrayed by her husband with another woman. What disturbs Niâni most about her husband's infidelity is the fact that he has chosen to leave her for a woman of a lower social ranking in the tribe.

Machado de Assis's third novel, *Helena* (1876; translated, 1984), also first appeared in installments in the popular press. Still working within the Romantic mode, Machado de Assis explores the theme of forbidden love, flirting with the notion of incest. Helena is supposedly the half sister of Estácio; she is brought into the family after the father dies and leaves word that he had a daughter by another woman. In spite of his strong desire to do what is right, Estácio cannot help falling in love with this mysterious young woman. It is perhaps the most Romantic of all of Machado de Assis's novels, for it is the only one in which the protagonist dies because of emotional turmoil. The next novel, *Iaiá Garcia* (1878; translated as *Yayá Garcia,* 1976), follows the same basic pattern as earlier efforts. The narrative presents a poor young woman who through friendly and quasi-familial relationships, good character, and personal attractiveness assures herself a better position in life through marriage.

The trajectory of Machado de Assis's career to 1878 might thus far seem to have been one of uninterrupted achievement and ascension. A crisis at the end of 1878, however, shows that such a view is probably far too simple. That year Machado de Assis was diagnosed with epilepsy, and for the first time in his life he was required to take a vacation for reasons of health. Machado de Assis and Carolina spent three months in the city of Nova Friburgo; Carolina, who came to Brazil to nurse her brother, now had to assume that role for her husband. For the first time in the historical

record Machado de Assis's infirmity becomes obvious, but it can hardly have been the first time symptoms manifested themselves. There is considerable speculation about when the seizures could have begun, including whether Machado de Assis knew he was epileptic before he married, and–if so–whether he revealed this bitter news to Carolina or concealed it from her. Machado de Assis also had other health problems around this time: a serious intestinal infection and an attack of amaurosis that threatened to leave him blind and from which he never fully recovered. But the great challenge of his life was epilepsy.

Additionally, some of Machado de Assis's associates referred to his problem with stuttering, and there is speculation about when this speech impediment may have emerged. Because stuttering so often has its onset in early childhood, some imagine that Machado de Assis must have struggled with the problem for most of his life. However, this theory seems inconsistent with the image of the youthful aspirant: the convivial young man who seems to have made friends easily, and the active participant in Paula Brito's Petalógica and other intellectual discussions. It seems more reasonable to suppose that the problem developed later in life as a result of the epileptic seizures, emerging after his many social ties were already established.

Although not exactly an illness, there was yet another physical condition that tempered Machado de Assis's many successes: he and his wife were never able to have children. Biographers have tried to show the writer's disappointment at this absence by quoting from his last novel, *Memorial de Aires* (1908; translated as *Counselor Ayres' Memorial,* 1972), where the narrator refers to the great sadness of the elderly Aguiar couple at their lack of children. Indeed, here and in other late works there are moments in which characters express an urgent desire for offspring. However, the cynical protagonist of *Memórias póstumas de Brás Cubas* (1881, The Posthumous Memoirs of Brás Cuba; translated as *Epitaph of a Small Winner,* 1952) claims as his greatest achievement the lack of progeny: "I did not have children; I did not transfer to any creature the legacy of our misery." On the issue of children the fictional record is contradictory, but the fiction is a highly unreliable indicator of the author's true feelings, regardless.

A simplistic biography might claim that the Machado de Assis who returned to Rio de Janeiro from Nova Friburgo after the period of recuperation was a different writer than the one who departed. It is probably not a good idea to try to establish such a definite watershed, however, especially considering the brilliance and daring demonstrated in short stories and essays before the recuperative vacation. But it is accu-

Drawing of Machado de Assis (from Ronald de Carvalho,
Pequena historia da literatura Brasileira, *1937;*
Thomas Cooper Library, University
of South Carolina)

rate to say that it was a different *novelist* who made his way back to the capital. Perhaps the struggle with serious illness had altered Machado de Assis's worldview. Perhaps it had helped him decide that life was too short to write for other peoples' tastes. Whatever the case, when Machado de Assis went back to work, he began a novel radically different from its predecessors. The previous books established Machado de Assis's name as a respected novelist. They had been successful with the public, but they were rather cautious efforts, pleasant and competent without creating any sparks.

Memórias póstumas de Brás Cubas began appearing in installments in 1880 and was published as a book the following year. With the early installments it became clear that Machado de Assis was finished with his previous models of sentimental Romanticism and that he had opted instead for mordant irony. The unobtrusive third-person narrators of the past were replaced by a brash and impudent first-person narrator, interacting aggressively with the reader: "If [this book] pleases you, fine reader, I'll consider myself well paid for my troubles; if it doesn't please you, I'll pay you with poke, and that's all there is to it." Overshadowing even these significant innovations was the book's daring conception. The book's idea is not that it consists of the posthu-

mously *published* memoirs of someone now deceased but indeed of the posthumously *written* memoirs of a man who has already arrived on the other side. This deceased narrator writes the following dedication for his book: "To the worm that first chewed the cold flesh of my cadaver, I dedicate with fond memories these posthumous memoirs."

Memórias póstumas de Brás Cubas generally describes the wasted life of a spoiled brat. Cubas describes the privileged childhood wherein he learned to abuse his slave, and he also describes his love affair with a Spanish flirt that costs much and ends badly, his elite education that is never used for anything productive, his aborted political career, and his on-again, off-again love affair with a politician's wife. The novel unfolds in a brilliant cascade of associative digressions. On the first page the narrator exposes his models for this practice: "It is, in truth, a diffuse work, in which I, Brás Cubas, although I adopted the free form of a Sterne or of a Xavier de Maistre, you could say that I also stuck in some pessimistic scratchings." *Memórias póstumas de Brás Cubas* reveals itself as a tour de force within the tradition of freely associative works. It uses the repetition of minute details to suggest a multitude of figurative associations among disparate motifs, and it employs an elaborate system of formal concatenations to bind short chapters together, even when they have little logical connection. The chapter "O delírio," which narrates the protagonist's last hallucination before dying, is an astounding piece of Surrealism *avant la lettre* (before the term existed).

Machado de Assis could see that Romanticism, even in Brazil, was past its prime; yet, he had problems with the values of realism or naturalism, which were coming into vogue in his country. In well-known essays such as "A nova geração" (1879, The New Generation), and in a critique of novels by the popular Portuguese novelist Eça de Queirós, he had condemned realism and naturalism for their crass objectivity and their excessive accumulation of detail, claiming that such tendencies were aesthetically ineffective. He also seems to have been bothered by the servile importation of whatever movement was carrying the day in France. With *Memórias póstumas de Brás Cubas,* Machado de Assis found an alternative by returning to narrative models from the eighteenth century, especially those involving a meandering, freely associative style.

One important aspect of Machado de Assis's refusal to adhere to the typical values of realism was the creation of problematic voices. This characteristic is especially apparant in *Memórias póstumas de Brás Cubas,* in which the narrator claims an extra measure of reliability: by virtue of being beyond the vicissitudes of life, he says he is able to view things dispassionately. However, it is hard not to think of the term "sour grapes" when reading his account of events. The narrator has achieved virtually nothing despite having had all the advantages that money can buy. But he justifies his uselessness with the claim that life is misery anyway, and all our efforts to achieve something of substance are mere vanity. The suggestion of vested interest contradicts the claim of disinterested veracity.

The foundation of Cubas's negative characterization of the world is expressed in "O delírio," one of the most famous chapters in Brazilian literature. But Cubas's philosophy is undermined by the fact that it is based on a delirium, and he is quick to inform us that his delirium belongs to the domain of mental incompetence. Later in the book there is an extended philosophical discussion between the narrator and a philosopher named Quincas Borba. Borba offers a view of the world that is in many ways consistent with the narrator's ideas about the vanity of life. The problem is that the philosopher is found in the end to be insane. By debilitating the judgment of the narrator and his philosophical ally, Machado de Assis creates an aesthetic that is squarely at odds with that of his fellow novelists. While most of his contemporaries were intent on creating fictions that spelled things out for the reader, creating clear pictures and showing solutions to problems, Machado de Assis was raising questions and posing problems through narrative voices that sowed seeds of doubt. The realists and naturalists generally wrote for relatively passive readers, but this type of reader was hardly what Machado de Assis had in mind.

Machado de Assis's readers, including his close friends, apparently had a hard time knowing what to make of *Memórias póstumas de Brás Cubas*. Capistrano de Abreu went so far as to ask if it was a novel at all. Noteworthy is Machado de Assis's response to that question, which appears in the preface to the third edition of the novel. Rather than directly answering the question, Machado de Assis quotes his narrator, saying that it would seem to be a novel to some but not to others. Responding to remarks about the book's pessimism, Machado de Assis again quotes his narrator, who characterizes his own account as pessimistic. Machado de Assis ends by saying "I will not say more, so as not to become involved in the analysis of a dead man, who painted himself and others in the way that to him seemed most fitting." Machado de Assis seems to have tried to draw an important line here. He wanted his readers not to look to him, the author, for the "real meaning" of the book. The book has a narrator, and the opinions expressed in the book are his. As that narrator himself says on the opening page, "The work in itself is everything." From this time forward, one of Machado de Assis's main enterprises was the positing

of controversial positions by problematic voices—for this reason, one of the primary dangers of Machadian criticism resides in the temptation to interpret positions found within fiction as the author's.

In 1882 Machado de Assis published another book of short stories titled *Papéis avulsos* (Detached Papers). In this volume the tales that are now considered true classics begin to appear. "O alienista" (translated as "The Psychiatrist," 1963), for example, is a long, highly allegorical story about the use and abuse of power and about what constitutes mental aberration. "Teoria do medalhão" (Theory of the Stuffed Shirt) is a study in irony in which a father counsels his son by upholding superficiality as a means of doing well in society. "O espelho" (The Mirror), one of Machado de Assis's most important philosophical stories, features a critique of both rationalism and empiricism. It also anticipates phenomenological models of thought through a character's story about his "exterior soul" and his "interior soul." Although it is generally less appreciated, another important story in the collection, "A chinela turca" (The Turkish Slipper), shows through a clever narrative trick "that the best drama is in the spectator and not on stage." First published in 1875, the tale illustrates how early Machado de Assis was at work on a more modern and balanced aesthetic model than his realistic or naturalistic contemporaries, one that gave considerable power to the reader in the literary dynamic.

Another collection of Machado de Assis's best stories, *Histórias sem data* (Stories Undated), appeared in 1884. One of these stories, "A igreja do diabo" (translated as "The Devil's Church," 1977), is a satire that can be read as Machado de Assis's critique of positivism and other excessively systematic projects. Meanwhile, "Cantiga de esponsais" (Espousal Song) is an ironic tale about a man who knocks himself out trying to compose the right musical phrase and a woman who hums the phrase he has been seeking without even thinking about it. The story may be seen as illustrating a Machadian theory of creative production. Meanwhile, "Noite de almirante" (Admiral's Night) is a song of praise for the human capacity for finding some solace in disappointment or failure. It relates the story of a young sailor whose long-anticipated night of passion with his girlfriend back home is frustrated when he learns that she has another lover. Despite his disappointment, when the young man rejoins his fellow sailors the next morning, he achieves no small satisfaction in allowing his friends to think he has been making love all night. Another story, "Singular ocorrência" (Singular Occurrence), shows Machado de Assis's perception of the human soul as essentially inconsistent. The tale involves a woman who is devoted to the man in her life, and entirely faithful to him—except for a single time.

Machado de Assis and Carolina made a series of moves over the years, each time to a nicer house in a nicer neighborhood, but around 1884 they moved to a home on Rua Cosme Velho that they would occupy for the rest of their lives. The house was a beautiful and spacious two-story abode located in what was one of the most affluent sections of Rio de Janeiro. Here Machado de Assis fell into a quiet and productive routine. He arose early to write, then he prepared for work and rode the mule-drawn streetcar to his downtown office while reading the newspaper. At the office he supervised a staff, reviewed matters of policy, and wrote memoranda. An example of his bureaucratic writing appears in *Terras: compilação para estudo* (1886, Lands: A Compilation for Study). On his way home from work, Machado de Assis stopped by the most popular bookstore in town, Livraria Garnier, where old friends greeted him, aspiring writers vied for his attention, and readers requested his autograph. Arriving home, he was greeted by Carolina and his dog, a bichon frise named Graziela. Evenings were devoted to writing, visits with friends where cards or chess were preferred entertainments, or the occasional public outing. Machado de Assis was especially fond of attending recitals at the Clube Beethoven, where he was a member, serving as librarian.

Machado de Assis's next novel, *Quincas Borba* (translated as *Philosopher or Dog?*, 1954), appeared in installments between 1886 and 1891 and was published in book form in 1891. Technically, the novel is a step backward from *Memórias póstumas de Brás Cubas*. Although Machado de Assis occasionally uses the first-person pronoun in the book, the narrator is perhaps most accurately defined as a third-person narrator because he is not involved in the plot and is generally unobtrusive. It can hardly be said, though, that in *Quincas Borba* Machado de Assis returns to the cautious lines of the Romantic novels. The novel carries forward several features of *Memórias póstumas de Brás Cubas*: a bold, digressive style of storytelling with an ironic tone, full of dark humor and keen to the contradictions and contingencies of life, and a skillful development of figurative language to provide semantic richness to the narrative.

Quincas Borba features the semidemented philosopher from the previous novel, who has now inherited a fortune and moved to the provincial town of Barbacena, Minas Gerais. There he acquires a dog, names the mutt after himself, becomes engaged to be married to a woman who dies before the wedding, and befriends the brother of his fiancée, a schoolteacher named Rubião. Rubião inherits the fortune of Quincas

Borba, along with the philosopher's dog, and moves to Rio de Janeiro. Another thing Rubião inherits, as it turns out, is the fate of demonstrating Borba's philosophy that individuals perish like bubbles in a broth, but all contribute to the continuation of life. According to Borba, one person's fall often leads to another's rise, but all that really matters is the forward march of the whole. Borba illustrates this contingency with the example of two hungry tribes at war over a field of potatoes: it doesn't matter who wins the war, only that someone does and that the potatoes go to good use. "To the victor, the potatoes" is Borba's conclusion. (With this ironic twist on a lapidary phrase, Machado de Assis anticipates the "anthropophagy" aesthetics of the Brazilian modernists of 1920, who would champion the roguish appropriation of consecrated models for unintended purposes.) Once Quincas Borba's philosophy is established, the main story of the novel becomes the demonstration of the relativity of rising and falling fortunes. Once he arrives in Rio de Janeiro, the heir of Borba's fortune is surrounded by friendly opportunists. By the end of the novel the "potatoes" are theirs and no longer his. One of the female characters, Sofia, who allows her husband to use her beauty to get close to Rubião, is considered one of Machado de Assis's most successful creations.

Quincas Borba may have taken so long to complete because other things in Machado de Assis's life were so demanding of his time and attention. At this time there was a fervent struggle in Brazilian politics. Liberals and conservatives were at odds over two main points: the institution of slavery and the monarchy. Because Dom Pedro II supported slaveholding landowners, the two issues were closely linked, and it is no accident that after slavery was abolished in 1888 it took only a year for the proclamation of a republic in Brazil. Unlike Castro Alves, Machado de Assis did not use the pen to advocate abolition, but it is highly unlikely that he was secluded in an ivory tower, as some have suggested; he could hardly have been uninvolved in the political turmoil of these years. Open participation in the abolitionist cause would have been contrary to Machado de Assis's quiet temperament, and as an appointee of the imperial government he would have felt strongly constrained against such action. According to Ubiratan Machado, Machado de Assis supported the cause of abolition in his own way. His office in the Agriculture Department was charged with arbitration of disputes pursuant to the Law of the Free Womb, established in 1871, which technically freed the newly born children of slaves. Questions regarding registration of children, their property, education, and care as minors were resolved by his office. As section head, Machado de Assis supplied information and wrote briefs that had direct bearing on ministerial decisions. As Ubiratan Machado explains, he "interpreted the regulations governing the registration of the exempted slaves, holding rigorously to the letter of the law. In this manner, he almost always opposed the interest of the landholders, who were the Empire's most powerful class."

In the midst of this political turmoil Machado de Assis still had time to assemble and publish some of his earlier stories. One of Machado de Assis's best collections of short stories appeared in 1896 under the title *Várias histórias* (Various Stories). One of the outstanding tales in the collection, "A cartomante" (The Fortune Teller), shows how desire breeds gullibility in spite of one's conscious resistance. "A causa secreta" (The Secret Heart) examines a man who enjoys suffering through the eyes of a man who enjoys watching people who enjoy suffering. Another noteworthy story, "Uns braços" (A Woman's Arms), explores the mysterious power of suggestion that takes hold when a woman feels herself being watched and admired.

Despite his successes, Machado de Assis was not without his detractors. A journalist named Diocleciano Mártir included him on a list of public officials who maintained their offices at high wages without sincere allegiance to the government or its policies. On the literary front, Sylvio Romero, a poet to whom Machado de Assis had been less than generous in a review, launched a series of attacks against his literary production. The target of these affronts did not say a word in his own defense. He didn't have to. Loyal friends, such as Lúcio de Mendonça in the former case and Lafaiete Rodrigues Pereira in the latter, went to Machado de Assis's aid, attacking their adversaries with an aggression of which Machado de Assis seems to have been incapable.

The formation of the Academia Brasileira de Letras (Brazilian Academy of Letters) began after the proclamation of the republic in 1889. The best writers in Brazil were brought together by José Veríssimo to contribute to *Revista Brasileira* (Brasilian Magazine). Within this group, there was a movement, driven principally by Lúcio de Mendonça, to establish an academy along the lines of the famous Academie Française (French Academy). When the academy was officially constituted in 1897, Machado de Assis was elected as its first president, and he offered the inaugural address at its opening session. Today a statue of the seated Machado de Assis greets visitors at the headquarters of the Brazilian academy of Letters in downtown Rio de Janeiro.

Machado de Assis's bureaucratic career was difficult under Brazil's new republic. In 1893 a reorganization at the ministerial level required a new appointment for Machado de Assis as general director of transporta-

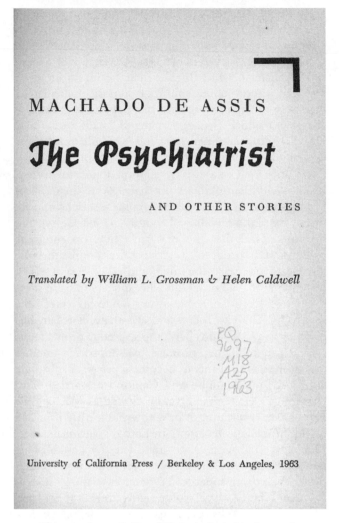

MACHADO DE ASSIS

The Psychiatrist

AND OTHER STORIES

Translated by William L. Grossman & Helen Caldwell

University of California Press / Berkeley & Los Angeles, 1963

Title page for a collection of Machado de Assis's short stories translated into English (Thomas Cooper Library, University of South Carolina)

tion within the Secretariate of Industry, Transportation, and Public Works. In 1897 a consolidation of offices sent Machado de Assis into involuntary retirement for approximately a year until he was called back into service, first as the secretary for the minister of transportation, and later as the general director of accounting for the Ministry, the post that Machado de Assis held until his death.

Machado de Assis used the forced furlough in 1897 to work on *Dom Casmurro*, which was published at the end of 1899 but did not reach bookstores until 1900. If *Memórias póstumas de Brás Cubas* is Machado de Assis's most virtuosic novel, *Dom Casmurro* is his most profound. Although the title of his masterpiece is not usually translated in foreign versions, it means something like "Lord Taciturn." The narrative is told by a digressive and eccentric first-person narrator. Bento Santiago has grown old and now finds himself alone and uneasy. He vows to recover the happier moments of his youth by writing a memoir. The narrator thus recounts the adolescent romance he experienced with Capitu, the girl next door. *Dom Casmurro* was a best-seller in Brazil, which means that the first printing of two thousand copies sold out almost immediately. Probably the main reason for this popularity is the lyricism with which Santiago remembers his early love. The Luso-Brazilian penchant for "saudade" (nostalgia) is certainly indulged to the maximum in this novel.

But *Dom Casmurro* is much more than a love story. Capitu and Bentinho (as the narrator is then called) promise to marry but must overcome a serious impediment. Bentinho's widowed mother, Dona Glória, has promised God that she will have her son enter the priesthood. In order to circumvent the promise the adolescent lovers seek the intervention of José Dias, a dependent of the household who appears to have some influence. Eventually, however, Bentinho enters the seminary. There, a friend and classmate, Escobar, hits upon a way around Bentinho's predicament: Dona Glória can fulfill her promise by sponsoring another young man who wants to become a priest. A substitute is found, and Bentinho and Capitu are married. This portion of *Dom Casmurro* can be viewed as Machado de Assis's demonstration of how to write a truly Brazilian novel. In the famous essay "Instinto de Nacionalidade," Machado de Assis had appealed for establishing national character in terms of an "intimate feeling" rather than using superficial references to things such as flora and fauna, local color, and ethnic types. Here Machado de Assis provides a story featuring folk Catholicism (the promise to God), the exercise of influence through favors (José Dias), and the "jeitinho" or clever maneuver (the substitute in the priesthood), all of which are considered typical aspects of the Brazilian personality.

The sweetness with which *Dom Casmurro* begins turns into bitterness; after several years of marriage and the birth of a son, Bentinho becomes convinced that Capitu has been unfaithful to him with his friend from the seminary, Escobar, and that Ezequiel, their son, is really Escobar's and not his. Bentinho then forces a separation. Machado de Assis's treatment of the theme of adultery, a favorite of nineteenth-century realists, may be viewed as his answer to the great Portuguese novelist Eça de Queirós. In 1878 Machado de Assis had written a scathing review of Eça de Queirós's *O primo Basílio* in which he argued that too much of what happens in the plot depends upon circumstances rather than upon the personality or moral fiber of the characters. Machado de Assis demanded, "Give me moral characters," by which he probably meant those who act according to well-established character traits. *Dom*

Casmurro is thoroughly consistent with Machado de Assis's position in the review. Capitu shows herself to be manipulative and driven to achieve whatever she desires. Likewise, Bentinho's character is typical of the accuser: insecure, suspicious, and patriarchal.

Dom Casmurro answers Eça de Queirós in another way, as well. Machado de Assis's critique of the foremost Portuguese novelist was in many ways a critique of an entire school, realism (including naturalism, which in Machado de Assis's mind was not clearly delineated from realism). The main emphasis of that criticism was that the realists insisted on spelling everything out—thoroughly, obsessively, ad infinitum. Machado de Assis abhorred such accumulation of detail. Instead, *Dom Casmurro* is by the narrator's own admission a "livro omisso," a book with gaps. Sounding rather prudish, Machado de Assis had criticized Eça de Queirós for revealing all the sordid details of his characters' adulterous encounters. These details are missing from *Dom Casmurro*, but their absence is not just a matter of "good taste" or narrative propriety. Machado de Assis is treading on much more revolutionary ground. *Dom Casmurro* is probably the first novel about adultery where the facts of the matter are dubious. The narrator, a lawyer by trade, carefully presents a case against his wife based on circumstantial evidence. But he also includes perspectives that do not seem consistent with his argument. Ever inclined to self-reference, he admits his account has lacunae that the reader can independently fill. In other words, the narrator openly confesses his limitations, laying the groundwork for a reading of the facts that runs contrary to his own version. Hence, with *Dom Casmurro*, Machado de Assis instills a story of domestic failure with a philosophical questioning that would later be taken up by writers such as Miguel de Unamuno and Borges. By shifting power from the writer to the reader, Machado de Assis produced a novel far different from those of his contemporaries and far ahead of his time.

The history of the reception of *Dom Casmurro* has involved diametrically opposed ways of reading the novel. Published reviews and analyses show that for generations readers accepted the narrator's perspective at face value, assuming that Capitu was guilty of adultery. The tide of opinion began to change in 1960, with Helen Caldwell's *The Brazilian Othello of Machado de Assis*, in which she claims that Capitu is the innocent victim of her husband's jealous and domineering mind. That view gained favor, particularly since Roberto Schwarz's "discovery" of Caldwell in *Duas meninas* (1997, Two Girls), and it seems to have become the prevailing opinion in Brazil. Both the reading of Capitu as adulterer and the reading of her as innocent victim, however, are partial and unbalanced. The more critically acute reading is that Machado de Assis wrote an ambiguous novel in which the truth of Santiago's claims against his wife cannot possibly be determined with any degree of confidence. In 1958 there was, in fact, an early assertion along these lines by Aloysio de Carvalho Filho that was apparently forgotten in Brazil. Since then, most of the proponents of this reading have been non-Brazilians (especially Keith Ellis, Arthur Brackel, Abel Barros Baptista, Paul B. Dixon, and Earl E. Fitz).

The year that *Dom Casmurro* appeared, Machado de Assis also published *Páginas recolhidas,* a combination of dramatic works, journalistic texts, and short stories. "O caso da vara" (Case of the Switch), a short story about how persecution begets persecution, is one of the few texts in which Machado de Assis makes mention of how race can be a factor in society's pecking order. Also, "Missa do galo" (Midnight Mass) is another classic case of ambiguity, where the narrator puzzles over the meaning of a midnight interview with his landlady.

In 1901 Machado de Assis published *Poesias completas* (Complete Poetry), which reprinted his early books of poetry and included a new collection of poems titled *Occidentaes* (Occidentals). In contrast to the tentative romantic verses of his youth, the poems of *Occidentaes* are grave and philosophical. Almost all of his poems that are now considered significant come from this collection. The sonnet "Círculo vicioso" (Vicious Circle) is notable for providing a vision of a world ruled by emptiness and desire. In the poem the lightning bug envies the star, the star envies the moon, and the moon envies the sun. But the sun, tired of the weight of its own glory, wishes it could be a mere lightning bug. Another oft-cited poem, "Uma criatura" (A Creature), shows the place of death and suffering in the forward march of life: "I know of a creature ancient and formidable, / Which devours its own limbs and entrails / With the urgency of unsatiable hunger, / . . .You will say that it is Death; I will say that it is Life." Machado de Assis's views on the ineffability of happiness are displayed in "A mosca azul" (The Blue Fly), a narrative poem set in the exotic world of mystical India. The text presents a pariah who finds beatitude in a vision of the sparkling wings of a fly. When he tries to capture the vision and analyze its source, however, he causes it to crumble before his eyes.

In 1904 Machado de Assis and Carolina took another recuperative vacation in Nova Friburgo. This time, however, Carolina was the ailing one, and there was no recovery from her intestinal cancer. She died in the couple's home on 20 October 1904. The gulf between Machado de Assis's intimate life and his texts closes somewhat when it comes to Carolina's death. Normally, even Machado de Assis's correspondence reveals little of his private self, but at this time letters to

Dust jacket for a 1977 collection of Machado de Assis's short stories translated into English (Thomas Cooper Library, University of South Carolina)

Joaquim Nabuco are different. In one he confesses, "As I myself am nearing the state of eternal rest, I will not have to spend much time remembering her. I shall go to see her. She awaits me." This statement, suggesting a belief in life after death, provides a glimpse of Machado de Assis that is different from the cynical and pessimistic narrators with whom he has been so often confused. Perhaps Machado de Assis's most confessional text is "A Carolina" (1906, To Carolina), a sonnet in which he speaks to his departed companion upon visiting her grave, recalling how her companionship made life not just bearable but even joyful. In the poem he claims that there can be no thoughts of continued earthly life now that she is gone. The sonnet is important not simply for its biographical significance but as a poem as well. It is a case in which the poem immortalized the biographical context, and the biographical context immortalized the poem. If Portuguese speakers know nothing else about Machado de Assis, they probably know of his marriage and "A Carolina."

Machado de Assis's eighth novel, *Esaú e Jacó* (translated as *Esau and Jacob,* 1965), appeared in 1904.

The narrator is Aires, a retired diplomat and aloof observer of humankind with all its foibles. The narrative perspective of the novel is curious, for the preface clearly states that the narrator is Aires, who will be a marginal participant in the action of the novel, but the narrative voice is more like that of an omniscient third-person narrator. In a sense, *Esaú e Jacó* is the author's most historically engaged novel, for it is set in Rio de Janeiro during and after the proclamation of the republic. It is an acutely satirical examination of people who during the governmental transition balance their political allegiances with their desires for insurance of continued prosperity whatever new form of government may appear. A famous anecdote from the novel is the shopkeeper Custódio, who debates about whether to change his existing sign from "Pastry Shop of the Empire" to "Pastry Shop of the Republic," and who, in view of the uncertainty of the whole situation, decides on "Pastry Shop of the Government." In another sense *Esaú e Jacó* is perhaps Machado de Assis's most abstract and formalistic novel, for it seems to experiment with the notion of a crystallized pattern revolving around a subject's mitigation of polar opposites, and the plot provides many conflicts that materialize the pattern, such as republic versus empire, orthodox versus unorthodox religion, and São Paulo versus Rio de Janeiro. The primary incarnation of this structure is the pair of twins Pedro and Paulo, one a republican and the other a monarchist, who fall in love with the same woman, Flora, who is never able to choose between the competing siblings.

In 1906 Machado de Assis published *Relíquias de casa velha* (Relics from an Old House), a collection of texts in a variety of genres. The book features Machado de Assis's immortal sonnet, "A Carolina." Beyond this poem the most notable selections from the book are its short stories. "Evolution" (translated as "Evolution," 1977), which first appeared in the popular press many years earlier, is about the development of Brazil's rail system and the development of one man's arsenal of socially impressive statements. It shows how a metaphor about the trains in Brazil is uttered by the narrator to another man but "evolves" or is gradually appropriated until the man claims the phrase as his own. A story about the strong but ambivalent bonds between two young men, "Pílades e Orestes" (translated as "Pylades and Orestes," 1977), has recently received attention for its suggestion of a homosexual relationship. Perhaps the greatest story of the collection is "Pai contra mãe" (Father against Mother), a gripping tale set during the time of slavery about a destitute young father who, in order to avoid giving up his child for adoption, must hunt down a pregnant escaped slave and collect her bounty. The tale clearly shows Machado de Assis's avoidance of moral simplism—acts in his world are hardly ever just good or bad.

Machado de Assis's final novel, *Memorial de Aires,* was published in 1908. Here Machado de Assis returns to the narrator of *Esaú e Jacó,* Aires, whose perspective is this time given in first person. The book has a tranquil, nostalgic, and gently ironic tone. Aires likes to observe and comment on the emotional ups and downs of his friends but seems unwilling at his age to become emotionally involved himself. The primary setting of the novel is the household of the Aguiars, an old and happily married, but childless couple. They pour all their parental affection upon their young friend Fidélia, a recently widowed woman. Tristão, the Aguiars' godchild, arrives from Portugal, and Aires begins to take special interest in the young man's interactions with Fidélia. The romance that develops delights the Aguiar couple until they realize that Tristão's budding political career is going to take him back to Portugal and that, by marrying Fidélia, he will take the closest thing they have to a daughter away from them. The interesting and unanswerable question for Aires is whether Tristão knew all the while that he would be returning to Portugal and hid that information, or whether it was an unexpected development, as he claims. Machado de Assis is ambiguous to the end, but his enigmas no longer have the urgency of what was seen in *Dom Casmurro.*

By the time the novel came out Machado de Assis had already retired from his ministerial position because of health issues. His epilepsy was advancing, his vision deteriorating, and his intestinal problems had returned. Additionally, seizures had caused a cancerous condition on his tongue that prevented him from eating solid food. In his last days Machado de Assis received visits from his closest friends, including many of Brazil's most important writers. Machado de Assis's refusal of last rites from the Catholic Church suggests that while he may have believed in God and the afterlife, he perhaps had little faith in organized religion. In the early morning of 29 September 1908 Machado de Assis died at home. His wake and funeral were attended by crowds of admirers, including many of Brazil's most prominent citizens. In the name of the Academy of Letters, Rui Barbosa, Brazil's foremost statesman, offered the funeral oration.

Bibliographies:

J. Galante de Sousa, *Bibliografia de Machado de Assis* (Rio de Janeiro: Ministério de Educação e Cultura/Instituto Nacional do Livro, 1955);

de Sousa, *Fontes para o estudo de Machado de Assis* (Rio de Janeiro: Ministério de Educação e Cultura/Instituto Nacional do Livro, 1958);

Alberto I. Bagby Jr., "Eighteen Years of Machado de Assis: A Critical Annotated Bibliography for 1956–74," *Hispania,* 58 (1975): 649–683;

Paul B. Dixon, "Fontes sobre o ensaio, a crônica e a correspondência: uma bibliografia anotada," *Espelho,* 2 (1996): 65–88.

References:

Abel Barros Baptista, *Em nome do apelo do nome: duas interrogações sobre Machado de Assis* (Lisbon: Litoral, 1991);

Baptista, "O legado Caldwell ou o paradigma do pé atrás," *Santa Barbara Portuguese Studies,* 1 (1994): 145–177;

Arthur Brackel, "Ambiguity and Enigma in Art: The Case of Henry James and Machado de Assis," *Comparative Literature Studies,* 19, no. 4 (1982): 442–449;

Helen Caldwell, *The Brazilian Othello of Machado de Assis: A Study of Dom Casmurro* (Berkeley: University of California Press, 1960);

Aloysio de Carvalho Filho, *O processo penal de Capitu* (Salvador: Regina, 1958);

Paul B. Dixon, *Reversible Readings: Ambiguity in Four Modern Latin American Novels* (University: University of Alabama Press, 1985);

Keith Ellis, "Technique and Ambiguity in 'Dom Casmurro,'" *Hispania,* 45 (1965): 76–81;

Luís Augusto Fischer, "Crônica dos vinte anos: estudo sobre as crônicas editadas em 1859," *Espelho,* 2 (1996): 5–37;

Earl E. Fitz, *Machado de Assis* (Boston: Twayne, 1989);

Carlos Fuentes, "O milagre de Machado de Assis," *Mais!: Folha de S. Paulo,* 1 October 2000, pp. 4–11;

Ubiratan Machado, "O enigma do Cosme Velho," in *Machado de Assis: uma revisão,* edited by Antônio Carlos Secchin and others (Rio de Janeiro: InFólio, 1998), pp. 17–30;

R. Magalhães Júnior, *Vida e obra de Machado de Assis,* 4 volumes (Rio de Janeiro: Civilização Brasileira/Instituto Nacional do Livro, Ministério de Educação e Cultura, 1981);

Roberto Schwarz, *Duas meninas* (São Paulo: Companhia das Letras, 1997);

José Luiz Foureaux de Souza Júnior, "O espelhamento do silêncio: literatura e homoerotismo num conto de Machado de Assis," *Espelho,* 5 (1999): 53–75.

Plínio Marcos
(Plínio Marcos de Barros)
(29 September 1935 – 19 November 1999)

Robert N. Anderson
University of North Carolina at Chapel Hill

BOOKS: *A navalha na carne* (São Paulo: Senzala, 1968);

Quando as máquinas param (São Paulo: Obelisco, 1971);

Histórias das quebradas do mundaréu (Rio de Janeiro: Nórdica, 1973);

O abajur lilás: peça em dois atos (São Paulo: Brasiliense, 1975);

Uma reportagem maldita–Querô: romance (São Paulo: Símbolo, 1976);

Barrela: peça em 1 ato (São Paulo: Símbolo, 1976);

Inútil canto e inútil pranto pelos anjos caídos (São Paulo: Lampião, 1977);

Dois perdidos numa noite suja: peça em dois atos (São Paulo: Global, 1978); translated by Elzbieta Szoka and Joe W. Bratcher III as *Two Lost in a Filthy Night,* in *3 Contemporary Brazilian Plays in Bilingual Edition* (Austin, Tex.: Host, 1988);

Homens de papel: teatro (São Paulo: Global, 1978);

Na Barra do Catimbó (São Paulo: Global, 1978);

Oração para um pé-de-chinelo (São Paulo: Global, 1979);

Jesus-homem: peça e debate (São Paulo: Grêmio Politécnico, 1981);

Prisioneiro de uma canção (São Paulo: P. Marcos, 1982);

Madame Blavatsky (São Paulo: P. Marcos, 1985);

A figurinha e soldados da minha rua (São Paulo: P. Marcos, 1986);

Canções e reflexões de um palhaço: textos curtos (São Paulo: P. Marcos, 1987);

A mancha roxa (São Paulo: P. Marcos, 1988);

A dança final (São Paulo: Maltese, 1994);

O assassinato do anão do caralho grande: Noveleta policial e peça teatral (São Paulo: Geração, 1996);

Figurinha difícil: pornografando e subvertendo (São Paulo: Senac, 1996);

O truque dos espelhos e outras histórias de pequenos artistas (Belo Horizonte: Una, 1999);

Jornada de um imbecil até o entendimento (São Paulo: Global, n.d.).

Editions and Collections: *Navalha na carne; Quando as máquinas param* (São Paulo: Global, 1978);

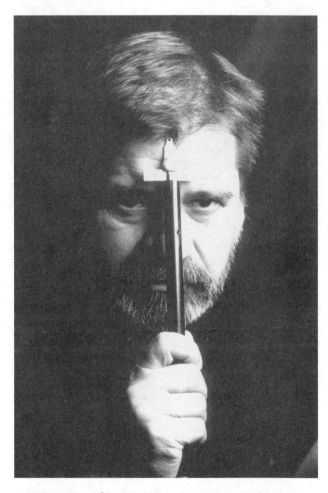

Plínio Marcos (from Fred Maia, Javier Arancibia Contreras, and Vinícius Pinheiro, Plínio Marcos: a crônica dos que não têm voz, *2002; Heard Library, Vanderbilt University)*

Prisioneiro de uma canção (São Paulo: Parma, 1984);

Teatro maldito (São Paulo: Maltese, 1992)—comprises *Navalha na carne, Dois perdidos numa noite suja,* and *O abajur lilás;*

Coleção melhor teatro, preface by Ilka Marinho Zanotto (São Paulo: Global, 2003)—comprises *Barrela, Dois perdidos numa noite suja, Navalha na carne, Abajur lilás,* and *Querô.*

PLAY PRODUCTIONS: *Barrela,* Santos, Centro Português, 1 November 1959;

Os Fantoches, Santos, Teatro de Camera de Santos, 1960; revised as *Jornada de um imbecil até o entendimento,* São Paulo, Teatro Opinião, July 1968;

Enquanto os navios atracam, São Paulo, Teatro de Arena, 1963; revised as *Quando as máquinas param,* São Paulo, Teatro de Arte, 14 October 1967;

Reportagem de um tempo mau, São Paulo, Teatro de Arena, 1965;

Dois perdidos numa noite suja, São Paulo, Bar Ponto de Encontro, 1966;

Dia Virá, São Paulo, Teatro do Colégio Des Oiseaux, 15 September 1967; revised as *Jesus-Homem,* São Paulo, Teatro Taib, December 1980;

Navalha na carne, São Paulo, Teatro Maria Della Costa, September 1967;

Homens de papel, São Paulo, Teatro Maria Della Costa, 10 October 1967;

Balbina de Iansã, São Paulo, Teatro São Pedro, November 1970;

Noel Rosa, o Poeta da vila e seus amores, São Paulo, Teatro Popular do SESI, 1977;

Feira livre, Rio de Janeiro, Teatro Opinião, 1 March 1979;

Oração para um pé-de-chinelo, São Paulo, TBC, July 1979;

Sob o Signo da discotéque, São Paulo, 1979;

O abajur lilás, Campinas, Teatro Municipal Castro Mendes, 25 June 1980;

Madame Blavatsky, São Paulo, Teatro Aliança Francesa, September 1985;

Balada de um palhaço, São Paulo, Teatro Zero Hora, October 1986;

O Coelho e a Onça, São Paulo, TBC, November 1988;

A mancha roxa, São Paulo, Teatro do Bixiga, 13 March 1989;

O assassinato do anão do caralho grande, São Paulo, Oficina Oswald de Andrade, November 1997;

A dança final, São Paulo, Teatro Itália, 25 April 2002.

PRODUCED SCRIPTS: "Réquiem de tamborim," television, *Tevê de Vanguarda,* Televisão Tupi, 9 February 1964;

"Macabô," adapted by Marcos and Benjamin Cattan from William Shakespeare's *Macbeth,* television, *Tevê de Vanguarda,* Televisão Tupi, 26 July 1964;

Uma história de subúrbio, television, TV Globo, 1972;

Coisas da cidade, television, Televisão Tupi, 1973;

A noite do desespero, television, Televisão Tupi, 1974;

"Somente uma vez na vida," television, *Fantástico,* TV Globo, 1974.

OTHER: Pedro Porfírio, *Canteiro de obra,* introduction by Marcos (Rio de Janeiro: Europa, 1978);

Gianni Ratto, *Hipocritando: fragmentos e páginas soltas,* introduction by Marcos (Rio de Janeiro: Bem-Te-Vi Produções Literárias, 2004).

Plínio Marcos is probably remembered mainly as the writer of shockingly vulgar and violent dialogue and, consequently, as Brazil's most often censored playwright. Unlike the explicitly political or ideological plays of Brazilian dramatists such as Gianfrancesco Guarnieri and Alfredo Dias Gomes, Marcos's works are naturalistic portrayals of life on the Brazilian margins, unadorned with satire or prescriptions for solutions. Marcos helped move Brazilian drama from the disjointedness and self-referentiality of the late 1960s and early 1970s to the rejuvenation of realism in the later 1970s and the 1980s. In the second act of Marcos's most highly acclaimed play, *Dois perdidos numa noite suja* (performed in 1966; published in 1978; translated as *Two Lost in a Filthy Night,* 1988), Paco tells his roommate, Tonho, that Tonho is "Cheio de grito, cheio de bafo, mas não era de nada" (Full of yelling, full of hot air, but good for nothing). The words are a paraphrase of the soliloquy of William Shakespeare's Macbeth on learning of the death of his wife—"Life's but a walking shadow, a poor player / That struts and frets his hour upon the stage, / And then is heard no more: it is a tale / told by an idiot, full of sound and fury, / Signifying nothing." But Lord and Lady Macbeth were of noble birth, even if they were of ignoble character; Paco and Tonho are ignoble on both counts. Underlying Marcos's drama is the tragedy of the underclass, in contrast both to Shakespeare's nobles and to Arthur Miller's "Common Man." Where Marcos's personae dwell, desperation is not as quiet as it is in Miller's world. Implicit—and occasionally explicit—in Marcos's work is the idea that social forces have robbed his characters of their dignity and, thus, of the glory of a tragic fall. Petty criminals and desperate victims inhabit Marcos's landscapes because more powerful criminals have created the conditions in which they must live.

Plínio Marcos de Barros was born in Santos, the port city of São Paulo, on 29 September 1935 to Armando Marcos, a bank clerk, and Hermínia Marcos; he had four brothers and a sister. Sources conflict about how much formal schooling he had, but Marcos complemented his education through self-study and lessons on the streets of Santos's seedier districts. His early jobs included handyman, soccer player for the Santos team, dockworker, and circus clown.

Marcos's theatrical career began in 1958 when the radical writer and director Patrícia Galvão, known as "Pagu," cast him at the last minute as the stuttering clown Frajola (Chic) in the children's play *Pluft, o fantasminha* (Pluft, the Little Ghost), by Maria Clara Machado. Marcos wrote his first play, *Barrela* (Gang Bang), at this time. *Barrela* shows how the prison system turns minor offenders into hardened criminals; it centers on the revenge that Portuga (a derogatory term for "Portuguese") exacts on his fellow inmates after they serially rape him. Galvão and Pascoal Carlos Magno, the most influential producer of the day, planned to stage the play at the 1958 National Festival of Student Theater in Santos under Marcos's direction; instead, the work landed its author-director in jail. *Barrela* was performed at the Centro Português in Santos on 1 November 1959, after which it was banned until 1980; in 1990 it was adapted for a movie directed by Marco Antonio Cury. Elzbieta Szoka notes that *Barrela* presents several features that are found in Marcos's more mature plays: the underworld context, colloquial language that is often violent or obscene, and the dynamic of oppressor versus oppressed in a claustrophobic setting. Szoka and Brazilian critic Décio de Almeida Prado point to the similarity of Marcos's drama to Antonin Artaud's "Theater of Cruelty."

In 1962 Marcos moved into São Paulo, settling in the downtown bohemian district. In 1963 he married the actress Walderez de Barros; they had three children: Kiko, Léo Lama, and Ana. He roamed the streets and bars, selling self-published editions of his plays, and his fans bought him drinks; according to Elma Lia Nascimento, he later claimed that street vendor was the only job he did well and that he probably should have become a thief. He thus knew intimately the world that he wrote about in his plays and that led to his various self-descriptions: The Accursed Playwright, The Poet of the Mean Streets, and The Reporter of Bad Times, the last of which derived from his second play, *Reportagem de um tempo mau* (1965, News Report from a Bad Time), about the 1964 military coup in Brazil.

Marcos's first major success was *Dois perdidos numa noite suja,* which opened in 1966 in a São Paulo bar but has since become the third most frequently staged Brazilian play. The two-act play is set in the flophouse apartment of Tonho and Paco. Tonho has illusions of succeeding within the economic system; Paco is a petty criminal. Paco's constant needling over a fine pair of shoes that Paco has stolen finally causes Tonho to snap, and he kills Paco with the latter's own revolver. *Dois perdidos numa noite suja* is a cautionary tale about the costs of degrading the human heart.

Navalha na carne (Razor in the Flesh) was written in 1967 and premiered that same year. Neusa Suely, an

aging prostitute, returns to her room in a fleabag hotel to find her pimp, Wado, in a bad mood because his money is missing. Suspecting Veludo, a homosexual hotel employee, of committing the theft, Suely and Wado trap him in the room and interrogate him in the style of sadistic police detectives. Veludo finally confesses and proposes restitution. Taking a cue from Veludo, Wado humiliates Suely on account of her age; then Suely threatens Wado with a razor and forces him to prostitute himself with Veludo. But Veludo seduces the razor away from Suely, and he and Wado leave the room together. Suely is left utterly alone.

In 1968 and 1969 the Brazilian military dictatorship enacted decrees that severely curtailed freedom of expression in most media. In 1968, when *Barrela* was once again barred from the stage, Marcos was quoted in the 19 March *Folha de São Paulo* (São Paulo News) venting his frustration at the censorship:

> Infelizmente, nós ainda não temos uma tradição de luta que nos permita responder com energia e rapidez a cada afronta que o governo faz à liberdade. É doloroso ver um país de analfabetos, famintos, desempregados, com um presidente que lê peças de teatro, não para aumentar sua cultura, mas para proibi-las. Tenho a impressão que o povo brasileiro está farto de mordaça.

> (Unfortunately, we do not yet have a tradition of struggle that allows us to respond energetically and quickly to each affront the government makes to liberty. It is sad to see a country of illiterate, starving, underemployed people with a president who reads theater plays, not to be more cultured, but to ban them. I think that the Brazilian people are tired of the muzzle.)

Marcos's early social dramas are neorealist; they include stark, documentary-style representations of characters' words and actions and scenes of sexual violence—in Marcos's works, sex is a form of power. Despite the realism of the plays, however, critics such as Szoka and Sabato Magaldi have noted that the characters are types rather than complex, psychologically nuanced personalities. Marcos's next important work, *O abajur lilás* (The Lilac Lamp), written in 1969 and published in 1975 but not performed until 1980, is set in an apartment occupied by Giro, a drug dealer; Oswaldo, his assistant; and three prostitutes. All are, again, types: Giro is the boss, the repository of power; Oswaldo is the sadistic enforcer; maternal Dilma is willing to fight and suffer for her son; Leninha is weak and timid; and Célia is alienated and embittered. In this play, however, Marcos, without abandoning social realism and the representation of power relations, explores female characters in depth and begins writing what have been called "existential" or "metaphysical" dramas. In *Balbina de Iansã* (1970) Balbina, an initiate of the Afro-Brazilian deity Iansã, struggles against abuse of power by Zefa, the head of the religious community. *Madame Blavatsky* (1985) is a sympathetic portrayal of Helena Blavatsky, the nineteenth-century esoteric philosopher and founder of the Theosophical Movement whom Marcos called "the first feminist." The choice of topic also reveals an attraction to mysticism that went back to Marcos's circus days, when he worked with gypsies and learned to read tarot cards. Marcos's wife starred in the premiere at the Teatro Aliança Francesa in São Paulo.

In 1986 Marcos wrote, and Teatro Zero Hora premiered, *Balada de um palhaço* (Ballad of a Clown). The sad clown Bobo Plim and the happy clown Menelão are trapped in an abstract space that, according to the stage directions, "pode ser um picadeiro de circo, um altar, a sala de um puteiro, o salão de um bar, uma praça" (could be a circus ring, an altar, a whorehouse waiting room, a barroom, a town square). The piece includes debates on performance, reflections on the role of the artist, and comments on the failure of communication amid conflicting subjectivities. Bobo Plim represents the artist who exhausts himself in performance, only to be misunderstood; he is melancholy because of his antiquated certainty about the world. In contrast, Menelão's cheer derives from his absurdism and relativism in the face of a chaotic reality. The clowns' conflict is a clash of the classical and the postmodern paradigms. Barros played Bobo Plim, and her son with Marcos, Léo Lama, wrote the music. Marcos considered the play his masterpiece, and Szoka sees it as his artistic manifesto and his most personal work.

Marcos's late work included a return to the harsh realism of the 1960s with *A mancha roxa* (1989, The Purple Spot), about prisoners who are vulnerable to HIV infection while incarcerated. The denouement uses the avant-garde technique of rupturing the barrier between actors and audience when the prisoners seductively make invitations to the spectators in an effort to infect them with the contagion. The message is that there can be no bystanders in this epidemic.

In 1997 Marcos and his second wife, journalist Vera Artaxo, moved from their longtime home in a modest apartment in downtown São Paulo to an upscale neighborhood. Marcos criticized the habits of his upper-middle-class neighbors and enjoyed scandalizing them by strolling around the neighborhood dressed as a bum. He died at the Hospital das Clínicas on 19 November 1999 of a heart attack, after battling diabetes and cardiovascular disease for several years.

Marcos's only comedy, *A dança final* (The Last Dance), had been published in 1994; it premiered at the

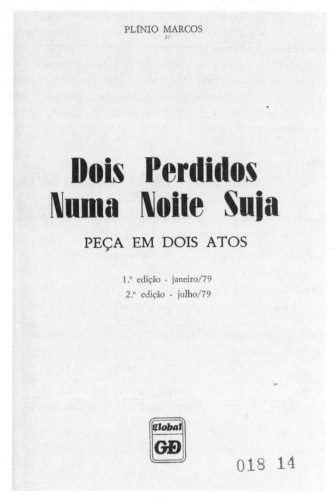

Title page for Marcos's play (translated as Two Lost in a Filthy Night, 1988), first performed in a São Paulo bar in 1966, about flophouse roommates whose bickering ends in murder (Heard Library, Vanderbilt University)

Teatro Itália in São Paulo in April 2002. The satire of bourgeois mores is about a happy and successful couple who have to confront the husband's impotence just before their silver wedding anniversary. The casting for the 2002 production was humorously ironic: the couple were played by Nuno Leal Maia and Aldine Müller, who had starred in the 1978 erotic movie comedy *O bem dotado: o homem de Itu* (The Well Endowed: The Man from Itu).

In a 1987 interview in English with Szoka that is included in *3 Contemporary Brazilian Plays in Bilingual Edition* (1988), translated by Szoka and Joe W. Bratcher III, Marcos said: "I have made one fundamental contribution to Brazilian theatre: I fought elitism, do you know what I mean? I made fun of THEIR culture. I gave interviews like: I am illiterate and I am the best, and so on. Because I considered THEIR culture nonsense."

Whether realistic and socially engaged or mystical and abstract, Marcos's dramas continue to resonate with audiences and critics. His works have enjoyed revivals such as the 1993 production of *Dois perdidos numa noite suja* at the Curitiba Festival, where Marcos was the only playwright representing his generation; the play has also been staged in France, Germany, England, Cuba, and the United States.

References:

David George, *The Modern Brazilian Stage* (Austin: University of Texas Press, 1992);

Mário Guidarini, *A desova da serpente: teatro contemporâneo brasileiro* (Florianópolis: UFSC, 1996);

Sabato Magaldi, *Moderna dramaturgia brasileira* (São Paulo: Perspectiva, 1998);

Fred Maia, Javier Arancibia Contreras, and Vinícius Pinheiro, *Plínio Marcos: a crônica dos que não têm voz* (São Paulo: Boitempo, 2002);

Jan Michalski, *O palco amordaçado: 15 anos de censura teatral no Brasil* (Rio de Janeiro: Avenir, 1979);

Elma Lia Nascimento, "Mean Streets Poet," *Brazzil* (November 1999) <http://www.brazzil.com/p10nov99.htm>;

"Plínio Marcos: Escrevo para incomodar," *Folha de São Paulo,* 19 March 1968;

Plínio Marcos: Sítio Oficial <http://www.pliniomarcos.com/>;

Décio de Almeida Prado, *Teatro em progresso: crítica teatral, 1955–1964* (São Paulo: Martins, 1964);

Peter Schoenbach, "Plínio Marcos: Reporter of Bad Time," in *Dramatists in Revolt: The New Latin American Theater,* edited by Leon F. Lyday and George W. Woodyard (Austin: University of Texas Press, 1976), pp. 243–257;

Elzbieta Szoka, *A Semiotic Study of Three Plays by Plínio Marcos* (New York: Peter Lang, 1995);

Paulo Vieira, *Plínio Marcos: a flor e o mal* (Petrópolis: Firmo, 1994).

Cecília Meireles

(7 November 1901 – 9 November 1964)

Darlene J. Sadlier
Indiana University, Bloomington

BOOKS: *Espectros* (Rio de Janeiro: Leite Ribeiro, 1919);

Nunca mais . . . e Poema dos poemas (Rio de Janeiro: Leite Ribeiro, 1923);

Criança, meu amor (Rio de Janeiro: Anuário do Brasil, 1924);

Balladas para El-Rei (Rio de Janeiro: Brasileira Lux, 1925);

O espírito vitorioso (Rio de Janeiro: Anuário do Brasil, 1929);

Batuque, samba e macumba (Lisbon: Mundo Português, 1935); translated in *Batuque, Samba, and Macumba: Drawings of Gestures and Rhythm, 1926–1934,* introduction by Lélia Gontijo Soares (Rio de Janeiro: Fundação Nacional de Arte, 1983);

Notícia da poesia brasileira (Coimbra: Coimbra Editora/ Biblioteca Geral da Universidade, 1935);

A festa das letras, by Meireles and Josué de Castro (Pôrto Alegre: Globo, 1937);

Rute e Alberto resolveram ser turistas (Pôrto Alegre: Globo, 1938); abridged and edited by Virginia Joiner and Eunice Joiner Gates as *Rute e Alberto* (Boston: D. C. Heath, 1945);

Viagem: poesia, 1929–1937 (Lisbon: Império, 1939);

Vaga música (Rio de Janeiro: Pongetti, 1942);

Mar absoluto e outros poemas (Pôrto Alegre: Globo, 1945);

Retrato natural (Rio de Janeiro: Livros de Portugal, 1949);

Rui: pequena história de uma grande vida (Rio de Janeiro: Livros de Portugal, 1949);

Amor em Leonoreta (Rio de Janeiro: Hipocampo, 1951);

Problemas da literatura infantil (Belo Horizonte: Imprensa Oficial, 1951);

Doze noturnos da Holanda e O aeronauta (Rio de Janeiro: Livros de Portugal, 1952);

Romanceiro da inconfidência (Rio de Janeiro: Livros de Portugal, 1953);

Pequeno oratório de Santa Clara (Rio de Janeiro: Philobiblion, 1955);

Pistóia, cemitério militar brasileiro (Rio de Janeiro: Philobiblion, 1955);

Canções (Rio de Janeiro: Livros de Portugal, 1956);

Cecília Meireles (from the back cover of Meireles, Mar absoluto/Retrato natural, *1983; Bruccoli Clark Layman Archives)*

Giroflê, giroflá (Rio de Janeiro: Philobiblion/Civilização Brasileira, 1956);

Oratório de Santa Maria Egipcíaca (Bahia: Escola de Teatro da Universidade da Bahia, 1957);

Romance de Santa Cecília (Rio de Janeiro: Philobiblion, 1957);

A rosa (Salvador: Dinamene, 1957);

Artes populares (Rio de Janeiro: Edições de Ouro, 1958);

Panorama folclórico dos Açores, especialmente da ilha de S. Miguel (Pôrto Alegre: Comissão Gaúcha de Folclore, 1958);

Eternidade de Israel (Rio de Janeiro: Centro Cultural Brasil-Israel, 1959);

Metal rosicler (Rio de Janeiro: Livros de Portugal, 1960);

Poemas escritos na India (Rio de Janeiro: São José, [1961]);

Rabindranath Tagore and the East West Unity, translated by Isabel do Prado (Rio de Janeiro: Brazilian National Commission for UNESCO, 1961);

Antologia poética, com poemas inéditos (Rio de Janeiro: Editora do Autor, 1963);

Solombra (Rio de Janeiro: Livros de Portugal, 1963);

Escolha o seu sonho: crônicas (Rio de Janeiro: Record, 1964);

Ou isto ou aquilo (São Paulo: Giroflê, 1964);

Crônica trovada da cidade de Sam Sebastião do Rio de Janeiro no quarto centenário de sua fundação pelo Capitão-Mor Estácio de Saa (Rio de Janeiro: J. Olympio, 1965);

O menino atrasado: auto de Natal (Rio de Janeiro: Livros de Portugal, 1966);

Inéditos (crônicas) (Rio de Janeiro: Bloch, 1967);

Notas de folclore gaúcho-açoriano (Rio de Janeiro: Campanha de Defesa do Folclore Brasileiro, 1968);

Poemas italianos, Italian translations by Edoardo Bizzarri (São Paulo: Instituto Cultural Italo-Brasileiro, 1968);

A Bíblia na poesia brasileira (Rio de Janeiro: Centro Cultural Brasil-Israel, 1969);

Poesias: ou isto ou aquilo & inéditos (São Paulo: Melhoramentos, 1969);

Ilusões do mundo: crônicas (Rio de Janeiro: Nova Aguilar, 1976);

Olhinhos de gato (São Paulo: Moderna, 1980);

O que se diz e o que se entende: crônicas (Rio de Janeiro: Nova Fronteira, 1980);

Janela mágica: crônicas (São Paulo: Moderna, 1981).

Editions and Collections: *Obra poética,* introduction by Darcy Damasceno (Rio de Janeiro: J. Aguilar, 1958);

Antologia poética, edited by Francisco da Cunha Leão and David Mourão-Ferreira (Lisbon: Guimarães, 1968);

Flor de poemas (Rio de Janeiro: J. Aguilar, 1972);

Seleta em prosa e verso de Cecília Meireles, edited by Damasceno (Rio de Janeiro: J. Olympio, 1973);

Poesias completas, 9 volumes (Rio de Janeiro: Civilização Brasileira, 1973–1974);

Cecília Meireles: poesia, edited by Damasceno (Rio de Janeiro: AGIR, 1974);

Flores e canções (Rio de Janeiro: Confraria dos Amigos do Livro, 1979);

Cânticos: oferenda (São Paulo: Moderna, 1982);

Cecília Meireles, edited by Norma Seltzer Goldstein and Rita de Cássia Barbosa (São Paulo: Abril, 1982);

Os melhores poemas de Cecília Meireles, edited by Maria Fernanda (São Paulo: Global, 1984);

Poesia completa, introduction by Walmir Ayala (Rio de Janeiro: Aguilar, 1994);

Cecília Meireles: obra em prosa, 5 volumes, edited by Leodegário A. de Azevedo Filho (Rio de Janeiro: Nova Fronteira, 1998–2001);

Poesia completa, 2 volumes, edited by Antonio Carlos Secchin (Rio de Janeiro: Nova Fronteira, 2001);

Melhores crônicas, edited, with a preface, by Azevedo (São Paulo: Global, 2003).

Edition in English: *Poemas em Tradução=Poems in Translation,* translated by Henry Hunt Keith and Raymond S. Sayers (Washington, D.C.: Brazilian-American Cultural Institute, 1977).

RECORDING: *Cecília Meireles; Guilherme de Almeida,* read by Meireles and Guilherme de Almeida, Festa LPP-009, n.d.

OTHER: *Poetas novos de Portugal,* edited, with a preface, by Meireles (Rio de Janeiro: Dois Mundos, 1944);

Homenagem: Rabindranath Tagore, edited by Meireles (Rio de Janeiro: Embaixada da India, 1961).

TRANSLATIONS: Rainer Maria Rilke, *A canção de amor e de morte do porta-estandarte Cristóvão Rilke* (Rio de Janeiro: Revista Acadêmica, 1947);

Virginia Woolf, *Orlando* (Pôrto Alegre: Globo, 1948);

Kathryn Hulme, *Os caminhos de Deus* (Rio de Janeiro: Seleções do *Reader's Digest,* 1958);

Taylor Caldwell, *Amado e glorioso médico* (Rio de Janeiro: Seleções do *Reader's Digest,* 1960);

Federico García Lorca, *Bodas de sangue* (Rio de Janeiro: AGIR, 1960);

Rabindranath Tagore, *Colheita de frutos, O jardineiro, Pássaros perdidos, Alua crescente, Sete poemas de Puravi, Minha bela vizinha* (Rio de Janeiro: MEC, 1962);

Poesia de Israel (Rio de Janeiro: Civilização Brasileira, 1962);

Tagore, *Çaturanga* (Rio de Janeiro: Delta, 1962);

García Lorca, *Yerma* (Rio de Janeiro: AGIR, 1963);

Moshé Smilansky, "Latife," in *Antologia da literatura hebraica moderna* (Rio de Janeiro: Biblos, 1969);

Li Bo and Du Fu, *Poemas chineses* (Rio de Janeiro: Nova Fronteira, 1996);

As mil e uma noites, 2 volumes (Rio de Janeiro: Anuário do Brasil, n.d.).

Cecília Meireles is one of the major poets of the Portuguese language and one of the few women authors to appear in the Lusophone literary canon. Often described as a postsymbolist, Meireles was a consummate stylist whose sense of poetic rhyme and meter was unequaled among her contemporaries. She is best known for her poems about the sea and other aspects of nature, as well as for her *Romanceiro da inconfidência*

(1953, Ballad of the Conspiracy), a collection inspired by an eighteenth-century Brazilian revolt against Portuguese rule known as the Inconfidência Mineira (Minas Conspiracy). Meireles was instrumental in bringing Portuguese poets, such as Fernando Pessoa, to the attention of Brazilian readers, and for many years she was the best-known Brazilian poet in Portugal. In addition to her volumes of poetry, she published essays, plays, children's literature, and *crônicas* (chronicles) for Brazilian newspapers. She also translated works by such authors as Virginia Woolf, Rainer Maria Rilke, and Federico García Lorca into Portuguese.

When Cecília Benevides de Carvalho Meireles was born on 7 November 1901, Brazil was a relatively young republic, established as a result of the overthrow of the imperial government in 1888. In 1901 Rio de Janeiro, Meireles's birthplace, had been the nation's political and cultural center for nearly a century, owing to the arrival of the court of the Portuguese regent, Dom João VI, who had fled Lisbon for Rio de Janeiro in 1808 in order to escape Napoleon Bonaparte's invasion of the Iberian Peninsula. Although Brazil was governed by Portuguese monarchs for nearly four centuries, the cultural and literary life of the country followed the French example. The same was not true for Meireles, who was raised by her maternal grandmother, Jacinta Garcia Benevides, an Azorean, whose songs and tales of her native São Miguel instilled within the child a deep and lasting interest in her Portuguese heritage and the traditions of that country. From her earliest poems to those written in her final years, Meireles was also attracted to images that expressed the transitory nature of life. Having lost her father, Carlos Alberto de Carvalho Meireles, and three siblings prior to her birth and having lost her mother, Matilda Benevides, when she was three years old, she returned time and again to contrast the fleeting aspect of existence with poetry and memory, which transform the ephemeral into the eternal.

Meireles was recognized early on as a gifted student. When she was nine years old, she was awarded a gold medal for her exceptional scholastic achievement at the Escola Normal in Rio de Janeiro. The occasion was all the more memorable since the medal was presented to her by Olavo Bilac, the district school inspector, who was also one of the most celebrated poets in Brazil. At school Meireles excelled in foreign languages, music, and design; she also attended the Conservatório de Música do Rio de Janeiro (Music Conservatory of Rio de Janeiro), where she studied voice and violin. Shortly after graduation in 1917, she found a position as a teacher in Rio de Janeiro. Two years later her first book of poems, *Espectros* (1919, Spectres), was published. A slim volume featuring seventeen sonnets, it

Front cover of Meireles's third poetry collection, published in 1925 (Joint University Libraries, Nashville)

included a preface by the distinguished academic Alfredo Gomes, author of one of the most influential studies of the Portuguese language, *Grammatica portugueza* (1910). Shortly after publication, *Espectros* was reviewed by the eminent scholar João Ribeiro. In his introduction to the first collected edition of Meireles's poetry, *Obra poética* (1958, Poetic Works), Darcy Damasceno, one of her chief biographers and author of the first book-length critical study of her poetry, quotes from Ribeiro's comments: "Com o talento e as qualidades poéticas, aqui reveladas, Cecília Meireles em breve, e sem grande esforço, poderá lograr a reputação de poetisa que de justiça lhe cabe" (With the poetic talent and qualities revealed here, Cecília Meireles will achieve shortly and without great effort, the reputation of poetess that rightly belongs to her). A close examination of Ribeiro's review, however, shows that he was perhaps more enthusiastic about Gomes's introduction than Meireles's sonnets. The fact that *Espectros* was written under Gomes's tutelage may explain why Ribeiro elected to publish a review of an unknown author's first book of poems.

Between 1919 and 1923, when Meireles's second collection of poems, *Nunca mais . . . e Poema dos poemas*

(Never More . . . and Poem of Poems), was published, Brazil was experiencing the beginnings of a new political era with the birth of the Partido Comunista Brasileiro (Brazilian Communist Party) and the attempted overthrow of the government by a group of young military officers under the leadership of Luís Carlos Prestes. These two events, among others, ultimately culminated in the revolution of 1930, a bloodless coup that ushered in a new president, Getúlio Vargas. In cultural terms, the late 1910s and early 1920s were a period of exhilaration and iconoclasm associated with the advent of literary modernism. Writers such as Ronald de Carvalho and Oswald de Andrade were already participating in efforts to "make it new" both in Brazil and abroad, and the 1922 Semana de Arte Moderna (Modern Art Week), which marked the official beginning of modernism in Brazil, was a major literary and artistic event in São Paulo. In the succeeding years, groups formed around special interests and agendas and founded their own literary reviews. One of these groups was the *espiritualistas* (spiritualists), writers who were drawn to Catholicism and whose works had more in common with Romantic symbolism than with the formal experiments and satiric verse that characterized the writings of poets such as Andrade and Mário de Andrade.

Meireles's association with the *espiritualistas* lasted into the 1930s. In 1927, two years after the publication of her third volume of poems, *Balladas para El-Rei* (1925, Ballads for the King), she and other members of the group founded *Festa* (Festival), their official journal, which was published until 1935. Both Meireles and her husband, the Portuguese artist Fernando Correia Dias, whom she married in 1922, were instrumental in organizing and publishing the review. According to poet and critic Andrade Muricy, who was also a member of the group, Correia Dias was responsible for designing the journal and suggested that it be printed in Portugal. There it attracted the attention of the Lisbon-based modernists known as the *presencistas* (those present), who were so impressed by the design of *Festa* that they used it as a model for their own publication, *Presença*.

In addition to prose and poetry by writers such as Adelino Magalhães, Gilka Machado, Muricy, Murilo Mendes, and Meireles, *Festa* featured the polemical writings of Tasso da Silveira, who was the principal spokesman of the group. According to Silveira, symbolism, not the primitivism associated with Oswald de Andrade's *Pau Brasil* (1925, Brazilwood), was the true source for the modernist movement. His proclamation was countered by Mário de Andrade, a central figure of the Semana de Arte Moderna and a major poet and critic, who asserted that modernism was not a continuation of the past but rather a break from it. Not surpris-

ingly, those who wrote for *Festa* were perceived as traditionalists, in contrast to writers such as Mário de Andrade, who wrote satiric verses about São Paulo and the bourgeois in his *Paulicéia desvairada* (1922; translated as *Hallucinated City,* 1968), and Oswald de Andrade, who advocated a literary *antropofagismo* (anthropophagy) as a means of dealing with foreign literary and cultural influences. In fact, this combination of traditionalism and radical experimentation characterized international modernism as a whole—a Janus-faced movement that looked both to the past and the future for its inspiration.

None of the three poetry volumes that Meireles published from 1919 to 1925 appear in her *Poesias completas* (1973–1974, Complete Poetry)—a fact that suggests her dissatisfaction with her earliest poems. From 1927 to 1935 she honed her craft in the pages of *Festa,* and her poems, which became a major selling point for the publication, appeared in nine of its twenty-one issues. During this time Meireles also wrote editorials on education for the *Diário de Notícias,* a major Rio de Janeiro newspaper, where she worked from 1930 to 1934. In May 1933 she presided over a special symposium dedicated to the works of the nineteenth-century black poet João da Cruz e Sousa, who was one of the foremost symbolist poets in Brazil. Meireles's participation in the symposium included an exhibition of her drawings inspired by Cruz e Sousa's *Últimos sonetos* (1905, Last Sonnets).

In 1934 Meireles responded to a request from the secretary of education of the federal district to serve as director of the children's center in Botafogo. As part of her activities with the center, she founded Brazil's first children's library, which operated until 1938, when the Estado Novo (New State), under the leadership of president-turned-dictator Vargas, ordered that it be closed for containing books such as Mark Twain's *The Adventures of Tom Sawyer* (1876). In 1934 Meireles was also invited by the Portuguese government to present a series of talks on Brazilian literature. Her lecture tour in Portugal was highly successful, and two of her presentations, *Notícia da poesia brasileira* (1935, Note on Brazilian Poetry) and *Batuque, samba e macumba* (1935), were published in Coimbra and Lisbon, respectively. This period of intense activity was also marked by a great personal loss. The death in 1936 of her husband, Correia Dias, whose bouts with depression led to his suicide, left Meireles alone to raise their three young daughters, Maria Elvira, Maria Matilde, and Maria Fernanda. In order to support her family, she continued to write for newspapers and literary journals, and in 1936 she accepted an invitation to teach Luso-Brazilian literature and literary theory and criticism at the Universidade do Distrito Federal (University of the Federal District), which had been founded the previous year.

Although Meireles gained considerable attention as an educator and founder of the first children's library in Brazil, critical recognition of her poetry was slow to come there. Of the reviews published prior to 1938, Agrippino Grieco's "Quatro poetisas" (Four Poetesses) perhaps best reflects the negative criticism directed toward Meireles's early works. Grieco complained that the poems in *Nunca mais . . .* include not a single note of happiness or hope. He was also critical of the verses in *Poema dos poemas,* which, he charged, were merely prose pieces formally disguised as poems. Grieco's remarks were somewhat tempered by Muricy's more favorable comments in his essay collection *A nova literatura brasileira* (1936, The New Brazilian Literature), although it should be noted that Muricy was one of the *espiritualistas* and that he devoted much of his book to an examination of writings by the group—especially those who had been ignored or poorly received by the critics. At that time, there was nothing to indicate the impending sensation that Meireles's 1939 volume, *Viagem: poesia, 1929–1937* (1929–1937, Voyage: Poetry), was to cause and that it was to launch her into the world of Brazilian letters as a major poet.

When *Viagem* was presented to the Academia Brasileira de Letras (Brazilian Academy of Letters) in 1939 along with literary works by other writers, it was placed in nomination for the first-place prize. That nomination sparked a lengthy and heated debate between two men of letters: Cassiano Ricardo, a recently elected academy member who was asked to judge the competition, and Fernando Magalhães, an older, established member. Ricardo's speech to the academy enraged Magalhães, because he not only nominated Meireles for the Prêmio Olavo Bilac (Olavo Bilac Prize), a nomination that Magalhães was against, but also proposed that the second-place and honorable mention awards be eliminated so that the prize bestowed upon her would be all the more prestigious. Magalhães responded to Ricardo by charging him with favoritism and with failure to read the works of the other twenty-nine candidates competing for the award. Ricardo answered the charge by publicly rejecting, one by one, each of the volumes, with the exception of those by Agnelo Machado and João Acioli, which, he declared, exhibited certain strengths. The debate did not end there, despite the fact that Ricardo left the academy in Rio de Janeiro for São Paulo. According to Ricardo's published memoir, *Viagem no tempo e no espaço* (1970), Magalhães prepared a speech critical of the nomination and of Ricardo personally, which he planned to deliver to the academy during Ricardo's absence. A São Paulo newspaper previewed the speech

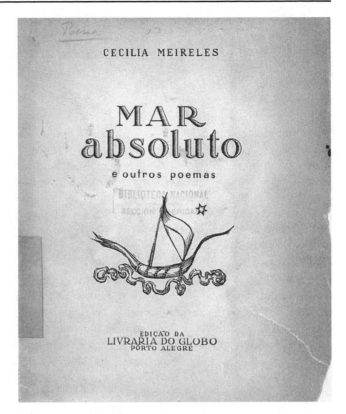

Front cover of Meireles's sixth poetry volume (1945), considered one of her strongest collections (Biblioteca Nacional de Chile)

the day before Magalhães was scheduled to address the academy, however, giving Ricardo sufficient time to return to Rio de Janeiro, attend the session, and respond to his opponent's attacks. Ricardo finally agreed to a second-place award for the Amazonian poet Wladimir Emanuel, whose work was supported by Olegário Mariano, an academy member whom Ricardo suspected had incited Magalhães to lead the charge against Meireles's sole nomination. Ricardo recounts in his memoir that his support of the second-place prize was a vote for Mariano, who proposed it, and not for Emanuel. When the final votes were cast, the first place was awarded to Meireles, and the second place, in Ricardo's words, went "indiretamente" (indirectly) to Mariano.

As the recipient of the Prêmio Olavo Bilac, Meireles was invited to address the Academia Brasileira de Letras at the awards ceremony. She declined to speak, however, because parts of her acceptance speech had been censored by a committee whose job was to read speeches in advance. One of the censored passages referred to the fact that awards tended not to be bestowed upon individuals but rather were fought for on the order of the mythical battle waged between good and evil. She was joined in her view by the leading figure of the Brazilian modernist movement, Mário de

Andrade, who published an article critical of the academy in which he playfully chided Meireles for having allowed herself to be nominated for the prize. A few months later, he wrote a glowing review of *Viagem* in which he praised her for her poetic independence, eclecticism, and sensitivity.

Viagem uses motifs and poetic forms that Meireles continued to rework throughout her career. Among the best-known poems in the collection is "Motivo" (Motif), which is a delicately wrought manifesto on the condition of being a poet. Other poems in the collection focus on the themes of transience, solitude, nature, and eternity. Meireles's fascination with music is apparent throughout the book, as indicated by her repeated use of poetic forms associated with music, such as the *cantiga,* the *canção,* and the *serenata.*

In 1940 Meireles married Heitor Grillo. She also made her first visit to the United States that year and spent several months at the University of Texas at Austin, where she conducted seminars on Brazilian literature and culture under the Departamento de Imprensa e Propaganda (DIP, the Department of the Press and Propaganda), an arm of the Vargas dictatorship that supported cultural exchanges between national and foreign writers (although it suppressed any intellectual activity considered harmful to Brazil). Following her visit to the United States, Meireles traveled to Mexico and then returned to Brazil to work for the DIP as editor of the promotional magazine *Travel in Brazil.* In 1942, at the invitation of her champion and friend Ricardo, then editor of *A Manhã* (The Morning), the official publication of the Estado Novo, she began writing a series of articles on folklore. Her studies appeared in *A Manhã* for the next two years.

Prior to the publication of *Viagem,* Meireles was more widely read and better known in Portugal than at home. With the appearance of *Viagem,* which was published in Portugal, her popularity in that country reached a new high. So great was the Portuguese public's interest in Brazilian poetry, and in Meireles's works in particular, that in 1942 two Luso-Brazilian reviews were founded: *Brasília,* published by the Instituto de Estudos Brasileiros (Institute for Brazilian Studies) in Coimbra; and *Atlântico,* funded by the Secretariado da Propaganda Nacional (Secretariat of National Propaganda). Both publications, as well as other reviews and newspapers in Portugal, regularly featured previously unpublished works by Meireles. For example, in 1942 an autobiographical work of fiction, *Olhinhos de gato* (Little Eyes of the Cat), was serialized in the Lisbon-based *Revista Ocidente.* (It was published in book form in 1980.) In 1943 the *Revista Ocidente* published Ricardo's speech supporting Meireles for the Prêmio Olavo Bilac. She continued to enjoy widespread popularity in Portugal,

not only as a result of publications such as *Brasília* and *Atlântico* but also because of the many favorable notices written about her work by some of the most distinguished writers and critics in Portugal, including João Gaspar Simões, Vitorino Nemésio, Adolfo Casias Monteiro, and David Mourão-Ferreira. Meireles also played an important role in presenting Portuguese writers such as Pessoa to a Brazilian readership by editing the anthology *Poetas novos de Portugal* (1944, New Poets from Portugal).

The years following the publication of *Viagem* were highly productive for Meireles. She continued writing for several journals and newspapers while publishing, on average, a book of poems every one to two years for the next twenty-five years. In 1942 her fifth volume of poems, *Vaga música* (Vague Music), was published and was immediately praised by the critic and writer Paulo Menotti del Picchia in *A Manhã.* Among the many fine poems in this collection are two of Meireles's most widely anthologized compositions: "Aluna" (Student) and "Epitáfio da navegadora" (Epitaph of the Navigator), both of which focus on the theme of solitude—a recurring preoccupation in her works. As the title of the book clearly indicates, the element of music is also strongly present in this volume, which is made up of *canções* and other musical forms.

Following a trip to Uruguay and Argentina, Meireles met in 1945 with the Chilean Gabriela Mistral, who was awarded the Nobel Prize in literature that year for her poetry. The two women had known each other ever since Mistral relocated to Rio de Janeiro to serve as her nation's cultural ambassador to Brazil. Meireles's sixth volume of poetry, *Mar absoluto e outros poemas* (Absolute Sea and Other Poems), published in Brazil in 1945, is regarded as one of her finest collections of verse. As the title suggests, the sea is a major motif. In the title poem, "Mar absoluto," the sea becomes a metaphor for whatever is both fleeting and eternal in life, forever eluding reason or explanation. The emphasis on the transitory and the eternal can also be found in a series of poems titled "Motivo da rosa" (Motif of the Rose) that appear at regular intervals throughout the book. The "other poems" referred to in the volume title refer to the collection "Os dias felizes" (The Happy Days), which features poems in praise of nature and the countryside, as well as the bittersweet "Elegia 1933–1937" (Elegy 1933–1937), Meireles's lyric tribute to the memory of her maternal grandmother. Four years later Meireles published *Retrato natural* (1949, Natural Portrait), which was praised by the poet Carlos Drummond de Andrade in the Rio de Janeiro newspaper *Jornal de Letras.* Drummond wrote enthusiastically of her skillful use of free verse as well as of the musicality of her compositions. There are some unusual selections in this volume that make a strong impression—in particular, "Balada das dez bailarinas do casino" (Ballad of the Ten Casino Dancers), which juxtaposes the audience's gaze with that of the poet and presents the dance not in terms of sensuality but in terms of death. "Canção romântica às virgens loucas" (Romantic Song to the Mad Virgins) is a subtle critique of the restraints that kept women from enjoying the carpe diem attitude and lifestyle granted to the other sex.

Although Meireles is known primarily as a poet, she was an enthusiastic student of folklore, and her interest in the topic can be traced through her writings for *A Manhã* as well as her work for the Comissão Nacional de Folclore (National Commission on Folklore), which was founded in 1948, and which, under her leadership, held its first meeting in Rio Grande do Sul in 1951. Meireles was especially interested in the folk culture of the Azores, the birthplace of her maternal grandmother, who was the inspiration for her fascination with the oral culture of the islands. At this time she made her first visit to the Azores—an emotional journey that, according to an interview she gave, was one of the most memorable events in her life. She also traveled to France, Belgium, and the Netherlands, where she wrote two short works, *Doze noturnos da Holanda* (Twelve Nocturnes of Holland) and *O aeronauta* (The Astronaut), both of which were published in one volume in 1952. The nocturnes combine Meireles's love of music with her attraction to the mysteries of the night. In *O aeronauta* one can find familiar elements, including the theme of solitude and a certain contented absence from the world around her.

For many years Meireles had the idea of composing a series of poems structured around one of the most important historical events in eighteenth-century Brazil, the Inconfidência Mineira. In 1789 a group of men, including the poets Tomás Antônio Gonzaga, Claúdio Manuel da Costa, and Inácio José de Alvarenga Peixoto, plotted to overthrow the imperial government in a rebellion along the lines of the French Revolution. The plot was uncovered, and the rebels were imprisoned. Manuel da Costa hung himself in his jail cell, while the other two poets were sent into exile in Africa. The person denounced as the leader of the conspiracy, the military lieutenant Joaquim José da Silva Xavier, also known as Tiradentes, was hung, and his corpse was quartered and placed on display in the towns where he had preached his revolutionary ideas. After years of research Meireles finally published her book about the conspiracy in 1953 under the title *Romanceiro da inconfidência*. The volume consists of five well-defined parts that convey the setting and atmosphere of the period, the trauma and frustration of the conspirators, the deaths of Manuel da Costa and Tiradentes, and the

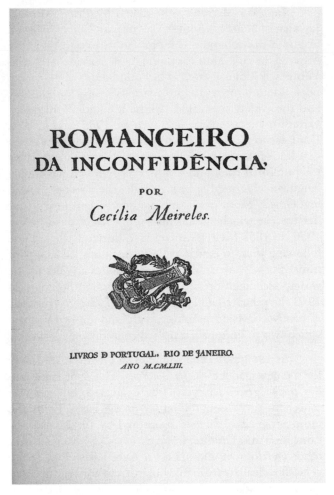

Title page for the 1953 collection of poems commemorating the Inconfidência Mineira (Minas Conspiracy), a 1789 revolt in Minas Gerais against Portuguese rule in Brazil (Joint University Libraries, Nashville)

exile of Gonzaga and Alvarenga Peixoto. The book ends with a temporal shift to describe the death of Dona Maria I, the mother of Dom João VI, some twenty years after the plot to overthrow the government was discovered. Maria had pronounced the men's sentences of death and exile—sentences that purportedly weighed heavily on her mind and drove her insane. What is especially compelling about *Romanceiro da inconfidência* is its formal composition, which is based on the *romanceiro*—a form cultivated by nineteenth-century scholars who sought to collect and record the ballads and tales associated with the oral culture of "o povo" (the people). Given Meireles's long-standing interest in history and folklore, it is easy to see why she opted for this poetic form, which allowed her to bring together a variety of poems employing dialogues, soliloquies, and lyric descriptions of individuals as well as of important historical places and events.

In 1953 Meireles was invited by Prime Minister Jawaharlal Nehru of India to participate in a symposium in honor of Mohandas Gandhi. Her trip to that country inspired the collection *Poemas escritos na India* (1961, Poems Written in India), as well as her translations of the Indian poet Rabindranath Tagore, various essays on Gandhi, and the widely translated "Elegia a Gandhi" (Elegy on Gandhi). In an interview given in 1955 (included in Damasceno's introduction to *Obra poética*), Meireles stated that one of the most moving events in her life was seeing the published translations of her elegy in various Indian languages. During her visit to India she also began writing *Giroflê, giroflá,* an autobiographical narrative about her travels, which she finished in Italy and published in 1956. In 1957 Meireles traveled to Puerto Rico and, the following year, to Israel; in 1962 she published a book of translations, *Poesia de Israel,* which includes artwork by the widely acclaimed Brazilian painter Cândido Portinari. In 1963 she prepared and published *Antologia poética, com poemas inéditos* (Poetic Anthology, with Unpublished Poems), which was to become a standard collection of her works.

In 1963 and 1964 Meireles wrote a weekly *crônica* for the newspaper *Folha de São Paulo.* Her contribution to the *crônica* genre has yet to be evaluated, but she was especially prolific in this area. In the early 1960s the radio program *Quadrante,* sponsored by the Ministry of Education and Culture, featured *crônicas* by Meireles and other well-known authors on a daily basis. The *crônicas* generally dealt with themes of current interest or daily life. In "Amada neve" (1968, Beloved Snow), one example of Meireles's work in this genre, she talked about the beauty and freshness of snow—an element foreign to most of her listeners, for whom she made snow almost palpable. In 1963 she published a small book of poems, *Solombra* (Sunshadow), in which she expresses a desire to recapture a lost love by moving beyond the constraints of day-to-day living. The book includes beautiful verses that describe a romantic longing as well as a sense of farewell to the world. In 1964 a book of Meireles's children's poetry, *Ou isto ou aquilo* (Either This or That), was published—the last volume of her work to appear prior to her death from cancer on 9 November 1964, just two days after her sixty-third birthday. A poem from the collection, "O último andar" (The Top Floor), describes the poet's desire to live in close contact with nature with a vista of the world around her. Although written in an engaging and playful way, the poem can be read as Meireles's invocation of a peaceful and all-encompassing afterlife.

In addition to her volumes of poetry and collections of *crônicas,* essays, articles, plays, and children's books, Meireles published translations of works by Rilke, Kathryn Hulme, García Lorca, Woolf, and Taylor Caldwell. Internationally renowned, Meireles's poetry has been translated into many languages, including English, Spanish, French, Italian, German, Hungarian, Hindi, and Urdu. Pulitzer Prize–winning poet James Merrill translated several of her poems into English. His translations appear in Elizabeth Bishop's *An Anthology of Twentieth-Century Brazilian Poetry* (1972).

Through the years Cecília Meireles's poetry has captured the attention not only of Brazilian and Portuguese critics but also of writers from Argentina, the Azores, Belgium, Bolivia, Cuba, Mozambique, Peru, Switzerland, Uruguay, and the United States. Among her many international awards, she received an honorary doctorate from the University of Delhi in India and was made a member of the Chilean Order of Merit. In 1965, the year after her death, the most distinguished of all literary prizes in Brazil, the Prêmio Machado de Assis, was conferred upon Meireles's complete works by the Academia Brasileira de Letras.

Letters:

A lição do poema: cartas de Cecília Meireles a Armando Côrtes-Rodrigues, edited by Celestino Sachet (Ponta Delgada, Portugal: Instituto Cultural de Ponta Delgada, 1998).

References:

Mário de Andrade, "Viagem," in his *O empalhador de passarinho,* second edition (São Paulo: Martins, 1955);

Neusa Pinsard Casscese, *Festa: contribuição para o estudo do modernismo* (São Paulo: Instituto de Estudos Brasileiros, 1971);

Fernando Cristóvão, "Compreensão portuguesa de Cecília Meireles," *Colóquio: letras,* 46 (1978): 20–27;

Darcy Damasceno, *Cecília Meireles: o mundo contemplado* (Rio de Janeiro: Orfeu, 1967);

Agrippino Grieco, "Quatro Poetisas," in his *Evolução da poesia brasileira,* third edition (Rio de Janeiro: J. Olympio, 1947);

Andrade Muricy, *A nova literatura brasileira* (Pôrto Alegre: Barcellos, Bertaso, 1936);

João Ribeiro, "Cecília Meireles: *Espectros,*" in his *Crítica,* volume 9 (Rio de Janeiro: Academia Brasileira de Letras, 1952), pp. 265–266;

Cassiano Ricardo, *Viagem no tempo e no espaço (memórias)* (Rio de Janeiro: J. Olympio, 1970);

Darlene J. Sadlier, *Cecília Meireles e João Alphonsus,* translated by M. A. Lopes Dean (Brasília: A. Quicé, 1984);

Sadlier, *Imagery and Theme in the Poetry of Cecília Meireles: A Study of Mar absoluto* (Madrid: J. Porrúa Turanzas, 1983);

Eliane Zagury, *Cecília Meireles* (Petrópolis: Vozes, 1973).

Vinicius de Moraes

(19 October 1913 – 9 July 1980)

Marta Almeida
Yale University

BOOKS: *O caminho para a distância* (Rio de Janeiro: Schmidt, 1933);

Forma e exegese (Rio de Janeiro: Pongetti, 1935);

Ariana, a mulher (Rio de Janeiro: Pongetti, 1936);

Novos poemas (Rio de Janeiro: J. Olympio, 1938);

5 elegias (Rio de Janeiro: Pongetti, 1943);

Poemas, sonetos e baladas (São Paulo: Gaveta, 1946);

Pátria minha (Barcelona: O Livro Inconsútil, 1949);

Antologia poética (Rio de Janeiro: A Noite, 1949; enlarged edition, Rio de Janeiro: Editora do Autor, 1960; revised and enlarged, 1962);

Orfeu da conceição: tragédia carioca (São Paulo: Dois amigo, 1956);

Livro de sonetos (Rio de Janeiro: Livros de Portugal, 1957; enlarged edition, Rio de Janeiro: Sabiá, 1967);

Novos poemas (II) (Rio de Janeiro: São José, 1959);

Para viver um grande amor (crônicas e poemas) (Rio de Janeiro: Editora do Autor, 1962);

Procura-se uma rosa: 3 peças em 1 ato, by Moraes, Pedro Bloch, and Claucio Gil (Rio de Janeiro: Massao Ohno, 1962);

Cordélia e o peregrino (Rio de Janeiro: Serviço de Documentação do Ministério da Educação, 1965);

Para uma menina com uma flor (Rio de Janeiro: Editora do Autor, 1966);

Obra poética, edited by Moraes and Afrânio Coutinho (Rio de Janeiro: Aguilar, 1968); enlarged as *Poesia completa e prosa* (Rio de Janeiro: Aguilar, 1974)– includes Eduardo Portella, "Do verso solitário ao canto coletivo," pp. 15–20, and Otto Lara Resende, "O caminho para o soneto," pp. 716–722;

O mergulhador: poemas (Rio de Janeiro: Atelier de Arte, 1968);

As feras: tragédia em três atos (Rio de Janeiro: Serviço Nacional de Teatro, Ministério da Educação e Cultura, 1968);

A arca de Noé: poemas infantis (Rio de Janeiro: Sabiá, 1970; enlarged edition, São Paulo: Companhia das Letras, 2003);

Vinicius de Moraes (photograph by Pedro de Moraes; from José Castello, Vinicius de Moraes: o poeta da paixão. Uma biografia, *1994; Howard-Tilton Memorial Library, Tulane University)*

A mulher e o signo (Rio de Janeiro: Rocco, 1980);

O Cinema de meus olhos, edited by Carlos Augusto Calil (São Paulo: Cinemateca Brasileira/Companhia das Letras, 1991);

Roteiro lírico e sentimental da cidade do Rio de Janeiro e outros lugares por onde passou e se encantou o poeta, introduction and additional texts by José Castello (São Paulo: Companhia das Letras, 1992);

Jardim noturno: poemas inéditos, edited by Ana Maria Miranda (São Paulo: Companhia das Letras, 1993);

Teatro em versos, edited by Calil (São Paulo: Companhia das Letras, 1993);

Poesia completa e prosa, edited by Alexei Bueno (Rio de Janeiro: Nova Aguilar, 1998).

Edition in English: *The Girl from Ipanêma,* translated by Gregory Rabassa, compiled by Roy Cravzow (Merrick, N.Y.: Cross-Cultural Communications, 1982).

PLAY PRODUCTION: *Orfeu da conceição,* music by Antônio Carlos Jobim, Rio de Janeiro, Municipal Theater, 25 September 1956.

PRODUCED SCRIPTS: *Arrastão,* by Moraes, Antoine d'Ormesson, and Lucile Terrin, motion picture, Sumer Films, 1966;

Garôta de Ipanema, by Moraes, Eduardo Coutinho, Leon Hirszman, and Glauber Rocha, motion picture, C.P.S. Produções Cinematográficas/Saga Filmes, 1967.

OTHER: Emil Ludwig, *Beethoven,* translated by Moraes (São Paulo: Nacional, 1945);

Chico Buarque, *Roda-viva (comédia musical em dois atos),* preface by Moraes (Rio de Janeiro: Sabiá, 1968);

Kuri (Maria Beatriz F. de Souza), *Lugar nenhum (poemas),* preface by Moraes (Rio de Janeiro: Pongetti, 1968);

Helena Jobim and Vânia Reis e Silva, *A chave do poço do abismo,* preface by Moraes (Rio de Janeiro: Record, 1968);

Antônio Maria, *O jornal de Antônio Maria,* edited by Ivan Lessa, introduction by Moraes (Rio de Janeiro: Saga, 1968);

Rio de Janeiro, photographs by Bernard Hermann, texts by Moraes and Ferreira Gullar (Papeete: Editions du Pacifique / Rio de Janeiro: Distribuidora Record, 1976); translated as *The Joy of Rio* (New York: Vendome Press, 1980);

Antonio Portinari, *Portinari menino,* includes poems by Moraes (Rio de Janeiro: J. Olympio, 1980).

Vinicius de Moraes is one of the most cherished personalities of Brazilian popular culture. Although he was one of the most important poets of his time, he wrote most of his poetry before the late 1950s and spent the next two decades writing, recording, and performing songs; thus, his public image is associated with song festivals and musical shows. Because of his success as a popular musician, some critics have not taken him seriously as a poet.

Moraes was born in Rio de Janeiro on 19 October 1913 to Clodoaldo Pereira da Silva Moraes and Lydia Santos Moraes, née Cruz; his Latin-loving father had

him christened Marcus Vinitius da Cruz de Melo. The father played the guitar and sang songs about Brazil's past for his four children; their mother played the piano and sang. For much of Moraes's childhood the family lived with his maternal grandparents. At age nine Moraes went to a notary public with his sister and legally changed his name to Vinicius de Moraes.

Moraes attended high school at the Colégio Santo Inácio, where he played guitar in a band and sang the songs he was beginning to compose; the lyrics declared love for all women and expressed despair at not being understood. His motto, "ser amigo de todos os homens e o amor de todas as mulheres" (being a friend to all men and the love of all women), guided his social life. After graduating from high school in 1931, Moraes enrolled in law school at the Faculdade de Direito of the Universidade Federal do Rio de Janeiro. He became a member of the Academic Center for Law Studies, where he met Almir Castro, a founder of the Charlie Chaplin Club. Moraes, who loved movies, spent hours copying the titles of motion pictures, the names of directors, and screenplays from Castro's files. His fellow law student, the future writer Otávio de Faria, inspired Moraes to publish his first poetry collection, *O caminho para a distância* (The Road into the Distance), in 1933. In the poems life hangs between light and darkness; the speaker is lonely and afraid and appeals for help as he confronts human misery and pain. His craving for maternal love is expressed in "Minha Mãe" (My Mother):

Minha mãe, minha mãe, eu tenho medo
Tenho medo da vida, minha mãe

(My mother, my mother, I am afraid
I'm afraid of life, my mother)

The modernist poet Oswald de Andrade told Moraes that his poetry would improve when he left behind his "antenna complex"—that is, when he stopped trying to capture something mysterious in the air and came down to earth.

Between 1935 and 1938 Moraes published *Forma e exegese* (1935, Forms and Exegeses), *Ariana, a mulher* (1936, Ariana, the Woman), and *Novos poemas* (1938, New Poems). *Ariana, a mulher* marks the end of his mystical and transcendental phase; up to this time Moraes had been seduced by the hermeticism of European poets such as Stéphane Mallarmé. Under the influence of his friend and fellow poet Manuel Bandeira the breath of real life and a more objective viewpoint begins to color Moraes's work; at a time when long, impersonal biblical verse was in fashion, Moraes wrote pieces such as "Soneto de inspiração" (Sonnet of Inspiration), which appears in *Novos poemas:*

> Amo-te como se ama todo o bem
> Que o grande mal da vida traz consigo.
>
> (I love you as one loves the good
> That the great evil of life brings.)

Antitheses such as "one loves the good that the evil of life brings" were censured by his fellow poets and critics, but these early attempts bore fruit in a masterpiece that includes a line that will forever be associated with Moraes: "a vida é a arte do encontro embora haja muitos desencontros pela vida" (life is the art of the encounter, although there are many nonencounters in life). "O falso mendigo" (The False Beggar) in *Novos poemas* is a plea to his family to help him make sense of his confused poetic drive:

> Quero fazer uma poesia
> . . . .
> Tenho um tédio enorme da vida
> Liga para vovó Nenem, pede a ela uma idéia bem
>   inocente.
>
> (I want to write a poem
> . . . .
> I have this enormous feeling of tediousness in my life
> Ask grandmother Neném for a very innocent idea.)

In 1938 the British Council granted Moraes a scholarship to study English language and literature at Magdalen College of the University of Oxford. While in England he worked for the British Broadcasting Corporation, broadcasting programs to Brazil. In 1939 he married Beatriz Azevedo de Mello by proxy. His stay in England cut short by the outbreak of World War II, Moraes returned to Brazil at the end of 1939. He and his wife settled in São Paulo; their first child, Susana, was born in 1940. In São Paulo, Moraes worked as a movie critic for the newspaper *A Manhã;* he also contributed to the literary supplement of the paper. His son, Pedro, was born in 1942. That year he met the Argentinean writer María Rosa Oliver and, through her, the poet Gabriela Mistral. In 1943 he began a course of training for a career with the Brazilian foreign service. In 1944 he edited the literary supplement of the newspaper *O Jornal,* publishing contributions from painters and architects, as well as from writers. During 1945 he wrote movie reviews for various newspapers.

In 1946 Moraes became Brazilian vice consul in Los Angeles; he remained in the post until 1950 and did not visit his homeland during that time. His *Poemas,*

THE GIRL FROM IPANÊMA
Vinícius de Moraes

Translated by Gregory Rabassa

...ltural Review   Chapbook 34

Paperback cover for the 1982 collection that includes an English translation of Moraes's best-known song, "A garôta de Ipanema" (1962), which was set to a bossa nova tune by Antônio Carlos Jobim. The popular 1964 recording by singer Astrud Gilberto used a much freer translation by Norman Gimbel (University of South Carolina Salkehatchie Libraries).

sonetos e baladas (1946, Poems, Sonnets and Ballads) filled the gap between the nostalgic treatment of the past by poets such as Carlos Drummond de Andrade and Augusto Frederico Schmidt and the free verse of the modernist poets. Moraes became the first mass-market poet in Brazil after his "Soneto de fidelidade" (Sonnet of Faithfulness) was set to music:

> Eu possa me dizer do amor (que tive)
> Que não seja imortal, posto que é chama
> Mas que seja infinito enquanto dure.
>
> (So that I can tell myself about the love [I had]
> Be it not immortal because its nature is flame
> But be it infinite while it lasts.)

Not only spiritual love but also a powerful and some-times explicit sensuality dominates the poetry in this volume, as in "Balada para Maria" (Ballad for Maria):

> Aprendi muita carícia . . .
> Para fazer-te a delícia
> Só terei gestos exatos.

> (I learned how to caress . . .
> For your delight
> I will have only the precise move.)

In this volume women are no longer disturbing and ethereal, as in *Ariana, a mulher,* but concrete and human: for example, in "Garotas de bicicleta" (Bicycle Girls) he depicts girls riding their bicycles through the streets of Rio de Janeiro. "A balada do Mangue" (The Ballad of Mangue [the Rio de Janeiro red-light district]) earned front-page status in national newspapers. Moraes deals with recent events in "A bomba atômica" (The Atomic Bomb) and "A rosa de Hiroxima" (The Rose of Hiroshima). "Pátria minha" (My Homeland) expresses more than melancholy homesickness in its realistic description of Brazil as "minha pátria sem sapatos e sem meias" (my country, without shoes or socks). "Dia da criação" (Day of Creation), another public favorite when it was set to music, has been compared to the verse of the Spanish poet Federico García Lorca. The speaker celebrates life in everything, from the sublime to the sordid:

> Neste momento todo os bares estão repletos de homens
>   vazios
> . . . .
> Todas as mulheres estão atentas
> Porque hoje é sábado

> (At this moment all the bars are full of empty men
> . . . .
> All the women are attentive
> Because today is Saturday)

Poemas, sonetos e baladas also includes "Saudades de Manuel Bandeira" (Missing Manuel Bandeira):

> Foste uma estrela em meu degredo
> Poeta, pai! Áspero irmão.

> (You were a star in my exile
> Poet, father! Harsh brother.)

In 1947 Moraes studied moviemaking with the actor and director Orson Welles and the cinematographer Gregg Toland, who had collaborated with Welles on *Citizen Kane* (1941). Moraes and his wife were divorced in 1949. That year he published *Antologia poética* (Poetic Anthology); it includes "Poema enjoa-dinho" (A Little Boring Poem), in which he portrays himself as a concerned and loving father:

> Filhos . . . Filhos?
> Melhor não tê-los!
> Mas se não os temos
> Como sabê-lo?

> Noites de insônia
> Cãs prematuras
> Prantos convulsos
> Meus Deus, salvai-o!

> (Children . . . Children?
> Better not have them!
> But if we don't have them
> How would we know it?

> Nights of insomnia
> Premature hair loss
> Convulsive weeping
> My God, save him!)

In 1950 Moraes traveled to Mexico to visit his friend the Chilean poet Pablo Neruda. The following year he married Lila Maria Esquerdo e Bôscoli. In 1952 he was sent by the foreign service as a delegate to the film festival in Punta del Este, Uruguay; afterward, he went to Europe to learn more about the organization of film festivals in Cannes, Berlin, Locarno, and Venice. His daughter Georgiana was born in 1953. That same year he was sent to Paris as second secretary of the Brazilian embassy. In 1954 he organized a film festival to celebrate the four hundredth anniversary of the city of São Paulo. The script for his play *Orfeu da conceição* (Orpheus of the Imagination) won an award in a contest held as part of the celebration; it was staged in Rio de Janeiro in 1956 with a score by Antônio Carlos Jobim, and an album of the songs from the play was released the same year. Also in 1956 Moraes's third daughter, Luciana, was born. The play was the basis for the 1959 French motion picture *Orfeo negro* (released in English as *Black Orpheus*), directed by Marcel Camus. Like the play, the movie sets the Greek tragedy of Orpheus and Eurydice in the slums of modern Rio de Janeiro during Carnaval and represents the underworld through Afro-Brazilian rituals. The entire cast of *Orfeo negro* is Afro-Brazilian, giving a voice to this largely ignored population.

In 1958 Moraes married Maria Lúcia Proença and was named first secretary of the Brazilian embassy in Montevideo, Uruguay. An album of his songs, *Canção do amor demais* (Song of Excessive Love), set to music by Jobim and sung by Elizete Cardoso, was a great success that year. In the late 1950s and early 1960s Moraes wrote many songs in the bossa nova

Moraes with Heloísa (Helô) Pinheiro. According to legend, the teenage Pinheiro inspired "A garôta de Ipanema" when she walked past the Veloso Bar in Rio de Janeiro on her way to the beach at Ipanema and was seen through the window by Moraes and Jobim, who were in the bar collaborating on a musical comedy (Collection of the Moraes family; from José Castello, Vinicius de Moraes: o pocta da paixão. Uma biografia, *1994; Howard-Tilton Memorial Library, Tulane University).*

(new trend) style of the samba that were set to music by Jobim, Carlos Lyra, and Pixinguinha. In 1962 he began composing sambas with the guitar player Baden Powell that reveal an Afro-Brazilian influence. In August of that year he gave his first show at the Rio de Janeiro nightclub AuBom Gourmet. For years thereafter he filled nightclubs with these shows, in which he read his poems and sang his songs.

The desire to possess the feminine ideal and the torture of trying to keep her is the theme of *Orfeu da conceição* and of many of Moraes's poems and songs. In "A mulher que passa" (The Woman Who Passes By) in *Novos poemas* the desire of the moment, the possibility of adventure, and the call of the unknown excite the speaker's imagination:

Oh! Como és linda, mulher que passas
Que me sacias e suplicias

(Oh, how beautiful it is, the woman who passes
That possesses me and tortures me)

One cannot help but compare this poem to the lyrics of Moraes's best-known song, "A garôta de Ipanema" (1962; translated as "The Girl from Ipanema," 1964), set to music by Jobim:

Olha que coisa mais linda
Mais cheia de graça
É ela, a menina
Que vem e que passa
Num doce balanço
Caminho do mar. . . .

(Look what a beautiful thing
So graceful
It is she, the girl
Who comes and passes by
In a sweet sway
On her way to the sea. . . .)

In 1963 Moraes married his fourth wife, Nelita Abreu Rocha, and went to Paris as a delegate to the United Nations Educational, Scientific, and Cultural

273

Organization (UNESCO). He returned to Brazil in 1964. In 1967 he collaborated on the screenplay for the movie *Garôta de Ipanema* (The Girl from Ipanema), inspired by his song. During the next decade he worked with some of Brazil's best-known musicians and composers, including Lyra, Powell, Chico Buarque, Toquinho, and Edu Lobo and wrote songs of every Brazilian musical style, including all forms of the samba. He and his various partners were often finalists at song festivals.

Moraes divorced Nelita in 1968; in 1969 he married Cristina Gurjão, only to divorce her a year later. His show-business career and his many marriages and love affairs were not considered the appropriate image for a diplomat, and he was asked to leave the foreign service. In 1970 he married the young actress Gesse Gessy; their daughter, Maria, was born that same year. In 1971 they moved to Bahia, where Moraes befriended some female shamans of the Afro-Brazilian ritual *candomblé*. In 1972 he and Toquinho traveled to Italy, where they recorded songs in Italian. In 1976 Moraes married Marta Rodrigues Santamaria. In 1977 he performed at the Canecão, Rio de Janeiro's great theater, with Jobim and Buarque's sister Miúcha; the performance made a monumental contribution to Brazilian music because of the many musical styles represented and their acceptance by the public. In 1978 Moraes married his seventh wife, Gilda Queirós Matoso, whom he had met in Paris. After being hospitalized several times for detoxification from alcohol, he died in his bathtub of pulmonary edema on 9 July 1980.

Moraes belonged to the generation of poets that included such literary giants as Bandeira, Faria, and Schmidt, all of whom were his close friends. While their contemporaries, the modernists, discarded meter and rhyme in favor of free verse and rejected the sonnet as outdated, cold in content, and rigid in form, Moraes's group revived this traditional form and made it fashionable again. Moraes was also recognized as a populist poet who wrote about social issues and concerns. The critic Eduardo Portella points out that Moraes's writing is essentially dramatic, in that he portrays conflict rather than fact; this tendency can be seen in the poet's propensity for using dichotomies. Rather than distancing himself from the world intellectually, Moraes participates in the scenes he portrays. His personal involvement in his work is revealed in the ballads he wrote to his family members and friends, such as "Soneto para Pablo Neruda" (Sonnet to Pablo Neruda) in *Livro de sonetos* (1957, Book of Sonnets):

Quantos caminhos não fizemos juntos

Neruda, meu irmão, meu companheiro . . .

(The many paths we did not cross together
Neruda, my brother, my friend . . .)

Moraes traveled widely in his career as a diplomat, and his work is marked by images from his life in England, France, and the United States. But he immortalized his beloved Rio de Janeiro in bossa nova such songs as "A garota de Ipanema" and an ode to the towering white statue of Christ that stands on the 2,400-foot Corcovado hill above Rio de Janeiro and can be seen from almost every part of the city. Moraes loved Rio de Janeiro, and in one of his many newspaper interviews he declared that being a Carioca has little to do with one's origin but "is a state of mind"; it means being enamored of the atmosphere surrounding the city, contemplating the ocean and the gentle mountains, and feeling at home in Rio's eternal, intoxicating disorder.

Moraes was the poet of love and women. His literary works are marked by a personal lyricism that resonates with two recurring themes: first, the dichotomy of love and death; and second, women—the pleasure he experienced with them and the torment he suffered because of them. Moraes's major contribution to the development of Brazilian poetry, according to the critic Antônio Cândido, is the development of a lexicon that establishes a connection among the ocean, the beach, and physical and nonphysical love. Because of his popularity, Moraes stands as a central figure in the literary Generation of 1945, and his image has become almost legendary. In his personal life he strived to fulfill his motto of being "charming to all men and loved by all women." He continues to be revered by younger generations as the father of the bossa nova, a musical rhythm that came to the fore in the late 1950s and early 1960s. Moraes is perhaps best known for writing the lyrics to the popular song, "The Girl from Ipanema," which portrayed the unattainable beauty of a Brazilian woman on her way to the sea. His torrid love affairs, some of which ended in marriage, earned him his reputation as the poet who held the key to women's hearts.

Four of Vinicius de Moraes's poems—"O soneto da Felicidade" (The Sonnet of Happiness), "Poema de Natal" (Christmas Poem), "A rosa de Hiroxima," and "Minha Pátria"—are included in the 2001 edition of Italo Moriconi's *Os cem melhores poemas brasileiros do século* (The One Hundred Best Brazilian Poems of the Century). This recognition ranks Moraes among Brazil's most representative poets. Nevertheless, the scope of Moraes's legacy of poetry, music, chronicles, plays, and movies has yet to be given the thorough examination it deserves. Bandeira's comment in a review of Moraes's first book, *O caminho para a distância,* in the Rio de Janeiro newspaper *Diário de Notícias* (13 November 1933) still holds true: "Moraes é uma força criativa da natureza, com o ar do romântico, a espiritualidade dos simbolistas, a arte dos parnasianos com um toque barroco, mas acima de tudo, um homem do seu tempo com todo seu cinismo e crenças" (Moraes is a creative force of nature, with the breath of the Romantic, spirituality of the Symbolists, skill of the Parnassians with a Baroque touch, but above all, a man of his time, with all its cynicism and beliefs).

Letters:

Querido poeta: correspondência de Vinicius de Moraes, edited by Ruy Castro (São Paulo: Companhia das Letras, 2003).

Interview:

Selden Rodman, *Tongues of Fallen Angels: Conversations with Jorge Luis Borges, Robert Frost, Ernest Hemingway, Pablo Neruda, Stanley Kunitz, Gabriel García Márquez, Octavio Paz, Norman Mailer, Allen Ginsberg, Vinícius De Moraes, João Cabral De Melo Neto, Derek Walcott* (New York: New Directions, 1974).

Biography:

José Castello, *Vinicius de Moraes: o poeta da paixão. Uma biografia* (São Paulo: Companhia das Letras, 1994).

References:

Carlos Afonso, *ABC de Vinícius de Moraes* (Rio de Janeiro: Novo Quadro, 1991);

Mário de Andrade, "Belo, forte, jovem," in his *O empalhador de passarinho* (São Paulo: Martins, 1946);

Geraldo Carneiro, *Vinícius de Moraes* (Rio de Janeiro: Espaço Cultural Toca do Vinícius, 1997);

José Castello, *Vinicius de Moraes: o poeta da paixão. Uma biografia* (São Paulo: Companhia das Letras, 1994);

Castello, *Vinicius de Moraes: uma geografia poética* (Rio de Janeiro: Relume Dumará/Rio Arte, 1996);

Otávio de Faria, *Dois poetas: Augusto Frederico Schmidt e Vinícius de Moraes* (Rio de Janeiro: Ariel, 1935);

Sonia Alem Marrach, *A arte do encontro de Vinícius de Moraes: poemas e canções de uma época de mudanças, 1932–1980* (São Paulo: Escuta/FAPESP, 2000);

Guaraciaba Micheletti, *A poesia, o mar e a mulher: um só Vinicius* (São Paulo: Escuta, 1994);

Vivi Nabuco and Lucia Braga, *Vinicius arquivinho* (Rio de Janeiro: Bem-Te-Vi, 2002);

João Carlos Pecci, *Vinicius sem ponto final* (São Paulo: Saraiva, 1994);

Carlos Swann, "Obra prima," *O Globo* (Rio de Janeiro), 23 June 2001;

Xoán Ignacio Taibo, *Vinícius de Moraes* (Madrid: Júcar, 1984).

Papers:

Vinicius de Moraes's manuscripts are in the Fundação Casa de Ruy Barbosa and in the Toca de Vinicius, both in Rio de Janeiro.

Nélida Piñon

(3 May 1937 –   )

Regina Igel
University of Maryland

See also the Piñon entry in *DLB 145: Modern Latin-American Fiction Writers, Second Series.*

BOOKS: *Guia-mapa de Gabriel Arcanjo* (Rio de Janeiro: GRD, 1961);

Madeira feita cruz (Rio de Janeiro: GRD, 1963);

Tempo das frutas: contos (Rio de Janeiro: Álvaro, 1966);

Fundador (Rio de Janeiro: Álvaro, 1969; revised edition, Rio de Janeiro: Labor do Brasil, 1976);

A casa da paixão (Rio de Janeiro: Sabiá, 1972);

Sala de armas: contos (Rio de Janeiro: Sabiá, 1973);

Tebas do meu coração (Rio de Janeiro: J. Olympio, 1974);

A força do destino (Rio de Janeiro: Record, 1977);

O calor das coisas (Rio de Janeiro: Nova Fronteira, 1980);

A república dos sonhos: romance (Rio de Janeiro: Alves, 1984); translated by Helen Lane as *The Republic of Dreams: A Novel* (New York: Knopf, 1989; London: Picador, 1994);

A doce canção de Caetana (Rio de Janeiro: Guanabara, 1987); translated by Lane as *Caetana's Sweet Song* (New York: Knopf, 1992);

O pão de cada dia: fragmentos (Rio de Janeiro: Nova Fronteira, 1994);

Discurso: Prêmio Juan Rulfo 1995 (São Paulo: Fundação Memorial da América Latina, 1996);

A roda do vento (São Paulo: Ática, 1998);

The Female Memory in Narrative: Lecture (Washington, D.C.: IDB Cultural Center, 1999);

Até amanhã, outra vez: crônicas (Rio de Janeiro: Record, 1999);

Cortejo do Divino: e outros contos escolhidos, edited by Maria da Glória Bordini (Pôrto Alegre: L & PM, 2001);

O presumível coração da América (São Paulo: Topbooks, 2002);

Vozes do deserto (Rio de Janeiro & São Paulo: Record, 2004).

Nélida Piñon (photograph by Nicolas Alagemovitz; Arquivo da Academia Brasileira de Letras)

Edition in English: "Adamastor," in *Latin American Writers: Thirty Stories,* edited by Gabriella Ibieta (New York: St. Martin's Press, 1993).

OTHER: *Fernando Casás: ocos. Marzo 1992, Casa da Parra, Santiago de Compostela,* texts by Piñon and others (Santiago de Compostela: Xunta de Galicia, 1992);

"Espanha: o passado da Europa à Baira-Mar," in *Viagem inteligente: as mais belas cidades do mundo na visão de sete autores Brasileiros* (São Paulo: Geração, 1994);

"Metamorphosis," in *Voice-overs: Translation and Latin American Literature,* edited by Daniel Balderston and Marcy E. Schwartz (Albany: State University of New York Press, 2002).

Nélida Piñon is known for her distinctive use of the Portuguese language in her novels and short stories. Through her language she achieves a poetic density that has led some critics to compare her work to the prose of the nineteenth-century writer Joaquim Maria Machado de Assis. This comparison is the highest compliment to which a Brazilian writer can aspire. Personal thoughts and comments, often ironic, are interspersed throughout her fiction.

Nélida Cuiñas Piñon was born on 3 May 1937 in the Vila Isabel district of Rio de Janeiro, to Lino Piñon Muiños, an immigrant from Galicia, Spain, and Olivia Carmen Cuiñas. Her first name is an anagram of Daniel, her paternal grandfather's name. Because books were one of her passions, Piñon's father gave her an open account in a bookstore. Her mother encouraged her love of opera and ballet and often accompanied her to performances. At age ten she was sent to her father's homeland for two years. Piñon attended Catholic elementary and high schools and received a degree in journalism from the Catholic University of Rio de Janeiro.

Piñon's first novel, *Guia-mapa de Gabriel Arcanjo* (1961, Guide-map of Archangel Gabriel), takes the form of a long dialogue between Mariella and the archangel Gabriel about the young woman's desire to be free from Christian dogmas. They discuss the concept of sin, divine pardon, and the relationship between humans and God. *Guia-mapa de Gabriel Arcanjo* is written in a baroque style filled with twisted sentences, multiple metaphors, and an abundance of descriptive minutiae.

In Piñon's next book, the novel *Madeira feita cruz* (1963, Wooden Cross), Pedro is a fanatic who creates a personal religion to hide his failures as a man; his wife, Maria, remains a virgin throughout their marriage; their young domestic servant, Ana, is an erotic flame, a silent but persistent personality reminiscent of a prophet. As a leitmotiv in the work, wood represents construction and destruction, a means of connection and of isolation, through images such as the door of Pedro and Maria's hut, a forest cut down by Ana's relatives, and a bridge built by Ana's brother. Piñon's first collection of short stories, *Tempo das frutas* (Time of the Fruit), appeared three years after *Madeira feita cruz*.

Piñon was assistant editor of the journal *Cadernos Brasileiros* in 1966–1967. In 1969, at the invitation of Afrânio Coutinho, chairman of the Department of Letters, she conducted the first workshop on literary creativity at the Federal University of Rio de Janeiro.

In the novel *Fundador* (1969, The Founder) the title character establishes a new religion in a village in the middle of a thick forest and persuades the inhabitants of the failures of their oppressors, who have always been considered unreachable idols. The rebellious message of the novel is obscured by a web of innuendos and allusions that typify Piñon's writing during the years of military dictatorship in Brazil. She received the Walmap Prize for the novel in 1970 and revised and republished the work in 1976.

A casa da paixão (1972, The House of Passions) is a feminist cry for recognition of women's sexual desires and for their freedom from social and religious chains. Marta, who is beginning to experience sexual feelings, channels her desires into worship of the sun. But her father is obsessed with her budding beauty, and they end up in an incestuous relationship. The towering trees surrounding the house symbolize the magnitude of the passions within. Piñon won the Mário de Andrade Prize of the Association of Art Critics of São Paulo for *A casa da paixão* in 1973.

Sala de armas (1973, Weapons Room) is Piñon's second collection of short stories. The sixteen narratives about self-doubts and conflicts of the heart combine reality with dreams. Throughout the volume Piñon integrates convolutions typical of the literary baroque with a linear and transparent style.

In *Tebas do meu coração* (1974, Thebes of My Heart) the inhabitants of the fictional city of Santíssimo are feverishly preparing for war because of their envy of the prosperous neighboring town. When the war breaks out, however, the contenders throw cookies at each other—a humorous twist in a narrative otherwise filled with apprehension and anguish.

Piñon was a member of the editorial board of the journal *Tempo Brasileiro* from 1976 to 1993. The sense of humor displayed in *Tebas do meu coração* is expanded in her next novel, *A força do destino* (1977, The Force of Destiny), a parody of Giuseppe Verdi's 1862 opera *La forza del destino*. Piñon inserts herself in the plot and disrupts the tragic sequence of events that were first depicted by the Spanish author Angel de Saavedra in his play *Don Álvaro, o La fuerza del sino* (1835, Don Álvaro, or the Power of Fate), the source of Verdi's work. Rewriting the drama on her own terms, Piñon allows the female characters to vent their frustration at the lofty behavior of the males.

In 1980 Piñon published *O calor das coisas* (The Warmth of Things), a collection of short fiction that includes the English-titled story "I love my husband." An atmosphere of silent despair permeates the piece, in which a housewife reflects on the monotony of her life. She resents the absence of a personal identity, and she gradually comes to see the ways in which society has

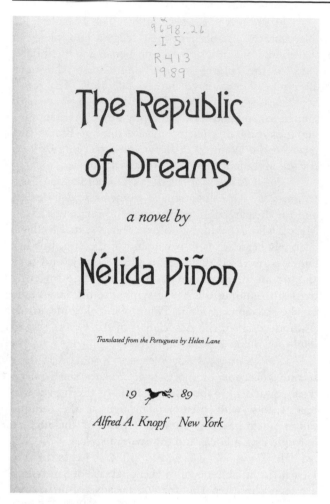

The Republic
of Dreams

a novel by

Nélida Piñon

Translated from the Portuguese by Helen Lane

19 🐎 89

Alfred A. Knopf   New York

Title page for the U.S. edition of the English translation of A república dos sonhos, *Piñon's 1984 novel about a Galician peasant who immigrates to Brazil and becomes a wealthy industrialist (Thomas Cooper Library, University of South Carolina)*

robbed her of individual freedom by imparting to her the feeling that she would be worthy as a woman only if she had a husband. Her intense analysis results in the ironic phrase, spelled out in a foreign language, that forms the title of the story. "I love my husband" was included in Italo Moriconi's *Os cem melhores contos brasileiros do século* (2000, The One Hundred Best Brazilian Short Stories of the Century).

In 1983 Piñon won the Premio Latinoamericano de Novela from Nicaragua and the Premio Casa de las Américas from Cuba. The following year she published *A república dos sonhos* (translated as *The Republic of Dreams,* 1989) to honor her Galician ancestors. The novel includes her personal memories and stories told by members of her family. Piñon wrote seven versions of the work—a total of five thousand pages—before submitting the manuscript to the publisher. The dense narrative follows the rise of Madruga from Galician peasant at the turn of the twentieth century to successful indus-

trialist in Brazil in the 1980s through the eyes of three women: Eulália, who describes the expatriates' experiences prior to their move to Brazil; her daughter, Esperança (Hope), whose name suggests the hopes nurtured by the immigrants; and Breta, who assimilates her predecessors' stories and reconstructs them from her own viewpoint. Piñon received the PEN Club and Association of Art Critics of São Paulo awards for *A república dos sonhos* in 1985.

A doce canção de Caetana (1987; translated as *Caetana's Sweet Song,* 1992), written during a visit to Barcelona, Spain, is set in the fictional Brazilian town of Trindade. The cattle baron Polidoro loved the singer Caetana, but she abandoned him many years ago. When she returns to Trindade, he has hopes of resuming their affair. After he prepares a room for her at the hotel, with the furnishings provided by local prostitutes, and even goes so far as to acquiesce in her demand that he build a theater as a venue for her performances, Caetana again suddenly departs from his life. After voicing their disbelief and anger at the behavior of the self-proclaimed diva, Polidoro and the ladies of ill repute return to the monotonous rhythm of life in the backwater town. Piñon won the Brazilian Union of Writers of São Paulo and the José Geraldo Vieira prizes for *A doce canção de Caetana.*

In 1988 Piñon served on the jury for the Neustadt Award in the United States and the panel for the Latin America Soap Opera Award in Nicaragua. On 27 July 1989 she was elected to the Brazilian Academy of Letters, replacing the late Aurélio Buarque de Holanda; she was inducted into the academy on 3 May 1990 and named director of the academy's archives later that year. Also in 1990 she won the State of Rio de Janeiro's Golfinho de Ouro prize for her contribution to Brazilian letters. In 1991 she received the Bienal Nestlé Prize and also became Henry King Stanford Distinguished Professor of Humanities at the University of Miami, where she teaches creative writing and Brazilian literature from January to May each year. She was awarded King Juan of Spain's Lazo de Dama de Isabel la Católica in 1992. In 1993 she was a member of the editorial boards of the journals *Cadernos Pedagógicos e Culturais* and *Imagen Latinoamericana,* the latter of which is published in Caracas, Venezuela.

O pão de cada dia: fragmentos (1994, Our Daily Bread: Fragments) is a nonfiction work in which Piñon describes her travels in Galicia, Nicaragua, and France; her encounters with such writers as Mario Vargas Llosa, Manuel Puig, Jorge Luis Borges, Julio Cortazar, Raquel de Queiroz, and Clarice Lispector; and her recollections of conversations with her father and grandfather. The work also includes her observations on poverty and comments on biblical passages and her

Cover for Piñon's 1987 novel (translated as Caetana's Sweet Song, *1992), about a cattle baron who is deserted
for the second time by the singer he loves (Thomas Cooper Library, University of South Carolina)*

view of writing as a mission that must be fulfilled at all costs.

Since 1995 Piñon has served on the editorial board of *Review: Latin American Literature and Arts* and has contributed a weekly column to the Rio de Janeiro newspaper *O Dia*. That year she received the Brazilian government's Order of the Southern Cross and became the first woman, and the first author writing in Portuguese, to win the Juan Rulfo International Prize for Latin American and Caribbean Literature. She was elected first secretary of the Brazilian Academy of Letters on 26 June 1995, general secretary on 12 July 1995, and acting president in August 1996. On 5 December 1996 Piñon became the first woman to be elected president of the academy of letters. Her term of office coincided with the institution's one-hundredth anniversary, which was celebrated throughout 1997 with events including conferences and new editions of works by Brazil's most eminent authors. Also in 1997 she served on the editorial board of the journal *Impressões*.

After many years of writing solely for adults, Piñon published a novel for a preadolescent audience. *A roda do vento* (1998, The Wind's Wheel) is the story of a magician who teaches her nephews to travel using their imagination. The day arrives when they embark on an adventurous voyage without their aunt's help.

Piñon has taught at the City University of New York, Columbia University, Johns Hopkins University, and Georgetown University in the United States; the Catholic University of Lima, Peru; the Sorbonne; and the Universidad Complutense of Madrid. She has participated in cultural organizations, debates, television programs, conferences, and symposia in Brazil and abroad. She has been honored by the establishment of the Nélida Piñon Library in the Brazilian consulate in Miami and by having a street named after her in the city of Lençóis Paulista in the state of São Paulo. In 2002 she received the prestigious Rosalía de Castro Prize from the PEN Club of Galicia, which recognizes lifetime achievements by authors writing in Spanish and Portuguese. That year she collected the speeches she had delivered on accepting some of her many awards as *O presumível coração da América* (The Possible Heart of America).

Nélida Piñon's contribution to Brazilian literature involves an intuitive ability to portray humanity's weaknesses and strengths and an acute awareness of the richness of the Portuguese language. Her thought-provoking plots revolve around such basic human elements as love, joy, solitude, pain, anger, jealousy, ambition, greed, and illusion. Throughout her fiction she sustains a balance between the spiritual and the mundane. For Piñon the Portuguese language is a gift to be preserved, honored, and bequeathed to future generations of Brazilians.

References:

Maria Alice Pires Cardoso de Aguiar, "A construção medieva dos personagens hierofantes em *Fundador* de Nélida Piñon," in *III Encontro Internacional de Estudos Medievais* (Rio de Janeiro: UERJ, 1999), pp. 33–34;

Aguiar, "Guia-Mapa de Gabriel-Arcanjo: o marco geográfico-existencial da obra de Nélida Piñon. 35 anos de produção literária," *Caderno Seminal*, 4 (1997);

Aguiar, "Nélida Piñon: fundação em tempo tríplice," in *Letras em tese (poesia, teatro, narrativa),* by Aguiar, Carlinda Fragale Pate Nuñez, and others (Rio de Janeiro: Relume-Dumará e Centro Cultural do Banco do Brasil, 1995), pp. 63–99;

Aguiar, "Rastreando a categoria do mito da origem e do sagrado em 'O pão de cada dia,' de Nélida Piñon," in *II Congresso Nacional de Lingüística e Filologia* (Rio de Janeiro: Universidade Federal do Rio de Janeiro, 1998), pp. 394–403;

Aguiar, "O resgate da origem através do mito do mar e da ilha em 'Finisterre' de Nélida Piñon," in *Congresso Internacional de Literaturas Lusófonas: As Vozes e as Vezes Oceânicas* (Brussels: Universidade Livre de Bruxelas, Bélgica, 1998), p. 42;

Aguiar, "A urdidura do mito e do sagrado em: 'O pão de cada dia,' de Nélida Piñon," *Paradoxa: Projetivas Múltiplas em Educação,* 4, no. 9 (1998): 5–10;

Vilma Areas, "Do adamastor camoniano à 'Sala de Armas' de Nélida Piñon," *Coloquio,* 27 (1974): 32–39;

Nelly Novaes Coelho, "A Casa da Paixão e as forças primordiais da natureza," *Convivium,* 16 (May–June 1973): 216–228;

Coelho, "'República dos Sonhos,' Prémio Ficção/84 APCA: Memória, historicidade, imaginário," *Convivium,* 28 (May–June 1985): 257–265;

Horácio Costa, "À margem de 'A República dos Sonhos,' de Nélida Piñon," *Luso-Brazilian Review,* 24 (Summer 1987): 1–15;

Naomi Hoki Moniz, "A Casa da Paixão: Ética, estética e a condição feminina," *Revista Ibero-americana,* 126 (January–March 1984): 129–140;

José Ornellas, "El mundo simbólico y filosófico de *Madeira Feita Cruz* de Nélida Piñon," *Nueva Narrativa Hispanoamericana,* 3, no. 1 (1973): 95–102;

Giovanni Pontiero, "Notes on the Fiction of Nélida Piñon," *Review,* 76, no. 19 (1976): 67–71;

Carmen Lúcia Tindó Secco, *Além da idade da razão: longevidade e saber na ficção brasileira* (Rio de Janeiro: Graphia, 1994);

Mario Vargas Llosa, "Presentación de un libro de Nélida Piñon," *Revista de Cultura Brasileña,* 48 (January 1979): 81–91.

Raul Pompéia
(Raul d'Ávila Pompéia)
(12 April 1863 – 25 December 1895)

Sérgio Nazar David
Universidade do Estado do Rio de Janeiro

BOOKS: *Uma tragédia no Amazonas* (Rio de Janeiro: Cosmopolita, 1880);

Microscópios (São Paulo: A Comédia, 1881);

O Ateneu (Rio de Janeiro: Gazeta de Notícias, 1888);

Carta ao autor das Festas nacionaes (Rio de Janeiro: Leuzinger, 1893);

Canções sem metro (Rio de Janeiro: Aldina, 1900);

Obras, 10 volumes, edited by Afrânio Coutinho and Eduardo de Faria Coutinho (Rio de Janeiro: Ministcrio da Educação e Cultura, Fundação Nacional de Material Escolar, Oficina Literária Afrânio Coutinho, Editora Civilização Brasileira, 1981–1984)—comprises volume 1: *Novellas;* volume 2: *O Ateneu;* volume 3: *Cantos;* volume 4: *Canções sem metro;* volume 5: *Escritos politicos;* volumes 6–9: *Crônicas;* and volume 10: *Miscelânea, Fotobiografia;*

Crônicas do Rio, edited by Virgílio Moretzsohn Moreira (Rio de Janeiro: Prefeitura da Cidade do Rio de Janeiro, Secretairia Municipal de Cultura, Departamento Geral de Documentação, 1996).

Collection: *Trechos escolhidos,* edited by Temístocles Linhares (Rio de Janeiro: AGIR, 1960).

OTHER: Rodrigo Octávio, *Festas nacionaes,* introduction by Pompéia (Rio de Janeiro: Briguiet, 1893).

Raul Pompéia's masterpiece *O Ateneu* (1888, The Ateneu) guaranteed his importance in Brazilian literature. Pompéia's writing distinguishes itself from that of the dominant realistic and naturalistic trends of the late nineteenth century. Poet, chronicler, and short-story writer, Pompéia had a solid foundation in the classics and knowledge of several different literatures, especially French. In *O Ateneu,* Pompéia questions the values of his time: the promises of positivism, the empty rhetoric that mediated social relations in the Second Empire (the reign of Emperor Pedro II), and the discipline exercised in schools like the one portrayed in the novel.

Raul Pompéia (Arquivo da Academia Brasileira de Letras)

Raul d'Ávila Pompéia was born in Angra dos Reis, in the Brazilian state of Rio de Janeiro, on 12 April 1863. Pompéia's parents were Antônio d'Ávila Pompéia e Castro and his wife, Rosa. Antônio d'Ávila Pompéia e Castro arrived in Angra dos Reis as a judge in 1859, and in 1873 he was transferred to Rio de Janeiro, the capital of the Brazilian Empire. That year he enrolled his son in the well-known Colégio Abílio (Abílio School), run by Doctor Abílio César Borges, Baron of Macaúbas. The young Pompéia later transferred to the Colégio Pedro II (Pedro II School), which in the nineteenth century was a school for the sons of noble families and the wealthy elite. The senior-year curriculum at the school provides a good sense of what the education for the upper class was like at that time: Latin, Greek, German, moral philosophy, history of philosophy, rhetoric, critical analyses of Portuguese classics, narration and declamation, history of Portuguese and Brazilian literatures, chemistry, mineralogy, and geology. Pompéia graduated in 1880. That year Pompéia was chosen to speak during one of composer Carlos Gomes's visits to Brazil, and he delivered an address at Teatro São Pedro de Alcântara (San Pedro de Alcantara Theater) in the name of the students in homage to the maestro. At the event, Pompéia put aside his republican ideals and warmly greeted the emperor, the empress, and Carlos Gomes. During this time Pompéia's writing for the journal *As Letras* (The Letters), which began in 1880, increased as he turned his poetic prose against the institution of slavery in Brazil.

Pompéia's first book, *Uma tragédia no Amazonas* (1880, A Tragedy in the Amazon) is a novella that fits the mold of Romantic regionalism. According to biographer Eloy Pontes, this work was written when the author was only fifteen years old. Although he was young, the writer was welcomed by literary critics of his time such as Carlos Laet and João Capistrano de Abreu.

In 1881 Pompéia enrolled in the Faculdade de Direito de São Paulo (The Law School of São Paulo) and began to advocate for the abolition of slavery in several small newspapers, including *A Comédia* (The Comedy), *Entr'acto (O Bohemio)* (The Bohemian [Intermission]), and *O Nove de Setembro* (The Ninth of September). With leading figures such as Luís Gama and, later, Antônio Bento, Pompéia joined the cause of the abolitionist movement. He extended his journalistic work to the *Gazeta do Povo* (The People's Newspaper), *Correio Paulistano* (The Newspaper of São Paulo), *A Idéia* (The Idea), *Çà Ira* (It Will Be), and the *Jornal do Comércio* (Commerce Newspaper).

Pompéia's novella *As jóias da coroa* (The Jewels of the Crown) was serialized anonymously in *A Gazeta de Notícias* (The News Journal) between March and May 1882. The work is a satire aimed at Pedro II. Around this time Pompéia began to write short stories for newspapers in Rio de Janeiro and São Paulo. Among these short stories two are noteworthy: "Durante a noite" (During the Night) and "Último castelo" (The Last Castle). In both of these stories Pompéia's style and approach to his themes are similar to those of his contemporary Joaquim Maria Machado de Assis, who is widely considered to be the greatest Brazilian writer.

In 1883 Pompéia began to write the prose poems of *Canções sem metro* (1900, Songs without Meter). The first versions of some of these works were published in the *Jornal do Comércio* and *Diário Mercantil* (The Market Journal). These early poems are gathered in a section

titled "Vibrações" (Vibrations), to which the author added the epigraph of Charles Baudelaire's poem "Correspondances" (1857, Correspondences). This epigraph suggests a harmony between the moral and physical world that pervades Pompéia's work. Pompéia finished the final version of these poems in 1889, but they were not published until 1900, after his death. Rodrigo Octávio, one of the author's best friends, wrote in *Minhas memórias dos outros* (1978–1979, My Memories of Others): "Dos seus trabalhos . . . a obra-prima, aquela a que dedicou mais cuidadoso desvelo e que, por certo, mais amava, é o livro *Canções sem metro,* em cujo lavor o artista trabalhava desde 1883" (Among all his works . . . the masterpiece, the one to which he dedicated the most careful devotion, and for sure the one he loved most, was the book *Canções sem metro,* on which the artist had been working since 1883).

Writer Lêdo Ivo included Pompéia's *Canções sem metro* in his study *O universo poético de Raul Pompéia* (1963, The Poetic Universe of Raul Pompéia), in which he compares the writer's work to that of Baudelaire and Victor Hugo. Ivo notes that in a century of science and religion Pompéia's curious and peculiar book portrays an empty-handed poet. As Pompéia states in "Solução" (Solution), one of the poems in *Canções sem metro:* "Aqui venho da grande derrota. Baixei ao fundo dos problemas; visitei, com o verme, as entranhas da terra . . . Sondei, sondei, sondei! Desafiei o gênio negro das metamorfoses; insultei as vertigens do abismo! . . . E o gênio negro respondeu-me: 'Nunca!' E eu li no abismo: 'Nunca!'" (Here I come from the great defeat. I went to the depths of problems, I visited the guts of the earth with the vermin . . . I dreamed, I dreamed, I dreamed! I challenged the dark genie of metamorphosis, I insulted the vertigo of the abyss! . . . And the genie told me: "Never!" And I read in the abyss: "Never!").

In March 1884 Pompéia was called to Rio de Janeiro because of his father's failing health. After his father's death he returned to São Paulo in May. Before Christmas that year Pompéia, Octávio, and many other students left São Paulo and went to the Faculdade de Direito de Recife (Law School of Recife) to finish their studies. The students left because of the school's reform of testing methods. According to Spencer Vampré, many students failed their exams, a strike occurred, and ninety-four students withdrew from school.

In Recife, Pompéia came into contact with the intellectual Tobias Barreto and his followers, especially Sílvio Romero. Unlike their counterparts in São Paulo, the intellectuals in Recife were concerned with general philosophy and not specifically the fight to end slavery. Camil Capaz claims that Romero's thesis in 1875 and the selection of Barreto to join the faculty in 1882 were landmarks in the introduction and adoption by the

Faculdade de Direito de Recife of theories of evolution, as well as the fight for the "religion of science" against metaphysics and natural law.

Pompéia graduated from law school and returned to Rio de Janeiro in November 1885. There he began to write for several newspapers: *A Gazeta da Tarde* (The Afternoon Journal), which was owned by José do Patrocínio, *Jornal do Comércio,* and the *Gazeta de Notícias,* the most important newspaper of the time, for which Joaquim Maria Machado de Assis and Ramalho Ortigão wrote. He also contributed to the *Diário de Minas* (Journal of Minas), a newspaper in the city of Juiz de Fora. Pompéia wrote about many topics affecting everyday life in Rio de Janeiro, including pieces in support of abolition, commentaries on literary events, reports on a crime on Uruguaiana street, the yellow fever epidemic, the water shortage, the suicide of a student at Colégio Pedro II, and the proclamation of the Republic. His biographers agree that the time between his return to Rio de Janeiro at the end of 1885 and 1892 were the most peaceful days of his life. He spent time with newspaper editors and frequented cafés, theaters, and bookshops, and he came to know about the most important happenings in the city and the country. During these years he had to live from his earnings as a reporter, as his political beliefs prevented him from obtaining any governmental position.

Pompéia wrote *O Ateneu* between January and March of 1888 and published it in the *Gazeta de Notícias* between 8 April and 18 May. It was published in book form that same year. The manuscript of the novel, held at the Biblioteca Nacional (National Library) in Rio de Janeiro, differs in many ways from both the serialized and published forms of the work. For instance, Sérgio, the adult first-person narrator who is telling the story of his adolescence, enrolls in the Ateneu boarding school at the age of nine in the manuscript; at the age of ten in the chapters published in the *Gazeta de Notícias;* and at the age of eleven in the final edition of the book.

On the publication of *O Ateneu* in 1888 Tristão de Alencar Araripe Júnior wrote that Pompéia was a philosopher and a thinker. He had created a distinct place for himself in nineteenth-century Brazilian literature, distancing himself from Romanticism; yet, his writing did not fall into the patterns established in the naturalism practiced by writers such as Aluísio Azevedo. Lúcia Miguel Pereira saw in *O Ateneu* "um romance estranho, diferente de tudo o que habitualmente se escrevia" (a strange novel, different from all the literary production of the time), and placed it as the lone companion of Machado de Assis's *Memórias póstumas de Brás Cubas* (1881, The Posthumous Memoirs of Brás Cubas; translated as *Epitaph of a Small Winner,* 1952), which renounced the tenets of naturalism.

Through the vengeful eyes of the narrator of *O Ateneu,* Sérgio, Pompéia gives the reader a portrait of what Brazil was like during the Second Empire: a period of hierarchy, empty rhetoric, and treason. The book's importance, however, lies not in its detailed descriptions of society but rather in its relationship to the literary trends of the time. Additionally, Pompéia goes to the heart of male affection and the field of sexuality and desire. *O Ateneu* is told from the perspective of an adult who seems to want to recall his adolescence in order to forget it, or perhaps to prove that he was influenced by a corrupt environment. Sérgio's beautiful style belies the ugly details of the narrative: the daylight promenades, the nightly escapades, the words whispered during study hours, the games, the fights, the baths, and all the cruel and arbitrary discipline exerted on the boys in the boarding school.

On 13 May 1888, as *O Ateneu* was being published in *Gazeta de Notícias,* slavery was abolished in Brazil. In the 20 May edition of *Gazeta de Notícias,* two days after the publication of the last chapter of *O Ateneu,* Pompéia praised those throughout Brazilian history who had fought for an end to slave labor.

Although he never had any formal studies in the fine arts, Pompéia had special talents for sculpture and drawing. The latter may be seen in his illustrations for *O Ateneu,* which are included in many editions of the novel. Pompéia also wrote *crônicas* about fine arts exhibitions in Rio de Janeiro; he was well acquainted with different painting styles but was particularly fond of landscaping.

In a piece for the *Diário de Minas* on 19 May 1889, Pompéia commented on the first anniversary of the abolition of slavery. The year, however, brought new problems: an epidemic of yellow fever in Rio de Janeiro, military crises, political crises, doubts concerning Pedro II's health, and resistance to Princess Isabel's possible reign. Although he was a republican, when the Republic was proclaimed on 15 November 1889, Pompéia wrote a deeply moving article about Pedro II's last days in Brazil. In 1889 he published short stories in the newspaper *A Rua* (The Street), which featured other important contributors, such as Olavo Bilac and Luís Murat. Among these short stories, two stand out: "Tílburi de praça" (Tilbury on the Square) and "A batalha dos livros" (The Battle of the Books), both published anonymously and signed with a question mark. Capaz asserts that such signatures provided a way for young writers to publish their more modern and daring works without receiving pressure from editors.

The establishment of the Republic brought a new national anthem, a new flag, reform of the education system and the Escola Nacional de Belas-Artes (National School of Fine Arts), and the creation of the

RAUL POMPÉIA, 1863-1895

OBRAS

Volume I

Organização de
Afrânio Coutinho
e assistência de
Eduardo de Faria Coutinho

Edição comemorativa do cinqüentenário da
criação do Ministério da Educação e Cultura (1980).

Rio de Janeiro
MEC — FENAME — OFICINA LITERÁRIA
AFRÂNIO COUTINHO (OLAC) —
Editora Civilização Brasileira
1981

472 04

*Title page for the first volume of Pompéia's collected works
(Joint University Libraries, Nashville)*

Instituto de Música (Institute of Music). Additionally, civil marriage became independent from the religious ceremony. Pompéia was very much concerned with these and other important social, moral, and political issues.

In 1890 Pompéia was appointed professor of mythology and secretary of the School of Fine Arts. When Floriano Peixoto became president of the Republic in 1891, Pompéia became more involved with political issues, making stronger attacks on the enemies of the Republic in his newspaper pieces. Those who opposed Floriano Peixoto for his dictatorial leadership, many of whom were Pompéia's former literary companions, turned against the writer. According to Pontes, the famous poet Bilac wrote an attack on Pompéia for the newspaper *O Combate,* saying, "Esse moço bem podia ganhar e ingerir o seu ordenado completamente, sem rebaixamento de caráter e sem alusões indignas. Ele, entretanto, prefere comer esse pão que o diabo

amassou, repassando-o pela manteiga do servilismo e da adulação" (This young man could well earn and digest his income without having to lower his character in such indignant claims. Instead, he would rather eat the enemy's stale bread, spreading it through the butter of servility and adulation). Bilac completes his statement with sarcasm: "Raul Pompéia masturba-se e gosta de, altas horas da noite, numa cama fresca, à meia luz e *veilleuse* mortiça, recordar, amoroso e sensual, todas as beldades que viu durante o seu dia, contando em seguida as tábuas do teto onde elas vaporosamente valsam" (Raul Pompéia masturbates at night, in a fresh bed, at half light, while he recalls all the beauties he saw during the day. Next he counts the ceiling battens where they warmly dance). Pompéia challenged Bilac to a duel. The weapons and witnesses were chosen, but when Pompéia and Bilac met at the appointed time and place, at the urging of one of the witnesses, navy officer Francisco de Matos, the two writers simply shook hands.

For Pompéia, defending Floriano Peixoto was the same as defending the nation from foreign capital, especially that of the British and Portuguese. His articles in the newspapers favored nationalism and the civic education of youngsters. In 1894, at the end of Floriano Peixoto's government, Pompéia was nominated director of the National Library.

Prudente de Morais became president in 1895 and brought back the political oligarchy, but this time without an emperor. Floriano Peixoto died that year, and during his funeral many important personalities gave speeches. When they began to attack the new government, Prudente de Morais left the ceremony. On the following day the newspapers disapproved of the excesses of the speakers. Pompéia was dismissed from his position at the National Library.

Pompéia's enemies increased in number. Murat, a former friend who years later accused Machado de Assis of having neglected the issue of slavery, called Pompéia a coward in an article published in the *Comércio de São Paulo* (Commerce of São Paulo) on 16 October 1895. Pompéia did not become aware of this article until December. That month Pompéia wrote two articles for *A Notícia* (The News). The first one, about a book by Leo Tolstoy, was published on 12 December 1895. Fifteen days later the second one, about Pierre Loti's *A Galiléia* (The Galileo), appeared. According to Pompéia's biographers, his inability to produce the article in a timely fashion triggered an acute depression. He committed suicide at 1:00 P.M. on 25 December 1895, at 116 São Clemente Street, where he had lived since November 1885 with his widowed mother and his sisters. He left the following message: "*À Notícia* e ao Brasil, declaro que sou um homem de honra" (I declare to *A Notícia* and the country that I am a man of honor).

Pompéia's radical act surprised his closest friends Octávio, Abreu, and Araripe Júnior. In an article published in *A Semana* (The Week) on 29 December 1895 Machado de Assis wrote:

> Raul era todo letras, todo poesia, todo Goncourts . . . A questão do suicídio não vem agora à tela. Este velho tema renasce sempre que um homem dá cabo de si, mas é logo enterrado com ele, para renascer com outro. Velha questão, velha dúvida. . . . Que solução se dará ao velho tema? A melhor é ainda a do jovem Hamlet: "The rest is silence."

> (Raul was all literature, all poetry, all Goncourts . . . The issue of suicide must not rise now. This old question revives whenever someone ends his own life, but it is soon buried with him, to be back again when someone else does the same. Old question, old doubt. . . . What solution can one give to the old issue? The best so far is still that of young Hamlet: "The rest is silence.")

Decades later critic Álvaro Lins offered an interesting hypothesis linking Raul Pompéia's interest in social issues to his suicide. Lins believed that the author was incapable of abandoning the artistic life to deal with issues of everyday reality. As a man Pompéia attempted to hide that which he clearly depicts in his books: the madness, revolt, and despair that are central to *O Ateneu,* the work for which he is most remembered and respected.

Biographies:

Eloy Pontes, *A vida inquieta de Raul Pompéia* (Rio de Janeiro: J. Olympio, 1935);

Camil Capaz, *Raul Pompéia: Biografia* (Rio de Janeiro: Gryphus, 2001).

References:

João Capistrano de Abreu, *Correspondência de Capistrano de Abreu,* 3 volumes (Rio de Janeiro: Instituto Nacional do Livro, 1954–1956);

Mário de Andrade, "O Ateneu," in his *Aspectos da literatura brasileira,* fifth edition (São Paulo: Martins, 1974), pp. 173–184;

Tristão de Alencar Araripe Júnior, *Teoria, crítica e história literária* (Rio de Janeiro: Livros Técnicos e Científicos / São Paulo: Editora da Universidade de São Paulo, 1978);

Joaquim Maria Machado de Assis, untitled *crônica* on Pompéia's death, in his *Obra completa,* volume 3: *Poesia, crônica, crítica, miscelânea e epistolario,* edited by Afrânio Coutinho (Rio de Janeiro: Aguilar, 1959), pp. 711–713;

Sérgio Nazar David, "Um Bentinho às Avessas," *O Globo,* 11 August 2001, p. 2;

Figueira Fernandes, *Digressões* (Rio de Janeiro: Annuário do Brasil, 1923);

Lêdo Ivo, *O universo poético de Raul Pompéia* (Rio de Janeiro: São José, 1963);

Álvaro Lins, "Dois adolescentes: Cocteau e Pompéia," in *O relógio e o quadrante: obras, autores e problemas de literatura estrangeira; ensaios e estudos, 1940–1960* (Rio de Janeiro: Civilização Brasileira, 1964), pp. 131–139;

Rodrigo Octávio, *Minhas memórias dos outros,* 3 volumes (Rio de Janeiro: Civilização Brasileira, 1978–1979);

Lúcia Miguel Pereira, *História da literatura brasileira: prosa de ficção, de 1870 a 1920* (Belo Horizonte: Itatiaia / São Paulo: Editora da Universidade de São Paulo, 1988);

Silviano Santiago, "O Ateneu: contradições e perquirições," in his *Uma literatura nos trópicos: ensaios sobre dependência cultural* (São Paulo: Perspectiva, 1978), pp. 67–100;

Roberto Schwarz, "O Atheneu," in his *A sereia e o desconfiado: ensaios críticos* (Rio de Janeiro: Paz e Terra, 1981), pp. 25–30;

Spencer Vampré, *Memórias para a história da Academia de São Paulo: edição comemorativa do sesquicentenário da instauração dos cursos jurídicos no Brasil, 1827–1977* (Brasília: Instituto Nacional do Livro, 1977).

Adélia Prado

(13 December 1935 –)

Eliana Yunes

Pontifícia Universidade Católica do Rio de Janeiro

BOOKS: *Lapinha de Jesus: presépio de Tiago Kamps,* by Prado and Lázaro Barreto (Petrópolis: Vozes, 1969);

Bagagem (Rio de Janeiro: Imago, 1976);

O coração disparado (Rio de Janeiro: Nova Fronteira, 1978);

Solte os cachorros (Rio de Janeiro: Nova Fronteira, 1979);

Cacos para um vitral (Rio de Janeiro: Nova Fronteira, 1980);

Terra de Santa Cruz (Rio de Janeiro: Nova Fronteira, 1981);

Os componentes da banda (Rio de Janeiro: Nova Fronteira, 1984);

O pelicano (Rio de Janeiro: Guanabara, 1987);

A faca no peito (Rio de Janeiro: Rocco, 1988);

O homem da mão seca (São Paulo: Siciliano, 1994);

Manuscritos de Felipa (São Paulo: Siciliano, 1999);

Oráculos de maio (São Paulo: Siciliano, 1999);

Filandras (São Paulo: Record, 2001).

Editions and Collections: *Poesia reunida* (São Paulo: Siciliano, 1991);

Prosa reunida (São Paulo: Siciliano, 1999).

Editions in English: *The Headlong Heart,* translated by Ellen Watson (Livingston, Ala.: Livingston University Press, 1988);

The Alphabet in the Park: Selected Poems of Adélia Prado, translated by Watson (Middletown, Conn.: Wesleyan University Press, 1990).

RECORDING: *Adélia Prado,* read by Prado (São Paulo: Instituto Moreira Salles, 1999).

OTHER: "Apresentação: observando as formigas," in *Poesia (e) filosofia: por poetas-filósofos em atuação no Brasil,* edited by Alberto Pucheu (Rio de Janeiro: Sette Letras, 1998);

"A arte como experiência religiosa," in *O simbólico e o diabólico: dramas e tramas,* edited by Waldecy Tenório (São Paulo: Editora da Pontifícia Universidade Católica de São Paulo, 1999);

Adélia Prado (Department of Spanish and Portuguese, University of Arizona)

Ecléa Bosi, *Velhos amigos,* introduction by Prado (São Paulo: Letras, 2003).

Adélia Prado came to the attention of the Brazilian public when renowned poet Carlos Drummond de Andrade announced in his 9 October 1975 column in the *Jornal do Brasil* that the country had a great woman poet whose work was about to be published. A devoted Catholic and mother, Prado continued her duties in the home as she wrote poetry. She once said, "sei que Deus mora em mim, mas esta letra é minha" (I know that God lives in me, but this writing is mine). She has lived her entire life in her hometown, the prophetically named Divinopolis (City of God), a small town dating from the colonial period in the interior state of Minas Gerais.

Born on 13 December 1935, the first daughter of João do Prado Filho and Ana Clotilde Corrêa, Adélia Luzia Prado began to write poetry on the death of her mother in 1950. She studied in the public schools of Divinopolis and became a schoolteacher. At the age of nineteen Prado married José de Freitas, a manager at a federal bank. While their two sons and two daughters were growing up, Prado continued to write poems and publish them in the literary supplements of local newspapers. In 1973 the writer Affonso Romano de Sant'Anna read her unpublished verses and became fascinated with her poetic abilities. He shared Prado's work with Drummond, who recommended her to an editor. The schoolteacher and mother of five who has created a highly personal philosophy in her poetry almost immediately became a national success in the bookstores. She decided, however, to maintain a private life in her small town. She refused many interviews, and she was highly selective in the invitations to travel that she accepted.

Prado's first book of poetry, *Bagagem* (1976, Baggage), was received enthusiastically by the critics. The work is characterized by an original feminine voice and style that stood out in the political context of the Brazilian military dictatorship of the 1970s. The verses, however, tend more toward domestic and religious themes than toward the political and the ideological. Prado did not identify or align herself with feminist writers, and she remained at a distance from the experimental trends in vogue in poetry at the time. Throughout the poems in this first book she establishes her own individual poetic voice as she reveals links with the great names in Brazilian literature.

In "Com licença poética" (With Poetic License), which constitutes a type of dialogue with a poem by Drummond, Prado is confident that her life is worthy poetic material:

Quando nasci um anjo esbelto
desses que tocam trombeta, anunciou:
vai carregar bandeira . . .
Vai ser coxo na vida, é maldição pra homem
Mulher é desdobrável. Eu sou.

(When I was born, an elegant angel
one of those who plays the trumpet, announced:
You will carry a banner . . .
To be lame in life, it is a curse for man
Woman is unfoldable. I am.)

The voice that dominates these lines has mystical qualities but maintains an awareness of the real. As the poet says of herself, she is not "Cornélia, mãe dos Gracos, mas Adélia mãe de filhos, mulher do povo" (Cornelia, mother of the Gracchus brothers, but rather Adélia,

mother, an ordinary woman). Through the rhyme of her name with Cornelia, Prado creates a poetic parallel between the mother of the famous Roman brothers and herself, who prefers to be the mother of normal children with a life free of pomp and circumstance. She confesses, "faço comida e como, quando dói, grito ai, quando é bom fico bruta, as sensibilidades sem governo" (I prepare meals and I eat, when I hurt, I cry out, when I am fine I am crude, with no sensitivities). Prado constantly reiterates her desire for a simple life in the subtleties of her sophisticated poetry. Rather than becoming involved in feminist politics and concerns, like many female poets of her day, she delves into the poetic aspects of ordinary life. With this focus on her poetry, Prado has discreetly avoided discussing the details of her personal life. Her husband and daughter often answer questions for her that do not deal specifically with her poems.

Throughout *Bagagem* Prado explores the past, giving new significance to women's place in history as she weaves elements from the Bible into the 113 poems that make up the volume. Her poetry is neither pedantic nor naive. Her poetic voice, while prophetic, is also epiphanic, filled with subtle revelations about everyday existence. The book, which foreshadows aspects of her later poetry, concludes with the long poem "Alfândega" (Customhouse). The verses consist of a lyrical litany in which Prado touches on themes that deal with her baroque heritage from the colonial history of the state of Minas Gerais and with the motif of the journey, which, rather than a physical trip, is more an internal one into her world of memories ("bagagem," her luggage).

Half of the poems in *O coração disparado* (1978, The Fearless Heart) had already appeared in *Bagagem*. In this second work there is a profound exploration of the state of grace that acts on everything and transforms the world into poetry. Prado discovers signs of God in all things. As she says, "a poesia [é] a passagem de Deus entre nós . . . Seu dedo na brutalidade das coisas" (Poetry [is] the passage of God among us . . . His finger on the brutishness of things). In various interviews Prado has reiterated that all things belong to God. To her, "a arte é uma mediaçao para a divindade" (art is mediation toward divineness). In *O coração disparado* she introduces a character who appears in her later works:

Vinte anos mais vinte é o que tenho
Mulher ocidental que se fosse homem
Amaria chamar-se Eliud Jonathan

(Twenty years plus twenty is my age
A western woman who if she were a man
Would love to be called Eliud Jonathan)

The identity of this figure is revealed only in *O pelicano* (1987, The Pelican), in the poem "Sacrifício" (Sacrifice):

> Desde a juventude canto.
> Desde a juventude desejo e desejo
> A presença que pra sempre me cale . . .
> Licor de romãs
> Sangue invisível pulsando na presença Santíssima.
> Eu canto muito alto:
> Jonathan é Jesus.
>
> (I have been singing since my youth.
> Since my youth I have so desired
> The presence that will silence me forever . . .
> Liqueur of pomegranate
> Invisible blood pulsating in the Holy presence.
> I sing loudly:
> Jonathan is Jesus.)

Several years before this revelation, however, Prado published *Solte os cachorros* (1979, Let the Dogs Loose), a book of short stories resembling a diary. In highly poetic language the work explores a woman's inner perceptions of daily life. The first section, which has the same title as the book, consists of a series of narratives in twenty-six short chapters. The remainder of the work is made up of two longer narratives and a section called "Afresco," a mixture of fragments from various genres, including prose and poetry. Prado maintains unity throughout the various sections of the book with the character of an anonymous woman from a city in the interior of Brazil. The woman contemplates life through her personal narratives, in which sexuality is presented as a natural and pleasurable part of living:

> Eu falo é sério e falo com crédito porque desde pequenininha eu gosto de homem. Nunca achei graça em brinquedo só de menina, não vou em chá de amizade, clube onde homem não entra. Penso que estou certa porque no livro da Bíblia, logo na primeira página, está escrito: "Deus fez o homem e o fez macho e fêmea" e isto quer dizer que somos igualzinho no valor. A boa diferença é só pra obrigação e amenidades. . . .
>
> (What I am saying is serious and I believe it because I have liked men since I was a little girl. I never really enjoyed girls' toys, I don't go for the tea and friendship thing, or clubs that don't allow men. I believe that I am right because in one of the books of the Bible, right there on the first page, it's written: "God made mankind and he made man and woman" and that means that we are all the same. Any difference between us is simply for social niceties. . . .)

As the title of *Solte os cachorros* suggests, the character speaks freely but without malice. The themes of love, marital relations, and beauty in the presence of God dominate "Afresco." Prado reworks these themes in her other prose writings, which are increasingly more delicate, subtle, and mystical.

Written in the third person, *Cacos para um vitral* (1980, Pieces for a Stained-Glass Window) is a reconstitution of small fragments of the simple life of Maria da Glória, a teacher of music and religion. With her husband, Gabriel, at her side, she contemplates the act of poetic creation: " um romance é feito de sobras, a poesia é o núcleo" (a novel is made of leftovers, poetry is the nucleus). Maria articulates a theory of writing in the form of a spiral linking the poetic and the prosaic, which reveals a baroque yet simple view. The image of the stained-glass window of the title, which is a whole composed of visually different parts, captures the sense of unity that emerges among the different types of writing Prado practices. The leftovers of poetry can be turned into a good novel, as a fragment of poetry can become a good piece of prose.

Prado juxtaposes the social and the personal in *Cacos para um vitral* when she narrates the events of two strikes—that of the metallurgists and that of the teachers, which Maria leads. Maria, along with Gabriel, reflects "a penosa descoberta do social" (the painful discovery of the social), which becomes more complex and difficult for her over the course of the story.

Terra de Santa Cruz (Land of the Holy Cross) was published in 1981. The title is the first name the Portuguese gave to Brazil after discovering the territory in 1500. Filled with obvious religious motifs, as is indicated by titles such as "Território, Catequese e Sagração" (Territory, Catechism and Consecration), this book is the only one in which Prado refers to the political events of the period from 1964 to 1984, when Brazil was under a military dictatorship. She was touched by an episode in which a young Dominican monk, Frei Tito, committed suicide as a result of the repressive policies of the regime. Prado refers to other Brazilian poets throughout the volume as she explores the themes of life, death, sadness, and happiness. She delves further into the erotic as a ritual of salvation: "eu descobri que o erótico é sagrado. Toda poesia mística é sensual, não precisa separar. O corpo é algo preciosíssimo, não é? Então só é erótico por isso, para animar a divindade" (I discovered that the erotic is sacred. All mystic poetry is sensual; there is no reason to separate the two. The body is something quite precious, isn't it? So it is only erotic for this, to encourage the divine).

The novel *Os componentes da banda* (The Members of the Band), published in 1984, is the saga of a female protagonist who explores the relationships between spiritual matters and material things. She discovers that the spiritual exists in the smallest, most humble things. In the joy of sex and the pain of birth the material aspects of life are transformed into spiritual moments.

Prado's next book was the poetry collection *O pelicano,* published in 1987. Filled with epigraphs from the Book of Job, Psalms, and the Song of Solomon, the work reveals a writer turned more inward and focused on the act of writing poetry. In this short book Prado mingles the religious and the personal as she transforms her experiences into poetry. The theme of the pelican returns at the end of *Oráculos de maio* (1999, Oracles of May), but until then the writer, in both her prose and poetry, continues her dialogue with Jonathan in which she explores the meaning of passion as passage.

In 1988 Prado published *A faca no peito* (A Knife in the Heart), in which the principal theme is poetry itself. The work has an open structure, without a title poem or synthesis, as in her other books. Although independent of each other, Prado's texts reveal a well-delineated unity. This organization has perhaps facilitated the poet's ability to move from verse to prose without losing her sense of the poetic. In Prado's point of view, poetry and prayer are the same thing, and in her poems she progressively assumes the role of mediator between poetic inspiration and the poem itself:

> Quero enfear o poema
> Pra te lançar meu desprezo, em vão.
> Escreve-o Quem me dita as palavras
> Escreve-o por minha mão. . . .
>
> (I want to make the poem ugly
> To hurl my disdain at you, in vain.
> Whoever dictates the words to me writes it
> And writes it with my hand. . . .)

The publication of *O homem da mão seca* (The Man with the Withered Hand) in 1994 completed the long spiritual and psychic formation of the anonymous woman who assumes different names in Prado's prose narratives. In this work she is Anônia, and she is reborn from the ashes. Although the process is not a true spiritual elevation, since she never leaves her body, the character does experience communion with all things and with her husband, Thomaz. He is like the "man with the withered hand" of the Gospel, to whom she must extend her hand in order to save herself and to save him from separation and isolation. As she says, "tem hora que Ele é eu" (there are moments when He is I). The liberation of her spirit, her intelligence, and her sensitivity lead to a state of grace in which everything is

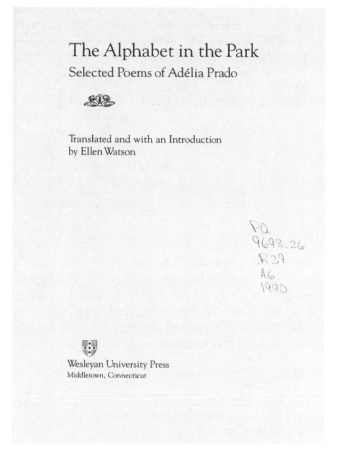

The Alphabet in the Park
Selected Poems of Adélia Prado

Translated and with an Introduction
by Ellen Watson

Wesleyan University Press
Middletown, Connecticut

Title page for the second collection of Prado's verse in English translation, published in 1990 (Thomas Cooper Library, University of South Carolina)

sanctified. As Prado concludes, "Deus não me fez até a cintura para o diabo fazer o resto" (God did not create me just to the waist so that the devil could do the rest).

Read as a group, Prado's prose narratives—*Solte os cachorros, Cacos para um vitral, Os componentes da banda,* and *O homem da mão seca*—seem to compose one long novel. Although the main characters have different names, and the point of view shifts between first and third person from one book to another, all four narratives focus on a lone female character in the process of constructing and revealing her identity. Like the Four Evangelists, the narrators follow the path of passion, death, and resurrection of a woman caught up in everyday domestic tasks. This female character, who has the aspirations of a great person, undergoes pain and suffering that climax in an epiphanic moment of discoveries of both her physical body and language. Much like her own life, according to interviews, Prado's work in prose resembles a novice's first novel in which the writer constantly suffers both pain and pleasure.

In *Oráculos de maio,* published in 1999, the mediating role is passed to the Virgin Mary as Prado opens the volume with a rebellious poem announcing that the poet has become tired:

Ó Deus
me deixa trabalhar na cozinha
nem vendedor, nem escrivão, me deixa fazer o teu pão.
Filha, diz-me o Senhor
Eu só como palavras.

(Dear God
Let me work in the kitchen
Neither vendor nor scribe, let me make your bread.
Daughter, You say to me
I only eat words.)

The verse forms in this collection vary, from the brief dedicatory poem to Drummond ("Arte: / Das tripas, / coração" [Art: / From the gut, / The heart]) to longer poems that deal with time and fear of death:

a vida inteira para estar aqui
neste domingo
nesta cidade sem história,
nesta chuva
mensageira de um medo
que não o dos relâmpagos, pois é mansa.
É inapelável morrer?

(an entire life to be here
this Sunday
in this city without history,
in this rain
messenger of a fear
not of the lightning, because it is meek.
Is death unappealable?)

In *Manuscritos de Felipa* (Felipa's Manuscripts), also published in 1999, the protagonist, Felipa, is married to Teodoro but has strong feelings for Silvino. She is besieged by doubts, which she shares with her friend Alba and with her sister Agnes. This prose work takes the form of a diary as the narrator reflects on language as sound and meaning. Like Prado, Felipa is both poet and prophet of ordinary, everyday things. As the narrator says, "Felipa, você é uma artista, sua roça é aqui, pega seu caderno, seu lápis de boa ponta e capina sem preguiça, Felipa, de sol a sol, conta o que te conto" (Felipa, you are an artist, your garden is here, take your notebook, your pencil with a sharp point and hoe tirelessly, Felipa, from sun to sun, tell what I tell you). Then, with a change of person in the same line, there follows a stream of consciousness that she hears and says: "Serei feliz porque estarei liberta, mais ainda porque a roça não é minha, sou trabalhador alugado para patrão exigente . . . ai de mim, os Evangelhos dão calafrios" (I will be happy because I will be free, but still because the garden is not mine, I am the worker hired for a demanding boss . . . alas! The Gospel makes one tremble).

In *Filandras* (2001) Prado continues her search for maximum intimacy and spiritual wholeness in the world to escape the Freudian sense of the sickness of civilization. There is a permanent epiphany in her verses in which the sense of discovery and bliss predominate. The great revelation of her poetry and novels, however, is the redemption available to a humanity graced by the ordinary aspects of life. The sacred and the profane are intermingled in Prado's feminine voice, placing the human into a union with the spiritual giver of life.

In Prado's work the prophetic and the mystical intermingle with the poetic and the erotic in such a way that any vestige of naive religiosity or reactive feminism is eliminated. She focuses her attention on the search for a truth of correspondence so that gender difference is dissolved. Prado's poetry, which finds the greatness and dignity of the feminine in all human beings, has not attracted a large following among feminist readers.

Using the intimate and the insignificant as the basis for her verses, Prado redefines the human condition as she searches for a harmonious balance of the profane and the prophetic. Through the ordinary details and aspects of everyday life that she treats in her poetry, she seeks a communion of the human and the divine. As she says, "Poesia sois vós, ó Deus" (Dear God, you are poetry).

Prado has continued to develop her poetic voice and style through the years. Her poetry, however, still includes a strong trace of the mystical experience characteristic of the medieval nuns and the poetry of the Spanish mystics St. Juan de la Cruz and St. Teresa de Ávila. Prado's poems express a communion with God in which nothing is lost and nothing escapes. As she says, "ou Deus salva tudo ou nada" (either God saves everything or nothing). To her the sensitivity of the body is a strong expression of God rather than a refuge for the devil. She glorifies common everyday acts, such as cooking, cleaning, bathing, and eating, as she transforms them into poetry.

Prado continues to live and write in Divinopolis, the town where she was born and married and where her children were born and raised. She spends her time reading and writing, and she continues to attract the attention of critics, who have compared her work to that of the modernist poet Cecília Meireles. Prado, like Meireles, has established herself not only as an outstanding feminine voice but also as one of the best lyric poets of twentieth-century Brazilian literature.

References:

Cadernos de Literatura Brasileira, special Prado issue, 9 (2000);

Ana Maria de Almeida Camargo, *Feminino singular: a participação da mulher na literatura brasileira contemporânea* (Rio Claro: GRD/Arquivo Municipal de Rio Claro, 1989);

Suzana Márcia Braga Camargos, "Poesia e psicanálise: uma leitura do texto de Adélia Prago," *Estudos de Psicanálise,* 13 (1990);

Gisela Simões Campos, "'O brilho que a razão não devassa': bliss e a experiência mística na prosa de Adélia Prado," M.A. thesis, Pontifícia Universidade Católica do Rio de Janeiro, 1995;

Luiz Dulci, "A insurgência do vivido," *Teoria e Debate,* 17 (1992);

Arnaldo Franco Jr., "Adélia Prado: a palavra do verso e o verso da palavra," *Travessia,* 21 (1990): 143–159;

Valéria Ribeiro Guerra, "A vertigem dos cacos: o feminino e a prosa de Adélia Prado," M.A. thesis, Pontifícia Universidade Católica do Rio de Janeiro, 1992;

Fábio Lucas, "Cacos para um vitral de Adélia Prado," in his *Mineiranças* (São Paulo: Oficina de Livros, 1991), pp. 181–182;

Cremilda Medina, "Adélia Prado: a poesia marco encontro em Divinópolis," in her *A posse da terra: escritor brasileiro hoje* (Lisbon: Nacional/Casa da Moeda / São Paulo: Secretaria da Cultura do Estado de São Paulo, 1985), pp. 417–425;

José Francisco Navarro Huamán, "La poesía, la más ínfima, es serva de la esperanza: la mística de la vida cotidiana en la poesía de Adélia Prado," dissertation, Universidad Iberoamericana, 1999;

Haquira Osakabe, "A ronda do anticristo," in *Os pobres na literatura brasileira,* edited by Roberto Schwarz (São Paulo: Braisiliense, 1983), pp. 226–231;

Carolyn Richmond, "The Lyric Voice of Adélia Prado: An Analysis of Themes and Structure in *Bagagem,*" *Luso-Brazilian Review,* 15 (1978).

Rachel de Queiroz

(17 November 1910 – 4 November 2003)

Sandra R. G. Almeida
Universidade Federal de Minas Gerais

BOOKS: *O quinze: romance* (Rio de Janeiro, 1930);

João Miguel (romance) (Rio de Janeiro: Schmidt, 1932);

Caminho de pedras: romance (Rio de Janeiro: J. Olympio, 1937);

As três Marias (Rio de Janeiro: J. Olympio, 1939); translated by Fred P. Ellison as *The Three Marias* (Austin: University of Texas Press, 1963);

Brandão entre o mar e o amor: romance, by Queiroz, José Lins do Rego, Graciliano Ramos, Anibal Machado, and Jorge Amado (São Paulo: Martins, 1942);

A donzela e a moura torta: crônicas e reminiscências (Rio de Janeiro: J. Olympio, 1948);

Lampião: drama em cinco quadros (Rio de Janeiro: J. Olympio, 1953);

A beata Maria do Egito: peça em 3 atos e 4 quadros (Rio de Janeiro: J. Olympio, 1958);

Cem crônicas escolhidas (Rio de Janeiro: J. Olympio, 1958); republished as *Um alpendre, uma rede, um açude: 100 crônicas escolhidas* (São Paulo: Siciliano, 1994);

O mistério dos MMM, by Queiroz, Amado, Viriato Correa, Dinah Silveira de Queirós, Lúcio Cardoso, Herberto Sales, José Condé, Guimarães Rosa, Antônio Callado, and Orígenes Lessa (Rio de Janeiro: Cruzeiro, 1962);

O brasileiro perplexo (Rio de Janeiro: Editôra do Autor, 1964);

Mapinguari (Rio de Janeiro: J. Olympio, 1964); republished as *O homem e o tempo: 74 crônicas escolhidas* (São Paulo: Siciliano, 1995);

O caçador de tatu, edited by Herman Lima (Rio de Janeiro: J. Olympio, 1967);

O menino mágico (Rio de Janeiro: J. Olympio, 1969);

Meu livro de Brasil: livro-guia para 3-4-5, by Queiroz and Nilda Bethlem (Rio de Janeiro: J. Olympio, 1971);

Luiz e Maria, by Queiroz and Marion Vilas Boas (São Paulo: Lisa, 1971);

Dôra, Doralina (Rio de Janeiro: J. Olympio, 1975); translated by Dorothy Scott Loos as *Dôra, Doralina* (New York: Avon, 1984);

Rachel de Queiroz (photograph by Richam Samir; Arquivo da Academia Brasileira de Letras)

As menininhas e outras crônicas (Rio de Janeiro: J. Olympio, 1976);

Discursos na Academia: em sessão realizada no dia 4 de novembro de 1977, by Queiroz and Adonias Filho (Rio de Janeiro: J. Olympio, 1978);

O jogador de sinuca e mais historinhas (Rio de Janeiro: J. Olympio, 1980);

O galo de ouro: romance (Rio de Janeiro: J. Olympio, 1985);

Cafute & Pena de Prata (Rio de Janeiro: J. Olympio, 1986);

Solenidade do centenário de nascimento de José Américo, by Queiroz and others (Rio de Janeiro: J. Olympio/ Fundação Casa de José Américo, 1988);

Matriarcas do Ceará: Dona Federalina de Lavras, by Queiroz and Heloísa Buarque de Hollanda (Rio de Janeiro: CIEC, 1990);

Andira (São Paulo: Siciliano, 1992);

Memorial de Maria Moura (São Paulo: Siciliano, 1992);

As terras ásperas (São Paulo: Siciliano, 1993);

O nosso Ceará, by Queiroz and Maria Luíza de Queiroz (Fortaleza: Fundação Demócrito Rocha/Consultor, 1994);

Tantos anos, by Queiroz and Maria Luíza de Queiroz (São Paulo: Siciliano, 1998);

A casa do morro branco (São Paulo: Siciliano, 1999);

O Não me Deixes: suas histórias e sua cozinha, by Queiroz and Maria Luíza de Queiroz (São Paulo: Siciliano, 2000);

Xerimbabo (Rio de Janeiro: J. Olympio, 2002);

Falso mar, falso mundo (São Paulo: Editorial Arx, 2002).

Editions and Collections: *Seleta de Rachel de Queiroz,* edited by Paulo Ronai (Rio de Janeiro: J. Olympio, 1973)—includes *O quinze, João Miguel, As três Marias, O galo de ouro, Lampião, A beata Maria do Egito;*

Obra reunida, 3 volumes (Rio de Janeiro: J. Olympio, 1989)—compriscs volumc 1: *O quinze, João Miguel, Caminho de pedras;* volume 2: *As três Marias; Dôra, Doralina;* volume 3: *O galo de ouro, A donzela e a moura torta;* volume 4: *Cem crônica escolhidas, O caçador de tatu;* and volume 5: *Mapinguari, Lampião, A beata Maria do Egito;*

Teatro: Lampião, A beata Maria do Egito (São Paulo: Siciliano, 1995);

Edição crítica em uma perspectiva genética de As rês Marias, *de Rachel de Queiroz,* edited by Marlene Gomes Mendes (Niterói: Editora da Universidade Federal Fluminense, 1998).

Edition in English: "Metonymy, or the Husband's Revenge," in *Other Fires: Short Fiction by Latin American Women,* edited by Alberto Manguel (New York: Potter, 1986).

PLAY PRODUCTIONS: *Lampião,* Rio de Janeiro, Municipal Theater, 1953;

A beata Maria do Egito, Rio de Janeiro, Teatro Serrador, 1958.

OTHER: Joaquim Manuel de Macedo, *A moreninha,* preface by Queiroz (Rio de Janeiro: Valverde, 1945);

Jean Manzon, *Flagrantes do Brasil,* introduction by Queiroz and Manuel Bandeira (Rio de Janeiro: Bloch, 1950);

José de Alencar, *Iracema: lenda do Ceará,* preface by Queiroz, Obras de ficção de José de Alencar, volume 8 (Rio de Janeiro: J. Olympio, 1951);

José Lins do Rêgo, *Eurídice,* notes by Queiroz (Rio de Janeiro: J. Olympio, 1956);

Herman Melville, *Moby Dick ou a baleia,* 2 volumes, translated by Berenice Xavier, preface by Queiroz (Rio de Janiero: J. Olympio, 1957);

Mário Palmério, *Vila dos confins: romance,* preface by Queiroz (Rio de Janeiro: J. Olympio, 1958);

Erich Joachim Hess, *Isto é o Brasil!* preface and captions by Queiroz (São Paulo: Melhoramentos, 1959);

Vivaldo Coaracy, *Paquetá: imagens de ontem e de hoje,* preface by Queiroz (Rio de Janeiro: J. Olympio, 1964);

David Nasser, *João sem mêdo,* preface by Queiroz (Rio de Janeiro: O Cruzeiro, 1965);

Leonardo Mota, *Sertão alegre: poesia e linguagem do sertão nordestino,* preface by Queiroz (Rio de Janeiro: Ouro, 1968);

Paulo Sarasate, *O rio Jaguaribe é uma artéria aberta: apontamentos sôbre a vida e a obra literária de Demócrito Rocha, à margem dos poemas o de algumas crônicas que o jornalista escreveu,* preface by Queiroz (Rio de Janeiro: Freitas Bastos, 1968);

Moreira Campos, *O puxador de têrço: contos,* preface by Queiroz (Rio de Janeiro: J. Olympio, 1969);

Ariano Suassuna, *Romance d' a Pedra do Reino e o Príncipe do sangue do vai-e-volta: romance armorial-popular brasileiro,* notes by Queiroz (Rio de Janeiro: J. Olympio, 1971);

Francisco Pereira da Silva, *O desejado,* preface by Queiroz (Rio de Janeiro: AGIR, 1973);

Chico Anísio, *O enterro do anão,* preface by Queiroz (Rio de Janeiro: J. Olympio, 1973);

Laís Corrêa de Araújo, *O grande blá-blá-blá,* preface by Queiroz (São Paulo: Fundação Movimento Brasileiro de Alfabetização/Instituto Nacional do Livro/Abril Cultural, 1974);

Literatura infanto-juvenil brasileira catálogo do exposição comemorativa do Ano Internacional da Criança, preface by Queiroz (Rio de Janeiro: La Biblioteca, 1979);

Mem de Sá, *Tempo de lembrar: memórias,* preface by Queiroz (Rio de Janeiro: J. Olympio, 1981);

Celina Bittencourt, *Verde verdade: poesia,* preface by Queiroz (Rio de Janeiro: J. Olympio, 1981);

Marcio Tavares d' Amaral, *Canção de vida e morte para o poeta,* preface by Queiroz (Rio de Janeiro: J. Olympio, 1983);

José Cândido de Carvalho, *O coronel e o lobisomem: deixados do Oficial Superior da Guarda Nacional, Ponciana de Azeredo Furtado, natural da praça de São Salvador de Campos dos Goitacases. Romance,* preface by Queiroz (Rio de Janeiro: J. Olympio, 1983);

Irene Tavares de Sá, *Fazenda da estrela: romance,* preface by Queiroz (Rio de Janeiro: AGIR, 1988);

Campos and João Alfredo de Sousa Montenegro, *Demócrito Rocha: o poeta e o jornalista,* preface by Queiroz (Fortaleza: Fundação Demócrito Rocha, 1989);

Mary Ann Leitão Karam, ed., *Antologia do conto cearense,* preface by Queiroz (Fortaleza: Tukano, 1990);

Raymundo A. C. Pinto, *Orfandade de um ideal: romance,* preface by Queiroz (Rio de Janeiro: Corpo da Letra Editora, 1993);

Campos, *Dizem que os cães vêem coisas,* preface by Queiroz (São Paulo: Maltese, 1993);

Denise Emmer, *O insólito festim: romance,* preface by Queiroz (Rio de Janeiro: Nova Fronteira, 1994);

Aderaldo Ferreira de Araujo, *Eu sou o cego Aderaldo,* introduction by Queiroz (São Paulo: Maltese, 1994);

Nenzinha Machado Salles, *Contos que te conto,* introductory note by Queiroz (Rio de Janeiro: Civilização Brasileira, 1995);

Charles Chaplin, *Minha vida,* translated by Queiroz, R. Magalhães Jr., and Genolino Amado (Rio de Janeiro: J. Olympio, 1998);

Pedro Rodrigues Salgueiro, *Brincar com armas (contos),* preface by Queiroz (Rio de Janeiro: Topbooks, 2000);

Suzana Flag (pseudonym of Nelson Rodrigues), *Minha vida: romance autobiográfico,* preface by Queiroz (São Paulo: Companhia das Letras, 2003).

TRANSLATIONS: Pearl S. Buck, *A exilada* (Rio de Janeiro: J. Olympio, 1943);

A. J. Cronin, *A família Brodie: romance* (Rio de Janeiro: J. Olympio, 1944); republished as *O castelo do homem sem alma (a família Brodie): romance* (Rio de Janeiro: J. Olympio, 1955);

Olive Higgins Prouty, *Stella Dallas: romance* (Rio de Janeiro: J. Olympio, 1945);

Buck, *A promessa, romance* (Rio de Janeiro: J. Olympio, 1946);

St. Teresa of Avila, *Vida de Santa Teresa de Jesus: escrita por ela própria* (São Paulo: J. Olympio, 1946);

John Galsworthy, *A crônica dos Forsythe: romance,* 3 volumes (São Paulo: J. Olympio, 1946);

Irving Stone, *Mulher imortal: biografia romanceada de Jessie* (Rio de Janeiro: J. Olympio, 1947);

Forrest Rosaire, *Os dois amores de Grey Manning: A leste da meia noite, romance = East of Midnight* (Rio de Janeiro: J. Olympio, 1948);

Cronin, *Os deuses riem* (Rio de Janeiro: J. Olympio, 1954);

Jane Austen, *Mansfield Park: romance* (Rio de Janeiro: J. Olympio, 1958);

Verner von Heidenstam, *Os Carolinos: crônica de Carlos XII* (Rio de Janeiro: Delta, 1963);

Agatha Christie, *A mulher diabólica* (Rio de Janeiro: J. Olympio, 1978).

Rachel de Queiroz's extensive oeuvre includes not only the several novels that largely account for her high literary reputation but also plays, children's books, essays, criticism, and a considerable number of collections of short stories and *crônicas* (brief humorous accounts of episodes of daily life). She has also contributed regularly to newspapers, journals, and magazines and translated into Portuguese works by writers such as Fyodor Dostoevsky, Leo Tolstoy, Honoré de Balzac, Emily Brontë, Jane Austen, and Samuel Butler. Queiroz belongs to the "Northeastern" or "Generation of 1930" group of writers who focused on realistic portrayals of life in the northeastern part of Brazil; other members of the group include José Lins do Rego, Jorge Amado, and Graciliano Ramos. Queiroz's works reveal a profound concern with the plight of the poor and struggling inhabitants of the region.

Queiroz was born in Fortaleza, in the northeastern state of Ceará, on 17 November 1910 to Daniel de Queiroz, a district attorney and geography teacher, and Clotilde Franklin de Queiroz; her maternal grandmother was a cousin of the nineteenth-century Brazilian writer José de Alencar. Her father taught Queiroz not only to read and write but also to ride horseback and swim. In 1917 the family moved to Rio de Janeiro to escape the drought that had begun in 1915. They returned to Ceará in 1919, at first settling in Guaramiranga and later moving to a farm near Quixadá. In 1921 Queiroz entered the Immaculate Conception boarding school; she graduated in 1925 with credentials as a teacher but returned to her parents' farm, where she spent most of her time reading French literature under her mother's direction. Her sister, Maria Luíza, with whom she co-authored three volumes of reminiscences (1994, 1998, and 2000), was born in 1926; their brothers—Roberto, Flávio, and Luciano—had all died young.

In 1927 Queiroz wrote a letter to the newspaper *O Ceará* under the pseudonym Rita de Queluz, satirizing a story that had appeared in the paper; the letter made such an impression on readers that the editor, Júlio Ibiapina, uncovered her true identity and hired her. Around this time she joined a group of writers representative of the modernist movement in Ceará that contributed regularly to the journal *Maracajá*.

Queiroz wrote her first novel while confined to bed by a lung condition that was suspected of being tuberculosis. Borrowing the money from her parents, she privately published one thousand copies of her novel *O quinze* (The Year 1915) in August 1930. Together with José Américo de Almeida's *A bagaceira*

(1928, The Husk-Pit), *O quinze* marks the beginning of the cycle of realistic novels from the northeast that predominated in Brazilian literature in the 1930s and 1940s. Queiroz's narrator, Conceição, an educated woman who is frustrated and unhappy in the repressive society in which she lives, spends 1915 on her grandmother's farm and witnesses the destruction by the drought of a destitute family. Torn between her desire for independence and societal expectations for women of marriage and motherhood, she ends up helping the poverty-stricken family and simultaneously fulfilling the maternal role by adopting one of the family's children. The clear, lean style of the work brought Queiroz praise from the writers Augustus Frederico Schmidt and Mário de Andrade, national acclaim, and, in 1931, the Graça Aranha Foundation literary prize. Her double criticism of human exploitation in the northeast and of women's social conditions has led critics to see her as a pioneer on the Brazilian intellectual scene.

In 1931 Queiroz joined the Brazilian Communist Party and helped to organize a branch of the party in Ceará. The following year she married José Auto da Cruz Oliveira, who was an employee of the Bank of Brazil, a journalist, a poet, and a bisexual. After reading the typescript for her next novel, *João Miguel* (1932), a three-man Communist Party committee in Rio de Janeiro ordered her not to publish it because it violated the party dogma of proletarian solidarity by depicting the killing of one worker by another: João Miguel, the only male central character in any of her novels, accidentally kills a man in a brawl and is sent to jail, leaving his lover, Santa, to fend for herself in the highly sexist Brazilian society. Queiroz told the committee that she would revise the work to make it acceptable; but when her typescript—the only copy she had—was returned to her, she walked to the door, turned and told the committee that she did not recognize its right to censor her work, kicked a chair, and ran from the room. The incident led her to resign from the party.

In 1932 Queiroz and her husband moved to São Paulo, where Queiroz joined a Trotskyite group. A daughter, Clotilde, was born in 1933. In 1935 the family moved to Maceió, where Clotilde died of septicemia at the age of eighteen months.

Queiroz's next novel, *Caminho de pedras* (1937, Stone Path), centers on a family of Communists. The main character, Naomi, is seeking liberation in a conservative society. She flees from the shackles of marriage only to discover that she cannot escape her biological function. Sexual and individual fulfillment are presented as opposed to motherhood.

In 1939 Queiroz was arrested and held for three months in a fire station in Fortaleza because of her political activities, and her books were publicly burned

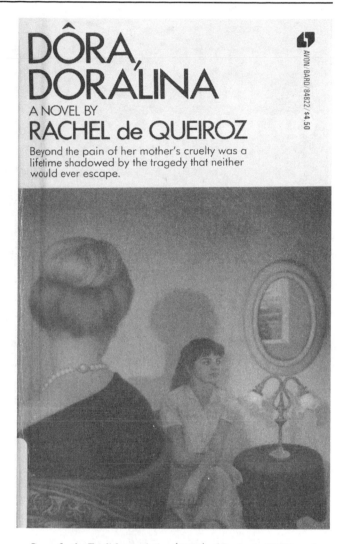

Cover for the English translation (1984) of Queiroz's 1975 novel, about a woman who learns the need for compromise between her desire for independence and society's demands (Thomas Cooper Library, University of South Carolina)

along with those of Amado, Lins do Rego, and Ramos. After her release she separated from her husband, moved to Rio de Janeiro, and published her fourth novel, *As três Marias* (1939; translated as *The Three Marias,* 1963). Queiroz's most autobiographical novel follows three friends, all named Maria, from boarding school to adulthood. Maria José and Maria da Glória take on the traditional roles of pious spinster and housewife, respectively; Maria Augusta (Guta), the narrator, searches for self-fulfillment through love but remains unfulfilled and empty, unable to reconcile her desires with societal demands. Critics see *As três Marias* as signaling Queiroz's literary maturity.

Queiroz became disillusioned with leftist politics when Leon Trotsky was murdered with an ice ax in Mexico on the orders of Joseph Stalin in 1940. In 1944

Paperback cover for Queiroz's 1985 novel (The Golden Rooster), about the exploitation of poor women in Rio de Janeiro (Thomas Cooper Library, University of South Carolina)

she wrote for the newspapers *Correio da Manhã, O Jornal,* and *Diário da Tarde* until becoming exclusively a writer of *crônicas* for the magazine *O Cruzeiro,* a position she held until 1975. In 1945 she married Oyama de Macedo, a physician with whom she had lived since 1940. Also in 1945 she returned to political activism, participating in the campaign that led to the fall of the repressive government of Getúlio Vargas. Her first collection of short stories, *A donzela e a moura torta: crônicas e reminiscências* (The Damsel and the Crooked Moorish Woman: Chronicles and Memoirs), came out in 1948. Her novel *O galo de ouro* (The Golden Rooster) was serialized in the popular magazine *O Cruzeiro* in the first months of 1950; it was not published in book form until 1985 and still has not received much critical attention. With *O galo de ouro,* Queiroz for the first time moves the setting of her narrative from her native Fortaleza to Rio de Janeiro. She depicts the city as a corrupt

place where women are exploited and trapped in poverty.

In 1953 Queiroz's *Lampião* was produced in Rio de Janeiro, São Paulo, and Fortaleza. The love story of the legendary northeastern outlaw Lampião and Maria Bonita, who abandoned her husband and children to follow the bandit and his group, received the Saci Prize from the newspaper *O Estado de São Paulo* as best play of the year.

In 1957 Queiroz received the prestigious Machado de Assis Prize from the Brazilian Academy of Letters for the body of her work. Her second play, *A beata Maria do Egito* (1958, The Pious Maria of Egypt), is based on a 1924 ballad by the Brazilian poet Manuel Bandeira. Queiroz's version transposes the story of the martyred saint from Egypt to northeastern Brazil. A pious nun gives herself to the lieutenant who arrests her to gain her release so that she may fulfill her sacred destiny of rescuing Padre Cícero from the soldiers who are planning to ambush him in Juazeiro.

In 1964 Queiroz, a cousin of General Humberto de Alencar Castelo Branco, supported the coup that ousted President João Goulart and established a military regime with Castelo Branco as president. In 1966 Castelo Branco appointed her to serve as a delegate to the United Nations Human Rights Commission; she was the first Brazilian woman to hold the position. Queiroz was a member of the Conselho Federal de Cultura (Federal Council of Culture) from 1967 to 1985. During this period she wrote two plays for children that were produced but remain unpublished: *O padrezinho santo* (The Little Saintly Priest) and *A sereia voadora* (The Flying Mermaid). In 1969 she published her first children's novel, *O menino mágico* (The Magic Boy).

Queiroz's next novel for adults, *Dôra, Doralina* (1975; translated, 1984) returns to the theme of a woman's search for self-fulfillment. Following the tradition of the novels of chivalry, the work is divided into three parts: "The Book of the Lady," "The Book of the Company," and "The Book of the Commander." Dôra leaves her farm in Ceará, becomes an actress and then a contented housewife, and finally returns to the farm, having learned to acknowledge the need for compromise between what she desires and what society demands from her as a woman. The novel received great acclaim.

In 1977 Queiroz became the first woman to be inducted into the Brazilian Academy of Letters. Her husband died in 1982. After publishing several collections of short stories and *crônicas* and two children's books, *Cafute & Pena de Prata* (1986, Cafute and Silver Feather) and *Andira* (1992), she brought out her novel *Memorial de Maria Moura* (Maria Moura's Memoirs) in 1992. Queiroz claimed that Dôra of *Dôra, Doralina* was an embryonic form of Maria Moura, her most revolutionary female character; she also said that *Memorial de Maria Moura* was partly based on the life of Queen Elizabeth I of England, who had her favorite suitor, Robert Devereux, second Earl of Essex, executed for betraying her. Maria Moura is a nineteenth-century outlaw in northeastern Brazil; to retain the land she has inherited, she dresses as a man, lives in a fortress, and leads a gang of bandits. She rejects love, marriage, and motherhood for a life of freedom and power. The novel is considered by many critics to be Queiroz's masterpiece and won several literary awards. In 1993 she received the Camões Prize, the most prestigious award for writers in the Portuguese language, from the governments of Brazil and Portugal. Never fully recovering from a stroke she suffered in August 1999, she died in her sleep from a heart attack in her home in Rio de Janeiro on 4 November 2003.

Rachel de Queiroz's reputation in Brazilian literature rests mainly on her innovative novels that focus on the challenges faced by women in a patriarchal society. Critics have observed in her novels a movement toward progressively stronger and more independent female protagonists, culminating in Maria Moura, a woman who refuses to compromise. Queiroz is also considered an important representative of the literature of northeastern Brazil, which chronicles the conflicts between the large landowners and the dispossessed who struggle in the hostile environment. Finally, Queiroz is highly regarded as a writer of *crônicas,* short stories, and children's books, a playwright, and a prolific translator.

Interviews:

Patricia Rosas Lopátegui, "A tradição oral em Rachel de Queiroz," *Hispanic Journal,* 17, no. 1 (1996): 17–29;

Hermes Rodrigues Nery, "Rachel de Queiroz: 'o meu recurso é a imaginação,'" *Jornal da Tarde,* 18 November 2000.

References:

Adonias Filho, *O romance brasileiro de 30* (Rio de Janeiro: Bloch, 1969);

Maria de Lourdes Dias Leite Barbosa, *Protagonistas de Rachel de Queiroz: caminhos e descaminhos* (Campinas: Pontes, 1999);

Haroldo Bruno, *Rachel de Queiroz: crítica, biografia, bibliografia, depoimento, seleção de textos, iconografia* (Brasília & Rio de Janeiro: Instituto Nacional do Livro/Cátedra, 1977);

Nelly Novaes Coelho, *A literatura feminina no Brasil contemporâneo* (São Paulo: Siciliano, 1993);

Joanna Courteau, "The Problematic Heroines in the Novels of Rachel de Queiroz," *Luso-Brasilian Review,* 22, no. 2 (1985): 123–144;

Fred P. Ellison, *Brazil's New Novel, Four Northeastern Masters: José Lins do Rego, Jorge Amado, Graciliano Ramos, Rachel de Queiroz* (Berkeley: University of California Press, 1954);

Heloisa Buarque de Hollanda, *A roupa de Rachel: um estudo sem importância* (Rio de Janeiro: CIEC, 1992);

Cristina Ferreira Pinto, *O bildungsroman feminino: quatro exemplos brasileiros* (São Paulo: Perspectiva, 1990);

Antônio Carlos Villaça, *Rachel de Queiroz: os oitenta* (Rio de Janeiro: J. Olympio, 1990);

Renata Wasserman, "A Woman's Place: Rachel de Queiroz's *Dôra, Doralina,*" *Brazil/Brasil,* 2 (1989): 46–58;

Elódia Xavier, *Declínio do patriarcado: a família no imaginário feminino* (Rio de Janeiro: Record/Rosa dos Ventos, 1998).

Graciliano Ramos

(27 October 1892 – 20 March 1953)

Joseph Abraham Levi
Rhode Island College

BOOKS: *Cahetés* (Rio de Janeiro: Schmidt, 1933); translated by Bernadette P. Guedes as *Caetés*, dissertation, University of South Carolina, 1976;

São Bernardo (Rio de Janeiro: Ariel, 1934); translated by R. L. Scott-Buccleuch (London: Owen, 1975; New York: Taplinger, 1979);

Angústia (Rio de Janeiro: J. Olympio, 1936); translated by L. C. Kaplan as *Anguish* (New York: Knopf, 1946);

Vidas secas (Rio de Janeiro: J. Olympio, 1938); translated by Ralph Edward Dimmick as *Barren Lives* (Austin: University of Texas Press, 1965);

A terra dos meninos pelados (Pôrto Alegre: Globo, 1939);

Histórias de Alexandre (Rio de Janeiro: Leitura, 1944);

Infância (Rio de Janeiro: J. Olympio, 1945); translated by Celso de Oliveira as *Childhood* (London: Owen, 1979);

Dois dedos (Rio de Janeiro: Revista Acadêmica, 1945);

Histórias incompletas (Pôrto Alegre: Globo, 1946);

Insônia (São Paulo: J. Olympio, 1947);

Sete histórias verdadeiras (Rio de Janeiro: Vitória, 1951);

Linhas tortas: crônicas escritas de 1915 a 1952 (São Paulo: Martins, 1952);

Memórias do cárcere, 4 volumes (Rio de Janeiro: J. Olympio, 1953);

Viagem: Tcheco-Eslováquia – U.R.S.S. (obra póstuma) (Rio de Janeiro: J. Olympio, 1954);

Alexandre e outros heróis: obra póstuma (São Paulo: Martins, 1962);

Viventes das Alagoas: quadros de costumes do Nordeste (São Paulo: Martins, 1962).

Editions and Collections: *Historias agrestes,* edited by Ricardo Ramos (São Paulo: Cultrix, 1960);

Trechos escolhidos, edited by Antônio Cândido (Rio de Janeiro: AGIR, 1961);

Graciliano Ramos: seleção de textos, notas, estudos biográficos, históricos e críticos e exercícios, edited by Vivina de Assis Viana (São Paulo: Abril Cultural, 1981);

Relatórios, edited by Mário Hélio Gomes de Lima (Rio de Janeiro: Record, 1994).

Graciliano Ramos (The website of Sérgio Godoy)

OTHER: José Carlos Cavalcanti Borges, *Neblina: contos,* preface by Ramos (Curitiba, 1940);

Booker T. Washington, *Memórias de um negro,* translated by Ramos (São Paulo: Nacional, 1940);

"Mário," in *Brandão entre o mar e o amor,* by Ramos, Jorge Amado, José Lins do Rego, Aníbal Machado, and Raquel de Queirós (São Paulo: Martins, 1942);

Raquel de Queirós, *Três Romances: O Quinze; João Miguel; Caminho de Pedras,* introduction by Ramos,

Augusto Frederico Schmidt, and Raquel de Queirós (Rio de Janeiro: J. Olympio, 1948);

Alina Paim, *Simão Dias,* preface by Ramos (Rio de Janeiro: Libraria Editora Da Casa, 1949);

Albert Camus, *A peste,* translated by Ramos (Rio de Janeiro: J. Olympio, 1950);

Contos e novelas: a apresentacão segue um critério geográfico, incluindo escritores antigos e modernos de todo o país, 3 volumes, edited by Ramos (Rio de Janeiro: Casa do Estudante do Brasil, 1957)–comprises volume 1: *Norte e nordeste;* volume 2: *Leste;* and volume 3: *Sul e centro-oeste.*

Graciliano Ramos is best known for the intense realism with which he represents scenes and characters from the arid northeast of Brazil, an area known for its *sertão* (hinterland) and constant droughts. Ramos's narratives vividly describe vegetation, animals, and humans all trying to survive the harsh and barren environment of northeastern Brazil. These works are generally placed within the larger context of Northeastern writers of the 1930s, a group of Brazilians who focused on the cultural and social problems of the region, including the multiethnic and multiracial component of the population, and the hardships and adversities of life in the area.

With the abolition of slavery in 1888 and the establishment of the Brazilian Republic in 1889, many artists, including writers, began to explore the complex and incongruent nation that Brazil had become. Prose fiction appeared to be one of the best means by which writers could pose questions about the individual regions and national identity. Euclides da Cunha's *Os sertões* (1902; translated as *Rebellion in the Backlands,* 1944), which in a sense is a manifesto of twentieth-century Brazilian regionalism, was the first work written on behalf of the "forgotten" Brazilian, the *sertanejo* (person from the *sertão*). A few years later José Pereira da Graça Aranha published *Canaã* (1902, Canaan), in which he ponders the effects of the recent immigration of Caucasians from Europe and the Middle East to Brazil, particularly the south and the south-central regions. Later, José Bento Monteiro Lobato, in his short-story collection *Urupês* (1918, White Agarics), speaks to a nation in search of its moribund native-Brazilian past and identity. These works preceded the Movimento Modernista Brasileiro (Brazilian Modernist Movement), which was embryonic between 1918 and 1921 and only manifested itself officially in 1922. The movement, which included literature, music, and the other fine arts, gave rise to a new cultural regionalism that flourished between 1922 and 1945. Ramos was one of the most important writers of this group, which included José Américo de Almeida, Jorge Amado, Amando Fontes, Gilberto Freyre, Jorge Mateus de Lima, Raquel de Queirós, and José Lins do Rego Cavalcanti.

Graciliano Ramos was born on 27 October 1892 in Quebrângulo, a hamlet in the northeastern state of Alagoas. His father was Sebastião Ramos de Oliveira, a retail merchant, and his mother was Maria Amélia Ferro Ramos. Both were of Portuguese descent, and Ramos was the first of their sixteen children. In 1894 Ramos's family moved to Maniçoba, in the state of Pernambuco, where his maternal grandparents owned a modest estate and raised cattle. The author's memoirs, *Infância* (1945; translated as *Childhood,* 1979), are based on his childhood memories of this area, a region cyclically stricken by droughts. A year after their move a drought put an end to the family's dream of raising cattle. In an effort to save the family from disaster, around 1895–1896 Ramos's father opened a fabric and soft-goods store in town. Six years later, in 1900, the family moved to the town of Viçosa, where Sebastião Ramos was later nominated to be a judge.

Ramos made his debut as a writer with his first short story, "Pequeno pedinte" (1904, Small Beggar), which was published in *O Dilúculo* (Dawn), a one-sheet biweekly journal founded in 1904 by the author himself. The magazine focused on children's literature. Using a pseudonym, Ramos soon tried his hand at literary writing with twenty-three sonnets and ten triolets (stanzas of eight lines with special rhyme) under the collective name *Trioletos* (1904, Triolets); he also wrote the special composition *Ritorno* (1904, Return). Ramos attended school first in Viçosa and Palmeira dos Índios, and then in 1905 he enrolled in the school of Professor Agnelo in Maceió. Between 1909 and 1915, under the pseudonyms S. de Almeida Cunha and Soeiro Lobato, he succeeded in publishing works in *O Malho* (Sledgehammer), a national journal based in Rio de Janeiro dedicated to the publication of original works.

In 1910 the Ramos family moved again, this time to Palmeira dos Índios, inland in the state of Alagoas. Ramos spent most of the next twenty years of his life in this location, and it left a mark on almost all of his works. He attended school in Pernambuco in 1910–1914, but he never completed his secondary education. While helping his father in the shop, particularly as a bookkeeper, Ramos had ample opportunity to read literature, Brazilian as well as foreign, including works by writers such as Eça de Queirós, Marcel Proust, Emile Zola, Fyodor Dostoevsky, and Maksim Gor'ky, considered by most to be the father of socialist realism. In 1914 Ramos moved to Rio de Janeiro, where he began working as proofreader for several newspapers: *O Correio da Manhã* (Morning Courier), *A Tarde* (The Afternoon), and *O Século* (The Century). During this time he

Cover for Ramos's first novel, the title of which is the generic name for several native-Brazilian tribes—known in the popular imagination for their cannibalism and cruelty—that dominated the Northeast until Portuguese settlers arrived in 1500 (Main Library, University of Arizona)

began writing for the newspaper *Paraíba do Sul* (Southern Paraíba) using the pseudonym R.O. He also began to write and publish in journals poetry, particularly sonnets, as well as children's stories.

In 1915 Ramos returned to Palmeira dos Índios for family reasons: a severe attack of bubonic plague claimed the lives of two of his sisters, a brother, and a nephew. That year he married Maria Augusta Barros and shortly afterward opened a general store. The couple had three children: Márcio, born in 1916; Júnio, born in 1917; and Maria Augusta, born in 1920. Márcio suffered from epilepsy. In 1920 Ramos was left a widower with three children.

In 1921, under the pseudonym J. Calixto, Ramos wrote a few articles for *O Índio* (Native Brazilian), a short-lived newspaper founded in Palmeiras dos Índios by his friend Father Francisco Xavier de Macedo.

Ramos's "Factos e fitas" (Facts and Ribbons) and "Traços a esmo" (Random Strokes), published between 30 January and 27 February, appear to have been among the few articles published by *O Índio* before the newspaper folded.

In 1925 Ramos began writing his first novel, *Cahetés* (1933; translated as *Caetés,* 1976), and in 1926 he was elected president of the Junta Escolar de Palmeira dos Índios (Board of Education of Palmeira dos Índios). On 7 October 1927 the writer was elected mayor of the city, a post he gave up in 1930. In 1927 Ramos met Heloísa Medeiros. They were married in a religious ceremony on 16 February 1928 in Maceió; four days later, in Palmeira dos Índios, they had the civil ceremony. The couple had four children: Ricardo, born in 1929; Roberto, who was born and died in 1930; Luísa, born in 1931; and Clara, known as Clarita, born in 1932.

In 1928 Ramos completed *Cahetés,* but he apparently had no intention of publishing it. Ramos started the narrative in 1925 as a short story. It became, however, so long and overcharged with characters and events that he turned it into a novel. Far from displaying any literary innovations, *Cahetés* exhibits many of the traits typical of nineteenth-century realist novels, particularly in its focus on adultery and Ramos's use of a refined language that does not reflect the language of the people who actually live in the setting of the book. The work features a novel within a novel, a device Ramos learned, either directly or indirectly, reading nineteenth-century Portuguese writer Eça de Queirós. Furthermore, it is possible that Eça de Queirós's posthumously published *A ilustre casa de Ramires* (1897; translated as *The Illustrious House of Ramires,* 1964) and *A cidade e as serras* (1900; translated as *The City and the Mountains,* 1955) served as the inspiration for Ramos's dissatisfaction with the corruption of the city environment.

The choice of the title *Cahetés* is significant; the word is a generic name applied to several different native-Brazilian tribes belonging to the Tupi-language branch who roamed throughout the Northeast before the arrival of the Portuguese in 1500. They were known for their alleged cruelty and cannibalism. Between 1534—when the Portuguese established the captaincy of Nova Lusitânia, soon renamed Pernambuco—and the last decade of the sixteenth century, the Caetés were exterminated by the Portuguese and the Tupinambás, one of the largest tribal nations still in existence in Brazil. From a literary point of view *Cahetés* was a throwback, its narrative techniques resembling more the realist novels of the nineteenth century than early-twentieth-century Brazilian modernists such as Rego and Amado.

Ramos found in Portuguese, Brazilian, French, and Russian authors–particularly Eça de Queirós, Joaquim Maria Machado de Assis, Aluísio Azevedo, Honoré de Balzac, Gustave Flaubert, Anatole France, Stendhal, Dostoevsky, and Leo Tolstoy–inspiration for the composition of a modern regional work. To this type of literature he brought personal experiences and imagination, and the result is a portrayal of a small northeastern town imbued with intrigues, ambitions, dreams, desires, envies, revenge, and personal defeats. Set in the city of Palmeira dos Índios, the plot revolves around adultery and its consequences. Closely resembling a stretch of the author's history, the narrator, João Valério, is a bookkeeper living in Palmeira dos Índios desperately trying to write a novel. At the same time, however, João is working for the commercial company Teixeira e Irmão (Teixeira and Brother), which is owned by Adrião and his brother. Adrião's young wife, Luísa, has a brief affair with João, who is considered by everyone, especially Adrião, to be a member of the family. Hence, João is overwhelmed by feelings of guilt. When the affair is discovered through an anonymous letter, Adrião shoots himself and dies seven days later. Meanwhile, João's project of an historical novel based upon the Caetés and their ties with one of his ancestors remains unwritten. João's ignorance about the pre-European history of Brazil makes him fear that his work will not be based on true historical facts. Furthermore, his knowledge of native-Brazilian tribes and their early ties with Europeans (Portuguese, Dutch, and French) is limited and dates back to his school days where he read António Gonçalves Dias's poems on Indianism, particularly *Os tymbiras* (1857, The Timbiras), as well as José Martiniano de Alencar's *O Guarany* (1857, The Guarani) and *Iracema* (1865; translated as *Iraçéma, the Honey Lips: A Legend of Brazil*, 1886), where native Brazilians are exalted and glorified for their principles, honesty, and values. The dialogues of these works are often imbued with a lexicon that would better suit people from a Portuguese rather than a Brazilian background, especially considering the modest origins of some of the characters who, for lack of means and exposure to the outer world, would have spoken and understood only the local vernacular.

The aspect of *Cahetés* that sets Ramos apart from his fellow modernists is João's descriptions of novel writing as a process, an unfinished product. Ramos shows awareness that writing a new text means borrowing, imitating, or at least re-creating something that has already been written. Even the most innovative novel is an "imitation" of a previous work of fiction, reproducing in a new key a preexisting set of rules and devices.

Ramos went on to write two nonliterary treatises, invaluable sources of historical information on the time

and the geographical area of northeastern Brazil, that were in a sense responsible for his future literary career. These two works, which originally circulated as typed manuscripts, are the "Relatório ao Governador do Estado de Alagoas" (1929, Report to the Governor of the State of Alagoas) and the "Segundo Relatório ao Sr. Governador Álvaro Paes, pelo Prefeito do Município da Palmeira dos Índios" (1930, Second Report to the Governor Álvaro Paes, by the Prefect of the Municipality of Palmeira dos Índios). The latter report was also published in article form in the Palmeira dos Índios newspaper. Ramos soon came to be known for his eloquence, clarity of style and content, and his honesty, despite the consequences.

In 1930 Ramos was in Maceió, where he was nominated director of the Imprensa Oficial do Estado (Official Printing Press of the State [of Alagoas]). During this time he published articles for various local and state newspapers, often under the pseudonym Lúcio Guedes. Two years later he resigned and returned to Palmeira dos Índios, where he founded a school in the sacristy of the main church, known as Igreja Matiz de Palmeira dos Índios (Mother Church of Palmeira dos Índios). During this time he began writing the first chapters of *São Bernardo* (1934; translated, 1975). In January 1933 Ramos was in Maceió, where he directed the Instrução Pública de Alagoas (Public Education for the State of Alagoas) and was nominated director of the Imprensa Oficial (Official Press). Here Ramos became part of a literary circle frequented by Valdemar Cavalcanti, Aurélio Buarque da Holanda Ferreira, Raul Lima, Rego, and Eça de Queirós.

In Rio de Janeiro the poet Augusto Frederico Schmidt stumbled upon Ramos's "Segundo relatório ao Sr. Governador Álvaro Paes, pelo Prefeito do município da Palmeira dos Índios" and was impressed by the young man's literary talent. Being also an editor and publisher–Schmidt's famous "discoveries" include Amado, Eça de Queirós, and Eddy Dias da Cruz (a Rio de Janeiro novelist who wrote under the pseudonym Marques Rebelo)–Schmidt befriended Ramos and in 1933 published *Cahetés*. That year Ramos began writing *Angústia* (1936; translated as *Anguish*, 1946).

Published in 1934, *São Bernardo* is Ramos's first novel to achieve the status of literary masterpiece in Brazil and worldwide. Like *Cahetés, São Bernardo* is set in the Brazilian northeast in the state of Alagoas, where Ramos spent his early years. Unlike *Cahetés,* however, *São Bernardo* starts at the end of the story, and the narrator uses flashbacks to work his way back to the beginning. Additionally, in *São Bernardo* the characters speak and act according to their status and place of origin. They speak and act as Brazilians from the broad spectrum of the middle class, including criminals, laborers,

Title page for the first edition of Ramos's 1936 novel about a husband who murders his unfaithful wife's lover and then descends into madness (Biblioteca Nacional de Chile)

servants, and those from the Afro-Brazilian population. Together the characters reflect small Brazilian cities' struggle for survival and adaptation to the modern era.

The main character of *São Bernardo,* Paulo Honório, is a middle-aged, self-made man who manages, through deceit and murder, to purchase the big ranch named São Bernardo, where he was once a laborer. Although the means by which he succeeds are not always honest and straightforward, in the interior of Brazil—as in any frontier culture of the New World, sub-Saharan Africa, Australia, or New Zealand—the ends justify the means, even at the cost of being ruthless and cruel. As a way of making sense of his own life and to justify his own actions, Honório decides to write his memoirs. Given his shortcomings in many fields, intellectual as well as stylistic, he feels compelled to enlist Padre Silvestre, João Nogueira, Arquimedes, and Lúcio Gomes de Azevedo Gondim to assist him with the moral content and Latin quotations, and also help him with his language, typesetting, and editing. Honório

contributes the general frame of the story, information on cattle raising and the farm, and he pays all expenses related to the production of the book.

Of lower-class background and without parents, Honório spent his childhood, adolescence, and early adulthood in poverty and delinquency. He spent almost four years in prison for stabbing a man in a jealous rage over a woman. The only positive thing that happened to him in jail was meeting a shoemaker, an older and gentler inmate who, using a Protestant Bible, taught him how to read and write. Once a free man, Honório continued his education, learning mathematics and accounting, skills that helped him survive and prosper. In Viçosa, where he settles, Honório takes over São Bernardo, buying it from Luís Padilha, a man in serious debt from his gambling habits. On many occasions Ramos inserts his personal views on the dangers of modern society that threaten to destroy the old system and disrupt the four-hundred-year-old harmony in the region.

Once he becomes the sole master of São Bernardo, Honório feels the need to turn his estate into a model for all farms. He opens a school so that his workers can master the basics of Portuguese language and mathematics and also learn how to contribute to the welfare of the entire community, that is, the productivity of the master's estate. Honório hires as teacher the former owner, Luís Padilha, who apparently is gifted at the work, although his "subversive" ideas, that is, his socialist views, are ultimately a threat to Honório's traditional values. In an attempt both to eliminate this problem and find a mate who eventually could bear him an heir, Honório befriends Glória, the aunt of a prospective bride named Madalena. The scheme works, and Madalena, who holds a degree in education, is lured into the position of teacher at São Bernardo and also accepts being Honório's wife. Soon the discrepancies in character and opinion bring the couple to an impasse: Madalena's modern views on justice and equality are at odds with the despotic and reactionary way of life of her husband.

With Honório, Ramos portrays the typical landowner of most parts of Brazil, especially in the Northeast: a corrupt individual, often with a criminal background, who built his fortune on trickery and theft, and is generally known by the pseudohonorific title of *coronel* (colonel). The gap between Madalena and Honório widens, even after the birth of their son, heir to São Bernardo. Madalena's friendship with Padilha, an intellectual tie rather than a physical attraction, eventually leads Honório to suspect an affair, and he ultimately takes a fragment of a letter written by Madalena as evidence of her betrayal. He confronts her in the estate chapel and almost kills her. Once in her bedroom, Madalena enacts what she had previously planned: escaping her entrapment at São Bernardo through suicide. She poisons herself, and the farewell message she leaves to her husband is missing a page. To his despair Honório realizes that what he took to be evidence of his wife's affair is actually the missing piece of her suicide note, proving her innocence. Honório is now alone, left with only memories and remorse.

Besides the personal conflicts, *São Bernardo* highlights the need for agrarian reform, especially in northeastern Brazil, where capitalism and technology were slow to enter and bring innovations. Throughout *São Bernardo* there are clear allusions to the Brazilian political scene of the time, particularly the fascism of the Vargas regime and the inadequacies of new reforms. Like the rest of the country, the Northeast had witnessed nothing more than a change of hands; the government did nothing to improve the living conditions of the average citizen still struggling to make ends meet in an environment where nature is hostile to growth and prosperity.

Statesman Getúlio Dornelles Vargas became president in 1930. Although Vargas was initially a republican, he soon showed signs of political intolerance, and as early as 1934 he began unleashing ferocious and relentless anticommunist propaganda. In 1937, after a strategically planned coup d'état, Vargas and his political entourage brought the country under a dictatorial, fascist regime that lasted until 29 October 1945.

Growing fears that Ramos's work and actions were "unpatriotic," "communist," and "subversive" led to the author's unfounded arrest. Ramos was not a member of any leftist group; he joined the Partido Comunista Brasileiro (Brazilian Communist Party) much later in his life, in 1945. In 1936 Ramos was named director of the Instrução Pública de Alagoas, and perhaps his attempts to institute several swift reforms within the Alagoas public education system raised suspicions. On 3 March 1936 he was arrested on charges of communism and having "subvervise ideas." Imprisoned for many months without a trial, Ramos was eventually sentenced to spend time in the state penitentiary of Pernambuco, but he was soon transferred to Recife, and then to the correction facility of Ilha Grande in Rio de Janeiro. In August 1936, while he was still in prison, the Rio de Janeiro–based Livraria José Olympio published *Angústia,* which in 1937 received the prestigious Prêmio Lima Barreto (Lima Barreto Prize), sponsored by the journal *Revista.* José Pereira Filho Olympio, simply known as José Olympio, soon became the promoter of most of Ramos's works.

Ramos's next novel, *Angústia,* features a more introspective approach. *Angústia* completes Ramos's trilogy centering on dysfunctional, jealous men operating within a society that alienates them. *Angústia* is about a crime of passion committed by Luís da Silva, who is tormented by the anguish of his act. Silva is a *sertanejo* who now lives in Maceió. Like João Valério and Paulo Honório, Silva is a writer, but he composes advertisements, announcements, and various insignificant articles rather than a novel, something that he will never achieve. Silva narrates episodes that either happen in the present or occurred in the past; the two conflate in his mind as details culled from different moments help him re-create alleged events.

A newly arrived neighbor, Marina, causes much distress for Silva, who is preoccupied with gaining her attention. Despite his disappointment at her simple-mindedness, he eventually marries her. Within a short period of time she depletes her husband's meager assets. Julião Tavares, an accomplished writer and shameless womanizer, a man Silva has always despised because he comes from a wealthy family, becomes Marina's lover. Silva's revenge comes in two ways. He calls Marina, pregnant with Tavares's child, a whore. Verbal abuse seems to be the right price for her crime; the punishment is to Silva's satisfaction. The worst punishment is reserved for Tavares, whom Silva blames for his unhappiness and public disgrace: he strangles him with a rope. Silva is then overcome with a feeling of great happiness, as if he is finally free, at least temporarily. To avoid any suspicion of foul play Silva ties the rope to a branch, thus giving the appearance of suicide.

Then, reluctantly and unwillingly, as if he were in a delirious mist, Silva recalls and relives his act of madness. Ramos succeeds in expressing Silva's pain when he, for example, compares the wires, strings, and cords in his mind with the infamous rope. The character's delirium derives from his frustration over his life as well as his physical isolation. He needs to be insane in order to come to terms with and expiate his crime. Tavares and Marina represent betrayal, but they also—and more importantly—represent the very system that failed Silva. In this Ramos was undoubtedly influenced by Dostoevsky—particularly his novels *Prestuplenie i nakazanie* (1866; translated as *Crime and Punishment,* 1886), the psychological and philosophical exposition of a murder, and *Zapiski iz polpol'ia* (1864; translated as *Letters from the Underworld,* in *Letters from the Underworld and Other Tales,* 1913). Luís da Silva's train of thought, obsession, and delirium make *Angústia* one of the most important psychological novels in early-twentieth-century Brazilian literature.

When he was freed from prison on 13 January 1937, Ramos chose to reside in Rio de Janeiro and continue his interrupted career as a federal inspector of education as well as a poorly paid editor and writer. In May 1937 he was honored with a special edition of the

*Cover for a 1947 Spanish-language edition of Ramos's 1938
novel (translated as* Barren Lives, *1965) about a family's
miserable struggle in Northeastern Brazil
(Biblioteca Nacional de Chile)*

pers and magazines, and when Ramos was subsequently asked to produce a new book, he put together what he had and added a few more characters: Fabiano's wife, Vitória, and their two unnamed sons.

Vidas secas shows how the barren Northeastern environment leads to complete misery as Fabiano and his family toil in impossible conditions. In fact, Ramos casts his characters as an integral part of the landscape. The author establishes this synthesis in part by keeping dialogue to a minimum. Additionally, with a semi-nomadic lifestyle imposed on them by frequent droughts, the family has almost no personal possessions that might distract the reader from their harsh surroundings. The novel instead centers on the harsh cyclical climate of the region and its effect on people. In the opening chapter, as Fabiano's family flees a drought, they come upon an abandoned farm and settle there for a year, during which time the drought abates. The following year, however, the drought returns and forces them to leave again in search of a better place. The intense, red-hot color of the *sertão* and the ever-present blue of the sky, all symbols of negativity and death, are counterbalanced by the green of the jujube trees, conveying hope for a better tomorrow, when rain and abundance will reign. This idea is central to the last chapter as the family once again flees drought and heads south toward the city. In the family's minds the move represents the hope of a better life in which they can own their own farm and the children can go to school. They see the south as a new promised land, which is the vision of many who flee the *sertão*.

Throughout the thirteen episodes of *Vidas secas,* Ramos uses the setting of the *sertão* to describe and define his characters, often likening them to vegetables and animals. Here humans, animals, and other parts of nature are brought together in their suffering, as everything in the barren world competes for survival. Feelings of fatalism, experienced by many in the generations before them, coupled with the overwhelming presence of completely parched land, turn Fabiano and his family into "desiccated" and "barren" individuals—hence, the title *Vidas secas*. Ramos even skillfully transfers these physical characteristics to Fabiano's personality: with the drought he becomes more taciturn than usual, almost mute. The language employed by Ramos in *Vidas secas* generally depicts the sterility of the environment, the torment of adaptation, and the characters' surrender to the forces of nature.

While Ramos was writing *Vidas secas,* the work that probably influenced him the most was Euclides da Cunha's *Os sertões*. This book is an historical account of the rebellion of Canudos, in the northeastern corner of the state of Bahia, which occurred between 1896 and 1897. The uprising involved a messianic group of

Revista Acadêmica (Academic Review), and in September his *A terra dos meninos pelados* (The Land of the Bald Boys), published in the Rio de Janeiro journal *Pan Infantil* (The Universal Child), received third place in the Concurso de Literatura Infantil do Ministério da Educação (Juvenile Literature Competition of the Ministry of Education).

In 1938 Ramos published *Vidas secas* (translated as *Barren Lives,* 1965), considered the last of his masterpieces and a classic of Brazilian modernism. *Vidas secas* is unusual because it is a succession of individual images, events, and scenes, rather than a linear account of events. The order of some of the chapters could, in fact, be rearranged without negatively affecting the individual chapters or the overall volume. Each chapter has its own coherence and unity, dependent upon the others only in the sense that they all belong to the same saga, namely, a family's attempt to survive the inhuman conditions of the Brazilian northeast. Ramos once admitted that *Vidas secas* began as a story about a dog, Baleia, followed by another story on its owner, Fabiano, a *caboclo* (person of mixed white and native-Brazilian ancestry) herdsman. These pieces appeared in several newspa-

almost eight thousand people, most of whom were homeless and poor. The group declared loyalty to the Portuguese Crown, condemning as evil the Brazilian Republic that had been formed in 1889. The group awaited the establishment in Canudos of a new Canaan under the command of Sebastião, the lost, or rather, "missing-in-action" king of Portugal, who was expected to return to earth after Judgment Day and reign undisturbed. Using his experience as a journalist, Cunha succeeded in reproducing the spirit of the *sertanejos* at Canudos at this point in history.

Like his predecessor, Ramos succeeds in documenting the *sertão* and its inhabitants for his readers. Ramos had an advantage over Cunha, however, because he was one of his subjects, having come from the *sertão*. With his personal knowledge of the conditions of the region, Ramos could best reproduce the pain and the feelings of the *sertanejos* forced to flee their homes, as well as their hopes for a better future. In many ways Fabiano is a symbol for all *sertanejos,* who were often illiterate and suspicious of everyone and everything, particularly the authorities. Given his ignorance, Fabiano cannot express his thoughts, not even when he should defend himself against the abuses of a local policeman. Through such incidents in the narrative Ramos cleverly attacks the social system and expresses dissatisfaction with the Vargas regime, which was more preoccupied with the political events of the large industrialized southern cities, dominated by the white upper and middle classes, than with the people of the interior.

In 1939 Ramos was named inspector federal do ensino secundário (federal inspector of secondary education). In the same year *A terra dos meninos pelados* was published in book form in Pôrto Alegre by the Livraria do Globo. In 1940 Ramos was asked to write the preface to José Carlos Cavalcanti Borges's book *Neblina* (Haze). Additionally, Ramos was comfortable enough with his command of English that he translated Booker T. Washington's 1901 autobiography *Up from Slavery* as *Memórias de um negro* (1940, Memoirs of a Negro); later, he took on a French text, translating Albert Camus's *La Peste* (1947) as *A peste* (1950, The Plague).

In 1942 Ramos contributed the chapter "Mário" to the volume *Brandão entre o mar e o amor* (Brandon between the Sea and Love), co-authored with Amado, Rego, Aníbal Machado, and Raquel de Queirós, and he also wrote the play *Idéias novas* (New Ideas), which was published in the journal *Revista do Brasil* (Brazilian Review). Later that year, on 27 October, a dinner at the Lido in Rio de Janeiro was held to celebrate the author's fiftieth birthday. On this occasion he was awarded the Prêmio Filipe de Oliveira (Filipe de Oliveira Prize), which included an honorarium of 5,000

cruzeiros. On 15 March 1943 the Oficinas Gráficas Alba published the proceedings of the papers presented at the dinner under the title *Homenagem a Graciliano Ramos* (Homage to Graciliano Ramos). The following year Ramos published *História de Alexandre* (Stories of Alexander). In 1945, the year he officially joined the Brazilian Communist Party, Ramos published *Infância* and *Dois dedos* (Two Fingers), the latter a deluxe and limited-edition collection of ten short stories (280 copies total, the first 55 including 10 xylographs by Axl Leskoschek).

Although different in theme and content from the novels, *Infância* features the same sensibility toward the human condition as the author focuses on the confining aspects of the political and natural environment. As memoirs, *Infância* combines real personal experiences with fiction. The imaginary is channeled through the perceptions of the world as it was seen by Ramos the child, including scenes from the Northeast that reveal the dichotomy between the urban and the rural; the narrative ends when the author reaches puberty. The child's hopes for a better future and uncertainty about tomorrow surface throughout the narrative.

The subhuman conditions in which many northeastern Brazilians live, typified in the character of the *caboclo sertanejo,* is represented in great detail in *Infância.* The suffering of generations of people exposed to harsh living conditions, fighting through adversity, and trying to survive at all costs is depicted through silence and apathy, bordering at times on passive resignation. This indifference is either understood as a fatalistic acceptance of one's lot or as a nonhuman trait of the *sertanejo,* who gradually becomes similar, at least on the surface, to the other living creatures that share his fate. In the region people, animals, and plants share degradation to a tenuous existence; the people and animals that populate all of Ramos's works as main characters and background figures are in a constant struggle for survival. The *sertanejo* is represented as an individual hardened by the harsh environment, whose fatalism, cynicism, and coldness are the only means by which he can overcome feelings of impotence against the forces of nature and destiny. Meanwhile, the *fazendeiro* (rich landholder), his counterpart, is represented as ruthless and greedy, at times equal to or more powerful than the government itself. Yet, the *fazendeiro* and his empire are eventually victims of the destructive powers of nature and the personal shortcomings of powerful patriarchs. Vices, financial troubles, political intrigues, and the winds of change brought by a capitalist and urban society are the ways in which an invisible supernatural force takes revenge against the power of the feudal barons in the interior of Brazil.

encouraged his son to read, as did Venâncio. It was ultimately in the private library of Barreto, however, that Ramos truly acquired a taste for literature.

In 1946 Ramos published *Histórias incompletas* (Incomplete Stories), a compilation of different stories, chapters from novels, and memoirs. Shortly afterward, Livraria José Olympio published *Insônia* (1947, Insomnia), a collection of thirteen short stories that can be grouped by theme. The first four stories are "Insônia," "O ladrão" (The Thief), "O relógio do hospital" (The Hospital Clock), and "Paulo" (Paul). The common denominator of the four stories is the irrational nightmare triggered by either insomnia or delirium. The unreal, at times surreal, elements of the stories are confronted or checked by the interruption of outer rational forces, such as the ticking of a clock. The next two stories, "Luciana" and "Minsk," are linked by the fact that they have a child, Luciana, as their central protagonist. "A prisão de J. Carmo Gomes" (The Prison of J. Carmo Gomes), the longest narrative of the collection, stands alone; like the later *Memórias do cárcere* (1953, Prison Memoirs), the story expresses the author's concerns with political ideologies and corruption. The next two stories, "Dois dedos" and "O testemunha" (The Witness), explore the guilt triggered when one is caught performing an illicit act. "Ciúmes" (Jealousy) is the only story that has as its main protagonist a woman, Zulmira, while the last three short stories, "Pobre diabo" (Poor Devil), "A visita" (The Visit), and "Silveira Pereira," deal with the theme of writing.

In *Insônia,* Ramos abandons traditional narrative techniques and adopts a more introspective approach. The stories are characterized by internal monologues and free, indirect speech. The characters are able to bare their souls, expressing their fears and their most intimate desires. *Insônia* is a mirror of life as an art form rather than a representation of events over which human beings have no control, as in *Vidas secas.* Although on the surface there seems to be no logical connection between them, the different stories that comprise *Insônia* actually are closely linked: the unifying feature is the author's focus on communication and the transmission of information rather than on continuity.

In 1948 Ramos, together with Schmidt and Raquel de Queirós, wrote a lengthy introduction to *Três Romances: O Quinze; João Miguel; Caminho de Pedras* (Three Novels: The Fifteen; John Miguel; Cobblestone Road), an edition of Raquel de Queirós's first three works. The first of the three stories describes in great detail the vicissitudes of the *sertanejos* during the horrible drought of 1915 in the Northeast of Brazil.

In 1949 Ramos was asked to write the preface to another novel, Alina Paim's *Simão Dias.* That year *São*

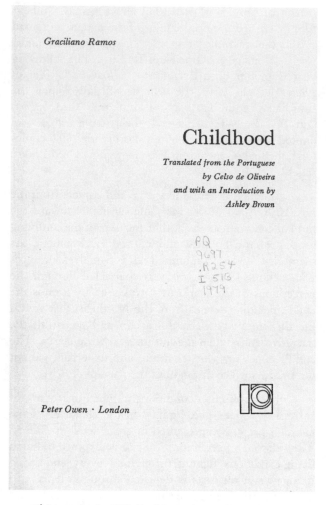

Graciliano Ramos

Childhood

*Translated from the Portuguese
by Celso de Oliveira
and with an Introduction by
Ashley Brown*

Peter Owen · London

Title page for the 1979 English translation of Ramos's 1945 memoirs focusing on his childhood experiences and observations, especially the subhuman conditions in which many in Northeast Brazil live (Thomas Cooper Library, University of South Carolina)

Infância can be considered Ramos's way of reconstructing for himself and for the reader the epiphanic moment in which he finally realized that writing was his calling in life. Throughout the narratives there are few references to time as a marker, such as the ages of characters or the dates of events. Instead, the emphasis is on the events and people that eventually marked or influenced Ramos—hence, the many people and events described, such as Ramos's parents, grandparents, his mentor Mário Venâncio, former slaves, slavery and its abolition in 1888, schoolmates, playmates, and relatives, including his cousin Emília, who introduced him to the notary Jerónimo Barreto, owner of the most prestigious library in the region. These people allow the reader to trace Ramos's development as a writer. Though stern and despotic, Ramos's father

Bernardo was broadcast on the radio, first by the Rio de Janeiro–based Rádio Globo and then by the Recife-based Rádio Jornal do Comércio. On 31 March 1951 Ramos became president of the Associação Brasileira de Escritores (Brazilian Guild of Writers), a position that was renewed the following year. That year the Rio de Janeiro–based publisher Vitória published *Sete histórias verdadeiras* (Seven True Stories), an adaptation of some of Ramos's stories that had previously appeared in the *Histórias de Alexandre*. The stories chosen for this volume were revised for a younger audience.

In 1952 a collection of Ramos's newspaper and journal articles composed between 1915 and 1952 was published for the first time under the title *Linhas tortas* (Crooked Lines), the title of one of the editorial columns for which Ramos was famous. In terms of style and content, these short pieces may be divided into three subgroups: 1915–1930, the juvenile years, in which Ramos explores the realm of writing; 1930–1937, when, more confident and prolix, his prose evolves into a style more appropriate for the novel; and 1937–1952, the mature period in which the author was mainly preoccupied with immediate needs and events.

Motivated by a desire to witness socialism first-hand, Ramos, Heloísa, and their friend Sinval Palmeira visited Czechoslovakia and the Soviet Union, with stops in Portugal and France, between 21 April and 16 June 1952. On 27 October 1952 Ramos's sixtieth birthday was celebrated in all pomp at the Câmara Municipal do Rio de Janeiro (City Hall of Rio de Janeiro). Speakers at the event included Rego, Amado, Haroldo de Oliveira Firmo Bruno, Afonso Félix de Sousa, Jorge de Lima, Ari de Andrade, and Peregrino Júnior. Clara Ramos spoke on behalf of her father, who was recovering from a 19 September cancer operation in Buenos Aires. Several months later, on 25 January 1953, Ramos was admitted to the clinic Casa de Saúde e Maternidade S. Vitor (House of Health and Maternity of Saint Victor) in Rio de Janeiro. He died there of lung cancer on 20 March 1953 and was buried in the Cemitério de São João Batista (Cemetery of Saint John the Baptist).

The year Ramos died his four-volume *Memórias do cárcere* (Prison Memoirs), including an afterword by his son Ricardo, was published in Rio de Janeiro. *Memórias do cárcere* is based on the author's recollection, or rather, reconstruction, of his prison notes, which he had to discard. Operating without his notes, Ramos relies on his memories of events and people, which are selectively filtered. Additionally, the author's fertile imagination is present throughout the memoirs. Hence, although it is a memoir, *Memórias do cárcere* reveals Ramos's talents in fiction, especially in those passages in which he vividly portrays characters and events. Through the mixture of the real and the fictional

Ramos relates terrible moments of his imprisonment; the reader feels the pain he experienced and is ultimately moved by it. *Memórias do cárcere* is divided into four parts: *Viagens* (Journeys), *Pavilhão dos recém-chegados* (Pavilion of the Newly Arrived), *Colônia penal* (Correctional Colony), and *Casa de correção* (House of Correction). Each part is made up of small chapters, a device that Ramos ultimately preferred over all other literary devices, since it best expressed his way of communicating: brief yet rich in meaning.

Memórias do cárcere was long in the making. Suffering from lung cancer and approaching the end of his life, Ramos wrote the book that he should have written during his imprisonment in 1936–1937. The inmates he met or had the opportunity to observe provided material that he adapted for similar nightmarish circumstances in works he wrote after his prison term. The prisoners' personae and deeds provide examples of Ramos's persistent theme of people adapting to an adverse and hostile environment. Throughout the text Ramos emphasizes time, focusing on the exact moment in which a specific action or word changes the course of events—in the case of one's imprisonment, the moment may be a crime of passion, a wrong decision, or a poor choice of words.

The year after Ramos's death Livraria José Olympio published *Viagem: Tcheco-Eslováquia – U.R.S.S.* (Trip: Czechoslovakia – U.S.S.R.), which was based on his "Anotações sobre a última viagem à U.R.S.S. em 1952" (Notes on the Last Trip to the U.S.S.R. in 1952). Ramos took extensive notes while traveling in the Soviet Union and Czechoslovakia, and his enthusiasm about the journey is reflected in these writings. Ramos began putting his notes in book form a few months prior to his death; the final chapters were still in draft form when he died. Like most of Ramos's works, *Viagem: Tcheco-Eslováquia – U.R.S.S.* is made up of a collection of short events linked by a common denominator.

In 1957 the three-volume collection edited by Ramos titled *Contos e novelas: a apresentacão segue um critério geográfico, incluindo escritores antigos e modernos de todo o país* (Short Stories and Novels) was published in Rio de Janeiro by the Casa do Estudante do Brasil, the first student organization in Brazil, founded in 1929 to aid students and to promote cultural events nationwide. In March and April 1960 the journal *Senhor* (Master) published Ramos's "Pequena história da República" (Small History of the Republic), and the São Paulo–based Cultrix published *Histórias agrestes* (Rural Stories), edited by his son Ricardo.

A few years after Ramos's death, when his popularity reached levels not achieved during his lifetime, Livraria Martins Editora, a leading publisher in São Paulo, acquired almost exclusive rights over the

GRACILIANO RAMOS

VIAGEM

(TCHECO-ESLOVÁQUIA - URSS)

(OBRA PÓSTUMA)

MARTINS

Title page for the 1970 edition of Ramos's 1954 exploration of communist countries based on notes taken while traveling in the Soviet Union and Czechoslovakia with his wife and Sinval Palmeira in 1952 (Thomas Cooper Library, University of South Carolina)

author's works. Along with many new editions of his most famous works, in 1962 the Livraria Martins Editora published *Viventes das Alagoas: quadros e costumes do Nordeste* (Inhabitants of the State of Alagoas: Pictures and Customs from the Northeast), which originally appeared as a series of articles in the journal *Cultura Política* (Political Culture) in January–March 1941 and October 1942 under the title "Quadros e costumes do Nordeste." That year Livraria Martins Editora was also responsible for the popular *Alexandre e outros heróis* (Alexander and Other Heroes), which comprises the *História de Alexandre, A terra dos meninos pelados,* and, for the first time in book form, the "Pequena história da república." A key feature of this collection is Ramos's use of old stories and legends from the Northeast; he allows his imagination free rein as he takes his young audience to a remote, magical world of native-Brazilian origin,

Tatipirum, "a terra dos meninos pelados." The not-so-distant past described is the time that elapsed between 1889, the year in which Brazil became independent, and 1930, the year in which Vargas took over and gradually made the country a stern dictatorship.

Another noteworthy event of 1962 occurred when the Biblioteca Nacional in Rio de Janeiro inaugurated the Exposição Graciliano Ramos (Graciliano Ramos Exposition). In 1963, in commemoration of the tenth anniversary of the author's death, the city of Curitiba held a retrospective show on Ramos. In 1964 *Vidas secas* was made into a movie by the famous Brazilian cinematographer Nelson Pereira dos Santos, and it received the Catholique International du Cinéma (International Catholic Movie) award as well as the Ciudad de Valladolid (City of Valladolid) prize.

Throughout his life Ramos kept an active correspondence with friends, family, and loved ones. First published in 1980, Ramos's *Cartas* (Letters) has gone through many editions, and his *Cartas de amor a Heloísa* (Love Letters to Heloísa) was published separately in 1994. Furthermore, Ramos left behind unfinished literary works: the unedited story "O ladrão" (The Thief), found in a manuscript signed "Rio de Janeiro, 27 June 1915," and a partly unedited document, "Manuscripto J. Carmo Gomes" (Manuscript J. Carmo Gomes), a continuation of the story "A prisão de J. Carmo Gomes" in *Insônia.* The latter was published in the prestigious Lisbon journal *Colóquio/Letras* in March–April 1971.

Ramos drew many of the features of his works from personal experience: versions of his homeland recur in the hard and bitter life he portrays in his novels. The Northeast, one of the five macroregions into which Brazil is divided, is formed by the nine states of Maranhão, Piauí, Ceará, Rio Grande do Norte, Paraíba, Pernambuco, Alagoas, Sergipe, and Bahia. It is mainly characterized by the *sertão,* the *caatinga* (brushwood), scarce rain, and disappearing rivers, and yet people there have tried against all odds to raise cattle, cultivate the land (including sugarcane and cotton plantations), and extract salt from areas along the northern littoral of Ceará and Rio Grande do Norte. Traditionally the Northeast was devoted to cattle raising, but recurring *secas* (droughts) pushed the *sertanejos* to migrate, particularly to the richer southern cities, where they often continued to toil in anguish. For this reason Ramos's writings often portray the survival instinct in a harsh environment. Beyond personal experiences, Ramos's vivid imagination contributed to his realist way of writing. Hence, along with the personal history recalled in *Infância* and *Memórias do cárcere,* the regionalist fiction of *Cahetés, São Bernardo,* and *Vidas secas* also bears witness to Ramos's daily encounter with the Northeast, from its *sertões* and *secas* to its typical *nordestino* characters.

In Ramos's works the psychological and the social are given equal treatment as he emphasizes the deep relationship between the people and the environment of the Northeast. Ramos's regional works have a universal aspect; he surpasses in quality and message those regionalist writers whose sole preoccupation was describing events and situations only visible on the surface. In terms of style, Ramos expresses the inner as well as the outer conflicts and dramas of his characters in a condensed and precise language. His sentences tend to be short and direct, as he uses the bare minimum—employing a carefully chosen vocabulary—to convey the exact feeling of the moment.

In all his works, it seems that Ramos is grappling with himself and his place in the world. For example, Ramos frequently expresses feelings of restlessness and anguish for not having completed the "proposed plan," his sense of what he was supposed to accomplish on Earth. Ramos was also self-conscious, a quality he transfers to most of his characters, especially those who are also writers, such as Valério, Honófrio, and Silva. Yet, whatever the parallels may be between Ramos and his protagonists, Ramos is only directly available in his *Infância,* his correspondence, and the posthumous *Memórias do cárcere.*

The theme of most of Graciliano Ramos's works, the human condition and how it is influenced by the environment, is expressed in a powerful language and style that makes the author one of the great figures of Brazilian letters. Unlike many of his famous contemporaries, Ramos cannot be exclusively labeled as a regionalist writer because all of his works feature a truly universal dimension, aspects not confined to a specific region or country. His message is timeless, recharging itself with each instance of human suffering. Ramos's works resonate because people cling to their collective history as a way of never forgetting the past and learning from it. Ramos's way of fusing personal experience with a universal, timeless, self-explanatory narrative, including the use of the story within a story, is one of his most important contributions to Brazilian fiction.

Letters:

"(Carta de um jurado a um cavalheiro de importância)," *O Índio,* 27 February 1921, p. 2;

Cartas, seventh edition (Rio de Janeiro: Record, 1992);

Cartas de amor a Heloísa (Rio de Janeiro: Record, 1994).

Bibliography:

Antônio C. R. Cunha, "Graciliano Ramos: An Annotated Bibliography," M.A. thesis, San Diego State College, 1970.

Cover for a 1962 collection of Ramos's newspaper and journal articles, writings that helped him develop and at times sustain his literary career (Daniel Library, The Citadel)

References:

Maria Isabel Abreu, "O protesto social na obra de Graciliano Ramos," *Hispania,* 48 (1965): 850–855;

Nola Kortner Aiex, "From Rural to Urban: A Painful Transition," *Proceedings—The Pacific Northwest Conference on Foreign Languages,* 30 (1979): 106–108;

Dorothy M. Atkins, "The Language of *Vidas Secas,*" in *Hispanic Studies in Honour of Joseph Manson,* edited by Dorothy Atkinson and Anthony H. Clarke (Oxford: Dolphin, 1972), pp. 9–20;

Sônia Brayner, ed., *Graciliano Ramos: coletânea* (Rio de Janeiro: Civilização Brasileira, 1977);

Nelson Cerqueira, "Hermeneutics and Literature: A Study of William Faulkner's *As I Lay Dying* and Graciliano Ramos's *Vidas Secas,*" dissertation, Indiana University, 1986;

Alexander Coleman, *Eça de Queirós and European Realism* (New York: New York University Press, 1980);

Joanna Courteau, "The World View in the Novels of Graciliano Ramos," dissertation, University of Wisconsin–Madison, 1970;

Afrânio Coutinho, *An Introduction to Literature in Brazil*, translated by Gregory Rebassa (New York: Cambridge University Press, 1969);

Ralph Edward Dimmick, "The Brazilian Literary Generation of 1930," *Hispania*, 34, no. 5 (1951): 181–187;

Fred P. Ellison, "Graciliano Ramos," in his *Brazil's New Novel: Four Northeastern Masters–José Lins do Rego, Jorge Amado, Graciliano Ramos, Rachel de Queiroz* (Berkeley: University of California Press, 1954), pp. 111–132;

Exposição Graciliano Ramos, 1892–1953 (Rio de Janeiro: Biblioteca Nacional, 1963);

Shepard Forman, *The Brazilian Peasantry* (New York: Columbia University Press, 1975);

Lynda Jentsch-Grooms, "Myth and Feminine Symbology in *Vidas Secas*," *Cincinnati Romance Review*, 8 (1989): 59–66;

Randal Johnson, "*Vidas Secas* and the Politics of Filmic Adaptation," *Ideologies and Literature*, 3 (1981): 3–18;

Robert M. Levine, *The Vargas Regime: The Critical Years, 1934–1938* (New York: Columbia University Press, 1970);

Wilson Martins, *The Modernist Idea: A Critical Survey of Brazilian Writing in the Twentieth Century*, translated by Jack E. Tomlins (New York: New York University Press, 1971);

Richard A. Mazzara, "The Odyssey of a Humanist: Graciliano Ramos' *Memórias do Cárcere*," *Journal of Evolutionary Psychology*, 8 (1987): 128–135;

John Nist, *The Modernist Movement in Brazil: A Literary Study* (Austin & London: University of Texas Press, 1967);

Celso Lemos De Oliveira, *Understanding Graciliano Ramos* (Columbia: University of South Carolina Press, 1988);

Augusto Frederico Schmidt, ed., *Homenagem a Graciliano Ramos* (Rio de Janeiro: Alba, 1943);

David J. Vieira, "Wastelands and Backlands: John dos Passos' *Manhattan Transfer* and Graciliano Ramos' *Angústia*," *Hispania*, 67, no. 3 (1984): 377–382;

John S. Vincent, "Graciliano Ramos: The Dialectics of Defeat," in *The Brazilian Novel*, edited by Heitor Martins, Luso-Brazilian Studies, no. 1 (Bloomington: Indiana University Press, 1976), pp. 43–58;

Linda M. Willem, "Narrative Voice, Point of View, and Characterization in Graciliano Ramos's *Vidas Secas*," *Mester*, 16 (1987): 18–28;

Sabrina Elizabeth Karpa Wilson, "Memory Against the Grain: Autobiographical Practice in Graciliano Ramos," dissertation, Harvard University, 1998.

José Lins do Rêgo
(3 June 1901 – 12 September 1957)

Maria Luci De Biaji Moreira
College of Charleston

BOOKS: *Menino de engenho* (Rio de Janeiro: Andersen, 1932); translated by Emmi Baum as *Plantation Boy,* in *Plantation Boy* (New York: Knopf, 1966);

Doidinho (Rio de Janeiro: Ariel, 1933); translated by Baum as *Doidinho,* in *Plantation Boy* (New York: Knopf, 1966);

Bangüê (Rio de Janeiro: J. Olympio, 1934); translated by Baum as *Bangüê,* in *Plantation Boy* (New York: Knopf, 1966);

O moleque Ricardo (Rio de Janeiro: J. Olympio, 1935);

Usina (Rio de Janeiro: J. Olympio, 1936);

Histórias da velha Totônia (São Paulo: J. Olympio, 1936);

Pureza (Rio de Janeiro: J. Olympio, 1937); translated by Lucie Marion (London & New York: Hutchinson International Authors, 1947);

Pedra bonita (Rio de Janeiro: J. Olympio, 1938);

Riacho doce (Rio de Janeiro: J. Olympio, 1939);

Água-mãe (Rio de Janeiro: J. Olympio, 1941);

Gordos e magros (Rio de Janeiro: Casa do Estudante do Brasil, 1942);

Fogo morto (Rio de Janeiro: J. Olympio, 1943);

Pedro Américo (Rio de Janeiro: Casa do Estudante do Brasil, 1943);

Poesia e Vida (Rio de Janeiro: Universal, 1946);

Conferências no Prata: Tendências do romance brasileiro–Raul Pompéia–Machado de Assis (Rio de Janeiro: Casa do Estudante do Brasil, 1946);

Eurídice (Rio de Janeiro: J. Olympio, 1947);

Bota de sete léguas (Rio de Janeiro: A Noite [1951]);

Homens, seres e coisas (Rio de Janeiro: Ministério da Educação e Saúde, 1952);

Cangaceiros (Rio de Janeiro: J. Olympio, 1953);

A casa e o homem (Rio de Janeiro: Organizações Simões, 1954);

Roteiro de Israel (Rio de Janeiro: Centro Cultural Brasil-Israel, 1955);

Meus verdes anos: memórias (Rio de Janeiro: J. Olympio, 1956);

Presença do Nordeste na literatura (Rio de Janeiro: Ministério da Educação e Cultura, 1957);

José Lins do Rêgo (Arquivo da Academia Brasileira de Letras)

Discursos de posse e recepção na Academia Brasileira de Letras, by Rêgo and Austragésilo de Athayde (Rio de Janeiro: J. Olympio, 1957);

Gregos e Troianos (Rio de Janeiro: Bloch, 1957);

O vulcão e a fonte, introduction by Lêdo Ivo (Rio de Janeiro: O Cruzeiro, 1958).

Editions and Collections: *Romances reunidos e illustrados de José Lins do Rego,* five volumes, introdcution by João Ribeiro, bibliography by Wilson Lousada, notes by Thiago de Mello, Almeida Sales, Cassiano Nunes, Antonio Candido, and Sergio Milliett, illustrations by Luís Jardin (Rio de Janeiro: J. Olympio, 1960–1962);

Fogo morto (Rio de Janeiro: J. Olympio, 1965)–includes an essay, "O brasileiríssimo José Lins do Rêgo," by Otto Maria Carpeaux;

Pedra bonita, seventh edition (Rio de Janeiro: José Olympio, 1968)–includes an essay, "De *Menino de engenho* a Pedra bonita," by Paulo Rónai;

José Lins do Rêgo: antologia e crítica, edited, with an introduction, by Edilberto Coutinho (Brasília: Coordenada-Editora de Brasília, 1971);

Menino de engenho, fourteenth edition (Rio de Janeiro: J. Olympio, 1973)–includes an essay, "Origem e significado de Menino de engenho," by José Aderaldo Castello;

O moleque Ricardo, ninth edition, introduction by M. Cavalcanti Proença (Rio de Janeiro: J. Olympio, 1973);

Ficçao completa de José Lins du Rêgo, 2 volumes, introduction by Josué Montello (Rio de Janeiro: Nova Aguilar, 1976);

O melhor da crônica Brasileira, by Rachel de Queiroz, Armando Nogueira, Sérgio Porto, and Rêgo (Rio de Janeiro: J. Olympio, 1979);

Antologia José Lins do Rêgo, O homem e a obra, edited by Eduardo Martins (João Pessoa: Secretaria de Educação e Cultura do Estado da Paraíba, 1980);–includes essays by José Américo de Almeida, Assis Chateaubriand, Carlos Lacerda, Valdemar Cavalcanti, Ariano Suassuna, Mário de Andrade, Aurélio Buarque de Hollanda, Otto Maria Carpeaux, José Aderaldo, and others;

Dias idos e vividos: antologia, edited by Ivan Junqueira (Rio de Janeiro: Nova Fronteira, 1981);

Eurídice, eighth edition (Rio de Janeiro: Nova Frontcira, 1986);

Fogo morto, fourth edition (Rio de Janeiro: J. Olympio, 1993)–includes an essay, "Breve notícia–Vida de José Lins do Rego," by Wilson Lousada;

Pureza, eleventh edition (Rio de Janeiro: J. Olympio, 1994)–includes an essay, "Pureza," by Antonio Carlos Villaça;

Zelins, Flamengo até morrer, edited by Edilberto Coutinho ([Rio de Janeiro], 1995);

Flamengo é puro amor: 111 crônicas escolhidas, edited by Marcos de Castro (Rio de Janeiro: J. Olympio, 2002).

OTHER: Julio Bello, *Memórias de um senhor de engenho*, second edition, preface by Rêgo (Rio de Janeiro: Olympia, 1938);

E. A. Rheinhardt, *A Vida de Eleanora Deese*, translated by Rêgo (Rio de Janeiro: José Olympio, 1940);

Gilberto Freyre, *Região e tradição*, preface by Rêgo (Rio de Janeiro: J. Olympio, 1941);

"Mistério de Brandão," in *Brandão Entre o Mar e o Amor*, by Aníbal Machado, Graciliano Ramos, Jorge Amado, Rêgo, and Rachel de Queiroz (São Paulo: Martins, 1942);

Os Gatos, edited by Rêgo and José Valentim Fialho de Almeida, Coleção Clássicos e contemporâneos, no. 6 (Rio de Janeiro: Livros de Portugal, 1942);

Freyre, *Ingleses*, preface by Rêgo (Rio de Janeiro: J. Olympio, 1942);

Mário Rodrigues, *Copa Rio Branco, 32*, preface by Rêgo (Rio de Janeiro: Irmãos Pongetti, 1943);

Rodolfo Maria de Rangel Moreira, *O morto debruçado*, preface by Rêgo (Rio de Janeiro: J. Olympio, 1947);

Eduardo Mallea, *Tôdo verdor perecerá*, translated by Rêgo and Henrique de Carvalho Simas (Rio de Janeiro: Globo, 1949);

José de Alencar, *Cinco minutos*, preface by Rêgo (Rio de Janeiro: J. Olympio, 1951);

Breno Accioly, *João Urso, contos*, second edition, preface by Rêgo (Rio de Janeiro: O Cruzeiro, 1953);

Luiz Cristóvão dos Santos, *Caminhos do Pajeú*, preface by Rêgo (Rio de Janeiro: Nordeste, 1954);

Zé da Luz, *Brasil caboclo*, third edition, preface by Rêgo (Rio de Janeiro: O Cruzeiro, 1956).

A series of coincidences led José Lins do Rêgo to write works describing the end of the Northeastern sugar aristocracy and the disappearance of rural patriarchal society in Brazil. Early in his career Rêgo met and was influenced by Brazilian writers Gilberto Freyre and José Américo de Almeida, who helped to change his life with their knowledge, wisdom, passion for the land, and search for their origins. A contemporary of Brazilian Modernism, Rêgo responded to the popular linguistic nationalism of the Modernists by creating a new movement. Rêgo's novels left an historical and sociological account of the Northeast, preserving the rural language and documenting his personal experiences with plantation life. Although Rêgo was not the first to focus on this region, critics consider him to be a first-generation writer of the Sugarcane Cycle, one of the important series of novels dealing with northeastern Brazil. Characterized by descriptive techniques of the nineteenth century, Rêgo's fiction made him one of the most representative Brazilian prose writers of the 1930s.

José Lins do Rêgo Cavalcanti was born 3 June 1901 on his grandfather's sugarcane plantation in the state of Paraíba in northeastern Brazil. Born to João and Amélia do Rêgo Cavalcanti, the author lost his mother to complications from childbirth before he was one year old. Rêgo was raised by his mother's relatives and the black nannies on his grandfather's plantation. He grew up hearing stories from black cooks, nurses, and caretakers, the living legacy of institutionalized slavery. At the age of eight Rêgo was sent to study at a boarding school in Itabaiana, Paraíba; when he was eleven years old he was transferred to the Colégio Marista (Marista School) in João Pessoa, where in 1912 he wrote an article on Joaquim Nabuco for the school newsletter *Revista Pio X.* By 1915 Rêgo had moved to Recife, where he attended the School of Law from 1919 to 1923; during this time he became friends with Américo de Almeida and Freyre. Américo de Almeida inspired him to revisit his roots to learn about his people and their past. Similarly, Freyre instilled in him a great passion for the land and the people, while also teaching him about the artistic value of writers such as D. H. Lawrence, Thomas Hardy, and Stendhal. Rêgo felt that these writers were closest to his personality and readily admitted their influence on him. Later, in a preface to Freyre's *Região e tradiçao* (1941, Region and Tradition), Rêgo confessed Freyre's enormous influence on both his life and works, such that writing about Freyre seemed much like writing about himself.

In 1920 Rêgo became the literary editor of *Diário do Estado,* a newspaper in Recife. With Osório Borba, Olívio Montenegro, and Freyre, he founded the weekly newsletter *Dom Casmurro.* In 1924 Rêgo married the daughter of Antonio Massa, senator of Paraíba state, Filomena Massa, with whom he had three daughters: Maria Elizabeth (born 17 July 1925), Maria da Glória (born 20 October 1926), and Maria Cristina (born 3 March 1933). Rêgo held several different jobs over the next ten years. He moved to Minas Gerais to work as a prosecutor but soon quit his job; he was not interested in the law. In the Northeast he worked in several jobs, including stints as a banker and as an income tax collector. It was during this period that he became friends with writers Graciliano Ramos, Rachel de Queiroz, Jorge de Lima, and Aurélio Buarque de Hollanda.

Rêgo's first book, *Menino de engenho* (translated as *Plantation Boy,* 1966), was published in 1932. Because publishers did not like the manuscript, Rêgo paid a little-known press to publish the first edition. The book was a surprising success and received the prestigious Fundação Graça Aranha (Graça Aranha Foundation) award, which is usually given to outstanding new authors. Over the next twenty-five years Rêgo published twelve novels, six books of essays and chronicles, three travel reports, two lectures, one children's book, and one book of memoirs.

In 1935 Rêgo moved to Rio de Janeiro, where he contributed to the newspapers *O Globo* (The Globe), *Diários Associados* (Associated Daily News), and *Jornal de Esportes* (Sports Newspaper). He made official visits to

Title page for the 1935 edition of Rêgo's 1933 novel centering on a man's memories of his boyhood in a Catholic boarding school (Biblioteca Nacional de Chile)

Argentina and Uruguay as a guest speaker; to France as a guest of the government; and to Portugal, Sweden, Denmark, and Peru as a member of the executive council of the Confederação Brasileira de Futebol (Brazilian Soccer Federation). In 1950 he became president of this organization, which dictates the rules and by-laws to all soccer teams in Brazil. Soccer had become one of Rêgo's great passions, and being a part of the executive council of the Confederação Brasileira de Futebol afforded political status and prestige. While living in Rio de Janeiro, Rêgo became intrigued by the powerful effect soccer had on the lives of Brazilians. He wrote more than 1,500 chronicles on Brazil's national pastime between 1940 and 1950. In 1995 critic Edilberto Coutinho collected and edited many of these writings. Rêgo was fanatical about the Flamengo soccer club, and in 1944, according to Eduardo F. Couthino and Ângela Bezerra de Castro, he wrote that a Flamengo championship was more important to the Brazilian people than the Battle of Stalingrad during World War II. He also declared that literature and soccer were the power of the people. These opinions became a national scandal. When asked about the possibility of becoming a member of the Academia Brasileira de Letras (Brazilian Academy of Letters), he replied that he was a common man and could not cheer Flamengo in the elegant uniform of the academy that was required during sessions. In one of his chronicles he asked "Como poderei torcer pelo Flamengo amarrado nos dourados arreios de luxo?" (How will I cheer on Flamengo tied down in a luxurious gold saddle?). He was saying that it seemed impossible to reconcile his irreverent passion for soccer with becoming a vaunted member of the academy. He later relented, however, and was inducted into the academy.

At times Rêgo's political beliefs were a hindrance to him. One of his novels, *O moleque Ricardo* (1935, The Black Boy Ricardo), expressed a political ideology seen by many as communist. In the mid 1940s, however, Rêgo joined the Integralist Party, a Brazilian fascist movement modeled on European fascism; his communist friends never forgave him for this move. Even Rêgo realized he had made a mistake in joining a political party affiliated with Hitler. In 1954 Rêgo wished to visit his daughter in the United States, but he was denied permission by the State Department because of *O moleque Ricardo*. Despite his controversial political alliances, Rêgo became a well-known author in Brazil and abroad. His books were translated and published in Italy, Argentina, England, France, and Germany. It was not until 1966, however, that his books were finally introduced to the United States.

The novels for which Rêgo is most celebrated are organized into "cycles." The first, known as the Sugarcane Cycle, includes the award-winning *Menino de engenho, Doidinho* (1933; translated as *Doidinho,* 1966), *Bangüê* (1934; translated as *Bangüê,* 1966), and *Usina* (1936, Sugar Refinery). *O moleque Ricardo,* though included by the author himself, usually is not considered part of the Sugarcane Cycle because it tells the story of political actions and communist movements in Recife as well as the title character's experiences there. On the other hand, *Fogo morto* (1943, Dead Fire), considered to be Rêgo's masterpiece, is a continuation of the Sugarcane Cycle. These books constitute a living record of a people immersed in the social world created by plantation mansions, and include explorations of the power struggles and personal conflicts that are part of that life.

Rêgo's two other novel cycles are The Cangaço Cycle (Banditry Cycle) and the Ciclo Independente (Independent Cycle) or Ciclo Lirismo Erótico (Erotic Lyricism Cycle). The Cangaço Cycle comprises *Pedra bonita* (1938, Pretty Stone) and *Cangaceiros* (1953, Bandits). These novels combine ecological and sociological elements of the Northeast. The Independent Cycle includes *Pureza* (1937; translated, 1947), *Riacho doce* (1939, Freshwater Stream), *Água-mãe* (1941, Water Mother), and *Eurídice* (1947). According to many critics, this cycle represents Rêgo's attempt to abandon themes dealing with the hinterlands and explore issues such as psychology and human nature. In 1941 *Água-mãe* won the Felipe d'Oliveira award for distinguished achievement, and in 1947 *Eurídice* earned the Prêmio Fábio Prado (Fábio Prado award).

The Sugarcane Cycle owes its name to ideas generated by the Congresso Regionalista de Recife (Congress of Brazilian Regionalism), which was organized by Freyre in 1926. Many people of different ages and professions attended, from plantation masters to medical doctors to old cooks. Freyre's goal was to expand the idea of regionalism, which he felt had been limited to bizarre language, style, and clothing. The Congress was the Northeastern writers' direct response to the Week of Modern Art, organized in São Paulo four years earlier. Freyre opposed the dynamic young artists of the South (that is, Rio de Janeiro and São Paulo) whose modernist ideas radiated from Brazil's cultural centers. Freyre's group, which included Rêgo, resisted the innovations of the modernists. They saw the modernists of the South as a threat to the roots of Brazil, which were in the Northeast. Freyre and Rêgo saw the modernists as bizarre, exotic, and noisy, and—even worse—they wrote in ungrammatical language. Freyre's idea was to develop and strengthen the characteristics of each state and region in order to strengthen the entire Brazilian people.

The Sugarcane Cycle essentially refers to a literary creation that focuses on the people of the hinterlands of the Northeast, featuring plantation mansions, the sugarcane plantations, and the mills. Rêgo once declared, in an interview quoted by Coutinho and Castro, "A terra é que manda nos meus romances" (the land is the one who gives orders in my novels). He created much of his fiction from his own biography, through which he simultaneously created a biography of all those who are a part of Northeastern culture. Some of Rêgo's characters were based on people he had known, while other characters were imagined products of the land. Rêgo's evocation of his childhood experiences with and impressions of the sugar mills are crucial to the novels of this cycle, which bring together the fundamental ideas of the author as he seeks to understand both the greatness and the misery of human nature.

The first book of the Sugarcane Cycle, *Menino de engenho,* illustrates Rêgo's narrative process, which is based on the oral traditions of the Northeastern storytellers. The book deals with social transformation in the

Brazilian Northeast, centering around cultural identity and human understanding as they relate to Rêgo's boyhood and family. Rêgo's childhood and the mills come alive in the author's search for a world that no longer exists. In narrating his memories, Rêgo relates the stories of many children who lived and worked in sugarcane mills. He portrays his grandfather, in the character José Paulino, as representative of the Northeastern rural patriarchal society. The symbolic depiction of the rural patriarchal system of the Northeast is a basic element in all the novels of the Sugarcane Cycle. José Paulino is the absolute master of the land and the mill, his family, and his servants. Thus, the splendor and colonial roots of the sugarcane mills, completely under the power of the owners, are revealed. In a synthesis of literature and life, Rêgo is represented in the character Carlinhos, who is a product of the rural elite. *Menino de engenho* was followed by another highly autobiographical novel, *Doidinho,* which relates the reminiscences of a plantation boy in a Catholic boarding school.

Rêgo's next book from the Sugarcane Cycle, *Bangüê,* is a romance of transition in which the author strays from his memoirs and focuses more on social issues. Specifically, *Bangüê* portrays the decadence of the patriarchal system. José Paulino is the last of the patriarchs, supported only by his pride and an unsustainable tradition. Carlos de Melo, Paulino's grandson, is the new generation. He is a young man who has graduated from law school and returned to the plantation. He does not, however, have the energy and power of his ancestors. *Bangüê* shows the end of the traditions of the rural patriarchy of the Northeast.

O moleque Ricardo, considered a sugarcane novel by Rêgo, is the first Brazilian novel in which a black man is portrayed as a good person. It is the story of Ricardo, a black contemporary of Carlos who is also the product of rural society. In the big city of Recife, Ricardo feels displaced and unhappy as he longs for rural life. When confronting spiritual values, Ricardo notices that African religions are just an escape for the poor in Recife. Similarly, sex in the mills is an escape for maids and young boys. The struggles of the migrants provide the background and basis for political action in the novel.

The next sugarcane novel, *Fogo morto,* is an essentially autobiographical narrative in which Rêgo creates social and psychological profiles of the people of the Northeast. He describes the pseudoaristocrats and their traditional values, mystics, and superstitious people, all of whom are involved in an unjust, arbitrary, and isolated world. *Fogo morto* constitutes a bridge between the Sugarcane Cycle and the Cangaço Cycle. In Rêgo's final Sugarcane Cycle book, *Usina,* rural inhabitants' physical and moral resistance, determination, resigna-

Title page for the 1937 edition of Rêgo's 1934 novel exposing the decadence of the patriarchal system in northeastern Brazil (Biblioteca Nacional de Chile)

tion, mysticism, and sense of fate are all represented. The workers feel compelled to attack and sack the sugar refinery. Ricardo, who left Recife in *O moleque Ricardo,* comes back to the sugarcane mill and his story ends in the first chapter. *Usina* conveys radical changes, portraying the death of the tradition of slave masters and the dehumanizing effect of the new economic order.

The two books of the Cangaço Cycle continue the saga of the rural inhabitants of the Northeast, focusing on peasant revolts. The history of *cangaço* is tied to the social history of the patriarchs. The Cangaço Cycle shows the social and economic consequences of the droughts that plague parts of northeastern Brazil and explores the revenge of the oppressed against society, the police, and the state. The atrocities practiced by the *cangaceiros* (bandits) are shown to result from the laws created and endorsed by powerful landowners and politicians. The first Cangaço Cycle novel, *Pedra bonita,* explores these elements during the misery of the long dry seasons. Both *Pedra bonita* and *Cangaceiros* are regionalist works that are filled with mysticism. Both novels explore moral and psychological problems, including

Rêgo in his library, 1955 (frontispiece for Eurídice, *1986; Thomas Cooper Library, University of South Carolina)*

sentimentalism and fatalism, and both depict the oppressive power of the police and the leadership of a fanatic. In Rêgo's novels the *cangaceiro* is a hero or a bandit; a victim or a revenger; admired or hated. He is a victim of his own existence.

The novels of the Independent Cycle are different from Rêgo's regionalist works. In the Independent Cycle a lyrical atmosphere predominates as the author explores collective and individual human psychology, involving hidden and painful dramas and tragic endings. *Pureza* belongs to this group as a novel with a simple, linear structure in which Rêgo focuses on male and female relationships. *Água-mãe, Riacho doce,* and *Eurídice* do not take place in the backlands, and *Eurídice* is Rêgo's only book that takes place in Rio de Janeiro. *Água-mãe* narrates the story of a famous soccer player and traces his apogee and decline. The novel also features the story of three different mothers who live in different social conditions and yet act the same way: they all fear the supernatural. Hence, the work documents the collective reality of human psychology. Additionally, in an attempt to get away from themes associated with the Northeast, Rêgo beautifully describes the coastal city of Cabo Frio and its lake, saltmines, and fishermen. *Riacho doce* deals with a human being's physical and spiritual self-destruction. It is the

story of a woman in search of her identity. For most of her life she struggles with personal relationships and attempts to adjust to social groups dominated by men or by popular mystical beliefs. Finally, the last novel of the Independent Cycle, *Eurídice,* is the only one of Rêgo's works to show the influence of Freudian theories.

Beyond the novel cycles, Rêgo wrote many other significant texts. In *Histórias da velha Totônia* (1936, Old Totônia's Stories), a children's book, Rêgo retells narratives related to him by Old Totônia during his childhood. In his preface to the book, Rêgo assures the reader that Old Totônia was a real person and his only source for the stories. He claims that he wanted to pass her image along to his grandson and to other children because the "Old Totônias" no longer exist. This sentiment is related to the nostalgic tone of the novels of the Sugarcane Cycle.

Another book, *Gordos e magros* (1942, Fat Men and Skinny Men), features Rêgo's interpretation of literary styles and his belief that literature is essential to the greatness of human beings. Rêgo gives physical attributes to the authors on whom he focuses, defining them as fat or skinny according to their style. In *A casa e o homem* (1954, The Home and the Man), Rêgo reconstructs the true story of Laurindo Rebelo, a black man who wrote a Portuguese grammar book that was widely used during the nineteenth century. In yet another book, *Presença do Nordeste na literatura* (1957, Presence of the Northeast in Literature), Rêgo published essays on the Jesuits in Brazil, Father Antonio Vieira, José de Alencar, Gilberto Freyre, Manuel Bandeira, and other important writers and poets of the Northeast. Additionally, Rêgo wrote about his travels in *Bota de sete léguas* (1951, The Boot of Seven Leagues), in which he sensitively captures the feeling of the places, the people, and landscapes visited.

While Rêgo's work has regionalist and memorialist characteristics, it also has modernist features in terms of its nationalism, use of oral traditions, and use of regional elements. Rêgo did not, however, embrace the tenets of the Southern modernists endorsed at the Week of Modern Art of 1922. Rêgo, along with Freyre and the Group of Paraíba, which included like-minded writers from Paraíba such as Valdemar Cavalcanti, Ramos, Aloísio Branco, Queiroz, Hollanda, and Lima rejected the modernists of São Paulo. For example, through his chronicles Rêgo attacked Mário de Andrade's use of language as the work of a philologist rather than a language for communication. Rêgo opposed the confusion of Andrade's "researched" and "invented" language with the spoken language of the illiterate Northeastern *Cantadores* (Popular Singers) and the workers of the backlands and sugar mills. (Despite this public debate,

Andrade and Rêgo later became good friends.) Rêgo's regionalism was an attempt to keep alive the popular culture of the Northeast that was being threatened by technological progress and change. Despite the tensions between them, both the modernists and the regionalists advocated historical, anthropological, and sociological studies and urged the Brazilian intelligentsia to incorporate Brazilian popular art, folklore, and traditions into their work.

Rêgo's narratives also feature cries for social justice in an unequal economic society. The Sugarcane Cycle provides an important example. These novels are a reconstitution of the rural patriarchal society, organized around the plantation house, the slave headquarters, and the remaining former slaves and their descendants. They capture the transformation of the region as the old sugar mills disappear and are replaced by modern sugar refineries. In the sugarcane novels Rêgo depicts the way in which the introduction of technology resulted in a dehumanization of the economy when workers—former slaves—were dispersed and not incorporated into the job market. The novels illustrate the historical, social, economic, and psychological changes that occurred when the sugarcane oligarchy disappeared, and explore the options that were available to the people who had been trapped in the system.

On 12 September 1957, after a three-month period of hospitalization, Rêgo died as a result of liver cirrhosis, hepatic-renal syndrome, and uremic acidosis. His coffin was covered with the flag of his beloved Flamengo soccer team. His body was mourned at the Brazilian Academy of Letters and then buried in Rio de Janeiro.

Rêgo was the product of both his country roots and his urban life. Through his characters, he searches for something lost in both worlds as he explores the past and the present; the mystical and the real; and the weak and the powerful. For these reasons Rêgo has been studied and analyzed in more than four hundred books and articles. All of his books have been reprinted, some of them many times. *Doidinho* has had twenty-five editions, and *Fogo morto* has had more than forty-three editions. By 1996 *Menino do engenho* had gone through sixty-four editions. These facts speak to Rêgo's impact on Brazilian literary history. The magazine *IstoÉ* considers Rêgo to be the seventeenth most important Brazilian writer of the century. Furthermore, then-Brazilian president Fernando Henrique Cardoso designated the year 2001 as "The Year of Literature," and Rêgo was one of the four Brazilian writers honored.

José Lins do Rêgo's literary work is predominantly memorialist and regionalist. The memorial aspects of his works result from the literary transformation of his personal experiences. His novels are regionalist in the sense that they focus on the sugarcane mills, the rural areas, the outlaws, and the mysticism of the Northeast. His characters, however, are both a part of and transcend the Northeast, having both specific and universal qualities. Rêgo's fictional universe, which features both regional and psychological elements, is influenced by and preserves folkloric traditions, the narratives of the popular storytellers, and his own personal participation in the life of the Brazilian Northeast.

References:

Mário de Andrade, *Macunaíma,* thirtieth edition (Belo Horizonte: Villa Rica, 1997);

David Brookshaw, *Race and Color in Brazilian Literature* (Metuchen, N.J.: Scarecrow Press, 1986);

Edilberto Coutinho, *Romance do açúcar. José Lins do Rêgo,* in *Vida e obra* (Rio de Janeiro: J. Olympio, 1980);

Eduardo F. Coutinho and Ângela Bezerra de Castro, eds., *José Lins do Rego: coleção fortuna crítica* (Rio de Janeiro: Civilização Brasileira, 1991);

"José Lins do Rego," *O Brasileiro do Século, IstoÉ* <http://www.terra.com.br/istoe/biblioteca/brasileiro/literatura/lit17.htm>.

Nelson Rodrigues

(23 August 1912 – 21 December 1980)

David S. George
Lake Forest College

BOOKS: *Álbum de família; e, Vestido de noiva* (Rio de Janeiro: Edições do Povo, 1946); *Vestido de noiva* translated by José de Mara Nogueira as *The Wedding Gown: Tragedy in 3 Acts* (Washington, D.C.: Brazilian-American Cultural Institute, 1978);

Anjo negro; Vestido de noiva; A mulher sem pecado (Rio de Janeiro: Seção de Livros da Emprêsa Gráfica *O Cruzeiro*, 1948);

Senhora dos afogados; e, A falecida (Rio de Janeiro: Seção de Livros da Emprêsa Gráfica *O Cruzeiro*, 1956);

Teatro, 2 volumes (Rio de Janeiro: Serviço Nacional de Teatro, 1959, 1960)—comprises volume 1, *A mulher sem pecado, Vestido de noiva, Álbum de família, Anjo negro, Dorotéia,* and *Valsa nº 6;* and volume 2, *A falecida; Senhora dos afogados; Perdoa-me por me traires; Viúva, porém honesta; Os sete gatinhos;* and *Boca de ouro;*

O beijo no asfalto (Rio de Janeiro: J. Ozon, 1961);

100 contos escolhidos: a vida como ela é, 2 volumes (Rio de Janeiro: J. Ozon, 1961);

Asfalto selvagem, 2 volumes (Rio de Janeiro: J. Ozon, 1962)—comprises volume 1, *Engraçadinha, seus amôres e seus pecados dos 12 aos 18;* and volume 2, *Engraçadinha, seus amôres e seus pecados, depois dos 30;*

Bonitinha mas ordinária (São Paulo: Brasiliense, 1965);

O casamento (Rio de Janeiro: Eldorado, 1966);

A menina sem estrêla (Rio de Janeiro: Correio da Manhã, 1967);

O óbvio ululante (Rio de Janeiro: Eldorado, 1968);

A cabra vadia (novas confissões) (Rio de Janeiro: Eldorado, 1969);

Toda nudez será castigada (Rio de Janeiro: Record, 1973); translated by Joffre Rodrigues and Toby Coe as *All Nudity Shall Be Punished* in *The Wedding Dress; All Nudity Shall Be Punished; Lady of the Drowned; Waltz #6; The Deceased Woman,* introduction by Sábato Magaldi (Rio de Janeiro: Fundação Nacional de Arte, 1998);

Elas gostam de apanhar (Rio de Janeiro: Bloch, 1974);

O reacionário: memórias e confissões (Rio de Janeiro: Record, 1977);

Meu destino é pecar (Rio de Janeiro: Tecnoprint, 1980);

A serpente (Rio de Janeiro: Nova Fronteira, 1980);

O homem proibido (Rio de Janeiro: Nova Fronteira, 1981);

Fla-Flu: —e as multidões despertaram! by Rodrigues and Mário Rodrigues Filho, edited by Oscar Maron Filho and Renato Ferreira (Rio de Janeiro: Edição Europa/Xerox, 1987);

A mentira, preface by Gerd Bornheim, afterword by Caco Coelho (São Paulo: Letras/Schwarcz, 2002);

Pouco amor não é amor: contos, edited, with an afterword, by Coelho (São Paulo: Letras, 2002);

O profeta tricolor: cem anos de Fluminense, crônicas, edited by Nelson Rodrigues Filho (São Paulo: Letras, 2002);

A mulher que amou demais, preface by Moacyr Scliar (São Paulo: Letras, 2003);

O baú de Nelson Rodrigues: os primeiros anos de crítica e reportagem (1928–35), edited by Coelho, preface by Carlos Heitor Cony (São Paulo: Letras, 2004).

Editions and Collections: *Teatro quase completo,* 4 volumes, afterword by L. Gilson Ribeiro (Rio de Janeiro: Tempo Brasileiro, 1965–1966);

Nelson Rodrigues, edited, with notes and a biographical study, by Maria Helena Pires Martins (São Paulo: Abril, 1981);

Teatro completo de Nelson Rodrigues, 4 volumes, edited, with an introduction, by Sábato Magaldi (Rio de Janeiro: Nova Fronteira, 1981–1989);

Coleção das obras de Nelson Rodrigues, 12 volumes, edited by Ruy Castro (São Paulo: Letras, 1992–1997);

O melhor do romance, contos e crônicas, edited by Castro (São Paulo: Schwarcz, 1993);

Teatro completo, edited, with a preface, by Magaldi (Rio de Janeiro: Nova Aguilar, 1993);

A dama do lotação e outros contos e crônicas, edited by Maura Sardinha (Rio de Janeiro: Ediouro, 1996).

Editions in English: *The Wedding Dress,* translated by Fred M. Clark (Valencia, Spain: Albatros Hispanófila, 1980);

The Wedding Dress; All Nudity Shall Be Punished; Lady of the Drowned; Waltz #6; The Deceased Woman, translated by Joffre Rodrigues and Toby Coe, introduction

Nelson Rodrigues, 1951 (photo by Manchete; from Ruy Castro, O anjo pornográfico, *1992; John C. Hodges Library, University of Tennessee)*

by Sábato Magaldi (Rio de Janeiro: Fundação Nacional de Arte, 1998);

The Theater of Nelson Rodrigues, translated by Joffre Rodrigues, Coe, and Flávia Carvalho, edited by Joffre Rodrigues (Rio de Janeiro: Fundação Nacional de Arte, 2001)–comprises *The Woman without Sin, Family Album, Black Angel, Dorotéia, A Widow but Chaste, Forgive Me for You Betraying Me,* and *The Seven Kittens.*

PLAY PRODUCTIONS: *A mulher sem pecado,* Rio de Janeiro, Teatro Carlos Gomes, 9 December 1942;

Vestido de noiva, Rio de Janeiro, Teatro Municipal, 28 December 1943;

Anjo negro, Rio de Janeiro, Teatro Fênix, 2 April 1948;

Dorotéia, Rio de Janeiro, Teatro Fênix, 7 March 1950;

Valsa nº 6, Rio de Janeiro, Teatro Serrador, 6 August 1951;

A falecida, Rio de Janeiro, Teatro Municipal, 8 June 1953;

Senhora dos afogados, Rio de Janeiro, Teatro Municipal, 1 July 1954;

Perdoa-me por me traíres, Rio de Janeiro, Teatro Municipal, 19 June 1957;

Viúva, porém honesta, Rio de Janeiro, Teatro São Jorge, 13 September 1957;

Os sete gatinhos, Rio de Janeiro, Teatro Carlos Gomes, 17 October 1958;

Boca de ouro, São Paulo, Teatro Federação, 13 October 1960;

O beijo no asfalto, Rio de Janeiro, Teatro Ginástico, 7 July 1961;

Bonitinha mas ordinária, Rio de Janeiro, Teatro da Maison de France, 28 November 1962;

Toda nudez será castigada, Rio de Janeiro, Teatro Serrador, 21 June 1965;

Álbum de família, Rio de Janeiro, Teatro Jovem, 28 July 1967;

Anti–Nelson Rodrigues, Rio de Janeiro, Teatro Nacional de Comédia, 28 February 1974;

A serpente, Rio de Janeiro, Teatro do BNH, 6 March 1980.

PRODUCED SCRIPTS: *Somos dois,* motion picture, by Rodrigues and others, Milton Rodrigues Produções/Cinédia, 1950;

Mulheres e milhões, motion picture, by Rodrigues, Jorge Ileli, and Flávio Tambellini, Inbracine Filmes, 1961;

O rei Pelé, motion picture, dialogue by Rodrigues, Decine Filmes/Denison Filmes, 1962;

A morta sem espelho, television, TV Rio, 1963;

Pouco amor não é amor, television, as Veronica Blake, TV Rio, 1963;

O desconhecido, television, TV Rio, 1964;

Sonho de amor, television, TV Rio, 1964;

O mundo alegre de Helô, motion picture, by Rodrigues and Carlos Alberto de Souza Barros, CASB Produções Cinematográficas, 1967;

Como ganhar na loteria sem perder a esportiva, motion picture, by Rodrigues and others, J. B. Tanko Filmes/ Produções Cinematográficas Herbert Richers, 1971;

A dama do lotação, motion picture, by Rodrigues and Neville De Almeida, Embrafilme/Regina Filmes/ Tecla Filmes, 1978.

OTHER: Hélio Carlos Sussekind, *Futebol em dois tempos: incluindo uma breve história do futebol carioca e uma ficção–crônica póstuma inédita de Nelson Rodrigues* (Rio de Janeiro: Relume-Dumará, 1996).

Brazilian theater celebrated several playwrights during the second half of the twentieth century. One of them, Nelson Rodrigues, is now almost universally considered the most important playwright in the history of Brazilian theater. In 2000 Gisele Kato and Renata Santos expressed this view clearly in the performing-arts magazine *Bravo:* "20 years after his death, . . . his genius is celebrated, his complete works are being republished, studied, staged, and filmed . . . Nelson Rodrigues is resuming the place that was always his; that of the greatest playwright in Brazilian history." Even *The New York Times* has recognized the playwright's importance, with an article by Larry Rohter titled "Reawakening the Giant of Brazilian Theater" (17 December 2000). After achieving renown as the modernizer of Brazilian theater with his 1943 play *Vestido de noiva* (translated as *The Wedding Gown,* 1978), Rodrigues subsequently fell into disrepute as a playwright, was deemed a pornographer and censored by the Right, was excoriated as a reactionary by the Left, and was scorned by the critical establishment. Although he was a widely read journalist and continued to write for the stage until shortly before his death, his theatrical exile endured until the end of his life. Today, however, his stature in Brazil is on the level of Eugene O'Neill, Tennessee Williams, and Arthur Miller in the United States.

Rodrigues's literary career followed as many twists and turns as a mystery novel. The threads running through the plot include a life as extravagant and mercurial as that of a pulp-fiction character, a flourishing journalistic calling that began at age thirteen and lasted until his death, and an epic playwriting voyage that took him from early renown to condemnation and ultimately to posthumous fame.

Born on 23 August 1912 in the northeastern Brazilian city of Recife, Nelson Falcão Rodrigues was the son of Mário Rodrigues and Maria Esther Falcão, the fifth of fifteen children born to the couple. Mário Rodrigues was a polemical journalist and politician whose articles incurred the wrath of local and national authorities and resulted in the death of his oldest son. His dangerous political battles led the Rodrigues family to pull up stakes and move two thousand miles south to Rio de Janeiro in 1916, where he edited a series of sensationalist newspapers. There, young Nelson witnessed events that shaped his later playwriting, such as the daily occurrence of death during the 1918 global influenza epidemic and the wakes held in neighborhood homes. From the village-like atmosphere of his working-class neighborhood in Rio de Janeiro's Zona Norte (North Zone) he later drew the diverse cast of characters that populate his dramas: the gossip who spares no one, criminal bosses who are heroes to many, and mothers grieving over lost children. This atmosphere was also the source of the sexual obsessions and taboos—including sexual abuse—that Rodrigues exposes in his plays.

As a child Rodrigues read widely, including melodramatic episodic novels that were serialized in newspapers, Fyodor Dostoevsky's *Crime and Punishment* (1867), and Alexandre Dumas *père*'s *The Count of Monte-Cristo* (1844–1845). As Ruy Castro notes, "The authors varied, but basically it was all the same thing: death punishing sex or sex punishing death." In spite of his love for reading, Rodrigues had problems in school that foreshadowed his behavior later in adulthood. He was expelled from classes at age fourteen for rebellious behavior, which at that time consisted of his insistent arguing of points of history and philosophy with his teachers. As an adult he was similarly punished for his iconoclasm. Rodrigues developed a passion for soccer in his youth and was a lifelong supporter of the Rio de Janeiro team known as Fluminense. He wrote about his beloved soccer team throughout his career, as did his brother Mário Rodrigues Filho, who became one of the best-known sportswriters in Brazil.

Family and personal tragedy marked Nelson Rodrigues's life. His father was jailed in 1924 for an item published in the newspaper for which he was then serving as editor, *Correio da manhã.* Mário Rodrigues then founded his own newspaper, *A manhã,* in 1925. At the age of thirteen Nelson began working for his father as a crime reporter. By age sixteen he had his own weekly column in the paper. His father, however, soon lost controlling interest in *A manhã* and opened another paper, *A crítica.* In 1929 Nelson witnessed the murder of an older brother, Roberto, who was shot by a society matron outraged by a salacious story his father had printed about her. Mário Rodrigues had been the intended target; already in bad health, he died soon afterward. His daring political views were not forgotten even after his death, and the offices of *A crítica* were trashed by thugs in the employ of Getúlio Vargas, the fascist dictator who took over the Brazilian government in 1930. The newspaper was a total loss, and the Rodrigues clan went from a life of comfort to one of poverty. The family survived on the pittances earned by the Rodrigues brothers, who obtained part-time newspaper work. To add to the family woes, Nelson came down with tuberculosis and was institutionalized in 1935. His many bouts with the disease—including relapses in 1937 and 1939—contributed to his death at age sixty-eight. His brother Joffre was also hospitalized for tuberculosis and died of the disease in 1936, with Nelson at his side. Tragedies such as these made their way into Rodrigues's writings.

Rodrigues's work as a crime reporter starting as a teenager allowed him to assemble an arsenal of dramatic—and melodramatic—stories to serve as raw material for his plays and other literary ventures. As was the practice of the day, he interspersed his crime reports with imaginary dialogue. Although this habit did not contribute to objective journalism, it did prepare him for a career in playwriting. It also equipped him to write one of the most popular series of newspaper columns in Brazilian history, titled "A vida como ela é" (Life as It Is), which he began writing in 1951.

Rodrigues married Elza Bretanha in 1940, and the first of his children, Joffre, was born the next year, when he began writing for the theater. The Brazilian stage at this time had not caught up with modernism. Beginning in 1922 the other arts in Brazil had been influenced by the modernist currents sweeping the world. This revolution produced artists whose names are recognized worldwide: Heitor Villa-Lobos in music, Cândido Portinari in painting, Manuel Bandeira in poetry, Jorge Amado in fiction, and the architect Oscar Niemeyer, who later designed the major structures in the new capital, Brasília. Brazilian theater was untouched by these currents, still offering a repertoire of nineteenth-century comedies of manners, melodramas, and thesis plays (or problem plays, in which social issues were presented). Technical production was equally outmoded. There was no concept of lighting design, sets consisted mostly of painted backdrops, and the role of the modern director had not yet been defined.

Rodrigues wrote his first play in 1941. His reasons for writing it had nothing to do with the revolutionary aesthetic with which he was later associated. Instead, he thought it would be a good way to make money; financial problems plagued him throughout his

Title page for the first edition of two of Rodrigues's controversial early plays (Family Album, 1946, and The Wedding Gown, 1943) that helped to modernize Brazilian theater. The 1946 play was banned by censors and not performed until 1967 (Joint University Libraries, Nashville).

life. The play, titled *A mulher sem pecado* (translated as *The Woman without Sin,* 2001), is about a man so obsessed with his wife's fidelity that he feigns paralysis. His fantastic scheme results in tragedy, a hallmark of most of Rodrigues's plays. The play produced a positive critical response and modest box-office returns when it premiered late in 1942, encouraging Rodrigues to continue pursuing this new craft.

In 1943 Rodrigues wrote *Vestido de noiva,* which is structured in the expressionist manner. The play is presented from the viewpoint of Alaíde, a woman dying on an operating table, the victim of a traffic accident. The audience witnesses her hallucinations and disintegrating memories. Structured episodically, the play includes scenes of Alaíde's failed marriage, her revolt against the stifling social conventions of Rio de Janeiro, her fantasies of murdering her husband, and her association with a long-dead prostitute, whose diary she had discovered in the attic of her parents' house. The final scene takes place in the realm of the supernatural, with Alaíde appearing as a ghost after her death. Scenes from external reality are interspersed throughout the action: the sound of sirens, newspapermen reporting on the accident, and doctors clinically discussing the young woman's injuries. The fragmented and multilevel plot structure, calling for complex and modern technical design, as well as the taboo themes of illicit sex, murderous desire, and revolt against patriarchal society, defied the prevailing conventions of Brazilian theater. The avant-garde theatrical structure of *Vestido de noiva* seems to have had two sources. Rodrigues frequently viewed touring European plays, and he was familiar with German expressionist movies such as Robert Wiene's *The Cabinet of Dr. Caligari* (1919).

World War II brought to Brazil Zbigniew Ziembinski, a Polish Jew fleeing the Holocaust. Ziembinski was a director who had worked in the European avant-garde theatrical revolution of the 1930s and had headed the Polish National Theater. He brought with him his experience as a director and as a coordinator of all aspects of theatrical production, including lighting design and modern acting styles, from expressionist techniques to the Stanislavsky method. Ziembinski became affiliated with a young but inexperienced theater company, Os Comediantes, which was imbued with the spirit of modernism. After a promising beginning with productions of European plays, Ziembinski began to look for a Brazilian play that suited his concept of theater. He found that play in Rodrigues's *Vestido de noiva,* which premiered on 28 December 1943.

Vestido de noiva was an immediate sensation. It outraged established critics and theater professionals, who were unable to decipher the meaning of the work. The play delighted the adherents of the modernist movement, young theater critics, and a new audience that had previously dismissed drama as something stale and old-fashioned. *Vestido de noiva* revolutionized the Brazilian stage. It ushered in an entirely new way of performing plays, enhancing the role of the director, introducing complex set and light design, adding modern technology, such as microphones and loudspeakers, and most important, encouraging a new kind of Brazilian playwriting that broke with the outmoded models of the past.

Vestido de noiva had a long run, so Rodrigues took a break from playwriting and embarked on a new moneymaking venture. He began writing *romances de folhetim,* steamy romances that were serialized in newspapers, under the pseudonym Suzana Flag. This seemingly odd practice was a lucrative enterprise for many Brazilian writers in the 1940s and 1950s. Rodrigues himself continued writing these serialized novels for many years under a variety of pseudonyms. Some of them have been republished in book form, including *Meu destino é pecar* (1944, My Destiny Is to Sin; republished, 1980), *A mulher que amou demais* (1949, The Woman Who Loved Too Much; republished, 2003), *O homem proibido* (1951, The Forbidden Man; republished, 1981), and *A mentira* (1953, The Lie; republished, 2002).

In 1945 Rodrigues suffered a relapse of tuberculosis and was again forced to stay in a sanatorium. That year also marked the birth of his second son, Nelson Rodrigues Filho, and a new production of *Vestido de noiva*. His first play, *A mulher sem pecado,* was restaged the following year. In 1946 Rodrigues returned to writing for the theater with *Álbum de família* (translated as *Family Album,* 2001). Expectations were high, and the theatergoing public waited anxiously to see how the playwright was going to advance the theatrical revolution he had begun. The play, however, was banned by the censors before it could be staged. (The ban lasted for two decades, and the play did not receive its premiere until 1967.) This prohibition was shocking to many, since Vargas's dictatorship had ended in 1945 and Brazil had supposedly entered a new age of democracy. The censors, however, acting in their role as "defenders of public decency," objected to the central theme of incest in the play. Although *Álbum de família* had supporters, many critics who read the script sided with the censors, deeming it a work of pornography. The same play, staged decades later, produced a different reaction. A 1981 production of *Álbum de família* by renowned director José Alves Antunes Filho revived the playwright's name and put him on the path to posthumous preeminence.

Rodrigues's next two plays, *Anjo negro* (1948; translated as *Black Angel,* 2001) and *Senhora dos afogados* (1948; produced, 1954; published, 1956; translated as *Lady of the Drowned,* 1998), were banned by the censors as well. *Anjo negro* was charged with obscenity for its frank treatment of sexual issues, but the most problematic aspect of the work was its dramatization of the marriage of a white woman and a black man. When the play was finally staged in 1948, the husband was played by a white man in blackface, over Rodrigues's objections, reinforcing his condemnation of a racist society. *Senhora dos afogados* is modeled after classical Greek tragedy, specifically, Aeschylus's *Oresteia* (458 B.C.). American playwright O'Neill's *Mourning Becomes Electra* (1931), also based on Aeschylus's work, was a further influence on Rodrigues's version. The subject that affronted the censors was incest.

Title page for Rodrigues's 1965 play (All Nudity Will Be Punished) about a deadly case of sibling rivalry; Nelson Xavier
and Luís Linhares in a 1965 performance of the play (left: Alderman Library, University of Virginia; right: from
Ruy Castro, O anjo pornográfico, 1992; John C. Hodges Library, University of Tennessee)

Rodrigues wrote another tragedy, *Dorotéia,* in 1949, and it was produced the following year. The critic Sábato Magaldi defines these plays as mythic, a designation the playwright himself embraced. Flush with the success of *Vestido de noiva,* Rodrigues attempted to study his characters and Brazilian society in greater depth. As a result of these mythic dramas, he came to be considered a failure as a playwright. He was also labeled a purveyor of obscenity by the guardians of morality in the press and the government. Rodrigues was compared unfavorably with another dramatist, Silveira Sampaio, during this period. Sampaio was immensely popular, and his piquant farces filled the theaters. Although Sampaio's plays have not survived—they are no longer staged or studied—critics in the late 1940s and 1950s saw them as a healthy alternative to Rodrigues's morbidity. Rodrigues's miseries were compounded in 1950 when his son Joffre developed tuberculosis. Instead of giving in and writing light farces in

the vein of Sampaio, he continued to write provocative plays that he termed "irresponsible farces." He also added, sarcastically, that his works were so pestilent that audiences could catch terrible diseases just from viewing them.

Rodrigues continued to receive a steady income from publishing serialized melodramas under female pseudonyms and from journalism. In 1951 newspaper editor Samuel Wainer invited Nelson to write a column for the Rio de Janeiro newspaper *Última hora.* The column was to be based on police reports, an apparently easy assignment for a writer who had begun working as a crime reporter when barely into his teens. Wainer suggested that the first column deal with an airplane accident that had taken the lives of a young couple on their honeymoon. Rodrigues dashed off a column that pleased the editor for its brilliance but also bothered him because the author had changed the names and other circumstances of the tragedy. When he asked

Rodrigues to be true to the facts, the writer answered that facts were not reality and that the important thing was "a vida como ela é" (life as it is). Wainer was persuaded and decided to use this phrase as the title of the column. While other Brazilian authors have worked successfully in this genre, known as the *crônica* (chronicle, a fusion of journalism and fiction), no one has ever mined it as fruitfully as Rodrigues. "A vida como ela é" became a sensation and was read faithfully by people of all walks of life for many years. Rodrigues became the most popular journalist in Brazil, even as his playwriting career languished.

Rodrigues did not, however, stop writing for the theater. In 1951 he composed a monologue, *Valsa n° 6* (translated as *Waltz #6,* 1998), about a young girl speaking from beyond the tomb after being cruelly murdered by her lover. Rodrigues hoped to cash in on the success of a wildly popular but now forgotten monologue by Pedro Bloch titled *As mãos de Eurídice* (Eurydice's Hands). While Bloch's play was mawkish melodrama, Rodrigues's *Valsa n° 6* was artfully constructed. Nevertheless, it was a box-office flop.

In 1953 Rodrigues initiated a new phase in his playwriting with a genre that later came to be known as the Carioca tragedy. He wrote several of these tragedies, which were better received than his mythic plays. This new genre was in part an attempt to modernize the traditional comedy of manners, a farcical and satirical play usually situated in Rio de Janeiro. (A Carioca is a native of Rio de Janeiro.) Rodrigues added the raw language of the street and the social problems of the city's working-class neighborhoods, especially the Zona Norte, located out of sight of the glamorous beaches of Copacabana and Ipanema and the spectacular scenery of the Pão de Açúcar (Sugar Loaf) and Morro do Corcovado (Mount Corcovado). The area, with its grinding poverty, was controlled by crime bosses. The first Carioca tragedy, *A falecida* (1953; translated as *The Deceased Woman,* 1998), tells the story of Zulmira, a woman from the Zona Norte whose only desire is to be buried in an expensive coffin.

The year 1955 brought a reversal of fortune for Rodrigues's family, which finally won a lawsuit against the government over the family newspaper *A crítica,* destroyed twenty-five years earlier by pro-Vargas mobs. The lawsuit was possible because Vargas, after serving briefly as an elected president, committed suicide in 1954. The next president, Juscelino Kubitscheck, was a friend and former classmate of Rodrigues's brother Mário Rodrigues Filho. The playwright composed two plays in 1957, the first of which was a Carioca tragedy with the paradoxical title *Perdoame por me traires* (translated as *Forgive Me for You Betraying Me,* 2001). The play, considered an affront to the tradi-

tional patriarchal code because a male character begs his wife to forgive him for her betrayal, was cut by the censors. It was adapted for the cinema by Braz Chediak in 1980, with the distinguished actress Vera Fischer in the lead role. The second play, *Viúva, porém honesta* (1957; translated as *A Widow but Chaste,* 2001), was classified by Rodrigues as an "irresponsible farce" and by Magaldi as a psychological play.

Dramatic events in Rodrigues's personal life continued to occur. In 1958 he underwent an operation that further compromised his health. In 1960 he witnessed and reported on the new national capital Brasília, which was both the capstone of President Kubitschek's political career and a monument to architectural modernism.

Between 1958 and 1960 Rodrigues wrote three more Carioca tragedies. In the first, *Os sete gatinhos* (1958; translated as *The Seven Kittens,* 2001), the protagonist, Noronha, feels humiliated by his lowly position as a gofer in the chamber of deputies. He is the father of five daughters, and he takes it as a source of honor that he upholds Brazilian society's ideal of feminine purity, not realizing that four of his daughters are prostitutes. Noronha is intent on ensuring that his youngest daughter will be a virgin upon her marriage. The other daughters donate the proceeds from their prostitution to finance their little sister's wedding. For them their sister's virginal marriage will constitute a kind of redemption, but she becomes pregnant before the wedding. Her pregnancy is discovered after she stabs a pregnant cat, which gives birth to the seven kittens of the title. When her anxious parents take her to the doctor, her pregnancy is discovered. The father then turns his house into a brothel. *Boca de ouro* (1960, Gold Tooth) opens with the death of the title character, a product of the slums who rose to become a powerful and ruthless gambling boss. Born in a dance-hall bathroom and abandoned, his life is a vindictive quest to gild his miserable origins, and to flaunt his newly minted status he has all his teeth pulled and replaced with gold inlays. Seen through the eyes of other characters, his life is remembered by his former wife. In the end, the formidable character has been reduced to a toothless cadaver in the morgue. *Boca de ouro,* like other Rodrigues plays, had censorship problems. Ziembinski both directed the play and played the lead character, a questionable choice since his thick Polish accent was jarring in the role of a Rio de Janeiro mob boss. *O beijo no asfalto* (1961; The Kiss on the Asphalt) concerns a man who gives another male, a dying stranger, a charitable kiss. The media picks up the story and treats it as a homosexual scandal, and the life of the charitable man is destroyed as a result. *Os sete gatinhos* and *Boca de ouro* have received significant productions since the 1980s.

In 1989 Antunes Filho staged *Os sete gatinhos,* along with *A falecida,* in a production titled *Paraiso Zona Norte* (North Zone Paradise; both plays are set in the Zona Norte of Rio de Janeiro). Another renowned director, José Celso, founder of one of the most celebrated and longest-running theaters in Brazil, Teatro Oficina, staged *Boca de ouro* in 2000. All three plays were made into movies, *Boca de ouro* twice (1963 and 1990).

The indictment of the media in *O beijo no asfalto* resulted in Rodrigues's losing his newspaper job. He was soon hired by another paper that was interested in his column, "A vida como ela é." Rodrigues added another popular column to his curriculum, this time dealing with soccer, a Brazilian passion. He also became a soccer commentator on television.

Rodrigues produced another Carioca tragedy in 1962, *Bonitinha mas ordinária* (Pretty but Uncouth), also known as *Otto Lara Resende, ou, Bonitinha mas ordinária.* The inclusion of the name was an in-joke, a reference to Rodrigues's friend the writer and critic Otto Lara Resende. The play, another Carioca tragedy, deals with a character named Edgar, the humble but ethical secretary of a corrupt and dissipated millionaire. Edgar is offered the hand of his boss's daughter in marriage. The daughter is a rape victim, a fact her father uses to test Edgar's character. His ethical standards are challenged when the millionaire offers him a huge sum of money. The play presents a merciless criticism of what Rodrigues saw as Brazil's lack of a moral center. *Bonitinha mas ordinária* was adapted for the cinema in 1963; a second adaptation, directed by Chediak, was released in 1981. In 1963 Rodrigues scripted the first ever *telenovela* (prime-time Brazilian soap opera), *A morta sem espelho.* Because of the writer's suspect reputation, the program was consigned to a late hour, ensuring a limited number of viewers. He continued to dabble in the medium of television, with limited success. He was hired to adapt works written by others and to host an interview show.

Rodrigues's personal life at this time was marked by his separation from his wife and his affair with another woman, Lúcia Cruz Lima, with whom he had a daughter, Daniela, who suffered from lifelong disabilities. Further chapters in Rodrigues's tragedy-marred life include the death of two of his brothers in the 1960s. Paulo Rodrigues perished, along with his entire family, when their apartment building collapsed under a landslide at the foot of one of the famed hillsides in Rio de Janeiro.

Rodrigues's next play, *Toda nudez será castigada* (1965; translated as *All Nudity Shall Be Punished,* 1998), is the culmination of his Carioca tragedies. The work recounts an incestuous tale of deadly sibling rivalry. Patricio sets out to destroy his older brother, the pro-

tagonist, Herculano, a well-heeled businessman who failed to rescue Patricio from his own folly and from a consequent bankruptcy. Patricio uses Geni, a prostitute, to seduce the chaste Herculano and involves the latter's son, Serginho, in what becomes a lethal plot combining fratricide, patricide, and matricide. As in *Álbum de família,* each case of seduction dooms the target of incest. Because Patricio seduces his brother through Geni, whom he later manipulates into an affair with Serginho, the incest is oblique. The annihilating power of incest, however, is plain, as in *Álbum de família.* By 1965 mores in Brazil had become more relaxed; *Toda nudez será castigada* was produced with some success at that time, and there have been several notable productions since then, including an acclaimed 1973 movie adaptation. Director Antunes Filho gave the play its definitive treatment in the 1980s with a production that toured Brazil, Spanish America, and several European countries. With these productions Rodrigues was introduced to worldwide audiences for the first time.

Rodrigues's 1966 novel, *O casamento* (The Wedding), was a huge commercial success, in spite of (or perhaps because of) attempts to censor it. Set in Rio de Janeiro in the 1960s, the plot deals with secret desires and violent death on the eve of a wedding. The novel was adapted as a movie in 1976. The 1960s brought another kind of renown to Rodrigues, which continued to cloud his reputation. After the brief nationalist euphoria of the period under Kubitscheck in the late 1950s, Brazil entered a difficult phase in the following decade. Not only had the economy taken a downward turn, but the Cold War descended on Brazil in the wake of Fidel Castro's victorious revolution in Cuba. Fears of further communist takeovers seized the United States government and intelligence community. The Brazilian military became increasingly restive, and many middle- and upper-class Brazilians began to support the idea of a military coup. Polarization between Left and Right intensified, and the president, João Goulart, moved Brazil closer to the Soviet bloc, openly defying the military. The armed forces took control of the nation on 1 April 1964. Although police-state repression was part of the dictatorship from the beginning, widespread human-rights abuses did not become egregious until a state of siege was declared in December 1968. From that time until the mid 1970s, censorship, arbitrary arrest, torture, and disappearances became routine. Rodrigues was one of the military regime's defenders. He believed that the generals had saved the nation from communist totalitarianism, and he stated his opinion openly in his widely read column "Confissões" (Confessions). Many artists and intellectuals from that period, victims of military repression, understandably ignored Rodrigues's work for years.

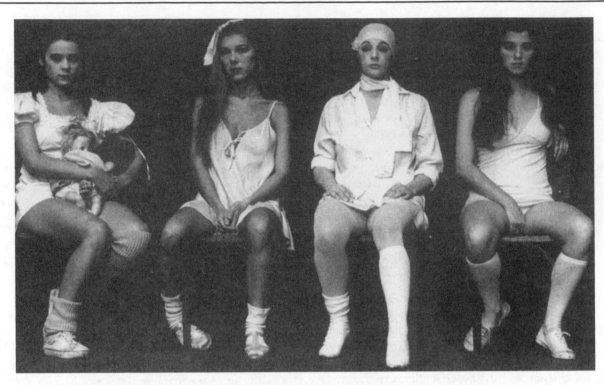

Scene from Nelson 2 Rodrigues, *a 1984 production comprising the plays* Álbum de família *and* Toda nudez será castigada,
staged by the Centro de Pesquisa Teatral/Grupo de Teatro Macunaíma in São Paulo (from David S. George,
The Modern Brazilian Stage, *1992; Thomas Cooper Library, University of South Carolina)*

Only after the end of the Cold War, when the old ideological battles had abated and Rodrigues's artistic reputation had rebounded, did they begin to take note of him.

After a ten-year absence from the stage Rodrigues wrote his last two plays, *Anti–Nelson Rodrigues* (1974) and *A serpente* (1980, The Serpent), both minor additions to his oeuvre. His health failing, he compiled his newspaper columns into a final book, *O reacionário: memórias e confissões* (1977, The Reactionary: Memoirs and Confessions). He died on 21 December 1980.

As a playwright Rodrigues was ahead of his time, and much of his fame came about only after his death. Several factors account for this posthumous fame. First, by the early 1980s it was no longer shocking in Brazil to speak openly about sexual abuse, women's desires, the degrading effects of poverty, the corruption engendered by power, the contradictions of the patriarchal system, racism, and the world of the unconscious. By then Brazil was well past the time when the language of the stage adhered to nineteenth-century models. The ideological battles of the Cold War and, concomitantly, of the military dictatorship were winding down.

To be truly appreciated as a dramatist, Rodrigues needed a visionary director to demonstrate the suitability of his works for the stage and a critic to give the full measure of his dramaturgical skills. Antunes Filho and his company had debuted in 1978 with a stage adaptation of Mário de Andrade's classic Brazilian novel *Macunaíma* (1928), a production that became a resounding national and international success. Antunes Filho opened his second production, *Nelson Rodrigues o Eterno Retorno* (Nelson Rodrigues the Eternal Return), on 6 May 1981. It included four works by the playwright—*A falecida*, *Álbum de família*, *Boca de ouro*, and *Toda nudez será castigada*—and the success of the production equaled that of *Macunaíma*. A shortened version, trimmed down to *Álbum de família* and *Toda nudez será castigada*, opened in 1984 with the title *Nelson 2 Rodrigues*. The production begins with an anecdote by the playwright. The audience listens to Rodrigues's voice telling a story from his childhood. He relates his initiation as a playwright, claiming that he wrote a prizewinning story about adultery and murder while still in elementary school. Apocryphal or not, the tale bears all the earmarks of Rodrigues's later scandalous career. His recorded voice also repeats a claim that he made all his life and that contradicts the pornographic reputation attributed to him by his detractors. He characterizes himself as a native sentimentalist who believes only in the redemptive power of love.

The two Antunes Filho productions were sensations. They had long runs in Brazil and toured the world, playing in the major capitals of Latin America, North America, Europe, and Asia, and at several international theater festivals. For Brazilians the stagings of Rodrigues's works were a revelation. They were now vehicles for stage magic, with possibilities for intricate choreography and artful design—in short, for imaginative stagecraft. The plays were moving, funny, timeless, and scathing social exegeses. They were reworkings of Brazil's own distinctive mythology, combined with universal myths of birth, death, and re-creation.

More directors have begun staging Rodrigues's works, and theaters have been named after him. Even his prose works have been adapted for the stage, and movie adaptations continue to appear. His leftist detractors from earlier decades have laid to rest their ideological differences and have produced his plays. Ruy Castro's *O anjo pornográfico: a vida de Nelson Rodrigues* (1992, The Pornographic Angel: The Life of Nelson Rodrigues) was a best-seller. All of Rodrigues's works—drama, journalism, and fiction—have gone through several new editions.

Brazil found in Nelson Rodrigues a playwright whose stature may be compared to that of Miller, Williams, and especially O'Neill in the United States because of their exposure of social ills. Rodrigues's analyses of what are now called dysfunctional families are uncannily similar to those of the American playwrights. *Álbum de família* stands beside O'Neill's *Long Day's Journey into Night* (1956) as a harrowing passage through the depths of familial calamity. In addition to being the most important Brazilian playwright of the twentieth century, Rodrigues ranks with the major figures of twentieth-century drama in general.

Biography:

Ruy Castro, *O anjo pornográfico: a vida de Nelson Rodrigues* (São Paulo: Campanhia das Letras, 1992).

References:

Fred M. Clark, *Impermanent Structures: Semiotic Readings of Nelson Rodrigues' Vestido de noiva, Álbum de família, and Anjo negro* (Chapel Hill: Department of Romance Languages, University of North Carolina, 1991);

S. Dennison, "Critical Responses to the Screening of Nelson Rodrigues," *Studies in Latin American Popular Culture,* 19 (2000): 129–144;

Eudinyr Fraga, *Nelson Rodrigues expressionista* (Cotia: Ateliê / São Paulo: Fundação de Amparo à Pesquisa do Estado de São Paulo, 1998);

Mário Guidarini, *Nelson Rodrigues: flor de obsessão* (Florianópolis: Editora da Universidade Federal de Santa Catarina, 1990);

J. Guinsburg, "Nelson Rodrigues: um folhetim de melodramas," *Travessia,* 28 (1994): 7–10;

Randal Johnson, "Nelson Rodrigues as Filmed by Arnaldo Jabor," *Latin American Theatre Review,* 16 (Fall 1982): 15–28;

Gisele Kato and Renata Santos, "À sombra do Nelson immortal," *Bravo,* 33 (June 2000): 44–49;

Ronaldo Lima Lins, *O teatro de Nelson Rodrigues: uma realidade em agonia* (Rio de Janeiro: F. Alves, 1979);

Angela Leite Lopes, *Nelson Rodrigues: trágico, então moderno* (Rio de Janeiro: Editora Universidade Federal do Rio de Janeiro/Tempo Brasileiro, 1993);

Sábato Magaldi, *Nelson Rodrigues: dramaturgia e encenações* (São Paulo: Perspectiva/Editora da Universidade de São Paulo, 1987);

Luiz Arthur Nunes, "The Conflict between the Real and the Ideal: A Study of the Elements of Naturalism and Melodrama in the Dramatic Works of Nelson Rodrigues," dissertation, City University of New York, 1987;

Victor Hugo Adler Pereira, *Nelson Rodrigues e a obs-cena contemporánea* (Rio de Janeiro: Editoria de Universidade do Estado do Rio de Janeiro, 1999);

Larry Rohter, "Reawakening the Giant of Brazilian Theater," *New York Times,* 17 December 2000.

João Guimarães Rosa

(27 June 1908 – 19 November 1967)

Eduardo F. Coutinho
Universidade Federal do Rio de Janeiro

See also the Rosa entry in *DLB 113: Modern Latin-American Fiction Writers, First Series.*

BOOKS: *Sagarana* (Rio de Janeiro: Universal, 1946; revised edition, São Paulo: J. Olympio, 1951); translated by Harriet de Onís as *Sagarana: A Cycle of Stories* (New York: Knopf, 1966);

Com o vaqueiro Mariano (Niterói: Hipocampo, 1956);

Corpo de baile: sete novelas, 2 volumes (Rio de Janeiro: J. Olympio, 1956); republished in 3 volumes as *Manuelzão e Miguilim: Campo geral; Uma estória de amor* (Rio de Janeiro: J. Olympio, 1964), *No Urubuquaquá, no Pinhém: O recado do morro. "Cara-de-Bronze." A estória de Lélio e Lina* (Rio de Janeiro: J. Olympio, 1965), and *Noites do sertão: Lão-Dalalão (Dão-Lalalão). Buriti* (Rio de Janeiro: J. Olympio, 1965);

Grande sertão: veredas (Rio de Janeiro: J. Olympio, 1956); translated by Onís and James L. Taylor as *The Devil to Pay in the Backlands: "The Devil in the Street, in the Middle of the Whirlwind"* (New York: Knopf, 1963);

Primeiras estórias (Rio de Janeiro: J. Olympio, 1962); translated by Barbara Shelby as *The Third Bank of the River and Other Stories* (New York: Knopf, 1968);

O mistério dos MMM, by Rosa, Viriato Correia, Dinah Silveira de Queiroz, Lúcio Cardozo, Herberto Salles, Jorge Amado, José Condé, Antonio Callado, Orígenes Lessa, and Rachel de Queiroz (Rio de Janeiro: O Cruzeiro, 1962);

Parabéns, cidade maravilhosa! (Rio de Janeiro: Minerva, 1965);

Tutaméia: terceiras estórias (Rio de Janeiro: J. Olympio, 1967);

Estas estórias (Rio de Janeiro: J. Olympio, 1969);

Ave, palavra (Rio de Janeiro: J. Olympio, 1970);

Fita verde no cabelo: nova velha estória (Rio de Janeiro: Nova Fronteira, 1992);

Magma, comments by Guilherme de Almeida (Rio de Janeiro: Nova Fronteira, 1997).

João Guimarães Rosa (photograph © Manchete; Arquivo da Academia Brasileira de Letras)

Collections: *Seleta de João Guimarães Rosa,* edited by Paulo Rónai (Rio de Janeiro: J. Olympio, 1973);

Guimarães Rosa, edited by Beth Brait (São Paulo: Abril Educação, 1982);

Ficção completa, 2 volumes (Rio de Janeiro: Nova Aguilar, 1994).

Edition in English: *The Jaguar and Other Stories,* translated by David Treece (Oxford: Boulevard, 2001).

OTHER: "Soberba: os chapéus transeuntes," in *Os sete pecados capitais* (Rio de Janeiro: Civilização Brasileira, 1964);

Antologia do conto húngaro, edited and translated by Paulo Rónai, revised by Aurélio Buarque de Hollanda Ferreira, preface by Rosa (Rio de Janeiro: Artenova, 1975).

One of the most distinguished authors of twentieth-century Brazilian literature, João Guimarães Rosa is best known by critics for the innovations he introduced into Brazilian narrative language—an accomplishment that has been seen by many as a landmark in the country's literature. Yet, Rosa's importance as a writer is not restricted to this aspect. Having produced most of his works in the last phase of the modernist movement, he effected a synthesis of all of the features that were formerly seen as antagonistic in Brazilian prose fiction—regionalism and universalism, aestheticism and social commitment, and myth and realism—and offered his readers an oeuvre of such great philosophical dimensions that it is only comparable in the canon of the country's literature to Joaquim María Machado de Assis's novels written half a century before. Despite their apparent difficulty, his works are some of the most widely read and frequently reprinted in Brazil, and they have been translated into several languages.

The first of six children of Florduardo Pinto Rosa and Francisca Guimaraes Rosa, Rosa was born on 27 June 1908 in Cordisburgo, a small town in the *sertão* (backlands) of the eastern Brazilian state of Minas Gerais. In 1918 he was sent away to school in Belo Horizonte, and in 1925 he was admitted to medical school at the University of Minas Gerais. While pursuing his studies, he began contributing short stories to the Rio de Janeiro magazine *O Cruzeiro;* he received four literary prizes for his writings. In June 1930 he married Lygia Cabral Pena, with whom he had two daughters, Agnes and Vilma. In December 1930 he was the speaker at his graduation ceremony from medical school. The following year he started his career as a physician in Itaguara, Minas Gerais, and participated in the revolution of 1932 against the dictatorship of President Getúlio Dornelles Vargas. He declared in a 1965 interview with Günter W. Lorenz, "Como médico conheci o valor místico do sofrimento; como rebelde, o valor da consciência; como soldado, o valor da proximidade da morte" (As a physician I came to know the mystical greatness of suffering; as a

rebel, the value of consciousness; and as a soldier, the importance of the proximity of death).

In 1934 Rosa entered the Ministry of Foreign Affairs; he also began to dedicate himself to literature. In 1936 he won the poetry award of the Brazilian Academy of Letters for his collection *Magma,* which was published posthumously in 1997. In 1937 he wrote a collection of short stories titled *Sagarana* and submitted it to the Humberto de Campos fiction contest, winning second place. In 1938 he married Aracy Moebius de Carvalho; that same year he was sent to Hamburg, Germany, as Brazilian consul. He helped several Jews to escape from the country and in 1942 was interned for several months in Baden-Baden along with the Brazilian intellectuals Cícero Dias and Cyro de Freitas Vale. He was then transferred to Bogotá, where he rewrote *Sagarana.* The book was published in 1946 (translated, 1966) and won a prize from the Society Felipe d'Oliveira.

The title is formed from the Germanic root *saga* and the Tupi Indian suffix *-rana.* By coining this hybrid word from languages that have no connection with each other, Rosa indicated his break with conventionality and proclaimed his adherence to a concept of aesthetic freedom. Thenceforth, he used whatever linguistic elements seemed to him the most appropriate to transmit his worldview, regardless of whether they were grammatical or described any extralinguistic reality. This practice is made explicit in *Sagarana* in the story "São Marcos" (St. Mark; translated as "Woodland Witchery"), in which Rosa describes, in a highly poetic way, his theory of the revitalization of literary language. Language in *Sagarana,* as well as in Rosa's later works, is not merely a vehicle for conveying ideas but is also identified with action: the word, for him, has the weight of an act and often determines the destinies of his characters. In "Sarapalha" (translated as "The Straw-spinners") the naive confession of a feeling causes a rupture in the protagonists' long friendship and condemns them to solitude; in "Duelo" (translated as "Duel") an oath made to a man at the moment of his death results in a murder; and in "São Marcos" the words of a prayer reveal to the protagonist the cause of his misfortune and, ultimately, save him.

Each of the nine stories in *Sagarana* is an independent narrative with its own characters and plot, but the worldview presented in the various stories is uniform: they are the physical, psychological, and sociological portrait of a particular area of the Brazilian backlands. In *Sagarana* the region is presented in all its rawness and concreteness: it is depicted in terms of its physical and geographical aspects, such as its fauna, flora, climate, and hydrography, as well as the customs and the social and economic systems of its people. In spite of the presence of these elements and the faithful and detailed manner in which they are often described, however, the book transcends regionalism in the strictest sense of the term: the region presented in its pages is less a specific geographical reality than a microcosm of the world. It is a mysterious, unlimited area where human beings constantly search for meaning. And the characters, rather than being particular types, are people of all times and places, living with their contradictions and experiencing situations that are the representation of everyone's daily life, especially in its moments of tension. Lalino Salãthiel in "A volta do marido pródigo" (translated as "The Return of the Prodigal Husband") and Augusto Matraga in "A hora e vez de Augusto Matraga" (translated as "Augusto Matraga's Hour and Turn"), as well as the characters in "Minha gente" (translated as "Mine Own People"), "Corpo fechado" (translated as "Bulletproof"), "Duelo," "Sarapalha," and "São Marcos," are typical inhabitants of the Brazilian backlands who confront a series of problems significant in that area: malaria in "Sarapalha," witchcraft in "São Marcos," superstition and banditry in "Corpo fechado," vengeance in "Duelo," machismo in "A volta do marido pródigo," and social exploitation and religious fervor in "A hora e vez de Augusto Matraga." Yet, they are also universal human beings whose conflicts are not exclusive to the region where they live but common to all human beings at all times and places—for example, Matraga's conflict between good and evil.

In this universe, where nature is not merely a setting but also the living expression of the collective character of its inhabitants, humans are not always the protagonists of the stories. This position is occupied by animals in "O burrinho pedrês" (translated as "The Little Dust-brown Donkey") and "Conversa de bois" (translated as "Conversation among Oxen"). And the animals are not thinly disguised human beings, as in fables or apologues, but real animals: they have acute intuitive knowledge or instincts, and the narrative is presented totally from their perspective—for example, in "Conversa de bois" the oxen create a sort of philosophical theory of humanity. Rosa's backlands is a region of art, a universe created in language. He is, above all, a storyteller, and one of his greatest achievements is to restore the old technique of narrating stories.

For Rosa, the ten years following the publication of *Sagarana* were marked by intense diplomat activities both in Brazil and abroad: he was secretary to the Brazilian delegation to the Paris Peace Conference in 1946, secretary-general of the Brazilian delegation to the Ninth Pan-American Conference in 1948, principal

secretary of the Brazilian Embassy in Paris from 1949 to 1951, and cabinet head in the Ministry of Foreign Affairs in Rio de Janeiro from 1951 to 1953, and was appointed budget director to the Ministry of State in Rio de Janeiro in 1953. Although he did a great deal of literary work during this period, the result was not made known until he published two major works in five months in 1956: the collection *Corpo de baile: sete novelas* (Corps de Ballet: Seven Novellas) in January and the novel *Grande sertão: veredas* (Great Backlands: Paths; translated as *The Devil to Pay in the Backlands: "The Devil in the Street, in the Middle of the Whirlwind,"* 1963) in May. The success he had achieved with *Sagarana,* which by then was in its fourth edition, was confirmed, and Rosa's reputation as a writer of high-quality works was established. Studies of his works appeared, and he won the Machado de Assis Prize from the Instituto Nacional do Livro, the Carmen Dolores Barbosa Prize from the city of São Paulo, and the Paula Brito Prize from the city council of Rio de Janeiro.

Corpo de baile originally came out in two volumes, but beginning with the third edition it was divided into three: *Manuelzão e Miguilim* (1964, Manuelzão and Miguilim), *No Urubuquaquá, no Pinhém* (1965, In Urubuquaquá, in Pinhém), and *Noites do sertão* (1965, Backlands' Nights). In *Corpo de baile* the elements that form the universe of *Sagarana* are more fully developed, and Rosa's linguistic and structural innovations are taken much further. The subjects of these stories are the same as the previous ones, but their themes are of a greater variety and more deeply explored. Humanity's existential conflicts acquire a greater dimension in these narratives, and reality is viewed from a wider perspective. Myth and fantasy play an important role, and justice is frequently on the side of those who question the status quo.

The backlands in *Corpo de baile,* as in *Sagarana,* is a multiple, ambiguous region, and its inhabitants live both in a logical-rational world and a mythical-sacred one. Yet, the importance of intuition is so stressed in Rosa's novellas that myth seems to dominate the author's worldview. It is present in all of its forms in the characters' attitude toward life, and it often constitutes the only way of approaching the mystery of existence. Predominantly intuitive beings largely populate the book, and are in many cases the focus of attention. In this universe where intuition plays a decisive role in the apprehension of reality, childhood is well represented; the first narrative in *Corpo de baile,* in fact, centers on an eight-year-old boy. Although the story deals with the child's process of growth and constantly points to the changes that take hold of him, his childish worldview is present throughout the narrative and is often contrasted with that of the adults. Whereas the latter are in general predominantly rationalistic and have a limiting view of the world, the child is imaginative, wise, and closer to the immediacy of things. The author's empathy for the child is extended to all of the other characters who, by not placing reason above everything else, are pushed to the fringes in the everyday world of adults. Among these characters, older people are prominent—for example, the wise old lady in "A estória de Lélio e Lina" (The Story of Lelio and Lina) and the couple Seu Camilo and Joana Xaviel in "Uma estória de amor" (A Love Story); other such characters include deranged people, criminals, sorcerers, and artists. "O recado do morro" (A Message from the Hill), in which a man is saved from being murdered by listening to a mysterious message transmitted by a chain of intuitive beings, can be read as an apology for antirationalistic thought.

Besides myth and intuition, another basic element of Rosa's novellas is emotion; emotional conflict is at the heart of several of the narratives in *Corpo de baile*. The tension of the story "Buriti" (The Buriti Palm Tree) is generated by passion and carnal love, and in "Dão-Lalalão (Dão-Lalalão)" (Ding-Ling-Ling [Ding-Ling-Ling]) the characters' actions are motivated by jealousy and insecurity. Love is present in each tale in a different form, and, as usual, preference rests with those who question the established order and transcend common sense. Emotion is, for Rosa, a total, almost sacred state; it is aesthetic experience at its utmost, for art is identified with life. Hence, the girl for whom the cowboy Grivo desperately searches in "Cara-de-Bronze" (The Bronze Face) is poetry in its full sense.

The linguistic and structural experiments Rosa initiated in *Sagarana* become more elaborate in *Corpo de baile*. One of the most developed aspects of this experimentation is the fusion of elements such as those that characterize prose as opposed to poetry or that distinguish one literary genre from another. Rosa never accepted such distinctions, seeing them as absurd limitations. His prose is filled with traits usually considered proper to poetry, such as onomatopoeia, alliteration, rhyme, and rhythm: these poetic devices are so exploited in *Corpo de baile* that in the third edition of the book he labeled the narratives poems. The mixture of genres reaches an extreme in "Cara-de-Bronze," which fuses the structures of a story, a poem, a drama, and even a screenplay. In *Corpo de baile*, as in *Sagarana*, Rosa's theoretical preoccupations are made explicit in the plots of his stories, and language is frequently an important thematic element: the protagonist of "Uma estória de amor" finds the clue to peace of mind in the words of an embedded story; through

the words of a popular song the hero of "O recado do morro" recognizes the trap that has been prepared for him; and "Cara-de-Bronze" centers on the relationship of poetry and life.

Rosa's only novel, *Grande sertão: veredas,* is not only his masterpiece, but also one of the most important works of twentieth-century Brazilian literature. It has gone through many editions and translations and is one of the most widely studied novels in Brazil. Breaking completely with traditional regionalism, Rosa presents the story of Riobaldo Tatarana, who is both a typical representative of the backlands and a common man of his century and who, tormented by doubt and insecurity, searches desperately for the meaning of existence. The novel consists of a monologue in which Riobaldo tells of his former life as a *jagunço* (a member of a group of outlaws who formed a sort of bodyguard to defend either their own interests or those of the landowners who supported them); his audience is a person from the city who is traveling through the backlands. Riobaldo says that he contracted a pact with the devil to obtain victory in war; he is now tortured by guilt for having sold his soul. Since the devil never appeared to him as a concrete entity, however, he cannot be sure of the demon's existence. Therefore, he has decided to narrate his life to a predominantly rationalistic interlocutor for the purpose of clearing up his doubts and finding some relief for his conscience.

Although Riobaldo's report is given in one extended narration, undivided into chapters, it is constructed around two periods in his life: the past, during which he had the experiences as a *jagunço* that he is describing; and the present, in which he reexperiences those events in the act of narrating them. The past episodes, in turn, are of two kinds: objective ones consisting of the succession of the battles and struggles in which Riobaldo was involved in the backlands, and subjective ones constituted by the inner conflicts he underwent—his hesitation between his love for the pure, idealized maiden Otacília and for the prostitute Nhorinhá, and his simultaneous feelings of attraction and repulsion for the warrior Diadorim. The aim pursued by the protagonist differs in the two kinds of episodes: in the objective ones he seeks the equilibrium of the *jagunço*'s world; in the subjective ones he searches for personal happiness. The two kinds of episodes are, nevertheless, similar in structure and merge into a single climax: a final battle that results in the death of Diadorim, who is revealed to be a woman who disguised herself as a man to avenge her father's murder. An incarnation of the principle of contradiction that rules Rosa's cosmos, Diadorim is the vital force that impels Riobaldo to act and reveals to him the beauty

*Cover for Rosa's first book (1946; translated, 1966), a collection
of nine stories set in the Brazilian backlands. The title is a word
invented by Rosa that combines the Germanic root* saga
and the Tupi Indian suffix -rana *(Biblioteca
Nacional de Chile).*

These two levels differ from those of the past in that they exist only in the act of narration. Since they are interwoven with the former ones, however, they imply an isomorphic relationship between art and life.

Riobaldo is in a constant state of uncertainty, and he uses narration to accomplish his search. But this process can be effected only if he finds a new type of language adequate to express his state, a language that inquires more than it affirms. As a result, an identification occurs between living and narrating, and his quest is represented through the search for a new means of expression. This identification of life and art is the meaning of the parallel construction that recurs as a leitmotiv throughout the novel: "Viver é muito perigoso" (Living is very dangerous), and "Contar é muito, muito dificultoso" (Narrating is very, very difficult). In the end, Riobaldo does not find any definite answers to his questions; he concludes that relativity is the only possible way to approach reality.

In 1961 Rosa was awarded a prize by the Brazilian Academy of Letters for the corpus of his work. In that same year *Sagarana* was published in Portugal, and three of the novellas of *Corpo de baile* were translated into French. The following year *Primeiras estórias* (First Stories; translated as *The Third Bank of the River and Other Stories,* 1968) was published and repeated the success of his previous books. *Estórias* is a neologism based on the English word *stories;* it is used in opposition to *conto,* the traditional Portuguese term for the short story. By employing this word, preceded by *primeiras* (first), Rosa intended to make clear the distinction between this book and *Sagarana:* the new stories are much more condensed, characterized by a sharper philosophical tone, more lyrical, and freer from traditional plot. The themes of the twenty-one stories are so similar that the unity of this book is even greater than that of *Sagarana.* The stories are sketches of life in the backlands, and the characters are trying to decipher the mystery of life and the meaning of human existence. Rationalism and common sense are called into question more vehemently here than ever before in Rosa's works: many of the stories center on a child's worldview, while others involve madness. The children are presented as endowed with a sensibility that adults can never possess; the madmen are depicted as prophets who can see beyond appearance and command respect on account of their wisdom.

The worldview of children is depicted in the first and last narratives, "As margens da alegria" (translated as "The Thin Edge of Happiness") and "Os cimos" (translated as "Treetops"), in which a boy experiences the conflict of good and evil in two extreme moments of his life. (Critics disagree as to whether the stories are about the same boy or two dif-

of life but at the same time makes him face the abyss of his own existence. Diadorim is, as her name suggests, dual: she is God and the devil, light and darkness, pain and pleasure, and man and woman. She constitutes, by means of the questioning she brings about, an image of Rosa's own questions about life and existence.

The second time period in the novel, the present of narration, is composed of the protagonist's experiences as he reports his life to his interlocutor. Here again, two levels can be distinguished: a speculative one in which Riobaldo is preoccupied with deciphering things he could not understand previously and dissipating the doubt that continues to torment him, and a critical and metalinguistic one in which he is concerned with finding the most suitable expressions to transmit those things with a maximum of faithfulness.

ferent ones.) In "A menina de lá" (translated as "The Girl from Beyond") a strange and lonely girl is thought to have become a miracle worker, while in "Partida do audaz navegante" (translated as "The Audacious Navigator") a girl sees things that are not perceived by anyone else. "Pirlimpsiquice" (translated as "Hocus Psychocus") is the story of a group of boys who create a play parallel to the one they are expected to perform, and in "Nenhum, nenhuma" (translated as "No Man, No Woman") the narration is filtered through the memory of a boy. In the narratives involving madness the barrier between sanity and insanity is eliminated. In "A benfazeja" (translated as "A Woman of Good Works") a madwoman who has murdered her husband is revealed as a sensible person whose feelings demand respect. The old madman of "Tarantão, meu patrão" (translated as "Tantarum, My Boss"), who undertakes a crusade to kill his doctor, is highly regarded by those he meets along the way. In "Darandina" (translated as "Much Ado") a madman hanging at the top of a palm tree drives an entire population to question their system of values. In "Sorôco, sua mãe, sua filha" (translated as "Sorôco, His Mother, His Daughter") the song of two madwomen at the moment of their departure to the sanatorium is the only true instance of communication among the inhabitants of the town. In other stories, madness is merely suggested and is confused with simple absurdity. Such are the cases of the old man who divides his property among his servants with no explanation to the daughters he sincerely loves in "Nada e a nossa condição" (translated as "Nothingness and the Human Condition") and of the suspicious foreigner who gives beer to his horse in "O cavalo que bebia cerveja" (translated as "The Horse Who Drank Beer"). The most intriguing such story is "A terceira margem do rio" (translated as "The Third Bank of the River"), about a man who abandons all he owns to spend the rest of his life in a canoe going up and down the same part of a river. This story, a jewel of narrative technique, is one of Rosa's sharpest criticisms of the supremacy of rationalist thought; on the other hand, it remains outside the realm of the marvelous or magical, for the protagonist's basic needs—food and clothing—are supplied by his family. The mystery and perplexity of life is a theme in the philosophical stories "Fatalidade" (translated as "My Friend the Fatalist"), "Seqüência" (translated as "Cause and Effect"), "Luas-de-Mel" (translated as "Honey-Moons"), "Um moço muito branco" (translated as "A Young Man, Gleaming White"), "Substância" (translated as "Substance"), and "O espelho" (translated as "The Mirror"). In these stories people try to understand the world, but the fac-

ets of reality are so many and the moment so ephemeral that all they can grasp is sheer relativity.

In *Primeira estórias* Rosa's experimentation with language reaches a previously unattained degree of elaboration. The innovations are many, and some are extremely sophisticated; again, his theories on the subject are explicitly presented in several of the stories. He uses a special language to characterize children's worldview in "A menina de lá" and "Partida do audaz navegante," and he makes language itself the theme of "Famigerado" (translated as "Notorious"), which revolves around the meaning of a word.

In August 1963 Rosa was unanimously elected to the seat in the Brazilian Academy of Letters left vacant by the death of his friend João Neves da Fontoura, with whom he had worked in the Ministry of Foreign Affairs, but he did not enter the academy at that time. By 1965 several of his books had been translated into French, Italian, English, and German, and some of the translations had gone into multiple editions. *Grande sertão: verdas* was filmed in 1965 and *A hora e vez de Augusto Matraga* in 1966.

In 1967 Rosa represented Brazil at the First Latin American Congress of Writers in Mexico. Later that year he published *Tutaméia: terceiras estórias* (Tutaméia: Third Stories); the title comes from *tuta-e-meia,* which means "trifle." Even shorter than those in *Primeiras estórias* and more philosophical in tone, these stories are a series of episodes, circumstances, and situations that display no commitment to rationalism. *Tutaméia* is divided into four parts, each of which is prefaced by a literary essay in which Rosa discusses his aesthetic theories; the stories in each section demonstrate the theories developed in the prefaces. The first preface deals with the opposition between *história* (history) and *estória* (story), both of which are signified in Portuguese by the word *história*: whereas history is the narration of facts that are supposed to have taken place, Rosa says, a story is a pure invention that has a logic of its own. The story is akin to the anecdote, in the sense that it requires originality and questions the limits of logic; but not every kind of anecdote serves this purpose. Rosa sketches a classification of anecdotes and concludes that the "anedota de abstração" (anecdote of abstraction) is the one that best defines the story because it involves a great deal of nonsense. He makes it clear that his writing proceeds on this level, not on that of common sense.

The second preface treats neologisms. Rosa defends his right to create words and affirms that doing so is a common trait in the language of the underprivileged social classes in the backlands. Educated people, he says, live in a pragmatic society dominated by materialistic preoccupations and do not feel the need to increase the expressiveness of their language. Such people limit themselves to ready-made ideas acquired in the process of education and do not bother to express the movements of their souls. Uncultivated people, on the other hand, have not lived under the influence of pragmatic society. Such people speak a language with a poor and simple vocabulary, have minds that are not dominated by the concepts and relationships of Western logic, view the world in a basically intuitive fashion, and feel the creation of words as an imperative. Yet, the necessity of producing neologisms is not exclusive to uneducated people: poets are also highly intuitive beings and must venture into this task whenever the forms of the existing language are inadequate to express their worldviews.

The third preface is a series of anecdotes about drunkards who try to escape from their existence by transforming the problems of everyday life into fantasy. In this preface the opposition between reality and unreality is eliminated, and everything becomes a matter of point of view: that which is traditionally considered real is revealed to be mere appearance, and fantasy—represented by drunkenness—is what brings consciousness to human beings. It is necessary, Rosa declares, to go behind the facades presented by common sense to find the hidden sides of things; he does so here by presenting the world from the perspective of a drunkard. The resulting nonsense brings into question the nature of objective reality and opens a path to the search for "suprasense." This preface makes it clear that traditional language and narrative logic only represent the external sides of things; from this consideration arises the search for a new mode of expression that characterizes Rosa's works.

The fourth preface deals with the problem of the creative act. Rosa asserts that a literary piece must be a synthesis of oppositions: the world is full of contrasts and contradictions, and the work of art must reflect them in its structure. He defends the artists's right to shake up the established order that supports apparent reality, and he states that everything acquires a new sense when language goes beyond the barrier of the supposed objective value of words. Doubt is the first step to aesthetic creation, because it opens the door to a deeper reality that cannot be explained in rational terms. Rosa confesses that his life has always been affected by strange occurrences—dreams, premonitions, coincidences, and intuitions—and contends that the work of art is often born in a sort of dream state that lies beyond the domain of reason. He describes how he conceived some of his stories and concludes by recalling a novel that he could never finish because he caught the illness of his protagonist.

On 16 November 1967 Rosa was inducted into the Brazilian Academy of Letters in a ceremony that he had postponed for four years. Three days later he died of a heart attack while writing in his study. His posthumously published works include the speech he gave when he entered the academy, which appears in the volume *Em memória de João Guimarães Rosa* (1968, In Memory of João Guimarães Rosa); *Estas estórias* (1969, These Stories) and *Ave, palavra* (1970, Hail, Word), collections of short stories that were either previously unpublished or never before gathered into book form—the only exception is the journalistic piece *Com o vaqueiro Mariano* (With the Cowboy Mariano) in *Estas estórias,* which was originally published in 1947 in the Rio de Janeiro newspaper *Correio da Manhã* and was republished in a limited edition as a book in 1956; his correspondence with Edoardo Bizzarri, the Italian translator of *Grande sertão: veredas* (1972); his letters to his friend Paulo Dantas (1975); his poetry book, *Magma,* which he had refused to publish in his lifetime; his letters to Vera and Beatriz Helena Tess from September 1966 to November 1967 (2003); his correspondence with his German translator, Curt Meyer-Clason (2003); and his letters to William Agel de Mello (2003). Movie versions of his works have continued to appear: *Cabaret mineiro* (1980), based on "Sorôco, sua mãe, sua filha"; *Noites do sertão* (1984), based on "Buriti"; *Cinema falado* (1986), based on *Grande sertão: veredas; A terceira margem do rio* (1994); and *Outras estórias* (1999, Other Stories). *Grande sertão: veredas* was also adapted as a television miniseries in 1985.

Critics usually classify Rosa as a member of the third generation of the modernist movement in Brazil, a generation characterized by its preoccupation with the means of literary expression. Rosa, however, took this preoccupation to such an extreme that he effected a revolution of narrative language that stands out as a landmark in twentieth-century Brazilian prose fiction. At the time he wrote the short stories of *Sagarana,* the novel of protest, which had found a fertile ground in the 1930s especially among the "Northeastern" writers, was predominant in Brazilian literature. Since the authors of this kind of fiction were primarily concerned with unmasking their country's social, political, and economic problems, they did not pay much attention to the role of language in their works but relied on worn-out, stereotyped formulas. Setting himself the task of breaking with the automatic character language had assumed in the works of the previous generation, Rosa revitalized writing on the levels of individual words, which had lost their primitive energy and acquired fixed meanings associated with specific contexts (for example, *selva* [jungle] and *sertão* in the regionalist novel); phrases, which had become vague and clouded with connotations that concealed their original strength; and syntax, the infinite possibilities of which had been abandoned and which had been limited to ready-made sentences and clichés. In spite of the great number of Rosa's linguistic innovations and the radical nature of some of them, the revitalization he effected does not involve the creation of a new language. He frequently violates specific grammatical rules of Portuguese, and, as a result, some of his works are rather hermetic; but at no point does he disregard the basic structure of the language. Instead, he exploits its potentialities and restores its poetic character. His language is an aesthetic creation, a fusion of elements derived from observation with others invented at the moment of expression. It has a regionalist component proper to the area of the backlands that forms the setting of his stories, but it is not an accurate reproduction of any specific dialect spoken in Brazil. It is, rather, an amalgamation of various dialects plus contributions from foreign languages, including Latin and Greek, and from the author's capacity for inventing words. His lexicon comprises archaisms and neologisms, regionalisms and foreign words, and erudite and colloquial terms. The combination of these elements forms a rich, dense, and complex discourse that at the beginning caused much perplexity both among critics and among ordinary readers; in both groups, perplexity has evolved into fascination.

Furthermore, Rosa's revitalization is not limited to language in the strict sense but extends to narrative discourse as a whole, which was also worn out in the novels of the 1930s. That is, he tried to break with the excessive linearity and causal coherence of the narrative and searched for new technical devices that would be better suited to expressing a dynamic and multifaceted reality. An example of these devices is the frequent use of metalanguage to indicate the self-conscious character of his works. This device, which places Rosa in the lineage of Brazilian literature represented by Machado de Assis, is extended from merely interrupting the narrative with comments on the author's technique to the insertion of entire theoretical reflections on the process of artistic creation. Such inserted passages, which constitute a real *ars poetica,* occur in the episode of the challenge in "São Marcos" in *Sagarana;* in the tales narrated by Joana Xaviel in "Uma estória de amor" and by the cowboy Grivo in "Cara-de-Bronze"; and in the prefaces of *Tutaméia,* which, although endowed with a certain independence, form a coherent whole with the stories they introduce.

Rosa engaged in considerable linguistic experimentation, but he never fell into mere verbal play or indulged in innovation for its own sake. His preoccu-

pation with form was a conscious political enterprise based on the premise that to express a revolutionary view of the world one must begin by revolutionizing the means of expressing that view. For Rosa, the language of a people is intimately connected with their way of thinking; thus, an author who wishes to alter his or her readers' worldview must start by changing the language that reflects this view. The writers of the 1930s were considered revolutionary because they denounced the Brazilian society of their time. But because they used the language of the establishment, their protest, though direct and vehement, lost a great deal of its strength. Rosa, by rejecting the forms of traditional narrative language and by restoring its poetic character, not only criticized the society of which this language was a manifestation but also reached the readers in a more effective manner, for by breaking with their crystallized structures of thought he induced them to reflect on their own reality.

Rosa is a regionalist writer in the sense that he uses the backlands as the setting for his stories, but he departs from traditional regionalism in the emphasis he places on the human being as the pivotal element of his fictional world. In traditional regionalist narratives the landscape is the core of the work, and human beings are relegated to a secondary status as representatives of the region—the gaucho or the backlands man, for example. In Rosa's prose, humans are the center of interest; they are depicted as multiple and contradictory beings, and the landscape is seen through them. The characters in Rosa's narratives are types in the sense that they express the collective consciousness of their region; yet, they transcend typicality by virtue of the human dimensions with which they are endowed, as can be seen by comparing Riobaldo, the protagonist of *Grande sertão: veredas,* with the *jagunço* type so frequently found in earlier Brazilian regionalist fiction. Whereas the latter can be defined by a series of clichés that conform to an abstract, a priori model, Riobaldo, in addition to possessing the characteristics of the *jagunço* type, is a universal character. One of his major concerns in the life journey he accomplishes in the novel is the question of good and evil—an issue that, while significant within the *jagunço's* world, is, above all, a human, existential preoccupation. Besides, Riobaldo continually questions the very condition of being a *jagunço;* this placing of a critical distance between himself and the type he embodies reinforces his transcendence of the model and accounts for his projection into a more nearly universal realm.

In the same way that human beings can be satisfactorily portrayed only when seen in their complexity and contradictoriness, so the landscape can be fully

— Té quando Deus quiser! O dinheiro *eu* lhe mando,
seu Ramiro.

Vai afadigado. Sobe para o lado do *chauffeur*.

— Não carece de buzinar, seu Miranda... Vamos
■■ *embora* !...

Brumadinho, enfim. Ainda não estão vendendo
passagens. — Vem *tomar* uma cerveja, seu Miranda. Ôi!
Que é *aquilo* meu-deus? Ah, a ciganada que está indo, *de vez.*
■■ Pegaram um dinheirão, levando gente de auto-
móvel p'r'a Santa Manoelina dos Coqueiros, que *agora* está no *bem*
Dom Silvério. Olha: tem uma ciganinha ■■ *muito* bonita. Mas isto é povo ■■ sujo, seu Miranda. ■
Não chegam aos pés das francesas... Seu Miranda,
escuta: vou lhe ■■ um favor. *pedir*

— Que é, seu Laio?

— Olha, fala com a Ritinha que eu não volto mais,
mesmo nunca *vou* *por* sair êsse mundo, zanzando. Como ■■
eu não presto, ela não perde... Diz a ela que pode
fazer o que entender....que eu não volto, nunca mais...

— Mas, seu Laio... Isso é uma ação de cachorro!
Ela é sua mulher!...

— Olha, seu Miranda: eu, com o senhor, de qualquer jeito isto é — ■■ não é?... ■■ bem, eu sei que *Então,*
não *a* por mal, que o senhor está falando. *E* agora eu não *estragar*
quero me amofinar, não tenho tempo p'ra a cabeça com
raiva nenhuma, atôa-atôa. Sou boi bravo nem cachorro
danado, *p'ra* me enraivar? Mas, *é bom* o senhor *pensar um*
■■ pouco, em antes de falar, ■ *hein*?

— Bom, eu *não* tenho nada com coisas dos outros...

— E, é. Quiser dar o recado, dá. Não quiser, faz
de conta.

Apitou. O trem.   *Me* *coisas pesadas)*

eu — Adeus, seu Miranda!... ■■ desculpe as ■■
que falei, que é porque *eu* estou meio ■■ *nervoso*...
está em
— Inda ■■ tempo de ter juízo, seu Laio! O
senhor pode merecer *um castigo* ■■ de Deus...

*: à mão, a tiro, ou a pau, o senhor
não pode comigo —*

Page from the fifth edition (1958) of Sagarana, *with Rosa's revisions (from Mary L. Daniel,* João Guimarães Rosa:
travessia literária, *1968; Thomas Cooper Library, University of South Carolina)*

represented only if it is captured in its multifaceted aspects. Rosa's depiction of the Brazilian backlands is not just an accurate description of a specific place but the re-creation, in as complete a manner as possible, of a wider reality that has no external boundaries; it is the representation of a region present and alive within the minds of the characters, a human, universal region that cannot be clearly delimited. Thus, Riobaldo is preoccupied throughout *Grande sertão: veredas* with defining the backlands but is unable to come up with a satisfactory definition. The novel includes a large number of attempted definitions, none of which can stand by itself; they complement and even contradict one another.

This wider regionalist perspective, based on the nonexclusive character of apparently opposed terms, is part of Rosa's general conception of reality as multiple and constantly changing, something that can only be fully represented in artistic terms if it is done in an all-encompassing manner that tries to express its dynamics and as many of its facets as possible. The world of Rosa's narratives is never static, nor is it ever built up on one level only. Myth and fantasy, as well as other levels of reality that transcend Western logic, are present in Rosa's narratives in many forms: superstitions, premonitions, apparitions, healers and fortune-tellers, mysticism, religious fears such as the terror of the devil, and wonder about mystery and the unknown. These elements are integral parts of the mentality of backlands people and can by no means be omitted; as Rosa told Lorenz, to understand the Brazilian way of life it is important to learn that knowledge is different from logic. Yet, he never completely abandoned the rationalist perspective. He was aware that the backlands person is an individual split between a mythical-sacred and a logical-rational world, and in his stories he condemns the supremacy of rationalism over the other ways of perceiving reality. He questions traditional realism but does not adopt the perspective either of the fantastic or of magical realism, and in this respect he distinguishes his works from those of the other great contemporary Latin American writers of fiction. Thus, he expresses a multiple worldview, in total accord with the cultural universe of the backlands inhabitant. The rejection of the dichotomic logic of the Cartesian tradition in favor of the search for a plurality of ways is represented by the leitmotiv "Tudo é e não é" (Everything is and is not) that is repeated throughout *Grande sertão: veredas.*

João Guimarães Rosa's work is plural, ambiguous, and marked by a constellation of different and often contradictory elements. In his writings imagination, rather than being opposed to "realism," is the basic condition of a more vital realism. In the same way, aestheticism, or formal concern, constitutes the proper way to express the writer's worldview. Regionalism, or the particular, is an indispensable element for attaining the universal. Regional and universal, mimetic and self-conscious, realist and antirealist, Rosa's work is, par excellence, an art of its century. It is an art of synthesis and relativity and represents perfectly the context from which it springs, a land that can only be fully apprehended when seen as hybrid and multicultural. There are no absolute values or pontifical assertions in his works; there are only paths to be traced, a wide spectrum of possibilities, all of which have the same chance of being actualized. Readers and critics have been venturing through these multiple paths of an inexhaustible wealth with increasing interest both in Brazil and abroad. Rosa's critical reputation continues to increase as does his reading public, and every new visit to his works is, as the author told Lorenz in regard to language, a "porta para o infinito" (door to the infinite).

Letters:

Rosa and Edoardo Bizzarri, *Correspondência com seu tradutor italiano* (São Paulo: Instituto Cultural Ítalo-Brasileiro, 1972);

Sagarana emotiva: cartas de João Guimarães Rosa a Paulo Dantas (São Paulo: Duas Cidades, 1975);

Ooó do Vovô! correspondência de João Guimarães Rosa, vovô Joãozinho, com Vera e Beatriz Helena Tess de setembro de 1966 a novembro de 1967 (São Paulo: EDUSP/ Imprensa Oficial, 2003);

Correspondência com seu tradutor alemão Curt Meyer-Clason (1958–1967), edited by Maria Apparecida Faria Marcondes Bussolotti, translated by Erlon José Paschoal (Rio de Janeiro: Nova Fronteira Belo Horizonte Ed. da UFMG, 2003);

Cartas a William Agel de Mello (Cotia: Ateliê, 2003).

Interviews:

Luis Harss and Barbara Dohmann, *Into the Main-stream: Conversations with Latin-American Writers* (New York: Harper & Row, 1967), pp. 137–172;

Günter W. Lorenz, "Guimarães Rosa," in his *Diálogo com a América Latina: panorama de uma literatura do futuro,* translated by Rosemary Costhek Abílio and Fredy de Souza Rodrigues (São Paulo: EPU, 1973), pp. 315–356.

Bibliographies:

Plinio Doyle, *Bibliografia de e sobre João Guimarães Rosa* (Rio de Janeiro: J. Olympio, 1968);

Doyle, "Bibliografia de João Guimarães Rosa" and "Bibliografia sôbre João Guimarães Rosa," in *Em memória de João Guimarães Rosa* (Rio de Janeiro: J. Olympio, 1968), pp. 199–217, 219–255;

Eduardo F. Coutinho, ed., *Guimarães Rosa, Fortuna Crítica,* volume 6 (Rio de Janeiro: Civilização Brasileira, 1983), pp. 19–34.

References:

Consuelo Albergaria, *Bruxo da linguagem no Grande sertão* (Rio de Janeiro: Tempo Brasileiro, 1977);

Sônia Maria Viegas Andrade, *A vereda trágica do "Grande sertão: veredas"* (Belo Horizonte: Loyola, 1985);

Leonardo Arroyo, *A cultura popular em* Grande sertão: veredas (Rio de Janeiro: J. Olympio, 1984);

Alaor Barbosa, *A epopéia Brasileira ou: para er Guimarães Rosa* (Goiânia: Imery, 1981);

Willi Bolle, *Fórmula e fábula: teste de uma gramática narrativa, aplicada aos contos de Guimarães Rosa* (São Paulo: Perspectiva, 1973);

Assis Brasil, *Guimarães Rosa* (Rio de Janeiro: Organização Simões, 1969);

Augusto de Campos, "Um lance de 'dês' do *Grande sertão,*" *Revista do Livro,* 4 (December 1959): 9–27;

Antônio Cândido, "O homem dos avessos," in his *Tese e antítese* (São Paulo: Nacional, 1964), pp. 119–140;

Maurice Capovilla, "'O recado do morro' de João Guimarães Rosa," *Revista do Livro,* 25 (March 1964): 131–142;

Manuel Antônio Castro, *O homem provisório no* Grande sertão (Rio de Janeiro: Tempo Brasileiro, 1976);

Nei Leandro de Castro, *Universo e vocabulário do Grande sertão* (Rio de Janeiro: J. Olympio, 1970; revised edition, Rio de Janeiro: Achiamé, 1982);

Nelly Novaes Coelho and Ivana Versiani, *Guimarães Rosa: dois estudos* (São Paulo: Quíron/INL, 1975);

Irlemar Chiampi Cortez, "Narração e metalinguagem em *Grande sertão: veredas,*" *Língua e literatura,* 2 (1973): 63–91;

Eduardo F. Coutinho, *The Process of Revitalization of the Language and Narrative Structure in the Fiction of João Guimarães Rosa and Julio Cortázar* (Valencia: Estudios Hispanófila, 1980);

Coutinho, *The "Synthesis" Novel in Latin America: A Study on João Guimarães Rosa's* Grande sertão: veredas (Chapel Hill, N.C.: NCSRLL, 1991);

Coutinho, ed., *Guimarães Rosa, Fortuna Crítica,* volume 6 (Rio de Janeiro: Civilização Brasileira, 1983);

Lenira Marques Covizzi, *O insólito em Guimarães Rosa e Borges* (São Paulo: Ática, 1978);

José Hildebrando Dacanal, "A epopéia riobaldiana," in his *Nova narrativa épica no Brasil* (Pôrto Alegre: Livraria Sulina, 1973), pp. 7–108;

Mary L. Daniel, "João Guimarães Rosa," *Studies in Short Fiction,* 8 (Winter 1971): 209–216;

Daniel, *João Guimarães Rosa: travessia literária* (Rio de Janeiro: J. Olympio, 1968);

Daniel, "Word Formation and Deformation in *Grande Sertão: veredas,*" *Luso-Brazilian Review,* 2 (Summer 1965): 81–97;

William Myron Davis, "Japanese Elements in *Grande sertão: veredas,*" *Romance Philology,* 29 (May 1976): 409–434;

Diálogo (Revista de Cultura), special Rosa issue, 8 (November 1956);

Lélia Parreira Duarte, ed., *Outras margens: estudos da obra de Guimarães Rosa* (Belo Horizonte: Autêntica, 2001);

Em memória de João Guimarães Rosa (Rio de Janeiro: J. Olympio, 1968);

Aglaêda Facó, *Guimarães Rosa: do icone ao símbolo* (Rio de Janeiro: J. Olympio, 1982);

Adonias Filho and others, *Guimarães Rosa* (Lisbon: Instituto Luso-Brasileiro, 1969);

David William Foster and Virginia Ramos Foster, eds., *Modern Latin American Literature,* 2 volumes (New York: Ungar, 1975), II: 282–295;

Fábio Freixeiro, *Da razão à emoção* (São Paulo: Nacional, 1968);

Walnice Nogueira Galvão, *As formas do falso* (São Paulo: Perspectiva, 1972);

Galvão, *Mitológica rosiana* (São Paulo: Ática, 1978);

José Carlos Garbuglio, *O mundo movente de Guimarães Rosa* (São Paulo: Ática, 1972);

Agrippino Grieco, *Poetas e prosadores do Brasil* (Rio de Janeiro: Conquista, 1968), pp. 276–278;

Russell G. Hamilton Jr., "The Contemporary Brazilian Short Story," in *To Find Something New: Studies in Contemporary Literature,* edited by Henry Grosshans (Pullman: Washington State University Press, 1969), pp. 118–135;

Dante Moreira Leite, *O amor romântico e outros temas* (São Paulo: Conselho Estadual de Cultura, 1964);

Luís Costa Lima, *A metamorfose do silêncio* (Rio de Janeiro: Eldorado, 1974);

Ana Maria Machado, *Recado do nome: leitura de Guimarães Rosa à luz do nome de seus personagens* (Rio de Janeiro: Imago, 1976);

Oswaldino Marques, "Canto e plumagem das palavras," in his *A seta e o alvo* (Rio de Janeiro: Instituto Nacional do Livro, MEC, 1957), pp. 9–128;

Wilson Martins, "Structural Perspectivism in Guimarães Rosa," in *The Brazilian Novel,* edited by Heitor Martins (Bloomington: Indiana University Publications, 1976), pp. 59–76;

Stephanie Merrim, *Logos and the Word* (New York: Peter Lang, 1983);

Adolfo Casais Monteiro, *O romance (teoria e crítica)* (Rio de Janeiro: J. Olympio, 1964), pp. 235–247;

Vera Novais, *Tutaméia: engenho e arte* (São Paulo: Perspectiva, 1989);

Benedito Nunes, "O amor na obra de Guimarães Rosa," in his *O dorso do tigre* (São Paulo: Perspectiva, 1969), pp. 203–210;

Franklin de Oliveira, "Guimarães Rosa," in *A literatura no Brasil,* second edition, volume 5: *Modernismo,* edited by Afrânio Coutinho (Rio de Janeiro: Editorial Sul Americana, 1968), pp. 402–449;

M. Cavalcanti Proença, *Trilhas no* Grande sertão (Rio de Janeiro: Serviço de Documentação MEC, 1958);

Myriam Ramsey and Paul B. Dixon, *Uma concordância do romance* Grande sertão, veredas *de João Guimarães Rosa* (Chapel Hill: University of North Carolina at Chapel Hill, Department of Romance Languages, 1989);

Júlia Conceição Fonseca Santos, *Nomes de personagens em Guimarães Rosa* (Rio de Janeiro: Instituto Nacional do Livro, 1971);

Paulo de Tarso Santos, *O diálogo no* Grande sertão: veredas (São Paulo: Hucitec, 1978);

Wendel Santos, *A construção do romance em Guimarães Rosa* (São Paulo: Ática, 1978);

Roberto Schwarz, "*Grande sertão* e *Dr. Faustus,*" in his *A sereia e o desconfiado: ensaios críticos* (Rio de Janeiro: Civilização Brasileira, 1965), pp. 28–36;

Suzi Frankl Sperber, *Caos e cosmos: leituras de Guimarães Rosa* (São Paulo: Duas cidades, 1976);

Sperber, *Guimarães Rosa: signo e sentimento* (São Paulo: Ática, 1982);

Alan Viggiano, *Itinerário de Riobaldo Tatarana* (Belo Horizonte: Comunicação/INL, 1974);

Jon S. Vincent, *João Guimarães Rosa* (Boston: Twayne, 1978);

Teresinha Souto Ward, *O discurso oral em* Grande sertão: veredas (São Paulo: Duas cidades, 1984);

Pedro Xistol, Augusto de Campos, and Haroldo de Campos, *Guimarães Rosa em três dimensões* (São Paulo: Conselho Estadual de Cultura, 1970).

Papers:

João Guimarães Rosa's manuscripts are at the Instituto de Estudos Brasileiros of the Universidade de São Paulo.

Murilo Rubião

(1 June 1916 – 16 September 1991)

Ana Cristina Pimenta da Costa Val
Faculdade de Pará de Minas

BOOKS: *O ex-mágico* (Rio de Janeiro: Universal, 1947);
A estrêla vermelha (Niterói: Hipocampo, 1953);
Os dragões e outros contos (Belo Horizonte: Movimento-Pespectiva, 1965); translated by Thomas Colchie as *The Ex-Magician and Other Stories* (New York: Harper & Row, 1979);
O convidado, preface by Jorge Schwartz (São Paulo: Quirón, 1974);
O pirotécnico Zacarias (São Paulo: Ática, 1974);
A casa do girassol vermelho (São Paulo: Ática, 1978);
O homem do boné cinzento e outras histórias (São Paulo: Ática, 1990).

Editions and Collections: *Murilo Rubião,* edited, with notes and a biographical study, by Jorge Schwartz (São Paulo: Abril, 1981);
Contos reunidos (São Paulo: Ática, 1998).

Murilo Rubião is credited with having introduced the genre of fantastic realism into Brazilian literature. His body of work as represented in his books consists of only thirty-three short stories, which were published in *O ex-mágico* (1947, The Ex-Magician), *A estrêla vermelha* (1953, The Red Star), and *Os dragões e outros contos* (1965, The Dragons and Other Stories; translated as *The Ex-Magician and Other Stories,* 1979). These same stories were later republished, with some revisions, in *O pirotécnico Zacarias* (1974, The Pyrotechnician Zacarias), *A casa do girassol vermelho* (1978, The House of the Red Sunflower), and *O homem do boné cinzento e outras histórias* (1990, The Man with the Gray Cap and Other Stories). *O convidado* (1974, The Guest) is Rubião's last original collection, with nine previously unpublished stories.

Murilo Eugênio Rubião was born on 1 June 1916 to Eugênio Rubião, a teacher and philologist, and Maria Antonieta Ferreira Rubião in Silvestre Ferraz (later renamed Carmo de Minas), in the state of Minas Gerais. The family lived there until Murilo was two, when they made a series of moves to other small towns in the state. When he was seven, the family settled in Belo Horizonte, the capital of Minas Gerais. During his school holidays Rubião often returned to the country-

Murilo Rubião (from the dust jacket for The Ex-Magician and Other Stories, *1979; Richland County Public Library)*

side, where he received the earliest influences on his writing: ghost stories, which were commonly told in rural communities, and circuses. The various attractions of circuses, such as magicians, clowns, and animals, are reflected in Rubião's use of magic and the fantastic transformations that people and animals undergo in his fiction. The family and intellectual experiences of his youth also had an important impact on his work.

Members of both sides of Rubião's family were writers. Two cousins on his mother's side, José Antônio Noronha and Godofredo Rangel, are well-known authors. On Rubião's father's side was a poet, cousin

Plínio Mota; an uncle, Álvares Rubião, and Rubião's paternal grandfather were also writers. Rubião's father was the author of several studies on linguistics and of poetry collections such as *No horto suave da legenda* (1923, In the Soft Garden of Legend) and *Trovas* (1938, Ballads). He was the owner of a large library that included the Bible, works on Greek mythology, Miguel de Cervantes' *Don Quixote* (1605, 1615), and the books of Joaquim Maria Machado de Assis. The availability of these books was important, since they gave Rubião his initial contact with fantastic literature. Eugênio Rubião also insisted that his son read the Portuguese classics, including works by João Batista de Almeida Garrett, Alexandre Herculano, and Camilo Castelo Branco.

Rubião began to write during his early years in school. He published love poems written for a girlfriend, but he destroyed these as soon as the relationship ended. The young poet admitted to the mediocrity of his writings. He broke with the Catholic religion at an early age and became an agnostic, a development that is expressed in some of his stories. In 1938 Rubião entered law school at the Universidade de Minas Gerais, and he worked as a journalist at the newspaper *Folha de Minas*.

Rubião published his first stories, such as "Eunice e as flores amarelas" (1941, Eunice and the Yellow Flowers) and "A Filosofia de Grão-Mogol" (1941, The Philosophy of Grão-Mogol), in the *Folha de Minas* and other periodicals. These stories focus on human abnormalities and madness. The atmosphere at the editorial room where Rubião worked was an important factor in his life at this time. It provided the opportunity for many discussions on literature and on the themes and processes of his own writings. His colleagues also recommended books that were not available in his father's library.

After Rubião started working at the *Folha de Minas*, he organized his stories into collections with the working titles "O dono do arco-íris" (The Owner of the Rainbow), "Grão-Mogol e outras histórias" (Grão-Mogol and Other Stories), "Marina, a intangível" (Marina, the Intangible), "As tentativas de João Eliotério" (The Attempts of João Eliotério), and "O ex-mágico da taberna Minhota" (The Ex-Magician from Minho's Tavern). He submitted the collections to eight different publishers, all of whom turned them down. The editors believed that the stories would not appeal to readers because of their unusual themes and would not be commercially successful.

Rubião then sent his stories to the writer Mário de Andrade, as many young authors did at the time. He wanted a more discerning opinion about his writing and felt that the respected author could offer such a judgment. Andrade responded, telling Rubião that he found the stories difficult to understand and saying that they reminded him of Franz Kafka's works. In one of his letters Andrade proposed that the author shorten the title of one collection from "O ex-mágico da taberna Minhota" to "O ex-mágico." In 1947 the collection was published in Rio de Janeiro with this shortened title.

Brazilian fiction up to 1947 was largely realist. Some authors, such as Aluísio de Azevedo and José Bento Monteiro Lobato, had made use of the unusual in their writings, but Rubião was the first Brazilian writer to devote his work entirely to the fantastic. With *O ex-mágico* fantastic realism had its true beginning in Brazilian fiction. The book consists of five parts, each preceded by a biblical epigraph: "Arco-íris" (Rainbow), "Mulheres" (Women), "Montanha" (Mountain), "Condenados" (Doomed), and "Família" (Family). The stories in the collection are "O ex-mágico"; "A casa do girassol vermelho"; "O pirotécnico Zacarias"; "Bárbara"; "Mariazinha"; "Elisa"; "A noiva da casa azul" (translated as "The Bride from the Blue Cottage," 1979); "Alfredo"; "O homem do boné cinzento"; "Marina, a intangível"; "Os três nomes de Godofredo" (translated as "Three Names for Godofredo," 1979); "O bom amigo Batista" (The Good Friend Batista); "Memórias do contabilista Pedro Inácio" (Memoirs of the Accountant Pedro Inácio); "Ofélia"; "Meu cachimbo e o mar" (My Pipe and the Sea); and "A cidade" (translated as "The City," 1979). The formal and thematic novelty introduced by the stories in *O ex-mágico* created a sharp debate among critics, who at first classified the work as Surrealistic, believing that madness was the subject of the stories. The innovative aspects of the stories were pointed out when Rubião was compared with two writers who had, in their own way, altered the structure and plot of the traditional short story: Eça de Queirós and Guy de Maupassant. These comparisons, however, became controversial when Kafka was mentioned. In their correspondence Andrade had informed Rubião of the similarity between his stories and Kafka's. Rubião was disappointed with this critique because he believed that he had created something unprecedented, both in a national and a worldwide literary context. He wanted to read the Czech writer's stories, but Andrade had only the original German version. Rubião finally read Kafka's works in 1957 in Spain.

In the early 1940s, while writing the stories that were published in *O ex-mágico*, Rubião started working in the civil service of the state of Minas Gerais. He often held positions of trust assigned by the governors of the state. From 1943 to 1951 he was appointed six times to the directorship of Rádio Inconfidência, a state-owned broadcasting service. In 1951 Rubião was appointed a cabinet officer by Governor Juscelino Kubitschek, over-

*Front cover of Rubião's 1974 collection (The Guest), his
last composed of entirely new stories (Joint
University Libraries, Nashville)*

"The Glass Flower," 1979); and "A lua" (translated as "The Moon," 1979). Each story is preceded by a biblical epigraph. The book itself opens with a similar epigraph, dedicated to all four stories. This distribution of epigraphs was maintained in *Os dragões e outros contos, O convidado,* and *A casa do girassol vermelho.* Rubião, however, removed the epigraphs to the stories as published in *O pirotécnico Zacarias* and *O homem do boné cinzento e outras histórias.*

In 1956 Rubião was sent to Madrid as chief officer of the Escritório Comercial do Brasil (Commercial Office of Brazil). His assignment was to develop commercial interchange between the two countries. He was also the cultural attaché at the Brazilian embassy in Spain. Rubião returned to Brazil in 1960 and was assigned to the editorial staff of *Minas Gerais,* the official daily paper of the state of Minas Gerais.

In 1965, twelve years after the publication of *A estrêla vermelha,* Rubião published *Os dragões e outros contos.* This collection is made up of twenty stories, four of which had not appeared in either *O ex-mágico* or *A estrêla vermelha:* "Os dragões" (translated as "The Dragons," 1979); "Teleco, o coelhinho" (translated as "Teleco, the Rabbit"); "A armadilha" (translated as "The Trap," 1979); and "O edifício" (translated as "The Edifice," 1979). The four stories of *A estrêla vermelha* were included in the volume, as well as twelve of the sixteen stories from *O ex-mágico:* "A noiva da casa azul"; "Bárbara"; "A casa do girassol vermelho"; "O homem do boné cinzento"; "Os três nomes de Godofredo"; "Alfredo"; "A cidade"; "Marina, a intangível"; "O ex-mágico" (with the longer version of the title, "O ex-mágico da taberna Minhota"); "Mariazinha"; "Elisa"; and "O pirotécnico Zacarias."

Rubião made a major contribution to both national and international literature when in 1966 he established *O suplemento literário de Minas Gerais* (The Literary Supplement of Minas Gerais). This supplement was associated with the official newspaper of Minas Gerais, initiated during the term of Governor Israel Pinheiro. Despite its title, the *Suplemento* also published articles on music, movies, and the plastic arts. It was a vanguard supplement, the principal aim of which was to further the careers of young writers and artists. Rubião published not only the works of young writers, however, but also those of famous ones. He wanted to give as many artists as possible the opportunity of being published and to provide a good weekly cultural section for the newspaper. The *Suplemento* had an important impact on the cultural life of Minas Gerais and encouraged an entire generation of writers from Belo Horizonte, which was dubbed the "Geração Suplemento" (Supplement Generation). These writers found in the paper a space for discussion of art and literature

seeing simultaneously the newspapers of the state press, *Folha de Minas* and *Imprensa Oficial.* In 1952 he was named Kubitschek's chief cabinet officer but resigned from this position that same year. In 1953 Rubião became the head of publicity for Kubitschek's electoral campaign to the state government.

Rubião published his second collection, *A estrêla vermelha,* in 1953. This book was one of twenty titles in the Hipocampo series, which included works by authors such as Carlos Drummond de Andrade, Manuel Bandeira, Jorge de Lima, Cecília Meireles, Cassiano Ricardo, and Henriqueta Lisboa. One hundred and twenty copies of each volume were printed for subscribers to the series, mostly authors and other intellectuals. *A estrêla vermelha* is made up of four previously unpublished stories: "A estrêla vermelha," later republished as "Bruma" (translated as "Misty," 1979) in *A casa do girassol vermelho;* "D. José não era" (translated as "Not Don José," 1979); "A flor de vidro" (translated as

as well as a place to publish their texts. This generation includes writers such as Humberto Werneck, Adão Ventura, Jaime Prado Gouvêa, Luiz Vilela, and Sérgio Sant'Anna.

As an independent, vanguard publication, *O suplemento literário de Minas Gerais* created a certain animosity among the provincial and more-traditional cultural organizations, such as the Academia Mineira de Letras (Minas Academy of Letters), the Academia Municipalista (Municipal Academy), and the Academia Mineira de Trovas (Minas Academy of Ballads). The supplement also faced several crises and was almost shut down. One of these crises was provoked by the publication of a poem that certain conservative politicians considered pornographic. These politicians put pressure on the governor of the state to close down the *Suplemento,* but he refused to do so. Because of these critical moments, the *Suplemento* began to lose its vigor, and, at times, publication ceased. Although *O suplemento literário de Minas Gerais* still exists, most writers consider Rubião's period as director to be the best phase of the publication. He remained in this position from 1966 to 1969, when he left to take over direction of the Departamento de Publicação e Divulgação da Imprensa Oficial (Publishing and Advertising Department of the Official Press). At this time Rubião was also appointed chairman of the Fundação de Arte de Ouro Preto (Art Foundation of Ouro Preto). In 1974 he became chairman of the Conselho Estatual de Cultura (Cultural State Council). In 1975 he retired as director of the Departamento de Publicação e Divulgação da Imprensa Oficial.

Before his retirement Rubião published two books in 1974, *O pirotécnico Zacarias* and *O convidado,* both of which reveal different nuances in the writer's approach to the fantastic. *O pirotécnico Zacarias* marked a turning point in Rubião's career as a writer because it was published by one of the major Brazilian publishing firms, Ática. This publication made his work known to a national reading public, whereas his previous books had been released by small, provincial publishers in limited editions. In 1974 Ática had begun a project of adapting works by Brazilian writers into texts for students and teachers of language and literature. They initiated this didactic series with *O pirotécnico Zacarias.* The mission of the series required fundamental changes in the format of Rubião's work. Each story was illustrated, and the text was published in sepia tones to highlight the mysterious atmosphere of the stories. The graphic changes made the stories more accessible to students. The selection of *O pirotécnico Zacarias* as a text represented in the admissions exams to the Universidade Federal de Minas Gerais (Federal University of Minas Gerais) and Pontifícia Universidade Católica de Minas

Gerais (Pontifical Catholic University of Minas Gerais) made the author's name better known to the general public. The PEN Clube do Brasil (PEN Club of Brazil) awarded Rubião a prize in the fiction category for the collection in 1975.

As Brazilian readers became more acquainted with Rubião's works, the critics reevaluated his importance to Brazilian literature. Many readers and critics noticed the similarities between his stories and the works of well-known Spanish American writers such as Jorge Luis Borges, Gabriel García Márquez, and Juan José Arreola. These authors were widely read in Brazil during the 1970s. Critics realized that Rubião had introduced fantastic literature in Brazil with the publication of *O ex-mágico* in 1947.

O pirotécnico Zacarias and the 1978 collection *A casa do girassol vermelho* emphasize two aspects of Rubião's work: his continuous rewriting of his stories and the excessive use of certain characteristics of the fantastic not found in the stories of *O convidado,* his last original collection. *O pirotécnico Zacarias* and *A casa do girassol vermelho* are both made up of stories previously published in *O ex-mágico, A estrêla vermelha,* and *Os dragões e outros contos.* The stories in *O pirotécnico Zacarias* are "O pirotécnico Zacarias"; "Bárbara"; "A cidade"; "O ex-mágico da taberna Minhota"; "A flor de vidro"; "Teleco, o coelhinho"; "O edifício"; and "Os dragões." *A casa do girassol vermelho* comprises "A casa do girassol vermelho"; "O homem do boné cinzento"; "Os três nomes de Godofredo"; "Marina, a intangível"; "Alfredo"; "D. José não era"; "A lua"; "A armadilha"; and "Bruma" (previously published as the title story of *A estrêla vermelha*).

Rubião spent a long time writing a story for the first time, as can be seen in the case of "O convidado," which took him twenty-six years to complete. One reason for this slow rate of work was the rigor with which he sought the right words and plots for his stories. His intense devotion to literature in his youth led to his decision not to marry. He considered the exercise of writing a solitary and exhaustive one, incompatible with the demands of marriage and family life.

Rubião's republishing of the twenty-four original stories from his first three collections involved a continuous exercise of writing and rewriting. Each republication of a story presented a new version, with an updating of language and a reworking of certain themes that delineate the characters' behavior. In the revised versions Rubião eliminated passages, replaced words or epigraphs, and ended up giving a new meaning to the stories. "A noiva da casa azul," first published in *O ex-mágico* and republished in *Os dragões e outros contos,* provides a good example. In the 1947 version the story ends with the protagonist's statement that he received,

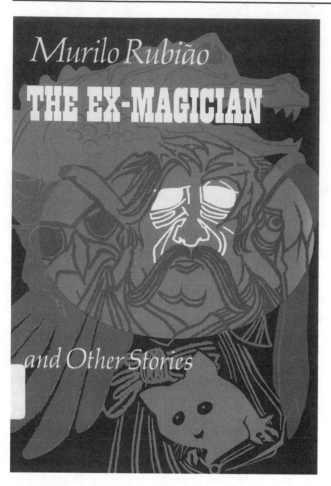

Dust jacket for the 1979 collection that is a translation of Rubião's
Os dragões e outros contos, *published in 1965*
(Richland County Public Library)

twenty years later, a letter from his fiancée, Dalila, who lived in the blue house of the title. This statement is a device to explain the protagonist's failures in meeting his fiancée. The elimination of this detail in the 1965 version of the story removes an explanation for the absurd events in the story, stressing the logic of the fantastic narrative. Besides changing the meaning of the stories, the rewriting allowed Rubião to change the language and update it.

In rewriting the stories, Rubião transformed his characters. Sometimes their names were changed, and sometimes their bodies were transformed. In "Teleco, o coelhinho," for example, Teleco is at first a naughty little rabbit who turns into different animals—a giraffe, a horse, a lion, a tiger, a peccary, or an extinct bird—to please his host, his neighbors, or children. Trying to become a human being, Teleco turns into a kangaroo called Barbosa, but his aim is only achieved when he finally transmutes into a dead child. The transformations of the little rabbit and the changes in its name

reflect Rubião's constant rewriting process of his stories.

The metamorphosis of characters is a recurring device in Rubião's fantastic fiction. This aspect of his work corresponds to the fantastic in many other twentieth-century narratives. Unlike fantastic literature of the nineteenth century, which employed ghosts and phantoms, Rubião's fiction introduces the unusual aspects of daily life and a critical attitude toward human beings and society.

Rubião frequently uses animals as characters in the stories of *O ex-mágico, A estrêla vermelha, Os dragões e outros contos, O pirotécnico Zacarias,* and *A casa do girassol vermelho.* They introduce the element of the unusual into the narratives and are a device for making critical observations on corrupt human behavior. The character metamorphoses and critical commentary reveal that, up to the publication of *A casa do girassol vermelho,* Rubião's notion of the fantastic was centered on individual human conflicts. This focus is not present in the stories of the 1974 collection *O convidado,* in which the fantastic assumes a social aspect and conflicts between humans and the social environment are emphasized. This social aspect is seen not only in the themes but also in the epigraphs for the stories.

There are nine stories in *O convidado:* "Epidólia," "Petúnia," "Aglaia," "A fila" (The Line), "O convidado," "Botão-de-rosa" (Rosebud), "O lodo" (The Mud), "O bloqueio" (The Blockade), and "Os comensais" (The Regular Guests). "A fila" and "Botão-de-rosa" focus on the search for employment, corruption, and social injustice. The protagonist of "A fila," Pererico, cannot find a job in the city, so he returns to his hometown. Corruption and lack of justice are seen when the attorneys make no effort to save the title character in "Botão-de-rosa" from the death penalty, which he was unjustly given.

The social aspect of the stories in *O convidado* is also seen in a change in the message of the epigraphs. In Rubião's earlier collections the epigraphs express perplexity, reflecting the characters' indignation at their absurd situations. In contrast, the epigraphs of *O convidado* foreshadow the characters' destiny, without a suggestion of their feeling indignant. The behavior of the characters in *O convidado* indicates that they cannot control their attitudes, which are determined by the social environment.

The prophetic tone of the epigraphs is suggested by the recurrence of involuntary acts committed by the protagonists of "Aglaia" and "Petúnia." These acts occur in a cyclical manner, without the possibility of an end. Rubião explained that this aspect of his stories reflected his own belief that eternity existed within life itself. He did not believe in life after death and had abandoned Catholicism in his youth. Religiosity is not exclusive to the stories in *O convidado;* it is also present in "O edifício," in which the uninterrupted construction of a building strangely moves toward heaven.

Some of Rubião's stories were republished in *Murilo Rubião* (1981), edited by Jorge Schwartz, and in the 1990 collection *O homem do boné cinzento e outras histórias.* In 1982 Rubião participated in the second Bienal Nestlé de Literatura (Nestlé Literature Biennial) and received an award in the short-story category. He achieved some international recognition after collections of his stories in translation were published in the United States, Germany, and Czechoslovakia. He announced plans for the publication of three novels— "O senhor Uber e o cavalo verde" (Mr. Uber and the Green Horse), "O esgoto" (The Sewer), and "O navio" (The Ship)—but he never completed these works.

Even after his retirement in 1975 Murilo Rubião continued to work as a civil servant of the state of Minas Gerais, serving as president and vice president of the Cultural State Council up to 1980. The Secretaria Municipal de Cultura da Prefeitura de Belo Horizonte (Belo Horizonte Municipal Secretary of Culture) organized the exhibition *Memória Viva* (Live Memory) in 1991 to honor the important living personalities representing the cultural life of Minas Gerais. Rubião was one of the first to be honored. On 12 September of that year the exhibition opened with the showing of a video made by Rodolfo Magalhães based on Rubião's story "O pirotécnico Zacarias." The writer was strongly touched by the video, as well as by the presence of his friends, who came to pay him homage. Rubião, however, died on 16 September 1991, before the conclusion of the homage. Brazil had lost its first and most important writer of fantastic literature.

Letters:

Mário e o pirotécnico aprendiz: cartas de Mário de Andrade e Murilo Rubião, edited, with an introduction and notes, by Marcos Antonio de Moraes (São Paulo: Instituto de Estudos Brasileiros/Giordano / Belo Horizonte: Editora Universidade Federal de Minas Gerais, 1995).

References:

Vera Lúcia Andrade, "A biblioteca fantástica de Murilo Rubião," in *A trama do arquivo,* edited by Wander Melo Miranda (Belo Horizonte: Editora Universidade Federal de Minas Gerais, 1995), pp. 45– 52;

David Arrigucci, "Minas, assombros e anedotas," *Suplemento literário de Minas Gerais,* 21 February 1987, pp. 1–4;

Audemaro Taranto Goulart, *O conto fantástico de Murilo Rubião* (Belo Horizonte: Lê, 1995);

Hélio Pellegrino, "Espelho dos escritores," *Suplemento literário de Minas Gerais,* 14 February 1987, p. 5;

Renard Perez, "A trajetória de um escritor," *Suplemento literário de Minas Gerais,* 7 February 1987, pp. 2–3;

Jorge Schwartz, *Murilo Rubião, a poética do uroboro* (São Paulo: Ática, 1981);

Humberto Werneck, *O desatino da rapaziada: jornalistas e escritores em Minas Gerais* (São Paulo: Letras, 1992).

Fernando Sabino
(Fernando Tavares Sabino)
(12 October 1923 – 11 October 2004)

Maria Angélica Lopes
University of South Carolina

BOOKS: *Os grilos não cantam mais: cantos* (Rio de Janeiro: Pongetti, 1941);

A marca: novela (Rio de Janeiro: J. Olympio, 1944);

A cidade vazia: crônicas e histórias de Nova York (Rio de Janeiro: O Cruzeiro, 1950);

A vida real: novelas (Rio de Janeiro: A Noite, 1952);

O encontro marcado: romance (Rio de Janeiro: Civilização Brasileira, 1956); translated by John Procter as *A Time to Meet* (London: Souvenir, 1967);

O homem nu (Rio de Janeiro: Editora do Autor, 1960);

A mulher do vizinho: sententa crônicas e histórias curtas (Rio de Janeiro: Editora do Autor, 1962);

A companheira de viagem: crônicas (Rio de Janeiro: Editora do Autor, 1965);

A inglêsa deslumbrada (Rio de Janeiro: Sabiá, 1967);

Gente: crônicas e reminiscências, 2 volumes (Rio de Janeiro: Record, 1975);

Deixa o Alfredo falar! (Rio de Janeiro: Record, 1976);

O encontro das águas: crônica irreverente de uma cidade tropical (Rio de Janeiro: Record, 1977);

O grande mentecapto—relato das aventuras e desventuras de Viramundo e de suas inenarráveis peregrinações: romance (Rio de Janeiro: Record, 1979);

A falta que ela me faz (Rio de Janeiro: Record, 1980);

O menino no espelho: romance (Rio de Janeiro: Record, 1982);

O gatu sou eu! (Rio de Janeiro: Record, 1983);

Macacos me mordam (Rio de Janeiro: Record, 1984);

A vitória da infância (São Paulo: Editora Nacional, 1984);

A faca de dois gumes (Rio de Janeiro: Record, 1985);

O pintor que pintou o sete (São Paulo: Berlendis & Vertechia, 1986);

Os melhores contos (Rio de Janeiro: Record, 1986);

As melhores histórias (Rio de Janeiro: Record, 1986);

As melhores crônicas (Rio de Janeiro: Record, 1986);

O tabuleiro de damas (Rio de Janeiro: Record, 1988);

De cabeça para baixo (Rio de Janeiro: Record, 1989);

A volta por cima (Rio de Janeiro: Record, 1990);

Zélia, uma paixão (Rio de Janeiro: Record, 1991);

Aqui estamos todos nus (Rio de Janeiro: Record, 1993);

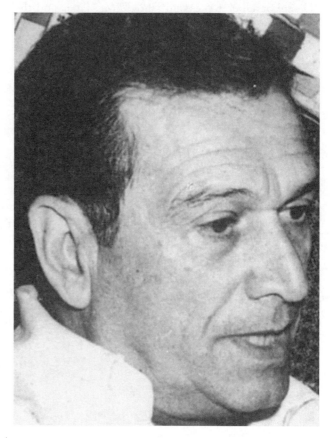

Fernando Sabino (from O tabuleiro de damas, *1988; Thomas Cooper Library, University of South Carolina)*

Com a graça de Deus (Rio de Janeiro: Record, 1994);

O outro gume da faca (Sao Paulo: Ática, 1996);

Obra reunida, 3 volumes (Rio de Janeiro: Nova Aguilar, 1996);

O homem feito (São Paulo: Ática, 1998);

Amor de Capitu—leitura fiel do romance de Machado de Assis sem o narrador Dom Casmurro: recriação literária (São Paulo: Ática, 1998);

No fim dá certo: se não deu, é porque não chegou ao fim (Rio de Janeiro: Record, 1998);

O galo músico: contos e novelas da juventude á maturidade, do desejo ao amor (Rio de Janeiro: Record, 1998);

A chave do enigma (Rio de Janeiro: Record, 1999);

Cara ou coroa?: antologia (São Paulo: Ática, 2000);

Livro aberto: páginas soltas ao longo do tempo (Rio de Janeiro: Record, 2001);

Os caçadores de mentira (Rio de Janeiro: Rocco, 2003);

Os movimentos simulados (Rio de Janeiro: Record, 2004).

Editions and Collections: *Fernando Sabino,* edited by Flora Christina Bender (São Paulo: Abril Educação, 1980);

Martini seco (São Paulo: Ática, 1987);

O bom ladrão (São Paulo: Ática, 1992);

Os restos mortais (São Paulo: Ática, 1993);

A nudez da verdade (São Paulo: Ática, 1994);

Um corpo de mulher (São Paulo: Ática, 1997).

OTHER: Gustave Flaubert, *Lugares-comuns,* translated by Sabino (Rio de Janeiro: Ministério da Educação e Saúde, Serviço de Documentação, 1952);

Shel Silverstein, *A árvore generosa,* translated by Sabino (Rio de Janeiro: Record, [1990s]).

Best known for his *crônicas* (short pieces for newspapers), Fernando Sabino was also the author of a major twentieth-century Brazilian novel, *O encontro marcado* (1956; translated as *A Time to Meet,* 1967). Sabino received prestigious awards for his works: the Brazilian Book Chamber's Jabuti (a popular indigenous name for "tortoise") Prize in 1980 for *O grande mentecapto—relato das aventuras e desventuras de Viramundo e de suas inenarráveis peregrinações* (1979, The Great Madman—A Report of the Adventures of Viramundo and his Indescribable Wanderings), a second Jabuti in 2002 for *Livro alberto: páginas soltas ao longo do tempo* (2001, Open Book: Loose Pages Throughout Time), and the foremost Brazilian literature prize, the Brazilian Academy of Letters' Machado de Assis, in 1999 for his body of work. Sabino's career as a writer, which spanned more than six decades, also included work in cinema. He wrote screenplays for documentaries on literature and the other arts and for a project on commercial fairs, for which he traveled extensively abroad. As the founder and part-owner of two publishing houses, Editora do Autor (The Author's Publishing House) and Sabiá, Sabino further played an important role in the literary world by helping to launch the works of many Brazilian and Spanish American writers.

Fernando Tavares Sabino was born 12 October 1923 in Belo Horizonte, the son of Domingos and Odete Sabino. Domingos Sabino was a small businessman, and Odete was a housewife. Sabino grew up in Minas Gerais, a state with long and proud political and artistic traditions. In elementary school Sabino was already concerned with grammar and syntax, and he was intent on reading Portu-

guese and Brazilian classics as practice toward becoming a writer. His efforts paid off—as a middle-school student he won prizes in several magazine and radio-sponsored writing contests. At thirteen he published a story in the state police magazine, *Argus.* In 1941 he published his first book, *Os grilos não cantam mais* (Crickets No Longer Sing), a collection of stories that received praise from established critics such as Tristão de Ataide, Sérgio Milliet, Álvaro Lins, and the great Mário de Andrade, the "papa do modernismo" (Pope of Modernism).

Resourceful and versatile, by his late teens Sabino had accomplished much. He was a champion swimmer, a private Portuguese tutor, a children's radio-show host, a part-time public servant, a newspaper reporter, and a member of a group of writers (with poet and psychiatrist Hélio Pellegrino, poet and *cronista* Paulo Mendes Campos, and short-story writer and journalist Otto Lara Resende) that eventually found an important place in Brazil's literary history. He started law school in Belo Horizonte in 1942, but he transferred to the Universidade do Brasil in Rio de Janeiro, where he graduated in 1946. At eighteen he became engaged to Helena, the beautiful younger daughter of Minas Gerais's governor, Benedito Valadares.

Sabino followed up the precocious *Os grilos não cantam mais* with the well-received *A marca* (1944, The Brand), the first of the many novellas he wrote. In 1946 Sabino, Helena, and their daughter Eliana, born 26 March 1945, moved to New York City, where Sabino worked at the Brazilian Consulate. He later published the pieces he wrote in New York in the volume *A cidade vazia: crônicas e histórias de Nova York* (1950, Deserted City: *Crônicas* and Tales of New York). In 1948 Sabino and his family returned to Rio de Janeiro. His second novella, *A vida real* (Real Life), appeared in 1952, as did *Lugares-comuns* (Commonplaces), a Brazilian dictionary based on Gustave Flaubert's *Dictionnaire des Idées reçues,* a text he had translated.

O encontro marcado, Sabino's first novel, was published in 1956. It is his most famous and appreciated book, and it has been translated into English, Dutch, German, Italian, and Spanish. The novel may be seen as a roman à clef since it tells the story of two young male friends who are composites of the author and his lifelong literary friends from Belo Horizonte, including Resende, Pellegrino, and Campos. Almost fifty years after its publication, *O encontro marcado* continues to receive critical and popular acclaim as an extraordinary portrait of a generation, written with rare courage and generosity. The novel is marked by the existential anguish that characterized much of the major fiction written in Brazil in the 1950s.

Over the years Sabino and Helena had three more children, daughters Eleonora and Virginia and a son, Pedro, but they eventually divorced. In 1964 Sabino married his second wife, the actress Ana Beatriz, with whom

*Cover for the 1986 collection (The Best Tales) of Sabino's tales
(Thomas Cooper Library, University of South Carolina)*

he had three children, Bernardo, Mariana, and Verônica. Sabino later chose to move abroad again, this time taking his wife and seven children to London, where he had been appointed the Brazilian cultural attaché. His autobiographical sketches in *O tabuleiro de damas* (1988, Checkerboard) examine several stages of his private and public lives during this time, including the genesis and fortune of his books and movies.

Over his career Sabino published many stories, novellas, and novels, as well as his correspondence with other writers. He also wrote children's literature, translated works, and produced screenplays for the Brazilian National Film Office. In 1973 he even founded a movie company, Bem-te-vi (Lovely Bird), and made documentary movies about Brazilian writers.

The bulk of Sabino's literary production, however, consists of *crônicas*. Regarded with a mixture of suspicion and condescension in more rigid literary circles, where they are seen as tainted by journalism, *crônicas* actually make great demands on the writer in terms of discipline and style. Brazilian examples resemble columns in United States newspapers, although they are more akin to the literary essay. The literary element does not, however, preclude the use of colloquial Brazilian Portuguese with a liberal sprinkling of slang, features stressed by modernist prose and poetry of the 1920s.

Although the name *crônicas* is reminiscent of long, dry Portuguese medieval and Renaissance chronicles, the best of these pieces are sensitive and humorous. At the turn of the twentieth century Joaquim Maria Machado de Assis became the first famous fiction *cronista,* and several other distinguished Brazilian writers followed in his footsteps. In the early 1900s *crônicas* were often didactic or polemic in their attempts to influence attitudes on subjects such as women's education and divorce or cast aspersions on writers or the clergy. Later, in the second half of the twentieth century, *crônicas* became lighter and more amusing. The genre not only provided Brazilian writers a living as journalists but also allowed them to hone their literary skills. The golden age of *crônicas* was the 1960s, and in the second half of the twentieth century significant authors, such as Carlos Drummond de Andrade, Clarice Lispector, Rubem Braga, and Rachel de Queiroz, excelled in the genre. Through *crônicas* these writers gained an immediate popularity that their other work, less accessible to many readers, would not have garnered, and major *cronistas* are still household names throughout Brazil.

Flexible in format, *crônicas* are stories, meditations, scenes, dialogues, poems, or a mixture of these forms and genres. Conveying the author's vision and temperament, they generally "chronicle" or tell of daily events, exploring relationships within and defining communities. For example, a favorite subject of Sabino and others, Cariocas (natives of the city of Rio de Janeiro), represent a fertile *crônica* matrix. Beyond Rio de Janeiro's historical importance as the capital of Brazil and the former seat of the Portuguese Empire, the city also possesses the beauty and local color necessary to keep not only its inhabitants but the rest of the country entertained. Furthermore, in the 1950s Rio de Janeiro experienced several events that provided fertile material for *crônicas,* including severe water rationing, the dawn of television with its soap operas, and Getúlio Vargas's resignation from the presidency and suicide.

Sabino was one of the outstanding post–World War II *cronistas* who became popular for their language and sense of humor, and Sabino was particularly masterful at capturing the spirit of his environment. Sabino's best *crônicas* are perceptive, straightforward, poetic, and linguistically exemplary. Like his friend and mentor Mário de Andrade, Sabino never ceased to work as a stylist in search of simplicity. Several of his pieces, including "O homem nu" (The Naked Man), "Passeio" (Stroll), "O gato sou eu!" (The Cat Is Me!), and "A companheira de viagem" (Travel Companion), have become famous. His *crônicas* often appeared every day of the week in the *Jornal do Brasil* (Brazilian Journal), as well as in other newspapers and magazines in Rio de Janeiro. They were also syndicated throughout Brazil, and finally collected by the author into several books.

Sabino classified his short pieces according to three categories: *crônica, história* (story), and *conto* (short story, tale). The difference, according to him, is that *crônicas* are reflections, whereas *histórias* relate the author's personal experience as a first-person narrative, and *contos* feature third-person narration. Sabino's collections of short journalistic works vary in their rubric: three are labeled as *crônicas,* seven as *crônicas e histórias,* ten as *crônicas e contos,* and two as *histórias.*

In 1960 Sabino published *O homem nu,* a group of *contos* and *crônicas* dealing with life in Rio de Janeiro. The title of the volume is taken from his most famous *crônica,* a skillful extended joke on nudity, a motif that recurred in Sabino's later work. Like Honoré de Balzac, Flaubert, Machado de Assis, and Autran Dourado, Sabino refashioned themes and motives. He explained that for him newspapers are a training ground for trying out topics and techniques for his fiction.

O homem nu and the next three collections of *crônicas* were published by Sabino's own publishing company, Editora do Autor. Sabino and his friend and fellow *cronista,* Braga, founded the firm in Rio de Janeiro in 1960. In 1962 he published *A mulher do vizinho* (The Neighbor's Wife). In 1965 *A companheira de viagem* was published. The title story of this collection has two traits typical of Sabino: the use of animals as characters and the use of jokes fashioned from daily life. A mysterious travel companion on a trip across the Atlantic Ocean turns out to be a female monkey. Next, *A inglêsa deslumbrada* (1967, The Starstruck Englishwoman), which features more *crônicas* and *contos,* brought stories based on English life to Brazilian readers. The publisher was Sabiá, founded in 1967, the new and successful publishing house where Sabino was director and partner. This publishing house, like its predecessor Editora do Autor, brought to light important new Brazilian writers and a few Spanish American authors.

Because he started his writing career as a teenager in the early 1940s, Sabino was able to meet many distinguished writers and artists. He corresponded with major authors such as Mário de Andrade, Drummond de Andrade, and Lispector. His biographical sketches in *Gente: crônicas e reminiscências* (1975, Persons: Crônicas and Reminiscences) are perceptive and well written. They are cited by critics and historians such as Wilson Martins in his *Historia da inteligência brasileira* (1976–1979, A History of Brazilian Intelligence). *Gente* and Sabino's subsequent books—with very few exceptions—were published by Editora Record in Rio de Janeiro.

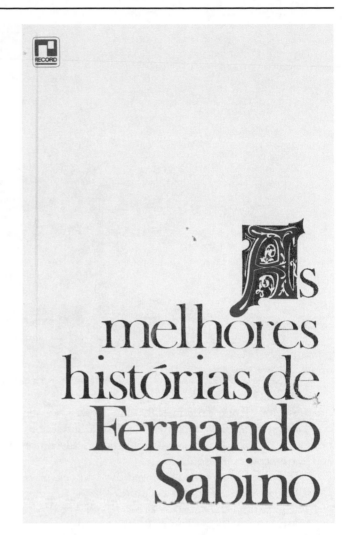

Cover for the 1986 collection (The Best Stories) of Sabino's short stories (Thomas Cooper Library, University of South Carolina)

Sabino's next book, *O encontro das águas* (1977, Meeting of the Waters), has the descriptive subtitle *crônica irreverente de uma cidade tropical* (irreverent crônicas about a tropical city). In Brazil "the meeting of the waters" refers to the merging of the Solimões and Negro Rivers as they form the Amazon River near the city of Manaus, the subject of the book.

In 1979 Sabino finished and published a picaresque novel, *O grande mentecapto,* that he had begun twenty-three years earlier. The novel develops the adventures of its protagonist, Geraldo Viramundo (World Voyager), in Sabino's home state of Minas Gerais. Part Don Quixote and part country bumpkin, Viramundo travels both in the world and against it. He can be seen as an affectionate and respectful take on Jesus Christ—the Jesus who did not shun the humble, the marginal, and the mad. In fact, Viramundo later appears briefly in the author's rendition of the gospel, *Com a graça de Deus* (1994, With God's Grace). *O grande mentecapto* was critically acclaimed and received

Sabino at Copacabana Beach (from Arnaldo Bloch, Fernando Sabino: reencontro, *2000; Bruccoli Clark Layman Archives)*

the prestigious Jabuti Prize in 1980. The work was a success because of Sabino's mixture of burlesque and seriousness in portraying his innocent protagonist's adventures and idiosyncratic philosophy.

O grande mentecapto was followed by *A falta que ela me faz* (1980, How I Miss Her), a collection of *contos* and *crônicas.* The next novel, *O menino no espelho* (1982, The Boy in the Mirror), is autobiographical, focusing on the author's childhood. This work was a commercial success, and it was well received by critics. In fact, childhood became an increasingly important theme for the author. A devoted father of seven children, he often made them the subject of his *crônicas,* and he began to write and translate stories for children.

In 1983 Sabino published another set of *contos* and *crônicas, O gato sou eu!* In the title story a patient resists his analyst's interpretations. *Macacos me mordam* (I'll Be Darned), a children's story, and *A vitória da infância* (Victory of Childhood), another collection of *crônicas* and *histórias,* appeared in 1984.

In 1985 Sabino tried his hand at the thriller, a genre that was becoming popular among Brazilian readers. The three novellas of *A faca de dois gumes* (The Two-Bladed Knife) explore the ambiguity and coincidences of different crimes ranging from robbery to murder. The following year Sabino published another children's book with a pun for a title, *O pintor que pintou o sete* (1986, The Painter Who Painted the Town Red). This year was a busy one for Sabino. He also published three anthologies under specific rubrics: *Os melhores contos* (The Best Tales), *As melhores*

histórias (The Best Stories), and *As melhores crônicas* (The Best Chronicles). Like his other collections, the distinction between *histórias* and *crônicas* is fluid here.

In 1988 Sabino published *O tabuleiro de damas,* which features a successful series of autobiographical sketches discussing the author's writing and touching discreetly on his personal life. Published the following year, *De cabeça para baixo* (Upside Down) is a collection of travel stories from a writer who enjoys traveling and has visited five continents. In 1990 *A volta por cima* (Successful Return) featured another round of *crônicas* and *histórias.*

Sabino's reputation was tested, however, by the publication of *Zélia, uma paixão* (Zelia, A Passionate Affair) in 1991. Written in forty days, the work is classified as a novel, but it is actually a fictional biography paid for by its subject, Zélia Cardoso de Mello, Brazil's secretary of economy under President Collor de Mello. Mello had been instrumental in an early-1990s financial measure that included the freezing of the population's savings and their subsequent return at a fraction of their original value. Deemed "repulsive," the book excited the ire of critics and readers. Neither the defense of Sabino by writers such as Jorge Amado, nor Sabino's bequeathing his substantial author's rights to needy children succeeded in pacifying an angry readership that felt betrayed. The author steadfastly insisted on his admiration for the book's subject and his belief in the book as a valid literary challenge. Sabino's choice of an unpopular public figure for the subject of a book was, however, an incident that impacted his personal life and career. After the problems surrounding the book,

Sabino temporarily became reclusive and distrustful of critics, fellow writers, and readers.

The writer's subsequent production consisted of more-ambitious works besides novellas, *crônicas,* and stories. *Aqui estamos todos nus* (We Are All Naked Here) was published in 1993. It consists of three novellas that were later published separately by Ática: *Um corpo de mulher* (1997, A Woman's Body), *A nudez da verdade* (1994, The Naked Truth), and *Os restos mortais* (1993, The Mortal Remains). Sabino then returned to tranquillity and optimism with *Com a graça de Deus* in 1994. Considered another tour de force for the author, the work is offered as "uma leitrua fiel do Evangelho, inspirada no humor de Jesus" (a faithful reading of the Gospel inspired by Jesus' humor). After an uncharacteristically erudite introduction in which he mentions his illustrious predecessors, Sabino proceeds to tell the life of Christ. He does so through a remarkable interweaving of the Gospels, his own interpretations of events, citations from his own and others' writings, and Brazilian jokes and diction. The work is written in a simple, flowing style.

After *Com a graça de Deus,* Sabino published more books with the São Paulo firm Ática: *O outro gume da faca* (1996, The Other Blade of the Knife) and *O homem feito* (1998, The Adult Male). In 1996 Aguilar in Rio de Janeiro brought out the three volumes of Sabino's *Obra reunida* (Collected Works). Two years later Ática published *Amor de Capitu—leitura fiel do romance de Machado de Assis sem o narrador Dom Casmurro: recriação literária* (Capitu's Love–A Faithful Reading of the Machado de Assis Novel Without the Narrator, Dom Casmurro: A Literary Recreation). This book features the most famous female character in Brazilian fiction, the protagonist of Machado de Assis's *Dom Casmurro* (1899; translated as *Dom Casmurro,* 1953). More *crônicas* and stories followed: *No fim dá certo* (1998, Everything Works Out in the End); *O galo músico* (1998, The Musical Rooster); and *A chave do enigma* (1999, The Key to the Riddle), all published by Record. In 2000 Sabino published another *crônica* and story collection, *Cara ou coroa?* (Heads or Tails?).

In 1999 Sabino was awarded the most prestigious literary prize in Brazil, the Machado de Assis. The award seems particularly appropriate because critics have long remarked that Sabino's concern with language has given his Portuguese a fluidity akin to that of Machado de Assis. Sabino's thank-you note for the prize was "minha obra póstuma antecipada" (the preview of my posthumous volume), an ambitious collection of different pieces covering the years 1939 (the date of his first *crônica*) to 1998. He titled it *Livro aberto: páginas soltas ao longo do tempo.* The volume includes *crônicas,* short stories, criticism, and letters from his literary mentors. In 2001 Sabino also published his correspondence with the late Lispector under the title *Cartas perto do coração* (Letters Near My Heart). Lispector,

one of the most prominent twentieth-century Brazilian fiction writers, had been Sabino's friend and colleague in Rio de Janeiro. After a long battle with cancer Sabino died in his Rio de Janeiro home on 11 October 2004.

A popular writer whose works have been reprinted often, Fernando Sabino is recognized as one of the creators of the modern *crônica.* Although many critics have remarked that Sabino's masterpiece novel *O encontro marcado* is enough to assure his place in literary history, his mastery of language and portrayal of daily life in both *crônicas* and short fiction have also played a major role in securing his distinguished place in twentieth-century Brazilian literature.

Letters:

Cartas a um jovem escritor e suas repostas de Fernando Tavares Sabino a Mário de Andrade (Rio de Janeiro: Record, 1981);

Cartas perto do coração, correspondência com Clarice Lispector (Rio de Janeiro: Record, 2001);

Cartas na mesa: correspondência com Paulo Mendes Campos, Otto Lara Resende e Hélio Pellegrino (Rio de Janeiro: Record, 2002).

References:

João de Almeida, "Da denotação a conotação," *Revista de Letras (São Paulo),* 28 (1988): 9–18;

Almeida, "Preconceito em disfarce," *Alfa: Revista de Linguística,* 39 (1970): 57–70;

Arnaldo Bloch, *Fernando Sabino: reencontro* (Rio de Janeiro: Relume Dumará/Secretaria Municipal de Cultura, 2000);

Odilon Helou Fleury, "A produção de sentido em uma narrativa de Fernando Sabino," *Alfa: Revista de Linguística,* 39 (1995): 71–85;

Victor Knoll, "O encontro marcado: falência de ser," *Revista da Faculdade de Filosofia e Ciências Humanas da Universidade Federal de Minas Gerais,* 15 (1962): 383–396;

Celeste Dolores Mann, "O Geraldo Viramundo de 'O grande mentecapto': um carnivalizador carnavalizado," *Torre de Papel,* 3, no. 2 (Summer 1993): 37–44;

Marco Aurelio Matos, "Fernando Sabino: o cotidiano como aventura," *Suplemento Literário de Minas Gerais,* 19, no. 918 (5 May 1984): 8–9;

Cremilda Medina, "O louco, o menino e o sonho estão soltos em Sabino," *Suplemento Literário de Minas Gerais,* 19, no. 942 (20 October 1984): 8;

Lygia Maria Moraes, "O encontro marcado," *Suplemento Literário de Minas Gerais,* 18, nos. 891–892 (5 November 1983): 6–7;

Eduardo Portella, "Fernando Sabino: dialéctica de la angustia," *Nueva Narrativa Hispanoamericana,* 3, no. 1 (1973): 51–55.

Affonso Romano de Sant'Anna

(27 March 1937 -)

Susan Canty Quinlan

University of Georgia

BOOKS: *4 poetas: Affonso Romano de Sant'Anna, Teresinha Alves Pereira, Silviano Santiago, Domingos Muchon* (Belo Horizonte: Faculdade de Filosofia, Universidade de Minas Gerais, 1960);

O desemprego do poeta (Belo Horizonte: Imprensa Universitária de Minas Gerais, 1962);

Violão de rua, by Sant'Anna and others, 3 volumes (Rio de Janeiro: Civilização Brasileira, 1962–1963);

Canto e palavra (Minas Gerais: Imprensa Oficial, 1965);

Poesia viva, edited by Moacyr Felix (Rio de Janeiro: Civilização Brasileira, 1968);

Drummond, o "gauche" no tempo (Rio de Janeiro: Lia, 1972); republished as *Carlos Drummond de Andrade: análise da obra* (Rio de Janeiro: Ário, 1977);

Análise estrutural de romances brasileiros (Petrópolis: Vozes, 1973);

Autores para vestibular: estrutura e interpretação de textos. Aluísio Azevedo, Machado de Assis, Autran Dourado, Carlos Drummond de Andrade, Manuel Bandeira, by Sant'Anna, Dirce Côrtes Riedel, and Marlene de Castro Correia (Petrópolis: Vozes, 1973);

Analíses de Xenócrates, o caçador de esmeraldas: Profissão de fé de Olavo Bilac (Rio de Janeiro: PUC, 1975);

Poesia sobre poesia (Rio de Janeiro: Imago, 1975);

Música popular e moderna poesia brasileira (Petrópolis: Vozes, 1977; revised and enlarged, 1980);

Por um novo conceito da literatura brasileira (Rio de Janeiro: Eldorado, 1977);

Lições de casa: exercícios de imaginação, by Sant'Anna and Julieta de Godoy Ladeira (São Paulo: Liveria Cultura, 1978);

A grande fala do índio Guarani perdido na história e outros derrotas: moderno Popol Vuh (São Paulo: Summus, 1978);

Que país é este? e outros poemas (Rio de Janeiro: Civilização Brasileira, 1980);

A morte da baleia (Rio de Janeiro: Berlindes & Vertecchia, 1981);

Estória dos sofrimentos, morte e ressureição do Senhor Jesus Cristo na pintura de Emeric Marcier (Rio de Janeiro: Pinakotheke, 1983);

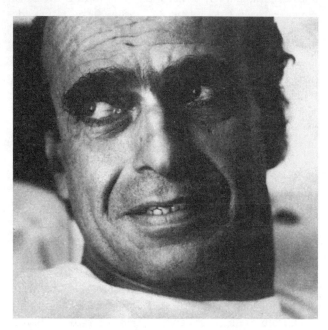

Affonso Romano de Sant'Anna (photograph by Romulo Fritscher; from the cover for Que país é este? *1990; Heard Library, Vanderbilt University)*

O livro do seminário: ensaios. Bienal Nestlé de Literatura Brasileira, 1982, by Sant'Anna and others, edited by Domício Proença Filho (São Paulo: LR, 1983);

Crônicas mineiras, by Sant'Anna and others (Rio de Janeiro: Ática, 1984);

Política e paixão (Rio de Janeiro: Rocco, 1984);

O canibalismo amoroso: o desejo e a interdição em nossa cultura através da poesia (São Paulo: Brasiliense, 1984);

Paródia paráfrase & cia (São Paulo: Ática, 1985);

Como se faz literatura (Petrópolis: Vozes, 1985); enlarged as *A sedução da palavra* (Brasília: Letraviva, 2000);

A catedral de Colônia e outros poemas (Rio de Janeiro: Rocco, 1985);

1950 almanaque, by Sant'Anna and others (Rio de Janeiro: João Fortes Engenharia / Editora Index, 1985);

A mulher madura (Rio de Janeiro: Rocco, 1986);

A poesia possível: poesia reunida (Rio de Janeiro: Rocco, 1987);

O imaginário a dois: textos escolhidos, by Sant'Anna and Marina Colasanti (Rio de Janeiro: Art Bureau, 1987);

O homem que conheceu o amor (Rio de Janeiro: Rocco, 1988);

A raiz quadrada do absurdo (Rio de Janeiro: Rocco, 1989);

Gente do aço, by Sant'Anna, Antônio Houaiss, Herculano Gomes Mathias, and Jamie Stewart-Granger (Rio de Janeiro: Index/Siderurgia Brasileira, 1989);

Ouro: sua história, seus encantos, seu valor, by Sant'Anna and others (Rio de Janeiro: Salamandra, 1989); translated as *Gold: Its History, Its Charm, Its Value* (Rio de Janeiro: Salamandra, 1997);

Anchieta, by Sant'Anna, Ana Maria de Bulhões Carvalho, and Hugo Leal (Rio de Janeiro: Salamandra/Samarco Mineração, 1989);

Hélio Pellegrino, a-Deus: psycanálise e religião. Textos e depoimentos, by Sant'Anna and others, edited by João Carlos Moura (Petrópolis: Vozes, 1990);

Agosto 1991: estavámos em Moscou, by Sant'Anna and Colasanti (São Paulo: Melhoramento, 1991);

De que ri a Mona Lisa? (Rio de Janeiro: Rocco, 1991);

O lado esquerdo do meu peito: livro de aprendiazgens (Rio de Janeiro: Rocco, 1991);

Os melhores poemas de Affonso Romano de Sant'Anna, edited by Donaldo Schüler (São Paulo: Global, 1991);

Auto-retratos, by Sant'Anna and Giovani Ricciardi (São Paulo: Martins Fontes, 1991);

Transformação, by Sant'Anna, Rosiska Darcy de Oliveira, and Carmen Lent (Rio de Janeiro: Diferença, 1993);

Cartas de Mário de Andrade, by Sant'Anna and others, edited by Fábio Lucas (Rio de Janeiro: Nova Fronteira, 1993);

Brasilianische Literatur, einzigartig und umfassend = Brazilian literature, singular and plural, by Sant'Anna and others (São Paulo: Câmara Brasileira do Livro, 1994);

O que aprendemos até agora? Constatações de fim de século (São Luís: EDUFMA/UFMA, 1994);

Mistérios gozosos (Rio de Janeiro: Rocco, 1994);

Fizemos bem em resistir: crônicas seleccionadas (Rio de Janeiro: Rocco, 1994);

Porta de colégio & outras crônicas (São Paulo: Ática, 1995);

O livro ao vivo, by Sant'Anna and others, edited by Candido José Mendes de Almeida, Claudia Roquette-Pinto, and Maria Elisa de Araújo (Rio de Janeiro: Centro Cultural Cândido Mendes/IBM Brasil, 1995);

Libraries, Social Inequality and the Challenge of the Twenty-first Century (Rio de Janeiro: Fundação Biblioteca Nacional, 1996); published in Portuguese as *Bibliotecas: desnível social e o desafio do século XXI* (Rio de Janeiro: Fundação Biblioteca Nacional, 1996);

A vida por viver: crônicas (Rio de Janeiro: Rocco, 1997);

Epitáfio para o século XX: antologia (São Paulo: Ediouro, 1997);

Intervalo amoroso: e outros poemas escolhidos (Pôrto Alegre: L & PM Pocket, 1999);

Textamentos (Rio de Janeiro: Rocco, 1999);

Barroco: do quadrado à elipse (Rio de Janeiro: Rocco, 2000);

Para entender o Brasil, by Sant'Anna and others, edited by Marisa Sobral Luiz Antonio Aguiar (São Paulo: Alegro, 2000);

Carlos Heitor Cony, by Sant'Anna and others (São Paulo: Instituto Moreira Salles, 2001);

Nós, os que matamos Tim Lopes (São Paulo: Expressão e Cultura, 2002);

Pequenas seduções: antología (Pôrto Alegre: Sulina, 2002);

Os homens amam a guerra (Rio de Janeiro: Alves, 2003);

Desconstruir Duchamp: arte na hora da revisão (Rio de Janeiro: Vieira & Lent, 2003);

Que fazer de Ezra Pound: ensaios (Rio de Janeiro: Imago, 2003).

Edition and Collection: *Que país é este?* (Rio de Janeiro: Rocco, 1990);

A grande fala do índio Guarani; e, Catedral de Colônia: edition commemorativa (Rio de Janeiro: Rocco, 1998).

RECORDINGS: *Cronicas escolhidas: com participação de Paulo Autran,* read by Sant'Anna, Luzdacidade, 1999;

O escritor por ele mesmo, Instituto Moreira Salles, 2001.

OTHER: T. S. Eliot, *A essência da poesia: estudos & ensaios,* translated by Maria Luiza Nogueira, introduction by Sant'Anna (Rio de Janeiro: Artenova, 1972);

Joaquim Manuel de Macedo, *A moreninha,* edited by Sant'Anna (Rio de Janeiro: Alves, 1975);

"Clarice: a epifania da escrita," in Clarice Lispector, *A legião estrangeira: textos críticos* (São Paulo: Ática, 1977), pp. 3–7;

Marcia Chagas Freitas, ed., *O Rosto do povo: foto-jornalismo,* contributions by Sant'Anna (Rio de Janeiro: Christiano, 1986);

Lispector, *A paixão segundo G.H.: edição crítica,* edited by Benedito Nunes (Paris: Association Archives de la Littérature latino américaine, des Caraïbes et africaine du XX siècle, 1988);

Cláudia Macedo, Angela Falcao, and Candido José Mendes de Almeida, eds., *TV ao vivo: depoimentos* (Rio de Janeiro: Brasiliense, 1988);

Maximiano de Carvalho e Silva, ed., *Homenagem a Manuel Bandeira* (Rio de Janeiro: Presença, 1989);

Denira do Rosário, ed., *Palavra de poeta* (Rio de Janiero: J. Olympio, 1989);

Carlos Drummond de Andrade, *Drummond: arte em exposição = Drummond: Art in Exhibition,* presentation text by Sant'Anna, translated by Annette J. Baughan (Rio de Janiero: Record/Salamandra, 1990);

Analdino Rodrigues Paulino, ed., *Crônicas de amor* (São Paulo: Ceres, 1990);

Cuentos brasileños, edited by Sant'Anna (Buenos Aires: Bello, 1994);

Barroco, alma do Brasil, photographs by Pedro Oswaldo Cruz, texts by Sant'Anna (Rio de Janeiro: Comunicação Máxima, 1997); translated by Diane Grosklau as *Baroque, the soul of Brazil* (Rio de Janeiro: Comunicação Máxima, 1998);

Roberto M. Moura, *MPB: caminhos da arte brasileira mais reconhecida no mundo,* preface by Sant'Anna (Rio de Janeiro: Vitale, 1998);

Fausto Henrique dos Santos, *Metodologia aplicada em museus,* introduction by Sant'Anna (São Paulo: Mackenzie, 2000);

Aluísio Azevedo, *The Slum: A Novel,* translated by David H. Rosenthal, afterword by Sant'Anna (Oxford & New York: Oxford University Press, 2000);

Gilda Santos, ed., *Brasil e Portugal: 500 anos de enlaces e desenlaces,* 2 volumes (Rio de Janeiro: Real Gabinete de Leitura, 2000, 2001);

Ronaldo Cagiano, ed., *Poetas mineiros em Brasília,* preface by Sant'Anna (Brasília: Varanda, 2002);

Bueno de Rivera, *Melhores poemas,* edited by Sant'Anna (São Paulo: Global, 2003).

Melding strong moral and religious convictions with a language that made his poetry accessible to the masses, Affonso Romano de Sant'Anna created a politically engaged verse that struggled against the censorship imposed by the Brazilian military dictatorship between 1964 and 1985. With the return to civilian government he became a leading member of the literary establishment, serving for seven years as head of Brazil's national library.

Sant'Anna was born on 27 March 1937 to Jorge Fermino de Sant'Anna, a captain in the military police, and Maria Romano in the city of Belo Horizonte in the interior state of Minas Gerais. Shortly after his birth, his parents moved to the smaller city of Juiz de Fora. The family was poor, and Sant'Anna paid for his own primary and secondary education at the Grupo Escolar Fernando Lobo and the private high school Instituto Granbury by carrying lunch boxes from homes to job sites, toting bundles of clothing for laundry women, and selling writing paper and candy to movie theaters and other businesses. As he rode his bicycle from place to place selling his merchandise, he stopped frequently to read books at the free libraries of the National Social Industrial Services.

Sant'Anna's parents were evangelical Protestants in an overwhelmingly Catholic country, and they intended him to become a Methodist minister. As a youth he spent many hours in church listening to the Scripture readings and fiery sermons of the local pastor, absorbing the biblical tones and nuances that later entered into his poetry. At seventeen he began to preach in various small towns throughout his home state. Among those to whom he ministered were people in slums, hospitals, and jails. Sant'Anna's experience among the poor and socially downtrodden is mirrored in his poetry and prose.

When he completed secondary school, Sant'Anna entered the Federal University of Minas Gerais in Belo Horizonte, paying for his education by working in banks and as a journalist. In 1956 he organized a group of young leftist intellectuals who were writing politically inspired literature that reflected their concern with disparities between social classes. That same year he made his operatic debut as the leading baritone in the group Madrigal Renasentista, directed by the conductor Isaac Karabtchevsky. He received a bachelor's degree in modern and classical literature in 1962.

In 1962 Sant'Anna published *O desemprego do poeta* (The Poet's Unemployment), a collection of four essays in which he maintains that a poet should not speak in a unique and personal voice but should serve as the voice of the people. He describes his life as a poet, the political climate of the time, and his frustration at not being understood by the intelligentsia. Sant'Anna was considered a bohemian, Romantic poet, out of step with his era, but this opinion changed after a military junta took control of the government in 1964 and the country entered a period of political repression.

Sant'Anna was a member of the faculty of the literature department at the Federal University of Minas Gerais in 1964–1965. In 1965 he published the poetry collection *Canto e palavra* (Song and Word). He lectured on Brazilian literature at the University of California at Berkeley from 1965 until 1967. In 1968 he returned to the United States on a Ford Foundation grant to spend two years at the International Writers' Workshop at the University of Iowa. In 1969 he defended his dissertation on the Brazilian poet Carlos Drummond de Andrade; it was published in 1972 as *Drummond, o "gauche" no tempo* and earned four of the most distinguished literary prizes in Brazil: the Mário de Andrade Prize, an award from the Cul-

Cover for the 1990 paperback edition of Sant'Anna's best-known poetry collection (What Kind of Nation Is This?), originally published during the Brazilian military dictatorship in 1980. The title poem, a protest against censorship, appeared on the editorial page of the newspaper Jornal do Brasil *(Heard Library, Vanderbilt University).*

tural Foundation of Brasília, the Guanabara State Prize, and the Union of Brazilian Writers' Award. Republished in 1977 as *Carlos Drummond de Andrade: análise da obra* (Carlos Drummond de Andrade: An Analysis of His Work), the book is considered a classic study of Sant'Anna's friend and colleague.

In 1971 Sant'Anna married the journalist Marina Colasanti, with whom he has co-authored two books. They have two daughters: Fabiana, born in 1965, and Alessandra, born in 1972. In 1972 Sant'Anna began teaching at the Federal University of Rio de Janeiro and at the Pontifical Catholic University of Rio de Janeiro; he was chairman of the literature department at the latter from 1973 to 1976. In *Poesia sobre poesia* (1975, Poetry about Poetry) he says that form needs to be separated from content in the creation of a poem so that the ideas will be of paramount importance. In 1975 Sant'Anna was instrumental in bringing the French philosopher and historian Michel Foucault to Brazil for the first time;

Foucault's ideas heavily influenced the study of Brazilian literature and history in the last half of the twentieth century.

Sant'Anna returned to the United States in 1976 as a visiting professor at the University of Texas at Austin. In 1978 he published *A grande fala do índio Guarani perdido na história e outras derrotas: moderno Popol Vuh* (The Secret Language of the Guarani Indian Lost in History and Other Defeats: A Modern Popol Vuh). The work is a return to epic poetry in the vein of colonial Brazilian poets such as Gregório de Matos, José Basílio da Gama, Bento Teixeira Santa Rita Durão, and Gonçalves Dias; imitating the bible of Mayan civilization that recounts the origin of creation and other oral traditions, it is an attempt to understand contemporary reality by looking at the mythical past through the eyes of a mysterious shaman. Critics have compared the work to Ezra Pound's *Cantos* (1928–1969) in both scope and style. Also in 1978 Sant'Anna lectured on Brazilian literature at the University of Cologne.

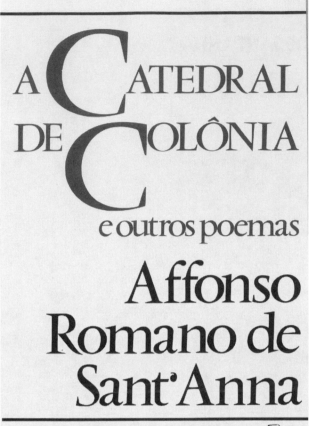

A CATEDRAL DE COLÔNIA
e outros poemas

Affonso Romano de Sant'Anna

Paperback cover for Sant'Anna's 1985 collection (Cologne's Cathedral and Other Poems), in which he uses medieval motifs to address present-day concerns (Ivy Stacks, University of Virginia Library)

In 1980 Sant'Anna published his best-known poetry collection, *Que país é este? e outros poemas* (What Kind of Nation Is This? and Other Poems). In the title poem, which appeared on the editorial page of the newspaper *Jornal do Brasil* on 6 January 1980, he points out that the censorship put in place by the military government limits the people's freedom to discuss basic questions, especially those having to do with national identity. The Brazilian literary critic Wilson Martins calls this piece the most Brazilian of all of Sant'Anna's poems and the one that marks him as the successor to Drummond de Andrade. The work incorporates the most distinctive qualities of contemporary Brazilian poetry: the words are simple, and the language is direct and clear, constantly recalling the reality of everyday life that surrounds the poet; there is an emphasis on the musicality of the words without recourse to classical poetic forms.

Sant'Anna spent the academic year 1981–1982 as a visiting professor at the University of Aix-en-

Provence. In 1984 he inherited the weekly column in the *Jornal do Brasil* that was formerly written by Drummond de Andrade. In this forum he crystallized his concern with the relationship between theory and praxis, seeing the poet's function as rediscovering his place within society. As it had "Que país é este?," the newspaper published Sant'Anna's poetry on the editorial page rather than in the literary supplement; often, as in the cases of "A implosão da mentira" (The Imploding Lie) and "Sobre a atual vergonha de ser brasileiro" (About the Real Shame of Being Brazilian), it was the only item on the page. Thus was Sant'Anna able to practice what he had been preaching since his early days as an itinerant minister: the necessity of making poetry accessible to the masses. Books were beyond the means of the working poor, but newspapers were not. The poems were reproduced on posters that were placed in homes, on beaches, and in offices and bars all over Brazil.

Civilian government returned to Brazil in 1985. That year Sant'Anna published the critically acclaimed epic-like poem, *A catedral de Colônia e outros poemas* (Cologne's Cathedral and Other Poems), in which he reverts to the Middle Ages to discuss the present. In the 1980s Sant'Anna wrote a series of poems that were broadcast on the Globo television network during the evening news to an audience of more than sixty million viewers. During the 1986 World Cup soccer tournament, Sant'Anna produced ten programs that joined the Brazilian national pastime with poetry: his poems about the matches were shown, with images from the games, after the broadcasts of the games themselves. The programs were so successful that the television executives commissioned him to write another series to accompany broadcasts of the Formula One automobile races.

In 1990 President Fernando Collor de Mello appointed Sant'Anna director of the Brazilian National Library. During his tenure, which lasted until 1996, Sant'Anna oversaw the modernization of the library; expanded the on-line catalogues; initiated a series of prizes for translation of Brazilian works into other languages; began the monthly newsletter *Recortes* and the journal *Poesia sempre;* created the Sistema Nacional de Bibliotecas (National System of Libraries), joining the resources of more than three thousand Brazilian libraries; and established PRO-LER (Programa de Promoção da Leitura [Program for the Promotion of Reading]), which sent more than thirty thousand volunteers into the poorer areas of three hundred cities to promote literacy among children and adults. Sant'Anna was elected in 1993 to a two-year term as president of CERLALC (Conselho do Centro Regional para o Fomento do Livro na

América Latina e no Caribe [Council of the Regional Center for the Promotion of Books in Latin America and the Caribbean]). In 1995–1996 he was president of the Association of Ibero-American National Libraries, an organization of twenty-two national libraries in Spain, Portugal, and Latin America. In addition to the Ford Foundation, Sant'Anna has received grants from the Guggenheim and Rockefeller Foundations.

In 1999 Sant'Anna published *Textamentos;* the title is a neologism created from *textos* (text) and *testamento* (testament). The poems in *Textamentos* are short and written in a conversational style that is completely different from his longer, more epic-like works. The themes include the fragility of life, the ways love changes, and the need for social action.

The style and the content of his poetry may have varied, but Affonso Romano de Sant'Anna's message has been constant throughout his long career. His works, many of which have been translated and read throughout the world, are a clear call for justice and salvation through love and action.

References:

Jorge de Aquinno Filho, "Os rumos da poesia brasileira, I: o poema do futuro deve falar do presente," *Suplemento Literário de Minas Gerais,* 18 (26 March 1985): 1–2;

Astolfo Araújo and Nader Wladyr, "Uma poesia que crescc apesar das vanguardas, ou o lixo do quintal na sala de visita," *Revista Mensal de Literátura,* 16 (1977): 3–10;

Serge Bourjea, "Lire le Brésildans la poésie d'Affonso Romano de Sant'Anna," in *Carrefour de Cultures,* edited by Régis Antoine (Tübingen: Narr, 1993);

Bourjea, "Le poète doit interferer dans le quotidian," *La Quinzaine Litterire,* no. 484 (1987): 26–28;

Golin Cida, "Affonso Romano de Sant'Anna: criação poética x teoria," *Brasil/Brazil,* 6, no. 4 (1991): 77–86;

Fred Ellison, "The Great Speech of the Guaraní Indian Lost to History and Other Defeats," *Dactylus,* 8 (Fall 1987): 31–35;

Ariel Krivichien Marques, "Que país é este?" *Revista brasileira de Língua e Literatura,* 3–4, no. 9 (1981–1982): 58;

Wilson Martins, "Affonso Romano de Sant'Anna: poeta do nosso tempo," *Jornal do Brasil,* 4 October 1980, section B;

Cremilda de Araújo Medina, "Affonso Romano de Sant'Anna," in her *A posse da terra: escritor brasileiro de hoje* (Lisbon: Casa de Moeda / São Paulo: Secretaria da Cultura do Estado, 1985), pp. 383–392;

Medina, "A praca maior para a poesia: Affonso Romano, um dos arautos," *Suplemento Literário de Minas Gerais,* 20, no. 6 (1985): 8;

João Camilo dos Santos, "Algumas reflexes sobre a poesia de Affonso Romano de Sant'Anna—uma poesia saída da 'Sombra da Música Popular,'" in *Amor das letras e das gentes: In Honor of Maria de Lourdes Belchior Pontes,* edited by Santos and Frederick G. Williams (Santa Barbara: Center for Portuguese and Brazilian Studies, University of California, Santa Barbara, 1995).

Ariano Suassuna

(16 June 1927 –   )

Elzbieta Szoka
Columbia University

BOOKS: *É de tororó,* by Suassuna, Capiba, and Ascenso Ferreira (Rio de Janeiro: Livraria Editora da Casa do Estudante do Brasil, 1950);

Ode (Recife: Amador, 1955);

Auto da Compadecida (Rio de Janeiro: AGIR, 1957); translated by Dillwyn F. Ratcliff as *The Rogues' Trial* (Berkeley: University of California Press, 1963);

O casamento suspeitoso (Recife: Igarassu, 1961);

Uma mulher vestida de sol (Recife: Imprensa Universitária, 1964);

O santo e a porca, imitação nordestina de Plauto (Recife: Imprensa Universitária, 1964);

A pena e a lei (Rio de Janeiro: AGIR, 1971)—includes Sábato Magaldi, "Auto da Esperança," pp. 9–20;

Romance d'A Pedra do Reino e o Príncipe do Sangue do vai-e-volta (Rio de Janeiro: J. Olympio, 1971);

Ferros do Cariri: uma heráldica sertaneja (Recife: Guariba Editora de Arte, 1974);

O Movimento Armorial (Recife: Universidade Federal de Pernambuco, Departamento de Extensão Cultural, Pró-Reitoria para Assuntos Comunitários, Editora Universitária, 1974);

Farsa da boa preguiça (Rio de Janeiro: J. Olympio, 1974)—includes José Laurenio de Melo, "Nota bibliográfica," pp. xi–xiv;

Seleta em prosa e verso de Ariano Suassuna, edited by Silviano Santiago (Rio de Janeiro: J. Olympio, 1974);

Iniciação à estética (Recife: Universidade Federal de Pernambuco, Editora Universitária, 1975);

História d'o rei degolado nas caatingas do sertão: romance armorial e novela romançal brasileira—ao sol da Onça Caetana (Rio de Janeiro: J. Olympio, 1977);

Fernando e Isaura (Recife: Bagaço, 1994);

Olavo Bilac e Fernando Pessoa: uma presença brasileira en Mensagem? (Lisbon: Aríon, 1998);

Poemas, edited by Carlos Newton Júnior (Recife: Editora Universitária UFPE, 1999).

Edition: *Auto da Compadecida,* preface by Henrique Oscar (Rio de Janeiro: AGIR, 1975).

Ariano Suassuna *(frontispiece for* Seleta em prosa e verso de Ariano Suassuna, *edited by Silviano Santiago, 1974; Joint University Libraries, Nashville)*

PLAY PRODUCTIONS: *Uma mulher vestida de sol,* 1947;

Cantam as harpas de Sião, 1948; revised as *O desertor de princesas,* 1948;

Os homens de barro, 1949;

Auto da Compadecida, Rio de Janeiro, Teatro Dulcina, 1957;

O casamento suspeitoso, São Paulo, Teatro Sérgio Cardoso, 1957;

Suassuna (in suit and tie) taking a bow during the curtain call at the premiere of his Auto da Compadecida *(Play of Our Lady of Mercy) at the Teatro Dulcina in Rio de Janeiro in 1957 (from* Cadernos de literatura brasileira: Ariano Suassuna, *2000; Bruccoli Clark Layman Archives)*

O santo e a porca, São Paulo, Teatro Sérgio Cardoso, 1957;

O homem da vaca e o poder da fortuna, 1958;

A pena e a lei, Recife, Teatro Popular do Nordeste, 1960;

Farsa de boa preguiça, Recife, Teatro Popular do Nordeste, 1961.

OTHER: Theresa Catharina de Góes Campos, *A TV nos tornou mais humanos? Princípios da comunicação pela TV,* preface by Suassuna (Recife: Universidade Federal de Pernambuco, 1970);

Sylvio Cavalcanti de Oliveira, *Inventário (poético) do Recife,* preface by Suassuna (Rio de Janiero: Civilização Brasileira, 1979);

José Lins do Rêgo, *Romances reunidos e ilustrados, 12: Cangaceiros,* edited by Suassuna (Rio de Janeiro: J. Olympio, 1980);

José Paulo Cavalcanti Filho, *O mel e o fel,* preface by Suassuna (Rio de Janeiro: Record, 1998);

Igarassu: origem, cenários e cores, photographs by José de Paula Machado, texts by Suassuna, José de Monterroso Teixeira, and Maria João Espírito Santo Bustorff Silva (Recife: Fundação Ricardo do Espírito Santo Silva / Rio de Janeiro: AGIR, 1998).

Critics have compared Ariano Suassuna's position in Brazilian literature to William Shakespeare's in English, Molière's in French, and Gil Vicente's in Portuguese literature. In his works Suassuna compares the Brazilian northeast—a region that is unfamiliar not only to foreign readers but also to many Brazilians from other regions—to Renaissance Europe. His worldview, aesthetics, and Roman Catholicism, to which he converted as a young adult, manifest themselves in his play *Auto da Compadecida* (1957, Play of Our Lady of Mercy; translated as *The Rogues' Trial,* 1963) and in his farces. The legends and folklore of northeastern Brazil are elevated in these plays to a universal level of dramatic discourse that can be understood anywhere in the Western world, as they draw from the sources of Western civilization without losing their Brazilian regional character.

Suassuna was born on 16 June 1927 in Paraiba in northeastern Brazil, one of nine children of João Urbano Pessoa de Vasconcelos Suassuna and Rita de Cássia Dantas Vilar Suassuna. After his father, who was governor of the state of Paraiba from 1924 until 1928, was assassinated in Rio de Janeiro in 1930, the family moved to the Acahuan, a relative's farm. Suassuna recalls another traumatic event from his early childhood in his

ARIANO SUASSUNA

THE ROGUES' TRIAL

Translated from the Portuguese by

DILLWYN F. RATCLIFF

1963 | UNIVERSITY OF CALIFORNIA PRESS
BERKELEY AND LOS ANGELES

Title page for the English translation of Auto da Compadecida,
*the work that is generally considered Suassuna's masterpiece
(Thomas Cooper Library, University of South Carolina)*

introduction to *Farsa da boa preguiça* (1974, The Farce of the Good Procrastination): his uncle, "a generous and brave man of the '*sertão*' [the hinterland area of the northeast], a friend of the People," went bankrupt as a result of the socio-economic changes caused by the influx of foreign capital. While these two events undoubtedly influenced the ideological stance of Suassuna's literary work, his formative years in the *sertão* familiarized him with a variety of themes and artistic expressions from the popular traditions of the northeast that also became an integral part of his vision.

In 1933 the family moved to Taperoá, where Suassuna completed his primary education. In 1942 they moved to Recife, and Suassuna continued his schooling there at the Colégio Americano Batista, the Ginásio Pernambucano, and the Colégio Osvaldo Cruz. Meanwhile, his literary education was supervised by his uncles Manuel Dantas Vilar, an atheist and a republican,

and Joaquim Duarte Dantas, a Catholic and a monarchist. His first poems, "Guabirabas" and "A morte do touro Mão-de-Pau" (The Death of the Bull Mão-de-Pau), were written during his years at the Colégio Osvaldo Cruz and published in the literary supplements of local newspapers.

In 1946 Suassuna began studying law at the Universidade Federal de Pernambuco. That same year he and other young artists and writers, including Hermilo Borba Filho, Joel Pontes, Gastão de Holanda, and Aloísio Magalhães, founded the Teatro do Estudante de Pernambuco (Pernambuco Student Theater). Taking theater to the people by staging shows in public spaces, the company produced plays by such dramatists as Sophocles, Shakespeare, Henrik Ibsen, Anton Chekhov, and Federico García Lorca. In 1947 Suassuna wrote his first play, *Uma mulher vestida de sol* (A Woman Dressed in Sunshine), which was awarded the Nicolau Carlos Magno Prize in a nationwide competition. The play was influenced by the poets and dramatists of Spain and Portugal, particularly the Golden Age masters. Suassuna says in the introduction to the published version of the work (1964) that his concern when he wrote the play was to show the similarities between the literary canons of Spain and the Brazilian northeast but that he rewrote it ten years later because he had to abandon his favorite Spanish masters in order to create within the Brazilian spirit. In "O dramaturgo do Nordeste" (The Dramaturgy of the Northeast), included in *Uma mulher vestida de sol,* Filho notes that this play was the first great tragedy ever produced in the northeast. It was the only tragedy Suassuna ever wrote. Two other plays from this period, which also show Suassuna's concern to reconcile the influence of Spanish and Portuguese classics with the themes and forms of expression belonging to the Brazilian northeastern tradition, are *Cantam as harpas de Sião* (1948, The Harps of Sion Sing), revised as *O desertor de princesas* (1948, The Seducer of Princesses), and *Os homens de barro* (1949, Men of Mud).

Suassuna graduated from law school in 1950 and spent the next two years in Taperoá recovering from a lung disease. During that period he converted to Roman Catholicism. He returned to Recife in 1952 to practice law. In 1955 he wrote *Auto da Compadecida,* his masterpiece and one of the most important plays in Brazilian dramaturgy. In 1956 he abandoned his legal career and became a professor of aesthetics at the Federal University of Pernambuco. *Auto da Compadecida* was performed in 1957 by the company Teatro Adolescente do Recife (Adolescent Theater of Recife) during an amateur theater festival in Rio de Janeiro and won the gold medal of the Brazilian Theatrical Critics Association.

Auto da Compadecida draws heavily on a mostly oral tradition of the Brazilian northeast known as *literatura de* cordel (string literature): ballads, self-published by the authors in three-to-thirty-page mimeographed *folhetos* (pamphlets), and traditionally sold hanging from a string tied between two stakes in marketplace booths. The first act is based on the "O enterro do cachorro" (The Burial of the Dog) episode in Leandro Gomes de Barros's *O dinheiro* (Money); the second act is based on Barros's *História do cavalo que defecava dinheiro* (The Story of a Horse that Defecated Money); and the third act is based on the short humorous play *O castigo da soberba* (The Punishment of an Arrogant Woman), by Anselmo Vieira de Souza. Other sources of inspiration that can be identified in *Auto da Compadecida* are religious plays by Vicente and other Iberian authors of the sixteenth and seventeenth centuries, as well as aspects of commedia dell'arte. Each act includes a prologue and an epilogue in which clowns comment on the plot and the quality of the performance. The main characters are Chicó, a master storyteller who during the first two acts narrates a series of tales from the *literatura de cordel* tradition, and João Grilo, a *malandro* (rogue) who is a master of cunning and double-dealing. In the third act, "O processo do Cristo Negro" (The Judgment of the Black Christ), most of the inhabitants of the village where the action takes place, including João Grilo, have been massacred by *cangaceiros* (roaming bandits of the *sertão*) and are judged by the black Christ and his mother, Nossa Senhora (Our Lady). The tone of the judgment is sarcastic at times, and the mockery is enhanced by the final revelation: João Grilo is absolved by Nossa Senhora only to discover after his resurrection that he owes this miracle to Chicó, who gave all their money to the church as a "lawyer fee" for Nossa Senhora.

In 1957 Suassuna wrote the farces *O casamento suspeitoso* (1961, The Suspicious Marriage) and *O santo e a porca, imitação nordestina de Plauto* (1964, The Saint and the Pig, a Northeastern Imitation of Plautus). Inspired by the ancient Greek New Comedy of Menander, commedia dell'arte, and Molière, the three-act *O casamento suspeitoso* deals with the greed and hypocrisy of characters involved in a marriage-for-money scheme. Suassuna here purposely distances himself from the northeastern tradition, and *O casamento suspeitoso* is his least rural text. *O santo e a porca* deals with the miser theme explored by Plautus in *Aulularia* (The Pot of Gold), the source for Molière's *L'Avare* (The Miser, produced in 1668, published in 1669). *O santo e a porca* returns to the northeastern flavor of *Auto da Compadecida,* which contributes to the appeal of the play.

In 1957 Suassuna married Zélia de Andrade Lima, an artist who illustrated several of his books. Two years later he and Filho founded Teatro Popular do Nordeste (Popular Theater of the Northeast) in Recife. Also in 1959 Suassuna wrote *A pena e a lei* (1971, The Punish-

Title page for Suassuna's second novel. The title means "Story of the King Beheaded on the Scrub Savanna of the Backlands: Armorial Fiction and Brazilian Romance Novel—to the Sun of the Jaguar Caetana" (Howard-Tilton Memorial Library, Tulane University).

ment and the Law), which he describes in the introduction as a "tragicomédia lírico-pastoril, drama cómico em três atos, farsa de moralidade e facécia de caráter bufonesco" (bucolic and lyrical tragicomedy, comedy in three acts, morality farce with comic flavor). The stage directions specify that the first act should be staged as if it were a *mamulengo* (marionette show), a form of theater developed in the northeast, with the actors performing in a mechanical fashion to represent human weaknesses and shortcomings. In the second act the performances are to be balanced between the actions of marionettes and of human beings, indicating the characters' oscillation between the material and transcendent worlds. In the third act the actors are to use normal gestures and facial expressions, indicating that only when faced with death do people become truly human. Directed by

Filho, *A pena e a lei* was staged for the first time in 1960 at the Teatro Popular do Nordeste; later it traveled to Rio de Janeiro and other major cities in Brazil.

In 1960 Suassuna received a degree in philosophy from the Catholic University of Pernambuco and wrote *Farsa de boa preguiça*. In the introduction to the 1974 edition he explains that he wanted to explore two themes in the play: "ócio criador" (creative laziness) as opposed to mindless robotic attitudes and the cultural differences and consequent prejudices between developed and underdeveloped societies. Another issue Suassuna treats is the dysfunctional coexistence of "two Brazils": the cosmopolitan bourgeoisie and the "Brazil of the People." In the play the cosmopolitan Brazil is represented by the wealthy Aderaldo Catacão and his wife, the false intellectual Dona Clarabela. The play, written in free verse, includes quotations from various popular sources, from the writings of the poet and playwright Luís de Camões, and from the Bible; it is divided into three relatively independent acts, each bearing its own title: "O peru do cão coxo" (The Turkey and the Lame Dog), "A cabra do cão caolho" (The Half-blind Devil's Nanny Goat), and "O rico avarento" (The Stingy Rich Man). Suassuna notes in the introduction that the first act is based on a news story and an anonymous *mamulengo* play; the second act is based on another anonymous *mamulengo* play; and the third act is based on a traditional story, "São Pedro e o queijo" (St. Peter and the Cheese), and another anonymous *mamulengo* play, *O rico avarento*. The marionette plays that served Suassuna as inspiration were performed in the northeast by the *mamulengo* companies Professor Tira-e-Dá and Benedito. When *Farsa da boa preguiça* was staged by Filho at the Teatro Popular do Nordeste in 1961, Marxist critics accused Suassuna of advising the Brazilian people to opt for laziness and conformity.

In 1967 Suassuna was a founding member of the Conselho Federal de Cultura (Federal Council for Culture). In 1969 he became president of the Departamento de Extensão Cultural (Department of Cultural Extension) of the Federal University of Pernambuco. In 1970 he inaugurated in Recife the group Movimento Armorial (Armorial Movement) to promote nationally the literature, theater, visual arts, crafts, music, and motion pictures of the northeast.

In 1971 Suassuna published his first novel, *Romance d'A Pedra do Reino e o Príncipe do Sangue do vai-e-volta* (A Tale about the Royal Stone and the Prince of Blood that Kept Coming and Going), based on the traditional northeastern belief that King Sebastian of Portugal would return to save the country. In 1974 he received the Prêmio Nacional de Ficção (National Fiction Award)

from the Ministry of Education and Culture; that same year a selection of his plays, poetry, short stories, and essays was published by Silviano Santiago. In 1977 Suassuna published the novel *História d'o rei degolado nas caatingas do sertão: romance armorial e novela romançal brasileira—ao sol da Onçao Caetana* (Story of the King Beheaded on the Scrub Savanna of the Backlands: Armorial Fiction and Brazilian Romance Novel—to the Sun of the Jaguar Caetana). *Auto da Compadecida* was adapted by Guel Arraes, a young movie director from the northeast, at the request of Rede Globo, the most powerful television network in Brazil, and became one of the most popular miniseries of the season.

Ariano Suassuna's plays have a universal appeal. The theatricality of his texts is vivid and is drawn from both sacred and profane sources: they are mixtures of church ritual and circus play. Suassuna's successful combination of the elaborate and the spontaneous, the erudite and the popular, and the literary and the colloquial have assured him an important place in twentieth-century Brazilian theater.

References:

Cadernos de literatura brasileira: Ariano Suassuna (São Paulo: Instituto Moretra Salles, 2000);

Mark Dinneen, *The Relationship between Erudite Literature and Popular Culture in the North East of Brazil: Ariano Suassuna and Armorial Art* (Glasgow: Institute of Latin American Studies, University of Glasgow, 1990);

Mário Guidarini, *Os pícaros e os trapaceir os de Ariano Suassuna* (São Paulo: Ateniense, 1992);

Sábato Magaldi, "Em busca do populário religioso," in his *Panorama do teatro brasileiro* (São Paulo: Global, 1997), pp. 236–244;

Elizabeth Marinheiro, *A intertextualidade das formas simples: aplicada ao Romance d'A Pedra do Reino de Ariano Suassuna* (Rio de Janeiro: Gráfica Olimpica, 1977);

Carlos Newton Júnior, *O circo da onça malhada: iniciaçao à obra de Ariano Suassuna* (Recife: Artelivro, 2000);

Newton Júnior, *O pai, o exílio e o reino: a poesia armorial de Ariano Suassuna* (Recife: Editora Universitária da UFPE, 1999);

Maria Aparecida Lopez Nogueira, *O cabreiro tresmalhado: Ariano Suassuna e a universalidade da cultura* (São Paulo: Palas Athena, 2002);

Idelette Muzart Fonseca dos Santos, *Em demanda da poética popular: Ariano Suassuna e o Movimento Armorial* (Campinas: Unicamp, 1999);

Ligia Vassallo, *O sertão medieval: origens européias do teatro de Ariano Suassuna* (Rio de Janeiro: Alves, 1993).

Lygia Fagundes Telles

(19 April 1923 –   )

Nancy T. Baden
California State University, Fullerton

See also the Telles entry in *DLB 113: Modern Latin-American Fiction Writers, First Series.*

BOOKS: *Porão e sobrado* (São Paulo: Privately printed, 1938);

Praia viva: contos (São Paulo: Martins, 1943);

O cacto vermelho (Rio de Janeiro: Mérito, 1949);

Ciranda de pedra (Rio de Janeiro: O Cruzeiro, 1954); translated by Margaret A. Neves as *The Marble Dance* (New York: Avon, 1986);

Histórias do desencontro (Rio de Janeiro: J. Olympio, 1958);

As pérolas ([Sá da Bandeira, Angola]: Imbondeiro, 1960);

Histórias escolhidas, introduction by Paulo Rónai (São Paulo: Boa Leitura, 1961);

Os mortos (Lisbon: Casa Portuguesa, 1963);

Verão no aquário (São Paulo: Martins, 1963);

A confissão de Leontina (Sá da Bandeira, Angola: Imbondeiro, 1964);

O jardim selvagem (São Paulo: Martins, 1965);

Antes do baile verde (Rio de Janeiro: Bloch, 1970; revised and enlarged edition, Rio de Janeiro: J. Olympio, 1971);

As meninas (Rio de Janeiro: J. Olympio, 1973); translated by Neves as *The Girl in the Photograph* (New York: Avon, 1982);

Seminário dos ratos (Rio de Janeiro: J. Olympio, 1977); translated by Neves as *Tigrela and Other Stories* (New York: Avon, 1986);

Filhos pródigos (São Paulo: Cultura, 1978); republished as *A estrutura da bolha de sabão: contos* (Rio de Janeiro: Nova Fronteira, 1991);

A disciplina do amor: fragmentos (Rio de Janeiro: Nova Fronteira, 1980);

Mistérios: ficções (Rio de Janeiro: Nova Fronteira, 1981);

Venha ver o pôr-do-sol & outros contos (São Paulo: Ática, 1988);

As horas nuas (Rio de Janeiro: Nova Fronteira, 1989);

Capitu, by Telles and Paulo Emílio Salles Gomes (São Paulo: Siciliano, 1993);

Lygia Fagundes Telles, 2002 (photograph by Richam Samir; Arquivo da Academia Brasileira de Letras)

A noite escura e mais eu: contos (Rio de Janeiro: Nova Fronteira, 1995);

A confissão de Leontina e fragmentos, edited by Maura Sardinha (Rio de Janeiro: Ediouro, 1996);

Oito contos de amor (São Paulo: Ática, 1996);

Invenção e memória (Rio de Janeiro: Rocco, 2000);

Durante aquele estranho chá: perdidos e achados, edited by Suênio Campos de Lucena (Rio de Janeiro: Rocco, 2002).

Editions and Collections: *Seleta,* edited, with an afterword, by Nelly Novais Coelho (Rio de Janeiro: J. Olympio, 1971);

Lygia Fagundes Telles, edited by Leonardo Monteiro (São Paulo: Abril, 1980);

Os melhores contos de Lygia Fagundes Telles, edited by Eduardo Portella (São Paulo: Global, 1984);

10 contos escolhidos (Brasília: Horizonte, 1984);

Pomba enamorada, ou, Uma história de amor, e outros contos escolhidos, edited by Léa Masina (Pôrto Alegre: L & PM, 1999).

Lygia Fagundes Telles is one of the most distinguished writers in Brazil. Her fiction reveals rich inner worlds in which reality and imagination seamlessly intermingle. In 1987 she became only the third woman to be elected to the Academia Brasileira de Letras (Brazilian Academy of Letters), the most prestigious literary society in the nation. Telles has received prestigious national and international awards, ranging from the 1958 Prêmio do Instituto Nacional do Livro (National Book Institute Prize) and the 1969 Cannes Prize in short fiction to the 2001 Prêmio Jabuti (Jabuti Prize) in fiction. Two of her novels and a short-story collection have been translated into English; her works have also been translated into French, German, Spanish, and Japanese.

Born in São Paulo on 19 April 1923, Lygia de Azevedo Fagundes was the youngest of four children. She was from a well-connected family whose fortune had disappeared over time. During the Brazilian Empire (1822–1889) her grandfather had been an honorary member of the Imperial Guard, an influential position. Lygia's childhood was rather unsettled. Her father, Durval de Azevedo Fagundes, was an attorney who headed several police precincts over the course of his career. A somewhat unstable man, he was a gambler and a dreamer. Because of his volatile nature, he often changed positions, and his family led a fairly nomadic existence, following him to different locations in the interior of the state of São Paulo. Lygia's mother, Maria do Rosário "Zizita" Azevedo Fagundes, was a pianist, a seemingly contented woman who played the music of Frédéric Chopin on the family piano.

In an interview published in *Seleta* (1971, Selected [Works]), edited by Nelly Novais Coelho, Telles recalled her childhood and described how she met both God and the devil on the nights when Maricota, her *pajem* (nursemaid), told ghost stories. These tales fired Telles's imagination, opening her eyes to a phantasmagoric kingdom that both attracted and terrorized her at the same time. The tales of afflicted souls moaning and throwing things off the roof were indelibly etched in her memory. Her adolescent reading included works by authors such as Edgar Allan Poe, Leo Tolstoy, Virginia Woolf, Franz Kafka, and William Faulkner. One does not have to look far to find their influence on Telles's writing. Brazilian literature, however, did not become an important part of her reading until later. Her first book of short stories, *Porão e sobrado,* was published in 1938 in an edition financed by her father, but Telles has dismissed it as an immature work.

Fagundes returned to the city of São Paulo and attended the Universidade de São Paulo, from which she earned a degree in physical education in 1941 and a law degree in 1946. She was a disciplined, serious student who tried to hide her natural beauty so as not to become sidetracked. She believed that writing was her true vocation. In 1950 she married Goffredo da Silva Telles, a law professor. She divorced him in 1961 but kept his name. Their son, now a movie director who lives in Paris, was named for his father. Her second husband, Paulo Emílio Salles Gomes, was a movie critic and founder of the Filmoteca do Museu de Arte de São Paulo (Cinematic Library of the São Paulo Museum of Art), later the Cinemateca Brasileira.

Telles's fiction leads the reader into the inner worlds of her characters. She is frequently described as a psychological writer who explores the problematical relationships of women and their family ties. Although her stories are set in urban São Paulo, Telles makes no attempt to describe the megalopolis. Rather, she focuses on intimate, enclosed spaces, such as gardens and boardinghouses. These settings are more in keeping with her themes and concerns. Her characters, condemned to solitude at birth, do not find redemption. Telles likes to delve into chance events, unexpected circumstances, and forms of madness. As a writer she is known for the female characters she creates, but her fiction is not limited to a single dimension. She explores larger issues related to the human condition and the problems of coping in a society in the throes of rapid urbanization. She shies away from realism and leans toward imagination, nuance, suggestion, ellipsis, and fantasy in elaborating her work. Her fiction looks at the imaginative side of the human experience, the supernatural, and what must remain unexplained.

Telles's protagonists often find themselves alone as they react to their world and circumstances. They experience misunderstanding, conflict, disillusionment, and deceit as their hopes and plans come face-to-face with reality. Fear, death, and fantasy are all part of these narratives. Conflicts are not happily resolved; rather, Telles's obsessive characters undergo a psychological self-analysis that maintains the narrative tension. For example, the novel *As horas nuas* (1989, The Naked Hours) concerns an aging actress who struggles with herself and her past. The problems of these lost souls are similar to those portrayed by many other twentieth-century writers. Telles's protagonists, usually women, retreat into an imaginary world as they search for meaning in life. She strongly identifies with characters such as Virgínia in *Ciranda de pedra* (1954; translated as *The Marble Dance,* 1986) and Lorena in *As meninas* (1973, The Girls; translated as *The Girl in the Photograph,* 1982). She has said that these characters are unfinished and may again appear in some later works.

In the interview from *Seleta,* Telles stated that she considers writing to be both "an act of love and mystery." Her stories well up from within her memory in a process she does not attempt to explain. As a writer she feels confident of her work; however, when she reads it, she feels compelled to correct it, prune it, and make adjustments to achieve greater emotional intensity. She does not change the content but concentrates on the language by modifying sentence structure, suppressing certain prepositions, and updating colloquial expressions. This continuous quest has led her to revise her work once published, a practice that has not pleased some critics. In Coelho's opinion, however, this search for the perfect expression leads Telles to a greater condensation of form and a stronger dramatic impact.

In the view of Brazilian critic Antônio Callado, *Ciranda de pedra* marks Telles's intellectual maturity as a writer. This 1954 novel is a bildungsroman that follows the path of the protagonist, Virgínia, a troubled young girl who later matures and decides to go on a journey to find herself. The first of the two parts of the novel reveals the fears and preoccupations of the young Virgínia as she tries to come to grips with her difficult life. She lives in a modest dwelling with her mentally ill mother; a servant, Luciana; and an uncle named Daniel, a doctor who cares for them. She is a nervous child who bites her nails and feels she is not pretty. She visits her father's house, a luxury home where her two sisters and brother reside with a governess to care for them. Next door to them live a brother and sister, Conrado and Otária, who are close to Virgínia's siblings. As a young girl she dreams of being able to be a part of this inseparable group of five, but she always feels excluded.

The second part of *Ciranda de pedra* begins with Virgínia's return from convent school after the death of her mother. At this point she lives in her father's house with her siblings. Although kind to her, her father is cold and does not love her. Virgínia now begins to gain the acceptance of her siblings and their friends, and she progressively comes to understand the relationships that exist among them. She contrasts

Front cover for the 1982 translation of Telles's As meninas (1973, The Girls), generally considered her best novel (Thomas Cooper Library, University of South Carolina)

the biblical teachings she received at her Catholic boarding school with the behavior of her family and the others around her. Over time Virgínia realizes that Daniel is not her uncle but her biological father and that her mother was an adulteress. This circumstance explains why Virgínia was separated from her siblings during childhood. As she integrates herself into the family, she learns that her sister Bruna has a lover, Rogélio; Letícia, her other sister, is a lesbian with an adolescent girlfriend; her brother, Afonso, is a farceur, and Conrado is impotent. After being seduced by Rogélio, Virgínia is on the verge of suicide, but she pulls herself together and decides to strike out on her own by taking a trip. As she departs, she reaches an understanding with Conrado, the one she has always loved.

Ciranda de pedra presents a devastating portrait of Brazilian middle-class values and women in a family situation. The title is significant: whereas *ciranda* (ring-around-a-rosy) is a children's game implying motion, a *pedra* (stone) is stationary. Thus, the title symbolizes the petrified relationships that exist among the characters in their family roles. Typical of Telles are the many symbols that help reveal the characters' situations. Physical descriptions are frequently impressionistic. Thoughts, dialogue, and situations reveal character. One can easily see how the novel speaks to young women growing up in urban Brazil. Telles was at the forefront of the group of Brazilian feminist writers who focused on the expression of the feminine condition. *Ciranda de pedra* has proved to be an enduring work; by the time of the thirtieth edition, published in 1997, it had sold fifty thousand copies. It appeared on a list of books that were distributed by the Ministério da Educação e Cultura (MEC, Ministry of Education and Culture) in 1997 to libraries across Brazil.

Telles's second novel, *Verão no aquário* (1963, Summer at the Aquarium), received widespread critical attention. The struggle to communicate is at the core of the work. The childhood of the heroine, Raiza, is seen as an obstacle to her liberation. Some critics consider her situation to be the embodiment of an entire generation.

Telles's short stories can be divided into two general categories: those dealing with psychological problems and those that involve the supernatural and the surreal. The themes in the short stories are the same as those in the novels; however, in her short fiction Telles employs more mystery, suspense, and elements of shifting reality. *Antes do baile verde* (1970, Before the Green Dance) features stories that she wrote over a twenty-year period, from 1949 to 1969. The first edition consists of sixteen stories; the revised and enlarged edition, published in 1971, has twenty. The narratives, ordered from the most recent to the oldest, were selected from her earlier books. The title story in the collection is typical of Telles's style. In it a young woman, Tatisa, and Lu, her black servant, converse as they prepare to celebrate Carnaval. In their inconsequential chatter they discuss the anticipated festivities as they glue sequins on Tatisa's costume. Suddenly, the mundane conversation is interrupted by the moans of Tatisa's ailing father in an adjoining room. Although the conversation continues, Tatisa begins to wrestle with her conscience. She is torn between her desire to participate in the celebration and her sense of filial responsibility. She tries to get Lu to stay with her father, but Lu has been promised this time off. Tatisa succumbs to the

lure of Carnaval and leaves her father alone. Some of the sequins from her costume roll down the stairs after her, as if to remind her of her duty.

In "A caçada" (The Hunt), reality shifts almost imperceptibly as the denouement unfolds. The setting is an antique store, with its musty smells and mysterious collections presided over by an old woman. A visitor to the store observes a hunt scene on a dusty tapestry at the back of the shop. As he identifies with the scene, what was exterior observation becomes interior reality with few overt signs of transition. The man becomes a part of the drama in the woods as time and space coalesce and the hunter is hunted.

In "Verde lagarto amarelo" (Green Yellow Lizard), included in the 1971 revised edition of *Antes do baile verde,* Telles paints an interesting psychological portrait. She presents the distrust and insecurity felt by Rodolfo, the overweight narrator, in his relationship with his younger brother, the outgoing and confident Eduardo. The crux of the story is revealed in a series of dialogues, flashbacks, and time shifts. Rodolfo's realization that he did not receive his mother's love, as did Eduardo, truncates his ability to reach out and communicate. The heat, odor, and a "transparent yellowish green" cling to Rodolfo's persona and prevent him from enjoying the spontaneous affection of his brother. The color green is frequently used symbolically in Telles's fiction; Fábio Lucas suggests that it may convey the image of youth prior to maturity.

As meninas is considered by most critics to be Telles's best novel. Written during the height of repression practiced by the military dictatorship in Brazil (1964–1985), this 1973 novel addresses the multiple problems of three young women who live at a boardinghouse under the watchful eye of nuns during turbulent times. The cramped physical space serves as a metaphor for the protagonists' lives. *As meninas* reveals the interwoven stories of Lorena Vaz Leme, a young woman who lives in a dreamworld; Lia, a student involved in revolutionary activities; and Ana Clara, a drug addict who suffers anguish in a drugged state until she commits suicide. Each character confronts reality in her own way, a technique that heightens reader involvement in their struggles. The novel also breaks new ground in both form and content. The young women, struggling with traditional societal constraints, also face the dangers and challenges of drugs, revolution, sex, love, and technology, all set against the backdrop of the chaotic early years of the military dictatorship. In terms of technique, the rapidly shifting points of views and the use of multiple narrators serve to intensify the confusion and struggle of the young protagonists. The novel was awarded the Prêmio Coelho Neto (Coelho Neto Prize) by the Academia Brasileira de Letras in 1973.

The publication of *As meninas* in the early 1970s was considered a courageous act because of the threat of censorship and other dangers of the times. Some writers were silenced, while others delivered their criticism of the government via allegory and deliberate vagueness. Telles's treatment of the revolutionary theme is direct but hidden in the complexity of the narrative. There is even a section in which she includes verbatim a manifesto she had received with regard to the torture of a political prisoner. She was willing to chance the consequences if the censors were to discover that the character Lia is involved in subversive activities. Telles's belief that the Third World writer must address social issues is evident in this novel.

In Telles's view, a writer in her situation could not be divorced from the harsh realities of living in a developing country. She felt that she must be a witness and a participant, as did many members of the Latin American intelligentsia. In 1977, at a crucial juncture during the years of the military dictatorship, Telles and other writers submitted a petition to Armando Falcão, the minister of justice, that was signed by 1,046 persons decrying the censorship imposed on Brazilian authors. These convictions find expression in some of Telles's fiction, particularly in *As meninas* and the story collection *Seminário dos ratos* (1977, Rat Seminar; translated as *Tigrela and Other Stories*, 1986). The title story in the collection uses the conventions of science fiction and horror to make a statement about morals and politics. A conference takes place in an isolated manor to discuss the elimination of rodents. As the discussion progresses, there is a growing noise and sense of unease. Suddenly, rodents invade the room. The rats are an obvious metaphor for the military. In effect, the narrative is a satirical fable that expresses opposition to the military regime then in power in Brazil.

"Tigrela" is the memorable tale of an apartment-raised tiger who is jealous of her mistress, Romana. The narrator meets Romana by chance in a café, and they converse over drinks. Romana, having divorced her fifth husband, is living with Tigrela, who happens to be two-thirds tiger and one-third human. Tigrela is a vegetarian like her owner and has a taste for jewels, the music of Johann Sebastian Bach, and whiskey. Over time Tigrela becomes increasingly jealous of Romana and watches her constantly. Romana matter-of-factly tells her tale as she consumes several whiskeys. In this story the outrageous is treated as ordinary, and the boundaries between imagination and

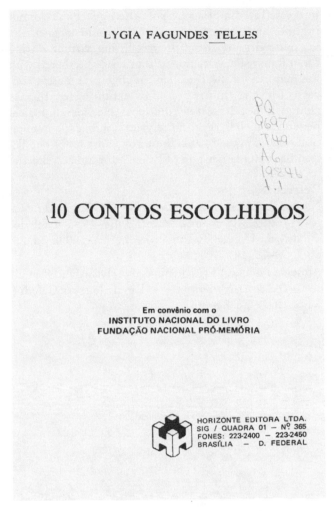

LYGIA FAGUNDES TELLES

10 CONTOS ESCOLHIDOS

Em convênio com o
INSTITUTO NACIONAL DO LIVRO
FUNDAÇÃO NACIONAL PRÓ-MEMÓRIA

HORIZONTE EDITORA LTDA.
SIG / QUADRA 01 – Nº 365
FONES: 223-2400 – 223-2450
BRASÍLIA – D. FEDERAL

Title page for one of two collections of Telles's stories (10 Selected Stories) published in 1984 (Thomas Cooper Library, University of South Carolina)

fantasy are blurred in an inventive way. Both "Tigrela" and "Seminário dos ratos" interweave the human-animal connection and transformation in such a seamless manner that the reader accepts the surreal at face value.

Lygia Fagundes Telles is a sought-after lecturer who invariably captivates audiences with her gracious style. She is a disciplined professional who gives interviews, supports writers, and has taken a leadership role in the social and political issues facing Brazil. Her works are well crafted and memorable. She deeply penetrates her characters' psyches, whether she is treating the theme of changing societal values, the role of women, or the psychological problems of isolation. Her language is carefully selected; she frequently employs the vernacular but does not resort to vulgar language, a characteristic practice of many Brazilian writers during the 1970s, who used such language to shock the establishment. While Telles is interested in the inner person, the mystery surrounding life, and the interplay of reality and fantasy, she introduced more-social themes in her writing during the military dictatorship. At that time she shared with the majority of the Brazilian intelligentsia a great concern for the future of the nation. Her themes changed, but her style did not. Her psychological penetration, her sense of mystery, her experimentation with language, and the strong impact of her fiction have made her one of Brazil's foremost writers.

References:

Nancy T. Baden, *The Muffled Cries: The Writer and Literature in Authoritarian Brazil, 1964–1985* (Lanham, Md.: University Press of America, 1999), pp. 26, 73–75, 154, 191;

Almeida Fischer, "Três meninas na selva asfática," in his *O áspero ofício, terceira série* (Rio de Janeiro: Cátedra, 1977), pp. 34–36;

Antônio Hohfeltdt, "O conto psicológico," in his *Conto brasileiro contemporâneo* (Pôrto Alegre: Mercado Aberto, 1981), pp. 119–121;

Maria Lúcia Lipecki, "*A disciplina do amor,*" *Colóquio-Letras,* 70 (November 1982): 100–102;

Luiza Lobo, "Women Writers in Brazil Today," *World Literature Today,* 61 (Winter 1987): 49–54;

Fábio Lucas, "Mistério e magia," *Estado de Sao Paulo, suplemento literario,* 5 September 1970, p. 1;

Malcolm Silverman, "O mundo ficcional de Lygia Fagundes Telles," in his *Moderna ficção brasileira 2: ensaios* (Rio de Janeiro: Civilização Brasileira, 1981), pp. 162–185;

Edla van Steen, "Lygia Fagundes Telles," in her *Viver & escrever,* volume 1 (Pôrto Alegre: L & PM, 1981), pp. 85–97.

Dalton Trevisan
(14 June 1925 –   )

Lesley Feracho
University of Georgia

BOOKS: *Serenata ao luar* (Curitiba: Gráfica Mundial, 1945);

Sete anos de pastor (Curitiba: Joaquim, 1948);

Novelas nada exemplares (Rio de Janeiro: Olympio, 1959; revised edition, Rio de Janeiro: Civilização Brasileira, 1970; revised, 1975; revised edition, Rio de Janeiro: Record, 1979);

Morte na praça: contos (Rio de Janeiro: Editora do Autor, 1964; revised and enlarged edition, Rio de Janeiro: Civilização Brasileira, 1975; revised edition, Rio de Janeiro: Record, 1979);

Cemitério de elefantes: contos (Rio de Janeiro: Civilização Brasileira, 1964; revised and enlarged, 1970; revised, 1975; revised again, 1977; revised edition, Rio de Janeiro: Record, 1980);

O vampiro de Curitiba (Rio de Janeiro: Civilização Brasileira, 1965; revised and enlarged, 1970); translated by Gregory Rabassa as *The Vampire of Curitiba and Other Stories* (New York: Knopf, 1972);

Desastres do amor: contos (Rio de Janeiro: Civilização Brasileira, 1968; revised, 1974; revised edition, Rio de Janeiro: Record, 1979);

Mistérios de Curitiba (Rio de Janeiro: Record, 1968; revised, 1979);

Os 18 melhores contos do Brasil (Rio de Janeiro: Bloch, 1968);

A guerra conjugal (Rio de Janeiro: Civilização Brasileira, 1969; revised, 1970; revised again, 1975; revised edition, Rio de Janeiro: Record, 1979);

O rei da terra: contos (Rio de Janeiro: Civilização Brasileira, 1972; revised, 1975);

O pássaro de cinco asas (Rio de Janeiro: Civilização Brasileira, 1974; revised, 1975; revised edition, Rio de Janeiro: Record, 1979);

A faca no coração (Rio de Janeiro: Civilização Brasileira, 1975; revised edition, Rio de Janeiro: Record, 1979);

Abismo de rosas: contos (Rio de Janeiro: Civilização Brasileira, 1976; revised edition, Rio de Janeiro: Record, 1976);

Dalton Trevisan *(from the dust jacket for* The Vampire of Curitiba and Other Stories, *translated by Gregory Rabassa, 1972; Bruccoli Clark Layman Archives)*

A trombeta do anjo vingador (Rio de Janeiro: Codecri, 1977; revised edition, Rio de Janeiro: Record, 1981);

Crimes de paixão (Rio de Janeiro: Record, 1978; revised, 1991);

Primeiro livro de contos: antologia pessoal (Rio de Janeiro: Record, 1979);

20 contos menores: antologia escolar (Rio de Janeiro: Record, 1979);

Virgem louca, loucos beijos (Rio de Janeiro: Record, 1979);

Lincha tarado (Rio de Janeiro: Record, 1980);

Chorinho brejeiro (Rio de Janeiro: Record, 1981);

Essas malditas mulheres (Rio de Janeiro: Record, 1982);

Meu querido assassino (Rio de Janeiro: Record, 1983);

Contos eróticos (Rio de Janeiro: Record, 1984);

A polaquinha (Rio de Janeiro: Record, 1985);

Pão e sangue (Rio de Janeiro: Record, 1988);

Vozes do retrato: quinze histórias de mentiras e verdades (São Paulo: Ática, 1991);

Em busca de Curitiba perdida (Rio de Janeiro: Record, 1992);

Dinorá: novos mistérios (Rio de Janeiro: Record, 1994);

Ah, é?: ministórias (Rio de Janeiro: Record, 1994);

234 ministórias (Rio de Janeiro: Record, 1997);

O grande deflorador: e outros contos escolhidos (Pôrto Alegre: L&PM, 2000);

Pico na veia (Rio de Janeiro: Record, 2002);

Capitu sou eu (Rio de Janeiro: Record, 2003);

Arara bêbada: ministórias (Rio de Janeiro & São Paulo: Record, 2004).

Collection: *Dalton Trevisan: seleção de textos, notas, estudos biográfico, histórico e crítico e exercícios,* edited by Alvaro Cardoso Gomes and Carlos Alberto Vechi (São Paulo: Abril Educação, 1981).

Edition in English: "Tres tiros na tarde," translated by Gregory Rabassa as "Three Shots in the Afternoon," in *Prospero's Mirror: A Translators' Portfolio of Latin American Short Fiction,* edited by Ilan Stavans (Willimantic, Conn.: Curbstone Press, 1998), pp. 232–235.

In any survey of the development of the short story in Brazil, a name that stands out for noteworthy and significant contributions is that of Dalton Trevisan. Trevisan's short stories have distinguished themselves as exercises in the minimalist portrayal of the human psyche. While writers such as Joaquim Maria Machado de Assis and Lygia Fagundes Telles provide detailed psychological studies of their characters, Trevisan allows his creations to reveal themselves through action and dialogue. Constantly returning to his native Curitiba in the state of Paraná for the setting of his stories, Trevisan explores eroticism, betrayal, violence, and isolation. The result is the development of a fictional Curitiba that is a metaphor for a site of physical and spiritual death and despair. The symbolic importance of the setting can be likened to those of Graciliano Ramos's arid northeast, João Guimarães Rosa's *sertão* (backlands), and Gabriel García Marquez's Macondo.

Trevisan shuns interviews and has allowed little information about himself to be published. He was born Dalton Jérson Trevisan in Curitiba on 14 June 1925. In the early 1940s he graduated from the law school of the Universidade Federal de Paraná and briefly practiced law in Curitiba before quitting to go to work in his family's ceramic factory. In 1945 he received a skull fracture in an accident and spent a month in the hospital; forced to confront his own mortality, he undertook a reevaluation of his life. The experience led him to begin writing. In 1945 he published his first book, the novel *Serenata ao luar* (Moonlight Serenade).

The following year Trevisan founded a literary journal, *Joaquim,* as a forum for the free exchange of ideas in the wake of Getúlio Vargas's authoritarian Estado Novo (New State) of 1937 to 1945. The journal published stories by Mário de Andrade, Oswald de Andrade, Carlos Drummond de Andrade, Antônio Cândido, and Otto Maria Carpeaux; articles on the nature of language by Jean-Paul Sartre; and studies of the works of André Gide by José Paulo Paes. Trevisan's own stories, such as "Rachel," were long narratives that were the opposite of what came to be his trademark concise style.

In 1948 Trevisan published a collection of his short stories titled *Sete anos de pastor* (Seven Years as a Shepherd). He later came to regard it and the novel *Serenata ao luar* as so unfocused, undeveloped, and different from his mature work that he prohibited them from being republished, omits them from his official bibliography, and has never discussed them in the few interviews he has given.

Joaquim ceased publication in December 1948. Trevisan traveled in Europe in 1950 and was married in 1953; he and his wife have two daughters. In the 1960s he began to explore the darker side of the human condition. Nelson H. Vieira notes that his stories are filled with imperfect human beings engaged in self-destructive behaviors from which they are powerless to escape. Those who are not the oppressors are the victims of violent attacks and are doomed to defeat. In 1964 Trevisan published the collection *Morte na praça* (Death in the Square), in which he develops his "técnica de reiteración" (technique of reiteration) or "técnica del indicio" (technique of indication). In this narrative strategy a developed moral profile of the characters is replaced by the repetition of names, descriptions, or behaviors. The technique can be seen in the various women with painted mouths and lips, such as the adulterous Anita in the title story, the prostitutes in "O velório" (The Wake), and Lili, who is abandoned by her lover, in "A casa de Lili" (Lili's House). An important effect of the technique is to highlight universalized reactions rather than individualized behavior. In his collection *O vampiro de Curitiba* (1965; translated as *The Vampire of Curitiba and Other Stories,* 1972) Trevisan incorporates archetypical models of everyman, antihero, heroine, and villain; many of his characters have the common names João (John) and Maria (Mary). Vieira, Berta Waldman, and Linda Ledford-Miller have all pointed out that while Trevisan's antiheroes and villains may perform malicious actions, the author does not pass moral judgments on them. Ledford-Miller notes that the personalized narrative style gives the reader the sense of "an authorless, or narrator-less narrative"; Vieira refers to this phenomenon as "mock absence." The lack of a narrative guide produces in the reader empathy for the characters because of an implied commonality of experience; the often ambiguous point of view demands an investment of the reader's emotions, knowledge, and experience.

In 1968 Trevisan published *Desastres do amor* (Disasters of Love). Like the pieces in *Morte na praça,* these short stories use a minimalist style to examine themes such as life in the city, the dehumanizing effects of industrialization, and the loss of a sense of the poetry of everyday life.

The beginning of the following decade brought greater emphasis in Trevisan's work on the spiritual aspects of human existence through his portrayals of Christ-like figures in what Ledford-Miller calls his "Passion/passion narratives." The 1970 revision of his 1959 collection *Novelas nada exemplares* (Novels Not at All Exemplary) illustrates this shift. In stories such as "A velha querida" (The Beloved Old Woman) he undermines and even parodies the Christian Passion narrative while at the same time reaffirming it. The stories use metaphorical language, dialogue-bound narration, interior monologues, parables, myths, and allegories from biblical, classical, and medieval sources. Trevisan focuses on women's experiences in the collection *O rei da terra* (1972, The King of the Land).

In the late 1970s Trevisan returned to a secular outlook but continued to set his stories in his native Curitiba. Curitiba is the site where his characters' attempts at connection with others are continuously thwarted. One of the principal characters in Trevisan's works is Nelsinho, the vampire who first appeared in the title story of *O vampiro de Curitiba.* He is the tragic aristocratic vampire of Bram Stoker's novel *Dracula* (1897) transformed into a middle-class man, the embodiment of depravity and the darker side of human nature in search of a fulfillment that it is never able to achieve.

In the late 1970s Trevisan's minimalist exploration of human suffering and alienation took the form of the microtext, a metonymic representation of individual experiences. The meaning of the microtext is deter-

DALTON TREVISAN

O VAMPIRO
DE CURITIBA

EDITORA CIVILIZAÇÃO BRASILEIRA S.A.
RIO DE JANEIRO

Title page for Trevisan's 1965 collection of stories set in his home state of Curitiba. The title piece features his recurring character Nelsinho, a middle-class vampire (Joint University Libraries, Nashville, Tennessee).

mined not only by the author's observations but also by the reader's desire to explore the symbolic meaning of the work. Trevisan was one of the major representatives of this form in Brazilian literature; it can also be found in the Mexican Juan José Arreola's *Confabulario* (1952; translated, 1964), the Argentine Jorge Luis Borges's *El hacedor* (1960, The Maker; translated as *Dreamtigers,* 1964), the Cuban Guillermo Cabrera Infante's *Vista del amanecer en el trópico* (1975; translated as *View of Dawn in the Tropics,* 1978), and the works of the American Donald Barthelme.

Trevisan's short stories of the 1980s develop another aspect of his examination of humanity: the exploration of the specifically feminine experience. In *Essas malditas mulheres* (1982, These Cursed Women) and *Meu querido assassino* (1983, My Dear Assassin) the

*Paperback covers for two of Trevisan's works: his second novel (The Little Polish Woman), published in 1985,
and a collection of short stories (Bread and Blood), published in 1988
(Thomas Cooper Library, University of South Carolina)*

reader is given a glimpse into the worlds of prostitutes, victims of spousal abuse, and unfaithful wives. The women are not just victims but find surprising sources of strength. Particularly in *Essas malditas mulheres,* Trevisan's "Marias" use the resources at their disposal to control the men in matters of sex, finances, and family life.

In 1985 Trevisan published his second novel, *A polaquinha* (The Little Polish Woman). Here he continues the portrayal of women of *Essas malditas mulheres* and *Meu querido assassino,* focusing on the loss of innocence of the young protagonist. Critics such as Eva Paulino Bueno have noted that the "Marias" and women such as the protagonist of *A polaquinha* are susceptible to abuse and victimization by the many villainous characters named "João," despite their moments of empower-

ment. Trevisan creates multifaceted heroines who are not merely paper dolls, angels or demons, or prostitutes or mothers; like their male counterparts, they struggle to escape their fragmented, hopeless existence.

With each successive work Trevisan's narratives have become increasingly succinct. The collections *Ah, é?* (1994, Is That Right?) and *234 ministórias* (1997, 234 Ministories) consist of microtexts and haiku in which the themes of loneliness, separation, betrayal, deception, strained family relationships, sexual abuse, and murder and the archetypal figures João and Maria are condensed into vignettes, some of which are as short as two lines; some are purely descriptive, and others consist solely of dialogue. A thread that runs throughout *234 ministórias* is that of the antihero, a sometime criminal whose solitary life on the margins of society is occasionally interrupted either by unfortunate encounters with others or by acts of physical, including sexual, violence.

His dedication to depicting the human experience places Dalton Trevisan among such renowned Brazilian writers as Machado de Assis, Telles, Mário de Andrade, Rubem Fonseca, Antonio Callado, Sergio Sant'Anna, and Clarice Lispector. His works have been translated into English, Spanish, German, Italian, Polish, and Swedish. Trevisan's contribution to Brazilian letters has been further confirmed by awards such as the Luís Cláudio de Sousa Prize of the PEN Club of Brazil for *Morte na praça* and the 1996 Prize of the Ministério da Cultura de Literatura for his work as a whole. In 2003 he shared with Bernardo Carvalho the first prize of the Portugal Telecom de Literatura Brasileira for *Pico na veia* (2002, Peak in the Vein). The narrator of the final piece in *234 ministórias* says, "O conto não tem mais fim que novo começo" (The story has more of a beginning than an ending). Trevisan's life work can be described as a never-ending attempt to articulate the most profound emotions and experiences of human beings.

References:

Vicente Ataide, "La técnica de la reiteración en el cuento de Dalton Trevisan," *Nueva narrativa hispanoamericana*, 3, no. 1 (1973): 123–131;

Eva Paulino Bueno, "Matrizes e filiais na ficção de Dalton Trevisan," *Chasqui*, 23 (November 1994): 12–21;

José Castelo, "Uma viagem no tempo nas páginas da *Joaquim*," *O Estado de S. Paulo*, February 2001, Caderno 2;

John J. Crocitte and Robert Levine, "The Vargas Era," in *The Brazil Reader: History, Culture, Politics*, edited by Crocitte and Levine (Durham, N.C.: Duke University Press, 1999), pp. 145–155;

David William Foster, "Major Figures in the Brazilian Short Story," in *The Latin American Short Story: A Critical History*, edited by Margaret Sayers Peden (Boston: Twayne, 1983), pp. 1–34;

Linda Ledford-Miller, "The Perverse Passions of Dalton Trevisan," in *Literature and the Bible*, edited by David Bevan (Amsterdam & Atlanta: Rodopi, 1993), pp. 61–77;

Ledford-Miller, "Shoes for Little Peter: Narrative Technique in Trevisan's Not-at-All Exemplary Novella, *Pedrinho*," *Brasil/Brazil*, 4 (April–May 1990): 37–50;

Nelson H. Vieira, "João e Maria: Dalton Trevisan's Eponymous Heroes," *Hispania*, 69 (March 1986): 45–52;

Vieira, "Narrative in Dalton Trevisan," *Modern Language Studies*, 14 (Winter 1984): 11–21;

Berta Waldman, "Dalton Trevisan: A linguagem roubada," *Revista Iberoamericana*, 43 (1977): 247–255.

Erico Veríssimo

(17 December 1905 – 28 November 1975)

Luciana Camargo Namorato
University of North Carolina at Chapel Hill

See also the Veríssimo entry in *DLB 145: Modern Latin-American Fiction Writers, Second Series.*

BOOKS: *Fantoches* (Pôrto Alegre: Globo, 1932);

Clarissa (Pôrto Alegre: Globo, 1933);

Caminhos cruzados (Pôrto Alegre: Globo, 1935); translated by Lewis C. Kaplan as *Crossroads* (New York: Macmillan, 1943); republished as *Crossroads and Destinies* (London: Arco, 1956);

Música ao longe (São Paulo: Nacional, 1935);

A vida de Joana d'Arc (Pôrto Alegre: Globo, 1935);

As aventuras do avião vermelho (Pôrto Alegre: Globo, 1936);

Um lugar ao sol (Pôrto Alegre: Globo, 1936);

Meu ABC (Pôrto Alegre: Globo, 1936);

Rosa Maria no castelo encantado (Pôrto Alegre: Globo, 1936);

Os três porquinhos pobres (Pôrto Alegre: Globo, 1936);

As aventuras de Tibicuera, que são também as aventuras do Brasil (Pôrto Alegre: Globo, 1937);

Olhai os lírios do campo (Pôrto Alegre: Globo, 1938); translated by Jean Neel Karnoff as *Consider the Lilies of the Field* (New York: Macmillan, 1947);

O urso com música na barriga (Pôrto Alegre: Globo, 1938);

Aventuras no mundo da higiene (Pôrto Alegre: Globo, 1939);

Outra vez os três porquinhos (Pôrto Alegre: Globo, 1939);

Viagem à aurora do mundo (Pôrto Alegre: Globo, 1939);

A vida do elefante Basílio (Pôrto Alegre: Globo, 1939);

Saga (Pôrto Alegre: Globo, 1940);

Gato preto em campo de neve (Pôrto Alegre: Globo, 1941);

Viagem através da literatura americana (Rio de Janeiro: Instituto Brasil-Estados Unidos, 1941);

As mãos de meu filho: contos e artigos (Pôrto Alegre: Meridiano, 1942);

O resto é silêncio (Pôrto Alegre: Globo, 1943); translated by Kaplan as *The Rest Is Silence* (New York: Macmillan, 1946; London: Arco, 1956);

Brazilian Literature: An Outline (New York: Macmillan, 1945); translated by Maria da Glória Bordini as

Erico Veríssimo (from the dust jacket for Veríssimo, His Excellency, the Ambassador, *1967; Richland County Public Library)*

Breve história da literatura brasileira (São Paulo: Globo, 1995);

A volta do gato preto (Pôrto Alegre: Globo, 1947);

O tempo e o vento, part 1: *O continente,* 2 volumes (Pôrto Alegre: Globo, 1949); individual chapters republished as *Ana Terra* (Brazil: Editores Associados, 1949; Pôrto Alegre: Globo, 1971) and as *Um certo Capitão Rodrigo* (Lisbon: Editores Associados,

1949; Pôrto Alegre: Globo, 1970); *O tempo e o vento,* part 1, translated by Linton Lomas Barrett as *Time and the Wind* (New York: Macmillan, 1951; London: Arco, 1954);

O tempo e o vento, part 2: *O retrato,* 2 volumes (Pôrto Alegre: Globo, 1951);

Lembrança de Pôrto Alegre (Rio de Janeiro: Globo, 1954); translated by Iris Strohschoen as *Souvenir of Pôrto Alegre* (São Paulo: Globo, 1960);

Noite (Pôrto Alegre: Globo, 1954); translated by Barrett as *Night* (New York: Macmillan, 1956; London: Arco, 1956); republished as *Evil in the Night* (Greenwich, Conn.: Fawcett, 1957);

Gente e bichos: histórias infantis (Pôrto Alegre: Globo, 1956);

México: história duma viagem (Pôrto Alegre: Globo, 1957); translated by Barrett as *Mexico* (New York: Orion Press, 1960; London: Macdonald, 1960);

O ataque (Rio de Janeiro: Globo, 1959)–includes "A ponte," republished as *A ponte* (Rio de Janeiro: Nova Fronteira, 1975);

O tempo e o vento, part 3: *O arquipélago,* 3 volumes (Pôrto Alegre: Globo, 1961–1962);

O Senhor Embaixador (Pôrto Alegre: Globo, 1965); translated by Barrett and Marie McDavid Barrett as *His Excellency, the Ambassador* (New York: Macmillan, 1967);

Ficção completa, 5 volumes (Rio de Janeiro: J. Aguilar, 1966–1967)–includes "O escritor diante do espelho";

O prisioneiro (Pôrto Alegre: Globo, 1967);

Israel em abril (Pôrto Alegre: Globo, 1969); translated by Virgil E. Bottom as *Israel in April* (Pôrto Alegre: Globo, 1993);

Incidente em Antares (Pôrto Alegre: Globo, 1971);

Um certo Henrique Bertaso: pequeno retrato em que o pintor também aparece (Pôrto Alegre: Globo, 1972);

Rio Grande do Sul (São Paulo: Brunner, 1973);

Solo de clarineta: memórias, volume 1 (Pôrto Alegre: Globo, 1973);

Artistas gaúchos (Pôrto Alegre: Sociedade Israelita Riograndense, 1975);

Solo de clarineta: memórias, volume 2, edited by Flávio Loureiro Chaves (Pôrto Alegre: Globo, 1976);

Galeria fosca (Pôrto Alegre: Globo, 1987);

O romance de um romance (Florianópolis: Museu/Arquivo da Poesia Manuscrita, 1999).

Editions and Collections: *Obras,* 17 volumes (Pôrto Alegre: Globo, 1953–1956);

Contos (Pôrto Alegre: Globo, 1978);

Histórias infantis de Erico Veríssimo (Pôrto Alegre: RBS, 1978);

As aventuras do avião vermelho e outras histórias (Lisbon: Verbo, 1980);

O urso com música na barriga e outras histórias (Lisbon: Verbo, 1980);

A Porto Alegre de Érico, edited by Josué Guimarães (Pôrto Alegre: Globo, 1984).

RECORDING: *Fragmentos de O tempo e o vento,* read by Veríssimo, Festa FP 7008, n.d.

OTHER: "Contemporary Trends in Brazilian Literature," in *Intellectual Trends in Latin America: Papers Read at a Conference on Intellectual Trends in Latin America* (Austin: University of Texas Press, 1945);

Albert Croissant, *El teatro americano: un análisis crítico,* preface by Veríssimo, translated by Rafael Trujillo (Pasadena: Keystone Press, 1945);

Moysés Vellinho, *Brazil South: Its Conquest & Settlement,* translated by Linton Lomas Barrett & Marie McDavid Barrett, preface by Veríssimo (New York: Knopf, 1968);

José Fernando Carneiro, *Psicologia do brasileiro e outros estudos,* preface by Veríssimo (Rio de Janeiro: AGIR, 1971);

Edgar Vasques, *Rango,* volume 1, preface by Veríssimo (Pôrto Alegre: L & PM, 1975);

Isaac Izecksohn, *Os judeus na atualidade,* preface by Veríssimo (Rio de Janeiro: Izecksohn, 1976);

Manoelito de Ornellas, *Gaúchos e beduínos: a origem étnica e a formação social do Rio Grand do Sul,* third edition, preface by Veríssimo (Rio de Janeiro: J. Olympio, 1976).

SELECTED TRANSLATIONS: Aldous Huxley, *Contraponto* (Pôrto Alegre: Globo, 1934);

John Steinbeck, *Ratos e homens* (Pôrto Alegre: Globo, 1940);

James Hilton, *Adeus, Mr. Chips* (Pôrto Alegre: Globo, 1941);

Hendrik Willem Van Loon, *Navios & de como êles singraram os sete mares* (Pôrto Alegre: Globo, 1941);

Robert Nathan, *O retrato de Jennie* (Pôrto Alegre: Globo, 1942);

Hilton, *Não estamos sós* (Pôrto Alegre: Globo, 1943);

W. Somerset Maugham, *Maquiavel e a dama* (Pôrto Alegre: Globo, 1948).

As an adolescent, Erico Veríssimo was called one evening to hold a lamp for a doctor performing surgery on a wounded man in an operating room at Veríssimo's father's pharmacy, where victims of fights and of attacks by assassins for hire were treated. The boy overcame his fear during the surgery by reflecting on the attitude of the victim. If the injured man was able to stand the pain without making a sound during his treatment, then Veríssimo figured that the least he could do was to hold

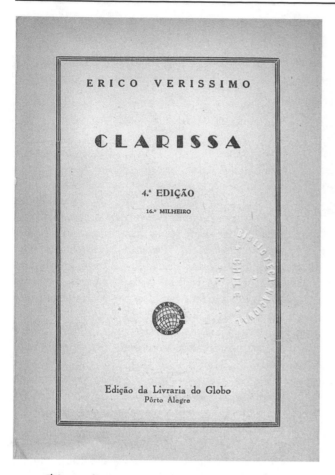

Title page for the 1942 edition of Veríssimo's 1933 novel
about the everyday life of a thirteen-year-old girl
(Biblioteca Nacional de Chile)

the light in order to help save his life. Over the years, Veríssimo compared his attitude toward the patient to his outlook as an author writing during a time of cruelty and injustice. He wrote to illuminate the reality of the world in which he lived, despite the nausea and horror that it caused him.

Veríssimo directed his attention to his home territory, recreating genealogically and socially the history of Rio Grande do Sul, the southernmost state of Brazil. His prose works reveal life on the pampas, the tricks of local political leaders, and the everyday lives of the gauchos and the strong women who were part of their lives. Veríssimo's trilogy *O tempo e o vento* (1949–1962; part 1 translated as *Time and the Wind*, 1951) brought the southern part of Brazil to the forefront in Brazilian literature at a time when most literary works focused on the cities of Rio de Janeiro and São Paulo. During this same period the Northeast of Brazil was becoming popular through the works of Jorge Amado. Veríssimo, however, was not known simply as a regionalist writer, a label he considered quite limiting and anachronistic. In his works he questioned the use of violence and wars as a way of solv-

ing man's problems and condemned acts of torture and tyranny, whether practiced by the political Left or the Right. He also wrote about the anguish of the modern man, divorced from religion and divided between his social requirements and his emotions. According to critic Wilson Martins, Veríssimo was able to achieve what no other writer of the Movimento Modernista Brasileiro (Brazilian Modernist Movement) of 1922 in São Paulo could do: to write modern urban romances with an emphasis on human beings. During his lifetime Veríssimo was, after Amado, the best-selling author in Brazil and, besides Amado, the only Brazilian author able to live solely on his earnings from his writings.

Erico Lopes Veríssimo was born to Sebastião Veríssimo da Fonseca and Abegahy Lopes Veríssimo on 17 December 1905 in Cruz Alta, Rio Grande do Sul. He belonged to a traditional family of farmers who had been economically ruined at the beginning of the twentieth century. Friends and acquaintances gathered at Veríssimo's father's pharmacy for drinks and conversation, a setting that offered the future writer countless examples for use as character types. Political officials, fight victims, liars, and storytellers served as inspirations for the characters in many of Veríssimo's works.

During his years of schooling Veríssimo had serious problems in learning mathematics. He was timid and enjoyed reading and drawing. By the age of seven he had become friends with the owner of the town cinema and was able to see many movies without paying. His future interest in and admiration for the United States derived from this passion for the cinema.

Generous and bohemian, Veríssimo's father never thought twice before helping relatives, friends, and even strangers in their time of need. A lover of opera and poetry, Sebastião Veríssimo led an extravagant life that included extramarital affairs and a problem with alcohol. His pharmacy was in constant financial difficulty, and when he was not able to pay off a promissory note, he turned to his father to ask for help. Erico Veríssimo's mother was the opposite of her husband by nature. Economically stable and selective in the friendships she kept, she worked as a dressmaker to help pay the household bills. The money she earned enabled Erico to attend an Episcopal boarding school founded and run by American missionaries in Pôrto Alegre, the capital of Rio Grande do Sul, where he finished three years of his secondary education.

When he returned home during his summer break from school in 1922, Veríssimo found his family in the middle of a crisis. His father persisted in his bohemian lifestyle, drinking too much and getting his family and the pharmacy deeper into debt. At this time Veríssimo's mother decided on a divorce and took him and his brother, Enio, to live with her parents. Veríssimo left school and began to work at a grocer's shop, where he wrote literature on the wrapping paper at the store. Dissatisfied with his job, he took a position at the Banco Nacional do Comércio (National Bank of Commerce) as a bookkeeper and, in 1924, asked to be transferred to a branch of the same bank in Pôrto Alegre. His mother had already decided to move there so that Enio could get a better education.

On his return to Cruz Alta in 1925, Veríssimo and a partner opened a pharmacy, which remained in business for four years. The business failed because of bad financial management, and it took Veríssimo seventeen years to pay off the debts. While working in his pharmacy, Veríssimo dedicated himself to reading the works of writers such as Henrik Ibsen, William Shakespeare, George Bernard Shaw, Oscar Wilde, and Joaquim Maria Machado de Assis. He also gave private classes in literature and English to help pay off his debts. During this same period the journalist Jacinto Prado Júnior convinced Veríssimo to have a short story about Christmas, titled "Chico," published in a local newspaper. In 1928 Veríssimo's story "Ladrão de Gado" (Cattles' Thief) was published in the Pôrto Alegre magazine *Revista do Globo*. After these first publications he submitted several manuscripts to various periodicals.

With the failure of the pharmacy, Veríssimo decided to attempt to earn a living by doing what he most enjoyed. In 1930 he went to Pôrto Alegre to work as a writer, taking with him borrowed money to pay for train fare and for his first month's rent. When this money and the hope he brought with him were almost gone, Veríssimo met with the director of the *Revista do Globo*, Mansueto Bernardi, who hired him as secretary to the publishing department of the recently created publishing firm Editora Globo. This company became known as a pioneer in the Brazilian publishing market during the 1930s and 1940s. Bernardi could not offer Veríssimo a good salary, but he still accepted the job. During the daytime he edited the magazine. Without a sufficient budget, the only solution was to copy articles from other magazines and newspapers. Veríssimo translated articles from American, French, British, Italian, and Argentinean magazines and reproduced black-and-white copies of illustrations from them. He also collaborated on the literary page of the newspapers *Diário de notícias* and *Correio do povo*, and he translated books from English into Portuguese to help pay his monthly bills. At night he met with influential writers and journalists to listen to their conversations.

Once his job was secure and his lifestyle more stable, Veríssimo returned to Cruz Alta to marry his girlfriend, Mafalda Volpe. They married in 1931 and returned together to Pôrto Alegre. Mafalda was Veríssimo's companion for life and, in his opinion, had the "better brains" of the couple. She understood her husband's periods of silence and distractions, and she provided much support to his career in writing.

Early in 1932 Veríssimo thought about publishing a collection of his best short stories. He knew, however, that it would be difficult to find an editor interested in publishing this form of literature. Short stories were not widely accepted in the literary market at that time, and Veríssimo was still an unknown author. He decided to publish the work himself and sought the help of Henrique Bertaso, the son of the owner of Editora Globo, concerning the costs of such a publication. In 1932 Bertaso supervised the publication of Veríssimo's *Fantoches* (1932, Puppets), a collection of eighteen short stories. The pieces in the collection ranged in theme from horror to comedy, and most were written as short theatrical pieces. The stories derived their inspiration from such authors as Ibsen, Shaw, Anatole France, and Luigi Pirandello. Of the 1,500 copies produced, only 500 were sold in the first year following publication. A fire at the publishing house destroyed the remainder of the books, and Veríssimo ended up receiving royalties on the total number of copies printed that first year.

During the 1930s Veríssimo wrote eleven books of children's literature, including *As aventuras do avião vermelho* (1936, The Adventures of the Red Airplane) and *Viagem à aurora do mundo* (1939, Trip to the Dawn of the World). In the following decades he wrote nothing more for children, but his early works for children were frequently reprinted. In 1934 he translated Aldous Huxley's *Point Counter Point* (1928) into Portuguese as *Contraponto*. The translation turned out to be a bad financial investment for Editora Globo, but it brought a certain level of prestige to the company. Some literary critics have found a similarity between the lack of a narrative center in Veríssimo's works and Huxley's style.

Clarissa (1933), Veríssimo's first novel, relates the life of a thirteen-year-old girl through a collection of scenes from her everyday life. The novel describes Clarissa's experiences as she enters the adult world, focusing on her discovery of desire and death and of the existence of misery and social discrimination.

In 1935 Veríssimo won the Prêmio Machado de Assis (Machado de Assis Prize) for *Música ao longe* (Distant Music), published that same year. Encouraged by writer Dyonélio Machado to compete for the prize, Veríssimo decided to write this novel in which the character Clarissa reappears. In it she is a sixteen-year-old girl who works as a teacher in her hometown of Jacarenga and lives with her family. Clarissa's interior world, unsettled and full of emotion, clashes with the exterior world, which is shown to be monotonous and decadent. The literary prize was shared by Marques Rebelo, João Alphonsus de Guimaraens, Machado, and Veríssimo because

Front cover for the 1940 edition of Veríssimo's 1935 satirical novel (translated as Crossroads, *1943) about life in the city of Pôrto Alegre (Biblioteca Nacional de Chile)*

the committee of judges could not select just one winner from among them.

In 1935 Veríssimo also published *Caminhos cruzados* (translated as *Crossroads,* 1943), a novel that revealed his satirical and caricaturist traits. It received the prize for best novel of the year from the Fundação Graça Aranha (Graça Aranha Foundation) of Rio de Janeiro. Written as a document of social protest, the novel deals with the everyday lives of characters from different social classes over a period of five days. *Caminhos cruzados* describes social life in the city of Pôrto Alegre during the 1930s, marked by violence and the power of money. Veríssimo shocked literary and political conservatives, along with the Catholic clergy, because the book showed such a strong contrast between rich and poor and revealed the moral decadence of the bourgeoisie. After the publication of the novel Veríssimo was listed as communist by the Departamento de Ordem Política e Social (Department of Political and Social Order) of Rio Grande do Sul. This action contributed to his signing an antifascist manifesto that was explicitly against the invasion of Abyssinia by

the Italian troops of Benito Mussolini. Also in 1935 Clarissa, Veríssimo's daughter, was born. In 1936 his son, Luís Fernando, was born.

Published in 1936, *Um lugar ao sol* (A Place in the Sun) tells of events and characters from *Clarissa* and *Caminhos cruzados.* The novel also introduces a group of new characters, young people who are dealing with affairs of the heart and existential conflicts while fighting to survive. During this same year Veríssimo accepted an invitation to create and maintain a program on Rádio Farroupilha that was dedicated to children. He also wrote six historical stories for children that later were collected as *Gente e bichos: histórias infantis* (1956, People and Animals: Children's Stories). Twice a week Veríssimo performed on radio, taking on the persona of a character named Amigo Velho (Old Friend) and telling stories. Because of a lack of time, he often improvised and made up the stories while he was on the air. Veríssimo was also in charge of the radio program *Clube dos três porquinhos* (Club of the Three Little Pigs). In 1937 the Brazilian government, led by Getúlio Vargas, became a dictatorship, known as the Estado Novo (New State). Veríssimo was informed that he had to submit his scripts for censorship to the Departamento de Imprensa e Propaganda (Department of Press and Propaganda). He could not agree to this imposition of censorship, mostly because the bulk of his material was created on air, so he decided to cancel the show. Veríssimo's departure from *Clube dos três porquinhos* demonstrated his opposition to the government, and the police of the Estado Novo began to distrust him.

During this period Veríssimo served as literary counsel for Editora Globo. He selected foreign works to be translated, and he was involved in the entire process of publishing books, which included choosing the cover and title of each volume and planning the release of the text after publication. In 1937 he published a children's book titled *As aventuras de Tibicuera, que são também as aventuras do Brasil* (Tibicuera's Adventures, Which Are Also the Adventures of Brazil). The book presents the life of an immortal Brazilian Indian, paralleling the official school version of the history of Brazil from 1500 to 1942. Veríssimo describes diverse historical episodes, including the expulsion of the Dutch from Brazil, certain wars that were fought internally, and the so-called revolution of 1930 that brought the future dictator Vargas to power.

Olhai os lírios do campo (1938; translated as *Consider the Lilies of the Field,* 1947) was a great success with the public, establishing Veríssimo as a well-known writer. In 1947 the novel was adapted in Argentina as a motion picture, *Mirad los lirios del campo.* The story relates the existential transformation of a young atheist and melancholic doctor who forgoes genuine love in order to marry for money. By this time Veríssimo had already left his job at the *Revista do Globo* and was dedicating all his time to the publishing department, working closely with Bertaso.

In 1940, while visiting São Paulo, Veríssimo participated in literary conferences. That year he published *Saga,* in his own opinion his worst book because of the cowardice of the main character. Narrated in the first person by the protagonist, Vasco Bruno, who served in the Spanish Civil War, *Saga* describes Bruno's return to Pôrto Alegre and his fight to survive in a bourgeois society. Veríssimo criticized this work mainly because of Bruno's decision to distance himself from society, exiling himself on a small farm to search for peace after marrying his cousin Clarissa.

In 1941 Veríssimo was invited by the consul of the United States in Brazil to visit America. The invitation was part of a good-neighbor program created by President Franklin Delano Roosevelt for writers and artists of Latin America. Veríssimo left Brazil by ship for a three-month stay in the United States. He traveled alone because he was unable to pay for his family to travel with him. Veríssimo visited many cities and delivered speeches about Brazilian literature. He also met important writers, such as Thomas Mann and W. Somerset Maugham, and famous people, including Walt Disney and Alfred Hitchcock. Veríssimo recorded his experiences in the United States in *Gato preto em campo de neve* (1941, Black Cat in a Snow Field), a book with an anecdotal and informative tone.

With the help of a loan Veríssimo bought a house in 1941, giving his family more stability. His purchase of the house, which was slowly furnished with the money from his publications, was his first step in finding his "lost home." According to Veríssimo, he had been searching for a place to call home since the divorce of his parents.

With the publication of *O resto é silêncio* (translated as *The Rest Is Silence,* 1946) in 1943, Veríssimo sued a clergyman for a virulent article attacking the novel. The idea for the book came from a suicide that Veríssimo witnessed. In the novel Joana Karewska, a young shop assistant, commits suicide, an act that strongly affects the lives of many people. Secondary characters include a young boy who sells newspapers, a woman in an existential crisis, and a writer. The investigation of the suicide connects the lives of the characters and motivates a discussion about the relationship between art and life. The clergyman's article, published in a Jesuit college journal in Pôrto Alegre, was motivated by certain erotic passages in *O resto é silêncio.* The author of the article accused Veríssimo of being a corrupter of morals, a baseless accusation in the opinion of Veríssimo, for whom the real pornography was violence and poverty, things that people saw in their everyday lives.

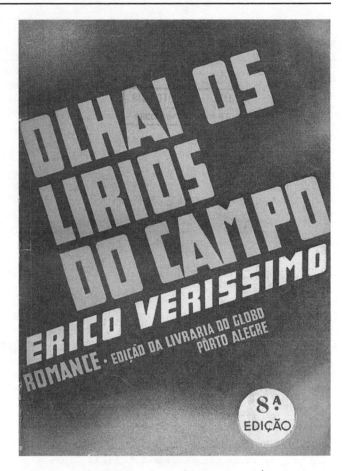

Dust jacket for the 1940 edition of the 1938 novel (translated as Consider the Lilies of the Field, *1947) about a melancholy doctor who marries for money, that established Veríssimo's reputation as an important writer in Brazil (Biblioteca Nacional de Chile)*

Some literary critics divide Veríssimo's works into two phases. The first, beginning with *Clarissa* and ending with *O resto é silêncio,* is characterized by the use of urban settings and an emphasis on life in Pôrto Alegre. Most of the main characters of this phase belong to the petty bourgeoisie. Their values and customs are emphasized, along with their struggles to survive in a big city. Veríssimo's novels written after the trilogy *O tempo e o vento* belong to his second phase. (The trilogy constitutes its own phase, that of the epic novel.) They are characterized by a more liberal consciousness and by political connotations that suggest international as well as national themes. These later works criticize the totalitarian ideologies of the period.

Veríssimo was invited to teach a course on Brazilian literature in the United States at the place of his choice in 1943. He selected the University of California, Berkeley, and moved to Berkeley with his family in September of that year. He also taught Brazilian literature and history classes at Mills College in Oakland, where he received an honorary doctorate. He traveled throughout

California, Oklahoma, Arizona, Indiana, and Texas, participating in various conferences. When World War II ended, Veríssimo was still in the United States. He heard the news of the Japanese surrender while on a train to New York; he and his family had to wait in Manhattan before returning to Brazil. When he returned to his country, Veríssimo felt pressure from leftist intellectuals to collaborate with them in their cause after the end of the Estado Novo in 1946. Although he sympathized with their cause, he had an aversion to any form of totalitarianism. During this time he made a political speech on a flight of stairs at the town hall of Pôrto Alegre, alongside a group of Communist Party deputies. Once again, Veríssimo felt pressure to conform to their specific political beliefs. He was accused of being too accommodating by the Left, and he was considered a communist by the Right.

In 1945 Veríssimo published *Brazilian Literature: An Outline* (translated as *Breve história da literatura brasileira,* 1995), in which he presents Brazilian literature from the perspective of a writer holding dialogues with other writers ranging from colonial times to the generation of 1945. Relationships between literature, history, and society are established. Veríssimo's visit to the United States in 1943 also led him to write a second book about his experiences there, *A volta do gato preto* (1947, The Return of the Black Cat), in which he discusses the difficulties of adapting to life in a foreign country. He describes daily contact with the American people and highlights the differences between the United States and Brazil.

After returning from the United States, Veríssimo continued to discuss Brazilian literature and culture in conferences, and he taught courses in countries such as Mexico, Ecuador, Peru, Uruguay, Spain, France, Portugal, and Germany. At the same time he was also working on *O tempo e o vento,* publishing the first part, *O continente* (The Continent), in 1949. The idea for this novel sequence came from his desire to write a saga about Rio Grande do Sul that would demystify its official history. Veríssimo believed that what was taught to children in schools was boring and full of prudent generalities. *O tempo e o vento* became a trilogy covering two hundred years of the history of Rio Grande do Sul, from 1745 to 1945. Veríssimo spent almost fifteen years writing the work. Besides having successful sales, like *Olhai os lírios do campo, O tempo e o vento* also won over literary critics.

The trilogy emphasizes the cyclical aspect of life through the succession of different generations of two families, the Terras and the Cambarás. These two families are united through marriage and are presented as archetypes of the founders of Rio Grande do Sul. On the Terra side, perseverance, obstinacy, and a love for the land dominate. On the Cambará side, dreams, adventure, and a love for freedom are most important. *O tempo*

e o vento is also known for its strong female characters, such as Ana Terra, one of the founders of the fictional city of Santa Fé. She fights to guarantee life in a world continually disfigured by violence. The title of the trilogy refers to the two main poles on which the narrative is based: time, representing movement and destruction; and the wind, which represents continuity and memory.

In the first part of the trilogy, *O continente,* Veríssimo presents a history of Rio Grande do Sul, from its origins in 1745 in the region of the missions to the end of the Revolução Federalista (Federalist Revolution) in 1895. This conflict was a fight for the government of Rio Grande do Sul led by politicians who opposed Floriano Peixoto, the president of Brazil. For the most part *O continente* was written in Verissimo's office at Editora Globo, where his work was frequently interrupted by the visits of friends or strangers. He stayed with the firm as a literary adviser until 1950. In reality, he never abandoned this post completely, although he opted at one time to dedicate himself wholly to his career as a writer, since he was now able to support his family with his writing alone. In his job Veríssimo translated more than fifty books from English, French, Spanish, and Italian into the Portuguese language. He also organized various literary series, such as the Biblioteca dos Séculos (Library of the Centuries).

In 1951 Veríssimo published the second part of *O tempo e o vento,* titled *O retrato* (The Portrait). The story in this part of the trilogy takes place in the period from approximately 1910 to 1945. Basing the narrative on his intense research of historical journals, Veríssimo focuses on one main character, Rodrigo Terra Cambará, a doctor and member of the revolution of 1930 that brought Vargas to power. Rodrigo opposes his own brother, Toríbio, who embodies the traditional values of patriotism and militarism. In critical commentary on *O retrato* one notices a tone of disappointment in comparison to the reception of *O continente.*

Veríssimo selected an uncle, Nestor Veríssimo, as the inspiration for the character of Toríbio. Nestor was an adventurous man who, in the author's opinion, had the best personality among his family members. Nestor was an assiduous reader of the works of Alexandre Dumas *père,* Xavier de Montepin, and Ponson du Terrail, and he participated in the political movement Coluna Prestes (Prestes Column, organized by Luis Carlos Prestes), which was active from 1925 to 1927. Members of the movement traveled throughout the interior of Brazil preaching communist ideals on social and political reforms and fighting against President Arthur Bernardes. These traits also inspired the creation of the character of Rodrigo, who reveals the characteristics of the gaucho stereotype—macho, brave, violent, adventurous, noble, generous, and given to womanizing. The author's father, Sebastião, was possibly an inspiration for this character.

In the beginning of *O tempo e o vento* corrosion and the provisional nature of human beings dominate the tone of the work. In the last part of the trilogy, *O arquipélago* (1961–1962, The Archipelago), Floriano Cambará, Rodrigo's son, is developed into a strong character who significantly changes the saga of his family's past through his writing. The beginning of his novel coincides with the first paragraph of *O continente,* confirming the cyclical aspect of the written work, already present in the epigraph, which cites a verse from Ecclesiastes on the passage of generations and the permanence of nature, always ready to begin another cycle.

Veríssimo wrote the novel *Noite* (1954; translated as *Night,* 1956) during his 1952 summer vacation. The action of the narrative takes places in one night, when a man loses his memory and finds himself lost in a city where he no longer recognizes anything. He meets two mysterious individuals who convince him that he is an assassin. Although not widely read in Brazil, *Noite* was translated for editions published in the United States, Britain, France, Norway, Germany, and Argentina and was adapted as a motion picture of the same title in 1985.

Toward the end of 1952 Veríssimo was invited by the Brazilian minister of foreign affairs to take the place of Alceu Amoroso Lima as director of the Department of Cultural Affairs with the Pan-American Union in Washington, D.C. The minister desired to have in this position someone who could speak knowledgeably about Brazilian literature and culture and could give classes and conferences in American universities. Veríssimo already had the required experience from having lived in the United States and participated in many conferences there and in other countries. As the new director, he visited various countries in Latin America, including Venezuela, Panama, Ecuador, Peru, and Mexico. He was unable, however, to complete work on the third part of *O tempo e o vento.* Veríssimo thought of leaving his post several times because he believed that his work in administrative functions lessened his literary creativity. In 1956, after serving as director of the Department of Cultural Affairs for three years and five months, he decided to resign and return to Brazil. Later that year he gave talks at the Pontifícia Universidade Católica de Pôrto Alegre (Catholic University of Pôrto Alegre) against the Soviet military intervention in Hungary. He decried all forms of oppression and violence. In 1956 and in 1959 Veríssimo also declared himself to be against the Portuguese dictator António de Oliveira Salazar.

While attempting to continue work on *O tempo e o vento,* Veríssimo decided to write about Mexico, a country he had visited briefly three times. The result, *México: história duma viagem* (1957, Mexico: Story of a Journey;

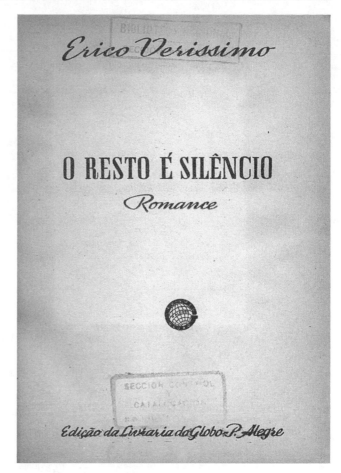

Title page for the first edition of Veríssimo's 1943 novel (The Rest Is Silence) about a shop girl's suicide that affects the lives of many people (Biblioteca Nacional de Chile)

translated as *Mexico,* 1960), recounts these visits and includes studies on Mexican culture and history. According to Veríssimo, *México* helped him to bring the characters of *O tempo e o vento* to life again. Most of *O arquipélago,* the third part of the trilogy, was written during his stay in the United States. In 1958 Veríssimo's first grandchild was born, the son of Clarissa and her husband, the American David Jaffe. Veríssimo returned to Washington, D.C., to meet his grandson and left in February 1960, when Clarissa's second child was born. During this period he also traveled throughout Europe with his wife and son, Luís Fernando, visiting Portugal, Spain, France, Italy, Germany, the Netherlands, and England.

In 1961 two volumes of *O arquipélago* were published. Veríssimo then had a heart attack that left him bedridden for two months. The third volume was finished in the United States, while the author was visiting his daughter again, and published in 1962. With the publication of the last volume of *O arquipélago,* which traces

Dust jacket for the 1967 English-language edition of Veríssimo's
O Senhor Embaixador *(1965), about a former guerrilla*
fighter who becomes the American ambassador for a
fictional South American country (Richland
County Public Library)

the lives of Rodrigo Cambará and Floriano, his son, up to the redemocratization of Brazil in 1945, Veríssimo completed *O tempo e o vento*.

With the trilogy completed, Veríssimo decided to emphasize social problems in his works. Inspired by his reflections on the dictatorships that dominated most Latin American countries during this period, he wrote *O Senhor Embaixador* (1965; translated as *His Excellency, the Ambassador,* 1967). This work presented a significant opportunity for him to comment on the relationships among the republics of Central and South America and the United States and to analyze the role of the intellectual in politics and revolutions. The novel takes place both in the American capital and in the fictional Latin American country of Sacramento, which is dominated by the corruption and abuse of a military dictatorship. *O Senhor Embaixador* tells the story of a former guerilla fighter, Dom Gabriele Heliodoro Alvarado, who

becomes the ambassador of Sacramento by promising to do what is right but later forgets his democratic promises.

In 1966 Veríssimo wrote an outline for an autobiography, "O escritor diante do espelho" (The Writer in Front of the Mirror), which was published in the collection *Ficção completa* (1966–1967, Complete Fiction). At the invitation of the Israeli minister of foreign affairs, he traveled throughout Israel for nineteen days, a visit that motivated him to write *Israel em abril* (1969; translated as *Israel in April,* 1993), his last book of travels. *Israel em abril* can be read as a discreet criticism of dictatorial political regimes because it includes enthusiastic praise for Israeli democracy at a time of political repression in Brazil.

In 1967 Veríssimo published *O prisioneiro* (The Prisoner), inspired by the Vietnam War. The story takes place in a country in Southeast Asia, and the events that it relates can be considered a metaphor both for the Vietnamese conflict and for the repression of guerrilla movements under the military dictatorship then in power in Brazil. The book is also an open criticism of imperialism and torture. In *O prisioneiro,* Veríssimo discusses questions of war and the position of powerful countries in relation to such conflicts. The protagonist is a man divided between his mission of torturing a prisoner and his inner feelings against violence and war. Always an opponent of any form of repression, Veríssimo wrote a text in 1970 against prior censorship that was read before the public by the legislative deputy Paulo Brossard. In the text Veríssimo calls censorship "uma paródia da Ide Média" (a parody of the Middle Ages).

In *Incidente em Antares* (1971, Incident in Antares) Veríssimo offers an allegory of the Brazilian military dictatorship. Through disputes between two traditional rural families, the Vacarianos and the Campolargos, he explores the nature of violence and causes the reader to question the concept of honor common among the gauchos. This code of honor often led the people of Rio Grande do Sul to act violently. Veríssimo also touches on economic exploitation through the main "incident" presented in the narrative, a gravediggers' strike that leaves seven corpses unburied. The dead come back to life, now completely aware of the lies, hypocrisy, and treachery that predominate in society.

In 1972 Veríssimo published *Um certo Henrique Bertaso: pequeno retrato em que o pintor também aparece* (A Certain Henrique Bertaso: A Brief Portrait in Which the Artist Also Appears) to celebrate the fiftieth anniversary of his friend and publisher's career. The work focuses on an account of Bertaso's entry into the Globo company, the creation of Editora Globo, and its transformation into one of the most important Brazilian publishing companies of the 1930s and 1940s. That same year Veríssimo received the prize

Veríssimo at home in 1970 with his cat, Snoopy, working on his 1971 novel Incidente em Antares *(Acervo Literário de Erico Veríssimo/Centro de Memória Literária da PUCRS, 1970; from* Cadernos de literatura brasileira, *2003; Bruccoli Clark Layman Archives)*

Personalidade do Ano (Personality of the Year) from the PEN Club of Brazil, and in 1973 he was awarded the Prêmio Literário da Fundação Moinhos Santista (Literary Prize of the Moinhos Santista Foundation) for his overall literary production.

Veríssimo was never a member of any political party, but his political position was clear. He always supported the cause of human rights, and he was always against any form of censorship. Along with fellow writer Amado, Veríssimo made clear his position against the military dictatorship that had come to power in Brazil in 1964.

Veríssimo died on 28 November 1975 of a heart attack. At the time he was working on the second volume of his autobiography, *Solo de clarineta: memórias* (Clarinet Solo: Memoirs). The first four chapters of the work had already been published in 1973; the second volume was published in the year following Veríssimo's death. Both volumes are composed of his memories of everyday life, his views on the work of the writer, and his opinion of his own books. The main focus, however, is on his trips throughout the world.

Erico Veríssimo's works concentrate on descriptions of people and customs of different regions and the expression of the inner feelings of characters. This latter aspect of his works is developed through the use of such modern techniques as interior monologues, nonlinear narratives, and flashbacks. Accused by some critics of being an "easy writer," Veríssimo was always proud of being a storyteller and emphasized that his main objective as a writer was to communicate with his readers. He did not consider himself a profound writer. Although he did not like to be interviewed, a collection of interviews with Veríssimo, *A liberdade de escrever: entrevistas sobre literatura e política* (The Freedom to Write: Interviews on Literature and Politics), was published in 1997, with an introduction by his son, the writer Luís Fernando Veríssimo. In this volume one notes the voice of an intellectual deeply involved in the political, social, and cultural issues of his time. Erico Veríssimo's books have been translated all over the world, and they express the humanitarian viewpoint of a man to whom a human being was always more important than property, religion, or political parties. The close interaction between the realm of fiction and reality is the hallmark of Veríssimo's works and the assertion of his action in the world. His books illuminate reality and bring readers to see what is sometimes nauseating and horrible.

Interviews:

A liberdade de escrever: entrevistas sobre literatura e política, edited by Maria da Glória Bordini, introduction by Luís Fernando Veríssimo (Pôrto Alegre: Editora da Universidade Federal do Rio Grande do

Sul/Editora da Pontifícia Universidade Católica do Rio Grande do Sul, 1997).

References:

Flávio Aguiar and Ligia Chiappini Moraes, eds., *Civilização e exclusão: visões do Brasil em Erico Veríssimo, Euclides da Cunha, Claude Lévi-Strauss e Darcy Ribeiro* (São Paulo: Boitempo/Fundação de Amparo à Pesquisa do Estado de São Paulo, 2001);

Lélia Almeida, *A sombra e a chama: as mulheres d'O tempo e o vento* (Santa Cruz do Sul: Editora da Universidade de Santa Cruz do Sul / Pôrto Alegre: Editora da Universidade Federal do Rio Grande do Sul, 1996);

Eliana Pibernat Antonini, *Incidentes narrativos: Antares e a cultura de massa* (Pôrto Alegre: Editora da Pontifícia Universidade Católica do Rio Grande do Sul/ Faculdade dos Meios de Comunicação Social, 2000);

Gilmar de Azevedo, *Na pele da imagem: o mito do gaúcho em O tempo e o vento* (Passo Fundo: Universidade de Passo Fundo, 2001);

Rebelo de Bettencourt, *Érico Veríssimo e o romance brasileiro* (Lisbon: *Gazeta dos Caminhos de Ferro*, 1950);

Maria da Glória Bordini, *Criação literária em Erico Veríssimo* (Pôrto Alegre: L & PM/Editora da Pontifícia Universidade Católica do Rio Grande do Sul, 1995);

Bordini, ed., *Erico Veríssimo, o escritor no tempo: homenagem aos 85 anos de nascimento* (Pôrto Alegre: Pontifícia Universidade Católica do Rio Grande do Sul/ Sulina, 1990);

Virginia Christine Burbridge, "A Study of the Novels of Érico Veríssimo, Contemporary Brazilian Author," dissertation, University of Illinois at Urbana-Champaign, 1967;

Wilson Chagas, *Mundo velho sem porteira: ensaio sobre a obra de Érico Veríssimo* (Pôrto Alegre: Movimento, 1985);

Flávio Loureiro Chaves, *Erico Veríssimo: o escritor e seu tempo* (Pôrto Alegre: Editora da Universidade Federal do Rio Grande do Sul, 2001);

Chaves, *Erico Veríssimo, realismo e sociedade* (Pôrto Alegre: Globo, 1976);

Chaves, ed., *O contador de histórias: 40 anos de vida literária de Erico Veríssimo* (Pôrto Alegre: Globo, 1972);

Ana Mariza Ribeiro Filipouski and Regina Zilberman, *Érico Veríssimo e a literatura infantil* (Pôrto Alegre: Universidade Federal do Rio Grande do Sul/Instituto Estadual do Livro, 1978);

Daniel Fresnot, *O pensamento político de Erico Veríssimo* (Rio de Janeiro: Graal, 1977);

Oswaldo Antônio Furlan, *Estética e crítica social em Incidente em Antares* (Florianópolis: Universidade Federal de Santa Catarina, 1977);

Robson Pereira Gonçalves, *O tempo e o vento: 50 anos* (Santa Maria: Editora da Universidade Federal de Santa Maria / Bauru: Editora da Universidade do Sagrado Coração, 2000);

Judith Grossmann, *O espaço geográfico no romance brasileiro* (Salvador: Fundação Casa de Jorge Amado, 1993);

Humberto Guimarães, *Um certo Erico Veríssimo* (Teresina: Universidade Federal do Piauí, 1990);

Antônio Hohlfeldt, *Erico Veríssimo* (Pôrto Alegre: Tchê! 1984);

Márcia Ivana de Lima e Silva, *A gênese de Incidente em Antares* (Pôrto Alegre: Editora da Pontifícia Universidade Católica do Rio Grande do Sul, 2000);

Carlos Alberto Antunes Maciél, *Richesse et évolution du vocabulaire d'Erico Veríssimo (1905–1975, Porto Alegre, Brésil),* preface by Maria Alice de Oliveira Faria (Paris: Champion / Geneva: Slatkine, 1986);

Luiz Marobin, *Imagens arquetípicas em O continente, de Erico Veríssimo* (São Leopoldo: Unisinos, 1997);

Wilson Martins, *O moderismo, 1916–1945* (São Paulo: Cultrix, 1965);

Louis L. Ollivier, "Synchrony, Amalgam and Communion: Erico Veríssimo's *O tempo e o vento* as a Symbolic Complex," dissertation, University of New Mexico, 1973;

Sandra Jatahy Pesavento and others, *Erico Veríssimo: o romance da história; artigo e entrevista inéditos de Antonio Candido sobre o autor de O tempo e o vento* (São Paulo: Nova Alexandria, 2001);

Malori J. Pompermayer, *Erico Veríssimo e o problema de Deus,* preface by Veríssimo (São Paulo: Loyola, 1968);

B. A. Richards, *The Brazilian Novels of Érico Veríssimo Assessed in the Context of Modernism and Latin American Fiction* (Pinner, U.K.: ITP, 1981);

Terezinha Cirene Rodrigues, *A poética das personagens em alguns romances de Érico Veríssimo* (Bauru: Faculdades do Sagrado Coração, 1983);

David Tullio Russo, "Erico Veríssimo's Two Faces of Life," dissertation, St. Louis University, 1968;

Joaquín Rodríguez Suro, *Érico Veríssimo: história e literatura* (Pôrto Alegre: D. C. Luzzatto, 1985);

Theodore Robert Young, *O questionamento da história em O tempo e o vento de Érico Veríssimo* (Lajeado: Fundação Alto Taquari de Ensino Superior, 1997).

Papers:
Erico Veríssimo's papers are held by the Fundação Erico Veríssimo in Cruz Alta.

António Vieira, S.J.
(Antonio Vieyra)
(6 February 1608 – 18 July 1697)

Joseph Abraham Levi
Rhode Island College

BOOKS: *Sermam que pregou o P. Antonio Vieira da Companhia de Iesus na caza professa da mesma companhia em 16 de Agosto de 1642. Na festa que fez a S. Roque Antoni Tellez da Silua* (Lisbon: Printed by Domingos Lopes Rosa da Silua, 1642);

Sermão que pregou o P. Antonio Vieyra . . . na igreja das Chagas, em a festa que se fez a S. Antonio, aos 14 de setembro deste anno de [1]642: tendo se publicado as Cortes pera o dia seguinte (Lisbon, 1642);

Proposta feita a El-Rei D. João IV, em que se lhe representava o miserável estado do reino e a necessidade que tinha de admitir os judeus mercadores que andavam por diversos pontos da Europa (Lisbon, 1643);

Sermam de S. Ioam Baptista, na profissam da Senhora Madre Soror Maria da Cruz, filha do Excellentissimo Duque de Medina Sydonia ([Lisbon]: Printed by Domingos Lopes Rosa da Silua, 1644);

Serman do esposo da May de Deus S. Ioseph: no dia dos annos del rey nosso senhor dom Ioam IV. da gloriosa memoria (Lisbon: Printed by Domingos Lopes Rosa, 1644);

Serman que pregou P. Antonio Vieira na misericordia da Bahia de todos os santos em dia da visitação de Nossa Senhora Orago da Casa: assistindo o Marquez de Montaluão, Visorrey daquelle estado do Brasil & foy o primeiro que ouuio naquella prouincia: anno 1646 (Lisbon: Printed by Domingos Lopes Rosa, 1646);

Sermâo que pregov o R.P. Antonio Vieira da Companhia de Iesus, na capella Real o primeiro dia de janeiro do anno de 1641 (Lisbon: Printed by Domingos Lopes Rosa, [1651?]);

Arte de furtar, espelho de enganos, theatro de verdades, mostrador de horas minugadas, gazúa dos reynos de Portugal: offerecida a Elrey Nosso Senhor d. João IV para que a emende (Amsterdam [i.e., Lisbon]: Printed by the Officina Elizeriana [sic], 1652);

Oraçam fvnebre qve disse o R.P. Antonio Vieira (Coimbra: Printed by Thome Carualho, 1658);

(from frontispiece for Charles Ralph Boxer, A Great Luso-Brazilian Figure: Padre António Vieira, S.J., 1608–1697, *1957; Thomas Cooper Library, University of South Carolina)*

Serman das Chagas de S. Francisco que pregou o R.P. Antonio Vieira da Companhia de Iesus, prégador de S. Alteza, no octauario da mesma festa, & na igreja da mesma inuocaçam em Roma. Traduzido de italiano em portuguez por Ioam de Mesqvita Arroyo, translated from Italian into Portuguese by João de Mesquita Arroyo (Lisbon: Miguel Manesçal, 1663);

Sermam nos annos da Serenissima Reyhna nossa Senhora (Zaragoza: Printed by Diego Iturbi, 1668);

Problema que o sempre memoravel padre Antonio Vieira da esclarecida Companhia de Jesus recitou em huma Academia em Roma; em que foy generoso assumpto; se o mundo he mais digno de rizo, ou de pranto: e assim quem acertava melhor, Democrito, que ria sempre, ou Heraclito, que sempre chorava (Lisbon, 1674);

Sermoens do p. Antonio Vieira da Companhia de Iesu, prégador de Sua Alteza, 16 volumes (Lisbon: Printed by João da Costa, 1679–1754);

Sermam nas exequias da rainha Nossa Senhora, D. Mara Francisca Isabel Saboya, que pregou o Padre Antonio Veüa ... na misericordia de Bahia em II de Setembro anno de 1648 (Lisbon: Printed by Miguel Deslandes, 1685);

Maria, Rosa Mystica. Excellencias, poderes e maravilhas do seu Rosario. Compendiados em treinta sermones aceticos, & Panegyricos sobre os dous evangelhos desta solemnidade novo, & antigo (Lisbon: Printed by Miguel Deslandes, 1686–1688);

Sermoens do P. Antonio Vieira, da Companhia de Jesu, visitador da Provincia do Brasil, Prègador de Sua Magestade. Quinta parte (Lisbon: Printed by Miguel Deslandes, [1689]);

Palavra de Deos empenhada, e desempenhada: empenhada no serman das exequias da rainha N.S. D. Maria Francisca Isabel de Saboya; desempenhada no serman de acçam de graças pelo nascimento do principe D. Joaõ Primogenito de SS. Magestades, que Deos guarde (Lisbon: Printed by Miguel Deslandes, 1690);

Sermoens do P. Antonio Vieyra da Companhia de Jesu, visitador da Provincia do Brasil, prégador de sua magestade, sexta parte (Lisbon: Printed by Miguel Deslandes, [1690]);

Sermam do felicissimo nacimento da serenissima infanta Teresa Francisca Josepha ([Lisbon], 169?);

Admodum reverendi patri Antonii Vieira e Societate Jesu (Cologne: Printed by Hermanni Demen, 1692);

Sermoens do P. Antonio Vieyra da Companhia de Jesu, prègador de Sua Magestade, septima parte (Lisbon: Printed by Miguel Deslandes, [1692]);

Xavier dormindo, e Xavier acordado (Lisbon: Printed by Miguel Deslandes, 1694);

Las cinco piedras de la honda de David en cinco discursos morales, predicados en Roma a la reyna de Suecia, Christina Alexandra, en lengua italiana, por el reverendissimo padre Antonio Vieira, translated into Spanish by Vieira (Lisbon: Printed by Miguel Deslandes, 1695); original Portuguese published as Cinco discursos moraes, fundados nas cinco padres de David; prègados em Roma na presença da rainha de Suecia (Lisbon: Printed by A. Pedrozo Galrão, 1754);

Sermam dos bons annos de Lisboa: na Capella Real, anno de 1642 (Lisbon: Printed by Miguel Deslandes, 1696);

Sermoens do P. Antonio Vieyra, da Companhia de Jesu, prègador de Sua Magestade. Undecima parte (Lisbon: Printed by Miguel Deslandes, 1696);

Sermoens do P. Antonio Vieyra da Companhia de Jesu, prègador de Sua Magestade, Parte duodecima (Lisbon: Printed by Miguel Deslandes, [1699]);

Papéis políticos que respeitão muitas das negociações deste reyno, e de muitos da Europa, 2 volumes (N.p., 17??);

Sermones selectissimi (Cologne: Printed by Hermanni Demen, 1707);

Sermões, e varios discursos do Padre Antonio Vieyra da Companhia de Jesu, prègador de Sua Magestade. Tomo XIV. Obra posthuma (Lisbon: Printed by Costa Deslandes, 1710);

Varios eloqvuentes libros, recogidos en vno (Valencia, Spain, 1711);

História do futuro. Livro anteprimeyro. Prolegomeno a toda a historia do futuro, em que se declara o fim, & se provão os fundamentos della. Escrito pelo padre Antonio Vieyra (Lisbon: António Pedrozo Galram, 1718);

Vozes saudadosas, da eloquencia, do espirito, do zelo, e eminenti sabedoria; a companhadas comhum felissimo echo, que sonoramente resulta do interior da obra Clavis prohetarum, concorda no sim a suavidades das musas em elogium raros (Lisbon: Printed by Miguel Rodrigues, 1736);

Rhetorica sagrada, ou, Arte de pregar (Lisbon: Printed by Luiz Jozé Correa Lemos, 1745);

Discurso catholico (Lisbon: Printed by António da Sylvia, 1747);

Sermões vários, e tratados, ainda não impressos, do grande padre Antonio Vieyra da Companhia de Jesus; offerecidos à magestade del rey D. João V. nosso senhor, pelo P. André de Barros da Companhia de Jesus. Tomo XV e de Vozes saudosas tomo II (Lisbon: Printed by Manoel da Sylva, 1748);

Voz sagrada, política, rhetorica, e métrica ou supplemento às vozes saudosas da eloquência, do espírito, do zelo, e eminente sabedoria (Lisbon: Printed by Francisco Luiz Ameno, 1748);

Relação exactissima instructiva, curioza, verdadeira e noticioza do procedimento das Inquiziçois de Portugal prezentada a o papa Ignocencio XI (Venice: Printed by João Mortein, 1750);

Sermam das obras de misericordia (Lisbon: Printed by the T.A.F. do S. Officio, 1753);

Serman, que pregou o Padre Antonio Viera. Ao enterro dos ossos dos enforcados, na misereicordia da cidade da Bahia (Lisbon, 1753);

Collecçam dos principaes sermoens, que pregou o p. Antonio Vieira, da companhia de Jesu: dedicada a Sto. Antonio de Lisboa, e offrecida a Antonio Martins (Lisbon: Published by the Officina dos Herdeiros de Antonio Pedrozo Galrão, 1754);

Noticias reconditas do modo de proceder a Inquisição de Portugal com os seus prezos (Lisbon: Imprensa Nacional, 1821);

Sermão da primeira dominga da Quaresma na cidade de S. Luis do Maranhão no ano de 1653, e uma carta a D. João IV, edited by Sebastião Morão Correira (Lisbon: Edição da "Revista de Portugal," 1946).

Editions and Collections: *Serman de Sto. Antonio pregado aos peixes, pelo Padre Antonio Vieira. Na cidade de S. Luiz do Maranham* (Lisbon, 1753);

História do futuro: livro ante-primeiro (Salvador da Bahia: Printed by F. C. O. Castilho, 1838);

Obras completas, 26 volumes, edited by Barnabé Maria Torres Canhão (Lisbon: J. M. C. Seabra & T. Q. Antunes, 1854–1858);

Sermões do padre Antonio Vieira, 15 volumes, edited by Torres Canhão (Lisbon: J. M. C. Seabra & T. Q. Antunes, 1854–1858);

Obras ineditas (Lisbon: J. M. C. Seabra & T. Q. Antunes, 1856–1857);

Vieira brasileiro, 2 volumes (Paris & Lisbon: Aillaud & Bertrand, 1921);

Os melhores sermões de Vieira, edited by Afrânio Peixoto (Rio de Janeiro: Americana, 1931);

Sermões patrióticos, edited by Pedro Calmon (Rio de Janeiro: Biblos, 1933); republished as *Por Brasil e Portugal, sermões comentados,* edited by Calmon (São Paulo: Companhia Editora Nacional, 1938);

Antologia de sermões, edited by Mário Gonçalves Viana (Porto: Educação Nacional, 1939; reprinted, 1947);

A invasao holandesa da Bahia (Salvador da Bahia: Livraria Progresso, 1955);

Defesa perante o Tribunal do Santo Oficio, 2 volumes (Bahia: Universidade da Bahia, 1957);

O fim do mundo e o juízo universal, edited, with an introduction, by Frederico Ozanam Pessoa de Barros (São Paulo: Luzes, [1961]);

Sermão de Sto. António aos peixes, e Carta a D. Afonso VI (20 de Abril de 1657), edited by Manuel Rodrigues Lapa, fifth edition (Lisbon [i.e., Porto]: Imprensa Portuguesa, 1961);

Trechos escolhidos (Rio de Janeiro: AGIR, 1971);

Livro anteprimeiro da História do futuro, edited by José [Joseph Jacobus] van den Besselaar (Lisbon: Biblioteca Nacional, 1983);

Sermão da sexagésima, edited by Gladstone Chaves de Melo (Niterói, Brazil: Núcleo Editora da Universidade Federal Fluminense, 1985);

Sermão pelo bom sucesso das armas de Portugal contra as de Holanda, edited by Frits Smulders (Middleburg, Netherlands: F. F. X. Smulders, 1989); translated by Smulders as *António Vieira's Sermons against the Dutch Arms (1640)* (Frankfurt am Main: Peter Lang, 1996);

Escritos instrumentais sobre os Índios, edited by José Carlos Sebe Bom Meihy (São Paulo: Loyola, Ediciones de la Universidad Católica, Editora da Pontifícia Universidade Católica de São Paulo, 1992);

História do futuro, edited by Maria Leonor Carvalhão Buescu, second edition ([Lisbon]: Imprensa Nacional-Casa da Moeda, 1992);

Ensaio sobre o termo da história: trezentos e cinquenta e três aforismos contra o incaracterístico (Lisbon: Hiena, 1994);

O rosário de Vieira, edited by Valério Alberton (São Paulo: Loyola, 1994);

De profecia e inquisição (Brasília: Senado Federal, 1998).

OTHER: "Annua ou annaes da provincia do Brazil dos dous anos de 1624, e de 1625," in *Annaes da biblioteca nacional do Rio de Janeiro,* volume 19 (Rio de Janeiro: Teuzinger, 1897), pp. 175–217.

In Father António Vieira, S.J., the seventeenth-century missionary and preacher works hand in hand with the baroque man of letters and the humanitarian and philanthropist. Vieira was deeply concerned with the physical and spiritual welfare of the less fortunate. Despite the consequences he felt a strong obligation to denounce all injustices and abuses of power. Because he lived in both Portugal and Portuguese America, Vieira can be seen as the typical figure of the colonial period: a man divided between the *Metrópole* (metropolis, a euphemism for Portugal) and its colony overseas, Brazil. He was a missionary caught between his loyalty to the Portuguese Crown and the Church, on the one hand, and the basic humanitarian ideals of justice, equality, and freedom for (almost) all people on the other. He defended tradition, and yet he advocated change and improvement. The turmoil of the times is clearly expressed in his language, which, despite the sometimes controversial and hard-hitting nature of his writings, makes Vieira one of the paradigms of prose in the Portuguese language and one of the major writers of baroque literature in colonial Brazil.

Vieira's most intriguing characteristic is the harmony between his thought and his action. This correlation is visible in his unusual, easily recognizable style, characterized by an overwhelming passion and dynamism, religious and humanitarian as well as secular and patriotic. Vieira's works comprise sixteen volumes of *Sermoens do p. Antonio Vieira da Companhia de Iesu, prégador de Sua Alteza* (Sermons of Father António Vieira, Society of Jesus, Preacher of Your Highness [that is, Royal Preacher]), published between 1679 and 1754; three volumes of *Cartas* (Letters), published between 1735 and

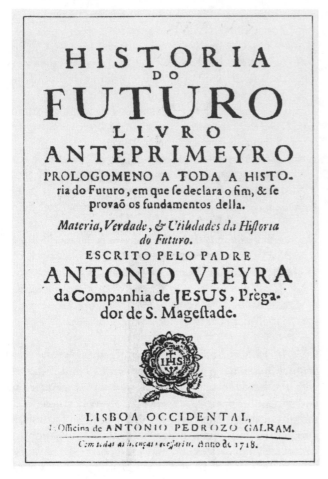

HISTORIA
DO
FUTURO
LIVRO
ANTEPRIMEYRO
PROLOGOMENO A TODA A HISTO-
ria do Futuro, em que fe declara o fim, & fe
provaõ os fundamentos della.

*Materia, Verdade, & Utilidades da Hiftoria
do Futuro.*

ESCRITO PELO PADRE
ANTONIO VIEYRA
da Companhia de JESUS, Prègador de S. Mageftade.

LISBOA OCCIDENTAL,
Na Officina de ANTONIO PEDROZO GALRAM.

Com todas as licenças necessarias, Anno de 1718.

Title page for the first edition of the only surviving part of Vieira's work that interprets the history of Portugal through biblical prophecies (from Ivan Lins, Para conhecer melhor padre Antônio Vieira *(Rio de Janeiro: Bloch, 1974; Woodruff Library, Emory University)*

1746; the *História do futuro* (written in 1665, History of the Future), although the only extant portion is the introduction, the *Livro anteprimeiro* (Preliminary Book), published as *História do futuro. Livro anteprimeyro. Prolegomeno a toda a historia do futuro, em que se declara o fim, & se provão os fundamentos della. Escrito pelo padre Antonio Vieyra* (History of the Future. Preliminary Book. Prolegomenon to the Entire History of the Future, in which the End is Announced and the Reasons for its Existence are Herein Proven. Written by Father António Vieira) in 1718; the *Esperanças: Esperanças de Portugal, quinto império do mundo, primeira e segunda vinda de El-Rei D. João IV* (written in 1659, Hope of Portugal, Fifth Empire of the World, First and Second Coming of King João IV), published in 1854–1855; and the *Clavis prophetica* (Prophetic Key), also known as *Clavis prophetarum* (The Key of the Prophets), which, although it was begun in or around 1659 and was reedited at the time of the

author's death, is extant today only in fragments. Vieira's works have been collected into the twenty-six-volume *Obras completas* (Complete Works), edited by Barnabé Maria Torres Canhão and published in Lisbon between 1854 and 1858. These volumes not only include the *Sermões* and *Cartas* but also travel accounts and political and literary works, as well as judicial treatises.

The literary production left by Vieira is extensive, comprising almost two hundred *sermões,* more than five hundred *cartas,* many *relatórios* (accounts), *representações* (petitions), *pareceres* (opinions), *panfletos* (pamphlets, political and diplomatic documents), religious booklets, treatises or writings with a strong prophetic exegesis, and defenses against the attacks of the Portuguese Inquisition. The common denominator among all of his works is his connection to and complete involvement with the public and political life of the time. The various aspects of Vieira's activism are indivisible; even his works on religion and sacred oratory include references to the political events of the time. His most persuasive works, such as the *Sermões,* the *Cartas,* and his harangues against the Inquisition and slavery, speak to the political atmosphere of the time.

António Vieira was born in Lisbon on 6 February 1608. His father, Cristóvão Vieira Ravasco, *escrivão oficial das devassas* (judicial clerk), was from Santarém, with roots in the Alentejo region; his mother, Maria de Azevedo, was from Lisbon. At the age of six Vieira accompanied his parents to the capital of the Portuguese colony in Brazil, Salvador da Bahia, because his father had been assigned the post of *escrivão da Relação do Salvador da Bahia* (secretary to the governor of the city of Salvador da Bahia). There Vieira attended the Colégio dos Jesuítas (Jesuit School), graduating in 1623 with the degree of Mestre em Artes (Master of Arts). On 5 May 1623, against his parents' wishes, Vieira became an *indiferente* (indifferent), entering the first stage of the Jesuit novitiate. Vieira spent his first year of apprenticeship in the hamlet of Espírito Santo (present-day Abrantes). After only two years he not only successfully passed his trial period but, given his remarkable writing and oratorical skills, he was also appointed secretary to the Jesuit missions in the area.

During this time the Dutch were trying to combat the Portuguese presence in Brazil, eventually occupying parts of the region between 1624 and 1654. On 8 May 1624 Dutch vessels appeared along the northern Brazilian coast; Salvador da Bahia was soon captured, but it was under Dutch control for only a year. In 1626 Vieira taught rhetoric, philosophy, and theology at the Colégio dos Jesuítas in Olinda and Pernambuco. That year he was also given the task of writing the annual report on the state of the Jesuit mission in Brazil, that is, the

Carta annuaao geral dos Jesuítas (Annual Letter to the General of the Jesuits), which not only refers to the Dutch invasion of the Portuguese colony but also marks the beginning of his famous Cartas. The Carta annuaao geral dos Jesuítas was first written in Portuguese and then translated into Latin, since all correspondence within the Jesuit order was executed in Latin.

In 1635 Vieira was finally ordained priest, and he soon gained the reputation for being a superb preacher and charismatic leader. Father Vieira spent the next five years preaching in many small towns around the Portuguese American capital. He also was appointed professor of theology at the Colégio dos Jesuítas in Salvador da Bahia.

Vieira's sermons were quite popular, both for their spiritual content and because they addressed the particular needs of the local population, composed of Amerindians, European settlers, and African slaves. The people's most important and imminent problem, however, was the threat that Holland posed to the young Portuguese colony in South America. In 1624 the troops of the Dutch West India Company succeeded in defeating the Portuguese colonial forces. Six years later, in 1630, the Dutch attacked again and took over the captaincies of Pernambuco, Itamaracá, Paraíba, and Rio Grande do Norte.

In 1633 Father Vieira gave his first public sermon in the Igreja de Nossa Senhora da Conccição (Church of Our Lady of the Conception), Maria, Rosa Mystica (1686–1688, Mary, Mystical Rose). In 1638 Salvador da Bahia suffered another attack from the Dutch, this time led by the Count Maurice of Nassau, Johannes Mauritius van Nassau-Siegen, governor of Dutch Brazil in 1637–1644. Among Vieira's most famous oratorical pieces given at that time are the Sermão de Santo António (1638, Sermon of St. Anthony), the Sermão da visitação de Nossa Senhora a Santa Isabel (1638, Sermon of the Visitation of Our Lady to Saint Isabel), and the Sermão pela vitória das nossas armas (1638, Sermon for the Victories of Our Arms), which was delivered right when the Dutch seemed to be on the verge of taking the town. In 1640 Vieira celebrated the Portuguese victory over the enemy with two powerful and inspirational sermons, the Sermão pelo bom sucesso das armas de Portugal contra as de Holanda (1989, Sermon for the Good Success of the Portuguese Army Against Holland; translated as António Vieira's Sermons against the Dutch Arms (1640), 1996), and the Sermão de Santo António (Sermon of Saint Anthony), preached in Salvador da Bahia on 13 July 1640.

Even though he employed many of the traditional oratorical techniques, Vieira realized that he was no longer addressing a medieval audience. Times had changed, and he had to adapt an old method and approach to a new era with "new" people and new needs. The Portuguese expansion overseas had created the colonist-native, thus modernizing the old concepts of slavery and indentured servitude, and subsequently opening the doors for transoceanic trade. In his sermons Father Vieira transformed traditional oratorical devices in order to convince "modern" people. It is not surprising that Father Vieira presented his sermons in a pragmatic way: first, the tema (topic), using the biblical passage as a point of departure; second, the intróito (introduction), his plan to develop the topic; third, the invocação (invocation), the cry for help, usually addressed to the Virgin Mary, whom he venerated more than Christ himself; fourth, the argumentação (argument), the body of the sermon; and fifth, the peroração, or final conclusion, in which he incites his audience to accept his teaching. Father Vieira addressed and interpreted the biblical text in such a way that the many mysteries therein had to be deciphered using real and concrete definitions in order for his audience to understand and follow with interest. Through a circular analytical process—fraught with many questions and answers, as well as similes and antitheses—the explicit eventually explained the abstract concept; that is, the hidden meaning of the biblical text. By means of a long chain of logical associations, Father Vieira thus convinced his listeners that they were being presented an infallible and indisputable truth, one that they were able to understand and easily accept as valid.

The Arte de furtar (Art of Stealing) was written in 1640. To this date its authorship has been the subject of at times violent disputes. Besides Father Vieira, the Arte de furtar has been attributed to various writers, jurists, and diplomats, including Tomé Pinheiro da Veiga, João Pinto Ribeiro, António de Sousa de Macedo, Duarte Ribeiro de Macedo, António da Silva e Sousa, Francisco Manuel de Melo, and Manuel da Costa. It is a well-written work describing Portuguese society during the reign of King João IV, a time in which, owing to fraud and corruption, the public treasury was in a troubled state. Father Vieira, or its rightful composer, thus offers possible solutions to these societal maladies. Style, content, and the sociopolitical message of the Arte de furtar, however, could be used as an indication of Father Vieira's authorship or perhaps his partial involvement in its composition.

Aside from the impending political and military threats, Vieira was concerned with the welfare of the local population, specifically the indigenous people and the way in which they were being treated by the European settlers, most of whom were Portuguese. Most of Vieira's sermões address human issues, namely, the defense of the rights of the Amerindians and the exposure of colonial abuse against them, the evil of the transatlantic slave trade, and the draconian power exercised by the colonial administration.

After sixty years of Spanish domination, Portugal was finally free of Spanish rule in 1640. In 1641 Vieira and Father Simão de Vasconcellos, S.J., accompanied the son of the sixteenth governor and viceroy of Brazil, Fernando José de Mascarenhas, Marquis of Montalvo, to Portugal as part of the Brazilian delegation welcoming the newly elected Portuguese monarch, King João IV. Their presence at court showed support for Portuguese supremacy in Brazil, although during the infamous eighty years of Spanish domination Brazil and other Portuguese colonies and possessions throughout the world never became de facto parts of the Spanish overseas empire. At the royal court Vieira's powerful communication skills were not only noticed for their use in remarkable religious messages—he was appointed court preacher and later offered a bishopric, which he readily declined—but also were seen as potential political tools.

Between 1646 and 1650 Vieira was sent on various diplomatic missions to Paris, The Hague, London, and Rome, with the goal of starting political and economic negotiations to strengthen the Portuguese Empire. Vieira's first missions were in France and Holland, since both countries were also enemies of Spain. He was tasked with forging a formal alliance with France in which that country would vow never to sign a peace agreement unless Portugal was also included. The French, however, asked that Portugal attack Spain. Vieira also invited France to intercede with Holland concerning Dutch intervention in Brazil. During the time of the Dutch occupation Pernambuco had been renamed the Republic of the Dutch United Provinces. Here, too, the French were uncooperative, and Vieira's mission to Paris was a complete failure. On 2 April 1646 he left for Calais and then for Rouen, where he met with the leaders of the Judeo-Portuguese communities, who gave him a letter of credit for Holland. On 18 April 1646 Vieira reached The Hague. On 14 March 1647 he gave King João IV his *Parecer sobre a compra de Pernambuco aos holandeses* (Opinion on the Purchase of Pernambuco from the Dutch), in which he advises Portugal to buy Pernambuco from Holland. His mission in Holland was just as unsuccessful as the one to Paris, and on 15 October 1648 he returned to Lisbon. Although his missions were highly ambitious, Vieria felt defeated. Yet, during his travels to Amsterdam, London, Paris, and Rome, Vieira had important opportunities to meet with rabbis and members of the Sephardic communities of the Diaspora, particularly those of Portuguese descent.

In 1643 Father Vieira wrote the *Proposta feita a El-Rei D. João IV, em que se lhe representava o miserável estado do reino e a necessidade que tinha de admitir os judeus mercadores que andavam por diversos pontos da Europa* (Proposal Presented to King João IV in which the Deplorable State of the Kingdom and the Need that it Had to Admit Jewish Merchants who Wandered through Different Points of Europe Was Explained), which was published that same year. Among the solutions proposed by Vieira in order to boost Portugal's presence as a world empire is basing all further enterprises on the economic power of the middle class. He argues that this strategy would allow an even flow of capital and goods between Portugal and its colonies and also between the Portuguese Empire and the rest of the European countries and city-states. Most of the members of the mercantile bourgeoisie, however, were either crypto-Jews—also known as *conversos* ([forced] converts), *marranos* (pigs), or *cristãos-novos* (new-Christians)—or openly declared Jews of the Sephardic Diaspora. People in both groups were instrumental in linking the Americas to the major European trade centers, such as Lisbon, Porto, Amsterdam, Antwerp, London, and Hamburg. Despite the many difficulties and restrictions they sometimes faced on both sides of the Atlantic, Jewish or crypto-Jewish businessmen succeeded in maintaining an important and economically successful position through the middle of the nineteenth century. Vieira argued that it was essential for the Portuguese Crown to take part in the transatlantic trade performed by the skilled Portuguese merchants who happened to be Jewish or of Jewish descent.

Despite general hostility to Veira's idea, which went against all the dictates of the Portuguese Inquisition, in 1649 King João IV granted Vieira the creation of the Companhia Geral para o Comércio com o Brasil (General Company for the Trade with Brazil). The Companhia Geral used as its model the Dutch East India Company and for a time was granted full monopoly over all revenues. Vieira's main political idea was to create a strong commercial center for the prosperity of the Portuguese Empire, with Portuguese Jews or *cristãos-novos* as key elements. In Vieira's view, for Jews to be attracted they had to be free from any danger from the Inquisition. Vieira advocated better treatment for the *cristãos-novos* to attract capital; the opening of the Inquisitorial prisons; a general pardon for all past "heresies" conferred upon Jews and/or Judaizers by the Holy See; and the repatriation of all the Portuguese Jews of the Diaspora, with the offer of security and immunity from any further inquisitorial attacks or intimidation and confiscation. Additionally, if a person were to be accused of Judaizing, Vieira proposed that the name(s) of the accuser(s) be made *abertos e publicados* (open and public), as was the case in the Roman Inquisition. Vieira strongly believed that Portugal could benefit greatly from receiving back into its fold the descendants of the Portuguese Jews expelled in 1496, those who escaped after the forced conversion (1497–1498), or those *cristãos-novos* who had more recently fled (1498 onward). Their centuries-old expertise in trade and their transoceanic ties with the Americas, India, and Africa made the Jews quite attractive, even necessary, for the Portuguese economy. Vieira hoped that they could reinvigorate Portuguese trade with Brazil and India, creating a system like the Dutch had with the Dutch East India Company.

In January 1650 Father Vieira went to Rome on a secret mission. The goal was to provoke the Kingdom of Naples, then under Spanish rule, to revolt against King Felipe IV, which would lead to a peace agreement between Portugal and Spain. The treaty would be sealed with the marriage between Felipe's son, Teodósio, and the daughter of King João, and in this way the two Iberian Crowns would once again be unified, this time with Lisbon as capital of the new Iberian empire. This mission also failed, but far from being discouraged, Vieira remained in Italy preaching and setting aside all monies from his honoraria and the royalties that he collected for the publication of his works for the Jesuit missions in Maranhão.

Because of Vieira's support of the king's policy, which at times went against the dictates of his own religious order, toward the end of 1652 he was sent to Brazil as one of the Jesuit missionaries to Maranhão. He remained there until 1661. The then-captaincy of Maranhão e Grão-Pará, which in 1751 became the captaincy of Grão-Pará e Maranhão, was separate from the rest of the Portuguese colony. Vieira was successful in this assignment. In 1653 he became superior of the Maranhão mission, preaching and defending the rights of the indigenous peoples. This position can be seen in the *Sermão de Santo Antonio.* Because of his dedication, linguistic talents, and commitment to helping the native populations and the African slaves, in a short time Vieira mastered seven of the many languages spoken in the area. Among these languages were some of the Tupi-Guarani group, as well as Kimbundu (a Bantu language spoken in present-day northern Angola). He used these languages in everyday life, including catechism and, at times, his sermons.

The *Sermão da primeira dominga da Quaresma na cidade de S. Luis do Maranhão no ano de 1653, e um carta a D. João IV* (1946, Sermon of the First Sunday of Lent, [Preached] in the City of São Luís in Maranhão in the Year 1653, and a Letter to Dom João IV), was preached in 1653 in the city of São Luís do Maranhão. Also known as the *Sermão dos captivos* (Sermon of the Captives), this sermon perhaps more precisely captures the double essence of Father Vieira. The preacher and

Title page for an anthology of Vieira's sermons (Z. Smith Reynolds Library, Wake Forest University)

the missionary/humanitarian here join forces, faith being at the service of human and social justice. The freedom of the Amerindian population is counterbalanced by the vicious attacks of the European settlers, especially in the Maranhão-Grão-Pará area. Moreover, Father Vieira not only attacks the practice of forced slavery but also proposes more humane ways of treating the indigenous tribes. Father Vieira understands that, since he cannot eradicate enslavement, at least he can offer a more practical and just solution to a long-term problem.

During his two sojourns in the Maranhão-Grão-Pará area in 1652 and 1655 Vieira strengthened his contacts with the native peoples. His sincere concern for the Amerindians caused many political complications, especially when he delivered strong sermons against slavery and the negative impact that a policy of mining–with the consequent dislocation of European settlers and African slaves–would have had for the economy of the colony and the rest of the Portuguese Empire. Vieira's religious and social stand eventually created many enemies for him and resulted in his exile and imprisonment. He was highly critical of the system and constantly questioned authority; he defended the Jews and *cristãos-novos* against the abuses of the Inquisition; he opposed African slavery and Amerindian enslavement; and he was in favor of the right of self-determination for all native peoples.

The *Sermão da sexagésima* (1985, Sermon of Sexagesima Sunday [the second Sunday before Lent]) was delivered in 1655 at the Royal Chapel in Lisbon. It is a clear expression of oratorical faith as well as being the first sermon to earn Father Vieira recognition for his oratorical skills. The *Sermão da sexagésima,* also known as *Sermão da palavra de Deus* (Sermon of the Word of God), touched upon oratory and sacred preachers. Father Vieira was in Lisbon trying to convince the Portuguese Crown to free the Amerindians, whom he was serving in the Maranhão-Grão-Pará area. The entire sermon is centered around the argument: why is it that today– that is, 1655–God's words bear little or no fruit at all? Father Vieira responds by saying that it is either the preachers' fault or it is owing to the listeners' overall indifference; or perhaps it is because of God's indifference. He then gradually concludes that the slight effect that preaching has on humankind is not the result of God's will, nor is it tied to the listeners' intentions. Hence, it has to be the deplorable state of the art of preaching in his time, since preachers are more preoccupied with flowery style than content and edification. On 9 April 1655 the king eventually granted the Jesuits the *Portaria* (Official Diploma), a decree that allowed the brothers of the Society of Jesus a more ample freedom when dealing with native Brazilian issues. Paragraph 19 of the *Portaria* also stated that members of any religious order could not own property where Indians (either free or enslaved) worked. On 14 April of the same year an addendum to the law declared that Amerindians could only work six months per year and that the missions could not use the native population for any kind of manual labor.

The disagreement between Jesuits and Portuguese settlers over the treatment of the indigenous population (Africans, Asians, and Amerindians) was an old one, dating back to the beginning of the Portuguese age of discoveries (circa 1415). The entire Amazon region was still unaffected by the Atlantic slave trade; hence, in order to obtain slaves, the local settlers had to perform *entradas* (expeditions into the interior of the country), hunt for indigenous peoples, and force them to *descer* (descend) from the Amazon region down to the Euro-

pean settlements, where they were enslaved or treated harshly. As a solution, the Jesuits of the Maranhão-Grão-Pará region reluctantly encouraged the importation of African slaves, hitherto confined to areas south of the Maranhão, into the captaincy. In this way the European settlers would still have slaves and the Jesuits could oversee the spiritual and physical well-being of the Amerindians.

When colonial delegates brought news of laws enacted in 1652 ordering the liberation of the Amerindians, the settlers refused to comply. By May 1654 a royal representative arrived from Lisbon with an addendum limiting the freedom of all Amerindian peoples living in Brazil. Before going to Lisbon to lodge a vehement protest, Vieira preached his famous satirical *Sermon de Sto. António pregado aos peixes.* In November 1654 he arrived in Lisbon, where he delivered caustic sermons that further provoked his enemies. As a way of finding common ground, King João IV appointed Vieira chief of the committee overseeing the Indian question. Vieira soon began writing prophesies of the future glory of Portugal, which he describes as becoming the Fifth Empire, a stable, perfect, and everlasting kingdom ruled by the resurrected King João IV. The work was completed in 1659 with the title "Esperanças de Portugal, quinto império do mundo, primeira e segunda vinda de El-Rei D. João IV." In the same year Vieira began writing the *Clavis prophetica,* also known as *Clavis prophetarum,* which he edited up to the last days of his life. He never completed the work.

Vieira and his religious order's sincere interest in the welfare of the Amerindian population, especially in the Maranhão area, caused serious rivalry between the Jesuits and the European settlers. The settlers' interests coincided with those of the Portuguese colonial authorities, whose intent was to exploit the land and its people to the fullest extent possible. Achieving this goal sometimes meant using forced labor by the indigenous population. Though not completely in favor of enslaving African peoples, particularly "Angolans" (then a loose term for West Africans), Vieira and his confreres endorsed this "alternative" over the total annihilation of the native populations already decimated by disease, harsh conditions of labor, and constant attacks by the colonists. Vieira's views on African slavery must be placed within the general framework of the times. He was not advocating the enslavement of Africans, but rather, since the rest of the colony was already deeply involved in the ignominious transatlantic slave trade (in full force since 1539), he saw no harm in extending it to this area. Vieira's rationale–which was shared by many people at the time–was his belief that, unlike Amerindians, Africans were physically and emotionally more likely to endure physical work and punishment. In his view, Africans were more gifted and more civilized than the native Brazilian peoples, who needed protection. Even though all men were born equal, Vieira believed that God allowed the subjugation of the African peoples because of their physical strength and endurance, and he feared for the survival of the entire native population, which he believed would soon be annihilated should the practice of enslavement be allowed to continue. Despite his tepid endorsement of the African slave trade, Vieira considered slavery as a contract that the Portuguese had made with the devil. In a sermon delivered to an Afro-Brazilian lay brotherhood, later published as *Sermão à Confraria do Rosário da Bahia* (written in 1683, Sermon to the Brotherhood of Our Lady of the Rosary of Salvador da Bahia), he remarked: "Oh comércio desumano, a tua mercadoria é composta de seres humanos!" (Oh inhuman trade! Your merchandise is made of human beings!) Vieira also recognized that Brazil existed and was sustained by Angola—that is, the African slave trade. In other words, the economy of the Portuguese colony in South America depended solely on slave labor from West Africa. As João Lúcio de Azevedo notes in *História de António Vieira* (1918–1920), more than once Father Vieira reiterated that Brazil was a place "com o corpo na América e a alma em África" (with its body in America and its soul in Africa).

In 1661 the local settlers, with the support of the other religious orders in the area—the Carmelite and Franciscan presence is attested to as early as 1627 and 1636, respectively—eventually succeeded in expelling the Jesuits from Maranhão. Although officially still under King Afonso VI, as a result of the 1662–1667 coup d'état Portugal was under the rule of Luís de Vasconcelos e Sousa, third Count of Castelo Melhor, a man wholly unsympathetic to the Indian issue. Accused of a palace intrigue, Vieira was first confined to Porto and then to Coimbra. In Coimbra he wrote the *História do futuro,* in which, through biblical prophesies, he interprets the future of Portugal; only the introduction, the *Livro anteprimeiro,* survives today.

In 1661 the High Tribunal of the Inquisition accused Vieira of being both a defender of the Jews and, for *Esperanças de Portugal, quinto império do mundo, primeira e segunda vinda de El-Rei D. João IV,* an unrepentant heretic. The allegorical way in which Vieira interpreted Scripture in this text gave easy ammunition to the Portuguese Inquisition as they accused him of disguised cabalistic beliefs in reincarnation. Using as his sources the Bible and Gonçalo Anes Bandarra's messianic *Trovas* (1530–1540, Ballads), Vieira interpreted the prophesies of the resurrection of the late King João IV as the future emperor of the Fifth Empire, or, rather, the Judeo-Christian Kingdom.

The myth of Portugal as the Fifth Empire, however, actually preceded Vieira. According to this theory, under the Portuguese Empire there would be a universal conversion to Catholicism, followed by the final advent of the Império Consumado de Cristo (Kingdom of Christ on Earth). It is a paradoxical combination of national messianism, chiefly informed by Sebastianism and Bandarism—that is, Bandarra's messianic theories—in combination with other European messianic movements or narratives (such as old Iberian traditions and Arthurian legends) and Jewish messianism, common among the *cristão-novo* communities of the Diaspora. Sebastianism itself is a multilayered system of myths, chiefly constructed around the deep belief in the return of a temporarily deceased charismatic leader who one day would restore the supremacy of Portugal as a world empire. Over time the leaders have shifted, going from King Sebastian, after whom the myth is named, to King João IV, King João VI, and King Miguel. Beyond the legend of the Fifth Empire, other myths deeply connected to Sebastianism include the myth of the Encoberto, a concealed king who would free his people from misery and oppression, and the belief in the Fundação da Nacionalidade (Establishment of Nationality). Vieira prophesied the general conversion of the Hebrew nation under the aegis of Rei Encoberto of the Quinto Império (Hidden King of the Fifth Empire). The Fifth Empire is envisioned as a great spiritual and temporal kingdom, ruled by the Portuguese following in the footsteps of the Assyrian-Babylonian, Persian, Greek, and Roman empires. According to the *História do futuro,* God's punishment befell Portugal in two ways. The first was the defeat of the Portuguese troops at Ksar-el-Kebir (in present day Morocco) in 1578. This defeat, which eventually triggered Sebastianism, was considered to be either a direct punishment for the invention of modern slavery or God's way of chastising the Portuguese nation for the expulsion of the Portuguese Jews in 1496 and the forced conversion to Catholicism in 1497–1498. The second divine punishment involved the establishment of the Portuguese Inquisition.

Vieira was challenged by the inquisitor general to speak on religion. On 1 October 1665, he was sent to the Inquisitorial Prison in Coimbra, where he remained until 24 December 1667. He was found guilty of heresy and sympathizing with the Jewish and *cristão-novo* cause. As a result he was confined to a teaching institution or a Jesuit convent. As for religious matters, he was placed under a permanent and irrevocable gag order. Vieira was, however, freed after the interventions of King Afonso VI and the quick actions of the prince regent and future king Pedro II. Pedro guaranteed Vieira's

*Cover for a 1971 edition of selected works by Vieira
(Howard-Tilton Library, Tulane University)*

safety and immediate reinstatement within the Jesuit order.

During Lent 1669 Vicira preached at the Royal Palace. Soon after, he left for Rome, where he remained between 1669 and 1675, conducting business on behalf of the Society of Jesus. At the Holy See, Vieira distinguished himself as a powerful preacher, this time giving his sermons in Italian and Latin. Because of his fame, Queen Christina of Sweden, who since her abdication and conversion to Catholicism in 1654 had chosen Rome as her residence, invited him to be confessor and preacher at her Italian court. Vieira, however, graciously declined. He felt his true mission in Rome was to convince the Holy See to abolish the establishment of the Holy Inquisition, thus putting an end to a legitimized form of abuse. He was somewhat successful, and an inquiry was started in 1674. Later, however, Pope Clement X succeeded in temporarily putting a halt to all investigations. Meanwhile, Vieira was triumphant in getting Rome and the Portuguese Crown to allow the formation of the Companhia Comercial da Índia (Commercial Company of India). This company, which was operated by Portuguese Jews or crypto-Jewish merchants, in turn agreed to assist Jesuit missions in the Far East. In April 1675 Clement X also granted Vieira an affidavit offering him immunity from any further attacks from the Inquisition.

Soon after his arrival in Lisbon that year, Vieira began editing his sermons, and in 1679 he published the first volume of these writings, *Sermoens do p. Antonio Vieira da Companhia de Iesu, prégador de Sua Alteza* (Sermons of Father António Vieira, Society of Jesus, Preacher of Your Highness [that is, Royal Preacher]). In 1681 he returned to Salvador da Bahia, where he was nominated superior of all the Jesuit missions in Brazil and the Maranhão area. In 1688 he was nominated Visitador (Visitor) of the Province of Bahia, a position he held until 1691. In this post his duties were to inspect, examine, and report back to Europe (Portugal and the Holy See) on the religious and social conditions of overseas missions. Vieira spent the remainder of his life in Salvador da Bahia, dividing his time between the Colégio dos Jesuítas in Salvador da Bahia and his estate, Quinta do Tanque, not far from the capital, preaching and completely dedicated to his evangelical ministry.

From 1679 until his death Vieira devoted time to editing all his sermons and revising old letters or writing new ones. He also reedited one of his earlier works, which he considered his masterpiece, namely the *Clavis prophetica,* an eschatological companion to *Esperanças de Portugal, quinto império do mundo, primeira e segunda vinda de El-Rei D. João IV,* which he continued to edit until his death. The work survives today only in fragments. Using disparate notes and editions he had gathered during his entire lifetime, Vieira edited the complete edition of his sermons, sending them regularly to Portugal to be printed. He died in Salvador da Bahia on 18 July 1697.

Among Vieira's many sermons, all characterized by an overall logical reasoning and force of expression, the following are worth mentioning: the *Sermão da sexagésima,* the *Eucaristia* (Eucharist), the *Sermão de São Francisco Xavier* (Sermon of Saint Francis Xavier; published as *Xavier dormindo, e Xavier acordado* [1694, Xavier Sleeping, and Xavier Awake]), and the *Sermão do N. Senhora Rosário* (1754, Sermon of Our Lady of the Rosary). These sermons feature moral reflections as well as accounts of natural and contemporary events.

The *Sermões* and the *Cartas* are a direct mirror of Vieira's strong political and religious ideas. The former rely more on oratorical and communicative skills, whereas the latter base their message on the power of the written word as it is being read, though exhibiting the same dynamism found in the *Sermões.* Given their aural nature, the *Sermões* were obviously written to be heard, hence the many repetitions and the vivid contrasts, aimed at shocking and captivating the attention of the audience. In a sense, Vieira's works are the typical example of a nation and world in transition, gradually moving away from the Renaissance and entering the modern age, though expressed in a baroque manner.

The *Sermões* are followed by other works on various topics, public as well as private, in which Vieira offers suggestions and religious, political, social, and economic solutions to the many issues at hand. One of the interesting features of Vieira's work is the fact that it is deeply tied to his public life, the latter giving more, if not complete, meaning and value to the former. Even his most religious speeches and treatises offer a plethora of information and insight on the political and social events of the time. Vieira's views on the Portuguese colonial policy, the enslavement of the indigenous population of Brazil, the Atlantic slave trade, and his invectives against the Inquisition (the latter published as *Defesa perante o Tribunal do Santo Ofício* [Defense against the Tribunal of the Holy Office of the Inquisition] for the first time in Salvador da Bahia only in 1957) are expressed with equal force in his sermons and letters as well as elsewhere in his writings.

What makes Vieira's works different from those of other preachers of his time is his use of baroque literary devices. Rather than being gongoristic, where the excessively ornate and obscure literary forms and style inevitably suffocate the message, Vieira's prose is clear and captivating, reserving ornate and embellished devices for specific needs. Logic prevails over style, although the latter perfectly obeys the literary conventions of the time. Rather than being a cultist, Vieira uses the nuances of the baroque language and style to convey with precision his social and religious messages. With his power of suggestive imagination, Father António Vieira, S.J., thus comments on faith, society, and the human condition of the oppressed, be they poor, Amerindian, or people of African or Jewish descent.

Letters:

Copia de huma carta para Elrey N. Senhor sobre as missões do Seará, do Maranham, do Parà, & do grande Rio das Almasónas (Lisbon: Printed by Henrique Valente de Oliveira, 1660);

Cartas, 3 volumes (Lisbon: Published by the Officina de Congregação de Oratorio, 1735–1746);

Esperanças: Esperanças de Portugal, quinto império do mundo, primeira e segunda vinda de El-Rei D. João IV (Lisbon: J. M. C. Seabra & T. Q. Antunes, 1854–1855);

Pe. Antônio Vieira

Escritos instrumentais sobre os Índios

Ensaio Introdutório pelo
Prof. José Carlos Sebe Bom Meihy

1992   educ
                                       editora da puc-sp

Title page for a collection (Instrumental Writings about the Native Brazilians) of Vieira's political works (Howard-Tilton Library, Tulane University)

Cartas (Lisbon: J. M. C. Seabra & T. Q. Antunes, 1854–1855);

Cartas do padre Antonio Vieira (Lisbon: Empreza Litteraria Fluminense, 1885);

Cartas do padre Antonio Vieira, edited by João Lúcio de Azevedo (Coimbra: Imprensa da Universidade, 1925);

Cartas: selecção de Novais Teixeira, edited, with a preface, by Luis de Paula Freitas (Rio de Janeiro: W. M. Jackson, [1949]);

Cartas, 3 volumes, edited by Azevedo ([Lisbon]: Imprensa Nacional-Casa da Moeda, [1997]);

Correspondência de Antônio Vieira (1646–1694): o decoro, edited by João Adolfo Hansen (São Paulo, 2003);

Cartas do Brasil: 1626–1697, Estado do Brasil e Estado do Maranhão e Grã Pará, edited by Hansen (São Paulo: Hedra, 2003).

References:

Dauril Alden, "Indian Versus Slavery in the State of Maranhão during the Seventeenth and Eighteenth Centuries," *Biblioteca Americana,* 13 (1983): 91–140;

João Lúcio de Azevedo, *História de António Vieira,* 2 volumes (Lisbon: A. M. Teixeira, 1918, 1920);

Azevedo, *Os jesuítas no Grão-Pará. Suas missões e a colonização,* second edition (Coimbra: Imprensa da Universidade de Coimbra, 1930);

José van den Besselaar, *António Vieira: Profecia e Polémica* (Rio de Janeiro: Editora da Universidade do Estado do Rio de Janeiro, 2002);

Charles Ralph Boxer, *The Dutch in Brazil, 1624–1654* (Oxford: Clarendon Press, 1957);

Boxer, *A Great Luso-Brazilian Figure: Padre António Vieira, S.J., 1608–1697* ([London: Hispanic & Luso-Brazilian Councils], 1957);

Edwin Blake Brownrigg, "Stylometry and the *Arte de Furtar:* The Case for Padre Vieira," dissertation, New York University, 1982;

Thomas M. Cohen, *The Fire of Tongues: António Vieira and the Missionary Church in Brazil and Portugal* (Stanford, Cal.: Stanford University Press, 1998);

Lewis Hanke, "Pope Paul III and the American Indians," *Harvard Theological Review,* 30 (1937): 65–102;

Mathias C. Kiemen, *The Indian Policy of Portugal in the Amazon Region, 1614–1693* (Washington, D.C.: Catholic University of America Press, 1954);

Sharon Bamberry Landers, "An Exploration of the Theory and Practice of Slavery in Seventeenth-Century Brazil in the Writings of Padre António Vieira," dissertation, Texas Christian University, 1995;

Serafim Leite, *Artes e ofícios dos jesuítas no Brasil, 1549–1760* (Lisbon: Brotéria, 1953);

Leite, *História da Companhia de Jesus no Brasil,* 10 volumes (Lisbon: Livraria Portugália, 1938–1950);

Leite, *Monumenta brasiliae [Cartas e outros documentos],* 5 volumes (Rome: Monumenta Historica Societatis Iesu, 1956);

Joseph Abraham Levi, "A Diáspora Sefardita nas Américas durante os séculos XVII–XVIII," *Cadernos de Estudos Sefarditas,* 1 (2002): 27–63, 133–158;

Levi, ed., *Survival and Adaptation: The Portuguese Jewish Diaspora in Europe, Africa, and the New World* (New York: Sepher-Hermon Press, 2002);

Ivan Lins, *Para conhecer melhor padre António Vieira* (Rio de Janeiro: Bloch, 1974);

Margarida Vieira Mendes, *A oratória barroca de Vieira* (Lisbon: Caminho, 1989);

Maria Lucília Pires Mendes and J. Costa Miranda, eds., *Vieira Escritor* (Lisbon: Cosmos, 1997);

Adma Fadul Muhana, *Os autos do processo de Vieira na inquisição* (São Paulo: Editora Universidade Estadual Paulista, 1996);

Luiz Felipe Baêta Neves Flores, ed., *Padre António Vieira: catálogo do acervo da Biblioteca Nacional* (Rio de Janeiro: Editora da Universidade do Estado do Rio de Janeiro, Ministério da Cultura, Fundação Biblioteca Nacional, Departamento Nacional do Livro, 1999);

Padre António Vieira, 1608–1697: catálogo da exposição Novembro 1997–Fevererio 1998 (Lisbon: Biblioteca Nacional, 1997);

José Pedro Paiva, *Padre António Vieira, 1608–1697: bibliografia* (Lisbon: Biblioteca Nacional, 1999);

António Alcir Bernardez Pécora, *Teatro do sacramento: a unidade teológico-retórico-política do sermões de António Vieira* (Campinas: Editora da UNICAMP, 1994);

Afrânio Peixoto and Constâncio Alves, *Vieira Brasileiro,* 2 volumes (Paris & Lisbon: Aillaud & Bertrand, 1921);

Afonso Júnior Pena, *A Arte de Furtar e o seu autor* (Rio de Janeiro: J. Olympio, 1946);

Sebastião da Rocha Pitta, *História da América portuguesa desde 1500 até 1724,* third edition (Salvador da Bahia: Progresso, 1950).

Papers:

Miscellaneous Writings of António Vieira: Portugal and Brazil: ms 1647–1700, a collection of twelve manuscript treatises by António Vieira, is held at the Bancroft Library, University of California, Berkeley.

Appendix

Colonial Literature
(Jesuit Literature, Baroque, Neoclassicism, Arcadianism)

Lúcia Helena Costigan
Ohio State University

Carta do achamento do Brasil (Letter of the Discovery of Brazil), written by Pero Vaz de Caminha in 1500 and first published in 1817, is generally considered the birth certificate of Brazilian literature. The letter describes the newly discovered land as an earthly paradise with abundant natural resources and beautiful, innocent natives. Caminha's enthusiastic account was emulated by later colonial writers seeking to attract immigrants to Brazil, and this encomiastic literature became known as *ufanismo*. When Caminha wrote his letter, however, the Portuguese empire's major interest was expansion in Africa and Asia, and Brazil was considered of secondary importance; this situation lasted for many decades. Only after other European explorers began to arrive in Brazil and take advantage of its natural resources did the Portuguese rulers decide to colonize it.

Literature and culture started to take shape in Portuguese America a half century after the year Pedro Álvares Cabral accidentally landed on the coast of Brazil and Caminha wrote his letter to King Dom Manuel announcing the discovery of the new land. Most of the literature produced in Brazil during the sixteenth and seventeenth centuries was written either by European-born Jesuits or by a few creole intellectuals with Jesuit educations. The Jesuit order, known formally as the Society of Jesus, was founded in Paris in 1540 by St. Ignatius Loyola. Defenders of the Spanish Counter-Reformation, the Jesuits quickly spread across Europe and to European colonies throughout the world and earned a reputation as excellent missionaries and educators. Soon after the order was founded, Portugal granted the Jesuits a monopoly on the conversion of "infidels" and "gentiles" in its Asian, African, and American colonies. King João III directed the Jesuits to establish the educational system in Portugal and in the colonies, and the University of Coimbra, which had been founded in Lis-

bon in 1290 and transferred to Coimbra in 1537, became one of the order's most important educational centers.

The Jesuits were the first missionaries charged with the catechization of the Brazilian natives. From the second half of the sixteenth century until the middle of the eighteenth century the Jesuits not only worked among the natives but also helped to shape the educational and the cultural development of the new society. The order became one of the wealthiest institutions in Portuguese America because it managed businesses that linked Brazil and Africa, particularly the slave trade; it received many donations; and it was exempt from taxation. Its patrimony included land, sugar plantations in the rural areas, and lavish schools and other buildings in the urban centers. Manuel da Nóbrega, José de Anchieta, and António Vieira are the most distinguished Jesuits of colonial Brazil. Like others of their order who were engaged in missionary work, they saw themselves as direct successors of the first Christians, who sought to convert Romans and barbarians alike.

The first Jesuit to arrive in Brazil, Nóbrega landed in the colony in 1549 with the first royal governor-general, Tomé de Sousa. Nóbrega's major contribution to colonial Brazil consisted of his missionary work promoting literature among the Tupi Indians in their *aldeias* (villages). His *Diálogo sobre a conversão do gentio* (1556, Dialogue on the Conversion of the Gentiles) presents arguments for and against the Christianization of the natives. Nóbrega says that the Indians are no better and no worse than any other people, and he has no illusions about their inherent innocence; the salvation of the natives will be accomplished not by a divine miracle but by hard work and sacrifice on the part of the missionaries. Nóbrega also wrote a large number of letters to his Jesuit colleagues abroad; most of this correspondence was not published until the twentieth century. The let-

Gold mining in Minas Gerais during the eighteenth century. The province was the center of Brazil's Arcadian literary movement. In 1789 members of the movement attempted an insurrection against Portuguese rule, the Inconfidência Mineira, *that was harshly put down (Biblioteca Nacional, Rio de Janeiro; from Robert M. Levine and John J. Crocitti, eds.,* The Brazil Reader, *1999; Collection of Jessica Reese Goudeau).*

ters dealing with his missionary experience in Brazil alternate between optimism and pessimism: at times the missionary expresses gentle affection for the Indians, while at other times he seems to despise them and recommends treating them with violent authoritarianism.

Nóbrega encouraged Anchieta to write and direct plays to facilitate the catechization of the natives. Known as the Apóstolo do Brasil (Brazilian Apostle) because of his work among the natives, Anchieta is the most distinguished literary and religious figure of sixteenth-century Brazil. Born in the Canary Islands in 1534 and educated at the University of Coimbra, Anchieta arrived in Brazil in 1553. His plays aimed at the evangelization of the natives are simple and straightforward *autos* (morality plays) based on Gil Vicente's didactic theater and written in verse in various combinations of Tupi, Portuguese, and Spanish. Since no formal theaters existed in the colony, they were performed in churchyards or in the central areas of towns and *aldeias;* the tropical forest was often used as a backdrop. The casts were made up of male colonists and of natives who lived in the missions. The *Auto da pregação universal* (Morality Play about the Universal Preaching), written around 1567 and published in 1672, is consid-

ered the first dramatic text composed in Brazil. Written in Portuguese and Tupi, it was intended to appeal to natives and settlers alike and was performed in various locations, with changes in the names of characters and references to local events and geography. One of Anchieta's few other surviving *autos* is the *Auto representado na festa de São Lourenço* (Morality Play Performed on Saint Lawrence's Day), written about 1583. Severino J. Albuquerque says that Anchieta's *autos* "reveal a remarkable feeling for spectacle, calling for the use of body paint, native costumes, song and dance, fights, torches, and processions." Aside from his plays, Anchieta is best known for two epic Latin poems: *De Beata Virgine Dei Matre* (On the Virgin Mother of God) was written in beach sand during Anchieta's captivity by the Tamoio Indians in 1563 and reconstructed after his release; *De gestis Mendi de Saa* (On Mem de Sá) praises the deeds of Mem de Sá, the third Portuguese governor-general of Brazil, who was instrumental in freeing Anchieta from captivity.

Toward the end of the sixteenth century Bento Teixeira composed *Prosopopéia* (Personification), the first epic poem written in Portuguese in Brazil. Teixeira was a "New Christian" (descendant of converted Jews) who immigrated to Brazil as a child and studied with the Jesuits; *Prosopopéia* was written at a time when he was being scrutinized by the Portuguese Inquisition on suspicion of secretly practicing Judaism. It was published in Portugal in 1601, shortly after the writer's death in an Inquisition jail in Lisbon. The publication indicates that Teixeira had influential connections, since the Inquisition usually prohibited the publication of texts by people it persecuted as heretics. The poem is dedicated to Jerônimo de Albuquerque Coelho, a relative of Duarte Coelho, who was a prestigious and influential individual both in Pernambuco, where Teixeira lived prior to his imprisonment in Lisbon, and in Portugal. He may have dedicated the poem to Albuquerque in an attempt to gain the latter's protection, and Albuquerque may have had something to do with the publication of the poem.

Using Luís de Camões's epic poem *Os Lusiadas* (1572, The Lusiads) as his model, Teixeira describes the beauty, wealth, and safety that immigrants will find in Pernambuco. He also praises the bravery of noble Portuguese such as Albuquerque, who fought the French and the Indians in Brazil. Because *Prosopopéia* was modeled on *Os Lusiadas,* some critics see Teixeira as an insignificant and mediocre poet. One can, however, detect in the poem a hidden message of resistance. Teixeira was persecuted because his ethnic and religious background did not fit in with mainstream European society. In terms of style, *Prosopopéia* can be situated at the crossroads of the Renaissance and the baroque.

In the late nineteenth century the critic Heinrich Wölfflin classified the lavishly ornate artistic, literary, and musical style that emerged in Europe between the Renaissance and the neoclassical period as the baroque. The baroque emerged in Spain during the period of the Council of Trent from 1545 to 1563. The Chiesa del Gesù in Rome, a church constructed by the Jesuits between 1568 and 1584, is considered the first example of the new style in architecture.

The best representative of baroque rhetoric among the Jesuits in seventeenth-century Brazil is Vieira. Born in Lisbon in 1608, Vieira moved with his family to Bahia at age six. When he was fifteen, he ran away to live with the Jesuits; two years later he was sent to the Jesuit college in Olinda, Pernambuco, to teach rhetoric. One of the great preachers, writers, and missionaries of the seventeenth century, Vieira was also important in European and Ibero-American politics. His writings consist primarily of sermons delivered in churches in Brazil and Europe. In content and in form the sermons are typical examples of Spanish baroque culture. Some address the political situation in Brazil during the period, beginning in 1580, when Portugal

and its colonies were part of the Spanish empire; in 1640 Portugal regained its independence from Spain, but there was still conflict in Brazil, this time with the Dutch. After this date Vieira's sermons deal with what he considers Portugal's fall from divine grace. These themes are particularly obvious in his *Sermão pelo bom sucesso das armas de Portugal contra as de Holanda* (1640, Sermon for the Success of the Portuguese Army against the Dutch), in which he asks why God deserted the Portuguese in favor of Protestant Dutchmen.

In 1641 Vieira went to Lisbon as part of a delegation of Brazilians to the court of King João IV, the new monarch who had been chosen to rule the independent Lusitanian empire. Vieira became João IV's adviser and one of the most powerful men in Portugal. In 1652 he gave up his position to return to Brazil and work among the natives in the northern region of Maranhão. Vieira and other Jesuits strongly opposed the exploitation of the natives by Portuguese colonizers; the conflict resulted in the expulsion of Vieira and his fellow Jesuit missionaries from Maranhão in 1661. Marked by the contradictions of the baroque era, many of Vieira's sermons reveal a crisis of faith and a disregard for religious and social orthodoxy. His open defense of Indians, the poor of Portugal, New Christians, and Jews brought him to the attention of the Inquisition. Prohibited from preaching, he returned to Bahia in 1681 and remained there until his death in 1697.

In 1759 the minister Sebastião José Carvalho de Melo, Marquis of Pombal, expelled the Jesuits from Portuguese lands. The official reasons were the Jesuit refusal to obey the Treaty of Madrid, signed between Spain and Portugal in 1750, and their instigation of the Indian uprising known as Guerra Guaranítica of 1750 to 1756. Clearly, however, the society's wealth and a desire to change the educational system in the Portuguese empire led the marquis and other members of the enlightened bourgeoisie to oppose the Jesuit order. The Jesuits were expelled from France in 1764 and from Spain in 1767, and in 1773 Pope Clement XIV abolished the Society of Jesus. That decision was reversed by Pius VII in 1814, resulting in the reemergence of the Jesuit order.

Non-Jesuit writers who produced baroque texts include the Portuguese New Christian Ambrósio Fernandes Brandão and the creoles Gregório de Matos Guerra and Manuel Botelho de Oliveira. Brandão's *Diálogos das grandezas do Brasil* (1618; translated as *Dialogues of the Great Things of Brazil*, 1986) seems to have been written with the purpose of attracting European immigrants to Portuguese America. The book consists of six dialogues between Brandônio, a longtime resident of Brazil, and Alviano, a skeptical newcomer from Portugal. Their discussions typify the conflict that extended over several centuries between Europeans who saw the New World as a land of innocence or promise and those who considered it savage, dangerous, and degenerate. The book also speculates about the possible Hebrew origin of the Indians and describes the various social groups and customs of the region. Brandônio argues that the immigrants should not seek to make quick profits and return to Portugal but should stay in Brazil and work for the benefit of the new society. An incomplete version of the *Diálogos das grandezas do Brasil* was published in Rio de Janeiro in 1930; a complete and definitive edition was not published until 1966. This edition includes a detailed analysis of the various theories of authorship of the work, an account of the known facts of Brandão's life, and a history of the various editions by the Brazilian critic José Antonio Gonsalves de Mello, who considers the *Diálogos das grandezas do Brasil* a significant work of Brazilian literature and one of the foundational documents in the history of the Brazilian northeast.

Matos was born in Bahia in 1636 into a wealthy family of sugar planters. He was sent to the University of Coimbra; on completing his education in 1661 he married a local woman and became a judge. Personal and political problems caused Matos to lose his judgeship, and he returned to Brazil in 1682. Matos wrote religious and lyrical poetry but is best known for his satirical verses, for which his models included Francisco de Quevedo y Villegas, Pedro Calderón de la Barca, and Luis de Góngora y Argote. Matos's satirical verses focus on what he saw in Bahia on his return from Portugal and portray the colony as an upside-down world. Like Quevedo, Matos sought to correct through satire the excessive liberty that he believed was the cause of the decadence of society. The aggressive and pornographic verses were addressed to the governor of Bahia, Luís Alves da Câmara Coutinho, and resulted in the writer being exiled to Angola in 1694. He was allowed to return to Brazil in 1695 on the conditions that he give up writing satirical verses and no longer live in Bahia. He died in Recife the following year. With the rise of the neobaroque and tropicalist movements since the 1960s, Matos's poems have been revived by the poet Harold de Campos and by the popular singer/songwriter Caetano Veloso.

Botelho de Oliveira was born in the same year as Matos and died in 1711. Although Antônio Cândido and José Aderaldo Castello contend that Botelho's production does not compare in quality to the writings of Vieira and Matos, his *Música do Parnaso* (1705, Music of Parnassus) does have the distinction of being the first volume of poetry published in Portugal by a native-born Brazilian. One of the most celebrated poems in the collection, "Ilha da Maré" (Island of Maré), is a good example of the *ufanista* spirit that characterized writings such as Caminha's *Carta do achamento do Brasil* and Teixeira's *Prosopopéia* that glorified the Brazilian landscape and resources. *Música do Parnaso* praises the natural beauty and delicious foods of Bahia, the poet's homeland.

In the field of historiography, names that stand out in colonial Brazil include Pero de Magalhães Gândavo, a Portuguese who lived in Brazil around 1570 and is thought to be the author of *História da província de Santa Cruz a que vulgarmente chamamos Brasil* (1576, History of Saint Cross Province Commonly Known as Brazil) and *Tratado da terra do Brasil* (Treatise of the Brazilian Land, written in 1570 and published in 1826), and Gabriel Soares de Sousa, a plantation owner who lived in Bahia at about the same time and is believed to have written *Tratado descritivo do Brasil* (Descriptive Treatise of Brazil), published in Rio de Janeiro in 1851. The work of these early historians can be considered exemplary of *ufanismo:* they portray Brazil as a land of beauty and wealth. Not all historians were so positive in tone, however. The creole Frei Vicente do Salvador's baroque *História do Brasil* (History of Brazil), written in 1627 but not published until 1889, details the political and military crises he observed in Brazil during the period that Portugal and its possessions were part of the Spanish empire. The creole Sebastião da Rocha Pita's baroque *História da América Portuguesa* (History of Portuguese America) was published in Portugal in 1730. The first two volumes describe the geography and the inhabitants of Brazil, while the remaining eight volumes discuss the political and administrative aspects of Brazilian colonial society.

The baroque style did not end with Vieira, Matos, and the other writers of the period but extended far beyond the seventeenth century; and the baroque influence remained strong not only in literature but also in architecture and art. In the early eighteenth century the town of Vila Rica de Ouro Preto became the center of the baroque architecture that characterized the Portuguese empire at the time.

The literature that emerged in Brazil in the second half of the eighteenth century shows the predominance of neoclassicism: a deference to ancient Greek and Roman models. The neoclassical style was favored by Pombal, and, following in the footsteps of their counterparts in Portugal, many Brazilian intellectuals who wanted the patronage of the powerful marquis wrote encomiastic poems praising him. The Jesuit-educated Brazilian José Basílio da Gama wrote laudatory verses to Pombal's daughter and also produced the epic poem *O Uraguai* (1769, Uruguay). Written a few years after Pombal expelled the Jesuits from the Portuguese territories, Basílio's epic supported the marquis's

Brazilians celebrating Carnaval in Rio de Janeiro during the late colonial period. Brazil declared its independence from Portugal in 1822 (Biblioteca Nacional, Rio de Janeiro; from Robert M. Levine and John J. Crocitti, eds., The Brazil Reader, 1999; Collection of Jessica Reese Goudeau).

action and saved the poet from being persecuted as a Jesuit.

José de Santa Rita Durão was an Augustinian priest who was born in Brazil in 1722 but lived in Portugal, where he had problems with the Portuguese elite. Perhaps to gain the sympathy of the members of the court, Durão wrote the wordy and pedestrian epic *Caramuru* (1781), which praises the Portuguese for bringing civilization to the Indians of Brazil. The hero of the poem, however, is not a figure like Anchieta, who spent his life teaching the Indians, but a Portuguese sailor, Diogo Álvares Correia, who was saved by Indians after being shipwrecked on the coast around 1510. Diogo Álvares is transformed into a hero and portrayed as responsible for transforming the natives into civilized people.

Arcadianism appeared in Europe with the advent of the Enlightenment and the formation of the first academies; the two movements arrived in Brazil almost simultaneously. Abandoning the baroque tradition, the followers of Arcadianism preached a return to the peaceful joys of nature and the purity and simplicity of thought and diction associated with Greek and Roman verse. Although marginalized in a colony such as Brazil, where printing presses were still prohibited, the first gatherings of intellectuals in Brazil occurred during the second decade of the eighteenth century. In 1724 the short-lived Brazilian Academia dos Esquecidos (Academy of the Forgotten) was founded in Bahia. Other groups of isolated intellectuals gathered sporadically to study and discuss literature, history, botany, and zoology. The adverse environment in which these intellectuals lived, without a press and cut off from contemporary developments in Europe, killed off the first Brazilian academies, and not until the last decades of the eighteenth century did the Arcadian movement gain strength in Brazil. Following the model of the philosophers of the French Enlightenment and the foundation of the Arcádia Lusitana (Lusitanian Arcadia) in Lisbon in 1756 under the patronage of King José I, a group of Brazilian clergymen, lawyers, doctors, and scientists began gathering to share ideas. These intellectuals were known as *árcades mineiros* (Mineiran Arcadians) because most of them lived in the state of Minas Gerais. The members included the writers Cláudio Manuel da Costa, Tomás Antonio Gonzaga, Inácio José de Alvarenga Peixoto, and Manuel Inácio da Silva Alvarenga, who were supported by Pombal. They adopted Arcadian pseudonyms and wrote poetry that associated them with Greek and Roman idyllic poets. Critics generally consider da Costa the best poet of the group. His poems, which incorporate aspects of both the baroque and the neoclassical styles, were published in *Obras* (1768, Works) and in *Obras poéticas* (1903, Poetic Works), edited by João Ribeiro. Gonzaga was a typical neoclassical poet; in addition to his love poetry, he is known as the author of the satirical poem *Cartas chilenas* (Chilean Letters), written around 1787. The work is a severe criticism of the corruption and abuses of power of Luis da Cunha Meneses, governor of Minas Gerais from 1783 until 1788.

Pombal fell from power in 1777 with the death of King José and the succession of Queen Maria I, and the Arcadian poets of Minas Gerais found themselves without a patron. Their poetry became less an emotional escape from reality than a catalyst for protest. The dissatisfaction of these intellectuals during the reign of Maria led them to start a movement, the *Inconfidência Mineira,* to free Brazil from Portugal. The movement was harshly put down by the Crown. Da Costa died in jail while awaiting trial in 1789, and one of the leaders of the movement, Joaquim José da Silva Xavier, known as Tiradentes, was executed in 1792. That same year Gonzaga was exiled to Mozambique, where he married into an important family of Portuguese colonizers and became a prosperous man. Alvarenga Peixoto and Silva Alvarenga were also exiled to Africa; Alvarenga Peixoto perished, but Silva Alvarenga survived and in 1797 was granted a pardon by the queen and returned to Brazil. When the royal family arrived in Brazil in 1808, Silva Alvarenga was working for the journal *O Pátrio* (The Patriot), one of the first magazines published in Brazil. Like the other Mineiran Arcadians, Silva Alvarenga is mostly known for his lyrical poetry, including *Glaura* (1799); his works were published by Joaquim Norberto Sousa e Silva in 1864. The literature written in Brazil between 1792, when the *Inconfidência Mineira* became public, and 1822, the year of independence, is usually considered inferior to the vibrant work produced by the Jesuits and by the baroque and neoclassical writers.

References:

Severino J. Albuquerque, "The Brazilian Theater up to 1900," in *Cambridge History of Latin American Literature: Brazilian Literature Bibliographies,* volume 3, edited by Roberto González Echevarría and Enrique Pupo-Walker (Cambridge: Cambridge University Press, 1996), pp. 105–125;

Dauril Alden, *The Making of an Enterprise: The Society of Jesus in Portugal, Its Empire, and Beyond, 1540–1750* (Stanford, Cal.: Stanford University Press, 1996);

Luiz Felipe de Alencastro, *O trato dos viventes: formação do Brasil no Atlântico Sul* (São Paulo: Companhia das Letras, 2000);

Antônio Cândido and José Aderaldo Castello, *Presença da literatura brasileira,* volume 1: *Das origens ao Romantismo,* sixth edition (São Paulo: Difusão Européia do Livro, 1974);

Thomas M. Cohen, *The Fire of Tongues: Antônio Vieira and the Missionary Church in Brazil and in Portugal* (Stanford, Cal.: Stanford University Press, 1998);

João Adolfo Hansen, *A sátira e o engenho: Gregório de Matos e a Bahia do século XVII* (São Paulo: Companhia das Letras/Secretaria de Estado da Cultura, 1989);

Ambrósio Fernandes Brandão, *Diálogos das grandezas do Brasil,* edited by José Antonio Gonsalves de Mello (Recife: Imprensa Universitária, 1962; revised, 1966); translated and annotated by Frederick Holden Hall, William F. Harrison, and Dorothy Winters Welker as *Dialogues of the Great Things of Brazil* (Albuquerque: University of New Mexico Press, 1986);

Robert M. Levine and John J. Crocitti, eds., *The Brazil Reader* (Durham, N.C.: Duke University Press, 1999);

Ivan Teixeira, *Mecenato pombalino e poesia neoclássica* (São Paulo: Editora da Universidade de São Paulo, 1999);

Heinrich Wölfflin, *Renaissance und Barock: Eine Untersuchung über Wesen und Entstehung des Barockstils in Italien* (Munich: Ackermann, 1888); translated by Kathrin Simon as *Renaissance and Baroque* (London: Collins, 1964; Ithaca, N.Y.: Cornell University Press, 1966).

Concrete Poetry

Reinhard Krüger
Technical University of Berlin and University of Stuttgart

Concrete poetry explores all aspects of language, with special emphasis on speech and graphic representation. The theoretical concepts underlying this form of poetry have been elaborated by an international group of poets who in many cases were polyglot and wrote poems in more than one language. Although the movement is global in scope, some individual artists and national groups, especially the Brazilian *Noigandres* group, have been in the forefront of the development of concrete poetry.

Concrete poetry officially began in 1955 as the result of a meeting between the German poet Eugen Gomringer and the Brazilian poet Décio Pignatari at the Hochschule für Gestaltung (School of Design) in Ulm, Germany, where Gomringer was secretary to Max Bill, the first director of the school. Pignatari and Gomringer combined two concepts. Gomringer's concept of poetry, published in 1955 in his manifesto *Konstellationen,* borrowed from Stéphane Mallarmé's idea in his poem "Un coup de dés jamais n'abolira le hasard" (1897, A Throw of the Dice Will Never Eliminate Chance): "Rien n'aura eu lieu que le lieu, exceptée, peut-être, une constellation" (Nothing will have happened than the place, with the exception, maybe, of a constellation). For Gomringer, poetry is the result of constellations of words arranged according to visual principles on the whiteness of the paper. Poetry, therefore, may be considered an ideographic work that retraces the poet's thoughts on paper. Pignatari contributed the notion of poetry based on the experience of concrete painting, a current that had emerged in the 1940s and of which Bill was a representative. The two artists agreed to call the new poetry "concrete poetry" in an analogy to concrete painting. (The Swedish poet Öyvind Fahlström had published "Manifest för konkret poesie" [Manifesto for Concrete Poetry] in 1953, but since his text was in Swedish and circulated in mimeograph form, it did not have an impact on the development of concrete poetry in Brazil, Germany, Austria, or Switzerland.)

Concrete poetry defies precise definition; the poets themselves have expressed the difficulty of arriving at a set of specific characteristics. In a 1996 interview in which Pignatari and Haroldo and Augusto de Campos discussed their forty years as concrete artists, Pignatari was asked for his definition; he replied by quoting Pablo Picasso, who, when asked in 1947 what cubism was, said "Connais pas" (I don't know); he then referred the readers of the interview to the 1965 anthology edited by the concrete poets, *Teoria da poesia concreta: textos críticos e manifestos, 1950–1960* (Theory of Concrete Poetry: Critical Texts and Manifestoes, 1950–1960). In the same interview Haroldo de Campos gave a provisional definition by quoting the Mexican writer Octavio Paz: "A melhor e mais sintética definição de 'poesia concreta' (correspondente à fase 'geométrica' ou, como se pode reconhecer a posteriori, 'minimalista' do movimento, aquela que traduz na prática as propostas do plano piloto de 58) é a formulada por Octavio Paz em *Transblanco:* 'Os senhores descobriram—ou inventaram—uma verdadeira topologia poética'" (The best and most comprehensive definition of concrete poetry [corresponding to the geometrical, or as one can recognize in retrospect, the minimalist phase of the movement that was translated into the proposals of the pilot plan of 1958] is the one formulated by Octavio Paz in *Transblanco:* "You have discovered—or invented—a true poetic topology"). Campos went on to give a more precise definition:

Tecnicamente, poesia concreta é a denominação de uma prática poética, cristalizada na década de 50, que tem como características básicas:

a) a abolição do verso;

b) a apresentação "verbivocovisual," ou seja, a organização do texto segundo critérios que enfatizem os valores gráficos e fônicos relacionais das palavras;

c) a eliminação ou rarefação dos laços da sintaxe lógico-discursiva em prol de uma conexão direta entre as palavras, orientada principalmente por associações paronomásticas.

(Technically, concrete poetry is the name of a poetic practice that came into being in the decade of the 1950s and has as basic characteristics:

a) elimination of the verse;

b) a "verbivocovisual" presentation, that is, the organization of the text according to criteria that emphasize the relational graphic and phonic values of words;

405

c) the elimination or rarefaction of the links of logical-discursive syntax in favor of a direct connection between words, oriented principally by paronomastic associations.)

The essay "Pilot Plan for Concrete Poetry," by Pignatari, Augusto de Campos, Haroldo de Campos, and Ronaldo Azevedo, was published in English in *Noigandres* in 1958. Among its more important points are:

Assuming that the historical cycle of verse (as formal-rhythmical unit) is closed, concrete poetry begins by being aware of graphic space as structural agent. Qualified space: space-time structure instead of mere linear-temporistical development. Hence the importance of ideogram concept, either in its general sense of spatial or visual syntax, or in its special sense . . . of method of composition based on direct-analogical, not logical-discursive juxtaposition of elements. . . .

Concrete Poetry aims at the least common multiple of language. Hence its tendency to nounising and verbification. . . . Hence its affinities with the so-called isolating languages (Chinese): . . . Chinese offers an example of pure relational syntax, based exclusively on word order. . . .

Renouncing the struggle for "absolute," Concrete Poetry remains in the magnetic field of perennial relativeness. Chronomicro-metering of hazard. Control. Cybernetics. The poem as a mechanism regulating itself: feed-back. Faster communication (problems of functionality and structure implied) endows the poem with a positive value and guides its own making.

Concrete Poetry: total responsibility before language. Thorough realism. Against a poetry of expression, subjective and hedonistic. To create precise problems and to solve them in terms of sensible language. A general art of the word. The poem-product: useful object.

The essay inspired a wave of concretist experiments not only in Brazil but also in the rest of Latin America and in Europe. The theoretical writings of Gomringer and Max Bense also provided a theoretical orientation for poets who wanted to experiment and invent.

The forerunners of concretism, according to Haroldo de Campos in the 1996 interview, were the early-twentieth-century vanguard movements futurism and Dada; the only aspect that was new to concrete poetry, he said, was its "rigor construtivista" (constructivist rigor). He also noted that, unlike their German counterparts, Brazilian concretists were interested in "a dimensão sonora" (the sonorous dimension) of the poem. He distinguished four phases in the development of concrete poetry: a "preconcretist" phase that lasted until the early 1950s; a phase that began with the founding of the review *Noigandres* in 1952; a phase marked by the insertion of nonverbal signs into the text in the late 1950s; and a phase in which visual possibili-

ties are offered by the computer, such as animation and the Internet, beginning in the 1990s.

The basic notions of concrete poetry can be found in trends that predate the official beginning of the movement in 1955. As early as the sixteenth century one can find evidence of an interest in the phonetic aspects of language in the poems of the Portuguese writer Gil Vicente. Vicente's plays present many examples of sound-poetry in ideophonic exclamations, such as "Hi hi hi hi hi hi hi!" "Hão! hão! hão! hão!" "Hãi! hãi! hãi! hãi!" and "Ha ah ah ah ah ah!" Vicente also explores the paronomastic aspects of words:

Diabo: Fradas?
Feiticeira: Fadas.
Diabo: Frades?

(Devil: Brathers?
Feiticeira: Fairies.
Devil: Brothers?)

Dadaist and Surrealist poets also demonstrated a critical attitude toward language similar to that of the concretists. They experimented with paradoxes and the unconscious as they analyzed the various dimensions and possibilities of individual words or groups of words.

In Brazil the most striking forerunners of concrete poetry are found in the writings of the two outstanding figures of Brazilian modernism, Mário and Oswald de Andrade. Unlike other avant-garde artists, the Brazilian concretists were careful not to stress the concept of rupture with the past; they had learned from the failures of former avant-garde artists, such as the Italian futurist Filippo Tommaso Marinetti and the French Surrealist André Breton, who claimed that their works represented a total break with what had gone before. In his "Informe sobre o modernismo" (1945, Essay on Modernism) Oswald de Andrade discusses the dialectics of modernism and classicism: "A palavra 'moderno' pertence a qualquer época. Foram modernos os iniciadores de todos os movimentos estéticos e filosóficos, de todos os movimentos científicos e políticos. O tempo encarrega-se de tornar os modernos clássicos ou se destruí-los" (The word "modern" belongs to any epoch. The founders of all aesthetic and philosophical movements and all political and scientific movements were modern. Time takes upon itself the task of making the moderns into classics or of destroying them). Andrade does not perceive an antagonistic tension between modernism and classicism; on the contrary, he sees modernist works as future classic. This notion corresponds to the ideas of Guillaume Apollinaire, Blaise Cendrars (pseudonym of Frédéric Sauser), and Louis Aragon in France.

Oswald de Andrade inserted a considerable number of poems in *Memórias sentimentais de João Miramar* (1924, Sentimental Memoirs of João Miramar), as Apollinaire had also done in his novels. In some of these poems, such as "Mont-Cenis," he reduces the narrative dynamics of the text to a "frozen verbal-scriptural representation" of a movement:

> O alpinista
> de alpenstock
> desceu
> nos
> Alpes
>
> (The alpinist
> of Alpenstock
> descended
> toward
> the Alps)

The verses are an ideographic construction, reducing the fact to be related to only fifteen syllables—even fewer than the seventeen syllables of a haiku.

In 1928 Andrade published a poem that Haroldo de Campos in his essay "Uma poética de radicalidade" (1964, A Poetics of the Radical) calls "uma verdadeira tomada pré-concreta" (a true preconcretist attack):

> América do Sul
> América do Sol
> América do Sal
>
> (America of the south
> America of the sun
> America of the salt)

The change of only one phoneme in one word radically changes the meaning of each successive line; at the same time, the similarity of the sounds of *sul* (south), *sol* (sun), and *sal* (salt) creates a link among them. In this poem one can see traces of a procedure that became important in concrete poetry: the construction of poetic expression through the construction of linguistic difference.

Andrade ends the poem "São José del Rei" (St. Joseph of the King) in *Pau Brasil* (1925, Brazilwood) with an annihilation of any movement in the text:

> Bananeiras
> O Sol
> O cansaço da ilusão
> Igrejas
> O ouro na serra de pedra
> A decadência
>
> (Banana-Trees
> The Sun
> The getting tired from illusion
> Churches

> The gold of the stone plain
> The decadence)

The poem resembles a gathering of verbal representations of simultaneous impressions and visions of a landscape. In the poems of Mário and Oswald de Andrade that reveal preconcretist characteristics the reader not only reads the words, but also becomes an observer of the linguistic functions that the poet puts into play. The reader has to invent a syntax for the words assembled on the page.

One of the most important examples of a preconcretist poem that makes a concretist use of space is "I treni" (1943, The Trains), by the Italian futurist Carlo Belloli. The Brazilian concretists "discovered" the poem and refer to it many times as an example of how futurist conceptions of a spatialized text can lead to the invention of poetic concretism:

> treni
>
> i treni
>
> i
>
> i i i i i i i i i i i i i

The interest in the sounds of language and their written representation that occur in Vicente's works can be found in Oswald de Andrade's play *O homem e o cavalho* (1934, Man and Horse), in which the Trojan Horse says, "Ploc! Ploc! Ploc!" and Napoleon's horse says, "Palá! Palá! Palá!" and "Ah! Ah! Ah! Ah! Ah! Ah! Ah!" In *Telefonema* (1927) Andrade uses the onomatopoetic words "Tá-tá-tá! Tátáritátátátá!" There are also preconcretist deconstructions of the word on the level of the phonology and sound in the work, such as "Uberaba-aba-aba. Tris-tris-tris-te."

In 1950 Bill had an exhibition at the Museu de Arte Moderna in São Paulo, and in 1951 he received the International Prize for Sculpture at the First São Paulo Art Biennial. Strongly influenced by Bill's works, Brazilian artists Mary Vieira and Almir Amvignier went to study under him in Basel. Also in 1951 Gomringer, who had been born in Bolivia and had mastered the Spanish language, published "Avenidas" (Venues). This poem is not simply German or Spanish but, because of its international linguistic content, is a Portuguese or Brazilian poem, as well. The poet successively adds motifs to the text in a combinatory way, and the reader has to reconstruct a possible image from the three main words that make up the poem. The reader is transformed into the *admirador* (admirer) of the last verse:

avenidas
avenidas y flores

flores
flores y mujeres

avenidas
avenidas y mujeres

avenidas y flores y mujeres y
un admirador

(Avenues
avenues and flowers

flowers
flowers and women

avenues
avenues and women

avenues and flowers and women and
an admirer)

In 1952 Waldemar Cordeiro, a Brazilian artist of Italian descent who was influenced by the Italian Marxist Antonio Gramsci, formed a group of concrete painters that included Lothar Charoux, Geraldo de Barros, Kazmer Fejer, Leopold Haar, Luís Sacilotto, and Anatol Wladyslaw. They launched the polemic manifesto *Ruptura* (Rupture), which became noted for its radically innovative ideas.

Cordeiro's group quickly made contact with the poets associated with the review *Noigandres,* founded in São Paulo in 1952 by Pignatari and Augusto and Haroldo de Campos. These poets shared the painters' interest in innovation and a desire to break with non-avant-garde artists. The name *Noigandres* was taken from Ezra Pound's *Canto XX* (1927): "Noigandres, eh noigandres / Now what the DEFFIL can that mean!" Thus, *Noigandres,* like *Dada,* was initially a playful creation, a meaningless word; but it came to signify some of the underlying tenets of the concrete-poetry movement, which emerged from the activities of the *Noigandres* group between 1953 and 1956.

In "Silencio" (1954, Silence) Gomringer tries to invent a graphic representation of the phenomenon of silence by working with the opposition of graphic text and no text. As a spoken word, *silencio* is not silent; only when the word no longer appears in the text does it truly become silent. The most striking aspect of this poem is that the poet has discovered a way of representing the meaning of a word without using words. The poem is characteristic of the concretists' method of structuring the space of the page with semantic antonyms and oppositions:

silencio silencio silencio
silencio silencio silencio
silencio   silencio
silencio silencio silencio
silencio silencio silencio

As can be seen in "Silencio," repetition is one of the most eye-catching methods of concretist poetic construction. Through its different positions on the page, the various occurrences of the word assume importance and thus acquire semantic difference. In fact, repetition in the strict sense does not occur, because no repetition is possible. Everything that seems to be identical with some other thing that has shown up in the past turns out to have been altered. Arthur Rimbaud's dictum in *Lettres du voyant* (1871), "Je est un autre" (Me is an other), refers to the continuous change of things and applies not only to humans and every form of life but also to the signs humans use. Therefore, "repetition" means that something seems to be identical without really being so. Repetition is a poetic strategy of showing things and signs in their characteristic of always being different.

The earliest poems that are considered completely consistent with the notions of concrete poetry are those in the series "Poetamenos," by Augusto de Campos, published in the second issue of *Noigandres* in 1955. Campos commented on their publication: "O segundo número da revista (1955) continha sua série de poemas em cores POETAMENOS, escritos em 1953, considerados os primeiros exemplos consistentes de poesia concreta no Brasil. O verso e a sintaxe convencional eram abandonados e as palavras rearranjadas em estruturas gráfico-espaciais, algumas vezes impressas em até seis cores diferentes, sob inspiração da Klangbarbenmelodie (melodia de timbres) de Webern" (The second number of the journal [1955] contained the series of poems in colors, *Poetamenos,* written in 1953, considered to be the first consistent examples of concrete poetry in Brazil. Conventional verse and syntax were abandoned and the words rearranged into graphico-spatial structures, at times printed in up to six different colors, under the inspiration of Webern's Klangbarbenmelodie [melody of colors]).

The *Noigandres* group organized the Exposição Nacional de Arte Concreta (National Exposition of Concrete Art), held in São Paulo from December 1956 through January 1957 and in Rio de Janeiro in February 1957. The artists Ferreira Gullar and Wladimir Dias Pinto of Rio de Janeiro, who were affiliated with the group Frente (Front), founded in 1954, participated in the exposition. Gullar later took part in many other important international events of the concretists.

Ronaldo Azeredo tries to make the difference that rules every repetition evident in his poem "como o vento" (1957, Like the Wind) by repeating the same word in a slightly altered form. The effect is that the poem appears as the unfolding of a paradigm of phonetically more or less equivalent words that operate a successive semantic shifting toward new linguistic realities—that is, new words:

como   o   vento
comovido
com   o   ouvido
como   o   vivo
locomovido
ou vindo

(like the wind
touched
like the forgetting
like the living
locomotioned
or the coming)

In his poem "ruasol" (1957, Sun-street) Azeredo again uses the technique of altered repetition. This time, however, he changes not the lexical status of the words but the location of the words in each new line:

ruaruaruasol
ruaruasolrua
ruasolruarua
solruaruarua
ruaruaruas

(streetstreetstreetsun
streetstreetsunstreet
streetsunstreetstreet
sunstreetstreetstreet
streetstreetstreets)

The displacement of the word *sol* in the poem corresponds to the astronomical spectacle that takes place every day: if the spectator is facing north, the sun rises on the right (the east) and moves to the left (the west), where it disappears.

This idea of representing movement by means of scriptographic expression, especially movement linked to velocity, had already been explored in the early twentieth century by the Italian futurists. Azeredo follows their lead in his "Velocidade" (1957, Velocity):

VVVVVVVVVV
VVVVVVVVVE
VVVVVVVVEL
VVVVVVVELO
VVVVVVELOC
VVVVVELOCI
VVVVVELOCID

VVVELOCIDA
VVELOCIDAD
VELOCIDADE

The line of *V*s imitates the sound of something moving slowly. With the progression of the poem from line to line, the phonetic ideogram dissolves and forms the word *velocidade* in the last line of the poem.

Also in 1957 Pignatari published "beba cloaca," which reflects the Dadaist and Surrealist interest in advertising. Pignatari's poem, however, is anti-advertising:

bebacocacola
babecola
bebacola
babecolacaco
caco
cola
cloaca

(drinkcocacola
drivelcola
drinkcola
drivelcolashit
shit
cola
cloaca)

Pignatari imitates an advertisement for Coca-Cola by printing the poem in white on a red background. Inverting the vowels in the word *beba* (drink) results in *babe* (drivel), while doing the same to *coca* results in *caco* (shit). Finally, Pignatari amalgamates *cola* and *caco*, inverting the consonants in *cola* and cutting *co* from *caco*, resulting in *cloaca*, or sewer. The political message of the poem is obvious: Pignatari is using the brand name *Coca-Cola* as a symbol of a lifestyle of which he does not approve for Brazil.

In Augusto de Campos's "Colocar a máscara" (1960, To Put on the Mask) the repetition of the title includes the Portuguese word for snail, *caracol:* "colocar a má**scara colo**car a máscara." The poet constructs a linguistic chain that represents ideographically the spiral structure of the snail:

colocaramas
caracolocar
amas**caracol**
ocaramas**car**
acolocarama
s**caracol**oca
ramas**caraco**
locaramas**ca**
racolocaram
as**caracol**oc
aramas**carac**
olocaramasc
aracolocara
mas**caracol**o
caramas**cara**

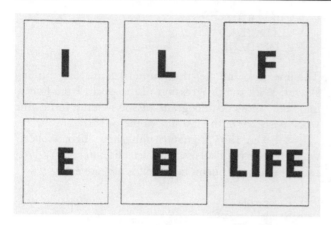

*Décio Pignatari's kinetic poem "Life" (1958), originally published
on six successive pages with one symbol per page
(Collection of Reinhard Krüger)*

Lettristic poetry–a term invented by Romanian and French avant-garde poets in the 1940s–takes into consideration the fact that poetry is made of letters. Pignatari's kinetic poem "Life" (1958) reveals the cabalistic background inherent in lettristic poetry. The poem proceeds through three phases. The first is a phase of chaos, in which four Latin letters appear in a random order: *I, L, F, E.* In the next phase the chaos undergoes a metamorphosis as the letters are superimposed in a graphic cluster that resembles a rectangular numeral *8,* the Chinese symbol for the sun–the origin of all life. Finally, from the Chinese ideogram Pignatari regenerates the four letters, which now spell out the word *LIFE.*

One notable technique of concrete poets is the reduction of given signs to a nonsignifying assembly and the creation of a new context in which these signs may be significant again. In Pignatari's "Organismo" (1960, Organism) each line of the poem is enclosed in a frame, as if it were on a new page:

o organismo quer perdurar
o organismo quer repet
o organismo quer re
o organismo quer
o organism
orgasm
oo
o

(the organism will keep alive
the organism will repeat
the organism will re
the organism will
the organism
orgasm
oo
o)

The idea behind the poem is that *organismo* (organism) and *orgasmo* (orgasm) are linked not only phonetically but also semantically. In the final verses *organismo* and *orgasmo* are reduced to the letters *oo* and *o,* which might be the phonetic representation of the sound made by a person experiencing an orgasm. In addition, Pignatari says in his commentary on the text, the letters *oo* and *o* have an ideographic relation to the female sexual organs. He notes that he used four techniques in constructing the poem. First, he changed the words of the first sentence morphologically from *o organismo quer perdurar* to *orgasmo* and then to *oo* or *o;* from *perdurar* to *repet[ar];* and from *orgasmo* to *o.* Second, he cut the original sentence by reducing it from line to line until the two verbs disappear, by deleting the noun *organismo,* and by generating a semantic shift from *organismo* to *orgasmo.* Third, he cut the syntactic structure of the phrase from a complete sentence to one word and then to metalinguistic exclamations. Fourth, he "zoomed in" on the typography as a means of maneuvering the cutting of the words and the sentence: with every step he put the text into bigger letters, which finally cover nearly the whole area circumscribed by the frame. This technique creates a cinematographic impression through the appearance of the letters "approaching" the reader.

The textual techniques employed by Pignatari lead to a semantic structuring of the poem. The initial sentence makes a biological claim: the organism will be durable. Durability is assured by repetition of the elementary vital functions. In a larger sense, the organism will be durable through the reproduction of its genes, which implies that the act of reproduction is tightly conjoined with the body. The desiring body tries to repeat and reproduce itself through the act that is rewarded by the orgasm. Finally, all of the multiple and complex meanings are reduced to one state, which is expressed by *oo* or *o.*

An underlying current of all the phases of development of concrete poetry is the poets' attempt to recognize and explore poetry's impact on all the human senses. As Haroldo de Campos indicates in the title of his 1985 collection, *A educação dos cinco sentidos,* the mission of concrete poets is "education of the five senses." The third phase of the movement began with the insertion of nonverbal signs into the texts and eventually led to the replacement of verbal expression with purely visual elements. This emphasis on nonverbal aspects was a result of the growing interest in the linguistic discipline of semiotics, which treats signs as a process of recognition and deciphering. Thus, every sign, including graphic ones, may be considered as belonging to the world of language and writing. Concretists engage in a philosophical and metaphysical tradition with roots in

Neoplatonic philosophy: if the shapes of things existed prior to creation in the mind of God, their material being must be a kind of writing that represents the ideas of God; the world is thus like a book, and each thing is like a word written in that book. Therefore, even non-verbal representations can be considered as words belonging to a hieroglyphic discourse of the world and the book of nature. All graphic representations of material beings, even if they are purely pictorial, acquire the status of Scripture. This idea of an artistic and poetic equivalence between all kinds of graphic expressions is also present in concrete music. Beginning with his composition *Bidule en Ut* in 1950, for example, Pierre Schaeffer has stressed his conviction of the equivalence of all kinds of sounds, whether they stem from classical music instruments such as the piano or from improvised percussion. Since the 1950s concrete poets have shown an increased interest in the phonetic aspect of language and in any possibilities that this area can offer for new explorations in poetic expression. Kurt Schwitters's futurist experiments in *Ursonate* (1921, Archaic Sonata) is one of the forerunners of this aspect of concrete poetry.

In 1964 Augusto de Campos published the visual poem "olho por olho" (eye for eye). The poem remains a riddle until one understands how to decipher the linguistic code in which graphic signs are substituted for written language. The first two lines are composed of pictures of Brazilian traffic signs, and the following eighteen are made up of pictures of apparently female eyes and mouths. The first line consists of a traffic sign with the triangle symbol that means "atenção!" (Attention!). The second line comprises three traffic signs with symbols that mean "não entrar" (Do Not Enter), "siga em frente" (Straight Ahead), and "sentido obrigatório" (obligatory direction [Right Turn Only]). The riddle of the relationship between these Brazilian traffic signs and the images of eyes and mouths can be resolved by reference to traditional Christian symbolism. The triangle is the symbol for God in Christian iconography; the three corners of the triangle represent the Trinity. The three round traffic signs of the second line can be seen as ideograms of the eye, which appears in the triangle that represents God in the baroque emblem tradition. (A pattern poem published in 1674 by the American Edward Taylor uses this symbolism; it was discovered and republished by Thomas H. Johnson in 1941, and Dick Higgins included it in his 1987 anthology *Pattern Poetry: Guide to an Unknown Literature*.) The circle is also the symbol for infinity and, therefore, of all aspects of the Trinity, since the Father, the Son, and the Holy Ghost are infinite. The third line responds to the symbolism of God's eye in the first two lines with four images cut from pictures of female faces: three of the

The visual poem "olho por olho/eye for eye" (1964), by Augusto de Campos (<http://www2.uol.com.br/augustodecampos/poemas.htm>)

images are eyes, and the fourth is a mouth. A visual joke emerges when the reader sees the analogy between a female eye and a female mouth. The final line is a sequence of three female eyes, responding to the three traffic-sign "eyes" on the second line.

The triangular shape of the poem is a continuation of the triangle in the first line, indicating that the first sign or first word of a text generates the rest of the text and has an impact on the whole. The triangular structure also produces an illusion of perspective: the large eyes at the bottom, tapering down to images at the top that are twenty times smaller, cause a three-dimensional effect, creating the image of a street plastered with pictures of eyes and mouths and with traffic signs at the far end.

This pop-art visual poem has a complicated semantic and semiotic structure that requires a precise description and an interpretation that considers the intertextual and historic relationships of the forms used in its construction. In other concrete poems the typographic characters attain a state of independence by representing the phonetic plan of a language; they are taken as pure graphic constructions that may be used for generating other graphic constructions. These graphic texts were especially plentiful in the 1960s. An example is *Text I 67* from *Visual Poems: 1967–1970*

"Text I 67" and "Text IV 68" from Clemente Padín's 1990 volume Visual Poems
1967–1970 *(Collection of Reinhard Krüger)*

(1990), by the Uruguayan Clemente Padín. In this text the letter *a* is used to organize the page, leaving no doubt that the page should be seen as a text even if it seems to say nothing in ordinary linguistic terms. Another example is *Text IV 68* from the same book. This text is related to Dadaist letter-constructions.

The fourth phase of concrete poetry is characterized by the creative possibilities offered by computer, especially by its capabilities for designing and animating texts through the use of GIF (Graphics Interchange Format) animations, and by the Internet. The application of these techniques to poetry is the realization of possibilities that concrete poets had envisaged in the 1960s. In Takahashi Shohachiro's *poesieanimations* (1968), for example, the text changes with the manipulation of the booklets. The idea of a mobile text can also be seen in the *poemobiles* that Augusto de Campos developed with Julio Plaza in the 1985 poem book of that title.

Pignatari's "O organismo quer perdurar" was the subject of one of the first applications of Internet techniques to a concretist poem. The cinematographic structure of the poem is fully realized in the animated version created by Elson Froés in 1997. Froés transformed the text into Web pictures and combined them into a GIF-formatted animated image for Internet application at <http://www.ubu.com/historical/pignatari/dporg.gif>.

Page by page and typographic picture by typographic picture, this GIF animation fully realizes the zooming-in process that the print version of 1960 approximated. Every picture/text appears for one second, which gives the viewer enough time to read the text and experience the movement produced by the zooming-in. The idea of a living *organismo* that desires *orgasmo* to assure its continuation is more obvious in the animated Internet format than in the printed version.

Other concretists, such as Augusto de Campos, have produced poems specifically for the Internet. Campos's "bombapoema" (1987–1992), at <www.ubu.com/historical/decampos_a/bombpoem.gif>, is an example of this new approach to the presentation of a concrete text. Campos arranges the typography in such a way that the letters appear to spill over the page as the result of a bomb having exploded in the center of the page. The impression of an explosion is created by having the background of the poem alternate between yellow and red, with each quarter-second yellow flash followed by two seconds of red. The poem stages typographically the notion of the "explosion of the text," which has been a tradition in poetry criticism and reflection on language since the futurists and Apollinaire. The explosion of the text is also a symbol of the arbitrary process of the creation of meaning as the putting together by the reader of fragmented elements. "Bombapoema" was undoubtedly influenced by futurist conceptions of the *parole in libertà* (words in freedom), and the composite noun in the title reflects Marinetti's advice to the futurist poet in his *Manifesto tecnico della letteratura futurista* (1912, Technical Manifesto of Futurist Literature) to create words such as *uomotorpediniera*. The poem may, therefore, be of interest only because of Campos's use of the new medium of a web page with a GIF animation; the remaining aspects of "bombapoema" are so closely linked to the futurist tradition that one might well doubt its originality.

Another poem by Campos, "coraçãocabeça/hearthead" (1980), is composed in Portuguese and English, reflecting the polyglot nature of the international community of concretists. Printed in yellow letters on a red background, the poem consists of two texts that are presented as enlargements of the words *heart* and *head*. Campos then inserts other words in the words *heart* and *head* by using parentheses:

COR(EM(COME(CA(MINHA)BEÇA)ÇA)MEU)AÇÃ
O
CABE(EM(NÃO(COR(MEU)AÇÃO)CABE)MINHA)Ç
A

he(in(st(hea(my)d)arts)my)art
he(in(h(he(my)art)eats)my)ad

Reading these texts requires profound concentration; it is difficult to make out the possible sentences hidden in the verbal constructions. For example, the reader may see "em minha cabeça começa meu coração"/"in my head starts my heart" or "em meu coração não cabe minha cabeça"/ "in my hart heats my head." Other possibilities include "em meu coração começa minha cabeça" (in my heart starts my head) and, in the English version, "in my head starts my art," "in my art heats my head," and so on.

In addition to the print version, Campos has produced a GIF animation of these two texts on the Internet at <www.uol.com.br/augustodecampos/images/coracaocabeca.gif> and at <www.ubu.com/historical/decampos_a/hearthead.html>, respectively.

Each text changes from one version to another every half second. The animation creates even more possible readings: the texts become unstable as they present themselves as linguistic clusters in which the reader may find a multitude of meanings.

A more striking example of the use of the Internet for exploring new ways of experiencing poetry is Campos's poem "ininstante" at his official Web site, <http://www2.uol.com.br/augustodecampos/clippoemas.htm>. Viewing this text properly requires the use of the Macromedia Shockwave Flash Player plug-in, which allows a complex presentation of a slide show with motion on the

slides accompanied by sound. Each slide contains one of six words on a black background in red, green, yellow, or blue characters: *instante* (instant) in red, *bastante* (sufficient) in red, *diminuto* (diminished) in green, *distante* (distant) in red, *infinito* (infinite) in yellow, and *restante* (staying) in green. Each word is segmented into lines of two characters; for example,

in
st
an
te

The text appears in four sequences of sixteen slides each, and each sequence ends with a different word. This procedure resembles the serpentine text-structures that poets such as Pignatari used in the early years of concrete poetry. The first sequence ends with *bastante,* the second with *distante,* the third with *restante,* and the final sequence with *infinito.* Through the quick overlapping of the words a new word emerges composed of fragments of *instante* and *infinito: ininstante,* the title of the poem. The word *infini* is then superimposed in blue over the animated yellow characters that form the final frame of *ininstante* in such a way that a new word, *infinistante,* appears. The reader can hear this new word if his or her computer has audio capabilities. Through this process the poet shows the fragility of words.

In keeping with their ideal of the education of all the human senses, and inspired by works such as Schwitters's *Ursonate,* concrete poets experiment not only with the spatio-typographical aspects of language but also with phonetic articulation. In 1979 Caetano Veloso recorded Augusto de Campos's poem "dias dias dias" (days days days) from the 1953 volume *Poetamenos.* In the printed version the poem is a spatialized text printed in four colors. Believing that each color indicated a different voice, Veloso produced a polyphonic work by adopting four speaking tones: loud, high, deep, and whisper. It is not clear whether this performance of the poem was the result of a collaboration between the poet and Veloso or if it was totally Veloso's idea.

In his own recording of his poem "Cidade City Cité" (1963, City, City, City) Campos reads his text twice, using two different phonologies: the first version is pure Brazilian Portuguese, and the second version is Portuguese with a French accent. The result is that the second text sounds French without the use of any French words. In his reading Campos stresses the idea that a phonology may be independent of any linguistic code; thus, the phonetic system of a language can be an independent medium of poetic expression. The text of "Cidade City Cité," in fact, is nothing but a sequence of roots of words from the Romance languages and some internationally recognizable prefixes, such as *plasti-, libri-, multipli-, organi-,* and *simpli-*:

atrocadapacaustiduplielastifeliferofugahistoriloqualubrimendimultipliorganiperiodiplastipubliraparecipororustisagasimplitenaveloveravivaunivoracidade

In his reading of his micropoem "Quazar" (1985) Campos explores, in fifteen seconds, several possibilities of phonetic relationships between the stellar phenomenon of the quasar and its name. At that time astrophysicists were trying to capture the sounds of the rays that were emitted from quasars, pulsars, and other astronomical objects. Veloso had made a recording of Campos's poem "Pulsar" in 1979 in which, using piano keys in the highest register, he evokes the casual beeps that astrophysicists have collected from scanning the universe. The new sounds of unknown objects in deep space were thus added to the human soundscape. The eternal quest for new possibilities in poetry and every other human activity has been and is still the primary mission of concrete poetry.

Bibliography:
Kathleen McCullough, *Concrete Poetry: An Annotated International Bibliography, with an Index of Poets and Poems* (Troy, N.Y.: Whitston, 1989).

References:

Joaquim de Sousa Andrade, *Sousândrade: poesia,* edited by Augusto de Campos and Haroldo de Campos, third edition (Rio de Janeiro: AGIR, 1995);

Oswald de Andrade, *O homem e o cavalo: espetáculo em 9 quadros* (São Paulo: Edição do Autor, 1934);

Andrade, *Pau Brasil: Cancioneiro de Oswald de Andrade,* preface by Paulo Prado (Paris: Sans Pareil, 1925);

Andrade, *Primeiro caderno do aluno de poesia Oswald de Andrade* (São Paulo: Mayença, 1927);

Stephen Bann, ed., *Concrete Poetry: An International Anthology* (London: London Magazine, 1967);

Claus Bremer, *Tabellen und Variationen,* konrete poesie—poesia concreta, no. 5 (Frauenfeld, Switzerland: Eugen Gomringer Press, 1960);

Augusto de Campos, *A margem da margem* (São Paulo: Companhia das Letras, 1989);

Campos, *Balanço da bossa e outras bossas,* second edition (São Paulo: Perspectiva, 1978);

Campos, *Ex poemas, 1980–1985* (São Paulo: Serigráficas Entretempo, 1985);

Campos, *Patricia Galvão, Pagu: vida-obra,* second edition (São Paulo: Brasiliense, 1982);

Campos, *Poesia 1949–1979* (São Paulo: Duas Cidades, 1979); republished as *Poesia 1949–1979: viva vaia* (São Paulo: Brasiliense, 1986);

Campos, *ReVisão de Kilkerry* (São Paulo: Brasiliense, 1985);

Campos, ed. and trans., *Irmãos germânos: poemas de Paul Fleming, Angelus Silesius, Hölderlin, Arno Holz, Hugo von Hoffmansthal, Rainer Maria Rilke, Christian Morgenstern, August Stramm, Kurt Schwitters* (Santa Cantina: Noa-Noa, 1992);

Campos and Haroldo de Campos, *Os sertões dos Campos: duas vezes Euclides* (Rio de Janeiro: Sette Letras, 1997);

Campos and Haroldo de Campos, eds., *ReVisão de Sousândrade: textos críticos, antologia, glossário, biobibliografia,* second edition, revised and enlarged (Rio de Janeiro: Nova Fronteira, 1982);

Campos, Décio Pignatari, and Haroldo de Campos, *Mallarmé* (São Paulo: Perspectiva/Editora da Universidade da São Paulo, 1974);

Campos, Pignatari, and Haroldo de Campos, *Teoria da poesia concreta: textos críticos e manifestos, 1950–1960* (São Paulo: Invenção, 1965); republished as *Textos críticos e manifestos 1950–1960: teoria da poesia concreta* (São Paulo: Brasiliense, 1987);

Campos, Pignatari, Haroldo de Campos, and Ronaldo Azeredo, "Pilot Plan for Concrete Poetry," *Noigandres,* 4 (1958);

Campos and Julio Plaza, *Poemobiles, 1968–1984* (São Paulo: Brasiliense, 1985);

Haroldo de Campos, *A arte no horizonte do prováel e outros ensaios,* fourth edition (São Paulo: Perspectiva, 1977);

Campos, *A educação dos cinco sentidos: poemas* (São Paulo: Brasiliense, 1985);

Campos, *A operação do texto* (São Paulo: Perspectiva, 1976);

Campos, *Deus e o diabo no Fausto de Goethe: marginália fáustica. Leitura do poema, acompanhada da transcriação em português das duas cenas finais da segunda parte* (São Paulo: Perspectiva, 1981);

Campos, *Galáxias* (São Paulo: Ex Libris, 1984);

Campos, *Metalinguagem & outras metas: ensaios de teoria e crítica literária,* fourth edition, revised and enlarged (São Paulo: Perspectiva, 1992);

Campos, *Morfologia do Macunaíma* (São Paulo: Perspectiva, 1973);

Campos, *Pedra e luz na poesia de Dante* (Rio de Janeiro: Imago, 1998);

Campos, "Uma poética de radicalidade" (1964), republished in Oswald de Andrade, *Pau-Brasil,* volume 3 of his *Obras completas* (São Paulo: Globo, 1990);

Campos, *Ruptura dos gêneros na literatura latino-americana* (São Paulo: Perspectiva, 1977);

Campos, *O sequestro do barroco na formação da literatura brasileira: o caso Gregório de Mattos* (Salvador: Fundação Casa de Jorge Amado, 1989);

Campos, *Signantia quasi coelum = Signância quase céu* (São Paulo: Perspectiva, 1979);

Campos, *Versuchsbuch Galaxien,* translated by Vilem Flusser and Anatol Rosenfeld (Stuttgart: Walther, 1966);

Campos and Octavio Paz, *Transblanco em torno a Blanco de Octavio Paz,* second edition (São Paulo: Siciliano, 1994);

Campos and Heloysa de Lima Dantas, eds., *Ideograma: lógica, poesia, linguagem,* third edition (São Paulo: Editora da Universidade de São Paulo, 1994);

G. J. de Rook, ed., *Anthologie visuele poëzie = Visual Poetry Anthology* (Utrecht: Bert Bakker Den Haag, 1975);

Klaus Peter Dencker, *Text-Bilder, visuelle Poesie international: von der Antike bis zur Gegenwart* (Cologne: M. DuMont Schauberg, 1972);

Wlademir Dias-Pino, *A separação entre inscrever e escrever (exposição): catalogo, 25 de novembro* (Cuiabá: Edições do Meio, 1982);

Paulo Franchetti, *Alguns aspectos da teoria da poesia concreta* (Campinas: UNICAMP, 1989);

Roland Greene, "From Dante to the Post-Concrete: An Interview with Augusto de Campos," *Harvard Library Bulletin,* 3 (Summer 1992);

Ferreira Gullar, Vinicius de Moraes, and Bernard Hermann, *Rio de Janeiro* (Papeete: Editions du Pacifique, 1977);

Ana Hatherly, *A experiência do prodígio: ases teóricas e antologia de textos-visuais portugueses dos séculos XVII e XVIII* (Lisbon: Imprensa Nacional-Casa da Moeda, 1983);

Dick Higgins, Herbert Francke, and Kalanath Jha, *Pattern Poetry: Guide to an Unknown Literature* (Albany: State University of New York Press, 1987);

K. David Jackson, ed., *One Hundred Years of Invention: Oswald De Andrade and the Modern Tradition in Latin American Literature. Centenary of Oswald de Andrade = Cem anos de invenção: Oswald de Andrade e a tradição moderna na literatura Latino-Americana. Centenário de Oswald de Andrade* (Austin: University of Texas, Department of Spanish and Portuguese/Abaporu Press, 1992);

Jackson, Eric Vos, and Johanna Drucker, eds., *Experimental Visual Concrete: Avant-Garde Poetry since the 1960s,* Avant-Garde Critical Studies, no. 10 (Amsterdam & Atlanta: Rodopi, 1996);

Milton Klonsky, ed., *Speaking Pictures: A Gallery of Pictorial Poetry from the Sixteenth Century to the Present* (New York: Harmony, 1975);

Susanne Lenz, "Literatur im Widerspruch: Zum Theorie-Praxis-Problem der Konkreten Poesie," dissertation, University of Cologne, 1976;

Filippo Tommaso Marinetti, *Manifesto tecnico della letteratura futurista* (Milan: Direzione del movimento futurista, 1912);

Philadelpho Menezes, *Poetics and Visuality: A Trajectory of Contemporary Brazilian Poetry* (San Diego: San Diego State University Press, 1994);

Kenneth B. Newell, *Pattern Poetry: A Historical Critique from the Alexandrian Greeks to Dylan Thomas* (Boston: Marlborough House, 1976);

Miguel d'Ors, *El caligrama, de Simmias a Apollinaire: Historia y antología de una tradición clásica* (Pamplona: Ediciones Universidad de Navarra, 1977);

Clemente Padín, *Visual Poems: 1967–1970* (Madison, Wis.: Xexoxial Editions, 1990);

Décio Pignatari, *Informação linguagem comunicação,* eleventh edition (São Paulo: Cultrix, 1982);

Pignatari, *Letras, artes, mídia* (São Paulo: Globo, 1995);

Pignatari, *Podbre brasil! crônicas políticas* (Campinas: Pontes, 1988);

Pignatari, *Poesia pois é poesia, 1950–1975; poetc, 1976–1986* (São Paulo: Brasiliense, 1986);

Pignatari, *O rosto da memória* (São Paulo: Brasiliense, 1986);

Pignatari, *Signagem da televisão* (São Paulo: Brasiliense, 1984);

Annymary Raminelli, "Die konkrete Poesie und ihr Verhältnis zur Avantgarde: Versuch einer Begriffserklärung und Untersuchung der Beziehungen zum Expressionismus, Dadaismus, Futurismus und Konstruktivismus anhand von Gedichten, Manifesten und Texten von Eugen Gomringer und der brasilianischen Gruppe Noigandres," M.A. thesis, University of Konstanz, 1997;

Stephen Scobie, *Earthquakes and Explorations: Language and Painting from Cubism to Concrete Poetry* (Toronto: University of Toronto Press, 1997);

David W. Seaman, *Concrete Poetry in France* (Ann Arbor, Mich.: UMI Research Press, 1981);

Mary Ellen Solt, *Concrete Poetry: A World View* (Bloomington: Indiana University Press, 1968);

Mike Weaver, "Concrete Poetry," *Journal of Typographical Research,* 1, no. 3 (1967);

Armando Zárate, *Antes de la vanguardia: Historia y morfología de la experimentación visual. De teócrito a la poesía concreta* (Buenos Aires: Alonso, 1976).

Tropicália

Christopher Dunn
Tulane University

Tropicália (also known as Tropicalismo) was a Brazilian cultural phenomenon of the late 1960s, coinciding with the advent of the most repressive phase of the military rule that lasted from 1964 to 1985. Although it coalesced as a formal movement only in the realm of popular music, cultural strategies associated with Tropicália were also manifest in theater, cinema, visual arts, and literature. Tropicália may be regarded as an exemplary case of cultural cross-fertilization in Brazilian artistic production. The dialogic impulse behind Tropicália generated an extraordinary flourish of artistic innovation during a period of political and cultural turmoil in Brazil. Although not reducible to any particular aesthetic or representational strategy, Tropicália may be identified with several general tendencies in Brazilian culture in the late 1960s, including a critical reevaluation of nationalist and populist cultural discourses and projects; a reconsideration of the modernist legacy; a skeptical view of left-wing artists and intellectuals as a political vanguard; an ironic embrace of lowbrow popular culture and kitsch; critical reflection on urban-industrial expansion; an ambiguous critique of the mass media; an allegorical treatment of Brazilian modernity; and an attempt to overcome the separation between art and life through participatory or experiential art.

Tropicália is associated primarily with a group of musicians from the northeastern state of Bahia who first attracted national attention in a series of televised music festivals in the late 1960s. The so-called *grupo baiano* (Bahian group) included singer-songwriters Caetano Veloso, Gilberto Gil, and Tom Zé; vocalist Gal Costa; and poets José Carlos Capinan and Torquato Neto.

Maria Bethânia, Veloso's younger sister, also belonged to the *grupo baiano* but did not participate in the Tropicalist movement. In the mid 1960s the Bahians migrated to Rio de Janeiro and later to São Paulo, where they forged a dynamic artistic relationship with several composers of the vanguard Música Nova group, most notably Rogério Duprat, who wrote the arrangements for most Tropicalist recordings. Duprat introduced the *grupo baiano* to the psychedelic rock band

Os Mutantes (The Mutants), consisting of vocalist Rita Lee, bass player Arnaldo Batista, and guitarist Sérgio Batista, which participated in several Tropicalist recordings. During this period the Bahian singer-songwriters also initiated a fruitful dialogue with the concrete poets, especially Augusto de Campos, who took a keen interest in their lyrical and musical innovations. Veloso has written that the concrete poets "liberaram nossa imaginação para certas experiências formais" (liberated our imagination for certain formal experiments that perhaps we wouldn't have otherwise risked). The Tropicalists experimented with various forms of wordplay, nondiscursive syntax, and what the concrete poets called "verbovocovisualidade" (verbi-voco-visuality). This alliance between artists from Bahia, a primary locus of Afro-Brazilian expressive culture, and from São Paulo, the largest, most industrialized Brazilian city, proved to be a potent combination and has had a lasting effect on Brazilian popular music and other arts.

Tropicália emerged in 1968, during a period of intense political conflict between the conservative military regime that had taken power in 1964 and a heterogeneous opposition composed of artists, intellectuals, students, workers, civilian politicians, and activists. At this time broad sectors of civil society coalesced in opposition to the regime. Factory workers carried out the first strikes since the inception of military rule. Leftist students battled with the military authorities and their ultrarightist allies in the universities. Around this time more-radicalized groups of the opposition went underground and initiated armed struggle against the regime. In December 1968 the government responded to civil protest and incipient armed resistance with a decree known as the Ato Institucional Número 5 (Institutional Act No. 5), or AI-5, which outlawed political opposition, purged and temporarily closed the Congress, suspended habeas corpus, established blanket censorship over the press, and effectively ended the protest movement. Thereafter, opposition to the regime was expressed primarily through disparate movements of armed resistance, which were ultimately suppressed by the regime.

Caetano Veloso, a key figure in the Tropicália movement, reading from his book Verdade tropical *(1997; translated as* Tropical Truth, *2002) at the Livro Vivo (Living Book) show in Rio de Janeiro, 1998 (photo by Cristina Granato; Agência o Globo; from Charles A. Perrone and Christopher Dunn, eds.,* Brazilian Popular Music & Globalization, *2001; Music Library, University of South Carolina)*

Cultural conflicts also came to a head in 1968, primarily within a largely middle-class urban milieu that opposed military rule. Artists and intellectuals began to reevaluate the failures of earlier political and cultural projects that sought to transform Brazil into an equitable and economically sovereign nation. Tropicália was both a mournful reflection on these defeats as well as an ironic celebration of Brazilian culture. As the name suggests, the movement referenced Brazil's tropical climate, which throughout history has been both exalted for generating lush abundance and lamented for impeding economic development like that found in societies located in temperate climates. The Tropicalists purposefully invoked stereotypical images of Brazil as a tropical paradise, only to subvert them with pointed references to political violence and social inequality.

In order to appreciate fully the significance of Tropicália, it is necessary to examine preceding literary movements and musical phenomena that contributed decisively to what was understood to be a "national culture." Of particular salience was *modernismo,* the Brazilian literary and cultural modernism that began in the 1920s. Two basic imperatives guided the members of

the modernist generation: they were oriented toward formal literary experimentation informed by the European avant-garde, and they were concerned with the articulation of what was distinctive about Brazil. The works of Oswald de Andrade were particularly important for the artists associated with Tropicália in the late 1960s.

Andrade is noted for his humorous and ironic interpretations of Brazilian history and culture, most famously expressed in two manifestos. In his "Manifesto da Poesia Pau Brasil" (1924, Brazilwood Manifesto) he exhorted his colleagues to create a "poesia de exportação" (poetry for export) that was neither deferential to nor ignorant of cosmopolitan literary currents. Oswald further radicalized his project in the "Manifesto Antropófago" (1928, Cannibalist Manifesto), which advanced a model for critically "devouring" cultural inflows from abroad. Cannibalism was a compelling and controversial metaphor for artists and critics of subsequent generations. Veloso claimed that Tropicália was a form of "neo-antropofagismo" (neo-cannibalism) relevant to the cultural context of the 1960s: "the idea of cultural cannibalism fit us, the Tropicalists, like a glove. We were 'eating' the Beatles and Jimi Hendrix."

The Tropicalists belonged to a generation of artists who reached adulthood in the late 1950s, a period of optimism under the democratic and developmentalist government of Juscelino Kubitschek. Emerging middle-class musicians of this generation had been profoundly inspired by bossa nova, a new musical style that synthesized elements of samba and modern jazz. Several musicians have claimed that they were moved to learn to play the guitar after hearing João Gilberto's famous 1958 recording of the song "Chega de Saudade" (No More Blues), written by the brilliant composer Antônio Carlos Jobim and the modernist poet Vinicius de Moraes. By the early 1960s, however, many young artists also aspired to raise political consciousness among urban and rural working classes and became increasingly disaffected with the introspective sentimentalism of early bossa nova. Many began to experiment with the musical traditions of the *povo* (masses), such as roots samba from the *favelas* (slums) of Rio de Janeiro and *moda-de-viola* from the rural interior. Under the aegis of the União Nacional dos Estudantes (UNE, National Students' Union), artists and intellectuals organized a national network of Centros Populares de Cultura (CPC, Peoples' Centers for Culture) that sought to foster a political alliance between middle-class students and workers. Cultural nationalism and social protest took on even greater urgency after the military coup of 1964.

At this time artists identified with an eclectic post-bossa-nova category, which was later denominated Música Popular Brasileira (MPB), generally opposed military rule, and espoused various forms of cultural nationalism. Like many other societies around the world, Brazil had a homegrown rock-music movement, known as the Jovem Guarda (Young Guard), which drew a large urban audience of people attracted to the consumer-oriented "youth culture" disseminated globally by the American culture industry. Many Brazilians associated rock music with the cultural imperialism of the United States and championed the MPB camp as the most appropriate musical expression of Brazilian modernity. The young Bahians were associated with MPB, but they were also interested in the Jovem Guarda as a pop phenomenon and were increasingly frustrated with sectors of the MPB camp that defined aesthetic priorities according to the imperatives of cultural nationalism. The young Bahians admired the bossa nova innovator Gilberto as an artist who engaged the tradition of Brazilian song while embracing musical modernity. In a roundtable discussion held in 1966, Veloso argued that it was necessary to return to the *linha evolutiva* (evolutionary line) of Brazilian popular music. In other words, MPB needed to evolve and be open to new trends instead of closing in on itself for the

sake of cultural authenticity. For Veloso, this "retomada da linha evolutiva" (retaking of the evolutionary line) ultimately led to Tropicália, which sounded like the antithesis of early bossa nova but was actually deeply informed by its attitude toward international musical modernity.

In response to a perceived impasse in MPB, Gil and Veloso proposed the "som universal" (universal sound), which they first presented at the 1967 Festival da Música Popular Brasileira (Festival of Brazilian Popular Music), hosted by TV Record. Gil's "Domingo no parque" (Sunday in the Park) best expressed the "som universal," a fusion of elements drawn from traditional Brazilian music and international pop. Gil performed with Os Mutantes and a percussionist who played the berimbau, a one-string bowed instrument used for performing *capoeira* music (Afro-Brazilian dance and martial art).

This musical event is generally considered to be an inaugural moment in the Tropicália movement that coincided with related developments in the cinema, theater, visual arts, and literature. Of particular salience was Glauber Rocha's 1967 movie *Terra em transe* (Land in Anguish), a watershed in the Brazilian Cinema Novo (New Cinema) movement. Rocha's masterpiece allegorized the collapse of populism and the ascension of authoritarian rule in Brazil. Veloso has noted that the movie represented a "momento traumático" (traumatic moment) for left-wing artists, creating the conditions for what was soon to be called "Tropicalismo." *Terra em transe* dramatized an historical moment of crisis for progressive artists and intellectuals living under a right-wing military dictatorship. Rocha's movie also influenced the "guerrilla theater" of São Paulo's Teatro Oficina, under the direction of José Celso Martinez Corrêa, which was quickly identified with the Tropicalist phenomenon. Around the time that Gil and Veloso presented their "som universal," Teatro Oficina staged *O rei da vela* (1933, The Candle King), Andrade's modernist farce about the Brazilian elite, reconfigured for the present context. Veloso has also cited José Agrippino de Paula's experimental "pop-Tropicalist" novel *Panamérica* (1967) as a key influence on the Tropicalist group.

The story behind the naming of Tropicália suggests the degree of dialogic cross-fertilization among several artistic realms. After hearing one of Veloso's untitled compositions in late 1967, the cinematographer Luís Carlos Barreto detected affinities with an art installation titled *Tropicália,* by the visual artist Hélio Oiticica. In this work Oiticica sought a "new language with Brazilian elements" by creating a three-dimensional ambient space inspired by the *favela* of Mangueira. The installation referenced the "organic architecture" of the *favelas,* the unfinished constructions, the vacant lots, and other material forms of an urban space in the process of formation. Oiticica described *Tropicália* as the "very first conscious, objective attempt to impose an obviously Brazilian image upon the current context of the avant-garde and national art manifestations in general." Despite Veloso's initial reluctance, he agreed to use "Tropicália" as the title of his composition, which subsequently became a key manifesto of the movement. Tropicália eventually served as the name for the entire movement, although Tropicália was the name more commonly used during the 1960s and 1970s.

The musical manifestations of Tropicália did not propose a new style or genre. Tropicalist music involved, instead, a pastiche of diverse styles, both new and old, national and international. Tropicalist music might be understood as a rereading of the tradition of Brazilian popular song in light of international popular music and avant-garde experimentation. The Tropicalists drew from diverse musical traditions, including samba, bossa nova, *baião* (a northeastern Brazilian dance rhythm), rock, the bolero, classical music, opera, *capoeira,* and the music of the Candomblé sect, an Afro-Brazilian religion. Tropicália is best understood as an approach, an attitude, or a cultural strategy that favors mixture and hybridity. In Brazil the Tropicalists elicited comparisons with their internationally famous contemporaries, the Beatles, a group that also created popular music in dialogue with art music, as well as with local popular traditions. In May 1968 the Tropicalist group released a concept album, *Tropicália, ou panis et circencis* (Tropicália, or Bread and Circuses), partly inspired by the Beatles' album *Sgt. Pepper's Lonely Hearts Club Band* (1967). Soon after the promulgation of AI-5 in December 1968, Veloso and Gil were arrested and subsequently exiled to England. During this time they participated in the vibrant London counterculture revolving around rock music and interacted with the Caribbean immigrant community, absorbing emerging styles from the African diaspora, such as reggae. Upon their return to Brazil the former leaders of the Tropicalist movement were celebrated as icons of a Brazilian countercultural movement.

In the latter part of the 1970s Gil and Veloso also became enthusiastic proponents of the emerging Afro-Brazilian cultural movements associated with soul, reggae, and the Afro-Bahian Carnaval in Salvador. During this period Costa achieved mass success as one of the most acclaimed female vocalists of her generation. Lee, of Os Mutantes, pursued a successful solo career as a leading proponent of Brazilian rock music. Following the Tropicalist experience, Zé fell from public view as he continued to develop more-experimental popular music. In the 1990s he regained visibility with the inter-

national release of a compilation of his works from the 1970s and two innovative albums featuring new material. In 1999 he toured the United States with the Chicago-based group Tortoise. Together with the other Tropicalists, Zé found new audiences outside Brazil, especially following a brief Tropicalist vogue in the United States and Europe during the late 1990s.

A considerable body of critical literature on Tropicália has accumulated in Brazil since the development of the movement. Cultural critics in the mainstream press of São Paulo and Rio de Janeiro published the earliest articles about Tropicália. As the movement unfolded, the concrete poet and theorist Campos wrote a series of enthusiastic articles praising Veloso and Gil for their brazen critique of musical nationalism. In one article Campos spoke of a "tropicaliança" (tropicalliance) based on a "comunidade natural de interesses" (natural community of interests). From the outset several journalists, such as Nelson Motta and Luiz Carlos Maciel, celebrated the movement in the press, although other critics, such as Eli Halfoun and José Ramos Tinhorão, expressed anxiety over the Tropicalists' unabashed enthusiasm for electric instrumentation, Anglo-American rock, mass-media exposure, and low-brow popular culture. In 1970 the literary critic Roberto Schwarz published a watershed essay about contemporary Brazilian culture and politics that became a fundamental reference for subsequent scholars of Tropicália. Drawing on the work of Walter Benjamin, Schwarz was the first critic to draw attention to the allegorical nature of Tropicália, noting its frequent allusions to anachronistic cultural emblems filtered through the "white light of ultramodernity" so as to convey the disjunctures of capitalist development in Brazil. While recognizing the critical potential of the Tropicalist allegory, Schwarz was troubled by its propensity to advance a fatalistic "atemporal idea of Brazil" that seemed to negate any potential for social transformation.

Several other critics returned to the question of Tropicalist allegory during the 1970s but drew different conclusions from Schwarz. Celso F. Favaretto, for example, argued that the Tropicalist allegory derived its critical effect precisely by leaving historical contradictions unresolved, thereby generating an indeterminate and fragmentary image of Brazil that could then be activated to satirize official culture. The literary critic Silviano Santiago criticized Schwarz for underplaying the specificity of Brazilian culture, which could not be adequately explained by Marxist dialectics: "O essencial é perceber que ás vezes certas posturas radicais carregam em si tal dose de eurocentrismo que ao se rebaterem contra o objeto 'brasileiro' revolucionário, simplesmente porque não segue de perto o modelo, minimiza-o, a ponto mesmo de aniquilar o seu potencial

Sérgio Batista, Arnaldo Batista, and Rita Lee, members of the rock band Os Mutantes (The Mutants), circa 1970. The band participated in several Tropicalist recording sessions (courtesy of the Arquivo Estadual de São Paulo; from Charles A. Perrone and Christopher Dunn, eds., Brazilian Popular Music & Globalization, *2001; Music Library, University of South Carolina).*

guerreiro" (It's essential to perceive that certain radical stances sometimes contain a dose of Eurocentrism that when confronted with the revolutionary "Brazilian" object, belittles it to the point of destroying its combative potential simply because it doesn't follow the model). Heloísa Buarque de Hollanda further contributed to the critique of Schwarz's position in an account of cultural politics during the 1960s and early 1970s. Hollanda asserts that Tropicália proposed a "nova linguagem crítica" (new critical language) that refused the redemptive claims of more-orthodox leftists but intervened directly on the level of individual attitudes and behavior, thereby paving the way for the countercultural practices of the 1970s. In her view, the Tropicalist movement signaled the decline of more-redemptive narratives of collective struggle and a turn toward new practices concerned with personal liberation and subjective experience. The radical skepticism of the Tropicalists in relation to the great themes of Brazilian modernity (national identity, industrial development, and social revolution) has led some critics to argue that Tropicália was the inaugural moment of postmodern culture in Brazil.

Tropicália has become the subject of a growing body of literature on contemporary Brazilian culture produced for a general reading public. Included in this category are scholarly analyses from several disciplines, cultural histories, didactic books, secondary-education texts, and lavishly illustrated coffee-table volumes. The Tropicalist phenomenon has also attracted the attention of artists, critics, and scholars outside of Brazil, especially in the United States. Although Tropicália has attracted primarily musical cognoscenti, it has also figured in contemporary discussions of Oiticica's work, which has received acclaim in international conceptual-art circles.

Since the late 1970s Tropicália has been regularly written about in the Brazilian press. The commemorative surge grew considerably in 1992–1993, when Veloso and Gil celebrated their fiftieth birthdays and recorded *Tropicália 2,* an album that reinterprets the movement within a contemporary context. A wave of memoir writing about the 1960s in Brazil has also contributed to ongoing debates around the Tropicalist experience. Most of the earliest memoirs were written by former urban guerrillas and tended to ignore cultural debates. More-recent memoirs have focused more broadly on the existential crises, political disputes, and cultural conflicts of artists and activists. In 1997 Veloso published *Verdade tropical* (translated as *Tropical Truth: A*

Story of Music and Revolution in Brazil, 2002), a book primarily focusing on his personal experiences in the Tropicalist movement. Veloso offers an insightful, although hardly disinterested, account of the political and cultural conflicts of the 1960s and the lasting importance of Tropicália. His memoir provoked yet another round of debate in the national press over the value and significance of Tropicália and how it relates to contemporary Brazilian culture in an era of economic and cultural globalization.

References:

Heloísa Buarque de Hollanda, *Impressões de viagem: CPC, vanguarda e desbunde, 1960–1970* (São Paulo: Brasiliense, 1980; third edition, Rio de Janeiro: Rocco, 1992);

Carlos Calado, *A divina comédia dos Mutantes* (Rio de Janeiro: Editora 34, 1995);

Calado, *Tropicália: a história de uma revolução musical* (São Paulo: Editora 34, 1997);

Antônio Callado, *Quarup* (Rio de Janeiro: Civilização Brasileira, 1967);

Augusto de Campos and others, *Balanço da bossa e outras bossas,* second edition (São Paulo: Perspectiva, 1974);

Christopher Dunn, *Brutality Garden: Tropicália and the Emergence of a Brazilian Counterculture* (Chapel Hill: University of North Carolina Press, 2001);

Dunn, "The Tropicalista Rebellion: A Conversation with Caetano Veloso," *Transition,* 70 (Summer 1996): 116–138;

Celso F. Favaretto, *Tropicália: alegoria, alegria* (São Paulo: Kairós, 1979; second edition, São Paulo: Ateliê, 1996);

Gilberto Gil, *Gilberto Gil: Expresso 2222,* edited by Antonio Risério (Salvador: Corrupio, 1982);

John Havey, "Cannibals, Mutants, and Hipsters: The Tropicalist Revival," in *Brazilian Popular Music & Globalization,* edited by Charles A. Perrone and Dunn (Gainesville: University Press of Florida, 2001), pp. 106–122;

Marisa Alvarez Lima, *Marginália: arte & cultura "na idade da pedrada"* (Rio de Janeiro: Salamandra, 1996);

Ivo Lucchesi and Gilda Korff Dieguez, *Caetano: por que não? Uma viagem entre a aurora e a sombra* (Rio de Janeiro: Leviatã, 1993);

Luiz Carlos Maciel, *Geração em transe: memórias do tempo do tropicalismo* (Rio de Janeiro: Nova Fronteira, 1996);

Bina Freidman Maltz, Jerônimo Teixeira, and Sérgio Ferreira, *Antropofagia e tropicalismo* (Pôrto Alegre: Editora da Universidade Federal do Rio Grande do Sul, 1993);

Chris McGowan and Ricardo Pessanha, *The Brazilian Sound: Samba, Bossa Nova, and the Popular Music of Brazil,* revised edition (Philadelphia: Temple University Press, 1998);

Frederick Moehn, "In the Tropical Studio: MPB Production in Transition," *Studies in Latin American Popular Culture,* 19 (2000): 57–66;

Nelson Motta, *Noites tropicais: solos, improvisos e memórias musicais* (Rio de Janeiro: Objetiva, 2000);

Enor Paiano, *Tropicalismo: bananas ao vento no coração do Brasil* (São Paulo: Scipione, 1996);

Charles A. Perrone, *Masters of Contemporary Brazilian Song: MPB, 1965–1985* (Austin: University of Texas Press, 1989);

Marcelo Ridenti, *Em busca do povo brasileiro: artistas da revolução, do CPC à era da tv* (São Paulo: Record, 2000);

Lúcia Santaella, *Convergências: poesia concreta e tropicalismo* (São Paulo: Nobel, 1986);

Affonso Romano de Sant'Anna, *Música popular e moderna poesia brasileira* (Petrópolis: Vozes, 1978);

Silviano Santiago, preface to Gilberto Vasconcellos, *Música popular: de olho na fresta* (Rio de Janeiro: Graal, 1977);

Roberto Schwarz, *Misplaced Ideas: Essays on Brazilian Culture,* edited, with an introduction, by John Gledson (London & New York: Verso, 1992);

Rebecca Liv Sovik, "Ponha seu capacete: uma viagem à tropicália pos-moderna," *Revista da Bahia,* 32 (May 1998): 60–67;

Sovik, "Tropicália, Canonical Pop," *Studies in Latin American Popular Culture,* 19 (2000): 113–128;

Vasconcellos, *Música popular: de olho na fresta;*

Caetano Veloso, *Alegria, alegria,* edited by Waly Salomão (Rio de Janeiro: Ronca, 1977);

Veloso, *Verdade tropical* (São Paulo: Letras, 1997); translated by Isabel de Sena as *Tropical Truth: A Story of Music and Revolution in Brazil,* edited by Barbara Einzig (New York: Knopf, 2002).

Books for Further Reading

Abdala Júnior, Benjamin. *Tempos da literatura brasileira*. São Paulo: Ática, 1985.

Alves, Henrique L. *Ficção de 30*. São Paulo: Sociedade Brasileira de Filosofia, Literatura e Ensino, 1978.

Alves Filho, F. M. Rodrigues. *O sociologismo e a imaginação no romance brasileiro*. Rio de Janeiro: J. Olympio, 1938.

Amora, Antônio Soares. *História da literatura Brasileira, séculos XVI–XX*. São Paulo: Saraiva, 1955.

Amora. *O romantismo, 1833–1838/1878–1881*. São Paulo: Cultrix, 1967.

Araripe Júnior, T. A. *Movimento de 1893: o crepusculo dos povos*. Rio de Janeiro: Democrática, 1896.

Araújo, Arturo Gouveia de. *Os homens cordiais: a representação da violência oficial na literatura dramática brasileira pós-64*. João Pessoa: Universitária, 1996.

Araújo, Murillo. *Quadrantes do modernismo brasileiro,* second edition. Rio de Janeiro: São José, 1972.

Armstrong, Piers. *Third World Literary Fortunes: Brazilian Culture and Its International Reception*. Lewisburg, Pa.: Bucknell University Press, 1999.

Avila, Henrique Manuel. *Da urgência à aprendizagem: sentido da história e romance brasileiro dos anos sessenta*. Londrina: UEL, 1997.

Azevedo, Fernando de. *A cultura brasileira: introdução ao estudo da cultura no Brasil,* second edition. São Paulo: Nacional, 1944.

Azevedo, Thales de. *Democracia racial: ideologia e realidade*. Petrópolis: Vozes, 1975.

Barbadinho Neto, Raimundo. *Tendências e constâncias da língua do modernismo*. Rio de Janeiro: Acadêmica, 1972.

Bastide, Roger. *A poesia afro-brasileira*. São Paulo: Martins, 1943.

Bastos, C. Tavares. *O simbolismo no Brasil e outros escritos*. Rio de Janeiro: São José, 1969.

Bernardes, Maria Thereza Caiuby Crescenti. *Mulheres de ontem? Rio de Janeiro, século XIX*. São Paulo: T. A. Queiroz, 1989.

Bernd, Zilá. *Introdução à literatura negra*. São Paulo: Brasiliense, 1988.

Bettencourt, Gastão de. *A inspiração folclórica na poesia brasileira*. Coimbra, 1954.

Boaventura, Maria Eugênia. *A vanguarda antropofágica*. São Paulo: Ática, 1985.

Bopp, Raul. *Movimentos modernistas no Brasil, 1922–1928*. Rio de Janeiro: São José, 1966.

Borelli, Silvia Helena Simões. *Ação, suspense, emoção: literatura e cultura de massa no Brasil.* São Paulo: Estação Liberdade, 1996.

Bosi, Alfredo. *Dialética da colonização.* São Paulo: Letras, 1992.

Bosi. *História concisa da literatura brasileira.* São Paulo: Cultrix, 1970.

Bosi. *O pré-modernismo,* third edition. São Paulo: Cultrix, 1969.

Brasil, Assis. *O modernismo.* Rio de Janeiro: Pallas, 1976.

Brasil. *A técnica da ficção moderna.* Rio de Janeiro: Nórdica/Instituto Nacional do Livro, 1982.

Brayner, Sônia. *Labirinto do espaço romanesco: tradição e renovação da literatura brasileira, 1880–1920.* Rio de Janeiro: Civilização Brasileira, 1979.

Broca, José Brito, and José Galante de Sousa. *Introdução ao estudo da literatura brasileira.* Rio de Janeiro: Instituto Nacional do Livro, Ministério da Educação e Cultura, 1963.

Brookshaw, David. *Race and Color in Brazilian Literature.* Metuchen, N.J.: Scarecrow Press, 1986.

Bueno, Eva Paulino. *Resisting Boundaries: The Subject of Naturalism in Brazil.* New York: Garland, 1995.

Cafezeiro, Edwaldo, and Carmem Gadelha. *História do teatro brasileiro: um percurso de Anchieta a Nelson Rodrigues.* Rio de Janeiro: Editora da Universidade Federal do Rio de Janeiro/Editora da Universidade do Estado do Rio de Janeiro/Fundação Nacional de Arte, 1996.

Campos, Augusto de. *Poesia, antipoesia, antropofagia.* São Paulo: Cortez & Morães, 1978.

Campos, Décio Pignatari, and Haroldo de Campos. *Teoria da poesia concreta: textos críticos e manifestos, 1950–1960.* São Paulo: Invenção, 1965.

Campos, Haroldo de. *Metalinguagem: ensaios de teoria e crítica literária,* second edition. Petrópolis: Vozes, 1970.

Cândido, Antônio. *O discurso e a cidade.* São Paulo: Duas Cidades, 1993.

Cândido. *Formação da literatura brasileira: momentos decisivos.* São Paulo: Martins, 1959.

Carbuglio, José C. *Literatura e realidade brasileira (a tentação e tentativa).* São Paulo: Conselho Estadual de Cultura, 1970.

Castello, José Aderaldo. *Aspectos do romance brasileiro.* Rio de Janeiro: Ministério da Educação e Cultura, 1960.

Castello. *Homens e intenções: cinco escritores modernistas.* São Paulo: Conselho Estadual de Cultura, Comissão de Literatura, 1959.

Castello. *A literatura brasileira: manifestações literarias da era colonial (1500–1808/1836).* São Paulo: Cultrix, 1962.

Castro, Sílvio. *A revolução da palavra: origens e estrutura da literatura brasileira moderna.* Petrópolis: Vozes, 1976.

Castro. *Teoria e política do modernismo brasileiro.* Petrópolis: Vozes, 1979.

Cavalheiro, Edgard. *Evolução do conto brasileiro.* Rio de Janeiro: Ministério da Educação e Cultura, 1954.

Cidade, Hernâni. *O conceito de poesia como expressão da cultura: sua evolução através das literaturas portuguesa e brasileira,* second edition. Coimbra: A. Amado, 1957.

Costa, Iná Camargo. *A hora do teatro épico no Brasil.* Rio de Janeiro: Graal, 1996.

Costa, J. Cruz. *A History of Ideas in Brazil: The Development of Philosophy in Brazil and the Evolution of National History,* translated by Suzette Macedo. Berkeley: University of California Press, 1964.

Coutinho, Afrânio. *An Introduction to Literature in Brazil,* translated by Gregory Rabassa. New York: Columbia University Press, 1969.

Coutinho, ed. *A literatura no Brasil,* second edition, 6 volumes. Rio de Janeiro: Sul Americana, 1968–1971.

Coutinho and Sousa, eds. *Enciclopédia de literatura brasileira,* second edition, 2 volumes. São Paulo: Global, 2001.

Coutinho, Edilberto. *Criaturas de papel: temas de literatura & sexo & folclore & carnaval & futebol & televisão & outros temas da vida.* Rio de Janeiro: Civilização Brasileira, 1980.

Cunha, Fausto. *A leitura aberta: estudos de crítica literária.* Rio de Janeiro: Cátedra, 1978.

Cunha. *Romantismo e modernidade na poesia.* Rio de Janeiro: Cátedra, 1988.

Cunha. *O romantismo no Brasil, de Castro Alves a Sousândrade.* Rio de Janeiro: Paz e Terra/Instituto Nacional do Livro, 1971.

Dacanal, José Hildebrando. *Nova narrativa épica no Brasil.* Pôrto Alegre: Sulina, 1973.

Damasceno, Benedita Gouveia. *Poesia negra no modernismo brasileiro.* Campinas: Pontes, 1988.

De Nicola, José. *Literatura brasileira, das origens aos nossos dias,* fifteenth edition. São Paulo: Scipione, 1998.

Del Fiorentino, Teresinha Aparecida. *Utopia e realidade: o Brasil no começo do século XX.* São Paulo: Cultrix, 1979.

DiAntonio, Robert E. *Brazilian Fiction: Aspects and Evolution of the Contemporary Narrative.* Fayetteville: University of Arkansas Press, 1989.

Ellison, Fred P. *Brazil's New Novel; Four Northeastern Masters: José Lins do Rego, Jorge Amado, Graciliano Ramos, Rachel De Queiroz.* Berkeley: University of California Press, 1954.

Fernandes, José. *O existencialismo na ficção brasileira.* Goiânia: Editora da Universidade Federal de Goiás, 1986.

Fernandez, Carmen M. *The Slave in Brazilian Romantic Poets.* Macao: Nacional, 1974.

Figueiredo, Guilherme. *Cobras e lagartos: rodapés de crítica literária, 1943 a 1945.* Rio de Janeiro: Nova Fronteira, 1984.

Fischer, Luís Augusto. *Poesia brasileira: do barroco ao pré-modernismo.* Pôrto Alegre: Novo Século, 2001.

Flores, Moacyr. *O negro na dramaturgia brasileira, 1838–1888.* Pôrto Alegre: Editora da Pontifícia Universidade Católica do Rio Grande do Sul, 1995.

Fonseca, Aleilton. *Enredo romântico, música ao fundo: manifestações lúdico-musicais no romance urbano do romantismo.* João Pessoa: Universidade Federal da Paraíba, 1996.

Foster, David William, and Roberto Reis. *A Dictionary of Contemporary Brazilian Authors.* Tempe: Center for Latin American Studies, Arizona State University, 1981.

França, Jean M. Carvalho. *Literatura e sociedade no Rio de Janeiro oitocentista.* Lisbon: Nacional/Casa da Moeda, 1999.

Franconi, Rodolfo A. *Erotismo e poder na ficção brasileira contemporânea.* São Paulo: Annablume, 1997.

Freyre, Gilberto. *Heróis e vilões no romance brasileiro: em torno das projeções de tipos sócio-antropológicos em personagens de romances nacionais do século XIX e do atual,* edited by Edson Nery da Fonseca. São Paulo: Cultrix/Editora da Universidade de São Paulo, 1979.

George, David S. *Flash and Crash Days: Brazilian Theater in the Postdictatorship Period.* New York: Garland, 2000.

George. *The Modern Brazilian Stage.* Austin: University of Texas Press, 1992.

Gomes, Eugênio. *Aspectos do romance brasileiro.* Salvador: Progresso, 1958.

Gomes, Heloisa Toller. *O negro e o romantismo brasileiro.* São Paulo: Atual, 1988.

Gonçalves, Augusto de Freitas Lopes. *Dicionário histórico e literário do teatro no Brasil,* 4 volumes. Rio de Janeiro: Cátedra, 1975–1982.

Grieco, Agrippino. *Evolução da prosa brasileira,* third edition. Rio de Janeiro: J. Olympio, 1947.

Guelfi, Maria Lúcia Fernandes. *Novíssima: estética e ideologia na década de vinte.* São Paulo: Instituto de Estudos Brasileiros, Universidade de São Paulo, 1987.

Gullar, Ferreira. *Cultura posta em questão.* Rio de Janeiro: Civilização Brasileira, 1965.

Helena, Lúcia. *Modernismo brasileiro e vanguarda.* São Paulo: Ática, 1986.

Houaiss, Antônio. *Drummond mais seis poetas e um problema.* Rio de Janeiro: Imago, 1976.

Igel, Regina. *Imigrantes judeus/escritores brasileiros: o componente judaico na literatura brasileira.* São Paulo: Perspectiva/Associação Universitária de Cultura Judaica, 1997.

Ivo, Lêdo. *Modernismo e modernidade.* Rio de Janeiro: São José, 1972.

Koshiyama, Alice Mitika. *Análise de conteúdo da literatura de cordel: presença dos valores religiosos.* São Paulo: Escola de Comunicações e Artes, Universidade de São Paulo, 1972.

Kothe, Flávio R. *O cânone colonial: ensaio.* Brasília: Editora Universidade de Brasília, 1997.

Kothe. *O cânone imperial.* Brasília: Editora Universidade de Brasília, 2000.

Lafetá, João Luiz. *1930: a crítica e o modernismo,* second edition. São Paulo: Duas Cidades, 2000.

Lajolo, Marisa, and Regina Zilberman. *A leitura rarefeita: livro e literatura no Brasil.* São Paulo: Brasiliense, 1991.

Leite, Sebastião Uchoa. *Participação da palavra poética, do modernismo à poesia contemporânea.* Petrópolis: Vozes, 1966.

Lima, Alceu Amoroso. *Introdução à literatura brasileira.* Rio de Janeiro: AGIR, 1956.

Lima. *Poesia brasileira contemporânea.* Belo Horizonte: P. Bluhm, 1941.

Lima, Luiz Costa. *Pensando nos trópicos: dispersa demanda II.* Rio de Janeiro: Rocco, 1991.

Lincoln, Joseph N. *Charts of Brazilian Literature.* Ann Arbor, 1947.

Linhares, Temístocles. *Diálogos sobre a poesia brasileira.* São Paulo: Melhoramentos/Instituto Nacional do Livro, 1976.

Linhares. *História crítica do romance brasileiro, 1728–1981,* 3 volumes. Belo Horizonte: Itatiaia, 1987.

Lins, Alvaro. *Poesia moderna do Brasil.* Rio de Janeiro: Edições de Ouro, 1967.

Lins. *Sagas literárias e teatro moderno do Brasil: Erico Veríssimo, Jorge Amado, Guimarães Rosa, Marques Rebêlo, Nelson Rodrigues.* Rio de Janeiro: Edições de Ouro, 1967.

Loos, Dorothy Scott. *The Naturalistic Novel of Brazil.* New York: Hispanic Institute in the United States, 1963.

Lopes, Maria Angélica Guimarães. *A coreografia do desejo: cem anos de ficção brasileira.* Cotia: Ateliê, 2001.

Lowe, Elizabeth. *The City in Brazilian Literature.* Rutherford, N.J.: Fairleigh Dickinson University Press, 1982.

Lucas, Fábio. *O caráter social da literatura brasileira.* Rio de Janeiro: Paz e Terra, 1970.

Luft, Celso Pedro. *Dicionário de literatura portuguêsa e brasileira.* Pôrto Alegre: Globo, 1967.

Lyra, Pedro. *Sincretismo: a poesia da geração 60; introdução e antologia.* Rio de Janeiro: Topbooks/Fundacao Rioarte, 1995.

Magaldi, Sábato. *Moderna dramaturgia brasileira.* São Paulo: Perspectiva, 1998.

Magaldi. *Panorama do teatro brasileiro,* third edition. São Paulo: Global, 1997.

Magalhães, Celso da Cunha. *A poesia popular brasileira,* introduction and notes by Braulio do Nascimento. Rio de Janeiro: Biblioteca Nacional, 1973.

Maligo, Pedro. *Land of Metaphorical Desires: The Representation of Amazonia in Brazilian Literature.* New York: Peter Lang, 1998.

Marobin, Luiz. *Estética das escolas literárias do Brasil (roteiro para o estudo teórico).* São Leopoldo: Universidade do Vale do Rios dos Sinos, 1971.

Marotti, Giorgio. *Black Characters in the Brazilian Novel,* translated by Maria O. Marotti and Harry Lawton. Los Angeles: Center for Afro-American Studies, University of California, 1987.

Martins, José V. de Pina. *Ensaio sobre o parnasianismo brasileiro, seguido de uma breve antologia.* Coimbra: Coimbra Editora, 1945.

Martins, Wilson. *The Modernist Idea: A Critical Survey of Brazilian Writing in the Twentieth Century,* translated by Jack E. Tomlins. New York: New York University Press, 1970.

Medina, Cremilda de Araújo. *A posse da terra, escritor brasileiro hoje.* Lisbon: Nacional/Casa da Moeda, 1985.

Mendes, Miriam Garcia. *O negro e o teatro brasileiro.* São Paulo: Editora de Humanismo, Ciência e Tecnologia, 1993.

Mendes. *A personagem negra no teatro brasileiro entre 1838 e 1888.* São Paulo: Ática, 1982.

Mendonça, Antônio Sérgio Lima, and Alvaro de Sá. *Poesia de vanguarda no Brasil: de Oswald de Andrade ao poema visual.* Rio de Janeiro: Antares, 1983.

Menezes, Philadelpho. *Poetics and Visuality: A Trajectory of Contemporary Brazilian Poetry,* translated by Harry Polkinhorn. San Diego: San Diego State University Press, 1995.

Menezes, Raimundo de. *Dicionário literário brasileiro,* 5 volumes. São Paulo: Saraiva, 1969.

Merquior, José Guilherme. *Razão do poema: ensaios de crítica e de estética.* Rio de Janeiro: Civilização Brasileira, 1965.

Moisés, Massaud, ed. *A literatura brasileira através dos textos.* São Paulo: Cultrix, 1971.

Montenegro, Olívio. *O romance brasileiro,* second edition, preface by Freyre. Rio de Janeiro: J. Olympio, 1953.

Moreira, Fernando. *Aspectos da dramaturgia brasileira contemporânea.* São Luís, 1979.

Mota, Leonardo. *Sertão alegre (poesia e linguagem do sertō nordestino).* Belo Horizonte: Imprensa Oficial de Minas, 1928.

Moutinho, José Geraldo Nogueira. *A fonte e a forma: 50 ensaios sobre a literatura brasileira contemporânea.* Rio de Janeiro: Imago, 1977.

Nist, John. *The Modernist Movement in Brazil: A Literary Study.* Austin: University of Texas Press, 1967.

Nunes, Cassiano. *Breves estudos de literatura brasileira.* São Paulo: Saraiva, 1969.

Octávio Filho, Rodrigo. *Simbolismo e penumbrismo.* Rio de Janeiro: São José, 1970.

Pacheco, João. *O realismo: 1870–1900.* São Paulo: Cultrix, 1963.

Pães, José Paulo. *Transleituras: ensaios de interpretação literária.* São Paulo: Ática, 1995.

Pães and Moisés, eds. *Pequeno dicionário de literatura brasileira,* second edition. São Paulo: Cultrix, 1980.

Parker, John M. *Brazilian Fiction: 1950–1970.* Glasgow: Institute of Latin American Studies, University of Glasgow, 1973.

Patai, Daphne. *Myth and Ideology in Contemporary Brazilian Fiction.* Rutherford, N.J.: Fairleigh Dickinson University Press, 1983.

Peixoto, Afrânio, ed. *Panorama da literatura brasileira,* second edition. São Paulo: Nacional, 1947.

Peixoto, Sérgio Alves. *A consciência criadora na poesia brasileira: do barroco ao simbolismo.* São Paulo: Annablume, 1999.

Pellegrini, Tânia. *A imagem e a letra: aspectos da ficção brasileira contemporânea.* São Paulo: Fundação de Amparo à Pesquisa do Estado de São Paulo / Campinas: Mercado de Letras, 1999.

Peregrino, Umberto. *Literatura de cordel em discussão.* Rio de Janeiro: Presença, 1984.

Pereira, Lúcia Miguel. *Prosa de ficção: de 1870 a 1920.* Rio de Janeiro: J. Olympio, 1950.

Perez, Renard. *Escritores brasileiros contemporâneos: biografias, seguidas de antologia,* 2 volumes. Rio de Janeiro: Civilização Brasileira, 1960, 1964.

Perrone, Charles A. *Seven Faces: Brazilian Poetry since Modernism.* Durham, N.C.: Duke University Press, 1996.

Pinto, Cristina Ferreira. *O bildungsroman feminino: quatro exemplos brasileiros*. São Paulo: Perspectiva, 1990.

Placer, Xavier, ed. *Modernismo brasileiro: bibliografia (1918–1971)*. Rio de Janeiro: Divisão de Publicações e Divulgação, 1972.

Portella, Eduardo. *Literatura e realidade nacional*. Rio de Janeiro: Tempo Brasileiro, 1963.

Prado, Décio de Almeida. *Apresentação do teatro brasileiro moderno: crítica teatral de 1947–1955,* second edition. São Paulo: Perspectiva, 2001.

Prado. *O drama romântico brasileiro*. São Paulo: Perspectiva, 1996.

Prado. *Teatro em progresso: crítica teatral, 1955–1964*. São Paulo: Martins, 1964.

Preti, Dino. *Sociolingüística, os níveis da fala: um estudo sociolingüístico do diálogo na literatura brasileira,* second edition. São Paulo: Nacional, 1975.

Proença Filho, Domício. *Pós-modernismo e literatura*. São Paulo: Ática, 1988.

Putnam, Samuel. *Marvelous Journey: A Survey of Four Centuries of Brazilian Writing*. New York: Knopf, 1948.

Py, Fernando. *Chão da crítica: jornalismo literário, 1962–1980*. Rio de Janeiro: F. Alves, 1984.

Quinlan, Susan Canty. *The Female Voice in Contemporary Brazilian Narrative*. New York: Peter Lang, 1991.

Rabassa. *O negro na ficção brasileira: meio século de história literária,* translated by Ana Maria Martins. Rio de Janeiro: Tempo Brasileiro, 1965.

Ramos, Clóvis. *Temas espíritas na poesia brasileira*. Rio de Janeiro: Sabedoria, 1969.

Ramos, Péricles Eugênio da Silva. *Do barroco ao modernismo: estudos da poesia brasileira*. São Paulo: Conselho Estadual de Cultura, 1967.

Reis, Roberto. *The Pearl Necklace: Toward an Archaeology of Brazilian Transition Discourse,* translated by Aparecida de Godoy Johnson. Gainesville: University Press of Florida/Center for Latin American Studies, 1992.

Reis. *A permanência do círculo: hierarquia no romance brasileiro*. Niterói: Universidade Federal Fluminense, 1987.

Resende, Vânia Maria. *O menino na literatura brasileira*. São Paulo: Perspectiva, 1988.

Ricardo, Cassiano. *Poesia praxis e 22*. Rio de Janeiro: J. Olympio, 1966.

Rocha Filho, Rubem. *Anjo ou demônio, malandro ou herói: aspectos do negro na dramaturgia brasileira*. Recife: Fundação de Cultura Cidade do Recife, 1998.

Romero, Sílvio. *História da literatura brasileira,* fifth edition, 5 volumes. Rio de Janeiro: J. Olympio, 1953.

Rosenfeld, Anatol. *O mito e o herói no moderno teatro brasileiro*. São Paulo: Perspectiva, 1982.

Salles, David. *Do ideal às ilusões: alguns temas da evolução do romantismo brasileiro*. Rio de Janeiro: Civilização Brasileira, 1980.

Salles, Fritz Teixeira da. *Das razões do modernismo*. Brasília: Editora Brasília, 1974.

Sampaio, Maria Lúcia Pinheiro. *História da poesia modernista.* São Paulo: J. Scortecci, 1991.

Santiago, Silviano. *Vale quanto pesa: ensaios sobre questões político-culturais.* Rio de Janeiro: Paz e Terra, 1982.

Santos, Olga de Jesus, and Marilena Vianna. *O negro na literatura de cordel.* Rio de Janeiro: Fundação Casa de Rui Barbosa, 1989.

Secco, Carmen Lúcia Tindó. *Além da idade da razão: longevidade e saber na ficção brasileira.* Rio de Janeiro: Graphia, 1994.

Sena, Jorge de. *Estudos de cultura e literatura brasileira.* Lisbon: Edições 70, 1988.

Sevcenko, Nicolau. *Literatura como missão: tensões sociais e criação cultural na Primeira República.* São Paulo: Brasiliense, 1983.

Silva, Domingos Carvalho da. *Vozes femininas da poesia brasileira: ensaio histórico-literário.* São Paulo: Conselho Estadual de Cultura, Comissão de Literatura, 1959.

Silveira, Homero. *Aspectos do romance brasileiro contemporâneo.* São Paulo: Convívio, 1977.

Silverman, Malcolm. *Moderna ficção brasileira 2 : ensaios,* translated by João Guilherme Linke. Rio de Janeiro: Civilização Brasileira, 1981.

Silverman. *Protesto e o novo romance brasileiro,* translated by Carlos Araújo, second edition. Rio de Janeiro: Civilização Brasileira, 2000.

Slater, Candace. *Dance of the Dolphin: Transformation and Disenchantment in the Amazonian Imagination.* Chicago: University of Chicago Press, 1994.

Slater. *Stories on a String: The Brazilian Literatura de Cordel.* Berkeley: University of California Press, 1982.

Sodré, Nelson Werneck. *História da literatura brasileira, seus fundamentos econômicos,* second edition. Rio de Janeiro: J. Olympio, 1940.

Sodré. *O naturalismo no Brasil.* Rio de Janeiro: Civilização Brasileira, 1965.

Sodré. *O que se deve ler para conhecer o Brasil.* Rio de Janeiro: Leitura, 1945.

Sousa. *O teatro no Brasil,* 2 volumes. Rio de Janeiro: Instituto Nacional do Livro, Ministério da Educação e Cultura, 1960.

Souto-Maior, Valéria Andrade. *Indice de dramaturgas brasileiras do século XIX.* Floriánopolis: Mulheres, 1996.

Souza, Magna Celi Meira de. *Misticismo e fanatismo na literatura de cordel.* João Pessoa: Universidade Federal de Paraíba, 1998.

Stern, Irwin, ed. *Dictionary of Brazilian Literature.* New York: Greenwood Press, 1988.

Süssekind, Flora. *Cinematograph of Words: Literature, Technique, and Modernization in Brazil,* translated by Paulo Henriques Britto. Stanford: Stanford University Press, 1997.

Süssekind. *O negro como arlequim: teatro & discriminação.* Rio de Janeiro: Achiamé/Socii, 1982.

Teles, Gilberto Mendonça. *A crítica e o romance de 30 do nordeste: ensaio.* Rio de Janeiro: Atheneu Cultura, 1990.

Teles. *A escrituração da escrita: teoria e prática do texto literário.* Petrópolis: Vozes, 1996.

Tinhorão, José Ramos. *A música popular no romance brasileiro,* 3 volumes. Belo Horizonte: Oficina de Libros, 1992–2002.

Tolman, Jon M., and Ricardo Paiva. *Brazilian Literature and Language Outlines.* Albuquerque: Latin American Institute, University of New Mexico, 1986.

Ventura, Roberto. *Estilo tropical: história cultural e polêmicas literárias no Brasil, 1870–1914.* São Paulo: Letras, 1991.

Veríssimo, José. *História da literatura brasileira de Bento Teixeira, 1601 a Machado de Assis, 1908,* third edition. Rio de Janeiro: J. Olympio, 1954.

Vieira, Nelson. *Jewish Voices in Brazilian Literature: A Prophetic Discourse of Alterity.* Gainesville: University Press of Florida, 1995.

Vincenzo, Elza Cunha de. *Um teatro da mulher: dramaturgia feminina no palco brasileiro contemporâneo.* São Paulo: Perspectiva, 1992.

Weber, João Hernesto. *Caminhos do romance brasileiro: de A moreninha a Os guaianãs.* Pôrto Alegre: Mercado Aberto, 1990.

Xavier, Elódia, ed. *Tudo no feminino.* Rio de Janeiro: F. Alves, 1991.

Zagury, Eliane. *A palavra e os ecos.* Petrópolis: Vozes, 1971.

Zilberman. *Do mito ao romance: tipologia da ficção brasileira contemporânea.* Caxias do Sul: Universidade de Caxias do Sul / Pôrto Alegre: Escola Superior de Teologia São Lourenço de Brindes, 1977.

Contributors

Marta Almeida . . . . *Yale University*

Sandra R. G. Almeida . . . . *Universidade Federal de Minas Gerais*

Robert N. Anderson . . . . *University of North Carolina at Chapel Hill*

Nancy T. Baden . . . . *California State University, Fullerton*

Zilá Bernd . . . . *Universidade Federal do Rio Grande do Sul*

Susan Canty Quinlan . . . . *University of Georgia*

Lúcia Helena Costigan . . . . *Ohio State University*

Eduardo F. Coutinho . . . . *Universidade Federal do Rio de Janeiro*

Sérgio Nazar David . . . . *Universidade do Estado do Rio de Janeiro*

Paul B. Dixon . . . . *Purdue University*

Christopher Dunn . . . . *Tulane University*

Alain-Philippe Durand . . . . *University of Rhode Island*

Lesley Feracho . . . . *University of Georgia*

David S. George . . . . *Lake Forest College*

Regina Igel . . . . *University of Maryland*

K. David Jackson . . . . *Yale University*

Sabrina Karpa-Wilson . . . . *Indiana University*

Reinhard Krüger . . . . *Technical University of Berlin and University of Stuttgart*

Joseph Abraham Levi . . . . *Rhode Island College*

Mark A. Lokensgard . . . . *St. Mary's University of San Antonio*

Maria Angélica Lopes . . . . *University of South Carolina*

Maria Luci De Biaji Moreira . . . . *College of Charleston*

Luciana Camargo Namorato . . . . *University of North Carolina at Chapel Hill*

Celso Lemos de Oliveira . . . . *University of South Carolina*

Alessandra M. Pires . . . . *University of Georgia*

Darlene J. Sadlier . . . . *Indiana University, Bloomington*

Regina Santos . . . . *University of North Carolina at Chapel Hill*

Vivaldo A. Santos . . . . *Georgetown University*

Marco G. Silva . . . . *University of North Carolina at Chapel Hill*

Elzbieta Szoka . . . . *Columbia University*

Carmen Chaves Tesser . . . . *University of Georgia*

Jon M. Tolman . . . . *University of New Mexico*

Ana Cristina Pimenta da Costa Val . . . . *Faculdade de Pará de Minas*

Richard Vernon . . . . *University of North Carolina at Chapel Hill*

Bruce Dean Willis . . . . *University of Tulsa*

Eliana Yunes . . . . *Pontifícia Universidade Católica do Rio de Janeiro*

Cumulative Index

Dictionary of Literary Biography, Volumes 1-307
Dictionary of Literary Biography Yearbook, 1980-2002
Dictionary of Literary Biography Documentary Series, Volumes 1-19
Concise Dictionary of American Literary Biography, Volumes 1-7
Concise Dictionary of British Literary Biography, Volumes 1-8
Concise Dictionary of World Literary Biography, Volumes 1-4

Cumulative Index

DLB before number: *Dictionary of Literary Biography,* Volumes 1-307
Y before number: *Dictionary of Literary Biography Yearbook,* 1980-2002
DS before number: *Dictionary of Literary Biography Documentary Series,* Volumes 1-19
CDALB before number: *Concise Dictionary of American Literary Biography,* Volumes 1-7
CDBLB before number: *Concise Dictionary of British Literary Biography,* Volumes 1-8
CDWLB before number: *Concise Dictionary of World Literary Biography,* Volumes 1-4

M

O

S

Cumulative Index

Cumulative Index